MW01052089

The Wiley Blackwell Handbook of Operant and Classical Conditioning

The Wiley Blackwell Handbook of Operant and Classical Conditioning

Edited by
Frances K. McSweeney and Eric S. Murphy

WILEY Blackwell

This edition first published 2014

Registered Office
John Wiley & Sons Ltd, The Atrium, Southern Gate, Chichester, West Sussex, PO19 8SQ, UK

Editorial Offices
350 Main Street, Malden, MA 02148-5020, USA

9600 Garsington Road, Oxford, OX4 2DQ, UK

The Atrium, Southern Gate, Chichester, West Sussex, PO19 8SQ, UK

For details of our global editorial offices, for customer services, and for information about how to apply for permission to reuse the copyright material in this book please see our website at www.wiley.com/wiley-blackwell.

Library of Congress Cataloging-in-Publication Data is available for this book.

The Wiley Blackwell handbook of operant and classical conditioning / edited by Frances K. McSweeney and Eric S. Murphy.
pages cm
Includes bibliographical references and index.
ISBN 978-1-118-46818-0 (cloth)
1. Operant conditioning. 2. Classical conditioning. I. McSweeney, Frances K., editor of compilation. II. Murphy, Eric S., editor of compilation.
BF319.5.O6W53 2014
153.1'526–dc23

2013051179

A catalogue record for this book is available from the British Library.

Cover image: Animal behaviour experiment, pigeon and Skinner box. © Photo Researchers / Science Photo Library
Cover design by Cyan Design

Set in 10/12.5 pt GalliardStd-Roman by Toppan Best-set Premedia Limited

1 2014

Contents

Contributors

William B. Abernathy received his master's in Experimental Psychology from Vanderbilt University and his Ph.D. in Industrial/Organizational Psychology from the Ohio State University. He taught Psychology at Ohio University and then left to join Edward J. Feeney & Associates, a consulting firm that specialized in applying behavioral principles in the workplace. He founded Abernathy & Associates in 1981 to assist client organizations in the design and management of organization-wide performance systems. His firm worked with more than 170 organizations in the United States and abroad. Aubrey Daniels International acquired Abernathy & Associates and Dr. Abernathy returned to teaching at Southeastern Louisiana University where he teaches Psychology and coordinates a master's degree program in I/O Psychology. Dr. Abernathy is the author of three books: *The sin of wages, Pay for profit*, and *Human performance diagnostics.*

Leonardo F. Andrade is currently completing a postdoctoral fellowship at the University of Connecticut School of Medicine. He earned his master's degree from the University of Brasilia (Brazil) and his doctorate from the University of Florida. His research focuses on impulsive decision-making, and its relationship to treatment and relapse. He has examined impulsivity from the context of delay and probability discounting in samples of alcohol and drug abusing patients as well as problem gamblers. His research interests also extend to the application of contingency management to promote abstinence from drugs and medication adherence, and to increase job-seeking activities and physical exercise.

Jonathan C. Baker is an Associate Professor in the Behavior Analysis and Therapy Program in the Rehabilitation Institute at Southern Illinois University (SIU) and coordinator of the Graduate Certificate in Gerontology at SIU. He received his Ph.D. from Western Michigan University (2009) in Behavioral Psychology, an M.S. (2005) in Applied Behavioral Sciences and a certificate in Gerontology from the University of Kansas. He is a Doctoral-level Board Certified Behavior Analyst and serves on the Editorial Board of *The Analysis of Verbal Behavior*, as well as a guest reviewer for *the Journal of Applied Behavior Analysis*, the *Journal of Organizational Behavior*

Management, and *The Psychological Record*. Dr. Baker is the current chair of the Behavioral Gerontology Special Interest Group with Association for Behavior Analysis International. Dr. Baker's interests in behavioral gerontology include the assessment/treatment of behavioral excesses and developing programs that remediate behavioral deficits in older adults with dementia, as well as treatment adoption.

Elizabeth L. Begej received her B.S in. Psychology from Sweet Briar College in 2013. As an undergraduate, she studied cognitive and behavioral processes and assisted in Daniel Gottlieb's animal learning laboratory. Elizabeth plans to pursue graduate study in Psychology.

Matthew C. Bell is an Associate Professor in the Psychology Department at Santa Clara University, where he has been a part of the faculty since 2001. He earned his B.S. in Psychology from the University of New Mexico and his M.A. and Ph.D. in Experimental Psychology at the University of California, San Diego. As an experimental psychologist and behavior analyst, he studies conditioned reinforcement, choice, and persistence using pigeons as subjects and also collaborates with Dr. Patti Simone studying remembering in older adults.

Mark E. Bouton, Ph.D, is the Lawson Green and Gold Professor of Psychology at the University of Vermont. He has studied extinction, and the effects of context on extinction learning and extinction performance, for over three decades. He is the author of a textbook on learning theory (*Learning and behavior: A contemporary synthesis*, published in 2007 by Sinauer Associates), of which he is busily writing a second edition, He has received a number of awards, including the Gantt Medal from the Pavlovian Society, and he is a Fellow of several scientific organizations, including the American Psychological Association, the Association for Psychological Science, and the Society of Experimental Psychologists.

Andrew R. Craig grew up in southwestern Pennsylvania and attended West Virginia University as an undergraduate. Under the mentorship of Drs. Kennon Lattal and Elizabeth Kyonka, he developed interests in behavior analysis, generally, and the quantitative analysis of behavior, particularly. Andrew earned his B.S. degree in Psychology in 2011. He then traded the rolling hills of Appalachia for the peaks of the Rocky Mountains when he enrolled as a doctoral student in the Psychology Department at Utah State University. His advisor is Dr. Timothy Shahan. His recent work focuses on examining the genesis of behavioral momentum and why momentum theory applies to some situations but not to others. He and Dr. Shahan are involved in collaborative efforts with Dr. John Nevin aimed at applying momentum theory to complex clinical situations and with Dr. Charles Gallistel aimed at quantifying the operant contingency in terms of information theory.

Kimberly A. Crosland, Ph.D., BCBA-D, is an Assistant Professor in the Applied Behavior Analysis Program in the Department of Child and Family Studies at the University of South Florida. Her research interests are in the area of behavioral assessment, caregiver training, child welfare, and developmental disabilities. She has received federal funding from the Department of Education to support her research to develop effective interventions to improve outcomes for youth in foster care.

Sabrina M. Darrow is currently a Postdoctoral Fellow in the Department of Psychiatry at the University of California, San Francisco. She received her doctorate in Clinical Psychology in 2011 from the University of Nevada, Reno where she developed expertise in third-wave behavior therapies, particularly Functional Analytic Psychotherapy, and psychotherapy outcome research methodology. During her postdoctoral fellowship in the Clinical Services Research Training Program at University of California, San Francisco she consulted on many mental health services research projects and built expertise in measurement development. Her primary research interests include the clinical utility of assessment, clinical behavior analysis, mechanisms of action in psychotherapy, and implementation research.

Michael S. Fanselow, Ph.D., is a Distinguished Professor in both the Psychology and Psychiatry Departments at University of California Los Angeles (UCLA). He currently holds the Eleanor Leslie Chair in Innovative Neuroscience through UCLA's Brain Research Institute. His research is on the neurobiology of learning and memory and focuses primarily on fear and stress related behavior. Dr. Fanselow is best known for his behavioral, neuropharmacological and anatomical characterization of contextual fear conditioning. One of his major early contributions to the field was the description of Pavlovian learning as an error-correcting circuit in which endogenous opioids perform an important error-calculating function. He has also explored the learning produced by experiences with drugs of abuse, particularly opioids. He uses rodent models with genetic, pharmacological, and surgical manipulations to pursue these questions. Dr. Fanselow also directs UCLA's Behavioral Testing Core where he provides instruction and support for investigators wishing to use rodent models.

Edmund Fantino received his B.A. in mathematics from Cornell University in 1961 and his Ph.D. in Psychology from Harvard University in 1964. After serving as Assistant Professor of Psychology at Yale University (1964–1967) he moved to the University of California, San Diego in 1967, where he has remained (now as Distinguished Professor of Psychology and the Neurosciences). His research has emphasized choice, irrational decisions, quantitative models of choice and foraging in humans and nonhumans, learning in educational contexts, and Comparative Psychology. He has served as Editor of the *Journal of the Experimental Analysis of Behavior* (1987–1991), on National Science Foundation and National Institute of Mental Health scientific advisory boards, and has promoted behavioral approaches at the U.S. House of Representatives. His books include *The Experimental analysis of behavior: A biological perspective*, and *Behaving well.*

William C. Follette is a Professor and member of the Clinical Faculty in the Department of Psychology at the University of Nevada, Reno. He received his Ph.D. in Psychology from the University of Washington. His interests include psychotherapy treatment development, outcome research design, program evaluation, functional analysis, assessment with clinical utility as a goal, and clinical behavior analysis.

He is particularly interested in the application of the principles of behavior analysis to outpatient adults with interpersonal deficits that result in diminished access to valued social reinforcement and that impede the individual in attaining his/her valued goals. Much of his intervention work focuses on helping people develop complex social repertoires through contingently shaped processes rather than rule-governed approaches often while studying Functional Analytic Psychotherapy as a vehicle to promote change. Dr. Follette has consulted with NIMH on the study of mechanisms of change, translational research, treatment dissemination, and programmatic research strategies.

Daniel A. Gottlieb received his B.S. in Psychology from Yale University, where he spent time in Allan Wagner's animal learning laboratory. He received his Ph.D. in Psychology from the University of Pennsylvania under the guidance of Robert Rescorla and spent two years as a postdoctoral researcher in C. R. Gallistel's laboratory at Rutgers University. He is now an Associate Professor of Psychology at Sweet Briar College, where he studies appetitive conditioning in rats and people.

Leonard Green is Professor of Psychology and Economics at Washington University in St. Louis. He received his undergraduate degree at the City College of New York (CCNY) and his Ph.D. at State University of New York—Stony Brook. His areas of research concern models of self-control and impulsivity, discounting, and behavioral economics. He was Editor of the *Journal of the Experimental Analysis of Behavior*, President of the Society for the Experimental Analysis of Behavior, on the Executive Board of the Society for the Quantitative Analysis of Behavior, and on the Editorial Boards of *Journal of Experimental Psychology: Animal Behavior Processes*, *Behavior and Philosophy*, *Pavlovian Journal of Biological Science*, *Journal of the Experimental Analysis of Behavior*, and *The Psychological Record*. In addition to more than 150 articles and chapters, Len Green is co-author of *Economic choice theory: An experimental analysis of animal behavior*, and co-editor of the series *Advances in Behavioral Economics*.

Steven R. Hursh (B.A., Wake Forest University, 1968; Ph.D., University of California, San Diego, 1972) is the President of the Institutes for Behavior Resources and Adjunct Professor of Behavioral Biology, Johns Hopkins University School of Medicine. Dr. Hursh has 40-years experience as a researcher and is author of more than 80 articles, book chapters, and books. He is a former Associate Editor of the *Journal of the Experimental Analysis of Behavior*. Dr. Hursh established Behavioral Economics as a major conceptual area. His research papers introduced into the behavioral vocabulary new concepts: open and closed economies, demand curves and elasticity, unit price, substitution and complementarity, P_{max}, O_{max}, and recently, exponential demand and essential value. His extensions to drug abuse and public policy have had a major impact on the research direction of programs supported by the National Institute of Health and other government agencies.

Kent Johnson is founder and Director of Morningside Academy a laboratory school for typical children and youth in Seattle. It investigates effective curricula and teaching methods, and has provided training to more than 125 schools throughout the world. Dr. Johnson's many publications about research-based curriculum and teaching methods include *The Morningside Model of generative instruction*, and *Response to intervention and precision teaching* with Dr. Elizabeth Street. More than 40,000 students and 1,000 teachers have implemented Morningside's Generative Instruction. Dr. Johnson received the Award for Public Service in Behavior Analysis from the Society for the Advancement of Behavior Analysis, the Anderson Award for Exemplary Contributions to Behavioral Education from the Cambridge Center for Behavioral Studies, the Award for Excellence in Evidence-based Education from the Wing Institute, the Allyn and Bacon Exemplary Program Award from the Council for Exceptional Children, and the Lindsley Lifetime Achievement Award in Precision Teaching from the Standard Celeration Society.

Alexander W. Kusnecov is Associate Professor of Psychology at Rutgers University. He obtained his Ph.D. in 1990 at the University of Newcastle, Australia, where he focused on the functional interface between the immune and nervous systems. Postdoctoral studies on Psychoneuroimmunology were conducted in the Department of Psychiatry, University of Rochester, New York. His research has continued to address different domains of neural-immune interactions. This has included behavioral conditioning of the immune system, as well as stressor effects on immune function. More recently, his research has addressed the neural, endocrine, and behavioral consequences of immunologic challenge with bacterial T cell superantigens, such as the staphylococcal enterotoxins.

Darnell Lattal received her Ph.D. in Clinical Psychology from West Virginia University. She is President of Aubrey Daniels International where she specializes in the design and implementation of behavioral-based business strategies to achieve core initiatives. Dr. Lattal is particularly effective in coaching individuals, from executives to line employees, to make sustained positive change, including corporate culture design and ethical practices. She has special expertise in the Psychology of Learning, designing sustainable yet rapid behavior change. Her publications include *Workplace ethics: Winning the integrity revolution*, coauthored with Ralph Clark; *Ethics at work*; *A good day's work: Sustaining ethical behavior and business results*; and *Reducing workplace stress through positive motivation strategies*, coauthored with Jun Ishida. She is currently coauthoring a book with Aubrey C. Daniels on how the science of behavior is influencing the workplace of the future.

Linda A. LeBlanc, Ph.D., BCBA-D, MI Licensed Psychologist is the Executive Director of Research and Clinical Services at Trumpet Behavioral Health. Trumpet Behavioral Health provides behavioral treatment services to consumers in school, home and center-based settings in 11 states. Dr. LeBlanc received her Ph.D. in 1996 from Louisiana State University and previously served as a Professor on the Psychology faculties at Claremont McKenna College (1997–1999), Western Michigan University (1999–2008), and Auburn University (2009–2012). Her current research interests include the behavioral treatment of autism and developmental disabilities across the lifespan, verbal behavior, and behavioral gerontology. She is a current Associate Editor of *Education and Treatment of Children, and The Analysis of Verbal Behavior* and *a former associate editor of the Journal of Applied Behavior Analysis and Behavior Analysis in Practice.*

Gwen J. Lupfer is an Associate Professor of Psychology at the University of Alaska Anchorage. She received her B.A., M.S., and Ph.D. from Kansas State University. Dr. Lupfer teaches courses in Behavioral Neuroscience and Evolutionary Psychology. Her research interests include social transmission of food preferences; sensory-specific satiety; measuring attitudes with implicit association tests; and operant behavior, food hoarding, and alcohol self-administration in hamsters.

James E. Mazur is a Professor of Psychology at Southern Connecticut State University, where he has taught since 1988. He obtained his B.A. at Dartmouth College in 1973, and his Ph.D. at Harvard University in 1977. He then taught at Harvard for several years and conducted postdoctoral research at Yale University. He has served as an Associate Editor for *Learning & Behavior* and as Editor for the *Journal of the Experimental Analysis of Behavior*. His research focuses on choice behavior in animals and people, examining how such variables as delay of reinforcement, variability, probability, and conditioned reinforcers affect choice. He is the author of *Learning & behavior*, a popular textbook for undergraduate and graduate courses on learning, which is currently in its 7th edition.

Margaret A. McDevitt is a Professor of Psychology at McDaniel College, a private college of the liberal arts and sciences located in Westminster, Maryland. She received her B.A. and M.S. in Psychology from California State University, Stanislaus, and her M.A. and Ph.D. in Experimental Psychology from the University of California, San Diego. She maintains a pigeon laboratory at McDaniel College where she studies basic learning processes with undergraduate students. Dr. McDevitt is particularly interested in conditioned reinforcement, and how the presence of stimuli affects the optimality of choice behavior. She lives near Baltimore with her husband and twin daughters.

Frances K. McSweeney is Regents Professor of Psychology and Vice Provost for Faculty Affairs at Washington State University. She received her B.A., Summa Cum Laude, from Smith College and her master's and Ph.D. from Harvard University. Dr. McSweeney has published on many topics, including the Matching Law, behavioral contrast and dynamic changes in reinforcer value. Her work has been supported by the National Science Foundation and the National Institute of Mental Health. She has served on grant review panels and on the editorial boards of several journals. She currently serves as an Associate Editor for *Learning and Motivation*. Dr. McSweeney is a Fellow of the Association for Behavior Analysis International (ABAI), of the American Psychological Association (APA), and of the Association for Psychological Science. She has served as President of ABAI and received the 2007 Med Associates Distinguished Contributions to Behavioral Research Award from Division 25 of APA.

Raymond G. Miltenberger, Ph.D., BCBA-D, is the Director of the Applied Behavior Analysis Program at the University of South Florida. He is a Fellow and past President of the Association for Behavior Analysis International (ABAI). His research focuses on safety skills, behavior analysis in health, fitness, and sports, and staff training and management. He has published more than 185 journal articles and chapters and has written a behavior modification textbook, now in its 5th edition. Dr. Miltenberger has received a number of teaching and research awards including the American Psychological Association Division 25 Award for Distinguished Contributions to Applied Behavioral Research and the ABAI Outstanding Mentorship Award.

Eric S. Murphy is an Associate Professor in the Department of Psychology at the University of Alaska Anchorage (UAA). He received his B.A. from UAA and M.S. and Ph.D. in Experimental Psychology from Washington State University. Dr. Murphy has research and teaching interests in behavior analysis. He and his students are currently studying the variables that regulate reinforcer effectiveness in laboratory rats. Dr. Murphy has published in the *Journal of the Experimental Analysis of Behavior* and *Journal of Applied Behavior Analysis* and is the recipient of UAA's Faculty Exemplar Award for his work in enhancing undergraduate research opportunities.

Joel Myerson is Research Professor of Psychology at Washington University in St. Louis. He received his undergraduate degree from the University of Michigan, his Ph.D. from Arizona State University, and did postdoctoral research in Neurophysiology and Behavioral Biology at the University of Wisconsin, the University of California, Berkeley, and the California Institute of Technology. His areas of research concern age and individual differences in cognitive abilities as well as behavioral economics, and the development of formal theoretical models in these areas. His research has been published in *Science*, *Psychological Review*, *Psychological Bulletin*, *Journal of Experimental Psychology: General*, *Psychological Science*, and *Psychonomic Bulletin & Review*, as well as more specialized journals.

John A. Nevin, known as Tony, received his Ph.D. from Columbia University in 1963. He taught at Swarthmore College until 1968, then returned to Columbia where he served two years as Department Chair. In 1972, he moved to the University of New Hampshire, where he remained until retirement in 1995. He now lives with his wife Nora on the island of Martha's Vineyard, and maintains research collaborations with colleagues at other institutions with the support of the National Institutes of Health. His recent work focuses on applications of the behavioral momentum metaphor, which he developed over several decades with data from pigeons trained on multiple schedules of reinforcement, to the persistence of severe problem behavior in children with intellectual and developmental disabilities. The postretirement persistence of his work is itself an instance of momentum, based on the many reinforcers he has enjoyed throughout his life.

Amy Odum is a Professor in the Department of Psychology at Utah State University. Her research interests are in basic behavioral phenomena, such as response persistence, sensitivity to delayed outcomes, conditional discriminations, and environmental influences on drug effects. Her work has been funded by the National Institute on Drug Abuse and the National Institute of Mental Health. She completed a postdoctoral fellowship at the University of Vermont's Human Behavioral Pharmacology Laboratory after earning her Ph.D. and M.A. in Psychology, specializing in Behavior Analysis, from West Virginia University. She received a B.S. in Psychology from the University of Florida. Dr. Odum has been Associate Editor for the *Journal of the*

Experimental Analysis of Behavior and President of the Society for the Experimental Analysis of Behavior and Division 25 of the American Psychological Association.

David C. Palmer studied inter-response times and conditioned reinforcement in pigeons at the University of Massachusetts under John Donahoe in the early 1980s. Upon graduation, he took a job teaching statistics and behavior analysis at Smith College, where he remains today. His interests in behavior analysis are broad, but his main contributions have all been attempts to extend Skinner's interpretive accounts of human behavior, particularly in the domains of language, memory, problem solving, and private events. He remains convinced that behavioral principles offer an adequate foundation for interpreting such phenomena. Together with John Donahoe, he authored the text, *Learning and complex behavior*, which was an attempt to justify such optimism.

Linda A. Parker is a Canada Research Chair in Behavioral Neuroscience and Professor of Psychology at the University of Guelph, Ontario, Canada. She focuses her research on chemicals found naturally in the human body that mimic chemicals in marijuana, the endogenous cannabinoids (endocannabinoids). These chemicals were only discovered in the 1990s, yet they are now known to play a role not only in control of nausea and vomiting, but also in learning, memory, neuroprotection against stroke and cancer, appetite, reward and addiction. Linda Parker's program of research cuts across the traditional boundaries of Psychology, Pharmacology, and Neurobiology, contributing not only to understanding basic processes of learning, but also to how those processes impact on food selection, addiction, and gastrointestinal malaise.

Caitlin S. Peplinski is a graduate student at the University of Wisconsin–Milwaukee (UWM). She completed her bachelor's degree at Bradley University in 2007 with a major in Psychology. She was admitted to UWM's program in 2008 and is developing clinical research expertise in the assessment and treatment of severe behavior disorders.

Nancy M. Petry earned a Ph.D. from Harvard University in 1994. In 1996, she joined the faculty of the University of Connecticut Health Center, where she is Professor of Medicine in the Calhoun Cardiology Center. Dr. Petry conducts research on the treatment of behavioral disorders, ranging from substance use to gambling disorders, and she developed the prize reinforcement system that has been widely applied and disseminated in the context of treating substance use disorders. She has published over 250 articles, and her work is funded by the National Institutes of Health. She serves as a consultant and advisor for the National Institutes of Health and the Veterans Administration and was a member of the Substance Use and Related Disorders Workgroup for the DSM-5.

Karen Pryor is a behavioral biologist and writer. Trained at Cornell, the University of Hawaii, and Rutgers, she has focused on learning and behavior in areas ranging from human lactation to marine mammal ethology to autism. Never an academic (though an active guest lecturer), she served three years as a presidential appointee to the federal Marine Mammal Commission, and a decade as a consultant on dolphin behavior to the tuna fishing industry. Since 1992, Pryor and her associates have played an important role in popularizing marker-based training in dog training, in zoos, and in human care and education. In addition to technical publications, her popular books include *Nursing your baby* (on breast feeding), *Lads before the wind* (on dolphin training), *Don't shoot the dog!* (on positive training for humans), and *Reaching the animal mind* (on training and neuroscience). Pryor has three children and seven grandchildren, and presently lives in Boston.

Brittany C. Putnam is a graduate student at the University of Wisconsin–Milwaukee (UWM). She completed her bachelor's degree at Fairfield University in 2011 with a double major in Psychology and French. She was admitted to UWM's program in 2011 and is developing clinical research expertise in the assessment and treatment of severe behavior disorders.

Kenneth Ramirez is Executive Vice-president of Animal Care and Animal Training at Chicago's Shedd Aquarium. A 35+ year veteran of animal care and training, he is a biologist and animal behaviorist who has worked professionally in both the zoological and the dog training fields. Ramirez has been active in several professional organizations, including the International Marine Animal Trainer's Association, of which he is a past president. Ken has also been on the faculty of Karen Pryor's Clicker Expos since 2004 and he teaches a graduate course on animal training at Western Illinois University. Ramirez has written many scientific publications and popular articles and has authored the book *Animal training: Successful animal management through positive reinforcement*, published in 1999.

William A. Roberts has carried out research on a number of problems in animal cognition, including working memory, spatial memory, timing, numerical processing, concept learning, episodic-like memory, and metamemory since 1970. His work has been continuously supported by discovery grants from the Natural Sciences and Engineering Research Council of Canada, and he has published approximately 150 articles and book chapters. He has served as editor of the journal *Learning and Motivation* since 2000. His textbook, *Principles of animal cognition*, was published in 1998. Recent high-profile publications include an article, "Are animals stuck in time," in the *Psychological Bulletin*, two review articles on episodic-like memory in *Current Biology*, a research report on the temporal basis of episodic-like memory published in *Science*, a review of the comparative study of mental time travel in *Current Directions in Cognitive Science*, and a review of the study of metacognition in animals in *Comparative Cognition and Behavior Reviews.*

John M. Roll is Senior Vice-chancellor at the Washington State University (WSU) Health Sciences Campus located in Spokane, WA. He has faculty appointments in Nursing, Psychology, Neuroscience, Health Policy, and Administration as well as in the University of Washington School of Medicine. He is the Director of the WSU Program of Excellence in Addictions Research and Co-Director of the WSU Translational Addiction Research Center. Dr. Roll's work has focused on human behavioral pharmacology, the development and refinement of behavioral interventions for addiction and other psychiatric disorders, as well as technology transfer issues.

Sarah R. Sterlace received her undergraduate degree from University of California, Los Angeles (UCLA) and is a doctoral candidate in the Department of Psychology at UCLA with a concentration of Behavioral Neuroscience. Her primary research interests include molecular mechanisms that underlie fear learning and how fear memories are formed. Sarah has been investigating specific amygdalar nuclei and their individual contributions to fear acquisition, consolidation, and retrieval.

Elizabeth M. Street, who was a member of the faculty at Central Washington University (CWU) for 33 years, is a board-certified behavior analyst. A graduate of West Virginia University, Dr. Street was a doctoral student under Julie Vargas who first introduced her to Ogden Lindsley and Precision Teaching. Prior to taking a faculty position at CWU, Dr. Street held positions at the University of Illinois Child Behavior Laboratory under Sidney Bijou, at Help and Education for the Emotionally Disturbed School in Champaign, Illinois, at the Adolph Meyer Mental Health Center in Decatur, Illinois, and at the University of Wisconsin–LaCrosse. She has served for more than 30 years as a consultant and trainer for Morningside Academy in Seattle Washington where Precision Teaching is integral to its educational approach. Dr. Street's most recent book, coauthored with Kent Johnson, is *Response to intervention and precision teaching: Creating synergy in the classroom.*

Richard F. Thompson is Emeritus Keck Professor and University Professor of Psychology, Biological Sciences and Neuroscience at the University of Southern California (USC). His research concerns mammalian brain substrates and mechanisms of learning and memory. He has written or edited many books and published 450 research papers. After earning his M.S. and Ph.D. in Psychology and holding a post-doctoral fellowship in Neurophysiology, he joined the faculty at the University of Oregon Medical School and then at the University of California, Irvine, Harvard and Stanford Universities, before joining USC in 1987. Dr. Thompson was elected to the National Academy of Sciences, the American Academy of Arts and Sciences, and the American Philosophical Society. He has received many honors including the Distinguished Scientific Contribution Award from the American Psychological Association, the Lashley Award from the American Philosophical Society, and the Gold Medal for Lifetime Achievement in the Science of Psychology from the American Psychological Foundation.

Travis Thompson received his Ph.D. From the University of Minnesota and served as a Postdoctoral Fellow at the University of Maryland. He was a Visiting Fellow at the University of Cambridge before serving as an Assistant to Full Professor at the University of Minnesota. He then held faculty positions at Vanderbilt University and the University of Kansas Medical School before returning to the University of Minnesota where he is currently a Professor in the Department of Special Education. Dr. Thompson has received awards from Divisions 25 and 33 of the American Psychological Association (APA) and from the Society for the Advancement of Behavior Analysis. He has served as president of Divisions 28 and 33 of APA and on the Executive Council of the Association for Behavior Analysis International. He has given invited addresses in 47 states and 16 countries. He has published 30 books and 243 professional articles and chapters.

Jeffrey H. Tiger in an Assistant Professor in the Psychology Department of the University of Wisconsin–Milwaukee. He received his Ph.D. from the University of Kansas and completed a postdoctoral fellowship at the Center for Autism Spectrum Disorders within the Munroe-Meyer Institute of the University of Nebraska Medical Center. His research has an emphasis on developing effective assessment and intervention practices for individuals with developmental and/or sensory disabilities, while at the same time extending our knowledge of the basic processes that result in behavior change. Dr. Tiger is a Board Certified Behavior Analyst and serves on the Board of Editors for the *Journal of Applied Behavior Analysis.*

Janet S. Twyman, Ph.D., BCBA, is a noted proponent of effective instruction and using technology to produce change. A career educator, she has been a preschool and elementary school teacher, a principal and administrator, and a university professor. Dr. Twyman has served on the boards of numerous organizations including the Cambridge Center for Behavioral Studies (chairing the Education Group) and PEER International (assisting township schools in Port Elizabeth, South Africa). In 2007–8, she served as President of the Association for Behavior Analysis International. Currently an Associate Professor of Pediatrics at the University of Massachusetts Medical School/Shriver Center, Dr. Twyman is also the Director of Innovation and Technology for the United States Department of Education's National Center on Innovations in Learning. She has published and presented internationally on evidence-based innovations in education and the systems that support them to produce meaningful difference in learners' lives.

Ariana Vanderveldt received her undergraduate degree from James Madison University and is an advanced graduate student in the Behavior, Brain, and Cognition program of the Department of Psychology at Washington University in St. Louis. Her primary research interests are in choice and decision-making. Ariana has been investigating how outcomes in choices are devalued when they are delayed in time and/or uncertain to occur, and how people make decisions that involve trade-offs among multiple attributes.

Drina Vurbic is a graduate student and National Institute of Drug Addiction Predoctoral Fellow in the Department of Psychology at the University of Vermont. She received her B.S. degree in Psychology from Baldwin-Wallace University and M.A. degree from the University of Vermont. Her research focuses mainly on the associative processes involved in the development and treatment of drug abuse, overeating/obesity, and anxiety disorders.

Stanley J. Weiss is Emeritus Professor of Experimental Psychology at American University and former Department Chair. He received his Ph.D. from Ohio State University (with Reed Lawson) and B.A. from the City College of New York. For almost 30 years, National Institute of Mental Health and/or National Institute of

Drug Abuse have funded his research. He was President of the Eastern Psychological Association and a Fulbright Scholar/Researcher at Pavlov Medical University in St. Petersburg, Russia. He was elected Fellow of the American Psychological Association's Divisions 3 (Experimental Psychology) and 25 (Experimental Analysis of Behavior), the Association for Psychological Science and the Eastern Psychological Association. He has been a Visiting Professor at Cambridge University, the Hebrew University, the University of St. Andrews, the University of New South Wales and the University of Colorado. Since 2002, he has convened the Winter Conference on Animal Learning & Behavior. His research is concerned with stimulus control and incentive motivation, the role of learning mechanisms in drug abuse and treatment plus biological constraints on learning.

Douglas A. Williams has maintained a nationally funded laboratory (Natural Sciences and Engineering Council of Canada) for some 20 years. Among his publications are more than a dozen articles in the prestigious *Journal of Experimental Psychology*, most coauthored with students from the mainly undergraduate University of Winnipeg. Many highly motivated undergraduates have made substantive contributions to his research program, later pursuing their own academic, research, or professional careers. He joined the faculty in 1991 after receiving a doctorate from the University of Minnesota under the guidance of J. Bruce Overmier and serving as a Killam Postdoctoral Fellow at Dalhousie University with Vincent M. LoLordo.

Preface

The *Wiley-Blackwell Handbook of Operant and Classical Conditioning* surveys the field of contemporary behavior analysis. The book is organized into four parts. Part I summarizes the basic principles, theories, and physiological substrates of classical conditioning. Habituation, a related fundamental form of learning, is also covered. Part II describes applications of classical conditioning. These applications include taste aversions, phobias, and immune system responses. Part III provides a review of the basic operant conditioning literature. Coverage ranges from traditional topics, such as basic operant principles and schedules of reinforcement, to the more contemporary topics of behavioral economics, behavioral momentum, and dynamic changes in reinforcer effectiveness. The final section of the book covers the growing field of applied behavior analysis. These applications range from intensive behavioral treatment for children with developmental disabilities to organizational behavior management to behavior analytic approaches to aging.

We chose to cover the topics of operant and classical conditioning in the same book because the basic principles of these two types of learning are similar. Therefore, an understanding of one type of conditioning can contribute to an understanding of the other type. As a result, the two types of learning are traditionally covered in a single volume. We chose to cover both basic principles and applications in the same book because we could not leave out either topic without ignoring a substantial part of the current literature on conditioning. In addition, we believe that applications cannot be properly understood without coverage of the principles on which they are based. Likewise, the understanding of basic principles is enriched and enhanced by a discussion of their applications.

There are many potential topics to cover in the broad areas of classical and operant conditioning. The choice of topics for this book is somewhat arbitrary. We have tried to select topics that are broad in coverage and, therefore, interesting to a relatively wide audience. This is particularly true in the section on applied behavior analysis in humans. With the exceptions of the chapters on autism and aging, we have tried to select topics that affect almost everyone, rather than concentrate on treatments for particular populations. We have also tried to select topics in which substantial research progress has been made since earlier conditioning handbooks were published and we gave priority to topics that were not covered recently in other books. Some topics were given a slightly lower priority because of less broad interest, slower recent research progress, or an ability to integrate these topics into other chapters. Our choices were also limited by our own prejudices and perspectives and by an occasional inability to find an appropriate and available author. We acknowledge that many worthy topics were omitted from this book.

The book is designed for advanced undergraduates and graduate students. It should provide a reference book for academicians, and professionals in behavior analysis including those who wish to conduct research in the area of conditioning, those who wish to use conditioning techniques as a baseline for understanding the effects of other variables (e.g., drugs), and those who wish to use conditioning techniques to either understand or treat challenging behaviors.

The chapters contained within this volume provide a summary of the chosen subfields within behavior analysis. Each author was chosen specifically for his or her expertise. Without the authors' dedication to this project, this book would not be possible. We are sincerely indebted to each contributor. We would also like to thank the dedicated staff at Wiley-Blackwell. Andrew Peart provided much-needed support and advice during the early stages of the project. We are also grateful to Karen Shield and Rosemary Morlin for their help with clearing copyright permissions and copyediting the book.

Frances K. McSweeney and Eric S. Murphy
January 2014

Part I
Basic Classical Conditioning

1

Principles of Pavlovian Conditioning

Description, Content, Function

Daniel A. Gottlieb and Elizabeth L. Begej

Although both early human memory researchers and behaviorists studied processes that today would be considered Pavlovian, Ivan Pavlov is credited with discovering classical conditioning and first officially describing the process to an English-speaking audience with the publication of *Conditioned reflexes* in 1927. Pavlov's systematic investigation of Pavlovian conditioning uncovered most of the primary phenomena, and his sharp and nuanced discussions are still relevant today.

Gottlieb (2011) defined Pavlovian, or classical, conditioning as the "adjustments organisms make in response to observing the temporal relations among environmental or proprioceptive stimuli." The most well-known form involves pairing a neutral conditioned stimulus (CS) with a biologically relevant unconditioned stimulus (US) that automatically elicits an unconditioned response (UR), leading the CS to elicit a conditioned response (CR) qualitatively similar to the UR. Pavlov's first reported example used dogs as subjects, a metronome CS, food as the US, and salivation as the UR and CR (Pavlov, 1927, p. 26).

Pavlovian conditioning is most clearly defined and constrained by its method, which involves maintaining strict control over the presentation of stimuli. There appear to be few clear principles that distinguish Pavlovian conditioning from other forms of associative learning, such as instrumental learning and human associative memory, and we agree with Rescorla and Solomon (1967)'s conclusion the Pavlovian conditioning is most distinct in how determined the form of the learned response is by the choice of US. Pavlovian responding is also characteristically resistant to instrumental contingencies. For example, it is difficult to prevent a pigeon from pecking (CR) at a discrete key light (CS) paired with food (US), even if pecking prevents the delivery of food (Williams & Williams, 1969).

The Wiley Blackwell Handbook of Operant and Classical Conditioning, First Edition.
Edited by Frances K. McSweeney and Eric S. Murphy.

Overview

Basic Excitatory Phenomena

Acquisition is the primary phenomenon of Pavlovian conditioning and refers to the growth in conditioned responding resulting from pairing a CS and US over time (Pavlov, 1927, p. 26). A CS that produces conditioned responding is sometimes referred to as an excitor. An example of an excitor is a brief tone that, due to repeated pairings with an air puff to the eye, elicits anticipatory eyeblinking.

An animal that has learned to blink to a tone may also blink when presented with a novel auditory stimulus. The magnitude of this generalized responding is a function of the similarity of the new stimulus to the originally trained CS (Pavlov, 1927, p. 111). Generalization functions can be modified by discrimination learning, in which some stimuli are reinforced while others are nonreinforced. For example, the generalized responding from a tone to a burst of white noise can be reduced by interspersing presentations of the noise alone.

A tone paired with an air puff to the eye gains more than the ability to elicit anticipatory blinking. It also develops the ability to serve as a conditioned reinforcer for another, second-order, CS (Pavlov, 1927, p. 33). Second-order conditioning tends to lead to lower levels of responding than does first-order conditioning. Thus, a light paired with a tone excitor will likely elicit less conditioned eyeblinking than will the tone itself. Conditioned reinforcers are contrasted with primary reinforcers that do not need prior training to be able to establish conditioned responding. Unlike in instrumental conditioning, Pavlovian reinforcers refer to stimuli that may be appetitive or aversive.

Basic Inhibitory Phenomena

Inhibitory phenomena are those that manifest in opposition to conditioned responding. When stimuli both reduce responding to simultaneously presented excitors and are slow to become excitors themselves, as compared to neutral stimuli, they are called inhibitors (Rescorla, 1969a). This type of inhibition is sometimes referred to as operational inhibition. It is contrasted with the theoretical inhibition that is used as an explanation for transient decreases in excitatory responding.

Extinction refers to the loss in conditioned responding that occurs when an excitor is subsequently presented in a manner that breaks the CS-US relationship (Pavlov, 1927, p. 49). For example, our tone excitor will stop eliciting conditioned eye-blinks if it is repeatedly presented alone. Although extinction is explained by appeal to inhibitory mechanisms, extinguished stimuli do not typically become operational inhibitors (Rescorla, 1969a).

Suppression of responding may also be observed when a nonreinforced stimulus is interspersed among the reinforced trials of another CS and a US. For example, if noise alone presentations are interspersed among tone-air puff pairings, generalized responding to the noise will be reduced. The suppression of responding observed in a discrimination procedure is referred to as differential inhibition. Unlike extinguished stimuli, differentially conditioned stimuli may become operational inhibitors (Pavlov, 1927, p. 120).

A particularly powerful form of differential inhibition results from a conditioned inhibition procedure in which a stimulus is nonreinforced in the presence of an excitor that is reinforced when presented alone. For example, if our tone signals an air puff except when it is presented together with a light, the light will become a conditioned inhibitor capable of passing the operational tests for inhibition (Pavlov, 1927, p. 68).

Perhaps it is not surprising that with extended training, organisms may come to withhold responding to a CS until closer to the time of the US. The decrease in responding to early parts of a CS that may result from extended training is referred to as inhibition of delay (Pavlov, 1927, p. 88).

Basic Framework

Early theorists most often adopted a contiguity view of learning, in which the pairing of stimuli in time and space was the necessary and sufficient condition for generating conditioned responding. Although Hull (1943) expanded on this view in arguing that drive reduction was also necessary for learning, it is his other contributions that have made him central to contemporary understandings of Pavlovian processes.

Hull (1943) adopted the view of Pavlovian conditioning as an associative process by which the magnitude of the association determined the magnitude of conditioned responding. He presented a simple mathematical learning rule that specified the change in associative (habit) strength that resulted from the pairing of a CS and a US. The vast majority of subsequent quantitative models developed within the associative framework contain Hull's simple learning algorithm (Mackintosh, 1975; Pearce, 1987; Rescorla & Wagner, 1972; Wagner, 1981).

Hull (1943) helped to cement a view of Pavlovian conditioning as an incremental trial-based process involving changes in the associative strength between stimuli. The parameters of his model are what were originally thought to be the determinants of Pavlovian learning. Primary was the number of trials. Secondary included three durations related to the CS-US interval: the length of the CS, the temporal gap between the CS and US, and the extension of the CS past the US; as well as two salience parameters, one for the CS and one for the US.

Hull's Choices

CS-US Interval

Delay Conditioning. Most demonstrations of acquisition use a delay conditioning procedure where CS offset coincides with US onset. As such, CS duration is the only determinant of the CS-US interval in delay conditioning. There appear to be two conflicting ideas related to effects of CS duration. The first is that there is an optimal CS-US interval that is highly procedure-dependent. For skeletal muscle CRs, like eyeblink conditioning, the optimal CS-US interval is often a fraction of a second (Gormezano & Kehoe, 1981), but for other types of CRs, such as sign-tracking and conditioned fear, the optimal interval may be multiple seconds (Gibbon, Baldock, Locurto, Gold, & Terrace, 1977; Yeo, 1974).

That there is an optimal CS-US interval conflicts with the other main idea about CS duration, that shortening it promotes acquisition (Lattal, 1999). This conflict is likely a result of optimal durations being at the low end of the range of durations that can establish conditioned responding. What appears most relevant is that certain procedures allow for conditioning with CS-US intervals much longer than others. In fear conditioning, CS durations of several minutes can be effective (Kamin, 1965), and in conditioned taste aversion, CS-US trace intervals of up to 24 hours can establish conditioned aversions (Etscorn & Stephens, 1973).

Trace Conditioning. When the CS terminates prior to US onset, acquisition of conditioned responding may be strongly impaired (Ellison, 1964). This procedure is known as trace conditioning, referring to one explanation for the conditioned responding that does occur: A memory trace of the CS is contiguously paired with the US. Although a gap between CS offset and US onset impairs conditioned responding, the impairment does not necessarily reflect a failure to learn. Trace conditioning can lead a CS to become inhibitory (LoLordo & Fairliss, 1985). It also may lead to increasing levels of responding during the time between CS offset and US onset (Marlin, 1981).

Simultaneous Conditioning. Early research suggested that simultaneous CS-US presentation did not lead to conditioned responding (Kimble, 1961), but it is clear that in many cases it does (Heth & Rescorla, 1973). Simultaneous conditioning may lead to different forms of learning than does forward conditioning. For example, in flavor conditioning, simultaneous, but not delay, conditioning prevents the reacquisition of an extinguished preference (Higgins & Rescorla, 2004).

Backward Conditioning. Backward conditioning refers to presenting the US prior to presenting the CS. Typically, US offset and CS onset coincide. After a small number of trials, it is not uncommon to observe excitatory conditioned responding, but after further trials, the responding diminishes and the CS may become an inhibitor (Heth, 1976). One complexity is that a backward CS may pass an operational test for inhibition while at the same time establishing excitatory second-order conditioning to another CS (Barnet & Miller, 1996). Romaniuk and Williams (2000) provided an explanation for this by demonstrating that the initial 3 s of a 30 s backwards CS was excitatory while the remaining 27 s was inhibitory. Adding a 3 s gap between US offset and CS onset eliminated excitatory responding, strengthened inhibition, and prevented second-order conditioning.

Stimulus Intensity

US Magnitude. Some argue that acquisition of conditioned responding should be broken down into components that include the point of acquisition and the asymptotic magnitude of responding (Gallistel, Fairhurst, & Gibbon, 2004). In general, increasing US intensity or number tends to increase the magnitude of conditioned responding (Mackintosh, 1974, pp. 70–71); however, although Morris and Bouton (2006) detected effects of US magnitude on the point of acquisition in aversive and appetitive procedures with rats, how strongly US magnitude influences the point of acquisition is still not clear. Unlike US intensity, the effects of increasing US duration are not consistent across procedures (Mackintosh, 1974).

CS Intensity. Razran (1957), in summarizing 161 Russian studies relevant to effects of CS intensity, concluded that there was abundant evidence that increasing CS intensity increased both the rate of acquisition and the asymptotic magnitude of performance. A caveat was that when CS intensity was very high, performance was sometimes impaired. Outside of Russia, results of varying CS intensity have been more equivocal (Mackintosh, 1974, pp. 41–45).

Mackintosh (1974) suggests that effects of CS intensity, like those of US duration, are more likely to be observed in within-subject than in between-subject experiments, perhaps explaining some of the earlier Russian findings. This explanation is consistent with findings showing that when stimuli are presented in a way in which they are available for comparison, higher valued ones are augmented (positive contrast) while lower valued ones are diminished (negative contrast) (Flaherty, 1996).

Form of Acquisition

A second aspect of Hull's (1943) model was that it predicted a particular geometric form of growth. Explicit is the mathematical form. Implicit is the gradual and increasingly slow progression of learning. The left side of Figure 1.1 shows a group-averaged learning curve for 16 pigeons in a 32 trials/day autoshaping procedure. Plotted is the rate/min of keypecking to a 5 s keylight CS that immediately preceded a 5 s access to grain US. The right side of Figure 1.1 shows a learning curve for one of the 16 pigeons. Both the learning curves start with a period characterized by the absence of conditioned responding, followed by a growth in conditioned responding until an asymptotic level is reached. The curves differ in that the individual curve shows a longer latency before conditioned responding emerges and a steeper rise. Gallistel et al. (2004) demonstrated that over a wide range of Pavlovian procedures,

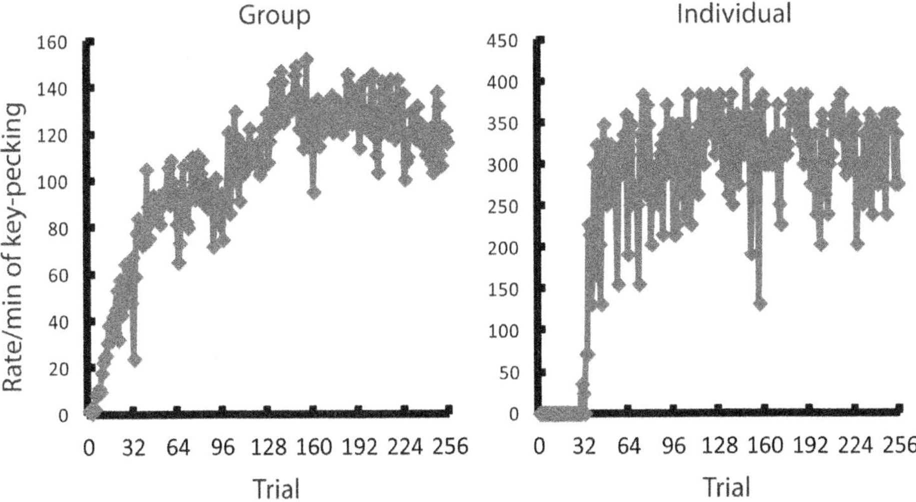

Figure 1.1 Left: group-averaged learning curve for 16 pigeons in a 32 trials/day autoshaping procedure. Right: learning curve for 1 of the 16 pigeons.

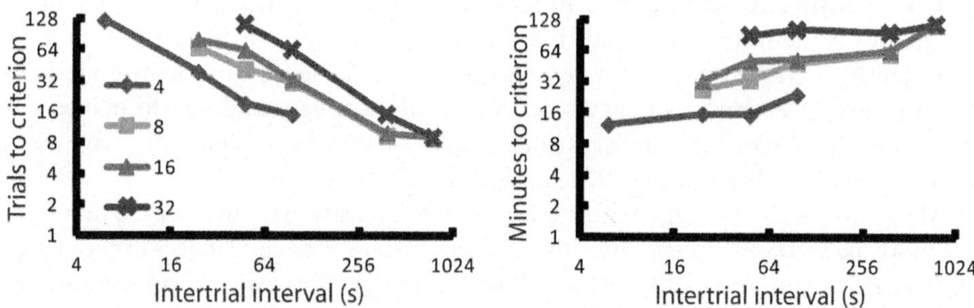

Figure 1.2 Replot of pigeon autoshaping data from Gibbon et al. (1977), Experiment 1. Left: # trials to criterion as a function of ITI. Right: # cumulative training hours to criterion as a function of ITI. Groups differed in CS duration (4–32 s).

group-averaged learning curves obscure the relative abruptness of individual learning curves. This abruptness suggests that two separate components of the learning curve can be meaningfully distinguished, the point of acquisition and the asymptotic magnitude of conditioned responding.

Trial Repetition

Repeatedly pairing a CS and a US leads to acquisition of conditioned responding. This does not mean that the number of repetitions is a primary determinant; increasing the number of trials is almost always accompanied by a corresponding increase in cumulative training time and number of sessions. It is reasonable to ask what is known about each of these factors in isolation.

Training Time. It is well established that increasing training time by lengthening the intertrial interval (ITI) increases the likelihood that an animal will develop conditioned responding, speeds acquisition, and promotes higher levels of conditioned responding. A particularly striking example is a quantitative analysis of the effects of ITI on pigeon autoshaping (Gibbon et al., 1977), replotted in Figure 1.2. The left side shows trials to criterion as a function of ITI. The right side shows hours of cumulative ITI to criterion. Cumulative ITI more strongly predicted rate of acquisition than did number of trials.

Number of Sessions. Kehoe and Macrae (1994) presented the most impressive evidence that increasing the number of sessions independently promotes acquisition. Their analysis of the literature that showed that rabbit eyeblink conditioning could be either fast or slow to develop depending on the number of trials per session. The left panel of Figure 1.3 replots their best-fitting function relating trials per session to trials to acquisition along with a new curve relating trials per session to sessions to criterion. As with cumulative ITI, number of sessions more strongly predicted rate of acquisition than did number of trials.

Number of Trials. Gottlieb (2008) assessed for the effects of number of trials on acquisition of conditioned approach behavior in mice and rats by varying the number of trials animals received in daily sessions of the same duration. In between-subject experiments, there was little evidence that up to 16-fold differences in the number

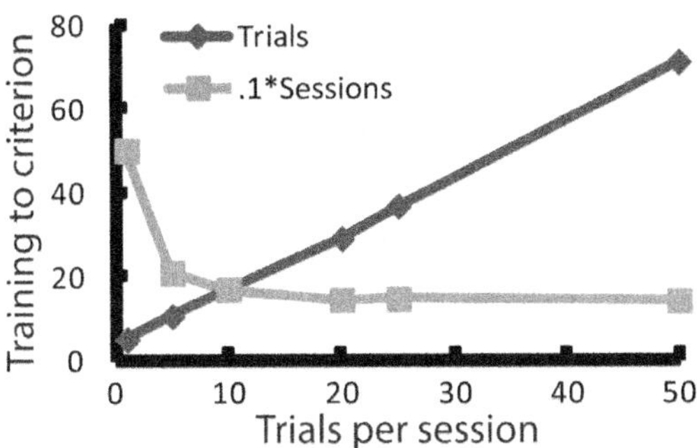

Figure 1.3 Replot of function determined by Kehoe and Macrae (1994) relating trials per session to trials to acquisition across a number of rabbit eyeblink conditioning studies. Overlaid is function relating trials per session to sessions to acquisition.

of trials per session promoted acquisition, although some impairment has been observed in the case of animals receiving only a single trial per session (Gottlieb & Prince, 2012). Gottlieb and Prince (2012) concluded that within a session, adding trials between any pair has little effect. As with US magnitude and CS intensity, within-subject effects of number of trials appear more readily obtainable than do between-subject effects (Gottlieb & Rescorla, 2010).

Figures 1.2 and 1.3 clearly point to repetitions over time being more important than number of repetitions in establishing conditioned responding. Figure 1.1 illustrates that the gradual nature of learning is still being called into question. Hull's (1943) choices may have been reasonable, but only those relating to the CS-US interval have received unequivocal support. Even there, Hull did not have a mechanism by which trace and backward conditioning could lead to inhibition.

Content of Learning

The simplest framework for understanding what is learned in Pavlovian conditioning is the Stimulus-Response (S-R) framework of behaviorism that pre-dated the first unambiguous reports of Pavlovian conditioning (Guthrie, 1935; Hull, 1943; Thorndike, 1911). Within this framework, animals come to reflexively respond to a CS that has been contiguously paired with a UR.

Pavlov (1927) envisioned learning as a process by which CS and US neural centers become linked through asynchronous mutual activation. As a result, the CS comes to activate the US center, leading to responding. This reflects a view from within the Stimulus-Stimulus (S-S) framework, in which learning results in representations of the CS and US becoming linked. From an S-S view, a tone activates the idea of shock, and so the rabbit blinks. From an S-R view, a tone elicits a blink. The *idea of shock* is a mental event that is not directly observable, and so S-S theories are inherently cognitive in nature, early attempts to model the mind to explain behavior. Even so, like the early behaviorists, Pavlov considered the CR to be automatic and identical to the UR in form.

Two strategies have been used to try to show evidence of S-S learning. The first attempted to demonstrate learning in the absence of a UR. For instance, Brogden

(1939), showed learning in a sensory preconditioning procedure that involved first pairing two neutral CSs before pairing one with the US and showing that the other also came to elicit conditioned responding. A more recent strategy has been to modify the value of the US after it has been used to train a CS. Any post-conditioning influence on the CS would be evidence for S-S learning.

One way to accomplish this is to use second-order conditioning and to modify the first-order stimulus through extinction. For example, one might first pair a tone with an air puff, then a light with the tone. The key question is whether the conditioned eyeblinking to the light is then affected by extinction of the tone. Supporting an S-R view, in a number of appetitive and aversive procedures and species, extinguishing the first-order stimulus has little effect on responding to the second-order stimulus and so provides no evidence of S-S learning (Rizley & Rescorla, 1972).

A second way to assess for S-S learning is to directly modify the primary reinforcer in a first-order conditioning experiment. Often, this is done by pairing a food reinforcer with illness (Holland & Straub, 1979). The results of primary reinforcer devaluation studies show decreased conditioned responding due to US devaluation and so provide evidence for S-S learning.

A way to reconcile these findings can be found in the few second-order conditioning studies that have devalued the primary reinforcer and assessed for effects on the second-order CS. Devaluation both through poisoning and motivational shifts has been found to reduce responding to a second-order CS (Ross, 1986; Winterbauer & Balleine, 2005). This suggests that in some cases the failure to adjust conditioned responding of a second-order CS after extinction of the first-order CS may not be due to exclusive S-R learning. Rather, organisms may have formed a direct association between the second-order CS and the primary US, despite those stimuli not having been contiguously paired.

Tolman (1932) adopted an S-S framework but rejected Pavlov's (1927) notion of stimulus substitution. He held instead that a CS predicts US occurrence and so leads to preparatory responding. One distinction between Pavlov's view and Tolman's is that for Pavlov the key element that determines behavior is the UR, while for Tolman it is the US. This allows Tolman to accommodate CRs that appear qualitatively different from URs. Although Mackintosh (1974) points out that most CRs look like URs, and that the exceptions may not prove fatal to the idea of CR-UR identity, there are a number of cases where the measured CR is either unrelated or superficially opposite to the UR. For example, the CR to shock is often freezing, whereas the UR involves vigorous motor activity. In conditioned tolerance procedures, the CR is may be exactly the opposite of the UR, as in the case of cues paired with morphine that lead to hyperalgesia and not analgesia (Siegel, 1983).

Contingency

Degraded Contingency

Partial Reinforcement. A major change in thinking about Pavlovian conditioning came about from studies that varied the proportion of trials in which the CS and US were paired. One way to vary this is to intersperse nonreinforced presentations of the CS. This has the effect of reducing the probability that the US will follow the CS and is referred to as partial reinforcement (Gottlieb, 2005).

Although the results from studies of partial reinforcement are not entirely consistent, reducing probability of reinforcement most often impairs acquisition of conditioned responding (Mackintosh, 1974). When the number of reinforced trials and the time between CS presentations are held constant, continuous reinforcement more often leads to higher levels of asymptotic responding than does partial reinforcement, though it has relatively little influence on the number of reinforced trials before conditioned responding emerges. There is also some evidence that deleterious effects of reducing the probability of reinforcement might manifest most strongly in whether organisms acquire the conditioned response at all and not in how rapidly it emerges or how vigorous it becomes (Gottlieb, 2005).

Intertrial USs and Explicit Unpairing. The effects on acquisition of presenting USs that are not preceded by CSs (unsignaled USs) are less ambiguous than the effects of partial reinforcement: Unsignaled USs strongly impair conditioned responding. This impairment is graded such that when sufficient USs are presented during the ITI to equate reinforcement rate during the CS and in its absence, a CS will not come to elicit conditioned responding (Rescorla, 1966, 1968). Furthermore, when the ITI reinforcement rate exceeds that during the CS, the CS will develop inhibitory properties (Rescorla, 1969b). This means that CS-US contiguity is not sufficient to generate conditioned responding. Nor may contiguity in the operational sense be necessary for learning. The explicitly unpaired condition, where USs are only delivered during the ITI, leads to inhibitory learning even though the CS and US are never contiguously paired. It appears that what most predicts conditioned responding is the relative likelihood of the US in the presence and absence of the CS, a quantity referred to as CS-US contingency.

Content: Additions to Associative Structure

It appears that what is essential in acquiring conditioned responding is discriminating the predictive value of the CS from that of the background. These findings necessitated that the associative structure expand to include associations between the background (context) and discrete stimuli, associations that either interfere with the acquisition or the expression of conditioned responding (Bouton, 1993; Gibbon & Balsam, 1981; Miller & Schachtman, 1985; Rescorla & Wagner, 1972).

Relative Contingency: Cue Competition Phenomena

Stimulus Compounds

Stimuli are never presented in isolation. When the experimenter lacks control over other stimuli in the environment, those stimuli are referred to as background or contextual stimuli. When the experimenter creates complexes of stimuli from individual elements, those stimuli are referred to as compounds. The study of compound conditioning reflects the understanding that organisms face the problem of discriminating stimuli that are informative from all the others that may be co-occurring.

When an excitor is first presented in compound with a neutral CS, it is not uncommon for there to be less responding than to the excitor alone. This is referred to as external inhibition, as the neutral stimulus appears to be inhibiting the conditioned response (Pavlov, 1927, p. 44). Alternatively, the decrement can be thought of as a result of the stimulus compound being represented as its own holistic stimulus that only partially generalizes to the excitor (Pearce, 1987). This distinction reflects two distinct views of Pavlovian processes. In one, stimuli can be reduced to elements that, when combined, maintain all their essential properties (Rescorla & Wagner, 1972). In the other, every stimulus, compound or not, is a distinct element (Guthrie, 1935; Pearce, 1987). Although this conceptual distinction is nontrivial, the quantitative realization of it appears to rely largely on the degree to which the predictive values of simultaneously presented stimuli are summed or averaged (Wagner, 2003). Reports of excitatory summation are common (Pavlov, 1927; Wagner, 1971), but less so are accounts that both compare compound responding to the maximal element and that attempt to rule out performance factors relating to greater stimulation when the compound stimulus, and not an element, is presented (Rescorla, 1997).

Compound Conditioning

Overshadowing. Overshadowing refers to a reduction in conditioned responding when a CS is reinforced in compound compared to if it were reinforced alone. For example, a light paired with an air puff may lead to substantially less anticipatory eyeblinking if it is conditioned in the presence of a tone than if it is conditioned alone. When stimuli differ in salience, one stimulus may completely overshadow the other (Mackintosh, 1971). Although overshadowing may not be complete, reports of mutual overshadowing in which both elements overshadow each other are uncommon (Kehoe, 1982).

Blocking. Blocking is one of the most important and well-established contemporary phenomena. It was first demonstrated by Kamin (1968) in a rat fear conditioning procedure. Kamin found that when a compound stimulus made up of a light and a noise was followed by shock, animals came to suppress ongoing bar pressing to the light alone. However, if the noise had previously been paired with shock, the light did not suppress bar pressing. Blocking provides strong evidence that contiguity is insufficient to generate conditioned responding, but it also suggests that contingency is insufficient, as well; in both of Kamin's groups, the contiguity and contingency between the light and the shock was equivalent.

Superconditioning. Blocking is an example of a more general principle by which individual CSs determine the acquisition of conditioned responding to other simultaneously presented stimuli. For example, if a light is established as a conditioned inhibitor of eyeblinking, subsequently conditioning a tone in the presence of the light can facilitate CR acquisition to the tone. This phenomenon is referred to as superconditioning (Williams & McDevitt, 2002; Wagner, 1971). A general principle to emerge is that the acquisition of conditioned responding to a CS trained in compound is an inverse function of the degree to which other simultaneously presented stimuli are predictive.

Protection from Extinction. If reinforcing a light in the presence of an excitatory tone can block the light from developing conditioned responding, nonreinforcing the light-tone compound may lead the light to become inhibitory (Holland, 1988). This phenomenon is referred to as protection from extinction, referring to the target CS preventing the blocking CS from fully extinguishing. When the target CS is an inhibitor, the protective effect may be even greater (Rescorla, 2003a).

Contingency Becomes Relative Contingency. Blocking and protection from extinction have their analogs in Rescorla's (1966, 1968, 1969b) contingency experiments. A random pairing procedure becomes a one-stage blocking procedure with the context playing the role of the blocker. Similarly, including the context as a CS turns the explicitly unpaired procedure into a one-stage protection from extinction procedure (the context is protected from extinction when the CS is present), which is the typical way of generating conditioned inhibition. Rescorla's contingency experiments, then, can be viewed as special cases of cue competition experiments.

Linear regression is the primary statistic researchers use to determine the relative contributions of predictor variables to particular outcomes. The outputs of regression analyses are measures of predictive strength (beta coefficients) that have been adjusted to take into account correlations amount predictor variables themselves. Cue competition phenomena suggest that in determining the predictive value of a stimulus, organisms take into account the predictive value of other co-present stimuli in a similar way. Indeed, the most influential associative model, the Rescorla-Wagner (R-W) Model (Rescorla & Wagner, 1972), is an algorithm that, when given enough information, asymptotically computes beta coefficients; when given insufficient information to parcel out predictive value to each element, as in the case of overshadowing, the R-W Model splits the difference among possible predictors. A more explicit regression mechanism is incorporated in the modeling of Gallistel and Gibbon (2000). It is informative that Pavlovian processes appear to be serving a similar function as a statistic developed to optimally allocate predictive value.

Overexpectation. If organisms are computing something like linear regression coefficients, then a compound made up of two predictors should lead to an expectation of an outcome that is greater than to either predictor alone. Returning to our example preparation, consider the situation in which both a light and a tone are separately trained to elicit conditioned eyeblinking. When they are then presented in compound, there should be a greater air puff expectation than when either CS is presented alone. But the compound is followed by the same air puff used to establish the individual CSs. This conflicting information should lead either to configuring (generation of an interaction term) or to a decrement in predictive value attributed to each element of the compound. Indeed, reinforcing a compound of two excitors can lead to a decrease in responding to either element, a phenomenon known as overexpectation (Lattal & Nakajima, 1998).

Relative Validity. Although the R-W Model was developed to account for cue competition, the phenomenon of relative validity poses a unique challenge (Rescorla & Wagner, 1972). Demonstrating relative validity involves comparing conditioned responding to a CS element that has been presented in two different kinds of discriminations. In one, the common element (X) has been reinforced in the presence of one CS and nonreinforced in the presence of another (AX+, BX−). In the other, the element is equally often reinforced and nonreinforced in the presence of the two other stimuli (AX+−, BX+−). Wagner, Logan, Haberlandt, and Price (1968) found that X leads to greater conditioned responding in the latter discrimination, demonstrating that the validity of a predictor depends on whether the other stimuli are better or worse predictors. Relative validity is clearly a cue competition phenomenon, but models like the R-W Model accommodate the effect only when the partially reinforced compounds have an asymptotic associative strength closer to that of a continuously reinforced stimulus than to that of a nonreinforced stimulus. However, recent evidence suggests that the associative strength of a partially reinforced stimulus is unbiased (Andrew & Harris, 2011).

Extinction of Conditioned Inhibibition. The most serious problem from a regression framework is that posed by conditioned inhibition: Nonreinforced presentations of an inhibitor do not extinguish the inhibition (Williams, 1986). Similarly, nonreinforcing a compound of an inhibitor and a neutral CS does not lead the neutral CS to become excitatory (Baker, 1974). Pavlovian theories find this intuitive finding difficult to accommodate.

Conditional Contingency

Occasion Setting

One complexity in viewing regression (or relative contingency) as a normative model of attributing predictive value is that it assumes a particular structure of the world in which the predictive values of stimuli do not systematically vary within a particular stimulus environment; however, it is possible for stimuli to have different predictive value depending on the local context. Consider, for example, a discrimination (A–, AX+) in which a tone-light compound (AX) is followed by air puff while the light (A) is separately nonreinforced. Although the regression solution attributes full predictive power to the tone (X), it is possible instead to frame the problem as one in which the light is predictive conditional on the presence of the tone. That is, instead of signaling the air puff, the tone signals that when the light is present the air puff is likely to occur. From this perspective, it is the light that controls conditioned eyeblinking and the tone that modulates this control.

To distinguish these possibilities, Ross and Holland (1981) took advantage of the fact that visual and auditory CSs paired with food evoke different behaviors in rats. They demonstrated that in an A–, AX+ simultaneous discrimination, the conditioned response was consistent with control by X. However, when X preceded and overlapped with A, the response was consistent with control by A. It appeared that in the serial discrimination, X did not gain the ability to elicit conditioned responding but rather set the occasion for A to elicit conditioned responding. This Pavlovian phenomenon of occasion setting has two common forms, positive and negative, referring to whether the occasion setter signals that a CS otherwise nonreinforced will be reinforced (positive occasion setting) or that a CS otherwise reinforced will be nonreinforced (negative occasion setting).

Holland (1992) distinguished occasion setters from simple CSs in three ways. The first, relating to response form, only applies to positive and not negative occasion setting. The second is that occasion setters do not lose their properties when they are either extinguished or reinforced on their own. The third distinguishing feature of occasion setters is that they tend to modulate responding to a smaller set of stimuli than do typical CSs. Holland (1992) originally concluded that occasion setters showed CS-US selectivity, as they failed to modulate responding to other CSs paired with the same US or to the original target CS paired with a different US. However, Rescorla (1985) showed that occasion setters can modulate responding to nontarget stimuli that have been targets of different occasion setters. This form of generalization reflects a level of abstraction that is more often associated with inferential accounts of information processing.

Interference Phenomena

The existence of occasion setting suggests that in attributing predictive value to stimuli, Pavlovian mechanisms are sensitive not only to relative but also to conditional contingencies. Behavior consistent with computations of conditional contingency can also be observed when the experimentally determined contingencies are solely conditional on time. This is the case when contingency is abruptly changed, for example when a tone signaling an air puff is suddenly presented alone. It is possible that organisms simply update their estimates as new information is acquired, but it is also possible that they maintain some form of conditional knowledge that certain contingencies are in effect at different times. Although there are a number of different treatments that involve abrupt changes in stimulus environment, we have chosen to focus on the three most common ways in which the predictive value of a single CS is abruptly changed.

CS Preexposure. Latent inhibition refers to a reduction in conditioned responding that is observed when nonreinforced CS trials are presented prior to conditioning (Lubow, 1973). Despite the name, latent inhibitors are slow to be established as appetitive or aversive excitors *or* inhibitors (Reiss & Wagner, 1972; Rescorla, 1971). That is, presenting a tone repeatedly without consequence makes it hard to learn *anything* about that tone. Context plays a large role. Latent inhibition is attenuated when a CS is preexposed in a different context from that of subsequent training and is also attenuated as a direct function of the amount of post-conditioning exposure to the preexposure/training context (Lubow, Rifkin, & Alek, 1976).

CS Pre-training. Counterconditioning refers to the procedure by which a CS is first trained with one US and then with another of opposite valence. This form of pre-training typically interferes with the acquisition of new conditioned responding (Konorski & Szwejkowska, 1956). For example, pairing a tone with shock makes it more difficult to then pair the tone with food and vice versa. Aversive-to-appetitive counterconditioning more reliably shows the interference effect than does appetitive-to-aversive counterconditioning (Bouton & Peck, 1992), though an impressive set of experiments by Nasser and McNally (2012) clearly establishes that appetitive-to-aversive interference can be consistently obtained.

CS Postexposure. Extinction refers to the procedure by which the contingency of an excitatory CS with a US is abruptly removed. It also refers to the reduction in conditioned responding that results (Vurbic & Bouton (this volume); Urcelay, 2012). Typically, extinction is accomplished by presenting the CS without the US, but it also occurs when the CS-US relationship is degraded in other ways, such as introducing a random relationship between CS and US (Delamater, 1996). Characteristic of extinction is that extinguished conditioned responding is highly susceptible to recovery, as with the passage of time (spontaneous recovery). An extinguished CS may also show recovery of responding when presented concurrently with a novel stimulus (disinhibition) or in a context in which an animal has had relatively little experience since an unsignaled US was last presented (reinstatement). Recent work has focused on the recovery that occurs when animals are tested outside the extinction context (renewal). Renewal is strongest when animals are trained and extinguished in different contexts and are tested in their training context (ABA renewal). It is weaker when training, extinction, and testing are conducted in different contexts (ABC renewal), and it is weakest, though still apparent, when training and extinction are conducted in the same context and testing occurs in a different one (AAB renewal) (Bouton, 2002).

It now appears that extinction is not unique. Whenever a second phase of training involves opposition of a response acquired in the first stage, as with counterconditioning and overexpectation, the first stage response shows recovery (Bouton & Peck, 1992; Peck & Bouton, 1990; Rescorla, 2007). These results strongly argue that excitatory learning is not fully erased but rather that its expression is selectively opposed by the superimposition of new inhibitory learning.

Findings such as these have led to the suggestion that inhibitory processes are particularly sensitive to disruption and may fade in time. Another possibility is that what is learned second is more sensitive to disruption than what is learned first. Distinguishing these possibilities depends on what happens to a stimulus that is first trained as a latent or conditioned inhibitor and then trained as an excitor. Although there is now some evidence for recovery of latent and conditioned inhibition (De La Casa & Lubow, 2002; Nelson, 2002), studies are few and there are notable failures to obtain (Rescorla, 2005).

The study of interference phenomena has shown that new learning does not fully erase old learning and that the subsequent expression of conditioned responding depends on temporal and physical context. Both occasion setting and the interference phenomena suggest that organisms are sensitive to conditional contingencies at different timescales.

Content: Hierarchical Associations

Within associative structure, conditional likelihoods are represented by hierarchical associations between modulators and CS-US associations. In occasion setting, modulators tend to be discrete stimuli, whereas in the interference phenomena, modulators tend to be contextual stimuli that may vary with the passage of time.

Time

Time is of central importance to Pavlovian conditioning, and there is evidence that organisms are not merely sensitive to it but that they encode specific durations. In the peak procedure, in which occasional nonreinforced probe trials with extended duration CSs are interspersed throughout acquisition, what is typically observed is normally distributed responding that peaks at the time of US delivery (Gallistel & Gibbon, 2000; Pavlov, 1927, p. 41). This timed behavior has been observed to emerge as soon as does conditioned responding (Balsam, Drew, & Yang, 2002) and to maintain throughout extinction (Guilhardi & Church, 2006). There is even evidence that this temporal encoding may precede the emergence of conditioned responding (Ohyama & Mauk, 2001).

In discussing the role of CS duration and ITI on acquisition, we did not mention another important regularity. If both the CS duration and the ITI are proportionately shortened or lengthened, the opposing beneficial and detrimental effects appear to cancel out. The ratio of ITI: CS-US interval (also called the C:T ratio) appears to be a powerful, though not perfect, predictor of the rate and magnitude of conditioned responding (Gibbon et al., 1977; Lattal, 1999).

Content: Addition of US Features

The growing acceptance of the importance of time as both a variable that influences conditioning as well as a variable that may be encoded has led to the most recent expansion of associative structure to include distinct features of the US (Delamater & Oakeshott, 2007). Although the view that USs have distinct sensory and motivational components is not new, that they may also have temporal features that represent when they occur relative to other stimuli, as well as hedonic and other features, marks a further departure from the view first proposed by Hull (1943). At the extreme are those who believe that the features of the US that are encoded include explicit statistical information about rates or probabilities of occurrence (e.g., Gallistel & Gibbon, 2000). From this perspective, associative strength is no longer a necessary construct, as the information provided by variations in associative strength is instead provided by representations of specific environmental quantities.

From Prediction to Performance

How Pavlovian Learning Translates into Conditioned Responding

Associative learning is inferred from amounts of conditioned responding, but how underlying learning manifests in behavior is neither well understood nor well specified. The typical assumption is that increases in responding reflect increases in estimates of associative strength. Unfortunately, the weakness of this assumption has made a number of important questions difficult to address. Recently, Rescorla (2000a) has described a compound testing technique that partially overcomes this limitation. He has used this technique to empirically address a number of important issues for the first time, such as the relative amounts of associative change when stimuli are conditioned in compound (Rescorla 2000a, 2001c), whether the superiority sometimes observed in retraining is due to difference in initial associative strength or difference in learning rate (Rescorla, 2002a), and whether the generalization gradient is broader for inhibition than excitation (Rescorla, 2002b). Although the questions Rescorla addressed are themselves important, it is the methodological advancement that will likely have the widest impact. We see no comparable situation where advancement in the logic of experimental design has allowed such a variety of theoretically important ideas to become testable. A sample of these designs and the first reported results from their use are presented in Table 1.1.

Table 1.1 Recent experimental designs that address previously untestable questions

Reference	*Phase 1*	*Phase 2*	*Phase 3*	*Test/Result*	*Interpretation*
Rescorla (2001a)	A+, C+, B−, D−	A+, B+		BC > AD	More change on early acquisition trials than on later trials
Rescorla (2001a)	A+, B+, C+, D+	A−, C−	A−, B−	BC < AD	More change on early extinction trials than on later trials
Rescorla (2002b)	A+, B−, C+, D−	A−, B−, C+, D+[1]		AD > BC	More change on reinforced trials than on nonreinforced trials
Rescorla (2002b)	A+, B−, C+, D−	A−, D+[2]		AD > BC	More inhibitory generalization than excitatory generalization
Rescorla (2002a)	A−, B−, C−, D−	A−, C−	A+, B+	BC > AD	Slower rate of learning with latent inhibitor than with novel CS
Rescorla (2002a)	A+, B−, C+, D−	A−, B−, C−, D−	A+, B+	BC > AD	Reacquisition faster due to head start and not faster learning rate
Rescorla (2003b)	A+, B−, C+, D−	A−, B−, C−, D−	AB+	AD > BC	Reacquisition also faster due to higher learning rate

Note: Letters refer to CSs, + = reinforcement, − = nonreinforcement.
[1] Brief training in Phase 2.
[2] Extended training in Phase 2.

How Pavlovian Learning Motivates Appetitive Instrumental Responding

The interaction of Pavlovian and instrumental processes has been a topic of interest throughout the study of learning and motivation. Although early interest focused on fear conditioning and avoidance learning, recent emphasis has been on the influence of appetitive CSs on instrumentally trained responses; this will be our focus, as well.

Pavlovian-Instrumental Transfer. Pavlovian to instrumental transfer (PIT) refers to the augmenting of an instrumentally trained response by a CS that has been separately trained with the same outcome. It is typically studied in rats where lever pressing for food may be increased by presentation of a CS separately paired with food. Appetitive PIT is both outcome specific and nonspecific. Nonspecific PIT refers to the ability of a CS to elicit more instrumental behavior than occurs in its absence. It is dependent on the strength of competing goal-directed responses directly elicited by the appetitive CS. More interesting is outcome-specific PIT, in which a CS acts selectively on instrumental responses trained with the CS's own US as opposed to responses trained with a different US. For example, a tone paired with a food pellet will lead rats to press a lever rewarded with food pellets more than a lever rewarded with liquid sucrose. Notably, a CS may elicit outcome-specific PIT while still suppressing instrumental responding and so failing to show nonspecific PIT (Holmes, Marchand, & Coutureau, 2010).

The most startling property of outcome-specific PIT is that it does not depend on the current predictive value of the CS, as its magnitude appears unaffected by both extinction and US devaluation (Delamater, 1996; Holland, 2004). Furthermore, Rescorla (2000b) demonstrated outcome-specific transfer to a CS randomly paired with a US, even when the CS did not come to elicit conditioned responding. It appears that outcome-specific transfer is established whenever there are surprising CS-US pairings and, once established, is resistant to change. Indeed, as far as we know, Delamater (2012) has provided the only report of a loss in transfer once the CS-US relationship has been established, the result of extinguishing a CS that had been given a small number of acquisition trials. This pattern of transfer implies that Pavlovian processes function as more than mechanisms of prediction.

If PIT reflects motivational properties of the CS, the motivation appears to be guided by an aspect of the reinforcer that is independent of obtaining and consuming it. This is consistent with a mechanism by which the CS activates a particular feature of the US representation that cannot be devalued and that subsequently activates the responses that brought it about (Balleine & Ostlund, 2007; Holland, 2004; Holmes et al., 2010).

Behavior Systems Approach to PIT. Timberlake (1994) promoted a behavior systems approach to conditioning that envisions CSs as eliciting a variety of species- and motivation-specific behaviors that depend on temporal proximity to the US. When food is more temporally distant, a CS elicits in a rat a general search mode characterized by increased attention to environmental stimuli relevant to food. As the US becomes more proximal, the general search mode gives way to a focal search mode which includes more specifically food-directed behavior (Silva & Timberlake, 1997).

It may be the case that outcome-specific PIT is a behavior characteristic of a general reward-directed search mode evoked in times when a proximal reward is not expected. This would explain why CS extinction may facilitate PIT and why it is easier to detect when the instrumental responses are being extinguished and the reinforcers are not proximal. The simultaneous facilitation of reinforcer-related behaviors and indifference toward the occurrence of the reinforcer suggests to us that the search behavior is not motivated toward directly obtaining reward. Rather, it may be aimed toward investigating which responses are effective in obtaining reward. Such a motivation toward focused exploration is consistent with a view of Pavlovian conditioning summarized by Domjan, Cusato, and Krause (2004, p. 232): an "adaptive process that promotes efficient interactions of the organism with significant biological events in its natural environment." It is also an adaptive understanding consistent with the mechanistic views of Balleine and Ostlund (2007) and Holland (2004).

Summary and Conclusion

Conditioned responding emerges as a function of observing contingent relationships among stimuli over time. It is sensitive to both relative and conditional contingencies. For the simplest form of associative formation, that between a single salient stimulus and a biologically relevant outcome, large numbers of observations are not needed, but observations must be separated in time. Predictive value, once established, is sensitive to changes in contingency. New contingencies are learned, but old ones are not forgotten, and old habits can reemerge in times of uncertainty. Once an association has been formed, it is hard to un-form, and that association will guide instrumental behavior independent of contingency.

Pavlovian processes are most strongly linked to predicting the likelihood that an important event will or will not occur at a certain time, allowing organisms to engage in complicated sequences of preparatory behavior that culminate in appropriately timed conditioned responding. Independent of this, Pavlovian processes may serve a role analogous to the hypothesis generating roles of theories in scientific research: to focus the search for additional control of the environment.

After almost a century of investigation, Pavlovian "simple learning" processes appear more and more like nonverbal analogs of many of the skills we spend countless hours trying to teach in statistics and research methods courses. In that context, we call them critical thinking.

Acknowledgments

We thank Robert Rescorla for advice and discussions as well as for his remarkable contributions to the study of mind and behavior. We also thank Peter Holland for useful discussion.

References

Andrew, B. J., & Harris, J. A. (2011). Summation of reinforcement rates when conditioned stimuli are presented in compound. *Journal of Experimental Psychology: Animal Behavior Processes, 37*, 385–393.

Baker, A. G. (1974). Conditioned inhibition is not the symmetrical opposite of conditioned excitation: A test of the Rescorla-Wagner model. *Learning and Motivation*, *5*, 369–379.

Balleine, B. W., & Ostlund, S. B. (2007). Still at the choice-point: Action selection and initiation in instrumental conditioning. *Annals of the New York Academy of Sciences*, *1104*, 147–171.

Balsam, P. D, Drew, M. R., & Yang, C. (2002). Timing at the start of associative learning. *Learning and Motivation*, *33*, 141–155.

Barnet, R. C., & Miller, R. R. (1996). Second-order excitation mediated by a backward conditioned inhibitor. *Journal of Experimental Psychology: Animal Behavior Processes*, *22*, 279–296.

Bouton, M. E. (1993). Context, time, and memory retrieval in the interference paradigms of Pavlovian learning. *Psychological Bulletin*, *114*, 80–99.

Bouton, M. E. (2002). Context, ambiguity, and unlearning: Sources of relapse after behavioral extinction. *Biological Psychiatry*, *52*, 976–986.

Bouton, M. E., & Peck, C. A. (1992). Spontaneous recovery in cross-motivational transfer (counterconditioning). *Animal Learning & Behavior*, *20*, 313–321.

Brogden, W. J. (1939). Sensory preconditioning. *Journal of Experimental Psychology*, *25*, 323–332.

De La Casa, L. G., & Lubow, R. E. (2002). An empirical analysis of the super-latent inhibition effect. *Animal Learning & Behavior*, *30*, 112–120.

Delamater, A. R. (1996). Effects of several extinction treatments upon the integrity of Pavlovian stimulus-outcome associations. *Animal Learning & Behavior*, *24*, 437–449.

Delamater, A. R. (2012). Issues in the extinction of specific stimulus-outcome associations in Pavlovian conditioning. *Behavioural Processes*, *90*, 9–19.

Delamater, A. R., & Oakeshott, S. (2007). Learning about multiple attributes of reward in Pavlovian conditioning. *Annals of the New York Academy of Sciences*, *1104*, 1–20.

Domjan, M., Cusato, B., & Krause, M. (2004). Learning with arbitrary versus ecological conditioned stimuli: Evidence from sexual conditioning. *Psychonomic Bulletin & Review*, *11*, 232–246.

Ellison, G. D. (1964). Differential salivary conditioning to traces. *Journal of Comparative and Physiological Psychology*, *57*, 373–380.

Etscorn, F., & Stephens, R. (1973). Establishment of conditioned taste aversions with a 24-hour CS-US interval. *Physiological Psychology*, *1*, 251–253.

Flaherty, C. F. (1996). *Incentive relativity*. New York: Cambridge University Press.

Gallistel, C. R., Fairhurst, S., & Balsam, P. (2004). The learning curve: Implications of a quantitative analysis. *Proceedings of the National Academy of Sciences of the United States of America*, *101*, 13124–13131.

Gallistel, C. R., & Gibbon, J. (2000). Time, rate, and conditioning. *Psychological Review*, *107*, 289–344.

Gibbon, J., Baldock, M. D., Locurto, C., Gold, L., & Terrace, H. S. (1977). Trial and intertrial durations in autoshaping. *Journal of Experimental Psychology: Animal Behavior Processes*, *3*, 264–284.

Gibbon, J., & Balsam, P. (1981). Spreading associations in time. In C. M. Locurto, H. S. Terrace, & J. Gibbon (Eds.), *Autoshaping and conditioning theory* (pp. 219–253). New York: Academic Press.

Gormezano, I., & Kehoe, E. J. (1981). Classical conditioning and the law of contiguity. In P. Harzem & M. D. Zeiler (Eds.), *Advances in analysis of behaviour: Vol. 2. Predictability, correlation, and contiguity* (pp. 1–45). Chichester, UK: John Wiley & Sons, Ltd.

Gottlieb, D. A. (2005). Acquisition with partial and continuous reinforcement in rat magazine-approach. *Journal of Experimental Psychology: Animal Behavior Processes*, *31*, 319–333.

Gottlieb, D. A. (2008). Is number of trials a primary determinant of conditioned responding? *Journal of Experimental Psychology: Animal Behavior Processes*, *34*, 185–201.

Gottlieb, D. A. (2011). Pavlovian conditioning. In *Encyclopedia of the Sciences of Learning*. New York: Springer.

Gottlieb, D. A., & Prince, E. B. (2012). Isolated effects of number of acquisition trials on extinction of rat conditioned approach behavior. *Behavioural Processes*, *90*, 34–48.

Gottlieb, D. A., & Rescorla, R. A. (2010). Within-subject effects of number of trials in rat conditioning procedures. *Journal of Experimental Psychology: Animal Behavior Processes*, *36*, 217–231.

Guilhardi, P., & Church, R. M. (2006). The pattern of responding after extensive extinction. *Learning & Behavior*, *34*, 269–284.

Guthrie, E. R. (1935). *The psychology of learning*. New York: Harper.

Heth, C. D. (1976). Simultaneous and backward fear conditioning as a function of number of CS-US pairings. *Journal of Experimental Psychology: Animal Behavior Processes*, *2*, 117–129.

Heth, C. D., & Rescorla, R. A. (1973). Simultaneous and backward fear conditioning in the rat. *Journal of Comparative and Physiological Psychology*, *82*, 434–443.

Higgins, T., & Rescorla, R. A. (2004). Extinction and retraining of simultaneous and successive flavor conditioning. *Learning & Behavior*, *32*, 213–219.

Holland, P. C. (1988). Excitation and inhibition in unblocking. *Journal of Experimental Psychology: Animal Behavior Processes*, *14*, 261–279.

Holland, P. C. (1992). Occasion setting in Pavlovian conditioning. In G. Bower (Ed.), *The psychology of learning and motivation* (Vol. 28, pp. 69–125). Orlando, FL: Academic Press.

Holland, P. C. (2004). Relations between Pavlovian-instrumental transfer and reinforcer devaluation. *Journal of Experimental Psychology: Animal Behavior Processes*, *30*, 104–117.

Holland, P. C., & Straub, J. J. (1979). Differential effects of two ways of devaluing the unconditioned stimulus after Pavlovian appetitive conditioning. *Journal of Experimental Psychology: Animal Behavior Processes*, *5*, 65–78.

Holmes, N. M., Marchand, A. R., & Coutureau, E. (2010). Pavlovian to instrumental transfer: A neurobehavioural perspective. *Neuroscience and Biobehavioural Reviews*, *34*, 1277–1295.

Hull, C. L. (1943). *Principles of behavior*. New York: Appleton-Century-Crofts.

Kamin, L. J. (1965). Temporal and intensity characteristics of the conditioned stimulus. In W. F. Prokasy (Ed.), *Classical conditioning: A symposium* (pp. 118–147). New York: Appleton-Century-Crofts.

Kamin, L. J. (1968). "Attention-like" processes in classical conditioning. In M. R. Jones (Ed.), *Miami symposium on the prediction of behavior: Aversive stimulation* (pp. 9–31). Miami, FL: University of Miami Press.

Kehoe, E. J. (1982). Overshadowing and summation in compound stimulus conditioning of the rabbit's nictitating membrane response. *Journal of Experimental Psychology: Animal Behavior Processes*, *8*, 313–328.

Kehoe, E. J., & Macrae, M. (1994). Classical conditioning of the rabbit nictitating membrane response can be fast or slow: Implications for Lennartz and Weinberger's (1992). two-factor theory. *Psychobiology*, *22*, 1–4.

Kimble, G. A. (1961). *Hilgard and Marquis' conditioning and learning*. New York: Appleton-Century-Crofts.

Konorski, J., & Szwejkowska, G. (1956). Reciprocal transformations of heterogeneous conditioned reflexes. *Acta Biologiae Experimentalis*, *17*, 141–165.

Lattal, K. M. (1999). Trial and intertrial durations in Pavlovian conditioning: Issues of learning and performance. *Journal of Experimental Psychology: Animal Behavior Processes, 25*, 433–450.

Lattal, K. M., & Nakajima, S. (1998). Overexpectation in appetitive Pavlovian and instrumental conditioning. *Animal Learning & Behavior, 26*, 351–360.

Lolordo, V. M., & Fairless, J. (1985). Pavlovian conditioned inhibition: The literature since 1969. In R. R. Miller & N. E. Spear (Eds.), *Information processing in animals: Conditioned inhibition* (pp. 1–50). Hillsdale, NJ: Erlbaum.

Lubow, R. E. (1973). Latent inhibition. *Psychological Bulletin, 79*, 398–407.

Lubow, R. E., Rifkin, B., & Alek, M. (1976). The context effect: The relationship between stimulus preexposure and environmental preexposure determines subsequent learning. *Journal of Experimental Psychology: Animal Behavior Processes, 2*, 38–47.

Mackintosh, N. J. (1971). An analysis of overshadowing and blocking. *Quarterly Journal of Experimental Psychology, 23*, 118–125.

Mackintosh, N. J. (1974). *The psychology of animal learning*. New York: Academic Press.

Mackintosh, N. J. (1975). A theory of attention: Variations in the associability of stimuli with reinforcement. *Psychological Review, 82*, 276–298.

Marlin, N. A. (1981). Contextual associations in trace conditioning. *Animal Learning & Behavior, 9*, 519–523.

Miller, R. R., & Schachtman, T. R. (1985). Conditioning context as an associative baseline: Implications for response generation and the nature of conditioned inhibition. In R. R. Miller & N. E. Spear (Eds.), *Information processing in animals: Conditioned inhibition* (pp. 51–88). Hillsdale, NJ: Erlbaum.

Morris, R. W., & Bouton, M. E. (2006). Effect of unconditioned stimulus magnitude on the emergence of conditioned responding. *Journal of Experimental Psychology: Animal Behavior Processes, 32*, 371–385.

Nasser, H. M., & McNally, G. P. (2012). Appetitive-aversive interactions in Pavlovian fear conditioning. *Behavioral Neuroscience, 126*, 404–422.

Nelson, J. B. (2002). Context specificity of excitation and inhibition in ambiguous stimuli. *Learning and Motivation, 33*, 284–310.

Ohyama, T., & Mauk, M. D. (2001). Latent acquisition of timed responses in cerebellar cortex. *Journal of Neuroscience, 21*, 682–690.

Pavlov, I. P. (1927). *Conditioned reflexes*. New York: Dover.

Pearce, J. M. (1987). A model for stimulus generalization in Pavlovian conditioning. *Psychological Review, 94*, 61–73.

Peck, C. A., & Bouton, M. E. (1990). Context and performance in aversive-to-appetitive and appetitive-to-aversive transfer. *Learning and Motivation, 21*, 1–31.

Razran, G. (1957). The dominance-contiguity theory of the acquisition of classical conditioning. *Psychological Bulletin, 54*, 1–46.

Reiss, S., & Wagner, A. R. (1972). CS habituation produces a "latent inhibition effect" but no active "conditioned inhibition." *Learning and Motivation, 3*, 237–245.

Rescorla, R. A. (1966) Predictability and number of pairings in Pavlovian fear conditioning. *Psychonomic Science, 4*, 383–384.

Rescorla, R. A. (1968). Probability of shock in the presence and absence of CS in fear conditioning. *Journal of Comparative and Physiological Psychology, 66*, 1–5.

Rescorla, R. A. (1969a). Pavlovian conditioned inhibition. *Psychological Bulletin, 72*, 77–94.

Rescorla, R. A. (1969b). Conditioned inhibition of fear resulting from negative CS-US contingencies. *Journal of Comparative and Physiological Psychology, 67*, 504–509.

Rescorla, R. A. (1971). Summation and retardation tests of latent inhibition. *Journal of Comparative and Physiological Psychology, 75*, 77–81.

Rescorla, R. A. (1985). Conditioned inhibition and facilitation. In R. R. Miller and N. E. Spear (Eds.), *Information processing in animals: Conditioned inhibition* (pp. 299–326). Hillsdale, NJ: Erlbaum.

Rescorla, R. A. (1997). Summation: Assessment of a configural theory. *Animal Learning & Behavior, 25*, 200–209.

Rescorla, R. A. (2000a). Associative changes in excitors and inhibitors differ when they are conditioned in compound. *Journal of Experimental Psychology: Animal Behavior Processes, 26*, 428–438.

Rescorla, R. A. (2000b). Associative changes with a random CS-US relationship. *Quarterly Journal of Experimental Psychology: Comparative and Physiological Psychology, 53B*, 325–340.

Rescorla, R. A. (2001a). Are associative changes in acquisition and extinction negatively accelerated? *Journal of Experimental Psychology: Animal Behavior Processes, 27*, 307–315.

Rescorla, R. A. (2001b). Experimental extinction. In R. R. Mowrer & S. B. Klein (Eds.), *Handbook of contemporary learning theories* (pp. 119–154). Mahwah, NJ: Erlbaum.

Rescorla, R. A. (2001c). Unequal associative changes when excitors and neutral stimuli are conditioned in compound. *Quarterly Journal of Experimental Psychology, 54B*, 53–68.

Rescorla, R. A. (2002a). Savings tests: Separating differences in rate of learning from differences in initial levels. *Journal of Experimental Psychology: Animal Behavior Processes, 28*, 369–377.

Rescorla, R. A. (2002b). Comparison of rates of associative change during acquisition and extinction. *Journal of Experimental Psychology: Animal Behavior Processes, 28*, 406–415.

Rescorla, R. A. (2003a). Protection from extinction. *Learning & Behavior, 31*, 124–132.

Rescorla, R. A. (2003b). More rapid associative change with retraining than with initial training. *Journal of Experimental Psychology: Animal Behavior Processes, 29*, 251–260.

Rescorla, R. A. (2005). Spontaneous recovery of excitation but not inhibition. *Journal of Experimental Psychology: Animal Behavior Processes, 31*, 277–288.

Rescorla, R. A. (2007). Renewal after overexpectation. *Learning & Behavior, 35*, 19–26.

Rescorla, R. A., & Solomon, R. L. (1967). Two-process learning theory: Relationships between Pavlovian conditioning and instrumental learning. *Psychological Review, 74*, 151–182.

Rescorla, R. A., & Wagner, A. R. (1972). A Theory of Pavlovian conditioning: Variations in the effectiveness of reinforcement and nonreinforcement. In A. H. Black & W. F. Prokasy (Eds.), *Classical conditioning: II. Current research and theory* (pp. 64–99). New York: Appleton-Century-Crofts.

Rizley, R. C. & Rescorla, R. A. (1972). Associations in second-order conditioning and sensory preconditioning. *Journal of Comparative and Physiological Psychology, 81*, 1–11.

Romaniuk, C. B., & Williams, D. A. (2000). Conditioning across the duration of a backward contioned stimulus. *Journal of Experimental Psychology: Animal Behavior Processes, 26*, 454–461.

Ross, R. T. (1986). Pavlovian second-order conditioned analgesia. *Journal of Experimental Psychology: Animal Behavior Processes, 12*, 32–39.

Ross, R. T., & Holland, P. D. (1981). Conditioning of simultaneous and serial feature-positive discriminations. *Animal Learning & Behavior, 9*, 293–303.

Siegel, S. (1983). Classical conditioning, drug tolerance, and drug dependence. In R. G. Smart, F. B. Glaser, Y. Israel, H. Kalant, R. E. Popham, & W. Schmidt (Eds.), *Research advances in alcohol and drug problems* (Vol. 7, pp. 207–246). New York: Plenum.

Silva, K. M., & Timberlake, W. (1997). A behavior systems view of conditioned states during long and short CS-US intervals. *Learning & Motivation, 28*, 465–490.

Tolman, E. C. (1932). *Purposive behavior in animals and men.* New York: Century.

Thorndike, E. L. (1911). *Animal intelligence: Experimental studies.* New York: Macmillan.

Timberlake, W. (1994). Behavior systems, associationism, and Pavlovian conditioning. *Psychonomic Bulletin & Review*, *1*, 405–420.

Urcelay, G. P. (2012). Exposure techniques: The role of extinction learning. In P. Neudeck & H. Wittchen (Eds.), *Exposure therapy* (pp. 35–63). New York: Springer.

Wagner, A. R. (1971). Elementary associations. In H. H. Kendler & J. T. Spence (Eds.), *Essays in neobehaviorism: A memorial volume to Kenneth W. Spence* (pp. 187–213). New York: Appleton-Century-Crofts.

Wagner, A. R. (1981). SOP: A model of automatic memory processing in animal behavior. In N. E. Spear & R. R. Miller (Eds.), *Information processing in animals: Memory mechanisms* (pp. 5–47). Hillsdale, NJ: Erlbaum.

Wagner, A. R. (2003). Context-sensitive elemental theory. *The Quarterly Journal of Experimental Psychology*, *56B*, 7–29.

Wagner, A. R., Logan, F. A., Haberlandt, K., & Price, T. (1968). Stimulus selection in animal discrimination learning. *Journal of Experimental Psychology*, *76*, 171–180.

Wagner, A. R., & Rescorla, R. A. Inhibition in Pavlovian conditioning: Application of a theory. In M. S. Halliday & R. A. Boakes (Eds.), *Inhibition and learning*. London: Academic Press, 1972.

Williams, B. A., & McDevitt, M. A. (2002). Inhibition and superconditioning. *Psychological Science*, *13*, 454–459.

Williams, D. A. (1986). On extinction of inhibition: Do explicitly unpaired conditioned inhibitors extinguish? *American Journal of Psychology*, *99*, 515–525.

Williams, D. R., & Williams, H. (1969). Automaintenance in the pigeon: Sustained pecking despite contingent nonreinforcement. *Journal of the Experimental Analysis of Behavior*, *12*, 511–520.

Winterbauer, N. E., & Balleine, B. W. (2005). Motivational control of second-order conditioning. *Journal of Experimental Psychology: Animal Behavior Processes*, *31*, 334–340.

Yeo, A. G. (1974). The acquisition of conditioned suppression as a function of interstimulus interval duration. *Quarterly Journal of Experimental Psychology*, *26*, 405–416.

2

Building a Theory of Pavlovian Conditioning From the Inside Out

Douglas A. Williams

Both Pavlovian/classical and instrumental/operant conditioning are powerful procedures for changing behavior, and many researchers have speculated on what learning mechanisms are involved. Theory building and testing have been especially intertwined in the study of Pavlovian conditioning. A good theory guides further empirical investigation and synthesizes seemingly disconnected facts into a coherent whole. The purpose of this chapter is to describe the main components of a reasonable theory of Pavlovian conditioning, explain why these components are necessary, and to suggest ways that learning might be translated into adaptive behavior.

How have current theories of conditioning tried to explain the contents of what is learned during Pavlovian conditioning and the conditions favoring learning and performance? Current theorizing owes a debt to early philosophers, such as Thomas Hobbes and David Hume, who speculated that animal and human minds operate in machine-like fashion to link together stimuli paired repeatedly in time or space. The relationship between a conditioned stimulus (CS) and an unconditioned stimulus (US) is believed to be the primary content of what is learned during Pavlovian conditioning. Associative models explain why certain conditions favor CS-US association formation, while others do not. Mathematical accounts have been widely used as a vehicle for making precise statements about learning, and how learning causes a conditioned response (CR). Knowing some of these principles has helped to ease the way towards understanding how Pavlovian conditioning supports evolutionarily adaptive changes in behavior (Domjan, 2005).

New CRs developing under response-independent contingencies often do not resemble the unconditioned response (UR). A rat expecting a grid shock may remain motionless (the CR), although the rat's initial reaction to shock is a scrambling and leaping UR rather than immobility (Fanselow & Lester, 1988). Evolution has shaped

The Wiley Blackwell Handbook of Operant and Classical Conditioning, First Edition.
Edited by Frances K. McSweeney and Eric S. Murphy.

age-old learning processes to deal with opportunity and danger. Leaping might draw the attention of a predator and decrease fitness, and thus freezing rather than leaping is a primary CR in the rat. Signals for appetitive USs elicit approach because they contribute to survival and reproduction. Drug tolerance develops in part because stimuli in the environment paired with deviations from homoeostasis trigger learned opponent-like conditioned reactions (Siegel, 1975).

The aim of this chapter is to apply associative and evolutionary thinking to understanding the mechanisms responsible for Pavlovian conditioning, and to discuss the salient experimental evidence they have sought to address. How learning mechanisms might be realized in the nervous system is also discussed. The chapter is organized in a similar way to the learning process it seeks to describe. New proposals are introduced in a gradual incremental fashion, and an attempt is made to integrate them into a coherent theory of how associations might lead to adaptive behavior. I begin with the error-correction approach, which emphasizes the importance of the US (e.g., surprise), and hybrid theories, which also consider changes in CS processing (e.g., associability). The initial emphasis is placed on the associative principles and processes derived from experiments, and moves outward towards situation-specific attributes of the CR that promote adaptation. The goal is to demonstrate how one might build a working account of Pavlovian learning from the inside out.

Associative Learning and Error-Correction

Associative models assume that conditioning is an incremental process in which CS-US connections are gradually strengthened in a cumulative fashion over trials until they reach an asymptote. Mathematical modeling is an especially precise approach to developing theoretical explanations. Clark Hull's (1943) *Principles of Behavior* was an ambitious first effort to explain all learning within a stimulus-response (S-R) framework. His system of postulates was not rigid, and his formulations were frequently altered in light of new experimental evidence. However, none of Hull's predictions were particularly unique or intuitively surprising, and many were incorrect. Although early tensions between S-R and cognitive theories did not produce a winner, they stimulated and advanced research (Holland, 2008).

US-processing Theories. It could be argued the most important theoretical advance occurred when Rescorla and Wagner (1972) introduced a slight modification to an algorithm previously introduced by Bush and Mosteller (1955). The new model not only simulated many facts already documented, but also led researchers to discover a number of new phenomena. The Rescorla-Wagner model describes a learning mechanism which strengthens associative connections on a trial-by-trial basis. The model simulates changes in the strength of a learned association between a CS and US, symbolized as $V_{CS\text{-}US}$. Learning in the model occurs "episodically" as a result of contiguity between events. Early in conditioning, the CS-US association is weak. As CS-US pairings accumulate, more learning takes place and the association is strengthened. Eventually, the CS-US association reaches a high level and a vigorous CR is observed. Equation 1 shows the algorithm used by the model to adjust the associative strength of a given CS on a trial:

$$\Delta V_{CS-US} = \alpha\beta\,(\lambda - V_{ALL}), \tag{1}$$

where $\Delta V_{CS\text{-}US}$ is the change in associative strength on the trial (positive or negative), α and β are the respective saliences of the CS and the US (allowed to vary between 0.0 and 1.0), λ is the asymptote supported by the US (usually 1.0 if the US is present and 0.0 if the US is absent), and V_{ALL} is the sum of the current associative strengths of *all* of the CSs *present* on the trial (based on past learning).

The key distinguishing feature of the model is its mathematical representation of the psychological concept of "surprise." The bracketed difference places emphasis on the intuitively appealing notion that learning occurs on the trial when something unexpected happens. Increments in associative strength occur if, and only if, the subject's US expectation based upon all present CSs (V_{ALL}) is not already asymptotic. In this case, the surprising occurrence of the US causes a prediction error, ($\lambda - V_{ALL}$), measured by the difference between the obtained and expected US. Prediction errors drive changes in associative strength. This assumption differentiated it from the model of Bush and Mosteller (1955) in which the strength of a given CS independently approached λ:

$$\Delta V_{CS-US} = \alpha\beta\,(\lambda - V_{CS-US}) \tag{2}$$

In Equation 2, V_{ALL} is replaced by $V_{CS\text{-}US}$, and thus learning can happen even if the US is already expected on the basis of other CSs. Consider an experiment in which an already well-conditioned CS, labeled A, is joined by a new CS, labeled B, and the compound is paired with the US. Equation 2 predicts learning about the added B should be unaffected by the associative strength of A. Contrary to this prediction, Kamin (1968) found B acquired very little strength.

Kamin's (1968) *blocking* effect is an example of a group of phenomena called *cue-interactions*. The general principle is the associative value of a cue (i.e., CS) trained in compound depends on the value of co-present cues. Another example is the *relative validity* effect. Wagner, Logan, Haberlandt, and Price (1968) found that if compound AB is reinforced (AB+, where "+" means the US follows the A and B), and compound BC is not (BC−, where "−" means no US follows the B and C), responding to B in a subsequent test is less than if both compounds were reinforced on a 50% basis. During the AB+ trials, B must compete with an always reinforced A.

Equation 1 permits negative prediction errors as well as positive ones (Wagner & Rescorla, 1972). For example, a CS trained to asymptote will lose strength in extinction because λ is zero and V_{ALL} is positive, leading to a negative prediction error. In the so-called conditioned inhibition procedure (A+, AB−), A is reinforced in isolation on some trials but not when it is accompanied by B on other trials. This procedure causes B to acquire below zero strength. In the absence of cue-interaction, there would be no mechanism for the excitatory A to engender negative strength to the inhibitory B. Negative surprises create conditioned inhibition. The initially neutral B is expected to accumulate negative associative strength until $V_{B\text{-}US}$ approaches −1.0. One conceptualization of conditioned inhibition that has enjoyed great success is to assume conditioned inhibition raises the threshold for US activation (Konorski, 1948). Thus, it is best not to take the Rescorla-Wagner conceptualization of conditioned inhibition as negative associative strength too literally (Williams, Overmier, & LoLordo, 1992).

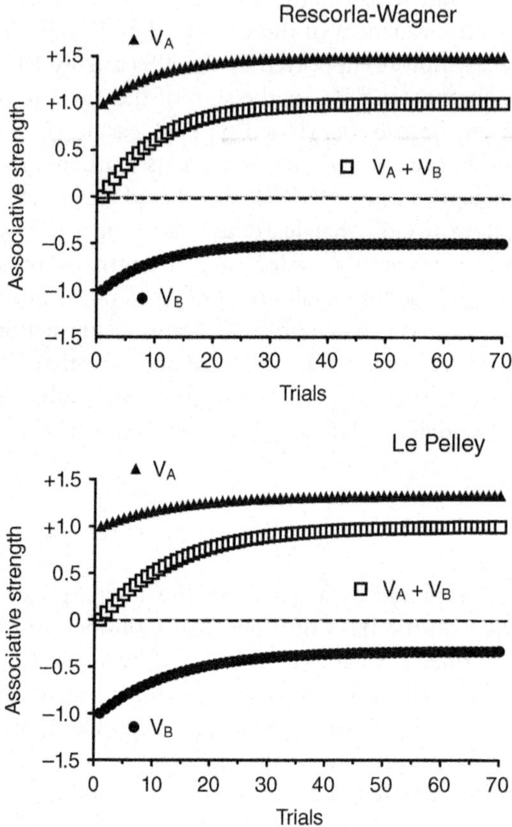

Figure 2.1 Predicted associative strengths for A (V_A) and B (V_B) and the combination ($V_A + V_B$) over trials when A and B are reinforced in compound. Predictions derived from Rescorla-Wagner (1972) model are shown in the top panel, whereas those derived from the Le Pelley (2004) model are shown in the bottom panel. Parameters used were $\lambda = 1.0$ (level of conditioning supported by US), $\alpha\beta = .05$ (product of CS and US salience), and $V_A = 1.0$, $V_B = -1.0$ (initial starting associative strengths entering Trial 1).

Like its predecessor, the Rescorla-Wagner model agrees that learning occurs incrementally rather than in an all-or-none fashion on the basis of the product of the salience of the CS ($0 < \alpha < 1.0$) and the US ($0 < \beta < 1.0$). Because the change in the associative strength of the CS on the trial ($\Delta V_{CS\text{-}US}$ or the amount learned) is a constant proportion of the prediction error, the absolute magnitude of the prediction error gradually diminishes over trials as the subject's expectations are adjusted to better approximate the actual US received. For illustration, the top panel of Figure 2.1 shows a simulation of responding to a reinforced AB compound that is comprised of two individual CSs with different starting values ($V_A = 1.0$, $V_B = -1.0$, and thus $V_{ALL} = 0$). The underlying associative strengths of A and B, which sum to determine the strength of the AB compound, are also shown. The simulation assumes the product of the saliences of the CS and US ($\alpha \times \beta$) is 0.05 and a large US is applied ($\lambda = 1.0$). Notice the increments in the AB curve become increasingly smaller over trials, the strengths of the two CSs increase in a lock-step fashion, and the associative strength of A climbs beyond 1.0.

That most learning curves are negatively accelerated is consistent with the trial-by-trial incremental learning found in Equation 1. However, an examination of individual acquisition curves often reveals a more abrupt onset of conditioned responding, which has traditionally been explained in terms of a threshold affecting response output. Incremental learning supplemented by a response threshold produces a sigmoidal learning curve (Hull, 1943). Increases in associative strength on early trials do not translate into performance. Harris (2011) reported that, after being delayed for a number of trials, there were gradual improvements in rates of responding in individual rats trained to approach a magazine for food cued by either auditory or visual CSs. Likewise, Kehoe, Ludvig, Dudeney, Neufeld, and Sutton (2008) reported that rabbit nictitating membrane conditioning, which often takes hundreds of trials to firmly establish, increases gradually to an asymptotic level. However, this popular interpretation is not universally accepted. For example, Gallistel, Fairhurst, and Balsam (2004) favor a model in which acquisition is step-like, and these abrupt changes are simply missed when the data are averaged across subjects. Their examination of the acquisition of key-peck responding in pigeons provided a measure of support for this suggestion.

As shown in the top panel of Figure 2.1, the final associative value of a CS may theoretically exceed 1.0. Because of ceiling effects, the prediction is verified by unusually slow extinction in a later test stage relative to controls (Pearce & Redhead, 1995). According to the Rescorla-Wagner model, the mismatch between the expected ($V_{ALL} = 0$) and obtained US ($\lambda = 1.0$) on the first AB+ trial should lead to increased associative strength for both A and B. When a CS's strength rises beyond 1.0, it is said to have become *supernormally* conditioned. Earlier, Rescorla (1971) reported a rather different form of supernormal conditioning in which associative strength was acquired rapidly, but the CS did not acquire above asymptotic strength. If A ($V_A = 0$) is initially neutral rather than excitatory (as assumed in Figure 2.1), the presence of the inhibitory B will simply facilitate the acquisition of excitatory strength by A.

One of the most compelling reasons for acceptance of the thinking in Equation 1 (the Rescorla-Wagner model) was research demonstrating a loss of responding with reinforcement (Kremer, 1978; Lattal & Nakajima, 1998). Negative surprises (rather than nonreinforcement per se) cause decrements in strength, just as positive surprises (rather than reinforcement per se) cause increments in strength. These considerations lead to a counterintuitive prediction. If two CSs are initially trained on separate trials to an asymptote of 1λ, the subsequent presentation of these stimuli in a reinforced compound should create *overexpectation* of the US, $V_{ALL} = 2\lambda$. Both CSs should lose strength despite being reinforced in compound. Thus, reinforcement in isolation is not the driving force behind associative learning as articulated in the theory of Bush and Mosteller (1955).

Equation 1 predicts that learning is not only gradual, but that the individual components of a reinforced compound should enjoy exactly the same changes in associative strength on each trial—all other factors equal (namely α). This prediction follows because learning is based on aggregated strength of all the stimuli on the trial (V_{ALL}). Thus, in a properly counterbalanced experiment in which physically different stimuli play all of the possible stimulus roles, there should be identical changes in the values of the components regardless of their starting values. Rescorla (2000) assessed this prediction in an ingenious set of experiments by testing two compounds, AD and BC, each comprised of one excitatory element (either A or C) and one inhibitory element (either B or D). A and C were independently reinforced in Stage 1 to create two interchangeable excitors, and B and D were independently non-reinforced in the presence of the excitatory X to create two equivalent inhibitors. In Stage 2, A and B were reinforced together. According to the Rescorla-Wagner model, A and B should each undergo an identical change because they share a common error term ($V_{ALL} = V_A + V_B$). If so, a test of AD versus BC in Stage 3 should reveal no difference. On the other hand, the inhibitory B might acquire more strength because it is the more discrepant predictor ($\lambda - V_B > \lambda - V_A$). Experimental findings revealed unequal associative changes as shown by more responding to BC than to AD in test. Rescorla concluded that although increments were related to the size of the aggregate prediction error, ($\lambda - V_{ALL}$), they also seemed to depend on the individual prediction error, $|\lambda - V_{CS\text{-}US}|$. Smaller individual errors lead to less associative change. Gottlieb and Begei in their chapter list a number of similar examples.

These results suggest that individual predictions errors, although they do not drive learning, must play some role in the acquisition process. One possibility is they moderate associative changes. Le Pelley (2004) quantified this idea by assuming increases in the strength in Equation 1 are down-modulated by the absolute value of individual CS error term, leaving us with:

$$\Delta V_{CS-US} = \alpha\beta\,(\lambda - V_{ALL})|\lambda - V_{CS-US}| \tag{3}$$

They also limited the range of the possible values of the individual error term, $|\lambda - V_{CS\text{-}US}|$ from 0.5 to 1.0 to insure that changes in the associative strength are neither over-corrected nor reduced to zero. Simulations of the predictions of the theory with this constraint are shown the bottom panel of Figure 2.1. The initial +1.0 positive prediction error on Trial 1 is eliminated by the last conditioning trial. The total gain is 0.33 units for A and 0.66 units for B. This prediction can be contrasted with identical total gains of 0.5 units for A and B in the top panel. Decrements in strength require a further modification in Equation 2, and the reader is referred to Le Pelley (2004) for more discussion. The reader also should be forewarned that incorporating a second term for the CS individual error is perhaps not the most expedient way to explain the results (see "CS Associability").

It is often said that animals are sensitive to the contingency between the CS and US. This idea derives from a series of fear conditioning experiments conducted by Rescorla (1968). He found that levels of fear conditioning tracked the degree to which the CS signaled an increase in the probability of the US. None of the USs in his experiments was predictable on a momentary basis, and only rates of US delivery were varied in the presence or absence of the CS. In a related set of experiments, Durlach (1983) found similar results when the US arrived at CS termination under a partial reinforcement schedule. Extra USs, if scheduled at sufficient rate during the intertrial interval (ITI), prevented CR acquisition. Interestingly, signaling the added USs in the ITI with a different CS eliminated the effect.

One of the most compelling aspects of the Rescorla-Wagner model is its ability to simulate sensitivity to CS-US contingency. Situational stimuli, for example, the visual appearance, the characteristic smell, and the background noises of the conditioning context are expected to acquire associative strength if they are paired with the US. Thus, USs in a conditioning experiment are never truly unsignaled. Instead, they are associated with the context. Recall, it is the *relative* and not the absolute predictive power that matters, such as shown by the Kamin blocking effect. A change in the level of contextual conditioning should then influence the level of associative strength acquired by the CS. For this reason, asymptotic predictions derived from the Rescorla-Wagner model are mathematically equivalent to calculating the CS-US contingency. In addition, the Rescorla-Wagner model also correctly predicts pre-asymptotic departures from conditioning (Quincey, 1971). This follows because a number of trials are required for the context, if independently paired with the US, to acquire its final level of associative strength. Signaling added USs in the ITI should reduce contextual conditioning, as Durlach (1983) found, permitting a partially reinforced CS to acquire more associative strength.

Basic CS-US contingency effects are equally well accommodated by another class of theories called time-accumulation models (Gibbon & Balsam, 1981; Gallistel & Gibbon, 2000). According to these models, the subject keeps track of average amount of time between US deliveries during the CS (T = trial time), and the average time between US deliveries over the whole experimental session (C = cycle time). It turns out the C/T ratio is often a rather good (but imperfect) predictor of how many trials it will take subjects to acquire the CR (Gibbon, Baldock, Locurto, Gold, & Terrace, 1977; Holland, 2000; Kirkpatrick & Church, 2000; Lattal, 1999). Higher ratios lead to faster acquisition. For example, a 10-s CS terminating with US delivery and an average 120-s interval between US deliveries would result in C/T = 12.0. Introducing unsignaled intertrial USs should decrease C/T by reducing the value of C. Explaining Durlach's (1983) findings is more challenging, and requires the awkward assumption that USs signaled by other nominal CSs are ignored (Cooper, Aronson, Balsam, & Gibbon, 1990), whereas those signaled by the context are not. Time-accumulation models have fared less successfully with the data from partially reinforced procedures. Deleting the US on some trials in a partial reinforcement group should effectively be the same as extending the duration of the CS in a continuously reinforced group. Both equally lengthen unreinforced CS exposure time, and should lead to a mathematical stalemate if acquisition is assessed across number of reinforcements rather than trials. This prediction has not been confirmed (Bouton & Sunsay, 2003; Gottlieb, 2004).

In closing this section it seems appropriate to mention the discovery of midbrain dopamine neurons with firing patterns that seem to follow the error-correction rules laid out in the Rescorla-Wagner model. The activity of these neurons has created quite a stir in the general scientific literature (Tobler, Dickinson, & Schultz, 2003; Waelti, Dickinson, & Schultz, 2001). Firing bursts in the ventral striatum of an awake monkey occur when an action is followed by the surprising delivery of a juice reward (positive prediction error). These bursts are diminished if the reward is already predicted by a CS paired with food (little or no error), and the firing rate may even become suppressed if an expected reward is omitted (negative prediction error). Thus, the bursts are not tied directly to the physical events received by the subject, but rather they seem to encode whether a prediction error has occurred, which depends both on previous learning and external events. Whether these dopamine neurons actually encode ($\lambda - V_{ALL}$) is controversial. They could instead be related to attentional processes (Redgrave & Gurney, 2006). That said, others have described how entire brain circuits rather than individual neurons might accomplish the same computational feat (Zelikowsky & Fanselow, 2011). That key aspects of the error-correction process are embodied in the neurology of the mammalian brain certainly lends support to approach taken by Rescorla and Wagner (1972).

CS-processing Theories. The Rescorla-Wagner model is a US-processing theory of learning. The US is conceptualized as supporting a limited amount of associative strength. Consequently, in compound conditioning, the elements of the compound will acquire less strength than they would otherwise had they been conditioned in isolation. According to CS-processing theories of conditioning, some (or all) of the effects attributed to prediction of the US might be caused by changes in attention. According to the theory of Mackintosh (1975), attention to A should increase if it is a better predictor of the US than a co-present B. The magnitude of the difference in the individual prediction errors for A, ($\lambda - V_A$), and B, ($\lambda - V_B$), is thought to determine the change in attention on a given trial. The theory receives some of its best support from experiments in which A is said to *overshadow* B (Pavlov, 1927). In overshadowing, the less salient B is found to evoke a smaller CR after AB+ compound conditioning than if B were conditioned alone. According to Mackintosh's theory, the effect of the several AB+ trials will be to severely limit conditioning to B by reducing attention towards it. As expected, overshadowing increases with increasing differences in saliences of A and B (Mackintosh, 1976).

Although overshadowing experiments have provided some basis for Mackintosh's (1975) approach, it would be fair to conclude changes in the attention cannot be the sole determinant of behavior in compound conditioning experiments. According to Mackintosh's theory, if we first expose hungry rats to light-food pairings (appetitive motivational system), followed in the second stage by pairings of both light and tone with footshock (aversive motivational system), the light is expected to become rapidly conditioned in the second stage. This prediction follows because light should have captured attention by virtue of predicting food, and thus the light rather than the tone should become the better predictor of shock. Dickinson (1977) found evidence of facilitated conditioning to the tone rather than transreinforcer blocking. It is also hard to explain overshadowing or blocking from this approach after only a single trial (Cole & McNally, 2007). A second learning trial is necessary so that any changes in attention taking place on Trial 1 can affect learning on Trial 2.

Most contemporary theories agree that attention is probably not the best way to understand changes in CS processing. Rather, they have adopted a related term, *associability*, first described by Pearce and Hall (1980). Associability is the ease of a specific CS entering into or increasing its association with a specific US. Associability is assumed to decline over the course of CS-US pairings as the US becomes less surprising, and further learning is unnecessary. Unlike attention, associability is specific to the US, and hence the prediction of appetitive to aversive blocking is retracted. Declines in associability of the CS eventually cause conditioning to slow as learning reaches an asymptotic level. Associability is restored when the CS is not followed by the expected US in simple extinction. Hall and Pearce (1979) state that negative transfer is explained by a loss of associability: Pairings of a CS with a weak shock may later interfere with later pairings of the same CS with a strong shock. The observation that some combinations of CSs and USs yield faster acquisition (LoLordo, 1979) suggests a factor beyond the CS and US salience is needed.

Changes in associability also explain the intriguing finding that blocking is sometimes preventable. Recall, Equation 1 predicts that prior learning about A may prevent conditioning to B if the magnitude of the US remains the same on the A and AB trials of a blocking experiment. Reducing the magnitude of the US on the AB trials in Stage 2 is predicted to cause a negative prediction error because λ is lower. However, the surprising result is that lowering the magnitude of the US during blocking may cause the added B to gain rather than lose strength (Dickinson, Hall, & Mackintosh, 1976). Only CS-processing theories are in a good position to explain this result. The surprising occurrence of a downshifted US is thought to cause a discrepancy between the obtained and expected US, which is thought to cause a surprise-induced enhancement of the associability of the added CS (Holland & Gallagher, 1993; cf. Holland & Kenmuir, 2005). Unblocking experiments demonstrate both CS and US processing must be considered to explain the totality of the data.

In keeping with this suggestion, Pearce and Mackintosh (2010) have recently described a hybrid model in which individual prediction error influences CS associability, while the aggregate prediction error determines the degree to which learning is available to all co-present CSs. The theory is based on a marriage of CS and US-processing theories. Pearce and Mackintosh (2010) introduced a new parameter σ, modifiable with experience, into the Rescorla-Wagner model to stand for the associability of the CS:

$$\Delta V_{CS-US} = \alpha\sigma\beta\,(\lambda - V_{ALL}),\ \text{where}\ \sigma = |\lambda - V_{CS-US}| \qquad (4)$$

Some evidence in favor of this hybrid approach comes from an experiment of Jones and Haselgrove (2011, Experiment 1). During the conditioning stage, A and B were trained in compound with each other, whereas X and Y were trained in isolation. In test, the rats received AY+, BY−, AX− discrimination learning. They withheld responding more quickly to the non-reinforced BY− than to the non-reinforced AX−. It seems the X and Y elements within AY+ vs. AX− subdiscrimination were simply harder to learn about than the A and B elements within the AY+ vs. BY− subdiscrimination. This suggests the individually trained CSs (X and Y) lost more associability than the compound trained CSs (A and B), which follows from Equation 4. Meanwhile, they also observed a standard overshadowing effect with more responding to X and Y individually than to A and B individually. Additional examples of the power gained by the addition of σ in Equation 4 are discussed by Pearce and Mackintosh (2010) and Haselgrove, Esber, Pearce, and Jones (2010).

If this hybrid approach has merit, we should expect to find brain circuitry underlying changes in associability to complement error-correction processes in the ventral striatum. More than a decade ago, Holland and Gallagher (1999) pointed to the amygdala as a likely target for this type of flexibility. Recent research has provided a good deal of experimental support for their idea (e.g., Belova, Paton, Morrison, & Salzman, 2007; Roesch, Calu, Esber, & Schoenbaum, 2010). In humans, activity in the ventral striatum but not in the amygdala, as measured by functional magnetic resonance imagery, is positively correlated with the prediction error. The opposite activation pattern is found for associability, which is positively correlated with activity in the amygdala but not the ventral striatum (Li, Schiller, Schoenbaum, Phelps, & Daw, 2011). In passing, it is worth noting the joint contribution of CS (associability) and US (error-correction) processing to Pavlovian conditioning was forecast long ago by Rescorla and Wagner (1972). At that time, it was well known that preexposure to the CS would subsequently retard conditioning (Lubow & Moore, 1959), a phenomenon dubbed *latent inhibition*. Rescorla and Wagner acknowledged that some modifiable quantity for processing of the CS would eventually have to be included in future models.

Equation 1 assumes responding to AB is determined solely by the sum of the associative values of its constituent parts, A + B. This view has not gone unquestioned (Rescorla, 1972). Solving the *negative pattering* discrimination (A+, B+, AB−), first studied by Woodbury (1943), requires less responding to AB than to either A or B. Notice the sum of the associative strengths of A and B is required to be lower than the strengths of either component alone—a mathematical impossibility. Woodbury found the discrimination was learned, although not quickly.

Is it possible all compound stimuli are treated as configurations? A rather powerful theory emerged when Pearce (1987) combined a configural learning assumption with a similarity rule of generalization. Pearce described a theory in which the entire stimulus complex enters into association with the US. In the negative patterning discrimination, A, B, and AB are viewed as three distinct complexes with AB being ½ similar to each of A and B. How might such a theory distinguish itself from the Rescorla-Wagner model? Consider an experiment in which subjects receive A+, AB− conditioned inhibition training in Stage 1, followed by B+ trials in Stage 2 (Wilson & Pearce, 1992). The elemental theory of Rescorla and Wagner predicts summation should occur in a final test stage, and responding to AB should exceed A and B individually. The model predicts B's negative strength should be replaced by positive strength in Stage 2, and thus A and B together should promote more responding than either CS alone. On the other hand, Pearce's configural theory does not predict elimination of the original discrimination. Generalized excitation received from the conditioning of B in Stage 2 should not completely mask the inhibition originally conditioned to the AB configuration in Stage 1. In test, responding to AB should not exceed B. This, and many other intriguing predictions of configural theory (Pearce, 2002; Pearce & Redhead, 1993, 1995; Redhead & Pearce, 1995; cf., Rescorla, 1997), have been confirmed at the expense of elemental theory of Rescorla and Wagner (1972).

In a critical development, a possible reconciliation of the elemental and configural approaches was introduced by Wagner and colleagues (Brandon, Vogel, & Wagner, 2000; Wagner, 2003). What would happen if internal representations for individual stimuli, A and B, were altered when they occurred in compound? One possibility is that some of the elements of A and B might be inhibited on compound trials (labeled Ai and Bi), whereas other elements might be activated whenever the relevant stimulus is presented, either singly or in compound (labeled simply A and B). This scheme called the *inhibited elements* approach is shown in Figure 2.2. In Figure 2.2, inhibition (blocked lines) is mediated by the units labeled Ab and Ba, which are activated only on AB trials (dashed lines). Thus, in negative patterning, the Ai and Bi elements are specifically inhibited on AB compound trials, but the Ai elements are activated

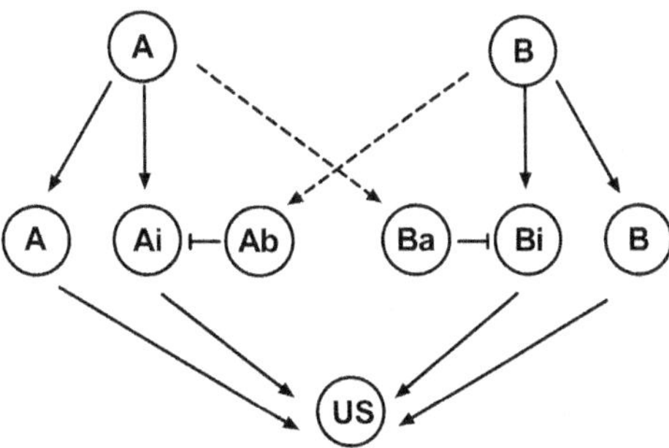

Figure 2.2 Internal representations evoked by A and B individually, and in compound, according to the inhibited elements model. The model holds a specified set of elements of A are inhibited on trials when B is present (Ai), and vice-versa for B (Bi). Inhibition (the blocked lines) is caused by the Ab (elements of A evoked only when B present) and Ba (elements of B evoked only when A present), which are activated only if the other CS is co-present (dashed lines). Elements tied to the presentation of a particular CS, presented individually or in compound (solid lines), are labeled A or B.

on A+ trials and the Bi elements are activated on B+ trials. Wagner and colleagues determined the inhibited elements approach made identical predictions as Pearce's configural theory.

A somewhat better model, they argued, resulted when the inhibited elements were allowed to be replaced. In the *replaced elements* model (Figure 2.3), the Ab and Ba units acquire direct associations with the US as well as inhibiting Ai and Bi, respectively. In this scheme, the Ai elements are essentially swapped for Ab elements (and Ba for Bi) on compound trials; hence, the term replaced elements. Interestingly, the replaced elements model correctly predicts more generalization from A to AB than from AB to A (Brandon et al., 2000). This is *asymetrical generalization* effect is shown in Figure 2.3. During the conditioning of A+ (top panel), both the A and Ai elements are conditioned (filled), although the latter are not activated (stripes) in the AB generalization test. Thus, of the previously conditioned elements (A, Ai), only one-half of the possible elements are activated during the A+ to AB+ generalization test. On the other hand, during the conditioning of AB+, the A, B, Ab, and Ba elements are linked with the US. Thus, of the previously conditioned elements present during AB+ conditioning (A, Ab, B, Ba), only one-quarter (namely A) are activated during the AB+ to A generalization test. Asymmetrical generalization decrements do not follow from the inhibited elements model. However, both models agree that the strength of any one element's activation in compound may well differ from its activation alone. Compound stimuli are more richly processed than simply AB = A + B.

How might this principle be combined with the others previously discussed to build a complete theory? Harris (Harris 2006; Harris & Livesey, 2010) intuited that changes in associability, σ, resulting from a capacity limitation could produce something like the patterns of activation shown in Figure 2.3. Because this theory is a hybrid, it recognizes a US-processing factor for cue-interactions (e.g., blocking,

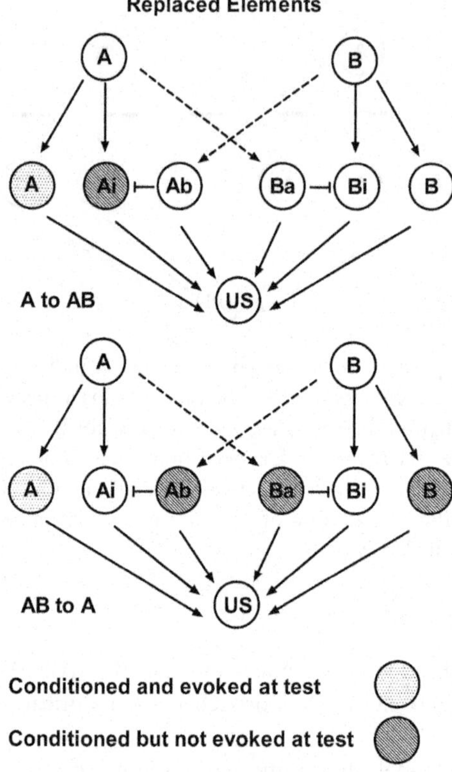

Figure 2.3 The replaced elements model assumes the inhibited elements Ai and Bi are replaced by elements Ab and Ba on compound trials. Element Ai is activated when A occurs without B, and element Bi is activated when B occurs without A. Elements A and B are activated whenever a specific CS, A and/or B, respectively, is presented. The top panel displays which elements are conditioned when A is reinforced (filled, A and Ai) and which of these will later be activated during an AB test (striped, A). The bottom panel displays which elements are conditioned when AB is reinforced (filled, A, Ab, B, and Ba) and which of these will later be activated during an A test (striped, A).

conditioned inhibition, relative validity, and contingency learning) as well as a CS-processing factor for associability (e.g., unblocking with US downshift, unequal changes during compound training, and overshadowing). In summary, a few principles applied broadly can account for a wealth of data.

Turning Associations Into Behavior

The previous sections reviewed Pavlovian conditioning divorced from behavior. What principles then determine how behavior is expressed? It was once thought that Pavlovian CRs might be autonomic whereas operants were skeletal. However, Brown and Jenkins (1968) discovered some time ago that pigeon key-pecking (skeletal response) in studies of operant conditioning can also be evoked by simply repeatedly pairing the illumination of a small plastic disc on the wall, with food. A new term autoshaping was coined to acknowledge the Pavlovian basis for response because the pigeons still pecked the illuminated disc even though a response was not required. Autoshaping is a form of sign-tracking. Conditioned behavior is directed toward a signal for an appetitve US. As such, it would be generally adaptive in the real world where the CS and the US are generally proximal.

One approach that has paid dividends is to ask what function the CR plays in promoting the animal's adaptive fitness. Conditioned responding takes on functional significance when it modifies the impact of US in the animal's normal environment. Predatory attack elicits strong unconditioned responses automatically or reflexively. Defensive responses that protect animals from encountering predators are perhaps even more useful (Bolles & Fanselow, 1980). For example, contexts associated with aversive events trigger hypoalgesia to prepare the animal for a possible injury. Being able to predict appetitive as well as aversive events is advantageous. Hollis, Pharr, Dumas, Britton and Field (1997) showed that male blue gourami sired more offspring when the signal presented in test stage had previously been paired with opportunity to engage in sexual activity. Similar results were reported by Mahometa and Domjan (2005) in Japanese quail.

In considering the questions about behavior, it would seem wise to attempt to synthesize evolutionary considerations within a formal theoretical approach based on error-correction. Questions about the mechanics of learning & behavior are intertwined, and answers to one naturally constrain the other. This section is divided into an examination of "when" the animal responds (timing) and what the animal does (response systems). Both of these aspects are crucial in understanding how associations translate into changes in behavior that benefit the animal.

Timing. Research in Pavlovian conditioning has demonstrated subjects learn "whether" the US will occur and also "when" it will happen (Bitterman, 1964). Equations 1–4 make predictions only about "whether" the US will follow the CS on a trial. However, subjects exposed to a fixed CS-US interval show temporally-based responding. The first CR occurrence in most preparations arises near the time of arrival of the US (Balsam, Drew, & Yang, 2002), although perhaps not in all conditions (Delamater & Holland, 2008). Examples include conditioned magazine-entries in rats (Kirkpatrick & Church, 2000) autoshaping in pigeons (Drew, Yang, Ohyama, & Balsam, 2004), and aversive conditioning in fish (Drew, Zupan, Cooke, Couvillon, & Balsam, 2005). That CRs are well timed in eye-blink conditioning in the rabbit is not too surprising from an evolutionary perspective. The eyelid CR ought to be maximal when the airpuff/shock US is scheduled, and the lid should normally remain open in the absence of the protective response to permit the animal to collect visual sensory information. Ohyama and Mauk (2001) reported that limited training at a designated CS-US interval in this preparation may result in temporal learning prior to the appearance of the first anticipatory CR. A latent temporal expectation was revealed by switching the arrival time of the US to an earlier point during the CS, and immediately terminating the trial. Although no further training occurred at the original CS-US interval, a timed CR emerged at the original CS-US interval when the CS was extended on test trials. Temporal specificity is also observed in fear conditioning. Even though rats may remain motionless for a long period of time (the conditioned freezing response), they learn the precise arrival time of the US as shown

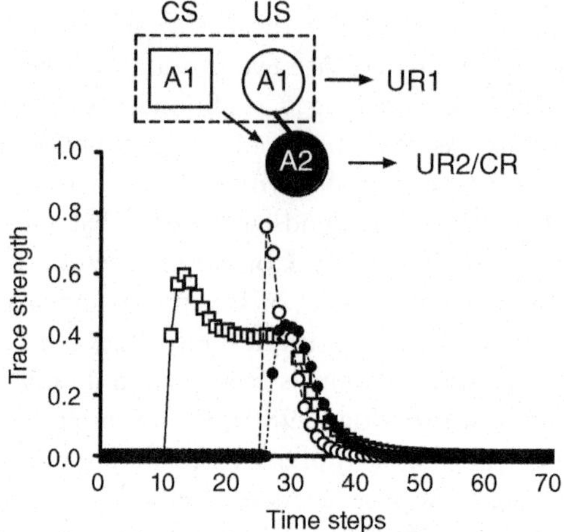

Figure 2.4 Memory trace strength (proportion of representational elements) for the CS (A1 state only) and the US (A1 and A2 states) is shown over the course of the first CS-US pairing. Elements of the CS begin to be evoked into the A1 state beginning at Step 10, and elements of the US begin to be evoked into the A1 state at Step 25 (from which they decay into the A2 state). The CS and US co-terminate at Step 26. Excitatory conditioning occurs to the extent that A1 processing of the CS and US overlap (dashed box), which causes evocation of the CR via A2 processing of the US. The CR resembles the secondary response to the US (UR2), which may or may not be similar to the primary response (UR1).

by increased startle responding measured down to the second (Davis, Schlesinger, & Sorenson, 1989).

There have been a number of attempts to extend the Rescorla-Wagner model to the temporal domain. Wagner (1981) described a model in which processing of the CS and US changed over time within the trial. The model assumes a hypothetical memory system in which the delivery of a stimulus probabilistically activates some proportion of the representation elements into a primary A1 state, from which they proceed to decay into a secondary A2 state, followed by a return to inactivity. The A1 state can be loosely described as stimulus registration, whereas the A2 state can result from the presentation of a recent stimulus or the future expectation of that stimulus (the "or" being a somewhat dicey proposition). With a fixed quantity of elements activated on a stochastic basis, it is easy to see this set of assumptions about stimulus processing will lead to different proportions of elements in the A1, A2, and inactive states over the trial. Figure 2.4 displays how elements are distributed when a CS is forward paired with the US on Trial 1 in a standard delay conditioning procedure (CS terminates with US). Because the CS is a less biologically salient biological event than the US, the figure sensibly assumes activity is ramped up more quickly in the US node than in the CS node.

Because the CS is not the actual US, Wagner (1981) reasoned the CS should activate elements of the US into the A2 state of activity, which in turn elicits the CR. This is how the model exploits a set of standard operating procedures (SOP) in memory to instantiate the concept of surprise. If a good proportion of the US are in the A2 state prior to the actual receipt of the US, there will be proportionately fewer inactive elements available to enter the A1 state upon US arrival. By making associative change dependent on whether CS and US elements are concurrently active in the A1 state (the dashed box in Figure 2.4), Wagner built positive prediction errors into his model.

One of the main contributions of SOP was to explain how the CS-US interval influences the overall magnitude of conditioning (Smith, 1968; Spence & Norris, 1950). As the onset of the US becomes increasingly remote from CS onset, there should be fewer elements of the CS in the A1 state of activity and a lesser chance that excitatory conditioning will be supported. Likewise, the model predicts that US delivery at CS termination (delay conditioning) will be more effective than if the CS terminates, and the US follows after a time gap (trace conditioning). Research has shown that backward conditioning (US before CS) is also correctly predicted to result in either conditioned excitation or conditioned inhibition, depending on the number of trials (Wagner & Larew, 1985).

The discerning reader will have noticed that Wagner's (1981) version of SOP is but a half-step to "real-time" learning: Animals are affected by the CS-US interval but they do not encode time (Savastano & Miller, 1998). Time affects learning, but time is not part of the contents of what is learned. For this reason, it has become more fashionable in recent years to build time directly into the contents of the learning. This is anything but a new idea. On the basis of his observations, Pavlov (1927) concluded that "it seems pretty evident that the duration of time has acquired the properties of a CS" (p. 41). In one of his experiments, dogs were given metronome-food pairings every 13 minutes. However, if the beating metronome was presented 5 or 8 minutes after the last reinforced trial it failed to produce a CR. Responding depended on the metronome being presented at the usual time. Pavlov's thinking encouraged theoreticians to consider the idea that predictive cues, like contexts and CSs, are temporally divisible.

Figure 2.5 shows some ways theories might incorporate time more directly into what is learned (adapted from Ludvig, Sutton, & Kehoe, 2012). Panel A has no representation for time within the CS, whereas Panel B is a graphical representation of Pavlov's thinking. He speculated that a chain of internal stimuli function as "miniature" CSs within the CS as a whole. In a real-time version of Wagner's SOP theory (Vogel, Brandon, & Wagner, 2003), for example, the CS is assumed to evoke temporally-defined patterns of activation in addition to the simple presence (A1), memory (A2), and absence (I) patterns of activation described in the earlier theory (Wagner, 1981). A version of the temporal difference (TD) model described by Sutton and Barto (1987) used this CS coding method, which they called a *complete serial compound.* Computer scientists sometimes refer to this coding as a delay line signaling. When the US occurs, it taps into the signal somewhere along the path. Panel C is a more realistic version of the same idea. Temporal stimuli ramp-up at certain times, and then slowly decline. Here, the onset of the CS produces a chain of events, and the US can tap into several overlapping "lines" at once (a cascade). The curves in Panel C are gamma functions. This function has several useful properties, one of which is that the standard deviation of a gamma function increases systematically with the mean, making the distribution Gaussian-like with a lower maximum at longer intervals (Gibbon, 1977). Many real-time conditioning theories

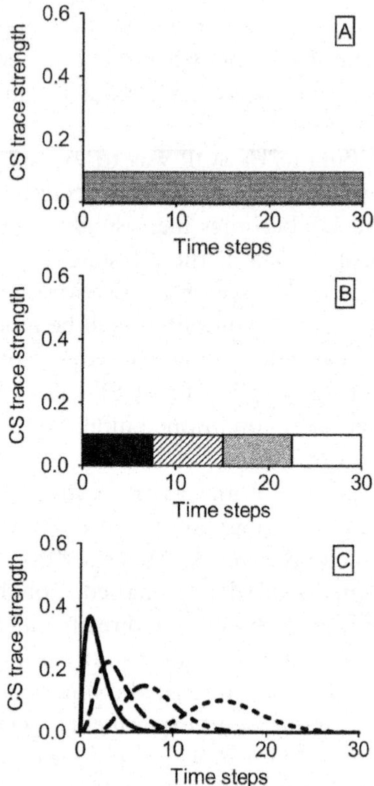

Figure 2.5 Three ways of thinking how the CS activation changes over time within a conditioning trial: (a) no change (uniform), (b) a chain of "miniature CSs" evoked in a series, or (c) a time-based cascade of discriminable but overlapping gamma functions triggered by CS onset.

invokes such functions (Schmajuk & DiCarlo, 1992), including a more recent version the TD model with micro-stimulus coding (Ludvig, Sutton, & Kehoe, 2008).

Defining the controlling stimulus as a time-based series of internal stimuli serves the intended purpose of introducing time into associative learning. However, the introduction of temporally-defined stimuli also solves another vexing question. Nervous systems operate in real time and continually update information on a moment-by-moment basis. How can a US delivered at Time X, reinforce temporal stimuli at Time X-1? Panels B and C suggest a possibility. If X is associated with the US, X should acquire the property of a secondary reinforcer. On the next trial, this learned expectation could bootstrap learning to X-1, the moment preceding X. TD learning is the process of taking the temporal difference in expectations between X and X-1. Bootstrapping occurs at a discount. Thus, the strength of X-1 will approach but never equal X, and associative strength should continue to spread from the learned US arrival time towards the CS onset as each time unit is paired with the next, again at a slightly discounted rate. The result is temporal conditioning first arising at the learned delivery time of the US, which is characteristic of many behavioral systems.

Raising the profile of time in associative learning has a number of other interesting implications. One is that observed levels of conditioned responding should not always reflect the overall CS-US contingency. When might such a result occur? If time is marked by internal stimuli within the CS, and the US is fixed in time, it should be possible for an animal to acquire a very strong conditioned response at the learned arrival time of the US even if the frequency of the US is higher during the ITI than during the whole CS (Williams, Lawson, Cook, Mather, & Johns, 2008). Temporal specificity in blocking (Barnet, Grahame, & Miller, 1993), overshadowing (Blaisdell, Denniston, & Miller, 1998), conditioned inhibition (Williams, Johns, & Brindas, 2008), and extinction (Kehoe & Joscelyne, 2005) is also consistent with this approach.

Timing of appetitive reinforcement in the seconds to minutes range is mediated by cortico-striatal circuits. Meck (2006) reported that dopamine depleting lesions in the dorsal striatum eliminated temporal control of responding, but the ability of the same rats to discriminate the appetitive value of two cues was spared. Conversely, lesions of the ventral striatum eliminated differences in the appetitive value of two cues as measured by maximum response rates, but temporal control was intact. This research ties nicely into work implicating midbrain dopamine in error-correction (see "US-processing Theories"). Timing in the milliseconds range has been extensively studied in cortico-cerebellar circuits in eye-blink conditioning in the rabbit (Christian & Thompson, 2003). It has been suggested that subsets of granule cells in the cerebellum active at different times during the CS may permit appropriate CR timing. Thus, timing may not always have a single neural substrate but may be embedded within multiple systems.

Response Systems. Konorski (1967) was the first to clearly distinguish two main classes of CRs. A rat expecting a water US experiences both a diffuse motivational reaction, which may trigger excited approach towards the location of the US (preparatory), and a more sensory anticipation, which causes licking (consummatory). The more specific adaptive response occurs within the background of the preparatory CR. Preparatory responses within this model are not specific to the US employed, but to the activation of a wider motivational system.

Wagner and Brandon (1989) postulated the same fundamental learning processes could underlie the generation of preparatory and consummatory CRs. They modified the earlier theory of Wagner (1981) by twinning the node for the US. One twin represented the motivational/emotive properties of the US (preparatory), whereas the other twin represented its sensory properties (consummatory). Called the affective extension (AESOP) model, it assumes preparatory CRs develop at much longer CS-US intervals than consummatory CRs. To enable this dichotomy, A1 processing of the US was assumed to decline more slowly for the motivational node than for the sensory node. A2 processing was likewise slower to develop and to decay into inactivity in the motivational node. In line with the theory, Vandercar and Schneiderman (1967) found a mild paraorbital shock US paired with a tone CS supported a consummatory (eye-blink) CR at short CS-US intervals, but a preparatory (heart-rate) CR at both short and long CS-US intervals. Preparatory responding might encourage general changes in autonomic arousal, which then enhances ongoing action initiated by sensory node (Brandon, Bombace, Falls, & Wagner, 1991). Tait and Saladin (1986) confirmed an interesting prediction of the theory. Backward pairings of a shock US followed by a tone CS had inhibitory associative effects in nictitating membrane conditioning (consummatory) and excitatory associative effects in fear conditioning (preparatory), suggesting a degree of independence.

It is worth noting that Wagner's (1981) earlier theory already permitted some malleability at the level of the CR. According to SOP, a CS-US association may translate into either a similar (stimulus substitution) or an opposite (compensatory) reaction. Some CRs promote activities which bear a strong resemblance to the primary effects of the US. Jenkins and Moore's (1973) beautiful still photographs of open beak (food US) and closed beak (water US) CRs come to mind. Others CRs serve to preserve homoeostatic balance by initiating a counter-reaction to the primary effects of the US. Many drug USs operate in this fashion (Siegel, 1975, 1977). Paletta and Wagner (1986) suggested that the secondary reaction on US-only trials is often (not always) predictive of the form of resulting CR. If the subject's initial reaction to the US is followed by a strong opponent reaction, the opponent is likely to become conditioned as the CR. Otherwise, the CR will tend to be anticipatory. Consistent with their thinking, morphine produces sedation or inactivity soon after its presentation which is followed by greater than normal activity levels. And, when morphine injection was paired with placement in a distinctive chamber, they observed hyperactivity as the CR. Likewise, freezing is a secondary reaction occurring after agitated leaping and scrambling to a footshock US. Freezing is the primary CR in the rat when exposed to a CS paired with shock. Contexts associated with a radiant heat US elicit hypoalgesia as a CR, which is an opioid-dependent secondary response blocked by naloxone (Fanselow & Baackes, 1982). Interestingly, the primary A1 reaction to the same US is non-opioid hypoalgesia, which is not conditioned.

How are behaviors organized within and across response systems? There is considerable evidence that a CS from one affective class (e.g., aversive) has an inhibitory influence on responses controlled by a CS from the other affective class (e.g., appetitive). Figure 2.6 shows a simplified flow diagram of this conceptualization for CSs paired with food or shock, adapted from Dickinson and Dearing (1979). Responding to appetitive signal (CS app) is mediated by general motivational system that encourages approach towards the US (Wasserman, Franklin, & Hearst, 1974), whereas responding to aversive signal (CS av) is mediated by a general motivational system that discourages approach to the US. These general systems are reciprocally inhibitory, which also explains why Pavlovian signals modulate instrumental conditioning. Consummatory CRs, such as salivation and flinching, depend on the specific qualities of the US. Blocking (discussed earlier in this chapter) is expected within but not across systems. Footshock and a loud noise can be exchanged as the US between stages of a blocking experiment without producing unblocking of a preparatory CR (Bakal, Johnson, & Rescorla, 1974). They are perceptually different but share aversive properties in common. The interactions shown in Figure 2.6 are surely oversimplified. Delamater and Oakeshott (2007; Delamater, 2012) list a number of other attributes of the US besides its motivational and sensory properties worthy of inclusion.

Response systems are presumably tailored to evoke individual behaviors within an organized system that contribute to the animal's fitness. According to the predatory imminence theory (Fanselow & Lester, 1988), animals' activities are organized by the degree of perceived danger over time. When the danger is temporally distant, the

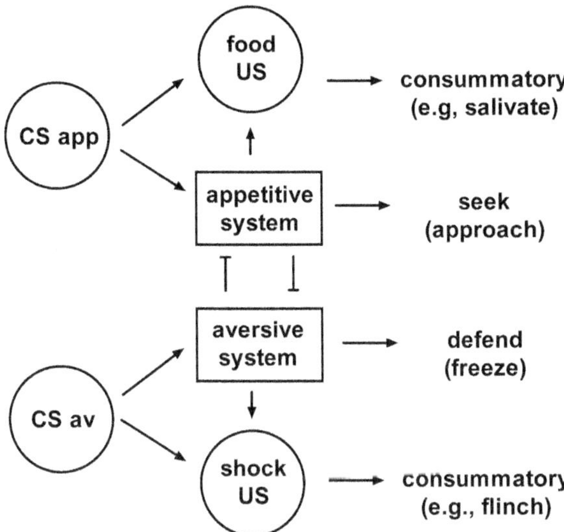

Figure 2.6 A simplified diagram of associations between a CS paired with an appetitive US (CS app, food US) and between a CS paired with an aversive US (CS av, shock US). The blocked lines show the reciprocal inhibitory relationship between the appetitive and aversive motivational states. Specific consummatory CRs are determined by the sensory properties of the US, which are primed by the motivational state of the US, which itself promotes general behavioral changes (seek or defend).

animal is free to engage in other activities relevant to survival and reproduction so long as they do not bring the animal into immediate danger. This is the pre-encounter mode. Should a sign of a predator be detected, the animal will quickly engage in species-specific defensive responses. These CRs are fairly stereotypical and driven by the avoidance of contact with predators. Lastly, if this strategy is unsuccessful, the predator-contact mode of defense is evoked. In the rat, these modes produce modified foraging behavior (pre-encounter), freezing and immobility (post-encounter), flight and fight (predatory contact). Others, most notably Timberlake (2001), have stressed how appetitive learning enhances a general search mode for more distal CSs and a focal-search mode for more proximal CSs. Distinct topographical CRs are sometimes observed as a function of the modality of the CS (Holland, 1977), an adaptive specialization accommodated by Timberlake's analysis.

Conclusions

Remarkable progress in building models of Pavlovian conditioning has occurred by first trying to understand principles of association, and then considering issues such as timing and the organization of behavior. It is often said that Pavlovian conditioning is the best studied example of associative learning. Associative models derive their influence because they have something to say about any situation which involves a predictive relationship. A key feature of modern associative models is correction based on a common error term (US processing). Feedback from the environment updates linkages between internal event representations if the state of the environment differs from pre-existing expectations. Building a complete model, however, is impossible without considering the CS may itself change during conditioning (CS processing). Here, I discussed the usefulness of constructs such as CS-US associability, and dividing the CS into subsets of elements (e.g., inhibited and replaced elements). Hybrid models combining aspects of CS and US models have culminated in reasonably simple but powerful theories.

Associative processes cannot be understood in isolation. A number of theorists have considered how CS-US learning translates into behavior. Some issues addressed include specifying when conditioned behavior is evoked (timing), and how different behaviors are organized into functional systems. Here, the preparatory/consummatory distinction has been historically influential. Progress has been aided by considering the functional significance of the CR, and trying to integrate functional, associative, and neurophysiological analysis.

Unfortunately, many topics have been glossed over or omitted in this review. Topics that come to mind include learning based on the memory of the CS or US (Hall, 1996; Holland, 1981), occasion-setting (Bouton, 1993), and retrieval processes (Stout & Miller, 2007). Nevertheless, although necessarily limited, this review has covered the rather broad territory needed to bring us from principles of associative learning (inside) to the emergence of well-timed adaptive CRs (outside).

References

Bakal, C. W., Johnson, R. D., & Rescorla, R. A. (1974). The effect of change in US quality on the blocking effect. *Pavlovian Journal of Biological Science*, *9*, 97–103.

Balsam, P. D., Drew, M. R., & Yang, C. (2002). Timing at the start of associative learning. *Learning and Motivation*, *33*, 141–155.

Barnet, R. C, Grahame, N. J., & Miller, R. R. (1993). Temporal encoding as a determinant of blocking. *Journal of Experimental Psychology: Animal Behavior Processes*, *19*, 327–341.

Belova, M. A., Paton J. J., Morrison, S. E., & Salzman, C. D. (2007). Expectation modulates neural responses to pleasant and aversive stimuli in primate amygdala. *Neuron*, *55*, 970–984.

Bitterman, M. E. (1964). Classical conditioning in the goldfish as a function of the CS-US interval. *Journal of Comparative and Physiological Psychology*, *58*, 359–366.

Blaisdell, A. P., Denniston, J. C., & Miller, R. R. (1998). Temporal encoding as a determinant of overshadowing. *Journal of Experimental Psychology: Animal Behavior Processes*, *24*, 72–83.

Bolles, R. C., & Fanselow, M. S. (1980). A perceptual-defensive-recuperative model of fear and pain. *Behavioral and Brain Sciences*, *3*, 291–301.

Bouton M.E. (1993). Context, time, and memory retrieval in the interference paradigms of Pavlovian learning. *Psychological Bulletin*, *114*, 80–99.

Bouton, M. E., & Sunsay, C. (2003). Importance of trials versus accumulating time across trials in partially reinforced appetitive conditioning. *Journal of Experimental Psychology: Animal Behavior Processes*, *29*, 62–77.

Brandon, S. E., Bombace, J. C., Falls, W. A., & Wagner, A. R. (1991). Modulation of unconditioned defensive reflexes by a putative emotive Pavlovian conditioned stimulus. *Journal of Experimental Psychology: Animal Behavior Processes, 17*, 312–322.

Brandon, S. E., Vogel, E. H., & Wagner, A. R. (2000). A componential view of configural cues in generalization and discrimination in Pavlovian conditioning. *Behavioural Brain Research, 110*, 67–72.

Brown, P. L., & Jenkins, H. M. (1968). Auto-shaping of the pigeon's key-peck. *Journal of Experimental Analysis of Behavior, 11*, 1–8.

Bush, R. R., & Mosteller, F. (1955). *Stochastic models for learning*. New York: John Wiley & Sons, Inc.

Christian, K. M., & Thompson, R. F. (2003). Neural substrates of eyeblink conditioning: Acquisition and retention. *Learning and Memory, 10*, 427–455.

Cole, S., & McNally, G. P. (2007). Opioid receptors mediate direct predictive fear learning. Evidence from one-trial blocking. *Learning and Memory, 14*, 229–235.

Cooper, L. D., Aronson, L., Balsam, P. D., & Gibbon, J. (1990). Duration of signals for intertrial reinforcement and nonreinforcement in random control procedures. *Journal of Experimental Psychology: Animal Behavior Processes, 16*, 14–26.

Davis, M., Schlesinger, L. S., & Sorenson, C. A. (1989). Temporal specificity of fear conditioning: Effects of different conditioned stimulus-unconditioned stimulus intervals on the fear-potentiated startle effect. *Journal of Experimental Psychology: Animal Behavior Processes, 15*, 295–310.

Delamater, A. R. (2012). On the nature of CS and US representations in Pavlovian learning. *Learning & Behavior, 40*, 1–23.

Delamater, A. R., & Holland, P. C. (2008). The influence of CS-US interval on several different indices of learning in appetitive conditioning. *Journal of Experimental Psychology: Animal Behavior Processes, 34*, 202–222.

Delamater, A. R., & Oakeshott, S. (2007). Learning about multiple attributes of reward in Pavlovian conditioning. *Annual of the New York Academy of Sciences, 1104*, 1–20.

Dickinson, A. (1977). Appetitive-aversive interactions: Superconditioning of fear by an appetitive CS. *Quarterly Journal of Experimental Psychology, 29*, 71–83.

Dickinson, A., & Dearing, M. F. (1979). Appetitive-aversive interactions and inhibitory processes. In A. Dickinson & R. A. Boakes (Eds.), *Mechanisms of learning and motivation. A memorial volume to Jerzy Konorski*. (pp. 203–231). Hillsdale, NJ: Erlbaum.

Dickinson, A., Hall, G., & Mackintosh, N. J. (1976). Surprise and the attenuation of blocking. *Journal of Experimental Psychology: Animal Behavior Processes, 2*, 313–322.

Domjan, M. (2005). Pavlovian conditioning: A functional perspective. *Annual Review of Psychology, 56*, 179–206.

Drew, M. R., Yang, C., Ohyama, T., Balsam, P. D. (2004). Temporal specificity of extinction in autoshaping. *Journal of Experimental Psychology: Animal Behavior Processes, 30*, 163–176.

Drew M. R., Zupan B., Cooke A., Couvillon P. A., Balsam P. D. (2005). Temporal control of conditioned responding in goldfish. *Journal of Experimental Psychology: Animal Behavior Processes, 31*, 31–39.

Durlach, P. J. (1983). The effect of signaling intertrial USs in autoshaping. *Journal of Experimental Psychology: Animal Behavior Processes, 9*, 374–389.

Fanselow, M. S., & Baackes, M. P. (1982). Conditioned fear-induced opiate analgesia on the formalin test: Evidence for two aversive motivational systems. *Learning and Motivation, 13*, 200–221.

Fanselow, M. S., & Lester, L. S. (1988). A functional behavioristic approach to aversively motivated behavior: Predatory imminence as a determinant of the topography of defensive behavior. In R. C. Bolles & M. D. Beecher (Eds.), *Evolution and learning* (pp. 185–212). Hillsdale, NJ: Erlbaum.

Gallistel, C. R., Fairhurst, S., & Balsam, P. (2004). The learning curve: Implications of a quantitative analysis. *Proceedings of the National Academy of Sciences, 101*, 13124–13131.

Gallistel, C. R., & Gibbon, J. (2000). Time, rate, and conditioning. *Psychological Review, 107*, 289–344.

Gibbon, J. (1977). Scalar expectancy theory and Weber's law in animal timing. *Psychological Review, 84*, 279–325.

Gibbon, J., Baldock, M. D., Locurto, C. M., Gold, L., & Terrace, H. S. (1977). Trial and intertrial durations in autoshaping. *Journal of Experimental Psychology: Animal Behavior Processes, 3*, 264–284.

Gibbon, J., & Balsam, P. D. (1981). The spread of association in time. In C. M. Locurto, H. S. Terrace, & J. Gibbon (Eds.), *Autoshaping and conditioning theory* (pp. 219–253). New York: Academic Press.

Gottlieb, D. A. (2004). Acquisition with partial and continuous reinforcement in pigeon autoshaping. *Learning & Behavior, 32*, 321–334.

Gottlieb, D. A., & Begej, E. L. (2014). Principles of Pavlovian conditioning. Description, content, function. In F. K. McSweeney & E. S. Murphy (Eds.), *The Wiley-Blackwell Handbook of Operant Conditioning* (pp. 3–26). Oxford: Wiley-Blackwell.

Hall, G. (1996). Learning about associatively-activated stimulus representations: Implications for acquired equivalence and perceptual learning. *Animal Learning & Behavior, 24*, 233–255.

Hall, G., & Pearce, J. M. (1979). Latent inhibition of a CS during CS-US pairings. *Journal of Experimental Psychology: Animal Behavior Processes, 5*, 31–42.

Harris, J. A. (2006). Elemental representations of stimuli in associative learning. *Psychological Review, 113*, 584–605.

Harris, J. A. (2011). The acquisition of conditioned responding. *Journal of Experimental Psychology: Animal Behavior Processes, 37*, 151–164.

Harris, J. A., & Livesey, E. J. (2010). An attention modulated associative network. *Learning & Behavior, 38*, 1–26.

Haselgrove, M., Esber, G. R., Pearce, J. M., & Jones, P. M. (2010). Two kinds of attention in Pavlovian conditioning: Evidence for a hybrid model of learning. *Journal of Experimental Psychology: Animal Behavior Processes, 36*, 456–470.

Holland, P. C. (1977). Conditioned stimulus as a determinant of the form of the Pavlovian conditioned response. *Journal of Experimental Psychology: Animal Behavior Processes, 3*, 77–104.

Holland, P. C. (1981). Acquisition of representation-mediated conditioned food aversions. *Learning and Motivation, 12*, 1–18.

Holland, P. C. (2000). Trial and intertrial durations in appetitive conditioning in rats. *Animal Learning & Behavior, 28*, 121–135.

Holland, P. C. (2008). Cognitive versus stimulus-response theories of learning. *Learning & Behavior, 36*, 227–241.

Holland P. C., & Gallagher, M. (1999). Amygdala circuitry in attentional and representational processes. *Trends in the Cognitive Sciences, 3*, 65–73.

Holland, P. C., & Gallagher, M. (1993). Effects of amygdala central nucleus lesions on blocking and unblocking. *Behavioral Neuroscience, 107*, 235–245.

Holland, P. C., & Kenmuir, C. (2005). Variations in unconditioned stimulus processing in unblocking. *Journal of Experimental Psychology: Animal Behavior Processes, 31*, 155–171.

Hollis, K. L., Pharr, V. L., Dumas, M. J., Britton, G. B. & Field, J. (1997). Classical conditioning provides paternity advantage for territorial male blue gouramis (*Trichogaster trichopterus*). *Journal of Comparative Psychology, 111*, 219–225.

Hull, C. L. (1943). *Principles of Behavior.* New York: Appleton-Century-Crofts.

Jenkins, H. M., & Moore, B. R. (1973). The form of the auto-shaped response with food or water reinforcers. *Journal of the Experimental Analysis of Behavior, 20,* 163–181.

Jones, P. M., & Haselgrove, M. (2011). Overshadowing and associability change. *Journal of Experimental Psychology: Animal Behavior Processes, 37,* 287–299.

Kamin, L. J. (1968). "Attention like" processes in classical conditioning. In M. R. Jones (Ed.), *Miami symposium on the prediction of behavior: Aversive stimulation* (pp. 9–31). Miami: Miami University Press.

Kehoe, E. J., & Joscelyne, A. (2005). Temporally specific extinction of conditioned responses in the rabbit (*Oryctolagus cuniculus*) nictitating membrane preparation. *Behavioral Neuroscience, 119,* 1011–1022.

Kehoe, E. J., Ludvig E. A., Dudeney, J. E., Neufeld, J., & Sutton, R. S. (2008). Magnitude and timing of nictitating membrane movements during classical conditioning of the rabbit (*Oryctolagus cuniculus*). *Behavioral Neuroscience, 122,* 471–476.

Kirkpatrick, K., & Church, R. M. (2000). Independent effects of stimulus and cycle duration on appetitive conditioning in rats: The role of timing processes. *Animal Learning & Behavior, 28,* 373–388.

Konorski, J. (1948) *Conditioned reflexes and neuron organization.* Cambridge, UK: Cambridge University Press.

Konorski, J. (1967). *Integrative activity of the brain.* Chicago: University of Chicago Press.

Kremer, E. F. (1978). The Rescorla-Wagner model: Losses in associative strength in compound conditioned stimuli. *Journal of Experimental Psychology: Animal Behavior Processes, 4,* 22–36.

Lattal, K. M. (1999). Trial and intertrial durations in Pavlovian conditioning: Issues of learning and performance. *Journal of Experimental Psychology: Animal Behavior Processes, 25,* 433–450.

Lattal, K. M., & Nakajima, S. (1998). Overexpectation in appetitive Pavlovian and instrumental conditioning. *Animal Learning & Behavior, 26,* 351–360.

Le Pelley, M. E. (2004). The role of associative history in models of associative learning: A selective review and a hybrid model. *Quarterly Journal of Experimental Psychology, 57B,* 193–243.

Li, J., Schiller D., Schoenbaum G., Phelps E. A., & Daw N. D. (2011). Differential roles of human striatum and amygdala in associative learning. *Nature Neuroscience, 14,* 1250–1252.

LoLordo, V. M. (1979). Constraints on learning. In M. E. Bitterman, V. M.LoLordo, J. B. Overmier, & M. E. Rashotte (Eds.), *Animal learning: Survey and analysis* (pp. 473–504). New York: Plenum Press.

Lubow, R. E., & Moore, A. U. (1959). Latent inhibition: The effect of non-reinforced pre-exposure to the conditioned stimulus. *Journal of Comparative and Physiological Psychology, 52,* 415–419.

Ludvig, E. A., Sutton, R. S., & Kehoe, E. J. (2008). Stimulus representation and the timing of reward-prediction errors in models of the dopamine system. *Neural Computation, 20,* 3034–3054.

Ludvig, E. A., Sutton, R. S., & Kehoe, E. J. (2012). Evaluating the TD model of classical conditioning. *Learning & Behavior, 40,* 305–319.

Mackintosh, N. J. (1975). A theory of attention: Variation in the associability of stimuli with reinforcement. *Psychological Review, 82,* 276–298.

Mackintosh, N. J. (1976). Overshadowing and stimulus intensity. *Animal Learning & Behavior, 4,* 186–192.

Mahometa, M. J., & Domjan, M. (2005). Classical conditioning increases reproductive success in Japanese quail, *Coturnix japonica. Animal Behaviour, 69,* 983–989.

Meck, W. A. (2006). Neuroanatomical localization of an internal clock: A functional link between mesolimbic, nigrostriatal, and mesocortical dopamingeric systems. *Brain Research, 1109*, 93–107.

Ohyama, T., & Mauk, M. D. (2001). Latent acquisition of timed responses in cerebellar cortex. *The Journal of Neuroscience, 21*, 682–690.

Paletta, M. S., & Wagner, A. R. (1986). Development of context-specific tolerance to morphine: Support for a dual-process interpretation. *Behavioral Neuroscience, 100*, 611–623.

Pavlov, I. P. (1927). *Conditioned reflexes.* New York: Dover.

Pearce, J. M. (1987). A model for stimulus generalization in Pavlovian conditioning. *Psychological Review, 94*, 61–73.

Pearce, J. M. (2002). Evaluation and development of a connectionist theory of configural learning. *Animal Learning & Behavior, 30*, 73–95.

Pearce, J. M., & Hall, G. (1980). A model for Pavlovian learning: Variations in the effectiveness of conditioned but not of unconditioned stimuli. *Psychological Review, 87*, 532–552.

Pearce, J. M., & Mackintosh, N. J. (2010). Two theories of attention: A review and a possible integration. In C. J. Mitchell & M. E. Le Pelley (Eds.), *Attention and associative learning: From brain to behaviour* (pp. 11–39). Oxford: Oxford University Press.

Pearce, J. M., & Redhead, E. S. (1993). The influence of an irrelevant stimulus on two discriminations. *Journal of Experimental Psychology: Animal Behavior Processes, 19*, 180–190.

Pearce, J. M., & Redhead, E. S. (1995). Supernormal conditioning. *Journal of Experimental Psychology: Animal Behavior Processes, 21*, 155–165.

Quincey, V. L. (1971). Conditioned-suppression with no CS-US contingency in the rat. *Canadian Journal of Psychology, 25*, 69–82.

Redgrave, P., & Gurney, K. (2006). The short-latency dopamine signal: A role in discovering novel actions? *Nature Reviews Neuroscience, 7*, 967–975.

Redhead, E. S., & Pearce, J. M. (1995). Stimulus salience and negative patterning. *Quarterly Journal of Experimental Psychology, 48B*, 67–83.

Rescorla, R. A. (1968). Probability of shock in the presence and absence of CS in fear conditioning. *Journal of Comparative and Physiological Psychology, 66*, 1–5.

Rescorla, R. A. (1971). Variation in the effectiveness of reinforcement and nonreinforcement following prior inhibitory conditioning. *Learning and Motivation, 2*, 113–123.

Rescorla, R. A. (1972). "Configural" conditioning in discrete trial bar pressing. *Journal of Comparative and Physiological Psychology, 79*, 307–317.

Rescorla, R. A. (1997). Summation: Assessment of a configural theory. *Animal Learning & Behavior, 25*, 200–209.

Rescorla, R. A. (2000). Associative changes in excitors and inhibitors differ when they are conditioned in compound. *Journal of Experimental Psychology: Animal Behavior Processes, 26*, 428–438.

Rescorla, R. A., & Wagner, A. R. (1972). A theory of Pavlovian conditioning: Variations in the effectiveness of reinforcement and nonreinforcement. In A. H. Black & W. F. Prokasy (Eds.), *Classical conditioning II: Current research and theory* (pp. 64–99). New York: Appleton-Century-Crofts.

Roesch, M. R., Calu, D. J., Esber, G. R., & Schoenbaum, G. (2010). All that glitters . . . dissociating attention and outcome expectancy from prediction error signals. *Journal of Neurophysiology, 104*, 587–595.

Savastano, H. I., & Miller, R. R. (1998). Time as content in Pavlovian conditioning. *Behavioural Processes, 44*, 147–162.

Schmajuk, N. A., & DiCarlo, J. J. (1992). Stimulus configuration, classical conditioning, and hippocampal function. *Psychological Review, 99*, 268–305.

Siegel, S. (1975). Evidence from rats that morphine tolerance is a learned response. *Journal of Comparative and Physiological Psychology, 89*, 498–506.

Siegel, S. (1977). Morphine tolerance acquisition as an associative process. *Journal of Experimental Psychology: Animal Behavior Processes, 3*, 1–13.

Smith, M. C. (1968). CS-US interval and US intensity in classical conditioning of the rabbit's nictitating membrane response. *Journal of Comparative and Physiological Psychology, 66*, 679–687.

Spence, K. W., & Norris, E. B. (1950). Eyelid conditioning as a function of the inter-trial interval. *Journal of Experimental Psychology, 40*, 716–720.

Stout, S. C., & Miller, R. R. (2007). Sometimes-competing retrieval (SOCR): A formalization of the comparator hypothesis. *Psychological Review, 114*, 759–783.

Sutton, R. S., & Barto, A. G. (1987). A temporal difference model of classical conditioning. In *Proceedings of the Ninth Annual Conference of the Cognitive Science Society* (pp. 355–378). Hillsdale, NJ: Erlbaum.

Tait, R. W., & Saladin, M. S. (1986). Concurrent development of excitatory and inhibitory associations during backward conditioning. *Animal Learning & Behavior, 14*, 133–137.

Timberlake, W. (2001). Motivated modes in behavior systems. In R. R. Mowrer & S. B. Klein (Eds.), *Handbook of contemporary learning theories* (pp. 155–209). Mahwah, NJ: Erlbaum.

Tobler, P. N., Dickinson, A., & Schultz, W. (2003). Coding of predicted reward omission by dopamine neurons in a conditioned inhibition paradigm. *Journal of Neuroscience, 23*, 10302–10410.

Vandercar, D. H., & Schneiderman, N. (1967). Interstimulus interval functions in different response systems during classical discrimination conditioning of rabbits. *Psychonomic Science, 9*, 9–10.

Vogel, E. H., Brandon, S. E., & Wagner, A. R. (2003). Stimulus representation in SOP II: An application to inhibition of delay. *Behavioural Processes, 62*, 27–48.

Waelti, P., Dickinson, A., & Schultz, W. (2001). Dopamine responses comply with basic assumptions of formal learning theory. *Nature, 412*, 43–48.

Wagner, A. R. (1981). SOP: A model of automatic memory processing in animal behavior. In N. E. Spear & R. R. Miller (Eds.), *Information processing in animals: Memory mechanisms* (pp. 5–47). Hillsdale, NJ: Erlbaum.

Wagner, A. R. (2003). Context-sensitive elemental theory. *Quarterly Journal of Experimental Psychology 56B*, 7–29.

Wagner, A. R., & Brandon, S. E. (1989). Evolution of a structured connectionist model of Pavlovian conditioning (AESOP). In S. B. Klein & R. R. Mowrer (Eds.), *Contemporary learning theories: Pavlovian conditioning and the status of traditional learning theory* (pp. 149– 189). Hillsdale, NJ: Erlbaum.

Wagner, A. R., & Larew, M. B. (1985). Opponent processes and Pavlovian inhibition. In R. R. Miller & N. E. Spear (Eds.), *Information processing in animals: Conditioned inhibition* (pp. 223–265). Hillsdale, NJ: Erlbaum.

Wagner, A. R., Logan, F. A., Haberlandt, K., & Price, T. (1968). Stimulus selection in animal discrimination learning. *Journal of Experimental Psychology, 76*, 171–180.

Wagner, A. R., & Rescorla, R. A. (1972). Inhibition in Pavlovian conditioning: Applications of a theory. In R. A. Boakes & M. S. Halliday (Eds.), *Inhibition and learning* (pp. 301–336). New York: Academic Press.

Wasserman, E. A., Franklin, S. R., & Hearst, E. (1974). Pavlovian appetitive contingencies and approach versus withdrawal to conditioned stimuli in pigeons. *Journal of Comparative and Physiological Psychology, 86*, 616–627.

Williams, D. A., Johns, K. W., & Brindas, J. L. (2008). Timing during inhibitory conditioning. *Journal of Experimental Psychology: Animal Behavior Processes, 34*, 237–246.
Williams, D. A., Lawson, C. L., Cook, R., Mather, A. A., & Johns, K. W. (2008). Timed excitatory conditioning under zero and negative contingencies. *Journal of Experimental Psychology: Animal Behavior Processes, 34*, 94–105.
Williams, D. A., Overmier, J. B., & LoLordo, V. M. (1992). A reevaluation of Rescorla's early dictums about Pavlovian conditioned inhibition. *Psychological Bulletin, 111*, 275–290.
Wilson, P. N., & Pearce, J. M. (1992). A configural analysis for feature negative discrimination learning. *Journal of Experimental Psychology: Animal Behavior Processes, 18*, 265–272.
Woodbury, C. B. (1943). The learning of stimulus patterns by dogs. *Journal of Comparative Psychology, 35*, 29–40.
Zelikowsky, M., & Fanselow, M. S. (2011). Conditional analgesia, negative feedback, and error correction. In T. R. Schachtman & S. Reilly (Eds.), *Associative learning and conditioning theory: Human and non-human applications* (pp. 305–320). New York: Oxford University Press.

3

A Contemporary Behavioral Perspective on Extinction

Drina Vurbic and Mark E. Bouton

The term *extinction* was introduced by Pavlov (1927), who first discovered and documented the phenomenon in classical conditioning. In a celebrated experiment, a dog learned to salivate to the sound of a beating metronome (the conditioned stimulus or CS) when Pavlov paired it with food (the unconditioned stimulus or US) several times. After establishing a conditioned salivation response, Pavlov repeatedly presented the metronome without any food, which caused the response to weaken. Since this early demonstration, extinction (which can refer not only to the gradual decline in behavior but also the experimental method that produces it) has become one of the most intensely studied behavioral phenomena in both classical and instrumental conditioning. This is due in part to its clinical importance, because extinction serves as the basis for exposure therapies for anxiety disorders (Bouton, Mineka, & Barlow, 2001; Maren, 2011) and may be a useful tool in the treatment of substance abuse (Conklin & Tiffany, 2002), and other behavioral problems such as overeating (Boutelle et al., 2011) and may be a useful tool in the treatment of substance abuse (Conklin & Tiffany, 2002) as well as other behavioral problems.

Extinction is a complex and multi-faceted phenomenon. One thing that has been emphasized in recent years is that it does not erase the original learning. For example, in his earliest experiments, Pavlov (1927) also showed that the extinguished response could return if time was allowed to pass following extinction. This phenomenon, known as *spontaneous recovery*, has been demonstrated many times in both classical and instrumental conditioning (Brooks & Bouton, 1993; Pavlov, 1927; Rescorla, 2004a). Because of spontaneous recovery and other phenomena that will be discussed later in the chapter, it is generally agreed that extinction does not destroy the original learning.

This chapter provides a review of the behavioral research literature on extinction. In the first part, we consider the mechanisms of extinction—the behavioral processes

The Wiley Blackwell Handbook of Operant and Classical Conditioning, First Edition.
Edited by Frances K. McSweeney and Eric S. Murphy.

that make it occur. In the second part, we consider certain "relapse" phenomena (including but not limited to spontaneous recovery) in which extinguished behavior can return after extinction has reduced responding. These phenomena are important because they can be taken as models (and mechanisms) of relapse after therapy (e.g., Bouton, 1988, 2000, 2002). They also support the idea that extinction involves a form of context-dependent new learning. In the final part of the chapter, we consider procedures that have been developed to facilitate extinction learning and perhaps its permanency. Throughout, in addition to emphasizing the clinical relevance of research on extinction, we emphasize the general role that the organism's knowledge of the background context plays in producing extinction and the various relapse phenomena.

Mechanisms of Extinction

Role of Prediction Error. Most contemporary learning theories have advanced the idea that conditioning (and extinction) is based on a process of error correction. This idea was popularized by the now-classic Rescorla-Wagner (1972) model. The main premise of this model is that learning occurs when a significant event (i.e., the US) is surprising. For instance, on the first few trials of conditioning, when the CS predicts nothing in particular, the occurrence of the US is surprising. The unexpected outcome generates an error signal that the learning mechanism incrementally corrects by strengthening an association between the CS and US. As a result, the CS excites a greater expectation of the US when it is presented the next time, and the predictive error is reduced. The process repeats itself over trials until the CS becomes a good predictor of the US, at which point no further learning occurs. The same idea is at work in extinction. According to the model, at the start of extinction, the non-occurrence of the US when the CS is presented is also surprising. To correct the prediction error, the association with the US is reduced until the CS accurately predicts the no-US outcome. Given a sufficient amount of extinction, the model assumes that associative strength can be eliminated entirely. Thus, the learning rule that forms the basis of the Rescorla-Wagner model provides a straightforward explanation for both acquisition and extinction through correction of prediction error.

The Rescorla-Wagner model actually assumes that an animal uses all available stimuli, and not merely the target CS, to predict the outcome of a trial. That is, the learning mechanism sums the predictive values of *all* the CSs that are presented on a trial. Based on this premise, the model makes several interesting predictions. For example, if two CSs are separately paired with a US and then combined in compound and paired with the same US, their prediction can sum to a value greater than the US—and thus generate negative prediction error. As a consequence, there is a loss of responding to the two CSs even though the compound is reinforced (e.g., Kremer, 1978; Lattal & Nakajima, 1998). The model also predicts that no-US extinction trials should be particularly effective when two or more separately-conditioned CSs are presented in compound, because the combined CSs should summate and create a large prediction error. Compound trials should thus lead to a greater loss of responding in extinction than the same number of trials conducted with each CS individually. Rescorla (2006) demonstrated this kind of "deepened extinction" using several conditioning preparations (see also Janak & Corbit, 2011; Kearns, Tunstall, & Weiss, 2012; Thomas & Ayres, 2004).

More recent theories of associative learning have continued to incorporate some kind of error correction mechanism (e.g., Pearce, 1994; Pearce & Hall, 1980; Sutton & Barto, 1981; Wagner, 2003). Importantly, these models have often assumed that the prediction error that occurs in extinction creates the learning of inhibition (rather than unlearning), and this has the same effect on reducing prediction error. As a result of the new inhibitory learning, a CS after extinction is predicted to have both an inhibitory and an excitatory association with the US (retained from conditioning).

Error correction approaches are also consistent with neurobiological studies investigating the substrates of associative learning. There is now considerable evidence that the brain encodes error signals during extinction. In appetitive learning, the firing of midbrain dopamine neurons appears to have several important roles, including detection of errors in reward prediction (Myers & Davis, 2002; Pan, Schmidt, Wickens, & Hyland, 2008). Studies with monkeys have shown that dopamine neurons encode both positive and negative prediction errors (Schultz, 1997; Waelti, Dickinson, & Schultz, 2001). Rewards that are greater than expected activate these neurons, whereas predictable rewards fail to activate them. In line with a prediction error mechanism, rewards that are smaller than expected (or are omitted entirely) depress activation below a baseline level of activity. The differential activation following expected versus unexpected rewards has also been shown in humans (Zaghloul et al., 2009). Prediction error processes in extinction are now widely investigated by behavioral neuroscientists (McNally, Johansen, & Blair, 2011; McNally & Westbrook, 2003; Tronson, Corcoran, Jovasevic, & Radulovic, 2008). Collectively, data from a number of neurobiological studies have supported a role for error correction in extinction, as well as the behavioral models founded on this view.

Importance of the Partial Reinforcement Extinction Effect (PREE). Like older views of conditioning, the more recent theories built on the basis of error correction assume that the strength of learned responding reflects the strength of the CS-US or response-reinforcer association, or so-called "associative strength." Perhaps ironically, one of the greatest problems for this general view is one of the most well-known phenomena in the extinction literature: the *partial reinforcement extinction effect* (*PREE*; see Mackintosh, 1974, for a review). First observed by Humphreys (1939), the PREE occurs when there is greater persistence during extinction of behaviors that have been intermittently reinforced relative to those that have always been reinforced. For example, rats that were trained to run down an alleyway for food ran faster in extinction if only half of the trials had been reinforced than if all the trials had been reinforced (Likely, Little, & Mackintosh, 1971). Although the PREE was initially investigated using mostly instrumental tasks, there have been demonstrations in classical conditioning as well (Haselgrove, Aydin, & Pearce, 2004; Rescorla, 1999). But importantly, the PREE implies that there is a sense in which partially-reinforced behaviors can be "stronger" than continuously reinforced ones, even when there have been fewer occasions on which the response (or CS) has been associated with the reinforcer.

Several contemporary views can accommodate the PREE. One example is rate estimation theory (RET), a theory of classical conditioning (Gallistel & Gibbon,

2000) that characterizes extinction as a form of discrimination. According to RET, an animal decides to stop responding during extinction when it detects a change in the rate of reinforcement during the CS. That decision is based on achieving a threshold ratio of the amount of time accumulated in the CS during extinction over the time accumulated in the CS between successive US presentations in conditioning. Under conditions of partial reinforcement, animals learn to expect the US after more accumulated time in the CS compared to continuous reinforcement. It thus requires more CS time in extinction for the ratio to exceed the decision threshold, which maintains responding across a larger number of extinction trials. An important point to note is that in contrast to more traditional trial-based approaches, RET calculates the reinforcement rate in acquisition according to the amount of CS time rather than the number of CS presentations. From this standpoint several predictions can be made, including one that has been tested in a number of experiments. Haselgrove et al. (2004) investigated whether the PREE could be obtained in situations where partially and continuously reinforced groups are equated on the accumulated CS time in acquisition. In one of their experiments, rats were given continuous reinforcement with a 20-s CS or partial reinforcement in which a 10-s CS was reinforced on half of the trials. Note that the reinforcement rate in the two conditions is the same; for both groups, the accumulated CS time between the US presentations is 20-s. According to RET, these conditions should result in equivalent responding in extinction. This was not the case, however, as the PREE was still observed. Related results were also obtained by Bouton, Woods, and Todd (2014), further questioning the main premise of RET (see also Bouton & Sunsay, 2003; Gottlieb, 2004; Haselgrove & Pearce, 2003; Morris & Bouton, 2006; Sunsay & Bouton, 2008; Sunsay, Stetson, & Bouton, 2004, for additional challenges).

An older set of theories also accounts for the PREE. At the center of both Amsel's frustration theory (Amsel, 1967, 1992) and Capaldi's sequential theory (Capaldi, 1966, 1994) is the idea that stimuli generated by the outcomes of conditioning trials can acquire some degree of control over responding. Frustration theory emphasized the frustrating consequences of not receiving an expected outcome, which can stop or suppress performance. According to Amsel (1967, 1992), the PREE occurs because training with partial reinforcement allows for the response to be reinforced in the presence of frustration. During extinction, frustration develops over trials with nonreinforcement. An animal that has been trained with continuous reinforcement has never experienced this kind of frustration and thus gives up in the absence of reward. On the other hand, frustration experienced during partial reinforcement serves as a cue for further responding. Capaldi's sequential theory (Capaldi, 1966, 1994) alternatively argued that the PREE can be explained by the fact that partial reinforcement allows animals to learn to respond under conditions that are more like extinction. During partial reinforcement, the animal is rewarded for responding in the presence of a memory of recent nonreinforced (N) trials. When it later encounters a string of N trials during extinction, the rat continues to respond because it had previously been rewarded for doing so. Thus, after partial reinforcement the memory for N trials serves a context in which responding is reinforced, and the similarities between that context and the one encountered in extinction encourages the same kind of persistence. In contrast, a rat that has been trained with continuous reinforcement stops responding more quickly because it has never been rewarded for responding in the presence of a memory of N trials.

Support for Capaldi's theory has come from studies investigating the effects on extinction of different sequences of reinforced and nonreinforced trials in acquisition (see Mackintosh, 1974, for a review). For instance, Spivey and Hess (1968) demonstrated that the PREE is observed only if reinforced (R) trials follow N trials. One group of rats was given two R trials followed by two N trials on each training day (RRNN), while for another the order was reversed (NNRR). All of the rats were then given extinction. Although both groups received equivalent rates of reinforcement, only Group NNRR demonstrated the PREE. This finding is consistent with sequential theory, because the RRNN group was never rewarded for responding after N trials. Sequential theory is in fact consistent with a great deal of research on the PREE (see Mackintosh, 1974).

Summary. It is now widely assumed that extinction is governed by the process of correcting prediction error. That is, learning is engaged by the surprisingness of a reinforcer when cues (or behaviors) predict one. Because (as developed further below), extinction is best characterized as a new form of learning, rather than erasure, one can assume that prediction error creates new learning that competes with or interferes with the original learning (e.g., Bouton, 1993). As noted earlier, several models of associative learning assume that extinction creates the conditions for inhibitory learning (e.g., Pearce, 1994; Pearce & Hall, 1980; Wagner, 2003). However, the importance of the PREE lies in the fact that it tells us that simple excitatory and/ or inhibitory strength (or habit strength in an older language) is not enough to explain behavioral persistence. Most views of the PREE have adopted the assumption that the inclusion of nonreinforced trials in conditioning increases the generalization of acquisition to extinction; or, in related terms, it makes extinction more difficult to discriminate from acquisition. Although some have claimed that this sort of discrimination process calls for a molar perspective on behavior (Baum, 2012), frustration theory and sequential theory successfully framed it in more molecular terms by assuming that the organism associates acquisition with background cues, such as the emotional state engendered by nonreinforcement or the memory of nonreinforced trials. In effect, the PREE has led many investigators to assume that generalization (or discrimination) between the contexts of acquisition and extinction plays a role in extinction.

Context and Relapse Effects after Extinction

As noted previously, researchers have uncovered several relapse phenomena in which a conditioned response returns after it has been extinguished. These effects have attracted attention in part because they are thought to be clinically relevant (e.g., Bouton et al., 2001; Conklin & Tiffany, 2002). Behavior therapies that incorporate the principles of extinction have shown some promise in treating these disorders, but the potential for relapse after extinction has taken place poses an obvious problem. Another reason for investigating these phenomena is that they help elucidate the behavioral processes that are involved in extinction. For example, it was Pavlov's

(1927) observation of spontaneous recovery that first led to the revelation that extinction is not merely the erasure of previous learning. As we will see, spontaneous recovery and other relapse effects are further consistent with the preceding section of this chapter in pointing to a role of context in understanding extinction.

The Renewal Effect. The renewal effect (e.g., Bouton & Bolles, 1979a; Bouton & King, 1983) is an especially important relapse phenomenon. In renewal, after extinction has eliminated responding, the response returns when the animal is removed from the context where extinction took place and responding is tested in another context. In an early demonstration of renewal, Bouton and King (1983; see also Bouton & Bolles, 1979a) trained rats in a fear conditioning preparation known as conditioned suppression. They first paired a tone CS with a shock US in one context (Context A), which caused the rats to suppress an ongoing behavior (i.e., lever pressing for food). Extinction was provided in a second context (Context B), which eliminated conditioned suppression and allowed lever pressing in the CS to return to baseline levels. However, when the rats were tested back in Context A, suppression returned (so-called *ABA renewal*). Although responding in this group was weaker on the renewal test than a control group that never received extinction, the increase in fear from the end of extinction was robust and large.

Renewal has now been shown in a large number of experimental methods. In classical conditioning, renewal has been demonstrated many times with conditioned fear (as described above; e.g., Bouton, Vurbic, & Woods, 2008; Thomas & Ayres, 2004). Most of this work has been done in laboratory animals; however, renewal of fear has also been shown in people undergoing extinction of preexisting fears (Mystkowski, Craske, Echiverri, & Labus, 2006), as well as extinction of CSs that were conditioned in the laboratory (Neumann, Lipp, & Cory, 2007; Vansteenwegen et al., 2005). The renewal effect has also been demonstrated in appetitive conditioning in which a CS is paired with food (e.g., Bouton & Peck, 1989; Brooks & Bouton, 1994), and more recently with drug USs (e.g., Chaudhri, Sahuque, & Janak, 2008). Collins and Brandon (2002) also demonstrated a renewal effect in human social drinkers after exposure to alcohol related cues (i.e., the sight and smell of beer) after extinction (but see MacKillop, & Lisman, 2008; Stasiewicz, Brandon, & Bradizza, 2007). Other preparations include taste aversion learning in which a flavor CS is paired with illness (e.g., Rosas & Bouton, 1998), eyeblink conditioning in humans (Grillon, Alvarez, Johnson, & Chavis, 2008), and human contingency learning, where people estimate the predictive value of cues associated with different events (e.g., Rosas & Callejas-Aguilera, 2006). Recent studies have begun to study the phenomenon in instrumental learning as well. Renewal has been demonstrated after the extinction of lever pressing for food (e.g., Bouton, Todd, Vurbic, & Winterbauer, 2011; Nakajima, Tanaka, Urushihara, & Imada, 2000; Todd, 2013), and for drugs of abuse, such as heroin (Bossert, Liu, Lu, & Shaham, 2004; Bossert et al., 2012), cocaine (Kearns & Weiss, 2007), and alcohol (Hamlin, Newby, & McNally, 2007).

In the examples of renewal cited above, the different contexts were provided by different rooms (in the human studies) or separate experimental chambers (in the animal studies), which were modified to look, feel, and smell differently from each other. It is important to note, however, that "context" includes other types of stimuli as well. Several kinds of internal cues have been shown to produce context effects in animals and humans, including changes in mood, deprivation state, hormonal state, as well as other subjective stimuli (see Bouton, 2002). For instance, Bouton, Kenney, and Rosengard (1990) reported that rats given a benzodiazepine drug during fear extinction showed a return of conditioned fear when tested without the drug (i.e., after receiving a placebo injection). Similar results have been shown when the extinction context is provided by alcohol (Cunningham, 1979; Lattal, 2007). The passage of time is also thought to function as a gradually changing internal context; when this context is sufficiently changed (as during a retention interval between extinction and testing, for example), extinguished responding can return. Thus, Pavlov's spontaneous recovery effect can be viewed as a renewal effect that occurs when the CS is tested outside its temporal extinction context (Bouton, 1988, 1993). Interestingly, recent work suggests that changes in external and internal contexts can summate to produce an even more powerful return of responding, such as when a change in the physical context is made following a retention interval (Laborda & Miller, 2012; Rosas & Bouton, 1998).

Renewal has been most commonly observed in the ABA paradigm described above, where acquisition and extinction occur in two different contexts (A and B), and renewal testing is performed in the original acquisition context (A). However, two other forms are at least as important. *ABC renewal* occurs when acquisition, extinction, and testing are each performed in different contexts. When testing occurs in Context C, extinguished responding returns (e.g., Bouton & Bolles, 1979a; Thomas, Larsen, & Ayres, 2003). And *AAB renewal* is observed when acquisition and extinction are conducted in the same context, and testing is performed in a second context, which again causes the response to return (e.g., Bouton & Ricker, 1994). ABC and AAB renewal are especially important theoretically, because they suggest that extinction transfers less effectively than conditioning to new contexts that have not been associated with either of them. Thus, mere removal from the extinction context can suffice.

Generally speaking, ABA renewal tends to be the strongest form of the renewal effect (Bouton & Swartzentruber, 1989; Harris, Jones, Bailey, & Westbrook, 2000). AAB designs often produce relatively weak recovery, and under some conditions AAB renewal has not been observed at all (e.g., Bossert et al., 2004; Crombag & Shaham, 2002; Nakajima et al., 2000). Until recently, there was uncertainty about whether ABC and AAB renewal occurred after the extinction of instrumental learning. However, Bouton et al. (2011) recently reported several experiments with instrumental (free operant) conditioning that demonstrated all three forms of renewal. In their experiments, hungry rats were first trained to lever press for food pellets and then extinguished. Every rat was then tested twice—once in the extinction context and once in the renewal context—in a counterbalanced order. Responding in the two contexts was then compared within subjects. The results indicated that although AAB renewal was weaker than ABA renewal, it was both reliable and replicable. In one experiment, for example, AAB renewal was observed when the rats were given twice as many sessions of extinction compared to acquisition. Todd, Winterbauer, and Bouton (2012a) have since demonstrated AAB renewal in nondeprived rats that were trained with sucrose and sweet/fatty food pellets. Todd, Winterbauer, and Bouton (2012b) have also shown that ABC renewal is strengthened by more extensive initial conditioning and by conditioning in more than one context. The results suggest that

ABC and AAB are replicable and apparently robust phenomena after the extinction of instrumental conditioning.

Research has also investigated the mechanisms through which the contexts control renewal. One possibility is that contexts acquire associative value during conditioning and extinction. Recall that according to Rescorla and Wagner's (1972) error correction model, the associative value of a CS (as well as that of co-present background stimuli) changes when there is a discrepancy between an animal's expectation and the actual outcome of a trial. During acquisition, the background stimuli in Context A, as well as the CS, are predicted to acquire a positive value when the US is presented. In a complementary way, extinction in a second context (i.e., ABA) should result in that context becoming inhibitory since its value at the start of extinction was zero. Thus, ABA renewal might occur because during testing the CS is (1.) released from inhibition in Context B and returned to (2.) an excitatory Context A. However, these mechanisms have not stood up well to empirical tests. In either classical or instrumental conditioning paradigms, extensive exposure to Context A prior to renewal testing, which should weaken the excitatory strength of Context A, has no apparent weakening effect on ABA renewal (Bouton & Peck, 1989; Bouton et al., 2011). And several studies have failed to find any evidence for conditioned inhibition in the extinction context (e.g., Bouton & King, 1983; Bouton & Swartzentruber, 1986, 1989; but see Polack, Laborda, & Miller, 2012).

Another possibility is that the meaning of a CS becomes ambiguous during extinction as a consequence of both conditioning and extinction (e.g., Bouton, 1984, 1988). (This idea acknowledges the fact that the original meaning is not erased by extinction.) The extinction context then acts to resolve this ambiguity by modulating the association that was learned there. More specifically, Bouton (e.g., 1994) has suggested that during extinction, animals learn an inhibitory association (i.e., CS-no US), which must be activated by the context in which it was acquired. The extinction context is thus thought to function as an *occasion setter* (see Holland, 1992), which allows this association to be expressed behaviorally. When testing occurs outside of that context, the CS-no US association is no longer in effect, and the original CS-US association is then expressed by default.

More recent research suggests that a somewhat different inhibitory process may be at work in the extinction and renewal of instrumental behavior. Although most reports of instrumental renewal can be explained with the occasion setting principles described above (e.g., Bouton et al., 2011), recent findings by Todd (2013) are more consistent with a different possibility. His experiments exploited a known property of occasion setting to test whether the extinction context operates this way. Previous research has shown that an occasion setter that is trained to modulate responding to one CS can also influence responding to another CS if the second CS has been similarly trained with a different occasion setter (Holland & Coldwell, 1993). Thus, an occasion setter can influence responding to a separately-trained CS. However, in instrumental extinction experiments, Todd (2013) contrastingly found no evidence that the extinction context transferred its inhibitory effect from one instrumental response to a second instrumental response that was similarly trained. Although an occasion setting mechanism could not be ruled out entirely, his findings suggested that the extinction context more likely inhibits the response directly (see also Rescorla,

1993, 1997). Thus, in instrumental extinction, the animal might learn to suppress performance of a specific response in the specific extinction context.

Reinstatement. Another recovery effect that has been observed in both classical and instrumental conditioning is reinstatement, in which an animal is reexposed to the US or reinforcer after extinction has taken place. As a result of this reexposure, responding returns when the CS is again presented or the instrumental response is made available (e.g., Pavlov, 1927; Rescorla & Heth, 1975). Careful investigation of this phenomenon has indicated that reinstatement depends importantly on conditioning of the context that occurs when the US is presented again. For one thing, reinstatement is not observed when the US is presented apart from the context where the response is tested (Baker, Steinwald, & Bouton, 1991; Bouton & Peck, 1989). For example, Bouton and Peck (1989) first presented rats with tone-food pairings and then extinguished the response to the tone. They then presented the food in the absence of the tone, which reinstated responding when the CS was subsequently tested in the same context. Reinstatement was not observed when US reexposure occurred in a different context. Similar results have been reported in fear conditioning, where the reinstating US presentations (shock exposures) demonstrably condition fear or anxiety to the context, which correlates with the strength of reinstatement (Bouton, 1984; Bouton & King, 1983). Additionally, other studies have shown that repeated exposure to the context between US reexposure and testing (which should extinguish conditioning of the context) reduces reinstatement (Baker et al., 1991; Bouton & Bolles, 1979b).

Baker et al. (1991) provided several forms of evidence that reinstated instrumental behavior is at least partly a result of contextual conditioning. However, there is also evidence that presentations of the reinforcer may also serve as a discriminative stimulus (S^D) that simply sets the occasion for the next response (Ostlund & Balleine, 2007; Reid, 1958; Winterbauer & Bouton, 2012). When the reinforcer is encountered after extinction, it may thus reinstate the response through its actions as an occasion setter, as well as its ability to condition the context.

In clinical terms, reinstatement suggests that exposure to a drug after a period of abstinence may cause a person to resume his or her drug use. Consistent with this, a growing number of investigations have shown reinstatement in the drug self-administration method. Reinstatement effects in animals have been demonstrated with a diverse set of drug reinforcers, including nicotine (Chiamulera, Borgo, Falchetto, Valerio, & Tessari, 1996), alcohol (Chiamulera, Valerio, & Tessari, 1995), cocaine (deWit & Stewart, 1981), heroin (Yue et al., 2012), and methamphetamine (Moffett & Goeders, 2007). Interestingly, the presentation of one drug can sometimes reinstate responding for a different drug (e.g., Spano et al., 2004; Stewart & Wise, 1992), perhaps because of generalization between drugs. In apparent contrast, studies with food reinforcers (Ostlund & Balleine, 2007) suggest that different reinforcers can have effects that are more specific. However, the reinforcer-specific reinstatement reported by Ostlund and Balleine (2007) was demonstrated after rats had learned in separate sessions that a specific response yielded a specific reinforcer. These conditions allowed the animals to learn that a specific reinforcer set the occasion for a specific response. This kind of discrimination training was not provided in the drug self-administration studies.

Rapid Reacquisition. A fourth recovery effect is rapid reacquisition, which occurs when the Pavlovian CS or instrumental response are paired with the reinforcer again after extinction. Here, the response is reacquired more quickly than when it was first learned. In an experiment reported by Napier, Macrae, and Kehoe (1992), one group of rabbits was initially given pairings of a tone and a weak electrical shock delivered to the nictitating membrane, which produced a conditioned eyeblink response to the tone. This was followed by multiple sessions of extinction. Another group was given exposure to the context during these two phases, but was not presented with any CS-US pairings. All of the rabbits were then given CS-US pairings in a final test phase. The rabbits given acquisition and extinction in the first two phases showed faster reacquisition than those given only context exposure. Reacquisition to an extinguished tone was thus more rapid than acquisition to a novel tone.

Rapid reacquisition suggests again that the originally learned association between the CS and US is "saved" during extinction. However, the problem is to explain specifically how the saved association causes responding to reemerge rapidly. One clue is provided by the fact that rapid reacquisition is not a universal finding; in some cases, reacquisition can be relatively slow rather than fast (e.g., Bouton, 1986; Bouton & Swartzentruber, 1989; Hart, Bourne, & Schachtman, 1995). Ricker and Bouton (1996), for example, demonstrated that reacquisition of appetitive conditioning can be *either* slower or faster than the original acquisition. They found that the speed of reacquisition depended on the number of extinction trials as well as the number of acquisition trials the animals received initially. For example, when few acquisition trials were given, reacquisition was relatively slow; when many were given, reacquisition was rapid. This finding may explain why reacquisition is typically rapid in the eyeblink conditioning paradigm, since it requires a large number of acquisition trials. More importantly, the finding suggests a possible mechanism for rapid reacquisition, which Ricker and Bouton (1996) referred to as "trial signaling." Consistent with sequential theory (Capaldi, 1966, 1994), described above, they proposed that animals learn during acquisition that reinforced trials occur in the context of other reinforced trials. A different context is created during extinction, however. There, animals learn that nonreinforced trials occur in the presence of other nonreinforced trials. When reinforced trials (CS-US pairings) are resumed, animals are in effect returned to the acquisition context, which promotes recovery of the response. According to this view, rapid reacquisition is an ABA renewal effect.

Ricker and Bouton's (1996) adaptation of sequential theory has been supported by a related set of findings in which reacquisition was slower when extinction included occasional reinforced trials among the many nonreinforced trials (Bouton, Woods, & Pineño, 2004; Woods & Bouton, 2007). For example, in two instrumental learning experiments, Woods and Bouton (2007) trained rats to lever press for food on a variable interval (VI)-30 s reinforcement schedule. Some rats then received simple extinction in which lever presses produced no further reinforcement, whereas others were trained with a leaner and leaner schedule of partial reinforcement. In the latter condition, the VI schedule was gradually lengthened from VI-4 min to VI-32 min over the course of several sessions. In a reacquisition phase, all of the rats were placed on a VI-2 min or VI-8 min schedule, both of which produced a slower return of responding among rats that had been given occasional response-reinforcer pairings during extinction compared to those given simple extinction. In these experiments, the lean reinforcement schedule in extinction gave animals the opportunity to learn that occasions of reinforcement occurred in the presence of (or in the "context" of) many nonreinforced responses, which generalized more readily to the context of reacquisition.

From a clinical perspective, these results suggest that strict abstinence may not be the most effective way to protect against relapse of instrumental behaviors like smoking, drinking, or drug use. Potentially, a more successful approach might be to arrange for an occasional "hit" so that users learn to associate isolated lapses with further abstinence, rather than with continued relapse. This is the idea behind the scheduled reduced smoking procedure developed by Cinciripini and colleagues (Cinciripini et al., 1995, 1994), in which smokers gradually reduce their smoking prior to a quit date by smoking only at predetermined intervals. Although further research is needed to determine whether these techniques are indeed useful in clinical populations, the findings suggest that, consistent with research with animals, occasional response-reinforcer pairings may be an effective tool for relapse prevention.

Resurgence. A final recovery phenomenon has been studied exclusively in instrumental conditioning (e.g., Leitenberg, Rawson, & Bath, 1970; Leitenberg, Rawson, & Mulick, 1975). In the main method for studying resurgence, an instrumental response is extinguished while a new alternative response is reinforced. When the second response is itself extinguished in a later phase, the first response can reemerge (or "resurge"). Resurgence was initially thought to occur because performance of the alternative response competed with the original one, which prevented animals from learning that the first response was no longer being reinforced (Leitenberg et al., 1970; Leitenberg et al., 1975). When the alternative response was later extinguished, the first response returned because it was no longer suppressed. Although such a mechanism could plausibly play a role in some conditions, Winterbauer and Bouton (2010) reported that resurgence can occur when there is no response suppression. These authors instead suggested that resurgence might be another example of the renewal effect. According to their argument, resurgence occurs because extinction takes place in the context of the second, alternative behavior being reinforced. When reinforcement of that response is discontinued, animals are effectively removed from the extinction context and placed in a new one. Resurgence of the first response would thus be a form of ABC renewal. Consistent with this view, resurgence is reduced when the schedule of reinforcement for the alternative behavior is "thinned" (made leaner and leaner) before entering resurgence testing (Winterbauer & Bouton, 2012). Theoretically, this allowed the organisms to associate extinction of the first behavior with longer periods between reinforcers, approximating the "context" that prevails in testing.

Shahan and Sweeney (2011) have alternatively provided a quantitative account of resurgence based on behavioral momentum theory (Nevin & Grace, 2000). In their model, resurgence occurs because extinction of the second behavior during final testing removes a source of disruption of the first behavior. The model can simulate (and account for) several facts about resurgence, including the effects of the thinning treatment just mentioned. However, it fails to predict the fact that under some conditions resurgence is not reduced by prolonged extinction and reinforcement of the second response (Winterbauer, Lucke, & Bouton, 2013). It also does not provide a ready explanation of the other relapse phenomena reviewed above—spontaneous recovery, renewal, reinstatement, and rapid reacquisition—which are integrated with resurgence by the contextual change point of view (see Bouton, Winterbauer, & Todd, 2012, for additional discussion).

Clinically, resurgence may represent a type of relapse in which an unwanted behavior returns when a deliberate replacement behavior (e.g., going to the gym instead of watching television; chewing gum in the place of smoking) is stopped. Importantly, replacing an undesirable behavior with alternative behaviors is one aspect of *contingency management* (CM), a technique in which monetary incentives (rewards) and other sources of reinforcement are provided by therapists to reinforce desirable behaviors. In clinical trials, CM has been shown to be successful at reducing illicit substance abuse (Higgins, Heil, & Lussier, 2004), and supporting weight loss (John et al., 2011), adherence to medication (Kimmel et al., 2012) and smoking cessation (Higgins et al., 2012). However, perhaps analogous to resurgence, these behaviors can return when the incentives are discontinued (e.g., John et al., 2011). The parallel between the resurgence effect and lapse and relapse after CM warrants further analysis.

Summary. The relapse phenomena described above each demonstrate that extinction does not erase what was originally learned, and that extinction is generally very context-dependent. Extinction performance is mainly expressed in the extinction context. At a theoretical level, the phenomena confirm and emphasize the point made in the previous section that extinction performance depends on a form of contextual discrimination. At a practical level, they suggest that even though a behavior may appear to have been erased during extinction, it can return when the context (broadly defined) is changed. The implication for patients undergoing exposure-based therapies is that the benefits may be restricted to the place where the therapy was provided. For instance, a drug addict undergoing cue-exposure therapy may experience renewed cravings when later confronted with drug-associated stimuli, particularly after returning to a place where he frequently used drugs in the past. Although extinction can be among the most successful methods for reducing unwanted behaviors (e.g., Conklin & Tiffany, 2002), its effects are not necessarily permanent.

Preventing Lapse and Relapse after Extinction

Given the ease with which lapse and relapse might occur after extinction, a number of investigators have begun to make relapse prevention a focus of their work. Much of the research in this area has focused on two main strategies for reducing relapse (Bouton, Woods, Moody, Sunsay, & García-Gutiérrez, 2006). The first strategy involves developing methods that might help strengthen or deepen the learning that occurs during extinction in the hope that better extinction learning might increase its permanence. The second is to accept what might be the inherent context-specificity of extinction and develop ways to "bridge" extinction learning from the context in which it is learned to other contexts. A third, newer strategy is to create new methods that might actually erase the original memory.

Deepening Extinction Learning. One way extinction learning might be strengthened is by conducting a very extensive amount of extinction training. Denniston, Chang, and Miller (2003) found that a "massive" number of extinction trials, far beyond the number of trials needed to eliminate fear responding during extinction, was effective at eliminating the renewal effect. Specifically, both ABA and ABC renewal were attenuated following 800 extinction trials, but not a more moderate number (160). In a similar method, Tamai and Nakajima (2000) found that AAB renewal was eliminated by 112 trials of extinction, but not 72. (ABA renewal was unaffected in their experiment.) It seems probable that extinction training must be truly extensive to eliminate the relapse effects. In instrumental learning, tripling the amount of extinction training had no demonstrable effect at weakening the AAB renewal effect (Bouton et al., 2011), and a nine-fold increase in the amount of extinction training did not weaken resurgence (Winterbauer et al., 2013).

Another way to strengthen extinction learning is to extinguish multiple cues at the same time. As described earlier, Rescorla (2006) reported that extinguishing multiple CSs in compound led to a greater amount of extinction, as well as reduced spontaneous recovery and reinstatement, and slower reacquisition. Although theoretically this approach should not change the fundamental nature of extinction learning (i.e., its context-specificity), others have shown that it can reduce relapse effects, including ABA renewal in fear conditioning (Thomas & Ayres, 2004) and spontaneous recovery of lever pressing in the presence of an S^D (Janak & Corbit, 2011; Kearns et al., 2012). One problem, however, is that extinction with multiple cues can fail to generalize efficiently to tests with one cue alone (Urcelay, Lipatova, & Miller, 2009; Vervliet, Vansteenwegen, Hermans, & Eelen, 2007).

Other ways to deepen extinction learning have been suggested by the neuroscience literature. For example, research has shown that administration of d-cycloserine (DCS), a partial agonist of the NMDA receptor that mediates long-term potentiation (a cellular model of learning), can facilitate extinction of fear in animals (e.g., Walker, Ressler, Lu, & Davis, 2002) and exposure therapy in humans (e.g., Guastella et al., 2008). For this reason, DCS has become one of the most widely-studied drugs in research on extinction. However, it may not be a silver bullet. Although extinction with DCS may occur more rapidly, Bouton et al. (2008) reported that it has no effect on ABA renewal of conditioned fear (see also Woods & Bouton, 2006). In effect, although DCS may increase the rate at which extinction is learned over trials, it might not qualitatively change its context-dependent nature.

Other studies have examined the effects of DCS on extinction after reinforcement with food or drugs. DCS can facilitate extinction of conditioned place preference, in which animals learn to associate a physical context with drug effects (e.g., Thanos, Bermeo, Wang, & Volkow, 2009), as well as instrumental lever-press responses reinforced by food (e.g., Leslie, Norwood, Kennedy, Begley, & Shaw, 2012), alcohol (e.g., Vengeliene, Kiefer, & Spanagel, 2008), and cocaine (e.g., Thanos et al., 2011). With regard to its effect on instrumental extinction, two recent studies suggest that DCS may have some limitations there as well. Vurbic, Gold, and Bouton (2011) investigated the effects of DCS on extinction and renewal in rats' lever pressing for food. In four experiments, they found no evidence that DCS had any effect on either extinction or ABA renewal. The authors suggested that the failure of DCS to enhance extinction might have been because DCS acts on Pavlovian processes rather than strictly instrumental (response-reinforcer) processes. In the studies that have demonstrated DCS enhancement of instrumental extinction, the procedures involved the presentation of conditioned reinforcers (i.e., explicit cues that were paired with the reinforcer in acquisition) during extinction; DCS could have facilitated the Pavlovian extinction of the ability of these cues to influence responding during the final test. (In contrast, the experiments reported by Vurbic et al. did not include explicit conditioned reinforcers.) Consistent with this idea, recent experiments with mice found that DCS enhanced extinction when a conditioned reinforcer was present during extinction and testing, but not when it was absent (Thanos et al., 2011).

Bridging Treatments. An alternative to the "strengthening" techniques described above is to "bridge" extinction learning to new contexts by enhancing the retrieval of extinction outside the extinction context. One such technique involves presenting subjects with cues that remind them of extinction during the tests for relapse. These retrieval cues, which are discrete stimuli that are presented intermittently during extinction, have been shown to reduce spontaneous recovery (e.g., Brooks, 2000; Brooks & Bouton, 1993) and renewal (Brooks & Bouton, 1994; Collins & Brandon, 2002). In a similar vein, an extinction method could try to arrange for extinction learning to be connected to the specific contexts in which relapse is most likely to be a problem for a client. For example, as described above, rapid reacquisition can be slowed to some extent by including occasional reinforced trials in extinction (Bouton et al., 2004; Woods & Bouton, 2007). And thinning the reinforcement schedule for an alternative behavior has reduced resurgence (Winterbauer & Bouton, 2012), in theory by connecting extinction of the target behavior with longer and longer intervals in which reinforcement for the alternative is not provided.

Another treatment that can be seen as a "bridging" treatment is to conduct extinction in multiple contexts. The idea is that, by associating extinction with multiple contexts, an animal is more likely to encounter an extinction-associated cue when tested in a new context (see Bouton, 1991). Gunther, Denniston, and Miller (1998) demonstrated that conducting fear extinction in three contexts attenuated ABC renewal compared to extinction in one context. Chaudhri et al. (2008) reported similar effects on ABA renewal with a CS that had been paired with alcohol. The effect has also been demonstrated in humans (e.g., Balooch & Neumann, 2011; Balooch, Neumann, & Boschen, 2012). Although several studies have failed to replicate these results (e.g., Bouton, García-Gutiérrez, Zilski, & Moody, 2006; Neumann et al., 2007), there is some evidence that the effectiveness of such training may depend on the amount of extinction provided in each context. For instance, Thomas, Vurbic, and Novak (2009) found that extinction in three contexts had no effect on ABA renewal if only 12 trials were given in each context, but had a strong effect when 36 trials were given in each context. More recently, Laborda and Miller (2012) extended these findings by demonstrating that conducting massive extinction (810 trials) in multiple contexts attenuated the deleterious effect of combining renewal with spontaneous recovery (i.e., a context switch after a retention interval). Their results also support the idea that using multiple strategies in combination may be more effective at preventing relapse than using any one strategy alone.

Erasure of Memory Through Reconsolidation. A final approach comes from the neuroscience literature researching how learning is encoded—or consolidated—in the brain. It has long been known that newly established memories are initially unstable and must undergo a consolidation process for several hours after acquisition. During this period, new memories can be disrupted by the administration of drugs that interfere with cellular consolidation processes (Schafe & LeDoux, 2000). At least one set of experiments suggested that extinction conducted immediately after fear conditioning, at a time before consolidation might be complete, might also disrupt the storage of conditioning (Myers, Ressler, & Davis, 2006). Although the finding suggested that immediate exposure therapy after a trauma might reduce fear learning, several other sets of experiments brought this conclusion into doubt by demonstrating that extinction conducted immediately after conditioning might actually be relatively ineffective (Maren & Chang, 2006; Rescorla, 2004b; Woods & Bouton, 2008).

Interestingly, once a memory has been consolidated, it can become vulnerable again when it is retrieved into an active state (e.g., Misanin, Miller, & Lewis, 1968). A reactivated memory is thought to need to undergo *reconsolidation* before it becomes stable again. However, before it is reconsolidated, the memory is vulnerable again to disruption by drugs and other treatments (e.g., Misanin et al., 1968; Nader, Schafe, & LeDoux, 2000). Several experiments suggest that after fear conditioning, if the CS is presented again, immediately administering a drug such as a protein synthesis inhibitor (Nader et al., 2000) or propranolol (Kindt, Soeter, & Vervliet, 2009) can disrupt the reconsolidation process and reduce conditioned fear. Although some research has suggested that the effects of this procedure are not permanent (e.g., Lattal & Abel, 2004), and are obtained only when the original conditioning is very weak or old (Wang, de Oliveira Alvares, & Nader, 2009), disrupting reconsolidation is thought by some to alter, or even erase, the original memory.

Monfils, Cowansage, Klann, and LeDoux (2009) have demonstrated a related effect when extinction is conducted within the reconsolidation window. In their first experiment, rats received three tone-shock pairings. Twenty-four hours after acquisition (when the fear memory was presumably consolidated), the authors reactivated the fear memory by presenting the tone CS one time. The rats were then given extinction either 10 min, 1 hr, 6 hrs or 24 hrs later. In the first two groups (10 min and 1 hr) extinction occurred within the reconsolidation window; in the latter two groups (6 hrs and 24 hrs), it was too late. Tests conducted later showed that fear was weakened and showed less relapse in the form of spontaneous recovery, renewal, and reinstatement in the 10-min and 1-hr groups. Similar results have also been reported in fear extinction in humans (Schiller et al., 2010), and extinction of heroin-associated cues in both rats and heroin-addicted people (Xue et al., 2012). These studies have generated considerable interest because of their theoretical implications and their practical significance, as they suggest that undesirable memories may be wiped out using a fairly simple drug-free behavioral manipulation. However, the findings raise important questions. First and foremost, one may wonder why the retrieval of the conditioning memory after the first trial of *any* extinction procedure does not always create the same effect (and prevent relapse in the form of renewal, spontaneous recovery, reinstatement, etc.). And at least as important, several other reports suggest some caution in interpreting these studies as proof of memory erasure. Discrepant findings have been reported in both rats (Chan, Leung, Westbrook, & McNally, 2010), and in humans (Kindt & Soeter, 2013; Soeter & Kindt, 2011). Thus, there is a need for continuing investigation.

Conclusion

Extinction has become a very active area of research in the last 20 years. There is now broad consensus that it is not a form of memory erasure, but instead depends on active new learning that interferes with or *inhibits*, rather than erases the original learning. One of the most important themes is that the context plays a central role in producing and maintaining it. Both historically and recently, phenomena like the partial reinforcement extinction effect have led investigators to emphasize the role of discrimination and generalization in explaining extinction performance. Thus, organisms given partial reinforcement in acquisition persist longer in extinction because they are more likely to generalize between the contexts of conditioning and extinction. The fall-off in performance can thus be seen as a result of discrimination between contexts. And research that has explicitly studied the impact of context on extinction has suggested that one important function of contexts is to set the occasion for conditioning and extinction performance. In effect, the response disappears because the organism learns that the CS-US relation, or the instrumental action itself, is inhibited by the current context. We suggest that it is most profitable to think that CSs or instrumental actions survive extinction with more than one meaning, and that the context in this way selects between them.

The fact that the various relapse phenomena can be integrated by understanding them as context effects also indicates the value and importance of considering the role of context in controlling extinction. In the long run, they are all consistent with the fact that extinction is relatively specific to the context in which it is learned. Their pursuit has thus helped us understand the mechanisms of extinction as well as give us potential mechanisms to understand relapse. This has in turn led to research that attempts to reduce relapse by making extinction more permanent or context-independent. Although some research suggests that deepening extinction or developing new methods to "erase" the original learning may be effective, another valuable approach is to develop methods that promote generalization of extinction across contexts. In the end, the two most important things to remember about extinction are that under normal conditions it does not involve erasure, and that the context plays an essential role.

Acknowledgments

Preparation of this chapter was supported by Grant 9RO1 DA033123 from the National Institute on Drug Abuse to MEB.

References

Amsel, A. (1967). Partial reinforcement effects on vigor and persistence. In K. W. Spence & J. T. Spence (Eds.), *The psychology of learning and motivation* (Vol. I, pp. 1–65). New York: Academic Press.

Amsel, A. (1992). *Frustration theory: An analysis of dispositional learning and memory.* New York: Cambridge University Press.

Baker, A. G., Steinwald, H., & Bouton, M. E. (1991). Contextual conditioning and reinstatement of extinguished instrumental responding. *The Quarterly Journal of Experimental Psychology, 43B*, 199–218.

Balooch, S., & Neumann, D. L. (2011). Effect of multiple contexts and context similarity on the renewal of extinguished conditioned behaviour in an ABA design with humans. *Learning and Motivation, 42*, 53–63.

Balooch, S., Neumann, D. L., & Boschen, M. J. (2012). Extinction treatment in multiple contexts attenuates ABC renewal in humans. *Behaviour Research and Therapy, 50*, 604–609.

Baum, W. M. (2012). Extinction as discrimination: The molar view. *Behavioural Processes, 90*, 101–110.

Bossert, J. M., Liu, S. Y., Lu, L., & Shaham, Y. (2004). A role of ventral tegmental area glutamate in contextual cue-induced relapse to heroin seeking. *Journal of Neuroscience, 24*, 10726–10730.

Bossert, J. M., Stern, A. L., Theberge, F. R. M., Marchant, N. J., Wang, H., Morales, M., & Shaham, Y. (2012). Role of projections from ventral medial prefrontal cortex to nucleus accumbens shell in context-induced reinstatement of heroin seeking. *Journal of Neuroscience, 32*, 4982–4991.

Boutelle, K. N., Zucker, N. L., Peterson, C. B., Rydell, S. A., Cafri, G., & Harnack, L. (2011). Two novel treatments to reduce overeating in overweight children: A randomized controlled trial. *Journal of Consulting and Clinical Psychology, 79*, 759–771.

Bouton, M. E. (1984). Differential control by context in the inflation and reinstatement paradigms. *Journal of Experimental Psychology: Animal Behavior Processes, 10*, 56–74.

Bouton, M. E. (1986). Slow reacquisition following the extinction of conditioned suppression. *Learning and Motivation, 17*, 1–15.

Bouton, M. E. (1988). Context and ambiguity in the extinction of emotional learning: Implications for exposure therapy. *Behaviour Research and Therapy, 26*, 137–149.

Bouton, M. E. (1991). A contextual analysis of fear extinction. In P. R. Martin (Ed.), *Handbook of behavior therapy and psychological science: An integrative ppproach* (pp. 435–453). Elmsford, NY: Pergamon Press.

Bouton, M. E. (1993). Context, time, and memory retrieval in the interference paradigm of Pavlovian learning. *Psychological Bulletin, 114*, 80–99.

Bouton, M. E. (1994). Conditioning, remembering, and forgetting. *Journal of Experimental Psychology: Animal Behavioral Processes, 20*, 219–231.

Bouton, M. E. (2000). A learning theory perspective on lapse, relapse, and the maintenance of behavior change. *Health Psychology, 19*, 57–63.

Bouton, M. E. (2002). Context, ambiguity, and unlearning: Sources of relapse after behavioral extinction. *Biological Psychiatry, 52*, 976–986.

Bouton, M. E., & Bolles, R. C. (1979a). Contextual control of the extinction of conditioned fear. *Learning and Motivation, 10*, 445–466.

Bouton, M. E., & Bolles, R. C. (1979b). Role of conditioned contextual stimuli in reinstatement of extinguished fear. *Journal of Experimental Psychology: Animal Behavioral Processes, 5*, 368–378.

Bouton, M. E., García-Gutiérrez, A., Zilski, J., & Moody, E. W. (2006). Extinction in multiple contexts does not necessarily make extinction less vulnerable to relapse. *Behaviour Research and Therapy, 44*, 983–994.

Bouton, M. E., Kenney, F. A., & Rosengard, C. (1990). State-dependent fear extinction with two benzodiazepine tranquilizers. *Behavioral Neuroscience, 104*, 44–55.

Bouton, M. E., & King, D. A. (1983). Contextual control of the extinction of conditioned fear: Tests for the associative value of the context. *Journal of Experimental Psychology: Animal Behavior Processes, 9*, 248–265.

Bouton, M. E., Mineka, S., & Barlow, D. H. (2001). A modern learning theory perspective on the etiology of panic disorder. *Psychological Review, 108*, 4–32.

Bouton, M. E., & Peck, C. A. (1989). Context effects on conditioning, extinction, and reinstatement in an appetitive conditioning preparation. *Animal Learning & Behavior, 17*, 188–198.

Bouton, M. E., & Ricker, S. T. (1994). Renewal of extinguished responding in a second context. *Animal Learning & Behavior, 22*, 317–324.

Bouton, M. E., & Sunsay, C. (2003). Importance of trials versus accumulating time across trials in partially-reinforced appetitive conditioning. *Journal of Experimental Psychology: Animal Behavior Processes, 29*, 62–77.

Bouton, M. E., & Swartzentruber, D. (1986). Analysis of the associative and occasion-setting properties of contexts participating in a Pavlovian discrimination. *Journal of Experimental Psychology: Animal Behavior Processes, 12*, 333–350.

Bouton, M. E., & Swartzentruber, D. (1989). Slow reacquisition following extinction: Context, encoding, and retrieval mechanisms. *Journal of Experimental Psychology: Animal Behavior Processes, 15*, 43–53.

Bouton, M. E., Todd, T. P., Vurbic, D., Winterbauer, N. E. (2011). Renewal after the extinction of free-operant behavior. *Learning & Behavior, 39*, 57–67.

Bouton, M. E., Vurbic, D., & Woods, A. M. (2008). d-Cycloserine facilitates context-specific fear extinction learning. *Neurobiology of Learning and Memory, 90*, 504–510.

Bouton, M. E., Winterbauer, N. E., & Todd, T. P. (2012). Relapse processes after the extinction of instrumental learning: Renewal, resurgence, and reacquisition. *Behavioural Processes, 90*, 130–141.

Bouton, M. E., Woods, A. M., Moody, E. W., Sunsay, C., & García-Gutiérrez, A. (2006). Counteracting the context-dependence of extinction: Relapse and some tests of possible methods of relapse prevention. In M. G. Craske, D. Hermans, & D. Vansteenwegen (Eds.), *Fear and Learning: Basic Science to Clinical Application*. American Psychological Association, Washington, DC.

Bouton, M. E., Woods, A. M., & Pineño, O. (2004). Occasional reinforced trials during extinction can slow the rate of rapid reacquisition. *Learning and Motivation, 35*, 371–390.

Bouton, M. E., Woods, A. M., & Todd, T. P. (2014). Trial-based vs. time-based accounts of the partial reinforcement extinction effect. Manuscript submitted for publication.

Brooks, D. C. (2000). Recent and remote extinction cues reduce spontaneous recovery. *Quarterly Journal of Experimental Psychology, 53B*, 25–58.

Brooks, D. C., & Bouton, M. E. (1993). A retrieval cue for extinction attenuates spontaneous recovery. *Journal of Experimental Psychology: Animal Behavior Processes, 19*, 77–89.

Brooks, D. C., & Bouton, M. E. (1994). A retrieval cue for extinction attenuates response recovery (renewal) caused by a return to the conditioning context. *Journal of Experimental Psychology: Animal Behavior Processes, 20*, 366–379.

Capaldi, E. J. (1966). Partial reinforcement: A hypothesis of sequential effects. *Psychological Review, 73*, 459–477.

Capaldi, E. J. (1994). The sequential view: From rapidly fading stimulus traces to the organization of memory and the abstract concept of number. *Psychonomic Bulletin & Review, 1*, 156–181.

Chan, W. Y., Leung, H. T., Westbrook, R. F., & McNally, G. P. (2010). Effects of recent exposure to a conditioned stimulus on extinction of Pavlovian fear conditioning. *Learning and Memory, 17*, 512–521.

Chaudhri, N., Sahuque, L. L., & Janak, P. H. (2008). Context-induced relapse of conditioned behavioral responding to ethanol cues in rats. *Biological Psychiatry, 64*, 203–210.

Chiamulera, C., Borgo, C., Falchetto, S., Valerio, E., & Tessari, M. (1996). Nicotine reinstatement of nicotine self-administration after long-term extinction. *Psychopharmacology, 127*, 102–107.

Chiamulera, C., Valerio, E., & Tessari, M. (1995). Resumption of ethanol seeking behaviour in rats. *Behavioural Pharmacology, 6*, 32–39.

Cinciripini, P. M., Lapitsky, L., Seay, S., Wallfisch, A., Kitchens, K., & Vunakis, H. V. (1995). The effects of smoking schedules on cessation outcome: Can we improve on common methods of gradual and abrupt nicotine withdrawal? *Journal of Consulting and Clinical Psychology, 63*, 388–399.

Cinciripini, P. M., Lapitsky, L. G., Wallfisch, A., Mace, R., Nezami, E., & Vunakis, H. V. (1994). An evaluation of a multicomponent treatment program involving scheduled smoking and relapse prevention procedures: Initial findings. *Addictive Behaviors, 19*, 13–22.

Collins, B. N., & Brandon, T. H. (2002). Effects of extinction context and retrieval cues on alcohol-cue reactivity among nonalcoholic drinkers. *Journal of Consulting and Clinical Psychology, 70*, 390–397.

Conklin, C. A., & Tiffany, S. T. (2002). Applying extinction research and theory to cue-exposure addiction treatments. *Addiction, 97*, 155–167.

Crombag, H. S., & Shaham, Y. (2002). Renewal of drug seeking by contextual cues after prolonged extinction in rats. *Behavioral Neuroscience, 116*, 169–173.

Cunningham, C. L. (1979). Alcohol as a cue for extinction: State dependency produced by conditioned inhibition. *Learning & Behavior, 7*, 45–52.

Denniston, J. C., Chang, R. C., & Miller, R. R. (2003). Massive extinction attenuates the renewal effect. *Learning and Motivation, 34*, 68–86.

deWit, H., & Stewart, J. (1981). Reinstatement of cocaine-reinforced responding in the rat. *Psychopharmacology, 75*, 134–143.

Gallistel, C. R., & Gibbon, J. (2000). Time, rate, and conditioning. *Psychological Review, 107*, 289–344.

Gottlieb, D. A. (2004). Acquisition with partial and continuous reinforcement in pigeon autoshaping. *Learning & Behavior, 32*, 321–334.

Grillon, C., Alvarez, R. P., Johnson, L., & Chavis, C. (2008). Contextual specificity of extinction of delay but not trace eyeblink conditioning in humans. *Learning and Memory, 15*, 387–389.

Guastella, A. J., Richardson, R., Lovibond, P. F., Rapee, R. M., Gaston, J. E., Mitchell, P., & Dadds, M. R. (2008). A randomized controlled trial of D-cycloserine enhancement of exposure therapy for social anxiety disorder. *Biological Psychiatry, 63*, 544–549.

Gunther, L. M., Denniston, J. C., & Miller, R. R. (1998). Conducting exposure treatment in multiple contexts can prevent relapse. *Behaviour Research and Therapy, 36*, 75–91.

Hamlin, A. S., Newby, J., & McNally, G. P. (2007). The neural correlates and role of D1 dopamine receptors in renewal of extinguished alcohol-seeking. *Neuroscience, 146*, 525–536.

Harris, J. A., Jones, M. L., Bailey, G. K., & Westbrook, R. F. (2000). Contextual control over conditioned responding in an extinction paradigm. *Journal of Experimental Psychology: Animal Behavior Processes, 26*, 174–185.

Hart, J. A., Bourne, M. J., & Schachtman, T. R. (1995). Slow reacquisition of a conditioned taste aversion. *Animal Learning & Behavior, 23*, 297–303.

Haselgrove, M., Aydin, A., & Pearce, J. M. (2004). A partial reinforcement extinction effect despite equal rates of reinforcement during Pavlovian conditioning. *Journal of Experimental Psychology: Animal Behavior Processes, 30*, 240–250.

Haselgrove, M., & Pearce, J. M. (2003). Facilitation of extinction by an increase or a decrease in trial duration. *Journal of Experimental Psychology: Animal Behavior Processes, 29*, 153–166.

Higgins, S. T., Heil, S. H., & Lussier, J. P. (2004). Clinical implications of reinforcement as a determinant of substance abuse disorders. *Annual Reviews of Psychology*, *55*, 431–461.

Higgins, S. T., Washio, Y., Heil, S. H., Solomon, L. J., Gaalema, D. E., Higgins, T. M., & Bernstein, I. M. (2012). Financial incentives for smoking cessation among pregnant and newly postpartum women. *Preventive Medicine*, *55*, S33–S40.

Holland, P. C. (1992). Occasion setting in Pavlovian conditioning. In D. L. Medin (Ed.) *The psychology of learning and motivation* (Vol. 28, pp. 69–125). San Diego, CA: Academic Press.

Holland, P. C., & Coldwell, S. E. (1993). Transfer of inhibitory stimulus control in operant feature-negative discrimination. *Learning and Motivation*, *24*, 345–375.

Humphreys, L. G. (1939). The effect of random alternation of reinforcement on the acquisition and extinction of conditioned eyelid reactions. *Journal of Experimental Psychology*, *25*, 141–158.

Janak, P. H., & Corbit, L. H. (2011). Deepened extinction following compound stimulus presentation: Noradrenergic modulation. *Learning and Memory*, *18*, 1–10.

John, L. K., Loewenstein, G., Troxel, A. B., Norton, L., Fassbender, J. E., & Volpp, K. (2011). Financial incentives for extended weight loss: A randomized control trial. *Journal of General Internal Medicine*, *26*, 621–626.

Kearns, D. N., Tunstall, B. J., & Weiss, S. J. (2012). Deepened extinction of cocaine cues. *Drug and Alcohol Dependence*, *124*, 283–287.

Kearns, D. N., & Weiss, S. J. (2007). Contextual renewal of cocaine seeking in rats and its attenuation by the conditioned effects of an alternative reinforcer. *Drug and Alcohol Dependence*, *90*, 193–202.

Kimmel, S. E., Troxel, A. B., Loewenstein, G., Brensinger, C. M., Jaskowiak, J., Doshi, J. A., Laskin, M., & Volpp, K. (2012). Randomized trial of lottery-based incentives to improve warfarin adherence. *American Heart Journal*, *164*, 268–274.

Kindt, M., & Soeter, M. (2013). Reconsolidation in a human fear conditioning study: A test of extinction as updating mechanism. *Biological Psychology*, *92*, 43–50.

Kindt, M., Soeter, M., & Vervliet, B. (2009). Beyond extinction: Erasing human fear responses and preventing the return of fear. *Nature Neuroscience*, *12*, 256–258.

Kremer, E. F. (1978). The Rescorla-Wagner model: Losses in associative strength in compound conditioned stimuli. *Journal of Experimental Psychology: Animal Behavior Processes*, *4*, 22–36.

Laborda, M. A., & Miller, R. R. (2012). Preventing return of fear in an animal model of anxiety: Additive effects of massive extinction and extinction in multiple contexts. *Behavior Therapy*, in press.

Lattal, K. M. (2007). Effects of ethanol on the encoding, consolidation, and expression of extinction following contextual fear conditioning. *Behavioral Neuroscience*, *121*, 1280–1292.

Lattal, K. M., & Abel, T. (2004). Behavioral impairments caused by injections of the protein synthesis inhibitor anisomycin after contextual retrieval reverse with time. *Proceedings From the National Academy of Sciences*, *101*, 4667–4672.

Lattal, K. M., & Nakajima, S. (1998). Overexpectation in appetitive Pavlovian and instrumental conditioning. *Animal Learning & Behavior*, *26*, 351–360.

Leitenberg, H., Rawson, R. A., & Bath, K. (1970). Reinforcement of competing behavior during extinction. *Science*, *169*, 301–303.

Leitenberg, H., Rawson, R. A., & Mulick, J. A. (1975). Extinction and reinforcement of alternative behavior. *Journal of Comparative Physiological Psychology*, *88*, 640–652.

Leslie, J. C., Norwood, K., Kennedy, P. J., Begley, M., & Shaw, D. (2012). Facilitation of extinction of operant behaviour in C57Bl/6 mice by chlordiazepoxide and D-cycloserine. *Psychopharmacology*, *223*, 223–235.

Likely, D., Little, L., & Mackintosh, N. J. (1971). Extinction as a function of magnitude and percentage of food or sucrose reward. *Canadian Journal of Psychology, 25*, 130–137.

MacKillop, J., & Lisman, S. A. (2008). Effects of a context shift and multiple context extinction on reactivity to alcohol cues. *Experimental and Clinical Psychopharmacology, 16*, 322–331.

Mackintosh, N. J. (1974). *The psychology of animal learning*. San Diego, CA: Academic Press.

Maren, S. (2011). Seeking a spotless mind: Extinction, deconsolidation, and erasure of fear memory. *Neuron, 70*, 830–845.

Maren, S., & Chang, C. H. (2006). Recent fear is resistant to extinction. *Proceedings From the National Academy of Sciences, 103*, 18020–18025.

McNally, G. P., Johansen, J. P., & Blair, H. T. (2011). Placing prediction into the fear circuit. *Trends in Neurosciences, 34*, 283–292.

McNally, G. P., & Westbrook, R. F. (2003). Opioid receptors regulate the extinction of Pavlovian fear conditioning. *Behavioral Neuroscience, 117*, 1292–1301.

Misanin, J. R., Miller, R. R., & Lewis, D. J. (1968). Retrograde amnesia produced by electroconvulsive shock after reactivation of a consolidated memory trace. *Science, 160*, 554–555.

Moffett, M. C., & Goeders, N. E. (2007). CP-154,526, a CRF type-1 receptor antagonist, attenuates the cue-and methamphetamine-induced reinstatement of extinguished methamphetamine-seeking behavior in rats. *Psychopharmacology, 190*, 171–180.

Monfils, M. H., Cowansage, K. K., Klann, E., & LeDoux, J. E., (2009). Extinction-reconsolidation boundaries: key to persistent attenuation of fear memories. *Science, 324*, 951–955.

Morris, R. W., & Bouton, M. E. (2006). Effect of unconditioned stimulus magnitude on the emergence of conditioned responding. *Journal of Experimental Psychology: Animal Behavior Processes, 32*, 371–385.

Myers, K. M., & Davis, M. (2002). Behavioral and neural analysis of extinction. *Neuron, 36*, 567–584.

Myers, K. M., Ressler, K. J., Davis, M. (2006). Different mechanisms of fear extinction dependent on length of time since fear acquisition. *Learning and Memory, 13*, 216–223.

Mystkowski, J. L., Craske, M. G., Echiverri, A. M., & Labus, J. S. (2006). Mental reinstatement of context and return of fear in spider-fearful participants. *Behavior Therapy, 37*, 49–60.

Nader, K., Schafe, G. E., & LeDoux, J. E. (2000). Fear memories require protein synthesis in the amygdala for reconsolidation after retrieval. *Nature, 406*, 722–726.

Nakajima, S., Tanaka, S., Urushihara, K., & Imada, H. (2000). Renewal of extinguished lever-press responses upon return to the training context. *Learning and Motivation, 31*, 416–431.

Napier, R. M., Macrae, M., & Kehoe, E. J. (1992). Rapid reacquisition in conditioning of the rabbit's nictitating membrane response. *Journal of Experimental Psychology: Animal Behavior Processes, 18*, 182–192.

Neumann, D. L., Lipp, O. V., & Cory, S. E. (2007). Conducting extinction in multiple contexts does not necessarily attenuate the renewal of shock expectancy in a fear-conditioning procedure with humans. *Behaviour Research and Therapy, 45*, 385–394.

Nevin, J. A., & Grace, R. C. (2000). Behavioral momentum and the law of effect. *Behavioral and Brain Sciences, 23*, 73–90.

Ostlund, S. B., & Balleine, B. W. (2007). Selective reinstatement of instrumental performance depends on the discriminative stimulus properties of the mediating outcome. *Learning & Behavior, 35*, 43–52.

Pan, W., Schmidt, R., Wickens, J. R., & Hyland, B. I. (2008). Tripartite mechanism of extinction suggested by dopamine neuron activity and temporal difference model. *Journal of Neuroscience, 28*, 9619–9631.

Pavlov, I. P. (1927). *Conditioned reflexes* (G. V. Anrep, Ed. & Trans.). London: Oxford University Press.

Pearce, J. M. (1994). Similarity and discrimination: A selective review and a connectionist model. *Psychological Review, 101*, 587–607.

Pearce, J. M., & Hall, G. (1980). A model for Pavlovian conditioning: Variations in the effectiveness of conditioned but not unconditioned stimuli. *Psychological Review, 87*, 332–352.

Polack, C. W., Laborda, M. A., & Miller, R. R. (2012). Extinction context as a conditioned inhibitor. *Learning & Behavior, 40*, 24–33.

Reid, R. L. (1958). The role of the reinforcer as a stimulus. *British Journal of Psychology, 49*, 202–209.

Rescorla, R. A. (1993). Inhibitory associations between S and R in extinction. *Animal Learning & Behavior, 21*, 327–336.

Rescorla, R. A. (1997). Response inhibition in extinction. *The Quarterly Journal of Experimental Psychology, 50B*, 238–252.

Rescorla, R. A. (1999). Within-subject partial reinforcement extinction effect in autoshaping. *Quarterly Journal of Experimental Psychology, 52B*, 75–87.

Rescorla, R. A. (2004a). Spontaneous recovery. *Learning and Memory, 11*, 501–509.

Rescorla, R. A. (2004b). Spontaneous recovery varies inversely with the training-extinction interval. *Learning & Behavior, 32*, 401–408.

Rescorla, R. A. (2006). Deepened extinction from compound stimulus presentation. *Journal of Experimental Psychology: Animal Behavior Processes, 32*, 135–144.

Rescorla, R. A., & Heth, C. D. (1975). Reinstatement of fear to an extinguished conditioned stimulus. *Journal of Experimental Psychology: Animal Behavior Processes, 1*, 88–96.

Rescorla, R. A., & Wagner, A. R. (1972). A theory of Pavlovian conditioning: Variations in the effectiveness of reinforcement and non-reinforcement. In A. H. Black & W. F. Prokasy (Eds.), *Classical conditioning II: Current theory and research* (pp. 64–99). New York: Appleton-Century Crofts.

Ricker, S. T., & Bouton, M. E. (1996). Reacquisition following extinction in appetitive conditioning. *Learning & Behavior, 24*, 423–436.

Rosas, J. M., & Bouton, M. E. (1998). Context change and retention interval can have additive, rather than interactive, effects after taste aversion extinction. *Psychonomic Bulletin & Review, 5*, 79–83.

Rosas, J. M., & Callejas-Aguilera, J. E. (2006). Context switch effects on acquisition and extinction in human predictive learning. *Journal of Experimental Psychology: Learning, Memory and Cognition, 32*, 461–474.

Schafe, G. E., & LeDoux, J. E. (2000). Memory consolidation of auditory Pavlovian fear conditioning requires protein synthesis and protein kinase A in the amygdala. *Journal of Neuroscience, 20*, RC96.

Schiller, D., Monfils, M. H., Raio, C. M., Johnson, D., LeDoux, J. E., & Phelps, E. A. (2010). Blocking the return of fear in humans using reconsolidation update mechanisms. *Nature, 463*, 49–53.

Schultz, W. (1997). Dopamine neurons and their role in reward mechanisms. *Current Opinion in Neurobiology, 7*, 191–197.

Shahan, T. A., & Sweeney, M. M. (2011). A model of resurgence based on behavioral momentum theory. *Journal of the Experimental Analysis of Behavior, 95*, 91–108.

Soeter, M., & Kindt, M. (2011). Disrupting reconsolidation: pharmacological and behavioral manipulations. *Learning and Memory, 18*, 357–366.

Spano, M. S., Fattore, L., Cossu, G., Deiana, S., Fadda, P., & Fratta, W. (2004). CB1 receptor agonist and heroin, but not cocaine, reinstate cannabinoid-seeking behaviour in the rat. *British Journal of Pharmacology, 143*, 343–350.

Spivey, J. E., & Hess, D. T. (1968). Effect of partial reinforcement trial sequences on extinction performance. *Psychonomic Science, 10*, 375–376.

Stasiewicz, P. R., Brandon, T. H., & Bradizza, C. M. (2007). Effects of extinction context and retrieval cues on renewal of alcohol-cue reactivity among alcohol-dependent outpatients. *Psychology of Addictive Behaviors, 21*, 244–248.

Stewart, J., & Wise, R. A. (1992). Reinstatement of heroin self-administration habits: Morphine prompts and naltrexone discourages renewed responding after extinction. *Psychopharmacology, 108*, 79–84.

Sunsay, C., & Bouton, M. E. (2008). Analysis of a trial spacing effect with relatively long intertrial intervals. *Learning & Behavior, 36*, 104–115.

Sunsay, C., Stetson, L., & Bouton, M. E. (2004). Memory priming and trial spacing effects in Pavlovian learning. *Learning & Behavior, 32*, 220–229.

Sutton, R. S., & Barto, A. G. (1981). Toward a modern theory of adaptive networks: Expectation and prediction. *Psychological Review, 88*, 135–170.

Tamai, N., & Nakajima, S. (2000). Renewal of formerly conditioned fear in rats after extensive extinction training. *International Journal of Comparative Psychology, 13*, 137–147.

Thanos, P. K., Bermeo, C., Wang, G. J., & Volkow, N. D. (2009). D-cycloserine accelerates the extinction of cocaine-induced conditioned place preference in C57BL/c mice. *Behavioral Brain Research, 199*, 345–349.

Thanos, P. K., Subrize, M., Lui, W., Puca, Z., Ananth, M., Michaelides, M., Wang, G. J., & Volkow, N. D. (2011). D-cycloserine facilitates extinction of cocaine self-administration in C57 mice. *Synapse, 65*, 1099–1105.

Thomas, B. L., & Ayres, J. J. B. (2004). Use of the ABA fear renewal paradigm to assess the effects of extinction with co-present fear inhibitors or excitors: Implications for theories of extinction and for treating human fears and phobias. *Learning and Motivation, 35*, 22–51.

Thomas, B. L., Larsen, N. J., & Ayres, J. J. B. (2003). Role of context similarity in ABA, ABC, and AAB fear renewal paradigms: Implications for theories of renewal and for treating human phobias. *Learning and Motivation, 34*, 410–436.

Thomas, B. L., Vurbic, D., & Novak, C. (2009). Extensive extinction in multiple contexts eliminates the renewal of conditioned fear in rats. *Learning and Motivation, 40*, 147–159.

Todd, T. P. (2013). Mechanisms of renewal after the extinction of instrumental behavior. *Journal of Experimental Psychology: Animal Behavior Processes, 39*, 193–207.

Todd, T. P., Winterbauer, N. E., & Bouton, M. E. (2012a). Contextual control of appetite: renewal of inhibited food-seeking behavior in sated rats after extinction. *Appetite, 58*, 484–489.

Todd, T. P., Winterbauer, N. E., & Bouton, M. E. (2012b). Effects of amount of acquisition and contextual generalization on the renewal of instrumental behavior after extinction. *Learning & Behavior, 40*, 145–157.

Tronson, N. C., Corcoran, K. A., Jovasevic, V., & Radulovic, J. (2008). Fear conditioning and extinction: Emotional states encoded by distinct signaling pathways. *Trends in Neurosciences, 35*, 145–155.

Urcelay, G. P., Lipatova, O., & Miller, R. R. (2009). Constraints on enhanced extinction resulting from extinction treatment in the presence of an added excitor. *Learning and Motivation, 40*, 343–363.

Vansteenwegen, D., Hermans, D., Vervliet, B., Francken, G., Beckers, T., Baeyens, F., & Eelen, P. (2005). Return of fear in a human differential conditioning paradigm caused by a return to the original acquisition context. *Behaviour Research and Therapy, 43*, 323–336.

Vengeliene, V., Kiefer, F., & Spanagel, R. (2008). D-cycloserine facilitates extinction of conditioned alcohol-seeking behavior in rats. *Alcohol and Alcoholism*, *43*, 626–629.

Vervliet, B., Vansteenwegen, D., Hermans, D., & Eelen, P. (2007). Concurrent excitors limit the extinction of conditioned fear in humans. *Behaviour Research and Therapy*, *45*, 375–383.

Vurbic, D., Gold, B., & Bouton, M. E. (2011). Effects of d-cycloserine on the extinction of appetitive operant learning. *Behavioral Neuroscience*, *125*, 551–559.

Waelti, P., Dickinson, A., & Schultz, W. (2001). Dopamine responses comply with basic assumptions of formal learning theory. *Nature*, *412*, 43–48.

Wagner, A. R. (2003). Context-sensitive elemental theory. *Quarterly Journal of Experimental Psychology*, *56*, 7–29.

Walker, D. L., Ressler, K. J., Lu, K. T., & Davis, M. (2002). Facilitation of conditioned fear extinction by systemic administration or intra-amygdala infusions of D-cycloserine as assessed with fear-potentiated startle in rats. *Journal of Neuroscience*, *22*, 2343–2351.

Wang, S. H., de Oliveira Alvares, L., & Nader, K. (2009). Cellular and systems mechanisms of memory strength as a constraint on auditory fear reconsolidation. *Nature Neuroscience*, *12*, 905–913.

Winterbauer, N. E., & Bouton, M. E. (2010). Mechanisms of resurgence of an extinguished instrumental behavior. *Journal of Experimental Psychology: Animal Behavior Processes*, *36*, 343–353.

Winterbauer, N. E., & Bouton, M. E (2012). Effects of thinning the rate at which the alternative behavior is reinforced on resurgence of an extinguished instrumental response. *Journal of Experimental Psychology: Animal Behavior Processes*, *38*, 279–291.

Winterbauer, N. E., Lucke, S., & Bouton, M. E. (2013). Some factors modulating the strength of resurgence after extinction of an instrumental behavior. *Learning and Motivation*, *44*, 60–71.

Woods, A. M., & Bouton, M. E. (2006). D-cycloserine facilitates extinction but does not eliminate renewal of the conditioned emotional response. *Behavioral Neuroscience*, *120*, 1159–1162.

Woods, A. M., & Bouton, M. E. (2007). Occasional reinforced responses during extinction can slow the rate of reacquisition of an operant response. *Learning and Motivation*, *38*, 56–74.

Woods, A. M., & Bouton, M. E. (2008). Immediate extinction causes a less durable loss of performance than delayed extinction following either fear or appetitive conditioning. *Learning and Memory*, *15*, 909–920.

Xue, Y., Luo, Y., Wu, P., Shi, H., Xue, L., Chen, C., Zhu, W., Ding, Z., Bao, Y., Shi, J., Epstein, D. H., Shaham, Y., & Lu, L. (2012). A memory retrieval-extinction procedure to prevent drug craving and relapse. *Science*, *336*, 241–245.

Yue, K., Ma, B., Ru, Q., Chen, L., Gan, Y., Wang, D., Jin, G., & Li, C. (2012). The dopamine receptor antagonist levo-tetrahydropalmatine attenuates heroin self-administration and heroin-induced reinstatement in rats. *Pharmacology, Biochemistry and Behavior*, *102*, 1–5.

Zaghloul, K. A., Blanco, J. A., Weidemann, C. T., McGill, K., Jaggi, J. L., Baltuch, G. H., & Kahana, M. J. (2009). Human substantia nigra neurons encode unexpected financial rewards. *Science*, *323*, 1496–1499.

4

Prologue to "Habituation: A History"

Richard F. Thompson

A truly extraordinary symposium on "Habituation" was held at the University of British Columbia in August of 2007, organized by Professor Catherine Rankin. The proceedings of this Symposium were published as a special issue of the journal *Neurobiology of Learning and Memory* (Rankin, 2009). My chapter "Habituation: A history" is reprinted from this issue (Thompson, 2009, pp. 127–134) with the kind permission of Elsevier Inc. In it, I summarize my views at the time of the Symposium. Thanks to the wide-ranging discussions at the Symposium, we agreed that certain of the nine "properties" of habituation listed in my article required some modifications (see Rankin et al., 2009). I note these briefly here.

Characteristic 1. Rather than just "response" we changed it to "some parameters of the response" and noted that although the decrement is often a negative exponential, other forms, such as linear and biphasic, can also occur.

Characteristic 4. We noted that the more rapid the frequency of stimulation, the more rapid spontaneous recovery may be.

Characteristic 6. We noted that habituation training beyond the asymptotic level may delay the onset of spontaneous recovery.

Characteristic 7. Here the group thought it best to refer to the effect as stimulus specificity rather than stimulus generalization. Personally I prefer stimulus generalization, or more correctly a generalization *gradient*.

Characteristic 8. We changed "another" stimulus to a "different" stimulus. We noted that sometimes a weak stimulus can dishabituate.

Finally, the group added a new Characteristic 10. Some stimulus repetition protocols may result in properties of the response decrement (e.g., more rapid rehabituation than baseline, smaller initial responses than baseline, smaller mean responses than baseline, less frequent responses than baseline) that last hours, days, or weeks. This persistence of certain aspects of habituation is termed long-term habituation.

The Wiley Blackwell Handbook of Operant and Classical Conditioning, First Edition.
Edited by Frances K. McSweeney and Eric S. Murphy.

A key issue concerns "dishabituation." As I note in my article, in mammalian systems to the extent studied to date, dishabituation is never a disruption of the process of habituation but rather a superimposed sensitization process. The habituated process remains habituated and must spontaneously recover. However, counter examples are seen in the invertebrate literature (see Rankin & Carew, 1988).

In terms of mechanisms, I now believe that the evidence is quite strong that for short-term within-session habituation, the basic process is a decrease in the probability of transmitter release at key synapses, first demonstrated by Eric Kandel and associates on *Aplysia* and supported by our work on the spinal cord. However, the mechanisms for long-term habituation (new Characteristic 10) remain obscure (see Glanzman, 2009).

The interested reader is urged to read the articles in the Symposium published in the *Neurobiology of Learning and Memory*. They range from genetic factors regarding habituation in *C. elegans* (Giles & Rankin, 2009) to the role of habituation in operant learning (McSweeney & Murphy, 2009) and many others as well. The field of habituation is very much alive and well today.

References

Giles, A. C., & Rankin, C. H. (2009). Behavioral and genetic characterization of habituation using *Caenorhabditis elegans*. *Neurobiology of Learning and Memory*, *92*, 139–146.

Glanzman, D. L. (2009). Habituation in *Aplysia*: The Cheshire Cat of neurobiology. *Neurobiology of Learning and Memory*, *92*, 147–154.

McSweeney, F. K., & Murphy, E. S. (2009). Sensitization and habituation regulate reinforcer effectiveness. *Neurobiology of Learning and Memory*, *92*, 189–198.

Rankin, C. H. (Ed.). (2009). Neurobiology of habituation [Special issue]. *Neurobiology of Learning and Memory*, *92*(2).

Rankin, C. H., Abrams, T., Barry, R. J., Bhatnagar, S., Clayton, D., Colombo, J., et al. (2009). Habituation revisited: An update and revised description of the behavioral characteristics of habituation. *Neurobiology of Learning and Memory*, *92*, 135–138.

Rankin, C. H., & Carew, T. J. (1988). Dishabituation and sensitization emerge as separate processes during development in *Aplysia*. *Journal of Neuroscience*, *8*, 197–211.

Thompson, R. F. (2009). Habituation: A history. *Neurobiology of Learning and Memory*, *92*, 127–134.

Habituation
A History[1]

Richard F. Thompson

Introduction

The notion of habituation is as old as humankind. As Ctesippus says in Plato's Lysis:

"Indeed, Socrates, he has literally deafened us and stopped our ears with the praises of Lysis; and if he is a little intoxicated, there is every likelihood that we may have our sleep murdered with a cry of Lysis."

To take an even older example:

> A fox who had never yet seen a lion, when he fell in with him for the first time in the forest was so frightened that he was near dying with fear. On his meeting with him for the second time, he was still much alarmed, but not to the same extent as at first. On seeing him the third time, he so increased in boldness that he went up to him and commenced a familiar conversation with him. (Aesop's Fables)

Experimental studies, or at least observations of phenomena of habituation for a variety of responses in a wide range of organisms from amoebas to humans literally exploded at the end of the 19th century and early 20th century. See Harris (1943) and Jennings (1906). I was unable to determine who first used the term habituation in this context, but it was in widespread use early in the 20th century. In his classic text on learning, Humphrey (1933) notes that a range of terms, "acclimatization," "accommodation," "negative adaptation", "fatigue" have been used to describe the phenomenon. Harris (1943) in his classic review adds the terms "extinction" and "stimulatory inactivation" to the list. As he notes,

> While none of the terms cited is especially appropriate to this type of response decrement, we shall use the term "habituation" throughout. Little can be said in favor of this term except that all the others imply an explanation which is unjustified by the facts, or

The Wiley Blackwell Handbook of Operant and Classical Conditioning, First Edition.
Edited by Frances K. McSweeney and Eric S. Murphy.

> have some more valid use in another connection. Perhaps the most commonly applied term, negative adaptation, seems to deny that response decrement may be an active process. Habituation on the other hand, has had in its favor that it is not ordinarily applied to other types of behavior, implies the knowledge of no specific or general mechanism underlying the phenomenon (of which we are as yet in almost total ignorance), and in addition has been freely used in referring to exactly the type of behavior modification of which we speak. (Harris, 1943, pp. 385–386)

The companion phenomenon of "dishabituation" or "dehabituation," the restoration of an habituated response by extraneous stimulation, was early studied by Holmes (1912) in the sea-urchin. Humphrey (1933) provides an example with human infants:

> The phenomenon may easily and prettily be demonstrated on a young baby. The hands are clapped behind the child's back every two seconds; blinking occurs several times, but has generally died down by the sixth or seventh stimulation. Habituation has set in. The cradle is then given a sharp blow, and the hands are once more clapped, keeping the proper interval by counting. The child will be observed to blink again. The explanation seems to be that the blow on the cradle requires a new adjustment on the part of the organism which is inconsistent with that involved in effecting the habituation. (p. 142)

Humphrey provides the following explanation:

> The peculiar process involved in the establishment of equilibrium are thus nullified and habituation has to be re-established. Dehabituation by lapse of time and by another stimulus are thus fundamentally the same, for they involve each of them the derangement of an established state of equilibrium by altered conditions, the alteration being one of increase of environmental energy in the one case, of decrease in the other. (p. 142)

Humphrey thus argues that dehabituation is an actual removal or elimination of the process of habituation, a restoration to the original unhabituated condition, a view that persisted at least into the 1960s.

In his classic text, *The integrative action of the nervous system* Sherrington (1906) analyzed fatigue of the scratch and flexion reflexes in the spinal dog. He was able to rule out sensory receptor adaptation as a mechanism of reflex fatigue by showing that stimulation of skin areas adjacent to the repeatedly stimulated area also exhibited fatigue, indeed he described the phenomena of stimulus generalization, the further separate the skin area was, the less the fatigue. Similarly he ruled out muscle fatigue by showing that the fatigued muscle response was in fact normal when activated by a different reflex. In short, fatigue was a central phenomenon. He also described several parametric features, i.e., weak stimulation led to more rapid fatigue (he notes this to be paradoxical). Reflex fatigue is in fact an example of habituation.

In an elegant series of experiments Proser and Hunter (1936) compared habituation (they used the term extinction) of the startle response in the intact rat and of spinal reflexes in the spinal rat, showing that they indeed exhibited common properties. By the time of Humphrey (1933) and Harris (1943) it was generally agreed that habituation was a central phenomenon, at least in organisms with nervous systems, and that it was an instance of elementary learning.

Modern interest in habituation really began with an extraordinarily influential paper by Sharpless and Jasper (1956) on habituation of EEG arousal. Using repeated presentations of brief tones they found that cortical EEG arousal of the normally sleeping cat (recorded through implanted electrodes) becomes progressively shorter and finally disappears. After cessation of stimulation the arousal response exhibits spontaneous recovery over a period of minutes or hours. Further, a strong sudden stimulus that differs markedly from the habituating stimulus causes dishabituation of the EEG arousal to the original stimulus. One very interesting aspect of Sharpless and Jasper's experiment was the specificity of the EEG arousal habituation in terms of stimulus characteristics. If the EEG arousal response of the sleeping animal was habituated to presentations of a 500-cycle tone to the point at which no arousal occurred, a 1000-cps tone would exhibit strong EEG arousal. However, if a 600-cps tone was presented after habituation to the 500-cps tone, no EEG arousal occurred. In behavioral terminology this could be described as an auditory frequency generalization gradient for EEG arousal.

The human alpha-blocking response, which resembles EEG arousal in the cat, was shown to habituate to tactile, auditory, and visual stimulation by Sokolov and his associates in the Soviet Union (Sokolov, 1960). Glickman and Feldman (1961) demonstrated that peripheral receptors are probably not involved in habituation of EEG arousal to sensory stimulation. They induced cortical EEG arousal by electrical stimulation through electrodes implanted in the midbrain reticular formation in animals. Under these conditions, habituation of EEG arousal occurred just as it did in earlier experiments using tones.

Following Sharpless and Jasper's study great interest developed in habituation as a fundamental form of behavioral plasticity. As noted earlier, it occurs for virtually all behavioral responses in virtually all organisms. A number of investigators reported evoked response habituation to various types of stimuli at most levels of the CNS, from first-order sensory nuclei to the cerebral cortex. The first experiment to report evoked response habituation was that of Hernández-Peón, Scherrer, and Jouvet (1956); they recorded responses to click stimulation at several levels of the auditory system. Trains of clicks were delivered once every 2 s for long periods of time and evoked responses of the cochlear nucleus (the first relay of the auditory system) were reported to habituate. This paper was also extremely influential in reviving interest in habituation.

Careful studies by Worden and associates (see Marsh, Worden, & Hicks, 1962; Worden & Marsh, 1963) demonstrated that click evoked responses at the cochlear nucleus do not show habituation. Instead, amplitudes of responses at this first relay nucleus in the auditory system are rigidly controlled by the physical properties of the sound stimulus. Because of acoustic factors, the intensity of a sound is often weaker at the floor of a test cage. If an animal gradually became bored and rested his head on the floor, the cochlear nucleus evoked response to click would decrease because of reduced sound intensity. If sound at the ear is held constant, there is no habituation of the evoked response at the cochlear nucleus.

Some of the basic properties of habituation were described in the classic works noted above (Harris, 1943; Humphrey, 1933; Jennings, 1906; Prosser & Hunter, 1936). In 1966, Thompson and Spencer surveyed the by then very extensive behavioral literature on habituation and identified some nine basic parametric properties or characteristics exhibited by behavioral habituation.

A few of personal remarks, if I may. William Alden Spencer and I were undergraduates together at Reed College in Portland Oregon and we became close friends. He went to Medical School (University of Oregon) and I went to graduate school (University of Wisconsin). Alden then did a postdoc at NIH, where he and Eric Kandel did their pioneering work on hippocampal physiology. Meanwhile I spent a several years postdoc in neurophysiology with Clinton Woolsey at the University of Wisconsin School of Medicine. Alden then did a further postdoc in Moruzzi's Laboratory at the University of Pisa. I had by that time accepted an assistant professorship at the University of Oregon Medical School in Psychiatry. Alden then accepted a position as Assistant Professor in the Physiology Department at the University of Oregon Medical School. We shared two adjoining basement laboratories.

Earlier, we had planned our initial joint project: spinal conditioning (i.e., classical conditioning) of the hindlimb flexion reflex in the acute spinal cat. This was a very controversial phenomenon then. But at that time more was known about the circuitry and physiology of the mammalian spinal cord than other regions of the nervous system, due largely to the work of John Eccles and his many associates. Initially, we used hindlimb paw shock as an unconditioned stimulus. However, each time we gave a series of shocks the flexion reflex habituated dramatically. It was such a robust phenomenon that we decided to study it instead of classical conditioning, and the rest is published history. (Later, junior colleagues and I did establish spinal conditioning as a genuine phenomenon; e.g., Patterson, Cegavske, & Thompson, 1973.) Alden was a brilliant and creative person and a superb neurophysiologist. He died tragically at an early age.

Below I list the parameters of habituation, together with some supporting evidence from the earlier literature. Note that the focus was on short-term or within-session habituation (characteristics 1, 2, 4, 5, 6, 7, and 8). Characteristic 3 dealt with long-term or between-session habituation and property 9 dealt with long-term or between-session dishabituation (sensitization).

(1) Given that a particular stimulus elicits a response, repeated applications of the stimulus result in decreased response (habituation). The decrease is usually a negative exponential function of the number of stimulus presentations.

> Examples of response habitation can probably be found in essentially all behaviorial studies where a stimulus is regularly presented. In earlier experiments devoted to habituation, per se, parametric characteristics were studied for a variety of responses (cf. Harris, 1943) ranging from postrotatory nystagmus (Griffith, 1920; Wendt, 1951) to startle (Prosser & Hunter, 1936) and galvanic skin response (GSR—Davis, 1934). With the exception of the "knee jerk" reflex (Lombard, 1887; Prosser & Hunter, 1936) habituation was a consistent finding, usually exhibiting an exponential course. (Thompson & Spencer, 1966, p. 18)

(2) If the stimulus is withheld, the response tends to recover over time (spontaneous recovery).

Spontaneous recovery is reported in most of the studies noted above and has come to be the most common method of demonstrating that a given response decrement is an example of habituation (Harris, 1943). The time course of spontaneous recovery is markedly influenced by many variables and is not necessarily characteristic of a given response. Thus, the habituated startle response to sound in the intact rat may recover in 10 minutes (Prosser & Hunter, 1936) or fail to recover in 24 hours (J. S. Brown, Personal communication, 1964), depending upon details of testing. Consequently any categorization of types of habituation based solely on recovery time is likely to be somewhat artificial. (Thompson & Spencer, 1966, p. 18)

(3) If repeated series of habituation training and spontaneous recovery are given, habituation becomes successively more rapid (this might be called potentiation of habituation).

Humphrey (1933) noted this effect in his studies on turtle leg withdrawal to shell tap. Konorski (1948) describes it for the orientating response, and it has been described in many studies where repeated habituation series were given (e.g., Davis, 1934). (Thompson & Spencer, 1966, p. 18)

(4) Other things being equal, the more rapid the frequency of stimulation, the more rapid and/or more pronounced is habituation.

Numerous examples of this were noted in the earlier reflex studies (Harris, 1943) as well as in more recent work on stimulus satiation and curiosity (Glanzer, 1953; Welker, 1961). The effect occurs in terms of real-time course and occurs within certain limits in terms of number of trials as well. (Thompson & Spencer, 1966, pp. 18–19)

(5) The weaker the stimulus, the more rapid and/or more pronounced is habituation. Strong stimuli may yield no significant habituation.

This relationship is characteristic of most types of responses ranging from simple reflexes (Harris, 1943) to complex exploratory behavior (Welker, 1961). Postrotatory optic nystagmus may be an exception in that under some conditions the degree of habituation is directly related to velocity of rotation (G. Crampton, personal communication, 1964). (Thompson & Spencer, 1966, p. 19)

(6) The effects of habituation training may proceed beyond the zero or asymptotic response level.

Additional habituation training given after the response has disappeared or reached a stable habituated level will result in slower recovery. Although relatively few experiments have studied "below-zero" habituation as such (Humphrey, 1933; Prosser & Hunter, 1936; Wendt, 1951), the observations may be viewed as an extension of the relationship between number of stimulus presentations and degree of habituation. Zero response level is of course to some degree dependent upon the particular response measures used. (Thompson & Spencer, 1966, p. 19)

(7) Habituation of response to a given stimulus exhibits stimulus generalization to other stimuli.

> Coombs (1938) demonstrated generalization of GSR habituation to different types of auditory stimulation, and Porter (1938) demonstrated cross-modal generalization of the habituated GSR for light and tone stimuli. Mower (1934) showed some generalization of postrotatory nystagmus habituation in the pigeon. In a recent study, Crampton and Schwam (1961) reported generalization of optic nystagmus habituation in the cat to different degrees of angular acceleration. (Thompson & Spencer, 1966, p. 19)

(8) Presentation of another (usually strong) stimulus results in recovery of the habituated response (dishabituation).

> This phenomenon appears to be as ubiquitous as habituation itself and is commonly used to demonstrate that habituation has occurred. Pavlov (1927) was perhaps the first to describe this process (i.e., disinhibition) in relation to an extinguished conditioned response (CR), but also applied it to the habituated orienting response. Humphrey (1933) studied dishabituation extensively in lower vertebrates. Essentially all responses of mammals that can be habituated can also be dishabituated (Harris, 1943). It is not always necessary for the dishabituatory stimulus to be strong. In fact Sokolov (1960) and Voronin and Sokolov (1960) reported that a decrease in the intensity of an auditory stimulus results in dishabituation of the habituated orienting response in humans. Dishabituation, viewed as neutralization of the process of habituation (Humphrey, 1933), has been perhaps the most important method of distinguishing between habituation and "fatigue". (Thompson & Spencer, 1966, p. 19)

(9) Upon repeated application of the dishabituary stimulus, the amount of dishabituation produced habituates (this might be called habituation of dishabituation).

> Most studies of dishabituation (see above) have noted its habituation. Lehner (1941) has done the most careful parametric studies, showing that habituation of dishabituation follows a negative exponential course for the startle response in the rat and the abdominal reflex in man. More recently, Hagbarth and Kugleberg (1958) and Hagbarth and Finer (1963) verified and extended Lehner's findings for the abdominal and leg flexion reflexes in humans. Crampton and Schwam (1961) have shown that dishabituation of postrotatory nystagmus in the cat by auditory or cutaneous stimuli habituates in a similar fashion.
>
> In reviewing the behavioral habituation literature, it is striking to find virtually complete agreement on the parametric characteristics of the phenomenon in such a wide variety of animals and responses. These nine common characteristics may consequently serve as the detailed operational definition of habituation, replacing the more general definition given above. The extent to which any other response decrements satisfy these characteristics will thus determine whether they can be called habituation. (Thompson & Spencer, 1966, pp. 19–20)

These nine defining properties of habituation were a major issue for discussion in this symposium and will be treated later (Rankin, this issue). I note that Davis and Wagner (1968) challenged the parameter concerning stimulus intensity. Recall that Sherrington, describing this effect that weaker stimuli yielded more rapid "fatigue" than stronger stimuli, felt it to be paradoxical. Davis and Wagner used the acoustic startle response in the rat and found that habituation to an intense stimulus caused a greater degree of absolute response decrement when tested with a weak stimulus than habituation to the weak stimulus. However, they also noted that if habituation and test stimuli were of identical intensities, then the relative degree of habituation increases as stimulus intensity is decreased, in accordance with Thompson and Spencer's characteristic number 5. So the key is absolute versus relative measures of habituation. As Groves and Thompson (1970) stressed, characteristic number 5 must refer to relative rather than absolute measures of response strength.

In an ingenious and rather complex study Davis and Wagner (1969) showed that a group given gradually increasing intensity of tone (rat-startle response) showed the greatest habituation, the constant loud intensity showed less habituation and a constant intermediate intensity group showed the least habituation and a marked rebound when tested at a loud intensity. As they noted, these results could not be accounted for by a Single-Process theory. However, Groves and Thompson (1970) were able to account for these results with their Dual-Process theory, and actually reproduced these results using the hind limb flexion reflex of the acute spinal cat (see below).

Using the spinal flexion reflex Spencer and I were able to rule out changes in skin receptors, cutaneous afferent nerve terminals and in motor neurons as loci of the decremental process underlying habituation, in accordance with Sherrington's earlier speculations. The decremental process must occur in interneurons. Perhaps their most important discovery was the fact that dishabituation was not a disruption of habituation but rather an independent superimposed process of sensitization. The decremental process underlying habituation was not disrupted at all by dishabituation. Indeed, in the flexion reflex, dishabituation (sensitization) always produces an increase in excitability of motor neurons. To the extent tested in mammalian systems, dishabituation is in fact a separate process of sensitization, but an exception has been noted in Aplysia (Rankin & Carew, 1988). These observations led Groves and Thompson (1970) to develop the Dual-Process theory (see below).

A number of theories, or at least hypotheses, concerning the process of habituation have been proposed over the years. A few examples are: Stimulus satiation (Glanzer, 1953); Reactive inhibition (Hull, 1943); Afferent neuronal inhibition (Hernández-Peón, 1960); Cholinergic inhibition (Carlton, 1968); Classical conditioning (Stein, 1966). Actually, many of these theories were more generally concerned with processes of learning and not developed specifically to deal with habituation. These and other views are treated at length in a number of publications (e.g., Groves & Thompson, 1970; Peeke & Herz, 1973a, 1973b; Thompson & Spencer, 1966). In most cases these theories collided with uncooperative facts. However, three theories have been relatively successful and are still prominent today: Eugene Sokolov's (1960, 1963a, 1963b) Stimulus–Model Comparator Theory; Allan Wagner's (1979) Revision of Konorski's Gnostic Hypothesis; and Groves and Thompson's (1970) Dual-Process Theory. I treat each of these briefly here.

Stimulus–Model Comparator Theory

Evgeny Sokolov (1960, 1963) developed a most influential Stimulus–Model Comparator theory of habituation (see Figure 4.1). It was based primarily on his observation of the orienting response, often measured as arousal in EEG activity. The

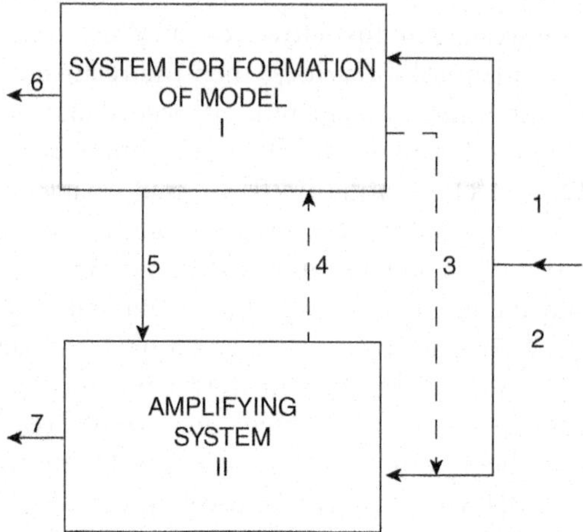

Figure 4.1 Sokolov's model of habituation. Sensory input through lines 1 and 2 project to both the model formation and the amplifying systems. With repeated stimulation, the model develops and inhibits the amplifying system. See text for details (from Sokolov, 1960).

basic notion is that as a result of repeated stimulation a stimulus model is formed in the brain, specifically in the cerebral cortex. In addition, there is an amplifying system that normally subverses behavioral output. A novel stimulus will result in a large orienting response, mediated by the amplifying system, identified with the ascending reticular activating system in lower brain regions. As the same stimulus is repeated, the stimulus model develops and as it develops, it exerts increasing inhibition on the amplifying system via descending corticofugal influences, thus yielding habituation. If a new or altered stimulus occurs which does not match the model, then inhibition is released and response strength recovers accordingly.

Wagner-Konorski Gnostic Unit Theory

Konorski briefly developed a theory of habituation that is in many ways analogous to Sokolov's theory (Konorski, 1967). Allan Wagner (1979) elaborated Konorski's notion with greater emphasis on the roles of short-term memory and the existing associative network. This model is shown in Figure 4.2. A stimulus (SO = stimulus object) is processed via afferent fields to project to a memory system, the Gnostic assembly, and to the arousal system. As the stimulus is repeated, a gnostic unit is formed, an increasingly accurate neuronal model or memory of the stimulus. As this model develops it increasingly activates an inhibitory system that inhibits the arousal system, resulting in habituation. Wagner added two processes to Konorski's model, a reverberating circuit of transient memory (short-term memory—the two solid circles in the gnostic assembly) and the influence of the preexisiting associative network. Indeed, Wagner's reformation of Konorski's model is in the main stream of information-processing theory (e.g., Anderson & Bower, 1973; Estes, 1976; Shiffrin & Schneider, 1977). A key notion introduced by Wagner is that contextual cues may act via the associative network to excite stimulus representations in memory

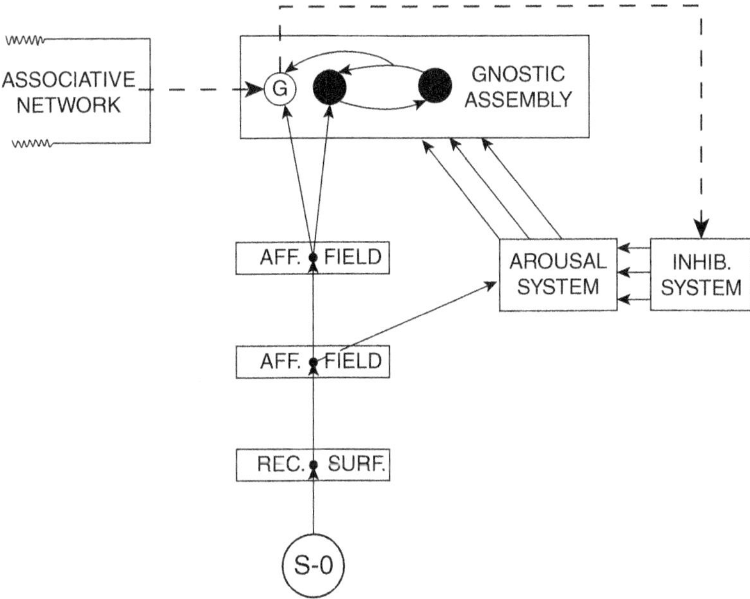

Figure 4.2 Wagner-Konorski's model of habituation. Sensory input forms a memory model in the Gnostic assembly. As the model develops it inhibits the arousal system. See text for details (from Wagner, 1979. Reproduced with permission from Taylor and Francis Group LLC Books).

(i.e., in the Gnostic assembly). An important implication of this view is that some response systems should show context-specific long-term habituation.

Groves and Thompson Dual-Process Theory

The basic assumption is that any effective stimulus will result in two independent processes in the central nervous system, one decremental (habituation) and one incremental (sensitization) that interact (see Figure 4.3). It is further assumed that habituation develops in the stimulus–response (S–R) pathway for whatever stimulus evoked response is being habituated and that sensitization develops in a separate state system which then acts on the S–R pathway to yield the final behavioral outcome (see Figure 4.4). Strong supporting evidence for this theory came from studies of the activity of interneurons in the spinal cord (see e.g., Glanzman, Groves, & Thompson, 1972; Groves, Demarco, & Thompson, 1969; Groves & Thompson, 1970, 1973).

It is not my purpose here to provide a detailed critique of these theories although my bias is obvious. Instead I will simply note a few observations.

All three theories have much in common. First, they all propose that a model of the stimulus develops as a result of repetition. This model is viewed more-or-less as a memory trace in the Sokolov and Wagner-Konorski models and simply as a decrement in synaptic transmission in the dual-process model. Such a synaptic decrement

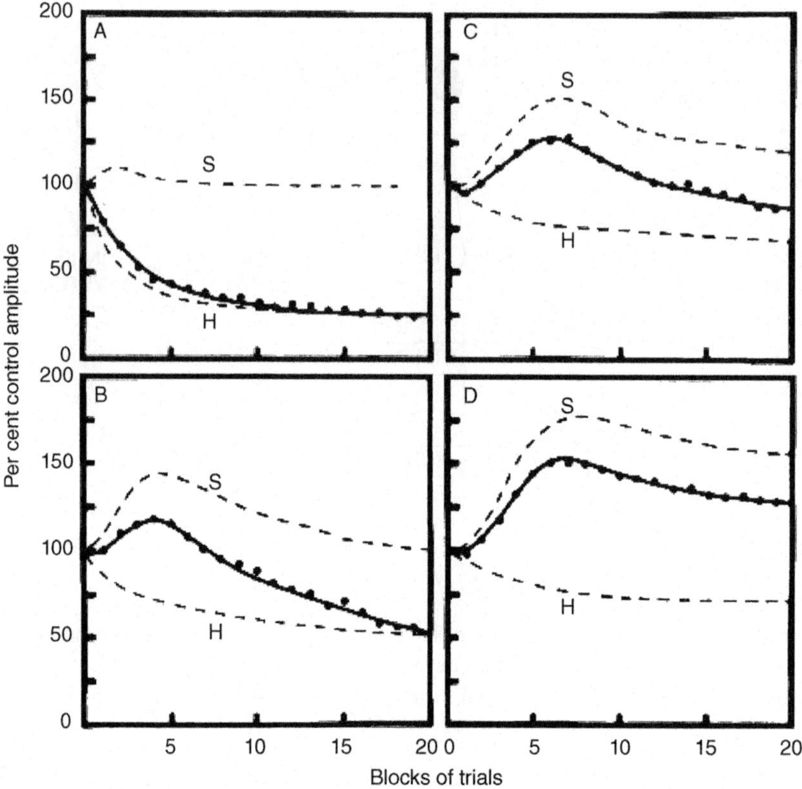

Figure 4.3 Basic notion of the dual process theory of habituation. Two processes (dashed lines) elicited by stimuli, one sensitizing and one habituating, interact to yield the behavioral response (solid line) (from Groves & Thompson, 1970). Reproduced with permission of APA.

can of course qualify as a memory. Second, all three theories have an arousal system ("amplifying" in Sokolov; "arousal" in Wagner-Konorski, "state" in dual-process).

In terms of differences, Both Sokolov and Wagner postulate a descending inhibitory system activated by the memory trace that inhibits the arousal system. The Dual-Process theory postulates no such inhibitory system. Instead, both the S–R pathway and the state system activated by stimulus repetition will habituate. In my view, this is a key difference. Another difference is that Sokolov, and particularly Wagner-Konorski, focus on long-term or between- session habituation whereas much of the focus in the Dual-Process theory is on short-term or within-session habituation.

Perhaps the most significant difference between dual-process and both Sokolov and Wagner-Konorski concerns the response measures used. The Dual-Process theory emphasizes discrete muscle responses whereas the other two focus on nonspecific or "state" measures (e.g., EEG arousal, GSR, vasoconstriction, etc.). One of the most dramatic predictions from Sokolov's theory (and also, I believe, the Wagner-Konorski theory) is the missing stimulus effect—if a stimulus is repeatedly presented at a fixed

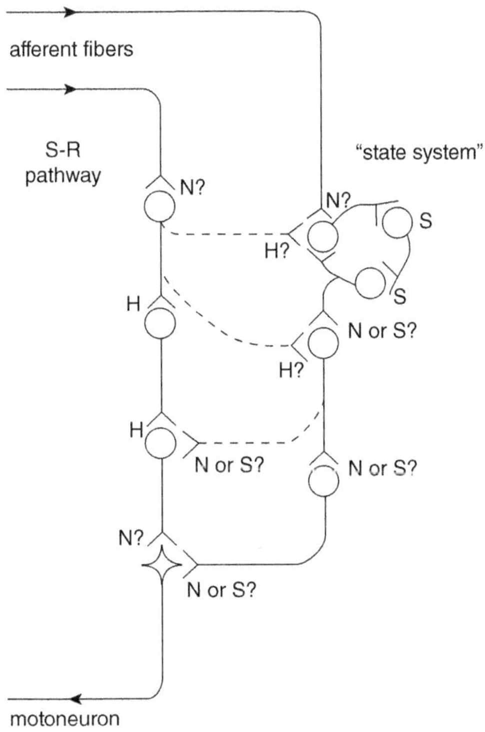

Figure 4.4 Neuronal model of the dual process theory. The S–R pathway develops habituation and the state pathway may develop sensitization. They interact to yield behavior. See text for details (from Groves & Thompson, 1970). Reproduced with permission of APA.

interval until the response has habituated, and if now the stimulus is omitted on one trial, the response will recur full-blown. Voronin and Sokolov (1960) reported this for the EEG alpha-blocking response (arousal) in humans.

Note that the missing stimulus effect is really an example of temporal conditioning. In general, temporal conditioning can be obtained most readily with nonspecific responses, salivation (Pavlov, 1927), EEG arousal (Jasper & Shagass, 1941), galvanic skin response (Lockhart, 1966). Hull (1934) found that regularly repeated shocks yielded temporal conditioning (in humans) of the galvanic response but not finger withdrawal, suggesting that in contrast to "state" measures, discrete muscle responses do not show temporal conditioning.

In 1973, when I was at Harvard, Sokolov joined me for two weeks and we attempted to establish temporal conditioning of the eyeblink response in rabbits. Animals were given a corneal airpuff every minute for 100 trials per day. On occasional trials, the US was omitted and there was no response—no evidence of temporal conditioning. So temporal conditioning seems primarily to be a phenomenon of "state" variables. In contrast to the classical conditioning of discrete muscle responses, it is easy to establish operant temporal avoidance conditioning of discrete motor responses (Herrnstein, 1969; Lockhart & Steinbrecher, 1963; Sidman, 1962).

Mechanisms of Habituation

In animals with nervous systems, the underlying processes yielding behavioral habituation are due to alteration in neurons and synapses (see below). But single-cell animals that behave (e.g., amoeba and paramecium) also show at least some phenomena of habituation (see Harris, 1943; Jennings, 1906) and they, of course, have no neurons. Perhaps the most simplified or reduced preparation used for habituation is the PC12 cell line, studied by Daniel Koshland and associates (McFadden & Koshland, 1990a, 1990b). The cells in this cell culture do not behave but they do secrete. The PC12 cell culture is a pheochromocytoma (cancer) cell line from the adrenal medulla. The cells are immortal in that they stop dividing until activated by nerve growth factor. When appropriately stimulated they secrete norepinephrine (NE) and other neurotransmitters. Koshland stimulated PC12 cells by pulses of potassium ions (K^+) and measured release of ^{3}HNE from the culture. The amount released showed clear habituation and exhibited both the frequency effect (more rapid and pronounced habituation with more rapid frequency of stimulation) and the intensity effect (the weaker the stimulus the more rapid and pronounced the habituation). Further, they showed both within-session and between-session habituation (i.e., both short- and long-term "memory"). Interestingly, NE release was also stimulated by acetylcholine (ACh) pulses and this also habituated. The habituation to K^+ pulses and ACh pulses were independent of each other, and treatment by PMA (a phorbal ester) dishabituated the habituated response to K^+ but not to ACh. So NE release by K^+ and Ach seems to involve differing mechanisms. The PC12 cell culture appears to be a most promising model for analysis of the physical–chemical bases of "habituation" like phenomena.

In animals with nervous systems, a consistent picture appeared to emerge in the 1970s of the basic synaptic mechanism of habituation. In a series of elegant experiments, Eric Kandel and associates analyzed within-session habituation of the monosynaptic gill-withdrawal response in Aplysia (see e.g., Kandel, 1975; Pinsker, Kuppermann, Catellucci, & Kandel, 1970). In brief, repeated stimulation resulted in a decrease in the probability of neurotransmitter release at the sensory–motor synapse, a presynaptic process, due in turn to a decrease in calcium ion influx at the sensory nerve terminals.

Spencer and I, working with the polysynaptic spinal flexion reflex, were unable to establish this but their results were certainly consistent with synaptic depression as a mechanism (see, e.g., Spencer, Thompson, & Neilson, 1966). Later, using the descending monosynaptic pathway from lateral column to motor neuron in the isolated frog spinal cord, the Thompson group was able to show habituation was due to a presynaptic decrease in synaptic efficacy, consistent with Kandel's earlier findings (Farel, Glanzman, & Thompson, 1973; Farel & Thompson, 1976; Glanzman & Thompson, 1979). So a clear picture seemed to emerge, at least for within-session habituation. Unfortunately, more recent work suggests that the mechanisms of both short and long-term habituation are far more complex than earlier believed (see, e.g., Ezzeddine & Glanzman, 2003; Li, Roberts, & Glanzman, 2005; Rose & Rankin, 2001).

In this brief review, I have attempted to highlight important historical developments in the study of habituation. But habituation is by no means just an historical curiosity. From 2000 to 2005, over 50,000 publications were concerned with habituation (pub-med citations).

Dedication

This chapter is dedicated to W. Alden Spencer (1931–1977)

Note

1 This chapter was published in *Neurobiology of Learning and Memory, 92*, *R. F. Thompson, Habituation: A history*, 127–134, Copyright Elsevier (2009). Reproduced with permission.

References

Anderson, J., & Bower, G. (1973). *Human associative memory*. New York: Winston.

Carlton, P. L. (1968). Brain acetylcholine and habituation. In P. B. Bradley & M. Fink (Eds.). *Progress in brain research. Anticholinergic drugs and brain functions in animals and man* (Vol. 28) (pp. 48–60). Amsterdam: Elsevier.

Coombs, C. H. (1938). Adaptation of the galvanic response to auditory stimuli. *Journal of Experimental Psychology, 22*, 244–268.

Crampton, G. H., & Schwam, W. J. (1961). Effects of arousal reaction on nystagmus habituation in the cat. *American Journal of Physiology, 200*, 29–33.

Davis, R. C. (1934). Modification of the galvanic reflex by daily repetition of a stimulus. *Journal of Experimental Psychology, 17*, 504–535.

Davis, M., & Wagner, A. R. (1968). Startle responsiveness after habituation to different intensities of tone. *Psychonomic Science, 12*, 337–338.

Davis, M., & Wagner, A. R. (1969). Habituation of startle response under incremental sequence of stimulus intensities. *Journal of Comparative and Physiological Psychology, 67*, 486–492.

Estes, W. K. (1976). Structural aspects of associative models for memory. In C. N. Cofer (Ed.), *The structure of human memory*. San Francisco: Freeman.

Ezzeddine, Y., & Glanzman, D. L. (2003). Prolonged habituation of the gillwithdrawal reflex in Aplysia depends upon protein synthesis, protein phosphatase activity and postsynaptic glutamate receptors. *Journal of Neuroscience*, *23*, 9585–9594.

Farel, P. B., Glanzman, D. L., & Thompson, R. F. (1973). Habituation of a monosynaptic response in the vertebrate central nervous system: Lateral column–motoneuron pathway in isolated frog spinal cord. *Journal of Neurophysiology*, *36*, 1117–1130.

Farel, P. B., & Thompson, R. F. (1976). Habituation of a monosynaptic response in frog spinal cord: Evidence for a presynaptic mechanism. *Journal of Neurophysiology*, *39*, 661–666.

Glanzer, M. (1953). Stimulus satiation: An explanation of spontaneous alternation and related phenomena. *Psychological Review*, *60*, 257–268.

Glanzman, D. L., Groves, P. M., & Thompson, R. F. (1972). Stimulus generalization of habituation to spinal interneurons. *Physiology & Behavior*, *8*, 155–158.

Glanzman, D. L., & Thompson, R. F. (1979). Evidence against conduction failure as the mechanism underlying monosynaptic habituation in frog spinal cord. *Brain Research*, *174*, 329–332.

Glickman, S. E., & Feldman, S. M. (1961). Habituation of the arousal response to direct stimulation of the brainstem. *Electroencephalography and Clinical Neurophysiology*, *13*, 703–709.

Griffith, C. R. (1920). The effect upon the white rat of continued bodily rotation. *American Naturalist*, *54*, 524–534.

Groves, P. M., Demarco, R., & Thompson, R. F. (1969). Habituation and sensitization of spinal interneuron activity in acute spinal cat. *Brain Research*, *14*, 521–525.

Groves, P. M., & Thompson, R. F. (1970). Habituation: A dual-process theory. *Psychological Review*, *77*, 419–450.

Groves, P. M., & Thompson, R. F. (1973). Dual-process theory of habituation: Neural mechanisms. In H. V. S. Peeke & M. J. Herz (Eds.). *Habituation: Behavioral studies and physiological substrates* (Vol. II) (pp. 175–203). New York: Academic Press.

Hagbarth, K. E., & Finer, B. L. (1963). The plasticity of human withdrawal reflexes to noxious skin stimuli in lower limbs. In G. Moruzzi, A. Fessard, & H. H. Jasper (Eds.). *Progress in brain research Brain mechanisms* (Vol. I, pp. 65–81). New York: Elsevier.

Hagbarth, K. E., & Kugleberg, E. (1958). Plasticity of the human abdominal skin reflex. *Brain*, *81*, 305–318.

Harris, J. D. (1943). Habituatory response decrement in the intact organism. *Psychological Bulletin*, *40*, 385–422.

Hernández-Peón, R. (1960). Neurophysiological correlates of habituation and other manifestations of plastic inhibition. *Electroencephalography and Clinical Neurophysiology, Supplement*, *13*, 101–114.

Hernández-Peón, R., Scherrer, H., & Jouvet, M. (1956). Modification of electrical activity in cochlear nucleus during ""attention" in unanaesthetized cats. *Science*, *123*, 331–332.

Herrnstein, R. J. (1969). Method and theory in the study of avoidance. *Psychological Review*, *76*, 49–69.

Holmes, S. J. (1912). Phototaxis in the sea-urchin, Arbacia ountulata. *Journal of Animal Behavior*, *2*, 126–136.

Hull, C. L. (1934). Learning II. The factor of the conditioned reflex. In C. Murchison (Ed.), *Handbook of general experimental psychology* (pp. 382–455). Worchester, MA: Clark University Press.

Hull, C. L. (1943). *Principles of behavior*. New York: Appleton-Century-Crofts.

Humphrey, G. (1933). *The nature of learning in its relation to the living system*. New York: Harcourt Brace.

Jasper, H. H., & Shagass, C. (1941). Conditioning the occipital alpha rhythm in man. *Journal of Experimental Psychology*, *28*, 373–388.

Jennings, H. S. (1906). *Behavior of the lower organisms*. New York: Columbia University Press.

Kandel, E. R. (1975). *The cellular basis of behavior: An introduction to behavioral neurobiology*. San Francisco: W. H. Freeman.

Konorski, J. (1948). *Conditioned reflexes and neuron organization*. New York: Cambridge University Press.

Konorski, J. (1967). *Integrative activity of the brain*. Chicago: University of Chicago Press.

Lehner, G. F. J. (1941). A study of the extinction of unconditioned reflexes. *Journal of Experimental Psychology*, *29*, 435–456.

Li, Q., Roberts, A. C., & Glanzman, D. L. (2005). Synaptic facilitation and behavioral dishabituation in Aplysia: Dependence upon release of Ca^{2+} from postsynaptic intracellular stores, postsynaptic exocytosis and modulation of postsynaptic AMPA receptor efficacy. *Journal of Neuroscience*, *25*, 5623–5637.

Lockhart, R. A. (1966). Temporal conditioning of GSR. *Journal of Experimental Psychology*, *71*, 438–446.

Lockhart, R. A., & Steinbrecher, D. C. (1963). Temporal avoidance conditioning in the rabbit. *Psychonomic Science*, *3*, 121–122.

Lombard, W. P. (1887). The variations of the normal knee jerk and their relation to the activity of the central nervous system. *American Journal of Physiology*, *1*, 5–71.

Marsh, J. T., Worden, F. G., & Hicks, L. (1962). Some effects of room acoustics on evoked auditory potentials. *Science*, *137*, 281–282.

McFadden, P. N., & Koshland, D. E. Jr., (1990a). Habituation in the single cell: Diminished secretion of norepinephrine with repetitive depolarization of PC12 cells. *Proceedings of the National Academy of Sciences of the United States of America*, *87*, 2031–2035.

McFadden, P. N., & Koshland, D. E. Jr., (1990b). Parallel pathways for habituation in repetitively stimulated PC12 cells. *Neuron*, *4*, 615–621.

Mower, O. H. (1934). The modification of vestibular systems by means of repeated elicitation. *Comparative Psychology Monographs*, *9*, 1–48.

Patterson, M. M., Cegavske, C. F., & Thompson, R. F. (1973). Effects of a classical conditioning paradigm on hindlimb flexor nerve response in immobilized spinal cat. *Journal of Comparative and Physiological Psychology*, *84*, 88–97.

Pavlov, I. P. (1927). *Conditioned reflexes* (trans., G. V. Anrep, Trans.). London: Oxford.

Peeke, H. V. S., & Herz, M. J. (Eds.). (1973a). *Habituation: Behavioral studies and physiological substrates* (Vol. 1). New York: Academic Press.

Peeke, H. V. S., & Herz, M. J. (Eds.). (1973b). *Habituation: Behavioral studies and physiological substrates* (Vol. 2). New York: Academic Press.

Pinsker, H., Kuppermann, I., Catellucci, V., & Kandel, E. (1970). Habituation and dishabituation of the gill withdrawal reflex in Aplysia. *Science*, *167*, 1740–1742.

Porter, J. M. (1938). Adaptation of the galvanic skin response. *Journal of Experimental Psychology*, *23*, 553–557.

Prosser, C. L., & Hunter, W. S. (1936). The extinction of startle responses and spinal reflexes in the white rat. *American Journal of Physiology*, *117*, 609–618.

Rankin, C. H., & Carew, T. J. (1988). Dishabituation and sensitization emerge as separate processes during development in Aplysia. *Journal of Neuroscience*, *8*, 197–211.

Rose, J. K., & Rankin, C. H. (2001). Analyses of habituation in Caenorhabditis elegans. *Learning and Memory*, *8*, 63–69.

Sharpless, S., & Jasper, H. (1956). Habituation of the arousal reaction. *Brain*, *79*, 357–388.

Sherrington, C. S. (1906). *The integrative action of the nervous system*. New Haven, CT: Yale University Press.

Shiffrin, R. M., & Schneider, W. (1977). Controlled and automatic information processing. II: Perceptual learning, automatic attending, and a general theory. *Psychological Review*, *84*, 127–190.

Sidman, M. (1962). Classical avoidance without a warning stimulus. *Journal of the Experimental Analysis of Behavior*, *5*, 97–104.

Sokolov, E. N. (1960). Neuronal models and the orienting influence. In M. A. Brazier (Ed.), *The central nervous system and behavior III* (pp. 187–276). New York: Macy Foundation.

Sokolov, Y. N. (1963a). Higher nervous functions: The orienting reflex. *Annual Review of Physiology*, *25*, 545–580.

Sokolov, Y. N. (1963b). *Perception and the conditioned reflex* (trans., S. Waydenfeld). Oxford: Pergamon Press.

Spencer, W. A., Thompson, R. F., & Neilson, D. R. Jr., (1966). Responses decrement of the flexion reflex in the acute spinal cat and transient restoration by strong stimuli. *Journal of Neurophysiology*, *29*, 221–239.

Stein, L. (1966). Habituation and stimulus novelty: A model based on classical conditioning. *Psychological Review*, *73*, 352–356.

Thompson, R. F., & Spencer, W. A. (1966). Habituation: A model phenomenon for the study of neuronal substrates of behavior. *Psychological Review*, *73*, 16–43.

Voronin, L. G., & Sokolov, Y. N. (1960). Cortical mechanisms of the orienting reflex and its relation to the conditioned reflex. *Electroencephalography and Clinical Neurophysiology, Supplement*, *13*, 335–346.

Wagner, A. R. (1979). Habituation and memory. In A. Dickinson & R. A. Boakes (Eds.), *Mechanisms of learning and motivation: A memorial volume for Jerry Konorski* (pp. 53–82). Hillsdale, NJ: Lawrence Earlbaum Associates.

Welker, W. I. (1961). An analysis of exploratory and play behavior in animals. In D. W. Fiskem & S. R. Maddi (Eds.), *Functions of varied experience* (pp. 175–226). Homewood, IL: Dorsey.

Wendt, G. R. (1951). Vestibular functions. In S. S. Stevens (Ed.), *Handbook of experimental psychology* (pp. 1191–1223). New York: John Wiley & Sons, Inc.

Worden, F. G., & Marsh, J. T. (1963). Amplitude changes of auditory potentials evoked at cochlear nucleus during acoustic habituation. *Electroencephalography and Clinical Neurophysiology*, *15*, 866–881.

Part II

Applied Classical Conditioning

5

Conditioned Taste Aversion Learning

Relationship to Nausea and Conditioned Disgust

Linda A. Parker

Conditioned taste avoidance (CTA) learning has profoundly influenced our understanding of the basic processes of learning and memory. It is accepted as one of the strongest forms of learning known today. Robust learning despite long taste (conditioned stimulus (CS))-illness (unconditioned stimulus (US)) delays after a single pairing has been the hallmark of taste avoidance learning. The historical development of CTA learning has been masterfully described in detail by Freeman and Riley (2009); therefore, here I will only briefly describe some of the early findings by the founders of the field, most notably John Garcia.

The Garcia Effect

John Garcia, while working in the Radiological Defense Laboratory at Hunters Point in San Francisco, CA (as richly described by Freeman & Riley, 2009), discovered that rats drank less water (than in their home cages) from bottles that were available in the irradiation testing apparatus. Noting that the bottles in the apparatus were made of plastic, but those in the rats' home cages were made of glass, he hypothesized that the plastic bottle gave the water a distinctive flavor that had been paired with illness induced by irradiation. When the rats were given water in the plastic bottles while in their home cages, they showed conditioned avoidance of the plastic-flavored water. This discovery led to a seminal paper in the taste avoidance literature, Garcia, Kimeldorf, and Koelling (1955), that appeared in *Science*. Rats received 6 hr exposure to sham, 30 or 75 roentgens of radiation with access to saccharin solution. Three days later, they were given access to both saccharin and water (in a two bottle test) in their home cage for two months with daily intake measured. Across the two-month period, rats displayed a dose-dependent avoidance of saccharin relative to water that

The Wiley Blackwell Handbook of Operant and Classical Conditioning, First Edition.
Edited by Frances K. McSweeney and Eric S. Murphy.

was maintained for at least 30 days of consumption. This was the first clear experimental evidence that ionizing radiation could act as an aversive unconditioned stimulus in a classical conditioning paradigm. Indeed, in subsequent work, Garcia and Kimeldorf (1957) showed that both trace (a temporal gap separates the CS and US) and simultaneous (presentation of the CS and the US at the same time) CS-US pairings produced CTA learning, but backward conditioning (presentation of the US before the CS) between the taste CS and the irradiation US did not, as would be predicted by the rules of Pavlovian conditioning (Pavlov, 1927).

Could stimuli other than tastes become avoided on the basis of aversive effects of irradiation? Garcia demonstrated that indeed rats would also avoid a conditioning context previously paired with irradiation, but this type of learning was not as robust as the single trial CTA learning (Garcia, Kimeldorf, & Hunt, 1957). This finding led Garcia to introduce the idea that CTA is an adaptive specialized form of learning of associations between information received by taste and internal states. These results published in the paper were the most highly cited in this literature (Relation of cue to consequence in avoidance learning, Garcia & Koelling, 1966), often called the "bright, noisy, tasty water experiment." Rats were presented with the compound CS of the taste of saccharin and an audiovisual cue (light and noise) that was available when the rat licked a spout. Half of these animals received a foot shock US and the other half received exposure to radiation. Then on a subsequent test, half of each US group was tested with saccharin water alone or with bright noisy water (in the absence of saccharin). Garcia and Koelling found that among the rats receiving radiation as the US, only those tested with the saccharin solution avoided consumption. On the other hand, among the rats receiving foot shock as the US, only those tested with the bright, noisy water avoided consumption. These different patterns of consumption reflected selective associations between taste and nausea and between audiovisual cues and foot shock.

This famous "bright, noisy, tasty water" experiment highlighted the importance of the relationship between the cue and consequence with which it is being paired. Subsequently, Garcia, Ervin, and Koelling (1966) demonstrated that when saccharin was paired with the nausea-producing drug, apomorphine, rats learned the association with delays between the CS and US (CS-US intervals) of up to 75 min. The concepts of selective association of cue to consequence and long delay learning were completely inconsistent with the traditional views of associative learning at the time (see Freeman & Riley, 2009 for a detailed review).

Such selective associations were shown to be an adaptive specialization arising from natural selection aiding in the survival of the organism. Biologically relevant stimuli are more likely to become associated, leading to the concept of stimulus relevance (Revusky & Garcia, 1970). Revusky and Garcia suggested that the concept of stimulus relevance provided a means by which a gustatory cue and subsequent illness, sharing stimulus relevance, could become associated over a long CS-US interval during which the animal would encounter many extraneous (but irrelevant) stimuli not likely to interfere with or overshadow the relevant association. Indeed, Revusky and Bedarf (1967) showed that if another novel taste was present during the CS-US interval, CTA learning was impeded by the relevant interfering stimulus. However, if the taste was made familiar to the animal, such interference did not occur. Furthermore, it was noted that CTA was subject to the phenomenon of latent inhibition shown in other learning paradigms (e.g., Lubow, 1973); that is, prior exposure to the to-be-conditioned flavor interfered with the establishment of a CTA (Siegel, 1974).

In contrast to Revusky and Garcia (1970) who made sense of CTA learning on the basis of general process learning and interference by biologically relevant cues, Rozin and Kalat (1971) argued that CTA is actually a specialized form of learning. To support this interpretation, they presented evidence that rats develop an aversion to diets which are missing essential nutrients necessary for survival; that is, they select beneficial foods because of their aversion to the deficient food. Rozin and Kalat interpreted long delay learning as a specific mechanism that evolved to causally link the taste and the delayed gastrointestinal consequences.

In the years that followed, the number of papers published in the CTA literature soared (see Freeman & Riley, 2009 for a review), as researchers explored the nature of CTA learning, how it could be produced and what manipulations affect the establishment and expression of CTA. In the present review, the focus will be on some issues that arose from this literature: (1) the nature of the US in flavor-illness associations, (2) the nature of the conditioned response (CR) in flavor-illness associations, (3) the effect of neurobiological manipulations of nausea on flavor-illness associations, and (4) the context-illness associations as a potential model of anticipatory nausea in chemotherapy patients.

Nature of the US: Nausea?

Earlier experiments investigated the associations between flavors and stimuli with known emetic properties such as radiation, apomorphine, or Lithium Chloride (LiCl; e.g., Gamzu, 1977). The robust associations formed led to the understanding that CTA is a unique learning process by which an organism rapidly associates a flavor with the emetic or nausea-inducing effects of a treatment. CTA learning was shown to be a highly sensitive means of detecting the nausea-inducing properties of a drug and could be induced at doses lower than those necessary to reduce food and water consumption (for review see Riley & Tuck, 1985). The importance of gustatory-visceral convergence in producing taste illness learning was eloquently described by Garcia, Lasiter, Bermudez-Rattoni, and Deems (1985).

After these initial investigations, researchers began to evaluate the potential of atypical agents to produce CTA learning. These investigations revealed that the ability of a drug to produce emesis in an animal capable of vomiting was not a necessary prerequisite for the potential of that drug to produce CTA (e.g., see Grant, 1987, for excellent review; Ionescu & Burešová, 1977; Nachman & Hartley, 1976). Indeed, paradoxically, even very low doses of drugs of abuse produce CTA, suggesting that nausea is not a prerequisite for this type of learning (Berger, 1972; Cappell & LeBlanc, 1973). The most convincing evidence of the paradoxical effects of rewarding drugs to produce CTA was simultaneously reported in the late 1970s. First, Wise, Yokel, and DeWit (1976) presented rats with saccharin solution prior to sessions of operant intravenous self-administration of amphetamine. When subsequently tested, the rats avoided the saccharin solution, but maintained responding for amphetamine. Second, Reicher and Holman (1977) injected rats intraperitoneally with amphetamine prior to placement in a distinctive chamber with access to a flavored solution. When later tested drug-free, the rats preferred the chamber, but avoided the flavored solution. Third, White, Sklar, and Amit (1977) trained rats daily to run down an alley to obtain a food reward. Immediately after they consumed the food in the goal box, the rats were injected with morphine, LiCl, or saline. In the subsequent test trial, in contrast to the rats injected with LiCl who reduced their running speed, the rats treated with morphine increased their running speed to the goal box, but both groups suppressed their consumption of food while in the box. Each of these important papers demonstrated that drugs of abuse produce paradoxical rewarding/aversive effects in rats.

This paradoxical potential of rewarding drugs to produce CTA led to hundreds of studies that have attempted to explain how a given drug injection could simultaneously produce both positive and negative consequences (see Hunt & Amit, 1987). One possibility that was addressed in this literature was that all doses of drugs that produce CTA also have an aversive side effect (e.g., see Davis & Riley, 2010 for review). The selective association between a taste and the aversive effects of the drug produces CTA (Reicher & Holman, 1977). The nature of the aversive effects of the drugs that produce CTA has not been well characterized, but it does not appear to be that of nausea (Parker, Limebeer, & Rana, 2009, for review; Parker, Rana, & Limebeer, 2008). Another possibility that was addressed in the literature was that any change in hedonic state, whether positive or negative, produces avoidance of a novel taste with which it is paired in rats which lack an emetic reflex (e.g., Gamzu, 1977; Hunt & Amit, 1987; Parker et al., 2009 for review). That is, tastes may be avoided because they signal danger to the "internal mileu" rather than because they elicit conditioned nausea. In support of this possibility, shrews, which are capable of vomiting in response to toxins, develop a conditioned taste preference, rather than avoidance, of a taste paired with rewarding doses of amphetamine or morphine, unlike rats (Parker, Corrick, Limebeer, & Kwiatkowska, 2002). A final suggestion that has also received considerable experimental support is that of reward comparison (Grigson, 1997; see Grigson, Twining, Freet, Wheeler, & Geddes, 2009 for review). The reward comparison hypothesis asserts that a palatable solution that is paired with a rewarding drug is avoided because the rewarding value of the drug devalues the rewarding effect of the flavored solution, resulting in suppression of its consumption. Although there is support for each of the above hypotheses, there is also evidence that is not supportive (for review see Davis & Riley, 2010; Verendeev & Riley, 2012). The issue of why rewarding drugs produce CTA remains unresolved.

Nature of the CR: Not all CTA is Accompanied by Conditioned Disgust

The early investigations of CTA learning were specifically directed towards understanding the nature of associations formed between flavors and toxic compounds with known emetic properties. According to Garcia, Hankins, and Rusiniak (1974), a conditioned taste aversion resulted when a novel flavored food or fluid was paired with nausea produced by activation of the emetic system of the gut and the brainstem. Typically, rats served as subjects in these experiments. Although rats are incapable of

Table 5.1 Conditioned taste avoidance learning versus conditioned disgust

Conditioned Taste Avoidance (CTA)	*Conditioned Disgust*
Assessed by consumption test	Assessed by taste reactivity test
Instrumental and classical conditioning	Only classical conditioning
Consummatory and preparatory responding	Only consummatory responding
Rat controls CS exposure	Experimenter controls CS exposure
Produced by both emetic and rewarding drugs	Produced only by emetic drugs

vomiting, they display conditioned disgust reactions (i.e., gaping, chin rubbing) when exposed to a taste previously paired with drug-induced nausea. Garcia et al. (1974) argued that conditioned disgust resulted in subsequent avoidance of the taste and that conditioned disgust is established by the association between the taste and activation of the emetic neural circuitry.

Although Garcia initially described conditioned disgust reactions during consumption tests, Grill and Norgren (1978a, 1978b) explicitly developed an assay for directly measuring these palatability driven reactions in rats, called the Taste Reactivity (TR) test. The typical measure of a flavor-illness association is the amount consumed from a bottle containing the flavored solution—a measure of CTA. This consumption measure requires that the rat approach the bottle in order to sample the flavored solution. Therefore, measuring taste avoidance involves both appetitive and consummatory responses (Konorski, 1967). Table 5.1 compares procedural differences between CTA and conditioned disgust measures. The TR test is an alternative measure of a flavor-illness association. In the TR test, the experimenter controls exposure to the CS flavored solution and the rat reacts with only the consummatory phase of responding. When intraorally infused with a flavored solution previously paired with drug-induced nausea, rats display conditioned disgust reactions. These disgust reactions are similar in form to those elicited by bitter quinine solution. During the intraoral infusion of a nausea-paired taste, rats display conditioned disgust reactions such as gaping, chin rubbing and paw treading which are specific and direct measures of conditioned taste aversion (Grill & Norgren, 1978a). The most reliable (Breslin, Spector, & Grill, 1992; Parker, 1995) measure is conditioned gaping (a wide opening of the mouth with lower incisors exposed). In fact, Travers and Norgren (1986) reported that the rat gaping reaction uses the same orofacial musculature that is required for vomiting in emetic species, and Parker (2003) reported that the gaping response is very similar in form to the orofacial component of the shrew retch (see Figure 5.1). Only drugs which produce nausea produce these conditioned disgust reactions when explicitly paired with a flavored stimulus (see Parker et al., 2009 for review). Also, anti-emetic drugs consistently reduce conditioned disgust reactions produced by high doses of LiCl, without attenuating CTA (e.g., Limebeer & Parker, 2000, 2003; Parker et al., 2008, 2009, for reviews; Pautassi, Arias, Molina, & Spear, 2008; Rudd, Ngan, & Wai, 1998).

According to Garcia et al.'s (1974; refined in Garcia, 1989) model, feedback from nausea produces conditioned disgust; therefore, a manipulation that produces nausea should establish conditioned disgust reactions. However, considerable evidence indicates that not all taste avoidance is accompanied by conditioned disgust to the taste

Figure 5.1 Rat gape and orofacial component of shrew retch. Unlike rats, shrews vomit in response to emetic stimulation.

when assessed with the TR test. The selectivity of conditioned disgust reactions to nausea-producing treatments was demonstrated by Pelchat, Grill, Rozin, and Jacobs (1983). Rats were conditioned to associate a sucrose solution with footshock, lactose (causing lower intestinal distress that produces a gaseous sensation) or LiCl-induced nausea, and the rats' orofacial and somatic responses to sucrose were measured in the TR test. The conditioning method was controlled across US treatments to produce equal strength conditioned sucrose avoidance in a traditional CTA test. However, when assessed in a TR test, only those rats that had received pairings of sucrose with LiCl-induced nausea displayed disgust reactions. Nausea was necessary to establish conditioned disgust. The authors suggested that CTA is the result of the flavor signaling danger, but conditioned disgust reflects conditioned nausea.

The paradoxical CTA produced by rewarding drugs is also not accompanied by conditioned disgust reactions. If taste avoidance produced by a rewarding dose of a drug is mediated by conditioned nausea, then the avoidance of the taste should be accompanied by conditioned disgust reactions (e.g., Garcia et al., 1974; Grill & Norgren, 1978b); however, considerable evidence indicates that it is not (Parker, 1982, 1995, 2003). In a series of experiments, Parker (1995, 2003 for reviews) demonstrated that, in contrast to LiCl, when rats were conditioned with doses of rewarding drugs (including amphetamine, cocaine, methamphetamine, methylphenidate, morphine, phencyclidine and low doses of nicotine), they did not display conditioned disgust reactions to an intraoral infusion of the flavored solution, but they did show a strong CTA. Therefore, drugs with rewarding properties produces a CTA (decreased consumption), but not conditioned disgust. Rewarding drugs do, however, produce suppressed ingestive responding and enhanced passive dripping (passive dripping of the fluid from the mouth), which may reflect a similar process as CTA (see Parker, 1995). The failure of rewarding agents to produce conditioned disgust reactions is not simply the result of the relative weakness of the acquired taste-drug association. When the dose of amphetamine was adjusted to produce stronger taste avoidance in a consumption test than a low dose of LiCl, the rats only displayed conditioned disgust reactions to the LiCl-paired flavor, but not to the amphetamine-paired flavor (Zalaquett & Parker, 1989). Therefore, the conditioned disgust reaction, but not CTA, is a reliable and selective measure of nausea in rats (Parker, 1998).

Recent evidence, however, suggests that when a flavor comes to predict delayed (but not immediate) self-administration of cocaine, rats eventually display disgust reactions to that flavor (Grigson & Twining, 2002; Wheeler & Carelli, 2009; Wheeler et al., 2011; Carelli & West, 2013). That is, the onset of the aversive process occurs when the taste cue comes to predict a waiting period before the administration of cocaine (Wheeler et al., 2011). Since naloxone-precipitated morphine withdrawal produces conditioned disgust reactions when paired with a taste (McDonald et al., 1997), the conditioned disgust following chronic, delayed cocaine exposure has been interpreted as a measure of the aversive properties of cocaine withdrawal (Carelli & West, 2013; Nyland & Grigson, 2013). Indeed, following extensive delayed pairings (but not immediate pairings) of a flavor with cocaine self-administration, dopamine signaling is reduced during the flavor exposure (Wheeler et al., 2008, 2011).

Human self-report studies also suggest that nausea plays a special role in the establishment of conditioned disgust, but not necessarily CTA. Hedonic ratings of dislike are more predictive of nausea than are consumption patterns in humans re-experiencing an illness-paired flavor (Pelchat & Rozin, 1982; Schwarz, Jacobsen, & Bjovberg, 1986). Schwarz et al. had human chemotherapy patients drink a novel flavored solution prior to their chemotherapy session during which they rated the severity of nausea that they experienced. When they were subsequently allowed to drink the chemotherapy-paired solution, their hedonic ratings of liking of the flavor were more predictive of self-reported ratings of nausea during the session than was the amount of the solution consumed. Nausea is a better predictor of the development of conditioned disgust than are other non-gastrointestinal aversive experiences as illustrated by a scenario described by Pelchat and Rozin. One person experiences food poisoning following eating shrimp, but another experiences an allergic reaction of hives following eating shrimp. Although both people avoid eating shrimp in the future, only the poisoned person comes to dislike the taste of shrimp. That is, the people avoid the shrimp for different reasons; one is based on distaste and the other on perceived danger.

Neurobiological Manipulation of Nausea: Effect on Conditioned Disgust and CTA

If CTA is motivated by conditioned nausea, then anti-nausea treatments would be expected to interfere with its establishment and/or expression. Early work indicated that classic anti-nausea drugs interfered with the expression of a previously established LiCl-induced CTA (Coil, Hankins, Jenden, & Garcia, 1978); however, more recent findings suggest that similar anti-nausea treatments (e.g., Goudie, Stollerman, Demellweek, & D'Mello, 1982; Parker & McLeod, 1991; Rabin & Hunt, 1983) and different anti-nausea treatments (e.g., Gadusek & Kalat, 1975; Limebeer & Parker, 2000, 2003) failed to interfere with the expression of an LiCl-induced CTA. There is also considerable evidence that anti-nausea treatments either do not interfere with the establishment of CTA learning (Limebeer & Parker, 2000, 2003; Rabin & Hunt, 1983; Rudd et al., 1998) or only interfere with the establishment of very weak LiCl-induced taste avoidance (Balleine, Garner, & Dickinson, 1995; Gorzolka, Hanson, Harrington, Killam, & Campbell-Meiklejon, 2003; Wegener, Smith, & Rosenberg, 1997). On the other hand, these treatments interfere with the establishment and/or the expression of conditioned disgust reactions (for review, see Parker et al., 2009; Parker, Rock, & Limebeer, 2011). The results of these experiments argue that conditioned disgust reflects conditioned nausea, unlike CTA. That is, treatments that reduce the US of nausea prevent the establishment of conditioned disgust reactions and can also prevent the expression of previously established conditioned disgust reactions. These treatments are not interfering with learning per se, however, because they do not interfere with the establishment or the expression of CTA learning.

Serotonin, Nausea, and Disgust

When cancer patients undergo cisplatin chemotherapy, the emetic response is mediated by serotonin (5-hydroxytryptamine, 5-HT) released from the gastrointestinal enterochromaffin cells (Andrews, Rappaport, & Sanger, 1988). Serotonin acts on 5-HT$_3$ receptors located on vagal afferents to trigger nausea and vomiting and 5-HT$_3$ receptor antagonists, such as ondansetron, exert their anti-emetic effects here to relieve the deleterious side effects that often accompany cancer chemotherapy. Similar mechanisms are believed to operate in the rat despite this animal's inability to vomit (Hillsley & Grundy, 1998). When intracranially delivered to the area postrema, a brainstem region critical for the emetic response, ondansetron also inhibits cisplatin-induced vomiting in ferrets (Higgins, Kilpatrick, Bunce, Jones, & Tyers, 1989). Serotonin plays a special role in the generation of vomiting and nausea. Indeed, drugs which elevate central levels of serotonin, such as the serotonin releaser, fenfluramine (Parker 1988), and the serotonin selective reuptake inhibitors, fluoxetine (Limebeer, Litt, & Parker, 2009) and paroxetine (Tuerke Leri, & Parker, 2009), produce conditioned disgust reactions when paired with a flavored solution in rats. These agents have also been reported to produce nausea in humans (Brambilla, Cipriani, Hotopf, & Barbui, 2005). Therefore, the conditioned disgust reaction model serves as an effective tool for detecting the side effects of nausea produced by newly developed pharmaceutical compounds.

If conditioned disgust reactions are only produced by nauseating treatments in rats, then pretreatment with drugs that attenuate toxin-induced vomiting in emetic species (e.g., Matsuki et al., 1988) might also attenuate conditioned disgust reactions in rats. Two such drugs that act on the serotonin system are the 5-HT$_3$ antagonist, ondansetron, and the 5-HT$_{1A}$ agonist, 8-OH-DPAT (e.g., Parker et al., 2008, 2011, for review). The central 5-HT system consists of two distinct subdivisions associated with the mid-sagittal seam (raphe) of the brainstem: a rostral division that projects to the forebrain, and a caudal division that projects to the spinal cord (see Figure 5 in Tork, 1990). The rostral division consists of the dorsal raphe nucleus (DRN) and the median raphe nucleus (MRN) which both project axons to multiple areas in the forebrain. At low doses (<0.5 mg/kg, ip), 8-OH-DPAT, acts selectively on the inhibitory 5-HT$_{1A}$ autoreceptors located on the soma and dendrites of neurons in the DRN and MRN exerting a negative feedback influence on their firing activity (Blier, Pineyro, Mansari, Bergeron, & de Montigny, 1998). The reduction in firing activity results in reduced 5-HT release in terminal forebrain regions. Both ondansetron and 8-0H-DPAT interfere with the establishment and the expression of LiCl-induced conditioned disgust reactions, but not CTA learning (Limebeer & Parker, 2000; Limebeer & Parker, 2003; see also Rudd et al., 1998). The effect of serotonin antagonism is specific to conditioned disgust reactions, because ondansetron pretreatment does not interfere with unconditional disgust reactions elicited by bitter quinine solution (Limebeer & Parker, 2000).

Central serotonin availability can also be reduced by selective serotonin neurotoxin-induced lesions of the raphe nuclei. The neurotoxin, 5,7-Dihyroxytryptamine (5,7-DHT), is taken up by the 5-HT containing neurons and produces degeneration of axons and terminals containing 5-HT. Since Grill and Norgren (1978b) previously demonstrated that an intact forebrain is necessary for the establishment and/or expression of LiCl-induced conditioned disgust reaction, Limebeer, Parker, and Fletcher (2004) reasoned that forebrain serotonin may be necessary for the generation of these conditioned disgust reactions. Therefore, they evaluated the potential of 5,7-DHT lesions of the DRN and the MRN to interfere with the establishment of LiCl-induced conditioned disgust reactions and CTA learning in rats. Indeed, depletion of forebrain serotonin prevented the establishment of LiCl-induced conditioned disgust reactions; however, the lesions did not prevent CTA learning (Limebeer et al., 2004). Other investigators have also reported that depletion of forebrain serotonin does not modify the strength of a CTA (e.g., Asin, Wirtshafter, & Kent, 1980; Bienkowski, Iwinska, Piasecki, & Kostowski, 1997). However, forebrain serotonin is critical for the establishment of these nausea-induced conditioned disgust reactions in rats. The critical forebrain region appears to be the insular cortex (IC) (Tuerke, Limebeer, Fletcher, & Parker, 2013).

Insular Cortex, Nausea, and Disgust

Considerable human research suggests that the IC is involved in the emotional reaction of disgust (e.g., Calder et al., 2007). The IC is engaged in humans who view facial expressions of disgust and pictures of disgusting scenes (e.g., Phillips et al., 1998; Wicker et al., 2003) or exposure to disgusting smells (Heining et al., 2003; Wicker et al., 2003). Calder, Keane, Manes, Antoun, and Young (2000) report that a patient, NK, with damage to the insula showed a marked and selective impairment in recognizing the facial expression and vocalization of disgust, as well as in his own responsiveness to disgust-provoking scenarios. Indeed, Rozin and Fallon (1987) claim that disgust has developed from a more primitive system involving distaste produced by nausea. Penfield and Faulk (1955) observed that electrical stimulation of the IC of conscious human patients undergoing surgery produced sensations of nausea, unpleasant tastes, and sensations in the stomach. As well, stimulation of the IC has been shown to produce vomiting in humans (Fiol, Leppik, Mireless, & Maxwell, 1988; Catenoix et al., 2008) and other animals (Kaada, 1951). In rats, inactivation of the visceral IC (granular) attenuated LiCl-induced malaise (Contreras, Ceric, & Torrealba, 2007) as measured by flattened lying on belly (Parker, Hills, & Jensen, 1984), which is also attenuated by lesions of the area postrema (Bernstein,

Chavez, Allen, & Taylor, 1992). Contreras et al. suggested that this region of the IC (which is also involved in craving for drugs; Naqvi, Rudrauf, Damasio, & Bechara, 2007) may be responsible for sensing strong deviations from a "well being state."

The literature on the effect of neurotoxin-induced or electrolytic lesions of the IC on the establishment of LiCl-induced CTA in rats is mixed. Damage to the gustatory area of input, the anterior dysgranular region (gustatory cortex, Kosar, Grill, & Norgren, 1986), has been reported to attenuate (but not eliminate) LiCl-induced taste avoidance (e.g., Bermúdez-Rattoni & McGaugh, 1991; Braun, Slick, & Lorden, 1972; Dunn & Everitt, 1988; Hankins, Garcia, & Rusiniak, 1974; Lasiter, 1982; Lasiter & Glanzman, 1985; Nerad, Ramirez-Amaya, Ormsby, & Bermúdez-Rattoni, 1996; Roman, & Reilly, 2007), but damage to the visceral area of input, the posterior granular region (visceral cortex; Cechetto & Saper, 1987) has been reported to be ineffective in attenuation of LiCl-induced CTA learning (Mackey, Keller, & van der Kooy, 1986; Nerad et al., 1996).

The role of the IC in the establishment of conditioned disgust reactions is less well investigated than CTA. Kiefer and Orr (1992) showed that rats with complete bilateral ablation of the IC learned to avoid drinking sucrose and salt that was paired with LiCl (albeit at a slower rate than controls), but they failed to display conditioned disgust to the tastes. This was not a function of their inability to make aversive responses or to detect aversive tastes, because they showed normal reactivity to quinine solution. Therefore, rats lacking an IC learned to avoid the taste, but not because it was conditionally disgusting. More recently, Tuerke et al. (2013) found that 5,7-DHT lesions which reduced 5-HT by 76% in the entire IC attenuated LiCl-induced conditioned disgust reactions. Furthermore, in a double dissociation, they found that intracranial administration of the 5-HT_3 receptor antagonist, ondansetron, to the visceral IC attenuated LiCl-induced conditioned disgust reactions, but not taste avoidance. On the other hand, ondansetron delivered to the gustatory IC attenuated LiCl-induced CTA, but not conditioned disgust. The direct delivery of a 5-HT_3 receptor agonist to these regions produced the opposite effect. Therefore, 5-HT_3 activity in the region of the IC with gastrointestinal input from the gut is critical for the establishment of nausea-inducing conditioned disgust reactions.

Although beyond the scope of this chapter, considerable evidence suggests that cannabinoids (in particular, CB_1 agonists such as Δ^9-tetrahydrocannabinol (THC) and drugs that enhance the action of the natural endocannabinoid system) regulate the nausea produced by serotonergic agonists (see Parker et al., 2011 for review). The visceral IC also responds to the inhibitory action of CB_1 agonists on conditioned disgust reactions, possibly by means of a CB_1 and 5-HT interaction. Limebeer, Rock, Mechoulam, and Parker (2012) found that the CB_1 agonist, HU-210, reduced conditioned disgust reactions (but not taste avoidance) when delivered to the visceral IC, but not to the gustatory IC. These data provide evidence that the visceral IC regulates the establishment of conditioned disgust reactions, but is not involved in the regulation of conditioned taste avoidance.

The gustatory IC appears to be more important in the regulation of conditioned taste avoidance. The effects of 5-HT_3 antagonism in the gustatory IC mirror the effects of NMDA lesions of the basolateral amygdala (BLA) on conditioned disgust and CTA (Rana & Parker, 2008; see Reilly, 2009 for review of CTA literature); that is, it reduced CTA, but not disgust. Indeed, the gustatory cortex and the BLA are directly interconnected (Allen et al., 1991), and they are functionally interrelated in the acquisition and retention of CTA (Burešová, 1978; Burešová, Aleksanyan & Bures, 1979; Yamamoto, Azuma, & Kawamura, 1981). Therefore, serotonergic activation of the visceral IC appears to mediate the production of nausea-induced conditioned disgust, but not taste avoidance. On the other hand, serotonergic activation of the gustatory IC at least plays a role in the generation of LiCl-induced taste avoidance, but not disgust.

Garcia et al. (1985) presented a model suggesting that gustatory-visceral convergence provides a substrate of gustatory-illness association learning. Indeed, considerable evidence indicates convergence between gustatory and visceral input in the CNS with topographical representation at the nucleus of the solitary tract (NTS), parabrachial nucleus of the pons (PBN), the thalamus and the insular cortex (see Figure 15.1 of Reilly, 2009 for review).

Nature of the CS: Contextually Elicited Conditioned Disgust Reactions-A Model of Anticipatory Nausea

Rats not only display conditioned disgust reactions to a flavor previously paired with a nauseating treatment, but they also display conditioned disgust reactions to a contextual cue previously paired with a nauseating treatment (e.g., Cloutier, Rodowa, Cross-Mellor, Chan, Kavaliers & Ossenkopp, 2012; Limebeer, Krohn, Cross-Mellor, Ossenkopp, & Parker, 2008; Meachum & Bernstein, 1992; Ossenkopp, Biagi, Cloutier, Chan, Kavaliers, & Cross-Mellor, 2011; Rock, Limebeer, Mechoulam, Piomelli, & Parker, 2008). Shrews also display conditioned retching to a context previously paired with LiCl (Parker & Kemp, 2001; Parker, Kwiatkowska, & Mechoulam, 2006). However, as previously demonstrated by Garcia et al. (1957), this type of learning is not as robust as the single trial flavor-nausea learning, requiring three or four pairings of the context with the nauseating treatment. Contextually elicited conditioned disgust serves as a model of anticipatory nausea (AN) evidenced in chemotherapy patients when they return to the treatment environment.

In human patients, AN often develops over the course of repeated chemotherapy sessions. Nesse, Carli, Curtis, and Kleinman (1980) reported that about 44% of patients in their study being treated for lymphoma developed AN, which is best understood as a classically conditioned response (Pavlov, 1927). Control over AN could be exerted at the time of conditioning or at the time of reexposure to the CS at test. Administration of an anti-emetic drug at the time of conditioning should attenuate the acute unconditioned response (UCR) of nausea, thereby reducing subsequent AN. Indeed, when administered during the chemotherapy session, the 5-HT_3 antagonist, granisetron, has been reported to reduce the incidence of AN in repeat cycle chemotherapy treatment (Aapro, Kirchner, & Terrey, 1994). On the other hand, if a drug is delivered prior to reexposure to cues previously paired with the toxin-induced nausea, then suppressed AN would be the result of attenuation of the expression of the CR (conditioned nausea); the 5-HT_3 antagonists are ineffective at this stage (e.g., Aapro et al.; Jordan, Kasper, & Schmoll, 2005).

Anecdotal, clinical and preclinical evidence suggests that the cannabis derived compound, Δ^9-THC, alleviates the expression of AN in chemotherapy patients

(Abrahamov, Abrahamov, & Mechoulam, 1995; Duran et al., 2010; Grinspoon & Bakalar, 1993; Iverson, 2000). The conditioned retching displayed by *S. murinus* when returned to a chamber previously paired with a dose of LiCl that produced vomiting (Parker & Kemp, 2001) is suppressed by pretreatment with Δ^9-THC, but (as in human patients) the 5-HT_3 antagonist ondansetron is completely ineffective (Parker et al., 2006). The doses employed were selected on the basis of their potential to interfere with toxin-induced vomiting in the *S. murinus* (Kwiatkowska, Parker, Burton, & Mechoulam, 2004; Parker, Kwiatkowska, Burton, & Mechoulam, 2004). As well, Δ^9-THC and drugs that enhance the action of the natural endocannabinoid system, unlike ondansetron, interfere with the expression of contextually elicited conditioned gaping reactions in rats (Limebeer et al., 2006; Rock et al., 2008). Finally, the primary non-psychoactive compounds found in the cannabis plant, cannabidiol and its acidic precursor, cannabidiolic acid (which is converted to cannabidiol upon heating), both are effective in suppressing contextually elicited conditioned gaping elicited by a LiCl-paired chamber (Bolognini et al., 2013; Rock et al., 2008). These results suggest that cannabinoid compounds may be effective agents in the treatment of AN in chemotherapy patients.

The potential of external contextual cues to become associated with the illness-inducing effects of drug treatments has been considered to be a form of "unprepared" learning (Seligman 1970), and indeed these associations generally require more conditioning trials than do associations between a flavor and illness (e.g. Garcia et al., 1957; Limebeer et al., 2008). However, not only do contextual cues (even in the absence of a distinctive odor; Limebeer et al., 2008) elicit conditioned disgust reaction of gaping, but they also are avoided in a place aversion paradigm when paired with LiCl (Parker, 1992). Such LiCl-induced place aversion learning can be produced even following a single trial (Parker, 1992), and it is highly resistant to extinction (Parker & McDonald, 2000).

Conditioned Taste Aversion Learning as a Preclinical Model of Nausea

The initial work on "conditioned taste aversion" learning based upon pairings of a novel taste with a sickness-producing drug has resulted in several preclinical animal models of nausea. CTA, as measured by amount consumed of the drug-paired flavored solution, has not served well to identify potential nauseating side effects of newly developed drugs because it is clearly not selectively produced by nausea (e.g., Gamzu, 1977; Grant, 1987; Parker et al., 2009). On the other hand, conditioned disgust reactions elicited by a drug-paired flavored solution, that were initially described by Garcia et al. (1974) and later characterized by Grill and Norgren (1978b) and Berridge, Grill, and Norgren (1981), do provide such a model. Drugs which produce nausea and vomiting in humans and other animals capable of vomiting collectively produce conditioned disgust in rats. The conditioned disgust reaction model, unlike CTA, also serves as an effective tool to measure the potential of newly developed pharmaceutical treatments to reduce nausea. Although less sensitive than the flavor-induced conditioned disgust preclinical model of nausea, the contextually-induced conditioned disgust preclinical model of AN experienced by chemotherapy patients has excellent face validity for the development of treatments for this distressing symptom. The behavioral measure of gaping is the most reliable conditioned disgust reaction in rats (Breslin et al., 1992; Parker, 1995). This measure is extremely easy to identify and score with inter-rater reliability ratings consistently falling in the range of r > 0.90 when the scores of highly experienced raters are compared with those of raters trained for only a few hours.

"Conditioned taste aversion learning" was initially measured by avoidance of consumption of the treatment paired flavored solution. However, it is not clear that CTA is always mediated by an aversion to the taste (e.g., Grigson, 1997; Parker, 1995, 2003; Pelchat et al., 1983). More recently, "Conditioned taste aversion" learning as measured by the CR of conditioned disgust (Berridge et al., 1981; Garcia et al., 1974; Grill & Norgren, 1978b; Parker, 2003; Pelchat et al.) clearly provides a promising preclinical measure of nausea. The conditioned disgust reaction model of nausea provides a new research tool to assist in understanding the neurobiological underpinnings of the elusive sensation of nausea.

Summary

John Garcia's initial discovery of conditioned taste aversion learning has greatly influenced our understanding of basic associations between biologically relevant cues and consequences. Dissection of the basic conditioned taste aversion learning phenomenon has revealed that this learning is not nearly as simple as it initially seemed to be. In non-emetic rats, nausea does not appear to be necessary for the production of conditioned taste avoidance, but it does appear to be necessary for the production of conditioned disgust to a flavor or to a contextual cue (a model of anticipatory nausea). Understanding the neurobiology of these conditioned disgust reactions provides clues about the neurobiology of nausea, which may be triggered by serotonin and suppressed by endocannabinoids. With the aid of the behavioral tool of conditioned disgust, we can expect new discoveries about how these two systems interact to regulate our experience of nausea.

References

Aapro, M. S., Kirchner, V., & Terrey, J. P. (1994). The incidence of anticipatory nausea and vomiting after repeat cycle chemotherapy: The effect of granisetron. *British Journal of Cancer*, *69*, 957.

Abrahamov, A., Abrahamov, A.. & Mechoulam, R. (1995). An efficient new cannabinoid antiemetic in pediatric oncology. *Life Sciences*, *56*, 2097–2102.

Asin, K. E., Wirtshafter, D., & Kent, E. W. (1980). The effects of electrolytic median raphe lesions on two measures of latent inhibition. *Behavioral and Neural Biology*, *28*, 408–417.

Andrews, P. L., Rappaport, W. G., & Sanger, G. J. (1988). Neuropharmacology of emesis induced by anti-cancer therapy. *Trends in Pharmacological Sciences*, *9*, 334–341.

Allen, G. V., Saper, C. B., Hurley, K. M., & Cechetto, D. F. (1991). Organization of visceral and limbicconnections in the insular cortex of the rat. *Journal of Comparative Neurology*, *311*, 1–16.

Balleine, B., Garner, C., & Dickinson, A. (1995). Instrumental outcome devaluation is attenuated by the anti-emetic ondansetron. *Quarterly Journal of Experimental Psychology, 48B*, 235–251.

Berger, B. (1972) Conditioning of food aversions by injections of psychoactive drugs. *Journal of Comparative and Physiological Psychology, 81*, 21–26.

Berridge, K. C., Grill, H. J., & Norgren, R. (1981). Relation of consummatory responses and preabsorptive insulin release to palatability and learned taste aversions. *Journal of Comparative and Physiological Psychology, 95*, 363–382.

Bermúdez-Rattoni, F., & McGaugh, J. L. (1991). Insular cortex and amygdala differentially effect acquisition on inhibitory avoidance and conditioned taste aversion. *Brain Research, 49*, 165–170.

Bernstein, I. L., Chavez, M., Allen, D., & Taylor, E. M. (1992). Area postrema mediation of physiological and behavioral effects of lithium chloride in the rat. *Brain Research, 575*, 132–137.

Bienkowski, P., Iwinska, K., Piasecki, J., & Kostowski, W. (1997). 5,7-Dihydroxytryptamine lesion does not affect ethanol-induced conditioned taste and place aversion in rats. *Alcohol, 14*, 439–443.

Blier, P., Pineyro, G., Mansari, M., Bergeron, R., & de Montigny, C. (1998). Role of somatodendritic 5-HT autoreceptors in modulating 5-HT neurotransmission. In G. R. Martin, R. M. Eglen, D. Hoyer, M. W. Hamblin, & F. Yocca (Eds.), Advances in serotonin receptor research: Molecular biology, signal transduction, and therapeutics. *Annals of the New York Academy of Science, 861*, 204–216.

Bolognini, D., Rock, E. M., Cluny, N. L., Cascio, M. G., Limebeer, C. L., Duncan, M., Stott, C. G., Javid, F. A., Parker, L. A., & Pertwee, R. G. (2013). Cannabidiolic acid prevents vomiting in *Suncus murinus* and nausea-induced behaviour in rats by enhancing 5-HT_{1A} receptor activation. *British Journal of Pharmacology, 168*, 1456–1470.

Braun, J. J., Slick, T. B. & Lorden, J. F. (1972). Involvement of gustatory neocortex in learning of taste aversions. *Physiology & Behavior, 9*, 637–641.

Brambilla, P., Cipriani, A., Hotopf, M., & Barbui, C. (2005). Side-effect profile of fluoxetine in comparison with other SSRIs, tricyclic, and newer antidepressants: A meta-analysis of clinical trial data. *Pharmacopsychiatry, 38*, 69–77.

Breslin, P. A., Spector, A. C.. & Grill, H. J. (1992). A quantitative comparison of taste reactivity behaviors to sucrose before and after lithium chloride pairings: A unidimensional account of palatability. *Behavioral Neuroscience, 106*, 820–836.

Burešová, O. (1978). Neocortico-amygdalar interaction in the conditioned taste aversion in rats. *Activitas Nervosa Superior (Praha), 20*: 224–230

Burešová, O., Aleksanyan, Z. A., &, Bures, J. (1979). Electrophysiological analysis of retrieval of conditioned taste aversion in rats. Unit activity changes in critical brain regions. *Physiologica Bohemoslovaca, 28*, 545–536.

Calder, A. J., Beaver, J. D., Davis, M. H., van Ditzhuijzen, J., Keane, J., & Lawrence, A. D. (2007). Disgust sensitivity predicts the insula and pallidal response to pictures of disgusting foods. *European Journal of Neuroscience, 25*, 3422–3428.

Calder, A. J., Keane, J., Manes, F., Antoun, N., & Young, A. W. (2000). Impaired recognition and experience of disgust following brain injury. *Nature Neuroscience, 3*, 1077–1078.

Cappell, H., & LeBlanc, A. E. (1973). Gustatory avoidance by drugs of abuse: Relationships to general issues in research on drug dependence. In N. W. Milgram, L. Krames, & T. M Alloway (Eds) *Food aversion learning* (pp. 133–167). New York: Plenum Publishing.

Carelli, R. M. & West, E. A. (2013). When a good taste turns bad: Neural mechanisms underlying the emergence of negative affect and associated natural reward devaluation by cocaine. *Neuropharmacology*, doi: 10.1016/j.neuropharm.2013.04.025.

Catenoix, H., Isnard, J., Guénot, M., Petit, J., Remy, C., & Mauguière, F. (2008). The role of the anterior insular cortex in ictal vomiting: A stereotactic electroencephalography study. *Epilepsy Behavior, 13*, 560–563.

Cechetto, D. F., & Saper, C. B. (1987). Evidence for a viscerotopic sensory representation in the cortex and thalamus in the rat. *Journal of Comparative Neurology, 262*, 27–45.

Cloutier, C. J., Rodowa, M. S., Cross-Mellor, S. K., Chan, M. Y., Kavaliers, M., & Ossenkopp, K. P. (2012). Inhibition of LiCl-induced conditioning of anticipatory nausea in rats following immune system stimulation: Comparing the immunogens lipopolysaccharide, muramyl dipeptide, and polyinosinic: polycytidylic acid. *Physiology & Behavior, 106*, 243–251.

Coil, J. D., Hankins, W. G., Jenden, D. J., & Garcia, J. (1978). The attenuation of a specific cue-to-consequence association by antiemetic agents. *Psychopharmacology, 56*, 21–25.

Contreras, M., Ceric, F., & Torrealba, F. (2007). Inactivation of the interoceptive insula disrupts drug craving and malaise induced by lithium. *Science, 318*, 655–658.

Davis, C. M., & Riley, A. L. (2010). Conditioned taste aversion learning: Implications for animal models of drug abuse. *Annals of the New York Academy of Sciences, 1187*, 247–275.

Dunn, L. T., & Everitt, B. J. (1988). Double dissociations of the effects of amygdala and insular cortex lesions on conditioned taste-aversion, passive-avoidance, and neophobia in the rat using the excitotoxin ibotenic acid. *Behavioral Neuroscience, 102*, 3–23.

Duran, M., Perez, E., Abanades, S., Vidal, X., Saura, C., Majem M., et al. (2010). Preliminary efficacy and safety of an oromucosal standardized cannabis extract in chemotherapy-induced nausea and vomiting. *British Journal of Clinical Pharmacology, 70*, 656–666.

Fiol, M., Leppik, I. E., Mireless, R., & Maxwell, R. (1988). Ictus emeticus and the insular cortex. *Epilepsy Research, 2*, 127–131.

Freeman, K. B. & Riley, A. L. (2009). The origins of conditioned taste aversion learning: A historical analysis. In S. Reilly & T. R. Schachtman (Eds.), *Conditioned taste aversion: Behavioral and neural processes.* (pp. 9–36). New York: Oxford University Press.

Gadusek, F. J., & Kalat, J. W. (1975). Effects of scopolamine on retention of taste-aversion learning in rats. *Physiological Psychology, 3*, 130–132.

Gamzu, E. (1977). The multifaceted nature of taste aversion inducing agents: Is there a single common factor? In L. Barker, M. Domjan, & M. Best (Eds.), *Learning mechanisms of food selection* (pp. 447–511). Waco, TX: Baylor University Press.

Garcia, J. (1989). Food for Tolman: Cognition and cathexis in concert. In T. Archer & L-G. Nilsson (Eds.), *Aversion, avoidance and anxiety* (pp. 45–85). Hillsdale, NJ: Erlbaum.

Garcia, J., Ervin, F. R., & Koelling, R. A. (1966). Learning with prolonged delay of reinforcement. *Psychonomic Science, 5*, 121–122.

Garcia, J., Hankins, W. G., & Rusiniak, K. W. (1974). Behavioral regulation of the milieu interne in man and rat. *Science, 185*, 824–831.

Garcia, J., & Kimeldorf, J. K. (1957). Temporal relationship within the conditioning of a saccharine aversion through radiation exposure. *Journal of Comparative and Physiological Psychology, 50*, 180–183.

Garcia, J., Kimeldorf, J. K., & Hunt, E. L. (1957). Spatial avoidance in the rat as a result of exposure to ionizing radiation. *British Journal of Radiology, 30*, 318–321.

Garcia, J., Kimeldorf, D. J., & Koelling, R. A. (1955). Conditioned aversion to saccharin resulting from exposure to gamma radiation. *Science, 122*, 157–158.

Garcia, J., & Koelling, R. A. (1966). Relation of cue to consequence in avoidance learning. *Psychonomic Science, 4*, 123–124.

Garcia, J., Lasiter, P. A., Bermudez-Rattoni, F., & Deems, D. A. (1985). A general theory of aversion learning. In N. S. Braveman and P. Bronstein (Eds.), Experimental assessments and clinical applications of conditioned food aversions. *Annals of the New York Academy of Sciences*, *443*, 8–22.

Gorzalka, B., Hanson, L., Harrington, J., Killam, S., & Campbell-Meiklejohn, D. (2003). Conditioned taste aversion: Modulation by 5-HT receptor activity and corticosterone. *European Journal of Pharamcology*, *47*, 129–134.

Goudie, A. J., Stollerman, I. P., Demellweek, C., & D'Mello, G. D. (1982). Does conditioned nausea mediate drug-induced conditioned taste aversion? *Psychopharmacology*, *78*, 277–282.

Grant, V. L. (1987). Do conditioned taste aversions result from activation of emetic mechanisms? *Psychopharmacology*, *93*, 405–415.

Grigson, P. S. (1997). Conditioned taste aversions and drugs of abuse: A reinterpretation. *Behavioral Neuroscience*, *111*, 129–136.

Grigson, P. S., & Twining, R. C. (2002). Cocaine-induced suppression of saccharin intake: A model of drug-induced devaluation of natural rewards. *Behavioral Neuroscience*, *116*, 321–333.

Grigson, P. S., Twining, R. C., Freet, C. S., Wheeler, R. A., & Geddes, R. I. (2009). Drug-induced suppression of conditioned stimulus intake: Reward, aversion and addiction. In S. Reilly & T. R. Schachtman (Eds.), *Conditioned taste aversion: Behavioral and neural processes* (pp. 74–91). New York: Oxford University Press.

Grill, H. C., & Norgren, R. (1978a). The taste reactivity test. I: Mimetic responses to gustatory stimuli in neurologically normal rats. *Brain Research*, *14*, 263–279.

Grill, H. C., & Norgren, R. (1978b). Chronically decerebrate rats demonstrate satiation but not bait shyness. *Science*, *201*, 267–269.

Grinspoon, L., & Bakalar, J. B. (1993). *Marijuana: The forbidden medicine*. New Haven, CT: Yale University Press.

Hankins, W. G., Garcia, J., & Rusiniak, K.W. (1974). Cortical lesions: Flavor-illness and noise shock conditioning. *Behavioral Biology*, *10*, 173–181.

Heining, M., Young, A.W., Ioannou, G., Andrew, C. M., Brammer, M. J., Gray, J. A., & Phillips, M. L. (2003). Disgusting smells activate human anterior insula and ventral striatum. *Annals of the New York Academy of Sciences*, *1000*, 380–384.

Higgins, G. A., Kilpatrick, G. J., Bunce, K. T., Jones, B. J., & Tyers, M. B. (1989). 5-HT_3 receptor antagonists injected into the area postrema inhibit cisplatin-induced emesis in the ferret. *British Journal of Pharmacology*, *97*, 247–255.

Hillsley, K., & Grundy, D. (1998). Serotonin and cholecystokinin activate different populations of rat mesenteric vagal afferents. *Neuroscience Letters*, *255*, 63–66.

Hunt, T., & Amit, Z. (1987). Conditioned taste aversion by self-administered drugs: Paradox revisited. *Neuroscience and Biobehavioral Reviews*, *11*, 107–130.

Ionescu, E., & Burešová, O. (1977). Failure to elicit CTA by severe poisoning. *Pharmacology, Biochemistry and Behavior*, *6*, 251–254.

Iversen, L. L. (2000). *The science of marijuana*. New York: Oxford University Press.

Jordan, K., Kasper, C., & Schmoll, H-J. (2005). Chemotherapy-induced nausea and vomiting: Current and new standards in the antiemetic prophylaxis and treatment. *European Journal of Cancer*, *41*, 199–205.

Kaada, B. R. (1951). Somato-motor, autonomic and electrocorticographic responses to electrical stimulation of rhinencephalic and other structures in primates, cat, and dog; A study of responses from the limbic, subcallosal, orbito-insular, piriform and temporal cortex, hippocampus-fornix and amygdala. *ACTA Physiological Scandinavian Supplement*, *24*,1–262.

Kiefer, S. W., & Orr, M. S. (1992). Taste avoidance, but not aversion, learning in rats lacking gustatory cortex. *Behavioral Neuroscience*, *106*, 140–146.

Konorski, J. (1967). *Integrative activity of the brain: An interdisciplinary approach*. Chicago: University of Chicago Press.

Kosar, E., Grill, H. J., & Norgren, R. (1986). Gustatory cortex in the rat. I. Physiological properties and cytoarchitecture. *Brain Research*, *379*, 329–341.

Kwiatkowska, M., Parker, L. A., Burton, P., & Mechoulam, R. (2004). A comparative analysis of the potential of cannabinoids and ondansetron to suppress cisplatin-induced emesis in the *Suncus murinus* (house musk shrew). *Psychopharmacology*, *174*, 254–259.

Lasiter, P. S. (1982). Cortical substrates of taste aversion learning: Direct amygdalocortical projections to the gustatory neocortex do not mediate conditioned taste aversion learning. *Physiological Psychology*, *10*, 377–383.

Lasiter, P. S., & Glanzman, D. L. (1985). Cortical substrates of taste aversion earning: Involvement of the dorsolateral amygdaloid neuclei and temporal neocortex in taste aversion learning. *Behavioral Neuroscience*, *99*, 257–276.

Limebeer, C. L., Hall, G., & Parker, L. A. (2006). Exposure to a lithium-paired context elicits gaping in rats: A model of anticipatory nausea. *Physiology & Behavior*, *88*, 398–403.

Limebeer, C. L., Krohn, J. P., Cross-Mellor, S., Ossenkopp, K-P., & Parker, L.A. (2008). Exposure to a context previously associated with toxin (LiCl)- or motion-induced sickness elicits conditioned gaping in rats: Evidence in support of a model of anticipatory nausea. *Behavioral Brain Research*, *187*, 33–40.

Limebeer, C. L., Litt, D. E., & Parker, L. A. (2009). Effect of 5-HT_3 antagonists and a 5-HT_{1A} agonist on fluoxetine-induced conditioned gaping reactions in rats. *Psychopharmacology*, *203*, 763–770.

Limebeer, C .L., & Parker, L. A. (2000). Ondansetron interferes with lithium-induced conditioned rejection reactions, but not lithium-induced taste avoidance. *Journal of Experimental Psychology: Animal Behavior Processes*, *26*, 371–384.

Limebeer, C. L., & Parker, L. A. (2003). The 5-HT_{1A} agonist 8-OH-DPAT dose-dependently interferes with the establishment and expression of lithium –induced conditioned rejection reactions in rats. *Psychopharmacology*, *166*, 120–126.

Limebeer, C. L., Parker, L. A., & Fletcher, P. J. (2004). 5,7-Dihydroxytryptamine lesions of the dorsal and median raphe nuclei interfere with lithium-induced conditioned gaping, but not conditioned taste avoidance, in rats. *Behavioral Neuroscience*, *118*, 1391–1399.

Limebeer, C. L., Rock, E. M., Mechoulam, R., & Parker, L. A. (2012). The anti-nausea effects of CB1 agonists are mediated by an action at the visceral insular cortex. *British Journal of Pharmacology*, *167*, 126–136.

Lubow, R. E. (1973). Latent inhibition. *Psychological Bulletin*, *79*, 398–407.

Mackey, W. B., Keller, J., & van der Kooy, D. (1986). Visceral cortex lesions block conditioned taste aversions induced by morphine. *Pharmacology, Biochemistry and Behavior*, *24*, 71–78.

Matsuki, N., Ueno, S., Kaji, T., Ishihara, A., Wang, C. H., & Saito, H. (1988). Emesis induced by cancer chemotherapeutic agents in the *Suncus murinus*: A new experimental model. *Japan Journal of Pharmacology*, *48*, 303–306.

McDonald, R. V., Parker, L. A., & Siegel, S. (1997). Conditioned sucrose aversions produced by naloxone-precipitated withdrawal from acutely administered morphine. *Pharmacology, Biochemistry and Behavior*, *58*, 1003–1008.

Meachum, C. L., & Bernstein, I. L. (1992). Behavioral conditioned responses to contextual and odor stimuli paired with LiCl administration. *Physiology & Behavior*, *52*, 895–899.

Nachman, M., & Hartley, P. L. (1976). The role of illness in inducing taste aversions in rats: A comparison of several rodenticides. *Journal of Comparative and Physiological Psychology*, *81*, 1010–1018.

Naqvi, N. H., Rudrauf, D., Damasio, H., & Bechara, A. (2007). Damage to the insula disrupts addiction to cigarette smoking. *Science*, *315*, 531–534.

Nerad, L., Ramirez-Amaya,V., Ormsby, C. D., & Bermúdez-Rattoni, F. (1996). Differential effects of anterior and posterior insular cortex lesions on the acquisition of conditioned taste aversion and spatial learning. *Neurobiology of Learning and Memory*, *66*, 44–50.

Nesse, R. M., Carli, T., Curtis, G. C., & Kleinman, P. D. (1980). Pretreatment nausea in cancer chemotherapy: A conditioned response? *Psychosomatic Medicine*, *42*, 33–36.

Nyland, J. E., & Grigson, P. S. (2013). A drug-paired taste cue elicits withdrawal and predicts cocaine self-administration. *Behavioral Brain Research*, *240*, 87–90.

Ossenkopp, K. P., Biagi, E., Cloutier, C. J., Chan, M. Y., Kavaliers, M., & Cross-Mellor, S. K. (2011). Acute corticosterone increases conditioned spontaneous orofacial behaviors but fails to influence dose related LiCl-induced conditioned "gaping" responses in a rodent model of anticipatory nausea. *European Journal of Pharmacology*, *660*, 358–362.

Parker, L. A. (1982). Nonconsummatory and consummatory behavioral CRs elicited by lithium- and amphetamine-paired flavors. *Learning and Motivation*, *13*, 281–303.

Parker, L. A. (1988). Positively reinforcing drugs may produce a different kind of CTA than drugs which are not positively reinforcing. *Learning and Motivation*, *19*, 207–220.

Parker, L. A. (1992). Place conditioning in a three- and four-choice apparatus: Role of stimulus novelty in drug-induced place conditioning. *Behavioral Neuroscience*, *106*, 294–306.

Parker, L. A. (1995). Rewarding drugs produce taste avoidance, but not taste aversion. *Neuroscience and Biobehavioral Reviews*, *19*, 143–151.

Parker, L. A. (1998). Emetic drugs produce conditioned rejection reactions in the taste reactivity test. *Journal of Psychophysiology*, *12*, 3–13.

Parker, L. A. (2003). Taste avoidance and taste aversion: Evidence for two different processes. *Learning & Behavior*, *31*, 165–172.

Parker, L. A., Corrick, M. L., Limebeer, C. L., & Kwiatkowska, M. (2002). Amphetamine and morphine produce a conditioned taste and place preference in the house musk shrew (*Suncus murinus*). *Journal of Experimental Psychology: Animal Behavior Processes*, *28*, 75–82.

Parker, L. A., Hills, K., & Jensen, K. (1984). Behavioral conditioned responses elicited by lithium- and amphetamine-paired contextual cues. *Animal Learning & Behavior*, *12*, 307–315.

Parker, L. A. & Kemp, S. W. (2001). Tetrahydrocannabinol (THC) interferes with conditioned retching in Suncus murinus: An animal model of anticipatory nausea and vomiting (ANV). *Neuroreport*, *12*, 749–751.

Parker, L. A., Kwiatkowska, M., Burton, P., & Mechoulam, R. (2004). Effect of cannabinoids on lithum-induced vomiting in the *Suncus murinus* (house musk shrew). *Psychopharmacology*, *171*, 156–161.

Parker, L. A., Kwiatkowska, M., & Mechoulam, R. (2006). Delta-9-tetrahydrocannabinol and cannabidiol, but not ondansetron, interfere with conditioned retching reactions elicited by a lithium-paired context in *Suncus murinus*: An animal model of anticipatory nausea and vomiting. *Physiology & Behavior*, *87*, 61–71.

Parker, L. A., Limebeer, C. L., & Rana, S. A. (2009). Conditioned disgust, but not conditioned taste avoidance, may reflect conditioned nausea in rats. In S. Reilly & T. R. Schachtman (Eds.), *Conditioned taste aversions: Behavioral and neural processes* (pp. 92–113). New York: Oxford University Press.

Parker, L. A., & McDonald, R. V. (2000). Reinstatement of both a conditioned place preference and a conditioned place aversion with drug primes. *Pharmacology, Biochemistry and Behavior*, *66*, 559–561.

Parker, L. A., & McLeod, K. B. (1991). Chin rub CRs may reflect conditioned sickness. *Pharmacology Biochemistry and Behavior*, *40*, 983–986.

Parker, L. A., Rana, S. A., & Limebeer, C. L. (2008). Conditioned disgust, but not conditioned taste avoidance: A measure of conditioned nausea in rats. *Canadian Journal of Experimental Psychology*, *62*, 198–209.

Parker, L. A., Rock, E. R., & Limebeer, C. L. (2011). Regulation of vomiting and nausea by cannabinoids. *British Journal of Pharmacology*, *163*, 1411–1422.

Pautassi, R. M., Arias, C., Molina, J. C., & Spear, N. (2008). Domperidone interferes with conditioned disgust reactions but not taste avoidance evoked by a LiCl-pared taste in infant rats. *Developmental Psychobiology, 50*, 343–352.

Pavlov, I. (1927) *Conditioned reflexes* (Trans. G. V. anrep,). Oxford University Press.

Pelchat, M. L., Grill, H. J., Rozin, P., & Jacobs, J. (1983). Quality of acquired responses to tastes by *Rattus norvegicus* depends on type of associated discomfort. *Journal of Comparative Psychology, 97*, 140–153.

Pelchat, M. L., & Rozin, P. (1982). The special role of nausea in the acquisition of food dislikes in humans. *Appetite, 3*, 343–351.

Penfield. W., & Faulk, M. E. (1955). The insula: Further observations on its function. *Brain, 78*, 445–470.

Phillips, M. L., Young, A. W., Senior, C., Brammer, M., Andrew, C., Calder, A. J., Bullmore, E. T., Perrett, D. I., & Rowland, D. S. (1998). Neural responses to facial and vocal expressions of fear and disgust. *Nature, 389*, 495–508.

Rabin, B. M., & Hunt, W. A. (1983). Effects of anti-emetics on the acquisition and recall of radiation and lithium chloride induced conditioned taste aversions. *Pharmacology, Biochemistry and Behavior, 18*, 629–636.

Rana, S. A., & Parker, L. A. (2008). Differential effects of neurotoxin-induced lesions of the basolateral amygdala and central nucleus of the amygdala on lithium-induced conditioned disgust reactions and conditioned taste avoidance. *Behavioral Brain Research, 189*, 284–297.

Reicher, M. A., & Holman, E. W. (1977). Location preference and flavor aversion reinforced by amphetamine in rats. *Animal Learning & Behavior, 5*, 343–346.

Reilly, S. (2009). Central gustatory system lesions and conditioned taste aversion. In S. Reilly & T. R. Schachtman (Eds.), *Conditioned taste aversion: Behavioral and neural mechanisms* (pp. 309–327). New York: Oxford University Press.

Revusky, S., & Garcia, J. (1970). Learned associations over long delays. In G. Bower & J. Spence (Eds.), *Psychology of learning and motivation: Advances in research and theory.* Vol. 4 (pp. 1–84). New York: Academic Press.

Revusky, S., & Bedarf, E. W. (1967). Association of illness with prior ingestion of novel foods. *Science, 155*, 219–220.

Riley, A. L., & Tuck, D.L. (1985). Conditioned taste aversions: A behavioral index of toxicity. *Annals of the New York Academy of Science, 443*, 272–292.

Rock, E. M., Limebeer, C. L., Mechoulam, R., Piomelli, D., & Parker, L. A. (2008) The effect of cannabidiol and URB597 on conditioned gaping (a model of nausea) elicited by a lithium-paired context in the rat. *Psychopharmacology, 196*, 389–395.

Roman, C., & Reilly, S. (2007). Effects of insular cortex lesions on conditioned taste aversion and latent inhibition in the rat. *European Journal of Neuroscience, 26*, 2627–2632.

Rozin, P., & Fallon, A. E. (1987). A perspective on disgust. *Psychological Review, 94*, 23–41.

Rozin, P., & Kalat, J. W. (1971).Specific hungers and poison avoidance as adaptive specializations of learning. *Journal of Comparative and Physiological Psychology, 64*, 237–242.

Rudd, J. A., Ngan, M. P., & Wai, M. K. (1998). 5-HT_3 receptors are not involved in conditioned taste aversions induced by 5-hydroxytryptamine, ipecacuanha or cisplatin. *European Journal of Pharmacology, 352*, 143–149.

Seligman, M. E. P. (1970). On the generality of the laws of learning. *Psychological Review, 77*, 406–418.

Siegel, S. (1974). Flavor preexposure and "learned safety." *Journal of Comparative and Physiological Psychology, 87*, 1073–1082.

Schwarz, M. D., Jacobsen, P. B., & Bjovberg, D. H. (1986). Role of nausea in the development of aversions to a beverage paired with chemotherapy treatment in cancer patients. *Physiology & Behavior, 59*, 659–663.

Tork, I. (1990). Anatomy of the serotonergic system. *Annals of the New York Academy of Science*, *600*, 9–34.

Tuerke, K. J., Leri, F., & Parker, L. A. (2009). Antidepressant-like effects of paroxetine are produced by lower doses than those which produce nausea. *Pharmacology, Biochemistry and Behavior*, *93*, 190–195.

Tuerke, K. J., Limebeer, C. L., Fletcher, P. J., & Parker, L. A. (2013). Double dissociation between regulation of conditioned disgust and taste avoidance by serotonin availability at the 5-HT_3 receptor in the visceral and gustatory insular cortex. *Journal of Neuroscience*, *32*, 13709–13717.

Travers, J. B., & Norgren, R. (1986). Electromyographic analysis of the ingestion and rejection of sapid stimuli in the rat. *Behavioral Neuroscience*, *100*, 544–555.

Verendeev, A., & Riley, A. L. (2012). Conditioned taste aversion and drugs of abuse: History and interpretation. *Neuroscience and Biobehavioral Reviews*, *36*, 2193–2205.

Wegener, G., Smith, D. F., & Rosenberg, R. (1997). 5-HT_{1A} receptors in lithium-induced conditioned taste aversion. *Psychopharmacology*, *133*, 51–54.

Wheeler, R. A., Aragona, B. J., Fuhrmann, K. A., Jones, J. L., Day, J. J., Cacciapaglia, F., Wightman, R. M., & Carelli, R. M. (2011). Cocaine cues drive opposing context dependent shifts in reward processing and emotional state. *Biological Psychiatry*, *69*, 1067–1074.

Wheeler, R. A., & Carelli, R. M. (2009). Dissecting motivational circuitry to understand substance abuse. *Neuropharmacology*, *56* (Suppl 1), 149–159.

Wheeler, R. A., Twining, R. C., Jones, J. L., Slater, J. M., Grigson, P. S., & Carelli, R. M. (2008). Behavioral and electrophysiological indices of negative affect predict cocaine self-administration. *Neuron*, *57*, 774–785.

White, N., Sklar, L., & Amit, Z. (1977). The reinforcing action of morphine and its paradoxical side effect. *Psychopharmacology*, *52*, 63–66.

Wicker, B., Keysers, C., Plailly, P., Royet, J.-R., Gallese,V., & Rizzolatti, G. (2003). Both of us disgusted in my insula: The common neural basis of seeing and feeling disgust. *Neuron*, *40*, 655–664.

Wise, R., Yokel, P., & DeWit, H. (1976). Both positive reinforcement and conditioned aversion from amphetamine and from apomorphine in rats. *Science*, *191*, 1273–1274.

Yamamoto, T., Azuma, S., & Kawamura, Y. (1981). Significance of cortical-amygdalar-hypothamic connections in retention of conditioned taste aversion in rats. *Experimental Neurology*, *74*, 758–768.

Zalaquett, C., & Parker, L. A. (1989). Further evidence that CTAs produced lithium and amphetamine are qualitatively different. *Learning and Motivation*, *20*, 413–427.

6

Pavlovian Fear Conditioning
Function, Cause, and Treatment

Michael S. Fanselow and Sarah R. Sterlace

Fear Conditioning Basics

Pavlovian fear conditioning refers to the learning of associations between nonthreatening environmental stimuli and painful, dangerous or threatening stimulation. With such an experience, these initially nonthreatening stimuli come to elicit a set of new responses that, for the species in question, have been phylogenetically successful in defending against threat (Bolles, 1970; Fanselow, 1984).

In the typical laboratory example of Pavlovian fear conditioning, initially neutral stimuli, such as a brief tone or light, or the conditioning environment itself, is followed closely by an aversive electric shock. These initially neutral stimuli are called conditional stimuli (CS) because they must be experienced in a dependent, or conditional, relationship with the initially aversive "unconditional" stimulus for an aversive response to develop (US; Pavlov, 1927; Rescorla, 1967). When the CS is a brief signal (e.g., a 30-second tone or light), it is referred to as *cued fear conditioning*; when the CS is the static feature of the conditioning environment (e.g., the conditioning chamber), it is referred to as *contextual fear conditioning*. After conditioning, the new learned responses to the CS are referred to as conditional responses (CR), because they are a result of experiencing the dependent relationship between CS and US. Because the responses generated by the US occur independently of experience, they are called unconditional responses (UR). As will be discussed below, CRs and URs are different responses that serve different functions. Rats, mice, and humans are the most frequently used subjects in these studies.

The first laboratory demonstration of fear conditioning is the famous (or infamous) "Little Albert" study conducted by Watson and Rayner (1920). In this study, an infant (Albert) received pairings of a white rat (CS) and loud clanging noise (US). Although discussion of the ethical conduct of this study and questions about the

The Wiley Blackwell Handbook of Operant and Classical Conditioning, First Edition.
Edited by Frances K. McSweeney and Eric S. Murphy.

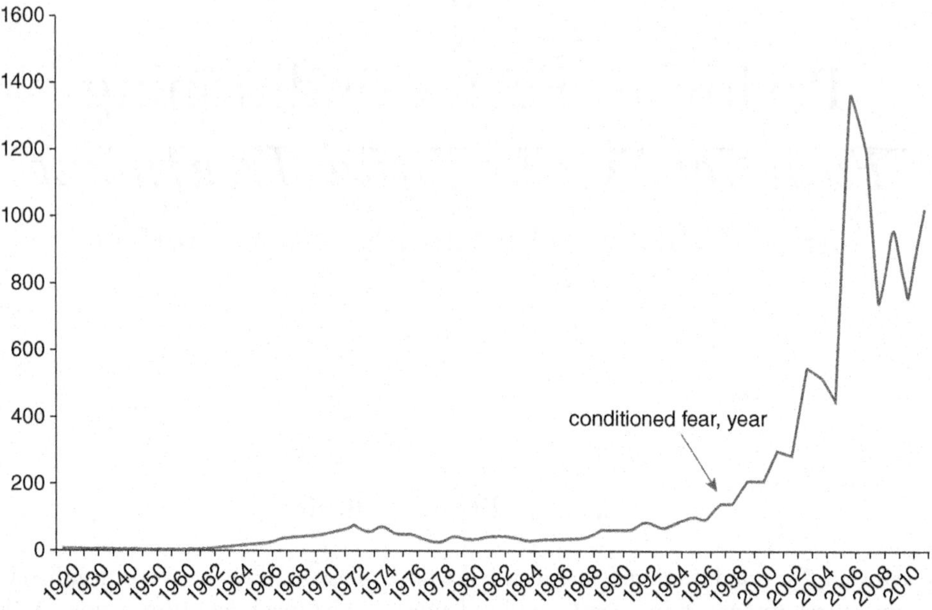

Figure 6.1 Annual number of publications on fear conditioning research since 1900. Data were generated by entering "conditioned," "fear", and a year into PubMed. Any retrieved publications not from the searched year were deleted.

identity of Albert persist to this day (Fridlund, Beck, Goldie, & Irons, 2012; Powell, 2010), one should not lose sight of the fact that the basic effect—learned fear to an initially innocuous stimulus—has been replicated in many species (including humans) under rigorously controlled conditions. Indeed, since 1920 there has been increasing use of the technique with an exponential growth in publications since the millennium, despite the crash of 2008 (see Figure 6.1). The cause of this growth in the rate of fear conditioning research is undoubtedly spurred by its relevance to clinical phenomena and its effectiveness in uncovering the mechanisms of learning. This chapter will deal with these two topics in detail.

Relevance to Anxiety Disorders: More than a Model

Why the prodigious growth in the use of fear conditioning as a research technique? A major reason for this is the relevance of fear to anxiety disorders, such as specific phobia and Post-Traumatic Stress Disorder (PTSD). As a class of psychiatric illness, anxiety disorders cause individuals to suffer from intense, chronic, and impairing anxiety. These disorders can be devastating to the individuals who suffer from them, and their families (McFarlane, 2010; Mendlowicz & Stein, 2000). Anxiety disorders are highly prevalent, with an estimate of 18% in any given year and 28% in the lifetime of an adult American (Kessler et al., 2005). The direct cost of these disorders is a staggering $42–47 billion annually, which jumps to over $100 billion when indirect costs such as long-term unemployment and co-morbidity with other health problems are taken into account (Greenberg et al., 1999). To gain scientific understanding of anxiety disorders and advancements of treatment, the value of a good animal model is paramount.

Pavlovian fear conditioning allows us to create and treat an anxiety disorder in animals. This might seem like a bold statement, but the core of an anxiety disorder is a powerful fear reaction in situations where such fear is unwarranted. For example, in PTSD, an intensely threatening experience results in aberrant fear responses to reminders of the trauma that last far beyond the event. For the rat, while the typical aversive US, such as a shock, is not particularly painful, it conditions potent fear reactions to innocuous stimuli that last for the lifespan of the animal (Gale et al., 2004). Indeed, one of the earliest laboratory studies of fear noted that the disruption of ongoing behavior produced by the CS far exceeded the disruption produced by the US itself (Estes & Skinner, 1941). Pavlovian fear conditioning in laboratory animals often shows similarities to the pattern of symptom expression found in humans. For example, it has been noted that there is a high correlation between traumatic brain injury and PTSD (Tanielian & Jaycox, 2008). Rats that have received an experimental diffuse traumatic brain injury show enhanced Pavlovian fear conditioning. Laboratory studies can go on to show the causal nature of this linkage between brain injury and how it causes a predisposition to heightened fear (Reger et al., 2012).

Pavlovian fear conditioning is not only relevant to find causes of anxiety disorders; it is also relevant to their treatment. The most effective form of treatment for anxiety disorders is exposure therapy (Norton & Price, 2007; Hofmann & Smits, 2008), which is primarily an application of Pavlovian extinction (Hermans, Craske, Mineka, & Lovibond, 2006; also see Vurbic & Bouton, this volume). Extinction is a new learning that interferes with but does not undo the original learning. This is accomplished by giving repeated presentation of the previously paired CS alone, so that the CS no longer is associated with the US. However, the original learning is not erased, because as time goes by, the original learning, and thus fear, returns (see Vurbic & Bouton, this volume). Thus Pavlovian fear conditioning is more than a model, it allows us to recreate both the cause and treatment of an anxiety disorder in a controlled laboratory setting.

Why are Anxiety Disorders So Prevalent?

The answer to this question requires us to think of fear in its ecological context: What are the costs and benefits of a fear response? Fear is the activation of the functional behavioral system responsible for defense and the principal Pavlovian fear CRs are species-specific defense reactions (Bolles, 1970; Bolles & Fanselow, 1980; Fanselow, 1994). Species-specific defense reactions (SSDRs) are innately organized action patterns that have successfully defended members of the species during their phylogenetic history (Bolles, 1970). Pavlovian fear conditioning activates one of the brain's "survival" circuits (LeDoux, 2012). Therefore, from an evolutionary perspective fear is a good thing; defense in the face of a life threatening danger is one of the greatest biological needs in terms of challenges to reproductive fitness. A single failure to defend against a predator could lead to death, eliminating all chances of future

Table 6.1 Signal detection analysis of the prevalence of anxiety disorders

	Presence of Life Threatening Event?	
	Danger Present	**Danger Absent**
Choose to Defend	Hit Cost: Defensive effort Survival: Possible	False Alarm Cost: Defensive effort Survival: Yes
Choose Not to Defend	Miss Cost: No reproductive future Survival: Unlikely	Correct rejection Cost: None Survival: Yes

reproductive success, while a single missed reproductive or feeding opportunity does not.

Danger must be predicted when possible and Pavlovian fear conditioning allows such prediction. Of course, prediction is rarely perfect in the complex world that mammals inhabit, a danger signal is only probabilistically related to harm. Signal detection theory provides a rubric for understanding prediction in an uncertain world (Peterson, Birdsall, & Fox, 1954; Tanner & Swets, 1954). Obviously, it is advantageous to predict danger when it is present; this is what signal detection theory calls a "hit" (see Table 6.1). Because fear disrupts ongoing behavior (Estes & Skinner, 1941) it has a cost. If no danger is present, it is best not to react fearfully (correct rejection). Both hits and correct rejections are desirable and advantageous. Since prediction is unlikely to be perfect, errors will be made. "Misses" occur when there is danger present but the organism in question does not react to it and the consequences are likely to be catastrophic (e.g., consumption by a predator).

False alarms, responding as if danger is present when there is none, has a cost. Defensive responses require energy and the time spent defending cannot be used for beneficial activities such as mating, feeding, and nesting. However, the evolutionary cost of a false alarm is far less than that of a miss. According to signal detection theory, this difference in cost will cause a shift in criterion leading to a bias in classifying situations with any ambiguity as dangerous, so behavior patterns that lead to a high probability of false alarms will be favored. In a fear situation, frequent false alarms mean frequently reacting to safe situations as if dangerous. The occurrence of such reactions is perhaps the major definitional component of an anxiety disorder, fear, or anxiety in inappropriate situations. Thus natural selection leaves us vulnerable to anxiety disorders (Nesse, 2005). The greater cost of a miss when danger is present leads to the high prevalence of anxiety disorders.

Laboratory Measures of Conditional Fear

Older stimulus-substitution views of Pavlovian conditioning suggested that the CR was a replica of the UR. Pavlov's dogs salivated to both the food and the bell. From this antiquated view, the choice of a measure is easy; simply see how the subject reacts to the US and look for that response when the CS is presented. However, it is well established that for Pavlovian conditioning there is no general invariant rule relating CR and UR; they may be the similar, they may be of opposing topographies, or they may simply be unrelated to each other (Rescorla, 1988). Rather, a CR can be any response that can be reliably attributed to the previous relationship the organism experienced with CS and US. Estes and Skinner (1941), who developed the first quantitative measure for fear conditioning, recognized both the importance of the CS-US relationship and the lack of correspondence between CR and UR when they stated that, "the disturbing stimulus which is principally responsible does not precede or accompany the state but is 'anticipated' in the future" and "in anxiety, the response which is developed to S1 (*CS*) need not be like the original response to S2 (*US*)" (p. 390).

Insight into choosing a measure of fear can again be obtained by considering the defensive function of fear. If something signals a potential threat to an animal, it needs to (a) stop whatever it is doing, (b) avoid detection or attack, and (c) prepare to react to the threat. These three behaviors underlie the three most common measures of fear. Estes and Skinner (1941), emphasizing the former, measured suppression of ongoing behavior. They did this by first training a rat to lever press for food and then observed the suppression of lever pressing produced by the CS after CS-US pairings. Because moving objects are easier to detect by visual systems, and movement is often the releasing stimulus for a predator's attack of a prey, a dramatic suppression of movement, referred to as freezing, is a reliable and easily quantifiable measure of fear (Fanselow, 1980a; Bolles & Collier, 1976). Freezing is now the most common measure of fear in rats and mice. It has also been shown in humans (Roelofs, Hagenaars, & Stins, 2010). If freezing is not successful and a predator attacks, defensive behavior shifts to explosive reactions to the predator's contact (Fanselow & Lester, 1988). This has been exploited by measuring startle to a loud noise substituted for the shock; fear CSs potentiate startle (Brown, Kalish, & Farber, 1951). This measure has also proven informative in rat and human studies and is currently the most frequently employed measure of fear in humans. Other measures of fear include autonomic changes such as increased blood pressure (e.g., Carrive & Gorissen, 2008), hyperthermia (Godsil, Quinn, & Fanselow, 2000), defecation (Fanselow, 1986) and heart rate (Schreurs, Smith-Bell, & Burhans, 2011), as well as ultrasonic vocalization to warn conspecifics of danger (Lee, Choi, Brown, & Kim, 2001) and analgesia to prevent pain from disrupting defensive behaviors (Bolles & Fanselow, 1980; Fanselow & Baackes, 1982).

In selecting a response measure, several factors need to be taken into consideration. First is the dynamic range of the response. Freezing is very sensitive to low levels of fear, such as those that occur after a single shock. Freezing, as a measure of fear, can discriminate well between different levels except when fear is very high (Fanselow & Bolles, 1979). Defecation can discriminate between no fear and some level of fear but the measure saturates quickly (Fanselow, 1986). Potentiated startle and several measures of avoidance are nonmonotonic with respect to the level of fear and appropriate caution must be used in interpreting the results (Warren & Bolles, 1965; Davis & Astrachan, 1978; Johnson & Church, 1965). Ultrasonic vocalizations are emitted under limited circumstances. Another consideration is that some measures of fear require a probe stimulus that may influence the behavior being measured. For example, analgesia requires administration of a painful stimulus (e.g., radiant heat, formalin injection, hot plate) that produces pain-related responses. The loud noise used to provoke a startle is sufficiently aversive to support fear conditioning in its own right (Leaton & Cranney, 1990). Some measures (e.g., heart rate, blood pressure, hyperthermia) require invasive manipulations, such as implantations. Conditioned suppression requires the presence of motivation for food or water. Therefore, care must be exerted when response measures are selected.

CS-US Relationships that Promote Cued and Contextual Fear Conditioning

Cued Conditioning

In a typical laboratory fear conditioning experiment, a tone or light will be presented for a period that usually ranges from a few seconds to a few minutes with the shock co-terminating at the end of the interval. Pavlov (1927) referred to this arrangement of stimuli as "delay conditioning" because there is a delay between the start of the CS and the start of the US (see Figure 6.2). The interval between the start of the CS and the start of the US is called the CS-US interval. As is true for most forms of conditioning, this arrangement produces the greatest amount of cued fear conditioning. There is some debate as to why having a short delay between CS and US produces more conditioning than the simultaneous presentation of both CS and US. One explanation is that prediction of the US is the critical factor and delay conditioning allows prediction, while in simultaneous conditioning the CS provides redundant information with the US itself (e.g., Egger & N. E. Miller, 1962). Others have suggested that it is not the amount of learning that causes the difference between delay and simultaneous conditioning but that the difference stems from factors related to the expression of fear. Blaisdell, Denniston, and Miller (1998), have argued that both procedures produce equivalent conditioning but that they are expressed in different

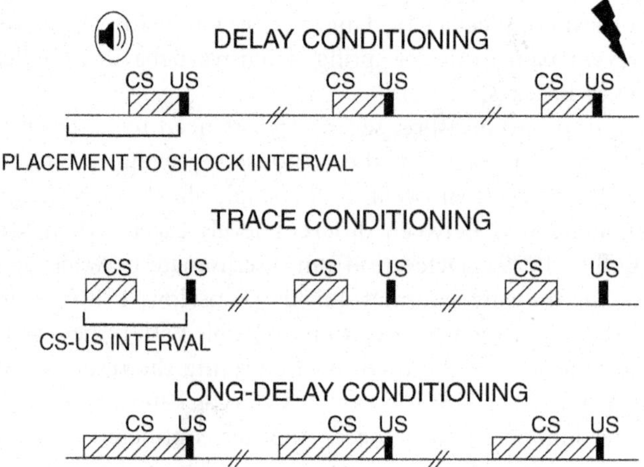

Figure 6.2 Types of Pavlovian conditioning.

responses. However, delay and simultaneous procedures provoke freezing and no one has discovered a response unique to simultaneous conditioning. Furthermore, Blaisdell et al. (1998) used conditioned suppression, and such a nonspecific measure should be disrupted by any fear response. Rescorla (1980) also argued that the superiority of delay conditioning is related to factors that operate at the time of testing. Tests for cued conditioning usually present the CS alone. Rescorla pointed out that means that for simultaneous conditioning the CS presented during test is experienced in a novel way; it is the CS without the US for the first time. This change between training and testing conditions may cause a loss of responding in simultaneously conditioned subjects (i.e., generalization decrement). This is not the case for delay conditioning as the subjects experience the CS alone prior to US delivery during training. Indeed, Rescorla presented evidence that when this change from training to testing is controlled for simultaneous conditioning actually produced better learning than delay. Rescorla's explanation fits well with the fact that although a short delay during training produces maximal expression of fear at test, the longer the delay the weaker the conditioning. The best conditioning will be at a point that strikes a balance between the strong learning that occurs with simultaneity of CS and US and the loss in performance caused by generalization decrement between training and testing conditions.

In delay conditioning there is contiguity between the end of the CS and the start of the US. Conditioning weakens if the CS ends before the US, even if the interval from start of the CS to start of the US is held constant. When the CS ends before the start of the US, there is a brief stimulus-free interval between CS and US. Pavlov (1927) argued that in order for such conditioning to occur some representation of the memory trace of the CS must remain in the brain until the US occurs. Therefore, he labeled this stimulus arrangement as "trace conditioning." While somewhat less robust than delay conditioning, trace fear conditioning can occur at trace intervals at least up to 30 seconds between the CS offset and the US occurring. The deficit in trace relative to delay conditioning is easily overcome if several conditioning trials are used (e.g., 7–10 trials; McEchron, Bouwmeester, Tseng, Weiss, & Disterhoft, 1998; Quinn, Oommen, Morrison, & Fanselow, 2002). As will be discussed later, trace conditioning has garnered attention because it recruits additional mechanisms that are not necessary for delay conditioning.

Context Conditioning

In the course of cued conditioning, contextual conditioning will also occur. Despite the fact that both cued and context conditioning occur at the same time, they proceed in very different manners. In general, things that enhance cued conditioning (e.g., shorter CS-US intervals, longer inter-trial intervals, selection of delay over trace procedures) will reduce context conditioning. A useful heuristic for predicting these competition-like effects is the Rescorla-Wagner rule (Rescorla & Wagner, 1972). The model aids in making realistic but counter-intuitive predictions about the effects of adjusting conditioning parameters. For example, by adding more trials one will favor cued over context conditioning. Therefore, if one is interested in maximizing context conditioning but not interested in cued conditioning, one can leave out the cue entirely as this will produce maximal context conditioning (e.g., Fanselow, 1980b).

A critical way that cued and context conditioning differ is with respect to manipulating the delay between the start of CS and start of the US. As described above, performance of cued conditioning degrades as the training CS-US interval lengthens. For context conditioning, the CS-US interval is the time between placement in the chamber and the delivery of shock (placement-to-shock interval, PSI). The PSI function for contextual conditioning is the reverse of the CS-US interval function for cued conditioning (Fanselow, 2010; Wiltgen, Sanders, Anagnostaras, Sage, & Fanselow, 2006). When the PSI is 0 there is no conditioning. This is called the immediate-shock deficit, and it has been demonstrated for freezing, defecation, analgesia, and potentiated startle (Fanselow, 1986; Fanselow, Landeira-Fernandez, DeCola, & Kim, 1994; Kiernan, Westbrook, & Cranney, 1995). Despite the name of the phenomenon, it also occurs with other USs such as a loud noise (Kiernan & Cranney, 1992). A testament to the robustness of the immediate-shock deficit is the finding that when rats received one immediate shock per day for three days they showed no contextual fear. When these same animals were switched to a delayed shock procedure, they acquired freezing at the same rate as shock-naïve rats; there were no savings from the prior three immediate-shock experiences (Landeira-Fernandez, DeCola, Kim, & Fanselow, 2006). The immediate-shock procedure is essentially simultaneous context conditioning, as CS and US onset occurs at the same time, but the absence of conditioning with this procedure contrasts strikingly with the relatively good conditioning that occurs with simultaneous presentation of tone and shock (Fanselow, 2010).

Conditioning increases gradually with lengthening PSI. The animal must configure the elements together into an integrated representation of context; reexposure to the context affords time for the formation of the integrated contextual representation prior to shock delivery, thereby eliminating the deficit. Importantly, pre-exposure to the context must include all features of that context together; separately pre-exposing the individual features (e.g., grid separate from walls) does not confer a benefit (Rudy & O'Reilly, 1999). Such data suggest that exposure allows the features of the context to become associated with each other (Iordanova & Honey, 2012) to form an integrated or conjunctive representation (Fanselow, 1990; Rudy & O'Reilly, 1999). The formation of this representation seems to require active exploration of the context, not simply a passive viewing of the features (McHugh & Tonegawa, 2007).

Biological Mechanisms of Fear Learning

Amygdala As the Hub Of the Circuit

The major components of the neural circuit mediating from environmental stimulation to fear behavior is well established and has been the subject of many reviews (see Figure 6.3; Fanselow & Poulos, 2005; Kim & Jung, 2006; Paré, Quirk, & LeDoux, 2004). Here is only a brief overview. Because fear learning involves the detection of the CS-US relationship, there need to be individual neurons that receive both CS and US information. There are several regions where this occurs but there is a general consensus that the basolateral amygdala complex (BLAC, consisting of lateral and basal nuclei) is the most critical region for this convergence. A long history

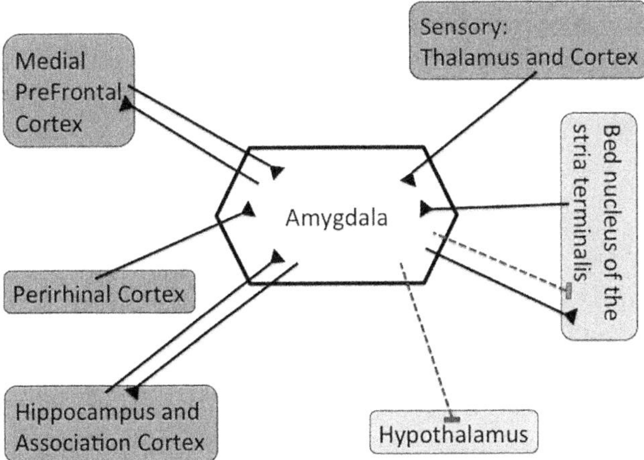

Figure 6.3 A brief overview of fear neural circuitry. Note that solid black lines indicate excitatory projections and dashed gray lines indicate inhibitory projections.

of studies showing that in both human and nonhuman animals, physical damage to the BLAC is devastating to conditional fear (Blanchard & Blanchard, 1972; Bechara et al., 1995; Hitchcock & Davis, 1986). Furthermore, temporarily inhibiting neural activity in the BLAC blocks both learning and expression of conditional fear (Helmstetter, 1992). These studies indicate that BLAC neurons do in fact play a causal role in mediating fear conditioning.

If BLAC neurons are involved in fear learning then it would be expected that BLAC neurons change in response to convergent CS and US information when associative learning occurs. The most promising candidate for the mechanism underlying associative learning is the long-term potentiation (LTP) of the efficacy of glutamatergic synapses (Rodrigues, Schafe, & LeDoux, 2004; Teyler & Discenna, 1984). Induction of LTP requires activation of N-methyl-D-aspartate type glutamate receptors (NMDAR) and application of NMDAR antagonists to the amygdala prior to conditioning prevents fear learning (Fanselow & Kim, 1994; Miserendino, Sananes, Melia, & Davis, 1990).

If NMDAR antagonists are infused into the BLAC prior to an extinction session, they block extinction of a previously conditioned fear response (Falls, Miserendino, & Davis, 1992). Because extinction is a form of associative safety learning (Vurbic & Bouton this volume) and NMDAR are thought to be critical for associative learning, these findings are consistent and suggest that the BLAC is an important site of extinction-related plasticity. However, because extinction does not erase previous fear learning, it is unlikely that acquisition and extinction act on the same glutamatergic synapses as acquisition. One possibility is that, during acquisition, the critical LTP is mediated by glutamatergic synapses on inhibitory neurons in the amygdala (Bauer & LeDoux, 2004; Barash, Bracewell, Fogassi, Gnadt, & Andersen, 1991).

Romanski, Clugnet, Bordi, and LeDoux (1993), provided compelling evidence of CS-US convergence in the BLAC when they made extracellular electrophysiological recordings from the lateral nucleus of the amygdala (LA) and found that both a tone

(CS) and footshock (US) increased spiking in individual neurons in that structure. More recently, Barot et al., (2008) revealed convergence of context and shock information on individual neurons in the BLAC using a very powerful molecular imaging technique for the immediate early gene activity-regulated cytoskeleton protein (Arc) (Guzowski & Worley, 2001). Arc protein is localized to activated glutamatergic NMDARs and is believed to mediate plasticity, as blockade of Arc using an antisense oligonucleotide impaired consolidation of long-term memory (Guzowski et al., 2000). Within a few minutes of relevant activity, projection neurons express Arc. After 20 minutes, Arc RNA is no longer in the nucleus but can be seen in the cytoplasm of the neurons. However, a second bout of neuronal activity will cause a new round of Arc transcription in the nucleus. Therefore, when brains are removed and labeled for Arc RNA, its presence in the nucleus indicates a neuron that was activated 1–5 min earlier and Arc in the cytoplasm indicates neurons activated 20–25 minutes earlier. To take advantage of this time course, Barot et al., (2008) placed rats in a novel context and 25 minutes later gave them a single shock. Compared to several control conditions, these rats showed substantial double-labeling for Arc in both the cytoplasm (corresponding to the onset of context exposure) and the nucleus (corresponding to the time of shock exposure) of basolateral nucleus neurons, indicating CS and US convergence on individual neurons.

Amygdala Afferents

Cued Conditioning. In order to act effectively as a hub structure for fear conditioning, the BLAC must receive the necessary environmental information. Conveniently, the BLAC is a cortex-like structure that receives highly processed information from several cortical and some thalamic regions (see Figure 6.3; Swanson & Petrovich, 1998). CS-evoked activity in several of these areas changes during conditioning (e.g., Edeline & Weinberger, 1992; Gdalyahu et al., 2012). For example, the preferred pitch of auditory responsive neurons shifts toward the frequency of the auditory CS during conditioning (Weinberger, 1993). While these changes probably add information to the fear memory, they do not seem necessary for conditioning to occur (Poremba & Gabriel, 2001; Maren, Yap, & Goosens, 2001).

Auditory information from both the auditory thalamus (medial geniculate nucleus) and auditory cortex arrive at the LA. Both of these routes can support conditioning and stimulation of either auditory pathway can induce LTP in the LA (Clugnet & LeDoux, 1990; Doyère, Schafe, Sigurdsson, & LeDoux, 2003). Visual and auditory information probably gain access to the BLAC via the perirhinal cortex (Kholodar-Smith, Allen, & Brown, 2008; Rosen et al., 1992).

Context Conditioning. The hippocampus also plays an important but relatively select role in fear conditioning. Hippocampal lesions will attenuate context conditioning but leave cued conditioning intact, even though both types of associative learning occurred at the same time (Phillips & LeDoux, 1992). This attenuation is most significant when lesions are made shortly after training (i.e., within a week; Kim & Fanselow, 1992). Lesions made before training or a long time after training have much less effect on contextual fear (see Figure 6.4; Kim & Fanselow, 1992; Maren, Aharonov, & Fanselow, 1997). The finding that increased time between training and lesion decreases the effects of the lesion is consistent with the temporally-graded

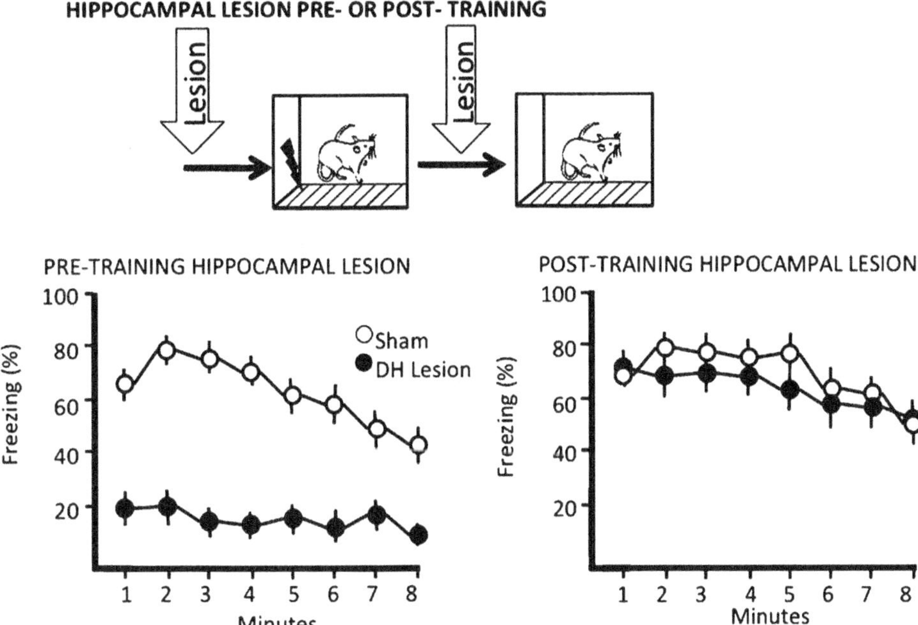

Figure 6.4 Comparing context freezing in rats pre- vs post-training hippocampal lesions. Based on Maren, Aharonov, and Fanselow, (1997) *Behavioural Brain Research, 88*, 261–274.

retrograde amnesia observed in humans for declarative memory following hippocampal loss of function or damage (Squire, 1992). These patients lose memories for events close to the time of brain insult, while older memories are preserved.

The previous section described how context conditioning requires a period of exploration to form an integrated representation of the context. The hippocampus is a good candidate for forming this representation. It is anatomically situated such that it receives highly processed information about the environment (Lavenex & Amaral, 2000). Additionally, rather than responding to simple sensory stimuli, neurons in the hippocampus respond to meaningful stimulus complexes such as being in particular section of a larger environment or a particular person irrespective of vantage point (O'Keefe & Dostrovsky, 1971; Quiroga, Reddy, Kreiman, Koch, & Fried, 2005).

The theory that emerges from these considerations is that long-term synaptic plasticity within the hippocampus underlies the formation of the integrated representation of context (Fanselow, 2000). If this is the case, then manipulations that prevent the acquisition or consolidation of LTP in the hippocampus during context pre-exposure should eliminate the benefit that context pre-exposure has for the immediate-shock deficit. This seems to be true, as both NMDA-antagonists prior to pre-exposure and protein synthesis inhibition immediately after pre-exposure attenuates the enhancement of context conditioning (Barrientos, O'Reilly, & Rudy, 2002; Matus-Amat, Higgins, Sprunger, Wright-Hardesty, & Rudy, 2007).

In this analysis of contextual fear conditioning, it has been suggested that successful context conditioning requires three processes of the animal (Table 6.2). Because

Table 6.2 Simplified environmental processes and brain regions involved in Pavlovian fear conditioning. Abbreviations: conditional stimulus, CS; long-term memory, LTM; medial geniculate nucleus of the thalamus, MGN; lateral geniculate nucleus of the thalamus, LGN; anterior cingulate cortex, ACC; prelimbic cortex, PL

PROCESSES	CUED CONDITIONING	CONTEXT CONDITIONING	TRACE CONDITIONING
	• brief CS signal (such as tone or light) coterminates with a shock	• sufficient time to explore the context to form a contextual representation and store it in LTM	• brief CS signal (such as tone or light)
SUPPORTING BRAIN REGION(S)	• Discrete CS: Thalamic nuclei (MGN, LGN) • CS with co-termination of shock. CS-US Association: Amygdala	• contextual representation: Hippocampus • representation of the context must be in active memory at time of shock: Hippocampus • active representation must be associated with shock. CS-US Association: Amygdala	• Discrete CS: Thalamic nuclei (MGN, LGN) • representation of the context must be in active memory at time of shock: Hippocampus/ prefrontal cortices (ACC, PL) • active representation must be associated with shock. CS-US Association: Amygdala
TEST	• Test cue alone in novel context with no shock	• Test subject in conditioning context with no shock	• Test cue alone in novel context with no shock • Test subject in conditioning context with no shock

hippocampal manipulations made during context pre-exposure influence later performance, the hippocampus is critical to the first process, forming the memory representation of the context. Given the period of exploration during pre-exposure is without shock, such experiments leave open the question of whether or not the hippocampus plays a role in formation of the context-shock association. Tests of this hypothesis took advantage of the fact that hippocampus-dependent memories eventually consolidate to a hippocampus-independent form (Anagnostaras, Gale, & Fanselow, 2001; Young, Boehenek, & Fanselow, 1994). Rats were pre-exposed to one context without shock and then the memory was allowed to age for a month. At that point, when the context representation was presumably consolidated into a hippocampus-independent form, the rats received a context-shock pairing. Lesions of the hippocampus made either before (Young et al., 1994) or after (Anagnostaras et al., 2001) training did not affect context conditioning in these context pre-exposed rats, while rats that were not pre-exposed to the conditioning chamber were adversely affected by the lesion. Thus context-shock associations can form without the hippocampus, provided the hippocampus previously aided in the formation and consolidation of a representation of the non-emotional features of the context.

As with tone-shock associations, the evidence on context-shock association formation also points to the amygdala (Phillips & LeDoux, 1992). Using the contextual pre-exposure design, one can isolate the time of context-shock association formation by conducting manipulations during the immediate-shock session that follows pre-exposure. Using that approach, Matus-Amat et al. (2007) infused an NMDA antagonist into either the amygdala or hippocampus either before context pre-exposure or immediate shock. The hippocampal manipulation affected test performance if injected before pre-exposure but not immediate shock. BLAC infusions produced the opposite pattern. This experiment provides a clear double dissociation between the amygdala and hippocampus's roles in contextual fear learning. Information about the contextual representations arrives at the amygdala via the ventral angular bundle and stimulation of these afferents supports LTP in the amygdala. Lesions within this pathway attenuate contextual but not auditory conditioning (Maren & Fanselow, 1995). While the hippocampus is important for forming the contextual representation, the amygdala is critical for the context-shock association.

Extinction: Medial prefrontal cortex is strongly interconnected with the BLAC. Rather than carrying simple information about the presence or absence of the CS, these regions typically modulate BLAC. Two adjacent medial prefrontal cortical areas, the infralimbic and prelimbic cortices (IL and PL, respectively), have garnered the most attention as they tend to repress or enhance BLAC activity, respectively (I. Vidal-Gonzalez, B. Vidal-Gonzalez, Rauch, & Quirk, 2006). It is not clear in what situations the prelimbic area acts to enhance fear. Neural activity in the IL occurs during extinction and mimicking this activity reduces responding to a CS (Milad & Quirk, 2002). Thus this region acts to orchestrate BLAC activity most likely by telling the BLAC to not react to CSs that no longer signal threat, particularly after extinction.

Amygdala Efferents

Once the BLAC recognizes that there is danger, it must trigger the full range of fear responses. The nearby medial division of the Central Nucleus of the Amygdala (CEAm) contains projection neurons to many of the downstream structures that generate fear responses including freezing, analgesia, autonomic, and respiration changes and potentiated startle (see Figure 6.5; Fendt & Fanselow, 1999 for a review). Several of the Bed Nuclei of the Stria Terminalis (BST), which communicates with the BLAC and central nucleus, also send parallel projections to these same effector systems (Nagy & Paré, 2008). Current data suggest that CEAm generates a fast but short-lived fear response. In contrast, the BST can produce a more prolonged activation of fear behavior (Waddell, Morris, & Bouton, 2006; Walker, Toufexis, & Davis, 2003).

If fear is recognized by the BLAC, but CEAm generates behavior, the two structures need to communicate. There are multiple routes of communication between BLAC and CEAm that likely serve both fear expression (after acquisition) and fear

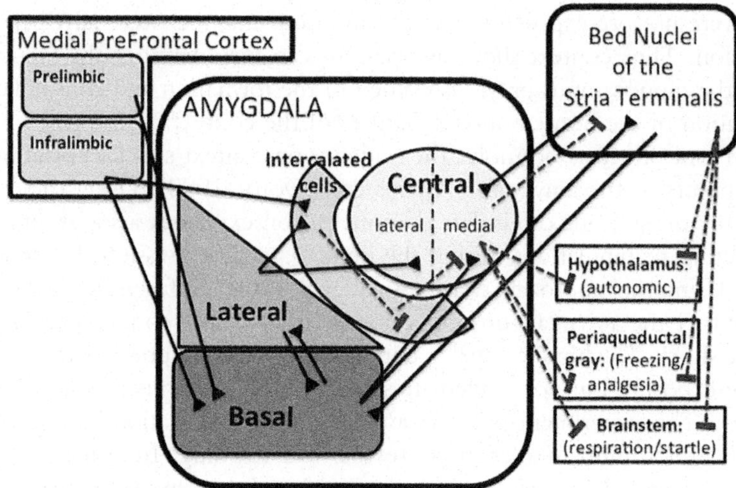

Figure 6.5 A more in-depth view of fear neural circuitry focusing on amygdalar nuclei. Note that solid black lines indicate excitatory projections and dashed gray lines indicate inhibitory projections.

inhibition (after extinction). While the BLAC and CEA are adjacent structures, the fiber tract that separates them contains small clumps of neurons called the paracapsular intercalated cells (PIC; Millhouse, 1986). To understand the function of this circuitry it must be recognized that the cortex-like BLAC consists of excitatory glutamatergic projection neurons and inhibitory interneurons (see Figure 6.5). The CEA is striatal-like and so its projection neurons release the inhibitory transmitter γ-Aminobutyric acid (GABA; Swanson & Petrovich, 1998). The PICs are also GABAergic (Nitecka & Ben-Ari, 1987).

This architecture offers a diverse set of possibilities for the BLAC to influence the CEAm (Carlsen, 1989; Paré et al., 2004). The dorsal part of the BLAC, the LA, does not project directly to the CEAm. However, because this nucleus is critical for auditory fear conditioning, it needs to enforce control of CEAm (Nader, Majidishad, Amorapanth, & LeDoux, 2001). There are three potential pathways for this. The first possibility relies on LA projections to the lateral portion of the Central Nucleus of the Amygdala (CEAl). There are two sets of GABAergic neurons in CEAl that reciprocally inhibit each other and can regulate CEAm output (Haubensak et al., 2010). The LA also projects to the basolateral nucleus and that region projects directly to CEAm (Pitkänen & Amaral, 1991). A third route is via the intercalated cells. The LA projects to a dorsal clump of these neurons, and exciting these neurons would cause an inhibition of the downstream cluster of PIC cells (Paré et al., 2004). This second cluster of PIC cells project to CEAm neurons, so the inhibition of these PIC cells leads to a disinhibition of CEAm neurons, thereby engaging a fear response.

This organization of the BLAC and CEA not only provides a substrate for eliciting fear, it also offers a target for executive regulation of fear by prefrontal cortex. Earlier it was noted that prelimbic (PL) and infralimbic (IL) cortex can upwardly or downwardly regulate fear responses, respectively (see Figure 6.5). Both of these prefrontal regions project to the basolateral nucleus. The IL, but not PL, also projects to the PIC cells (Berretta, Pantazopoulos, Caldera, Pantazopoulos, & Paré, 2005; Pinard, Mascagni, & McDonald, 2012). Activation of these inhibitory neurons by the IL is one way that the IL may produce the inhibition of fear needed for extinction (Paré et al., 2004).

The Dynamic Origins of Memory Systems (DOMS)

The foregoing section provided a brief overview of how fear circuitry takes in environmental information, processes and stores that information and then generates adaptive behavior. It is important to note that there is no fear "center." Rather, fear is generated by a complex circuit with different aspects of the circuit performing specific tasks (e.g., hippocampus incorporating context and time, the IL inhibiting fear). Often specific locations are described as essential or necessary. The "essential" or "necessary" terminology suggests that if one of these regions is lost the animal should be incapable of performing the function of that brain region. However, the brain is remarkably adaptable and considerable compensation can occur in the face of damage. Rather, these brain regions may be best viewed as normally serving these functions. The compensation is revealed when pre-training and post-training damage are compared.

This pattern first became apparent in studies of hippocampal control over context conditioning. The initial studies used either strong training parameters (15 trials) and made post-training lesions (Kim & Fanselow, 1992) or pre-training lesions with weak training parameters (three or fewer trials; Phillips & LeDoux, 1992). The effectiveness of hippocampal lesions in these early studies led to the interpretation that the hippocampus was essential for contextual fear. However, subsequent studies found the pre-training lesion effect to be variable (Frankland, Cestari, Filipkowski, McDonald, & Silva, 1998). Indeed, Maren et al. (1997) using identical training parameters either before or after a lesion found that pre-training hippocampal lesions had no effect even though post-training lesions abolished contextual fear memory. In general, post-training lesions are uniformly effective regardless of training parameters, while pre-training lesions are very training parameter dependent (Maren et al., 1997). Pre-training hippocampal lesions only affect context fear with minimal training parameters (i.e., when few trials or short context exposures were used). For example, Wiltgen et al (2006) gave 10 conditioning trials to rats and then completely ablated the entire hippocampus. These animals showed no context fear but they were easily retrained to the same level as unlesioned controls. In other words, retrograde amnesia was far greater than anterograde amnesia.

The hippocampus is not the only region where this difference between pre- and post-training lesions was found. Rats with large lesions of the amygdala can acquire fear if substantial overtraining is provided (e.g., 75 shocks; Kim & Davis, 1993; Maren, 1999). Interestingly, rats that receive the same overtraining while intact will completely lose fear if they receive a post-training amygdala lesion or a pretest inactivation of the amygdala (Maren, 1999; Ponnusamy, Poulos, & Fanselow, 2007). Similarly, pre-training lesions limited to the basal nucleus of the amygdala

(Anglada-Figueroa & Quirk, 2005) or the auditory cortex (Boatman & Kim, 2006) do not affect auditory conditioning but post-training lesions of these structures eliminate auditory cued fear.

This pattern of findings has led to a model proposing that there is a dynamic origin to the incorporation of particular neural structures into specific memory systems (Fanselow, 2010). The Dynamic Origin of Memory Systems (DOMS) model starts with the assumption that there are multiple pathways that have potential to mediate between environmental stimulus and adaptive behavior. A common assumption to virtually all theories of memory including DOMS is that these pathways must undergo increases in synaptic efficacy to mediate learned behavior. DOMS assumes that the efficiency of synaptic strengthening varies between these pathways. Unpredicted USs will drive plasticity in these pathways and with each trial the amount of plasticity in a pathway is proportional to the efficiency of the pathway. If the US is fully predicted, that US presentation does not drive synaptic plasticity. If one pathway is highly efficient, it will come to predict the US rapidly leaving little chance for the other pathways to strengthen. We refer to these highly efficient pathways as *primary pathways* because normally they will be the ones that support the majority conditional behavior. If the primary pathway is not available at the time of conditioning (e.g., it has been lesioned or inactivated), the less efficient pathways have the ability to compensate as they are no longer competing with the rapid learning primary pathway. We call these *alternate pathways* as they come into play only when competition with the primary pathway is alleviated. The alternate pathways come to predict the US but because of their reduced synaptic efficiency, they need more training to do so. One should recognize that these ideas are virtually identical to competitive error-correction algorithms that account for stimulus selection in Pavlovian conditioning (Rescorla & Wagner, 1972; Williams, this volume), except that in DOMS, the selection is of neural pathways rather than environmental stimuli. The circuits that perform error-correction in fear conditioning have been characterized elsewhere (Young & Fanselow, 1992; Fanselow, 1998; Bolles & Fanselow, 1980).

DOMS also provides insight into situations where pre-training manipulations are effective. Hippocampally damaged animals that receive minimal training (e.g., one shock) show learning deficits (Rudy, Barrientos, & O'Reilly, 2002) demonstrating the lowered efficiency of the alternate pathways. Genetic or pharmacological manipulations that target long-term synaptic plasticity rather than synaptic transmission also produce profound learning deficits if administered prior to training (Miserendino et al., 1990; Nakazawa et al., 2006). For example, NMDA and cholinergic antagonists, which are both known to prevent LTP, cause profound contextual fear learning deficits if they are infused into the hippocampus prior to conditioning (Gale, Anagnostaras, & Fanselow, 2001; Young et al., 1994). In this case, the primary pathway functions well during learning coming to predict the US and therefore outcompeting the alternate pathways, but the memory formed in the primary circuit cannot be maintained resulting in long-term memory deficits. A nice example of this is provided by Ploski et al. (2008) who used an antisense oligonucleotide to interfere with the immediate early gene Arc. Arc protein accumulates at activated synapses to regulate the expression of AMPA-type glutamate receptors there. Antisense was injected into the LA just prior to conditioning. When tone fear was tested 3 hours after training, fear expression was normal in the antisense-treated rats. Thus, the primary pathway appeared to be functional during learning. However, when these rats were tested 24 hours later contextual fear was gone. As normally occurs, the primary pathway learned to predict the US giving no opportunity for the alternate pathway to learn. However, the loss of Arc activity in the amygdala meant that the necessary plasticity was not maintained and the result was a loss of long-term memory.

Translational Significance

At the start of this chapter, a case was made for the relevance of Pavlovian fear conditioning to anxiety disorders. The substantial body of research on Pavlovian conditioning has provided detailed insight into the processes and mechanisms that underlie this form of learning. Given these two points, the field should be in a position to apply this knowledge clinically. One arena where this is coming to fruition is combining an understanding of the neural mechanisms with the processes that underlie extinction. As stated earlier, extinction is a new learning that interferes with, but does not undo, the original learning. One clinically problematic aspect of this new learning is that it is context bound. It does not transfer well outside of the original extinction context (see Vurbic & Bouton this volume). Unfortunately, the original fear memory is not so limited and fear will return if the fear CS is presented in any context other than the extinction context (Bouton, 1993). This phenomenon is called renewal and it provides some of the strongest evidence that extinction does not undo the original fear learning. If that were the case, fear should not renew after extinction. This poses a problem for clinical efficacy, as the loss of fear may not generalize out of the therapy context.

One possible way to make extinction more effective is to increase the strength of the extinction learning. Since extinction is mediated by NMDAR in the amygdala, facilitating activity at NMDAR should enhance extinction (Falls et al., 1992). Such a result has been reported for D-Cycloserine (DCS), a positive modulator of NMDAR (Walker, Ressler, Lu, & Davis, 2002). Given that extinction is the source of therapeutic benefit from cognitive-behavioral therapy, the ability to enhance extinction has potential translational impact. Initial reports in human patients have met with some, albeit mixed, success (Guastella, Lovibond, Dadds, Mitchell, & Richardson, 2007; Wilhelm et al., 2008). However, even when DCS treatment facilitates extinction, it does not prevent renewal when the context is changed (Woods & Bouton, 2006; also see Vurbic & Bouton this volume).

To address the context specificity of extinction, a logical candidate is the hippocampus. The hippocampus's role in renewal parallels its role in contextual fear conditioning. Manipulations of the hippocampus can block renewal (Ji & Maren, 2005) and the effects are greater for post-extinction than pre-extinction lesions (Zelikowsky, Pham, & Fanselow, 2012). Obviously, invasive and/or permanent manipulations of the hippocampus cannot be used in a clinical setting. However, systemic administration of very low doses of the cholinergic antagonist scopolamine mimics the effects of hippocampal infusions of the drug on contextual fear conditioning (Anagnostaras, Maren, & Fanselow 1999; Gale et al., 2001). This drug has been used clinically in humans for years to treat sea-sickness, Parkinson's disease and previously, drug addiction. Giving a very low systemic dose of scopolamine during extinction treatment prevented later fear renewal when rats were tested out of the extinction context (Zelikowsky et al., 2013). It seems that because the rats could not effectively process context during extinction, the extinction memory was encoded in a context independent way. Thus, this treatment holds promise as an adjunct to behavior therapy with the goal of making the loss of fear more general. Ideally, a combined treatment that facilitated extinction learning (such as D-cycloserine in the amygdala), while eliminating its context specificity (like scopolamine in the hippocampus) could be developed.

Conclusions

Fear is a double-edged sword. Because of the evolutionary importance of defense, it must be rapidly turned on when needed and utterly dominate behavior to ensure survival. But there is a downside: fear can be on a hair trigger, especially in those who have experienced previous trauma (Rau, DeCola, & Fanselow, 2005). This, in turn, leads to a high incidence of anxiety disorders. Advances in fear conditioning research have led to an excellent understanding of the behavioral processes and neural mechanisms that mediate fear. Fortunately, this knowledge is being translated to enhance clinical treatment, most notably in terms of adjuncts to extinction-based exposure treatments. Therefore, thanks to fear conditioning research, we should be optimistic that the next years will see a new generation of more efficacious treatments for anxiety disorders.

References

Anagnostaras, S., Gale, G., & Fanselow, M. S. (2001). Hippocampus and contextual fear conditioning: recent controversies and advances. *Hippocampus, 11*, 8–17.

Anagnostaras, S., Maren, S., & Fanselow, M. S. (1999). Temporally graded retrograde amnesia of contextual fear after hippocampal damage in rats: Within-subjects examination. *Journal of Neuroscience, 19*, 1106–1114.

Anglada-Figueroa, D., & Quirk, G. J. (2005). Lesions of the basal amygdala block expression of conditioned fear but not extinction. *Journal of Neuroscience, 25*, 9680–9685.

Barash, S., Bracewell, R., Fogassi, L., Gnadt, J., & Andersen, R. A. (1991).Inhibitory transmission in the basolateral amygdala. *Journal of Neurophysiology, 66*, 1109–1124.

Barot, S. K., Kyono, Y., Clark, E. W., & Bernstein, I. L. (2008). Visualizing stimulus convergence in amygdala neurons during associative learning. *Proceedings of the National Academy of Sciences of the United States of America, 105*, 20959–20963.

Barrientos, R., O'Reilly, R., & Rudy, J. (2002). Memory for context is impaired by injecting anisomycin into dorsal hippocampus following context exploration. *Behavioural Brain Research, 134*, 299–306.

Bauer, E., & LeDoux, J. E. (2004). Heterosynaptic long-term potentiation of inhibitory interneurons in the lateral amygdala. *Journal of Neuroscience, 24*, 9507–9512.

Bechara, A., Tranel, D., Damasio, H., Adolphs, R., Rockland, C., & Damasio, A. (1995). Double dissociation of conditioning and declarative knowledge relative to the amygdala and hippocampus in humans. *Science New York NY, 269*, 1115–1118.

Berretta, S., Pantazopoulos, H., Caldera, M., Pantazopoulos, P., & Paré, D. (2005). Infralimbic cortex activation increases c-Fos expression in intercalated neurons of the amygdala. *Neuroscience, 132*, 943–953.

Blaisdell, A., Denniston, J., & Miller, R. R. (1998).Temporal encoding as a determinant of overshadowing. *Journal of Experimental Psychology Animal Behavior Processes, 24*, 72–83.

Blanchard, D. C., & Blanchard, R. J. (1972). Innate and conditioned reactions to threat in rats with amygdaloid lesions. *Journal of Comparative and Physiological Psychology, 81*, 281–290.

Boatman, J., & Kim, J. J. (2006). A thalamo-cortico-amygdala pathway mediates auditory fear conditioning in the intact brain. *European Journal of Neuroscience, 24*, 894–900.

Bolles, R. C. (1970). Species-specific defense reactions and avoidance learning. *Psychological Review, 77*, 32–48.

Bolles, R. C., & Collier, A. (1976). The effect of predictive cues on freezing in rats. *Animal & Learning Behavior, 4*, 6–8.

Bolles, R. C., & Fanselow, M. S. (1980). A perceptual-defensive-recuperative model of fear and pain. *Behavioral and Brain Sciences, 3*, 291–323.

Bouton, M. E. (1993). Context, time, and memory retrieval in the interference paradigms of Pavlovian learning. *Psychological Bulletin, 114*, 80–99.

Brown, J., Kalish, H., & Farber, I. (1951). Conditioned fear as revealed by magnitude of startle response to an auditory stimulus. *Journal of Experimental Psychology, 41*, 317–328.

Carlsen, J. (1989). New perspectives on the functional anatomical organization of the basolateral amygdala. *Acta neurologica Scandinavica Supplementum, 122*, 1–27.

Carrive, P., & Gorissen, M. (2008). Premotor sympathetic neurons of conditioned fear in the rat. *European Journal of Neuroscience, 28*, 428–446.

Clugnet, M., & LeDoux, J. E. (1990). Synaptic plasticity in fear conditioning circuits: Induction of LTP in the lateral nucleus of the amygdala by stimulation of the medial geniculate body. *Journal of Neuroscience, 10*, 2818–2824.

Davis, M., & Astrachan, D. (1978). Conditioned fear and startle magnitude: Effects of different footshock or backshock intensities used in training. *Journal of Experimental Psychology Animal Behavior Processes, 4*, 95–103.

Doyère, V., Schafe, G., Sigurdsson, T., & LeDoux, J. E. (2003). Long-term potentiation in freely-moving rats reveals asymmetries in thalamic and cortical inputs to the lateral amygdala. *European Journal of Neuroscience, 31*, 250–262.

Edeline, J., & Weinberger, N. (1992). Associative retuning in the thalamic source of input to the amygdala and auditory cortex: receptive field plasticity in the medial division of the medial geniculate body. *Behavioral Neuroscience, 106*, 81–105.

Egger, M., & Miller, N. (1962). Secondary reinforcement in rats as a function of information value and reliability of the stimulus. *Journal of Experimental Psychology, 64*, 97–104.

Estes, W. K., & Skinner, B. F. (1941). Some quantitative properties of anxiety. *Journal of Experimental Psychology, 29*, 390–400.

Falls, W., Miserendino, M., & Davis, M. (1992). Extinction of fear-potentiated startle: Blockade by infusion of an NMDA antagonist into the amygdala. *Journal of Neuroscience, 12*, 854–863.

Fanselow, M. S. (1980a).Conditioned and unconditional components of post-shock freezing. *Pavlovian Journal of Biological Science, 15*, 177–182.

Fanselow, M. S. (1980b) Signaled shock-free periods and preference for signaled shock. *Journal of Experimental Psychology: Animal Behavior Processes, 6*, 65–80.

Fanselow, M. S. (1984). What is conditioned fear? *Trends in Neurosciences, 7*, 460–462.

Fanselow, M. S. (1986). Associative versus topographical accounts of the immediate shock-freezing deficit in rats: Implications for the response selection rules governing species-specific defensive reactions. *Learning and Motivation, 17*, 16–39.

Fanselow, M. S. (1990). Factors governing one-trial contextual conditioning. *Learning & Behavior, 18*, 264–270.

Fanselow, M. S. (1994). Neural organization of the defensive behavior system responsible for fear. *Psychonomic Bulletin Review, 1*, 429–438.

Fanselow, M. S. (1998). Pavlovian conditioning, minireview negative feedback and blocking: mechanisms that regulate association formation, *Neuron, 20*, 625–627.

Fanselow, M. S. (2000). Contextual fear, gestalt memories, and the hippocampus. *Behavioural Brain Research, 110*, 73–81.

Fanselow, M. S. (2010). From contextual fear to a dynamic view of memory systems. *Trends in Cognitive Sciences, 14*, 7–15.

Fanselow, M. S., & Baackes, M. (1982) Conditioned fear-induced opiate analgesia on the formalin test: Evidence for two aversive motivational systems. *Learning and Motivation, 13*, 200–221.

Fanselow, M. S., & Bolles, R. C. (1979). Naloxone and shock-elicited freezing in the rat. *Journal of Comparative and Physiological Psychology, 93*, 736–744.

Fanselow, M. S., & Kim, J. J. (1994). Acquisition of contextual Pavlovian fear conditioning is blocked by application of an NMDA receptor antagonist D, L-2-amino-5-phosphonovaleric acid to the basolateral amygdala. *Behavioral Neuroscience, 108*, 210–212.

Fanselow, M. S, Landeira-Fernandez, J., DeCola, J., & Kim, J. J. (1994). The immediate-shock deficit and postshock analgesia: Implications for the relationship between the analgesic CR and UR. *Animal Learning & Behavior, 22*, 72–76.

Fanselow, M. S., & Lester, L. (1988). A functionalistic behavioristic approach to aversively-motivated behavior: Predatory imminence as a determinant of the topography of defensive behavior. In R. C. B. M. D. Denny (Ed.), *Evolution and Learning* (pp. 185–212). Hillsdale, NJ: Erlbaum.

Fanselow, M. S., & Poulos, A. (2005). The neuroscience of mammalian associative learning. *Annual Review of Psychology, 56*, 207–234.

Fendt, M., & Fanselow, M. S. (1999). The neuroanatomical and neurochemical basis of conditioned fear. *Neuroscience and Biobehavioral Reviews, 23*, 743–760.

Frankland, P., Cestari, V., Filipkowski, R., McDonald, R., & Silva, A. (1998). The dorsal hippocampus is essential for context discrimination but not for contextual conditioning. *Behavioral Neuroscience, 112*, 863–874.

Fridlund, A., Beck, H., Goldie, W., & Irons, G. (2012). Little Albert: A neurologically impaired child. *History of Psychology,15*, 302–327.

Gale, G., Anagnostaras, S., & Fanselow, M. S. (2001). Cholinergic modulation of Pavlovian fear conditioning: Effects of intrahippocampal scopolamine infusion. *Hippocampus, 11*, 371–376.

Gale, G., Anagnostaras, S., Godsil, B., Mitchell, S., Nozawa, T., Sage, J., Wiltgen, B., et al. (2004). Role of the basolateral amygdala in the storage of fear memories across the adult lifetime of rats. *Journal of Neuroscience, 24*, 3810–3815.

Godsil, B., Quinn, J. J., & Fanselow, M. S. (2000). Body temperature as a conditional response measure for Pavlovian fear conditioning. *Learning and Memory, 7*, 353–356.

Greenberg, P., Sisitsky, T., Kessler, R., Finkelstein, S., Berndt, E., Davidson, J., Ballenger, J., et al. (1999). The economic burden of anxiety disorders in the 1990s. *Journal of Clinical Psychiatry, 60*, 427–435.

Guastella, A., Lovibond, P., Dadds, M., Mitchell, P., & Richardson, R. (2007). A randomized controlled trial of the effect of D-cycloserine on extinction and fear conditioning in humans. *Behaviour Research and Therapy, 45*, 663–672.

Gdalyahu, A., Tring E., Polack, P. O., Gruver, R., Golshani, P., Fanselow, M. S., Silva, A. J., Trachtenberg, J. T. (2012). Associative fear learning enhances sparse network coding in primary sensory cortex. *Neuron, 75,* 121–132.

Guzowski, J., Lyford, G., Stevenson, G., Houston, F., McGaugh, J., Worley, P., & Barnes, C. (2000). Inhibition of activity-dependent arc protein expression in the rat hippocampus impairs the maintenance of long-term potentiation and the consolidation of long-term memory. *Journal of Neuroscience, 20,* 3993–4001.

Guzowski, J. F., & Worley, P. F. (2001). Cellular compartment analysis of temporal activity by fluorescence in situ hybridization (catFISH). *Current Protocols in Neuroscience Chapter, 1*: 1–8. doi: 10.1002/0471142301.ns0108s15.

Haubensak, W., Kunwar, P., Cai, H., Ciocchi, S., Wall, N., Ponnusamy, R., Biag, J., et al. (2010). Genetic dissection of an amygdala microcircuit that gates conditioned fear. *Nature, 468,* 270–276.

Helmstetter, F. J. (1992).Contribution of the amygdala to learning and performance of conditional fear. *Physiology & Behavior, 51,* 1271–1276.

Hermans, D., Craske, M., Mineka, S., & Lovibond, P. (2006). Extinction in human fear conditioning. *Biological Psychiatry, 60,* 361–368.

Hitchcock, J., & Davis, M. (1986). Lesions of the amygdala, but not of the cerebellum or red nucleus, block conditioned fear as measured with the potentiated startle paradigm. *Behavioral Neuroscience, 100,* 11–22.

Hofmann, S., & Smits, J. (2008). Pitfalls of meta-analyses (letter to the editor). *Journal of Nervous and Mental Disease, 196,* 716–717.

Iordanova, M., & Honey, R. (2012). Generalization of contextual fear as a function of familiarity: The role of within- and between-context associations. *Journal of Experimental Psychology: Animal Behavior Processes, 38,* 315–321.

Ji, J., & Maren, S. (2005). Electrolytic lesions of the dorsal hippocampus disrupt renewal of conditional fear after extinction. *Learning Memory, 12,* 270–276.

Johnson, J., & Church, R. (1965). Effects of shock intensity on non-discriminated avoidance learning of rats in a shuttle box. *Psychonomic Science, 3,* 497–498.

Kessler, R., Berglund, P., Demler, O., Jin, R., Merikangas, K., & Walters, E. (2005). Lifetime prevalence and age-of-onset distributions of DSM-IV disorders in the National Comorbidity Survey Replication. *Archives of General Psychiatry, 62,* 593–602.

Kholodar-Smith, D., Allen, T., & Brown, T. (2008). Fear conditioning to discontinuous auditory cues requires perirhinal cortical function. *Behavioral Neuroscience, 122,* 1178–1185.

Kiernan, M., & Cranney, J. (1992). Immediate-startle stimulus presentation fails to condition freezing responses to contextual cues. *Behavioral Neuroscience, 106,* 121–124.

Kiernan, M., Westbrook, R., & Cranney, J. (1995). Immediate shock, passive avoidance, and potentiated startle: Implications for the unconditioned response to shock. *Animal Learning & Behavior, 23,* 22–30.

Kim, J. J., & Fanselow, M. S. (1992). Modality-specific retrograde amnesia of fear. *Science, 256,* 675–677.

Kim, J. J., & Jung, M. (2006). Neural circuits and mechanisms involved in Pavlovian fear conditioning: a critical review. *Neuroscience and Biobehavioral Reviews, 30,* 188–202.

Kim, M., & Davis, M. (1993). Electrolytic lesions of the amygdala block acquisition and expression of fear-potentiated startle even with extensive training but do not prevent reacquisition. *Behavioral Neuroscience, 107,* 580–595.

Landeira-Fernandez, J., DeCola, J., Kim, J. J., & Fanselow, M. S. (2006). Immediate shock deficit in fear conditioning: Effects of shock manipulations. *Behavioral Neuroscience, 120,* 873–879.

Lavenex, P., & Amaral, D. (2000). Hippocampal-neocortical interaction: A hierarchy of associativity. *Hippocampus, 10,* 420–430.

LeDoux, J. E. (2012). Rethinking the emotional brain. *Neuron, 73*, 653–676.

Leaton, R., & Cranney, J. (1990). Potentiation of the acoustic startle response by a conditioned stimulus paired with acoustic startle stimulus in rats. *Journal of Experimental Psychology Animal Behavior Processes, 16*, 279–287.

Lee, H., Choi, J., Brown, T., & Kim, J. J. (2001). Amygdalar nmda receptors are critical for the expression of multiple conditioned fear responses. *Journal of Neuroscience, 21*, 4116–4124.

Maren, S. (1999). Neurotoxic basolateral amygdala lesions impair learning and memory but not the performance of conditional fear in rats. *Journal of Neuroscience, 19*, 8696–8703.

Maren, S., Aharonov, G., & Fanselow, M. S. (1997). Neurotoxic lesions of the dorsal hippocampus and Pavlovian fear conditioning in rats. *Behavioural Brain Research, 88*, 261–274.

Maren, S., & Fanselow, M. S. (1995). Synaptic plasticity in the basolateral amygdala induced by hippocampal formation stimulation in vivo. *Journal of Neuroscience, 15*, 7548–7564.

Maren, S., Yap, S., & Goosens, K. (2001). The amygdala is essential for the development of neuronal plasticity in the medial geniculate nucleus during auditory fear conditioning in rats. *Journal of Neuroscience, 21*, RC135 (1–6).

Matus-Amat, P., Higgins, E., Sprunger, D., Wright-Hardesty, K., & Rudy, J. (2007). The role of dorsal hippocampus and basolateral amygdala NMDA receptors in the acquisition and retrieval of context and contextual fear memories. *Behavioral Neuroscience, 121*, 721–731.

McEchron, M., Bouwmeester, H., Tseng, W., Weiss, C., & Disterhoft, J. (1998). Hippocampectomy disrupts auditory trace fear conditioning and contextual fear conditioning in the rat. *Hippocampus, 8*, 638–646.

McFarlane, A. (2010). The long-term costs of traumatic stress: Intertwined physical and psychological consequences. *Journal of the World Psychiatric Association, 9*, 3–10.

McHugh, T., & Tonegawa, S. (2007). Spatial exploration is required for the formation of contextual fear memory. *Behavioral Neuroscience, 121*, 335–339.

Mendlowicz, M., & Stein, M. (2000). Reviews and overviews quality of life in individuals with anxiety disorders. *Psychiatry Interpersonal and Biological Processes, 157*, 669–682.

Milad, M. R., & Quirk, G. (2002). Neurons in medial prefrontal cortex signal memory for fear extinction. *Nature, 420*, 713–717.

Millhouse, O. (1986). The intercalated cells of the amygdala. *Journal of Comparative Neurology, 247*, 246–271.

Miserendino, M., Sananes, C., Melia, K., & Davis, M. (1990). Blocking of acquisition but not expression of conditioned fear-potentiated startle by NMDA antagonists in the amygdala. *Nature, 345*, 716–718.

Nader, K., Majidishad, P., Amorapanth, P., & LeDoux, J. E. (2001). Damage to the lateral and central, but not other, amygdaloid nuclei prevents the acquisition of auditory fear conditioning. *Learning and Memory, 8*, 156–163.

Nagy, F., & Paré, D. (2008). Timing of impulses from the central amygdala and bed nucleus of the stria terminalis to the brain stem. *Journal of Neurophysiology, 100*, 3429–3436.

Nakazawa, T., Komai, S., Watabe, A., Kiyama, Y., Fukaya, M., Arima-Yoshida, F., Horai, R., et al. (2006). NR2B tyrosine phosphorylation modulates fear learning as well as amygdaloid synaptic plasticity. *The EMBO Journal, 25*, 2867–2877.

Nesse, R.(2005). Natural selection and the regulation of defenses. *Evolution and Human Behavior, 26*, 88–105.

Nitecka, L., & Ben-Ari, Y. (1987). Distribution of GABA-like immunoreactivity in the rat amygdaloid complex. *Journal of Comparative Neurology, 266*, 45–55.

Norton, P., & Price, E. (2007). A meta-analytic review of adult cognitive-behavioral treatment outcome across the anxiety disorders. *Journal of Nervous and Mental Disease*, *195*, 521–531.

O'Keefe, J., & Dostrovsky, J. (1971). The hippocampus as a spatial map. Preliminary evidence from unit activity in the freely-moving rat. *Brain Research*, *34*, 171–175

Paré, D., Quirk, G., & LeDoux, J. E. (2004). New vistas on amygdala networks in conditioned fear. *Journal of Neurophysiology*, *92*, 1–9.

Pavlov, I. (1927). Conditioned reflexes. (Ivan Petrovich Pavlov, Ed.) *Oxford University Press* (Vol. 17, p. 448). Oxford: Oxford University Press.

Peterson, W., Birdsall, T., & Fox, W. (1954) The theory of signal detectability (J. V. Tobias, Ed.), *4 IRE Professional Group on Information Theory* (pp. 171–212). New York: Academic Press.

Phillips, R., & LeDoux, J. E. (1992). Differential contribution of amygdala and hippocampus to cued and contextual fear conditioning. *Behavioral Neuroscience*, *106*, 274–285.

Pinard, C., Mascagni, F., & McDonald, A. (2012).Medial prefrontal cortical innervation of the intercalated nuclear region of the amygdala. *Neuroscience*, *205*, 112–124.

Pitkänen, A., & Amaral, D. (1991). Demonstration of projections from the lateral nucleus to the basal nucleus of the amygdala: A PHA-L study in the monkey. *Experimental Brain Research*, *83*, 465–470.

Ploski, J., Pierre, V., Smucny, J., Park, K., Monsey, M., Overeem, K., & Schafe, G. (2008). The activity-regulated cytoskeletal-associated protein (Arc/Arg3.1) is required for memory consolidation of Pavlovian fear conditioning in the lateral amygdala. *Journal of Neuroscience*, *28*, 12383–12395.

Ponnusamy, R., Poulos, A., & Fanselow, M. S. (2007). Amygdala-dependent and amygdala-independent pathways for contextual fear conditioning. *Neuroscience*, *147*, 919–927.

Poremba, A., & Gabriel M. (2001) Amygdalar efferents initiate auditory thalamic discriminative training-induced neuronal activity. *Journal of Neuroscience*, *21*, 270–278.

Powell, R. (2010). Little Albert still missing. *American Psychologist*, *65*, 299–300.

Quiroga, R., Reddy, L., Kreiman, G., Koch, C., & Fried, I. (2005). Invariant visual representation by single neurons in the human brain. *Nature*, *435*, 1102–1107.

Quinn, J. J., Oommen, S., Morrison, G., & Fanselow, M. S. (2002). Post-training excitotoxic lesions of the dorsal hippocampus attenuate forward trace, backward trace, and delay fear conditioning in a temporally specific manner. *Hippocampus*, *12*, 495–504.

Rau, V., DeCola, J., & Fanselow, M. S. (2005). Stress-induced enhancement of fear learning: An animal model of post-traumatic stress disorder. *Neuroscience and Biobehavioral Reviews*, *29*, 1207–1223.

Reger, M., Poulos, A., Buen, F., Giza, C., Hovda, D., & Fanselow, M. S. (2012). Concussive brain injury enhances fear learning and excitatory processes in the amygdala. *Biological Psychiatry*, *71*, 335–343.

Rescorla, R. A. (1967). Pavlovian conditioning and its proper control procedures. *Psychological Review*, *74*, 71–80.

Rescorla, R. A. (1980). Simultaneous and successive associations in sensory preconditioning. *Journal of Experimental Psychology Animal Behavior Processes*, *6*, 207–216.

Rescorla, R. A. (1988). Pavlovian conditioning. It's not what you think it is. *American Psychologist*, *43*, 151–160.

Rescorla, R. A., & Wagner, A. R. (1972). A theory of Pavlovian conditioning: Variations in the effectiveness of reinforcement and nonreinforcement. In A. H. Black & W. F. Prokasy (Eds.), *Classical Conditioning II Current Research and Theory* (Vol. 20, pp. 64–99). New York: Appleton-Century-Crofts.

Rodrigues, S., Schafe, G., & LeDoux, J. E. (2004). Molecular mechanisms underlying emotional learning and memory in the lateral amygdala. *Neuron*, *44*, 75–91.

Roelofs, K., Hagenaars, M., & Stins, J. (2010). Facing freeze: Social threat induces bodily freeze in humans. *Psychological Science*, *21*, 1575–1581.

Romanski, L., Clugnet, M., Bordi, F., & LeDoux, J. E. (1993). Somatosensory and auditory convergence in the lateral nucleus of the amygdala. *Behavioral Neuroscience*, *107*, 444–450.

Rosen, J., Hitchcock, J., Miserendino, M., Falls, W., Campeau, S., & Davis, M. (1992). Lesions of the perirhinal cortex but not of the frontal, medial prefrontal, visual, or insular cortex block fear-potentiated startle using a visual conditioned stimulus. *Journal of Neuroscience*, *12*, 4624–4633.

Rudy, J., & O'Reilly, R. (1999). Contextual fear conditioning, conjunctive representations, pattern completion, and the hippocampus. *Behavioral Neuroscience*, *113*, 867–880.

Rudy, J. W., Barrientos, R. M., & O'Reilly, R. C. (2002). Hippocampal formation supports conditioning to memory of a context. *Behavioral Neuroscience*, *116*, 530–538.

Schreurs, B., Smith-Bell, C., & Burhans, L. (2011). Incubation of conditioning-specific reflex modification: Implications for Post-Traumatic Stress Disorder. *Journal of Psychiatric Research*, *45*, 1535–1541.

Squire, L. R. (1992). *Encyclopedia of learning and memory*. New York: Maxwell Macmillan International.

Swanson, L. W., & Petrovich, G. (1998). What is the amygdala? *Trends in Neurosciences*, *21*, 323–331.

Tanielian, T. L., & Jaycox, L. (Eds.). (2008). Invisible wounds of war: Psychological and cognitive injuries, their consequences, and services to assist recovery (Vol. 720). Rand Corporation.

Tanner, W., & Swets, J. (1954). A decision-making theory of visual detection. *Psychological Review*, *61*, 401–409.

Teyler, T. & Discenna, P. (1984). Long-term potentiation as a candidate mnemonic device. *Brain Research*, *319*, 15–28.

Vurbic, D., & Bouton, M. E. (2014). A contemporary behavioral perspective on extinction. In F. K. McSweeney & E. S. Murphy (Eds.), *The Wiley-Blackwell Handbook of Operant Conditioning* (pp. 53–76). Oxford: Wiley-Blackwell.

Vidal-Gonzalez, I., Vidal-Gonzalez, B., Rauch, S., & Quirk, G. (2006). Microstimulation reveals opposing influences of prelimbic and infralimbic cortex on the expression of conditioned fear. *Learning and Memory*, *13*, 728–733.

Waddell, J., Morris, R., & Bouton, M. E. (2006). Effects of bed nucleus of the stria terminalis lesions on conditioned anxiety: Aversive conditioning with long-duration conditional stimuli and reinstatement of extinguished fear. *Behavioral Neuroscience*, *120*, 324–336.

Walker, D., Ressler, K., Lu, K., & Davis, M. (2002). Facilitation of conditioned fear extinction by systemic administration or intra-amygdala infusions of D-cycloserine as assessed with fear-potentiated startle in rats. *Journal of Neuroscience*, *22*, 2343–2351.

Walker, D., Toufexis, D., & Davis, M. (2003). Role of the bed nucleus of the stria terminalis versus the amygdala in fear, stress, and anxiety. *European Journal of Pharmacology*, *463*, 199–216.

Warren, J., & Bolles, R. C. (1965).Effects of delayed UCS termination on classical avoidance learning of the bar-press response. *Psychological Reports*, *17*, 687–690.

Watson, J., & Rayner, R. (1920). Conditioned emotional reactions. *American Psychologist*, *3*, 313–317.

Weinberger, N. (1993). Learning-induced changes of auditory receptive fields. *Current Opinion in Neurobiology*, *3*, 570–577.

Wilhelm, S., Buhlmann, U., Tolin, D., Meunier, S. A., Pearlson, G., Reese, H., Cannistraro, P., et al. (2008). Augmentation of behavior therapy with D-cycloserine for obsessive-compulsive disorder. *American Journal of Psychiatry*, *165*, 335–341.

Williams, D. A. (2014). Building a theory of Pavlovian conditioning from inside out. In F. K. McSweeney & E. S. Murphy (Eds.), *The Wiley-Blackwell Handbook of Operant Conditioning* (pp. 27–52). Oxford: Wiley-Blackwell.

Wiltgen, B., Sanders, M., Anagnostaras, S., Sage, J., & Fanselow, M. S. (2006). Context fear learning in the absence of the hippocampus. *Journal of Neuroscience*, *26*, 5484–5491.

Woods, A., & Bouton, M. E. (2006). D-cycloserine facilitates extinction but does not eliminate renewal of the conditioned emotional response. *Behavioral Neuroscience*,, 1159–1162.

Young, S., Bohenek, D., & Fanselow, M. S. (1994). NMDA processes mediate anterograde amnesia of contextual fear conditioning induced by hippocampal damage: Immunization against amnesia by context preexposure. *Behavioral Neuroscience*, *108*, 19–29.

Young, S., & Fanselow, M. S. (1992). Associative regulation of Pavlovian fear conditioning: Unconditional stimulus intensity, incentive shifts, and latent inhibition. *Journal of Experimental Psychology Animal Behavior Processes*, *18*, 400–413.

Zelikowsky, M., Pham, D., & Fanselow, M. S. (2012). Temporal factors control hippocampal contributions to fear renewal after extinction. *Hippocampus*, *22*, 1096–1106.

Zelikowsky, M., Hast, T. A., Bennett, R. Z., Merjanian, M., Nocera, N. A., Ponnusamy, R., & Fanselow, M. S. (2013). Cholinergic Blockade Frees Fear Extinction from Its Contextual Dependency. *Biological Psychiatry*, *73*, 345–352.

7

Behavioral Conditioning of Immune Responses

An Overview and Consideration of Clinical Applications

Alexander W. Kusnecov

Introduction

The immune system is a biological defense mechanism with similar properties of adaptation as the central nervous system (CNS). It is a "sensory" system that evolved to combat molecular and cellular invaders—such as viruses and bacteria—and in so doing, developed a repertoire of responses that involve learning and memory, the underlying principle exploited by vaccinations. This much was understood throughout the history of immunology, until the mid-1970s when there began to emerge a formal and concerted effort to demonstrate the existence of a functional interaction between the brain and the immune system. Within the behavioral sciences, this was most explicitly shown through conditioning studies, whereby classically conditioned behavioral responses reenlisted immunological changes associated with the immunopharmacologic unconditioned stimulus (UCS) that was first presented during the conditioning or learning trial. Although this was by no means the first time the immune system was being linked to neural or behavioral processes, it was nonetheless, the beginning of a systematic program of research (labeled as "psychoneuroimmunology" by Robert Ader (1981)). Psychoneuroimmunology relied on several different experimental and methodological approaches and used stringent controls. As a result, it generated considerable interest in how the CNS modified immune function, and conversely, how the immune system altered brain and behavioral functions. Over the years, the distinction between the CNS and immune system has become blurred, as it has become obvious that CNS-immune system interactions are inseparable elements of a defense network promoting adaptation in the face of threat.

The purpose of this chapter is to consider how conditioning fits into the general scheme of normal neural-immune interactions, and to consider whether it is possible that immune-related phenomena can be behaviorally conditioned for clinical purposes.

The Wiley Blackwell Handbook of Operant and Classical Conditioning, First Edition.
Edited by Frances K. McSweeney and Eric S. Murphy.

In allowing various experiments and concepts to unfold, immunological terminology will arise, and may require explanation. Therefore, at the outset, a brief rudimentary synopsis of the immune system will be provided. This will render various terms and measures discussed in the conditioning sections more meaningful to readers less familiar with parameters of immunological function.

Overview of the Immune System

The immune system is composed of specialized cells (e.g., leukocytes or "white blood cells") that patrol the body and organs (the *host*) for signs of injury and/or infection due to replication of foreign microorganisms (e.g., bacteria, viruses). Typically, the immune system is segregated into functional modes of performance that are either adaptive (or acquired) or innate (or natural). Acquired immunity possesses classic hallmarks of stimulus specificity and memory for encounters with pathogenic molecules. In contrast, natural immunity is rapid, involving nonspecific reactivity to pathogens, with no requirement for memory. Of the multiple cell types in the immune system, two groups define these two forms of immunity: lymphocytes (T and B cells), related to acquired immunity, and macrophages (as well as related monocytes and granulocytes), which are associated with innate immunity. Although the immune system is too complex to describe in a few pages, the key point to appreciate is the cooperative nature of immune cells, as they generate a response against a pathogen. This is schematically summarized in Figure 7.1. Key terms provided in Figure 7.1 are defined further below, but as the interactions within the immune system are described, the reader will be asked to refer back to Figure 7.1 to gain a sense of the relationship between the cellular and molecular interactions taking place.

All cells of the immune system derive from pluripotent hematopoietic ("blood-forming") stem cells, from which emerge divergent lymphoid and myeloid cell lines that differentiate into lymphocytes and macrophages, respectively. Macrophages, the primary mediators of innate immunity, typically reside in tissues, and originate from a precursor myeloid cell, the monocyte, which circulates in blood. Tissue macrophages are phagocytic (i.e. from *phagocytosis*: "to eat"), and are also referred to as polymorphonuclear phagocytes. Phagocytosis is a critical feature of immune function that clears cellular debris (e.g., necrotic tissue) and bacterial cells through intracellular ingestion and enzymatic degradation. The ability of macrophages to remove bacterial microorganisms is based on recognition of pathogen-associated molecular patterns (PAMPs) that are expressed on the bacterial cell surface. These PAMPs are recognized by various receptors on macrophages such as the Toll-like receptors (TLRs). Indeed, the most common immune stimulus used in psychoneuroimmunological investigations is a lipopolysaccharide (LPS) molecule that is derived from the cell walls of gram negative bacteria, such as *Escherichia coli* (E. coli). Lipopolysaccharide (which is also referred to as *endotoxin*) targets surface molecules on macrophages, which include CD14 and TLR4. This results in the synthesis and release of a class of molecules called cytokines ("cell messengers") that regulate various tissue functions, including those within the immune system, and are generally considered promoters of inflammation (hence, such cytokines are referred to as "proinflammatory"). Inflammation is a clinical term for a condition caused by tissue injury or infection,

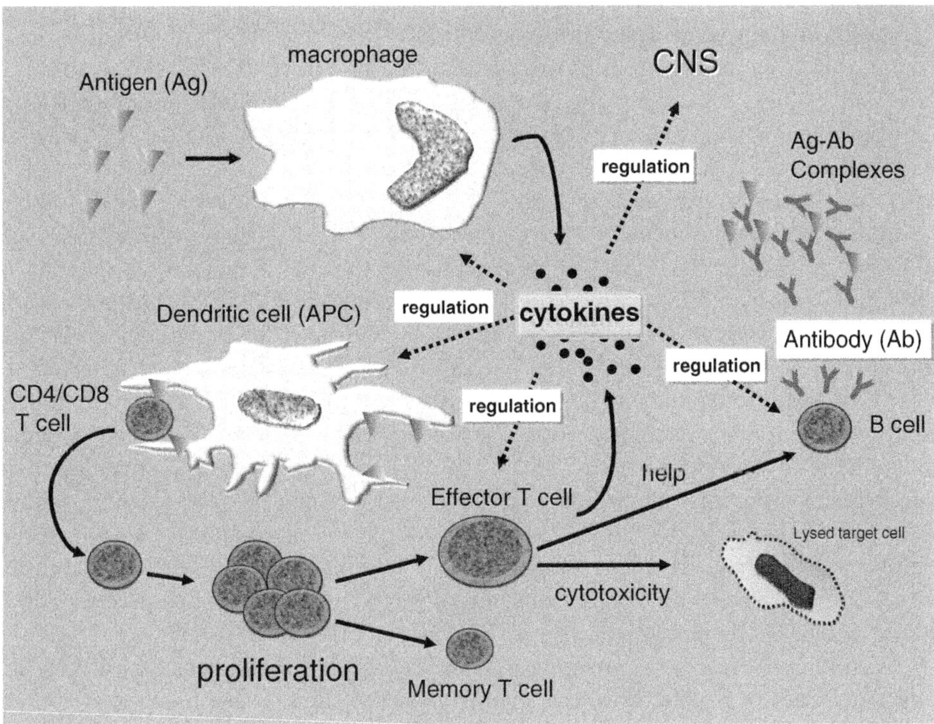

Figure 7.1 A schematic illustration of the functional relationships between the innate and acquired components of the immune system. Phagocytic cells, such as macrophages, can ingest and degrade bacterial pathogens, and act as antigen-presenting cells (APCs). However, professional APCs, such as dendritic cells, can similarly interact with antigens (Ag) and present them to T lymphocytes (i.e. T cells). Upon activation by Ag, the T cells proliferate and become effector cells. Effector function can be defined by the presence of cytokine production, cytotoxicity, or assistance ("help") of the B cell antibody response. Some of the activated T cells (and B cells) become memory cells, and are more easily activated by future encounters with the same Ag that activated the cells initially. The antibody produced by B cells binds Ag and forms complexes that consist of antibodies bound to different parts of an antigenic molecule. These complexes can be bound by macrophages, which can then degrade the antigen. Cytokines are produced by all types of cells of the immune system, especially macrophages and T cells. The term "regulation" encompasses a number of different effects that have been attributed to different cytokines: stimulation of cell growth and proliferation, augmentation of antibody production, suppression of proliferation and cytokine production, and induction of cell death to reduce the number of cells that have proliferated, since they are no longer needed after the antigen has been removed. In recent decades, it has become evident that cytokines can also regulate central nervous system (CNS) function, producing a range of neural, endocrine, and behavioral effects.

and which involves the immune system. Indeed, cutaneous indicators of inflammation (e.g., skin swelling and redness) are considered consequences of an immune response. Internal inflammation in bodily organs similarly relies on the recruitment and responsiveness of lymphocytes, monocytes, macrophages and other cellular components of the immune system.

Cytokines serve various effector functions, acting on cells by selectively binding to receptors on lymphocytes and macrophages, as well as non-immune cells, and altering their function (e.g., causing cells to divide or die, or allowing B cells to make more antibodies). All cells of the immune system secrete cytokines, although T lymphocytes, monocytes, and macrophages are the predominant source of these proteins (see Figure 7.1). Many cytokines are called interleukins (i.e. to reflect the observation that they act "between leukocytes," and are abbreviated to IL). For example, cytokines produced by T lymphocytes include interleukin-2 (IL-2), which promotes T cell mitosis and proliferation. Another prominent cytokine produced by T cells is interferon-gamma (IFNγ), which can aid in the elimination of infectious pathogens, and enhances antigen-presenting functions (see below). Other cytokines that are produced by macrophages include interleukin-1 (IL-1β), tumor necrosis factor (TNFα), and interleukin-6 (IL-6). These cytokines can be induced by LPS, and as such, are often referred to as *proinflammatory* cytokines; indeed, the administration of LPS, and other agents that stimulate the innate immune system, is referred to as an *inflammatory* challenge, by virtue of the induction and release of these cytokines. However, the same cytokines can also be produced by many other cell types of the immune system (e.g., IL-6 can be produced by macrophages and T cells). Therefore, this brief overview of cytokines and some of their functions, should serve to clarify the meaning of the term, "regulation," in Figure 7.1.

Most immune responses progress as a consequence of interactions between innate immune cells and lymphocytes. For example, macrophages, as a consequence of their phagocytic ability, can also present *antigens* (short peptide sequences derived from degraded pathogens) on their cell surface to T cells, and in this capacity is called an antigen-presenting cell (APC). Other APCs include dendritic cells and B lymphocytes (e.g., Figure 7.1 shows a dendritic cell presenting antigen). Lymphocytes, as the primary recipients of antigen serve the adaptive properties of immunity. They specifically recognize the "foreignness" of antigen and then through a process of clonal expansion generate a cohort of cells that will become memory lymphocytes capable of responding to the antigen in any future encounters. This is the basis of vaccination procedures against hepatitis, tetanus, and other deadly viruses, such as the seasonal influenza virus.

The term "antigen" (or Ag) was coined as an abbreviation of "*<u>anti</u>*body-*<u>gen</u>*erating." Therefore, any substance that can bind antibody is considered an antigen. With regard to T lymphocyte recognition of particular antigens, the term is restricted to a short peptide sequence that is derived from the breakdown of a larger protein molecule. Antigen-presenting cells, like macrophages, can perform this breakdown by enzymatic means, and then express the short antigenic peptides on their cell surface. Commonly, however, any protein molecule, virus, or cellular mixture (e.g., sheep red blood cells) may, as matter of convenience, be called an "antigen," if this molecule has the capability of stimulating T and B lymphocytes and generating an adaptive immune response. This more inclusive use of the term appears to have developed out of the practical need to communicate the nature of the immune response being investigated (adaptive vs. innate). Acquired or adaptive immunity, therefore, involves antigenic stimulation of lymphocytes (e.g., Figure 7.1 shows T lymphocytes responding to antigen presented by dendritic APCs). The antigens can be derived from toxins and other bacterial or viral proteins, and once the lymphocytes respond to the antigens, the *immunity* (or "protection") is a product of learning and memory by the responding lymphocytes. Memory is tested by re-exposing the lymphocytes to the antigen to which they had responded, and is reflected by a more rapid and increased response to that antigen (e.g., 10-fold more antibody than during the initial response). For these reasons, the initial exposure to antigen is referred to as a primary response, while reexposure to the antigen generates a secondary response (or even a tertiary response if there is a third antigenic reexposure).

When a lymphocyte responds to an antigen, it progresses through a series of recognizable but continuous phases. Initial binding and recognition of antigen by a lymphocyte is the *inductive* phase, in which intracellular processes are initiated to allow for progression into the *activation* phase. Once activated, lymphocytes divide, multiply (or proliferate), and then differentiate (i.e. change form and function). Differentiation serves to endow cells with effector functions (hence, this is referred to as the **effector** phase) that include the production and release of various soluble products, such as cytokines and antibodies. These soluble mediators promote the recruitment and expansion of more lymphocytes (and other types of cells), as well as the neutralization and elimination of antigen either through cytotoxic or antibody-mediated functions. See Figure 7.1, which shows a T cell in the enlarged state of being an effector cell (cytokine-producing and/or cytotoxic).

Lymphocytes are rarely stationary, and circulate throughout the body, although they do accumulate in well-defined and widely distributed organs called lymph nodes. In addition, there are small lymphoid nodules that traverse the small intestine, and the lung and upper respiratory tract contain depots of lymphocyte populations. These form the common mucosal immune system. The spleen, which is located adjacent to the liver and which is heavily vascularized, more directly samples the cellular and molecular contents of the circulatory system. It is the most commonly used lymphoid organ in experimental animal studies.

Because they mediate antigen-specific acquired immunity, lymphocytes are the preeminent adaptive cells of the immune system, with all other cells (e.g., monocytes/macrophages, dendritic cells, granulocytes) interacting with lymphocytes to either present particular antigens or to eliminate antigens in a nonspecific, innate manner. The B lymphocyte (or B cell) is derived from a common progenitor hematopoietic stem cell. It matures during fetal life in the liver and then in the bone marrow. The major function of B lymphocytes is the production of antibody, which in its molecular form is an immunoglobulin protein (abbreviated Ig), of which there are five major classes or isotypes: IgA, IgD, IgE, IgM, and IgG. Measurement of antibody, therefore, will involve identifying each of these different isotypes. The production by B cells of antibodies against an antigen is called the *humoral* immune response. In Figure 7.1, the B cell has achieved an effector state in which it is producing antibodies that bind the antigen that stimulated the B cell in the first place. Although the isotype of the antibody will be a mixture of different isotypes, during later phases of the primary immune response, and especially during the secondary response that follows reexposure to antigen, the major isotype will be IgG.

T lymphocytes (or T cells) are so-called because of their maturation in the thymus gland (located just above the heart). All T cells emigrating from the thymus express an antigen-recognizing receptor, which is referred to as the T cell receptor (TCR). The TCR of each T cell will recognize a specific antigenic peptide and initiate intracellular signals which will result in cell division (mitosis) and differentiation. However, T lymphocytes also differentially express on their cell surface molecules (CD4 and CD8) that are the basis of their segregation into two major functional subtypes. Hence, mature T cells are designated as either $CD4^+$ or $CD8^+$. The CD4 T cell helps or promotes antigen-specific B cell responses, and is called a T-helper cell (in Figure 7.1, the cytokine production of stimulated T cells aids the B cells in producing antibody); while CD8 T cells mediate cytotoxic responses against foreign cells or host cells infected with viruses, and are therefore called cytotoxic T cells (in Figure 7.1, the cytotoxicity is demonstrated by the lysed cell).

Finally, there is another class of cytotoxic lymphocyte (not shown in Figure 7.1), known as a large granular lymphocyte, which is also referred to as a natural killer (NK) cell. These cells spontaneously lyse (i.e. degrade or destroy) bacterial cells, virally-infected cells of the host, and tumor cells, and are considered to serve both innate and acquired immune functions.

Conditioning of the Immune System

Conditioned physiologic effects were the province of original Pavlovian experiments that included the now classic salivary responses, but had been extended to basic immune phenomena, such as phagocytosis. These early reports were not well recognized, nor were they conclusive, given the absence of adequate controls, as reported in a historical review of the early 20th century Soviet literature (Ader, 1981). Nonetheless, they provided an encouraging precedent for the more rigorous approach of Ader and Cohen (1975) who provided the seminal observations in the West for conditioned immunomodulatory effects. Indeed, the story of how this classic experiment was conceived deserves telling. As reported by Ader (1974), the hypothesis that the immune system might be capable of being conditioned was arrived at serendipitously. Rats conditioned in a taste aversion paradigm using an immunosuppressive drug, cyclophosphamide, were unexpectedly succumbing to illness and had increased mortality. The choice of cyclophosphamide as a UCS was made in ignorance of its immunosuppressive properties, but full knowledge of its powerful ability to produce a conditioned taste aversion (Wright, Foshee, & McCleary, 1971). Because animals that died had initially been given a larger volume of the conditioned stimulus (CS, saccharin solution) during the learning trial than the animals that did not die, it was hypothesized that some link between the magnitude of CS ingestion and the immunosuppressive properties of the drug had been formed and led to a conditioned immunosuppression (Ader, 1974). This hypothesis was tested and confirmed (Ader & Cohen, 1975).

In their experiment, Ader and Cohen (1975) presented rats with a novel saccharin-flavored solution (the CS), that was subsequently paired with an injection of the immunosuppressive drug, cyclophosphamide (the UCS). As expected, the pairing of saccharin and cyclophosphamide resulted in a conditioned taste aversion, whereby reexposure to the CS several days after the CS-UCS pairing resulted in a significant reduction in saccharin consumption. Most importantly, however, at the time of this CS presentation, animals were injected with sheep red blood cells (SRBC) to induce an immune response, and were sacrificed at various times (three or six days) afterward for measurement of the humoral antibody response to SRBC. The results revealed that the antibody titer of the conditioned animals was significantly reduced relative to the control groups (especially animals that received cyclophosphamide and water, instead of saccharin). The strength of these early experiments was the inclusion of a number of groups that controlled for the impact of the conditioning trial per se, as well as the residual immunosuppressive effects of the drug. Additional non-contingent pairings of CS/UCS and conditioned, but not CS reexposed, groups were also used. Therefore, reduced antibody levels for conditioned animals reexposed to the CS could not be due to anything other than the behavioral response to the CS.

Because this effect could only be attributed to the conditioned behavioral response (taste aversion), the observation was interpreted as a behaviorally conditioned immunosuppression. Moreover, the findings were quickly replicated using essentially the same experimental design and immunosuppressive drug (Rogers, Reich, Strom, & Carpenter, 1976; Wayner, Flannery, & Singer, 1978), and led to a growing interest in conditioned effects on the immune system. Experiments were conducted successfully in rats, mice, guinea pigs, and ultimately, humans; and the choice of CS ranged from gustatory stimuli to novel odors, auditory stimuli, contextual cues, and tactile stimulation (for reviews see Ader, 2003; Schedlowski & Pacheco-Lopez, 2010). In general, most studies supported the notion that the immune system could be conditioned.

In the early studies, cyclophosphamide was the most common UCS, although other immunopharmacologic or immunomodulatory agents were used. The list included cyclosporine, levamisole, methotrexate, and antilymphocyte serum (Ader & Cohen, 1993; Husband, King, & Brown, 1987; Kusnecov et al., 1983; Wirth et al., 2011). In addition, epinephrine has been used to condition increases in immune activity in human subjects (Buske-Kirschbaum, Kirschbaum, Stierle, Jabaij, & Hellhammer, 1994; Buske-Kirschbaum, Kirschbaum, Stierle, Lehnert, & Hellhammer, 1992), while in rats, opiates like morphine and heroin have been shown to produce conditioned immunosuppressive effects (Saurer, Ijames, Carrigan, & Lysle, 2008; Szczytkowski & Lysle, 2008). In all these studies, the direction of the conditioned immune response was in the same direction as the unconditioned response produced by the UCS. For example, the effect of opiates is to suppress the immune response, and this suppression was reenlisted when animals were exposed to the CS after the conditioning trial. These studies show that agents with endogenous receptor targets (viz., adrenergic and opioid receptors) can modify immune function, which can be linked in a learned manner to reenlist the immune effects of associated conditioned stimuli. The implications of such effects for drug addiction and how immune changes may be associated with cue-induced craving and drug-seeking, a well-documented phenomenon (Drummond, 2001), is an important area that needs closer investigation.

Conditioned Immunopharmacologic Effects and Stress

Over the years, there have been many demonstrations of conditioned effects on immune function. Conditioning has been shown to alter basic immune parameters like antigen-specific antibody production, T lymphocyte proliferation and cytokine production, natural killer cell activity and changes in immune cell numbers. This has been observed using both *in vitro* and *in vivo* (e.g., delayed-type hypersensitivity or DTH) measures of immune function (Ader, 2003). Moreover, the effects are not universally immunosuppressive, as conditioned enhancement of immune responses have been reported even when using an immunosuppressive drug (D. Bovbjerg, Cohen, & Ader, 1987). The latter is particularly important in light of initial criticism that the conditioned immunosuppressive effects were an epiphenomenon of stress-induced elevations of corticosterone.

The use of an aversive UCS can result in a conditioned behavioral effect that is emotional in nature. In the case of the conditioned taste aversion (CTA) paradigm, subjects display avoidance or aversion to the UCS presumably due to the threat of illness. Other aversive learning paradigms, such as shock-induced fear conditioning to contextual cues also result in immunosuppressive effects after CS reexposure in rats and mice (Lysle, Cunnick, & Maslonek, 1991; Shanks, Kusnecov, Pezzone, Berkun, & Rabin, 1997; Shurin, Kusnecov, Riechman, & Rabin, 1995; Zalcman, Richter, & Anisman, 1989). These studies suggested that once a CS becomes a stressor, its effects on the immune system may be due to stressor-activated neural and hormonal systems. This interpretation would be in contrast to the notion that immune changes that are part of the unconditioned response, become linked to the CS, and are then reenlisted when the animal is reexposed to the CS. Interestingly, the notion that a link between the CS and an immune change produced by an aversive non-pharmacologic stimulus serving as the UCS, such as electric shock , has not been demonstrated. For example, exposure to shock suppresses spleen cell proliferation to mitogenic stimulation (Kusnecov & Rabin, 1993), and this is prevented by the beta-adrenergic antagonist, propranolol (Cunnick, Lysle, Kucinski, & Rabin, 1990; Lysle et al., 1991). However, when propranolol was given to rats during a CS-UCS trial, a conditioned immunosuppression was still observed upon CS reexposure (Lysle et al., 1991). Therefore, conditioned fear effects on the immune system are unlikely to have evolved from direct interaction between the brain and immunomodulation by the shock UCS.

The likely inapplicability of the conditioned fear paradigm to explaining conditioned immunopharmacologic effects that suppress the immune system still does not answer the question of whether the CTA paradigm might similarly involve a stressor-like effect of the CS on immune function. Since treatment with cyclophosphamide can produce an elevation in corticosterone, an index of physiological stress, a gustatory CS previously paired with the drug should also show this elevation. This was, in fact, the case. Rats that previously had received saccharin followed by cyclophosphamide, showed a significant elevation in blood corticosterone when tested for taste aversion (Ader, 1976). Similar effects could be observed with lithium chloride (LiCl) as the UCS (Ader, 1976; Smotherman, Hennessy, & Levine, 1976). However, in spite of this conditioned elevation in corticosterone, a dissociation between the immunosuppressive effects of CS reexposure and corticosterone elevations has been observed (Kusnecov, Husband, & King, 1988; Roudebush & Bryant, 1991). Moreover, injection of LiCl or corticosterone does not suppress the antibody response (Ader, Cohen, & Grota, 1979), although CTA using LiCl can suppress delayed-type hypersensitivity, a measure of T cell mediated immune function, in mice (Kelley, Dantzer, Mormede, Salmon, & Aynaud, 1985). In addition, stressors have been shown to both suppress and enhance antigen-specific T cell and B cell-mediated immune responses (Kusnecov & Rabin, 1993; Zalcman et al., 1989). Consequently, it is likely that the historical struggle to establish conditioned immunomodulation as a phenomenon that is independent of stressor effects will remain unresolved. What is clear, however, is that stress as a unitary explanation for conditioning effects on immune function is not particularly useful, because acute and even repeated stressor exposure is not universally immunosuppressive, can actually be immunoenhancing, and in some cases, has no impact at all on certain immune parameters (Kusnecov & Rabin, 1994).

In spite of the evidence against the idea that conditioned stress fully accounts for behaviorally conditioned immunomodulation, evidence for an actual link between immune perturbation by the pharmacologic UCS (such as cyclophosphamide) and the CS has been elusive. A solution to this problem arose in literature on the neuromodulatory effects of immune responses, which is discussed next.

The Use of Antigen as a UCS

Behavioral conditioning of the immune system using an immunopharmacologic agent suggested that variations in immune status can serve as a UCS. Identifying the relevant stimuli that arise from the immune system after, say, cyclophosphamide injection, is difficult to isolate from the illness-inducing effects of the drug, which ostensibly arise from extra-immune effects, and affect illness-inducing neural pathways such as the vagus (Andrews et al., 1990). Consequently, alternative approaches are necessary to demonstrate that activation or change in the immune system could serve as a UCS, and represent the necessary signal that forms links between the neurally-processed CS and the immune system.

Fortunately, immunophysiological studies that began in the 1970s led the way to an understanding of how the immune system can alter neural and behavioral functions (Besedovsky & Rey, 2007). This early research showed that the immune response to various cellular and protein antigens altered CNS function, including increased neuronal firing rate, turnover of catecholamine neurotransmitters, and activation of the neuroendocrine system (Anisman, Zalcman, & Zacharko, 1993). Ultimately, while antibodies can modify behavior, cytokines, the soluble regulatory molecules of the immune system, have a significant impact on CNS function, reproducing many of the neuroendocrine and neurotransmitter effects of protein antigens. Cytokines also produce a range of behavioral changes known as sickness behaviors (e.g., anorexia, reduced social exploration, anxiety-like effects, lethargy/immobility; Dantzer, O'Connor, Freund, Johnson, & Kelley, 2008; Anisman, 2009). To the extent that antigens are able to stimulate lymphocytes and innate immune cells to produce cytokines, antigen challenge might serve as a UCS in conditioning studies of the immune system.

In the first test of this idea, Ader and colleagues set out to demonstrate that an antibody response to various antigens could actually be conditioned. In their study (Ader, Kelly, Moynihan, Grota, & Cohen, 1993), mice were exposed to a novel gustatory CS (viz., chocolate milk) in conjunction with exposure to low doses of a protein antigen (viz., keyhole limpet hemocyanin, KLH). The injections of antigen

(Ag) did not produce any overt behavioral effects nor any taste aversion. However, after a series of monthly pairings of the CS and Ag, exposure to the CS in conjunction with a suboptimal dose of Ag that normally would not elicit a significant elevation in antibody, produced a significant enhancement in the IgG and IgM isotypes of antibody specific to KLH (the Ag). The control groups (e.g., previously conditioned, but not given the CS on the test day) which also received the suboptimal dose of Ag, showed only marginal increases in antibody production (significantly lower than conditioned animals reexposed to the CS). As a result, the CS could be interpreted as providing a "boosting" effect on antibody levels. This use of antigen as a UCS has been replicated in other laboratories in both rats and mice, with different gustatory or contextual stimuli serving as the CS (Chen et al., 2004; Espinosa et al., 2004; Madden et al., 2001; Ramirez-Amaya & Bermudez-Rattoni, 1999).

Measures of antigen-specific cell mediated cytotoxicity (i.e. cellular lethality) are also subject to conditioning (Gorczynski, Macrae, & Kennedy, 1982). These studies go beyond the conditioned immunopharmacologic studies that have involved cyclophosphamide and cyclosporine, and support not only the notion of antigen-specific, immunologically-mediated actions on the brain, but the concept that such effects may engage an underlying cognitive process that subsequently impacts the immune system.

The mechanism by which the response to antigen results in CNS changes is not known at this time. It could include cellular proliferation, circulating antibody that breaches the blood-brain barrier or stimulates afferent neural processes (e.g., via the vagus), or elevations in the concentration of cytokines, which are known to act on the vagus, as well as to cross the blood-brain barrier (Dantzer, O'Connor, Freund, Johnson, & Kelley, 2008). While these mechanisms remain to be explored, it is difficult to detect cytokine elevations or cell proliferation in response to low doses of immunogenic, but benign, protein antigens. At the immune level, the responses to Ag in the foregoing experiments is modest, but nonetheless initiates sufficient neural changes for there to be some link with the neural processing of the CS. Indeed, one can envisage the opportunity to design studies in which vaccinations against various infectious hazards (e.g., influenza virus) might be aided by conditioning procedures. Most certainly responses to vaccinations in humans can be variable and psychosocial factors can influence the magnitude of the immune response to viral antigens in vaccines (Moynihan et al., 2004). However, there currently are no studies addressing whether a conditioning approach to vaccinations might serve to boost or augment the natural antibody response to specific antigens.

In addition to the use of specific protein antigens as UCSs, several studies have used bacterial toxins. These toxins have a more pronounced inflammatory response and a more dramatic impact on the CNS and behavior when compared to antigens like KLH. The most commonly tested toxin is lipopolysaccharide (LPS) (also referred to as endotoxin), which has the ability to stimulate macrophages and cause the release of the proinflammatory cytokines IL-1β, IL-6 and TNFα (Urbach-Ross & Kusnecov, 2007). These particular cytokines are perhaps the most potent modulators of CNS function and behavior. They have been shown to participate in the induction of sickness behavior (Dantzer et al., 2008), as well as modulate learning and memory (Cunningham & Sanderson, 2008; Dantzer et al., 2008; Yirmiya & Goshen, 2011).

It is notable that LPS, IL-1, and TNF have been used as UCSs in the generation of CTA (Bernstein, Taylor, & Bentson, 1991; Mormede, Palin, Kelley, Castanon, & Dantzer, 2004; Tazi, Dantzer, Crestani, & Le Moal, 1988). The behavioral avoidance that is observed when LPS is used to produce CTA is associated with its metabolic effects (e.g., changes in body temperature). Endotoxin (LPS) exposure can result in an initial reduction (hypothermia) and then increase (hyperthermia) in core body temperature. In rats, this effect occurs in response to CS reexposure seven days after a single pairing of saccharin solution and an injection of LPS (Bull, Brown, King, & Husband, 1991; Exton, Bull, King, & Husband, 1995).

In addition to temperature, endotoxin-induced changes in slow wave sleep have been conditioned (Exton et al., 1995). The development of TNFα tolerance to endotoxin has also been conditioned (Oberbeck, Kromm, Exton, Schade, & Schedlowski, 2003). The latter finding is particularly important, because the immune system develops a natural capacity to reduce cytokine output after repeated stimulation (Urbach-Ross & Kusnecov, 2007). In the case of repeated LPS exposure, this results in lower production of TNFα, which in high amounts can produce lethal shock. Therefore, the ability to condition reductions in TNFα production after LPS exposure can have potentially beneficial effects and prevent the onset of shock. Interestingly, in a recent study using mice, backward conditioning using LPS as a UCS and saccharin as a CS, also resulted in conditioned tolerance of TNFα production, in spite of an absence of taste aversion to the CS (Washio, Hayes, Hunter, & Pritchard, 2011).

Overall, studies using endotoxin point to a variety of different outcomes, metabolic and cytokine, that can be classically conditioned. Moreover, the use of other bacterial toxins, such as staphylococcal enteroxin B, derived from gram positive bacteria, has also been successful in producing conditioned taste aversions and a conditioned reenlistment of the T cell-stimulating effects of this protein antigen (Pacheco-Lopez et al., 2004).

Human studies designed to produce conditioned immune changes as a function of *antigenic* stimulation are rare, relative to the number of studies employing non-human animals. In an older study, explicit manipulation of cues was used to produce alterations in the cutaneous response to tuberculin injections (Smith & McDaniel, 1983). In this study, no drugs were actually administered, but the context, nurse participant, and vials from which the sensitizing antigens were extracted, may have served as CSs in conditioning trials. Subjects were administered antigen intradermally to elicit a hypersensitivity response characterized by redness (erythema) and hardening (induration) that could be measured. On each of five days, antigen was repeatedly given in one arm, while saline was always given to the opposite arm. Subjects always received the injection from a vial that was a constant shape and color (e.g., red). This color differed from the color of the other vial (e.g., green) that contained contents that went into the unresponsive arm which would not show any signs of a reaction. On day 6, the contents of the vials were switched and the previously non-reactive arm received antigen (but still from the green vial), while the previously reactive arm (the "antigen arm") received saline (still from the red vial).

Most subjects showed dramatically diminished erythema and induration to the antigen. One interpretation of the results was a conditioned diminution of the hypersensitivity response developed because the vial from which the injected substance had been removed was always associated with a non-reaction (Smith & McDaniel, 1983). What was interesting, however, was that the injection of saline from the vial that had always been associated with an immune reaction (i.e. the erythema and induration) did not result in an immunological reaction. This might have been predicted from the animal studies discussed earlier, in which antigen injection served as the UCS (Ader, Kelly, Moynihan, Grota, & Cohen, 1993). This outcome, however, is perhaps reasonable given that immune responses occur only to antigens. Indeed, in some of the animal work (e.g., Ader, Kelly, Moynihan, Grota, & Cohen , 1993), a CS associated with antigen exposure is more likely to reenlist immune reactivity (e.g., increase antibody production) only if a suboptimal dose of Ag is provided.

Nonetheless, the value of the Smith and McDaniel's (1983) observation is that it showed that human subjects can display conditioned suppression of immune changes when the UCS fails to be immunogenic. That is, when a CS is linked with an absence of immune reactivity, actual antigen may fail to induce an optimal immune response. This is more akin perhaps to the endotoxin-tolerance conditioning cited above. Interestingly, in a recent human study that involved injections of endotoxin and pairing of a novel gustatory CS, no reenlistment of cytokine production normally induced by LPS was produced by the CS, in spite of the development of a flavor aversion (Grigoleit et al., 2012).

Therapeutic Effects of Behaviorally Conditioned Immunomodulation

Given the large number of studies confirming that the immune system can be conditioned, it was natural to address the potential clinical applicability of this phenomenon. There are a number of disease states that are associated with immunological dysregulation, including autoimmune disease and cancer, as well as clinical interventions in which suppression of the immune system is needed (e.g., organ transplantation). Indeed, the clinical utility of conditioned immune effects was recognized quickly. For example, Ader and Cohen (1982) applied a conditioning protocol to the treatment of pathological symptoms of proteinuria (i.e. a condition in which there is an abnormal concentration of protein in the urine) in an animal model of systemic lupus erythematosus (SLE). In addition, they monitored mortality. The design of the study included one group of mice that was consistently given exposure to saccharin solution (the CS) that was always paired with cyclophosphamide (the UCS). This group was designated as the C100 group to reflect that they received the CS-UCS pairing 100% of the time. Another group received saccharin that was paired 50% of the time with cyclophosphamide and the remaining 50% of the time with a saline injection (C50 group). A third group was given exposure to saccharin and the same number of injections of cyclophosphamide as the C50 group, but these injections were not paired with saccharin (NC50 group). All these cyclophosphamide groups were compared to a no-treatment group, which showed the earliest onset of proteinuria, as well as early death.

As expected, delay in proteinuria and mortality was greatest in the C100 group, which received the maximal drug dosage. However, the most interesting observation was that the C50 group showed significantly later onset of proteinuria and mortality than the NC50 group. This occurred in spite of the same number of saccharin exposures and drug exposures, and suggested the influence of conditioned immunosuppressive effects in the C50 animals (Ader & Cohen, 1982). This would be consistent with other findings in mice that pairing of saccharin and cyclophosphamide suppresses T and B cell functions (Ader & Cohen, 1993). Therefore, conditioned suppressive immune effects were hypothesized to account for the therapeutic benefits in the SLE disease model (Ader & Cohen, 1982).

Such findings indicate that conditioning may improve the efficacy of immunotherapeutic drugs that to some extent are highly toxic and difficult to tolerate when given in frequent and high dosage amounts. Additional animal studies provided similar results. In one study, the autoimmune inflammatory condition of rheumatoid arthritis was attenuated by conditioning in rats (Klosterhalfen & Klosterhalfen, 1983). This latter study used cyclosporine, a drug frequently used to reduce inflammatory responses in patients with autoimmune disease.

Cyclosporine is also used to inhibit the T cell mediated immune response against organ transplants, allowing time for tolerance to develop and tissue transplants to be accepted by the recipient. Grochowicz et al. (1991) tested whether conditioned immunosuppressive effects might prolong the survival of organ transplants. They found that mice that received a mouse heart transplant, showed delayed rejection of transplanted cardiac tissue when they were reexposed twice to a saccharin solution CS that had previously been followed immediately by the UCS of a cyclosporine injection.

In another study of tissue transplantation (Gorczynski, 1990), mice received skin grafts from genetically dissimilar mice (referred to as allografts). Prior to grafting, mice had received several paired presentations of a saccharin solution CS and cyclophosphamide UCS. Once grafts were applied, mice were reexposed to the CS, but without any cyclophosphamide injections. Compared to control, non-conditioned mice that had prior unpaired drug exposure, conditioned mice reexposed to the CS retained their allografts for a longer period of time (Gorczynski, 1990). This finding, and the preceding studies, speak to a potentially powerful clinical influence provided by environmental stimuli that are explicitly associated with immunosuppressive drugs.

These findings are also consistent with a recent discussion of the significant presence of placebo effects that are potentially evident in most pharmacotherapeutic situations (Tausk, Ader, & Duffy Smith, 2013). It is now a federal requirement for clinical drug trials to include a placebo control (administration of substances that are inert or biologically inactive), because expectations of therapeutic efficacy may improve health and recovery from disease without any biological modifications brought about by the drug. There has been much written about placebo effects recently, both in terms of known neurobiological changes that occur during presentation of a placebo and in terms of whether placebo effects can be conditioned (Vits et al., 2011). If placebo effects can be conditioned, they might be useful for double-blind cross-over design treatments, in which a given drug regimen is gradually replaced by an inert substance (the placebo), or the converse, in which placebo is replaced by drug administration. To the extent that conditioned immunopharmacologic effects have been observed when initial drug administration is followed by exposure to the stimulus cues associated with drug treatment, this conditioned immunopharmacological effect could be capitalized on in clinical situations in a way similar to the previously mentioned studies in animals. That is, there is good scientific reason to suspect that introducing explicit conditioning strategies into immunotherapeutic settings may provide added benefits to the patient.

This reasoning was applied by Ader and colleagues (Ader et al., 2010) to patients suffering from psoriasis. This dermatological disease is particularly stressful and/or anxiogenic, associated with depression, and is mediated by a recognized inflammatory condition in the skin that results in skin ulcerations characterized by induration (hardening of the skin) and erythema (reddening). Topical administration of ointments containing steroid drug (e.g., corticosterone) is provided as a pharmacotherapy. As reported by Ader et al., incorporating unique color and odor cues that can serve as CSs may be helpful when treating this condition.

In their study, which they reported as being preliminary, a protocol was introduced similar to the Ader and Cohen (1982) study of animals with SLE (see above). Subjects were recruited into one of two cohorts in either California (studied at Stanford) or New York (studied at the University of Rochester). Each cohort was treated identically, and in each cohort, there were three distinct treatment groups. One group of patients received Standard Therapy in which consistent exposure was provided (twice daily for up to eight weeks) to a corticosteroid drug (Aristocort: 0.1% triamcinolone acetonide in aquaphor). In conditioning terms, this group received 100% pairing of the CS and UCS. Two remaining groups received 25–50% of the total drug exposure. The first of these (the Partial Reinforcement group) applied the uniquely fragrant and colored ointment for the same number of days as the Continuous Reinforcement group, but the drug was present in the ointment on only 25–50% of the occasions when ointment was applied. As a result, only the CS (without the drug) was applied on 50–75% of occasions. The final group (Dose Control group) controlled for the dosage amount that the Partial Reinforcement group received. That is, this group received the drug repeatedly, and this amounted to the same cumulative drug exposure as the Partial Reinforcement group.

No biological or immunological measures were taken, but severity of psoriasis was quantified clinically and found to differ among the groups. Consistent with the hypothesis of a conditioned pharmacotherapeutic effect , the Standard Therapy and Partial Reinforcement groups did not differ in psoriatic lesion severity for the cohort of subjects studied at the University of Rochester. However, the Dose Control group, which received the same amount of drug as the Partial Reinforcement group, showed greater severity of lesions than the other two groups. While this provided support for the possible contribution of a conditioning effect, the California cohort did not show these particular differences, neither supporting nor refuting the conditioning interpretation of the Rochester cohort. The data were reported as providing preliminary support for the utility of partial reinforcement procedures that conform to a learning model of drug reinforcement.

While valuable as a practical demonstration of the potential for conditioned pharmacotherapeutic effects, this recent study by Ader et al. (2010) only implies the possibility of a conditioned immunomodulatory effect. What renders it feasible for use in human clinical studies is that there have already been demonstrations of conditioning of the immune system in human subjects. Studies of behaviorally conditioned immunomodulation in human subjects have been rare, but they exist. As noted earlier, epinephrine was used as a UCS to condition an increase in natural killer (NK) cell activity (Buske-Kirschbaum et al., 1992). Historically, NK cells have been associated with tumor surveillance. In recent years, NK cells have been shown to take on an adapative phenotype (including formation of memory) and to be cytotoxic during viral infections and in response to tissue injury. Epinephrine unconditionally enhances the number and cytotoxic activity of NK cells (normally measured by incubating NK cells with tumor cells *in vitro*). Therefore, in their study, Buske-Kirschbaum et al. (1992), gave young human subjects paired presentations of a novel taste (a taste of sherbet) that was followed by a bolus intravenous infusion of epinephrine, which resulted in the unconditioned response of increased NK cell function in blood. Interestingly, some days later after the unconditioned response had subsided, reexposure of conditioned subjects to the CS (viz., sherbet) resulted in an enhanced blood NK cell activity when compared with the blood NK cell activity of conditioned subjects previously given epinephrine but not reexposed to the CS on the test day (Buske-Kirschbaum).

In a follow-up of this study (Buske-Kirschbaum et al., 1994), a compound stimulus (CS^+: consisting of a novel sherbet taste combined with white noise) was paired with epinephrine, while a second, and different compound stimulus (CS^-: also taste+noise) was non-contingently presented with epinephrine. In keeping with the earlier study, reexposure to the CS^+ led to a conditioned enhancement of NK cell activity, whereas CS^- was without influence on NK function.

The benefit of augmenting NK cell activity is to sustain optimal surveillance of the body for virally-infected, tumorigenic, and distressed or unwanted cells. Although knowledge about these conditioning studies has been around for some time, concerted efforts to apply them to the enhancement of cytotoxic cell functions in clinical situations have yet to be reported.

In more recent years, Schedlowski's group has demonstrated repeatedly that a conditioned alteration in measures of cellular immunity and cytokine production (e.g., interleukin 2 and interferon-gamma) can be produced when unique taste solutions are paired with administration of cyclosporine (Goebel et al., 2002; Wirth et al., 2011). Such studies provide potentially promising avenues for clinical studies.

Cancer and Conditioning. Conditioned anticipatory nausea and vomiting in cancer patients can arise due to the toxic chemotherapy and radiation used to eliminate malignant tumors (Roscoe, Morrow, Aapro, Molassiotis, & Olver, 2011). Development of this anticipatory nausea results from cancer patients forming associations between chemotherapy and hospital-related cues, including the nursing staff, building, rooms, consistent odors. Moreover, the physical presence of suspected conditioning cues is not necessary. Out-patients undergoing chemotherapy merely have to think or conjure up images of the clinical environment in order to trigger conditioned anticipatory nausea (Dadds, Bovbjerg, Redd, & Cutmore, 1997). During chemotherapy and radiation, the immune system of cancer patients is particularly vulnerable, and most likely suppressed (Pruitt, 2012). Although there have been investigations of the behavioral component, the conditioned nausea (Roscoe et al., 2011; Dadds et al., 1997), little evidence exists for immunological changes in response to these conditioned reactions.

In one early study, women with ovarian cancer who were undergoing chemotherapy every four weeks were recruited for testing of potential conditioned immune alterations (D. H. Bovbjerg et al., 1990). Measurement of behavior indicated that greater anxiety and nausea was evident during hospital stay. Immune assays were conducted on blood samples obtained approximately three to eight days prior to hospital arrival (sample 1), the night before each scheduled chemotherapy (sample 2), and followed by a blood sample just prior to drug infusion (sample 3). The results showed that NK cell function did not differ between baseline (sample 1) and pre-infusion (sample 2) assessments. However, mitogen-induced lymphocyte proliferation was significantly lower just prior to chemotherapy (sample 3), when compared with that obtained at home. This could not be accounted for by changes in blood lymphocyte numbers, as these did not differ between baseline and pre-infusion samples (Bovbjerg et al., 1990).

This latter study suggested that anticipatory nausea could result in functional changes in lymphocyte function. In contrast, another study of women with breast cancer measured anxiety and anticipatory nausea and observed no conditioning-related changes in mitogenic function of peripheral blood lymphocytes (Fredrikson, Furst, Lekander, Rotstein, & Blomgren, 1993). The discrepancy between the two studies may have been due to the Frederickson et al. study providing more aggressive chemotherapeutic treatment, and most importantly, administration of sedatives to 80% of patients, as part of routine treatment for anxiety and psychological distress, during their hospital visit. This can be an important issue, given that psychopharmacologic drugs, such as anxiolytics, can modify immune function (Miyawaki et al., 2012; Roquilly, Josien, & Asehnoune, 2011).

These studies involved opportunistic sampling of blood during ongoing patient care and treatment. A more experimental protocol was instituted by Bovbjerg and colleagues in breast cancer patients, who were given a novel gustatory stimulus (a distinctive beverage) that was paired with chemotherapy (D. H. Bovbjerg et al., 1992). Subsequent to presentation of the gustatory CS, reexposure to the CS was provided in a separate context unrelated to treatment. The results showed that pairing of the CS with chemotherapy produced conditioned nausea when patients were reintroduced to the beverage (D. H. Bovbjerg et al., 1992). Although no immune measures were taken, their design offers several advantages that might be used to determine the degree to which well-controlled conditioned effects occur in cancer patients, and how they might be avoided if treatment involved suppression of critical immune mediators. Blood draws and CS reexposures can be carried out remotely from the hospital setting, and subjects could be assigned to different treatment groups that can be given the CS, denied the CS, or provided with a different gustatory stimulus never associated with the hospital and chemotherapy. No such studies have been carried out. However, efforts to minimize the development of conditioned anticipatory nausea have been ongoing (Roscoe et al., 2011).

Conclusion

The current chapter selectively highlighted evidence for conditioned modulation of immune function. The notion of conditioning the immune system was first conceived when Pavlov demonstrated the physiological sequelae of classical conditioning. This idea was revived by the conditioned taste aversion studies first published by Ader and

Cohen (1975). Better methodology and more knowledge about the immune system in the modern era has firmly established the existence of conditioning effects on immune function. In some cases, studies have provided evidence that conditioned immune responses can be incorporated into pharmacotherapeutic settings. However, this particular movement has been slow, and has as yet, failed to make the impact that it should have given the enormous evidence for placebo effects, as well as the existence of quite sophisticated and real communication between the brain and the immune system. Future studies, thoughtfully designed, and with the interests of the patient in mind, may one day alter this situation and produce a better and more effective therapeutic approach to the treatment of immune-related conditions.

Dedication

In memory of, and recognition for, the achievements of Robert Ader (1932–2011) Professor of Psychiatry, University of Rochester, NY

References

Ader, R. (1974). Letter: Behaviorially conditioned immunosuppression. *Psychosomatic Medicine, 36*, 183–184.

Ader, R. (1976). Conditioned adrenocortical steroid elevations in the rat. *Journal of Comparative Physiological Psychology, 90*, 1156–1163.

Ader, R. (1981). A historical account of conditioned immunobiologic responses. In R. Ader (Ed.), *Psychoneuroimmunology* (pp. 321–352). New York: Academic Press.

Ader, R. (2003). Conditioned immunomodulation: Research needs and directions. *Brain Behavioral and Immunity, 17*, S51–57.

Ader, R., & Cohen, N. (1975). Behaviorally conditioned immunosuppression. *Psychosomatic Medicine, 37*, 333–340.

Ader, R., & Cohen, N. (1982). Behaviorally conditioned immunosuppression and murine systemic lupus erythematosus. *Science, 215*, 1534–1536.

Ader, R., & Cohen, N. (1993). Psychoneuroimmunology: conditioning and stress. *Annual Review Psychology, 44*, 53–85. doi: 10.1146/annurev.ps.44.020193.000413.

Ader, R., Cohen, N., & Grota, L. J. (1979). Adrenal involvement in conditioned immunosuppression. *International Journal Immunopharmacology, 1*, 141–145.

Ader, R., Kelly, K., Moynihan, J. A., Grota, L. J., & Cohen, N. (1993). Conditioned enhancement of antibody production using antigen as the unconditioned stimulus. *Brain Behavioral Immunology, 7*, 334–343. doi: 10.1006/brbi.1993.1033.

Ader, R., Mercurio, M. G., Walton, J., James, D., Davis, M., Ojha, V., & Fiorentino, D. (2010). Conditioned pharmacotherapeutic effects: A preliminary study. *Psychosomatic Medicine, 72*, 192–197. doi: 10.1097/PSY.0b013e3181cbd38b.

Andrews, P. L., Davis, C. J., Bingham, S., Davidson, H. I., Hawthorn, J., & Maskell, L. (1990). The abdominal visceral innervation and the emetic reflex: Pathways, pharmacology, and plasticity. *Canadian Journal of Physiological Pharmacology, 68*, 325–345.

Anisman, H. (2009). Cascading effects of stressors and inflammatory immune system activation: Implications for major depressive disorder. *Journal of Psychiatry & Neuroscience, 34*, 4–20.

Anisman, H., Zalcman, S., & Zacharko, R. M. (1993). The impact of stressors on immune and central neurotransmitter activity: Bidirectional communication. *Review of Neuroscience, 4,* 147–180.

Bernstein, I. L., Taylor, E. M., & Bentson, K. L. (1991). TNF-induced anorexia and learned food aversions are attenuated by area postrema lesions. *American Journal of Physiology, 260,* R906–910.

Besedovsky, H. O., & Rey, A. D. (2007). Physiology of psychoneuroimmunology: A personal view. *Brain Behavioral Immunology, 21,* 34–44. doi: 10.1016/j.bbi.2006.09.008.

Bovbjerg, D., Cohen, N., & Ader, R. (1987). Behaviorally conditioned enhancement of delayed-type hypersensitivity in the mouse. *Brain Behavioral Immunology, 1,* 64–71.

Bovbjerg, D. H., Redd, W. H., Jacobsen, P. B., Manne, S. L., Taylor, K. L., & Surbone, A., et al. (1992). An experimental analysis of classically conditioned nausea during cancer chemotherapy. *Psychosomatic Medicine, 54,* 623–637.

Bovbjerg, D. H., Redd, W. H., Maier, L. A., Holland, J. C., Lesko, L. M., Niedzwiecki, D., & Hakes, T. B. et al. (1990). Anticipatory immune suppression and nausea in women receiving cyclic chemotherapy for ovarian cancer. *Journal of Consulting Clinical Psychology, 58,* 153–157.

Bull, D. F., Brown, R., King, M. G., & Husband, A. J. (1991). Modulation of body temperature through taste aversion conditioning. *Physiological Behavior, 49,* 1229–1233.

Buske-Kirschbaum, A., Kirschbaum, C., Stierle, H., Jabaij, L., & Hellhammer, D. (1994). Conditioned manipulation of natural killer (NK) cells in humans using a discriminative learning protocol. *Biological Psychology, 38,* 143–155.

Buske-Kirschbaum, A., Kirschbaum, C., Stierle, H., Lehnert, H., & Hellhammer, D. (1992). Conditioned increase of natural killer cell activity (NKCA) in humans. *Psychosomatic Medicine, 54,* 123–132.

Chen, J., Lin, W., Wang, W., Shao, F., Yang, J., Wang, B., & Ju, G. (2004). Enhancement of antibody production and expression of c-Fos in the insular cortex in response to a conditioned stimulus after a single-trial learning paradigm. *Behavior Brain Researc, 154,* 557–565. doi: 10.1016/j.bbr.2004.03.024.

Cunnick, J. E., Lysle, D. T., Kucinski, B. J., & Rabin, B. S. (1990). Evidence that shock-induced immune suppression is mediated by adrenal hormones and peripheral beta-adrenergic receptors. *Pharmacological Biochemical Behavior, 36,* 645–651.

Cunningham, C., & Sanderson, D. J. (2008). Malaise in the water maze: Untangling the effects of LPS and IL-1beta on learning and memory. *Brain Behavio Immunology, 22,* 1117–1127. doi: 10.1016/j.bbi.2008.05.007.

Dadds, M. R., Bovbjerg, D. H., Redd, W. H., & Cutmore, T. R. (1997). Imagery in human classical conditioning. *Psychological Bulletin, 122,* 89–103.

Dantzer, R., O'Connor, J. C., Freund, G. G., Johnson, R. W., & Kelley, K. W. (2008). From inflammation to sickness and depression: When the immune system subjugates the brain. *Nat Rev Neurosci, 9,* 46–56. doi: 10.1038/nrn2297.

Drummond, D. C. (2001). Theories of drug craving, ancient and modern. *Addiction, 96,* 33–46. doi: 10.1080/09652140020016941.

Espinosa, E., Calderas, T., Flores-Mucino, O., Perez-Garcia, G., Vazquez-Camacho, A. C., & Bermudez-Rattoni, F. (2004). Enhancement of antibody response by one-trial conditioning: Contrasting results using different antigens. *Brain, Behavior, and Immunity, 18,* 76–80.

Exton, M. S., Bull, D. F., King, M. G., & Husband, A. J. (1995). Modification of body temperature and sleep state using behavioral conditioning. *Physiological Behavior, 57,* 723–729.

Fredrikson, M., Furst, C. J., Lekander, M., Rotstein, S., & Blomgren, H. (1993). Trait anxiety and anticipatory immune reactions in women receiving adjuvant chemotherapy for breast cancer. *Brain, Behavior, and Immunity, 7*, 79–90. doi: 10.1006/brbi.1993.1008.

Goebel, M. U., Trebst, A. E., Steiner, J., Xie, Y. F., Exton, M. S., Frede, S., & Schedlowski, M. (2002). Behavioral conditioning of immunosuppression is possible in humans. *FASEB Journal, 16*, 1869–1873. doi: 10.1096/fj.02-0389com.

Gorczynski, R. M. (1990). Conditioned enhancement of skin allografts in mice. *Brain, Behavior, and Immunity, 4*, 85–92.

Gorczynski, R. M., Macrae, S., & Kennedy, M. (1982). Conditioned immune response associated with allogeneic skin grafts in mice. *Journal of Immunology, 129*, 704–709.

Grigoleit, J. S., Kullmann, J. S., Winkelhaus, A., Engler, H., Wegner, A., Hammes, F., & Schedlowski, M. (2012). Single-trial conditioning in a human taste-endotoxin paradigm induces conditioned odor aversion but not cytokine responses. *Brain, Behavior, and Immunity, 26*, 234238. doi: 10.1016/j.bbi.2011.09.001.

Grochowicz, P. M., Schedlowski, M., Husband, A. J., King, M. G., Hibberd, A. D., & Bowen, K. M. (1991). Behavioral conditioning prolongs heart allograft survival in rats. *Brain, Behavior, and Immunity, 5*, 349–356.

Husband, A. J., King, M. G., & Brown, R. (1987). Behaviourally conditioned modification of T cell subset ratios in rats. *Immunology Letters, 14*, 91–94.

Kelley, K. W., Dantzer, R., Mormede, P., Salmon, H., & Aynaud, J. M. (1985). Conditioned taste aversion suppresses induction of delayed-type hypersensitivity immune reactions. *Physiological Behavior, 34*, 189–193.

Klosterhalfen, W., & Klosterhalfen, S. (1983). Pavlovian conditioning of immunosuppression modifies adjuvant arthritis in rats. *Behavioral Neuroscience, 97*, 663–666.

Kusnecov, A. W., Husband, A. J., & King, M. G. (1988). Behaviorally conditioned suppression of mitogen-induced proliferation and immunoglobulin production: Effect of time span between conditioning and reexposure to the conditioning stimulus. *Brain, Behavior, and Immunity, 2*, 198–211.

Kusnecov, A. W., & Rabin, B. S. (1993). Inescapable footshock exposure differentially alters antigen- and mitogen-stimulated spleen cell proliferation in rats. *Journal of Neuroimmunology, 44*, 33–42.

Kusnecov, A. W., & Rabin, B. S. (1994). Stressor-induced alterations of immune function: Mechanisms and issues. *International Archives Allergy Immunology, 105*, 107–121.

Kusnecov, A. W., Sivyer, M., King, M. G., Husband, A. J., Cripps, A. W., & Clancy, R. L. (1983). Behaviorally conditioned suppression of the immune response by antilymphocyte serum. *Journal of Immunology, 130*, 2117–2120.

Lysle, D. T., Cunnick, J. E., & Maslonek, K. A. (1991). Pharmacological manipulation of immune alterations induced by an aversive conditioned stimulus: Evidence for a beta-adrenergic receptor-mediated Pavlovian conditioning process. *Behavioral Neuroscience, 105*, 443–449.

Madden, K. S., Boehm, G. W., Lee, S. C., Grota, L. J., Cohen, N., & Ader, R. (2001). One-trial conditioning of the antibody response to hen egg lysozyme in rats. *Journal of Neuroimmunology, 113*, 236–239.

Miyawaki, T., Kohjitani, A., Maeda, S., Higuchi, H., Arai, Y., Tomoyasu, Y., & Shimada, M. (2012). Combination of midazolam and a cyclooxygenase-2 inhibitor inhibits lipopolysaccharide-induced interleukin-6 production in human peripheral blood mononuclear cells. *Immunopharmacology and Immunotoxicology, 34*, 79–83. doi: 10.3109/08923973.2011.577783.

Mormede, C., Palin, K., Kelley, K. W., Castanon, N., & Dantzer, R. (2004). Conditioned taste aversion with lipopolysaccharide and peptidoglycan does not activate cytokine gene expression in the spleen and hypothalamus of mice. *Brain Behavior and Immunity, 18*, 186–200. doi: 10.1016/s0889-1591(03)00133-8.

Moynihan, J. A., Larson, M. R., Treanor, J., Duberstein, P. R., Power, A., Shore, B., & Ader, R. (2004). Psychosocial factors and the response to influenza vaccination in older adults. *Psychosomatic Medicine, 66*, 950–953. doi: 10.1097/01.psy.0000140001.49208.2d.

Oberbeck, R., Kromm, A., Exton, M. S., Schade, U., & Schedlowski, M. (2003). Pavlovian conditioning of endotoxin-tolerance in rats. *Brain Behavior and Immunity, 17*, 20–27.

Pacheco-Lopez, G., Niemi, M. B., Kou, W., Harting, M., Del Rey, A., Besedovsky, H. O., & Schedlowski, M. (2004). Behavioural endocrine immune-conditioned response is induced by taste and superantigen pairing. *Neuroscience, 129*, 555–562. doi: 10.1016/j.neuroscience.2004.08.033.

Pruitt, A. A. (2012). CNS infections in patients with cancer. *Continuum (Minneapolis Minnesota), 18*, 384–405. doi: 10.1212/01.CON.0000413665.80915.c4.

Ramirez-Amaya, V., & Bermudez-Rattoni, F. (1999). Conditioned enhancement of antibody production is disrupted by insular cortex and amygdala but not hippocampal lesions. *Brain, Behavior, and Immunity, 13*, 46–60. doi: 10.1006/brbi.1998.0547.

Rogers, M. P., Reich, P., Strom, T. B., & Carpenter, C. B. (1976). Behaviorally conditioned immunosuppression: Replication of a recent study. *Psychosomatic Medicine, 38*, 447–451.

Roquilly, A., Josien, R., & Asehnoune, K. (2011). Midazolam impairs immune functions: It's time to take care of dendritic cells. *Anesthesiology, 114*, 237–238. doi: 10.1097/ALN.0b013e3182070ee6.

Roscoe, J. A., Morrow, G. R., Aapro, M. S., Molassiotis, A., & Olver, I. (2011). Anticipatory nausea and vomiting. *Support Care Cancer, 19*, 1533–1538. doi: 10.1007/s00520-010-0980-0.

Roudebush, R. E., & Bryant, H. U. (1991). Conditioned immunosuppression of a murine delayed-type hypersensitivity response: Dissociation from corticosterone elevation. *Brain Behavior, and Immunity, 5*, 308–317.

Saurer, T. B., Ijames, S. G., Carrigan, K. A., & Lysle, D. T. (2008). Neuroimmune mechanisms of opioid-mediated conditioned immunomodulation. *Brain, Behavior, and Immunity, 22*, 89–97. doi: 10.1016/j.bbi.2007.06.009.

Schedlowski, M., & Pacheco-Lopez, G. (2010). The learned immune response: Pavlov and beyond. *Brain, Behavior, and Immunity, 24*, 176–185. doi: 10.1016/j.bbi.2009.08.007.

Shanks, N., Kusnecov, A., Pezzone, M., Berkun, J., & Rabin, B. S. (1997). Lactation alters the effects of conditioned stress on immune function. *American Journal of Physiology, 272*, R16–25.

Shurin, M. R., Kusnecov, A. W., Riechman, S. E., & Rabin, B. S. (1995). Effect of a conditioned aversive stimulus on the immune response in three strains of rats. *Psychoneuroendocrinology, 20*, 837–849.

Smith, G. R. Jr., & McDaniel, S. M. (1983). Psychologically mediated effect on the delayed hypersensitivity reaction to tuberculin in humans. *Psychosomatic Medicine, 45*, 65–70.

Smotherman, W. P., Hennessy, J. W., & Levine, S. (1976). Plasma corticosterone levels as an index of the strength of illness induced taste aversions. *Physiological Behavior, 17*, 903–908.

Szczytkowski, J. L., & Lysle, D. T. (2008). Conditioned effects of heroin on proinflammatory mediators require the basolateral amygdala. *European Journal of Neuroscience, 28*, 1867–1876. doi: 10.1111/j.1460-9568.2008.06472.x.

Tausk, F., Ader, R., & Duffy Smith, N. (2013). The placebo effect: Why we should care? *Clinical Dermatology, 31*, 86–91. doi: 10.1016/j.clindermatol.2011.11.012.

Tazi, A., Dantzer, R., Crestani, F., & Le Moal, M. (1988). Interleukin-1 induces conditioned taste aversion in rats: A possible explanation for its pituitary-adrenal stimulating activity. *Brain Research*, *473*, 369–371.

Urbach-Ross, D., & Kusnecov, A. W. (2007). Effects of acute and repeated exposure to lipopolysaccharide on cytokine and corticosterone production during remyelination. *Brain Behavior and Immunity*, *21*, 962–974. doi: 10.1016/j.bbi.2007.03.010.

Vits, S., Cesko, E., Enck, P., Hillen, U., Schadendorf, D., & Schedlowski, M. (2011). Behavioural conditioning as the mediator of placebo responses in the immune system. *Philosophical Tranactions of the Royal Society London Bulletin of Biological Science*, *366*, 1799–1807. doi: 10.1098/rstb.2010.0392.

Washio, Y., Hayes, L. J., Hunter, K. W., & Pritchard, J. K. (2011). Backward conditioning of tumor necrosis factor-alpha in a single trial: Changing intervals between exposures to lipopolysaccharide and saccharin taste. *Physiological Behavior*, *102*, 239–244. doi: 10.1016/j.physbeh.2010.11.010.

Wayner, E. A., Flannery, G. R., & Singer, G. (1978). Effects of taste aversion conditioning on the primary antibody response to sheep red blood cells and Brucella abortus in the albino rat. *Physiology & Behavior*, *21*, 995–1000.

Wirth, T., Ober, K., Prager, G., Vogelsang, M., Benson, S., Witzke, O., & Schedlowski, M. (2011). Repeated recall of learned immunosuppression: Evidence from rats and men. *Brain, Behavior, and Immunity*, *25*, 1444–1451. doi: 10.1016/j.bbi.2011.05.011.

Wright, W. E., Foshee, D. P., & McCleary, G. E. (1971). Comparison of taste aversion with various delays and cyclophosphamide dose levels. *Psychonomic Science*, *22*, 55–56.

Yirmiya, R., & Goshen, I. (2011). Immune modulation of learning, memory, neural plasticity and neurogenesis. *Brain Behavior, and Immunity*, *25*, 181–213. doi: 10.1016/j.bbi.2010.10.015.

Zalcman, S., Richter, M., & Anisman, H. (1989). Alterations of immune functioning following exposure to stressor-related cues. *Brain Behavior, and Immunity*, *3*, 99–109.

Part III
Basic Operant Conditioning

8

Basic Principles of Operant Conditioning

Eric S. Murphy and Gwen J. Lupfer

Operant conditioning is a form of learning in which the frequency of a behavior is controlled by its consequences (Skinner, 1953). The term *operant* is the combination of two common terms: operate and environment. Thus, the term operant refers to a special class of behavior that operates on the environment to produce consequences. Consequences, such as reinforcers, increase the frequency of behavior. Punishers decrease the frequency of behavior.

This chapter outlines the fundamental principles of operant conditioning and the primary methods used to study it. It should be viewed as an introduction and as a reference tool for understanding the chapters that follow. It is not a comprehensive review of basic principles. Subsequent chapters in this volume will expand on the basic ideas presented here.

A Brief History

The study of operant conditioning was pioneered by B. F. Skinner. In 1938, he published the *Behavior of organisms*, an early account of the effects of antecedents and consequences on nonhuman operant behavior. In this book, Skinner used a natural science approach to discover fundamental behavioral principles. His discoveries inspired the ground-breaking textbook *Principles of psychology* (Keller & Schoenfeld, 1950) and led to the founding of the *Journal of the Experimental Analysis of Behavior* (*JEAB*), the flagship outlet for basic operant research, in 1958. As the field grew, applications of operant conditioning became an important research focus (e.g., Aylion & Michael, 1959) and the *Journal of Applied Behavior Analysis* was founded in 1968 to publish applications of operant conditioning to problems of social importance

The Wiley Blackwell Handbook of Operant and Classical Conditioning, First Edition.
Edited by Frances K. McSweeney and Eric S. Murphy.

(Baer, Wolf, & Risley, 1968). In 1974, the Association for Behavior Analysis International was established as the leading professional organization for researchers and practitioners of operant conditioning. More recently, the Behavior Analyst Certification Board was established to provide professional qualifications for applied behavior analysts (Shook & Favell, 2008). Many universities have, or are currently developing curricula, that lead to these credentials.

Conceptual Foundations of Behavior Analysis

A New Goal for Psychology

Skinner (1938, 1953) argued that the goal of psychology was the prediction and control of behavior. In formulating this goal, he dismissed the hypothesis as a critical feature of scientific inquiry. Instead, behavior analysis is best characterized as an inductive approach because it gives prominence to the data rather than to theory. As Chiesa (1994) noted, psychology usually begins with a theory and then develops an experiment to test the theory. Skinner (1950) argued against this method of inquiry because theories are eventually discarded and by consequence, so are the data that were collected to test the theory. Instead, Skinner suggested that experiments should be driven by the results of past experiments. After many data have been collected, regularities should emerge. These regularities may lead to formal statements about important environmental variables and their effects on behavior. A formal statement, regardless if it is proposed mathematically or using precise language, should lead to the prediction and control of behavior in new situations.

Skinner (1987, 1990) ardently argued that psychology should be the science of behavior, and behavior only. He defined behavior as anything that an organism does (Skinner, 1938, p. 6). Skinner's definition transcends more traditional ways of viewing behavior as a discrete, overt phenomenon. That is, Skinner's definition also includes events within the organism, such as "thinking" (Skinner, 1953, 1974) and language (see Palmer, this volume; Skinner, 1957). Furthermore, Skinner argued that behavior should be at the forefront of inquiry rather than as a symptom of events taking place at some other level, or on some other dimension. These other events and dimensions are hypothetical constructs that often substitute for an explanation of the behavior that they are said to explain (Skinner, 1977). The problem with using hypothetical constructs as causes of behavior is that these hypothetical constructs need to be explained. Therefore, they complicate an adequate conception of behavior, rather than clarifying it. Skinner called these types of explanations "explanatory fictions." Skinner's definition of psychology circumvents this problem by arguing that internal processes are part of what an organism does and therefore, are dependent variables in their own right (i.e., not a cause, but a dimension of the organism's behavior).

By adopting this assumption, behavior analysis makes behavior amenable to scientific inquiry and therefore, assumes that principles of behavior will be discovered if appropriate methods are adopted. This assumption is particularly relevant to the modification of problem behaviors. For example, an understanding of environment-behavior relations will yield techniques for modification of behavior by changing the controlling variables.

Measurement of Behavior

Because Skinner's interest was in psychology as an experimental science, he argued that it should search for the functional relationships between controlling variables and behavior.

Functional relations are those relations that occur when a change in an independent variable results in a corresponding change in the dependent variable. The process of experimentation that leads to the identification of functional relations is called a functional analysis. The results of these functional analyses reveal the controlling variables of behavior and therefore, allow for the prediction and control of that behavior. To aid accurate observations, operational definitions are used to specify the behavior (e.g., Skinner, 1945). Operational definitions specify the operations used to produce the phenomenon. For example, an operational definition of "hunger" may stipulate that a rat was food deprived for 23 hours.

In an early demonstration of a functional analysis, Skinner (1938) systematically changed the interval between food reinforcers from 3 to 9 minutes and measured the effect on the rate of lever pressing using four rats. He noted that rates of responding systematically decreased as the interval between reinforcers increased. In doing this careful functional analysis, Skinner discovered a principle of operant conditioning: Rate of reinforcement is a key variable in controlling the rate of a response.

Single-Subject Research Designs

Because the goal of behavior analysis is the prediction and control of behavior at the individual level, behavior analysts often employ single-subject experimental designs rather than group designs (e.g., Sidman, 1960). At the most basic level, a single subject is exposed to a baseline and treatment condition (Johnston & Pennypacker, 2008). The baseline condition is the period of the experiment without the treatment. The treatment condition occurs when the independent variable is introduced. A common single-subject research design is the reversal or ABA design. During baseline, the behavior is observed for several sessions until stable responding is observed (i.e., very little fluctuation in responding between sessions). Next, the treatment condition is introduced until stability is reached. Finally, the original baseline condition is reinstituted. If the behavior changes during the treatment condition and returns to its original baseline level during the baseline reversal, the results provide strong evidence that the independent variable produced the change. That is, it is unlikely that other events coincided with the replication of the baseline condition. For example, Hall, Lund, and Jackson (1968) studied the effects of reinforcement on the studying of elementary school children. During baseline conditions, studying was ignored. During the treatment conditions, studying was reinforced by contingent teacher attention. Figure 8.1 shows the results from one of Hall et al.'s participants. In the first baseline condition, the participant studied in approximately 25% of the intervals. During the treatment conditions, the percentage of studying intervals increased to 75%. Hall et al.'s results rule out alternative explanations because studying decreased and increased appropriately with each replication of the conditions.

The multiple-baseline is a second, frequently-used, experimental design. As the reversal design, there is a baseline and treatment condition; however, the treatments

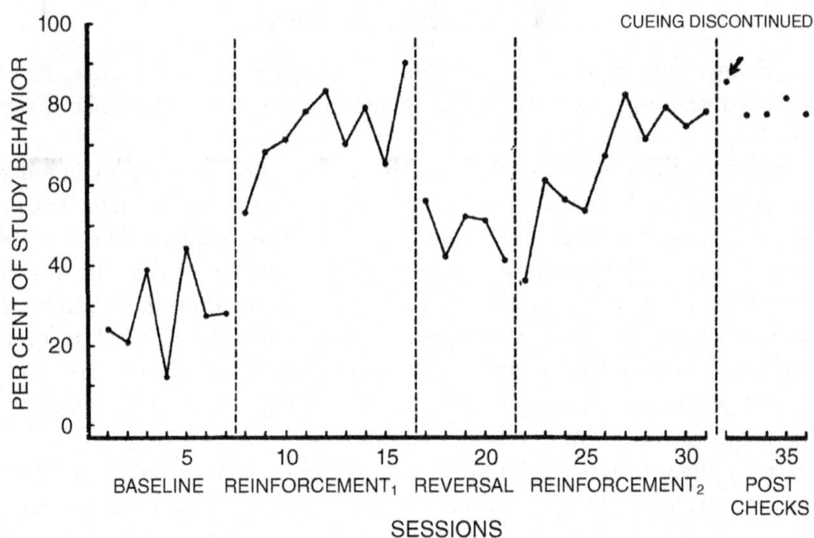

Figure 8.1 Percentage of intervals in which studying occurred in one participant. In the baseline conditions, studying was ignored. In the reinforcement conditions, studying was contingently reinforced by the teacher. From "Effects of teacher attention on study behavior," by R. V. Hall, D. Lund, and D. Jackson (1968), *Journal of Applied Behavior Analysis, 1*, p. 3. Copyright 1968 by the Society for the Experimental Analysis of Behavior, Inc. Reprinted with permission.

are introduced at different times for different individuals or behaviors (Miller, 2006). The multiple-baseline design is used when the behavior is not reversible or when it is not ethically feasible to do a reversal. Like the reversal design, the multiple-baseline design rules out alternative explanations for the change in behavior because the independent variable was introduced at different times for different individuals or behaviors. If each behavior (or each individual's behavior) changes when the treatment is introduced, then it is likely that the independent variable was responsible for the change.

A third experimental design assesses the effects of several levels of the independent variable (e.g., several rates of reinforcement) on an individual's behavior (Kazdin, 2011). Although there are many variations of this multiple-treatment design, each level of the independent variable is studied until stable responding is observed. The multiple-treatment design can be used with or without an initial baseline, and the order of treatment conditions may be systematic (e.g., ABCDE) or random (e.g., DCEAB).

Summary

Behavior analysis has several features that make it distinct from other areas of psychology. Its goals, such as the prediction and control of behavior, separate its research strategies from the hypothetico-deductive strategies of many other areas of psychology. Its subject matter is behavior in its own right, not as a symptom of an internal construct. Methodologically, behavior analysis is the search for functional relations between the environment and behavior, not for relationships between hypothetical constructs and overt behavior. Finally, behavior analysis assumes that behavior is a lawful subject and therefore, amenable to scientific inquiry.

Reinforcement and Punishment

There are four types of consequences in operant conditioning. These consequences can be placed into two distinct categories: reinforcement and punishment.

Reinforcement

Reinforcement refers to a procedure that increases the rate of a response. There are two types of reinforcement: positive and negative.

Positive Reinforcement. Positive reinforcement is, perhaps, the most familiar operant conditioning procedure because it delivers what lay people call a "reward." For a rewarding stimulus to be called a "reinforcer," however, it must follow a behavior and increase the frequency of that behavior (Miller, 2006). If both requirements are not met, the stimulus is not a positive reinforcer. A rat, for example, may be given a food pellet after each lever press and the rate of lever pressing may increase. The food pellet is said to serve as a positive reinforcer because it follows an instance of behavior and increases the rate of that behavior.

In applied settings, praise may be used as a positive reinforcer to increase the frequency of target behaviors in individuals with disabilities (e.g., Dozier, Iwata, Thomason-Sassi, Worsdell, & Wilson, 2012). In the real world, positive reinforcers include money, social attention, and the opportunity to engage in preferred activities.[1]

Negative Reinforcement. Like positive reinforcement, negative reinforcement procedures increase the frequency of a behavior, but the response removes or prevents the presentation of a stimulus. In order for a procedure to qualify as negative reinforcement, a stimulus must be terminated or prevented by a response and that termination or prevention must increase the frequency of the response (Miller, 2006).

Researchers have identified two types of negative reinforcement procedures. If the stimulus is terminated by the response, the procedure is called escape. If the stimulus is prevented by the response, the procedure is called avoidance. For example, an early preparation for studying negative reinforcement involved pairing a conditioned stimulus (e.g., buzzer) with the delivery of foot shocks to rats. Initially, the rats escaped the shock by jumping over a barrier in the apparatus. After several trials, however, the rats learned to avoid the shock by jumping over the barrier in the presence the buzzer. Early researchers (e.g., Mowrer & Lamoreaux, 1946) interpreted the negative reinforcer as "fear" reduction. That is, they argued that the buzzer elicited conditioned fear through its association with the shocks, and the rats jumped over the barrier to reduce that fear. Later researchers, however, disputed this claim. Sidman (1953) presented shocks to rats after fixed intervals of time (e.g., 5 s). The shock was postponed (i.e., avoided) for a period of time (e.g., 10 s) when they pressed the lever. Because no external stimulus predicted the delivery of shock, fear reduction was an inadequate explanation for avoidance responding. Instead, shock reduction was the controlling variable (see Hineline, 1977, for an early review of this work).

In applied settings, people may behave inappropriately to escape or avoid the demands of the task (e.g., LaRue et al., 2011). Governments may use negative reinforcement to control the behavior of their citizens (see Sidman, 1989; Skinner, 1953). For example, people may pay their taxes to avoid a fine or going to jail, rather than because paying taxes yields a positive reinforcer.

Punishment

The term punishment refers to a procedure that decreases the frequency of a response. As in reinforcement, there are two types of punishment: positive and negative.

Positive Punishment. For a stimulus to qualify as a positive punisher, it must follow a behavior and decrease the probability of that behavior (Miller, 2006). A rat, for example, may be shocked after each lever press. If the rate of lever pressing decreases, the shock is a positive punisher for lever pressing. In applied settings, punishment has been used to decrease self-injurious behavior (SIB). In a classic example, Risley (1968) applied a brief electrical shock to a young girl with autism when she climbed high objects, such as a bookcase or chair. As a result, the rate of dangerous climbing decreased to zero, while the rate of appropriate behavior, such as eye contacts with the experimenter, increased.

Positive punishment is ubiquitous in the real world. For example, if a person places his or her hand too close to a hot stove, he or she may get burned. As a result, it is less likely the person will place his or her hand near a stove in the future.

Negative Punishment. Negative punishment refers to the contingent removal of a stimulus that decreases the rate of a response. In order for a stimulus to qualify as a negative punisher, stimulus removal must follow a behavior and that removal must decrease the probability of the behavior (Miller, 2006). For example, a food-deprived rat may be given free access to food, but lever presses may remove the food. If the contingent removal of food decreases the rate of lever pressing, food removal serves as a negative punisher.

A common application of negative punishment is the time-out procedure (e.g., Wolf, Risley, & Mees, 1964). The time-out procedure involves moving an individual from a reinforcing environment to a less reinforcing one after an instance of inappropriate behavior. In a recent example, Donaldson and Vollmer (2011) investigated the use of time-out on inappropriate playground and classroom behavior in young children with developmental disabilities. When the children engaged in inappropriate behavior (e.g., jumping from swings or throwing academic materials), they were placed in time-out for four minutes. Rates of inappropriate behavior decreased when the time-out contingency was in effect, and increased when it was not. Real-world examples of negative punishers may include traffic fines and bank fees for late credit card payments.

Shaping

The procedure of shaping by successive approximations is used in both basic and applied research to create new behavior (Skinner, 1951). The procedure starts with defining the behavior that one wants to train, the "target behavior." For example, in a basic research laboratory, lever pressing might be defined as any force exerted on the lever that activates a microswitch. A more precise definition might include the minimum force required to operate the lever, such as .25 N. An even more precise definition might specify the response topography. For example, a lever press might require the rat to push the lever with .25 N of force with both paws simultaneously. The definition of the target behavior can be as specific as required, depending on the nature of the response and the research question (see Johnston & Pennypacker, 2008, for a comprehensive discussion of this issue). Next, approximations to the target response are identified and systematically reinforced. For example, proximity to the lever might be the first approximation that is reinforced. Once that behavior occurs with some frequency, the rat may be required to rear up, the next approximation to be reinforced. The next approximation may involve touching the lever with its paw. This process continues until the target behavior is emitted.

Shaping techniques are used widely in applied settings. For example, shaping has been used to train many socially-important behaviors such as appropriate toilet use (e.g., Smeets, Lancioni, Ball, & Oliva, 1985), verbal responses (e.g., Kelley, Shillingsburg, Castro, Addison, & LaRue, 2007), and academic skills (Athens, Vollmer, & St. Peter Pipkin, 2007).

Reinforcers must quickly follow the desired response for shaping to be effective. As a result, conditioned reinforcers may be used to decrease the delay between the behavior and the delivery of a primary reinforcer. Conditioned reinforcers are previously neutral stimuli that acquire the ability to reinforce after being paired with a primary reinforcer (see Bell & McDevitt, this volume). The use of conditioned reinforcers is common in animal training. For example, commercially-available "clickers" are used for shaping behaviors of a wide variety of pets, including dogs, cats, and horses (e.g., Pryor, 2001; see Pryor & Ramirez, this volume). In applied settings with people, social reinforcers, such as "Good job!." may serve as an effective conditioned reinforcer.

Schedules of Reinforcement

Schedules of reinforcement[2] are rules that specify which responses will be followed by a reinforcer. Although Skinner conducted early investigations in the 1930s (e.g., Skinner, 1938), schedules of reinforcement were not widely investigated until Ferster and Skinner (1957). Ferster and Skinner showed that schedules of reinforcement produce predictable and characteristic patterns in operant responding. They used a cumulative recorder to measure moment-to-moment changes in the behavior of pigeons and rats. A cumulative record presents the cumulative number of responses on the y-axis as a function of time on the x-axis (see Figure 8.2). High rates of responding are indicated by a steep slope on the cumulative record, whereas no responding is indicated by a horizontal line. Reinforcers are represented by a dash (i.e. oblique pip).

Reinforcers can be delivered on a continuous (CRF) or partial (PRF) reinforcement schedule. A CRF schedule delivers a reinforcer after each response. PRF schedules do not deliver a reinforcer after each response. Common PRF schedules deliver reinforcers after a certain number of responses have been emitted (ratio schedules)

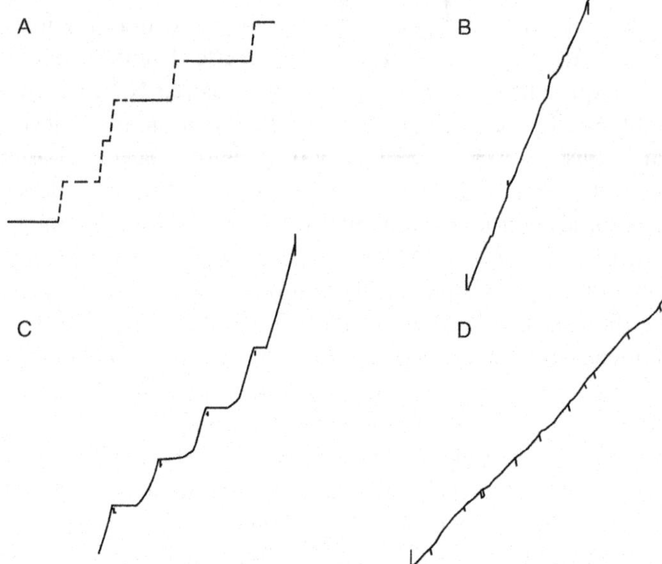

Figure 8.2 Individual pigeon's responding on a FR 120 (A), VR 360 (B), FI 4 min (C), and VI 2 min (D) schedule of reinforcement. From "Schedules of reinforcement," by C. B. Ferster and B. F. Skinner (1957), pp. 51, 159, 332, & 393. Copyright 1997 by the B. F. Skinner Foundation. Reprinted with permission.

or according to the passage time (interval schedules). Four common simple schedules of reinforcement will be described here.

Ratio Schedules

Fixed-ratio Schedules. During fixed-ratio (FR) schedules, reinforcers are delivered after a certain number of responses are emitted (Ferster & Skinner, 1957). The number of responses required for reinforcement is used to describe the schedule. A continuous reinforcement schedule is technically an FR 1 because each response is followed by a reinforcer. In contrast, an FR 15 schedule requires 15 responses to be emitted for every reinforcer delivered. Rate of reinforcement, therefore, is dependent upon how fast an organism responds, and the probability of reinforcement increases with successive responses (Mazur, 1982).

Fixed-ratio schedules produce a characteristic pattern of responding in a variety of species with many types of reinforcers, including tokens and money (Mazur, 1983; Tatham, Wanchisen, & Hineline, 1993). A postreinforcement pause (PRP) occurs immediately after reinforcement and the length of the PRP depends on the schedule requirement. For example, FR schedules with larger ratio requirements will produce longer PRPs than FR schedules with smaller ratio requirements (Powell, 1968). A rapid run of responses follows the PRP. This classic break-and-run pattern is known as a "stair-step" on the cumulative record (see Figure 8.2A). In the real world, an

FR schedule might involve a person getting paid (reinforcer) after he or she produced a certain number of items (responses; see Note 1).

Variable-ratio Schedules. During variable-ratio (VR) schedules, responding is reinforced after a randomly determined number of responses have been emitted (Ferster & Skinner, 1957). The average number of responses required to produce reinforcement is used to describe the schedule. For example, a VR 15 indicates the average number of responses required to produce reinforcement is 15. Nevertheless, the schedule requirement could vary between extreme values so that 29 responses may be required during one interreinforcement interval and one response may be required during the next interval.

The rate of responding generated by VR schedules is typically faster than during FR schedules which require the same number of responses for reinforcement. A PRP is typically not observed for responding on a VR schedule, and response rates are usually relatively constant over time (see Figure 8.2B).

A potential example of a VR schedule in the real world is fishing. The probability of catching a fish (reinforcer) is dependent (to some extent) on the number of casts of the fishing line (responses). However, the number of casts required to catch each fish can vary from one successful attempt to the next.

Interval Schedules

Fixed-interval Schedules. During fixed-interval (FI) schedules, the first response emitted after a designated amount of time is followed by a reinforcer (Ferster & Skinner, 1957). For example, FI 60-s schedules reinforce the first response emitted after 60 s usually measured since the last reinforer was obtained.

Fixed-interval schedules produce a characteristic pattern of responding in a variety of species with both primary and conditioned reinforcers (Barnes & Keenan, 1993; Dews, 1978). The pattern is a PRP followed by slow rates of responding early in the interval and high rates of responding toward the end of the interval (Ferster & Skinner, 1957; Innis, Mitchell, & Staddon, 1993). On a cumulative record, this characteristic pattern is known as a "scallop" (see Figure 8.2C).

Assuming one has a reliable postman, checking one's mailbox (response) and finding mail (reinforcer) can be construed as an FI schedule. The snail mail delivery happens at approximately the same time every day, and it takes only one response to obtain the mail.

Variable-interval Schedules. During variable-interval (VI) schedules, responding is reinforced after a randomly determined amount of time usually measured since the last reinforcer (Ferster & Skinner, 1957). The average of these time intervals is used to describe the schedule. A VI 60-s schedule, for example, reinforces responding on the average of every minute, although individual interreinforcement intervals will differ from one occasion to the next.

The response rates produced by a VI schedule are usually relatively constant and moderate (Ferster & Skinner, 1957). The PRP commonly observed in FI and FR schedules does not appear with VI schedules, except at unusually low rates of reinforcement (e.g., Baum, 1993). The VI schedule is, perhaps, one of the most commonly used schedules in operant research because it produces steady, predictable performances (see Figure 8.2D). If one uses a variable amount of water or a variable heat source each time he or she boils water, the response of looking to see if the water is boiling may be reinforced by seeing boiling water on a VI schedule.

In general, VI schedules are better choices than VR schedules when using schedules to assess the effect of some other variable, such as drugs. As mentioned, rate of reinforcement is proportional to rate of responding on a ratio schedule. Therefore, if a drug changes the rate of responding on a ratio schedule, it will also change the obtained rate of reinforcement. It will then be impossible to determine how much of the change in response rates was produced by administration of the drug and how much was produced by the change in the obtained rate of reinforcement. In contrast, the rate of reinforcement obtained from an interval schedule is relatively constant over a wide range of rates of responding. As a result, observed changes in response rates on VI schedules can be clearly attributed to the administration of the drug, rather than to changes in the obtained rate of reinforcement.

Complex Schedules

The simple schedules[3] discussed above are the most commonly used in the laboratory, but complex schedules of reinforcement are required to investigate complicated behaviors, such as choice (e.g., Baum, 1974; see Mazur & Fantino, this volume), behavioral momentum (see Craig, Nevin, & Odum, this volume; Nevin & Grace, 2000), and behavioral contrast (e.g., Reynolds, 1961). Complex schedules involve the use of two or more simple schedules that operate concurrently or in succession. Each simple schedule is referred to as a component of the complex schedule. Although Ferster and Skinner (1957) described six complex schedules of reinforcement, only two schedules will be discussed here.

Concurrent Schedules. Ferster and Skinner (1957) studied choice by presenting pigeons with two or more operanda associated with independent simple schedules of reinforcement. The two operanda were available at the same time. This concurrent schedule procedure allows an animal to allocate its responses between two or more alternatives. Concurrent schedules of reinforcement have proven useful in formulating theories of choice, such as Herrnstein's (1961, 1970) matching law (see Mazur & Fantino, this volume). The matching law is a quantitative description stating that relative rates of responding to two or more alternatives tends to match (equal) the relative rates of reinforcement obtained from those alternatives.

Multiple Schedules. Multiple schedules of reinforcement involve the successive presentation of two or more simple schedules of reinforcement with clearly different discriminative stimuli present during each simple schedule. Each simple schedule constitutes a component of the multiple schedule and qualitative aspects of responding (e.g., cumulative records) during each component are characteristic of the component's prevailing simple schedule. For example, a food-deprived rat might respond on a FI 60-s schedule of reinforcement signaled by a light. After reinforcement on that schedule, the schedule might be replaced by a FR 10 signaled by white noise. If the animal demonstrates the typical FI scallop in the presence of the light and the FR stair-step in the presence of the noise, *multiple control* is said to be established.

Rate of responding in one component of a multiple schedule also depends on the schedule available in the other component. The ability of these simple schedules to influence each other through time is known as a *multiple-schedule interaction* (e.g.,

Reynolds, 1961). These interactions have been studied extensively (e.g., McSweeney & Weatherly, 1998) and have implications for behavioral treatment in humans (Gross & Drabman, 1981).

Variables Influencing Reinforcer Effectiveness

In addition to schedules of reinforcement, several other procedures influence the rate of operant behavior by altering the effectiveness of the reinforcer.

Reinforcer Characteristics

Reinforcer Rate. Rate of reinforcement (number of reinforcers per time period) is a critical variable influencing the rate of an operant response (number of responses per time period). For example, Catania and Reynolds (1968) studied the keypecking of pigeons on VI schedules of food reinforcement. They varied the programmed rates of reinforcement from 8.4 to 300 reinforcers per hour in different conditions. They reported that rate of responding was an increasing, negatively accelerated, function of reinforcement rate.

Reinforcer Amount. In general, although not always, the rate of an operant response is directly related to the size of the reinforcer. That is, larger reinforcers tend to maintain higher response rates than smaller reinforcers. Reed and Wright (1988), for example, studied the operant leverpressing of rats on a VR 30 schedule of food reinforcement. In different conditions, they delivered 1 to 4 food pellets per reinforcer delivery. They reported a systematic increase in rate of responding as a function of the number food pellets delivered per reinforcer.

Reinforcer Quality. Reinforcers also differ in quality. Quality is somewhat difficult to define, but higher quality reinforcers are usually preferred to lower quality reinforcers. In general, higher quality reinforcers are also more effective in supporting operant responding than are lower quality reinforcers.

Reinforcers of varying quality have been used in applied settings. For example, Lee, Yu, Martin, and Martin (2010) studied operant responding for six qualitatively-different food reinforcers (e.g., orange juice, pretzels, & cookies) in adults with developmental disabilities. Next, they assessed each participant's preference for each stimulus by requiring 10 choices between that stimulus and every other stimulus. They reported that rates of responding were highly correlated with the participant's preference for the item. That is, higher rates of responding were observed for stimuli that were more preferred than for those that were less preferred.

Contingencies

A contingency of reinforcement refers to the difference between the probability that a behavior will be followed by a reinforcer and the probability that the reinforcer will be delivered in the absence of that behavior (Catania, 2007). In order for a consequence to be effective, the first probability should be higher than the second probability.

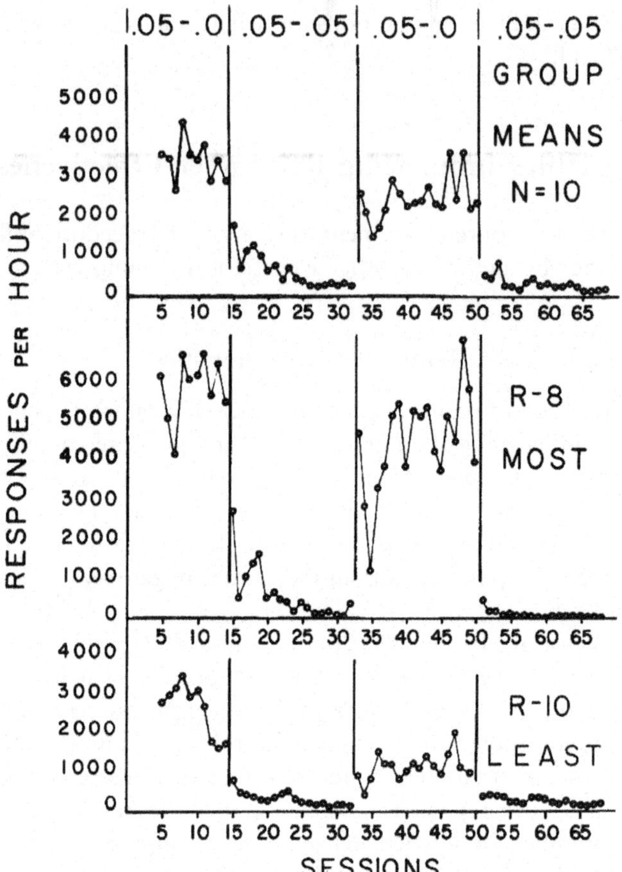

Figure 8.3 Responses per hour as a function of condition. In the first condition, the probability of receiving a water reinforcer following a lever press was .05 and the probability of receiving a reinforcer in the absence of lever pressing was 0.0. In the second condition, the first probability remained the same, but the probability for the delivery of reinforcement in the absence of lever pressing was changed to .05. From "The effect of contingency upon the appetitive conditioning of free-operant behavior," by L. Hammond (1980), *Journal of the Experimental Analysis of Behavior, 34*, p. 300. Copyright 1980 by the Society for the Experimental Analysis of Behavior, Inc. Reprinted with permission.

In a classic demonstration of the effect of reinforcer contingencies, Hammond (1980) exposed rats to two conditions. In the first condition, the probability of receiving a water reinforcer following a lever press was 0.05 and the probability of receiving a reinforcer in the absence of lever pressing was 0.0 (a positive contingency). In the second condition, the first probability remained the 0.05, but the probability of the delivery of reinforcement in the absence of lever pressing was changed to 0.05 (a zero contingency). Hammond's results showed that when the probability of receiving a reinforcer was higher for lever pressing than it was for not lever pressing, higher response rates were maintained than when the two probabilities were the same (see Figure 8.3).

Identifying contingencies may be important in the treatment of problem behaviors in applied settings. Once the reinforcer maintaining a problem behavior is identified, that reinforcer can be delivered noncontingently to reduce the behavior (Carr, Severtson, & Lepper, 2009). Such a procedure may be preferred to punishment, another method for reducing problematic behaviors, because it involves the delivery of positive, rather than aversive, stimuli.

Delayed Consequences

In general, the effectiveness of a reinforcer decreases as a function of the delay between the response and the delivery of the reinforcer (Mazur, 1987). This phenomenon is called delay discounting and it is a rich area of behavior-analytic research (see Green, Myerson, & Vanderveldt, this volume). Individuals who may develop behavioral problems, such as pathological gambling (Dixon, Marley, & Jacobs, 2003) and drug abuse (Carroll, Anker, Mach, Newman, & Perry, 2010) may show relatively steep discounting of delayed reinforcers.

Delay discounting is also used to study problems of self-control. Self-control can be defined as a preference for a larger later (LL) reinforcer than for a smaller sooner (SS) reinforcer (Logue, 1995). Impulsiveness can be defined as choosing the SS reinforcer over the LL reinforcer. The relative sizes of the reinforcers are important in the development of self-control. For example, increasing the relative size of the LL reinforcer or decreasing the size of the SS reinforcer will increase self-control (Logue, 1995, 2000).

Motivating Operations

Reinforcer effectiveness can be altered by motivating operations. A motivating operation is "an environmental event, operation, or stimulus condition that affects an organism by momentarily altering (a) the reinforcing effectiveness of other events and (b) the frequency of occurrence of that part of the organism's repertoire relevant to events as consequences" (Michael, 1993, p. 192). Establishing operations increase, and abolishing operations decrease, the effectiveness of a consequence.

Perhaps the most common procedure for increasing the effectiveness of a reinforcer is deprivation. That is, depriving an organism of a stimulus (i.e., food) establishes that stimulus as a reinforcer and increases the frequency of the behavior that it follows (e.g., Michael, 1982). A common procedure for decreasing the effectiveness of a stimulus is increasing the amount of exposure that an animal has to it. In practice, increasing exposure to a reinforcer might involve using dense schedules of reinforcement and increasing the reinforcer magnitude (i.e., size).

McSweeney and Murphy (this volume; McSweeney & Murphy, 2009) describe how the processes of habituation and sensitization to the sensory properties of the reinforcer can alter the effectiveness of that reinforcer. Habituation is a decrease in responsiveness to a repeatedly-presented stimulus (R. F. Thompson, this volume). Sensitization is the opposite effect, an increase in responsiveness to a repeatedly-presented stimulus that occurs under specific conditions. Procedures that decrease habituation (e.g., variability in the delivery of the stimulus), or enhance senstitization (e.g., introduction of a novel stimulus) can increase reinforcer effectiveness. Enhancing habituation (e.g., increasing stimulus exposure) or decreasing sensitization (e.g., decreasing unpredictable stimuli), can decrease reinforcer effectiveness. The sensitization–habituation description of reinforcer effectiveness offers novel predictions about how environmental events may alter the effectiveness of reinforcers.

Extinction

Extinction is a procedure used to weaken operant control. If a response was previously reinforced, then extinction will decrease its frequency. If a response was previously punished, then extinction will increase its frequency. Extinction can be produced in two ways. First, the delivery of the consequence (i.e., reinforcers and punishers) can be stopped. For example, Skinner (1938) reinforced 100 lever presses by rats with food. Then, he discontinued the delivery of food (extinction). Lever pressing was quite fast when extinction was first introduced, but it eventually decreased to zero following one hour of extinction (see Figure 8.4). Second, the consequence (reinforcer or punisher) can be presented independently of the behavior. Hammond's (1980) zero contingency condition described earlier provides an example of this procedure (see Figure 8.3).

Behavior undergoing extinction shows some complicated and unexpected characteristics. For example, extinguished behavior spontaneously recovers after a period of time elapses since an extinction session. Extinguished behavior also increases after the presentation of a sudden stimulus such as a tone or light (disinhibition). The restoration of part of the conditioning episode will restore a previously extinguished

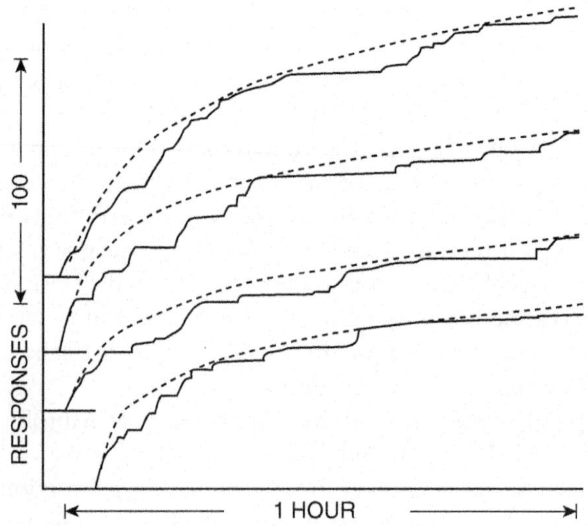

Figure 8.4 Cumulative lever pressing of four rats during extinction as a function of time. From "The behavior of organisms: An experimental analysis," by B. F. Skinner (1938), p. 75. Copyright 1991 by the B. F. Skinner Foundation. Reprinted with permission.

response (reinstatement). In addition, an operant response will recover when the original context is reintroduced if the response is conditioned in one context and extinguished in a different context (renewal; Bouton & Peck, 1989). The partial reinforcement extinction effect (PREE; e.g., Humphreys, 1939) also refers to the finding that responses that have been partially reinforced extinguish more slowly than those that have been continuously reinforced. The PREE has been considered to be paradoxical because its observation suggests that behaviors that have been reinforced less frequently have higher response strength (i.e., as indicated by greater resistance to extinction) than those that have been reinforced continually. Because of the complexity of these characteristics, it is challenging to theoretically explain why extinction occurs even though it seems intuitively obvious that extinction should occur (see Vurbic & Bouton, in this volume for the current understanding of extinction).

Other characteristics of behavior undergoing extinction are extinction bursts and behavioral variability. An extinction burst refers to a temporary increase in frequency of the response at the beginning of extinction (Alessandri, Sullivan, & Lewis, 1990). Additionally, the topography of a response undergoing extinction will vary more than if the same response was followed by a reinforcer (Antonitis, 1951). These properties of extinction have important implications in applied settings (Lerman & Iwata, 1996). For example, a common way to decrease SIB maintained by social reinforcement is to place the behavior on extinction. Extinction bursts of SIB, however, could lead to more injury. Therefore, researchers often equip the participant with self-protective gear during extinction or they use extinction in conjunction with other procedures (Lerman & Iwata, 1996). In contrast, the behavioral variability induced by extinction may aid in shaping new, more appropriate, responses (Duker & van Lent, 1991).

Extinction is often useful for decreasing the strength of an operant behavior, but its use may not always be appropriate. For example, extinction by ignoring the behavior might not be the best way to decrease crying in an infant. When extinction begins, crying will generally increase (extinction burst). A parent may resist comforting the infant for a while in response to the increased crying. If the parent eventually yields and comforts the child, however, the behavior of crying will have been placed on an intermittent reinforcement schedule. The PREE will then make crying even more resistant to further extinction. Even if the parents are able to ignore the increased crying, they may not be able to control the grandparents who may rush in to comfort the child and, therefore, reinforce crying. Extinction is easiest to use when a slow loss of behavioral strength can be tolerated and when all of the reinforcers that support the behavior have been identified and are under the control of the behavior analyst.

Stimulus Control

Stimuli in the environment may come to control operant behavior. When this happens it is referred to as stimulus control. There are two basic types of stimulus control: generalization and discrimination.

Generalization

Generalization occurs when a response that has been reinforced in presence of one stimulus also occur in the presence of other, similar, stimuli. In a classic experiment, Guttman and Kalish (1956) trained pigeons to peck a key for food only in the presence of a colored key light of 530, 550, 580 or 600 nanometers. Pigeons were then tested with multiple wavelengths. An examination of response rate as a function of wavelength revealed that the peak rate of responding occurred in the presence of the training stimulus. Response rates to new stimuli decreased as a normal function of the distance in nanometers between that new stimulus and the training stimulus.

Discrimination

Discrimination occurs when a behavior produces reinforcers in the presence of some stimuli, but not in the presence of other stimuli. The behavior will occur in the presence of the stimuli that signaled reinforcer availability and not in the presence of the other stimuli. Stimuli that are present when the behavior is reinforced are abbreviated S^D; stimuli that are present when performing that behavior has no consequence are S-deltas (abbreviated S^Δ). For example, hailing a taxi that is already occupied is ineffective. Therefore, most taxicabs have a sign on the roof that can be illuminated when the cab is available. The lighted taxi sign is an S^D for the response of hailing that cab; an unlit sign is an S^Δ for hailing that cab. Individuals who are accustomed to riding in taxis only hail a cab when its sign is illuminated. The behavior of hailing the taxi is said to be under the stimulus control of the lighted sign.

Discriminative stimuli can also indicate that performing a behavior will produce punishers. In that case, the behavior will decrease in frequency in the presence of stimuli that signal punishers, and not in the presence of stimuli that do not signal punishers. For example, children may quickly learn that many of their lively behaviors will be punished when their mother frowns, but not when she smiles. As a result, they may carefully restrain their behavior in the presence of her frown, but not in the presence of her smile.

Learning to discriminate can affect the stimulus generalization gradient around the S^D. For example, Hanson (1959) trained pigeons with a 550 nm wavelength keylight (S^D). Some subjects then received discrimination training with keylights of 555 nm, 560 nm, 570 nm, or 590 nm as the S^Δ. All subjects displayed stimulus generalization, but their highest levels of responding did not occur in the presence of the S. Instead, peak responding occurred to a stimulus that was similar to the S but in the direction away from the S^Δ . That is, pigeons trained with longer-wavelength S^Δ stimuli exhibited significantly higher responding to a 540 nm keylight than did pigeons trained only with 550 nm S^D. This phenomenon is referred to as *peak shift*.

Relatively complex stimuli can serve as effective discriminative stimuli even in nonhuman animals, such as pigeons. For example, Watanabe, Sakamoto, and Wakita (1995) used paintings by Monet and Picasso as the S^D and S^Δ (counterbalanced across subjects). Pigeons' pecking not only came under stimulus control, but also exhibited impressive stimulus generalization. Subjects trained to respond to Monet pecked when presented with unfamiliar Monet paintings and to paintings by other Impressionists (i.e., Cézanne and Renoir). Subjects trained with Picasso as the S^D

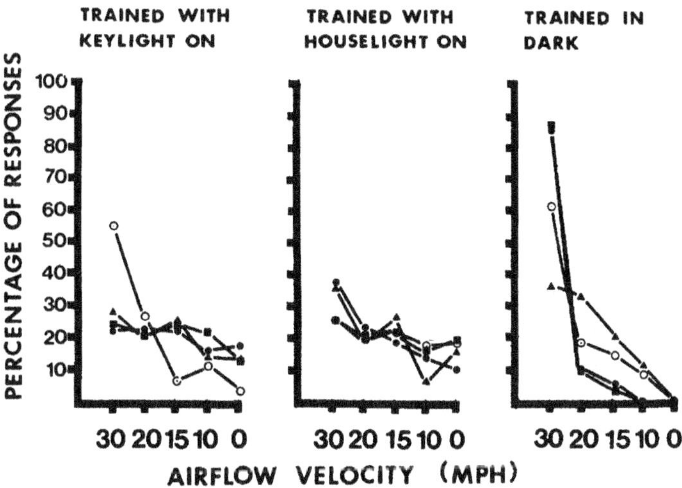

Figure 8.5 Percentages of total responses emitted in the presence of different airflow velocities during a generalization test for pigeons trained with a compound keylight-airflow S, a compound houselight-airflow S^D, or only an airflow S^D with no light present. Training airflow velocity S^D was always 30 mph, and different lines represent individual responses of individual subjects. From "The development of stimulus control with and without a lighted key," by R. Van Houten & R. Rudolph (1972), *Journal of the Experimental Analysis of Behavior, 18*, p. 219. Copyright 1972 by the Society for the Experimental Analysis of Behavior, Inc. Reprinted with permission.

responded to new paintings by Picasso and to paintings by other Cubists (i.e., Matisse and Braque).

The internal states produced by drugs can also serve as discriminative stimuli. Rats received injections of delta^9-THC (i.e., the active ingredient in marijuana) and nicotine as the S^D and S^Δ (counterbalanced across subjects) in a food reinforcement task. They discriminated between the drugs as indicated by responding faster following injections of the S drug than following injections of the S^Δ drug (Troisi, LeMay, & Järbe, 2010). Because the experimenters injected both drugs in the same manner, the animals must have based their discriminations on the subjective effects produced by those drugs, indicating that they could distinguish between those subjective states.

Generalization and discrimination may both be affected by the salience of the discriminative stimuli. One clear determinant of stimulus salience is intensity. Other things being equal, a loud noise or a bright light are more salient than a soft noise or a dim light. Stimulus salience is also affected by the presence of other stimuli. Van Houten and Rudolph (1972) trained pigeons to peck in total darkness only when a 30-mph airflow was present. The subjects readily learned the task and displayed stimulus generalization to similar airflow velocities (see Figure 8.5). Pigeons that learned the task with either a houselight or keylight present in the operant chamber failed to exhibit stimulus generalization and also learned more slowly to discriminate 10-mph from 20-mph compared to birds trained in darkness. That is, the presence of light reduced the stimulus control of the airflow. With more training, however, subjects learned to respond only to the presence of the airflow that signaled the behavior-reinforcer contingency.

Practical Applications

Discrimination procedures provide a useful technique for asking questions of nonverbal animals (e.g., infants, nonhuman animals). For example, the Watanabe et al. (1995) experiment, described earlier, answered the question of whether pigeons can distinguish between paintings by Monet and Picasso. Drug discrimination studies provide a way to assess what a drug "feels" like to an animal. When responding generalizes from one drug to another (i.e., when one drug can substitute for another as the S^D), this usually indicates that the two drugs produce similar subjective effects possibly because they act at the same neural synapses. For example, rats trained to discriminate diazepam from saline also responded on the drug lever when injected with the barbiturate drug pentobarbital (see Lelas, Spealman, & Rowlett, 2000, for a review of such drug substitutions) These results suggest that diazepam and pentobarbital produce somewhat similar subjective effects which might be expected because both drugs act on receptors for the same neurotransmitter (i.e., GABA). Studies of drug discriminations can be a useful tool when new drug reinforcers with unknown receptor actions substitute for drugs with known synaptic effects.

Discrimination procedures are often used to teach new behaviors in applied settings. When individuals have difficulties discriminating between the S^D and S^Δ, a technique called *stimulus fading* can help. In stimulus fading, differences between the S^D and S^Δ are exaggerated early in training to facilitate successful discrimination. As the learner progresses, the exaggerated differences are reduced or faded out. A recent study used stimulus fading to teach two children with autism to rock-climb in an indoor gymnasium (Kaplan-Reimer, Sidener, Reeve, & Sidener, 2011). In this study, the gymnasium rock wall contained several routes that varied in difficulty and were marked by small pieces of tape extending from each synthetic rock (called a "hold"). The dark blue tape served as the S^D and indicated a successful route. Any other color tape was the S^Δ. The discrimination task was too difficult for the children, so researchers made it simpler by framing each hold with a large, cardboard colored square. The cardboard frame made color more salient than a small piece of tape, and with the competing color of the holds concealed, both children learned to climb the rock wall with few errors. In subsequent phases of the study, the frames were faded out by making them progressively smaller, and the masking tape was removed. Importantly, both children's rock-climbing generalized to other situations. Testing indicated they were able to follow new route colors, that their climbing was not disrupted by a noisy environment, and that they no longer required verbal or edible reinforcers for correct hold choices.

Stokes and Baer (1977) identified tactics to increase generalization from a learning environment to a real-world setting. The most dependable of these tactics involves taking advantage of natural contingencies, which can be accomplished by "trapping" (p. 353). Trapping involves temporarily changing the natural contingencies so that the desired behavior produces reinforcement from a teacher or experimenter. After the target behavior occurs more frequently, natural reinforcers should be sufficient to maintain it in the person's usual environment. For example, if the target behavior is an increase in social interactions with peers, the experimenter might increase the rate of social reinforcement for engaging in peer interactions by enlisting a confederate. Later, the natural contingencies present in human social interaction should maintain the behavior. In the rock-climbing example above, parents reported that both children asked to go climbing outside of the experiment. This suggests that the rock-climbing shifted to the control of naturally-occurring reinforcers.

Chaining and Conditioned Reinforcement

When a task consists of a sequence of behaviors (a behavioral chain), the behaviors may be learned better using a step-by-step, rather than using an all-at-once, procedure. During chaining, a series of linked behaviors is taught one by one. In *forward chaining*, a subject or participant first learns the first step in a sequence, and subsequent steps are added, in order, after that. For example, in a task consisting of four behaviors A, B, C, and D, using forward chaining would consist of, "teach A, teach AB, teach ABC, teach ABCD" (Walls, Zane, & Ellis, 1981, p. 62). In *backward chaining*, the final behavior in a sequence is taught first before additional behaviors are added onto the beginning of the chain (i.e., "teach D, teach CD, teach BCD, teach ABCD"; Walls et al., p. 63). A behavioral chain (a chain of responses) is similar to a *chained schedule* which successively presents an organism with two or more schedules of reinforcement, each correlated with a different discriminative stimulus (a chain of schedules; Ferster & Skinner, 1957). Only the final schedule in this chain produces primary reinforcement.

In either a chained schedule or a behavioral chain, primary reinforcement may be far removed from performance of the initial link. Conditioned reinforcers (i.e., stimuli that acquire reinforcing properties due to their association with primary reinforcers; see Bell & McDevitt, this volume) may, therefore, play important roles in the execution of the task. After the first link in the chain is completed, the stimuli accompanying the second link may serve as conditioned reinforcers for completing the first behavior. In addition, those stimuli may also function as discriminative stimuli signaling an opportunity to earn another conditioned reinforcer by completing the next behavior in the chain. In this manner, conditioned reinforcement and stimulus control lead the subject through all links in the chain until performance of the terminal behavior produces primary reinforcement.

Both forward and backward chaining may result in superior performance compared to learning all steps in a task at once. For example, Walls et al. (1981) taught developmentally-disabled adults to assemble a carburetor, a bicycle brake, and a meat grinder. When participants were taught using the whole task method, their proportions of incorrect responses were more than twice as high as when they learned via either forward or backward chaining (Walls et al., 1981).

Chaining is also effective with nonhuman subjects. For example, Pisacreta (1982) trained pigeons to perform a four-component sequence of key pecks using either forward or backward chaining. Subjects training via backward chaining made most of their errors in the first link of a chain, whereas subjects trained by forward chaining tended to make errors on the final link. The overall proportion of incorrect key pecks, however, was similar for both groups.

Comparing Forward and Backward Chaining

It is unclear whether backward or forward chaining produces better learning. For example, Spooner and Spooner (1984) reviewed studies in which developmentally-disabled individuals were taught to perform tasks using forward or backward chaining. Which technique yielded the best performance varied, with no consistent advantage for using one method over another across studies. More recently, Slocum and Tiger (2011) compared forward and backward chaining when teaching sequences of simple body movements (e.g., clap, touch head) to a group of children with learning disabilities. Results again indicated no clear advantage for either technique, and also no evidence that particular individuals consistently learned better or preferred one type of chaining over the other.

Although results comparing the overall efficacy of forward versus backward chaining have been mixed, each procedure may possess some specific advantages. Weiss (1978) pointed out that when learning by forward but not backward chaining, successful completion of each step produces a primary reinforcer at some point in training. Such immediate primary reinforcement may produce better learning. Indeed, Weiss reported far fewer errors committed by college students who learned a sequence of key presses by forward than by backward chaining.

Other researchers have identified potential advantages for backward chaining. For example, backward chaining enables individuals to concentrate on new links before they must perform the other recently learned links. Rushall and Ford (1982) argued that the requirement in forward chaining for learners to perform relatively unfamiliar skills before attempting a completely new behavior can interfere with learning new steps in the chain. They advocated for the use of backward chaining for coaching various aspects of sports, including swinging a golf club and tackling or pinning opponents in football or wrestling.

An example of the efficacy of backward chaining for coaching golf was illustrated by Simek and O'Brien (1981), who compared it with traditional instruction in two experiments with novice golfers. Both teaching methods included demonstrations and verbal instructions. However, traditional instruction began at the tee and worked toward the hole, whereas backward chaining instruction began 6 inches away from the hole and progressed backwards. Participants in the backward chaining group mastered putting before advancing to chipping, then pitching, then longer drive shots, and finally club selection. Following eight training lessons, participants in both groups played an 18-hole round of golf. Backward chaining proved to be a superior coaching procedure for the game of golf; participants trained by backward chaining outperformed those in the traditional instruction group by an average of 17 strokes.

Social Learning

Imitation/R-S Learning

Much of what humans learn comes from observation of others rather than from direct exposure to reinforcement contingencies. One form of observational learning is imitation, which occurs when a subject's behavior approximates the actions of a model. The term imitation is generally reserved for goal-directed behaviors in which behavior-consequence associations are acquired by observation. Another term, social facilitation, describes behavior that is simpler or reflexive, such as yawning or applauding. When observation of a reinforced behavior increases the likelihood that an

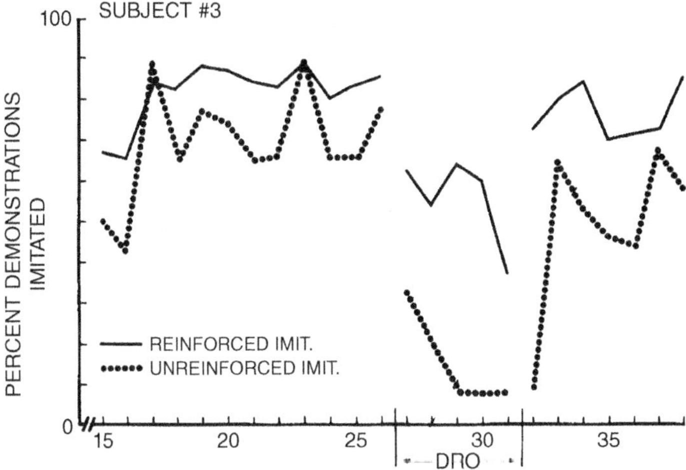

Figure 8.6 Percentages of demonstrations imitated during reinforcement, DRO, and a return to reinforcement in one subject. The solid line indicates imitative behaviors that produced (or prevented, during DRO) reinforcement. The dotted line represents inconsequential imitative behaviors. From "The development of imitation by reinforcing behavioral similarity to a model," by D. Baer, R. Peterson, & J. Sherman (1967), *Journal of the Experimental Analysis of Behavior, 10*, p. 413. Copyright 1967 by the Society for the Experimental Analysis of Behavior, Inc. Reprinted with permission.

observer will perform that behavior, the procedure is sometimes referred to as vicarious reinforcement.

In one study of imitation, 3-year-old children either observed a model use a tool to push a toy out of a tube (experimental condition) or observed a model push the tool through the air over the tube without inserting it (control condition). Children in the experimental condition were more successful at using the tool to push the toy out of the tube than those in the control condition (Horner & Whiten, 2007; Want & Harris, 2001). Some children also benefited from observing what not to do (vicarious punishment). That is, those who watched a model demonstrate both a correct and an incorrect method of inserting the tool into the tube outperformed children who only viewed the correct method, at least when the task was not overly difficult.

Sometimes children imitate without an obvious reinforcer. Baer and colleagues (Baer, Peterson, & Sherman, 1967) exposed three developmentally-disabled children with no imitative ability to demonstrations of many actions and vocalizations. Imitation of most of these behaviors (e.g., "Point gun and say 'Bang'" and "walk and hold book on head") produced food reinforcement. The solid line in Figure 8.6 shows the percentage of the reinforced imitative behaviors emitted by one child across sessions. Certain other behaviors, however, (e.g., "stab self with rubber knife" and "put hat on hobby horse") were modeled even though they were never reinforced. Imitation of these non-reinforced actions is shown by the dotted line in Figure 8.6.

A differential reinforcement of other behavior (DRO) phase was then implemented in which the previously reinforced actions now prevented reinforcement. The previously unreinforced actions still had no effect. During this phase, children ceased imitating both types of actions. Finally, the initial contingency was reestablished, and the children once again imitated all of their model's actions. Baer et al. (1967) explained the imitation of the unreinforced behaviors by arguing that once children have experience with receiving positive reinforcement for copying a model's behavior, the act of successfully imitating may itself become a conditioned reinforcer.

Mirror Neurons Contribute to Imitation

Several studies point to an important role of mirror neurons in imitation. Mirror neurons are neurons that fire when one both executes and observes a particular action. For example, Buccino et al. (2004) found that observing a model play chords on a guitar neck activated brain areas known to contain mirror neurons to a greater extent if participants attempted to imitate the hand action themselves than if they simply observed it. Additionally, inhibiting mirror neuron activity disrupts one's ability to imitate. When transcranial magnetic stimulation was used to inhibit the posterior section of Broca's area (believed to contain mirror neurons), participants were impaired at repeating a model's finger movements on a keyboard but not at pressing the keys indicated by a red dot (Heiser, Iacoboni, Maeda, Marcus, & Mazziotta, 2003).

It is well-known that individuals affected by autism spectrum disorder are poor imitators (e.g., Hobson & Lee, 1999). Because of the relationship between mirror neurons and imitation, some researchers have proposed a role for mirror neuron dysfunction in autism spectrum disorder (e.g., Rizzolatti & Fabbri-Destro, 2010). Some support for this "mirror neuron hypothesis of autism" has been documented. For example, children with autism exhibited much less mirror neuron activation than typically developing children when they observed and imitated facial expressions. The amount of this activation was negatively correlated with autism severity (Dapretto et al., 2006).

Although imitation in general, and imitation of facial expressions specifically, is often difficult for children with autism, they can learn to imitate facial displays of emotion with positive reinforcement. For example, DeQunzio, Townsend, Sturmey, and Poulson (2007) used tokens (which could be exchanged for snacks) to reinforce imitation of smiling, frowning, and looking surprised in three boys with autism. All three boys dramatically increased their imitation of facial expressions. For two of the three boys, imitation generalized to a facial expression that had not been reinforced. This result is similar to that reported by Baer et al. (1967) in Figure 8.6.

Another promising intervention for children with autism involves training the imitation of hand gestures and object manipulations. Children who received Reciprocal Imitation Training (a technique including modeling, reinforcement for imitation, and also imitation of the child's actions by the model) for 10 weeks increased both "elicited" (i.e., verbally requested) and "spontaneous" (i.e., occurring with specific instruction) imitation compared to a randomized control group (Ingersoll, 2010).

Finally, observation and imitation of hand actions has recently been used to supplement traditional physical therapies after stroke. Ertelt et al. (2007) exposed participants suffering from upper limb mobility dysfunction to daily videos of common hand actions such as turning a faucet on and off before the participants practiced these actions themselves. These participants improved significantly more than a control group who practiced the same actions but did not observe videos of the actions beforehand. Ertelt and colleagues attributed this improvement to the activation of mirror neurons involved in representing and executing the observed actions.

Conclusion

Operant conditioning began as a basic science to discover fundamental behavioral principles in nonhuman animals (e.g., Skinner, 1938). As research findings accumulated and key principles, such as reinforcement and punishment, were identified, they were systematically applied to improve behavior of social importance (e.g., Baer et al., 1968). Because of the generality of operant principles, they are now being applied in a wide variety of settings, including animal training (e.g., Pryor & Ramirez, this volume), the treatment of autism (T. Thompson, this volume), parenting (Miltenberger & Crosland, this volume), education (Twyman, this volume), and the behavior of organizations (Abernathy & Lattal, this volume), to name a few. A mighty field has grown from the discovery of a few simple principles. In a fitting tribute to the number and importance of these developments, B. F. Skinner was identified as the most influential psychologist of the 20th century (Hagbloom, et al., 2002).

Notes

1 Translating a laboratory concept into a real-world example is always risky. Therefore, we encourage the reader to use caution when interpreting our examples. A more detailed analysis might prove many of them wrong.
2 Negative reinforcers, positive punishers, and negative punishers can also be delivered according to schedules. Due to space constraints, we will only describe schedules of positive reinforcement.
3 There are several other simple schedules of reinforcement used to investigate operant conditioning. For example, differential reinforcement of low response rate, differential reinforcement of high response rate, differential reinforcement of other behavior, differential reinforcement of alternative behavior, differential reinforcement of incompatible behavior, fixed-time, and variable-time schedules are often used in basic and applied research. Unfortunately, we do not have the space to cover them here. We refer the interested reader to Lattal (1991) for more details on simple and complex schedules of reinforcement.

References

Abernathy, W. B., & Lattal, D. (2014). Organizational behavior management: Past, present, and future. In F. K. McSweeney & E. S. Murphy (Eds.), *Wiley-Blackwell handbook of operant and classical conditioning* (pp. 645–668). Oxford: Wiley-Blackwell.

Alessandri, S. M., Sullivan, M. W., & Lewis, M. (1990). Violation of expectancy and frustration in early infancy. *Developmental Psychology, 26*, 738–744.

Antonitis, J. J. (1951). Response variability in the white rat during conditioning, extinction, and re-conditioning. *Journal of Experimental Psychology, 42*, 273–281.

Athens, E. S., Vollmer, T. R., & St. Peter Pipkin, C. C. (2007). Shaping academic task engagement with percentile schedules. *Journal of Applied Behavior Analysis, 40*, 475–488.

Ayllon, T., & Michael, J. (1959). The psychiatric nurse as a behavioral engineer. *Journal of the Experimental Analysis of Behavior, 2*, 323–334.

Baer, D., Peterson, R., & Sherman, J. (1967). The development of imitation by reinforcing behavioral similarity to a model. *Journal of the Experimental Analysis of Behavior, 10*, 405–416.

Baer, D. M., Wolf, M. M., & Risley, T. R. (1968). Some current dimensions of applied behavior analysis. *Journal of Applied Behavior Analysis, 1*, 91–97.

Barnes, D., & Keenan, M. (1993). Concurrent activities and instructed human fixed-interval performance. *Journal of the Experimental Analysis of Behavior, 59*, 501–520.

Baum, W. M. (1974). On two types of deviation from the matching law: Bias and undermatching. *Journal of the Experimental Analysis of Behavior, 22*, 231–342.

Baum, W. M. (1993). Performances on ratio and interval schedules of reinforcement: Data and theory. *Journal of the Experimental Analysis of Behavior, 59*, 245–264.

Bell, M. C., & McDevitt, M. A. (2014). Conditioned reinforcement. In F. K. McSweeney & E.S. Murphy (Eds.) *Wiley-Blackwell handbook of operant and classical conditioning.* (pp. 221–248) Oxford: Wiley-Blackwell.

Bouton, M. E., & Peck, C. A. (1989). Context effects on conditioning, extinction, and reinstatement in an appetitive conditioning preparation. *Animal Learning & Behavior, 17*, 188–198.

Buccino, G., Vogt, S., Ritzl, A., Fink, G. R., Zilles, K., Freund, H. J., & Rizzolatti G. (2004). Neural circuits underlying imitation learning of hand actions: An event-related fMRI study. *Neuron, 42*(2), 323–334.

Carr, J. E., Severtson, J. M., & Lepper, T. L. (2009). Noncontingent reinforcement is an empirically supported treatment for problem behavior exhibited by individuals with developmental disabilities. *Research in Developmental Disabilities, 30*, 44–57.

Carroll, M. E., Anker, J. J., Mach, J. L., Newman, J. L., & Perry, J. L. (2010). Delay discounting as a predictor of drug abuse. In G. J. Madden & W. K. Bickel (Eds.), *Impulsivity: The behavioral and neurological science of discounting* (pp. 243–271). Washington, DC: American Psychological Association.

Catania, A. C. (2007). *Learning* (interim 4th ed.). Cornwall-on-Hudson, NY: Sloan.

Catania, A. C., & Reynolds, G. S. (1968). A quantitative analysis of the responding maintained by interval schedules of reinforcement. *Journal of the Experimental Analysis of Behavior, 11*, 327–383.

Chiesa, M. (1994). *Radical behaviorism: The philosophy and the science.* Boston: Authors Cooperative.

Craig, A. R., Nevin, J. A., & Odum, A. L. (2014). Behavioral momentum and resistance to change. In F. K. McSweeney & E. S.Murphy (Eds.), *Wiley-Blackwell handbook of operant and classical conditioning* (pp. 249–274). Oxford: Wiley-Blackwell.

Dapretto, M., Davies, M. S., Pfeifer, J. H., Scott, A. A., Sigman, M., Bookheimer, S. Y., & Iacoboni, M. (2006). Understanding emotions in others: Mirror neuron dysfunction in children with autism spectrum disorders. *Nature Neuroscience, 9*(1), 28–30.

DeQuinzio, J., Townsend, D., Sturmey, P., & Poulson, C. L. (2007). Generalized imitation of facial models by children with autism. *Journal of Applied Behavior Analysis, 40*(4), 755–759.

Dews, P. B. (1978). Studies on responding under fixed-interval schedules of reinforcement: II. The scalloped pattern of the cumulative record. *Journal of the Experimental Analysis of Behavior*, *290*, 67–75.
Dixon, M. R., Marley, J., & Jacobs, E. A. (2003). Delay discounting by pathological gamblers. *Journal of Applied Behavior Analysis*, *36*, 449–458.
Donaldson, J. M., & Vollmer, T. R. (2011). An evaluation and comparison of time-out procedures with and without release contingencies. *Journal of Applied Behavior Analysis*, *44*, 693–705.
Dozier, C. L., Iwata, B. A., Thomason-Sassi, J., Worsdell, A. S., & Wilson, D. M. (2012). A comparison of two pairing procedures to establish praise as a reinforcer. *Journal of Applied Behavior Analysis*, *45*, 721–735.
Duker, P. C., & van Lent, C. (1991). Inducing variability in communicative gestures used by severely retarded individuals. *Journal of Applied Behavior Analysis*, *24*, 379–386.
Ertelt, D., Small, S., Solodkin, A., Dettmers, C., McNamara, A., Binkofski, F., & Buccino, G. (2007). Action observation has a positive impact on rehabilitation of motor deficits after stroke. *Neuroimage*, *36*(Suppl 2), T164–T173.
Ferster, C. B., & Skinner, B. F. (1957). *Schedules of reinforcement*. New York: Appleton-Century-Crofts.
Green, L., Myerson, J., & Vanderveldt, A. (2014). Delay and probability discounting. In F. K. McSweeney & E. S. Murphy (Eds.), *Wiley-Blackwell handbook of operant and classical conditioning* (pp. 307–337). Oxford: Wiley-Blackwell.
Gross, A. M., & Drabman, R. S. (1981). Behavioral contrast and behavioral therapy. *Behavior Therapy*, *12*, 231–246.
Guttman, N., & Kalish, H. I. (1956). Discriminability and stimulus generalization. *Journal of Experimental Psychology*, *51*, 79–88.
Hagbloom, S. J., Warnick, R., Warnick, J., Jones, V., Yarbrough, G., Russell, T., Brorecky, C., McGahhey, R., Powell, J., Beavers, J., & Monte, E. (2002). The most eminent psychologists of the twentieth century. *Review of General Psychology*, *6*, 139–152.
Hall, R. V., Lund, D., & Jackson, D. (1968). Effects of teacher attention on study behavior. *Journal of Applied Behavior Analysis*, *1*, 1–12.
Hammond, L. (1980). The effect of contingency upon the appetitive conditioning of free-operant behavior. *Journal of the Experimental Analysis of Behavior*, *34*, 297–304.
Hanson, H. M. (1959). Effects of discrimination training on stimulus generalization. *Journal of Experimental Psychology*, *58*(5), 321–334.
Heiser, M., Iacoboni, M., Maeda, F., Marcus J., & Mazziotta J. C. (2003). The essential role of Broca's area in imitation. *European Journal of Neuroscience*, *17*(5), 1123–1128.
Herrnstein, R. J. (1961). Relative and absolute strength of responses as a function of frequency of reinforcement. *Journal of the Experimental Analysis of Behavior*, *4*, 267–272.
Herrnstein, R. J. (1970). On the law of effect. *Journal of the Experimental Analysis of Behavior*, *13*, 243–266.
Hineline, P. N. (1977). Negative reinforcement and avoidance. In W. K. Honig & J. E. R. Staddon (Eds.) *Handbook of operant behavior* (pp. 364–414). Englewood Cliffs, NJ: Prentice Hall.
Hobson, R., & Lee, A. (1999). Imitation and identification in autism. *Journal of Child Psychology and Psychiatry*, *40*(4), 649–659.
Horner, V., & Whiten, A. (2007). Learning from others' mistakes? Limits on understanding a trap-tube task by young chimpanzees and children. *Journal of Comparative Psychology*, *121*, 12–21.
Humphreys, L. G. (1939). The effect of random alternation of reinforcement on the acquisition and extinction of conditioned eyelid reactions. *Journal of Experimental Psychology*, *25*, 141–158.

Ingersoll, B. (2010). Brief report: Pilot randomized controlled trial of reciprocal imitation training for teaching elicited and spontaneous imitation to children with autism. *Journal of Autism and Developmental Disorders, 40*(9), 1154–1160.

Innis, N. K., Mitchell, S. K., & Staddon, J. E. R. (1993). Temporal control on interval schedules: What determines the postreinforcement pause? *Journal of the Experimental Analysis of Behavior, 60*, 293–311.

Johnston, J. M., & Pennypacker, H. S. (2008). *Strategies and tactics of behavioral research* (3rd ed.). London: Routledge.

Kaplan-Reimer, H., Sidener, T. M., Reeve, K. F., & Sidener, D. W. (2011). Using stimulus control procedures to teach indoor rock-climbing to children with autism. *Behavioral Interventions, 26*(1), 1–22.

Kazdin, A. E. (2011). *Single-case research designs: Methods for clinical and applied settings* (2nd ed.). New York: Oxford University Press.

Keller, F. S., & Schoenfeld, W. N. (1950). *Principles of psychology*. New York: Appleton-Century-Crofts.

Kelley, M. E., Shillingsburg, M. A., Castro, M. J., Addison, L. R., & LaRue Jr., R. H. (2007). Further evaluation of emerging speech in children with developmental disabilities: Training verbal behavior. *Journal of Applied Behavior Analysis, 40*, 431–445.

LaRue, R. H., Stewart, V., Piazza, C. C., Volkert, V. M., Patel, M., & Zeleny, J. (2011). Escape as reinforcement and escape extinction in the treatment of feeding problems. *Journal of Applied Behavior Analysis, 44*, 719–735.

Lattal, K. A. (1991). Scheduling positive reinforcers. In I. H. Iverson & K. A. Lattal (Eds.), *Experimental analysis of behavior* (Vol. 1, pp. 87–134). New York: Elsevier.

Lee, M. S. H., Yu, C. T., Martin, T. L., & Martin, G. L. (2010). On the relation between reinforcer efficacy and preference. *Journal of Applied Behavior Analysis, 43*, 995–100.

Lelas, S., Spealman, R. D., & Rowlett, J. K. (2000). Using behavior to elucidate receptor mechanisms: A review of the discriminative stimulus effects of benzodiazepines. *Experimental and Clinical Psychopharmacology, 8*(3), 294–311.

Lerman, D. C., & Iwata, B.A. (1996). Developing a technology for the use of operant extinction in clinical settings: An examination of the basic and applied literature. *Journal of Applied Behavior Analysis, 29*, 345–382.

Logue, A. W. (1995). *Self-control: Waiting until tomorrow for what you want today*. Englewood Cliffs, NJ: Prentice Hall.

Logue, A. W. (2000). Self-control and health behavior. In W. K. Bickel & R. E. Vuchinich (Eds.), *Reframing health behavior change with behavioral economics* (pp. 167–192). Mahwah, NJ: Erlbaum

Mazur, J. E. (1982). A molecular approach to ratio schedule performance. In M. L. Commons, R. J. Herrnstein, & H. Rachlin (Eds.), *Quantitative analyses of behavior (Vol. 2). Matching and maximizing accounts*. Cambridge, MA: Ballinger.

Mazur, J. E. (1983). Steady-state performance on fixed-, mixed-, and random-ratio schedules. *Journal of the Experimental Analysis of Behavior, 39*, 293–307.

Mazur, J. E. (1987). An adjusting procedure for studying delayed reinforcement. In M. L. Commons, J. E. Mazur, J. A. Nevin, & H. Rachlin (Eds.), *Quantitative analyses of behavior: Vol. 5. The effect of delay and of intervening events on reinforcement value* (pp. 55–73). Hillsdale, NJ: Erlbaum.

Mazur, J. E., & Fantino, E. (2014). Choice. In F. K. McSweeney & E. S. Murphy (Eds.) *Wiley-Blackwell handbook of operant and classical conditioning* (pp. 195–220). Oxford: Wiley-Blackwell.

McSweeney, F. K., & Murphy, E. S. (2009). Sensitization and habituation regulate reinforcer effectiveness. *Neurobiology of Learning and Memory, 92*, 189–198.

McSweeney, F. K., & Murphy, E. S. (2014). Characteristics, theories, and implications of dynamic changes in reinforcer effectiveness. In F. K. McSweeney & E. S. Murphy (Eds.)

Wiley-Blackwell handbook of operant and classical conditioning (pp. 339–368). Oxford: Wiley-Blackwell.

McSweeney, F. K., & Weatherly, J. N. (1998). Habituation to the reinforcer may contribute to multiple-schedule behavioral contrast. *Journal of the Experimental Analysis of Behavior, 69*, 199–221.

Michael, J. (1982). Distinguishing between the discriminative and motivational functions of stimuli. *Journal of the Experimental Analysis of Behavior, 37*, 149–155.

Michael, J. (1993). Establishing operations. *The Behavior Analyst, 16*, 191–206.

Miller, L. K. (2006). *Principles of everyday behavior analysis* (4th ed.). Belmont, CA: Thomson Wadsworth.

Miltenberger, R. G., & Crosland, K. A. (2014). Parenting. In F. K. McSweeney & E. S. Murphy (Eds.), *Wiley-Blackwell handbook of operant and classical conditioning* (pp. 509–531). Oxford: Wiley-Blackwell.

Mowrer, O. H., & Lamoreaux, R. R. (1946). Fear as an intervening variable in avoidance conditioning. *Journal of Comparative and Physiological Psychology, 39*, 29–50.

Nevin, J. A., & Grace, R. C. (2000). Behavioral momentum and the Law of Effect. *Behavioral and Brain Sciences, 23*, 73–130.

Palmer, D. C. (2014). Verbal behavior. In F. K. McSweeney & E. S. Murphy (Eds.), *Wiley Blackwell handbook of operant and classical conditioning* (pp. 369–391). Oxford: Wiley-Blackwell.

Pisacreta, R. (1982). A comparison of forward and backward procedures for the acquisition of response chains in pigeons. *Bulletin of the Psychonomic Society, 20*(4), 233–236.

Powell, R. W. (1968). The effect of small sequential changes in fixed-ratio size upon the post reinforcement pause. *Journal of the Experimental Analysis of Behavior, 11*, 589–593.

Pryor, K. (2001). *Getting started: Clicker training for cats.* Waltham, MA: Sunshine Books.

Pryor, K., & Ramirez, K. (2014). Modern animal training. In F. K. McSweeney & E. S. Murphy (Eds.), *Wiley-Blackwell handbook of operant and classical conditioning* (pp. 455–482). Oxford: Wiley-Blackwell.

Reed, P., & Wright, J. E. (1988). Effects of magnitude of food reinforcement on free-operant response rates. *Journal of the Experimental Analysis of Behavior, 49*, 75–85.

Reynolds, G. S. (1961). Behavioral contrast. *Journal of the Experimental Analysis of Behavior, 4*, 57–71.

Risley, T. R. (1968). The effects and side effects of punishing the autistic behaviors of a deviant child. *Journal of Applied Behavior Analysis, 1*, 21–34.

Rizzolatti, G., & Fabbri-Destro, M. (2010). Mirror neurons: From discovery to Autism. *Experimental Brain Research, 200*(3–4), 223–237.

Rushall, B. S., & Ford, D. (1982). Teaching backwards—an alternate skill instruction progression. *CAHPER Journal, 48*(5), 16–20.

Shook, G. L., & Favell, J. E. (2008). The Behavior Analyst Certification Board and the profession of behavior analysis. *Behavior Analysis in Practice, 1*(1), 44–48.

Sidman, M. (1953). Two temporal parameters in the maintenance of avoidance behavior of the white rat. *Journal of Comparative and Physiological Psychology, 46*, 253–261.

Sidman, M. (1960). *Tactic of scientific research: Evaluating experimental data in psychology.* New York: Basic Books.

Sidman, M. (1989). *Coercion and its fallout.* Boston, MA: Authors Cooperative.

Simek, T. C., & O'Brien, R. M. (1981). *Total golf: A behavioral approach to lowering your score and getting more out of your game.* New York: Doubleday.

Skinner, B. F. (1938). *Behavior of organisms: An experimental analysis.* New York: Appleton-Century-Crofts.

Skinner, B. F. (1945). The operational analysis of psychological terms. *Psychological Review, 52*, 270–277.

Skinner, B. F. (1950). Are theories of learning necessary? *Psychological Review, 57*, 193–216.

Skinner, B. F. (1951). How to teach animals. *Scientific American, 185*(12), 26–29.

Skinner, B. F. (1953). *Science and human behavior.* New York: Macmillan.

Skinner, B. F. (1957). *Verbal behavior.* New York: Appleton-Century-Crofts.

Skinner, B. F. (1974). *About behaviorism.* New York: Knopf.

Skinner, B. F. (1977). Why I am not a cognitive psychologist. *Behaviorism, 5,* 1–10.

Skinner, B. F. (1987). Whatever happened to psychology as the science of behavior? *American Psychologist, 42,* 780–786.

Skinner, B. F. (1990). Can psychology be a science of mind? *American Psychologist, 45,* 1206–1210.

Slocum, S. K., & Tiger, J. H. (2011). An assessment of the efficiency of and child preference for forward and backward chaining. *Journal of Applied Behavior Analysis, 44*(4), 793–805.

Smeets, P. M., Lancioni, G. E., Ball, T. S., & Oliva, D. S. (1985). Shaping self-initiated toileting in infants. *Journal of Applied Behavior Analysis, 18,* 303–308.

Spooner, F., & Spooner, D. (1984). A review of chaining techniques: Implications for future research and practice. *Education and Training of the Mentally Retarded, 19*(2), 114–124.

Stokes, T. F., & Baer, D. M. (1977). An implicit technology of generalization. *Journal of Applied Behavior Analysis, 10*(2), 349–367.

Tatham, T. A., Wanchisen, B. A., & Hineline, P. N. (1993). Effects of fixed and variable ratios on human behavioral variability. *Journal of the Experimental Analysis of Behavior, 59,* 349–359.

Thompson, R. F. (2014). Habituation revisited. In F. K. McSweeney & E. S. Murphy (Eds.), *Wiley-Blackwell handbook of operant and classical conditioning* (pp. 79–94). Oxford: Wiley-Blackwell.

Thompson, T. (2014). Autism and behavior analysis: History and current status. In F. K. McSweeney & E. S. Murphy (Eds.), *Wiley-Blackwell handbook of operant and classical conditioning* (pp. 483–508). Oxford: Wiley-Blackwell.

Troisi, J., LeMay, B. J., & Järbe, T. C. (2010). Transfer of the discriminative stimulus effects of Δ^9-THC and nicotine from one operant response to another in rats. *Psychopharmacology, 212*(2), 171–179.

Twyman, J. (2014). Behavior analysis in education. In F. K. McSweeney & E. S. Murphy (Eds.), *Wiley-Blackwell handbook of operant and classical conditioning* (pp. 553–558). Oxford: Wiley-Blackwell.

Van Houten, R., & Rudolph, R. (1972). The development of stimulus control with and without a lighted key. *Journal of the Experimental Analysis of Behavior, 18*(2), 217–222.

Vurbic, D., & Bouton, M.E. (2014). A contemporary behavioral perspective on extinction. In F. K. McSweeney & E. S. Murphy (Eds.) *Wiley-Blackwell handbook of operant and classical conditioning* (pp. 53–76). Oxford: Wiley-Blackwell.

Walls, R. T., Zane, T., & Ellis, W. D. (1981). Forward and backward chaining, and whole task methods: Training assembly tasks in vocational rehabilitation. *Behavior Modification, 5*(1), 61–74.

Want, S. C., & Harris, P. L. (2001). Learning from other people's mistakes: Causal understanding in learning to use a tool. *Child Development, 72*(2), 431–443.

Watanabe, S., Sakamoto, J., & Wakita, M. (1995). Pigeons' discrimination of painting by Monet and Picasso. *Journal of the Experimental Analysis of Behavior, 63*(2), 165–174.

Weiss, K. M. (1978). A comparison of forward and backward procedures for the acquisition of response chains in humans. *Journal of the Experimental Analysis of Behavior, 29*(2), 255–259.

Wolf, M. M., Risley, T. R., &, Mees, H. (1964). Application of operant conditioning procedures to the behaviour problems of an autistic child. *Behaviour Research and Therapy, 1,* 305–312.

9

Choice

James E. Mazur and Edmund Fantino

Introduction

Throughout the history of research on operant conditioning, psychologists have shown great interest in the question of how organisms make choices. Since the 1950s, thousands of experiments on choice have been conducted in operant conditioning chambers with two or three identical manipulanda (e.g., response keys for pigeons, levers for rodents). It is not surprising that those who study operant conditioning are interested in choice, because outside the laboratory these two topics are almost inseparable. On any ordinary day, a person makes countless choices about such matters as what clothes to wear, what food to eat, what people to speak to and what to say, what chores to perform at home and at work, and how much time to spend on each activity. Although their daily routines are very different, animals in their natural environments also continually make choices among the many options that are currently available. Psychologists who study choice have examined such topics as how organisms choose between different behaviors, when and why they switch from one behavior to another, and how much time they devote to different behaviors.

This chapter will focus on three categories of choice procedures that have been used extensively by behavioral researchers. The first major section will focus on *concurrent schedules*—situations in which two or more reinforcement schedules are available simultaneously. In concurrent schedules, choice is an ongoing process—at any moment, the individual can continue with one response or switch to another response, either of which might or might not result in the delivery of a reinforcer. The second major section will examine *concurrent-chain schedules*, which are more complex procedures that alternate between initial links and terminal links. The initial links are similar to simple concurrent schedules—typically, two variable-interval (VI) schedules

The Wiley Blackwell Handbook of Operant and Classical Conditioning, First Edition.
Edited by Frances K. McSweeney and Eric S. Murphy.

operating concurrently. However, responding in the initial links does not lead directly to primary reinforcers, but rather to the terminal links—additional schedules in which reinforcers can be collected. Concurrent-chain schedules therefore separate choice behavior into a choice period (the initial links) and a consequences period (the terminal links). Finally, the third major section will examine discrete-trial choice procedures, in which an individual makes a choice by producing a single, brief response (e.g., a single key peck) and then usually cannot switch choices for a certain period of time. As will be shown, each of these different categories of choice procedures has yielded many valuable empirical findings, and each has led to important theoretical advances.

Concurrent Schedules

Herrnstein's Experiment and the Matching Law

Herrnstein (1961) conducted a classic experiment with three pigeons that led to his development of the matching law. The experiment was conducted in a chamber with two response keys and a food hopper that delivered controlled access to grain. Each key was associated with its own VI schedule that operated continuously throughout each session—each VI schedule set up reinforcers at irregular and unpredictable intervals, after which a response on the appropriate key was required to collect the reinforcer. A pigeon could switch between keys at any time. The pigeons were presented with a series of conditions, each lasting at least 17 sessions, and in each condition a different pair of VI schedules was in effect. For example, in one condition, the VI schedule for the left key delivered about 26 reinforcers per hour, and the VI schedule for the right key delivered about 13 reinforcers per hour. The pigeons typically made several thousand responses per hour, but in this condition, where two-thirds of the reinforcers were delivered by the left key, the pigeons made about two-third of their responses on the left key. As shown in Figure 9.1, similar results were obtained in other conditions with other pairs of VI schedules: In all cases, the pigeons' response percentages approximately equaled (matched) the reinforcement percentages.

Based on these data, Herrnstein (1961) proposed the most basic version of the matching law:

$$\frac{B_1}{B_1 + B_2} = \frac{R_1}{R_1 + R_2}, \tag{1}$$

where B_1 and B_2 are response rates on alternatives 1 and 2 (number of responses divided by total session time), and R_1 and R_2 are the reinforcement rates for the two alternatives. Equation 1 states that the percentage of responses on one alternative will equal the percentage of reinforcers delivered by that alternative. The matching law can also be written in a form that emphasizes response ratios and reinforcement ratios:

$$\frac{B_1}{B_2} = \frac{R_1}{R_2}. \tag{2}$$

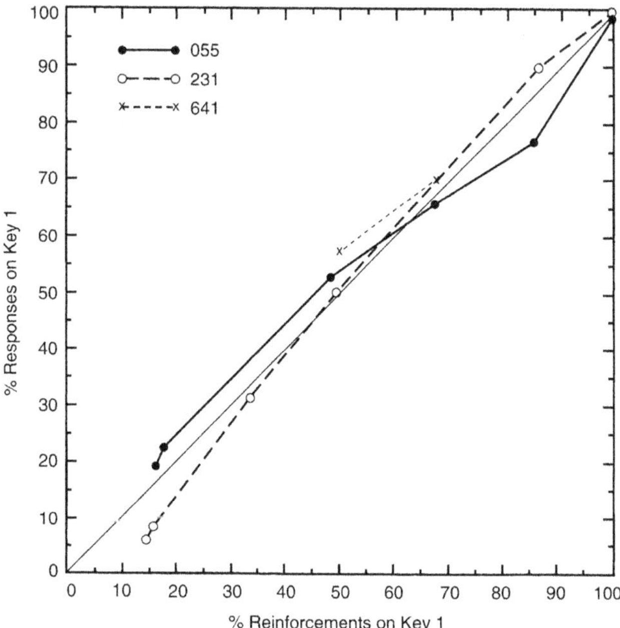

Figure 9.1 Response percentages on Key 1 are plotted as a function of the reinforcement percentages for the three pigeons in the experiment. From "Relative and absolute strength of response as a function of frequency of reinforcement," by R. J. Herrnstein (1961), *Journal of the Experimental Analysis of Behavior, 4*, p. 268. Copyright 1961 by the Society for the Experimental Analysis of Behavior. Reprinted with permission.

One important additional feature of Herrnstein's (1961) procedure was that it included a 1.5-s changeover delay (COD): Each time a pigeon switched from responding on one key to the other, a minimum of 1.5-s had to elapse before a subsequent keypeck could be reinforced. The purpose of the COD was to decrease the possibility of inadvertently reinforcing switching behavior, and it turns out that the presence of a COD can make a big difference. Without a COD, animals tend to exhibit more frequent switching between alternatives, and this results in *undermatching*—their response percentages are closer to 50% than are the reinforcement percentages (e.g., Shull & Pliskoff, 1967).

Deviations from Matching and the Generalized Matching Law

Whether or not a COD is used, undermatching has been a frequent finding in experiments with concurrent VI schedules (e.g., Koffarnus & Woods, 2008; Myers & Myers, 1977). Several explanations of undermatching have been proposed, including the hypothesis that animals may sometimes fail to discriminate or fail to remember which response produced a reinforcer (Davison & Jenkins, 1985), and a model based on the principle of selection by consequences (McDowell & Caron, 2007). Undermatching is just one of several ways in which an animal's choice behavior may depart from the predictions of Equation 1. Baum (1974, 1979) described two other types of deviations from matching—overmatching and bias. *Overmatching* occurs when the animal's choice proportions are more extreme than the reinforcement proportions (e.g., making 80% of its responses on one alternative when that alternative delivers only 70% of the reinforcers). Overmatching has been observed when switching from one alternative to the other is punished (Todorov, 1971) or when switching takes time or effort (Baum, 1982): In such circumstances, animals will spend more time responding on the alternative with the higher rate of reinforcement, seldom switching to the other alternative. *Bias* refers to cases where an animal consistently makes more responses on one alternative than predicted by the matching law. This could be the result of a position preference, a color preference, a subtle difference in the amount of effort required to make one response compared to the other, and so on.

To accommodate these deviations from Equation 1, Baum (1974, 1979) proposed an equation now known as the generalized matching law:

$$\frac{B_1}{B_2} = b\left(\frac{R_1}{R_2}\right)^s, \tag{3}$$

where b is a measure of bias for one alternative or the other, and the exponent s reflects sensitivity to the differences in reinforcement rates for the two alternatives. Values of s less than 1 reflect undermatching, and values greater than 1 reflect overmatching. If both b and s are equal to 1, Equation 3 reduces to the original version of the matching law (Equation 2).

The generalized matching law has been successfully applied to the results from numerous experiments on concurrent schedules, with species as diverse as humans (e.g., Ecott & Critchfield, 2004; Rasmussen & Newland, 2008; Pierce & Epling, 1983), goats (Foster, Matthews, Temple, & Poling, 1997), and quail neonates (Schneider & Lickliter, 2010). The basic form of Equation 3 can be easily modified to handle choices where the two alternative reinforcers differ in amount or quality rather than rate of delivery (see Davison & McCarthy, 1988). The generalized matching law has proven to be a versatile and useful framework for modeling behavior on concurrent VI schedules.

Theoretical Analyses of Matching

Having established that matching (Equations 1 and 2) or generalized matching (Equation 3) are very general results in concurrent VI schedules, theorists attempted to explain why this is so. In his early writings, Herrnstein (1961, 1970) suggested that the matching law provided not only a description of behavior on concurrent VI schedules, but an explanation as well. That is, he proposed that matching is a fundamental principle of choice: When animals are faced with two or more alternatives that deliver reinforcers at different rates, they tend to distribute their responses so that their response percentages approximately match the reinforcement percentages. However, results from other procedures soon questioned the adequacy of this viewpoint. These include experiments with concurrent variable-ratio (VR) schedules. In VR schedules, a variable and unpredictable number of responses is required for each reinforcer. If an animal is presented with concurrent VR schedules, it is easy to show that there are only two ways that the animal can exhibit matching—by responding exclusively on the schedule with the shorter VR schedule, or by responding exclusively on the longer VR schedule. To see why, notice that the response:reinforcer ratio is fixed on any VR schedule. For example, with concurrent VR 20 VR 40 schedules, the response:reinforcer ratios are fixed at 20:1 for the first schedule and 40:1 for the second. The only way that Equation 1 can be satisfied is if $B_1/(B_1 + B_2) = 0$ or if $B_1/(B_1 + B_2) = 1$. The problem for the matching law is that both animals (Herrnstein & Loveland, 1975) and humans (Shah, Bradshaw, & Szabadi, 1989) almost always respond exclusively on the shorter VR schedule, never on the longer one. Choosing the schedule with the smaller response requirement makes intuitive sense, but the matching law cannot explain why this happens (though it is not contradicted by this finding).

Based on these and other findings, Herrnstein and Vaughan (1980) developed the theory of *melioration*. Melioration means "making better," and the essence of melioration theory is that an organism will shift its behavior to whichever alternative currently has a better reinforcer/response ratio. Another way to express the basic matching relation is:

$$\frac{R_1}{B_1} = \frac{R_2}{B_2}. \tag{4}$$

This form of the equation emphasizes the fact that when matching occurs, the number of reinforcers to responses is equal for the two alternatives. Melioration theory states that if these two ratios are unequal, the individual will continue to shift more of its responses to the alternative with the larger reinforcer/response ratio until the ratios become equal, or until the individual is responding exclusively on one alternative. This theory gives a straightforward explanation for why animals almost always show exclusive preference for the shorter of two VR schedules: The reinforcer/response ratio does not change on VR schedules no matter how an animal distributes its responses. For example, the ratio is always 1/25 for a VR 25 schedule, and it is always 1/50 for a VR 50 schedule. Because the reinforcer/response ratio is greater for the VR 25 schedule, the animal's responding should continue to shift to the VR 25 schedule until it is responding on that schedule exclusively.

A very different approach to choice behavior is provided by optimization theories (or molar maximization theories). The basic premise of these theories is that in choice situations, organisms tend to distribute their responses in a way that maximizes the total amount of reinforcement, or minimizes the amount of time or effort involved in obtaining reinforcers. Rachlin, Green, Kagel, and Battalio (1976) used the results of computer simulations to argue that in concurrent VI schedules, matching response rates to reinforcement rates maximizes the overall rate of reinforcement. In short, they proposed that matching occurs because it is the optimal way to distribute responses in concurrent VI schedules. To evaluate whether optimization theory does indeed account for matching behavior, various studies with both humans and nonhumans have arranged choice situations for which the matching law and optimization theory make distinctly different predictions. Although some data seem to be consistent with optimization theory (e.g., Sakagami, Hursh, Christensen, & Silberberg,

1989), most studies have obtained results that favored the matching law (e.g., Davison, 1992; Mazur, 1981). One way to compare the two theories is to examine choice distributions on concurrent VI VR schedules. According to optimization theory, individuals should exhibit a bias for the VR schedule. This is because the number of reinforcers delivered by the VR schedule is directly proportional to the number of responses, but this is not the case on a VI schedule, so the animal can earn more reinforcers (optimize) by responding more on the VR than on the VI schedule. However, studies with pigeons (DeCarlo, 1985; Vyse & Belke, 1992) and with college students (Savastano & Fantino, 1994) did not find the bias toward the VR schedule that is predicted by optimization theory; instead, response proportions approximately matched reinforcement proportions. Other studies have arranged complex response/reinforcer feedback functions (i.e., functions that specify what reinforcement rate will occur for every different response rate) to distinguish between the predictions of matching and optimization, and these studies have also supported matching (or melioration) rather than optimization (e.g., Herrnstein, Loewenstein, Prelec, & Vaughan, 1993; Herrnstein & Prelec, 1992; Vaughan, 1981).

Other theorists have attempted to account for matching behavior by taking a molecular approach—that is, by analyzing the moment-to-moment patterns in an animal's choices and how they might reflect short-term changes in the reinforcement probabilities for the two alternatives. For example, Silberberg, Hamilton, Ziriax, and Casey (1978) used a discrete-trial analogue to a concurrent VI VI procedure, in which a short inter-trial interval (ITI) separated each response. Because of the nature of VI schedules, as a pigeon made several consecutive responses on one VI schedule, the probability of reinforcement for a switch to the other VI steadily increased. The key finding of Silberberg et al. was that the pigeons' trial-by-trial response probabilities changed in ways that mirrored the trial-by-trial changes in the reinforcement probabilities. They argued that these results supported the principle of *momentary maximizing*, which states that at each moment, an animal tends to choose whichever response has the higher momentary probability of reinforcement. Furthermore, they asserted that following the principle of momentary maximizes results in matching behavior at the molar level. Subsequent studies looking for evidence of momentary maximizing have obtained mixed results. Nevin (1979) conducted a similar discrete-trial experiment but found no evidence for momentary maximizing, but his pigeons exhibited matching at the molar level (cf. Heyman, 1979). However, other researchers have found evidence supporting the principle of momentary maximizing (e.g., Brown & Cleaveland, 2009; Hinson & Staddon, 1983; Todorov, Souza, & Bori, 1993). Although matching at the molar level may not always be the result of momentary maximizing, there is now abundant evidence for systematic moment-to-moment changes in behavior in concurrent VI schedules.

Rapid Schedule Changes and Fine-Grain Response Patterns

A large body of research conducted by Davison, Baum, and their colleagues has demonstrated consistent short-term fluctuations in response proportions that depend on which alternative delivered the last few reinforcers. Whereas most previous experiments on matching kept the same pair of VI schedules in effect for many sessions, Davison and Baum (2000) used a procedure in which pigeons were presented with

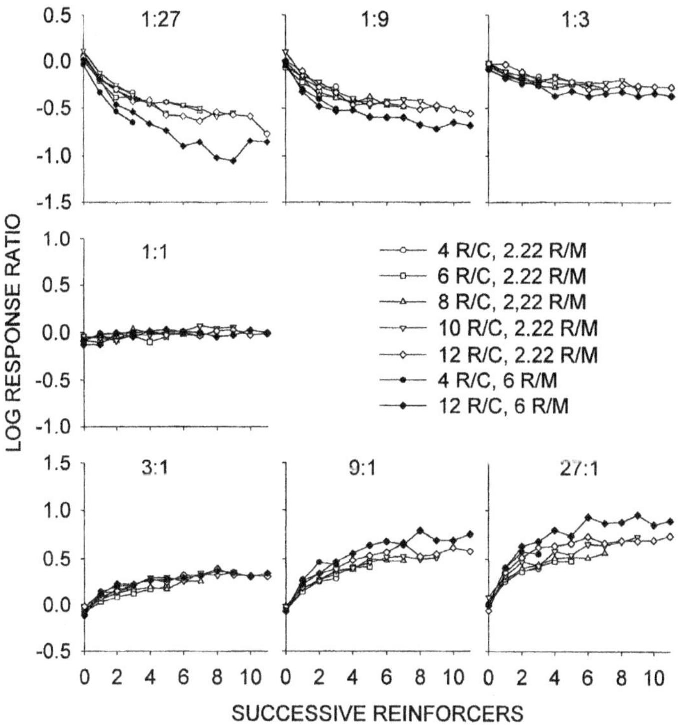

Figure 9.2 Mean log response ratios are shown for the seven different reinforcer ratios (labeled in each panel), plotted as a function of the number of reinforcers delivered since the beginning of the component. R/C = reinforcers per component; R/M = reinforcers per minute. From "Choice in a variable environment: Every reinforcer counts," by M. Davison and W. M. Baum, 2000, *Journal of the Experimental Analysis of Behavior*, *74*, p. 11. Copyright 2000 by the Society for the Experimental Analysis of Behavior. Reprinted with permission.

seven different pairs of VI schedules in a single session. Each daily session was divided into seven components (separated by 10-s blackouts), and the reinforcer ratios (R_1:R_2) in these components were 27:1, 9:1, 3:1, 1:1, 1:3, 1:9, and 1:27. The order of components varied randomly each day, and there were no stimuli to indicate which schedules were in effect, so at the start of each new component there was no way for a pigeon to know which pair of VI schedules was in effect. Davison and Baum could therefore observe how preference for the richer schedule developed as successive reinforcers were delivered. They found that with these rapid changes in the reinforcement schedules, there were rapid changes in preference. Figure 9.2 shows mean log response ratios with the seven different reinforcer ratios, plotted as a function of the number of reinforcers delivered since the beginning of the component. (We will not consider the different procedural variations represented by the different symbols in each panel, but only the main trends.) As can be seen, the pigeons began each component with a log response ratio near zero (indicating equal responding on the two schedules). As successive reinforcers were delivered, responding quickly shifted toward the richer schedule, and the magnitude of the shift depended on the reinforcer ratio (i.e., more extreme shifts in preference with a reinforcer ratio of 27:1 than with 3:1).

Based on their detailed data analyses, Davison and Baum (2000) concluded that "every reinforcer counts"—every reinforcer has an effect on subsequent choice behavior. One piece of evidence comes from what are called *preference pulses.* Various studies using the procedure of Davison and Baum have found that after each reinforcer delivery, there is a temporary increase in response proportions for the alternative that just delivered the reinforcer, which may last for approximately 20 to 30 seconds (e.g., Aparicio & Baum, 2009; Boutros, Elliffe, & Davison, 2009). When reinforcer amounts are varied, larger reinforcers lead to preference pulses that are larger and last longer (Landon, Davidson, & Elliffe, 2003). The effects of a single reinforcer do not end with the disappearance of the preference pulse, however. Davison and Baum showed, in exquisite detail, how momentary choice proportions depended on which response key had delivered the last few reinforcers. For example, if the last three reinforcers were delivered from the left, left, and right keys, respectively, the left-key response ratio increased after the two left-key reinforcers and then dramatically decreased after the right-key reinforcer. Other data presented by Davison and Baum indicated that there were measurable effects of at least the last six reinforcers on current choice proportions.

This research on rapidly changing choice contingencies has demonstrated that reinforcer deliveries in a choice situation have effects that can be measured at several different levels, ranging from the immediate shifts seen as preference pulses to the long-term response distributions that are well described by the generalized matching law (Aparicio & Baum, 2009). Baum (2010) has argued that a complete understanding of choice behavior requires analyses at many different levels, and the data on concurrent-schedule choice certainly support this viewpoint.

Matching Outside the Laboratory

The matching law has been used in many reports of translational and applied research, and only a few examples can be presented here. Some researchers have attempted to demonstrate that the behaviors of individuals or groups in natural environments can be described by the generalized matching law. For example, Alferink, Critchfield, Hitt, and Higgins (2009) examined college and professional basketball players' choices of two-point versus three-point shots, and found that their choice percentages matched their reinforcement percentages (i.e., percentages of shots made), but with a bias for 3-point shots (which makes sense, because 3-point shots are worth more). An example of matching at a group level comes from an analysis of football teams' selections of running versus passing plays. Critchfield and colleagues (Reed, Critchfield, & Martens, 2006; Stilling & Critchfield, 2010) compared the play selection of American professional football teams. Different teams used different mixtures of passing versus running plays, probably because of factors such as the talents of their players and coaching philosophies. However, the researchers found a consistent pattern within this variability: With each team treated as one data point, the percentage of passing plays approximately matched the relative gains (yards per passing play versus yards running play). In research on consumer purchases, a few studies have applied the matching law to people's choices among different brands of products (e.g., Foxall, James, Oliveira-Castro, & Ribier, 2010; Oliveira-Castro, Foxall, & Wells, 2010). For example, Oliveira-Castro et al. (2010) found that they could use the generalized matching law to analyze consumers' choices among different brands of food products (e.g., baked beans, fruit juices) by taking into account such factors as the quality, price, and reputation of the different brands.

In applied research on children and adults with various behavior problems, the matching law has been used to analyze choices between socially appropriate and inappropriate behaviors. McDowell and Caron (2010) analyzed the spontaneous conversations of pairs of delinquent boys, classifying their statements into two classes—rule-break talk and normative talk. As measures of reinforcement, they counted the number of times a boy's statement was met with some statement of approval or agreement by the other boy in the conversation. They found that the boys' proportions of appropriate and inappropriate speech could be described by the generalized matching law, although there was substantial undermatching and a strong bias toward normative speech. Borrero et al. (2010) found that the rates of socially appropriate versus disruptive behaviors exhibited by individuals with developmental disabilities approximately matched the rates of reinforcement for these two classes of behaviors. They then developed an intervention strategy designed to lower the rate of reinforcement for disruptive behaviors, and the rates of these behaviors decreased.

Because of the complexities inherent in natural environments, applying quantitative models, such as the matching law, can be challenging. Matters that are usually straightforward in laboratory research (such as deciding how to count responses and reinforcers, or how to compare qualitatively different responses or reinforcers) can be a major source of concern. Despite these problems, studies in a variety of settings have shown that the generalized matching law can serve as a useful framework for analyzing the relationships between reinforcement and behavior.

Concurrent-Chain Schedules

The Matching Law Redux

Soon after Herrnstein (1961) and colleagues developed the matching law describing choice in simple concurrent schedules, he and his student Autor sought to extend the matching law to choice situations in which the choice was between different rates of conditioned reinforcement (Autor, 1960; Herrnstein, 1964). For example, instead of choosing between a VI 30-s schedule and a VI 90-s schedule (concurrent VI 30-s VI 90-s), the organism would respond on two (generally equal) concurrent schedules each leading to a particular "outcome schedule" that, in turn, led to food. Typically the two outcome schedules were different and the subject's preference was reflected in the proportion of responses made to each of the equal schedules (the initial links); whichever schedule was completed first led to the outcome schedule (terminal link) corresponding to that completed schedule. For example, for choice between VI 30-s and VI 90-s outcome schedules, equal VI schedules (e.g., VI 120-s schedules) would lead to either of the two outcome schedules, depending on which was chosen. Both studies supported a pleasing generality: in concurrent-chains too, choice proportions (initial links or choice phase) matched proportions of reinforcement (terminal link or outcome phase). Thus, for the values given above, where the reinforcement proportions were .75 for the VI 30-s outcome, pigeons' choice proportions for that outcome were also about .75. The "matching law" appeared to have considerable generality.

Delay-Reduction Theory

The early research on the matching law and conditioned reinforcement led to a question with at least three plausible answers. Which of the following primarily controls choice responding: rate of conditioned reinforcement, rate of primary reinforcement, or both? Rate of conditioned reinforcement is the rate at which the terminal link is produced, that is, the rate at which initial-link responding produces terminal-link entry. Rate of primary reinforcement is the rate at which terminal-link responding produces primary reinforcement (here food). Fantino (1969) approached this question by exploring whether the proportion of responses in the initial links ("choice phase") is primarily a function of the rate of conditioned reinforcement, as measured by the duration of the (here) unequal initial links, the rate of primary reinforcement, as measured by duration of the unequal terminal links, or by the overall rate of reinforcement, which was equal for the two alternatives. One route to reward consisted of a VI 90-s initial link leading to a VI 30-s outcome link, whereas the alternative consisted of a VI 30-s initial link leading to a VI 90-s outcome link. Note that the overall rate of reinforcement is one reinforcement every 120 seconds for either alternative. Thus, if overall rate of reinforcement is the critical variable, choice should be equal for the two alternatives. If rate of conditioned reinforcement is the critical variable more choice responding should be emitted to the initial link of the chain VI 30-s VI 90-s alternative since it offers a rate of conditioned reinforcement that is three times as great as the chain VI 90-s VI 30-s alternative (predicted choice proportion of .75). Finally, if rate of primary reinforcement is the critical variable then more choice responding should be emitted to the initial link of the chain VI 90-s VI 30-s alternative. Of course intermediate outcomes were possible, even likely, since more than one variable might play a role in choice responding. Thus, the choice proportion for the VI 30-s outcome might be anywhere from .25, suggesting dominance by rate of conditioned reinforcement, to .75, suggesting dominance by rate of primary reinforcement.

The results, however, did not conform to any of these outcomes. Instead, the mean choice proportion for the schedule leading to the shorter terminal-link outcome was 94%. This result (see also McDevitt & Williams, 2010) suggested that another approach was called for. Specifically, it appeared that choice in this situation might be controlled by some other variable than a straightforward one such as rate of conditioned reinforcement or of primary reinforcement, or a mixture of both. For none of those variables predicted choice proportions exceeding .75. Another perspective was called for.

It appeared that the critical variable might be the improvement, in terms of proximity to primary reinforcement, correlated with the onset of the stimulus signaling the terminal (outcome) link of the chain. For example, consider the case in which both initial-link stimuli are associated with equivalent VI 120-s schedules, one leading to a VI 30-s outcome (terminal link) and the other to a VI 90-s outcome. Owing to the nature of VI schedules, the two VI schedules will "pay off" at about the same rate over a wide range of preference. The overall expected time to reinforcement from the onset of a trial to receipt of food is 120 s (1/2 × 120 s in the choice phase—since the initial links operate concurrently—and ½ x 30 s + ½ × 90 s in the outcome—or terminal-link phase sums to 120 s). Therefore onset of the VI 30-s outcome is correlated with a 120–30 or a 90-s reduction in average time to reinforcement whereas the 90-s outcome is correlated with only a 30-s reduction in average time to reinforcement (120–90). Thus, for these values the delay-reduction approach makes a choice prediction similar to that of the matching law and nothing is seemingly gained by introducing it. However, consider somewhat longer and shorter initial-link values, say VI 600-s and VI 40-s. With equal VI 600-s initial links, and the same VI 30-s and VI 90-s terminal links as in the previous example, the predicted choice proportion is now sharply different from that of the matching law, or .55 instead of .75. Similarly, with equal VI 40-s initial links the choice proportion predicted by this approach is exclusive preference for the richer VI 30 s outcome. Both the data of Fantino (1969) and Squires and Fantino (1971) supported this delay-reduction (or relative improvement to reinforcement) view. According to the Squires and Fantino equation, choice is described as follows:

$$\frac{R_L}{R_L + R_R} \begin{cases} = \dfrac{r_L(T - t_{2L})}{r_L(T - t_{2L}) + r_R(T - t_{2R})} & (\text{when } t_L < T,\ t_R < T) \\ = 1 & (\text{when } t_L < T,\ t_R > T) \\ = 0 & (\text{when } t_L > T,\ t_R < T) \end{cases} \qquad (5)$$

where T represents the expected time to primary reinforcement from the onset of the initial links, r_L equals the rate of primary reinforcement on the left key, r_R equals the rate of primary reinforcement on the right key, and $t2_L$ and $t2_R$ represent the expected time to reinforcement in the terminal link for the left and right keys respectively.

While these results complicated the elegant simplicity of a choice world in which the same general law (matching) applied to choice in both simple concurrent and more complicated concurrent-chain schedules, they also led to a broader view of choice behavior as we shall see when discussing more recent models of choice (e.g., Grace, 1994; Mazur, 2001). The results also make important contact with the literature on self-control. The fact that acceptability of the less preferred of two acceptable outcomes increases as the time to any reward increases (corresponding to increasing equal initial-link values in concurrent-chains schedules as discussed above) is comparable to early studies of self-control (Navarick & Fantino, 1976; Rachlin & Green, 1972). Consistent with delay-reduction theory, these studies showed that the shorter the choice phase duration, the greater impulsivity in the sense of choosing the more immediate reward. Self-control is enhanced when time to the effective choice is increased. People may find sacrifices (e.g., regarding abstinence from fattening foods) or increases in the price of a commodity (such as fuel) more palatable when delayed.

The early research reviewed so far was supplemented by the papers of Killeen and Fantino (1990) and by Luco (1990). The former paper showed the close correspondence between Killeen's (1982) incentive theory and delay-reduction theory (DRT).

Killeen and Fantino also compared their joint model to other major approaches, such as Mazur's (1984) equivalence rule and Vaughan's (1985) melioration theory. The primary thrust of Luco's paper was to integrate the central points of the various models. He proved that "in the case of equal initial links, the model derived from melioration coincided with Fantino's original model for full (reliable) reinforcement and with the model proposed by Spetch and Dunn (1987) for percentage (unreliable) reinforcement. In the general case of unequal initial links, the model derived from melioration differs from the revised model advanced by Squires and Fantino (1971) only in the factors affecting the delay-reduction terms ($T - t_L$) and ($T\text{-}t_R$)" (Luco, 1990, p.53).

The Contextual Choice and Hyperbolic Value-Added Models

Two viable alternatives to the delay-reduction view were proposed subsequently by Grace (1994) and by Mazur (2001). Grace's contextual choice model (CCM) was applied to 10 data sets previously analyzed in an influential paper by Davison (1987). Whereas DRT is based on the idea that choice is determined by the relative improvement in the time to reward correlated with the onset of the stimuli being chosen, CCM is relatively atheoretical, generalizing Baum's (1974) generalized matching law by incorporating context effects. For example, it includes free parameters that reflect bias for one alternative over the other, sensitivity to differences in the initial-link schedules, and sensitivity to differences in the terminal-link schedules. Applying his model to a total of 92 data sets from individual organisms in 19 experiments, Grace found that CCM could account for roughly 90% of the data variance, a clear improvement over extant alternative models. However, Mazur (2001) pointed out that the superiority of CCM might reflect the greater number of free parameters introduced. Thus, Mazur added the same number of free parameters to DRT and to his own hyperbolic value-added model (HVA) and showed that the superiority of CCM was then eliminated. In other words, he asked how these two models would fare when applied to the very same data sets that Grace (1994) had applied to assess his CCM model. We have already introduced DRT. But the HVA model requires introduction.

A cornerstone of HVA theory is that reinforcer value decreases with increasing delay to primary reinforcement. With respect to concurrent-chains schedules, HVA theory asserts that: the value of the terminal-link stimulus is a function of the time from the terminal-link onset to onset of primary reinforcement; and the value of the initial (or choice) link depends on the time between the onset of the initial link and the onset of primary reinforcement. The dependent variable, or choice proportion, is a function of the amount of value added when the organism achieves entry into the terminal link (or outcome phase). Mazur (2001) showed that the principle of value added is in many ways similar to the principle of delay reduction. Value added stresses the increase in value associated with terminal-link onset, whereas delay reduction stresses the increased proximity to reinforcement associated with terminal-link onset. While the theories are conceptually distinct they make comparable predictions in many situations. Each theory has been extended outside the realm of concurrent-chains schedules, in each case supporting their generality.

Mazur (2001) discussed important similarities and differences of the three models (CCM, DRT, and HVA) and they need not be repeated here. However the reader with some familiarity with the models may ask how the models may begin with different assumptions and yet make similar quantitative predictions. Mazur dealt with this issue (e.g., Mazur, 2001, p. 109). He showed that his principle of value addition accounts for the same set of predictions made by DRT concerning how changes in the duration of either initial or terminal links affect choice. But the two models have also given rise to unique predictions in domains outside of concurrent-chains schedules to which we now turn. For example, one advantage of the HVA model is that it was derived from a simpler model that makes accurate predictions for discrete-trial choice. This model will be discussed later under "Theoretical analyses and applications." Here we note only that a relatively simple and conceptually straightforward hyperbolic expression captures critical aspects of a number of experiments involving the discrete-trials adjusting-delay procedure.

Optimal Foraging

As with HVA theory, delay-reduction theory has been shown to have generality beyond the perhaps somewhat arcane world of concurrent-chains procedures. For example, DRT has been applied with some success to situations mimicking (and assessing) optimal foraging theory (OFT). George Collier developed an experimental analogue to OFT that proved influential in theory of both operant choice (psychology) and of behavioral ecology (biology). Early research by behavioral ecologists had shown support for models suggesting that organisms choose optimally. However, the results of several studies showed only modest, even unimpressive, quantitative support for OFT (reviewed in Fantino & Logan, 1979). By assessing OFT with the well-controlled procedures developed in the operant laboratory, a fairer test of OFT might be possible. The first influential effort in this area was a series of studies performed at Rutgers University by George Collier and his associates. For example, Collier (1977) suggested that research conducted in the laboratory should better simulate crucial aspects of field research but with much tighter experimental control. Research by Collier and his associates constituted a broad experimental analysis of the complete behavior chain involved in the behavior of feeding. Collier and his group experimentally analyzed several portions of the feeding chain, including the effect of different response requirements (schedule) on both the search and procurement stages of feeding. For example, in seminal studies from Collier's laboratory reviewed by Collier (1977) and by Fantino and Logan (1979), the subjects (rats) lived in experimental chambers where they were provided with their food and other needs. Typically two response levers were available. When the rat made a fixed number of responses (fixed-ratio schedule or FR) on the first ("search") lever, the light associated with that lever was extinguished and the onset of a second light (one of two) indicated the availability of food for responding on a second lever (the "procurement" lever). Each of these procurement lights was correlated with its own FR schedule leading to food. The difference was that when one of the procurement schedules was in effect food became available after only 5 responses (FR 5) whereas on the leaner procurement schedule food became available only after 200 responses (FR 200). It is important to note that—unlike the concurrent-chains procedure—in Collier's "successive encounters" procedure the alternatives are available successively, not simultaneously. The FR 5 and FR 200 outcomes were equally probable; the rat could accept the offered procurement condition by responding on the lever or reject it by not responding for 7.5 seconds. If the procurement condition was rejected, the subject returned to the search phase with the possibility of getting a better opportunity on the next trial. As the search cost increased, would rats be more likely to accept opportunities on the larger procurement ratio (FR 200)? In one manipulation, the cost of search (that is the cost to enter the procurement stage) was varied over conditions between FR 5 and FR 200. If the rats were behaving optimally, they should accept only the richer (FR 5) outcome when the search phase required as many responses as FR 100 or (especially) FR 200. On average, only when response costs in the search phase were more than 97½ responses, was accepting the FR 200 schedule superior to rejecting that outcome and returning to a new search.

While the results with rats generally supported Collier's predictions, and, hence, optimal foraging theory, the fit to the data was very approximate. For example in conditions where OFT predicted exclusive preference for the richer outcome, often as much as 40% acceptance of the inferior outcome was found. Studying pigeons and instituting procedural changes, Lea (1979) and later Abarca and Fantino (1982) and Fantino and Abarca (1985) obtained close fits between predictions of OFT and the data. Moreover, as the Abarca and Fantino papers showed, the predictions of OFT, developed in the behavioral ecology laboratory (biology) were virtually identical to those of DRT developed in the behavior-analytic laboratory (psychology), an exciting convergence.

The extension of DRT to choice for uncertain outcomes (the choice results, unpredictably, in one of usually two possible outcomes) has been developed successfully by Dunn, Spetch, and their colleagues (e.g., Dunn & Spetch, 1990; Spetch, Belke, Barnet, Dunn, & Pierce, 1990). Fantino, Preston, and Dunn (1993) have summarized other extensions of DRT to foraging situations including:

1. As search duration (initial-link duration) is increased, pigeons shift from rejecting to accepting the less profitable of two outcomes at the duration required by the models (Abarca & Fantino, 1982).
2. As equal outcome durations (terminal link) are increased, pigeons shift from accepting to rejecting the less preferred of two outcomes (Ito & Fantino, 1986).
3. In choice between a lean schedule always leading to food and a richer schedule leading to food on only a percentage of food trials, pigeons opted for whichever alternative provided the higher overall mean rate of reinforcement (Abarca, Fantino, & Ito, 1985).
4. Changing accessibility of the more profitable alternative has a greater effect on choice than changing accessibility of the less profitable alternative (Fantino & Abarca, 1985). By "accessibility" we mean the ease or difficulty—in length or effect—of reaching the outcome.
5. Preference for the more profitable outcome decreases as travel time (the time between a response on one alternative and the next response on the other alternative) between alternatives increases (i.e., pigeons become less selective; Fantino & Abarca, 1985).

6. Increased accessibility of the less profitable alternative leads to decreased acceptability of that alternative when accessibility is manipulated by varying the search time leading to the less profitable alternative (Fantino & Preston, 1988). Many have found this finding counterintuitive.

The commonality of predictions from OFT and DRT as well as the broad predictive powers of these models and of HVA, not only suggests a broad convergence or synthesis of choice models but also offers the promise of a richer and more precise understanding of choice. This theme has been echoed by behavioral ecologists such as Alasdair Houston and colleagues (e.g., Houston, McNamara, & Steer, 2007). They suggest that although DRT may not describe strictly optimal choice, "it is likely to be a good principle, given that errors occur" (Houston et al., 2007, p. 1539). Indeed, Williams and Fantino (1994) showed that in situations where OFT and DRT make divergent predictions, the (non-optimal) predictions of DRT were supported. This finding echoes those of Fantino and Dunn (1983) and of Mazur (2000b) who showed that adding a third alternative in the concurrent-chains procedure would inevitably and predictably alter the choice proportion between the two original options (except for a specific set of values, as shown by Houston et al., 2007). In conclusion, Houston et al. (2007) aver that DRT "is linked to optimality and the costs of making errors. This might suggest that it is a good rule—even though it was proposed as, and is still primarily, a descriptive model of choice it has a normative basis" (p. 1535).

While most research on operant analogues to foraging has been conducted with nonhumans, there has been some work with humans (e.g., Fantino & Preston, 1989). Perhaps the most intriguing human study assessed DRT's counterintuitive prediction, discussed above with pigeons, that increased accessibility may lead to decreased acceptability of an outcome. Ursula Stockhorst assessed this prediction with students at Heinrich-Heine University in Düsseldorf. The students were exposed to a successive-choice schedule under which responses interrupted an aversive tone. The response requirement to access the more profitable alternative (which turned off the tone on a VI 3-s schedule) was held constant (fixed-interval 7.5-s; the first response after 7.5 seconds had elapsed accessed the more profitable alternative), while the requirement to access the less profitable alternative (which turned off the tone only on a VI 18-s schedule) was varied. The results dovetailed with those from previous work exploring the same variables with pigeons: increased accessibility of the less profitable outcome led to *decreased* acceptability of that outcome (Stockhorst, 1994). Thus, these results contribute to the likelihood that the substantial body of research on choice with pigeons and other nonhumans has direct relevance for humans (but see Sih & Christensen's, 2001 suggestion that theories of foraging are best at predicting the behavior of organisms that feed on immobile prey).

Discrete-trial and Other Choice Procedures

Adjusting-Delay, Adjusting-Amount, and Progresssive-Delay Procedures

Basic Procedures. The purpose of each of these procedures is to estimate *indifference points*—pairs of alternatives that an individual chooses about equally often (e.g.,

Mazur, 1987). Because the alternatives are chosen equally often, researchers infer that they have equal reinforcing value. A representative example of an adjusting-delay procedure was used by Mazur and Biondi (2009), who conducted parallel experiments with pigeons and rats on choice between alternatives that differed in delay and amount of reinforcement. Each daily session included 64 trials, divided into 4-trial blocks of two forced trials followed by two choice trials. On forced trials, only one alternative was available, and these trials were included to ensure that the animals continued to receive exposure to both alternatives. A detailed description of one choice trial in a typical condition will illustrate how the procedure worked. In a three-key chamber, a response on the center key was required to start a trial, and then the side keys were lit green and red, respectively. The green key was the standard key: A single peck always led to a 10-s delay with green houselights, followed by one 2.5-s presentation of grain. The red key was the adjusting key: A single peck on this key led to an adjusting delay with red houselights, followed by three 2.5-s presentations of grain. After both adjusting and standard trials, there was an inter-trial interval (ITI) of a duration that was set so as to keep the total time from a choice response to the start of the next trial at 50 s.

The duration of the adjusting delay could change after every 4-trial block, depending on the pigeon's choices. If a pigeon chose the adjusting key on both choice trials, the adjusting delay was increased by 1 s for the next 4-trial block. If it chose the standard key on both choice trials, the adjusting delay was decreased by 1 s. This procedure continued for a minimum of 12 sessions per condition. Once certain stability criteria were met, the mean adjusting delay from the last several sessions was treated as the indifference point. For instance, the mean indifference point for the eight pigeons tested in this condition was about 27 s, suggesting that three grain deliveries after a 27-s delay were equal in value to 1 grain delivery after a 10-s delay.

In different conditions, Mazur and Biondi (2009) used different combinations of reinforcer amounts (1 versus 2, 1 versus 3, and 3 versus 2 grain deliveries) and different standard delays ranging from 1 to 15 s. The indifference points from the group of eight pigeons are shown in Figure 9.3, and they display a very clear and orderly pattern. As the standard delays increased, the mean adjusting delays increased according to linear functions with slopes that depended on the relative reinforcer amounts for the two alternatives. The theoretical implications of these results will be discussed later in this section.

Adjusting-amount procedures are similar in overall design and purpose, except that the size of one reinforcer is systematically increased or decreased over trials rather than one of the delays. For example, Richards, Mitchell, De Wit, and Seiden (1997) gave rats choices between a fixed amount of water delivered after a delay versus an adjusting amount of water delivered immediately. In some conditions, the fixed amount was 100 μL of water, and the adjusting amount began at 50 μL. After each choice trial, the adjusting amount was increased or decreased by 10%, depending on which alternative was chosen. The use of percentage increments (rather than the fixed 1-s increments used by Mazur (1987; Mazur & Biondi, 2009), along with the use of fewer forced trials, allowed for a rapid convergence on the indifference point. Richards et al. used the mean adjusting amount from the last 30 choice trials of each session as a measure of the indifference point. Therefore, with this procedure they could obtain an indifference point estimate in a single session, whereas Mazur's

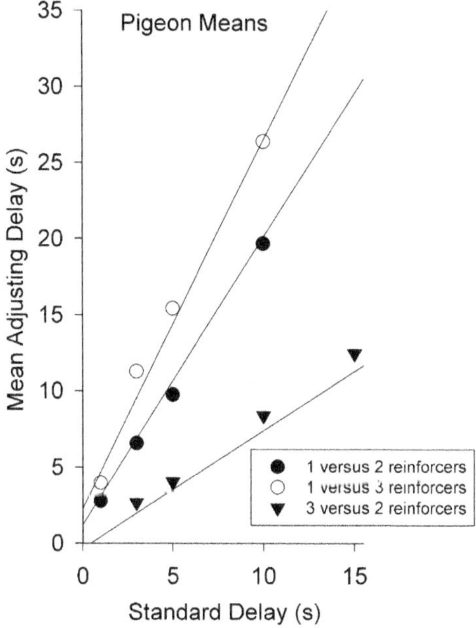

Figure 9.3 Group means of the indifference points are shown for the pigeons in the experiment. The lines are the best-fitting predictions of Equation 6. From "Delay-amount tradeoffs in choices by pigeons and rats: Hyperbolic versus exponential discounting" by J. E. Mazur and D. R. Biondi (2009), *Journal of the Experimental Analysis of Behavior, 91*, p. 204. Copyright 2009 by the Society for the Experimental Analysis of Behavior. Reprinted with permission.

(1987) adjusting-delay procedure typically requires 12 or more sessions to obtain one indifference point. They found very systematic decreases in the adjusting amounts as the delay for the fixed, 100-μL amount was increased from 0 s to 16 s. The decreases in reinforcer value were well described by a hyperbolic discounting function, as discussed in the next section.

Progressive-delay procedures can also be used to estimate indifference points. The delay for one alternative is constant throughout a session, whereas the delay for the other alternative is progressively increased across trial blocks within a session. Bezzina et al. (2007) used this procedure to examine how lesions to the nucleus accumbens affected rats' choices with delayed reinforcers. Each session was divided into six blocks of trials. Pressing one lever always led to a fixed delay (e.g., 8 s) followed by 50 μL of a sucrose solution. Pressing the other lever led to a progressive delay followed by 100 μL of sucrose. In the first block of each session, the progressive delay was equal to the fixed delay, but the progressive delay increased by 75% in each successive block. Interpolation methods were then used to estimate the indifference point—the delay at which a rat would choose the progressive alternative 50% of the time. Bezzina et al. found shorter indifference points for rats with the nucleus accumbens lesions compared to sham-operated controls, and they concluded that these lesions increased the rates of delay discounting (the rates at which a reinforcer's effectiveness declines with increasing delay). Other studies have also obtained useful results from progressive-delay procedures (e.g., da Costa Araújo et al., 2009).

Theoretical Analyses and Applications. Mazur (1987) showed that the results such as those displayed in Figure 9.3 are consistent with the following hyperbolic equation:

$$V = \frac{A}{1 + KD}, \tag{6}$$

where V is the value or strength of a reinforcer, D is the delay between a choice response and the reinforcer, A reflects the amount or size of the reinforcer, and K is a parameter that determines how rapidly V decreases with increases in D. If the reinforcer with the greater amount is plotted on the y-axis, Equation 6 predicts linear functions with slopes greater than 1 and y-intercepts greater than 0. If the reinforcer with the smaller amount is plotted on the y-axis (as in the conditions with 3 versus 2 reinforcers in Figure 9.3), Equation 6 predicts linear functions with slopes less than 1 and y-intercepts less than 0. Mazur also showed that the pattern of results in Figure 9.3 was inconsistent with an exponential decay function, a finding that has been confirmed in studies with pigeons (e.g., Rodriguez & Logue, 1988), rats (e.g., Richards et al., 1997), and humans (e.g., Green, Fry, & Myerson, 1994; van der Pol & Cairns, 2002).

Because Equation 6 usually provides a good description of the effects of delay on reinforcer value, the parameter K can be used as a measure of the rate of delay discounting, and comparisons can be made among different individuals, different species, and different reinforcer types and amounts (see Odum, 2011). For instance, data from a variety of different studies suggest that values of K for pigeons are approximately four or five times larger than for rats (e.g., Mazur, 2000a, 2007), which means that the value of a delayed reinforcer decreases much more rapidly for pigeons. There is also a curious difference between humans and other animals when different reinforcer amounts are compared. In studies where human participants choose between hypothetical amounts of money with different delays, estimates of K decrease (indicating slower delay discounting) when the choices involve larger amounts of money (Green, Myerson, & McFadden, 1997). In contrast, studies with nonhumans have found no consistent effects of reinforcer amount on the rates of delay discounting (Green, Myerson, Holt, Slevin, & Estle, 2004; Richards et al., 1997). The reason for this difference between humans and nonhumans is not known. However, it probably involves the fact that different nonhumans have different requirements. For example, pigeons do not generally "save" food but typically eat when food is available or, if sated, likely miss out on the currently available food.

These discrete-trial procedures have been used by neuroscientists to study brain mechanisms related to delay discounting, and in psychopharmacology research to examine the effects of different drugs. The study by Bezzina et al. (2007) described previously used a progressive-delay procedure to demonstrate the role of the nucleus accumbens in choices between delayed reinforcers. Adjusting-delay procedures have been used to examine the relationships between impulsivity (as measured by the rate of delay discounting) and addictive drugs. Gipson and Bardo (2009) found that long-term exposure to amphetamine led to increased rates of delay discounting in rats. Other pharmacological agents seem to have the opposite effect. Using an adjusting-delay procedure with pigeons, Wolff and Leander (2002) found that pigeons given fluoxetine (a serotonin-specific reuptake inhibitor) had increased tolerance for long delays to reinforcement in an adjusting-delay task. There is also evidence from animal studies that individual differences in delay discounting can be used as predictors of susceptibility to drug use. Perry, Nelson, and Carroll (2008) first used an adjusting-delay task to identify rats as high or low in impulsivity, and then the rats were given the opportunity for intravenous cocaine self-adminstration. The rats classified as high in impulsivity were faster to acquire cocaine self-administration. This work parallels that of studies with humans that have found higher rates of delay discounting in individuals who use addictive drugs (e.g., Hamilton & Potenza, 2012).

Observing Responses

Stimuli that are correlated with upcoming reinforcement act as conditioned reinforcers. Is this because they have an informative function or because they are correlated with positive (but not negative) reinforcement?

An informative procedure, developed by Wyckoff (1969), and refined by Dinsmoor and his associates (e.g., Dinsmoor, Browne, & Lawrence, 1972) is known as the observing-response procedure. In this procedure the organism has the opportunity to make "observing responses" the only consequence of which is production of the "observing stimulus" which is uniquely correlated with the schedule of reinforcement in effect (typically either EXT or a food schedule such as an FI). The observing response has no effect on the actual arrival of food; rather, its function is strictly informative. Many types of organisms emit such observing responses, including humans, other primates, pigeons, rats, and goldfish. Are these organisms information-seekers as some have maintained or are their observing responses maintained by conditioned reinforcement? In either event, what are the conditions that promote observing?

Despite its popularity, there is little empirical support for the information hypothesis. When the reinforcing potency of news about positive and about negative events is assessed under the same circumstances and with the same individual subjects, it has been shown many times that only news about positive events maintains observing. In other words, "bad news," or a stimulus correlated with EXT, despite being informative, does not maintain observing (Figure 9.4, from Dinsmoor, et al. 1972). In order to maintain observing, a stimulus must be differentially correlated with "good news" (positive reinforcement). In fact even a stimulus associated with food that is the poorer of two possible stimuli does not maintain observing (Auge, 1974). Auge's study, as well as more recent ones, have shown that a stimulus will maintain observing if and only if its appearance is correlated with an improvement in the prospects for reinforcement as required by delay-reduction theory.

Perhaps because of its intuitive appeal, numerous efforts have been made to revive the information theory of observing, including its central notion that information is reinforcing, at least for humans, even when the information concerns impending bad news and even though the information cannot be utilized. These efforts are

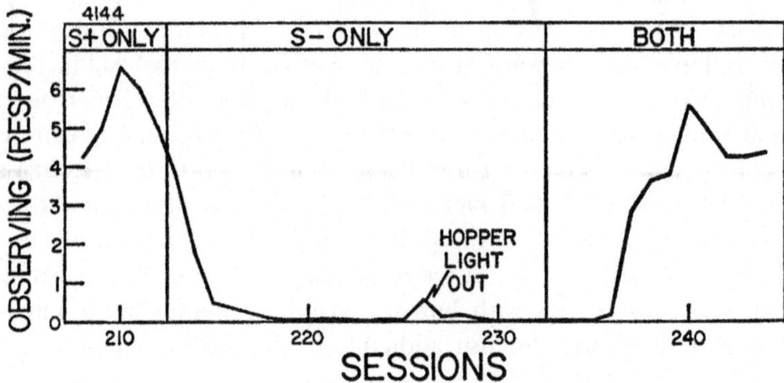

Figure 9.4 Rate of pecking the observing key on successive sessions by one pigeon when pecking produced S+ only, S- only, or both stimuli. From "A test of the negative discriminative stimulus as a reinforcer of observing" by J. A. Dinsmoor, M. P. Browne, and C. E. Lawrence (1972), *Journal of the Experimental Analysis of Behavior, 18*, p. 84. Copyright 1972 by the Society for the Experimental Analysis of Behavior. Reprinted with permission.

summarized in more recent papers by Escobar and Bruner (2009) and by Fantino and Silberberg (2010) both of which have again put this notion to rest. For example, Fantino and Silberberg showed that humans preferred "bad news" only when the putative bad news was correlated with good news ("information leakage" in the argot of information processing theory). "Pure" bad news did not maintain observing. Thus, information is reinforcing if and only if it is correlated with positive events and/or it has utility. Otherwise observing is not maintained.

In conclusion, while the large body of research on observing behavior compels rejection of the original (and popular) information—or "uncertainty-reduction"—hypothesis, this conclusion in no way detracts from the central importance of information. But it is only useful information that should be sought after. Indeed it would be extremely inefficient if we were reinforced by useless information. Such useless information should indeed be ignored, as the literature reviewed here suggests.

Conclusions

This chapter has described techniques for studying choice by people or by organisms of other species. By using these methods in the laboratory, researchers have been able to discover—and develop models of—the effects of factors such as time, effort, and amount of reinforcement on choice behavior and to extend their findings in novel basic and applied areas. Based on current research trends, we predict that the coming years will see significant progress in both basic and applied research on choice. Basic researchers will likely gain a better understanding of the dynamics of choice, and how short-term interactions between reinforcement and behavior affect both local and global patterns of choice responses. Those who conduct translational and applied research will develop increasingly sophisticated and effective ways to apply the behavioral principles of choice in real-world settings.

References

Abarca, N., & Fantino, E. (1982). Choice and foraging. *Journal of the Experimental Analysis of Behavior, 38*, 117–123.

Abarca, N., Fantino, E., & Ito, M. (1985). Percentage reward in an operant analogue to foraging. *Animal Behaviour, 33*, 1096–1100.

Alferink, L. A., Critchfield, T. S., Hitt, J. L., & Higgins, W. J. (2009). Generality of the matching law as a descriptor of basketball shot selection. *Journal of Applied Behavior Analysis, 42*, 592–605.

Aparicio, C. F., & Baum, W. M. (2009). Dynamics of choice: Relative rate and amount affect local preference at three different time scales. *Journal of the Experimental Analysis of Behavior, 91*, 293–317. doi:10.1901/jeab.2009.91-293.

Auge, R. J. (1974). Context, observing behavior, and conditioned reinforcement. *Journal of the Experimental Analysis of Behavior, 22*, 525–533.

Autor, S. M. (1960). *The strength of conditioned reinforcers as a function of frequency and probability of reinforcement.* Unpublished doctoral dissertation, Harvard University.

Baum, W. M. (1974). On two types of deviation from the matching law: Bias and undermatching. *Journal of the Experimental Analysis of Behavior, 22*, 231–242.

Baum, W. M. (1979). Matching, undermatching, and overmatching in studies of choice. *Journal of the Experimental Analysis of Behavior, 32*, 269–281.

Baum, W. M. (1982). Choice, changeover, and travel. *Journal of the Experimental Analysis of Behavior, 38*, 35–49.

Baum, W. M. (2010). Dynamics of choice: A tutorial. *Journal of the Experimental Analysis of Behavior, 94*, 161–174. doi:10.1901/jeab.2010.94-161.

Bezzina, G. G., Cheung, T. C., Asgari, K. K., Hampson, C. L., Body, S. S., Bradshaw, C. M., & Anderson, I. M. (2007). Effects of quinolinic acid-induced lesions of the nucleus accumbens core on inter-temporal choice: A quantitative analysis. *Psychopharmacology, 195*, 71–84. doi:10.1007/s00213-007-0882-0.

Borrero, C. W., Vollmer, T. R., Borrero, J. C., Bourret, J. C., Sloman, K. N., Samaha, A. L., & Dallery, J. (2010). Concurrent reinforcement schedules for problem behavior and appropriate behavior: Experimental applications of the matching law. *Journal of the Experimental Analysis of Behavior, 93*, 455–469. doi:10.1901/jeab.2010.93-455.

Boutros, N., Elliffe, D., & Davison, M. (2009). Time versus response indices affect conclusions about preference pulses. *Behavioural Processes*, doi:10.1016/j.beproc.2009.11.007.

Brown, E., & Cleaveland, J. (2009). An application of the active time model to multiple concurrent variable-interval schedules. *Behavioural Processes, 81*, 250–255. doi:10.1016/j.beproc.2008.10.014.

Collier, G. (1977). Optimal feeding strategies in animals: Laboratory simulation. Paper presented at the meetings of the Eastern Psychological Association, Boston.

da Costa Araújo, S. S., Body, S. S., Hampson, C. L., Langley, R. W., Deakin, J. W., Anderson, I. M., & Szabadi, E. E. (2009). Effects of lesions of the nucleus accumbens core on inter-temporal choice: Further observations with an adjusting-delay procedure. *Behavioural Brain Research, 202*, 272–277. doi:10.1016/j.bbr.2009.04.003.

Davison, M. C. (1987). The analysis of concurrent-chain performance. In M. L. Commons, J. E. Mazur, J. A. Nevin, & H. A. Rachlin (Eds.), *Quantitative Analyses of Behavior*: Vol. 5. *The effect of delay and of intervening events on reinforcement value* (pp. 225–241). Hillsdale, NJ: Erlbaum.

Davison, M. (1992). Choice between repleting/depleting patches: A concurrent-schedule procedure. *Journal of the Experimental Analysis of Behavior, 58*, 445–469. doi:10.1901/jeab.1992.58-445.

Davison, M., & Baum, W. M. (2000). Choice in a variable environment: Every reinforcer counts. *Journal of the Experimental Analysis of Behavior, 74*, 1–24.

Davison, M., & Jenkins, P. E. (1985). Stimulus discriminability, contingency discriminability, and schedule performance. *Animal Learning & Behavior, 13*, 77–84. doi:10.3758/BF03213368.

Davison, M., & McCarthy, D. (1988). *The matching law: A research review.* Hillsdale, NJ: Erlbaum.

DeCarlo, L. T. (1985). Matching and maximizing with variable-time schedules. *Journal of the Experimental Analysis of Behavior, 43*, 75–81.

Dinsmoor, J. A., Browne, M. P., & Lawrence, C. E. (1972). A test of the negative discriminative stimulus as a reinforcer of observing. *Journal of the Experimental Analysis of Behavior, 18*, 79–85.

Dunn, R., & Spetch, M. L. (1990). Choice with uncertain outcomes: Conditioned reinforcement effects. *Journal of the Experimental Analysis of Behavior, 53*, 201–218.

Ecott, C. L., & Critchfield, T. S. (2004). Noncontingent reinforcement, alternative reinforcement, and the matching law: A laboratory demonstration. *Journal of Applied Behavior Analysis, 37*, 249–265. doi:10.1901/jaba.2004.37-249.

Escobar, R., & Bruner, C.A. (2009). Observing responses and serial stimuli: Searching for the reinforcing properties of the S-. *Journal of the Experimental Analysis of Behavior, 92*, 215–231.

Fantino, E. (1969). Choice and reinforcement. *Journal of the Experimental Analysis of Behavior, 12*, 723–730.

Fantino, E., & Abarca, N. (1985) Choice, optimal foraging, and the delay-reduction hypothesis. *The Behavioral and Brain Sciences, 8*, 315–362 (including commentary).

Fantino, E., & Dunn, R. (1983). The delay-reduction hypothesis: Extension to three-alternative choice. *Journal of Experimental Psychology: Animal Behavior Processes, 9*, 132–146.

Fantino, E., & Logan, C. A. (1979). *The experimental analysis of behavior: A biological perspective.* San Francisco: Freeman.

Fantino, E., & Preston, R. A. (1988). Choice and foraging: The effects of accessibility on acceptability. *Journal of the Experimental Analysis of Behavior, 50*, 395–403.

Fantino, E., & Preston, R. A. (1989). The delay-reduction hypothesis: Some new tests. In N. W. Bond & D. A. T. Siddle, (Eds.), *Psychology: Issues and applications* (pp. 457–467). Amsterdam: Elsevier.

Fantino, E., Preston, R. A., & Dunn, R. (1993). Delay reduction: Current status. *Journal of the Experimental Analysis of Behavior, 60*, 159–169.

Fantino, E., & Silberberg. A. (2010). Revisiting the role of bad news in maintaining human observing behavior. *Journal of the Experimental Analysis of Behavior, 93*, 157–170.

Foster, T., Matthews, L. R., Temple, W., & Poling, A. (1997). Concurrent schedule performance in domestic goats: Persistent undermatching. *Behavioural Processes, 40*, 231–237. doi:10.1016/S0376-6357(97)00018-1.

Foxall, G. R., James, V. K., Oliveira-Castro, J. M., & Ribier, S. (2010). Product substitutability and the matching law. *The Psychological Record, 60*, 185–216.

Gipson, C. D., & Bardo, M. T. (2009). Extended access to amphetamine self-administration increases impulsive choice in a delay discounting task in rats. *Psychopharmacology, 207*, 391–400. doi:10.1007/s00213-009-1667-4.

Grace, R. C. (1994). A contextual model of concurrent-chains choice. *Journal of the Experimental Analysis of Behavior, 61*, 113–129.

Green, L., Fry, A. F., & Myerson, J. (1994). Discounting of delayed rewards: A life-span comparison. *Psychological Science, 5*, 33–36.

Green, L., Myerson, J., Holt, D. D., Slevin, J. R., & Estle, S. J. (2004). Discounting of delayed food rewards in pigeons and rats: Is there a magnitude effect? *Journal of the Experimental Analysis of Behavior*, *81*, 39–50.

Green, L., Myerson, J., & McFadden, E. (1997). Rate of temporal discounting decreases with amount of reward. *Memory and Cognition*, *25*, 715–723.

Hamilton, K. R., & Potenza, M. N. (2012). Relations among delay discounting, addictions, and money mismanagement: Implications and future directions. *The American Journal of Drug And Alcohol Abuse*, *38*, 30–42. doi:10.3109/00952990.2011.643978.

Herrnstein, R. J. (1961). Relative and absolute strength of response as a function of frequency of reinforcement. *Journal of the Experimental Analysis of Behavior*, *4*, 267–272.

Herrnstein, R. J. (1964). Secondary reinforcement and rate of primary reinforcement. *Journal of the Experimental Analysis of Behavior*, *7*, 27–36.

Herrnstein, R. J. (1970). On the law of effect. *Journal of the Experimental Analysis of Behavior*, *13*, 243–266. doi:10.1901/jeab.1970.13-243.

Herrnstein, R. J., Loewenstein, G. F., Prelec, D., & Vaughan, W. (1993). Utility maximization and melioration: Internalities in individual choice. *Journal of Behavioral Decision Making*, *6*, 149 185. doi:10.1002/bdm.3960060302.

Herrnstein, R. J., & Loveland, D. H. (1975). Matching and maximizing on concurrent ratio schedules. *Journal of the Experimental Analysis of Behavior*, *24*, 107–116.

Herrnstein, R. J., & Prelec, D. (1992). Melioration. In G. Loewenstein, J. Elster, G. Loewenstein, J. Elster (Eds.), *Choice over time* (pp. 235–263). New York: Russell Sage Foundation.

Herrnstein, R. J., & Vaughan, W. (1980). Melioration and behavioral allocation. In J. E. R. Staddon (Ed.), *Limits to action: The allocation of individual behavior* (pp. 143–176). New York: Academic Press.

Heyman, G. M. (1979). A Markov model description of changeover probabilities on concurrent variable-interval schedules. *Journal of the Experimental Analysis of Behavior, 31*, 41–51.

Hinson, J. M., & Staddon, J. E. R. (1983). Hill-climbing by pigeons. *Journal of the Experimental Analysis of Behavior*, *39*, 25–47.

Houston, A. I., McNamara, J. A., & Steer, M. D. (2007). Do we expect natural selection to produce rational behaviour? *Philosophical Transactions of the Royal Society*, *362*, 1531–1543.

Ito, M., & Fantino, E. (1986). Choice, foraging, and reinforcer duration. *Journal of the Experimental Analysis of Behavior*, *46*, 93–103.

Killeen, P. R. (1982). Incentive theory: II. Models for choice. *Journal of the Experimental Analysis of Behavior*, *38*, 217–232.

Killeen, P. R., & Fantino, E. (1990). Unification of models for choice between delayed reinforcers. *Journal of the Experimental Analysis of Behavior*, *53*, 189–200.

Koffarnus, M. N., & Woods, J. H. (2008). Quantification of drug choice with the generalized matching law in rhesus monkeys. *Journal of the Experimental Analysis of Behavior*, *89*, 209–224.

Landon, J., Davidson, M., & Elliffe, D. (2003). Concurrent schedules: Reinforcer magnitude effects. *Journal of the Experimental Analysis of Behavior*, *79*, 351–365. doi:10.1901/jeab.2003.79-351.

Lea, S. E. G. (1979). Foraging and reinforcement schedules in the pigeon: Optimal and non-optimal aspects of choice. *Animal Behavior*, *27*, 875–886.

Luco, J. E. (1990). Matching, delay-reduction, and maximizing models for choice in concurrent-chains schedules. *Journal of the Experimental Analysis of Behavior*, *54*, 53–67.

Mazur, J. E. (1981). Optimization theory fails to predict performance of pigeons in a two-response situation. *Science*, *214*, 823–825. doi:10.1126/science.7292017.

Mazur, J. E. (1984). Tests of an equivalence rule for fixed and variable reinforcer delays. *Journal of Experimental Psychology: Animal Behavior Processes*, *10*, 426–436.

Mazur, J. E. (1987). An adjusting procedure for studying delayed reinforcement. In M. L. Commons, J. E. Mazur, J. A. Nevin, & H. Rachlin (Eds.), *Quantitative analyses of behavior*: Vol. 5. *The effect of delay and of intervening events on reinforcement value* (pp. 55–73). Hillsdale, NJ: Erlbaum.

Mazur, J. E. (2000a). Tradeoffs among delay, rate and amount of reinforcement. *Behavioural Processes*, *49*, 1–10.

Mazur, J. E. (2000b). Two- versus three-alternative concurrent-chain schedules: A test of three models. *Journal of Experimental Psychology: Animal Behavior Processes*, *26*, 286–293.

Mazur, J. E. (2001). Hyperbolic value addition and general models of choice. *Psychological Review*, *198*, 96–112.

Mazur, J. E. (2007). Rats' choices between one and two delayed reinforcers. *Learning & Behavior*, *35*, 169–176.

Mazur, J. E., & Biondi, D. R. (2009). Delay-amount tradeoffs in choices by pigeons and rats: Hyperbolic versus exponential discounting. *Journal of the Experimental Analysis of Behavior*, *91*, 197–211.

McDevitt, M. A., & Williams, B. A. (2010). Dual effects on choice of conditioned reinforcement frequency and conditioned reinforcement value. *Journal of the Experimental Analysis of Behavior*, *93*, 147–155.

McDowell, J. J., & Caron, M. L. (2007). Undermatching is an emergent property of selection by consequences. *Behavioural Processes*, *75*, 97–106.

McDowell, J. J., & Caron, M. L. (2010). Bias and undermatching in delinquent boys' verbal behavior as a function of their level of deviance. *Journal of the Experimental Analysis of Behavior*, *93*, 471–483.

Myers, D. L., & Myers, L. E. (1977). Undermatching: A reappraisal of performance on concurrent variable-interval schedules of reinforcement. *Journal of the Experimental Analysis of Behavior*, *27*, 203–214.

Navarick, D. J., & Fantino, E. (1976). Self-control and general models of choice. *Journal of Experimental Psychology: Animal Behavior Processes*, *2*, 75–87.

Nevin, J. A. (1979). Overall matching versus momentary maximizing: Nevin (1969) revisited. *Journal of Experimental Psychology: Animal Behavior Processes*, *5*, 300–306. doi:10.1037/0097-7403.5.3.300.

Odum, A. L. (2011). Delay discounting: I'm a *K*, you're a *K*. *Journal of the Experimental Analysis of Behavior*, *96*, 427–439.

Oliveira-Castro, J. M., Foxall, G. R., & Wells, V. K. (2010). Consumer brand choice: Money allocation as a function of brand reinforcing attributes. *Journal of Organizational Behavior Management*, *30*, 161–175. doi:10.1080/01608061003756455.

Perry, J. L., Nelson, S. E., & Carroll, M. E. (2008). Impulsive choice as a predictor of acquisition of IV cocaine self-administration and reinstatement of cocaine-seeking behavior in male and female rats. *Experimental and Clinical Psychopharmacology*, *16*, 165–177. doi: 10.1037/1064-1297.16.2.165.

Pierce, W., & Epling, W. (1983). Choice, matching, and human behavior: A review of the literature. *The Behavior Analyst*, *6*, 57–76.

Rachlin, H., & Green, L. (1972). Commitment, choice, and self-control. *Journal of the Experimental Analysis of Behavior*, *17*, 15–22.

Rachlin, H., Green, L., Kagel, J. H., & Battalio, R. C. (1976). Economic demand theory and psychological studies of choice. In G. H. Bower (Ed.), *The psychology of learning and motivation*, *10*, 129–154.

Rasmussen, E. B., & Newland, M. (2008). Asymmetry of reinforcement and punishment in human choice. *Journal of the Experimental Analysis of Behavior, 89*, 157–167. doi:10.1901/jeab.2008.89-157.

Reed, D. D., Critchfield, T. S., & Martens, B. K. (2006). The generalized matching law in elite sport competition: Football play calling as operant choice. *Journal of Applied Behavior Analysis, 39*, 281–297. doi:10.1901/jaba.2006.146-05.

Richards, J. B., Mitchell, S. H., De Wit, H., & Seiden, L. S. (1997). Determination of discount functions in rats with an adjusting-amount procedure. *Journal of the Experimental Analysis of Behavior, 67*, 353–366. doi:10.1901/jeab.1997.67-353.

Rodriguez, M. L., & Logue, A. W. (1988). Adjusting delay to reinforcement: Comparing choice in pigeons and humans. *Journal of the Experimental Analysis of Behavior, 14*, 105–111.

Sakagami, T., Hursh, S. R., Christensen, J., & Silberberg, A. (1989). Income maximizing in concurrent interval-ratio schedules. *Journal of the Experimental Analysis of Behavior, 52*, 41–46.

Savastano, H. I., & Fantino, E. (1994). Human choice in concurrent ratio-interval schedules of reinforcement. *Journal of the Experimental Analysis of Behavior, 61*, 453–463.

Schneider, S. M., & Lickliter, R. (2010). Choice in quail neonates: The origins of generalized matching. *Journal of the Experimental Analysis of Behavior, 94*, 315–326. doi:10.1901/jeab.2010.94-315.

Shah, K. K., Bradshaw, C. M., & Szabadi, E. E. (1989). Performance of humans in concurrent variable-ratio variable-ratio schedules of monetary reinforcement. *Psychological Reports, 65*, 515–520. doi:10.2466/pr0.1989.65.2.515.

Shull, R. L., & Pliskoff, S. S. (1967). Changeover delay and concurrent schedules: Some effects on relative performance measures. *Journal of the Experimental Analysis of Behavior, 10*, 517–527.

Sih, A., & Christensen, B. (2001). Optimal diet theory: When does it work, and when and why does it fail? *Animal Behaviour, 61*, 379–390.

Silberberg, A., Hamilton, B., Ziriax, J. M., & Casey, J. (1978). The structure of choice. *Journal of Experimental Psychology: Animal Behavior Processes, 4*, 368–398.

Spetch, M. L., Belke, T. W., Barnet, R. C., Dunn, R., & Pierce, W. D. (1990). Suboptimal choice in a percentage-reinforcement procedure: Effects of signal condition and terminal-link length. *Journal of the Experimental Analysis of Behavior, 53*, 219–234.

Spetch, M.L., & Dunn, R. (1987). Choice between reliable and unreliable outcomes: Mixed percentage reinforcement in concurrent chains. *Journal of the Experimental Analysis of Behavior, 47*, 57–72.

Squires, N., & Fantino, E. (1971). A model for choice in simple concurrent and concurrent-chains schedules. *Journal of the Experimental Analysis of Behavior, 15*, 27–38.

Stilling, S. T., & Critchfield, T. S. (2010). The matching relation and situation-specific bias modulation in professional football play selection. *Journal of the Experimental Analysis of Behavior, 93*, 435–454.

Stockhorst, U. (1994). Effects of different accessibility of reinforcement schedules on choice in humans. *Journal of the Experimental Analysis of Behavior, 62*, 269–292.

Todorov, J. C. (1971). Concurrent performances: Effect of punishment contingent on the switching response. *Journal of the Experimental Analysis of Behavior, 16*, 51–62. doi:10.1901/jeab.1971.16-51.

Todorov, J. C., Souza, D. G., & Bori, C. M. (1993). Momentary maximizing in concurrent schedules with a minimum interchangeover interval. *Journal of the Experimental Analysis of Behavior, 60*, 415–435. doi:10.1901/jeab.1993.60-415.

van der Pol, M., & Cairns, J. (2002). A comparison of the discounted utility model and hyperbolic discounting models in the case of social and private intertemporal preferences for health. *Journal of Economic Behavior and Organization, 49*, 79–96.

Vaughan, W., Jr. (1981). Melioration, matching, and maximization. *Journal of the Experimental Analysis of Behavior*, *36*, 141–149. doi:10.1901/jeab.1981.36-141.

Vaughan, W., Jr. (1985). Choice: A local analysis. *Journal of the Experimental Analysis of Behavior*, *43*, 383–405.

Vyse, S. A., & Belke, T. W. (1992). Maximizing versus matching on concurrent variable-interval schedules. *Journal of the Experimental Analysis of Behavior*, *58*, 325–334.

Williams, W. A., & Fantino, E. (1994). Delay reduction and optimal foraging: Variable-ratio search in a foraging analogue. *Journal of the Experimental Analysis of Behavior*, *61*, 465–477.

Wolff, M. C., & Leander, J. (2002). Selective serotonin reuptake inhibitors decrease impulsive behavior as measured by an adjusting-delay procedure in the pigeon. *Neuropsychopharmacology*, *27*, 421–429. doi:10.1016/S0893-133X(02)00307-X.

Wyckoff, L. B., Jr. (1969). The role of observing responses in discrimination learning. In D. P. Hendry (ed.), *Conditioned reinforcement*. Homewood, IL: Dorsey Press.

10

Conditioned Reinforcement

Matthew C. Bell and Margaret A. McDevitt

Introduction

The idea that a neutral stimulus can function as a learned (i.e., conditioned) reinforcer has a long and venerated place in learning theory. These conditioned reinforcers are sometimes said to have acquired conditioned *value*, a term we use to indicate that the stimulus has acquired the ability to function as a reinforcer for behavior. One of the first textbook accounts of conditioned reinforcement appeared in Keller and Schoenfeld (1950):

> In reaching our goal [of understanding human behavior], the principle of secondary [conditioned] reinforcement will be of great analytical assistance. When added to the other functions of stimuli, it gives us a powerful and indispensable tool for the solution of many vexing and absorbing problems of human actions. (Keller & Schoenfeld, 1950, p. 260)

Skinner also recognized the importance in his seminal textbook,

> Although it is characteristic of human behavior that primary reinforcers may be effective after a long delay, this is presumably only because intervening events become conditioned reinforcers. (Skinner, 1953, p. 76)

In general terms, learning processes have evolved in humans and other animals because of the survival advantage they offer. Although there is some cost to an organism (and a species) to have the capacity to learn, learning provides virtually unlimited behavioral flexibility. Imagine what would happen if most of our behaviors were genetically determined. Specific behavior patterns might be very useful in one environment, but what works in one environment might easily prove to be a hindrance

The Wiley Blackwell Handbook of Operant and Classical Conditioning, First Edition.
Edited by Frances K. McSweeney and Eric S. Murphy.

in another. If you consider how drastically human life has changed in the last few hundred years, you quickly realize the importance of learning. Without the capacity to learn, we would not be able to adapt quickly to a rapidly changing environment. The ability to learn is one of the most important contributions of evolution.

Conditioned reinforcers help navigate and guide our behavior through a complex world. Food and other primary reinforcers are crucial for the survival of humans and other animals, and learning about how they function is quite important. In order to respond effectively, though, it is equally important to learn about the myriad of other events and stimuli that provide information about those primary reinforcers. They have survival value as well. In fact, as Skinner (1953) pointed out above, most human behavior is guided by conditioned reinforcement. Most of what motivates our behavior is not direct access to primary reinforcers like food and water, but rather things that lead to those primary reinforcers.

Defining Characteristics of Conditioned Reinforcement

Conditioned reinforcers are previously neutral stimuli that gain reinforcing effectiveness either by their association with primary reinforcers or by association with already-established conditioned reinforcers. For example, the sound of a food hopper (a grain delivery mechanism) being raised may become a conditioned reinforcer for a pigeon that has been working for food in an experimental chamber. The sound of the hopper being raised immediately precedes access to and consumption of grain, and therefore over time that sound itself becomes a reinforcing stimulus. Similarly, the sound of our friend's voice may become a conditioned reinforcer over time, as the presence of their voice often signals the reinforcing aspects of the friendship.

Conditioned reinforcers are traditionally assumed to have one essential characteristic: When presented as a consequence immediately following a response, the conditioned reinforcer functions to increase the probability of future responding. This function is thought to be due to its history of association with already-established reinforcers.

Zimmerman, Hanford, and Brown (1967) provide one example of an early experiment designed to demonstrate conditioned reinforcement effects. Pigeons were presented with a two-component multiple schedule (where two or more simple schedules are arranged in sequence; see, for example, Ferster & Skinner, 1957). In both components food delivery was not contingent upon responding and any food presentation that was scheduled required 6 s without a key peck. Response keys were illuminated blue and yellow, respectively, for the two components. Responding to the illuminated keys resulted in brief presentations of the food magazine sound (the conditioned reinforcer). The first component delivered reinforcement according to variable interval (VI) schedules ranging from a VI 1-min to a VI 12-min across conditions in addition to two extinction conditions (key pecks never produced the conditioned reinforcer). A VI schedule provides reinforcement for a single response following a varying period of time across opportunities. The second component delivered food according to a VI 1-min schedule as well. Responding was well maintained over a substantial period of time (the study lasted for over 100 sessions) even though pecking at the keys was never reinforced with food.

Zimmerman et al.'s (1967) findings seem to necessitate an explanation in terms of conditioned reinforcement; the concept's use as an explanatory concept has been more controversial for other behavioral procedures, some of which we will describe below. It is important to clarify when conditioned reinforcement is a necessary and/or sufficient explanation for a behavioral finding and when other explanatory frameworks are required. For example, many of the findings attributed to conditioned reinforcement have alternatively been interpreted in terms of discriminative functions. We do not advocate conditioned reinforcement as a one-stop catch-all explanatory mechanism. Multiple behavioral procedures are involved in most behavioral phenomena, and it is a mistake to view them as mutually exclusive.

Zimmerman et al.'s (1967) procedure is but one example of several procedures used to investigate conditioned reinforcement. In the next section, we describe a number of different procedures that have been used to study conditioned reinforcement. As we will see, there are a number of challenges in studying pure conditioned reinforcement effects. Although there is no single definitive procedure for studying conditioned reinforcement effects, the data from a rich variety of procedures provide considerable evidence of the nature of the effect and the importance of the concept.

In addition to reinforcing properties, stimuli may also have discriminative properties. In other words, a stimulus may signal a particular operant contingency and, functioning as a discriminative stimulus (S^D), it may lead to differential responding independent of any reinforcing properties. Distinguishing between the discriminative and reinforcing functions of stimuli has proven difficult. Early theorists suggested that in order for a neutral stimulus to become a conditioned reinforcer that it would have to become a discriminative stimulus for an operant contingency (see, for example, Schoenfeld, Antonitis, & Bersh, 1950; Skinner, 1938; Wyckoff, 1952), although later work suggests this may not be a necessary condition (see, Jenkins & Boakes, 1973; Kendall, 1973a, 1973b). The interplay between conditioned reinforcing and discriminative properties of stimuli is an important topic, but it is largely beyond the scope of this chapter.

Studying Conditioned Reinforcement

Several procedures have been used to study conditioned reinforcement. In this section, we describe a variety of procedures to illustrate both some historical approaches and to show the challenges presented in the study of conditioned reinforcement. While this list is not exhaustive, it does cover the major approaches.

Train a New Response

One of the earliest approaches to studying conditioned reinforcement effects focused on demonstrating the response-strengthening aspect of conditioned reinforcement. In an initial condition, a neutral stimulus is repeatedly paired with a primary reinforcer and then, in extinction, that previously neutral stimulus is tested to see if it functions as a reinforcer for a new response. Skinner (1938) provided one of the earliest demonstrations of this approach: he trained rats to approach a food cup when the mechanism operated. (Its operation produced a sound which was used as the conditioned reinforcer.) Following 60 sound-food presentations, he stopped presenting food in the situation and introduced a lever. Responding on the lever produced the sound. Skinner successfully shaped bar pressing and reported increased response rates over a brief period. Responding then decreased, presumably as the conditioned reinforcing value of the sound extinguished.

Another early example with a more applied emphasis was reported by Wolfe (1936) who compared the effectiveness of primary and conditioned reinforcement in establishing and maintaining the behavior of chimpanzees. While there was some decrement associated with the use of conditioned reinforcement (tokens), the conditioned reinforcement was generally similar to food in its effectiveness.[1]

Although it provided some interesting and useful data, this general procedure proved to be problematic for two reasons. First, it is an extinction procedure. Any existing conditioned value diminishes during testing because the stimulus functioning as a conditioned reinforcer is no longer paired with primary reinforcement, and therefore it is no longer paired with the source of conditioned value. Second, the change from the baseline conditions to the conditioned reinforcement tests produced stimulus generalization decrement effects. This is because removal of the primary reinforcer made the testing condition noticeably different from the training condition. In other words, responding might decrease not merely because of any change in conditioned value per se, but rather because the change of conditions can be discriminated. Regardless of which of these factors might be implicated, effects found using this paradigm were typically fleeting and thus this approach proved to be quite limited.

Extinction Rates for an Established Response

A similar approach is to maintain a response with both a conditioned reinforcer and primary reinforcer. The primary reinforcer is then removed (extinction) and responding is compared across conditions with or without the putative conditioned reinforcer present. Higher, more persistent responding in conditions where the stimulus followed a response would suggest that the stimulus functioned as a conditioned reinforcer.

An early example of this approach was reported by Zimmerman (1957) using water-deprived rats. In the training phase, a 2-s buzzer was followed immediately by presentations of water using a dipper. Trials occurred approximately once a minute. Zimmerman began with a 1:1 buzzer-water pairing and thinned out the schedule until buzzer presentations were followed by water on approximately 10% of the trials. Then, in the test phase, Zimmerman tested whether or not the buzzer would function as a conditioned reinforcer by using it as a consequence for lever pressing (according to an intermittent reinforcement schedule). Importantly, water was never presented during these sessions. Zimmerman found that responding was maintained by the conditioned reinforcing properties of the buzzer. Zimmerman also reported that lever pressing extinguished when the buzzer was removed, providing additional evidence that the buzzer functioned as a conditioned reinforcer (but see Wyckoff, Sidowski, & Chambliss, 1958, for an alternative interpretation).

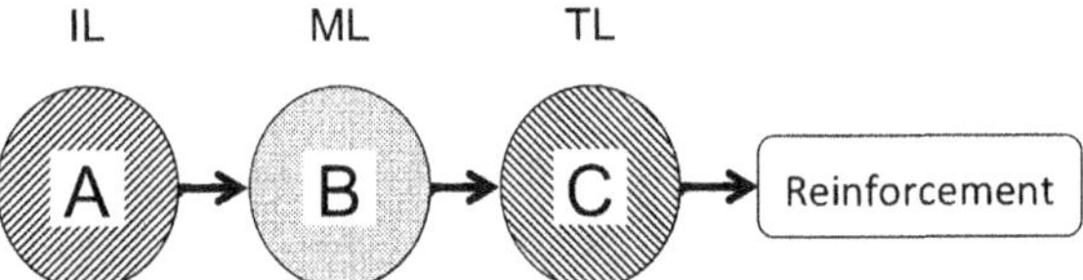

Figure 10.1 Procedure schematic of a typical three-link chain schedule used to study conditioned reinforcement effects. Each link of the chain is correlated with a specific schedule of reinforcement. When the schedule requirement is satisfied, responding to the initial link (IL) stimulus (A) leads to the middle link (ML) stimulus (B) which then leads to the terminal link (TL) stimulus (C) and finally primary reinforcement.

Chain Schedules

A chain schedule is a fixed sequence of stimuli correlated with different reinforcement schedules where the final link of the chain ends in primary reinforcement (see Figure 10.1). Each link in the chain is presented successively and operates according to its own independent schedule of reinforcement. Imagine, for example, that a pigeon is presented with a three-link chain schedule, in which green, yellow, and red colored keylights are presented in sequence. Food is presented following completion of the schedule requirement correlated with the red stimulus, but to get to the red stimulus, our pigeon must respond to first the green, and then the yellow stimulus, completing the schedule requirements in each of those links. What reinforces responding to the green and yellow stimuli?

One possibility could be the delayed primary reinforcer at the end of the chain. However, depending on the schedule values used in the chain schedule, the overall delay to food might be so long that responding may not be adequately maintained by the food at the end of the chain. Another possibility is that responding to green is reinforced by the presentation of yellow, and responding to yellow is reinforced by the presentation of red. In this way, conditioned reinforcement value is traditionally believed to extend backwards through the chain. Because red is directly associated with food, it quickly gains value as a conditioned reinforcer. As red gains in reinforcing strength, yellow begins to gain value as well, through its association with red (and so on, back through the chain). The stimulus at the end of the chain is always the most valuable conditioned reinforcer (due to its direct association with the primary reinforcer), and reinforcing effectiveness decreases with each prior link of the chain, as you get further away from the primary reinforcer at the end (see, for example, Williams, Ploog, & Bell, 1995; Williams, 1997). The stimuli in the chain appear to have acquired conditioned value and function as conditioned reinforcers for responding in earlier links of the chain.

This approach avoids the problems associated with testing during extinction by examining steady-state behavior maintained by primary reinforcement at the end of the chain. Conditioned reinforcement effects are seen by examining performance in links of the chain not directly paired with primary reinforcement.

Chain schedule performance has been compared to a variety of control conditions, often tandem schedules. Tandem schedules differ from chain schedules in that there are no stimulus changes between links; they are otherwise functionally identical to chain schedules. Control of responding in early links of a chain schedule was typically thought to be under direct control of the immediate consequences. In other words, the conditioned reinforcement value of the following stimulus functions to reinforce responding in the preceding link. Eliminating the stimulus transition should eliminate conditioned reinforcement and, therefore, lower the response rate.

An early failure to show conditioned reinforcement effects in the chain schedule demonstrates the difficulties encountered in studying these effects. Gollub (1958, as described in Gollub, 1977 and Fantino & Logan, 1979) compared responding across three groups. He used fixed-interval (FI; for more, see Ferster & Skinner, 1957) schedules of reinforcement, in which only the first response that occurred after a fixed amount of time resulted in delivery of the reinforcer. In the first group, pigeons were presented with a simple FI 5-min schedule. The second group of pigeons was presented with a chain schedule with five FI 1-min links. The third group of pigeons was presented a tandem schedule with five FI 1-min links. Responding on the simple and tandem schedules were comparable, but responding on the chain schedule was weakly maintained, if at all. The problem with this particular procedure, and a challenge associated with chain schedules more generally, is that stimuli in early links of a chain function as signals for nonreinforcement. Thus, responding in earlier links of a chain will typically be slower than responding in later links. Responding is difficult to maintain in the early links of chains with three or more links.

Despite the failure of Gollub's (1958) study to demonstrate support for conditioned reinforcement within a chain schedule, later research which employed shorter chains (i.e., fewer than five links) and VI schedules (instead of FI) have successfully investigated the conditioned reinforcement relationship between links in a chain schedule. For example, Royalty, Williams, and Fantino (1987) systematically included an unsignaled delay of reinforcement in different links of a three-link chain schedule. In the typical chain schedule, the response that satisfies the schedule requirement is immediately followed by a stimulus change. When an unsignaled delay is included, that same response is followed by a brief delay prior to the stimulus change (note that additional responses have no effect). Royalty et al. found evidence that unsignaled delays can have substantial effects on responding in the link associated with the unsignaled delay. In their study, pigeons responded to a three-link chain where, in baseline conditions, each link was a VI 33-s schedule. They systematically inserted a 3-s unsignaled delay between the response and the consequence—in other words, the VI 33-s schedule was changed to a tandem VI 30-s fixed-time (FT, an FT schedule delivers reinforcers independently of responding after a fixed amount of time) 3-s schedule—for each of the links. One important feature of this design is that the overall time to primary reinforcement was held constant. That is, the relationship between each stimulus and primary reinforcement remained unchanged. Their results showed lower responding in only the link with the unsignaled delay (Figure 10.2) caused by the degraded contingency between the response and the conditioned reinforcer in the following link of the chain (and not by any changes in timing of stimulus changes or in time to reinforcement). The results of this study suggest that responding in chain schedules is, in part, maintained by conditioned reinforcement.

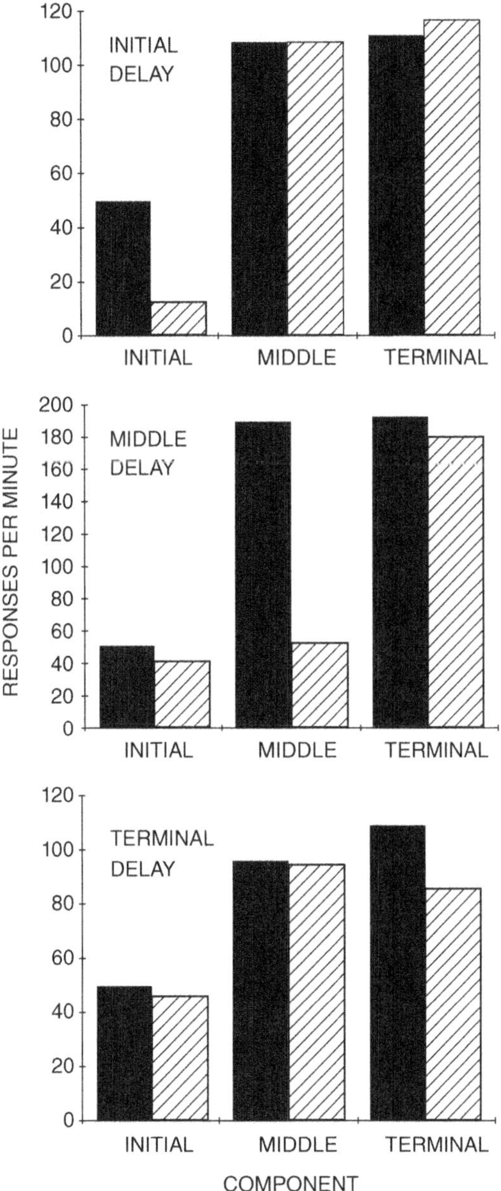

Figure 10.2 Mean response rate (response/min) for each chain component. The dark bars represent baseline responding. Hashed bars represent responding during the various delay conditions, with the initial-link delay condition shown in the top graph, middle-link delay condition shown in the middle graph, and terminal-link delay condition shown in the bottom graph. Ordinate scaling varies among panels. (Royalty, Williams, and Fantino, 1987, Figure 7. Reproduced with permission from Wiley).

Observing Responses

The observing response procedure takes a different approach. This procedure assesses the degree to which a conditioned reinforcer has value (recall that this term is used to indicate the ability of a reinforcer to maintain behavior). Wyckoff (1952, 1969) presented pigeons with two schedules of reinforcement, an FI 30-s schedule of food reinforcement and extinction. These schedules alternated within experimental sessions. Initially, the schedules were correlated with the same white key light stimulus (a mixed schedule). A separate observing response (a pedal press) changed the key light stimulus from white to red if food was available or from white to green if extinction was in effect. Thus, observing responses converted the mixed schedule to a multiple schedule, but had no other consequence. In control conditions, the stimuli were not correlated with reinforcement (i.e., red and green were equally associated with the FI 30-s schedule and the extinction schedule). When the stimuli were correlated with reinforcement, subjects reliably responded to the pedal and to the red stimulus and responded at a much lower rate to the green stimulus. When the stimuli were uncorrelated, the observing rate was low and subjects responded equally to the two schedules. This study shows that subjects will respond for the signal indicating which reinforcement schedule is in effect when the signals are correlated with the reinforcement and extinction schedules (top graph in Figure 10.3) and will respond differentially to the two schedules. When the signals are uncorrelated, subjects make very few observing responses and responding to the two schedules is not different (bottom graph in Figure 10.3). Thus, when the signals are correlated, it appears that the signal for the reinforcement schedule functions as a conditioned reinforcer. One alternative interpretation of these findings is that subjects are responding because of the information value of the signal, independent from any association with reinforcement. However, the information hypothesis was not supported by subsequent research (e.g., Fantino 1977).

Concurrent Chains

The concurrent chains procedure (Figure 10.4) was developed to address the challenges of discriminating between schedule-related effects (like the scallop pattern of responding often seen in FI schedules) and conditioned reinforcement effects (Fantino, 1977). That is, in simple choice situations there is a confound between any putative conditioned reinforcement effects and schedule demands. For example, if subjects were presented with a choice between a differential reinforcement of high rate schedule (DRH; this is a schedule where the response rate must be higher than a pre-defined response rate threshold for reinforcement to be delivered), and a differential reinforcement of low rate schedule (DRL; a schedule where the response rate must be lower than a pre-defined response rate threshold for reinforcement to be delivered), it would appear as if the DRH were highly preferred. Clearly, the high rate of responding in the DRH is not necessarily an indication of preference for that schedule.

The concurrent chains procedure addressed this problem by presenting subjects with a choice between alternatives with two equal initial links, typically equal VI schedules available concurrently. Any differences seen in initial-link responding are then attributable to differences in what follows those choice alternatives.[2]

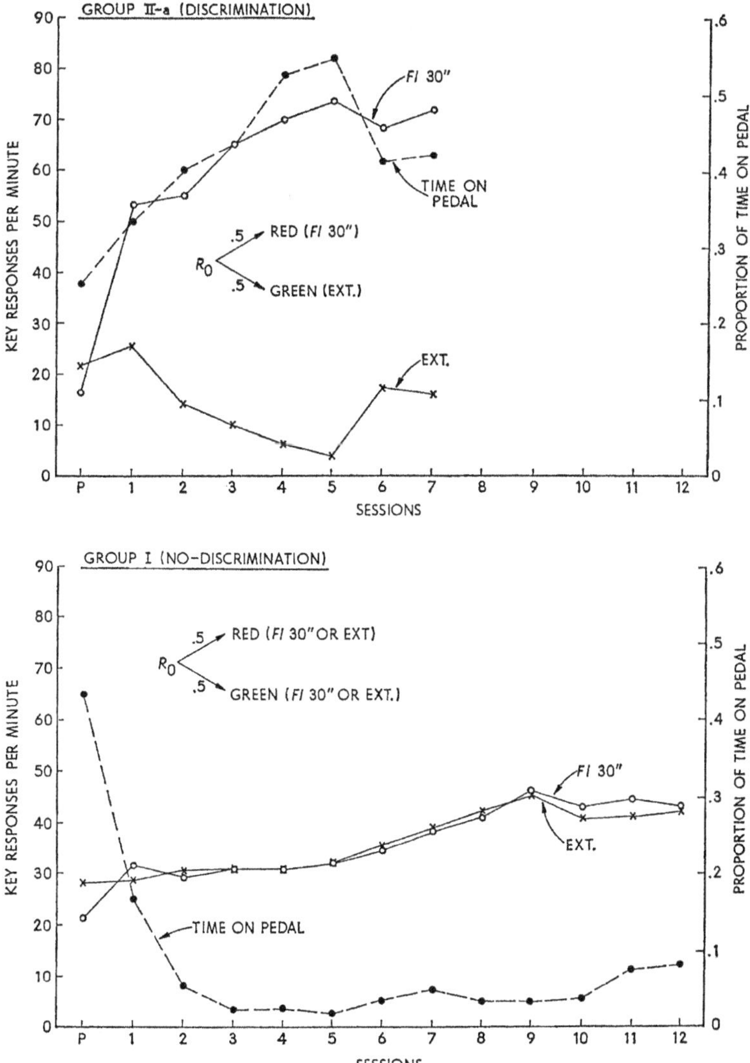

Figure 10.3 The top graph shows mean responding when pedal presses produced signals (red and green stimuli) correlated with the fixed-interval (FI) 30-s and extinction (EXT) schedules. The bottom graph shows mean responding when the pedal presses produced signals uncorrelated with the two schedules. When the signals were correlated, subjects made observing responses and responded differentially to the two schedules. When the signals were uncorrelated, subjects made very few observing responses and did not respond differently to the two schedules (reprinted from Wyckoff, 1969, Figures 9.1 [bottom panel] and 9.2 [top panel]).

A counterintuitive example of how conditioned reinforcement effects are tied to the schedule of primary reinforcement is illustrated by studies that evaluated preference between a reliable alternative (one that leads to food 100% of the time) and an unreliable alternative (one that leads to food 50% of the time and blackout 50% of the time; Belke & Spetch, 1994; Dunn & Spetch, 1990; Kendall, 1974; McDevitt,

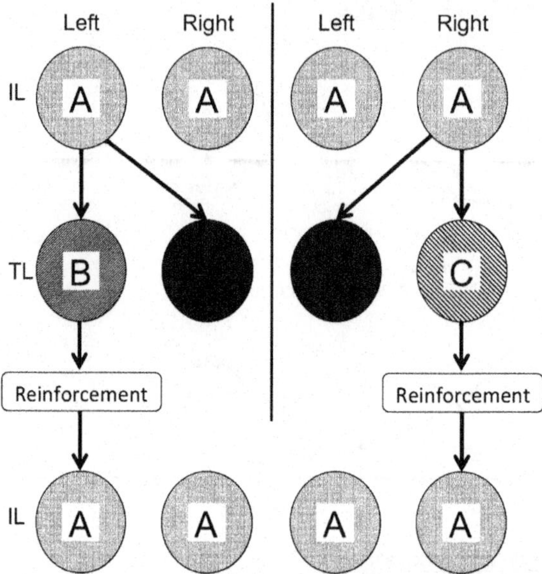

Figure 10.4 Procedure schematic of a typical concurrent chains schedule used to study conditioned reinforcement effects. When subjects complete the schedule requirement on the left initial link (IL) (shown in the left panel), the IL stimuli extinguish and the left terminal-link (TL) schedule begins. Completing the terminal-link schedule results in reinforcement. The right side functions in a similar fashion. Typically IL schedules consist of equal VI schedules. TL schedules vary by experiment. Since IL schedules are equal, any differences in performance to those is presumed to be a function of what follows those links.

Spetch, & Dunn, 1997; Spetch, Belke, Barnet, Dunn, & Pierce, 1990). In a replication of the basic finding, McDevitt et al. showed that pigeons were largely indifferent between a 100% reinforcement alternative and a 50% alternative when the food and blackout outcomes were signaled by the terminal-link stimulus on the 50% alternative (i.e., when one stimulus was correlated with trials ending in food and a different stimulus was correlated with trials ending in blackout). It was hypothesized that the signal for food on the 50% alternative served as a stronger conditioned reinforcer than the signal for food on the 100% alternative, since subjects should have exclusively preferred the 100% alternative because it provided twice as much food. In a series of conditions, McDevitt et al. assessed the strength of the terminal-link stimuli as conditioned reinforcers by interposing a short gap (a 5-s period in which the keylights were darkened) between the choice response and some or all of the terminal-link stimuli. If a terminal–link stimulus functioned as a conditioned reinforcer, the imposition of the gap should reduce its effectiveness, and choice behavior should shift away from the alternative with the gap. The results supported the notion that conditioned reinforcement underlies the finding of suboptimal preference in probabilistic (100% vs. 50%) reinforcement procedures (i.e., when the gap was placed at the beginning of the signal for food on the 50% alternative, choice shifted more than when the gap was placed at the beginning of the signal for food on the 100% alternative). Thus, the evidence indicated that the signal for food on the 50% reinforcement alternative functioned as a stronger conditioned reinforcer than the signal for food on the 100% reinforcement alternative.

McDevitt and Williams (2010) used a concurrent chains procedure to provide evidence that both the frequency and the value of conditioned reinforcers influence choice in a concurrent chains procedure. In their study, pigeons responded on a concurrent chain where one choice option presented a VI 30-s VI 60-s chain and the other option presented a VI 60-s VI 30-s chain. Again, only the initial links were concurrent. This manipulation equated total time to reinforcement for the two alternatives. Importantly, McDevitt and Williams manipulated whether the terminal links of the two chains had different or identical signals. In conditions with different signals, subjects preferred the chain with the shorter terminal link, a finding consistent with other research (e.g., Duncan & Fantino, 1970). When identical stimuli were used for the terminal links, preference reversed in favor of the alternative with the shorter initial link (i.e., the VI 30-s VI 60-s). They concluded that the reversal in preference occurred because the shorter initial link produced the common terminal-link stimulus more frequently. In other words, the conditioned reinforcer occurred more frequently.

Discrimination Learning

Although most studies of conditioned reinforcement have used free-operant procedures (which focus on response rate as the dependent variable), Williams and Dunn (1991b) examined the effects of conditioned reinforcement on the acquisition of a discrimination task. Rats were presented with trials in which one of two S^Ds, a light or a noise, was presented. Responding to one lever was reinforced in the presence of the light, and responding to the other lever was reinforced in the presence of noise. After a learning criterion was reached, the contingencies for the S^Ds were reversed. In baseline conditions, food always followed correct responses. In other conditions, food followed correct responses only 50% or 30% of the time. The critical manipulation involved presenting a conditioned reinforcer on the unreinforced correct trials. When the conditioned reinforcer was presented on those trials, learning occurred more quickly. When the conditioned reinforcer was not presented, learning occurred more slowly. Williams and Dunn's results show that conditioned reinforcers could substitute for primary reinforcers in a discrimination learning task.

Despite the weaknesses inherent in individual approaches, taken together, these findings offer strong support for the notion that conditioned reinforcers are just that, stimuli that acquire reinforcement strength of their own. Next, we consider the determinants of conditioned reinforcement.

Determinants of Conditioned Value

The exact quantitative relationship that best describes the critical factors determining conditioned reinforcement is still a matter of some debate (see Preston & Fantino, 1991, for a review). Fantino's (1977; Fantino, Preston, & Dunn, 1993) *delay-reduction theory*, for example, proposes that the value of a conditioned reinforcer is a function of the reduction in the waiting time to reinforcement signaled by a stimulus. More specifically, delay-reduction theory posits that choice responding in the initial link of a concurrent chains schedule is determined by the relative improvement in time to reinforcement signaled by the terminal-link onsets (Fantino, 1969), as shown in Equation 1. B_L and B_R represent the number of responses to the left and right initial links, T represents the average time to primary reinforcement from the onset of the initial links, and t_L and t_R represent the average durations of the left and right terminal links.

$$\frac{B_L}{B_R} = \frac{T - t_L}{T - t_R} \tag{1}$$

Others have emphasized the information value of the conditioned reinforcer—in other words, the degree to which a stimulus signals availability of primary reinforcement and reduces the uncertainty about the availability of reinforcement (referred to as either the *information hypothesis* or the *uncertainty-reduction hypothesis*; Berlyne, 1960; Bloomfield, 1972; Rachlin, 1976). Fantino (1977) provided a summary of the literature focused on discriminating between these accounts, and suggested that delay-reduction theory, and thus a conditioned reinforcement account, better accounts for the data.

Autoshaping (sometimes referred to as sign-tracking) procedures (Brown & Jenkins, 1968) provide some evidence that neutral stimuli paired with food and water acquire value. In the typical autoshaping procedure, naïve pigeons are trained to eat from a food hopper. They are then presented with an illuminated response key for 10 s followed by 4-s access to food which is then followed by a 60-s intertrial interval. In this procedure, the illuminated response key functions as a conditioned stimulus (CS) and the food as an unconditioned stimulus (US). Even though there is no requirement that the pigeons respond, most will come to peck at the illuminated response key.

Jenkins and Moore (1973) provided compelling evidence that the CS acquires some of the properties of the associated US. Across a series of experiments, they exposed pigeons to an autoshaping procedure. The critical manipulation was the type of US employed. In some cases the US was food and in others it was water. The difference in the US is important because of the different beak positions: when pigeons eat, they do so with an open gape and when they drink it is with a closed gape. Jenkins and Moore reported that the pecking topography toward the key (the CR) differed as a function of the US used. When food was used as the US, the conditioned pecks were open-gaped. When the US was water, the conditioned pecks were close-gaped (see Figure 10.5). This finding suggests that some of the properties of the US have transferred to the CS as indicated by the type of conditioned pecks that occur. It is important to note that a CR need not be similar to a UR as shown by these results. In fact, in many cases of Pavlovian conditioning the UR and CR differ dramatically.

Autoshaping suggests that conditioned stimuli acquire some of the properties of the unconditioned stimuli that they are paired with as evidenced by pigeons pecking at keys and doing so in a very specific way even though there is no contingency for doing so. If stimuli functioning as conditioned reinforcers acquire their function

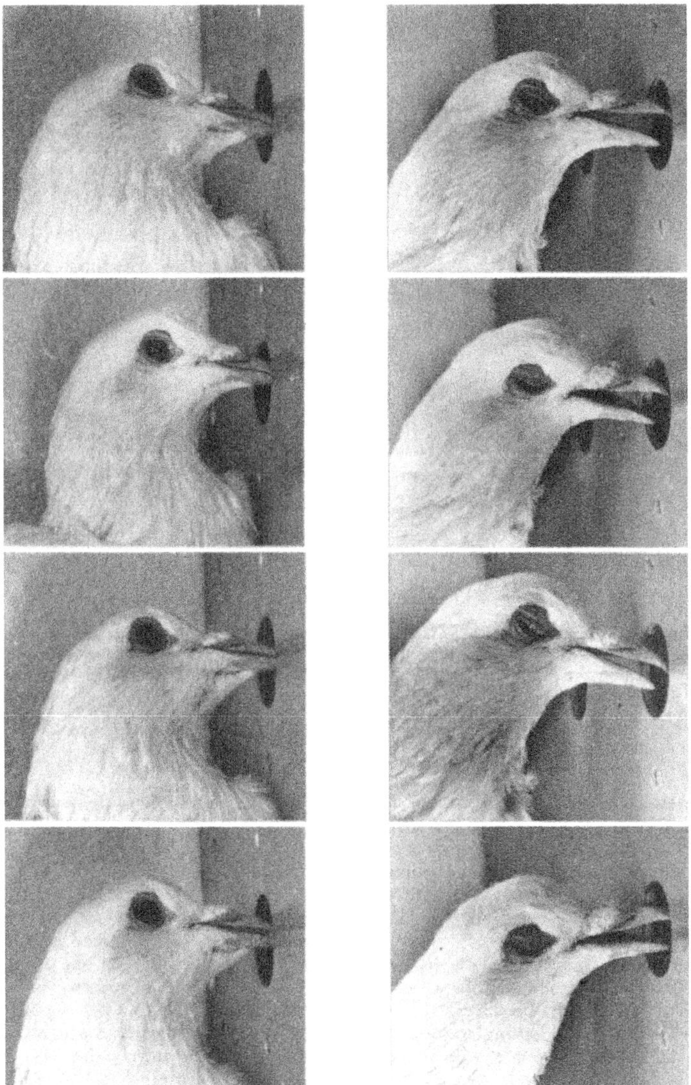

Figure 10.5 Typical food and water autoshaped responses for pigeons. Photos were taken at the moment of key contact. The left column shows responses to the water-paired key. The right column shows responses to the food-paired key. Reprinted from Jenkins and Moore (1973, Figure 2).

through Pavlovian conditioning process, it follows that the development of conditioned reinforcers should conform to the rules of Pavlovian conditioning. Furthermore, it suggests that the properties of those conditioned stimuli could be similar to the properties of the associated primary reinforcers.

Behavioral Momentum Theory

One example of a theory that explicitly connects conditioned reinforcement value to Pavlovian contingencies is *behavioral momentum theory* (Nevin, 1992; Nevin &

Grace, 2000). Behavioral momentum theory describes behavior both under steady-state conditions and, more importantly, under conditions in which behavior is disrupted. The theory uses a metaphor of momentum from physics which says that responding in a discriminated operant is a function of two separate factors analogous to the factors that control the velocity of a body in motion. The first factor, resistance to change (persistence) under conditions of disruption, is likened to inertial mass in classical mechanics of physics. Resistance to change is said to be determined by the rate of food in the presence of a stimulus—in other words, by the Pavlovian stimulus-reinforcer relationship—and independent from any operant response-reinforcer contingencies. The second factor is the rate of occurrence of the operant response, likened to velocity of an object in motion and is well-described by the matching law (e.g., Herrnstein, 1961).

Nevin, Tota, Torquato, and Shull (1990) provide evidence for the role of Pavlovian contingencies in determining stimulus value. Their Experiment 1 presented pigeons with a multiple schedule in which two 3-min components alternated during experimental sessions. In both components (of most conditions) reinforcement was available according to equal VI 1-min schedules. Components were separated by a 1-min inter-component interval (ICI). The critical manipulation was the addition of free food (using a VT schedule) added to one of the VI 1-min components. This manipulation had the effect of both disrupting the operant (response-reinforcer) contingency and increasing the Pavlovian (stimulus-reinforcer) relationship. The increase in the Pavlovian relationship, according to behavioral momentum theory, should increase resistance to change, which is what they reported when they disrupted behavior using prefeeding and extinction manipulations. The findings are consistent with the general claim that Pavlovian contingencies function to determine the conditioned reinforcing properties of a stimulus (although note that other interpretations of these results are possible).

The Pavlovian conditioning and resistance to change relationship described in behavioral momentum theory is not the final word on the matter. Thus, while Nevin's theory attributes differences in resistance to change to Pavlovian conditioning, there is research challenging this conclusion (see, for example, Grace, Schwendiman, & Nevin, 1998 and Bell, 1999). Although beyond the scope of this chapter, alternative interpretations should be taken into consideration when considering the viability of using Pavlovian conditioning to explain resistance to change.

Comparing Conditioned and Primary Reinforcers

A final issue to consider is whether or not conditioned reinforcers, once established, are qualitatively different from primary reinforcers. One way this has been assessed was to determine if variables affect primary reinforcement and conditioned reinforcement differently. We provide three examples of commonalities. First, early work with chain schedules of reinforcement (e.g., Ferster & Skinner, 1957) show, for example, that response patterns in earlier links (i.e., links not paired directly with primary reinforcement) of a chain schedule reflect response patterns seen in simple schedules with the same response contingencies. Second, Royalty et al. (1987), described above, showed effects of unsignaled delays for conditioned reinforcers. Williams (1976) showed a similar effect using unsignaled delays to primary reinforcement. Finally,

Shahan, Podlesnik, and Jimenez-Gomez (2006) presented pigeons a choice between two concurrently available observing responses. They showed that the ratio of delivery of conditioned reinforcers predicted the ratio of observing responses and that the data were well-described by the generalized matching law which was developed to describe the relationship between primary reinforcement ratios and response ratios (Baum, 1974; Baum & Rachlin, 1969). Taken together, these examples show that there are a number of shared features between conditioned and primary reinforcers.

There are of course differences between conditioned and primary reinforcers. However, it is not critical that conditioned reinforcers possess all of the functional capabilities of the primary reinforcer with which it is associated. In Pavlovian conditioning, CSs may elicit only a subset of the response that the associated US elicits (Mazur, 2006). Conditioned reinforcers may also show differences in function compared to the primary reinforcers with which they have been associated. For example, some researchers have found that conditioned reinforcers seem to be less "transsituational" than primary reinforcers (Keehn, 1962; Schuster, 1969; Reinforcers are considered to have the property of transsituationality when they work in different situations. See Meehl, 1950 for more on this concept).

Alternative Views: Challenges to Conditioned Reinforcement

Experimental evidence supporting conditioned reinforcement has often had alternative interpretations, and other theoretical constructs have been proposed as possible alternatives or supplements to the concept of conditioned reinforcement. We will briefly describe three: marking, bridging, and timing. All of these alternatives focus on the discriminative properties of a stimulus and how it signals distance to primary reinforcement.

Marking and Bridging

Marking is a procedure in which a brief stimulus signals a delay that follows a choice response. The signal and the delay occur regardless of whether or not a correct choice was made. Bridging is similar to the marking procedure except that the stimulus is present during the entire delay. Both marking (Lieberman, McIntosh, & Thomas, 1979) and bridging (Rescorla, 1982) can facilitate acquisition of behavior relative to an unsignaled delay control group. Superficially, conditioned reinforcement, marking, and bridging procedures are quite similar: they all allow a connection between an event (stimulus or behavior) and its temporally distant consequence. Somehow they function to link the temporal gap between two events.

The critical distinction between conditioned reinforcement and marking/bridging procedures is that in conditioned reinforcement procedures the stimulus occurs only after a correct response (i.e. a response leading to primary reinforcement) has been made, whereas with marking and bridging the stimulus occurs regardless of the choice response. (Note that brief stimuli and stimuli that fill the entire delay are both considered in conditioned reinforcement accounts, with no distinguishing terminology.) One view is that marking effects "perceptually isolate the choice response, thus making it more salient in memory at the time the response consequence is eventually delivered" (Williams, 1991, p. 264).

Williams (1991) directly compared marking and bridging procedures with a conditioned reinforcement procedure using rats in a two-choice conditional discrimination. Two different discriminative stimuli, a noise and a light, were used to indicate which response lever would result in food after a delay (3- to 12-s, depending upon the condition). Thus, the S^D was presented, and subjects chose. The S^D terminated, and a delay occurred. If subjects made a correct choice, the delay ended in food. If they made an incorrect choice, the delay ended without a food delivery. The critical manipulation was what occurred during the delay. In marking and bridging conditions, a tone stimulus followed both correct and incorrect responses. In marking conditions, the stimulus was presented briefly (0.5-1 s at the beginning of the delay) and in bridging conditions, the stimulus filled the entire delay. In the conditioned reinforcement conditions, a tone stimulus followed correct responses only. After subjects reached a training criterion, the contingencies were reversed (i.e., if the noise signaled that the left key was correct and the light that the right key was correct, in the subsequent condition, noise signaled the right key was correct and light signaled the left key was correct). Williams failed to find a marking or bridging effect, but did find that the conditioned reinforcement conditions resulted in fewer trials to criterion (i.e., faster learning) compared to all other conditions (no signal, bridging and marking conditions). Although marking and bridging procedures do appear to enhance learning under some conditions, they do not eliminate the need for the concept of conditioned reinforcement, as we will describe later.

Timing

Timing explanations serve as an alternative approach to conditioned reinforcement and have attracted a good deal of attention. Timing accounts explain the effects of delays as a function of connections to primary reinforcement and rely upon the ability of a subject to maintain an accurate memory of the temporal relationship between events. In other words, rather than acquiring the functional properties of reinforcers, stimulus changes function to mark passage of time with respect to the primary reinforcer. One goal of this approach is to provide a unified theoretical approach to explaining operant behavior. As yet, these accounts have failed to provide a more parsimonious or complete account of operant conditioning compared to the theoretical construct of conditioned reinforcement (see Williams, 2003). Royalty et al. (1987), which was described above, provides some evidence to support this claim. Recall that they showed differences in responding within the link of a chain schedule as a function of the unsignaled delays associated with that link. The fact that they demonstrated this effect while holding time to primary reinforcement constant is problematic for timing theories. In other words, if time is the only controlling variable, then there should be no difference in responding between links with an unsignaled delay and links with no delay (for additional evidence challenging a timing account, see Bell & Williams, 2013).

Cronin (1980) also provides a clear example of the difficulties encountered by accounts based solely on timing. The basic procedure involved a simple discrimination in which pigeons chose between two keys, one illuminated red and the other green

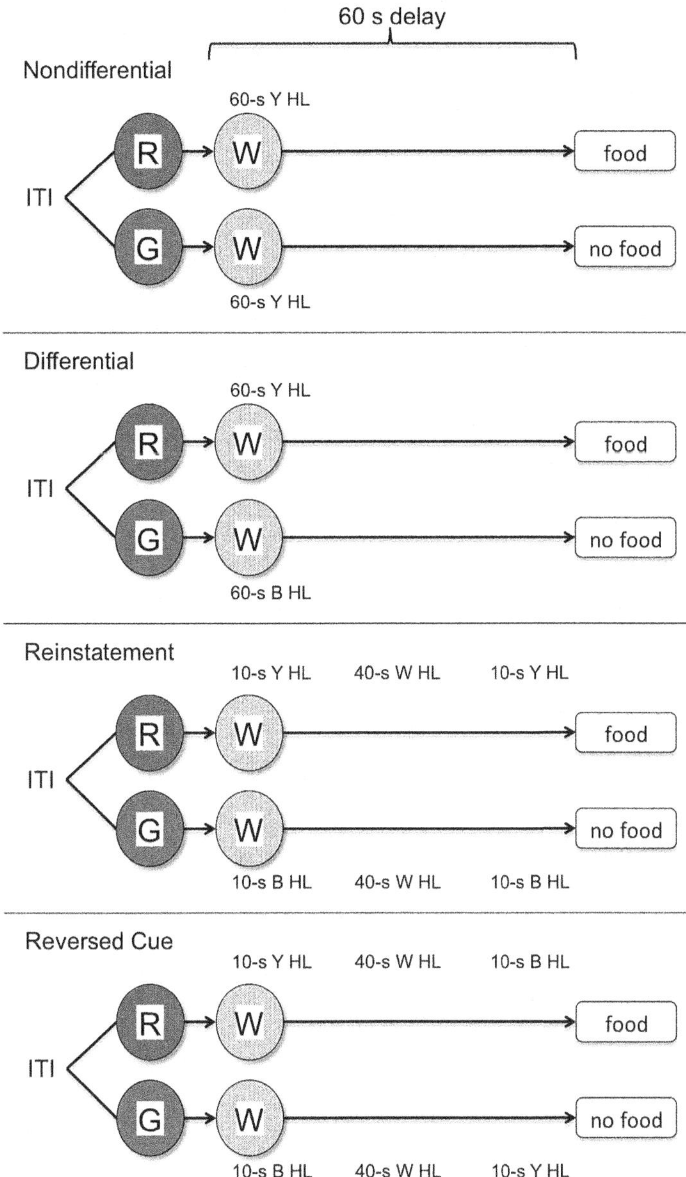

Figure 10.6 Procedure schematic of Cronin (1980). Following a 2-min intertrial interval (ITI), a trial began with a choice between a red and green key light (KL). In this example, responses to red always led to food reinforcement and responses to green never did (i.e., extinction). Pecks to the red and green KL stimuli were followed by a change in KL color and house light (HL) color. Additional procedural details are provided in the text.

(see Figure 10.6). Responding to either stimulus was followed by a 60-s delay. A peck to the red stimulus led to food while pecks to the green stimulus resulted in no food. In the baseline condition, the delay period was signaled with a yellow house light and a white keylight. In the differential signal condition, the 60-s delay period was segmented as follows: Following a peck to the red stimulus a yellow houselight

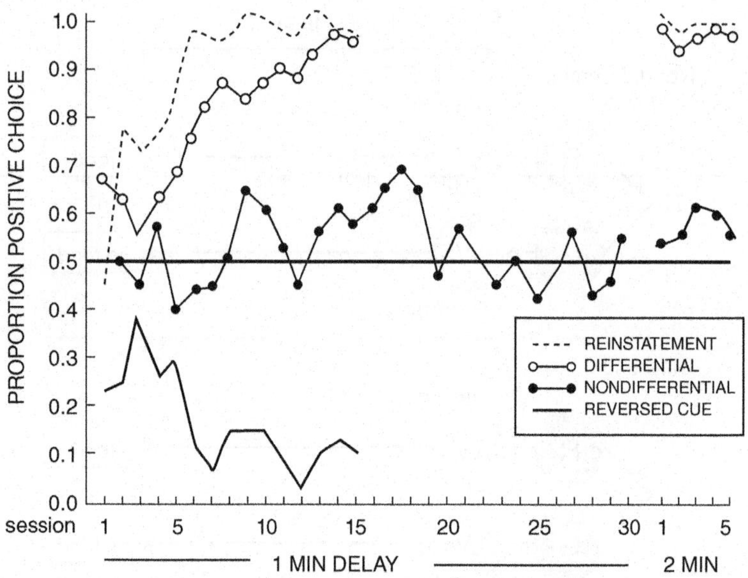

Figure 10.7 Mean choice proportion for the alternatives leading to food reinforcement for the four training groups in Cronin (1980, showing Figure 2 reprinted). The reinstatement and differential groups quickly learned to respond to the stimulus leading to food. The nondifferential group remained at chance levels of performance, and never learned the task. Interestingly, the reverse cue group responded most to the stimulus that did not lead to food.

was illuminated for 10-s, followed by a white houselight for 40-s, and again followed by the yellow houselight for 10 s and then food. Pecks to the green stimulus were followed by a blue houselight for 10 s, the white houselight for 40 s, and the blue houselight for 10 s, then the end of the trial without food. In the reversed cue condition, the delays were also signaled, but choice of the red stimulus led to yellow, white, then blue, and choice of the green stimulus led to blue, white, and then yellow. The results (Figure 10.7) showed that birds in the baseline condition chose red about 50% of the time, and never learned the task. Birds in the differential signal condition quickly learned the task, approaching 100% correct. Birds in the reversed cue condition, however, went below chance to 9% correct (i.e., the pigeons were choosing the option that did not lead to food 91% of the time). This last finding offers compelling support of a conditioned reinforcement interpretation over a timing interpretation (or bridging or marking). If the stimuli merely mark the passage of time, one stimulus should be as good as any other—they should be functionally identical and completely interchangeable. The fact that responding went below chance accuracy in the inconsistent signal condition suggests that the blue stimulus acquired conditioned reinforcement value as a function of being paired, albeit infrequently, with reinforcement when birds chose the red alternative. Thus, choice between red and green essentially involved pitting a long delayed outcome of a conditioned reinforcer (blue) and food against an immediate conditioned reinforcer.

Other Challenges

Schuster (1969) reported a series of studies often cited as evidence contradicting conditioned reinforcement and worth some consideration here. The first two experiments were multiple VI VI schedules in which a brief stimulus presentation was added to one schedule on a fixed ratio (FR) 11 schedule. FR schedules require a certain number of responses for re-inforcer delivery (Ferster & Skinner, 1957). The brief stimulus presentations were either paired or unpaired with primary reinforcement deliveries across conditions. He found that when the brief stimulus presentations were regularly paired with reinforcement, relative response rates increased for all subjects. Schuster claimed, however, that this finding did not constitute a conditioned reinforcement effect as the results lacked a clear contrast effect—in other words, there was not an accompanying decrease in responding to the schedule without the brief signal presentations. Although it is well known that an increase in reinforcement rate in one component can reduce responding in other components (Reynolds, 1961), this relationship is complex (see, for example, Williams, 1989, 1988, 2002; Williams & McDevitt, 2001).

Schuster (1969) also reported studies using a concurrent chains procedure in which an additional stimulus was presented on only one of two terminal links. Schuster reported no effects of the added stimulus presentations, and thus his results do not support a conditioned reinforcement interpretation. However, Williams and Dunn (1991a) raised several noteworthy criticisms of this procedure, and suggested that Schuster's results should be interpreted with caution. The most critical issue they identified was that the added stimulus presentations were never presented contingent upon choice responding. Thus, any conditioned reinforcement effect would have to have been mediated through the terminal-link stimulus and would require the stimulus to acquire conditioned value through second-order conditioning (as opposed to being directly paired with the primary reinforcer).

Williams and Dunn (1991a) carried out an extension of the Schuster (1969) procedures. In their procedure (Figure 10.8), pigeons chose between two equal VI initial-link schedules, each leading to an FI terminal link. The key manipulation was adding non-reinforced FT terminal-link presentations differentially to the two-choice alternatives. This manipulation makes terminal-link stimulus presentations contingent upon choice responding, addressing the flaw in Schuster's design. The distribution of additional terminal-link presentations was systematically varied across conditions. In some conditions the presentations were 50/50 across the two alternatives. In others, the distribution was 80/20. Initial-link preference varied as a function of the distribution of the additional terminal-link stimulus presentations, with higher responding occurring to the alternative paired with 80% of the additional stimulus presentations. In other words, subjects preferred the alternative that led to more terminal-link presentations and, as a result, proportionally fewer primary reinforcers. These results demonstrate that the additional terminal-link presentations functioned as conditioned reinforcers.

On another front, Staddon (1983, 2010; see also Staddon & Ettinger, 1989; Staddon & Cerutti, 2003) suggests that there are other problems with a traditional conditioned reinforcement account, which hinge upon a few specific issues. First,

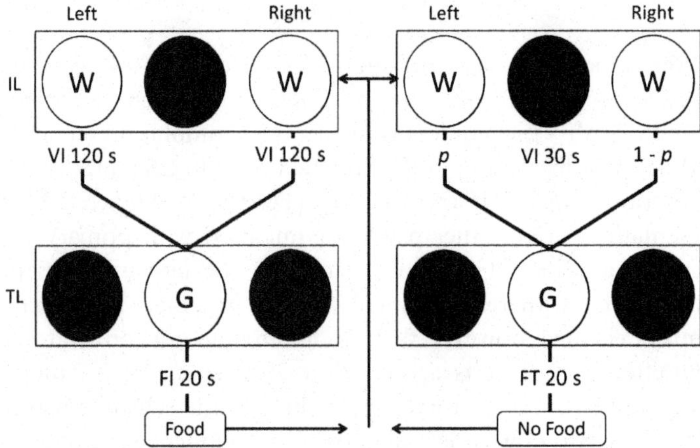

Figure 10.8 Schedules of center key light presentations. The left panel shows the concurrent chain schedule leading to food reinforcement. Initial links were equal VI 120-s schedules followed by equal FI 20-s terminal links, after which food was delivered. The conditioned reinforcement schedule, shown on the right, was superimposed on the food schedule. Here initial-link responding moved subjects to the terminal link according to a single VI 30-s schedule where entry to the terminal link from the left or right keys was varied with a probability p across conditions. When subjects entered this terminal link, the center key light terminated on a fixed-time (FT) 20-s schedule (and did not end in food). Reprinted from Williams and Dunn (1991a).

some experiments fail to demonstrate conditioned reinforcement effects. For example, Catania, Yohalem, and Silverman (1980) used pigeons to compare responding on three-link chain schedules (with FI 30-s links) with several yoked control conditions, including a tandem schedule control. As responding did not differ between the chain and tandem schedules, they concluded that the stimulus changes in the chain schedule did not function as conditioned reinforcers. This conclusion has been challenged by Royalty et al. (1987), described earlier, who suggested that the control conditions were not appropriate because, in part, they failed to control for overall time to reinforcement and, as we noted earlier, the response rates drop in early links of long chains thus extending the overall delay to primary reinforcement. In other words, the overall rate of primary reinforcement decreased in the chain schedules.

Second, Staddon (1983, 2010) discusses the finding that increasing the number of links in a chain can eliminate responding. Typically chain schedules with four or more links will not maintain much, if any, responding in early links. Staddon suggests this failure challenges a conditioned reinforcement account and that mere proximity to primary reinforcement is the key variable controlling responding. Contrary to this claim, low rates of responding in early links are compatible with a conditioned reinforcement account. Again, stimuli in the early links of a chain schedule are distant from reinforcement and therefore signal extinction. Any conditioned reinforcement effects would have to be mediated through the following links. (Davison & Baum, 2010, provide an alternative perspective.) The related Pavlovian literature also shows that conditioning beyond the second order is difficult, at best, to achieve (e.g.,

Murphy & Miller, 1957). Finally, Staddon claims that simple temporal proximity to food is sufficient to explain responding in chain schedules. Once again, Royalty et al. (1987) provided clear evidence that the contingencies between links of the chain play a key role.

Recently, it has been argued that the very notion of conditioned reinforcement needs to be reconsidered (Shahan, 2010, 2013), and this argument is certainly not new. In fact, Hendry (1969) suggested that it would perhaps be "more prudent and objective to avoid the connotations of the word 'reinforcer'" (p. 401). However, no superior concept has yet been proposed to replace it. In any case, research into conditioned reinforcement will continue. The concept of conditioned reinforcement appears indispensable. For any theory of learning to be complete, it must include an explanation of how a (previously) neutral stimulus acquires the ability to reinforce responding.

Applications of Conditioned Reinforcement

Notwithstanding the theoretical issues that have surrounded conditioned reinforcement, its importance as a key concept in the development of techniques to change and maintain both human and nonhuman behavior has been enormous. Our daily lives consist of sequences of events and responses and chains of behavior, and conditioned reinforcement propels us through those chains (and lack of it impedes our progress).

Conditioned reinforcement can also make delayed reinforcement more effective. There are times when it is not possible (or desirable) for a primary reinforcer to immediately follow our behavior, but a conditioned reinforcer can be applied quickly and effectively. For example, a simple "thank you" might be all that is necessary to strengthen a behavior. Of course, life often involves layers of conditioned reinforcers. For example, our work might evoke a "good job" from a colleague, but is also reinforced by the conditioned reinforcement associated with a direct deposit notice from our employer, which then leads to a succession of other conditioned and primary reinforcers. Learning to use conditioned reinforcers effectively is a vital part of learning to effectively change and maintain behavior.

Animal Training

Animal trainers rely heavily on conditioned reinforcers. In fact, the recent popularity of "clicker training" attests to this (Pryor, 2004). The first step in these programs is to pair the clicker or other sound with a particularly delicious treat. The pet owner "clicks," and then immediately gives the pet a small morsel of food. Once the sound of the clicker has become an established conditioned reinforcer, it can then be used to reinforce particular behaviors.

Conditioned reinforcers have a number of benefits compared to primary reinforcers. First, they are often more portable, and easily dispensed. A parent can easily apply a verbal conditioned reinforcer, such as the verbal response "Nice sharing!" to a child, regardless of where they are, as the response needs no direct environmental support, except the periodic pairing with primary or other reinforcers. Conditioned reinforcers can also be more effective than primary reinforcers in terms of pinpointing the portion or characteristic of a response that was responsible for producing reinforcement. For example, a clicker that has developed conditioned reinforcing properties can be presented at the point at which a dog's hind legs clear a bar during a jump, indicating the part of the response that was deemed favorable by the trainer. Finally, conditioned reinforcers can effectively lengthen animal training sessions, as they do not result in satiation the way food reinforcers do.

Interestingly, in spite of the widespread popularity of clicker training, we were unable to find much research reported on its use with pets. Meyer and Ladewig (2008), for example, report what appears to be one of the first systematic studies of dog clicker training. For more information on training, see Pryor's chapter in this volume.

Token Economies

To see the enormous power of conditioned reinforcement, one must only consider the potent effects of money on human behavior. A "token" is an object that can be exchanged for other reinforcers. It is also called a "generalized reinforcer," as it does not need to rely on a single reinforcer in order to be effective. Money is one such token and maintains much of our behavior, but other kinds of tokens can be used to establish or maintain specific behaviors.

Token economies have been used in a variety of work environments in order to support particular behavioral goals. For example, Fox, Hopkins, and Anger (1987) used a token economy to successfully increase safety at two open-pit mines. Employees at the mines earned stamps for working without accidents and injuries, and could exchange their stamps for tangible items. Token economies have also been used effectively to maintain appropriate classroom behavior (e.g., Boniecki & Moore, 2003), treat drug addiction (Eriksson, Götestam, Melin, & Ost, 1975), reduce disruptive noise in a group living situation (Meyers, Artz, & Craighead, 1976), and modify countless other behaviors. See Hackenberg (2009) and Kazdin & Bootzin (1972) for reviews of the research related to and application of token economies, as well as a discussion of the challenges faced in implementing them.

Future Directions

As we have seen in this chapter, the concept of conditioned reinforcement holds a central place the field of learning. The power of operant conditioning lies in the use of consequences to change future behavior. Because much of what reinforces our behavior is not primary reinforcement, conditioned reinforcement plays an even more important role in understanding human behavior although interest in conditioned reinforcement appears to have dropped off in recent decades (Williams, 1994). However, some issues relating to our understanding of conditioned reinforcement remain unresolved.

One issue relates to how to best estimate the value of a conditioned reinforcer and model the effects of conditioned reinforcement on choice behavior. There are several possible approaches, including models based on the degree to which stimuli function to signal a reduction in the waiting time to reinforcement (Fantino, 1969, 1977, 1981) or models that estimate the conditioned value based on time to reinforcement (Mazur, 1993). While the field surely benefits from the variety of approaches, there is no theoretical approach that can be considered a clear winner.

There also appears to be quite a divide between the basic research on conditioned reinforcement and applications based on that construct. The utility of clicker training and other token economies is clear, but the applications and the basic research are not clearly connected. This disconnect is a problem, as applications that are not based on a clear connection to the basic science are at best incomplete and at worst antithetical to the fundamental properties of behavior analysis.

Summary

Conditioned reinforcement has an esteemed position in the experimental analysis of behavior, appearing in the earliest texts in the field. The early procedures provided evidence for conditioned reinforcement but were plagued with small, quickly-disappearing effects, confounding variables, and alternative interpretations. These early findings led to refined procedures for establishing the importance of conditioned reinforcement. The literature, taken as a whole, provides substantial and converging evidence that conditioned reinforcement continues to play an important role in learning theory. Some work has suggested alternative interpretations, including explanations focused exclusively on timing. However, timing-based explanations as yet do not provide a more parsimonious explanation for the literature than does conditioned reinforcement. Conditioned reinforcement continues to have enormous utility, providing a straightforward explanation for a variety of experimental results. Furthermore, the usefulness of the construct is shown in the ubiquity and central importance of conditioned reinforcement in applications such as animal training and token economies.

Author Note

One challenge we faced in writing this chapter was the sheer corpus of work on this topic. Conditioned reinforcement has a long and varied history warranting serious consideration. It is an important and necessary conceptual construct (although, as you see, some disagree). A single chapter cannot adequately cover the topic in depth; that is not our goal. Rather, we want to provide an introduction to the topic, touching on key issues and present examples of important research in the area to provide a broad overview of the topic. We have provided a few review references at the end of the chapter for anyone interested in pursuing the topic. We thank Roger Dunn and Ben A. Williams for comments on an earlier version of this chapter.

Notes

1 However, as Williams (1994) notes, neither Skinner (1938) nor Wolfe (1936) are definitive demonstrations of conditioned reinforcement.

2 There is a substantial literature on the concurrent chains procedure and various theories related to that procedure that is beyond the scope of this chapter (see, e.g., Fantino, 1977 and Davison & McCarthy, 1987, for reviews; see also Williams, 1988, 1994). Our purpose is to present this procedure specifically in the context of conditioned reinforcement.

References

Baum, W. M. (1974). On two types of deviation from the Matching law: Bias and undermatching. *Journal of the Experimental Analysis of Behavior, 22*, 231–242.

Baum, W. M., & Rachlin, H. C. (1969). Choice as time allocation. *Journal of the Experimental Analysis of Behavior, 12*, 861–874.

Belke, T. W., & Spetch, M. L. (1994). Choice between reliable and unreliable reinforcement alternatives revisited: Preference for unreliable reinforcement. *Journal of the Experimental Analysis of Behavior, 62*, 353–366.

Bell, M. C. (1999). Pavlovian contingencies and resistance to change in a multiple schedule. *Journal of the Experimental Analysis of Behavior, 72*, 81–96.

Bell, M. C., & Williams, B. A. (2013). Conditioned reinforcement in chain schedules when time to reinforcement is held constant. *Journal of the Experimental Analysis of Behavior, 99*, 179–188. doi: 10.1002/jeab.10.

Berlyne, D. E. (1960). *Conflict, arousal, and curiosity.* New York: McGraw Hill.

Bloomfield, T. M. (1972). *Reinforcement schedules: contingency or contiguity?* In R. M. Gilbert & J. R. Millenson (Eds.), *Reinforcement* (pp. 65–208). New York: Academic Press.

Boniecki, K. A., & Moore, S. (2003). Breaking the silence: Using a token economy to reinforce classroom participation. *Teaching of Psychology, 30*, 224–227. doi:10.1207/S15328023TOP3003_05.

Brown, P. L., & Jenkins, H. M. (1968). Auto-shaping of the pigeon's keypeck. *Journal of the Experimental Analysis of Behavior, 11*, 1–8.

Catania, A. C., Yohalem, R., & Silverman, P. J. (1980). Contingency and stimulus change in chained schedules of reinforcement. *Journal of the Experimental Analysis of Behavior, 33*, 213–219.

Cronin, P. B. (1980). Reinstatement of postresponse stimuli prior to reward in delayed-reward discrimination learning by pigeons. *Animal Learning & Behavior, 8*, 352–358.

Davison, M., & Baum, W. M. (2010). Stimulus effects on local preference: Stimulus-response contingencies, stimulus-food pairing, and stimulus-food correlation. *Journal of the Experimental Analysis of Behavior, 93*, 45–59. doi:10.1901/jeab.2010.93-45.

Davison, M., & McCarthy, D. (1987). The interaction of stimulus and reinforcer control in complex temporal discrimination. *Journal of the Experimental Analysis of Behavior, 48*, 97–116.

Duncan, B., & Fantino, E. (1970). Choice for periodic schedules of reinforcement. *Journal of the Experimental Analysis of Behavior, 14*, 73–86.

Dunn, R., & Spetch, M. L. (1990). Choice with uncertain outcomes: Conditioned reinforcement effects. *Journal of the Experimental Analysis of Behavior, 53*, 201–218.

Eriksson, J. H., Götestam, K. G, Melin, L., & Ost, L-G. (1975). A token economy treatment of drug addiction. *Behaviour Research and Therapy, 13*, 113–225.

Fantino, E. (1969). Choice and rate of reinforcement. *Journal of the Experimental Analysis of Behavior, 12*, 723–730.

Fantino, E. (1977). Conditioned reinforcement: Choice and information. In W. K. Honig & J. E. R. Staddon (Eds.), *Handbook of operant behavior* (pp. 313–339). Englewood Cliffs, NJ: Prentice Hall.

Fantino, E. (1981). Contiguity, response strength, and the delay-reduction hypothesis. In P. Harzem & M. D. Zeiler (Eds.), *Advances in analysis of behaviour: Vol. 2. Predictability, correlation, and contiguity* (pp. 169–201). Chichester, UK: John Wiley & Sons, Inc.

Fantino, E. J., & Logan, C. A. (1979). *The experimental analysis of behavior: A biological perspective.* San Francisco: Freeman.

Fantino, E., Preston, R. A., & Dunn, R. (1993). Delay reduction: Current status. *Journal of the Experimental Analysis of Behavior, 60,* 159–169.

Ferster, C. B., & Skinner, B. F. (1957). *Schedules of reinforcement.* New York: Appleton-Century-Crofts.

Fox, D. K., Hopkins, B. L., & Anger, W. K. (1987). The long-term effects of a token economy on safety performance in open-pit mining. *Journal of Applied Behavior Analysis, 20,* 215–224. doi:10.1901/jaba.1987.20-215.

Gollub, L. R. (1958). *The chaining of fixed-interval schedules.* Unpublished doctoral dissertation, Harvard University.

Gollub, L. R. (1977). Conditioned reinforcement: Schedule effects. In W. K. Honig & J. E. R. Staddon (Eds.), *Handbook of operant behavior* (pp. 288–312). Englewood Cliffs, NJ: Prentice Hall.

Grace, R. C., Schwendiman, J. W., & Nevin, J. A. (1998). Effects of unsignaled delay of reinforcement on preference and resistance to change. *Journal of the Experimental Analysis of Behavior, 69,* 247–261.

Hackenberg, T. D. (2009). Token reinforcement: A review and analysis. *Journal of the Experimental Analysis of Behavior, 91,* 257–286.

Hendry, D. P. (1969). *Conditioned reinforcement.* Oxford: Dorsey.

Herrnstein, R. J. (1961). Relative and absolute strength of response as a function of frequency of reinforcement. *Journal of the Experimental Analysis of Behavior, 4,* 267–272.

Jenkins, H. M., & Boakes, R. A. (1973). Observing stimulus sources that signal food or no food. *Journal of the Experimental Analysis of Behavior, 20,* 197–207.

Jenkins, H. M., & Moore, R. A. (1973). The form of the autoshaped response with food or water reinforcers. *Journal of the Experimental Analysis of Behavior, 20,* 163–181.

Kazdin, A. E., & Bootzin, R. R. (1972). The token economy: An evaluative review. *Journal of Applied Behavior Analysis, 5,* 343–372.

Keehn, J. D. (1962). The effect of post-stimulus conditions on the secondary reinforcing power of a stimulus. *Journal of Comparative and Physiological Psychology, 55,* 22–26. doi: 10.1037/h0042005.

Kelleher, R. T., & Gollub, L. R. (1962). A review of positive conditioned reinforcement. *Journal of the Experimental Analysis of Behavior, 5,* 543–597.

Keller, F. S., & Schoenfeld, W. N. (1950). *Principles of psychology: A systematic text in the science of behavior.* New York: Appleton-Century-Crofts.

Kendall, S. B. (1973a). Effects of two procedures for varying information transmission on observing responses. *Journal of the Experimental Analysis of Behavior, 20,* 73–83.

Kendall, S. B. (1973b). Redundant information in an observing-response procedure. *Journal of the Experimental Analysis of Behavior, 19,* 81–92.

Kendall, S. B. (1974). Preference for intermittent reinforcement. *Journal of the Experimental Analysis of Behavior, 21,* 463–473.

Lieberman, D. A., McIntosh, D. C., & Thomas, G. V. (1979). Learning when reward is delayed: A marking hypothesis. *Journal of Experimental Psychology: Animal Behavior Processes, 5,* 224–242.

Mazur, J. E. (1993). Predicting the strength of a conditioned reinforcer: Effects of delay and uncertainty. *Current Directions in Psychological Science, 2,* 70–74.

Mazur, J. E. (2006). *Learning & behavior* (6th ed.). Upper Saddle River, NJ: Prentice Hall.

McDevitt, M. A., Spetch, M. L., & Dunn, R. (1997). Contiguity and conditioned reinforcement in probabilistic choice. *Journal of the Experimental Analysis of Behavior, 68*, 317–327.

McDevitt, M. A., & Williams, B. A. (2010). Dual effects on choice of conditioned reinforcement frequency and conditioned reinforcement value. *Journal of the Experimental Analysis of Behavior, 93*, 147–155. doi:10.1901/jeab.2010.93-147.

Meehl, P. E. (1950). On the circularity of the law of effect. *Psychological Bulletin, 47*, 52–75. doi: 10.1037/h0058557.

Meyer, I., & Ladewig, J. (2008). The relationship between number of training sessions per week and learning in dogs. *Applied Animal Behaviour Science, 111*, 311–320.

Meyers, A. W., Artz, L. M., & Craighead, W. E. (1976). The effects of instructions, incentive, and feedback on a community problem: dormitory noise. *Journal of Applied Behavior Analysis, 9*, 445–457. doi: 10.1901/jaba.1976.9-445.

Murphy, J. V., & Miller, R. E. (1957). Higher-order conditioning in the monkey. *The Journal of General Psychology, 56*, 67–72.

Myers, J. L. (1958). Secondary reinforcement: A review of recent experimentation. *Psychological Bulletin, 55*, 284–301.

Nevin, J. A. (1992). An integrative model for the study of behavioral momentum. *Journal of the Experimental Analysis of Behavior, 57*, 301–316.

Nevin, J. A., & Grace, R. C. (2000). Behavioral momentum and the law of effect. *Behavioral and Brain Sciences, 23*, 73–130.

Nevin, J. A., Tota, M. E., Torquato, R. D., & Shull, R. L. (1990). Alternative reinforcement increases resistance to change: Pavlovian or operant contingencies? *Journal of the Experimental Analysis of Behavior, 53*, 359–379.

Preston, R. A., & Fantino, E. (1991). Conditioned reinforcement value and choice. *Journal of the Experimental Analysis of Behavior, 55*, 155–175.

Pryor, K. (2004). *Getting started: Clicker training for dogs.* Dorking, UK: Interpet Publishing.

Rachlin, H. (1976). *Behavior & learning.* San Francisco: W H. Freeman.

Rescorla, R. A. (1982). Effect of a stimulus intervening between CS and US in autoshaping. *Journal of Experimental Psychology: Animal Behavior Processes, 8*, 131–141.

Reynolds, G. S. (1961). An analysis of interactions in a multiple schedule. *Journal of the Experimental Analysis of Behavior, 4*, 107–117.

Royalty, P., Williams, B. A., & Fantino, E. (1987). Effects of delayed conditioned reinforcement in chain schedules. *Journal of the Experimental Analysis of Behavior, 47*, 41–56.

Shahan, T. A. (2010). Conditioned reinforcement and response strength. *Journal of the Experimental Analysis of Behavior, 93*, 269–289.

Shahan, T. A. (2013). Attention and conditioned reinforcement. In G. J. Madden, W. V. Dube, T. D. Hackenberg, G. P. Hanley, K. A. Lattal (Eds.), *APA handbook of behavior analysis, Vol. 1: Methods and principles* (pp. 387–410). Washington, DC: American Psychological Association.

Shahan, T. A., Podlesnik, C. A., & Jimenez-Gomez, C. (2006). Matching and conditioned reinforcement rate. *Journal of the Experimental Analysis of Behavior, 85*, 167–180. doi:10.1901/jeab.2006.34-05.

Schoenfeld, W. N., Antonitis, J. J., & Bersh, P. J. (1950). A preliminary study of training conditions necessary for secondary reinforcement. *Journal of Experimental Psychology, 40*, 40–45.

Schuster, R. H. (1969). A functional analysis of conditioned reinforcement. In D. P. Hendry (Ed.), *Conditioned reinforcement* (pp. 192–235). Homewood, IL: The Dorsey Press.

Skinner, B. F. (1938). *The behavior of organisms: An experimental analysis*. New York: Appleton-Century-Crofts.
Skinner, B. F. (1953). *Science and human behavior*. New York: Free Press.
Spetch, M. L., Belke, T. W., Barnet, R. C., Dunn, R., & Pierce, W. D. (1990). Suboptimal choice in a percentage-reinforcement procedure: Effects of signal condition and terminal-link length. *Journal of the Experimental Analysis of Behavior, 53*, 219–234.
Staddon, J. E. R. (1983). *Adaptive behavior and learning*. New York: Cambridge University Press.
Staddon, J. E. R. (2010). *Adaptive behavior and learning* (Internet ed.) New York: Cambridge University Press.
Staddon, J. E. R., & Cerutti, D. T. (2003). Operant behavior. *Annual Review of Psychology, 54*, 115–144.
Staddon, J. E. R., & Ettinger, R. H. (1989). *Learning: An introduction to the principles of adaptive behavior*. Orlando, FL: Harcourt.
Williams, B. A. (1976). The effects of unsignalled delayed reinforcement. *Journal of the Experimental Analysis of Behavior, 26*, 441–449.
Williams, B. A. (1988). The effects of stimulus similarity on different types of behavioral contrast. *Animal Learning & Behavior, 16*, 206–216.
Williams, B. A. (1989). Component duration effects in multiple schedules. *Animal Learning & Behavior, 17*, 223–233.
Williams, B. A. (1991). Marking and bridging versus conditioned reinforcement. *Animal Learning & Behavior,19*, 264–269.
Williams, B. A. (1994). Conditioned reinforcement: Neglected or outmoded explanatory construct? *Psychonomic Bulletin & Review, 1*, 457–475.
Williams, B. A. (2002). Behavioral contrast redux. *Animal Learning & Behavior, 30*, 1–20.
Williams, B. A. (1997). Conditioned reinforcement dynamics in three-link chained schedules. *Journal of the Experimental Analysis of Behavior, 67*, 145–159.
Williams, B. A. (2003). Challenges to timing-based theories of operant behavior. *Behavioural Processes, 62*, 115–123.
Williams, B. A., & Dunn, R. (1991a). Preference for conditioned reinforcement. *Journal of the Experimental Analysis of Behavior, 55*, 37–46.
Williams, B. A., & Dunn, R. (1991b). Substitutability between conditioned and primary reinforcers in discrimination acquisition. *Journal of the Experimental Analysis of Behavior, 55*, 21–35.
Williams, B. A., & McDevitt, M. A. (2001). Competing sources of stimulus value in anticipatory contrast. *Animal Learning & Behavior, 29*, 302–310.
Williams, B. A., Ploog, B. O., & Bell, M. C. (1995). Stimulus devaluation and extinction of chain schedule performance. *Animal Learning & Behavior, 23*, 104–114.
Wolfe, J. B. (1936). Effectiveness of token rewards for chimpanzees. *Comparative Psychological Monographs, 12*, 1–72.
Wyckoff Jr., L. B. (1952). The role of observing responses in discrimination learning: Part I. *Psychological Review, 59*, 431–442.
Wyckoff Jr., L. B. (1969). The role of observing responses in discrimination learning. In D. P. Hendry (Ed.), *Conditioned reinforcement* (pp. 237–260). Homewood, IL: Dorsey.
Wyckoff Jr., L. B., Sidowski, J., & Chambliss, D. J. (1958). An experimental study of the relationship between secondary reinforcing and cue effects of a stimulus. *Journal of Comparative Physiological Psychology, 51*, 103–109.
Zimmerman, D. W. (1957). Durable secondary reinforcement: Method and theory. *Psychological Review, 64*, 373–383.

Zimmerman, J., Hanford, P. V., & Brown, W. (1967). Effects of conditioned reinforcement frequency in an intermittent free-feeding situation. *Journal of the Experimental Analysis of Behavior, 10*, 331–340.

Additional Reading

There are several excellent reviews (e.g., Myers, 1958; Kelleher & Gollub, 1962; Gollub, 1977; Fantino, 1977; Williams, 1994) and a text (Hendry, 1969) describing early work on conditioned reinforcement.

11

Behavioral Momentum and Resistance to Change

Andrew R. Craig, John A. Nevin, and Amy L. Odum

Persistence is an important dimension of behavior for both theoretical and practical reasons. Persistence of behavior, in itself, is neither good nor bad. If the behavior in question were completing math problems in a 3rd grade classroom, then persistence would be a desirable attribute. If the behavior in question were cigarette smoking, then persistence would be an undesirable attribute. The context and function of the behavior will determine whether the individual, her family, and others concerned would *wish* it to continue. Basic learning factors, though, determine whether it *will* continue, and for how long, and in the face of what challenges.

Nevin (1974) conducted a groundbreaking experiment on the basic processes that contribute to the persistence of behavior (this experiment will be described briefly here, and in more detail later in the chapter). He used pigeons pecking lit disks (conventionally called "keys") to earn food as his subjects, and a sound-and light-attenuated chamber (a so-called "Skinner box" or "operant chamber") as his setting, but the findings have long since been shown to have broad applicability. In Nevin's experiment, the pigeons could peck the key when it was lit either of two colors. When the key was lit one color (the "rich" component of the reinforcement schedule), they could earn relatively more food (which served as the reinforcer). When the key was lit another color (the "lean" component of the schedule), they could earn relatively less food. Nevin employed various ways to make one component richer than the other, as well as various ways of challenging and disrupting the performance engendered by the schedule. The result was the same: Behavior maintained by a richer schedule of reinforcer delivery was more resistant to change than behavior maintained by a leaner schedule of reinforcer delivery.

These basic findings, along with findings from a number of related studies (see Nevin, 1992a; Nevin & Grace, 2000, for review), led Nevin and his colleagues to draw parallels between the resistance to disruption of voluntary (i.e., "operant") behavior and Newton's second law of motion (see Nevin, Mandell, & Atak, 1983).

The Wiley Blackwell Handbook of Operant and Classical Conditioning, First Edition.
Edited by Frances K. McSweeney and Eric S. Murphy.

Newton's second law states that when some outside force acts on a moving object, the resulting change in the velocity of the object will be directly related to the magnitude of the force that is applied, and inversely related to the mass of the object (Newton, 1686). That is, larger external forces tend to slow down an object more quickly, and heavier objects are harder to slow down. Objects that are more massive, then, are more resistant to changes in velocity. Building on the metaphor between behavior and Newton's second law of motion, Nevin et al. suggested that the rate of responding (i.e., the number of responses emitted by an organism across some period of time) in a given situation is analogous to the velocity of a moving object. Based on the observation that behavior that is maintained by higher reinforcer rates generally is more resistant to change (i.e., more persistent in the face of disruption) than behavior that is maintained by lower reinforcer rates, Nevin et al. continued this metaphor by suggesting that behavior also possesses a mass-like quality that contributes to resistance to change, and that reinforcer deliveries in a stimulus situation contribute to this "behavioral mass." Nevin and colleagues called this metaphor "behavioral momentum theory."

The overarching goal of this chapter is to provide a general review of behavioral persistence from the perspective of behavioral momentum theory. In the following sections, we first will describe the basic theoretical underpinnings of behavioral momentum, the procedures that historically have been used to investigate behavioral persistence, and some general findings from the resistance-to-change literature. Second, we will detail some conceptually problematic findings that may not be well captured by the metaphor offered by Nevin and colleagues (1983). Finally, we will discuss recent extensions of momentum theory to more complex behavioral phenomena.

Behavioral Momentum Theory: An Overview

As it currently is understood, behavioral momentum theory contends that response rate and resistance to change are two separate aspects of operant behavior. Further, distinct relations between reinforcers and (1) the responses that produce them and (2) the stimuli in the presence of which they are delivered contribute to response rate and resistance to change (Nevin, 1992a). The separability of these relations can be illustrated by considering the operant three-term contingency (Skinner, 1938; for an illustration, see Figure 11.1).

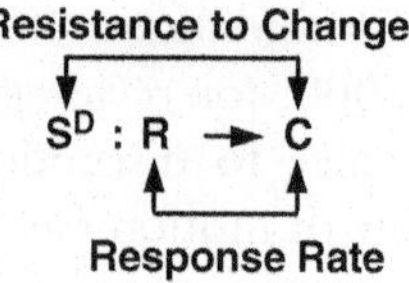

Figure 11.1 The operant three-term contingency. Here, S^D represents a discriminative stimulus, R is a response in the presence of the S^D, and C is the delivery of a consequence. The response-consequence and stimulus-consequence relations are outlined with indication to which aspect of operant behavior these contingencies are thought to contribute.

According to the three-term contingency, a discriminative stimulus (S^D, in Figure 11.1) in the organism's environment sets the occasion for a response (R), and dependent on that response, a consequence (C) may be delivered. In this chapter, we will limit our consideration of consequences to that of reinforcers. One can derive a number of two-term contingencies from the overall three-term contingency. The first contingency, that between the response and the reinforcer, governs the rate at which responding occurs in the stimulus situation. The second contingency, known as the Pavlovian stimulus-reinforcer relation, is that between the discriminative stimulus and the presence of reinforcers. This stimulus-reinforcer relation contributes to resistance to change independently of the response-reinforcer relation.

In this section, we will provide an overview of the foundational work underlying behavioral momentum theory. First, we will discuss the methods that traditionally have been used to study behavioral persistence. We then will present some findings that support both the basic predictions and theoretical underpinnings of behavioral momentum.

Traditional Methods for Studying Behavioral Persistence

When a single behavior is trained and subsequently disrupted, the decrease in behavior that occurs may tell the observer little about the factors that influence resistance to change. Indeed, determining the functional relation between an independent variable (in this case, reinforcer rate) and a dependent variable (here, resistance to change) requires contrasts between the effects of different levels of the independent variable on the dependent variable (see Baron & Perone, 1998, for further discussion). To clarify the contribution of reinforcers to behavioral persistence, comparisons must be made between behavior that is maintained in the presence of two or more stimuli that are associated with different reinforcer frequencies or magnitudes (see Nevin, 1974; Nevin et al., 1983). This arrangement, known as a multiple schedule (Ferster & Skinner, 1957), provides a useful tool for studying resistance to change.

In the multiple-schedule paradigm, two or more separate discriminative stimuli, each of which is associated with a distinct schedule of reinforcement, alternate successively within an experiment; each stimulus and its associated schedule of reinforcement defines a multiple-schedule component (see Figure 11.2 for a schematic depiction of a basic two-component multiple-schedule preparation; see also Nevin & Grace, 2000). In the case of a pigeon in an operant chamber, these separate components are signaled by different key colors. The pigeon's pecking the response key when it is lit one color (C1, in Figure 11.2) may produce food relatively frequently, while pecking the key when it is lit another color (C2) may produce food relatively infrequently.

In resistance-to-change research, variable-interval (VI) schedules historically have been the preferred rule by which reinforcers are delivered within multiple schedules (for reviews, see Nevin, 1992a; Nevin & Grace, 2000). Typically, researchers have used reinforcer-rate ratios between the rich and lean components between 3:1 and 12:1. For example, a VI 60-s schedule providing 60 reinforcers per hr could be used in the rich component, and a VI 240-s schedule providing 15 reinforcers per hr could be used in the lean component. In this example, the reinforcer-rate ratio would be 4:1. The rate at which responding produces reinforcers according to VI schedules

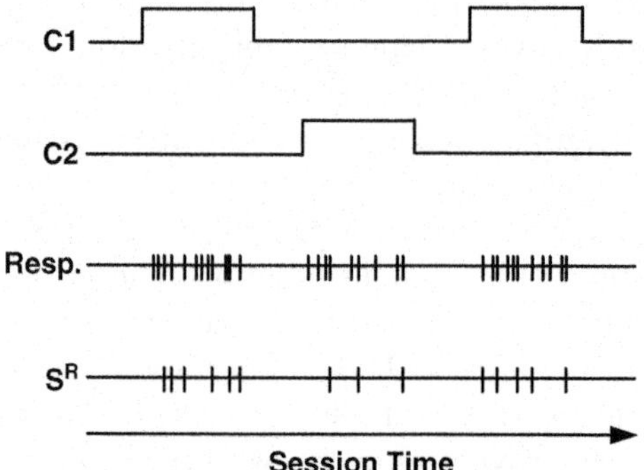

Figure 11.2 A schematic representation of a two-component multiple schedule. "C1" represents the first component, and "C2" represents the second. Raised bars are periods during which the stimuli correlated with each component are present. Note that C1 and C2 components are separated by periods of blackout (inter-component intervals).

tends to be fairly constant despite potential variations in rate of responding, thereby ensuring that obtained reinforcer rates closely approximate the reinforcer rates that are programmed by the experimenter (see Nevin, Grace, Holland, & McLean, 2001, for detailed discussion). This is an important consideration, given that baseline reinforcer rates typically are the major independent variables in momentum studies.

Another important detail of the multiple-schedule preparation is that the distinct components of the schedule sometimes are separated by brief (e.g., 30-s) inter-component intervals (ICIs). During ICIs, the chamber is typically in blackout and the operandum is unavailable. Inter-component intervals tend to decrease interactions between the components of the multiple schedule, such as those that produce behavioral-contrast effects in response rate (see Nevin, 1992b, for discussion). Inter-component intervals, therefore, help to ensure that the separate components of the multiple schedule represent distinct stimulus situations.

The meaningful comparison in resistance-to-change research is between the relative contributions of different reinforcer rates to behavioral persistence. The multiple schedule allows for such comparisons to be arranged both within subjects and within a single experimental condition. This feature limits the need to conduct lengthy, multi-phase or between-groups experiments (for a discussion of other relative advantages of within-subjects designs, see Baron & Perone, 1998). Further, because disruptors can be applied to various stimulus situations of the multiple schedule within the same session, this paradigm eliminates any potential confounds that may be associated with exposing subjects to conditions of disruption multiple times. For example, repeated exposure to extinction, a commonly used disruptor in which responding no longer produces reinforcers, may change the discriminability of nonreinforcement and thereby affect data from subsequent extinction tests (see Baum, 2012).

Once stable responding is achieved in the various components of the multiple schedule, resistance to change may be assessed by applying a disruptor to all of the multiple-schedule components within a session. In the animal laboratory, such disruptors as operant extinction, pre-feeding (providing hungry animals with some portion of their daily ration of food prior to sessions), and the presentation of response-independent food during ICIs traditionally have been used (e.g., Harper, 1996; Nevin, 1974, 2012; Nevin & Grace, 2000).

One can classify disruptors by whether they alter the motivation of the organism to respond for reinforcers or change the baseline contingencies under which the organism responded (see Nevin & Grace, 2000, for review). On one hand, pre-feeding and the presentation of free, ICI food may be classified as "external disruptors." These disruptors alter the motivation of the organism to respond for reinforcement while the internal workings of the experimental situation, like reinforcer availability for performing some behavior, remain intact. External disruptors tend to result in decreases in behavior that are proportional to the magnitude of the disruptor. For example, if a hungry pigeon is pre-fed prior to a session in which it typically would respond for food, the decrease in behavior that is observed during the session generally is greater when they are given more food than when they are given less food (cf. Nevin, 1992b; Nevin, Tota, Torquato, & Shull, 1990). Extinction, on the other hand, is an "internal disruptor." It alters the response-reinforcer relation that previously maintained responding. Because the baseline contingencies necessarily are altered during extinction, behavior typically decreases across time with continued exposure to extinction contingencies (see Nevin, 2012, for review).

Aside from the methodological considerations just reviewed, thought also must be given to the manner in which data are analyzed when studying behavioral persistence. One challenge for studying the effects of reinforcer rate on resistance to change is that different reinforcer rates tend to maintain different rates of responding. More specifically, higher reinforcer rates typically produce higher response rates. This finding is ubiquitous in behavioral psychology (see Shull, 2005, for review). Describing the resistance to change of one behavior relative to that of another behavior might be difficult if the two behaviors occurred at different rates prior to disruption. For example, if behavior in one multiple-schedule component occurs at a higher rate (e.g., 100 responses per min) than behavior in the other component (e.g., 50 responses per min), disruption potentially could decrease responding in both components by a similar *absolute* amount (e.g., 25 responses per min). The *relative* change in responding produced by disruption, however, would be larger in the component that occasioned lower response rates. In this example, behavior in the component with lower rates would be reduced by 50%, whereas behavior in the component with the higher rates would be reduced by only 25%. From the perspective of behavioral momentum theory, then, absolute response rate in the face of disruption might not be the ideal measure of resistance to change. A standardized unit of measurement is advantageous.

Converting absolute rates of responding during disruption to proportion-of-baseline response rates helps to address the issue present when comparing decreases in behavior between different stimulus situations in which behavior occurred at different rates (see Nevin et al., 1983). Proportion-of-baseline rates of responding typically are calculated by dividing the rate of responding in a given session of disruption by the average rate of responding obtained in the last few sessions during baseline. This measure can range from zero when no responses occurred during that session of disruption to one when responding occurred at the same rate during that session of disruption as it had during the final sessions of baseline. Occasionally, responding

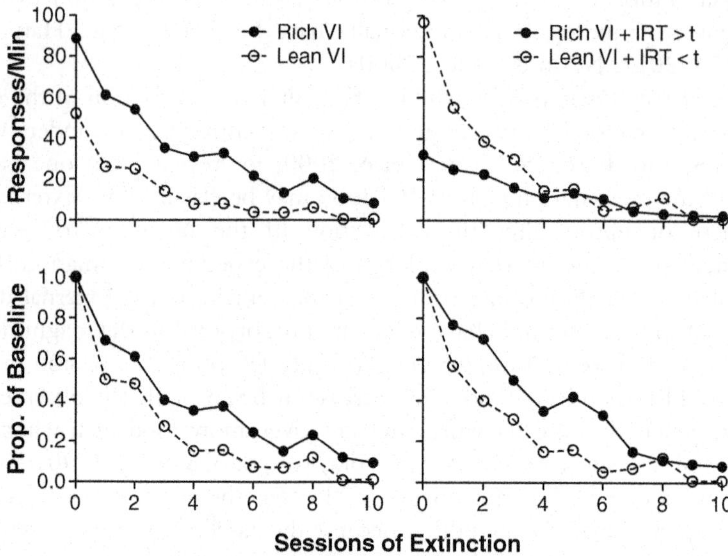

Figure 11.3 Hypothetical extinction data demonstrating the utility of proportion of baseline as a measure of resistance to change. The left panels represent data from a typical rich/lean multiple schedule using variable-interval (VI) schedules, while the right panel represents data from a rich/lean multiple schedule with VI schedules in which additional constraints on responding were arranged. Here, the response that earned reinforcement had to have occurred following either a relatively long inter-response time (IRT > t) or a relatively short IRT (IRT < t) in the rich and lean components, respectively. The top graphs depict absolute response rates in the rich and lean components of a multiple schedules, and the bottom graphs depict proportion-of-baseline rates for the same data.

briefly will increase in frequency relative to baseline when disruption is applied, resulting in a proportion-of-baseline value that is greater than one. A common example of this result is the extinction burst (e.g., Lerman, Iwata, & Wallace, 1999). This effect, though, is usually transient.

Proportion-of-baseline response rates describes the frequency at which behavior is occurring now (during disruption) *relative to how fast it was, then* (during baseline). Figure 11.3 presents hypothetical extinction data from two multiple-schedule situations to illustrate the advantages of this measure of resistance to change. These data were modeled after those reported in Nevin's (1974) Experiment 5 (to be discussed later). The left panel depicts extinction data from a typical rich-VI/lean-VI multiple schedule in which responding occurred more frequently in the rich component than in the lean component during baseline. The right panel depicts extinction data from a rich-VI/lean-VI multiple schedule in which additional constraints were placed on the form of responding that was eligible for reinforcement. Here, inter-response times (IRTs) had to be greater than (IRT > t) or less than (IRT < t) some specified duration (these schedule arrangement also are referred to as differential reinforcement of low-rate (DRL) and high-rate (DRH) behavior, respectively; Ferster & Skinner,

1957). With these additional constraints, behavior occurred more frequently in the *lean* component during baseline despite its producing reinforcers less frequently in this stimulus situation. Comparing data from the bottom panels to those from the top panels, it is easier to determine the persistence of behavior in the rich-schedule component relative to that of behavior in the lean-schedule component when the data are represented as proportion of baseline. Indeed, in the case of the right panel, converting responding across days of extinction to proportion of baseline reveals greater persistence in the rich-schedule component that might not have been apparent otherwise. The advantages of converting response-rate data from conditions of disruption to proportion of baseline are clear: Doing so provides a quantitative measure of responding in the face of disruption that is robust with respect to variations in baseline response rates.

Some Representative Findings

Now that we have discussed the methods that traditionally have been used to study behavioral persistence, we will describe some general findings from studies that have used these methods and variations on them. Many data sets have supported the notion that reinforcers contribute to behavioral persistence in the face of disruption (see Nevin, 1992b; Nevin, 2012; Nevin & Grace, 2000, for reviews). As described briefly above, Nevin (1974) conducted an example of this work demonstrating that higher reinforcer rates yielded more persistent behavior. In his Experiments 1 and 2, pigeons pecked keys for food in a two-component multiple schedule. In the rich component, food was available three times as often as in the lean component. After responding had stabilized in both components of the multiple schedule, behavior was disrupted either by presenting response-independent variable-time (VT) schedule food at various frequencies during ICIs (Experiment 1) or by extinction (Experiment 2). In both experiments, key-pecking in the component associated with the richer schedule of reinforcement was more resistant to disruption than was key-pecking in the component associated with the leaner schedule. Further, in Experiment 1, larger amounts of ICI food resulted in more disruption in both components.

The positive relation between reinforcer presentations during baseline and resistance to change is not limited to the *frequency* with which reinforcers are delivered. Resistance to change also is affected by the *amount* of each reinforcer that is delivered (i.e., variations in reinforcer magnitude). Shettleworth and Nevin (1965) offered an early demonstration of this effect. Here, pigeons pecked keys for food in a two-component multiple schedule in which both components arranged food according to VI 120-s schedules (providing on average 30 reinforcers per hr). The critical difference between the components was that one component delivered 1 s of access to food while the other component delivered 9 s of access to food. When resistance to extinction was assessed following baseline, behavior in the component associated with 9-s hopper presentations was more persistent than behavior in the component associated with 1-s hopper presentations. Nevin (1974, Experiment 3) subsequently replicated these findings using a different disruptor. Here, pigeons responded under a multiple VI 60-s VI 60-s schedule in which the components differed in the reinforcer magnitudes that they arranged. Reinforcers consisted of 2.5 s of access to food in one component and 7.5 s of access in the other. Across different phases of disruption, different frequencies of response-independent (VT) food were introduced into the dark-key periods that separated the components of the multiple schedule. Resistance to change was greater in the component that was associated with 7.5 s of access to food and higher frequencies of free ICI food resulted in more disruption to behavior in both multiple-schedule components.

The findings just reviewed provide support for the general observation that higher reinforcer rates and/or magnitudes during baseline produce behavior that is more persistent in the face of disruption. These general findings have been demonstrated in a number of species other than pigeons, including rats (e.g., Blackman, 1968; Grimes & Shull, 2001; Shahan & Burke, 2004), goldfish (Igaki & Sakagami, 2004), and different human populations (Cohen, 1996; Mace et al., 1990; Mace et al., 2010). Furthermore, as will be noted in detail below, these observations hold with a variety of different reinforcers and settings.

In addition to the generality of the basic empirical findings associated with behavioral momentum theory, various studies have provided support for the conceptual underpinnings of the theory as well. As previously noted, behavioral momentum theory states that baseline response rate (velocity) and resistance to change (related to a mass-like aspect of behavior) are independent dimensions of discriminated operant behavior. We now consider the support for the conjecture that the response-reinforcer relation governs response rate while the Pavlovian stimulus-reinforcer relation governs resistance to change (refer to Figure 11.1).

The Stimulus-reinforcer Relation: Support for Momentum Theory

When all of the reinforcers that are delivered in the presence of a discriminative stimulus are dependent on a response, increasing the reinforcer rate strengthens both the stimulus-reinforcer and the response-reinforcer relations. Under most circumstances, one would expect that adding more reinforcers to a multiple-schedule component should result in higher rates of responding *and* behavior that is more resistant to change. How, then, might one tease apart these aspects of behavior to empirically test whether response rates and resistance to change depend on two separate relations?

Possibly the most straightforward method for answering the question just posed is by manipulating either the stimulus-reinforcer or the response-reinforcer relation independently of the other. Nevin et al. (1990) conducted a series of experiments that elegantly addressed this issue by strengthening the stimulus-reinforcer relation independently of the response-reinforcer relation. In their first experiment, pigeons pecked keys for food in a two-component multiple schedule. One component, signaled by a green key, arranged food according to a VI 60-s schedule. In the other component, signaled by a red key, food was available according to the same VI schedule, *but additional food also was given independently of responding* according to VT schedules. The addition of this extra food had two effects. First, because responding produced only a portion of the food in the VI+VT component, the relation between responding and reinforcer deliveries was weakened to some extent. Second, the Pavlovian stimulus-reinforcer relation in that component was strengthened because more food was delivered in the presence of the discriminative stimulus. Therefore, Nevin et al. predicted that response rates would be lower (due to the weaker response-reinforcer relation), but resistance to change would be higher (due to the stronger stimulus-reinforcer relation), in the component with added VT food. This prediction was exactly what was observed: Response rates in the red-key component tended to be lower than in the green-key component during baseline. When resistance to change was assessed by either pre-feeding or extinction, however, behavior was more persistent in the component with the added food than in the other, VI-only, component.

In a second, admittedly complex, experiment, Nevin et al. (1990) asked whether adding food to a stimulus context *dependent on an alternative response* would increase the resistance to change of a target behavior. Here, Nevin et al. arranged a three-component multiple-concurrent schedule of reinforcement. In all of the components, two response keys, each of which was associated with different contingencies, were available simultaneously to the pigeons. In Component A, the two response keys were illuminated green. Food was delivered according to a VI 240-s schedule (15 reinforcers per hr) for a target response on one key while food was delivered concurrently according to a VI 80-s schedule (45 reinforcers per hr) for an alternative response on a second key. In Component A, therefore, there were 60 possible reinforcers per hr. In Component B, two red response keys were available. The target response key again delivered food according to a VI 240-s schedule (15 reinforcers per hr) while responding on the alternative-response key had no consequences (i.e., extinction; 0 reinforcers per hr). In Component B, therefore, there were 15 possible reinforcers per hr. In Component C, two white response keys were available, and responding on the target key produced food according to a VI 60-s schedule (60 reinforcers per hr) while responding on the alternative-response key was on extinction (0 reinforcers per hr), thus providing the same reinforcer rate as the sum of rates in Component A (60 reinforcers per hr). Baseline response rates on the target key in Component A (the component with additional food for alternative responding) were lower than in Components B and C with no alternative reinforcement. Resistance to both pre-feeding and extinction of target responding, however, was greater in Component A than in Component B, which arranged the same rate of response-dependent food for the target response, and about the same as in Component C, which arranged the same overall reinforcer rate. In summary, the findings of Nevin et al. demonstrate that increasing the rate of reinforcement in a stimulus situation increases behavioral persistence, even when some reinforcers are delivered independently of responding or dependent on another response. In other words, behavioral persistence is independent of the source of reinforcers in the situation, but instead depends simply on the sum total of reinforcers in the situation.

Other experiments subsequently have replicated and extended the results reported by Nevin et al. (1990). For example, Mace et al. (1990; Experiment 2) delivered edibles to adults with intellectual disabilities for sorting different colors of dinnerware. These differently colored stimuli served to distinguish the separate components of a multiple schedule. The same rate of response-dependent edible presentations was delivered for sorting in both components, but in the presence of one color of dinnerware, response-independent edibles also were delivered. Resistance to change was assessed by distracting the participants with access to a video program during the sorting task. The adults sorted at a lower rate, but more persistently, in the component with added reinforcers.

Recent studies show that these findings extend to situations in which the response-independent reinforcer differs from the response-dependent reinforcer. For example, in Grimes and Shull (2001), rats pressed levers for food pellets. Sweetened condensed milk, when delivered independently of responding in one component of the multiple schedule, decreased the rate of lever pressing but increased resistance to extinction. Shahan and Burke (2004) replicated these results with drug reinforcement by demonstrating that adding response-independent food deliveries into one component of a two-component multiple schedule increased the persistence of alcohol-maintained responding in rats. Together, these results show that response-independent reinforcers, which enhance the stimulus-reinforcer relation, increase resistance to change even when those reinforcers are different from those produced by responding.

Above, we discussed the effects of augmenting the stimulus-reinforcer relation, alone, on resistance to change. Another approach to studying the separable nature of response rate and resistance to change is to place the response-reinforcer relation into opposition with the stimulus-reinforcer relation. Nevin (1974, Experiment 5) investigated exactly this arrangement. In this experiment, pigeons responded under a multiple VI 60-s VI 180-s schedule of reinforcement. Across conditions, additional constraints were added to the underlying VI schedules such that, when an interval elapsed, the IRT had to be either less than or greater than 3 s (IRT < 3 s and IRT > 3 s contingencies, respectively) for a response to earn a reinforcer. If separate reinforcer relations governed response rates and resistance to change, Nevin reasoned that behavioral persistence in the separate multiple-schedule components should be positively related to baseline reinforcer rates, regardless of the additional constraints (i.e., IRT < 3 s or IRT > 3 s) placed on responding. This is precisely what Nevin observed. The IRT < 3-s and IRT > 3-s arrangements produced high-and low-rate responding, respectively. When responding was disrupted by either free ICI food presentations or by extinction, however, behavior maintained in the context that was associated with the VI 60-s schedule consistently was more resistant to disruption than behavior maintained in the context associated with the VI 180-s schedule (see Figure 11.3 for an illustration of this finding using hypothetical data).

The experiments described thus far have enhanced the stimulus-reinforcer relation by increasing the amount of food in one component. Nevin (1992b) offered a different approach to demonstrate the dependency of resistance to change on the Pavlovian stimulus-reinforcer relation. The relation between reinforcers and a target discriminative stimulus, by definition, reflects the reinforcer rate in the presence of that stimulus *relative to* the reinforcer rate in the absence of that stimulus (i.e., in the context within which the target stimulus appears; see Rescorla, 1968). This definition of the stimulus-reinforcer relation suggests that resistance to change should be governed both by the absolute reinforcer rate in a given multiple-schedule component and by the reinforcer rate in that component *relative to* the reinforcer rate in other components in the experimental session. Put more simply, resistance to change should be susceptible to behavioral-contrast effects. Nevin demonstrated precisely this effect. In his experiment, pigeons pecked keys for food in a multiple schedule in various conditions. In all of these conditions, responding in the presence of a red key was reinforced according to a VI 60-s schedule (60 reinforcers per hr). Responding in the presence of the other, green, key was reinforced according to either a VI 12-s (300 reinforcers per hr) or a VI 360-s (10 reinforcers per hr) schedule across conditions. When food was delivered in the green-key component according to the VI 12-s schedule, the food rate in the red-key component was relatively lean, and when the green-key component delivered VI 360-s food, the food rate in the red-key component was relatively rich. Following baseline, resistance to both prefeeding and extinction was assessed.

The critical comparison in this experiment was between the resistances to change of responding in the red-key component, which was always associated with VI 60-s food, across conditions. Nevin (1992b) reported a behavioral-contrast effect in resistance to change between conditions in that responding in the red-key component was more persistent when the green-key component arranged VI 360-s food than when it arranged VI 12-s food. In other words, resistance to change depended on the reinforcer rate in the constant red-key component *relative* to the reinforcer rate in the alternative green-key component.

In summary, when either the response-reinforcer relation or the stimulus-reinforcer relation is manipulated alone (or the two relations are placed in opposition to one another), separate effects on response rate and resistance to change may be observed. Therefore, in terms of momentum theory, resistance to change generally is a function of the relative reinforcer rate that is delivered in the presence of a discriminative stimulus, and this relation largely is independent of the response-reinforcer relation. In the cases just discussed, this relation was independent of the source of reinforcers (i.e., whether or not reinforcers were delivered dependently on responding; Grimes & Shull, 2001; Nevin et al., 1990; Shahan & Burke, 2004), the type of reinforcers (Grimes & Shull; Shahan & Burke), and the rate at which responding was maintained during baseline (Nevin, 1974, Experiment 5). Further, resistance to change can be affected by manipulating the relative rates of reinforcer presentations between a component and its surrounding context (Nevin, 1992b) in addition to by manipulating the absolute rates of reinforcer presentation in a component.

These results demonstrate the broad applicability of the simple metaphor offered by behavioral momentum theory. This metaphor accurately describes the general finding that higher relative reinforcer rates (or amounts) produce behavior that is more resistant to disruption, independently of baseline response rates. There are, however, a number of findings that might be considered problematic for behavioral momentum theory. While these findings might not have implications for most situations outside of the laboratory, they provide insights into the accuracy of the fundamental metaphor of behavioral momentum. In the following section, we will describe some of these challenges.

Challenges to Behavioral Momentum Theory

Behavioral momentum theory proposes that the resistance to change of response rate in the presence of a stimulus situation depends directly on the reinforcer rate or amount signaled by that stimulus after extended training (i.e., the Pavlovian stimulus-reinforcer relation), regardless of whether all reinforcers are dependent on the target response. Although several lines of evidence support that proposition, as described above, there are some challenges to its generality. Much as Newtonian physics works well under most conditions that would be encountered in daily life, but may fail to predict what happens under extreme conditions (like the physics of objects approaching the speed of light or of objects on the molecular scale; see Feynman, 1994), these challenges to behavioral momentum theory may pose little difficulty and have few implications in many applied and clinical situations. Ultimately, however, these problems suggest that behavioral momentum theory might profitably be replaced or supplemented by a theory that more accurately captures a wider range of situations and outcomes. The main areas in which discrepancies have emerged are different response-reinforcer relations, extreme differences in reinforcer rates, and single schedules of reinforcement.

Different Response-reinforcer Relations

If resistance to change depends on stimulus-reinforcer relations, there should be no difference in resistance to change between multiple-schedule components when stimulus-reinforcer relations are the same, regardless of what response-reinforcer relations are arranged. To the contrary, several studies have found that when obtained reinforcer rates are matched between components but response-reinforcer relations differ between components, high response rates are generally *less* resistant to disruption than low response rates. A study by Blackman (1968) provides an early example. Rats were trained in multiple schedules with identical VI schedules of food reinforcement but with different constraints on response rate in the components. For example, in Component A, Rat 1 obtained reinforcers on a schedule that reinforced only those responses occurring within 0.2 s of the previous response (IRT $< t$, or DRH), and in Component B, only those responses that were spaced between 1.5 and 3.0 s apart were reinforced (a pacing schedule). As a result, response rates in Component A were about double those in Component B, even though obtained reinforcer rates were essentially identical. When a 1-min tone signaling an unavoidable shock was presented in the middle of each 8-min component, responding was suppressed much more in Component A (high-rate IRT $<$ t) than in Component B (low-rate pacing). These results should be contrasted with those obtained by Nevin (1974, Experiment 5) discussed above. In his experiment, Nevin arranged similar constraints on response rates but a two-component multiple schedule that arranged *different* reinforcer rates. Nevin's experiment, unlike Blackman's, provided support for behavioral momentum.

The finding that relatively low response rates are more resistant to change in multiple schedules has been confirmed in subsequent experiments. For example, Lattal (1989) had pigeons respond on VI schedules with fixed-ratio (FR) or IRT $>$ t (DRL) contingencies that produced different response rates in components with equated reinforcer rates. When responding was disrupted by introducing food during ICIs, response rate decreased less in the DRL component than in the FR component. Similarly, Nevin et al. (2001, Experiment 2) evaluated resistance to change with VI versus variable-ratio (VR) schedules, where the VR value was adjusted every few sessions so that higher-rate VR responding yielded the same obtained reinforcer rate as that in the VI component. Lower-rate VI responding was less disrupted by ICI food, extinction, and ICI food plus extinction, than higher-rate VR responding. The common feature of these studies is that when reinforcer rates were the same in two multiple-schedule components, resistance to change was greater in the component with the lower response rate.

Another area of research on the effect of response-reinforcer contingencies on resistance to change also reveals a relation between response rate and persistence, but in the opposite direction as described above. When reinforcers are presented immediately after eligible responses, the rate of responding is usually higher than when unsignaled delays intervene between responses and reinforcers (see Lattal, 2010, for review). Bell (1999) and Grace, Schwendiman, and Nevin (1998) confirmed this result in components of multiple schedules with obtained reinforcer rates equated between components, and then compared resistance to pre-feeding, ICI food, and extinction between components. Both studies obtained greater resistance to change in the component that arranged immediate reinforcers. The results not only challenge the role of Pavlovian factors (stimulus-reinforcer relations) in determining resistance to change, because reinforcer rates were equated between components, but also question the generality of the findings cited above that low response rates are more resistant to change than high response rates.

In summary, differential stimulus-reinforcer relations between the component stimuli in multiple schedules evidently are not necessary to produce differential resistance to change. Resistance to change may be influenced by contingencies that generate different response rates in the absence of differences in reinforcer rates. The critical differences, however, between response-reinforcer relations that require higher or lower response rates (pacing contingencies) and those that delay reinforcers remain obscure. Both procedures affect response rate, but in one case (pacing contingencies), lower response rates are more persistent, and in the other case (delaying reinforcers), lower response rates are less persistent. Both lines of research show, however, that response persistence can be affected by factors other than reinforcer rate, which challenges one of the basic tenets of behavioral momentum theory – that persistence is affected only by the stimulus-reinforcer relation of the 3-term contingency.

Extremely Different Reinforcer Rates

In addition to challenges when reinforcer rates are the same, the generality of Pavlovian determination of resistance to change recently has been challenged from the opposite direction, when reinforcer rates are very different. McLean, Grace, and Nevin (2012) arranged standard two-component multiple VI VI schedules that covered a far greater range of reinforcer-rate ratios than any previous study. The studies reviewed above that reported greater resistance to change in a multiple-schedule component with more-frequent reinforcement arranged VI schedules with reinforcer-rate ratios between 3:1 and 12:1. By contrast, McLean et al. covered a range from about 1:100 to 100:1 and assessed resistance to change using pre-feeding.

Figure 11.4 depicts a summary of the results of this (admittedly complex) study. In this figure, the x-axis is log (base 10) reinforcer-rate ratios for Components 1 and 2 (r1 and r2, respectively). The y-axis in the top panel shows log response-rate ratios in Components 1 and 2 (B1 and B2), and the y-axis in the bottom panel shows log proportion-of-baseline response rates during disruption for both components. These

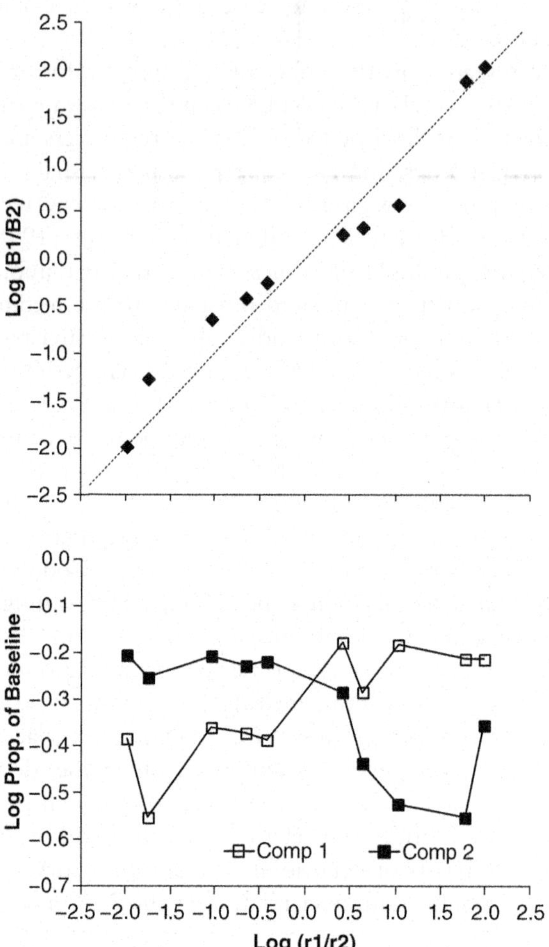

Figure 11.4 Log response-rate ratios and log proportion of baseline, both plotted as a function of log reinforcer-rate ratios across multiple-schedule conditions used by McLean, Grace, and Nevin (2012). Note that as the reinforcer-rate ratios became more extreme (closer to the left or right side of the x-axis), log proportion-of-baseline response rates were more similar between the two components than they were at less extreme ratios. Average data adapted from McLean et al. (2012).

data were log-transformed because this technique has the advantage of rendering equal unit changes for proportional differences. For example, a decrease in responding form 0.4 to 0.2 proportion of baseline (a 50% decrease) will be reflected in an equal change in log units as a change from 0.2 to 0.1. McLean et al. (2012) found that response rates were always higher in the richer component, and that the ratio of response rates between the two components increased and approached matching to the most extreme reinforcer-rate ratios (see the top panel of Figure 11.4). Resistance to pre-feeding, however, became less differentiated between rich and lean components at those extreme ratios (see the bottom panel of Figure 11.4), suggesting that differential Pavlovian stimulus-reinforcer relations are not sufficient to account for differential resistance to change.

McLean et al. (2012) noted that when response ratios match reinforcer ratios, it is necessarily true that the probability of reinforcement per response is the same in both components. Therefore, there should be little or no difference in resistance to change at extreme reinforcer ratios if probability rather than rate of reinforcement determines resistance to change. In standard multiple VI VI schedules, such as those that were used in this experiment, reinforcer probability and rate are generally confounded, so support for this notion must be sought elsewhere.

The findings of greater resistance to change of lower than higher response rates with pacing contingencies with equated reinforcer rates, described above, are consistent with determination by reinforcer probability. The effects of reinforcer delays described above, however, are contrary to expectation because the higher response rates observed with immediate reinforcers necessarily correspond to lower reinforcer probabilities per response. Neither can reinforcer probability account for the effects of reinforcer context found by Nevin (1992b) because in that study, lower response rates in a constant component when the alternated component was rich were less resistant to change than when the alternated component was lean—a result consistent with Pavlovian determination of resistance to change. At least to our current knowledge, no single principle can account for all of these findings that challenge momentum theory.

Resistance to Change in Single Schedules

Another situation in which behavioral momentum theory has difficulty predicting response persistence has to do with how the schedules of reinforcement are arranged. As previously described, virtually all laboratory research on resistance to change has used multiple schedules. This arrangement allows baseline response rates and resistance to change to be compared within subjects and sessions, and resistance to extinction is usually greater in the rich component than in the lean component. By contrast, when different conditions of reinforcement are arranged in single schedules for entire sessions and compared across successive conditions, the usual positive relation between resistance to change and reinforcer rate may not be obtained. For example, with rats as subjects, Cohen, Riley, and Weigle (1993) found that resistance to pre-feeding was about the same for VI 30-s, VI 60-s, and VI 120-s schedules arranged singly across successive conditions (i.e., not in a multiple schedule). If resistance to change followed the usual result, behavior should have been most persistent in the richest schedule (VI 30-s) and least persistent in the leanest schedule (VI 120-s).

Cohen (1998) suggested that the difference between resistance to change in single and multiple schedules arose from the frequency of alternating exposure to different reinforcer rates. He compared resistance to both pre-feeding and extinction after training with VI 30-s and VI 120-s schedules in different arrangements. Schedules were arranged singly across successive conditions (Part 1), on alternating days (Part 2), and in a standard multiple schedule (Part 3). Distinctive stimuli accompanied the schedules throughout all three phases.

Cohen (1998) found that resistance to pre-feeding was about the same for both schedules in Part 1 (successive conditions) but was greater for the richer component in Part 3 (the standard multiple schedule); results for Part 2 were mixed. Relatedly, resistance to extinction was greater in the richer component during Phase 3 (the standard multiple schedule), but differed in the opposite direction (i.e., behavior maintained by the leaner schedule was more persistent) in Phases 1 (successive conditions) and 2 (alternating days). The latter findings essentially replicate the well-known "partial-reinforcement extinction effect" that routinely is observed in single schedules (see Sutherland & Mackintosh, 1971). That is, in single schedules, behavior that is intermittently reinforced (or reinforced at a relatively low rate) tends to be more persistent than behavior that is reinforced continuously or relatively frequently. Cohen's and other authors' (e.g., Shull & Grimes, 2006) finding resistance to extinction is *negatively* related to baseline reinforcer rate in single schedules is not easily reconciled with momentum theory (see Nevin, 2012, for a discussion).

A recent study by Lionello-DeNolf and Dube (2011) compared the effects of added VT reinforcement (cf. Nevin et al., 1990) in successive conditions and in multiple schedules with separate groups of children with various developmental disabilities. In different stimulus conditions, participants tapped pictures on a touch screen to gain access to either edibles or tokens exchangeable for various preferred items. In both conditions, reinforcers were delivered dependently on tapping the touch screen according to VI 12-s schedules. In one condition, free reinforcers also were delivered independently of responding according to a VT 6-s schedule. Tapping the touch screen was disrupted by presenting a different stimulus that signaled VI 8-s reinforcement for an alternative response presented concurrently with the target response. The results were striking: Responding was less disrupted in the VI+VT component than in the VI component for all six children trained and tested with multiple schedules, consistent with many previous findings described above, but the same ordering was observed with only two of six children experiencing the schedules in successive conditions. Evidently, the difference between single and multiple schedules extends to translational settings and includes the effects of added response-independent reinforcers.

In summary, the direct relation between resistance to change and the rate of reinforcement that is characteristic of behavior maintained in multiple-schedule components does not appear to generalize to behavior maintained by single schedules. As we know from Nevin (1992b), resistance to change in a constant component depends inversely on the reinforcer rate in an alternated component; equivalently, resistance to change depends directly on the relative rate of reinforcement in a component. In single schedules, where environmental conditions and reinforcer rates are uniform throughout the session, relative rate of reinforcement cannot be meaningfully calculated. In that sense, behavioral momentum theory is not challenged by single-schedule data. More importantly, virtually any distinctive situation in daily life is embedded in an array of other irregularly alternating situations with their own contingencies and reinforcers, and thus resembles a multiple-schedule component more than an isolated single schedule. Therefore, behavioral momentum theory should be applicable to clinical, educational, and other applied settings where the persistence of learned behavior is important.

The preceding discussion has highlighted some findings that are problematic for behavioral momentum theory, as it historically has been used to describe the contribution of the Pavlovian stimulus-reinforcer relation to resistance to change. Theoretical development continues within the framework of behavioral momentum theory, however, and recently it has been extended to more complex aspects of behavior (i.e., relapse and stimulus control). In the following section, we hope to demonstrate that despite some empirical challenges to behavioral momentum theory, its applicability outside of these challenging situations is robust.

Extensions of Behavioral Momentum Theory

Most research on resistance to change has employed multiple schedules of reinforcement and measured the rate of a response in the steady state and during disruption. As reviewed above, many studies have shown that baseline response rate is more resistant to change in a multiple-schedule component with larger or more-frequent reinforcers. Given the generality of this finding, one reasonable question is: To what extent does reinforcer rate or magnitude govern other aspects of behavior?

In light of this question, behavioral momentum theory recently has been extended to account for more complex behavioral phenomena. One extension of behavioral momentum is to the recurrence (or "relapse") of previously reinforced behavior. Behavioral momentum also has been applied to studying the resistance to change of a qualitative dimension of operant behavior (remembering). In the following section, we will describe both of these recent extensions.

Behavioral Momentum and Relapse

In clinical situations, extinction often is used in conjunction with other behavioral interventions as a method for decreasing the frequency of undesirable behavior (see Lerman & Iwata, 1996). One characteristic of behavior that demonstrates persistence is the propensity of that behavior to relapse when the conditions of disruption that were established during treatment are altered in some way (see Podlesnik & Shahan, 2009; 2010; Shahan & Sweeney, 2011). Just as it is important to understand the factors that contribute to the resistance to change of behavior, it is also important to understand the conditions under which one might anticipate that behavior will return, and to what degree.

There are several general relapse paradigms: reinstatement, renewal, and resurgence (see Vubric & Bouton, this volume). Reinstatement, the most commonly investigated relapse phenomenon, occurs when a stimulus that was previously associated with reinforcement (or the reinforcer itself) is presented following the extinction of a target response (e.g., Reid, 1958; see also Katz & Higgins, 2003, for a review of the reinstatement paradigm in the context of drug use). For example, an ex-smoker, after months of abstinence and under normal circumstances, may no longer crave cigarettes. If he is exposed to cigarette-related cues (e.g., cigarette smoke, the sound of a match striking, etc.), he may experience intense cigarette cravings and potentially relapse to, or "reinstate," cigarette smoking.

In the renewal paradigm, behavior first is maintained in one stimulus context (Context A) and then is extinguished in a separate stimulus context (Context B). Once behavior is extinguished, a return to the context in which it was trained (Context A) typically results in the reoccurrence of the target responding. For example, a child may learn to aggress against others to gain access to attention. In the setting of a clinic, a behavioral intervention may be implemented that effectively extinguishes his aggressing. When the child is returned to the environment in which aggressing previously was reinforced, however, its occurrence may be reoccasioned or "renewed." Other variations of this basic procedure, namely "AAB" (training and extinction in one context, then a change to a second context) and "ABC" (training in one context, extinction in a second context, and then a change to a third context) renewal, exist as well. Relapse of operant behavior has been observed in each of these preparations (see Bouton, Todd, Vurbic, & Winterbauer, 2011).

Finally, resurgence entails the reoccurrence of a previously reinforced and since extinguished behavior when reinforcement for a more recently trained alternative response is withheld (see Leitenberg, Rawson, & Mulick, 1975; see also Lattal & St. Peter Pipkin, 2009, for review). Consider the child mentioned above. In treatment, he might have been taught to appropriately request attention instead of engaging in problem behavior. If the therapist were not to reinforce these requests, appropriate behavior might decrease in frequency and aggressing might reoccur or "resurge."

Based both on the observation that relapse tends to be positively related to the rate of reinforcement in a stimulus context (cf. Leitenberg et al., 1975; see Winterbauer, Lucke, & Bouton, 2013, Experiment 1, for a more recent example) and on insights from momentum theory, Podlesnik and Shahan (2009) investigated whether the Pavlovian stimulus-reinforcer relation that governs resistance to change also governs the magnitude of relapse that is obtained in basic reinstatement, renewal, and resurgence preparations. In their first experiment, Podlesnik and Shahan investigated the role of baseline reinforcer rates on reinstatement in pigeons. Here, they arranged a two-component multiple schedule in which both components delivered food according to VI 120-s schedules (30 reinforcers per hr). In one component, VT 20-s food (180 per hr) concurrently was available in addition to the VI 120-s food. After behavior in both components was extinguished, a few food presentations were made available at the beginning of sessions to test for reinstatement. Experiment 2 investigated the effects of baseline rates of food on resurgence. The procedure was the same as that of Experiment 1, but VI 30-s food (180 per hr) was made available for responding on an alternative-response key during extinction in both components. Alternative food was discontinued during resurgence testing. In their final experiment, Podlesnik and Shahan arranged an ABA renewal preparation in which baseline stimulus conditions were identical to those of the previous experiments, with steady house lights throughout the session (Context A). During extinction, the house lights in the pigeons' chambers flashed constantly, thereby establishing a separate stimulus context (Context B). Once behavior had been eliminated in both components, the pigeons were returned to Context A for renewal testing.

In all three relapse preparations that Podlesnik and Shahan (2009) arranged, two findings were general. First, responding in the context that was associated both with VI and VT food (and thus had an overall higher rate of food delivery) was more persistent during extinction than was behavior in the other, VI-only, component (cf. Grimes & Shull, 2001; Nevin et al., 1990; Shahan & Burke, 2004). Second, and most importantly for the current discussion, behavior in the component that was associated with both VI and VT food relapsed to a greater degree than did behavior in the VI-only component. Though reinstatement, renewal, and resurgence entail the reoccurrence of extinguished behavior through different environmental manipulations, one underlying effect appears to be common among them: More reinforcement during baseline conditions (and thus enhanced stimulus-reinforcer relations in those conditions) yields greater relapse following extinction.

The findings of Podlesnik and Shahan (2009) have been replicated in a number of species using a variety of procedures. For example, Mace et al. (2010) either reinforced the targeted problem behavior of children at relatively low rates (lean reinforcement) or differentially reinforced an alternative behavior (DRA) at relatively high rates (rich reinforcement, but for an alternative behavior), across conditions. Problem behavior in the DRA condition decreased to low levels during treatment, analogous to the decrease in target responding observed in the second phase of a standard resurgence preparation. When the target and alternative behaviors were extinguished, problem behavior resurged to a higher level following the relatively rich DRA condition than following relatively lean reinforcement of problem behavior. In other words, adding reinforcers for alternative behavior made the problem behavior occur at a lower rate, but when the additional reinforcers were removed after the problem behavior was extinguished, the problem behavior came back at a higher rate than when no reinforcers were added for alternative behavior.

Two recent experiments with laboratory animals have extended the initial experiments on behavioral momentum and relapse. Pyszczynski and Shahan (2011) demonstrated that adding food to one component of a multiple schedule in which rats responded for dippers full of alcohol solutions produced behavior that was more susceptible to reinstatement. Further, Thrailkill and Shahan (2011) showed that, in pigeons, the renewal, reinstatement, and resurgence of responding maintained by conditioned reinforcement (i.e., stimuli predictive of food in an observing-response preparation; see Wyckoff, 1952) was positively related to the rate at which food was delivered prior to relapse testing.

In summary, behavioral momentum theory offers not only an approach to understanding the factors that contribute to the persistence of behavior in the face of disruption, but also helps us to understand factors that contribute to the return of extinguished responding. The implications for this extension of momentum theory are clear: It provides a formalized approach to understanding how environment and reinforcers interact to contribute to the recurrence of prior behavior. It also addresses a longstanding issue in learning theory: Does extinction abolish learning or merely affect performance? The persistence of differential strengthening effects of baseline reinforcement that are revealed in testing for relapse suggests that extinction, although characterized as an internal disruptor, leaves intact at least some aspects of a reinforcement history, expressed as behavioral mass in momentum theory. In other words, extinction does not abolish prior learning (see Vurbic & Bouton, this volume). Moreover, using momentum theory as an approach to understanding relapse may inform treatment strategies for problematic behaviors that are susceptible to relapse (i.e., drug taking, aggressive behavior, etc.).

All of the results reviewed in this chapter so far have focused on the resistance to change of one dimension of operant behavior: response rate. Recent investigations, however, suggest that the metaphor of behavioral momentum is not limited to understanding the resistance to change of response rate in the face of disruption: It may also be extended to qualitative dimensions of behaviors. In particular, momentum theory has been used to describe the effects of reinforcer rates on the accuracy and persistence of delayed stimulus control in procedures used to assess remembering.

Measuring Resistance to Change of Accuracy and Response Rate

Delayed matching-to-sample (DMTS) procedures historically have been used to assess the stimulus control over responding across time (cf. Maki, Moe, & Bierly, 1977). In DMTS preparations, a pigeon might first be presented with a sample stimulus (say, a green key). After some delay (called the "retention interval"), two comparison stimuli are presented, one that matches the sample stimulus and one that does not. If the pigeon chooses the stimulus that matches the sample stimulus, it may gain access to food according to some schedule. The proportion of correct matches emitted during a DMTS procedure reflects the extent to which the pigeon (or rat, or person) remembers the sample stimulus given a delay. If the DMTS procedure permits the study of delayed stimulus control (or remembering), how might it be adapted to study the *resistance to change* of stimulus control?

Schaal, Odum, and Shahan (2000) developed a paradigm that incorporated DMTS and that permits measurement of both response rate and accuracy of stimulus control (and of the resistance to change of both of these aspects of behavior). Briefly, the paradigm arranges that a pigeon may respond to produce DMTS trials (instead of food) on a VI schedule; accordingly, the paradigm is designated VI DMTS. Food reinforcers for correct matches maintain responding both in the VI and DMTS portions of the preparation, and the probability or magnitude of the reinforcer can be varied between signaled multiple-schedule components. After stable baseline performances have been established in both components, resistance to change of both VI response rate and DMTS accuracy can be examined within subjects and sessions and related to the conditions of reinforcement exactly as in standard multiple schedules.

Nevin, Milo, Odum, and Shahan (2003) reported the first study to employ the multiple VI DMTS paradigm in this way. They arranged a two-component multiple schedule in which pigeons produced matching-to-sample trials according to VI 30-s schedules. The center key was lit red or green during the VI to signal the probability of reinforcement for a correct match. When the VI timed out, a center-key peck turned off the color and produced a vertical or slanted line as a sample stimulus. After 2 s, the sample was extinguished and the side keys were lit with the comparison stimuli, vertical and slanted lines displayed randomly on the left and right keys (DMTS with 0-s delay). A peck to the side key with the same orientation as the sample produced food with a probability either of .8 (rich) or .2 (lean), depending on the key color during the VI. Key colors and the correlated reinforcer probabilities alternated after four such cycles, separated by a 30-s ICI. After baseline response rates and matching accuracies were stable, resistance to change was evaluated by pre-feeding, free ICI food, extinction, and the abrupt insertion of a short delay between sample offset and comparison onset.

During baseline, both response rates and matching accuracies generally were higher in the rich component, and during disruption by pre-feeding, ICI food, and extinction, both response rates and matching accuracies generally were more resistant to change. When matching performance was disrupted by a 3-s delay, response rate was largely unaffected but matching accuracy was drastically reduced, more so in the lean component. Overall, though, matching accuracy under disruption was positively correlated with VI response rate under disruption, suggesting that these separate aspects of behavior were similarly strengthened by reinforcement.

Odum, Shahan, and Nevin (2005) modified the Nevin et al. (2003) procedure to study the resistance to change of forgetting functions—the relation between accuracy and duration of the delay between sample offset and comparison onset (see White, 1985; 1991, for quantification and discussion of forgetting functions). Specifically, they arranged identical VI 20-s schedules in the initial segments of the VI DMTS with reinforcer probabilities of .9 (rich) or .1 (lean) signaled by red or green center key lights. They used yellow and blue key lights as samples and comparisons. Samples remained on until the first peck after 3 s, after which the center key returned to its color during the VI for 0.1, 2, 4, or 8 s before onset of the side-key comparison stimuli. Correct matches were reinforced with the signaled probability. Components alternated after four such cycles, separated by 15-s ICIs. After both VI response rates and DMTS forgetting functions were judged to be stable, resistance to change was tested by presenting free ICI food and by extinction. As expected, Odum et al. observed that responding in the VI portion of the VI DMTS was more resistant to disruption in the rich component than in the lean component. Further, relative to baseline, the rate of forgetting was more resistant to disruption in the rich component than in the lean component. Thus, both response rates and the accuracy of remembering were strengthened similarly in relation to relative reinforcement in a component, extending the results of Nevin et al. (2003).

Separating Baseline Accuracy and Resistance to Change

Early studies of free-operant responding in typical multiple schedules found that resistance to change was correlated with baseline response rate, as in Experiment 1 by Nevin (1974). Subsequent research, described above, has suggested that baseline response rate and resistance to change may be separately determined by response-reinforcer and stimulus-reinforcer relations. The studies with the VI DMTS paradigm described above found that the resistance to change of accuracy was correlated with baseline accuracy, in that higher probabilities of reinforcement maintained higher levels of accuracy and also established greater resistance to change. An extension of behavioral momentum theory to DMTS, based on findings with free-operant responding, would suggest that response-reinforcer relations within DMTS trials may control baseline accuracy whereas stimulus-reinforcer relations (i.e., relative reinforcer rate in a component) may control resistance to change.

To explore this possibility, Nevin, Ward, Jimenez-Gomez, Odum, and Shahan (2009) exploited the Differential Outcomes Effect (DOE), whereby DMTS accuracy is higher when different outcomes are arranged for the two correct side-key responses. In an early study, for example, Peterson, Wheeler, and Trapold (1980) trained a group of pigeons in red-green matching to sample in which correct responses to green comparisons were followed by a tone plus food, but correct responses to red comparisons were followed by the tone only (differential outcomes for correct green responses vs. correct red responses). A second group received tone plus food for all correct side-key responses (same outcomes for correct green responses and correct red responses). Despite the fact that the same outcomes group obtained more-frequent reinforcers, accuracy was higher for the differential outcomes group, especially at longer delays between samples and comparisons.

Nevin et al. (2009) compared differential outcomes with more-frequent same outcomes in the multiple-schedule VI DMTS paradigm. Reinforcer probabilities were .9 and .1 for correct responses to yellow and blue comparisons in the different-outcome (DO) component and probabilities were .9 and .9 for responses to both colors in the same-outcome (SO) component. Thus, the overall probability of reinforcers was greater in the SO component. The DO or SO components were signaled by lighting the center key red or green during the VI and the DMTS retention interval; components alternated after four completed DMTS trials, and were separated by 15-s ICIs. After 50 training sessions, resistance to disruption by pre-feeding, ICI food, and extinction were evaluated.

In baseline, VI response rate was higher in the SO component, consistent with the greater overall reinforcer probability in that component, but the forgetting function was substantially higher (showing better accuracy) in the DO component, replicating the standard DOE. Nevertheless, during disruption by pre-feeding, ICI food, and extinction, decreases relative to baseline in both VI response rate and DMTS accuracy were greater in the DO component. Thus, the higher level of DMTS accuracy maintained by differential response-reinforcer relations in the DO component was weaker than the lower level in the SO component with overall richer reinforcement—clear evidence of the dissociability of baseline performance and resistance to change.

In a final part of the study, reinforcer probabilities in the SO component were changed to .5, .5, so the overall probability of reinforcement was now the same in both the SO and DO components. Baseline accuracy remained higher in the DO component, with reinforcer probabilities of .1 and .9. Resistance to change was essentially the same in DO and SO components, confirming the importance of relative reinforcement in determining resistance to change.

In summary, in addition to response rates, remembering appears to follow the basic tenets of behavioral momentum theory. Greater reinforcer availability during baseline produces relatively more persistent remembering, just as greater reinforcer availability during baseline produces relatively more persistent response rates (e.g., Nevin, 1974). Further, how accurate remembering is during baseline can be dissociated from how perseverant it will be, just as how fast response rates are at baseline can generally be dissociated from how perseverant they will be (e.g., Nevin et al., 1990).

Conclusions

Human and nonhuman animals alike persist in performing tasks despite disruptors every day. Behavioral momentum theory is concerned with the contribution of the Pavlovian stimulus-reinforcer relation to the persistence of behavior in the face of disruption. Like the topography, patterning, or frequency of a response, resistance to change is a fundamental dimension of operant behavior. Persistence also is a fundamental part of life. Returning to the vignettes offered in the introduction of this chapter, for example, a 3rd grade student may persist in performing math problems despite noisy classmates, or a cigarette smoker may persist in smoking despite disapproval from friends and loved ones. Regardless of the behavior in question, *that* it persists in the face of disruption is a simple observation. *To what degree* or *under what circumstances* behavior persists are the more precise attributes of behavior that are addressed by behavioral momentum theory.

In this chapter, we provided a historical and contemporary overview both of the study of resistance to change and of the theoretical underpinnings of behavioral momentum. This overview included a description of the methods that typically are used to study behavioral persistence, some findings that have generated support for behavioral momentum theory, and some challenges to the simple metaphor. Further, we described the various facets of behavioral persistence (i.e., the resistance to change of response rates, remembering, and the relapse of previously extinguished responding), and how momentum theory has been extended to each. Clearly, the basic tenets of behavioral momentum theory are generalizable (e.g., across species, types of reinforcers, settings, behavioral dimensions, etc.), despite the practical limitations to the theory noted above.

The literature concerning the persistence of behavior in the face of disruption and behavioral momentum theory is extensive and oftentimes highly conceptual. Therefore, the overarching purpose of this chapter was to provide a *general* review of behavioral momentum and resistance to change. Because of our general approach, much of the preceding discussion focused on the ability of momentum theory to *describe*, qualitatively, the relation between stimulus-reinforcer relations and resistance to change in various situations. That is, relatively rich reinforcer rates tend to enhance the stimulus-reinforcer relation in a given stimulus situation and thereby produce behavior that is more resistant to disruption.

Another important quality of momentum theory worth noting is its power to *predict* the degree to which a behavior will persist in a given circumstance. That is, given information about the magnitude of the behavioral disruptor and baseline reinforcer rates, one can make precise predictions about resistance to change. This predictive capability of momentum theory is dependent on its quantitative underpinnings (see Nevin & Grace, 2000; Nevin et al., 1983; Podlesnik & Shahan, 2009; 2010; Shahan & Sweeney, 2011). A complete discussion of these models, however, is outside of the scope of this chapter. The general concepts of behavioral momentum theory as well as these more specific quantitative models have implications, though, for work outside of the animal laboratory. For example, they provide insights into how one might promote persistence when it is a desirable attribute of behavior (e.g., completing school work) and deter persistence when it is undesirable (e.g., smoking).

To summarize, behavioral momentum theory is a conceptual framework that can be used to describe *why* and *to what degree* behavior will persist in a given stimulus situation. It also may be considered a practical framework that can be used to extend the fundamental principles of resistance to change to clinical or everyday situations. Thus, there are many theoretical and real-world implications of momentum theory. This chapter outlined a few of these implications, but it will be up to future researchers to continue to determine its conceptual boundaries and clinical relevance.

Acknowledgments

Preparation of this chapter was supported in part by R01 HD064576 from the NICHD. The authors thank Timothy Slocum and Frances McSweeney for helpful comments and suggestions.

References

Baron, A., & Perone, M. (1998). Experimental design and analysis in the laboratory study of human operant behavior. In K. A. Lattal & M. Perone (Eds.), *Handbook of research methods in human operant behavior* (pp. 45–91). New York: Plenum Press.

Baum, W. M. (2012). Extinction as discrimination: The molar view. *Behavioural Processes, 90*, 101–110.

Bell, M. C. (1999). Pavlovian contingencies and resistance to change in a multiple schedule. *Journal of the Experimental Analysis of Behavior, 72*, 81–96.

Blackman, D. E. (1968). Response rate, reinforcement frequency, and conditioned suppression. *Journal of the Experimental Analysis of Behavior, 11*, 503–516.

Bouton, M. E., Todd, T. P., Vurbic, D., & Winterbauer, N. E. (2011). Renewal after the extinction of free operant behavior. *Learning & Behavior, 39*, 57–67.

Cohen, S. L. (1996). Behavioral momentum of typing behavior in college students. *Behavior Analysis and Therapy, 1*, 36–51.

Cohen, S. L. (1998) Behavioral momentum: The effects of temporal separation of rates of reinforcement. *Journal of the Experimental Analysis of Behavior, 69*, 29–47.

Cohen, S. L., Riley, D. S., & Weigle, P. A. (1993) Tests of behavior momentum in simple and multiple schedules with rats and pigeons. *Journal of the Experimental Analysis of Behavior, 60*, 255–291.

Ferster, C. B., & Skinner, B. F. (1957). *Schedules of reinforcement.* Englewood Cliffs, NJ: Prentice Hall.

Feynman, R. P. (1994). *The character of physical law*. New York: Modern Library.

Grace, R. C., Schwendiman, J. W., & Nevin, J. A. (1998). Effects of unsignaled delay of reinforcement on preference and resistance to change. *Journal of the Experimental Analysis of Behavior, 69*, 247–261.

Grimes, J. A., & Shull, R. L. (2001). Response-independent milk delivery enhances persistence of pellet-reinforced lever pressing by rats. *Journal of the Experimental Analysis of Behavior, 76*, 179–194.

Harper, D. N. (1996). Response-independent food delivery and behavioral resistance to change. *Journal of the Experimental Analysis of Behavior, 65*, 549–560.

Igaki, T., & Sakagami, T. (2004). Resistance to change in goldfish. *Behavioural Processes, 66*, 139–152.

Katz, J. L., & Higgins, S. T. (2003). The validity of the reinstatement model of craving and relapse to drug use. *Psychopharmacologia, 168*, 21–30.

Lattal, K. A. (1989). Contingencies on response rate and resistance to change. *Learning and Motivation, 20*, 191–203.

Lattal, K. A. (2010). Delayed reinforcement of operant behavior. *Journal of the Experimental Analysis of Behavior, 93*, 129–139.

Lattal, K. A., & St. Peter Pipkin, C. (2009). Resurgence of previously reinforced responding: Research and application. *The Behavior Analyst Today, 10*, 254–266.

Leitenberg, H., Rawson, R. A., & Mulick, J. A. (1975). Extinction and reinforcement of alternative behavior. *Journal of Comparative and Physiological Psychology, 88*, 640–652.

Lerman, D. C., & Iwata, B. A. (1996). Developing a technology for the use of operant extinction in clinical settings: An examination of basic and applied research. *Journal of Applied Behavior Analysis, 29,* 345–382.

Lerman, D. C., Iwata, B. A., & Wallace, M. D. (1999). Side effects of extinction: Prevalence of bursting and aggression during the treatment of self-injurious behavior. *Journal of Applied Behavior Analysis, 32,* 1–8.

Lionello-DeNolf, K. M., & Dube, W. V. (2011). Contextual influences on resistance to disruption in children with intellectual disabilities. *Journal of the Experimental Analysis of Behavior, 96,* 317–327.

Mace, F. C., Lalli, J. S., Shea, M. C., Lalli, E. P., West, B. J., Roberts, M., & Nevin, J. A. (1990). The momentum of human behavior in a natural setting. *Journal of the Experimental Analysis of Behavior, 54,* 163–172.

Mace, F. C., McComas, J. J., Mauro, B. C., Progar, P. R., Ervin, R., & Zangrillo, A. N. (2010). Differential reinforcement of alternative behavior increases resistance to extinction: Clinical demonstration, animal modeling, and clinical test of one solution. *Journal of the Experimental Analysis of Behavior, 93,* 349–367.

Maki, W. S., Moe, J. C., & Bierly, C. M. (1977). Short-term memory for stimuli, responses, and reinforcers. *Journal of Experimental Psychology: Animal Behavior Processes, 3,* 156–177.

McLean, A. P., Grace, R. C., & Nevin, J. A. (2012). Response strength in extreme multiple schedules. *Journal of the Experimental Analysis of Behavior, 97,* 51–70.

Nevin, J. A. (1974). Response strength in multiple schedules. *Journal of the Experimental Analysis of Behavior, 21,* 389–408.

Nevin, J. A. (1992a). An integrative model for the study of behavioral momentum. *Journal of the Experimental Analysis of Behavior, 57,* 301–316.

Nevin, J. A. (1992b). Behavioral contrast and behavioral momentum. *Journal of Experimental Psychology: Animal Behavior Processes, 18,* 126–133.

Nevin, J. A. (2012). Resistance to extinction and behavioral momentum. *Behavioural Processes, 90,* 89–97.

Nevin, J. A., & Grace, R. C. (2000). Behavioral momentum and the law of effect. *Behavioral and Brain Sciences, 23,* 73–130.

Nevin, J. A., Grace, R. C., Holland, S., & McLean, A. P. (2001). Variable-ratio versus variable-interval schedules: Response rate, resistance to change, and preference. *Journal of the Experimental Analysis of Behavior, 76,* 43–74.

Nevin, J. A., Mandell, C., & Atak, J. R. (1983). The analysis of behavioral momentum. *Journal of the Experimental Analysis of Behavior, 39,* 49–59.

Nevin, J. A., Milo, J., Odum, A. L., & Shahan, T. A. (2003). Accuracy of discrimination, rate of responding, and resistance to change. *Journal of the Experimental Analysis of Behavior, 79,* 307–321.

Nevin, J. A., Tota, M. E., Torquato, R. D., & Shull, R. L. (1990). Alternative reinforcement increases resistance to change: Pavlovian or operant contingencies? *Journal of the Experimental Analysis of Behavior, 53,* 359–379.

Nevin, J. A., Ward, R. D., Jimenez-Gomez, C., Odum, A. L., & Shahan, T. A. (2009). Differential outcomes enhance accuracy of delayed matching to sample but not resistance to change. *Journal of Experimental Psychology: Animal Behavior Processes, 35,* 74–91.

Newton, I. (1686). *Philosophia naturalis principia mathematica.* London: S. Pepys.

Odum, A. L., Shahan, T. A., & Nevin, J. A. (2005). Resistance to change of forgetting functions and response rates. *Journal of the Experimental Analysis of Behavior, 84,* 65–75.

Peterson, G. B., Wheeler, R. L., & Trapold, M. A. (1980). Enhancement of pigeons' conditional discrimination performance by expectancies of reinforcement and nonreinforcement. *Animal Learning & Behavior, 8,* 22–30.

Podlesnik, C. A., & Shahan, T. A. (2009). Behavioral momentum and relapse of extinguished operant responding. *Learning & Behavior*, *37*, 357–364.

Podlesnik, C. A., & Shahan, T. A. (2010). Extinction, relapse, and behavioral momentum. *Behavioural Processes*, *84*, 400–411.

Pyszczynski, A. D., & Shahan, T. A. (2011). Behavioral momentum and relapse of ethanol seeking: Nondrug reinforcement in a context increases relative reinstatement. *Behavioural Pharmacology*, *22*, 81–86.

Reid, R. L. (1958). The role of the reinforcer as a stimulus. *British Journal of Psychology*, *49*, 202–209.

Rescorla, R. A. (1968). Probability of shock in the presence and absence of CS in fear conditioning. *Journal of Comparative and Physiological Psychology*, *66*, 1–5.

Schaal, D. W., Odum, A. L., & Shahan, T. A. (2000). Pigeons may not remember the stimuli that reinforced their recent behavior. *Journal of the Experimental Analysis of Behavior*, *73*, 125–139.

Shahan, T. A., & Burke, K. A. (2004). Ethanol-maintained responding of rats is more resistant to change in a context with added non-drug reinforcement. *Behavioural Pharmacology*, *15*, 279–285.

Shahan, T. A., & Sweeney, M. M. (2011). A model of resurgence based on behavioral momentum theory. *Journal of the Experimental Analysis of Behavior*, *95*, 91–108.

Shettleworth, S., & Nevin, J. A. (1965). Relative rate of response and relative magnitude of reinforcement in multiple schedules. *Journal of the Experimental Analysis of Behavior*, *8*, 199–202.

Shull, R. L. (2005). The sensitivity of response rate to the rate of variable-interval reinforcement for pigeons and rats: A review. *Journal of the Experimental Analysis of Behavior*, *84*, 99–110.

Shull, R. L., & Grimes, J. A. (2006). Resistance to extinction following variable-interval reinforcement: Reinforcer rate and amount. *Journal of the Experimental Analysis of Behavior*, *85*, 23–39.

Sutherland, N. S., & Mackintosh, N. J. (1971). *Mechanisms of animal discrimination learning*. New York: Academic Press.

Skinner, B. F. (1938). *The behavior of organisms*. Englewood Cliffs, NJ: Prentice Hall.

Thrailkill, E. A., & Shahan, T. A. (2011). Resistance to change and relapse of observing. *Journal of the Experimental Analysis of Behavior*, *97*, 281–304.

Vurbic, D., & Bouton, M. E. (this volume). A contemporary behavioral perspective on extinction. In F. K. McSweeney & E. S. Murphy (Eds.), *The Wiley-Blackwell Handbook of Operant Conditioning* (pp. 53–76). Oxford: Wiley-Blackwell.

White, K. G. (1985). Characteristics of forgetting function in delayed matching to sample. *Journal of the Experimental Analysis of Behavior*, *44*, 15–34.

White, K. G. (1991). Psychophysics of direct remembering. In M. L. Commons, J. A. Nevin, & M. C. Davison (Eds.), *Signal detection: Mechanisms, models, and applications* (pp. 221–237). Hillsdale, NJ: Erlbaum.

Winterbauer, N. E., Lucke, S., & Bouton, M. E. (2013). Some factors modulating the strength of resurgence after extinction of an instrumental behavior. *Learning and Motivation*, *44*, 60–71.

Wyckoff Jr., L. B. (1952). The role of observing responses in discrimination learning. Part I. *Psychological Review*, *59*, 431–442.

12

Behavioral Economics and the Analysis of Consumption and Choice

Steven R. Hursh

The relatively new field of behavioral economics represents a concrete attempt to apply the science of behavior to understand the data of economics, as proposed by Skinner (1953). The concepts from micro-economic theory are explored with methods to study consumption by a range of species in the laboratory and the concepts of operant conditioning are extended to an understanding of demand for economic commodities. The blending of behavioral principles with micro-economic theory has been a fruitful area of research (Hursh, 1980; Kagel et al., 1975; Kahneman, Slovic, & Tversky, 1982; Lea, 1978; Rachlin, Green, Kagel, & Battalio, 1976; Rachlin & Laibson, 1997; Thaler & Mullainathan, 2008) and provides a translational framework for extending principles derived from laboratory studies to an understanding of consumer choice observed in whole communities. Practical application of these methods pave the way for empirical research to test the implications of public policy that seek to influence the choices of people in society (Magoon & Hursh, 2011).

There are several points of converge between economics and behavioral psychology. One is a common interest in the value of goods, defined as reinforcers by the behaviorist, and defined as objects of scarce consumption by economists. A second point of convergence is an interest in the process of choice: for the economist, the allocation of limited resources for the consumption of alternative goods (consumer choice), and for the behaviorist the division of operant behavior among different competing reinforcers. In this review, we will focus more on the utility of economic methods of analysis and consistent functional relationships than on hypothetical economic concepts, such as utility functions, indifference curves, and optimal choices. What emerges is an important extension of behavioral principles and a functional analysis of economic processes (Hursh, 1980, 1984).

Concepts of behavioral economics have proven useful for understanding the environmental control of overall levels of behavior for a variety of commodities in closed

The Wiley Blackwell Handbook of Operant and Classical Conditioning, First Edition.
Edited by Frances K. McSweeney and Eric S. Murphy.

systems (Bickel, DeGrandpre, Higgins, & Hughes, 1990; Bickel, Madden, & DeGrandpre, 1997; Foltin, 1992; Hursh, 1984; Lea, 1978; Lea & Roper, 1977; Rashotte & Henderson, 1988) and the factors that control the allocation of behavioral resources among available reinforcers (Hursh, 1980, 1984; Hursh & Bauman, 1987). A closed system or *closed economy*, as it is called, is a situation in which there is no other source of the commodity of interest, outside of the environment being studied. Behavioral economics, as practiced by students of operant conditioning and behavior analysis, has borrowed concepts from micro-economics, especially consumer demand theory and labor supply theory (Allison, 1983; Allison, Miller, & Wozny, 1979; Lea, 1978; Kagel, Battalio, & Green, 1995; Rachlin, Green, Kagel, & Battalio, 1976; Staddon, 1979; see Watson & Holman, 1977, for a review of relevant micro-economic theory). When applied in laboratory experiments, economic concepts are operationalized in special ways that build on more fundamental behavioral processes, such as reinforcement, discrimination, differentiation, and the like. These experiments have directed our attention to new phenomena previously ignored and new functional relations previous unnamed. In this chapter, behavioral economics is applied to the analysis of consumption of various reinforcers and the responding that produces that consumption. This chapter provides some basic groundwork that will serve as a primer for understanding behavioral-economic concepts that could be applied to understanding of a range of behaviors in the laboratory and clinical settings and we will illustrate extensions to human behavior that could advance empirical public policy.

Value of Reinforcers

One of the most important contributions of behavioral economics has been to redirect our attention to total daily consumption of reinforcers as a primary dependent measure of behavior and the way consumption varies with the cost of reinforcers provides a fundamental definition of the value of those reinforces. In this context, responding is regarded as a secondary dependent variable that is important because it is instrumental in controlling consumption of valued reinforcers. Consideration of consumption as a primary factor required a major methodological shift. In most behavioral experiments, the practice has been to control "drive" by imposing some deprivation schedule. For example, animals reinforced by food are held to 80% of free feeding weight by limiting daily consumption and supplementing the amount of food earned in the test session with just enough food to hold body weight within a restricted range. This strategy was designed to hold "drive" constant and eliminate a confounding factor. Inadvertently, the practice also eliminated one of the major factors controlling behavior in the natural environment, defense of consumption. Under conditions of controlled drive, responding is not instrumental in determining daily consumption and is directly related to the rate of reinforcement in the experimental session (Herrnstein, 1961). This strategy of controlling deprivation or daily consumption, independent of behavioral changes, is what Hursh has defined as an "open economy" (Hursh, 1980, 1984); the situation is not a closed system with regard to sources of the reinforcers. In more recent experiments, control of deprivation has been eliminated and subjects have been allowed to control their own level of consumption, what Hursh has termed a *closed economy*, or a closed system in which there is no outside source of the reinforcer under study. The finding is that radically different sorts of behavioral adjustments occur in these two types of economies, especially when the reinforcer is a necessary commodity like food or water (see Bauman, 1991; Collier, 1983; Collier, Johnson, Hill, & Kaufman, 1986; Foster, Blackman, & Temple, 1997; Hall & Lattal, 1990; Hursh, 1978, 1984; Hursh & Natelson, 1981; Hursh, Raslear, Bauman, & Black, 1989; Hursh, Raslear, Shurtleff, Bauman, & Simmons, 1988; LaFiette & Fantino, 1989, 1989; Lucas, 1981; Raslear, Bauman, Hursh, Shurtleff, & Simmons, 1988; Roane, Call, & Falcomata, 2005; Zeiler, 1999).

Most studies of food reinforcement have been conducted in open economies and suggest that food consumption is easily reduced by changes in effort or rate of reinforcement. However, studies of food reinforcement in closed economies provide a striking contrast of persistent behavior that is very resistant to the effects of reinforcer cost (see Hursh, 1978; Bauman, 1991; Foltin, 1992). On the other hand, for those interested in drugs as reinforcers, most experiments involving drug self-administration have arranged a closed economy for the drug reinforcer; all drug administrations are response dependent during the period of experimentation (Johanson, 1978; Griffiths, Bradford, & Brady, 1979; Griffiths, Bigelow, & Henningfield, 1980; Hursh & Winger, 1995). It is important that when comparing drug-reinforced behavior to behavior reinforced by another reinforcer, such as food, that a closed economy be arranged for that reinforcer as well. The behavioral difference between open and closed economies is best understood in terms of demand for the reinforcer, discussed next.

Demand Curve Analysis

The relationship between reinforcer cost and reinforcer consumption is termed a "demand curve." As the cost of a commodity increases, consumption decreases, illustrated in Figure 12.1, left panel. The rate of decrease in consumption (sensitivity to price) relative to the initial level of consumption, is called "elasticity of demand." When consumption declines slowly with proportionately large increases in price, we define that as "inelastic demand." For this to occur, total responding must increase as cost increases (Figure 12.1, right panel). For example, when the price of gasoline increased three-fold during the 1970s from 33 cents a gallon to over one dollar a gallon, consumption decreased by only 10% (Nicol, 2003). This was an example of inelastic demand and the result was that a larger share of household budgets was allocated to gasoline than was before. Other commodities, such as luxury goods (unnecessary for survival, for example) or goods with many substitutes (such as one brand of peanut butter, for example), have steeply sloping demand curves. Demand for such goods are generally "elastic" and consumption is highly sensitive to price.

The difference in demand between inelastic and elastic goods is easily demonstrated in the laboratory. Figure 12.2 depicts the consumption by monkeys of saccharin sweetened water with an alternative source of water and consumption of food pellets without alternative food. The demand curve for saccharin is generally elastic and is steeply sloping, while the curve for food is generally inelastic and decreases more slowly. In the figure, the price of each commodity (food or saccharin) was

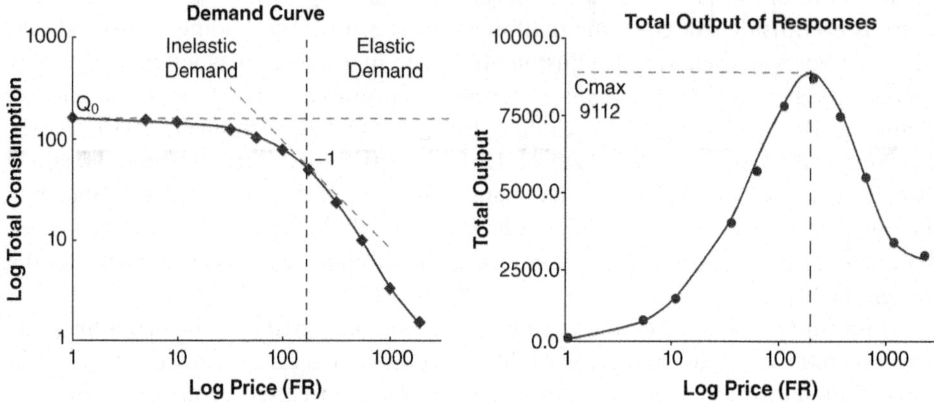

Figure 12.1 Left panel: diagrammatic demand curve showing the usual shape and increasing elasticity across the demand curve. The vertical line marks the point of unit elasticity (slope = −1) which is the transition from inelastic to elastic demand. The level of demand is denoted as the y-intercept or the quantity consumed at zero price (Q_0). Right panel: diagram of total daily consumption that would be required to support the levels of demand shown in the left panel. The vertical line marks the point of unit elasticity and the peak response output. The price at that point is called P_{max}.

gradually increased from ten responses per reinforcer to over 372 responses per reinforcer in a closed economy. As a corollary to the differences in the demand curves, total responding for food increased over a broad range while responding for saccharin generally decreased over the same range. The distinction between elastic and inelastic reinforcers defines a continuum. Consumption of all reinforcers becomes elastic if the price is elevated sufficiently; the difference between reinforcers can be specified in terms of the price at the point of transition between inelastic and elastic demand and coincides with the peak of the response rate functions (P_{max}) shown in the right panel of Figure 12.2 (dashed lines). If that transition occurs at relatively low prices, then demand for that reinforcer is generally more elastic than demand for a reinforcer that sustains response increases over a broad range of prices. As we will see later, there is a mathematical model that fits these curves and a single rate constant in the model that determines the P_{max} value.

Carroll (1993) used demand curves to demonstrate that the addition of a saccharin reinforcer concurrent with a PCP (Phencyclidine) reinforcer had the effect of increasing the elasticity of demand for PCP, increasing the slope of the demand curve and decreasing the price at which responding reached its peak. In general, demand curves for drug reinforcers conform to the same nonlinear, decreasing function typified by those in Figure 12.2 and responding is an inverted U-shaped function of price (see below for details; also see review by Bickel, DeGrandpre, Hughes, & Higgins, 1991). As discussed by Bickel, DeGrandpre, and Higgins (1993), elasticity of demand may be a useful basic metric for comparing the value of different reinforcers, such as the abuse liability of drug reinforcers, and for assessing the potency of interventions to reduce demand for drugs and other reinforcers.

Measuring Demand

In order to use elasticity of demand as a basic yardstick for evaluating "motivation" for reinforcers, the conditions for measuring demand must be precisely specified. This includes clear definitions of the two primary variables, consumption, and price. Hursh (1980, 1984, 1991; Hursh et al., 1988) has proposed that consumption be measured in terms of total daily intake. The simplest measure of total daily consumption is a count of the number of reinforcers that have been consumed—total number of food pellets, drinks of water, or injections of a drug, for example. This approach naturally leads to a simple definition of price as the cost in terms of responses (or amount of time) required to obtain each reinforcer, which is normally specified as the value of the fixed-ratio (FR) schedule of reinforcement. For human subjects, it may be specified as the amount of money for each package of the reinforcer. The demand curve is simply the change in the number of reinforcers earned as a function of increases in the FR schedule, the cost of each reinforcer. In some experiments, the cost may be the amount of time spent working for the reinforcer and would be the value of the fixed-interval (FI) schedule of reinforcement.

As depicted in Figure 12.2, demand curves are seldom linear so precisely specifying slope requires a nonlinear function. A basic exponential function appears to adequately describe most demand curves when plotting the log of consumption as a function of cost (Hursh & Silberberg, 2008):

$$\log Q = \log Q_0 + k(e^{-\alpha \cdot (Q_0 \cdot C)} - 1) \tag{1}$$

The independent variable is Cost (C) measured either as responses or units of time per reinforcer. Log of consumption (log Q) is a function of Cost and is maximal at

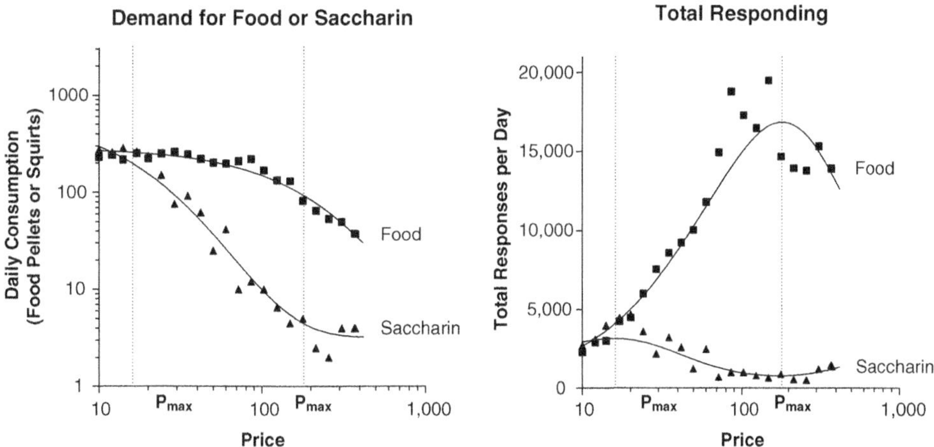

Figure 12.2 Left panel: two demand curves by rhesus monkeys working for either food (squares) or saccharin sweetened water (triangles). The functions show the total number of reinforcers earned (consumption) each day under a series of fixed-ratio (FR) schedules (crices) that ranged from FR 10 to FR 372. Right panel: daily output of responding that accompanied the levels of consumption shown in the left panel. The curves were fit with an exponential equation (Hursh & Roma, 2013).

zero cost (log Q_0) and specifies the highest level of demand. The rate constant, α, determines the rate of decline in relative consumption (log consumption) with increases in cost (C). The value of k is a scaling constant that reflects the range of the data and is generally set to a common constant across comparisons. The slope of the demand curve, elasticity, when k is constant is determined by the rate constant, α. The value of α determines the ***essential value*** of the reinforcer or the sensitivity of consumption to changes in cost.

It should be noted that the form of a demand curve may be critically dependent on the dimensions of the good purchased. In a study by Hursh et al. (1988), two groups of rats earned their daily food ration responding under FR schedules ranging in size from 1 to 360. For one group, the reinforcer size was one food pellet; for the other, it was two. Although the only difference between groups was the size of their food reinforcer, the demand curves that were generated differed in Q_0 and in slope. Equation 1 applied to those data provides a single estimate for the rate constant α because the equation considers differences in reinforcer size that change baseline consumption at zero price (Q_0) and incorporates the value of Q_0 in the exponent of the exponential as a component of price.

Stated another way, when commodities differ in size, it takes varying amounts of each to reach satiation reflected in Q_0 and, therefore, differences in the true cost required to defend the level of baseline demand; it takes more small packages to equal the quantitative value of a larger package. By standardizing price as ($Q_0 \times C$), Equation 1 isolates that component of elasticity due entirely to differences in essential value, α.

This consideration of the size of the reinforcer as a component of price is identical to the practice of providing unit price equivalence values in the grocery store—the true price of a good can be raised by charging more for each package or by reducing the size of each package forcing the customer to buy more packages to meet their needs. Equation 1 automatically considers both of these kinds of price manipulation in the expression $Q_0 \times C$.

Hursh and Winger (1995) proposed a similar way to eliminate scalar differences by expressing price in terms of the number of responses per 1% of maximal consumption, what we call Q_0 (see also Peden & Timberlake, 1984). The approach used here does not require rescaling the data since the conversion is inherent in the demand equation. More importantly, the exponential equation fulfills the goal of having a single parameter (α) to scale elasticity of demand, our basis for defining essential value considering the range of consumption (k).

Sensitivity to price is specified by α and is inversely proportional to essential value (EV). In order for EV to be a valid metric of value across experiments, the formulation must consider the value of k that establishes the span of the consumption data in the experiment. That formula is given in Equation 2:

$$\mathrm{EV} = 1/(100 \cdot \alpha \cdot \mathrm{k}^{1.5}) \tag{2}$$

This definition of value may be used to scale essential value for different reinforcers across a range of experiments and is closely related to the price at which demand elasticity is −1 and overall responding is maximal, the price point called P_{max}. This P_{max} is defined for demand in normalized units of consumption with all levels of consumption expressed as a percent of maximal consumption ($Q_0 = 100\%$), and price is in normalized units of cost per 1% unit of consumption ($C \times Q_0 / 100$). For an approximation of P_{max} for non-normalized demand, replace the 100 in the formula with the estimated value of Q_0.[1]

Comparing Reinforcers in Terms of Demand

The demand for three drugs self-administrated by monkeys were compared by Winger, Hursh, Casey, and Woods (2002). The study compared demand for three NMDA antagonists that differed systematically in time of onset to peak drug effect. Ketamine, PCP, and dizocilpine were measured to have times to peak visible physiological effects of 1, 10, and 32 min, respectively. The exponential demand equation permitted a direct comparison of elasticity of demand for these three drugs, shown in Figure 12.3. The figure compares best-fit demand curves for the three drugs using Equation 1. First, note that each drug was delivered using two or three different doses and that separate demand curves are fit to each dose. However, the exponential demand equation isolated the dose differences in the Q_0 parameter so that sensitivity to price, α, was constant across doses of the same drug. Second, Figure 12.3 shows that essential value was not directly related to potency; the lowest potency drug, ketamine, was reinforcing at unit doses 10 times higher than the highest dose of dizocilpine, yet had an α (sensitivity to price) that was one-fourth that for dizocilpine and a higher essential value. Figure 12.3 illustrates the utility of using demand curve analysis and exponential demand to scale psychoactive drugs for essential value and abuse liability. Hursh and Roma (2013) reported the results of demand curve studies of a range of drug and non-drug reinforcers and the results suggest a direct relationship between essential value and the abuse potential of drugs. Put another way, drugs with comparatively high sensitivity to price (large values of α and low essential value) would be expected to have lower abuse liability in the open market because of competition from cheaper or more potent substitutes.

Sensitivity to price or α is inversely related to *essential value* and P_{max}. That relationship appears to hold for the three drugs reported in Figure 12.3. The essential value or EV (Equation 2) was 252, 212, and 51 for ketamine, phencyclidine, and dizocilpine, respectively. Interestingly, EV was inversely related to the average time to onset of peak effect, shown in Figure 12.4. In other words, the value of these drugs as a reinforcer and the sensitivity of consumption to the prevailing price was controlled by the speed with which the drugs had their psychoactive effect, a relationship that mirrors numerous studies showing that the strength of reinforcement is modulated by delay of reinforcement using food and other reinforcers (Hursh & Fantino, 1973; Grace, Schwendiman, & Nevin 1998; Mazur, 1985; Mazur et al., 1985; Tarpy & Sawabini, 1974; Woolverton & Anderson, 2006). In behavioral terms, essential value is an inverse function of delay to drug reinforcement. This leads to the practical implication that pharmaceutical manipulations that delay the onset of drug effects may be useful manipulations to reduce abuse liability of therapeutic drugs, such as opiates for treatment of pain.

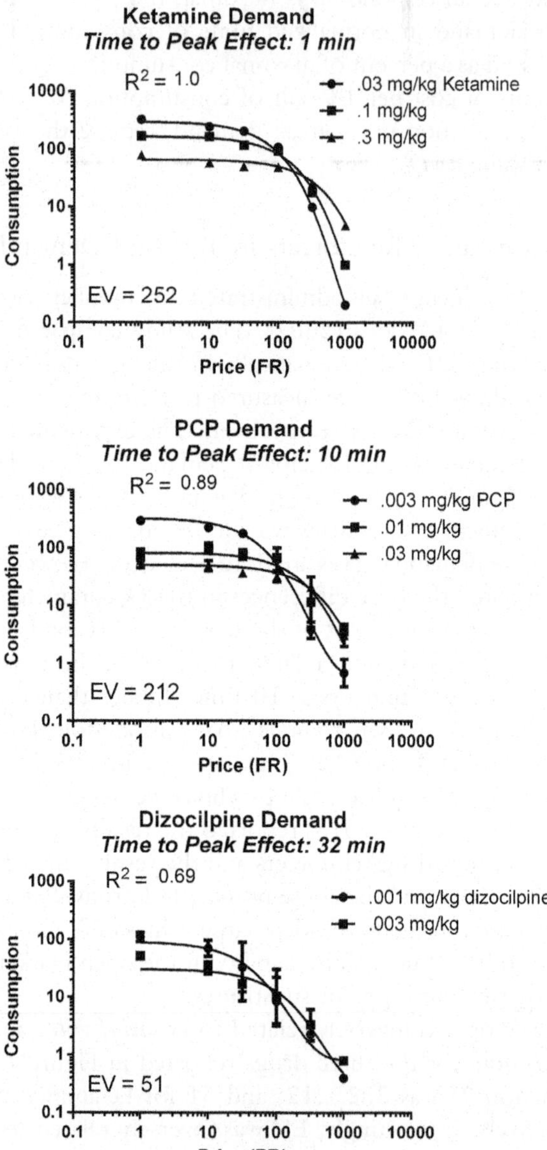

Figure 12.3 Demand curves (see Equation 1) fit to average consumption of three drugs self-administered by rhesus monkeys. The drugs were ketamine, phencyclidine, and dizocilpine. Also shown are the essential value for each drug (Equation 2).

Factors That Alter Demand and Choice

Elasticity of demand is not an inherent property of the reinforcer. For example, one of the primary differences between open and closed economies is elasticity of demand. While demand for food is inelastic in a closed economy (see Figure 12.2) where the subject controls its own intake and no supplemental food is provided, demand for

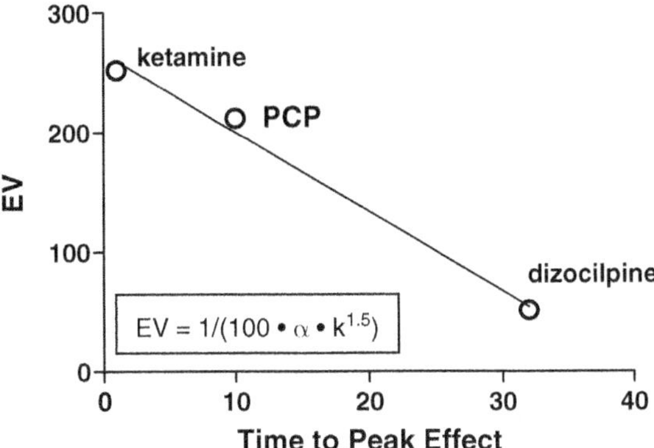

Figure 12.4 Essential value (EV) as a function of the average time to peak physiological effect of ketamine, PCP, and dizocilpine.

food in an open economy can be quite elastic. To illustrate this point, we provided a monkey access to low-cost food requiring only one response per pellet (FR 1) for 20 minutes after a 12-hour work period for food at higher prices. The price of food in the work period was increased to assess demand (Figure 12.4). The subject could work for food in the work period at the prevailing price or wait and obtain food at a lower price later, analogous to obtaining low cost food in the home cage within an open economy. Compared to demand for food when no low cost food was available, demand when an alternative source was available was much more elastic with α value 2.5 times greater than that for food without an alternative source. As a consequence, responding reached a peak at a much lower price, indicated as P_{max}. Comparing Figure 12.5 with Figure 12.2, one can conclude that the addition of a substitute food source functioned to convert food in the work period into an elastic commodity, very similar to the non-nutritive saccharin solution shown in Figure 12.2 and discussed above. In general, elastic demand is typical for all reinforcers studied in an open economy.

One way to understand the difference between open and closed economies is to observe that the reinforcers provided outside the work period can substitute for reinforcers obtained during the work period. This is just one example of a more general set of interactions that can occur among commodities available simultaneously or sequentially in the course of the subject's interaction with the environment. Within a behavioral-economic framework, reinforcer interactions are classified into several categories, illustrated in Figure 12.6. If we think of reinforcers as collections of attributes, we can represent those attributes as a "set" or circle in Figure 12.6. Each quadrant illustrates two sets of reinforcer properties as Venn diagrams. Most studies of choice with animals have arranged for the alternative behaviors to provide the same, perfectly substitutable reinforcer, usually food, shown as two perfectly congruent reinforcer sets. This yields a specific kind of interaction in which the amount of behavior to each roughly matches the amount of reinforcement received from each (*the matching law*, see Davison & McCarthy, 1988). When the two alternatives require a specific number of responses per reinforcer delivery, the subjects

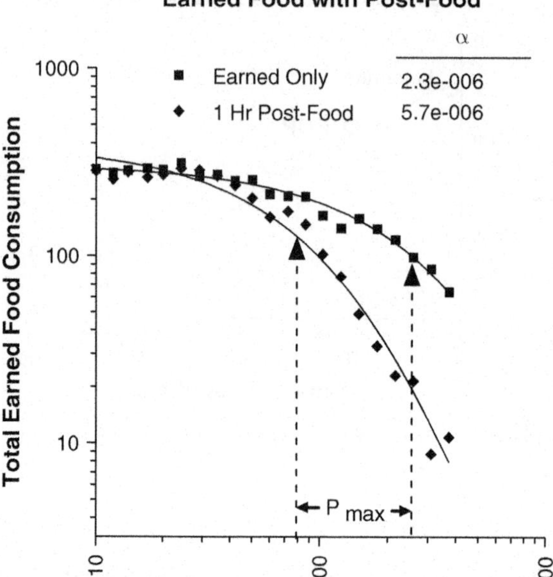

Figure 12.5 Two demand curves by a rhesus monkey for food during a 12-hr work period, either with no other source of food (closed squares) or with a 1-hr period of FR 1 food reinforcement immediately following the work period (closed diamonds). Consumption is shown as a function of the FR schedule that ranged from FR 10 to FR 372 (Hursh, 1993).

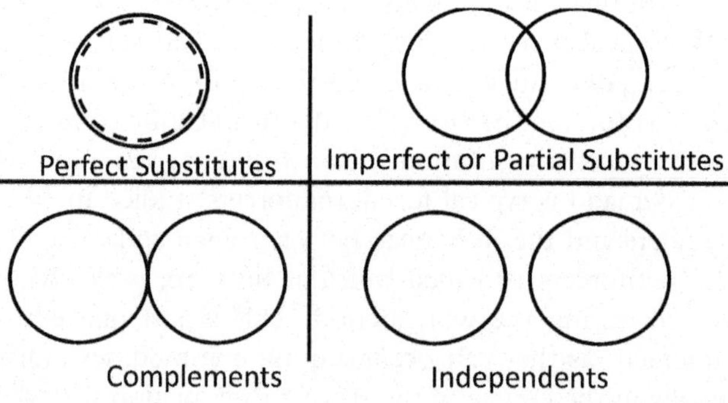

Figure 12.6 Diagram of four hypothetical forms of reinforcer interactions (see text for explanation).

generally show exclusive preference for the least costly of the alternatives (Herrnstein, 1958; Herrnstein & Loveland, 1975). This situation is much like comparison shopping for identical items from different stores; all else being equal, one will go to the store with the lowest price.

Most choices are between commodities that are not perfect substitutes (Green & Freed, 1993, 1998). The other interactions depicted in Figure 12.6 are imperfect

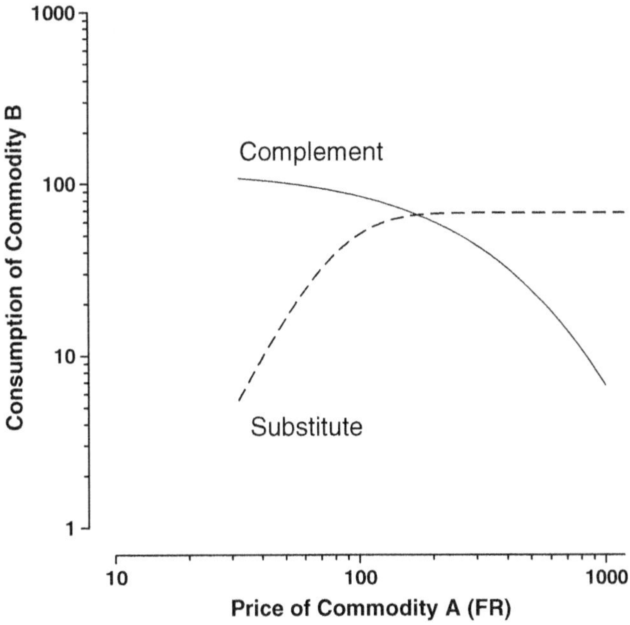

Figure 12.7 Diagram of hypothetical changes in consumption of commodity B as a function of the price of commodity A. The solid line indicates a complementary relation; the dashed line indicates a substitutable relation (Hursh & Roma, 2013).

substitutes, complements, and independent reinforcers. *Imperfect substitutes* share many features but each also poses unique features not contained in the other reinforcer. *Complements* are a special kind of reinforcer interaction in which the presence of the features of one reinforcer enhance the value of the features of the other reinforcer, that is, their individual values are "connected." Finally, *independent* reinforcers share no common functional properties, nor does the presence of one alter the value of the other; hence the sets are disconnected.

Figure 12.7 illustrates the difference between imperfect substitutes and complements. Along the x-axis is the price of commodity A; along the y-axis is the quantity of consumption of the alternative commodity B with fixed price. As the price of A increases, consumption of A decreases, the usual demand relation. If, at the same time, the consumption of B increases in response to these increases in the price of A, then B is defined as a substitute for A. If the consumption of B decreases, then B is defined as a complement of A.

Substitution

Choice between two imperfect substitutes is illustrated in Figure 12.8 (Spiga, based on unpublished data). Using a procedure similar to that reported by Spiga, Martinetti, Meisch, Cowan, and Hursh (2005), human subjects chose between methadone available after pressing one lever under an increasing series of FRs. The other alternative was a different opiate, hydromorphone, available under a constant FR schedule. Even

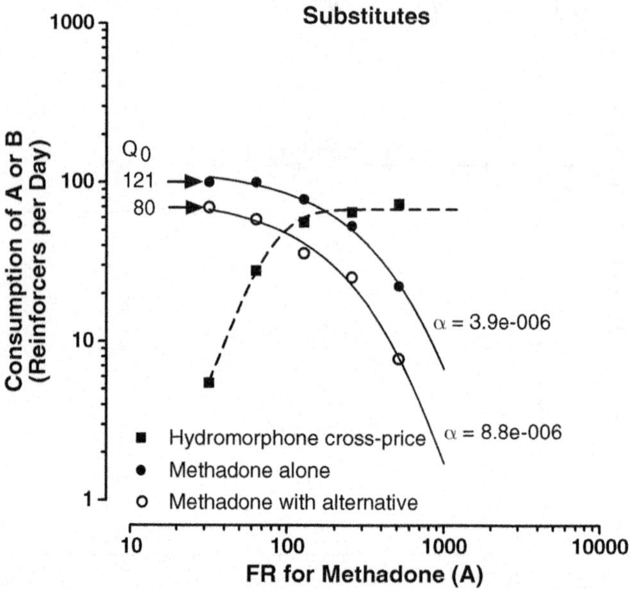

Figure 12.8 Mean daily consumption by human subjects of methadone (commodity A) and hydromorphone (commodity B) as a function of the unit price (FR schedule) for methadone, in log-log coordinates (Spiga, based on unpublished data).

at the lowest price of methadone (FR 30), some hydromorphone was consumed; as the price of methadone increased and methadone consumption decreased, consumption of hydromorphone increased as a partial substitute. The decline in methadone consumption was greater with hydromorphone available than when methadone was offered alone. However, even at the highest price of methadone (FR 512), some methadone was consumed despite the lower price of hydromorphone. This reciprocal trade-off between consumption of two reinforcers is typical of imperfect substitutes.

Of further note is the change in elasticity of methadone when hydromorphone was available as a substitute shown in Figure 12.8. Sensitivity to methadone price (α) was more than doubled when hydromorphone was available as an alternative and level of demand (Q_0) was reduced by a third (79 vs. 120). In the context of drug abuse therapy, an alternative drug reinforcer such as methadone may be used as a medical intervention designed to reduce demand or increase elasticity of demand for the drug of abuse. In this experimental model of the therapeutic process, the methadone demand is like demand for an illicit drug and the hydromorphone is like the drug therapy. Behavioral economics provides an approach to evaluation of the behavioral efficacy of this sort of drug therapy. The efficacy of different therapies would be measured in terms of their effects on the elasticity of demand for the target drug. As described above, fitting the demand equation to the observed demand curves provides a quantitative tool for specifying these changes in terms of the parameters of the demand Equation 1. In order to determine the demand for the illicit drug using actual patients requires an indirect approach using hypothetical demand curves.

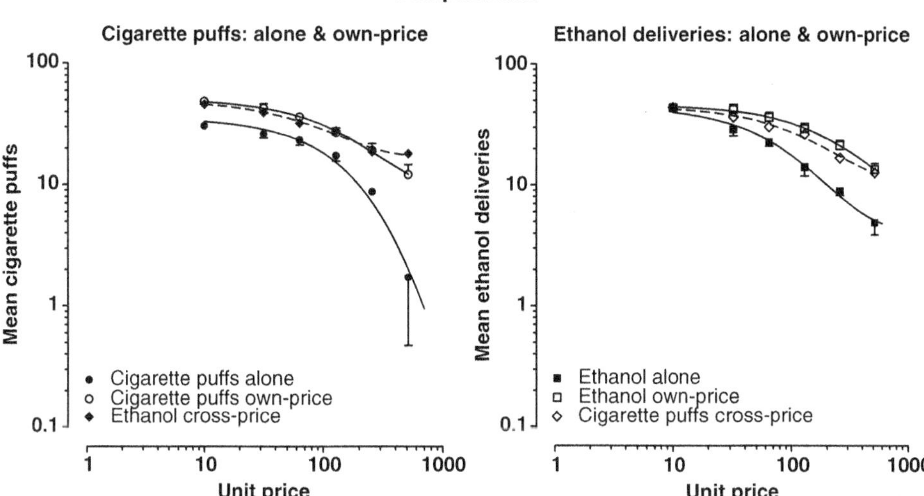

Figure 12.9 For human subjects, consumption of fixed price alternatives (commodity B, dashed lines) ethanol drinks (left filled diamond) or cigarette puffs (open diamond right) and the variable price alternative (commodity A) as a function of the fixed ratio for commodity A (open circle or open square) in log-log coordinates. Demand for cigarettes or ethanol drinks alone are shown as filled circles (left) or filled squares (right), respectively (Spiga, unpublished).

Instead of actually measuring levels of consumption under real prices, we ask subjects to estimate their levels of consumption of various illicit drugs under a series of increasing hypothetical monetary prices. The slopes of these hypothetical demand curves conform to the same exponential demand equation as actual demand curves (Hursh & Silberberg, 2008) and shifts in the rate constant of the demand curve—or changes in elasticity—can be used to track the influence of therapy to reduce overall demand (Q_0) and increase sensitivity to price (α).

Complementarity

Choice between two complements is illustrated in Figure 12.9 (Spiga, based on unpublished data). The two alternatives were ethanol drinks and cigarette puffs. In the right panel, ethanol drinks were offered at a constant price (commodity B) and the price of cigarette puffs (commodity A) was varied, either with the ethanol or alone. In the left panel, cigarette puffs were offered at a fixed price (commodity B) and the price of ethanol drinks (commodity A) was varied, either with cigarette puffs or alone. As the price of the variable price commodity A increased, decreasing consumption of that commodity, daily consumption of the fixed price alternative (B) decreased. The value of ethanol or cigarettes as a reinforcer declined as the consumption of the alternative declined. This kind of parallel decline in consumption for one commodity as the price of an alternative is increased defines the alternative as a complement. Referring back to Figure 12.6, the two reinforcers share no specific properties, but the value of each is connected to the value of the other such that one enhances the other. Note also that the demand for the variable price alternative (cigarettes on the left and ethanol on the right) was less elastic when the complement was available; the demand curves for these offered alone were consistently below the demand curves with the alternative. This further illustrates the complementary relationship between ethanol consumption and cigarette smoking.

Determining Own-Price and Cross-Price Elasticity

Own-price elasticity of demand refers to the slope of the demand curve for a commodity when plotted in the usual log-log coordinates and reflects proportional changes in consumption of the commodity with proportional changes in its own price. As noted above, demand curves are usually nonlinear and elasticity increases with price. No single number can be used to represent elasticity of demand for comparison across experiments. The demand Equation 1 provides two methods for comparing elasticities. The first is to compare the rate of change in elasticity with price. The faster elasticity increases with price, the greater the elasticity is at any given price. The *a* parameter of the demand equation represents the rate of change in elasticity of demand and is a convenient parameter for comparison across conditions and experiments. The second method uses the demand equation to compute the price that produces maximum responding, P_{max}. This is the price at which the demand curve has a slope of -1 and represents a convenient common point of reference across conditions and studies. Generally, if demand becomes more elastic, then one will observe a decrease in the price associated with an elasticity of –1 and maximum responding (P_{max}).

Cross-price elasticity of demand is the slope of the function relating the consumption of a second commodity at fixed price to the changes in price of an alternative commodity (see Figures 12.8 and 12.9). As noted above, if this function has positive slope, then the second commodity is termed a substitute for the first (Figure 12.8); if the slope is negative, then the second is termed a complement of the first (Figure 12.9); if the slope is zero, they are considered independent. An extension of exponential demand was used to fit the cross-price demand curves (commodity B) in Figures 12.8 for hydromorpone (substitute for methadone) or in Figure 12.9 for ethanol and cigarettes (complements to each other):

$$Q_B = \log(Q_{alone}) + Ie^{-\beta \cdot C_A} \tag{3}$$

where Q_{alone} is the level of demand for the constant-price commodity B at infinite price (C) for commodity A (zero consumption of commodity A), *I* is the interaction constant, β is the sensitivity of commodity B consumption to the price of commodity A, and C_A is the cost of commodity A. In Figure 12.8, the interaction term *I* was negative (-3), indicating a reciprocal or substitution relationship between consumptions of the two commodities; in Figure 12.9, the interaction terms *I* were positive (0.5 for ethanol and 0.6 for cigarettes) indicating a parallel or complementary relationship between consumptions of ethanol and cigarettes.[2]

To summarize, essential value may be dramatically affected by the availability of alternative reinforcers. When substitutes are available, the essential value of a reinforcer declines relative to when no other source of reinforcer is available. Low-priced concurrently available perfect substitutes produce the largest decrease in essential value with imperfect substitutes and delayed alternatives producing more modest declines in essential value. At the other end of the continuum, concurrently available complements increase the essential value of a reinforcer. These reinforcer interactions are not traditionally incorporated into approaches to prominent models of decision-making such as Herrnstein's (1970) matching law, although extensions to qualitatively different reinforcers and to choices in the "market place" have been described (Green & Rachlin, 1991; Herrnstein & Prelec, 1992).

The Behavioral Economics of Addiction and Treatment

There are a number of economic theories suggested to explain the development of an addiction—an increasingly strong tendency to seek and consume a specific commodity (Foxall & Sigurdsson, 2011; Vuchinich & Heather, 2003). Here, the application of the demand law offers a systematic and longitudinal way to describe the neurobehavioral changes that are described as addition. Rather than attempt to construct a hypothetical process to explain the development of an addiction, we merely provide a convenient way to measure and track the process (Bickel et al., 1993; Hursh, 1991, 1993). The underlying process that leads to addiction are likely both genetic and developmental (ontogenetic) but there is no consensus on the exact balance of the two processes. Nevertheless, there is a growing literature that indicates that for some commodities extended exposure to the reinforcing properties of the item lead to progressive changes in demand (Ahmed & Koob, 1998). In a recent experiment with rodents, demand curves for infusions of cocaine were determined after a brief familiarization with the drug and then later after a two-week long history of infusions (Christensen, Silberberg, Hursh, Roma, & Riley, 2008). In parallel, demand curves for food were also obtained.

Figure 12.10 illustrates the effect of the extended history for cocaine. There was both an increase in the level of demand and a change in elasticity of demand following the extended history. Here, we focus on the change in elasticity of demand; the demand curve for cocaine has been plotted as changes in consumption, with Q_0 set as the 100% level of consumption at the lowest price (see Hursh & Winger, 1995). This figure shows that the additional history with cocaine reinforcement led to a 50% reduction in sensitively to price (α) and an increase in essential value with P_{max} increasing from 19 to 37 responses per unit reinforcement, dashed lines in Figure 12.10. Hence, the fundamental nature of addiction may be defined as a shift in the essential value of a commodity resulting from increased experience with the effects of the reinforcer.

If addiction can be defined as an increase in the essential value of a commodity and a decrease in elasticity of demand, then, perhaps, treatment for addiction can be defined as the reversal of that process—a reduction in essential value and an increase in elasticity of demand. Consistent with this expectation, Madden and Kalman (2010) reported that for individuals using bupropion to assist with smoking cessation, changes in elasticity (α from Equation 1) from the first to the second week of treatment were predictive of subsequent success in smoking cessation.

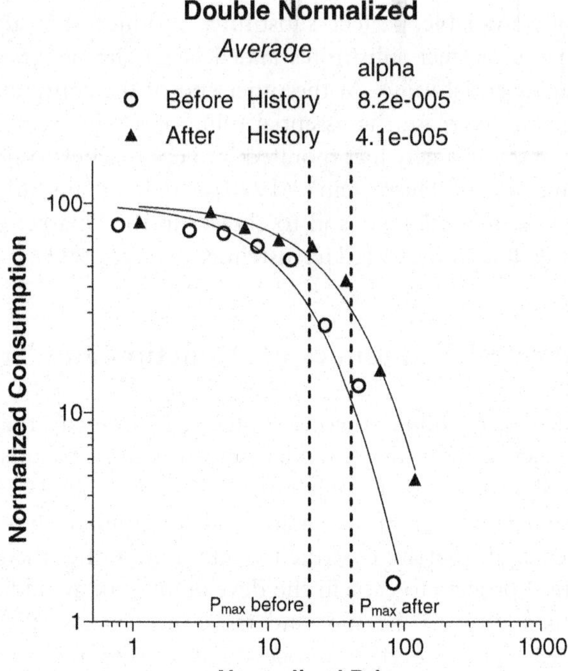

Figure 12.10 For the mean of a group of rodents, consumption of cocaine infusions as a function of increasing fixed-ratio schedule before (open circles) and after an extended history of exposure to cocaine (filled triagles), in log-log coordinates. The shift in P_{max} is shown as the two vertical dashed lines (Hursh & Roma, 2013).

Demand Elasticity in Open and Closed Economies

The literature on demand curves contains examples of situations that span a range of research paradigms, from non-human primates working in an environment with restricted access to alternative drug and non-drug reinforcers, to humans in a laboratory setting with limited access to alternative reinforcers during the period of the experimental session, to humans in a more clinical setting with unrestricted access to alternative reinforcers. As pointed out above (Hursh, 1980, 1984,1993), conditions that permit the reinforcer under study to be consumed outside the experimental setting are called *open economies* and demand curves are generally more elastic compared to conditions that restrict access to the experimental setting, *closed economies,* (see Hursh, 1991, Figures 13 and 14). For this reason, one would expect that the demand curves obtained in non-human primate studies *using closed economies* would be generally less elastic than those found in human studies with less restricted access or *open economies.* Nevertheless, *relative changes in elasticity* with changes in the availability of alternative reinforcers or resulting from pharmacotherapy should generalize across these research paradigms.

To illustrate the influence of contextual variables on elasticity, Spiga (personal communication) reported differences in the elasticity of demand for methadone in

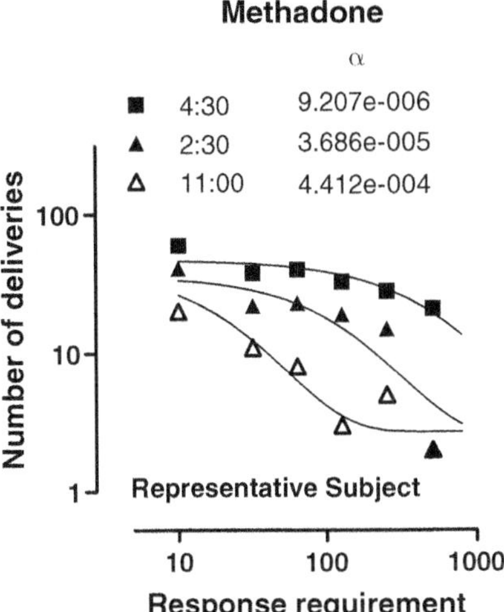

Figure 12.11 Methadone consumption by a human subject working for small deliveries of methadone under a series of fixed-ratio schedules arranged in separate sessions. The experiment was run at about 9 a.m. and unearned methadone was provided later at 11 a.m., 2:30 p.m. or 4:30 p.m. The number of earned doses by a representative subject are shown for the three times to the remaining dose.

human subjects working for methadone doses in morning sessions that occurred at about 9 a.m. The total daily dose of methadone for each subject was constant and any unearned methadone was provided later in the day, hence an open economy. However, the time to that second methadone dose was systematically varied, as shown in Figure 12.11 for a representative subject. When the second dose occurred at 11 a.m., α was large—consumption was quite sensitive to price; when it was provided in the afternoon at 2:30 or 4:30 p.m., the α parameter of the demand curve systematically declined to a level several orders of magnitude smaller. This illustrates that there is a temporal dimension to substitution; parallel to the concept of delay of reinforcement, delayed substitutes have reduced influence on demand elasticity relative to substitutes that are proximal in time (Hursh, 1991).

The difference between inpatient and outpatient treatment for addictive behavior is an obvious parallel to the distinction between closed and open economies, respectively. Patients who undergo drug detoxification, for example, in an inpatient clinic frequently fail to maintain abstinence when they return to their community and undergo outpatient treatment (Wikler, 1977, 1980). It is safe to say that detoxification does not "cure" addiction (see Koob & Le Moal, 2001; McLellan, Lewis, O'Brien, & Kleber, 2000). In part, this may be due to long lasting behavioral conditioning: Cues in the client's neighborhood elicit conditioned drug effects. This explains the subjective sensations reported by the subject and, perhaps, the initial attraction to the prior drug-taking pattern. However, the ultimate breakdown in abstinence that often occurs during outpatient treatment may simply be a reflection of the unfavorable economic conditions that skew preference toward the illicit commodity: higher reinforcing value, greater convenience of use (economies of time and distance), and strong collateral social reinforcement. Yet, outpatient treatment is a necessary step in the treatment or rehabilitation process; successful progress will depend on a realization that outpatient treatment is an open economy in which the benefits of treatment are economic goods evaluated in a competitive market. Innovations that improve the economic utility and reduce the psychological costs of therapy will serve to swing more clients toward compliance with the outpatient protocol. This generalization is applicable for a range of outpatient programs including treatment for drug and alcohol abuse, smoking, and obesity.

Therapy and Demand Interactions

The concepts of substitution and complementarity provide some insights into important limitations of individual therapy programs for the control or elimination of behaviors in excess in individual clients. Within a behavioral framework, one can conceptualize the therapeutic situation as one in which the therapist or the clinic attempts to shape new behavior under the control of acceptable reinforcers that compete with and reduce the occurrence of behavior to obtain unhealthy commodities, be it illicit drugs, alcohol, cigarettes, or excessive amounts of food. Thus, the reinforcers arranged by the therapeutic process interact with those from the target commodity (see Carroll, 1993; Thompson, Koerner, & Grabowski, 1984). For example, when monkeys were allowed to work for a sweet saccharin solution concurrently with consumption of PCP, elasticity of demand for PCP is increased and P_{max} moved to the left; however, considerable amounts of PCP were still consumed despite the presence of a competing reinforcer (Carroll, 1993).

The effectiveness of the competition between a drug reinforcer, for example, and other reinforcers will depend, at least in part, on several economic factors: the amount of direct substitution between the two sources of reinforcement, the availability of desirable complements to the therapeutic reinforcers that will maximize their effectiveness, and the amount of direct competition that exists between the two sources of reinforcement, i.e. does performance for one preclude or prevent reinforcement from the other (Greenwald, 2010). These factors can be illustrated by considering the effectiveness of methadone therapy for users of heroin.

Agonist Therapy

Methadone is an imperfect substitute for heroin; it is an opiate agonist and has many of the psychoactive properties of heroin and morphine. It is explicitly formulated so that an oral dose will prevent opiate withdrawal but will not produce a pronounced euphoria or "high." It substitutes for heroin to prevent withdrawal symptoms, the aversive consequences of non-drug use, but does not substitute for the immediate positive reinforcing consequences of euphoria. One could predict, then, that even if a large price differential existed between the two commodities, some heroin would still be purchased from illicit sources for its unique reinforcing features (see Stitzer, Grabowski, & Henningfield, 1984). A recent study has demonstrated that the exponential demand model may be used to explore the effects of agonists on the abuse liability of opiates (Banks, Roma, Folk, Rice, & Negus, 2011).

In addition, heroin is often consumed as part of a social ritual and these social events serve as complements to the primary reinforcing consequences of the drug (Matto, 2004). To the extent that the substitute, methadone, must be consumed in a clinical, non-social environment, its value will be diminished as an adequate substitute for heroin because it is not accompanied by important complementary social reinforcers (see Hunt, Lipton, Goldsmith, & Strug, 1984).

Antagonist Therapy

The use of methadone as a treatment for heroin is an example of the use of an agonist to substitute for the drug of abuse and drive up elasticity of demand. An alternative approach is to provide a drug therapy that is a specific antagonist for the drug of abuse; the antagonist binds to the neurochemical receptor and blocks the action of the drug without itself producing a psychoactive effect. A common antagonist for opiate drugs is naltrexone or naloxone; it is used in emergency rooms to rapidly block the action of opiates in patients that have taken an overdose. As a therapy, the antagonist partially or completely blocks the action of the target drug and presumably would reduce demand.

This presumption has been tested in a study reported by Harrigan and Downs (1978). Monkeys worked for morphine under a series of increasing unit prices for morphine, arranged by decreasing the morphine dose per reinforcer. Morphine self-administration was studied either alone or when combined with one of three doses of intravenous doses of naltrexone. This yielded four separate consumption curves. Generally, the level of consumption of morphine at the lowest unit price *increased* in direct relation to the dose of naltrexone and sensitivity to the effects of increasing the unit price also increased with the dose of naltrexone. This apparently complicated effect of naltrexone can be resolved by examining exponential demand for morphine alone and in combination with naltrexone. Fitting exponential demand revealed that sensitivity to price (α) was unchanged but rather, there was an upward shift in Q_0 such that the demand curves with naltrexone were uniformly shifted to the right to higher effective prices considering the larger baseline levels of consumption required to reach satiation. To state it another way, naltrexone did not change the essential value of morphine but did lower the potency of each morphine infusion and raised the effective price of the drug.

At first, one might conclude that this indicates that antagonist therapy has no utility for the treatment of opiate "drug seeking" since it does not alter sensitivity to environmental price variables. In fact, this is not precisely true. The effect of naltrexone was to reduce the functional potency of the morphine. This had the effect of *increasing* the functional cost of morphine under each environmental cost, i.e. unit dose of morphine. Hence, increases in naltrexone moved the demand curve to the right and to lower daily levels of consumption. A sufficiently high dose of naltrexone would virtually eliminate any reinforcing value of morphine and, consequently, would move the functional price sufficiently far to the right that all consumption would cease under all levels of environmental cost. In effect, the morphine would be rendered ineffective as a reinforcer and the cost-benefit ratio for expending any effort to obtain it would approach infinity. This would occur, not because the fundamental demand for morphine was changed, but because the functional potency of morphine as a reinforcer was changed.

The clinical value of antagonist therapy is complicated by several considerations. As indicated above, the initial effect of an antagonist when the environmental price is low and the dose of the antagonist is insufficient to eliminate drug reinforcement is an increase in the total number of injections per day (increase in Q_0). This increase is motivated by the need to compensate for the functional decrease in the potency of the drug of abuse that brings with it several undesirable side effects. First, the number of doses of the drug required per day increases, and this potentially increases the need for funds to obtain the drug and to engage in illegal activities to raise the funds. Second, it increases the revenues to the drug suppliers. Third, for self-injected drugs, it may increase the use of dirty needles and increases the risk of needle transmitted diseases such as HIV/AIDS. But the primary challenge for any antagonist therapy is that it requires that the subject voluntarily administer a drug that will drive up the functional cost of another reinforcer. Ordinarily, consumers choose to minimize cost so such a choice would have to be compensated by a correlated increase in benefit from other sources of reinforcement, such as the retention of a well-paying job by a physician addicted to morphine. For many drug users, however, such alternatives may not be available unless provided by the therapeutic process itself.

From Science to Public Policy

In the previous sections, I discussed the factors that serve to control the choices of a person to work for and consume drugs of various sorts. Many other policy decisions relate to similar choices for other commodities. For example, in the arena of environmental and energy policy, tax incentives and rebates are often provided to encourage citizens to purchase more fuel-efficient cars, to increase the insulating properties of homes, or to adopt alternative energy sources for home electricity. The power of such policies depends on the price sensitivity of the commodities at issue. When attempting to encourage alternative energy choices, high price sensitivity is a virtue because it suggests that small reductions in price (using rebates, for example) will have relatively large effects on consumption. When attempting to discourage wasteful use of resources, such as taxes on the use of paper bags, high price sensitivity is again a virtue because a small cost, such as 5 cents per bag, might be expected to have a relatively powerful effect on consumption. When attempting to reduce drug use, provision of medically administered alternatives like methadone are expected to increase price sensitivity of demand for substitutable illicit alternatives, resulting in an overall decrease in consumption of the illicit commodity in favor of the lower cost (and legal) medical alternative.

When formulating such policies, it is important to understand the demand elasticities of the commodities at issue; in effect, it is important to be able to establish the value of α for the various alternatives. This requirement presents a challenge because often there are not naturalistic data available to allow for the mapping of the basic demand curve. When naturalistic data are available based on market fluctuations or differences in supply (and price) across different geographic locations, the range of prices is often very limited. This makes it difficult to precisely map the demand curve

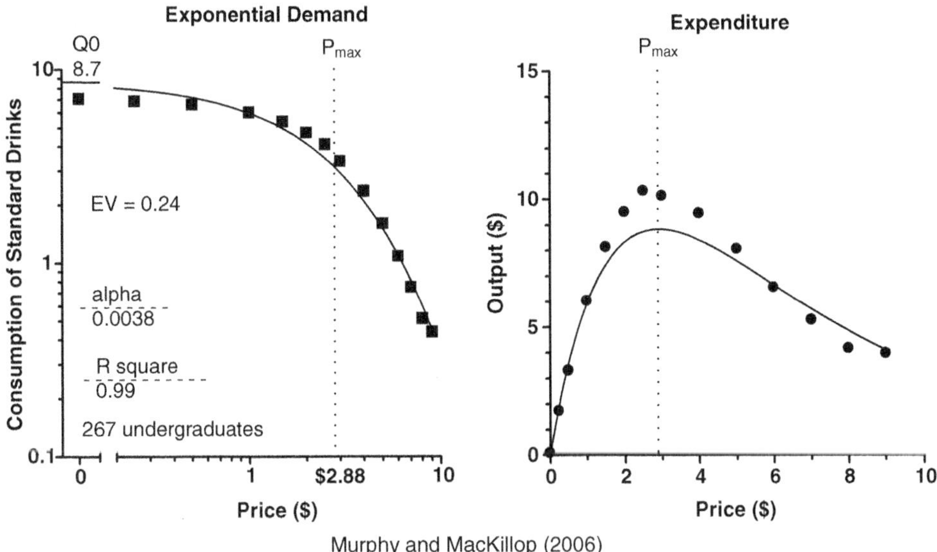

Figure 12.12 The reported consumption of standard alcoholic drinks as a function of the cost of each drink from a group of 267 college undergraduates responding to a set of questions about hypothetical alcohol consumption (from Murphy & MacKillop, 2006).

and determine the value of α. Along with other economics-oriented approaches (e.g., Roddy, Steinmiller, & Greenwald, 2011), recent experiments have been conducted using "hypothetical" demand curves constructed by asking subjects to indicate the levels of consumption that they would adopt if confronted with different prices for the commodity in question. Typically such experiments involve describing a scenario that defines the purchase setting, the commodity offered for sale, the availability of other possible alternatives and their prices, limits on when the commodities can be consumed to prevent hypothetical savings or reselling, limits on how much money the subject has to spend, and other possible environmental constraints. These experiments have shown that such hypothetical demand curves (1) have a consistent shape well described by the exponential demand equation and (2) have values of α that vary with hypothetical contextual variables.

Murphy and MacKillop (2006) surveyed alcohol consumption as a function of price in 267 undergraduate students. Figure 12.12 is the resulting demand curve (left panel) and response output function (right panel). The line through the hypothetical consumption curve is the best fitting exponential demand curve, and accounted for 99% of the variance in consumption. The expenditure function also was well described by the function, and the point of maximum consumption (P_{max}) coincided closely with the maximum of the exponentially derived output function. While we have no independent way to assess the true levels of consumption of alcohol in these students, the systematic relationship obtained using the hypothetical method is encouraging.

One way to assess the usefulness of such functions is to determine if they vary in a rational way with other ecologically valid variables. To that end, Murphy and

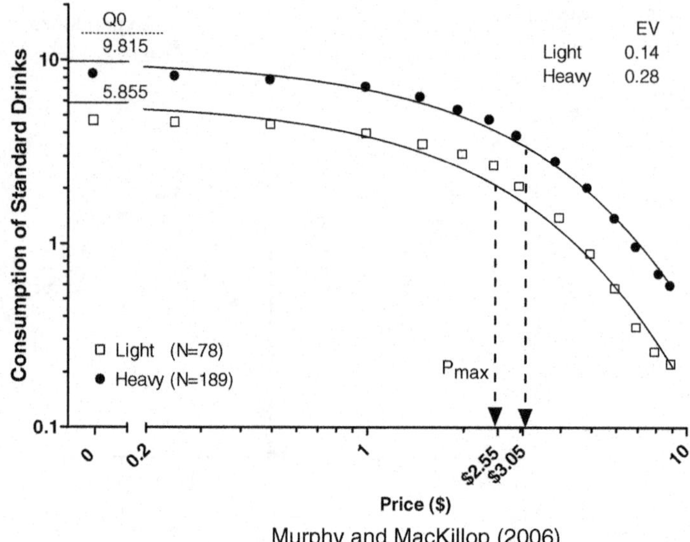

Figure 12.13 The reported consumption of standard alcoholic drinks as a function of the cost of each drink from two groups of college undergraduates, one group self-reporting light consumption (n = 78), and one group reporting heavy consumption (n = 189). Subjects responded to a set of questions about hypothetical alcohol consumption (from Murphy & MacKillop, 2006).

MacKillop (2006) related the demand curves in these students to their reported overall use of alcohol. They divided the 267 students into two groups defined as light and heavy alcohol users. The two resulting demand curves (Figure 12.13) differed from each other in both Q_0 and α. Heavy drinkers had higher levels of consumption, as might be expected from their self-assessment of overall use, but they also showed less sensitivity to alcohol price, with an α value about half that of light drinkers. In a similar study, MacKillop et al., (2008) reported that minimal users of nicotine products had price sensitivity (α) that was five times higher than that reported by those with moderate nicotine use.

These findings suggest that hypothetical demand curves may be used as a tool for demand curve assessment to inform public policy that will use taxes to increase prices to discourage certain behaviors, or use incentives and rebates to encourage other behaviors (see Bidwell, Mackillop, Murphy, Tidey, & Colby, 2012; MacKillop, Few, Murphy, Wier, Acker, Murphy, Stojek, Carrigan, & Chaloupka, 2012). Such research will provide two important bits of information. First, it will help define the overall shape of the underlying demand curves and the associated α values. Second, it will help define where the current prevailing price is relative to P_{max}, i.e., is demand elasticity in the vicinity of the current price elastic or inelastic. This will lead to directly verifiable predictions of the policy's (price increase or decrease) effect size on resulting consumption.

A recent study reported by Roma et al. (2013) demonstrates that with a relatively small number of subjects (8), meaningful hypothetical demand curves can be obtained that differentiate between a range of commodities in important ways. The subjects in this study were all former opiate (heroin) users enrolled in a methadone treatment program. All reported experience using prescription opiate pills, such as OxyContin, and manipulating them, for example, crushing them to be inhaled or dissolved for injection. They were asked to estimate the level of consumption of a range of commodities across a wide range of prices, including several forms of opiate pills. The commodities were: standard opiate pills that could be crushed, opiate pills that could not be crushed and could only be swallowed (tamper resistant formulation), alcoholic drinks, cigarettes (nicotine), and a non-drug control, chicken nuggets or wings. Figure 12.14 shows the results for all five commodities. Shown are the demand curves and beneath the curves are two bar graphs, one showing maximum consumption at zero price, and one showing the *essential value* (Equation 2) of each commodity. Most importantly, the standard opiate pills that could be crushed had the highest essential value and the tamper resistant opiate pills that had to be swallowed had significantly lower essential value. Oral opiate pills had a higher maximum consumption than the standard pills at the lowest price, presumably because the subjects would have taken more of them to compensate for the oral route of administration. Nevertheless, consumption of the oral opiate pills was more sensitive to price and declined more quickly across increasing prices, indicating that a tamper resistant formulation would reduce the essential value and illicit demand for prescription opiates pills in the street market.

On the other end of the continuum, in these same subjects, chicken would have been purchased at about the same level when free as opiate pills but, as we would expect, consumption was much more sensitive to price so that the essential value of chicken was about one-seventh that of standard opiate pills. Between these two extremes were alcohol and cigarettes. About as many cigarettes would be purchased as opiate pills when free, but consumption declined more quickly with increasing price so that essential value was about one-fourth that of the standard opiate pills. Alcohol would be purchased at a level lower than cigarettes but had about the same essential value. These data taken together illustrate how hypothetical demand can be used to assess both the level of consumption and the abuse potential of a range of commodities and can be used to test the value of tamper resistant formulations as a deterrent to illicit prescription drug use.

The previous charts illustrate how hypothetical demand can be used to compare consumption patterns across subjects and commodities. It is also important to establish that hypothetical demand can reflect the context of alternatives and disincentives that might alter demand. This is important because some policy initiatives impose non-monetary costs. For example, consider a policy that would encourage the use of an alternative ethanol-based fuel for automobiles. Even if the price of the fuel were equivalent to the price of regular gasoline, other costs might have a dramatic impact on utilization, such as the travel time and distance to the alternative fuel station, the potential to travel to a location that does not have such fuel, and a possible reduction in fuel mileage necessitating increased frequency of refueling. If the vehicle would run on both kinds of fuel (i.e., if the two fuels were functionally substitutable), the much higher convenience of using the standard fuel might outweigh any environmental benefit. To combat this disincentive, the policy maker may have to provide counteracting incentives to the consumer, such as refueling rebates and tax incentives.

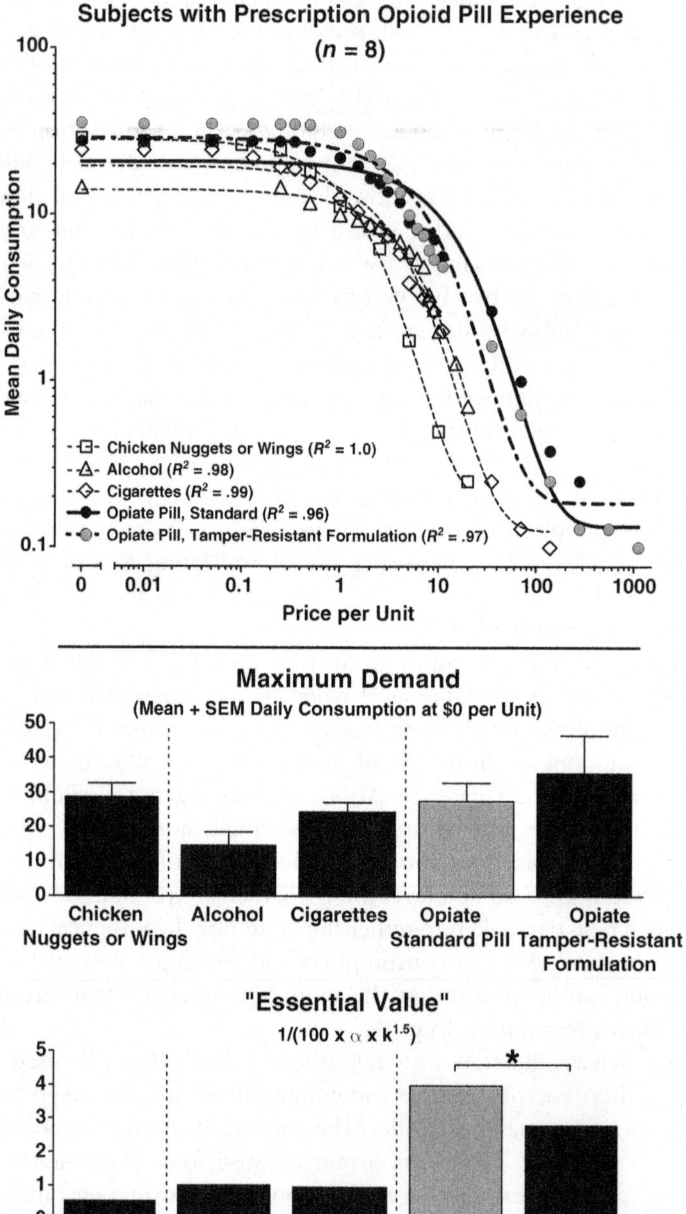

Figure 12.14 The reported consumption of five commodities as a function of the cost of each from former heroin users in methadone treatment (N = 8) chosen based on prior experience using opiates in pill form (from Roma et al., 2012). The top panel shows reported consumption as a function of price of five commodities; the bottom two panels show maximum reported consumption and essential value (Equation 2) for each commodity: chicken nuggets or wings, alcohol drinks, cigarettes, standard opiate pill, and tamper resistant opiate pill (Roma et al., 2013).

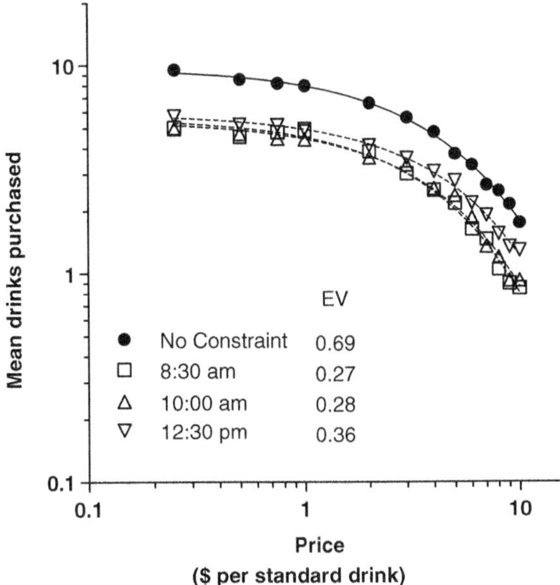

Figure 12.15 The reported consumption of standard alcoholic drinks as a function of the cost of each drink from college undergraduates (N = 164) randomly assigned to one of three hypothetical academic constraints (academic classes scheduled at 8:30 a.m., 10:00 a.m., and 12:30 p.m.) or a control condition: no constraint. The curves fit to the data are from the exponential demand model and the values of EV (Equation 2) are shown for each condition (from Gentile et al., 2012).

In addition, the policy maker may need to take steps to reduce the disincentives, such as encouraging producers to increase availability of the alternative fuel. But the question ultimately becomes one of how much compensation is required to have a beneficial impact on alternative fuel use. The method of hypothetical demand curves provides an empirical approach for evaluating the impact of these incentives on expected consumption, providing an empirical basis for a rational cost-benefit analysis of the proposed policy. While the results in Figure 12.14 are encouraging, future research should seek to further establish the validity of hypothetical demand curves as predictors of actual consumption in the natural economy.

To illustrate how disincentives and contextual variables may be evaluated with hypothetical demand curves, Gentile, Librizzi, and Martinetti (2012) used an alcohol purchase task similar to that used by Murphy and MacKillop (2006) to assess the effects of academic constraints (next-day class time and next-day class requirement) on alcohol demand among college students. The three "academic constraint" conditions involved scenarios that included a next-day class that differed by scheduled time (8:30 a.m., 10:00 a.m., or 12:30 p.m.), or a control condition (no next-day class). Exponential demand analyses revealed that participants in all three of the academic constraint conditions reported fewer drinks consumed and displayed lower "essential value" of alcohol, or greater sensitivity to price increases, compared with the no-constraint control. The results are plotted in Figure 12.15 and show excellent fits to the exponential demand model and progressively decreasing sensitivity to price (α) as the delay to the next-day class increased, with the lowest sensitivity occurring when no class was scheduled (no constraint).

These results confirm that hypothetical demand curves are sensitive to modulating variables such as the potential disincentive of attending an academic class after the consumption of the commodity, here alcoholic drinks. From a policy perspective, this opens the possibility of investigating a range of public policy variables that might involve the combination of price and contextual incentives and disincentives.

Conclusions

At its heart, behavioral economics attempts to apply concepts developed by micro-economists studying human economic markets, such as consumer demand and labor supply theories, to understand how the behavior of individual organisms is maintained by various commodities. This theoretical framework has proven useful for understanding the environmental control of overall levels of behavior for a variety of reinforcing "commodities" in the laboratory, including self-administered drugs in animals and humans. One of the most important contributions of behavioral economics has been to direct attention to total daily consumption as a primary dependent measure. Changes in consumption in relation to the prevailing price—elasticity of demand—is a key indicator of consumer motivation and serves to define the "essential value" of commodities. Essential value, then, is a useful metric to categorize differences between commodities, differences between individuals toward similar commodities, and differences in the value of commodities across different contexts of available alternatives and disincentives (see Oliveira-Castro, Foxall, Yan, & Wells, 2011). The overarching value of this framework is an ability to understand behavioral tendencies that are quantitatively precise at the level of individual organisms and scalable to understanding factors that control the motivation of many individuals within an entire community. Behavioral economics makes the science of behavior a practical evidentiary foundation for decision-making and is a common language for translational research in support of empirical public policy (Magoon & Hursh, 2011).

Notes

1 The exact value of P_{max} varies slightly with the value of k so that a closer approximation is achieved by correcting eq (2) with an adjustment for the value of k: $P_{max} = m/(Q_0 \cdot \alpha \cdot k^{1.5})$, where $m = 0.083k + 0.65$.

2 If both the prices of commodity B and commodity A are changing, then Equation 3 can be expanded by replacing the $\log(Q_{alone})$ term for commodity B consumption at a fixed price with Equation 1 for commodity B consumption with variable price. This expanded form provides an economic foundation for determining choice ratios as the ratio of several such expanded demand equations, a topic beyond the scope of this chapter.

References

Ahmed, S. H., & Koob, G. F. (1998). Transition from moderate to excessive drug intake: Change in hedonic set point. *Science, 282*, 298–301.

Allison, J. (1983). *Behavioral Economics*. New York: Praeger.

Allison, J., Miller, M., & Wozny, M. (1979). Conservation in behavior. *Journal of Experimental Psychology: General, 108*, 4–34.

Banks, M. L., Roma, P. G., Folk, J. E., Rice, K. C., & Negus, S. S. (2011). Effects of the delta-opioid agonist SNC80 on the abuse liability of methadone in rhesus monkeys: A behavioral-economic analysis. *Psychopharmacology, 216*, 431–439.

Bauman, R. (1991). An experimental analysis of the cost of food in a closed economy. *Journal of the Experimental Analysis of Behavior, 56*, 33–50.

Bickel, W. K., DeGrandpre, R. J., & Higgins, S. T. (1993). Behavioral economics: A novel experimental approach to the study of drug dependence. *Drug and Alcohol Dependence, 33*, 173–192.

Bickel, W. K., DeGrandpre, R. J., Higgins, S. T., & Hughes, J. R. (1990). Behavioral economics of drug self-administration. I. Functional equivalence of response requirement and drug dose. *Life Sciences, 47*, 1501–1510.

Bickel, W. K., DeGrandpre, R. J., Hughes, J. R., & Higgins, S. T., (1991). Behavioral economics of drug self-administration. II. A unit-price analysis of cigarette smoking. *Journal of the Experimental Analysis of Behavior, 55*, 145–154.

Bickel, W. K., Madden, G. J., & DeGrandpre, R. J. (1997). Modeling the effects of combined behavioral and pharmacological treatment on cigarette smoking: Behavioral-economic analyses. *Experimental and Clinical Psychopharmacology, 5*, 334–343.

Bidwell, L. C., Mackillop, J., Murphy, J. G., Tidey, J. W., & Colby, S. M. (2012). Latent factor structure of a behavioral economic cigarette demand curve in adolescent smokers. *Addictive Behaviors, 37*, 1257–1263.

Carroll, M. E. (1993).The economic context of drug and non-drug reinforcers affects acquisition and maintenance of drug-reinforced behavior and withdrawal effects. *Drug and Alcohol Dependence, 33*, 201–210.

Christensen, C. J., Silberberg, A., Hursh, S. R., Roma, P. G., & Riley, A. L. (2008). Demand for cocaine and food over time. *Pharmacology, Biochemistry and Behavior, 91*, 209–216.

Collier, G. H. (1983). Life in a closed economy: The ecology of learning and motivation. In M. D. Zeiler & P. Harzem (Eds.), *Advances in analysis of behaviour: Vol. 3. biological factors in learning* (pp. 223–274). Chichester, UK: John Wiley & Sons, Ltd.

Collier, G. H., Johnson, D. F., Hill, W. L., & Kaufman, L. W. (1986). The economics of the law of effect. *Journal of the Experimental Analysis of Behavior, 46*, 113–136.

Davison, M., & McCarthy, D. (Eds.). (1988). *The matching law: A research review*. Hillsdale, NJ: Erlbaum.

Foltin, R. W. (1992). Economic analysis of the effects of caloric alternatives and reinforcer magnitude on "demand" for food in baboons. *Appetite, 19*, 255–271.

Foster, M., Blackman, K., & Temple, W. (1997). Open versus closed economies: performance of domestic hens under fixed-ratio schedules. *Journal of the Experimental Analysis of Behavior, 67*, 67–89.

Foxall, G. R., & Sigurdsson, V. (2011). Drug use as consumer behavior. *Behavioral and Brain Sciences, 34*, 313–314.

Gentile, N. D., Librizzi, E. H., Martinetti, M. P. (2012). Academic constraints on alcohol consumption in college students: A behavioral economic analysis. *Experimental and Clinical Psychopharmacology, 20*, 390–399.

Grace R., Schwendiman J., & Nevin J., (1998). Effects of unsignaled delay of reinforcement on preference and resistance to change. *Journal of the Experimental Analysis of Behavior, 69*, 247–261.

Green, L., & Freed, D. E. (1993). The substitutability of reinforcers. *Journal of the Experimental Analysis of Behavior, 60*, 141–158.

Green, L., & Freed, D. E. (1998). Behavioral economics. In W. O'Donohue (Ed.), *Learning and behavior therapy* (pp. 274–300). Boston: Allyn & Bacon.

Green, L., & Rachlin, H. (1991). Economic substitutability of electrical brain stimulation, food, and water. *Journal of the Experimental Analysis of Behavior, 55*, 133–143.

Greenwald, M. K. (2010). Effects of experimental unemployment, employment and punishment analogs on opioid seeking and consumption in heroin-dependent volunteers. *Drug and Alcohol Dependence, 111*, 64–73.

Griffiths, R. R., Bigelow, G. E., & Henningfield, J. E. (1980). Similarities in animal and human drug-taking behavior. In N. K. Mello (Ed.), *Advances in substance abuse* (Vol. 1, pp. 1–90). Greenwich, CT: JAI Press.

Griffiths, R. R., Bradford, L. D., & Brady, J. V. (1979). Progressive ratio and fixed ratio schedules of cocaine-maintained responding in baboons. *Psychopharmacology (Berl), 65*, 125–136.

Hall, G. A., & Lattal, K. A. (1990). Variable-interval schedule performance in open and closed economies. *Journal of the Experimental Analysis of Behavior, 54*, 13–22.

Harrigan, S. E., & Downs, D. A. (1978). Continuous intravenous naltrexone effects on morphine self-administration in rhesus monkeys. *Journal of Pharmacology and Experimental Therapeutics, 204*, 481–486.

Herrnstein, R. J. (1958). Some factors influencing behavior in a two-response situation. *Transactions of the New York Academy of Sciences, 21*, 35–45.

Herrnstein, R. J. (1961). Relative and absolute strength of response as a function of frequency of reinforcement. *Journal of the Experimental Analysis of Behavior, 4*, 267–272.

Herrnstein, R. J. (1970). On the law of effect. *Journal of the Experimental Analysis of Behavior, 13*, 243–266.

Herrnstein, R. J., & Loveland, D. H. (1975). Maximizing and matching on concurrent ratio schedules. *Journal of the Experimental Analysis of Behavior, 24*, 107–116.

Herrnstein, R. J., & Prelec, D. (1992). A theory of addiction. In G. Loewenstein & J. Elster (Eds.), *Choice over time* (pp. 331–360). New York: Russell Sage Foundation.

Hunt, D. E., Lipton, D. S., Goldsmith, D. S., & Strug, D. L. (1984). Problems in methadone treatment: The influence of reference groups. *NIDA Research Monographs, 46*, 8–22.

Hursh, S. R. (1978). The economics of daily consumption controlling food- and water-reinforced responding. *Journal of the Experimental Analysis of Behavior, 29*, 475–491.

Hursh, S. R. (1980). Economic concepts for the analysis of behavior. *Journal of the Experimental Analysis of Behavior, 34*, 219–238.

Hursh, S. R. (1984). Behavioral economics. *Journal of the Experimental Analysis of Behavior, 42*, 435–452.

Hursh, S. R. (1991). Behavioral economics of drug self-administration and drug abuse policy. *Journal of the Experimental Analysis of Behavior, 56*, 377–393.

Hursh, S. R. (1993). Behavioral economics of drug self-administration: An introduction. *Drug and Alcohol Dependence, 33*, 165–172.

Hursh, S. R., & Bauman, R. A. (1987). The behavioral analysis of demand. In L. Green & J. H. Kagel (Eds.), *Advances in behavioral economics* (Vol. 1, pp. 117–165). Norwood, NJ: Ablex.

Hursh, S. R., & Fantino, E. (1973). Relative delay of reinforcement and choice, *Journal of the Experimental Analysis of Behavior, 19*, 437–450.

Hursh, S. R., & Natelson, B. H. (1981). Electrical brain stimulation and food reinforcement dissociated by demand elasticity. *Physiology & Behavior, 26*, 509–515.

Hursh, S. R., Raslear, T. G., Bauman, R., and Black, H. (1989). The quantitative analysis of economic behavior with laboratory animals. In K. G. Grunert and F. Ölander (Eds.), *Understanding economic behavior*. Dordrecht: Kluwer.

Hursh, S. R., Raslear, T. G., Shurtleff, D., Bauman, R., & Simmons, L. (1988). A cost-benefit analysis of demand for food. *Journal of the Experimental Analysis of Behavior, 50*, 419–440.

Hursh, S. R., & Roma, P. G. (2013). Behavioral economics and empirical public policy. *Journal of the Experimental Analysis of Behavior, 99*, 98–124.

Hursh, S. R., & Silberberg, A. (2008). Economic demand and essential value. *Psychological Review, 115*, 186–198.

Hursh, S. R., & Winger, G. (1995). Normalized demand for drugs and other reinforcers. *Journal of the Experimental Analysis of Behavior, 64*, 373–384.

Johanson, C. E. (1978). Drugs as reinforcers. In D. E. Blackman & D. J. Sanger (Eds.), *Contemporary research in behavioral pharmacology* (pp. 325–390). New York: Plenum Press.

Kagel, J. H., Battalio, R. C., & Green, L. (1995). *Economic choice theory: An experimental analysis of animal behavior*. Cambridge: Cambridge University Press.

Kagel, J. H., Battalio, R. C., Rachlin, H., Green, L., Basmann, R. L., & Klemm, W. R. (1975). Experimental studies of consumer demand behavior using laboratory animals, *Economic Inquiry, 13*, 22–38.

Kahneman, D., Slovic, P., & Tversky, A. (1982). *Judgment under uncertainty: Heuristics and biases*. New York: Cambridge University Press.

Koob, G. F., & Le Moal, M. (2001). Drug addiction, dysregulation of reward, and allostasis. *Neuropsychopharmacology, 24*, 97–129.

LaFiette, M. H., & Fantino, E. (1989). Responding on concurrent-chains schedules in open and closed economies. *Journal of the Experimental Analysis of Behavior, 51*, 329–342.

Lea, S. E. G. (1978). The psychology and economics of demand. *Psychological Bulletin, 85*, 441–466.

Lea, S. E. G., & Roper, T. J. (1977). Demand for food on fixed-ratio schedules as a function of the quality of concurrently available reinforcement. *Journal of the Experimental Analysis of Behavior, 27*, 371–380.

Lucas, G. A. (1981). Some effects of reinforce availability on the pigeon's responding in 24-hour sessions. *Animal Learning & Behavior, 9*, 411–424.

MacKillop, J., Few, L. R., Murphy, J. G., Wier, L. M., Acker, J., Murphy, C., Stojek, M., Carrigan, M., & Chaloupka, F. (2012). High-resolution behavioral economic analysis of cigarette demand to inform tax policy. *Addiction, 107*, 2191–2200.

MacKillop, J., Murphy, J. G., Ray, L. A., Eisenberg, D. T., Lisman, S. A., Lum, J. K, & Wilson, D. S. (2008). Further validation of a cigarette purchase task for assessing the relative reinforcing efficacy of nicotine in college smokers. *Experimental and Clinical Psychopharmacology, 16*, 57–65.

Madden, G. J., & Kalman, D. (2010). Effects of bupropion on simulated demand for cigarettes and the subjective effects of smoking. *Nicotine and Tobacco Research, 12*, 416–422.

Magoon, M., & Hursh, S. R. (2011). *The behavioral economics of transportation travel time, mode choice and carbon impact*. Presented at the 5th annual Behavior, Energy and Climate Change Conference (BECC). Washington, DC.

Matto, H. C. (2004). Applying an ecological framework to understanding drug addiction and recovery. *Journal of Social Work Practice in the Addictions, 4*, 5–22.

Mazur, J. E. (1985). Probability and delay of reinforcement as factors in discrete-trial choice. *Journal of the Experimental Analysis of Behavior, 43*, 341–351.

Mazur, J. E., Snyderman, M., & Coe, D. (1985). Influences of delay and rate of reinforcement on discrete-trial choice. *Journal of Experimental Psychology: Animal Behavior Processes, 11*, 565–575.

McLellan, A. T., Lewis, D. C., O'Brien, C. P., & Kleber, H. D. (2000). Drug dependence, a chronic medical illness, *Journal of the American Medical Association, 284*, 1689–1695.

Murphy, J. G., & MacKillop, J. (2006). Relative reinforcing efficacy of alcohol among college student drinkers. *Experimental and Clinical Psychopharmacology, 14*, 219–227.

Nicol, C. J. (2003). Elasticities of demand for gasoline in Canada and the United States. *Energy Economics, 25*, 201–214.

Peden, B. F., & Timberlake, W. (1984). Effects of reward magnitude on key pecking and eating by pigeons in a closed economy. *The Psychological Record, 34*, 397–415.

Oliveira-Castro, J. M., Foxall, G. R., Yan, J., & Wells, V. K. (2011). A behavioral-economic analysis of the essential value of brands. *Behavioural Processes, 87*, 106–114.

Rachlin, H., Green, L., Kagel, J. H., & Battalio, R. C. (1976). Economic demand theory and psychological studies of choice. In G. Bower (Ed.), *The psychology of learning and motivation* (Vol.10, pp. 129–154). New York: Academic Press.

Rachlin, H., & Laibson, D. (1997). *The matching law: Papers on psychology and economics by Richard Herrnstein.* Cambridge, MA: Harvard University Press.

Rashotte, M. E., & Henderson, D. (1988). Coping with rising food costs in a closed economy: Feeding behavior and nocturnal hypothermia in pigeons. *Journal of the Experimental Analysis of Behavior, 50*, 441–456.

Raslear, T. G., Bauman, R. A., Hursh, S. R., Shurtleff, D., & Simmons, L. (1988). Rapid demand curves for behavioral economics. *Animal Learning & Behavior, 16*, 330–339.

Roane, H. S., Call, N. A., & Falcomata, T. S. (2005). A preliminary analysis of adaptive responding under open and closed economies. *Journal of the Experimental Analysis of Behavior, 38*, 335–348.

Roddy, J., Steinmiller, C. L., & Greenwald, M. K. (2011). Heroin purchasing is income and price sensitive. *Psychology of Addictive Behaviors, 25*, 358–364.

Roma, P. G., Henningfield, J. E., Hursh, S. R., Cone, E. J., Buchhalter, A. R., Fant, R. V., & Schnoll, S. H. (2013, June). *Applied behavioral economics for evaluating potential labeling claims of abuse-deterrent opioids: A pilot study.* Paper presented at the annual meeting of the International Study Group Investigating Drugs as Reinforcers, San Diego, CA.

Spiga, R., Martinetti, M. P., Meisch, R. A., Cowan, K., & Hursh, S. (2005). Methadone and nicotine self-administration in humans: A behavioral economic analysis. *Psychopharmacology (Berl), 178*, 223–231.

Spiga, R., Wilson, K., & Martinetti, M. P. (in press). Human drug self-administration: An exponential analysis of nicotine and ethanol interactions.

Skinner, B. F. (1953). *Science and human behavior.* New York: Macmillan.

Staddon, J. E. R. (1979). Operant behavior as adaptation to constraint. *Journal of Experimental Psychology: General, 108*, 48–67.

Stitzer, M. L., Grabowski, J., & Henningfield, J. E. (1984). Behavioral intervention techniques in drug abuse treatment: Summary of discussion. *NIDA Research Monographs, 46*, 147–157.

Tarpy, R. M., & Sawabini, F. L. (1974). Reinforcement delay: A selective review of the last decade. *Psychological Bulletin, 81*, 984–997.

Thaler, R. H., & Mullainathan, S. (2008). Behavioral economics. *The Concise Encyclopedia of Economics.* Library of Economics and Liberty. Retrieved January 8, 2014 from http://www.econlib.org/library/Enc/BehavioralEconomics.html.

Thompson, T., Koerner, J., & Grabowski, J. (1984). Brokerage model rehabilitation system for opiate dependence: A behavioral analysis. *NIDA Research Monographs, 46*, 131–146.

Vuchinich, R. E. & Heather, N. (2003). *Choice, behavioural economics and addiction.* Oxford: Elsevier.

Watson, D. S., & Holman, M. A. (1977). *Price theory and its uses* (4th ed.). Boston: Houghton Mifflin.

Winger, G., Hursh, S. R., Casey, K. L., & Woods, J. H. (2002). Relative reinforcing strength of three N-methyl-D-aspartate antagonists with different onsets of action. *Journal of Pharmacology and Experimental Therapeutics, 301*, 690–697.

Wikler, A. (1977). The search for the psyche in drug dependence. A 35-year retrospective survey. *Journal of Mental Disorders, 165*, 29–40.

Wikler, A. (1980). *Opioid dependence: Mechanisms and treatment* (pp. 167–218). New York: Plenum Press.

Woolverton, W. L., & Anderson, K. G. (2006), Effects of delay to reinforcement on the choice between cocaine and food in rhesus monkeys, *Psychopharmacology, 186*, 99–106.

Zeiler, M. (1999). Reversed effects in closed and open economies. *Journal of the Experimental Analysis of Behavior, 71*, 171–186.

13

Delay and Probability Discounting

Leonard Green, Joel Myerson, and Ariana Vanderveldt

Many of our everyday decisions involve tradeoffs. For example, we frequently encounter situations in which we have to choose between something that we really like but which we would have to wait for, and something else that is not quite so desirable but which is available immediately. So, too, we often have to choose between taking a chance on getting something we really want and being certain of getting something that is not quite as desirable. Such choices involve tradeoffs between the amount or quality of a reward and its immediacy or certainty. Interestingly, people often do not choose the larger, more desirable option if it is more delayed or uncertain. In such cases, it is said that they "discounted" the value of the delayed or probabilistic option, as if delay or uncertainty decreased the subjective value of an otherwise more desirable alternative. *Delay discounting* may be defined as the decrease in the subjective value of an outcome as the time until its occurrence increases, whereas *probability discounting* may be defined as the decrease in subjective value as the likelihood of an outcome decreases (Rachlin, 2006; Rachlin, Raineri, & Cross, 1991).

In addition to its role in everyday decision making, discounting may be a factor in various problem behaviors. For example, some researchers have argued that discounting is at the heart of impulse control problems such as substance abuse. That is, the choice of whether to take a drug may be viewed as a choice between a smaller, but immediate reward and the much greater, but also much more delayed, consequences of alternative behaviors. In large part because substance abusers typically show steeper delay discounting than controls (i.e., they devalue delayed rewards to a greater extent), it has been suggested that delay discounting measures impulsivity (e.g., Bickel & Marsch, 2001). In keeping with this view, choosing the smaller,

The Wiley Blackwell Handbook of Operant and Classical Conditioning, First Edition.
Edited by Frances K. McSweeney and Eric S. Murphy.

immediate outcome is often thought of as the impulsive choice, whereas choosing the larger, delayed outcome is often thought of as reflecting self-control.

As with delay discounting, probability discounting also has been interpreted as a measure of impulsivity (e.g., Yi, Mitchell, & Bickel, 2010). In this case, those who choose the smaller, certain reward may be viewed as more risk-averse, whereas those who choose the larger, probabilistic reward are being more impulsive, in the sense of being more risk-taking. As we will show, however, the relation between discounting and impulsivity appears to be far more nuanced than was previously thought.

We begin with a presentation of the theoretical framework that has emerged from research on delay and probability discounting. Next, we summarize findings regarding the discounting of delayed rewards and the discounting of probabilistic rewards from the perspective of this framework, and we discuss the similarities and differences between these two types of discounting when the outcomes are positive (i.e., rewards or gains). This is followed by consideration of the discounting of delayed and probabilistic losses, and the similarities and differences between the discounting of losses and the discounting of gains. We then review the relevant literature on discounting by nonhuman animals and similarities and differences with the human literature. We consider the implications of current findings for our understanding of the processes and traits that underlie discounting and present evidence for multiple "impulsivities." Finally, we discuss the future of discounting research, including the emerging field of social discounting and the neuroeconomic approach to decision making.

The Discounting Framework

Research on discounting has focused on the tradeoffs that individuals make when choosing between "packages" that have at least two aspects or dimensions. Most typically in such research, the packages have had the dimensions of amount of reward and duration of the delay. For example, a participant in a delay discounting experiment might be asked to choose between two packages, one corresponding to $25 now and the other corresponding to $75 in six months. It is assumed that the package chosen is the one of greater value to the participant. In an experiment like the one just described, researchers often manipulate the amount of the immediate reward to find out what amount makes it equally likely that the participant will choose either package. This amount may be termed the present equivalent value of the package corresponding to the delayed reward.

Similarly, a participant in a probability discounting experiment might be asked to choose between $25 for sure and a 50% chance of $75. In such an experiment, researchers also usually manipulate the amount of the certain reward to find out what amount makes it equally likely that the participant will choose either package, and in this case, that amount may be termed the certain equivalent value of the package that corresponds to the probabilistic reward. Following Rachlin et al. (1991), both the certain equivalent value of a probabilistic reward and the present equivalent value of a delayed reward are termed the subjective value of the corresponding package, a term that is meant simply to distinguish the value the participant places on a package (i.e., its certain or present equivalent) from the amount of the reward (e.g., $75) that is part of that package.

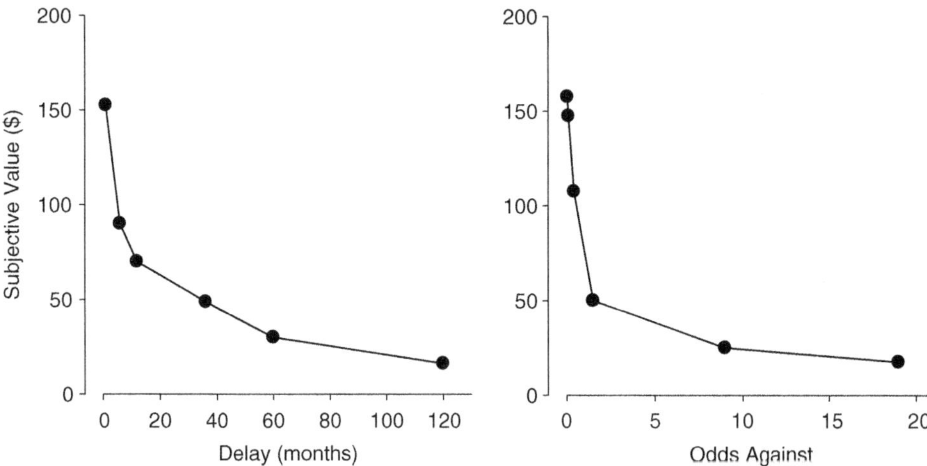

Figure 13.1 Subjective value of a \$200 reward plotted as a function of the time until its receipt (left panel) and the odds against its receipt (right panel). Data are from Experiment 2 of "Amount of reward has opposite effects on the discounting of delayed and probabilistic outcomes," by L. Green, J. Myerson, and P. Ostaszewski (1999), *Journal of Experimental Psychology: Learning, Memory, and Cognition, 25*, p. 423.

Discounting Functions

Typically, a discounting experiment will estimate the subjective values of a series of packages, each of which contains the same reward amount but in which the delay until or the probability of that reward is systematically varied. Typical data from such experiments may be seen in Figure 13.1: The left panel shows the subjective value of a \$200 reward plotted as a function of the time until its receipt, and the right panel shows the subjective value of a \$200 reward plotted as a function of the odds against its receipt. In each panel, the subjective values map out a discounting function that describes the decrease in subjective value as a function of the packages' other dimension, either delay (left panel) or probability (right panel).

Both delay and probability discounting functions have been shown to be well described by a hyperboloid model,

$$V = A/(1 + bX)^s, \tag{1}$$

where V is the subjective value of a delayed or probabilistic reward, A is the amount of that reward, and X is either the delay until a reward in the case of delay discounting or the odds against its receipt in the case of probability discounting. Note that the odds against receipt of a reward equals $(1-p)/p$, where p is the probability of reward. The hyperboloid model has two free parameters: the parameter b, which reflects the degree of discounting (with higher values of b being associated with steeper discounting), and the parameter s, which determines the shape of the discounting function.

The hyperboloid model may be contrasted with two other well-known models that have been proposed for the delay discounting function. One of these is the simple hyperbola (Ainslie, 1975, 1992; Mazur, 1987), which is actually a special case of the hyperboloid, corresponding to Equation 1 when $s = 1.0$. Another prominent form of discounting function, one that traditionally has been favored by economists, is an exponential function:

$$V = Ae^{-bX}, \tag{2}$$

in which b again reflects the discounting rate. Numerous studies have compared the fits of these three functions to discounting data, and almost invariably, the exponential function provides the poorest fit (e.g., Mazur & Biondi, 2009; Rachlin et al., 1991; Rodriguez & Logue, 1988). In cases where the fits of the hyperbola and hyperboloid differ, the hyperboloid always provides the better fit, often even after controlling for the fact that it has an additional free parameter (e.g., McKerchar et al., 2009; Myerson & Green, 1995). Fits of the three models to the same delay discounting data may be seen in Figure 13.2.

The hyperboloid model also may be contrasted with two other models of the probability discounting function. Again, one of these is the simple hyperbola (Rachlin et al., 1991); the other is the formula for expected value, which is simply the product of amount and probability. For purposes of direct comparison with the other two models, the expected value model may be rewritten in terms of odds against:

$$V = A[1/(1 + X)], \tag{3}$$

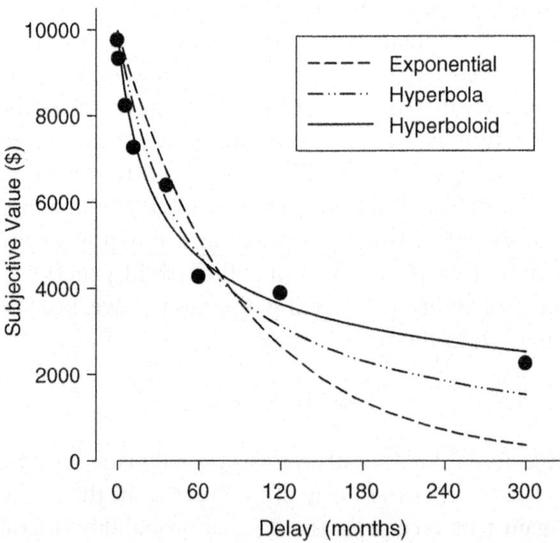

Figure 13.2 Subjective value of a delayed $10,000 reward plotted as a function of the time until its receipt. The curved lines represent fits of the exponential, hyperbolic, and hyperboloid functions to the data. Data are from "Discounting of delayed rewards: A life-span comparison," by L. Green, A. F. Fry, and J. Myerson (1994), *Psychological Science, 5*, p. 35. The figure is adapted from "A discounting framework for choice with delayed and probabilistic rewards," by L. Green and J. Myerson (2004), *Psychological Bulletin, 130*, p. 773. Copyright 2004 by the American Psychological Association.

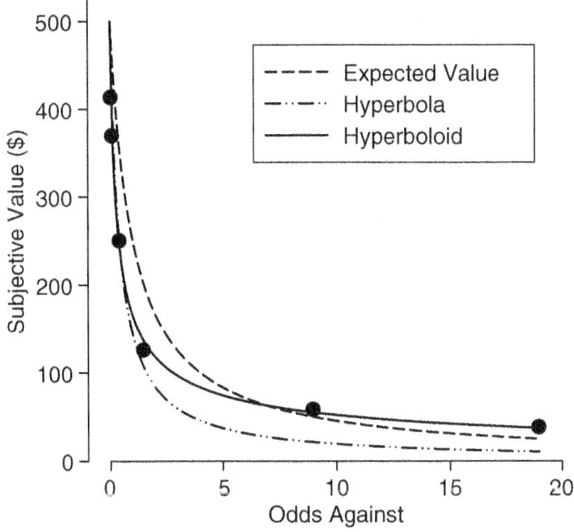

Figure 13.3 Subjective value of a probabilistic $500 reward plotted as a function of the odds against its receipt. The curved lines represent the fits of the hyperbolic and hyperboloid functions to the data as well as the expected value of the probabilistic reward. Data are from Experiment 1 of "Amount of reward has opposite effects on the discounting of delayed and probabilistic outcomes," by L. Green, J. Myerson, and P. Ostaszewski (1999), *Journal of Experimental Psychology: Learning, Memory, and Cognition, 25*, p. 421. The figure is adapted from "A discounting framework for choice with delayed and probabilistic rewards," by L. Green and J. Myerson (2004), *Psychological Bulletin, 130*, p. 779. Copyright 2004 by the American Psychological Association.

where X is again the odds against receiving a reward, and $[1/(1 + X)] = p$. It should be noted that Equation 3 is the special case of the simple hyperbola in which $b = 1.0$. These three models are contrasted in Figure 13.3, which shows them fitted to the same probability discounting data. Notably, the hyperboloid model provides a significantly better fit even after controlling for the difference in the number of free parameters (e.g., McKerchar et al., 2009).

The fact that the hyperboloid function provides a very good description of both delay and probability discounting data provides the basis for a discounting framework that allows for unconfounded comparisons of these two types of discounting. Using analogous procedures to estimate subjective value and fitting both delay and probability discounting data to the same hyperboloid function are both essential to this enterprise. If analogous procedures and analytic approaches are not used, then any differences that are observed are difficult to interpret. This is because any divergence in the results could be due to the differences in either the procedure or the approach rather than being a reflection of a true difference in the decision-making processes underlying delay and probability discounting.

In subsequent sections, in addition to using the discounting framework to contrast delay and probability discounting, we also use the framework to compare discounting of gains and losses, both delayed and probabilistic. Finally, we would note that the framework and its underlying logic apply to comparisons involving different kinds of outcomes (e.g., monetary rewards, health changes) and, in principle, to other types of discounting (e.g., social and effort discounting), as well.

Estimating Subjective Value

The establishment of a discounting function depends upon the validity and reliability of the estimates of subjective value. Several types of experimental procedures have been used to assess how delay and probability affect the subjective value of an outcome. For simplicity, we focus here on procedures used to study the discounting of delayed rewards, but it should be noted that similar procedures have been used to study delayed losses as well as to study the discounting of probabilistic outcomes. The relative advantages and disadvantages of various delay discounting procedures used with both humans and other animals are discussed by Madden and Johnson (2010).

Most of the procedures used to estimate the subjective value of a reward have a similar structure. Participants typically make a series of choices between a smaller and a larger reward, with the smaller reward available immediately or after a short delay, and the larger reward available after a longer delay. One aspect of the outcomes is varied (e.g., the amount of the smaller reward) until a point is reached at which the participant is indifferent between (i.e., equally likely to choose) the smaller, sooner reward and the larger, later reward. The amount of the smaller, sooner reward at this indifference point is taken to be the subjective (i.e., present) value of the larger, delayed reward. The procedure then is repeated varying another aspect of the outcomes (e.g., the delay to the larger reward). The resulting indifference points, when plotted as a function of delay, reveal a decreasing, decelerating curve describing the effect of delay on subjective value (see Figure 13.1).

Several variations of this basic discounting task have been used. Mazur (1987) introduced the first procedure for establishing indifference points. In his procedure, originally developed for use with pigeons, the amounts of the smaller and larger rewards are held constant, and the delay to the larger one is adjusted until indifference is observed. These adjustments are continued until each alternative is chosen approximately 50% of the time. The Mazur adjusting-delay procedure, in essence, begins with an estimate of subjective value (i.e., with an amount of smaller, sooner reward) and then determines the duration of the delay to the larger reward at which the larger reward has that value. This task was later adapted for use with humans by Rodriguez and Logue (1988).

Rather than adjusting the delay to the larger reward to obtain a specified subjective value, Rachlin et al. (1991) developed an adjusting-amount procedure in which the delay and the larger amount are held constant, and the smaller amount is adjusted until participants switch their preference from the smaller, immediate reward to the larger, delayed reward or vice versa. As Rachlin et al. noted, their procedure was borrowed from psychophysics, and indeed, the study of discounting may be viewed as a kind of psychophysics of reward value.

From this perspective, the original Rachlin et al. (1991) procedure is like the method of limits (D'Amato, 1970; Kantowitz, Roediger, & Elmes, 2009) in which one starts with a stimulus well above (or below) threshold, and decreases (or increases) the magnitude of the stimulus until threshold is reached. In contrast, the original

Mazur (1987) procedure is like a psychophysical staircase procedure in which the stimulus presented on a specific trial is determined by a participant's responses on previous trials. We would note, however, that the linkage between the type of psychophysical procedure (e.g., method of limits vs. staircase) and the choice of which variable to vary (e.g., immediate amount vs. delay to the larger reward) is arbitrary. For example, Du, Green, and Myerson (2002) developed a staircase adjusting-amount procedure in which the amount of immediate reward was adjusted based on participants' previous choices.

Kirby and Maraković (1996) introduced a brief pencil-and-paper test, the Monetary Choice Questionnaire (MCQ), to estimate indifference points. Each test item presents a choice that corresponds to a specific value of the discounting rate parameter, b, in a simple hyperbola (e.g., Equation 1 with $s = 1.0$) when the two rewards are equal in subjective value. Note that the k associated with indifference between a given immediate reward amount and a given amount of reward available after a specific delay may be obtained by rearranging the terms of the simple hyperbola: $k = [(A/V) - 1]/D$.

The pattern of an individual's choices between immediate and delayed rewards on the MCQ provides an estimate of that individual's discounting rate. For example, indifference between \$27 now and \$50 in 21 days corresponds to a discounting rate parameter of approximately 0.04 (Kirby, Petry, & Bickel, 1999). Therefore, if an individual were to choose the immediate \$27 reward, that individual's discounting rate parameter would be assumed to be greater than 0.04. If, on a subsequent item, given the choice between \$33 now and \$80 in 14 days (for which indifference corresponds to a discounting rate of 0.10), the individual chose the larger, later reward, then this would suggest that the individual's rate parameter is greater than 0.04 but less than 0.10.

Holt, Green, and Myerson (2012) compared the adjusting-delay procedure and two adjusting-amount procedures, one in which the immediate amount was adjusted (Du et al., 2002) and another in which the delayed amount was adjusted, and found that the different procedures yielded qualitatively similar patterns of results: Larger delayed rewards were discounted less steeply than smaller ones on all three procedures, and a hyperboloid function described discounting on both the adjusting-immediate-amount and adjusting-delay procedures. The third, adjusting-delayed-amount procedure, which is often used in neuroeconomics (e.g., Kable & Glimcher, 2007), has the drawback that it does not permit estimation of discounting functions unless one assumes, incorrectly, that the amount of the delayed reward does not affect the discounting rate.

Holt et al. (2012) did find that the adjusting-immediate-amount procedure yielded the most consistent estimates of the degree of discounting and that these estimates were unaffected by the order in which choices were presented. Although the exact degree of discounting may vary between procedures (e.g., Epstein et al., 2003), there appear to be no fundamental differences in the pattern of results obtained using various discounting procedures (Green, Myerson, Shah, Estle, & Holt, 2007; Lagorio & Madden, 2005; Robles & Vargas, 2007), and the steepness with which an individual discounts delayed rewards has been shown to be highly correlated across procedures (Holt et al., 2012; Kowal, Yi, Erisman, & Bickel, 2007; Rodzon, Berry, & Odum, 2011).

Measures of individual discounting are not only consistent across different procedures involving the same types of rewards, they also have been shown to be reliable and stable across test-retest intervals in both young adults (e.g., Kirby, 2009; Simpson & Vuchinich, 2000) as well as in older adults (Jimura et al., 2011). Indeed, a longitudinal study involving over 1,000 participants reported stability in discounting rates from age 15 through 20 and across three testing occasions (Audrain-McGovern et al., 2009). Having measures of discounting that are both reliable and stable is important both for addressing theoretical questions regarding the nature of tradeoffs in decision making and for addressing issues of applied significance, such as group differences and the effects of interventions on degree of discounting. Reliable, stable measures, moreover, are essential for addressing questions about individual differences, such as whether degree of discounting is a more trait-like or state-like phenomenon.

Discounting of Delayed Rewards

Although it is well established that a delayed reward is valued less than the same amount of reward available immediately, it also is clear that the rate at which an outcome is devalued differs across different reward amounts, different types reward, and different choice contexts.

Amount of Delayed Reward

One of the most robust and well-studied findings in the discounting literature is the effect of reward amount on delay discounting: Larger delayed rewards are discounted less steeply than smaller rewards. More specifically, the decrease in the *relative* subjective value of a large delayed reward (i.e., subjective value expressed as a proportion of its actual amount) is less than the decrease for a smaller delayed reward, a finding commonly referred to as the *magnitude effect* (Benzion, Rapoport, & Yagil, 1989; Green, Fry, & Myerson, 1994; Kirby, 1997; Raineri & Rachlin, 1993). For example, Raineri and Rachlin found that if the delay was one year, the subjective value of $100 was $58, a decrease in value of 42%, whereas the subjective value of $10,000 in one year was $7,500, a decrease of only 25% (see Figure 13.4). Green, Myerson, Oliveira, and Chang (2013) examined delay discounting over an extremely wide range of amounts (from $20 to $10 million) and found that the rate of discounting decreased as the delayed amount was increased up to $50,000, with little, if any, further decrease beyond that amount.

Hypothetical and Real Rewards

The majority of research on discounting has involved hypothetical monetary rewards, and one might wonder whether choices between hypothetical outcomes accurately represent everyday decisions involving real outcomes. To investigate this issue, Kirby and Maraković (1995) compared discounting of hypothetical and "potentially real" monetary rewards. That is, participants choosing between potentially real rewards were instructed that at the end of their experimental session, one of their choices

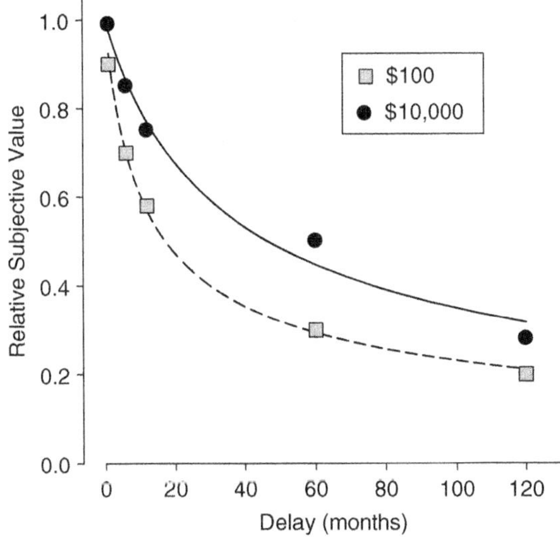

Figure 13.4 Relative subjective value of $100 and $10,000 rewards as a function of time until receipt. The curved lines represent the best-fitting hyperboloid functions. Data are from Experiment 2 of "The effect of temporal constraints on the value of money and other commodities," by A. Raineri and H. Rachlin (1993), *Journal of Behavioral Decision Making, 94*, p. 85.

would be randomly selected and they would actually receive that reward after the specified delay. Because they did not know which choice would be selected, it was assumed that participants would respond on every trial as if they were really to receive that outcome, and indeed, qualitatively similar patterns of discounting were observed with both hypothetical and potentially real rewards. Johnson and Bickel (2002) also had participants make choices involving both hypothetical and potentially real monetary rewards and found little difference in the rate at which the two types of rewards were discounted. Moreover, Johnson and Bickel varied the amount of delayed reward between $20 and $250, and reported similar magnitude effects with both types of reward.

In a series of experiments, Madden and colleagues (Lagorio & Madden, 2005; Madden, Begotka, Raiff, & Kastern, 2003; Madden et al., 2004) found that the lack of difference between the discounting of hypothetical and potentially real rewards persisted across various changes in experimental procedure, including one in which participants obtained money to buy real food rewards. In the real rewards condition of this experiment (Lagorio & Madden, 2005), participants made only one choice per day and had to purchase snack foods and beverages as soon as they obtained their reward (i.e., after they made their choice or when they returned on a subsequent day, depending on their choice between the immediate or delayed outcome). No systematic difference was observed in the degree to which participants discounted the real and hypothetical rewards. There also is evidence suggesting that discounting hypothetical and potentially real monetary rewards activates the same areas of the brain (Bickel, Pitcock, Yi, & Angtuaco, 2009), although there is evidence that real rewards activate these areas to a greater degree than hypothetical rewards (Kang, Rangel, Camus, & Camerer, 2011).

Nonmonetary Rewards

The hyperboloid discounting function describes the discounting of various types of rewards, both monetary and nonmonetary (Green & Myerson, 2004). The list of types of rewards whose discounting is well described by a hyperboloid is extensive, and includes such varied hypothetical outcomes as vacations (Raineri & Rachlin, 1993), alcohol, and food (Odum & Rainaud, 2003), social policy outcomes such as legalization of gay marriage (Weatherly, Plumm, & Derenne, 2011), and sexual and companionate relationship outcomes (Lawyer, 2008; Lawyer, Williams, Prihodova, Rollins, & Lester, 2010; Tayler, Arantes, & Grace, 2009). Moreover, the hyperboloid accurately describes data from substance abusers (e.g., heroin addicts and cigarette smokers) discounting hypothetical delayed receipt of their substance of abuse (Madden, Petry, Badger, & Bickel, 1997; Mitchell, 1999; for a review, see MacKillop et al., 2011). Real non-alcoholic, caffeine-free liquid rewards (e.g., apple juice) that participants actually received on each trial also have been shown to be discounted in a hyperboloid manner (Jimura, Myerson, Hilgard, Braver, & Green, 2009).

Although the same form of discounting function applies to various types of delayed reward, the degree of discounting appears to differ across types. In general, delayed monetary rewards are discounted less steeply than nonmonetary ones (see Figure 13.5, left panel). For example, using hypothetical outcomes, Raineri and Rachlin (1993) found that people discounted money less steeply than both vacation time and free use of a car, and Odum and Rainaud (2003) found that money was discounted

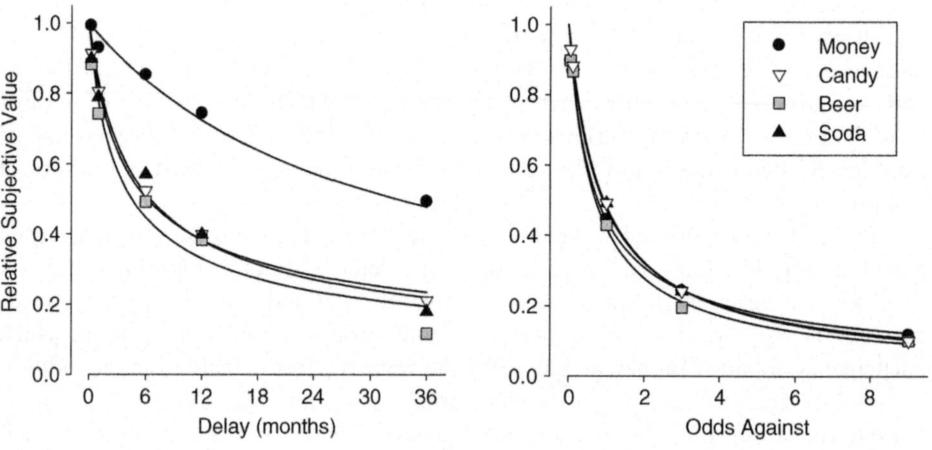

Figure 13.5 Relative subjective value of money and three directly consumable rewards as a function of time until receipt (left panel) and odds against receipt (right panel). Figure is adapted from "Discounting of monetary and directly consumable rewards," by S. J. Estle, L. Green, J. Myerson, and D. D. Holt, 2007, *Psychological Science, 18*, p. 60. Copyright 2007 by Sage Publications. Adapted with permission.

less steeply than either alcohol or food, whereas alcohol and food were discounted at similar rates. Similar results have been found when delayed money was compared with other consumable rewards such as beer, pizza, chips, candy, and soda (Estle, Green, Myerson, & Holt, 2007; Kirby & Guastello, 2001; Tsukayama & Duckworth, 2010).

Differences among some types of nonmonetary rewards have been reported. Charlton and Fantino (2008) observed that money was discounted less steeply than books, CDs, and DVDs, which all were discounted at similar rates, and that these all were discounted less steeply than food. Petry (2003) found that money was discounted more than freedom (defined as not going to jail), which in turn was discounted more than health. Real liquid rewards have been shown to be discounted the most steeply of all of the reward types studied with humans, losing half their value with delays as brief as one minute or less (Jimura et al., 2009).

It is important to note that when comparing the discounting of different types of rewards one must avoid confounding differences in reward type with differences in reward magnitude. This has often been done by equating the different rewards in terms of their dollar value. For example, Madden et al. (1997) had heroin addicts discount two types of delayed reward, $1,000 and one thousand dollars' worth of heroin. Chapman (1996) had participants match hypothetical health and money outcomes on their attractiveness, and then had them discount delayed outcomes whose equivalent utility had been established at the individual level. Importantly, differences in the rates at which different types of rewards are discounted are observed even when they are equated in terms of value.

Overall, these studies converge on two important findings. First, the discounting of delayed nonmonetary rewards, like the discounting of monetary rewards, is well described by a hyperboloid function, thereby extending the discounting framework to a wide variety of delayed outcomes. Second, there are important differences in rates of discounting across types of reward. These differences raise the possibility that there also are other kinds of differences between reward types with respect to discounting, a topic to which we return below (see "Impulsivity or Impulsivities?").

Discounting of Probabilistic Rewards

Just as delay discounting refers to the devaluing of a reward as a function of the time until its receipt, probability discounting correspondingly refers to the devaluing of a reward as a function of the likelihood of receipt. As the odds against receipt increase (i.e., the probability decreases), the subjective value of the reward decreases, and the hyperboloid discounting function describes the discounting of various types of probabilistic rewards, both monetary and nonmonetary (Green & Myerson, 2010).

As with delay discounting, research has examined the influence of reward amount on probability discounting. Contrary to what is observed with delayed rewards (i.e., larger amounts are discounted less steeply), larger amounts of probabilistic reward are discounted more steeply than smaller amounts (see Figure 13.6). The majority of research on probability discounting, like that on delay discounting, has focused on hypothetical monetary rewards. To date, only a handful of studies have compared hypothetical and real probabilistic outcomes, and the results have been somewhat

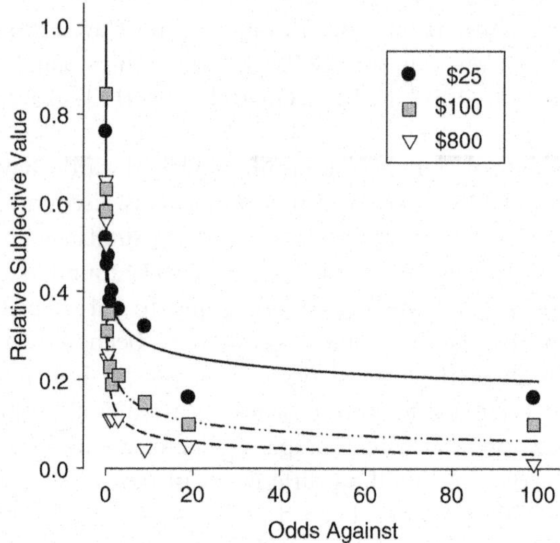

Figure 13.6 Relative subjective value of \$25, \$100, and \$800 rewards as a function of the odds against their receipt. Data are from "On the shape of the probability weighting function," by R. Gonzalez and G. Wu, 1999, *Cognitive Psychology, 130*, pp. 769–792. The figure is adapted from "Modeling the effect of reward amount on probability discounting," by J. Myerson, L. Green, and J. Morris (2011), *Journal of Experimental Analysis of Behavior, 95*, p. 182. Copyright 2011 by the Society for the Experimental Analysis of Behavior. Adapted with permission.

mixed and difficult to interpret due to order effects (Hinvest & Anderson, 2010; Jikko & Okouchi, 2007; Lawyer, Schoepflin, Green, & Jenks, 2011). What is clear, however, is that the hyperboloid discounting function describes the discounting of both hypothetical and real probabilistic monetary rewards (Lawyer et al., 2011).

The few studies that have examined discounting of nonmonetary probabilistic outcomes have found that the hyperboloid function also describes the discounting of diverse probabilistic rewards, including edible and drinkable items (Estle et al., 2007; Rasmussen, Lawyer, & Reilly, 2010), sexual outcomes (Lawyer et al., 2010), and individuals' preferred sedentary activities (Manwaring, Green, Myerson, Strube, & Wilfley, 2011). The Estle et al. study directly compared discounting rates across money and various types of consumable rewards (candy, soda, and beer), all approximately equal in monetary value to the monetary rewards. Estle et al. found that, unlike what they observed with delayed rewards, discounting rates did not differ between probabilistic money and consumable rewards (see Figure 13.5, right panel), but clearly more research with more varied types of rewards is needed before firm conclusions can be reached.

Comparison of Delay and Probability Discounting

Although the same hyperboloid function describes the discounting of delayed and probabilistic rewards, the effects of reward amount on delay and probability

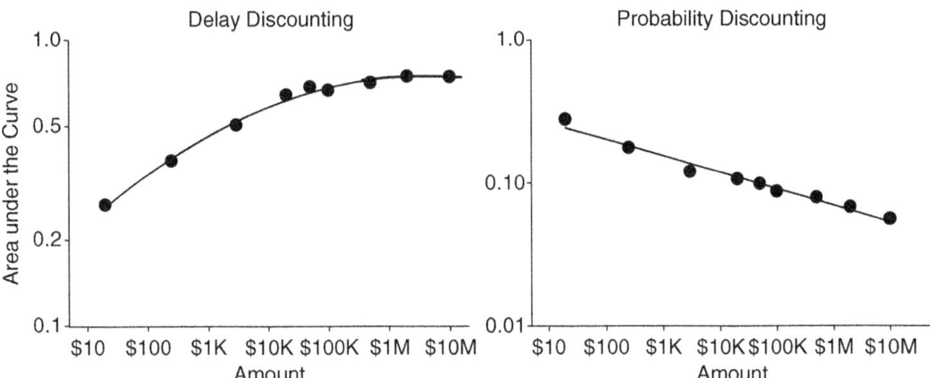

Figure 13.7 Area under the curve (AuC) as a function of amount for delay discounting (left panel) and probability discounting (right panel). Note that all axes are logarithmically scaled. AuCs are calculated based on group mean subjective values. The left panel is adapted from "Delay discounting of monetary rewards over a wide range of amounts," by L. Green, J. Myerson, L. Oliveira, and S. Chang, (2013), *Journal of the Experimental Analysis of Behavior, 100*, p. 275. The right panel is adapted from "Modeling the effect of reward amount on probability discounting," by J. Myerson, L. Green, and J. Morris (2011), *Journal of Experimental Analysis of Behavior, 95*, p. 180. Copyright 2011 by the Society for the Experimental Analysis of Behavior. Adapted with permission.

discounting clearly differ. The question of the degree of parallelism between choices involving delayed rewards and choices involving probabilistic rewards has a long history in psychology, behavioral biology, and economics (Benzion et al., 1989; Green & Myerson, 1996; Quiggin & Horowitz, 1995; Rachlin et al., 1991). Prelec and Loewenstein (1991) pointed out that for a number of anomalies observed with choices involving delayed outcomes, there are analogous anomalies with choices involving probabilistic outcomes, where an anomaly represents an empirical violation of normative theories of economic decision making. For example, Prelec and Loewenstein argued that the fact that people overvalue immediate outcomes, an anomaly from the perspective of discounted utility (Koopmans, 1960), is analogous to people's overvaluing of certain outcomes, an anomaly from the perspective of expected utility theory (von Neumann & Morgenstern, 1953). Prelec and Loewenstein suggested that the observed parallelism implies that there may be common decision-making processes that underlie choices with both delayed and risky outcomes.

Despite the appearance of a single process, however, recent evidence suggests that delay and probability discounting involve at least some fundamentally different processes. Perhaps the most notable example of a difference between delay and probability discounting is the difference in the effects of reward amount. As mentioned earlier, larger delayed rewards are discounted less steeply than smaller delayed rewards, whereas larger probabilistic rewards are discounted more steeply than smaller probabilistic rewards. This may be seen in Figure 13.7, which shows area under the curve (AuC), a measure of the degree of discounting, plotted as a function of reward amount. The AuC is the numerical integral of the observed indifference points (normalized here as proportions of the actual amount and as proportions of the maximum

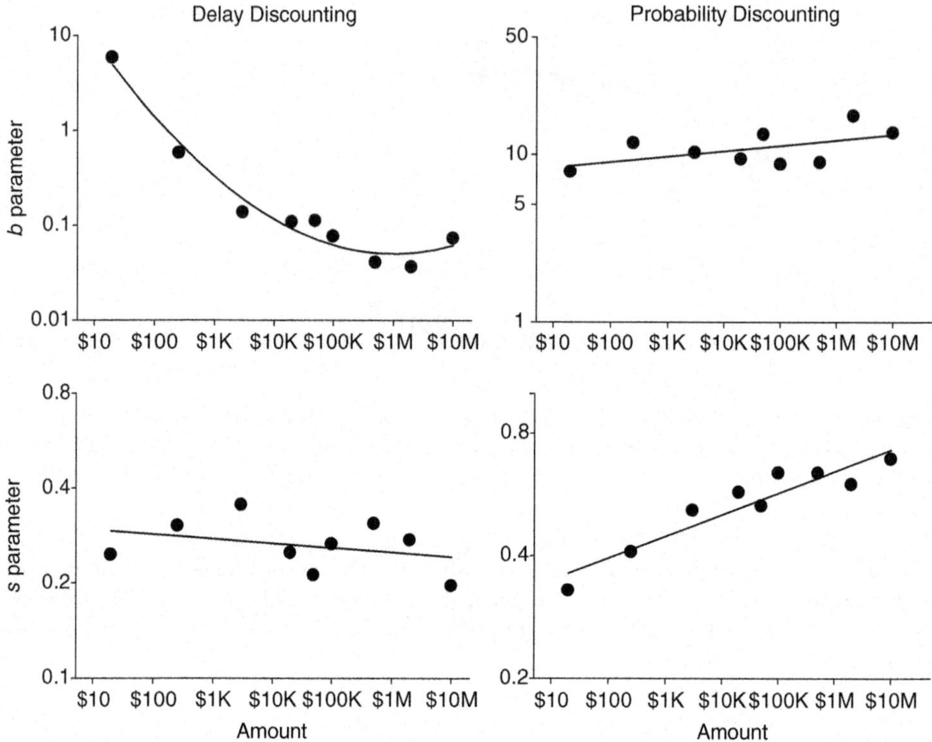

Figure 13.8 Values of the *b* (top) and *s* (bottom) parameters in the hyperboloid discounting function (Equation 1) as a function of amount for delay discounting (left panels) and probability discounting (right panels). Parameter estimates are based on fits to group mean subjective values. The left panels are adapted from "Delay discounting of monetary rewards over a wide range of amounts: Comparisons," by L. Green, J. Myerson, L. Oliveira, and S. Chang (2013), *Journal of the Experimental Analysis of Behavior*, *100*, p. 275. The right panels are adapted from "Modeling the effect of reward amount on probability discounting," by J. Myerson, L. Green, and J. Morris (2011), *Journal of Experimental Analysis of Behavior*, *95*, p. 180. Copyright 2011 by the Society for the Experimental Analysis of Behavior. Adapted with permission.

delay or odds against). Thus, the smaller the AuC, the greater the degree of discounting (Myerson, Green, & Warusawitharana, 2001).

The difference between the effects of reward amount on delay and probability discounting goes beyond the fact that the effects are opposite in direction (Estle, Green, Myerson, & Holt, 2006; Myerson, Green, & Morris, 2011). To begin with, the form of the relation between degree of discounting and amount differs: For delayed rewards, the AuC increases fairly rapidly up to point and tends to level off as amount increases further, whereas for probabilistic rewards, the AuC decreases continuously. In addition, amount of reward selectively affects different parameters of the delay and probability discounting functions, *b* (the discounting rate parameter) in the case of delay, and *s* (the exponent) in the case of probability. Moreover, these parameters are affected in different ways (see Figure 13.8). For delay discounting, *b* decreases as the reward amount increases, leveling off as the amount gets very large, while *s* shows little or no systematic change, whereas for probability discounting, *s* increases continuously as amount increases, with *b* showing little or no systematic change.

In addition to amount, a number of other variables differentially affect delay and probability discounting. For example, inflation appears to affect the rate of delay, but not probability discounting of monetary rewards (Ostaszewski, Green, & Myerson, 1998). In addition, Estle et al. (2007) found that although delayed nonmonetary rewards (hypothetical candy, beer, and soda) were discounted at a much steeper rate than delayed money, the probabilistic nonmonetary rewards were discounted at rates equivalent to that for probabilistic money (compare the left and right panels of Figure 13.5). It also has been reported that degree of delay discounting, but not probability discounting, differs between younger children and older children and adolescents (Olson, Hooper, Collins, & Luciana, 2007; Scheres et al., 2006), and that in cigarette smokers, delay but not probability discounting of money was affected by nicotine deprivation (although surprisingly, neither delay nor probability discounting of cigarettes were affected; Yi & Landes, 2012). Taken together, the findings showing differential effects of amount on both degree of discounting and the parameters of the delay and probability discounting functions, as well as the evidence of selective or differential effects of a number of other variables on delay and probability discounting, provide strong support for the view that, despite the similarity in the mathematical form of the discounting function, delay and probability discounting involve at least some fundamentally different processes.

Why is There a Magnitude Effect?

It is well established that larger delayed rewards are discounted less steeply than smaller rewards, whereas the opposite is observed with probabilistic rewards. Despite the general consensus, however, these findings remain among the most perplexing in the discounting literature. From the standpoint of economic theory, moreover, these magnitude effects are anomalies (Loewenstein & Prelec, 1992; Loewenstein & Thaler, 1989; Prelec & Loewenstein, 1991), and several hypotheses have been proposed to account for them.

Thaler (1985) suggested that people keep different "mental accounts," and smaller amounts of money are categorized as "spending money" whereas larger amounts are categorized as "savings." From this perspective, Thaler argued that waiting for a smaller reward (i.e., "spending money") entails forgoing consumption, whereas waiting for a larger reward entails forgoing incurring interest on "savings." Steeper discounting of smaller rewards occurs because people are more willing to forgo earning interest than to forgo consuming (Loewenstein & Thaler, 1989). One problem with this approach is that because the rate of delay discounting changes continuously as a function of amount, at least for amounts up to tens of thousands of dollars, one would have to posit many, many different mental accounts. Another problem is that magnitude effects have been observed with nonmonetary rewards such as health (Chapman & Elstein, 1995), and one would have to posit multiple mental accounts for health as well as for any other type of reward (e.g., vacations of different durations; Raineri & Rachlin, 1993) for which magnitude effects are observed.

Prelec and Loewenstein (1991) later proposed that the magnitude effect arises from a property of the shape of the value function that they termed *increasing proportional sensitivity*, according to which the ratio of a pair of small amounts appears to be less than the ratio of a larger pair even when the actual ratio is the same for both pairs. Raineri and Rachlin (1993) proposed instead that larger and smaller reward amounts are consumed at different rates. Although the person receiving $1,000 may spend a greater absolute amount of money within a given time period than the person receiving only $100, it will not be *proportionally* more, and this could account for the different degrees of discounting. Finally, Myerson and Green (1995) proposed that there is some minimum delay to even "immediate" rewards, and that the shallower discounting of larger reward amounts reflects larger minimum times to their consumption. This interpretation is consistent with the finding that in a study of choice between two delayed rewards, the rate at which the later one was discounted decreased as the time to both rewards (i.e., the minimum delay) increased (Green, Myerson, & Macaux, 2005).

Although one or more of the hypothesized mechanisms may explain the magnitude effect in delay discounting, these accounts do little to illuminate the opposite effect that reward amount has on probability discounting, increasing rather than decreasing how steeply rewards are discounted. Recognizing this problem, Prelec and Loewenstein (1991) proposed that a different mechanism is responsible for the magnitude effect in probability discounting. They argued that in the case of probabilistic rewards, people anticipate the possibility of "disappointment" if they do not receive a reward, with larger amounts being associated with disproportionately more disappointment. So, too, Green and Myerson (2004) have suggested that the effects of amount on delay and probability discounting reflect different mechanisms, and they proposed that these mechanisms are localized in separate weighting functions for delay and probability, rather than in the value function that is common to all rewards. In sum, as the evidence accumulates that delay and probability discounting involve separate processes, it becomes increasingly likely that at least some of these separate processes are responsible for the differences in the effects of amount on these two types of discounting.

Delayed and Probabilistic Losses

Although the vast majority of discounting experiments have concerned rewards (gains), many of the choices people make involve delayed or possible losses, with decisions regarding insurance being a classic example: People choose to pay money now rather than take the chance that they will have to pay more money later. As is the case with gains, both the delay and probability discounting of monetary losses are well described by hyperboloid functions (Estle et al., 2006; Mitchell & Wilson, 2010; Murphy, Vuchinich, & Simpson, 2001; Ostaszewski & Karzel, 2002). Although few studies have addressed this issue, the delay discounting of nonmonetary losses has been shown to be well described by a hyperboloid function (Baker, Johnson, & Bickel, 2003; Odum, Madden, & Bickel, 2002).

With losses (as with gains), preference reversals occur when the same amount of time is added to the delays until occurrence of a smaller, sooner loss and a larger, later loss (Holt, Green, Myerson, & Estle, 2008). With gains, for example, people tend to prefer the smaller, sooner gain when the times until both outcomes are relatively brief; as time is added to the delay before both outcomes, however, preference tends to switch to the larger, later gain (Ainslie & Haendel, 1983; Green, Fristoe, & Myerson, 1994). The opposite pattern is observed with losses: People tend to prefer the larger, later loss so long as the times until both outcomes are relatively brief, but as time is added to the delay before both outcomes, preference tends to switch to the smaller, sooner loss (Holt et al., 2008). This experiment is analogous to situations like the one in which someone, despite having previously planned to pay off the entire debt, ends up making only the minimum payment on his credit card balance, thereby incurring a greater loss later.

Despite the similarities between the discounting of gains and losses, there are at least two important differences. One is the classic finding (sometimes referred to as the *gain-loss asymmetry* or as the *sign effect*) that both delayed and probabilistic losses are discounted less steeply than the same amount of delayed and probabilistic gain (Benzion et al., 1989; Kahneman & Tversky, 1979; Thaler, 1981). The other prominent difference concerns the effect of amount of loss. Amount has opposite effects on the degree to which delayed and probabilistic gains are discounted, but little or no effect on the discounting of either delayed or probabilistic losses (Estle et al., 2006; Green, Myerson, Oliveira, & Chang, 2014; Holt et al., 2008; McKerchar, Pickford, & Robertson, 2013; Mitchell & Wilson, 2010; Ostaszewski & Karzel, 2002; Yi & Landes, 2012).

The finding that discounting varies as a function of outcome sign (i.e., gain vs. loss) has implications for a variety of public health issues. For example, cigarette smokers make choices that have both immediate and delayed consequences: between nicotine intake versus nicotine withdrawal in the short term, followed by an increased likelihood of poor health versus better health in the long term. The question is whether public health efforts should frame such health decisions as choices between gains (e.g., the pleasure of a cigarette now or the benefit of good health later) or as choices between losses (e.g., nicotine withdrawal now or possibly serious illness later), or as some combination of the two. Chapman (1996) found that, consistent with the sign effect observed with monetary outcomes, people discounted health losses less steeply than health gains. She suggested, therefore, that framing health decisions in terms of future health losses, rather than future gains, might be more effective. It is possible, of course, that specific health decisions (e.g., whether to smoke; whether to exercise), which often have positive and negative consequences specific to the behavior in question, may differ in the relative rates at which these consequences are discounted, or that different groups (e.g., smokers, older adults) may differ in their relative discounting rates (e.g., Odum et al., 2002), and further research will illuminate these possibilities.

Discounting in Nonhuman Animals

Nonhuman animals, like humans, discount the value of delayed rewards, and their choices are well described by the same hyperboloid function that describes human delay discounting (e.g., Freeman, Green, Myerson, & Woolverton, 2009; Green, Myerson, Holt, Slevin, & Estle, 2004; Mazur, 1987; Richards, Mitchell, de Wit, & Seiden, 1997). Also like humans, nonhuman animals show preference reversals (Ainslie & Herrnstein, 1981; Green & Estle, 2003; Green, Fisher, Perlow, & Sherman, 1981), a finding frequently attributed to their hyperbolic discounting. In addition to rats and pigeons, discounting has been found in nonhuman primates, including lemurs (Stevens & Mühlhoff, 2012), marmosets, and tamarins (Stevens, Hallinan, & Hauser, 2005), capuchins (Addessi, Paglieri, & Focaroli, 2011), and rhesus monkeys (Woolverton, Myerson, & Green, 2007), as well as in chimpanzees and bonobos (Rosati, Stevens, Hare, & Hauser, 2007). Although the majority of animal work in discounting has focused on delayed reinforcers, a hyperboloid function also describes animals' choices with probabilistic reinforcers (Green, Myerson, & Calvert, 2010) as well as with delayed punishers (Woolverton, Freeman, Myerson, & Green, 2012).

Quantitative and Qualitative Properties of Rewards

Studies that investigated the effect of reinforcer amount on degree of discounting in nonhuman animals have, with one exception (Grace, Sargisson, & White, 2012), failed to find a magnitude effect. Richards et al. (1997) reported no effect of amount on rats' discounting of delayed water; Grace (1999) found no amount effect with pigeons discounting delayed food; Green et al. (2004) found no effect of amount on the discounting of delayed food in either pigeons or rats; and Freeman et al. (2009) found no amount effect in rhesus monkeys with delayed saccharin.

Despite the absence of an effect of amount of delayed reinforcer, it is possible that nonhuman animals discount more desirable types of reinforcers less steeply than less desirable ones. When Calvert, Green, and Myerson (2010) examined this possibility, however, they found that rats discounted both highly preferred (sucrose pellets) and dispreferred (cellulose pellets) food reinforcers at equivalent rates. Calvert et al. then replicated this finding with highly preferred (saccharin) and dispreferred (quinine) liquid reinforcers. In a related study using a novel discounting procedure, Freeman, Nonnemacher, Green, Myerson, and Woolverton (2012) varied the concentration of an immediate sucrose solution until monkeys chose it as often as a delayed sucrose solution whose concentration was fixed. Similar rates of discounting were observed regardless of whether the concentration of the delayed reinforcer was 10% or 20%, despite the fact that all of the monkeys preferred the higher sucrose concentration.

This is not to say that monkeys (or other nonhuman animals) discount all types of reinforcer at similar rates. Freeman et al. (2012) compared the discounting rates for delayed sucrose solutions in their study with the rates at which the same monkeys discounted delayed saccharin and delayed cocaine in previous studies (Freeman et al., 2009; Woolverton et al., 2007) and found that cocaine was discounted at the lowest rate, saccharin at the highest rate, and sucrose at an intermediate rate. Because of procedural differences among the studies with different types of reinforcers, one must be cautious in interpreting these findings. Moreover, these findings appear inconsistent with those of Calvert et al. (2010) who found that rats discounted different types (and amounts) of delayed food and liquid reinforcers at similar rates.

Further studies of the discounting of qualitatively different reinforcers are needed, if only because the conclusions from a comparison of reinforcer A with reinforcer B might not generalize to comparisons of A or B with C (Green & Freed, 1993).

Perhaps more importantly, research is needed in which the reinforcers available after shorter and longer delays are of different types. Choice under such circumstances is a fundamental issue in the study of foraging. Moreover, such circumstances are similar to many faced every day, particularly those of applied interest (e.g., choice between immediate nicotine consumptions and later health).

Comparisons of Discounting Across Species

Despite many similarities, there are important differences between discounting in human and nonhuman animals. In addition to the issue of the apparent absence of a magnitude effect in nonhuman animals, the other most notable issue is the fact that the rates of discounting in animal studies are much steeper than those typically observed in human studies, and it has been shown repeatedly that pigeons discount at a greater rate than rats (Green et al., 2004; Mazur & Biondi, 2009). These findings indicate that species differ in degree of discounting, even though delay discounting by each species is described by a hyperboloid. Great apes such as chimpanzees and bonobos appear to discount delayed food at lower rates than monkeys like macaques and marmosets, which in turn have lower discounting rates than rats and pigeons (Addessi et al., 2011; Stevens & Mühlhoff, 2012). These differences appear to be associated with differences in body mass, with smaller animals showing steeper discounting than larger animals. This may be seen in Figure 13.9, which shows measures of discounting that were all obtained using adjusting-delay procedures and (with the exception of the pigeon data) using an immediate reward that was one-third the size of the delayed reward (e.g., two versus six food items).

Stevens and Mühlhoff (2012) speculated that factors correlated with body mass, such as metabolic rate and life expectancy, underlie the observed correlation with

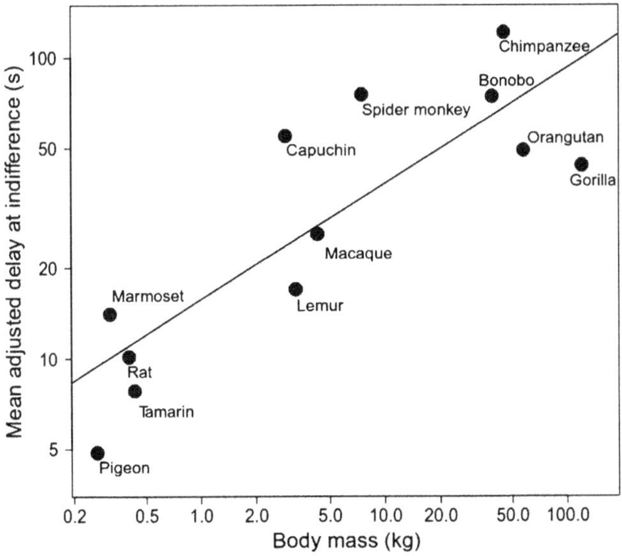

Figure 13.9 Delay at indifference as a function of body mass. Longer delays indicate shallower discounting. Note that the axes are logarithmically scaled. Figure is from "Intertemporal choice in lemurs," by J. R. Stevens and N. Mühlhoff (2012), *Behavioural Processes, 89*, p. 126. Copyright 2012 by Elsevier. Reprinted with permission.

discounting rate, but their analyses also revealed some interesting inconsistencies. Lemurs (prosimians) and capuchins (New World monkeys) have similar body mass, yet capuchins discount less steeply than would be predicted based on their body mass, whereas lemurs discount more steeply than would be predicted. Discounting rates may be related to foraging and feeding styles (e.g., Addessi et al., 2011). Stevens et al. (2005) found that marmosets had lower discounting rates than tamarins (both New World monkeys), despite the similar body weights and brain-body ratios of these closely related species. They noted that tamarins primarily feed on insects, which requires acting quickly when the opportunity arises, whereas marmosets feed on slowly flowing gum and sap. Stevens et al. suggested that this difference in feeding ecology might have selected for greater patience in marmosets and greater impulsivity in tamarins, at least when making decisions regarding food.

When a species difference is reported, there always is the concern that the observed difference really might be due to procedural or motivational differences (Calvert, Green, & Myerson, 2011; Mazur & Biondi, 2011). With regard to differences between human and nonhumans, this problem is particularly acute, and in the case of discounting experiments, several obvious differences come to mind. Nonhuman subjects in delay discounting experiments typically make choices in which the outcomes are real, consumable reinforcers that are delivered after a delay. In contrast, the choices faced by humans in discounting experiments typically involve monetary rewards, and in addition, these rewards are usually hypothetical as are the delays until their receipt. Any or all of these differences potentially could be responsible for the much steeper discounting rates observed in nonhuman animals.

As already discussed, however, humans appear to discount hypothetical and potentially real monetary rewards at similar rates even when they actually have to wait for the real rewards (e.g., Johnson & Bickel, 2002; Madden et al., 2003). The fact that the outcomes in human studies are usually monetary whereas those in animal studies are directly consumable is more problematic, however, because humans discount hypothetical consumable rewards more steeply than hypothetical money (Estle et al., 2007). Indeed, humans have been reported to discount real, consumable rewards very rapidly (McClure, Ericson, Laibson, Loewenstein, & Cohen, 2007; Rosati et al., 2007), and Jimura et al. (2009) found that even a 30-s delay was sufficient to reduce the subjective value of a liquid reward to half its objective value, bringing human discounting rates more in line with those reported for nonhuman animals discounting liquid rewards (e.g., Freeman et al., 2009; Richards et al., 1997). Thus, differences in the type of outcomes appear to at least partially explain the difference between humans' and nonhumans' discounting rates. As for the lack of a magnitude effect in animals, it should be noted that when directly consumable hypothetical rewards are used with humans, the magnitude effect is much smaller than that observed with monetary rewards, and it remains possible that procedural differences ultimately may explain this apparent species difference as well (Grace et al., 2012).

Impulsivity or Impulsivities?

It is well established that those with substance abuse problems tend to discount delayed rewards steeply (for a meta-analytic review, see MacKillop et al., 2011). For example, cigarette smokers (Mitchell, 1999), alcoholics (Petry, 2001), and heroin addicts (Kirby et al., 1999), all discount delayed monetary rewards more steeply than do controls. Furthermore, substance abusers discount their drug of addiction more steeply than they discount monetary rewards (e.g., Madden et al., 1997). Moreover, there is evidence that steep delay discounting rates are a predictor, rather than an outcome, of substance abuse (Audrain-McGovern et al., 2009) as well as a predictor of drug relapse following treatment (Yoon et al., 2007). Such findings frequently are taken as evidence that substance abusers are impulsive.

The issue is complicated, however, by evidence suggesting that discounting may not really measure what personality psychologists usually mean by impulsiveness. Although psychologists differ in their views regarding the relative importance of traits versus situations as determinants of behavior, there is a general consensus regarding the definition of a trait (e.g., Fleeson & Noftle, 2009; Larsen & Buss, 2010). Notably, a trait like impulsiveness (e.g., Barratt & Patton, 1983; Eysenck & Eysenck, 1977) is typically understood to be a relatively enduring cross-situational pattern of behavior. It is unclear, however, how discounting fits into this conception.

Consistent with the view of discounting as a trait or as a facet of the trait of impulsiveness, delay-discounting rates have been found to be relatively stable across time (Audrain-McGovern et al., 2009; Jimura et al., 2011; Kirby, 2009; Ohmura, Takahashi, Kitamura, & Wehr, 2006; Simpson & Vuchinich, 2000). However, discounting rates often are not stable across situations, particularly those involving different types of rewards. For example, Chapman (Chapman, 1996; Chapman & Elstein, 1995) found that the degree to which individuals discounted delayed money was only weakly correlated with the degree to which they discounted delayed health outcomes. Similarly, Jimura et al. (2011) found that the discounting of delayed hypothetical monetary rewards was uncorrelated with the discounting of real delayed liquid rewards. Although there clearly are some cases in which the degree to which an individual discounts one type of reward does predict the degree to which that individual will discount another type of reward (e.g., food and money, Odum, 2011), based on the low correlations across other types of reward (e.g., health and money) some have argued for the domain independence of discounting rates (e.g., Chapman, 1996).

Further, delay and probability discounting are at best weakly correlated, and the correlation, when significant, is always positive (Holt, Green, & Myerson, 2003; Myerson, Green, Hanson, Holt, & Estle 2003; Mitchell, 1999; Mitchell & Wilson, 2010; for a review, see Green & Myerson, 2010). If the same underlying trait (i.e., impulsivity) were responsible for both delay and probability discounting, then a strong negative correlation between delay and probability discounting rates would be expected. That is, one would have expected that impulsive individuals would be both unable to wait for a reward and prone to gamble and take risks, in which case they would show both steep delay discounting and shallow probability discounting (i.e., a negative correlation).

Despite the consistent finding of steep delay discounting by individuals with substance abuse problems, different types of discounting and the discounting of different types of rewards appear to be dissociable within this special population just as they are within the general population. For example, it has been reported that brief smoking abstinence leads to an increase in delay discounting but has no effect on probability discounting (Yi & Landes, 2012). Further, there is evidence to suggest that cigarette smokers discount delayed money more steeply than controls, but do not differ in their discounting rate of delayed health outcomes (Johnson, Bickel, & Baker, 2007).

Taken together, the evidence argues in favor of there being multiple "impulsivities" and against a single, unitary trait of impulsivity (Green & Myerson, 2013). One important corollary is that researchers seeking to develop an animal model of impulsive behavior might be better served by developing multiple models for the study of different impulsive behaviors.

Future Directions

To this point, our focus has been on discounting in choice situations that involve tradeoffs between something smaller but sooner and something larger but later, or between something smaller but more likely and something larger but less likely. However, the concept of discounting is much broader than this (Rachlin, 2006), and research is beginning to explore tradeoffs involving other important dimensions on which outcomes differ. Research on effort discounting, for example, examines tradeoffs between something smaller but easier to obtain and something larger but harder to obtain, where effort is the critical dimension. Just as delaying an outcome or making it less likely leads to its devaluation, so, too, increasing the effort associated with an outcome reduces the subjective value of that outcome, and such devaluation also can be examined within the discounting framework. The effort dimension can be either physical (e.g., force of muscular contraction; Mitchell, 1999, 2004) or cognitive (e.g., number of choice alternatives; Reed, Reed, Chok, & Brozyna, 2011), and in either case, increased effort decreases preference.

Research on social discounting examines the tradeoff between keeping more for oneself and keeping less but sharing more with others, where the critical dimension is the social distance between oneself and the others (Jones & Rachlin, 2006). People are willing to forgo more of a reward for themselves so that another person to whom they are close, such as a relative or good friend, can receive more of a reward, but will forgo much less for an acquaintance and even less for a stranger. Similar to delay and probability discounting, a hyperboloid function describes the relation between the amount of monetary reward that an individual will forgo and the social distance of the other (Jones & Rachlin, 2006; Rachlin & Jones, 2008a). Also consistent with the results for delay discounting, Locey, Jones, and Rachlin (2011) found no significant difference in degree of discounting depending on whether the reward to be shared was real or hypothetical.

Jones and Rachlin (e.g., 2006; Rachlin & Jones, 2008a) have suggested that the degree of social discounting exhibited by an individual may provide a behavioral index of altruism (where shallower discounting is more altruistic). Interestingly, the type of relationship one has with the other person has been found to modulate the degree of social discounting. People tended to forgo more money for relatives than for nonrelatives, even when the relatives and nonrelatives are at the same social distance (Rachlin & Jones, 2008b), a finding consistent with inclusive fitness accounts of altruism.

Another potentially fruitful area of research closely related to discounting is the emerging field of neuroeconomics, which uses neuroscientific methods to study economic decision making (e.g., Glimcher, Camerer, Poldrack, & Fehr, 2008). Data from behavioral experiments reveal that delay and probability discounting involve at least some separate processes (Green & Myerson, 2004), and the results of recent experiments using functional magnetic resonance imaging (fMRI) are consistent with this view. For example, Weber and Huettel (2008) observed that delay and probability discounting activated different areas of the brain. More specifically, whereas delay discounting activated areas (posterior cingulate cortex) that have been associated with imagining the future (Szpunar, Watson, & McDermott, 2007), probability discounting activated areas (posterior parietal cortex) that have been associated with numerical estimation and calculation (Dehaene, Piazza, Pinel, & Cohen, 2003). Peters and Büchel (2009), too, observed differential activation, but they also found that the ventral striatum and orbitofrontal cortex were active during both tasks, suggesting a common neural signal of subjective value.

McClure and colleagues have argued that two competing valuation systems are involved in delay discounting (McClure et al., 2007; McClure, Laibson, Loewenstein, & Cohen, 2004). They postulate a β system, reflected in limbic (e.g., ventral striatal) activation, that is responsive to immediate rewards, and a δ system, reflected in activation of lateral prefrontal and posterior parietal cortex, that responds to both delayed and immediate rewards. The difference in activity in these two systems is hypothesized to be the basis for choice between immediate and delayed rewards. However, Kable and Glimcher (2007) observed that the brain areas hypothesized to correspond to the β system, like the areas hypothesized to correspond to the δ system, respond to delayed rewards, and moreover, that activity in both sets of areas decreases as a function of delay. In addition, Kable and Glimcher reported that increasing delay results in a hyperbolic decrease in brain activation, rather than an exponential decrease, as predicted by the McClure et al. β-δ model. The controversy involving neural mechanisms has yet to be resolved, but behavioral data clearly support Kable and Glimcher.

While neuroeconomic research on discounting is still at an early stage, such studies have the potential to differentiate between alternative models of the mechanisms underlying economic decision making (for recent reviews, see Hayden, Heilbronner, & Platt, 2010; Redish & Kurth-Nelson, 2010; Winstanley, 2010). The observation that delay and probability discounting activate both common and unique brain areas is a case in point. Another example comes from a neuropsychological study of the role of "mental time travel" in delay discounting. Kwan et al. (2012) observed normal delay discounting in an individual with extensive medial temporal lobe damage that left him with an inability to imagine future experiences. These results suggest, perhaps surprisingly, that the anticipation of what future events will be like is not a necessary part of future-oriented decision making, and, contrary to what is often assumed (e.g., Boyer, 2008; Loewenstein, Weber, Hsee, & Welch, 2001; Loomes & Sugden, 1987; Peters & Büchel, 2010), may not be required for evaluation of either delayed or probabilistic outcomes.

Conclusions

Many choices involve tradeoffs between the amount or quality of a reward and its immediacy or certainty. These tradeoffs are reflected in the decrease in subjective value of an outcome as a function of both the time until and the odds against its occurrence, and a review of the literature reveals that these decreases (termed delay discounting and probability discounting, respectively) are each well-described by the same (hyperboloid) form of mathematical function. Moreover, the degree to which subjective value decreases as the delay or the odds-against increases is influenced by the amount of the outcome and the nature of the tradeoff. For delay discounting, larger rewards are discounted less steeply than smaller rewards. In contrast, larger probabilistic rewards are discounted more steeply than smaller probabilistic rewards. The degree of discounting may also be influenced by the type of outcome. For example, delayed monetary rewards are discounted less steeply than delayed non-monetary rewards, and both delayed and probabilistic losses are discounted less steeply than delayed and probabilistic gains.

The finding that amount differentially affects delay and probability discounting illustrates the advantage of studying choice within the discounting framework (Green & Myerson, 2004). Within this framework, analogous procedures and analyses are used to study both delayed and probabilistic outcomes, thus allowing for more direct comparisons. For example, the study of choice within a discounting framework has revealed how amount differentially affects the parameters of the hyperboloid functions describing delay and probability discounting, thereby strengthening the case that, contrary to earlier suggestions, delay and probability involve different processes. The case for separate processes is further strengthened by the finding that there is little relation between the degree to which an individual discounts delayed rewards and the degree to which that individual discounts probabilistic rewards. Thus, discounting research argues against the notion of a unitary trait underlying individual differences in self-control and, instead, for a more nuanced view of impulsivity.

Although much is known about the way in which delay and probability affect the subjective value of rewards, there remain significant gaps in the discounting literature. Previous research has tended to focus on relatively simple forms of delay and probability discounting. Whereas this is arguably the best way to approach a new research area, research is needed that, building on the insights obtained from studying simpler situations (e.g., the similarities and differences between delay and probability discounting), now examines more complicated situations, notably the discounting of outcomes that involve probability and delay and/or gains and losses, as well as trade-offs involving qualitatively different types of delayed and probabilistic outcomes. Such research is not only of theoretical importance but also of considerable applied significance, given that health-related and economic decisions, as well as everyday choices, typically involve such combinations.

Acknowledgments

Preparation of this chapter was supported by National Institutes of Health Grant RO1 MH055308. We thank Pascal Boyer for his helpful comments on an earlier draft.

References

Addessi, E., Paglieri, F., & Focaroli, V. (2011). The ecological rationality of delay tolerance: Insights from capuchin monkeys. *Cognition*, *119*, 142–147.

Ainslie, G. (1975). Specious reward: A behavioral theory of impulsiveness and impulse control. *Psychological Bulletin, 82*, 463–496.

Ainslie, G. (1992). *Picoeconomics: The strategic interaction of successive motivational states within the person.* Cambridge, UK: Cambridge University Press.

Ainslie, G., & Haendel, V. (1983). The motives of the will. In E. Gottheil, K. A. Drulry, T. E. Skoloda, & H. M. Waxman (Eds.), *Etiological aspects of alcohol and drug abuse* (pp. 199–240). Springfield, IL: Charles C. Thomas.

Ainslie, G., & Herrnstein, R. J. (1981). Preference reversal and delayed reinforcement. *Animal Learning & Behavior, 9*, 476–482.

Audrain-McGovern, J., Rodriguez, D., Epstein, L. H., Cuevas, J., Rodgers, K., & Wileyto, E. P. (2009). Does delay discounting play an etiological role in smoking or is it a consequence of smoking? *Drug and Alcohol Dependence, 103*, 99–106.

Baker, F., Johnson, M. W., & Bickel, W. K. (2003). Delay discounting in current and never-before cigarette smokers: Similarities and differences across commodity, sign, and magnitude. *Journal of Abnormal Psychology, 112*, 382–392.

Barratt, E. S., & Patton, J. H. (1983). Impulsivity: Cognitive, behavioral, and psychophysiological correlates. In M. Zuckerman (Ed.), *Biological bases of sensation seeking, impulsivity and anxiety* (pp. 77–116). Hillsdale, NJ: Erlbaum.

Benzion, U., Rapoport, A., & Yagil, J. (1989). Discount rates inferred from decisions: An experimental study. *Management Science, 35*, 270–284.

Bickel, W. K., & Marsch, L. A. (2001). Toward a behavioral economic understanding of drug dependence: delay discounting processes. *Addiction, 96*, 73–86.

Bickel, W. K., Pitcock, J. A., Yi, R., & Angtuaco, E. J. C. (2009). Congruence of BOLD response across intertemporal choice conditions: Fictive and real money gains and losses. *The Journal of Neuroscience, 29*, 8839–8846.

Boyer, P. (2008). Evolutionary economics of mental time travel? *Trends in Cognitive Sciences, 12*, 219–224.

Calvert, A. L., Green, L., & Myerson, J. (2010). Delay discounting of qualitatively different reinforcers in rats. *Journal of the Experimental Analysis of Behavior, 93*, 171–184.

Calvert, A. L., Green, L., & Myerson, J. (2011). Discounting in pigeons when the choice is between two delayed rewards: Implications for species comparisons. *Frontiers in Neuroscience, 5*, 96.

Chapman, G. B. (1996). Temporal discounting and utility for health and money. *Journal of Experimental Psychology: Learning, Memory, and Cognition, 22*, 771–791.

Chapman, G. B., & Elstein, A. S. (1995). Valuing the future: Temporal discounting of health and money. *Medical Decision Making, 15*, 373–386.

Charlton, S. R., & Fantino, E. (2008). Commodity specific rates of temporal discounting: Does metabolic function underlie differences in rates of discounting? *Behavioural Processes, 77*, 334–342.

D'Amato, M. R. (1970). *Experimental psychology: Methodology, psychophysics, and learning.* New York: McGraw-Hill.

Dehaene, S., Piazza, M., Pinel, P., & Cohen, L. (2003). Three parietal circuits for number processing. *Cognitive Neuropsychology, 20*, 487–506.

Du, W., Green, L., & Myerson, J. (2002). Cross-cultural comparisons of discounting delayed and probabilistic rewards. *The Psychological Record, 52*, 479–492.

Epstein, L. H., Richards, J. B., Saad, F. G., Paluch, R. A., Roemmich, J. N., & Lerman, C. (2003). Comparison between two measures of delay discounting in smokers. *Experimental and Clinical Psychopharmacology, 11*, 131–138.

Estle, S. J., Green, L., Myerson, J., & Holt, D. D. (2006). Differential effects of amount on temporal and probability discounting of gains and losses. *Memory and Cognition, 34*, 914–928.

Estle, S. J., Green, L., Myerson, J., & Holt, D. D. (2007). Discounting of monetary and directly consumable rewards. *Psychological Science*, *18*, 58–63.

Eysenck, S. B. G., & Eysenck, H. J. (1977). The place of impulsiveness in a dimensional system of personality description. *British Journal of Social and Clinical Psychology*, *16*, 57–68.

Fleeson, W., & Noftle, E. E. (2009). In favor of the synthetic resolution to the person-situation debate. *Journal of Research in Personality*, *43*, 150–154.

Freeman, K. B., Green, L., Myerson, J., & Woolverton, W. L. (2009). Delay discounting of saccharin in rhesus monkeys. *Behavioural Processes*, *82*, 214–218.

Freeman, K. B., Nonnemacher, J. E., Green, L., Myerson, J., & Woolverton, W. L. (2012). Delay discounting in rhesus monkeys: Equivalent discounting of more and less preferred sucrose concentrations. *Learning & Behavior*, *40*, 54–60.

Glimcher, P. W., Camerer, C., Poldrack, R. A., & Fehr, E. (Eds.). (2008). *Neuroeconomics: Decision making and the brain*. London: Academic Press.

Gonzalez, R., & Wu, G. (1999). On the shape of the probability weighting function. *Cognitive Psychology*, *38*, 129–166.

Grace, R. C. (1999). The matching law and amount-dependent exponential discounting as accounts of self-control choice. *Journal of the Experimental Analysis of Behavior*, *71*, 27–44.

Grace, R. C., Sargisson, R. J., & White, K. G. (2012). Evidence for a magnitude effect in temporal discounting with pigeons. *Journal of Experimental Psychology: Animal Behavior Processes*, *38*, 102–108.

Green, L., & Estle, S. J. (2003). Preference reversals with food and water reinforcers in rats. *Journal of the Experimental Analysis of Behavior*, *79*, 233–242.

Green, L., Fisher, E. B., Perlow, S., & Sherman, L. (1981). Preference reversal and self-control: Choice as a function of reward amount and delay. *Behaviour Analysis Letters*, *1*, 43–51.

Green, L., & Freed, D. E. (1993). The substitutability of reinforcers. *Journal of the Experimental Analysis of Behavior*, *60*, 141–158.

Green, L., Fristoe, N., & Myerson, J. (1994). Temporal discounting and preference reversals in choice between delayed outcomes. *Psychological Bulletin and Review*, *1*, 383–389.

Green, L., Fry, A., & Myerson, J. (1994). Discounting of delayed rewards: A life-span comparison. *Psychological Science*, *5*, 33.

Green, L., & Myerson, J. (1996). Exponential versus hyperbolic discounting of delayed outcomes: Risk and waiting time. *American Zoologist*, *36*, 496–505.

Green, L., & Myerson, J. (2004). A discounting framework for choice with delayed and probabilistic rewards. *Psychological Bulletin*, *130*, 769–792.

Green, L., & Myerson, J. (2010) Experimental and correlational analyses of delay and probability discounting. In G. J. Madden & W. K. Bickel (Eds.), *Impulsivity: The behavioral and neurological science of discounting* (pp. 67–92). Washington, DC: American Psychological Association.

Green, L., & Myerson, J. (2013). How many impulsivities? A discounting perspective. *Journal of the Experimental Analysis of Behavior*, *99*, 3–13.

Green, L., Myerson, J., & Calvert, A. L. (2010). Pigeons' discounting of probabilistic and delayed reinforcers. *Journal of the Experimental Analysis of Behavior*, *94*, 113–123.

Green, L., Myerson, J., Holt, D. D., Slevin, J. R., & Estle, S. J. (2004). Discounting of delayed food rewards in pigeons and rats: Is there a magnitude effect? *Journal of the Experimental Analysis of Behavior*, *81*, 39–50.

Green, L., Myerson, J., & Macaux, E. W. (2005). Temporal discounting when the choice is between two delayed rewards. *Journal of Experimental Psychology: Learning, Memory, and Cognition*, *31*, 1121–1133.

Green, L., Myerson, J., Oliveira, L., & Chang, S. (2013). Delay discounting of monetary rewards over a wide range of amounts. *Journal of the Experimental Analysis of Behavior, 100*, 269–281.

Green, L., Myerson, J., Oliveira, L., & Chang, S. (2014). Discounting of delayed and probabilistic losses over a wide range of amounts. *Journal of the Experimental Analysis of Behavior, 101*, 186–200.

Green, L., Myerson, J., & Ostaszewski, P. (1999). Amount of reward has opposite effects on the discounting of delayed and probabilistic outcomes. *Journal of Experimental Psychology: Learning, Memory, and Cognition, 25*, 418–427.

Green, L., Myerson, J., Shah, A. K., Estle, S. J., & Holt, D. D. (2007). Do adjusting-amount and adjusting-delay procedures produce equivalent estimates of subjective value in pigeons? *Journal of the Experimental Analysis of Behavior, 87*, 337–347.

Hayden, B. Y., Heilbronner, S. R., & Platt, M. L. (2010). Ambiguity aversion in rhesus macaques. *Frontiers in Neuroscience, 4*, 166.

Hinvest, N. S., & Anderson, I. M. (2010). The effects of real versus hypothetical reward on delay and probability discounting. *The Quarterly Journal of Experimental Psychology, 63*, 1072–1084.

Holt, D. D., Green, L., & Myerson, J. (2003). Is discounting impulsive? Evidence from temporal and probability discounting in gambling and non-gambling college students. *Behavioural Processes, 64*, 355–367.

Holt, D. D., Green, L., & Myerson, J. (2012). Estimating the subjective value of future rewards: Comparison of adjusting-amount and adjusting-delay procedures. *Behavioural Processes, 90*, 302–310.

Holt, D. D., Green, L., Myerson, J., & Estle, S. J. (2008). Preference reversals with losses. *Psychonomic Bulletin & Review, 15*, 89–95.

Jikko, Y., & Okouchi, H. (2007). Real and hypothetical rewards in probability discounting. *The Japanese Journal of Psychology, 78*, 269–276.

Jimura, K., Myerson, J., Hilgard, J., Braver, T. S., & Green, L. (2009). Are people really more patient than other animals? Evidence from human discounting of real liquid rewards. *Psychonomic Bulletin & Review, 16*, 1071–1075.

Jimura, K., Myerson, J., Hilgard, J., Keighley, J., Braver, T. S., & Green, L. (2011). Domain independence and stability in young and older adults' discounting of delayed rewards. *Behavioural Processes, 87*, 253–259.

Johnson, M. W., & Bickel, W. K. (2002). Within-subject comparison of real and hypothetical money rewards in delay discounting. *Journal of the Experimental Analysis of Behavior, 77*, 129–146.

Johnson, M. W., Bickel, W. K., & Baker, F. (2007). Moderate drug use and delay discounting: A comparison of heavy, light, and never smokers. *Experimental and Clinical Psychopharmacology, 15*, 187–194.

Jones, B. A., & Rachlin, H. (2006). Social discounting. *Psychological Science, 17*, 283–286.

Kable, J. W., & Glimcher, P. W. (2007). The neural correlates of subjective value during intertemporal choice. *Nature Neuroscience, 10*, 1625–1633.

Kahneman, D., & Tversky, A. (1979). Prospect theory: An analysis of decision under risk. *Econometrica, 47*, 263–291.

Kang, M. J., Rangel, A., Camus, M., & Camerer, C. F. (2011). Hypothetical and real choice differentially activate common valuation areas. *The Journal of Neuroscience, 31*, 461–468.

Kantowitz, B. H., Roediger, H. L., III, & Elmes, D. G. (2009). *Experimental psychology* (9th ed.). Belmont, CA: Wadsworth Publishing.

Kirby, K. N. (1997). Bidding on the future: Evidence against normative discounting of delayed rewards. *Journal of Experimental Psychology: General, 126*, 54–70.

Kirby, K. N. (2009). One-year temporal stability of delay-discount rates. *Psychonomic Bulletin & Review, 16*, 457–462.

Kirby, K. N., & Guastello, B. (2001). Making choices in anticipation of similar future choices can increase self-control. *Journal of Experimental Psychology: Applied, 7*, 154–164.

Kirby, K. N., & Maraković, N. N. (1995). Modeling myopic decisions: Evidence for hyperbolic delay-discounting within subjects and amounts. *Organizational Behavior and Human Decision Processes, 64*, 22–39.

Kirby, K. N., & Maraković, N. N. (1996). Delay-discounting probabilistic rewards: Rates decrease as amounts increase. *Psychonomic Bulletin & Review, 3*, 100–104.

Kirby, K. N., Petry, N. M., & Bickel, W. K. (1999). Heroin addicts have higher discount rates for delayed rewards than non-drug-using controls. *Journal of Experimental Psychology: General, 128*, 78–87.

Koopmans, T. C. (1960). Stationary ordinal utility and impatience. *Econometrica, 28*, 287–309.

Kowal, B. P., Yi, R., Erisman, A. C., & Bickel, W. K. (2007). A comparison of two algorithms in computerized temporal discounting procedures. *Behavioural Processes, 75*, 231–236.

Kwan, D., Craver, C. F., Green, L., Myerson, J., Boyer, P., & Rosenbaum, R. S. (2012). Future decision-making without episodic mental time travel. *Hippocampus, 22*, 1215–1219.

Lagorio, C. H., & Madden, G. J. (2005). Delay discounting of real and hypothetical rewards III: Steady-state assessments, forced-choice trials, and all real rewards. *Behavioural Processes, 69*, 173–187.

Larsen, R. J., & Buss, D. M. (2010). *Personality psychology: Domains of knowledge about human nature* (4th ed.). New York: McGraw-Hill.

Lawyer, S. R. (2008). Probability and delay discounting of erotic stimuli. *Behavioural Processes, 79*, 36–42.

Lawyer, S. R., Schoepflin, F., Green, R., & Jenks, C. (2011). Discounting of hypothetical and potentially real outcomes in nicotine-dependent and nondependent samples. *Experimental and Clinical Psychopharmacology, 19*, 263–274.

Lawyer, S. R., Williams, S. A., Prihodova, T., Rollins, J. D., & Lester, A. C. (2010). Probability and delay discounting of hypothetical sexual outcomes. *Behavioural Processes, 84*, 687–692.

Locey, M. L., Jones, B. A., & Rachlin, H. (2011). Real and hypothetical rewards in self-control and social discounting. *Judgment and Decision Making, 6*, 552–564.

Loewenstein, G. F., & Prelec, D. (1992). Anomalies in intertemporal choice: Evidence and interpretation. *The Quarterly Journal of Economics, 107*, 573–597.

Loewenstein, G. F., & Thaler, R. H. (1989). Anomalies: Intertemporal choice. *The Journal of Economic Perspectives, 3*, 181–193.

Loewenstein, G. F., Weber, E. U., Hsee, C. K., & Welch, N. (2001). Risk as feelings. *Psychological Bulletin, 127*, 267–286.

Loomes, G., & Sugden, R. (1987). Testing for regret and disappointment in choice under uncertainty. *The Economic Journal, 97*, 118–129.

MacKillop, J., Amlung, M. T., Few, L. R., Ray, L. A., Sweet, L. H., & Munafò, M. R. (2011). Delayed reward discounting and addictive behavior: A meta-analysis. *Psychopharmacology, 216*, 305–321.

Madden, G. J., Begotka, A. M., Raiff, B. R., & Kastern, L. L. (2003). Delay discounting of real and hypothetical rewards. *Experimental and Clinical Psychopharmacology, 11*, 139–145.

Madden, G. J., & Johnson, P.S. (2010). A delay discounting primer. In G. J. Madden, & W. K. Bickel (Eds.), *Impulsivity: The behavioral and neurological science of discounting* (pp. 11–37). Washington, DC: American Psychological Association.

Madden, G. J., Petry, N. M., Badger, G. J., & Bickel, W. K. (1997). Impulsive and self-control choices in opioid-dependent patients and non-drug-using control participants: Drug and monetary rewards. *Experimental and Clinical Psychopharmacology*, *5*, 256–262.

Madden, G. J., Raiff, B. R., Lagorio, C. H., Begotka, A. M., Mueller, A. M., Hehli, D. J., & Wegener, A. A. (2004). Delay discounting of potentially real and hypothetical rewards: II. Between- and within-subject comparisons. *Experimental and Clinical Psychopharmacology*, *12*, 251–261.

Manwaring, J. L., Green, L., Myerson, J., Strube, M. J, & Wilfley, D. E. (2011). Discounting of various types of rewards by women with and without binge eating disorder: Evidence for general rather than specific differences. *The Psychological Record*, *61*, 561–582.

Mazur, J. E. (1987). An adjusting procedure for studying delayed reinforcement. In M. L. Commons, J. E. Mazur, J. A. Nevin, & H. Rachlin (Eds.), *Quantitative analyses of behavior: Vol. 5. The effect of delay and of intervening events on reinforcement value* (pp. 55–73). Hillsdale, NJ: Erlbaum.

Mazur, J. E., & Biondi, D. R. (2009). Delay-amount tradeoffs in choices by pigeons and rats: Hyperbolic versus exponential discounting. *Journal of the Experimental Analysis of Behavior*, *91*, 197–211.

Mazur, J. E., & Biondi, D. R. (2011). Effects of time between trials on rats' and pigeons' choices with probabilistic delayed reinforcers. *Journal of the Experimental Analysis of Behavior*, *95*, 41–56.

McClure, S. M., Ericson, K. M., Laibson, D. I., Loewenstein, G. F., & Cohen, J. D. (2007). Time discounting for primary rewards. *The Journal of Neuroscience*, *27*, 5796–5804.

McClure, S. M., Laibson, D. I., Loewenstein, G., & Cohen, J. D. (2004, October 15). Separate neural systems value immediate and delayed monetary rewards. *Science*, *306*, 503–507.

McKerchar, T. L., Green, L., Myerson, J., Pickford, T. S., Hill, J. C., & Stout, S. C. (2009). A comparison of four models of delay discounting in humans. *Behavioural Processes*, *81*, 256–259.

McKerchar, T. L., Pickford, S., & Robertson, S. R. (2013). Hyperboloid discounting of delayed outcomes: Magnitude effects and the gain-loss asymmetry. *The Psychological Record*, *63*, 441–451.

Mitchell, S. H. (1999). Measures of impulsivity in cigarette smokers and non-smokers. *Psychopharmacology*, *146*, 455–464.

Mitchell, S. H. (2004). Effects of short-term nicotine deprivation on decision-making: Delay, uncertainty and effort discounting. *Nicotine and Tobacco Research*, *6*, 819–828.

Mitchell, S. H., & Wilson, V. B. (2010). The subjective value of delayed and probabilistic outcomes: Outcome size matters for gains but not for losses. *Behavioural Processes*, *83*, 36–40.

Murphy, J. G., Vuchinich, R. E., & Simpson, C. A. (2001). Delayed reward and cost discounting. *The Psychological Record*, *51*, 571–588.

Myerson, J., & Green, L. (1995). Discounting of delayed rewards: Models of individual choice. *Journal of the Experimental Analysis of Behavior*, *64*, 263–276.

Myerson, J. Green, L., Hanson, J. S., Holt, D. D., & Estle, S. J. (2003). Discounting delayed and probabilistic rewards: Processes and traits. *Journal of Economic Psychology*, *24*, 619–635.

Myerson, J., Green, L., & Morris, J. (2011). Modeling the effect of reward amount on probability discounting. *Journal of the Experimental Analysis of Behavior*, *95*, 175–187.

Myerson, J., Green, L., & Warusawitharana, M. (2001). Area under the curve as a measure of discounting. *Journal of the Experimental Analysis of Behavior*, *76*, 235–243.

Odum, A. L. (2011). Delay discounting: Trait variable? *Behavioural Processes*, *87*, 1–9.

Odum, A. L., Madden, G. J., & Bickel, W. K. (2002). Discounting of delayed health gains and losses by current, never- and ex-smokers of cigarettes. *Nicotine and Tobacco Research, 4*, 295–303.

Odum, A. L., & Rainaud, C. P. (2003). Discounting of delayed hypothetical money, alcohol, and food. *Behavioural Processes, 64*, 305–313.

Ohmura, Y., Takahashi, T., Kitamura, N., & Wehr, P. (2006). Three-month stability of delay and probability discounting measures. *Experimental and Clinical Psychopharmacology, 14*, 318–328.

Olson, E. A., Hooper, C. J., Collins, P., & Luciana, M. (2007). Adolescents' performance on delay and probability discounting tasks: Contributions of age, intelligence, executive functioning, and self-reported externalizing behavior. *Personality and Individual Differences, 43*, 1886–1897.

Ostaszewski, P., Green, L., & Myerson, J. (1998). Effects of inflation on the subjective value. *Psychological Bulletin and Review, 5*, 324–333.

Ostaszewski, P., & Karzel, K. (2002). Discounting of delayed and probabilistic losses of different amounts. *European Psychologist, 7*, 295–301.

Peters, J., & Büchel, C. (2009). Overlapping and distinct neural systems code for subjective value during intertemporal and risky decision making. *The Journal of Neuroscience, 29*, 15727–15734.

Peters, J., & Büchel, C. (2010). Episodic future thinking reduces reward delay discounting through an enhancement of prefrontal-mediotemporal interactions. *Neuron, 66*, 138–148.

Petry, N. M. (2001). Delay discounting of money and alcohol in actively using alcoholics, currently abstinent alcoholics, and controls. *Psychopharmacology, 154*, 243–250.

Petry, N. M. (2003). Discounting of money, health, and freedom in substance abusers and controls. *Drug and Alcohol Dependence, 71*, 133–141.

Prelec, D., & Loewenstein, G. F. (1991). Decision making over time and under uncertainty: A common approach. *Management Science, 37*, 770–786.

Quiggin, J., & Horowitz, J. (1995). Time and risk. *Journal of Risk and Uncertainty, 10*, 37–55.

Rachlin, H. (2006). Notes on discounting. *Journal of the Experimental Analysis of Behavior, 85*, 425–435.

Rachlin, H., & Jones, B. A. (2008a). Social discounting and delay discounting. *Journal of Behavioral Decision Making, 21*, 29–43.

Rachlin, H., & Jones, B. A. (2008b). Altruism among relatives and non-relatives. *Behavioural Processes, 79*, 120–123.

Rachlin, H., Raineri, A., & Cross, D. (1991). Subjective probability and delay. *Journal of the Experimental Analysis of Behavior, 55*, 233–244.

Raineri, A., & Rachlin, H. (1993). The effect of temporal constraints on the value of money and other commodities. *Journal of Behavioral Decision Making, 94*, 77–94.

Rasmussen, E. B., Lawyer, S. R., & Reilly, W. (2010). Percent body fat is related to delay and probability discounting for food in humans. *Behavioural Processes, 83*, 23–30.

Redish, A. D., & Kurth-Nelson, Z. (2010). Neural models of delay discounting. In G. J. Madden, & W. K. Bickel (Eds.), *Impulsivity: The behavioral and neurological science of discounting* (pp. 123–158). Washington, DC: American Psychological Association.

Reed, D. D., Reed, F. D. D., Chok, J., & Brozyna, G. A. (2011). The tyranny of choice: Choice overload as a possible instance of effort discounting. *The Psychological Record, 61*, 547–560.

Richards, J. B., Mitchell, S. H., de Wit, H., & Seiden, L. S. (1997). Determination of discount functions in rats with an adjusting-amount procedure. *Journal of the Experimental Analysis of Behavior, 67*, 353–366.

Robles, E., & Vargas, P. A. (2007). Functional parameters of delay discounting assessment tasks: Order of presentation. *Behavioural Processes, 75*, 237–241.

Rodriguez, M. L., & Logue, A. W. (1988). Adjusting delay to reinforcement: Comparing choice in pigeons and humans. *Journal of Experimental Psychology: Animal Behavior Processes*, *14*, 105–117.

Rodzon, K., Berry, M. S., & Odum, A. L. (2011). Within-subject comparison of degree of delay discounting using titrating and fixed sequence procedures. *Behavioural Processes*, *86*, 164–167.

Rosati, A. G., Stevens, J. R., Hare, B., & Hauser, M. D. (2007). The evolutionary origins of human patience: Temporal preferences in chimpanzees, bonobos, and human adults. *Current Biology*, *17*, 1663–1668.

Scheres, A., Dijkstra, M., Ainslie, E., Balkan, J., Reynolds, B., Sonuga-Barke, E., & Castellanos, F. X. (2006). Temporal and probabilistic discounting of rewards in children and adolescents: Effects of age and ADHD symptoms. *Neuropsychologia*, *44*, 2092–2103.

Simpson, C. A., & Vuchinich, R. E. (2000). Reliability of a measure of temporal discounting. *The Psychological Record*, *50*, 3–16.

Stevens, J. R., Hallinan, E. V., & Hauser, M. D. (2005). The ecology and evolution of patience in two New World monkeys. *Biology Letters*, *1*, 223–226.

Stevens, J. R., & Mühlhoff, N. (2012). Intertemporal choice in lemurs. *Behavioural Processes*, *89*, 121–127.

Szpunar, K. K., Watson, J. M., & McDermott, K. B. (2007). Neural substrates of envisioning the future. *Proceedings of the National Academy of Sciences of the United States of America*, *104*, 642–647.

Tayler, S., Arantes, J., & Grace, R. C. (2009). Temporal discounting for monetary and close relationship outcomes. *Personal Relationships*, *16*, 385–400.

Thaler, R. H. (1981). Some empirical evidence on dynamic inconsistency. *Economics Letters*, *8*, 201–207.

Thaler, R. H. (1985). Mental accounting and consumer choice. *Marketing Science*, *4*, 199–214.

Tsukayama, E., & Duckworth, A. L. (2010). Domain-specific temporal discounting and temptation. *Judgment and Decision Making*, *5*, 72–82.

von Neumann, J., & Morgenstern, O. (1953). *Theory of games and economic behavior.* Princeton, NJ: Princeton University Press.

Weatherly, J. N., Plumm, K. M., & Derenne, A. (2011). Delay discounting and social policy issues. *The Psychological Record*, *61*, 527–546.

Weber, B. J., & Huettel, S. A. (2008). The neural substrates of probabilistic and intertemporal decision making. *Brain Research*, *1234*, 104–115.

Winstanley, C. A. (2010). The neural and neurochemical basis of delay discounting. In G. J. Madden, & W. K. Bickel (Eds.), *Impulsivity: The behavioral and neurological science of discounting* (pp. 95–121). Washington, DC: American Psychological Association.

Woolverton, W. L., Freeman, K. B., Myerson, J., & Green, L. (2012). Suppression of cocaine self-administration in monkeys: Effects of delayed punishment. *Psychopharmacology*, *220*, 509–517.

Woolverton, W. L., Myerson, J., & Green, L. (2007). Delay discounting of cocaine by rhesus monkeys. *Experimental and Clinical Psychopharmacology*, *15*, 238–244.

Yi, R., & Landes, R. D. (2012). Temporal and probability discounting by cigarette smokers following acute smoking abstinence. *Nicotine and Tobacco Research*, *14*, 547–558.

Yi, R., Mitchell, S. H., & Bickel, W. K. (2010). Delay discounting and substance abuse-dependence. In G. J. Madden, & W. K. Bickel (Eds.), *Impulsivity: The behavioral and neurological science of discounting* (pp. 191–211). Washington, DC: American Psychological Association.

Yoon, J. H., Higgins, S. T., Heil, S. H., Sugarbaker, R. J., Thomas, C. S., & Badger, G. J. (2007). Delay discounting predicts postpartum relapse to cigarette smoking among pregnant women. *Experimental and Clinical Psychopharmacology*, *15*, 176–186.

14

Characteristics, Theories, and Implications of Dynamic Changes in Reinforcer Effectiveness

Frances K. McSweeney and Eric S. Murphy

The formulation of the Matching Law (Herrnstein, 1970) changed the dependent variable in many studies of operant conditioning from the moment-by-moment changes in responding studied by Skinner (e.g., Skinner, 1938) and others to response rate averaged over the experimental session. The use of averaged responding rests on the assumption that responding does not change systematically within sessions. If it does, then average measures will obscure significant changes in behavior at a more molecular level.

Recent evidence shows that operant response rates are not constant within experimental sessions, but may increase, decrease, or increase and then decrease within the session (e.g., McSweeney, 1992; see Figure 14.1). These within-session changes in responding may appear during the first session of training and persist after many sessions (e.g., 60) of exposure to schedules that provide a flat distribution of reinforcers within the session (e.g., variable-interval (VI) schedules; McSweeney & Hinson, 1992). The changes are not transitional effects (e.g., acquisition curves).

Within-session changes in responding deserve study because they are not anticipated by existing theories. The changes are also at least as large as those usually studied by operant psychologists. For example, McSweeney, Roll, and Weatherly (1994) reported that rate of responding changed by a factor of 92 from the beginning to the end of the session. Admittedly, the reported size of the change would be different if the changes had been measured over different time intervals, but within-session changes in responding are clearly large.

Within-session changes in responding are also highly general. McSweeney and Roll (1993) found such changes in approximately 200 studies that used procedures such as positive reinforcement, avoidance, punishment, extinction, discrimination, delayed matching to sample (DMTS), concept formation, maze and alley running, and laboratory analogues of foraging. The studies employed a wide variety of schedules

The Wiley Blackwell Handbook of Operant and Classical Conditioning, First Edition.
Edited by Frances K. McSweeney and Eric S. Murphy.

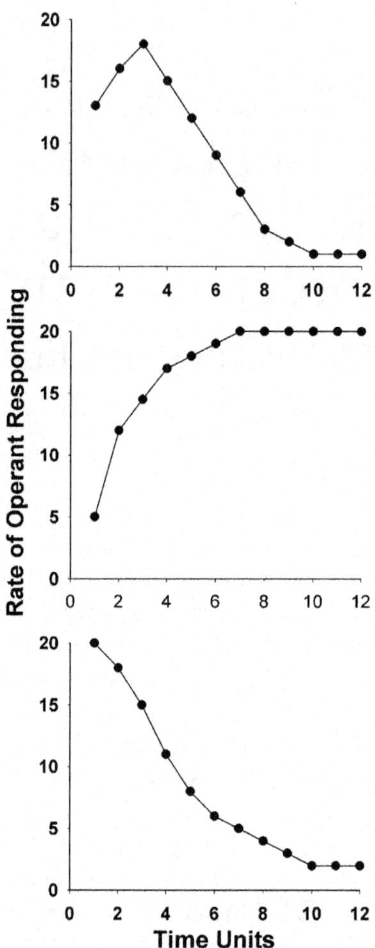

Figure 14.1 Three common within-session patterns of operant responding as a function of time. The units of time and behavior are arbitrary. The results show that operant response rate may increase (middle graph), decrease (bottom graph), or increase and then decrease (top graph) within the experimental session even when the conditions of reinforcement are held constant across the session. From "Dynamic changes in reinforcer effectiveness: Theoretical, methodological, and practical implications for applied research," by E. S. Murphy, F. K. McSweeney, R. G. Smith, and J. J. McComas (2003), *Journal of Applied Behavior Analysis, 36*, p. 422. Copyright 2003 by the Society for the Experimental Analysis of Behavior, Inc. Reprinted with permission.

including continuous reinforcement, fixed interval (FI), fixed ratio (FR), VI, differential reinforcement of low rates of responding (DRL), differential reinforcement of other behavior, multiple, concurrent, and second-order. The changes occurred for a wide variety of species, including mice, rats, pigeons, goldfish, raccoons, rhesus and cebus monkeys, greater galagos, and slow loris.

In this chapter, we will review the empirical characteristics of within-session changes in operant responding and then consider potential theoretical explanations for them. We conclude that sensitization (increases in responding) and habituation (decreases in responding) to the sensory properties of the reinforcer alter the ability of the reinforcer to support behavior with its repeated delivery. We discuss some methodological, applied, and theoretical implications of this idea for the basic and applied conditioning literatures and beyond. The predictions of the habituation hypothesis are interesting because they differ markedly from those of more traditional concepts, such as satiation.

Empirical Characteristics

Reinforcer Rate (Stimulus Rate)

Changing the rate of reinforcement changes the form of the within-session pattern of responding. Within-session changes usually peak earlier in the session and are larger when reinforcers are presented at higher, than at lower, rates. Figure 14.1 illustrates this finding. Delivering reinforcers at the intermediate rate used in many studies (e.g., 60 reinforcers/hour) usually produces the bitonic response pattern (top graph). Delivering no reinforcers (see "Extinction") or delivering reinforcers at high rates (e.g., 120 reinforcers/hour or more) usually produces the decreasing response pattern (bottom graph). Responding usually does not change within sessions when reinforcers are delivered at low rates (e.g., fewer than 15 reinforcers per hour). Although primarily increasing patterns are sometimes found (middle graph), the factors that produce these patterns are not known (see McSweeney, 1992; McSweeney, Roll, & Cannon, 1994; McSweeney, Roll, & Weatherly, 1994; McSweeney, Swindell, & Weatherly, 1996b; 1998; Murphy, McSweeney, & Kowal, 2007).

Presentation, Not Amount

Weatherly, McSweeney, and Swindell (1995, Experiment 1) reported that changing the rate of reinforcement exerted its effect because of changes in the number of reinforcers presented, not because of changes in the amount of food delivered. Pigeons responded on five different multiple schedules that provided scheduled rates of reinforcement from 15 to 240 reinforcers per hour. The size of the food reinforcers changed with the schedule so that subjects obtained at most 300 seconds of reinforcement per session during all schedules. The within-session pattern of responding changed with the change in schedule even though the total amount of food presented per session was constant (see also "Reinforcer Size," "Prefeedings").

Reinforcer Effectiveness

The ability of the reinforcer to control behavior (its effectiveness or value) changes systematically within sessions when measured by a probe preference test (e.g., Williams, 1991). In McSweeney, Weatherly, and Swindell (1996a), pigeons' left-key pecking was reinforced by mixed grain delivered by VI 15-second, VI 30-second, VI 60-second, VI 120-second or VI 240-second schedules in different conditions. Every

30 seconds, the right key was also illuminated for 30 seconds with a probability of 0.1. When the right key was illuminated, pecking that key yielded wheat according to a VI 60-second schedule. The ratio of the response rates for mixed grain and wheat changed systematically within the session during schedules that provided high rates of mixed grain reinforcement (e.g., 60–240 reinforcers/hour). Because the rate of responding for wheat remained relatively constant across the session, the changes in these ratios were attributed to changes in the effectiveness of the mixed grain reinforcers within the session.

Absolute, Not Relative, Time or Number

Within-session patterns of responding depend on absolute, not relative, time in the session. For example, McSweeney, Weatherly, and Swindell (1995a) varied session duration from 20 to 100 minutes in 5 steps. Within-session patterns were identical for sessions of different lengths when the patterns were plotted in terms of successive 5-minute intervals in the session (absolute time), not in terms of proportion of total-session time (relative time; see also McSweeney, 1992; McSweeney, Roll, & Cannon, 1994). However, these experiments confounded time with number of reinforcers because they delivered reinforcers at the same rate at all times in the session. Therefore, the within-session pattern may depend on absolute number of reinforcer deliveries and/or absolute time.

Response-Independent Reinforcers (Classical Conditioning)

Within-session patterns of responding are observed when reinforcers are delivered independently of responding (classical conditioning). For example, McSweeney, Swindell, and Weatherly (1996b) exposed pigeons to an autoshaping procedure in which an 8-second key light was followed by response-independent food. The average intertrial interval varied from 7 to 232 seconds in different conditions. Rates of responding usually changed within sessions during the autoshaping procedures in a manner similar to that observed during operant conditioning (e.g., McSweeney, 1992; McSweeney, Roll, & Cannon, 1994. See also McSweeney, Swindell, & Weatherly, 1999).

Response Rate, Not Accuracy

Response accuracy usually does not change within sessions. McSweeney, Weatherly, and Swindell (1996c, Experiment 1) studied responding by pigeons on a DMTS procedure. A trial started when a sample stimulus (red or green light) was presented for at least 5 seconds. A choice period in which two keys were illuminated with white light followed the sample after a delay of 1, 5, 12, 8 or 3 seconds in different conditions. During the choice period, a peck on one key was correct if one sample stimulus was presented; a peck on the other key was correct if another sample was presented. A 20-second intertrial interval followed each trial and sessions ended after 60 minutes. Rate of responding on the sample stimulus changed systematically within sessions when the delay between the stimulus and the choice period was short (1–5 seconds; i.e., high reinforcer rate), but not when it was long (8–12 seconds; i.e., low reinforcer rate). The percentage of responses that were correct (response accuracy) did not change within sessions (see also Edhouse & White, 1988; Wilkie, 1986; but see also McSweeney, Weatherly, & Swindell, 1996c, Experiment 2; Olton & Samuelson, 1976).

Unconsumable and Unconsumed Reinforcers

Within-session changes in responding occur for reinforcers that are not consumed. Early studies showed that punishers (e.g., Azrin, 1960) and negative reinforcers (e.g., Jerome, Moody, Connor, & Ryan, 1958) may lose their effectiveness late in the session. Running in wheels by rats decreases within sessions (Aoyama & McSweeney, 2001a). Large within-session decreases in responding are reported during extinction when no reinforcers are delivered (see "Extinction"). Temple, Giacomelli, Roemmich, and Eptstein (2008) also reported systematic within-session changes in operant responding when human subjects played a computer game for potato chip reinforcers. Within-session changes in responding were observed regardless of whether subjects consumed the reinforcers during the session or only after the session ended (see Figure 14.2B).

Reinforcer Intensity (Stimulus Intensity)

Within-session patterns of responding may be steeper for less intense, than for more intense, reinforcers. Melville, Rue, Rybiski, and Weatherly (1997) reported that rats'

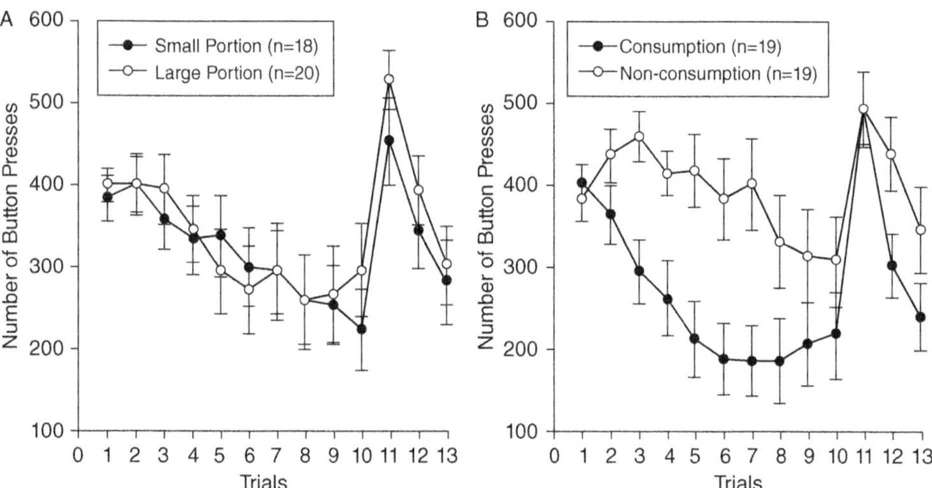

Figure 14.2 Stimulus specificity of operant responding in humans. Results are presented as mean number of responses for potato chips (trials 1–10) and M&M's (trials 11 –13) for individual subjects assigned to (A) small (75 kcal; black circles) and large (225 kcal; white circles) portions of food and (B) who consumed the food throughout the duration of the experiment (black circles) and those who had to delay consumption until the end (white circles). Error bars represent the standard error of the mean. From "Habituation and within-session changes in motivated responding for food in children," by J. L. Temple, A. M. Giacomelli, J. N. Roemmich, and L. H. Epstein (2008), *Appetite, 50,* p. 394. Copyright 2007 by Elsevier Ltd. Reprinted with permission.

responding sometimes decreased more steeply late in the session when less concentrated, rather than more concentrated, sucrose solutions served as reinforcers.

Experimental Context

Brief exposure to the experimental context may alter the within-session response pattern during a following session. McSweeney, Swindell, and Weatherly (1998) placed rats and pigeons in the experimental enclosure 0, 5, 10, 15 or 30 minutes before the start of an experimental session. Exposure to the experimental context for 5 minutes altered the within-session response pattern relative to the pattern shown when the session started immediately after the subject was placed in the enclosure. Increasing exposure from 5 to 30 minutes did not increase the effect beyond that seen with a 5-minute preexposure (see also Weatherly & McSweeney, 1995; but see also McSweeney & Johnson, 1994). Large within-session changes in responding also occur during sessions of extinction. Exposure to the experimental context may contribute to these changes (see "Extinction").

Recovery (Spontaneous Recovery)

Within-session patterns of responding recover if enough time elapses between sessions. The amount of recovery may increase with increases in time between sessions. For example, Murphy, McSweeney, Kowal, McDonald, and Wiediger (2006) reported that within-session patterns of responding were identical during two consecutive sessions that were separated by 24 hours, but not by 5 minutes or 2 hours when alcohol-preferring rats' lever pressing was reinforced by ethanol (see also Aoyama & McSweeney, 2001a; but see McSweeney & Johnson, 1994).

After Stimulus Change (Dishabituation)

Introducing an arbitrary stimulus, such as a light or noise, increases responding once the baseline is restored. For example, in Aoyama and McSweeney's (2001a) baseline condition, rats ran in a wheel for 30 minutes. In experimental conditions, a new stimulus was applied for 5 seconds at 20 min and 55 seconds into the session. The new stimulus was either an intermittently-applied brake or a flashing houselight. Rate of running was faster immediately after the new stimulus than it had been at a comparable time in the baseline condition (see Figure 14.3; McSweeney, Kowal, Murphy, & Varao, 2005; Murphy et al., 2006).

Changing some aspect of the experimental conditions for a brief time in the session has a similar effect. For example, in Aoyama and McSweeney's (2001b) baseline condition, rats' lever pressing was reinforced by food on an FR 4 schedule. During experimental conditions, the situation was changed for 3 minutes in the middle of the session in four ways: the lever was withdrawn; lever pressing was reinforced on an FR 6 schedule and two Noyes pellets were delivered per reinforcer; the schedule was changed to an FR 8; and two FR schedules (2 and 6) alternated. In all four cases, response rate increased relative to baseline after the changed condition was removed and subjects once again responded on the FR 4 schedule. This increase in responding was observed regardless of whether rate of responding decreased (e.g., no lever) or

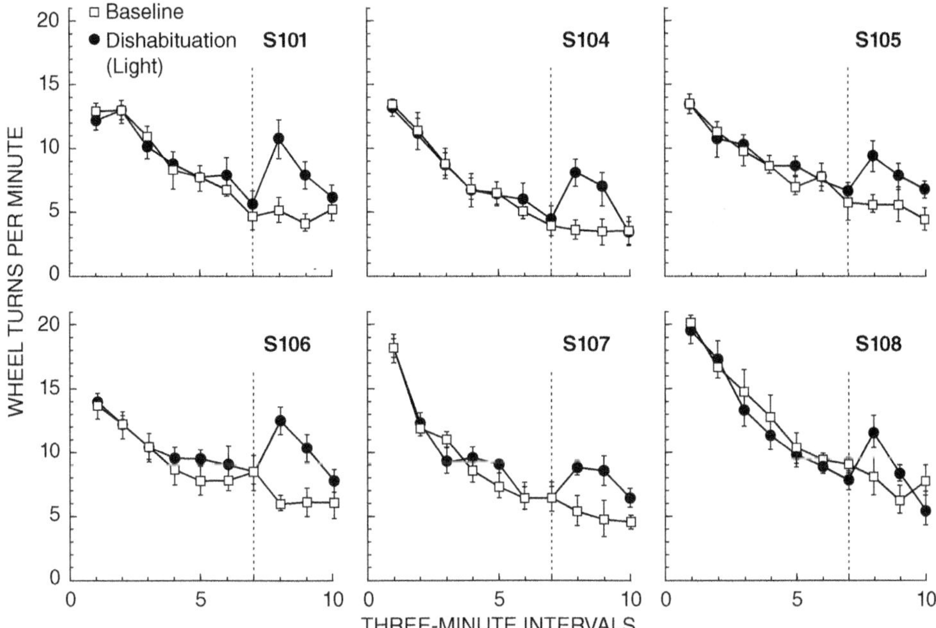

Figure 14.3 Dishabituation of wheel running in rats. Results are presented as rate of responding (responses/minute) during successive 3-minute intervals in the session. Each set of axes presents the results for an individual subject responding during baseline (open circles) and experimental (filled squares) conditions. The dotted vertical line indicates the time at which the stimulus was briefly changed in the experimental conditions. During the stimulus change, the houselight went off for 1 second, on for 1 second. Error bars represent the standard error of the mean. When error bars are not apparent, the bars were smaller than the diameter of the data symbol. From "Habituation contributes to within-session changes in free wheel running," by K. Aoyama and F. K. McSweeney (2001), *Journal of the Experimental Analysis of Behavior, 76*, p. 294. Copyright 2001 by the Society for the Experimental Analysis of Behavior, Inc. Reprinted with permission.

increased (e.g., FR 8) relative to baseline while the stimulus was changed. The increase also occurred regardless of whether subjects obtained more (e.g., FR 6-2 pellets) or less (e.g., no lever) food relative to baseline while the stimulus was changed (see also McSweeney & Roll, 1998; McSweeney, Kowal, Murphy, & Varao, 2005; but see also Ernst & Epstein, 2002).

During Stimulus Change (Stimulus Specificity)

Changing stimulus conditions also increases responding while that change is in effect, not just after baseline is restored (previous section). For example, Aoyama and McSweeney (2001a) examined wheel running in rats. Rats ran faster in the second half of the session when the wheel was changed in the middle of the session than when it was not (see also Figure 14.2; Epstein et al., 2003; Ernst & Epstein, 2002; McSweeney, Swindell, & Weatherly, 1996c; McSweeney, Weatherly, & Swindell,

1996a; Murphy et al., 2006; Temple, Giacomelli, Kent, Roemmich, & Epstein, 2007; Temple et al., 2006.)

Variety (Variety Effects)

Within-session decreases in responding occur more slowly to stimuli that are presented in a variable, than in a fixed, manner. For example, Ernst and Epstein (2002) allowed human participants to play a computer game for food delivered on a VR 32 schedule. In one condition, the food was always pieces of turkey sandwiches. In another condition, the food varied among three different foods that provided the same number of calories and macronutrient content as the constant food (pieces of turkey or roast beef sandwiches, potato chips). Within-session decreases in responding were steeper for those given the same food each time a reinforcer was delivered than for those given a variety of foods (see Figure 14.4; see also Aoyama & McSweeney, 2001b; Lupfer-Johnson, Murphy, Blackwell, LaCasse, & Drummond, 2010; Melville, Rue, Rybiski, & Weatherly, 1997; Murphy et al., 2007).

Reinforcer Size

Altering reinforcer size alters within-session response patterns, but only when the size change is large. Temple et al. (2008) reported no effect on within-session patterns when they changed reinforcer size by a factor of 3 for human participants (see Figure 14.2A). Cannon and McSweeney (1995) and Roll, McSweeney, Johnson, and

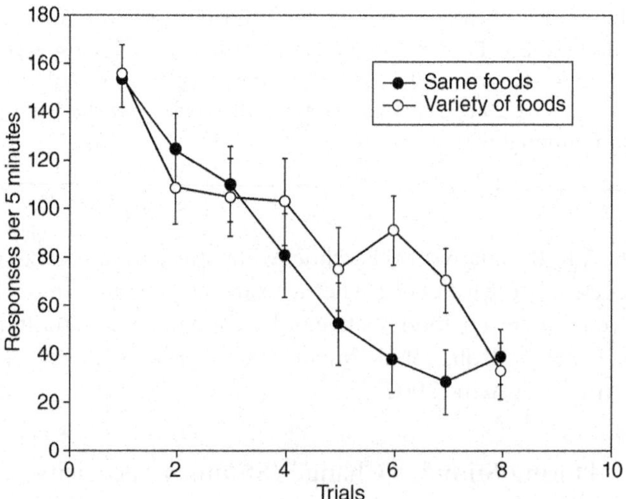

Figure 14.4 Variety effects in humans. Results are presented as the number of responses per 5-minute trial as a function of successive trials for the mean of all human subjects responding for turkey sandwiches (filled circles) or for three different isolcaloric foods (open circles). Error bars represent the standard error of the mean. From "Habituation of responding for food in humans" by M. M. Ernst and L. H. Epstein (2002), *Appetite*, 38, p. 229. Copyright 2002 by Elsevier Ltd. Reprinted with permission.

Weatherly (1995, Experiment 3) found that changing reinforcer size by a factor of 5, but not by a factor of 3, altered within-session patterns. For example, in Roll et al. (1995, Experiment 3), each reinforcer was 0.20 ml of condensed milk plus 0, 0.40 or 0.80 ml of condensed milk infused directly into the stomach in different conditions. The within-session response pattern changed when reinforcer size increased from 0.20 to 1.0 ml, but not from 0.20 to 0.60 ml (see also, Bizo, Bogdanov, & Killeen, 1998, Experiment 1; DeMarse, Killeen, & Baker, 1999, Experiment 2; Palya & Walter, 1997, Experiment 2).

Prefeedings

Feedings delivered before the session may alter within-session response patterns, but only when the pre-session food is eaten, not infused. DeMarse et al. (1999, Experiment 3; see also Murphy, McSweeney, & Kowal, 2003) fed pigeons 0, 5, 15 or 25 g of milo prior to a session in which pigeons' key pecks were reinforced by milo. The within-session decreases in responding were steeper for larger pre-feedings than for smaller ones. In contrast, Roll et al. (1995, Experiment 2) examined responding by rats when no prefeedings were given. Then the amount of condensed milk reinforcer consumed up to the point in the session at which the peak response rate occurred was calculated for each rat. Subjects were divided into two groups that received either 1.0 or 2.0 times their predetermined amount of milk infused directly into the stomach, immediately before the session. Prefeeding the subjects did not alter the within-session pattern of responding from its baseline form for either group. An explanation for the differences in results between these studies will be offered in "Reinforcer Delivery."

Factors That Do Not Alter the Within-Session Response Pattern

To date, manipulating several factors has failed to alter within-session patterns of responding. These factors include: handling the subject before the session (McSweeney & Johnson, 1994); deprivation for the reinforcer (Roll et al., 1995, Experiment 2); the caloric density of the reinforcer (McSweeney et al., 1990; Roll et al., 1995; but see Melville et al., 1997, in "Reinforcer Intensity (Stimulus Intensity)"—a potential explanation for the different results of these studies will be offered in "Reinforcer Delivery"); and the nature and rate of responding (Aoyama & McSweeney, 2001a; 2001b; Ernst & Epstein, 2002; McSweeney, 1992; McSweeney, Hatfield, & Allen, 1990; McSweeney & Johnson, 1994; McSweeney, Roll, & Cannon, 1994; McSweeney, Roll, & Weatherly, 1994; McSweeney, Weatherly, & Roll, 1995; McSweeney, Weatherly, Roll, & Swindell, 1995; Melville, Rybiski, & Kamrani, 1996). Of course, negative results are difficult to interpret. Future experiments might show an effect of these variables if, for example, the variables were manipulated over a wider range.

Quantitative Descriptions

Two equations have described within-session patterns of responding well (see also E. G. Bittar, Del-Claro, L. G. Bittar, & da Silva, 2012, for a new model that deserves further evaluation). McSweeney, Hinson, and Cannon (1996) proposed Equation 1.

P is the predicted proportion of total-session responses that should occur during a time interval in the session. T is the ordinal number of that time interval in the session; e is the base of the natural logarithm and a, b, and c are free parameters. We will argue later that a and b govern habituation and c applies to sensitization (see "Reinforcer Delivery").

$$P = \frac{b}{e^{aT}} - \frac{c}{c+T} \tag{1}$$

Aoyama and McSweeney (2001b; see also Aoyama, 1998, 2000) proposed Equation 2 where R_r is rate of operant responding, R_c is cumulative number of reinforcers delivered, and a and b are free parameters. Parameter b is the y-axis intercept of the regression line (i.e., response rate at the beginning of the session) and a is the slope of the regression line (i.e., the decrease in response rate produced by an obtained reinforcer).

$$R_r = b - aR_c \tag{2}$$

Both equations fit the data well. For example, Equation 1 accounted for a median of 92% of the variance in 106 data sets (McSweeney, Hinson, & Cannon, 1996). As will be discussed, this equation also describes data taken from the literatures on extinction (see "Extinction"), habituation (see "Habituation"), and motivation (see "Motivation"). Equation 2 has the advantage of parsimony because it is a simple linear equation. It also fits the data well when within-session decreases in responding are observed (e.g., Aoyama, 1998, 2000; Aoyama & McSweeney, 2001b). However, it must be supplemented by other equations to describe the often-observed early-session increases in responding.

Potential Theoretical Explanations

Responding

Operant responding might increase early in the session as subjects' muscles warm up. Responding might decrease later in the session because of fatigue (e.g., Mosso, 1906). Contradicting this idea, many studies have shown that changing the nature, or rate, of the response over a wide range does not alter the within-session pattern of responding (see "Factors That Do Not Alter the Within-Session Response Pattern").

Interfering Responses

A response (e.g., exploration) might wane early in the session (e.g., Bindra, 1959), allowing operant responding to increase. Another response (e.g., falling asleep; e.g., Pavlov, 1928) might develop as the session progresses, forcing operant responding to decline.

To date, studies have ruled out two potential candidates for these interfering responses: exploration (Roll & McSweeney, 1997) and adjunctive behaviors (e.g.,

Falk, 1971). For example, McSweeney, Swindell, and Weatherly (1996a) examined rats' lever pressing that was reinforced by food delivered by different FI schedules in different conditions. A drinking spout (Experiment 1) or running wheel (Experiment 2) was also available during some conditions, but not during others. Within-session patterns of lever pressing did not differ when either drinking or running was available than when it was not. The correlation between the amount of lever pressing and the amount of drinking or running at a particular time in the session was also positive for some schedules and subjects, and negative for others. Within-session changes in adjunctive drinking and running were not consistently negatively correlated with within-session changes in operant responding, as predicted by the interfering response theory.

A General Motivational State

Within-session patterns of responding might be attributed to changes in a general motivational state, such as arousal (e.g., Killeen, Hanson, & Osborne, 1978). Arousal has been defined in many ways (e.g., Anderson, 1990; Duffy, 1962; Neiss, 1988), but the most common definition is probably a state of the animal that determines the "energy" level of its behavior (e.g., Duffy, 1962). If a general motivational state changed within the session, then changes in all behaviors would be positively correlated during that session. Instead, as just argued, McSweeney, Swindell, and Weatherly (1996a) reported that the correlation between rate of lever pressing and the rate of drinking or running at a particular time in the session was inconsistently positive or negative (see also McSweeney, Swindell, & Weatherly, 1996c).

Time

Responding might increase early in the session if subjects required time to recover from the handling that brought them to the experimental enclosure. Responding might decrease late in the session in anticipation of the session's end. For example, a conditioned emotional response might interfere with operant responding as subjects anticipate being handled again after the session (e.g., Estes & Skinner, 1941).

McSweeney and Johnson's (1994) results question a contribution from recovery from handling. In their experiment, pigeons' key-pecking was reinforced by food delivered by a VI 1-minute schedule in two successive 50-minute sessions. Subjects were handled during the intersession interval in some conditions, but not in others. Early-session increases in responding occurred in the second of their 50-minute sessions even if subjects were not handled between the first and second sessions.

McSweeney, Weatherly, and Swindell's (1995a) results question a contribution from anticipation of the end of the session. They reported that within-session response patterns were identical regardless of whether the end of the session was predictable (constant-length sessions) or unpredictable (randomly-ended sessions). If anticipatory factors produced the late-session decreases in responding, then these late-session decreases should have been eliminated when the end of the session could not be anticipated (see also the within-session patterns of responding during the first session of conditioning in McSweeney, 1992).

Cognitive Factors

Within-session changes in responding might be caused by within-session changes in several cognitive factors, including memory (Spear, 1973), attention (Blough, 1983), or information overload (e.g., Richardson & Campbell, 1992) or underload (e.g., boredom). Results to date have ruled out two potential definitions of changes in attention as causes of within-session changes in responding.

First, changes in the accuracy of responding during DMTS procedures are often taken as an index of changes in attention to the task (e.g., McCarthy & Voss, 1995). McSweeney, Weatherly, and Swindell (1996c, Experiment 1) reported that the accuracy of responding (percentage correct) during a DMTS procedure did not change within sessions even when the rate of responding on the sample stimulus did change systematically within sessions (see "Response Rate, Not Accuracy").

Second, the operant contingency might exert greater control over behavior when subjects attend to the experimental task than when they do not. During discrimination tasks, increasing control by the operant contingency should produce an increase in responding during S+ (responding is reinforced) and a decrease in responding during S– (responding is not reinforced). Therefore, response rates should change in the opposite directions during S+ and S– if attention to the task changes within the session. Instead, McSweeney, Weatherly, and Swindell (1996c, Experiment 2) reported that rate of responding during the S+ and S– of multiple VI extinction schedules changed in similar, not opposite, ways within the session (see also McSweeney, Roll, & Weatherly, 1994).

Reinforcer Delivery

Factors related to the delivery of reinforcers contribute to the within-session changes in responding. For example, changing the rate of reinforcement changes the within-session pattern (see "Reinforcer Rate (Stimulus Rate)"). In addition, the ability of the reinforcer to control behavior also changes systematically within sessions (see "Reinforcer Effectiveness").

The question then becomes, what variable produces these systematic changes in reinforcer effectiveness? Because food served as the reinforcer in most of our experiments, we initially thought that satiation causes the within-session decreases in reinforcer effectiveness. In fact, a definition of satiation that is often used in the operant literature identifies these changes as satiation. For example, Millenson (1967, p. 367) states, "Satiation is . . . repeatedly presenting the reinforcer until it loses its power to reinforce." Unfortunately, this definition of satiation provides a redundant description, not an explanation for within-session changes in operant responding. To avoid this problem, we turned to the satiety literature for a more substantive definition.

Those who study satiation often use that term to describe the collection of factors that contribute to the termination of ingestive behaviors such as feeding and drinking (e.g., Mook, 1996). However, many variables that help to terminate ingestive behaviors play little or no role in producing within-session changes in responding. Manipulating such classic satiety factors as caloric density, deprivation for the reinforcer (see "Factors That Do Not Alter the Within-Session Response Pattern"), intubated stomach loading (see "Prefeedings"), and reinforcer size (see "Reinforcer Size") failed to alter within-session response patterns, altered them only when large changes were made, or altered them in the wrong direction (see "Reinforcer Intensity (Stimulus Intensity)"). Within-session decreases in operant responding also occurred even when subjects did not eat the food reinforcer or responded for reinforcers that are not consumable (see "Unconsumable and Unconsumed Reinforcers").

One satiety factor remained untested, however. Habituation to the sensory properties of food contributes to satiety for food (e.g., Swithers & Hall, 1994). "Habituation" is a decline in responsiveness to a stimulus when that stimulus is presented repeatedly or for a prolonged time (e.g., Groves & Thompson, 1970). "Sensitization" is an increase in responsiveness to a stimulus early in its presentation or after the presentation of a strong, different, or extra stimulus (e.g., Groves & Thompson, 1970).

We hypothesized that sensitization and habituation occur to the sensory properties of repeatedly presented reinforcers and that those processes alter the ability of that reinforcer to control behavior. According to this idea, sensitization increases the effectiveness of reinforcers during their first few presentations leading to an early-session increase in operant responding. Habituation decreases the effectiveness of later reinforcers leading to a late-session decrease in operant responding.

Many arguments support the idea that sensitization and habituation to the reinforcer primarily cause within-session changes in operant responding. McSweeney, Hinson, and Cannon (1996), McSweeney and Roll (1998), and McSweeney and Murphy (2000) provided reviews. To recap, we believe that the habituation hypothesis is compatible with the evidence that others have offered to support the satiety hypothesis (e.g., Bizo et al., 1998; DeMarse et al., 1999; Hinson & Tennison, 1999). The habituation hypothesis also explains some conflicting data reported earlier. For example, prefeedings alter the form of the within-session patterns when the food is eaten but not when it is infused (see "Prefeedings"). Subjects are exposed to all of the stimulus properties of the food when they eat that food. Subjects are not exposed to many of the stimulus properties of food when that food is infused (e.g., its taste, smell, shape, color). As a result, eaten prefeedings should produce some habituation to the food, but infused prefeedings should produce little habituation to the food. The large habituation produced by eaten, but not by the infused, prefeedings should alter later within-session patterns if those patterns are caused by habituation to the reinforcer.

Melville et al. (1997) reported that within-session changes in responding were steeper for lower, than for higher, calorie reinforcers when calories were manipulated by changing sucrose concentration (see "Reinforcer Intensity (Stimulus Intensity)"). In contrast, Roll et al. (1995) reported that altering caloric density had no effect when calories were manipulated across different types of reinforcers (e.g., sucrose, saccharin). Neither of these results is easy to reconcile with the idea that satiation produces within-session decreases in responding. Higher caloric foods should produce quicker satiety. In contrast, the divergent results are compatible with habituation. Habituation is more rapid for weaker than for stronger stimuli (e.g., Thompson & Spencer, 1966). Therefore, Melville et al.'s results are compatible with habituation if manipulating sucrose concentration produced its effect by altering the perceived intensity of sucrose, rather than by altering its caloric content. If this reasoning is correct, then it should be possible to reproduce Melville et al.'s results by altering the intensity of the reinforcer in ways that do not manipulate calories (e.g., by altering the concentration of a non-nutritive flavoring).

Nevertheless, the strongest argument in favor of habituation is that the empirical characteristics of within-session changes in responding are strikingly similar to the empirical characteristics of habituation (e.g., McSweeney, Hinson, & Cannon, 1996; McSweeney & Roll, 1998). Since the time of Thompson and Spencer (1966), conformity to a list of empirical properties has been used as a test for the presence of habituation (e.g., Leaton & Tighe, 1976). Table 14.1 provides such a list. The list is adapted from the consensus list proposed by Rankin et al. (2009). Some of Rankin et al.'s definitions have been slightly revised in Table 14.1 to shorten them without changing their meaning. Rankin et al.'s characteristics have also been increased from 10 to 15 as follows. First, two characteristics of sensitization, taken from Groves and Thompson (1970), have been added to Rankin et al.'s list which applies only to habituation. An additional characteristic of habituation, generality (see Characteristic 13), has been added because habituation is so often observed for different stimuli, responses and species (e.g., Thorpe, 1966). Rankin et al.'s Characteristic 4 has been divided into two parts "stimulus rate" and "stimulus rate and recovery" because stimulus rate has been frequently studied in the literatures that we review, but the effect of stimulus rate on spontaneous recovery has not been studied. Listing these two characteristics as one would leave the mistaken impression that both have been confirmed. Finally, variety effects (e.g., Broster & Rankin, 1994) have been added to Rankin et al.'s list (see our Characteristic 9). Rankin et al. may have omitted this characteristic because variety effects are a direct prediction of their Characteristic 7, stimulus specificity, so adding it may be redundant. We have included it because many authors address stimulus specificity by studying variety effects.

To date, within-session changes in operant responding have shown 12 of the 15 characteristics of sensitization and habituation listed in Table 14.1. The other characteristics have not been studied. Several of the confirmed characteristics were tested as true predictions of the habituation hypothesis and are difficult to reconcile with an explanation in terms of satiation. These characteristics include dishabituation, faster habituation for less intense than for more intense stimuli, stimulus specificity, and variety effects. We have used the labels of the characteristics listed in Table 14.1 to head earlier sections of this chapter to make it easy to find the data supporting each of these conclusions. The similarities between habituation and within-session changes in responding are also quantitative as well as qualitative. When McSweeney, Hinson, and Cannon (1996) fit Equation 1 to 145 data sets taken from the habituation literature, it accounted for a median of 89% of the variance in the data.

As a result of these similarities, we believe that the contribution of habituation to within-session changes in responding has been established. In fact, researchers have applied the term habituation to phenomena that share as few as three of the characteristics of habituation (e.g., Eisenstein & Peretz, 1973). Nevertheless, we are not arguing that factors other than sensitization-habituation never contribute to within-session changes in responding. Most of our studies used easy-to-manipulate operanda and intermediate rates of reinforcement. Other variables might contribute under more extreme conditions.

Implications for Conditioning

Although the distinction between satiation and habituation may seem trivial, the implications of these two ideas actually differ substantially. We will discuss some of

Table 14.1 Empirical characteristics of sensitization and habituation

#	*Characteristic*	*W*	*D*	*E*	*M*
1	Responding decreases. Repeated or prolonged presentation of a stimulus results in a progressive decrease in some parameter of a response to an asymptotic level.	x	x	x	x
2	Spontaneous recovery. Responsiveness to a habituated stimulus recovers at least partially when that stimulus is not presented for a time.	x	x	x	x
3	Potentiation of habituation. Habituation may become more rapid and/or pronounced with repeated habituations.	x		x	
4	Stimulus rate. Faster rates of stimulus presentation yield faster and more pronounced habituation than slower rates.	x	x	x	
5	Stimulus rate and recovery. Spontaneous recovery may be faster after faster, than after slower, rates of stimulus presentation.				
6	Stimulus intensity. The weaker the stimulus, the more rapid and pronounced the habituation.	x			
7	Habituation below zero. Repeated stimulus presentations after the response reaches asymptote may alter subsequent behavior.			x	
8	Stimulus specificity. Habituation is disrupted by changes in the presented stimulus.	x	x	x	x
9	Variety effects. Habituation occurs more slowly to stimuli presented in a variable, rather than a fixed, manner.	x	x		x
10	[a]Dishabituation. Presenting a strong, different or extra stimulus restores responsiveness to a habituated stimulus.	x	x	x	x
11	Dishabituation habituates. The amount of dishabituation decreases with repeated applications of the dishabituating stimulus.		x		
12	Long-term habituation. Some habituation is learned and persists over time.	x	x	x	
13	Generality. Habituation occurs for many, if not all, stimuli and species of animals.	x	x	x	x
14	Sensitization by early-stimulus presentations. An increase in responsiveness may occur during the first few presentations of a stimulus.	x	x	x	x
15	[a]Sensitization by stimuli from another modality. An increase in responsiveness to a stimulus may be produced by the introduction of a stimulus from another modality (e.g., a light or noise).	x	x	x	x

Note. The table is based on the characteristics listed in Rankin et al. (2009) with the exceptions noted in the text. An x in the column under the heading of within-session changes (**W**, see "Empirical Characteristics"), drug consumption (**D**, McSweeney, Murphy, & Kowal, 2005), extinction (**E**, McSweeney & Swindell, 2002) and motivated behavior (**M**, McSweeney & Swindel, 1999b) indicates that this characteristic had been shown for that phenomenon at the time of the cited literature review.

[a] Both sensitization (Characteristic 15) and dishabituation (Characteristic 10) may involve the introduction of a stimulus from another modality. Results are conventionally described as "dishabituation" if the added stimulus restores responsiveness to an already habituated stimulus and as "sensitization" if the added stimulus increases responding before substantial habituation occurs to the other stimulus (e.g., Marcus, Nolen, Rankin, & Carew, 1988).

the potential implications of the habituation hypothesis in the following sections. The role of habituation in understanding any one of the following phenomena is far from proven. Nevertheless, the presence of many of the striking characteristics of habituation in most of the following literatures convince us that the contribution of habituation to these phenomena is worth examining.

Methodological Implications

Within-session Designs. Within-session procedures present different values of an independent variable in different parts of a single session rather than in different sessions (e.g., Ettinger & Staddon, 1983; Heyman, 1983). Unfortunately, within-session changes in responding may create problems for using this methodology. Within-session changes in responding may be confounded with the independent variable, thus complicating the interpretation of the data (see also McSweeney, Weatherly, & Swindell, 1995b).

Group or Single-subject Designs. Finding that within-session changes in responding occur and are governed by absolute session time (see "Absolute, Not Relative, Time") suggests that group or single-subject designs should not confound session length with other experimental variables. For example, when studying the effect of rate of reinforcement on rate of responding, the experimenter must confound either session length or number of reinforcers delivered per session with rate of reinforcement. Session length is often confounded because it is assumed not to alter response rates (e.g., Catania & Reynolds, 1968). If, however, responding changes systematically with absolute time in the session, then the rate of responding averaged over the session will differ for sessions of different lengths. As a result, the answer to some theoretical questions may vary with session length. For example, McSweeney (1992) reported that response rate at the beginning of an operant session increased monotonically with increases in the rate of reinforcement, confirming some theories (e.g., Herrnstein, 1970). Responding later in the session increased up to a point and then decreased, confirming other theories (e.g., Baum, 1981; Staddon, 1979). Experimenters should be wary of drawing theoretical conclusions when sessions of different lengths are conducted for different values of their independent variable.

Applied Implications

Murphy, McSweeney, Smith, and McComas (2003) discussed several implications of changes in reinforcer effectiveness for applied behavior analysis. We will give only one example here. If sensitization and habituation alter the strength of reinforcers, then the characteristics listed in Table 14.1 can be used to maintain the effectiveness of needed reinforcers (increase sensitization and decrease habituation) and to weaken the effectiveness of problematic reinforcers (decrease sensitization and increase habituation).

For example, food is often used as a reinforcer for autistic children. To preserve the effectiveness of this reinforcer, a behavior analyst might offer a variety of foods instead of only one (Table 14.1, Characteristic 9). He or she should present the reinforcers according to a variable, rather than a fixed, schedule (Table 14.1, Characteristic 9). He or she should deliver sensitizers by introducing extraneous stimuli or by working in a noisy, busy, environment (Table 14.1, Characteristic 15). Finally, giving the child a nibble of food might restore the effectiveness of food as a reinforcer once that effectiveness has been lost (Table 14.1, Characteristic 14). Murphy et al. (2003) reviewed evidence that these techniques will work.

Theoretical Implications

Because of space limitations, we will omit a discussion of behavioral economics. The interested reader can find such a discussion in McSweeney and Swindell (1999a) and in McSweeney, Swindell, and Weatherly (1996c). We will also omit a discussion of theories of absolute response rates because we discussed them briefly in "Methodological Implications."

The Matching Law. The generalized matching law (GML) provides a leading description of operant choice behavior (Baum, 1974; Herrnstein, 1970; Equation 3). The rates of responding emitted on, the time spent responding on, and the values of the reinforcers obtained from, one schedule (component) of a concurrent schedule are symbolized by P_1, T_1, and V_1, respectively. The same variables for the other component are symbolized by P_2, T_2, and V_2. Many factors contribute to reinforcer value including the size of the reinforcers, the immediacy of their delivery, and their rate of delivery (e.g., Baum, 1974). The *a* and *b* parameters are "bias" and "sensitivity to reinforcement," respectively. Bias represents preference for an alternative that is not explained by differences in the values of the reinforcers provided by the alternatives (e.g., a position, operandum, or color preference). Sensitivity represents the degree to which preference changes with changes in reinforcer ratios.

$$\frac{P_1}{P_2} = \frac{T_1}{T_2} = a\left(\frac{V_1}{V_2}\right)^b \qquad (3)$$

Unfortunately, within-session changes in responding will create problems for assessing the validity of the GML if within-session response patterns differ for the two components of a concurrent schedule. For example, suppose that the peak rate of responding occurs earlier in the session and the within-session changes are larger for components that provide higher, than for those that provide lower, rates of reinforcement (e.g., McSweeney, 1992). In that case, the ratio of the more preferred to the less preferred response rate would not be constant, but would increase to a peak and then decrease, within the session. If the peak rate of responding was reached at a constant time after the beginning of the session regardless of session length, as it is for simple schedules (e.g., McSweeney, 1992; McSweeney, Roll, & Cannon, 1994), then the ratio of response rates would also differ for sessions of different lengths when that ratio was calculated across the entire session (see McSweeney, Swindell, & Weatherly, 1996c for more details).

Within-session changes in responding would not cause problems for the GML if the changes occurred similarly for the two components. Suppose, for example, that within-session changes are related to changes in a multiplier that modulates the absolute rates at which subjects respond. If this multiplier changed in the same way within the session for the two components of a concurrent schedule, then its effect would cancel when the ratios of the response rates were calculated.

To date, within-session patterns of responding have been similar for the two components of a concurrent schedule even when the components differ in the rates of reinforcement they provide, the types of responses they require, or the simple schedules they deliver (McSweeney, Murphy, & Kowal, 2001; McSweeney, Weatherly, & Roll, 1995; McSweeney, Weatherly, & Swindell, 1996b). Neither the parameters, nor goodness of fit, of Equation 3 changed systematically within sessions for these types of concurrent schedules (McSweeney et al., 2001; McSweeney, Weatherly, & Roll, 1995).

In contrast, within-session patterns of responding differ for the components of concurrent schedules when those components provided qualitatively different reinforcers (food and water for rats or wheat and mixed grain for pigeons; McSweeney, Swindell, & Weatherly, 1996c). For most subjects, the bias and sensitivity to reinforcement parameters of the GML, as well as the percentage of variance accounted for, decreased within the session. Negative sensitivity parameters were sometimes found late in the session for concurrent schedules that provided food in one component and water in the other component.

These results suggest that the mechanism that determines within-session changes in responding integrates (e.g., sums) the reinforcers obtained from the two components of a concurrent schedule as long as the two components provide qualitatively-similar reinforcers. The mechanism does not integrate those reinforcers when the components provide qualitatively different reinforcers. As a result, within-session changes in responding cause problems for assessing the validity of the GML only when the components provide qualitatively different reinforcers (see also Heyman, 1993).

Extinction. Extinction refers to a decrease in operant responding that occurs when a conditioned response is no longer followed by the reinforcer. It also refers to a decrease in a classically conditioned response when the conditioned stimulus (CS) no longer predicts the unconditioned stimulus (US). Extinction is one of the longest known and most fundamental properties of conditioned behavior (e.g., Pavlov, 1927). Nevertheless, there is no generally accepted theory of extinction. Many theories are challenged because behavior undergoing extinction shows some complicated and unexpected characteristics.

McSweeney and Swindell (2002; see also e.g., Humphrey, 1930; Thompson & Spencer, 1966) argued that many of the puzzling characteristics of extinguished behavior could be understood if habituation occurs to some of the stimuli that support conditioned responding. These stimuli help to support conditioned responding either directly (the CS) or by acting as a discriminative stimulus for, or a facilitator of, that responding (the context). Responding should decrease during a session of extinction as habituation occurs to the stimuli that support conditioned responding. Responding should also decrease across sessions of extinction as long-term or learned habituation develops to those stimuli (Table 14.1, Characteristic 12).

Table 14.1 summarizes the characteristics of extinction that are consistent with this idea (McSweeney & Swindell, 2002; see also McSweeney, Murphy, & Kowal, 2004a; McSweeney, Swindell, & Weatherly, 1999). Equation 1 also accounts for more than 90% of the variance in 149 data sets on extinction.

Enough evidence supports the habituation hypothesis to suggest that it is worth testing. Nevertheless the habituation hypothesis cannot explain all of the characteristics of extinction (McSweeney & Swindell, 2002). Similar to other authors (e.g., Mackintosh, 1974), McSweeney and Swindell (2002) suggested that extinction is multiply determined and that habituation is only one of several factors that may contribute.

Behavioral Contrast. Multiple-schedule behavioral contrast refers to the fact that the rate of responding during a constant component of a multiple schedule may vary inversely with reinforcement in the other component (e.g., McSweeney & Norman, 1979). For example, a multiple VI 1-minute VI 1-minute schedule might be changed to a multiple VI 1-minute extinction schedule. If rate of responding during the VI 1-minute component increased with this worsening of the alternative reinforcement, the increase would be labeled "positive contrast." A multiple VI 1-minute VI 1-minute schedule might be changed to a multiple VI 1-minute VI 15-second schedule. If rate of responding during the VI 1-minute component decreased with this improvement in the alternative reinforcement, the decrease would be labeled "negative contrast."

McSweeney and Weatherly (1998) argued that habituation to the reinforcer may provide a parsimonious explanation for some multiple-schedule contrast. They reasoned that reducing the rate of reinforcement in one component of a multiple schedule (e.g., changing a VI 1-minute schedule to extinction) also reduces the amount of habituation that occurs to the reinforcer across the session. The reinforcers provided in the constant component should be more effective (less habituation) and support a higher rate of responding (positive contrast). Providing more reinforcers in one component (e.g., changing a VI 1-minute, to a VI 15-second, schedule) increases habituation to the reinforcer, reducing the effectiveness of the constant-component reinforcers. Less effective reinforcers should support a lower rate of responding (negative contrast).

McSweeney and Weatherly (1998) reported that many results in the literature on multiple-schedule behavioral contrast are compatible with this idea. Some of these results provide relatively strong support for the theory because they are consistent with the habituation hypothesis but not with most other theories and because they were reported in experiments specifically designed to test the habituation hypothesis (e.g., McSweeney, Kowal, Murphy, & Isava, 2004; McSweeney, Murphy, & Kowal, 2003). For example, as predicted, contrast is largest when habituation is strongest (e.g., later, rather than earlier, in the experimental session; McSweeney, Murphy, & Kowal, 2004b; McSweeney, Swindell, Murphy, & Kowal, 2004; Swindell, McSweeney, & Murphy, 2003). Nevertheless, some results in the literature on behavioral contrast are not predicted by habituation. Because of these incompatible findings, McSweeney and Weatherly argued that habituation is only one of several contributors to behavioral contrast, a common assumption in the contrast literature (e.g., Williams, 1983).

Classical Conditioning Phenomena. Similar stimuli serve as reinforcers in operant conditioning and as USs in classical conditioning. In fact, the term "reinforcer" is often used to refer to the US in Pavlovian procedures (e.g., Davidson & Rescorla, 1986). If habituation occurs to reinforcers, then it should also occur to USs and some phenomena in the classical conditioning literature might be attributed to habituation to the US. For example, the size of the UR may decrease during conditioning (conditioned diminution of the UR; e.g., Kimmel, 1966). Classical conditioning may be weaker when several USs are presented before conditioning begins than when they are not (the US preexposure effect; e.g., Mis & Moore, 1973).

Conditioning may be weaker when a US is presented immediately before a CS-US pairing than when it is not (priming by the US; e.g., Terry, 1976). Conditioning is usually also weaker when a CS is paired with a weak US before it is paired with a strong US than when it is not (the Hall-Pearce Effect; Hall & Pearce, 1979).

Several phenomena might also be attributed, at least partially, to habituation to the CS in classical conditioning. For example, the salience of the CS may change during conditioning (e.g., Pearce & Hall, 1980). Classical conditioning may be weaker when several CSs are presented before conditioning begins than when they are not (latent inhibition; e.g., Lubow, 1989). Conditioning may be weaker when a CS is presented immediately before a CS-US pairing than when it is not (priming by the CS; e.g., Pfautz & Wagner, 1976). In addition, habituation to both the CS and US may contribute to learned irrelevance (e.g., Mackintosh, 1973), the finding that conditioning is retarded following uncorrelated presentations of the CS and US (e.g., Bonardi & Hall, 1996).

Although habituation has been proposed as an explanation for many of these phenomena, the present hypothesis differs from, for example, Wagner's (1976) theory because we take an empirical, not a theoretical, approach to habituation. The predictions of the habituation hypothesis for each of these phenomena has not yet been examined.

Not Preference for Variability. Animals often prefer variable to fixed outcomes (see Kacelnik & Bateson, 1996, for a review.) Slower habituation to variable, than to fixed, outcomes (Table 14.1, Characteristic 9) is one of many potential explanations for this preference (see e.g., McSweeney, Kowal, & Murphy, 2003). McSweeney, Kowal et al. reasoned that if habituation contributes to preferences for variability, then this preference should be strongest when differences in habituation to the fixed and variable outcomes are largest. Differences in habituation should be larger later in the session than earlier because these differences should accumulate with successive reinforcer presentations. Differences in habituation should also be larger when reinforcers are presented at higher than at lower rates (Table 14.1, Characteristic 4). McSweeney et al.'s results failed to confirm these predictions. Instead preference for variability, as measured in the initial link of a concurrent chain schedule, was usually stronger for lower than for higher rates of reinforcement and preference did not change systematically within the session.

McSweeney, Kowal et al.'s (2003) results could be explained by the earlier idea that all qualitatively-similar reinforcers contribute to a single number that represents the total amount of habituation that has occurred to that reinforcer at any one point in the session (see "The Matching Law"). Consistent with this idea, the within-session patterns of responding were similar for the initial links of the concurrent chain-schedule that provided fixed and variable reinforcers.

Implications Beyond Conditioning

Habituation

The present argument expands the domain of habituation. To begin with, most studies of habituation examine the waning of a reflexive response (e.g., leg flexion,

Thompson & Spencer, 1966). Arguing that habituation occurs to reinforcers means that habituation may also be observed in "voluntary" or "goal-directed" operant behavior, not just in reflexive behavior. But also, most studies of habituation present a neutral stimulus, such as a light or tone (e.g., Thompson & Spencer, 1966). Arguing that habituation occurs to reinforcers means that habituation also occurs to many biologically significant stimuli that are needed for survival (e.g., food, water).

Motivation

McSweeney and Swindell (1999b) argued that sensitization-habituation may help to explain the initiation and termination of many motivated behaviors. The term "motivation" usually applies to behaviors such as feeding, drinking, aggression, exploration, escape, curiosity and drug taking that are energetic and goal-directed. Early theories of motivation explained these behaviors in terms of a single general process such as homeostasis, instincts, or drives. However, this general-process approach was abandoned as each of these theories encountered problems. For example, motivated behaviors appear to be a heterogeneous class. The class includes some basic biological behaviors (e.g., feeding, drinking, sexual, and maternal behavior), as well as behaviors that are directed at more arbitrary stimuli (e.g., exploration, curiosity). Theories that dealt well with biologically important behaviors (e.g., instincts) tended to fail for more arbitrary behaviors and vice versa.

With the rejection of general-process theories, research on motivation turned to determining the specific factors that govern specific behaviors. For example, termination of ingestion (e.g., eating, drinking) is usually attributed to satiation (e.g., Bizo et al., 1998); termination of energetic responding (e.g., running), to fatigue (e.g., Belke, 1997); termination of cognitive behaviors (e.g., studying), to the waning of attention (e.g., Hinson & Tennison, 1999); termination of drug taking, to pharmacodynamic factors (e.g., Ahmed & Koob, 1999). Unfortunately, the use of different terms to explain different behaviors is unparimonious and is contradicted by the many common characteristics possessed by different motivated behaviors (McSweeney & Swindell, 1999b).

McSweeney and Swindell (1999b) argued that two simple assumptions may contribute to understanding motivated behaviors. First, assume that the goal objects of motivated behaviors (e.g., food) are reinforcers (e.g., Teitelbaum, 1966). Second, assume that sensitization and habituation alter the ability of these goal objects to control behavior with repeated contact. As animals habituate to a goal, the goal loses its ability to control behavior, and behavior directed toward that goal stops. Because spontaneous recovery occurs when the animal is not in contact with the goal (Table 14.1, Characteristic 2), the effectiveness of the goal increases with deprivation and the animal becomes more likely to pursue that goal. McSweeney and Swindell did not argue that habituation is the sole regulator of all motivated behavior. Instead, they argue that habituation is one of serveral variables that contribute to the regulation of many motivated behaviors, just as habituation is one of several variables that help to regulate eating (e.g., Swithers & Hall, 1994).

McSweeney and Swindell (1999b) showed that the characteristics of habituation are found for many motivated behaviors (see Table 14.1). Several predictions of this hypothesis were also confirmed (see Aoyama & McSweeney, 2001a for wheel running;

Murphy et al., 2006; 2007, for alcohol consumption). Finally, Equation 1 accounted for more than 90% of the variance in the data when it was fit to 95 examples of temporal changes in feeding, 16 cases of drinking, 44 cases of exploration, 17 cases of escape, and 27 cases of aggression.

Some of the characteristics of motivated behaviors are surprising. For example, Rolls and her colleagues showed that people eat more when served a variety of foods than when fed constant foods (e.g., B. J. Rolls, van Duijvenvoorde, & E. T. Rolls, 1984) even if the foods differ only in sensory properties such as color or shape (B. J. Rolls, Rowe, & E. T. Rolls, 1982) and even when the foods have no nutritive value (B. J. Rolls, Wood, & E. T. Rolls, 1980). Similar variety effects (Table 14.1, Characteristic 9) have also been reported for drinking (B. J. Rolls et al., 1980) and for sexual behavior (e.g., the Coolidge effect; e.g., Fisher, 1962). In addition, introducing an arbitrary stimulus from another modality strengthens motivated behaviors (Table 14.1, Characteristics 10 and 15). For example, pinching the tail of rats facilitates eating, gnawing, licking, drinking, grooming, locomotion, sniffing, rearing, sexual behavior, maternal behavior and pup retrieval, exploration, vocalization, eating feces or gnawing the cage (e.g., Antelman, Rowland, & Fisher, 1976; Antelman & Szechtman, 1975; Guder & Kornblith, 1979; Robbins & Fray, 1980; Rowland & Antelman, 1976). Bolles (1980) was so perplexed by this phenomenon that he wrote, "Consider the tail-pinch as a source of eating. It is an interesting phenomenon precisely because it does not make much sense; it is the exception to the rule that motivational systems are well-adjusted and independent" (p. 229). This phenomenon is expected, not perplexing, if habituation contributes to the regulation of motivated behavior.

This analysis of motivated behaviors has many interesting applications. We will use obesity as an example here (see McSweeney, Murphy, & Kowal, 2005, for an application to drug taking). Many data support the idea that habituation to the reinforcer contributes to the dysregulation of food consumption that leads to obesity. To give just a few examples, a constant food is more reinforcing for obese subjects than for normal weight subjects (Saelens & Epstein, 1996). Obese subjects also habituate more slowly to food cues than nonobese subjects (Epstein, Paluch, & Coleman, 1996). Obese participants, unlike those of normal weight, fail to slow food intake late in a meal (i.e., show no or slow habituation; Bellisle & Le Magnen, 1981). Raynor and Epstein (2001) also argued that obesity develops and is maintained by the increasing variety of the food supply.

The traditional approach to the control of obesity suggests that a person who wants to lose weight should eat fewer and lower calorie foods and should exercise more to burn excess calories. The habituation model does not deny the importance of these variables, but it emphasizes other variables such as the sensory properties of the food and the environment in which the person eats. The model predicts that a person should eat relatively constant foods to avoid over-consumption. As noted, variety in food reduces the rate of habituation and therefore, can lead to over-consumption (e.g., Ernst & Epstein, 2002). People should avoid eating in places with many environmental distractors (e.g., in front of the television, in a noisy restaurant; e.g., Temple et al., 2007). These unpredictable stimuli will slow habituation by acting as dishabituators or sensitizers. A person should put away food once (s)he has stopped eating. A nibble of an easily available food may produce sensitization, which will briefly increase the reinforcing effectiveness of food and lead to a resumption of eating.

Recently, Morewedge, Huh, and Vosgerau (2010) confirmed another surprising prediction of this idea. They showed that people who repeatedly imagined eating a food (e.g., cheese) many times subsequently consumed less of the imagined food than did people who repeatedly imagined eating that food fewer times, imagined eating a different food (e.g., candy), or did not imagine eating a food. These results were predicted by the habituation hypothesis. If imagining food generates any of the stimuli associated with eating food, then some habituation to the sensory properties of food should be generated by imagining that food. Of course, this exposure to the sight and/or taste of food should be long enough to ensure that habituation, rather than sensitization, occurs.

Summary

Response rates may increase, decrease, or increase and then decrease within conditioning sessions even when the distribution of reinforcers or USs does not vary across the session. Sensitization and habituation to the sensory properties of the reinforcers mainly produce these within-session changes in responding. Because of sensitization-habituation, the ability of the reinforcer or US to control behavior changes with its successive presentation. This idea has a wide variety of implications for methods, applications, and theory in conditioning and beyond. Dinsmoor (2001) argued that " . . . the goal of scientific theory is to discover and describe the common characteristics that link together seemingly unrelated observations" (p. 324). We believe that the habituation hypothesis has enormous potential for tying together seemingly unrelated phenomena in the conditioning literature and beyond. Because the properties of sensitization and habituation are relatively well known, the model makes many predictions that differ strongly from the predictions made by traditional concepts such as satiation.

References

Ahmed, S. H., & Koob, G. F. (1999). Long-lasting increase in the set point for cocaine self-administration after escalation in rats. *Psychopharmacology*, *146*, 303–312.

Anderson, K. J. (1990). Arousal and the inverted-u hypothesis: A critique of Neiss's "Reconceptualizing arousal." *Psychological Bulletin*, *107*, 96–100.

Antelman, S. M., Rowland, N. E., & Fisher, A. E. (1976). Stimulation bound ingestive behavior: A view from the tail. *Physiology & Behavior*, *17*, 743–748.

Antelman, S. M., & Szechtman, H. (1975). Tail pinch induces eating in sated rats which appears to depend on nigrostriatal dopamine. *Science*, *189*, 731–733.

Aoyama, K. (1998). Within-session response rate in rats decreases as a function of amount eaten. *Physiology & Behavior*, *64*, 765–769.

Aoyama, K. (2000). Effects of hunger state on within-session response decreases under CRF schedule. *Learning and Motivation*, *31*, 1–20.

Aoyama, K., & McSweeney, F. K. (2001a). Habituation contributes to within-session changes in free wheel running. *Journal of the Experimental Analysis of Behavior*, *76*, 289–302.

Aoyama, K., & McSweeney, F. K. (2001b). Habituation may contribute to within-session decreases in responding under high-rate schedules of reinforcement. *Animal Learning & Behavior, 29*, 79–91.

Azrin, N. H. (1960). Sequential effects of punishment. *Science, 131*, 605–606.

Baum, W. M. (1974). On two types of deviation from the matching law: Bias and undermatching. *Journal of the Experimental Analysis of Behavior, 22*, 231–242.

Baum, W. M. (1981). Optimization and the matching law as accounts of instrumental behavior. *Journal of the Experimental Analysis of Behavior, 36*, 387–403.

Belke, T. W. (1997). Running and responding reinforced by the opportunity to run: Effect of reinforcer duration. *Journal of the Experimental Analysis of Behavior, 67*, 337–351.

Bellisle, F., & Le Magnen, J. (1981). The structure of meals in humans: Eating and drinking patterns in lean and obese subjects. *Physiology & Behavior, 27*, 649–658.

Bindra, D. (1959). Stimulus change, reactions to novelty and response decrement. *Psychological Review, 66*, 96–103.

Bittar, E. G., Del-Claro, K., Bittar, L. G., & da Silva, M. C. P. (2012). Towards a mathematical model of within-session operant responding. *Journal of Experimental Psychology: Animal Behavior Processes, 38*, 292–302.

Bizo, L. A., Bogdanov, S. V., & Killeen, P. R. (1998). Satiation causes within-session decreases in instrumental responding. *Journal of Experimental Psychology: Animal Behavior Processes, 24*, 439–452.

Blough, D. S. (1983). Alternative accounts of dimensional stimulus control. In M. Commons, R. Herrnstein, & A. Wagner (Eds.), *Quantitative analyses of behavior* (Vol. 4, pp. 59–72). Cambridge, MA: Ballinger.

Bolles, R. C. (1980). Stress-induced *over*eating? A response to Robbins and Fray, *Appetite, 1*, 229–230.

Bonardi, C., & Hall, G. (1996). Learned irrelevance: No more than the sum of CS and US preexposure effects? *Journal of Experimental Psychology: Animal Behavior Processes, 22*, 183–191.

Broster, B. S., & Rankin, C. H. (1994). Effects of changing interstimulus interval during habituation in *Caenorhabditis elegans*. *Behavioral Neuroscience, 108*, 1019–1029.

Cannon, C. B., & McSweeney, F. K. (1995). Within-session changes in responding when rate and duration of reinforcement vary. *Behavioural Processes, 34*, 285–292.

Catania, A. C., & Reynolds, G. S. (1968). A quantitative analysis of responding maintained by interval schedules of reinforcement. *Journal of the Experimental Analysis of Behavior, 11*, 327–383.

Davidson, T. L., & Rescorla, R. A. (1986). Transfer of facilitation in the rat. *Animal Learning & Behavior, 14*, 380–386.

DeMarse, T. B., Killeen, P. R., & Baker, D. (1999). Satiation, capacity, and within-session responding. *Journal of the Experimental Analysis of Behavior, 72*, 407–423.

Dinsmoor, J. A. (2001). Stimuli inevitably generated by behavior that avoids electric shock are inherently reinforcing. *Journal of the Experimental Analysis of Behavior, 75*, 311–333.

Duffy, E. (1962). *Activation and behavior*. New York: John Wiley & Sons, Inc.

Edhouse, W. V., & White, K. G. (1988). Cumulative proactive interference in animal memory. *Animal Learning & Behavior, 16*, 461–467.

Eisenstein, E. M., & Peretz, B. (1973). Comparative aspects of habituation in invertebrates. In H. V. S. Peeke & M. J. Herz (Eds.), *Habituation. Volume II: Physiological substrates* (pp. 1–31). New York: Academic Press.

Epstein, L. H., Paluch, R., & Coleman, K. J. (1996). Differences in salivation to repeated food cues in obese and nonobese women. *Psychosomatic Medicine, 58*, 160–164.

Epstein, L. H., Saad, F. G., Handley, E. A., Roemmich, J. N., Hawk, L. W., & McSweeney, F. K. (2003). Habituation of salivation and motivated responding for food in children. *Appetite*, *41*, 283–289.

Ernst, M. M., & Epstein, L. H. (2002). Habituation of responding for food in humans. *Appetite*, *38*, 224–234.

Estes, W. K., & Skinner, B. F. (1941). Some quantitative properties of anxiety. *Journal of Experimental Psychology*, *29*, 390–400.

Ettinger, R. H., & Staddon, J. E. R. (1983). Behavioral competition, component duration and multiple schedule contrast. *Behavioural Analysis Letters*, *2*, 31–38.

Falk, J. L. (1971). Theoretical review: The nature and determinants of adjunctive behavior. *Physiology & Behavior*, *6*, 577–588.

Fisher, A. E. (1962). Effects of stimulus variation on sexual satiation in the male rat. *Journal of Comparative and Physiological Psychology*, *55*, 614–620.

Groves, P. M., & Thompson, R. F. (1970). Habituation: A dual-process theory. *Psychological Review*, *77*, 419–450.

Guder, L. D., & Kornblith, C. L. (1979). Tail pinch-induced eating does generalize to a nonpreferred but familiar food. *Physiology & Behavior*, *22*, 179–183.

Hall, G., & Pearce, J. M. (1979). Latent inhibition of a CS during CS-US pairings. *Journal of Experimental Psychology: Animal Behavior Processes*, *5*, 31–42.

Herrnstein, R. J. (1970). On the law of effect. *Journal of the Experimental Analysis of Behavior*, *13*, 243–266.

Heyman, G. M. (1983). A parametric evaluation of the hedonic and motoric effects of drugs: Pimozide and amphetamine. *Journal of the Experimental Analysis of Behavior*, *40*, 113–122.

Heyman, G. M. (1993). Ethanol regulated preference in rats. *Psychopharmacology*, *112*, 259–269.

Hinson, J. M., & Tennison, L. R. (1999). Within-session analysis of visual discrimination. *Journal of the Experimental Analysis of Behavior*, *72*, 385–405.

Humphrey, G. (1930). Extinction and negative adaptation. *Psychological Review*, *37*, 361–363.

Jerome, E. A., Moody, J. A., Connor, T. J., & Ryan, J. (1958). Intensity of illumination and the rate of responding in a multiple-door situation. *Journal of Comparative and Physiological Psychology*, *51*, 47–49.

Kacelnik, A., & Bateson, M. (1996). Risky theories – the effects of variance on foraging decisions. *American Zoologist*, *36*, 402–434.

Killeen, P. R., Hanson, S. J., & Osborne, S. R. (1978). Arousal: Its genesis and manifestation as response rate. *Psychological Review*, *85*, 571–581.

Kimmel, H. D. (1966). Inhibition of the unconditioned response in classical conditioning. *Psychological Review*, *73*, 232–240.

Leaton, R. N., & Tighe, T. J. (1976). Comparisons between habituation research at the developmental and animal-neurophysiological levels. In T. J. Tighe & R. N. Leaton (Eds.), *Habituation: Perspectives from child development, animal behavior and neurophysiology* (pp. 321–340). New York: John Wiley & Sons, Inc.

Lubow, R. E. (1989). *Latent inhibition and conditioned attention theory.* Cambridge: Cambridge University Press.

Lupfer-Johnson, G., Murphy, E. S., Blackwell, L. C., LaCasse, J. L., & Drummond, S. (2010). Effects of rate of reinforcement and reinforcer flavor variety on within-session changes in operant responding in dwarf hamsters (*Phodopus campbelli*). *Behavioural Processes*, *84*, 573–580.

Mackintosh, N. J. (1973). Stimulus selection: Learning to ignore stimuli that predict no change in reinforcement. In R. A. Hinde & J. S. Hinde (Eds.), *Constraints on learning* (pp. 75–96). London: Academic Press.

Mackintosh, N. J. (1974). *The psychology of animal learning*. New York: Academic Press.

Marcus, E. A., Nolen, T. G., Rankin, C. H., & Carew, T. J. (1988). Behavioral dissociation of dishabituation, sensitization, and inhibition in *Aplysia*. *Science*, *241*, 210–213.

McCarthy, D., & Voss, P. (1995). Delayed matching-to-sample performance: Effects of relative reinforcer frequency and of signaled versus unsignaled reinforcer magnitudes. *Journal of the Experimental Analysis of Behavior*, *63*, 33–51.

McSweeney, F. K. (1992). Rate of reinforcement and session duration as determinants of within-session patterns of responding. *Animal Learning & Behavior*, *20*, 160–169.

McSweeney, F. K., Hatfield, J., & Allen, T. M. (1990). Within-session responding as a function of post-session feedings. *Behavioural Processes*, *22*, 177–186.

McSweeney, F. K., & Hinson, J. M. (1992). Patterns of responding within sessions. *Journal of the Experimental Analysis of Behavior*, *58*, 19–36.

McSweeney, F. K., Hinson, J. M., & Cannon, C. B. (1996). Sensitization-habituation may occur during operant conditioning. *Psychological Bulletin*, *120*, 256–271.

McSweeney, F. K., & Johnson, K. S. (1994). The effect of time between sessions on within-session patterns of responding. *Behavioural Processes*, *31*, 207–217.

McSweeney, F. K., Kowal, B. P., & Murphy, E. S. (2003). The effect of rate of reinforcement and time in session on preference for variability. *Animal Learning & Behavior*, *31*, 225–241.

McSweeney, F. K., Kowal, B. P., Murphy, E. S., & Isava, D. (2004). Dishabituation produces interactions during multiple schedules. *Learning and Motivation*, *35*, 419–434.

McSweeney, F. K., Kowal, B. P., Murphy, E. S., & Varao, R. S. (2005). Stimulus change dishabituates operant responding supported by water reinforcers. *Behavioural Processes*, *70*, 235–246.

McSweeney, F. K., & Murphy, E. S. (2000). Criticisms of the satiety hypothesis as an explanation for within-session decreases in responding. *Journal of the Experimental Analysis of Behavior*, *74*, 347–361.

McSweeney, F. K., Murphy, E. S., & Kowal, B. P. (2001). Within-session changes in responding during concurrent variable interval variable ratio schedules. *Behavioural Processes*, *55*, 163–179.

McSweeney, F. K., Murphy, E. S., & Kowal, B. P. (2003). Dishabituation with component transitions may contribute to the interactions observed during multiple schedules. *Behavioural Processes*, *64*, 77–89.

McSweeney, F. K., Murphy, E. S., & Kowal, B. P. (2004a). Extinguished responding shows stimulus specificity. *Behavioural Processes*, *65*, 211–220.

McSweeney, F. K., Murphy, E. S., & Kowal, B. P. (2004b). Varying reinforcer duration produces behavioral interactions during multiple schedules. *Behavioural Processes*, *66*, 83–100.

McSweeney, F. K., Murphy, E. S., & Kowal, B. P. (2005). Regulation of drug taking by sensitization and habituation. *Experimental and Clinical Psychopharmacology*, *13*, 163–184.

McSweeney, F. K., & Norman, W. D. (1979). Defining behavioral contrast for multiple schedules. *Journal of the Experimental Analysis of Behavior*, *32*, 457–461.

McSweeney, F. K., & Roll, J. M. (1993). Responding changes systematically within sessions during conditioning procedures. *Journal of the Experimental Analysis of Behavior*, *60*, 621–640.

McSweeney, F. K., & Roll, J. M. (1998). Do animals satiate or habituate to repeatedly presented reinforcers? *Psychonomic Bulletin & Review*, *5*, 428–442.

McSweeney, F. K., Roll, J. M., & Cannon, C. B. (1994). The generality of within-session patterns of responding: Rate of reinforcement and session length. *Animal Learning & Behavior*, *22*, 252–266.

McSweeney, F. K., Roll, J. M., & Weatherly, J. N. (1994). Within-session changes in responding during several simple schedules. *Journal of the Experimental Analysis of Behavior*, *62*, 109–132.

McSweeney, F. K., & Swindell, S. (1999a). Behavioral economics and within-session changes in responding. *Journal of the Experimental Analysis of Behavior*, *72*, 355–371.

McSweeney, F. K., & Swindell, S. (1999b). General-process theories of motivation revisited: The role of habituation. *Psychological Bulletin*, *125*, 437–457.

McSweeney, F. K., & Swindell, S. (2002). Common processes may contribute to extinction and habituation. *The Journal of General Psychology*, *129*, 364–400.

McSweeney, F. K., Swindell, S., Murphy, E. S., & Kowal, B. P. (2004). The relation of multiple-schedule behavioral contrast to deprivation, time in session, and within-session changes in responding. *Learning & Behavior*, *32*, 190–201.

McSweeney, F. K., Swindell, S., & Weatherly, J. N. (1996a). Within-session changes in adjunctive and instrumental responding. *Learning and Motivation*, *27*, 408–427.

McSweeney, F. K., Swindell, S., & Weatherly, J. N. (1996b). Within-session changes in responding during autoshaping and automaintenance procedures. *Journal of the Experimental Analysis of Behavior*, *66*, 51–61.

McSweeney, F. K., Swindell, S., & Weatherly, J. N. (1996c). Within-session changes in responding during concurrent schedules with different reinforcers in the components. *Journal of the Experimental Analysis of Behavior*, *66*, 369–390.

McSweeney, F. K., Swindell, S., & Weatherly, J. N. (1998). Exposure to context may contribute to within-session changes in responding. *Behavioural Processes*, *43*, 315–328.

McSweeney, F. K., Swindell, S., & Weatherly, J. N. (1999). Within-session response patterns during variable interval, random reinforcement, and extinction procedures. *Learning and Motivation*, *30*, 221–240.

McSweeney, F. K., & Weatherly, J. N. (1998). Habituation to the reinforcer may contribute to multiple-schedule behavioral contrast. *Journal of the Experimental Analysis of Behavior*, *69*, 199–221.

McSweeney, F. K., Weatherly, J. N., & Roll, J. M. (1995). Within-session changes in responding during concurrent schedules that employ two different operanda. *Animal Learning & Behavior*, *23*, 237–244.

McSweeney, F. K., Weatherly, J. N., Roll, J. M., & Swindell, S. (1995). Within-session patterns of responding when the operandum changes during the session. *Learning and Motivation*, *26*, 403–420.

McSweeney, F. K., Weatherly, J. N., & Swindell, S. (1995a). Prospective factors contribute little to within-session changes in responding. *Psychonomic Bulletin & Review*, *2*, 234–238.

McSweeney, F. K., Weatherly, J. N., & Swindell, S. (1995b). Within-session response rates when reinforcement rate is changed within each session. *Journal of the Experimental Analysis of Behavior*, *64*, 237–246.

McSweeney, F. K., Weatherly, J. N., & Swindell, S. (1996a). Reinforcer value may change within experimental sessions. *Psychonomic Bulletin & Review*, *3*, 372–375.

McSweeney, F. K., Weatherly, J. N., & Swindell, S. (1996b). Within-session changes in responding during concurrent variable-interval schedules. *Journal of the Experimental Analysis of Behavior*, *66*, 75–95.

McSweeney, F. K., Weatherly, J. N., & Swindell, S. (1996c). Within-session changes in responding during delayed matching-to-sample and discrimination procedures. *Animal Learning & Behavior*, *24*, 290–299.

Melville, C. L., Rue, H. C., Rybiski, L. R., & Weatherly, J. N. (1997). Altering reinforcer variety or intensity changes the within-session decrease in responding. *Learning and Motivation*, *28*, 609–621.

Melville, C. L., Rybiski, L. R., & Kamrani, B. (1996). Within-session responding as a function of force required for lever press. *Behavioural Processes*, *37*, 217–224.

Millenson, J. R. (1967). *Principles of behavioral analysis.* New York: Macmillan.

Mis, F. W., & Moore, J. W. (1973). Effect of preacquisition UCS exposure on classical conditioning of the rabbit's nictitating membrane response. *Learning and Motivation*, *4*, 108–114.

Mook, D. G. (1996). *Motivation: The organization of action* (2nd ed.). New York: W.W. Norton.

Morewedge, C. K., Huh, Y. E., & Vosgerau, J. (2010). Thought for food: Imagined consumption reduces actual consumption. *Science*, *330*, 1530–1533.

Mosso, A. (1906). *Fatigue* (M. Drummond, Trans.). New York: Putnam.

Murphy, E. S., McSweeney, F. K., & Kowal, B. P. (2003). Within-session decreases in operant responding as a function of pre-session feedings. *The Psychological Record*, *53*, 313–326.

Murphy, E. S., McSweeney, F. K., & Kowal, B. P. (2007). Motivation to consume alcohol in rats: The role of habituation. In P. W. O'Neal (Ed.), *Motivation of health behavior* (pp. 111–126). Hauppauge, NY: Nova Science.

Murphy, E. S., McSweeney, F. K., Kowal, B. P., McDonald, J., & Wiediger, R. V. (2006). Spontaneous recovery and dishabituation of ethanol-reinforced responding in alcohol-preferring rats. *Experimental and Clinical Psychopharmacology*, *14*, 471–482.

Murphy, E. S., McSweeney, F. K., Smith, R. G., & McComas, J. J. (2003). Dynamic changes in reinforcer effectiveness: Theoretical, methodological, and practical implications for applied research. *Journal of Applied Behavior Analysis*, *36*, 421–438.

Neiss, R. (1988). Reconceptualizing arousal: Psychological states in motor performance. *Psychological Bulletin*, *103*, 345–366.

Olton, D. S., & Samuelson, R. J. (1976). Remembrance of places passed: Spatial memory in rats. *Journal of Experimental Psychology: Animal Behavior Processes*, *2*, 97–116.

Palya, W. L., & Walter, D. E. (1997). Rate of a maintained operant as a function of temporal position within a session. *Animal Learning & Behavior*, *25*, 291–300.

Pavlov, I. P. (1927). *Conditioned reflexes.* London: Oxford University Press.

Pavlov, I. P. (1928). *Lectures on conditioned reflexes.* New York: International.

Pearce, J. M., & Hall, G. (1980). A model of Pavlovian learning: Variations in the effectiveness of conditioned but not unconditioned stimuli. *Psychological Review*, *87*, 532–552.

Pfautz, P. L., & Wagner, A. R. (1976). Transient variations in responding to Pavlovian conditioned stimuli have implications for the mechanisms of "priming." *Animal Learning & Behavior*, *4*, 107–112.

Rankin, C. H., Abrams, T., Barry, R. J., Bhatnagar, S., Clayton, D., Colombo, J., Coppola, G., Geyer, M. A., Glanzman, D. L., Marsland, S., McSweeney, F., Wilson, D. A., Wu, C.- F., & Thompson, R. F. (2009). Habituation revisited: An updated and revised description of the behavioral characteristics of habituation. *Neurobiology of Learning and Memory*, *92*, 135–138.

Raynor, H. A., & Epstein, L. H. (2001). Dietary variety, energy regulation, and obesity. *Psychological Bulletin*, *127*, 325–341.

Richardson, R., & Campbell, B. A. (1992). Latent habituation of the orienting response in the preweanling rat. *Animal Learning & Behavior*, *20*, 416–426.

Robbins, T. W., & Fray, P. J. (1980). Stress-induced eating: Reply to Bolles, Rowland and Marques, and Herman and Polivy. *Appetite*, *1*, 231–239.

Roll, J. M., & McSweeney, F. K. (1997). Within-session changes in operant responding when gerbils (*Meriones unguiculatus*) serve as subjects. *Current Psychology: Developmental, Learning, Personality, and Social*, *15*, 340–345.

Roll, J. M., McSweeney, F. K., Johnson, K. S., & Weatherly, J. N. (1995). Satiety contributes little to within-session decreases in responding. *Learning and Motivation*, *26*, 323–341.

Rolls, B. J., Rowe, E. A., & Rolls, E. T. (1982). How sensory properties of foods affect human feeding behavior. *Physiology & Behavior*, *29*, 409–417.

Rolls, B. J., van Duijvenvoorde, P. M., & Rolls, E. T. (1984). Pleasantness changes and food intake in a varied four-course meal. *Appetite*, *5*, 337–348.

Rolls, B. J., Wood, R. J., & Rolls, E. T. (1980). Thirst: The initiation, maintenance, and termination of drinking. In J. M. Sprague & A. N. Epstein (Eds.), *Progress in psychobiology and physiological psychology* (pp. 263–321). New York: Academic Press.

Rowland, N. E., & Antelman, S. M. (1976, January 23). Stress-induced hyperphagia and obesity in rats: A possible model for understanding human obesity. *Science*, *191*, 310–312.

Saelens, B. E., & Epstein, L. H. (1996). Reinforcing value of food in obese and non-obese women. *Appetite*, *27*, 41–50.

Skinner, B. F. (1938). *The behavior of organisms.* New York: Appleton-Century-Crofts.

Spear, N. E. (1973). Retrieval of memory in animals. *Psychological Review*, *80*, 163–194.

Staddon, J. E. R. (1979). Operant behavior as adaptation to constraint. *Journal of Experimental Psychology: General*, *108*, 48–67.

Swindell, S., McSweeney, F. K., & Murphy, E. S. (2003). Dynamic changes in the size of behavioral contrast. *The Behavior Analyst Today*, *4*, 199–208.

Swithers, S. E., & Hall, W. G. (1994). Does oral experience terminate ingestion? *Appetite*, *23*, 113–138.

Teitelbaum, P. (1966). The use of operant methods in the assessment and control of motivational states. In W. K. Honig (Ed.), *Operant behavior: Areas of research and application* (pp. 565–608). New York: Appleton-Century-Crofts.

Temple, J. L., Giacomelli, A. M., Kent, K. M., Roemmich, J. N., & Epstein, L. H. (2007). Television watching increases motivated responding for food and energy intake in children. *American Journal of Clinical Nutrition*, *85*, 355–361.

Temple, J. L., Giacomelli, A. M., Roemmich, J. N., & Epstein, L. H. (2008). Habituation and within-session changes in motivated responding for food in children. *Appetite*, *50*, 390–396.

Temple, J. L., Kent, K. M., Giacomelli, A. M., Paluch, R. A., Roemmich, J. N., & Epstein, L. H. (2006). Habituation and recovery of salivation and motivated responding for food in children. *Appetite*, *46*, 280–284.

Terry, W. S. (1976). Effects of priming unconditioned stimulus representation in short-term memory on Pavlovian conditioning. *Journal of Experimental Psychology: Animal Behavior Processes*, *2*, 354–369.

Thompson, R. F., & Spencer, W. A. (1966). Habituation: A model phenomenon for the study of neuronal substrates of behavior. *Psychological Review*, *73*, 16–43.

Thorpe, W. H. (1966). *Learning and instinct in animals.* Cambridge, MA: Harvard University Press.

Wagner, A. R. (1976). Priming in STM: An information-processing mechanism for self-generated or retrieval-generated depression in performance. In T. J. Tighe and R. N. Leaton (Eds.), *Habituation: Perspectives from child development, animal behavior and neurophysiology* (pp. 95–128). New York: John Wiley & Sons, Inc.

Weatherly, J. N., & McSweeney, F. K. (1995). Within-session response patterns when rats press levers for water: Effects of component stimuli and experimental environment. *Behavioural Processes*, *34*, 141–152.

Weatherly, J. N., McSweeney, F. K., & Swindell, S. (1995). On the contributions of responding and reinforcement to within-session patterns of responding. *Learning and Motivation*, *26*, 421–432.

Wilkie, D. M. (1986). Pigeons' spatial memory: V. Proactive interference in the delayed matching of key location paradigm occurs only under restricted conditions. *Animal Learning & Behavior, 14*, 257–266.

Williams, B. A. (1983). Another look at contrast in multiple schedules. *Journal of the Experimental Analysis of Behavior, 39*, 345–384.

Williams, B. A. (1991). Behavioral contrast and reinforcement value. *Animal Learning & Behavior, 19*, 337–344.

15

Verbal Behavior

David C. Palmer

A behavioral interpretation of language differs from the many alternative approaches to the topic by restricting its analytical tools to those that have emerged from experimental analyses *and to nothing else*. Therefore in this chapter I will discuss language as behavior and with a few exceptions will limit myself to those topics to which the principles of behavior are relevant. I will assume that my reader is a behavior analyst who wishes to review the assumptions, the analytical units, and the technical vocabulary that have become standard in the field as well as to explore some of the ways in which the topic poses special conceptual challenges to a behavior analytic account. I will make no attempt to review the vast literature on language, even within a behavior analytic perspective, lest there be space for nothing more. The reader primarily interested in language acquisition can find many suitable resources, but I particularly recommend, Horne and Lowe (1996), Locke (1993), Novak and Pelaez (2004), Schlinger (1995), and Tomasello (2003, 2008). In the past two decades the behavioral approach to teaching children with language deficits has flourished, and the associated literature is now substantial. I will cover none of this work; the reader can find good overviews elsewhere, written by scholars with greater expertise (e.g., Carr & Miguel, 2012; degli Espinosa, 2011; Greer & Ross, 2008; Sundberg, 2008). The success of such work provides a kind of validation of the approach, but in contrast, I will identify topics where the behavioral account is weakest and most speculative, for the adequacy of such an account cannot be evaluated simply by rehearsing its strengths. Consequently, this chapter will be like a photographic negative of other behavior analytic overviews; I will cover familiar topics lightly, or not at all, but will discuss in greater detail tentative interpretations of thorny empirical problems about which there is as yet no consensus within behavior analysis, because I think such topics will be of greater service to the likely reader.

The Wiley Blackwell Handbook of Operant and Classical Conditioning, First Edition.
Edited by Frances K. McSweeney and Eric S. Murphy.

On the grounds of consistency and conceptual adequacy, I will take Skinner's interpretation of verbal behavior as a foundation (Skinner, 1957). I will discuss alternative perspectives within behavior analysis only in passing, but I will point the reader to other sources for more complete treatments. Following Skinner, I will adopt the term *verbal behavior* as an alternative to *language* in order to emphasize the restricted domain of the discussion. I will occasionally use familiar terms such as *word, sentence, noun,* and *verb,* but I do not intend them to be taken as behavioral units or as technical terms in the analysis. I will confine most of my examples to vocal and written English, but only for the purpose of illustrating an interpretive approach. The details of any interpretation of verbal behavior will vary from one verbal community to another and will even vary within verbal communities from one speaker to another. Nevertheless, I believe that all such interpretations will have many common features, and it is the goal of this chapter to identify them.

I will open the chapter by defining the domain of interest and offering some reasons to consider verbal behavior special. I will then briefly summarize some technical terms that have become standard in the field and will point out the implications of a behavioral interpretation for the everyday notions of reference, meaning, and truth. Next, I will challenge the reader to consider what I regard as the central puzzle of verbal behavior, namely, its abundant structural regularities that seem to be devoid of function. I devote the remainder of the chapter to an attempt to show how the tools of the behavior analyst can be deployed to provide at least the outline of a solution to this puzzle: The concepts of multiple control, joint control, automatic shaping, and autoclitic frames are identified as versatile and powerful interpretive tools. I then offer the conditioning of the behavior of the listener as not only one of the most commonplace effects of verbal behavior but one for which we can, in the present state of science, offer only the most tentative of accounts.

Definition of Verbal Behavior

As a first approximation, we may adopt Skinner's definition of verbal behavior as behavior whose consequences are mediated by other organisms, organisms whose behavior, in this respect, has been conditioned specifically to reinforce the behavior of the speaker (Skinner, 1957). This is a descriptive definition, not a prescriptive definition (Palmer, 2008), and therefore has fuzzy boundaries: Once acquired, verbal behavior can be emitted under many conditions, even in the absence of a listener. Moreover, the speaker can be, and usually is, also a listener to his own verbal behavior. One important source of reinforcement for verbal behavior is the effect on the speaker himself in problem-solving, recall, and subsequent verbal behavior. Finally, many electronic systems and devices from automated telephone systems to notepad computers can now respond appropriately to some verbal responses, but the engineering of such devices is functionally analogous to conditioning the behavior of a listener. Nevertheless, Skinner's definition captures the generalization that verbal behavior arises in communities that maintain contingencies of reinforcement for behavior that reflects conventional but arbitrary relationships between behavior and its consequences, and if it violates these conventions, it ceases to be effective.

Because the relationship between verbal behavior and its consequences is solely a matter of convention, the magnitude of a verbal response is usually wholly unrelated to the magnitude of its effect. A whispered command can set armies in motion, and a skilled orator can whip a crowd into a frenzy. A religious tract on a roll of parchment can affect the behavior of millions of worshipers over thousands of years. Perhaps as a result, verbal behavior, in all of its forms, tends to consist of highly efficient, small magnitude responses. Speakers typically utter several words per second, and can do so for hours at a time with little fatigue. Thus the ratio of reinforcement to effort can be immense, and even trivial reinforcers can be sufficient to maintain verbal behavior in strength. Consequently, elementary speech sounds commonly recede to the simplest forms that can be discriminated by the verbal community. They can be chained and permuted to generate countless discriminable units of behavior lasting no more than a fraction of a second. Thus verbal behavior is commonly fast, flexible, and powerful.

The Physical Substrate of Vocal Behavior

Verbal behavior in its modal form, that is, vocal behavior, is distinctive by its complexity, the number of muscle groups recruited, and its competition with reflexive behavior. Uttering even the simplest of verbal operants requires the finely coordinated action of diaphragm, intercostal and abdominal muscles, larynx, oral cavity, velum, tongue, lips, and the muscles of the throat (Lieberman, 2006). Speaking must then be coordinated with the competing functions of respiration and ingestion, with their associated reflexes of breathing, coughing, sneezing, salivating and swallowing. Thus articulation alone, to say nothing of the temporal arrangement of verbal operants, is an engineering marvel.

Languages of the world vary considerably, not just in vocabulary, but in articulatory character. Relative pitch plays a strong role in some languages, a minor role in others. Most language families use some idiosyncratic speech sounds not found elsewhere. Xhosa and some other Bantu languages, for example, employ a variety of click consonants, most of which can be executed without the participation of subglottal mechanisms. Moreover, even within members of a verbal community, the physical articulation of speech sounds differs somewhat from one speaker to another (Nearey, 1980). Different configurations of articulators can produce the same speech sound; that is, they will produce speech sounds indiscriminable to a listener in that verbal community. It is clear then, from both the variability of the practices of different verbal communities and the variability in articulation from speaker to speaker, that vocal verbal behavior is operant behavior, shaped by experience.

But a complete account of vocal behavior must consider the competing demands of other processes. For most languages, speech sounds occur only during the expiration phase of breathing. Vocalization requires maintaining fairly constant air pressure in the lungs, which is incompatible with normal patterns of respiration. Specifically, unlike normal breathing, speech is characterized by rapid inspiration and prolonged expiration (Lieberman, 2000). Typically, the cycles of inspiration and expiration coincide with extended verbal units (usually sentences). Since such units can vary greatly in length, the depth of inspiration must be determined, at least roughly, before the unit is uttered. In order to maintain steady subglottal air pressure, the intercostal and abdominal muscles must initially work against the elastic recoil of the distended lungs, but after the lungs contract to their resting volume, they must work in the other direction to contract the lungs still further until the verbal unit is completed and inspiration can occur again. The capacity to make the full range of human speech sounds depends further on an elongated pharynx, the configuration of the rib cage, the shape of the oral and nasal cavities, and a highly flexible tongue. Presumably, the ability to temporarily subordinate the demands of respiration to that of speech is another example of an evolutionary adaptation that permits speech as we know it (Lieberman, 2006). Thus, as a physical act, speech is behavior, a highly complex behavior that depends in part on distinctive anatomical characteristics, some of which are shared by our closest relatives, some of which are found only in humans.

Analytical Units of Verbal Behavior

Starting from the axiom that language is behavior, Skinner (1957) identified ways in which concepts derived from the behavioral laboratory were relevant to language. To avoid the surplus connotations of existing terms, he coined new terms for the various classes of behavior that emerged from his analysis. His terms have become part of the technical vocabulary of the field, and for that reason I briefly review the major ones here. However, the reader should be warned that the purpose of the terms is simply to identify types of controlling relationships for purposes of understanding the provenance and dynamic properties of verbal behavior. There is no point to classification for its own sake. Moreover, pure examples of Skinner's verbal operants are rare outside the laboratory or educational setting; almost all verbal behavior is under multiple control, and almost all verbal behavior requires a complex interpretation.

The Mand

The mand is a verbal response that leads to a characteristic reinforcing consequence: If, when water deprived, saying *Water!* has led to getting water, the verbal response will be under control of water deprivation and would be classified as a mand. A phrase or clause, such as *Please pass the salt,* could be a mand if it were acquired and emitted as a unit.

Mands are functional in that they extend the reach of the speaker in myriad ways, but they also play an important role in the transmission of cultural practices. Listeners typically acquire fine-grained differentiated responses, each under the control of distinctive verbal stimuli: *Raise your hand; Push the handle down; Add a teaspoon of vanilla; Walk forward two steps; Knit two, purl two;* and so on. Such an atomic repertoire confers a distinctive advantage: An indefinitely large number of permutations of behavior can be evoked in a single trial by the presentation of corresponding stimuli. Mands, in the form of instructions, can thus short-circuit the long process of shaping through successive approximations. When one person acquires an adaptive pattern of behavior, possibly through long and difficult experience, that pattern can rapidly diffuse throughout a verbal community through instructed behavior. (Skinner, 1963, 1969, called such instructed behavior *rule-governed behavior* to distinguish it from *contingency-shaped behavior*, that is, behavior shaped through successive approximations to a final form. See Palmer (2012) for an extended discussion of the various types and uses of atomic repertoires. By *atomic repertoire* I mean a set of fine-grained units of behavior, each under control of a distinctive stimulus, which can be evoked in any permutation by the arrangement of corresponding stimuli. Skinner (1957) used the term interchangeably with *minimal repertoire*, but I prefer the former, as it emphasizes the combinatorial power of such a repertoire.)

The Echoic

An echoic response is a vocal or subvocal response that is formally similar to a prior vocal stimulus, for example, the repetition of the name *Jones* upon being introduced to him. Rehearsing a telephone number in the interval before dialing it would be an example of self-echoic behavior. The echoic is conceptually trivial, and Skinner (1957) devoted only a few pages of his book to the topic, but it is of great importance in human affairs: Echoic behavior is a second illustration of an atomic repertoire. Children presumably acquire an atomic echoic repertoire implicitly through response differentiation: *big* not *bag*; *cap* not *tap*. As a consequence, we can usually repeat novel words or expressions at once, without shaping. Thus echoic responses serve a simple but important function: They transduce verbal stimuli into verbal responses. As a result, they facilitate the rapid transmission of effective response forms throughout a verbal community.

Textual Behavior

Textual behavior is analogous to echoic behavior, but the antecedent stimulus is visual rather than auditory. The antecedent stimulus is commonly a text, but it can take other forms such as hieroglyphs, pictograms, the dots and dashes of Morse code, smoke signals, semaphore flags, and so on. Like echoic behavior, textual behavior is commonly covert; only rarely do adults read aloud, except when they are reading to an audience. Textual behavior is another example of an atomic repertoire. Novel verbal responses can be induced in a reader simply by a novel arrangement of letters. Whereas auditory stimuli are only rarely preserved in recordings, textual stimuli tend to endure indefinitely and can therefore affect many readers over long periods of time. Consequently texts are especially influential in transmitting cultural practices.

The Intraverbal

The intraverbal is a verbal response occasioned by a prior verbal stimulus that lacks point-to-point correspondence with that stimulus. This is the standard definition of the term, but if it is to serve an explanatory function, the term must be subject to the further qualification that the control of the response by an antecedent verbal stimulus arises from a history of contiguous or correlated usage. That is, the antecedent verbal stimulus must be a discriminative stimulus, not merely a prior stimulus. This qualification is not always honored in the discourse of behavior analysts, but the term is useless if it embraces all behavior that indirectly follows from a prior verbal stimulus. Thus, the reply *144* in response to *12 times 12* is an intraverbal; . . . *and seven years ago* in response to *Four score* . . . is an intraverbal, but for most people the reply *1,722* in response to *41 times 42* is not an intraverbal, even though it is, in a sense, occasioned by the prior verbal stimulus, for, with very rare exceptions, there is no history of contiguous or correlated usage. The verbal stimulus occasions mediating behavior that in turn occasions the response *1,722.* Among other possibilities, the mediating behavior may consist of a set of operations with a paper and pencil, the manipulation of a calculator, or merely some overt or covert verbal responses. Without the mediating behavior, the target response would have almost no strength at all. Answers to questions are seldom directly evoked by the question itself, and conversation is only rarely so banal as to be directly under the control of antecedent remarks. In short, to call something an intraverbal is to assert, or assume, a history that is sufficient to *explain* the strength of the verbal operant at the moment that it occurs. Without the qualification of contiguous usage, or correlated usage, the term embraces a heterogeneous grab-bag of behavior and serves no explanatory function at all.

Some intraverbal control is established, not by strictly contiguous usage, but by correlated usage. The stimulus *bull* will increase the probability of saying *cow*, and *leash* may occasion *dog*, but we seldom say, or hear, *bull-cow* or *leash-dog*. But terms that are occasioned by a common context will typically be intraverbally related, as suggested by word-association experiments and priming experiments to be discussed later.

We speak of *an intraverbal* as a type of operant when the response is conspicuously under the control of an antecedent stimulus, but *intraverbal control* is a more important concept, for it presumably varies continuously; moreover, it must be virtually ubiquitous in verbal behavior. We can assume that every reinforced utterance establishes some measure of intraverbal control among terms in the verbal stream and between those terms and any verbal antecedents. Thus intraverbal relations are likely to contribute some measure of control to most utterances, however slight. Skinner (1957) devoted just a few pages to the intraverbal, but its contributions to the moment-to-moment control of verbal behavior must almost always be considered. We will see later that intraverbal control will emerge as an important concept in the sequential ordering of verbal operants (i.e., "grammar").

The Tact

As defined by Skinner, a tact is a verbal response "evoked (or at least strengthened) by a particular object or event or property of an object or event" (1957, p. 82). The tact embraces the traditional concepts of labels, names, and descriptions, but is not restricted to them. When one answers a telephone, the remark *It's for you* can be a unitary response to the state of affairs, but we would not ordinarily call this a "description." Verbal communities tend to maintain appropriate stimulus control of tacts by supplying generalized reinforcement or punishment for conformity to or deviations from the norm: *No, that's not poison ivy; it's woodbine.* Because the reinforcement is generalized, the tact tends to be "objective" in the sense of being relatively free of special motivating variables. Objectivity is important to the verbal community. The boy who cries *Wolf!* is punished, whereas the rider who warns that *The British are coming!* is given a hero's welcome. When additional motivational variables come to bear, tacts can become distorted, to the detriment of listeners. The speaker may engage in wishful thinking, exaggeration, or outright lies.

The Autoclitic

A clitic is a standard grammatical term meaning a word or fragment whose pronunciation depends on words that precede or follow it. Of the technical terms introduced by Skinner (1957), the last that we will review here is the *autoclitic*, which he defined as verbal behavior that alters the listener's response to other verbal behavior of the speaker. Apart from this common property, it is a heterogeneous category encompassing function words, such as *and, but,* and *through;* qualifiers, such as *some* or *all*; inflections and grammatical tags, such as markers of possession and grammatical tense; negation, assertion, and predication; mands on the listener, such as *note that* . . .; tacts of response strength, such as *I hesitate to say that* . . .; and other remarks about one's own verbal behavior, such as, *I have already pointed out that*. . . . Although autoclitics are clearly central to the puzzle of verbal behavior, the topic is too broad to be covered here, and with the exception of autoclitic frames, I refer the reader to Skinner (1957) for further discussion.

A verbal operant composed of alternating fixed and variable terms is called an autoclitic frame (Skinner, 1957) or an intraverbal frame (Palmer, 1998): *If X, then Y; X gave the Y to the Z; X promised Y that Z; On the X; In front of X; The boy's X.* In each case, some term entails one or more variable terms that play distinctive roles in the expression. Prepositions and possessives invariably require such variables, and verbs often require several. In a random sample of 200 verbs, 88% occurred in characteristic frames (Palmer, 2007). Much of the novelty in verbal behavior arises from the interweaving of relatively fixed intraverbal frames occasioned by one feature of the context with variable terms provided by other features of the context. A context that brings to strength the word *give* typically entails a giver, a recipient, and something given. These terms are woven together in one or another autoclitic frame.

Function, Not Structure

These verbal operants are not essences. If a garbled attempt to repeat a foreign phrase lacks formal similarity, is it *really* an echoic? The question is not worth debating. Once we understand the relationship between behavior and its controlling variables, we need not waste time quibbling about terminology. We speak of *a* mand, *a* tact, or *an* autoclitic as labels for certain words, expressions, or frames, but each term entails a relationship between an utterance and its controlling variables. No dictionary could specify the type of verbal operant of a word. First, verbal operants do not necessarily correspond with words; second, the form of a word by itself is not a verbal operant. The word *water* could be a mand, tact, echoic, textual, or transcription, depending on its controlling variables. Thus the form of a verbal response plays only a secondary role in a behavioral interpretation; function is paramount.

The Sentence

The sentence is not a technical term in behavior analysis. Skinner used the term liberally in his text, but informally. After reviewing traditional definitions, he concluded that the term was too heterogeneous to warrant a behavioral translation (1957, p. 354). Nevertheless, a behavioral analysis must accommodate the orderliness to be found in strings of verbal operants. Speech frequently consists of fragments, discontinuities, and erratic intrusions that would be difficult for any grammarian to parse into sentences, as traditionally conceived, but order remains, and we must account for it, even if our analytical unit does not correspond to the traditional term. To illustrate the point, put your finger at random on any page of text. Then look at windows of varying widths around the point you have selected, and read them to a patient listener. For example, if you selected the word *page* in the previous sentence, you might select the window yielding, *random on any page of text look at windows of.* In almost every case, the exercise will yield strings that the listener reports as gibberish. Most of the exceptions (but not all) occur when our window captures a string conventionally called a sentence. That is, strings of words conventionally called sentences will be effective on listeners in a way that arbitrarily chosen sequences of verbal behavior will not. This observation offers a behavioral alternative to the grammatical definition of a sentence. As a first approximation, we may define a sentence as a sequence of verbal responses that effectively controls the behavior of the listener. When supported by the context, phrases, gestures, and single words can be functionally complete in the sense of being effective to a listener, e.g., *There; Not today; Next to the Jeep.* When the context exerts no relevant control, only more elaborate strings will be effective on a listener; these more closely correspond to the traditional concept of "complete sentence." That is, the verbal response by itself has to be sufficient to effectively control the behavior of the listener: *I put the keys there; I don't want coffee today; I left the folding chair next to the Jeep.* On the other hand, some "complete sentences," traditionally defined, are not functionally complete by themselves. Riddles, anecdotes, and limericks must be emitted in full before they are effective, whatever their grammatical structure. Thus the behavioral unit, so defined, does not correspond to the traditional unit, but it appears to capture much of the behavioral regularity of interest.

Verbal behavior has at least two kinds of effects on the listener, and both are relevant in determining whether a verbal string is functionally complete. The first effect is easily understood: a behavioral "sentence" exerts immediate discriminative control over the listener's behavior. But verbal behavior also may have latent effects on the repertoire of the listener. Verbal behavior commonly conditions the behavior of the listener with respect to an object, condition, or state of affairs. An utterance of this sort is, in a sense, "functionally complete" when it does so:

> Almost any salient verbalization brings about some conditioning. If I announce "The boy's bicycle . . ." my listeners are likely to be able to report, some half-hour later, that I brought up the boy's bicycle. In this case, their behavior has been conditioned with respect to my behavior as a stimulus, as it might have been conditioned by witnessing any salient event: a frog on the porch, a salt-shaker in the shape of a nutcracker, a jogger with a ponytail. However their behavior has not been modified with respect to the boy's

> bicycle. But if I announce "The boy's bicycle is blocking the driveway," they can report what I said, as they would with respect to any other event, but they will also behave in a new way with respect to the boy's bicycle. (Palmer, 2007, p. 168)

It is important to note that the conditioning permits the effect to be long delayed. That is, we might not respond with respect to the boy's bicycle until we get home from a trip, but in the interim we can be said to "know the fact that it is blocking the driveway" and can measure this knowledge in a variety of ways. Thus we must include such effects in our behavioral definition of sentence:

> In traditional terms, a sentence consists of a subject and a predicate. In behavioral terms, the subject is the stimulus, condition, or state of affairs, with respect to which the listener's behavior is conditioned, and the predicate brings about the conditioning of new behavior with respect to the subject. It is this effect, among others, that listeners discriminate when they label something as a "sentence," or mark it "acceptable," or say they "understand it." In effect, they are saying, "My repertoire has been successfully altered with respect to the subject at hand." (Palmer, 2007, p. 168)

Such conditioning is perhaps the most important function of verbal behavior, but how verbal behavior brings it about remains a formidable challenge. I will return to this challenge later.

On Reference, Meaning, and Truth

A distinctive feature of a behavioral interpretation of verbal behavior is that no role is played by certain conventional concepts, among which are *meaning*, *reference*, and *truth*. From a behavioral perspective, these concepts become superfluous once the relationship between a response and its controlling variables is established. *The old man is snoring* could be an echoic, a textual response, an intraverbal, or several tacts in an autoclitic frame, or it could be the result of randomly drawing words from bins labeled *noun, adjective, article,* and so on. Stripped of its controlling variables, the string has no meaning at all. We can impute a meaning, but only by inferring a plausible set of controlling variables. Thus if the phrase is an intraverbal, there is no point in asking what the referent of *old man* is, or whether the statement is true. Likewise, there is no point in puzzling over paradoxes, such as *This statement is false*. When the variables responsible for the statement are analyzed, it becomes clear that *false* is not a tact, and there is no autoclitic of assertion. Any tendency to be baffled arises from considering strings of words as independent objects, not as products of behavior. We can dispose of these troublesome terms by analyzing the relevant behavior in other ways.

The Structural Complexity of Verbal Behavior: The Puzzle of Lawful Novelty

Following Skinner (1957), I devoted the previous sections of this chapter to showing how principles of behavior can be recruited to organize our understanding of verbal behavior, but in the remaining pages I will discuss topics at the fringes of our understanding. The adequacy of a behavioral account will ultimately rest upon our ability to interpret such phenomena.

Verbal behavior poses a special challenge to the behavior analyst, and indeed to the scientist of any other persuasion, for it often entails patterns of responses that have never been emitted before but which nevertheless serve an adaptive function in the particular context in which they occur. Moreover, other patterns, seemingly equally plausible, are commonly rejected by members of a verbal community. Consider the following examples (adapted from Pinker, 1994):

I gave the money to the campaign.
I gave the campaign the money.
I donated the money to the campaign.
I donated the campaign the money.

Native speakers of English typically find the first three examples "acceptable" but balk at the fourth. That is, although it is perfectly sensible, it "sounds odd"; they cannot imagine themselves or anyone else putting it quite that way. This judgment is but one of countless similar oddities that any scientific account must wrestle with (see Chomsky, 1965, 1975, 1980, and Pinker, 1989, 1994 for many other examples). It is surely not the case that people have uttered the fourth sentence and been punished for it. The absurdity of such a claim is exposed by noting that *money* can be changed to great number of other things, and the grammatical intuition remains. It is equally absurd to suppose that parents or teachers have inculcated a general rule about dative verbs, like *give* and *donate*. Hardly anyone is aware of the puzzle until it is pointed out to them. In the sequencing of verbal elements, people somehow pick up regularities that transcend particular examples. Strings of verbal responses are typically novel, but still orderly. Explaining orderliness amidst novelty is a challenge to the scientist, behaviorist or otherwise, but I will attempt to show that it is not insurmountable.

Language acquisition poses a problem even for commonplace remarks. Studies of parent-child interactions reveal that parents tend to fuss about the truth of a child's utterance, but shrug off deficits in grammar (e.g., Brown & Hanlon, 1970, but see Schoneberger, 2010). Moerk (1983), has shown that although children tend to get little formal instruction, their interactions with others are nevertheless densely packed with unstructured contingencies. However, even his analysis did not reveal evidence of the kind of detailed discrimination training necessary to establish fine-grained grammatical distinctions. Such considerations have fueled speculation that grammar—that is, regularities in the sequencing of verbal operants—is largely innate (e.g. Chomsky, 1980; Fodor, 1975, 1983; Jackendoff, 2002; Pinker, 1994; Gordon, 1986). Every behavior analyst with an interest in language should read Chomsky's critique of Skinner's account and MacCorquodale's rebuttal (Chomsky, 1959; MacCorquodale, 1970; see Palmer 2006 for an overview). I have argued elsewhere that the nativist hypothesis is empty (Palmer, 1986, 2000), but the formidable challenge of offering a substantive alternative account remains.

The Additivity of Stimulus Control

The variables controlling verbal behavior almost never occur alone. Verbal responses may be partly under the control of an audience, motivational variables, and the context; in addition responses are often subject to intraverbal control or echoic control by preceding verbal behavior. To illustrate the point Skinner proposed the following strategy for getting someone to say *pencil*:

> To strengthen a mand of this form, we could make sure that no pencil or writing instrument is available, then hand our subject a pad of paper appropriate to pencil sketching, and offer him a handsome reward for a recognizable picture of a cat . . . Simultaneously we could strengthen other responses of the same form by providing echoic stimuli (a phonograph in the background occasionally says *pencil*) and textual stimuli (signs on the wall read *PENCIL*). We scatter other verbal stimuli among these to produce intraverbal responses: the phonograph occasionally says *pen and* . . . and there are other signs reading *PEN AND*, . . . We set up an occasion for a tact with the form *pencil* by putting a very large or unusual pencil in an unusual place clearly in sight—say, half submerged in a large aquarium or floating freely in the air near the ceiling of the room. We indicate our own audience-character as an English-speaking person by the simple device of speaking English. Under such circumstances it is highly probable that our subject will say *pencil*. (1957, pp. 253–254)

Such a strategy would work, according to Skinner (1957), because stimulus control is additive. This has been shown to be true for reflexes (Sherrington, 1906), conditioned reflexes (Pavlov, 1927), operant conditioning (Wolf, 1963) and for both operant and classical conditioning in a wide variety of preparations by Weiss and his colleagues (e.g., Emurian & Weiss, 1972; Panlilio, Weiss, & Schindler, 2000; Van Houten, O'Leary, & Weiss, 1970; Weiss 1964, 1967, 1977). The additivity of stimulus control has profound implications for our understanding of verbal behavior and behavior generally.

The additive control of a single response by multiple stimuli, as in the example above, has been dubbed convergent multiple control. The converse—that is, the control of a variety of responses by a single stimulus—is called divergent multiple control (Michael, Palmer, & Sundberg, 2011). A reddish brown dog might evoke any of a variety of responses such as *dog, Fido, here boy, Irish Setter, bird dog, shedding, goofy,* and so on. (The particular response usually depends upon convergent control by other variables.) Of course one typically remains silent upon sight of a dog, but data from priming experiments suggests that even if no response is actually emitted, a variety of responses are potentiated by the stimulus. Many different experimental procedures are used to study priming, but in a typical procedure, a word is flashed on a screen for a fraction of a second. Then a second word is presented, and the experimental subject must respond to it, perhaps by reading it aloud, or by judging whether it is an English word or not, and striking a corresponding key. The dependent measure is response latency, and the relevant finding is that latency to respond to the second word usually decreases when the words are intraverbally related. Thus in the pairs *Bread-Butter* and *Bread-Bottle*, responses are faster to *Butter* than to

Bottle (see Krisjánsson & Campana, 2010; Neely, 1991; and van den Bussche, van den Noortgate, & Reynvoet, 2009, for reviews of this and a variety of other priming effects). Of particular relevance to the present point, category terms like *Fruit* simultaneously potentiate a variety of exemplars of the category, such as *Apple, Banana,* and *Orange.* The potentiation must be *simultaneous* because the second term of the pair cannot be predicted in advance. That is, when *Fruit* is displayed on a screen, one has no reason to expect that *Banana* will follow on that trial, as opposed to any other word; if potentiation occurs on separate trials for many exemplars of a category, we must assume that it occurs for them all on every trial.

The significance of such findings is that, in addition to overt behavior, our conceptual toolbox must include not just covert behavior but latent behavior as well—that is, behavior which has not actually been emitted but which is nevertheless fluctuating in strength according to variations in discriminative stimuli. If the single textual stimulus *Fruit* has a simultaneous potentiating effect on a number of mutually incompatible exemplars of the category, we can assume that during conversation, or when reading a text, when verbal stimuli may be presented at the rate of several words per second, the effect on one's repertoire over the course of a few minutes must be highly complex, with myriad responses fluctuating in strength. Only one response in any response system can be emitted, but the smoothness and orderliness of overt behavior masks bewildering complexity (see Palmer, 2009 for a fuller treatment of this topic).

Consideration of changes in strength of latent behavior may seem out of place in a science devoted to measurable changes in observable variables, but an interpretation of much complex human behavior requires just such a consideration. Verbal, gestural, and physical prompts, the mainstays of many procedures in applied settings, tend to work for the very reason that the control supplied by the prompt supplements control by the task. A parlor game requires one player to provide a succession of faint hints until another player correctly guesses the target word. For example, *cherry tree, false teeth, Martha,* might be sufficient together to evoke *George Washington*, but no clue alone would do so. In problem-solving and in recall, which I have argued is merely an instance of problem-solving (Donahoe & Palmer, 2004; Palmer, 1991), the individual does something perfectly analogous: He prompts himself with a succession of supplementary stimuli each of which sums with prevailing stimuli until the target response is emitted (Skinner, 1953). The game of "20 Questions" is a model: Is it an animal? Is it a mammal? Is it native to North America? Is it nocturnal? Each successive answer raises the probability of a narrower and narrower set of verbal responses until the answer is emitted as such. In recall we employ similar strategies: When trying to recall the name of an acquaintance, we rehearse the names of mutual friends, visualize the context in which we met them, go through the alphabet to provide formal prompts, and so on. The additive effect of stimuli on latent behavior is central to a behavioral interpretation of such everyday behavior.

The skilled use of multiple control distinguishes the work of the great writer, artist, and composer, as well as the poet and humorist. To open *Richard III,* Shakespeare might have written, *Everyone sure is pleased with King Edward, now that he's won the battle*, but he chose instead to write, *Now is the winter of our discontent made glorious summer by this sun of York.* The line is memorable because of the multiple interacting sources of control: The cadence; the thematic elements of winter and discontent; the intraverbal relation between winter and summer, summer and sun; the parallel between winter and summer, war and victory; Edward as both the son of York and, metaphorically, the sun of York who brought the warmth of peace in time of war; the theme of discontent and Richard's jealousy. In addition, Shakespeare's contemporaries would likely have known that Edward's emblem was the sun and that the antithesis of the imagery was historically mirrored by the physical contrast between the hunchbacked Richard and the imposing Edward, England's tallest king. Such relationships do more than keep literary critics busy; they have complicated effects on listeners.

Humor often arises from bringing an unexpected secondary source of control to bear on a response that is strong for other reasons. The pun may be the lowest form of humor, but it illustrates the principle. In poetry, responses which would be semantically weak come to strength by their metrical and rhyming properties. In Lewis Carroll's *Jabberwocky*, rhythm and rhyme carry much of burden of establishing response strength, for the rest is nonsense embedded in autoclitic frames. The thumping rhythms of Poe's poetry are often more memorable than the imagery itself. Semantically esoteric poetry that lacks both rhythm and rhyme may be judged harshly by readers if secondary sources of control are ineffective for them.

Joint Control

A special case of multiple control appears to be relevant to matching-to-sample, pattern recognition, and other tasks that entail a search among stimuli for those with particular properties. In such tasks, the relevant stimulus will tend to evoke behavior that is already strong. Under such conditions we speak of *joint control* (Lowenkron, 1991, 1998; Lowenkron & Colvin, 1992; see degli Espinosa, 2011, for an overview of the concept and a discussion of its application to children with autism). The subsequent jump in response strength may be discriminable, and if so, can control subsequent behavior. For example, when scanning a page in a telephone book for the name *McDermott,* we may read many items before encountering the name, but as soon as we do, we go no further. This is such a commonplace phenomenon that we are inclined to overlook the need for an explanation: We stop when we have found what we are looking for. But how do we *know* that we have found it? Lowenkron's answer is that the response *McDermott* is already strong in the context; when we encounter the name in a list, control by the text sums with control by these other variables, and the discrepancy in stimulus control signals that the item has been found. The effect is clearest when both sources of control are conspicuous. For example, suppose you are told to find the name in a book corresponding to the phone number 413-658-8819, a number that is wholly new to you. Simply scanning the page will not work because when the number is encountered, it has no special effect. That is, it is not "recognized" as the target number. The only source of control arises from the text itself, and that does not set it apart from any other number on the page. Of course, most of us have learned what to do in such cases: we rehearse the number as we search. This establishes a second source of control: Self-echoic control and textual control evoke the same topography of behavior only when the target number is reached. The onset of joint control, presumably causing a discriminable saltation in response strength, is sufficient to explain the selection response, and no other explanations have been offered. Lowenkron (1998) spoke of the joint control by exactly two stimuli, but there is no reason to suppose that the effect is limited to such cases. That is, any time a new stimulus is encountered that adds to the evocative effects of existing stimuli, however many, the saltation in stimulus control may be discriminable.

Given the putative ubiquity of multiple control, it may seem implausible that the onset of joint control should be special. However, the claims are not incompatible. The onset of joint control is only useful to us in certain kinds of tasks, such as identity judgments, discrepancy judgments, matching-to-sample, recall, problem-solving, and other tasks in which recognition is required. I am suggesting that the effect of joint control is conditional upon such tasks. That is, we learn to exploit the onset of joint control only in certain contexts; it is not an innate ability. Usually any shift in orientation is typically followed by stimulus change rather than stimulus identity. For example, if we look from one face to another in a crowd, or shift our gaze over any scene, we are accustomed to stimulus discrepancy. When stimulus discrepancy is the norm, seeing an identical stimulus from one glance to the next may be "surprising," hence more discriminable. For example, when we happen to look at identical twins, we are surprised; we experience a saltation in response strength rather than a decrement. Likewise, when we scan a list of telephone numbers, we are accustomed to a decrement in stimulus control, as each successive number evokes incompatible behavior. When two numbers are identical, or when a textual stimulus is supplemented by a self-echoic stimulus, the effect is in the opposite direction from the customary effect. Thus, our exploitation of joint control or multiple control may be restricted to contexts where discrepancy is the norm.

Automatic Shaping

A distinctive feature of vocal behavior is that the behavior itself has stimulus properties that, under normal conditions, affect the speaker at least as faithfully and as promptly as they affect others. This feature is not shared by signing or other motor behavior: A manual sign looks somewhat different to an observer than to the person performing the sign. As a result, in order for a verbal community of signers to maintain sharp control over sign topography, the verbal community must shape the behavior of signers. However, much of the fine-grained shaping of vocal behavior can be accomplished without explicit shaping by other people. Children are commonly discriminating listeners long before they become articulate speakers. Toddlers with vocabularies of only a few words can understand complex commands that they cannot utter. That is, many verbal stimuli serve as discriminative stimuli for children who cannot yet formulate the responses that produce such stimuli. However, as their repertoire expands, and they begin to make such responses, they can tell whether they have done so correctly. That is, they can tell whether they have matched the normative practices of the verbal community by whether the stimulus properties of their own behavior exert appropriate stimulus control. In other words, they can recognize when they have matched (Baer & Deguchi, 1985; Palmer, 1996; Skinner, 1957).

It is easy to demonstrate automatic shaping in an analog task: I programmed a computer so that each key produced a different tone, rather like the keys of a piano, except that the order of position of the keys was unrelated to the pitch of the tones (Palmer, 1998) I then asked a naïve subject to play the tune, *Mary Had a Little Lamb*. As she had no experience with the device, her initial behavior was merely exploratory, but within a few minutes of working at the keyboard, she produced the tune with only one false note. The shaping was accomplished "automatically," that is, without any social reinforcement. Because the tune was familiar to her, she could instantly hear any discrepancy between her performance and the tune. Correct keystrokes were thus reinforced and incorrect ones punished. Needless to say, this process of automatic shaping would have been impossible if the tune had been unfamiliar to her. No doubt people learn to whistle through an analogous kind of automatic shaping, just as children learn to imitate the noises of motorcycles, trains, airplanes, with appropriate Doppler shift, all without explicit shaping by others.

I should emphasize that the reinforcement in the previous example was not the tune itself but evidence of matching. That is, the tinny sound of a computer playing *Mary Had a Little Lamb* is not a reinforcer for a typical adult, and it is implausible that my subject would have eagerly listened to the tune if it had been played by someone else. Rather, the demand to produce the tune established evidence of accomplishing the feat as a reinforcer. Thus, "recognizing the tune" was the reinforcer, not the tune itself. To make the point another way, if her random poking at the keyboard had accidentally produced the divine *Moonlight Sonata*, her behavior would have been punished, not reinforced, at least with respect to the task at hand. "Recognizing a tune" is a kind of pattern matching, and as I pointed out earlier, joint control is a possible variable controlling such performances. That is, the sound of the correct note would sum with the tendency to "sing" that note, presumably covertly. An incorrect note would be incompatible with our behavior.

Automatic Shaping and Grammar

The concept of automatic reinforcement is an important element of a possible behavioral resolution of the puzzle of structural regularities in verbal behavior (cf. Donahoe & Palmer, 2004; Palmer, 1996, 1998). That children learn subtle features of their language without explicit instruction (e.g., Brown & Hanlon, 1970) is not troublesome for a behavioral account. Automatic shaping may play an important role in the acquisition of a verbal repertoire for at least two reasons. First, it is instantaneous, unlike social reinforcement, which is usually slightly delayed. Second, it can occur virtually every time the child speaks. Contingencies of automatic reinforcement vastly outnumber those of social reinforcement.

To illustrate the power of automatic shaping, relative to social reinforcement, Silvestri, Davies-Lackey, Twyman, and Palmer (2000) conducted a demonstration that pitted the two sources of control against one another. This experiment has been replicated twice, with appropriate controls, once in English (Wright, 2006) and once in Norwegian (Østvik, Eikeseth, & Klintwall, 2012). The essential features were these: Young children took turns with the experimenter in describing a series of pictures. The experimenter consistently modeled a particular construction in the passive voice, namely, the autoclitic frame *The X is being Y-ed by the Z.* For example, one picture might occasion the response *The zebra is being painted by the peacock*, another the response *The elephant is being pulled by the mouse.* No constraints were imposed on the children, and no instruction was provided. If they used the active voice, some mild reinforcement was provided: The experimenter made an approving comment or gave the child a sticker. If they used the passive voice, no social reinforcement was provided. Nevertheless, all children in all three studies acquired all or part of the passive autoclitic frame and applied it to novel pictures. Since the frame was not initially in the children's repertoires, this extremely complex performance was presumably shaped by the reinforcing effect of conforming to a model. That the contingencies were effective in the face of explicit social and tangible reinforcement for using the active voice illustrates the strength of reinforcement by conformity with models (see Goldberg, Casenhiser, & Sethuraman, 2004 for an analogous example of the rapid acquisition of a nonsense frame through modeling).

Autoclitic Frames, Novelty, and "Grammatical Intuitions"

These studies suggest a way of interpreting "grammatical intuitions" of novel strings that pose such puzzles to the scientist. It is true that most sentences are novel, but the autoclitic frames at the heart of sentences are not. We can assume that an autoclitic frame comes to strength in characteristic contexts; in the experiments on the passive voice, the context in which the passive frame was emitted and reinforced included a particular room, a particular person, and a picture of two animals interacting. The presentation of a novel picture and the attentive expression of the experimenter set the occasion for responding. The autoclitic frame came to strength, for, by hypothesis, it had repeatedly been emitted as a covert echoic in that context; then variable terms occasioned by the picture were interwoven with the frame, creating a novel sentence, perhaps never uttered before by anyone. Novelty lies in the combination of controlling variables for verbal behavior. The orderliness we speak of as "grammar" arises from the structure of autoclitic frames—that is, each element of the frame occurs in a fixed position relative to other elements. Our "intuitions" about the acceptability of certain constructions depends in part on whether we have acquired the corresponding autoclitic frame. Thus the verb *donate* occurs in fewer contexts than *give*, and it occurs in frames like *X donated Y to the Z*, but seldom, or never, in the frame *X donated Z Y.* In contrast, *give* occurs in both frames. So our "grammatical intuition" arises from the familiarity of the autoclitic frame, not from the novel string as a whole. Although this argument is post hoc, something of the sort must surely be true, for the terms *give* and *donate* are purely arbitrary. In principle, their functions could be reversed (see Palmer, 1998, 2007 for elaboration of these points).

Rapid Shifts in Stimulus Control in Autoclitic Frames

Thus the interweaving of autoclitic frames with other verbal operants occasioned by some context may be sufficient to explain the novelty of much verbal behavior, but much remains mysterious, for the interweaving of verbal elements requires rapidly shifting stimulus control. A child in the passive voice study is emitting sequences of the form *frame-tact-frame-tact-frame-tact* (*The X is being Y-ed by the Z.*). The ordering of the frame itself was fixed, but how did stimulus control switch from the variables evoking the frame to the variables evoking the appropriate tact?

Although this is among the most commonplace of performances, it is surely one of the most formidable challenges to the behavior analyst. That the general context is essentially constant over the time course of such utterances suggests that the controlling variables for transitions between verbal operants are to be found in the verbal behavior itself and perhaps in the speaker's discriminative responses to his own verbal behavior as it is being emitted. The plausibility of such a claim is supported by studies of delayed auditory feedback. Usually speakers hear themselves immediately and faithfully, but when such stimulation is electronically delayed by a fraction of a second, most people find it difficult to speak (e.g., Fabbro & Darò, 1995). However, on the assumption that the sequence is novel, it cannot be the particular words that are controlling the transitions; the elements of the frame may be fixed, but the variable terms (*X*, *Y*, and *Z*) are not. Moreover, the variable terms themselves can differ considerably in form: In place of the variable term *pig*, a child might say *pig with a funny tail*, but the terms would serve the same function in controlling a transition in stimulus control. That is, the particular phonemes do not seem to be sufficient to control the next element in the string.

However, there is an important feature of speech that may be relevant to transitions in stimulus control, specifically, prosody. Prosody is the song of speech, its cadence and stress. Prosody serves several different functions in speech, such as determining emphasis, distinguishing questions, assertions, and exclamations, marking clause boundaries, and differentiating words. But another important function may be to mark transitions in autoclitic frames. In the passive voice examples, the stress falls on all of the variable terms; the elements of the autoclitic frame are unstressed: *The <u>pig</u> is being <u>pushed</u> by the <u>rat</u>*; or *The <u>pig with the funny tail</u> is being <u>pushed</u> by the <u>rat</u>*. It is possible, then, that for some autoclitic frames—perhaps all—prosodic cues become controlling variables for transitions between verbal elements for speakers themselves. The controlling stimulus may be the auditory property of the stress, the proprioceptive property of emitting stress, or perhaps the controlling variable that causes an element to be stressed at all (see Palmer, 1998, 2007 for a more extensive discussion of this topic).

Conditioning the Behavior of the Listener

Conditioning the behavior of the listener is both the most commonplace of phenomena and the greatest puzzle (Palmer, 2005, 2007; Schlinger, 2008a; Skinner, 1957). When we observe someone respond "144" to "What is 12 times 12?" we infer that they encountered the question before, responded correctly, and that some reinforcement followed. The conclusion is plausible, for most children have encountered this three-term contingency in grammar school. But it is easy to demonstrate the acquisition of novel verbal behavior in the apparent absence of contingencies of reinforcement: Make up some nonsense fact, and announce it to a group of people. For example, tell them that you were born on an island called Bingwich and that you plan to retire there as an ermine-robed emperor some day. Fifteen minutes later, a day later, perhaps a week later, most of your audience will be able to report that "fact," including the name of the island. But how can *Bingwich* be in someone's repertoire *as a response* if they have never uttered the word before? The puzzle arises from the apparent absence of contingencies. To an observer, the listener appears to have emitted no behavior and to have participated in no contingencies of reinforcement. In many cases, mere exposure to verbal stimuli seems to be sufficient to effect an enduring change in human behavior. But this is untenable. This example illustrates, not just a change in the stimulus control of an existing response, but the establishment of a novel response at a future time.

The explanation, of course, is that the listener is not a passive vessel. The listener's repertoire changes only when he or she is "paying attention." The term is intuitively appealing but difficult to operationalize, as it seems to embrace, not just subtle orienting responses, but covert behavior as well. If we assume that attentive listeners engaged in covert echoic behavior at the time of your statement, much of the mystery dissolves. Your audience *has* emitted the response *Bingwich* before, at the time you presented it as a verbal stimulus. They were able to do so immediately, without shaping, because, as we have seen, echoic behavior is an example of an atomic repertoire. It is true that we must also infer that some reinforcement followed, but this is not implausible. Simply successfully following a speaker into a new domain is likely to be a conditioned reinforcer. We say we "get the point" when such a response evokes a wealth of other relevant behavior in our repertoire. This effect too is likely to be a conditioned reinforcer, for, in our experience, understanding is correlated with reinforcement, confusion with extinction. Compare those cases in which we are unable to echo the foreign phrase, the incomprehensible jargon, or the inarticulate mumbling of a speaker. By assuming that listening entails echoic behavior, we are able to begin to explain a great deal of human behavior, specifically, the acquisition of "information" simply by listening to others (Palmer, 2005; Schlinger, 2008b). The hypothesis that listening entails echoic behavior is supported by research on activity in the motor cortex (e.g., Fadiga, Craighero, Bucchino, & Rizzolatti, 2002; Watkins, Strafella, & Paus, 2003; Wilson, Saygin, Sereno, & Iacoboni, 2004) as well as studies of auditory perception (e.g., Liberman, Cooper, Shankweiler, & Studdert-Kennedy, 1967). It is closely related to the motor theory of speech perception (Liberman, et al., 1967), a theory influential to the Soviet school of psychology (see Žinkin, 1968 for a review and Horne & Lowe, 1996, for an analysis of the role of echoic behavior in the acquisition of listener behavior, tacting, and naming).

The concept of echoic behavior implies a temporal order, with the listener following the speaker. This is plausible when the verbal response is novel, or is otherwise weak in the listener's repertoire, but often the listener speaks along with the speaker, or even a little ahead, as when the listener finishes the remark of a hesitant speaker or supplies a word for a fumbling one. Under many conditions an important function of speech is simply to set up conditions that induce verbal behavior in the listener. Evoking echoic behavior is an effective way of doing so, but not the only way. Listener behavior doubtless includes other relevant activities as well: cascades of discriminative responses, mnemonic strategies, elaborations, imagery, intraverbal chains, and so on. Echoic behavior is sufficient to establish a verbal response of novel topography in one's repertoire, thereby disposing of the puzzle of the first instance, but all listener behavior must be considered if we are to have a comprehensive account.

Verbal stimuli sometimes alter the function of other stimuli (Schlinger & Blakeley, 1987; Skinner, 1957). If we are told to turn left when we come to a stone church, we are likely to do so. The church appears to have acquired discriminative control over turning left. But such an account is inadequate by itself, as it omits relevant mediating behavior: We turn left only if we are "paying attention," that is, responding discriminatively to the verbal stimulus and again to the buildings along the road. The importance of such behavior becomes clear when the example becomes more complex: If told to turn left at 82 Gower Street, we will do so only if we scrutinize the storefronts and engage in textual behavior as we pass along the street; the verbal stimulus does not magically endow the building with evocative control over our behavior. Thus, the phenomenon of conditioning the behavior of the listener is of central importance to human behavior, but unfortunately, our accounts of it remain highly speculative, owing to the inaccessibility of much of the relevant behavior.

Equivalence Classes and Relational Frames

In this chapter I have neglected to discuss two major empirical threads within behavior analysis that are sometimes assumed to be central to an understanding of verbal behavior, or perhaps even to define behavior that is distinctively verbal. I speak of work on equivalence classes and relational frames. The reader can find good treatments of the former in Sidman (1994, 2000) and of the latter in Hayes, Barnes-Holmes, and Roche (2001). The important feature of such work is that subjects who are posed a series of analogical tasks can often generalize to novel tasks of the same sort without further training. Moreover, stimulus functions often transfer as well (e.g., Dougher et al., 2007). However, the research paradigms that are used to study these phenomena typically study verbal subjects and measure just one bit of behavior (usually a keystroke or a mouse-click) terminating trials that can last many seconds and often feature complex and abstract stimuli. When subjects are forced to respond quickly, that is, within two seconds of stimulus presentations, subjects fail at the tasks (Holth & Arntzen, 2000), suggesting that successful performance is at least partly under control of unmeasured events within the trials (e.g., Dugdale & Lowe, 1990; Horne & Lowe, 1996; Miguel, Þétursdóttir, Carr, & Michael, 2008; Randell & Remington, 2006). Research with nonverbal subjects has met with little success and then only with the simplest of relationships and after prolonged training. When relationships are complex, even adult verbal subjects often fail at the tasks. These research preparations are important in themselves, but they may be too complex to shed light on fundamental processes in verbal behavior. Rather, they seem to illustrate contextually controlled problem-solving: The phenomena of interest may arise from unmeasured verbal behavior or nonverbal mediating behavior that is conditioned during training.

Conclusion

I have reviewed some of the ways in which verbal behavior is distinctive. Although producing even the simplest of speech sounds requires precise coordination among disparate muscle groups, once a repertoire of such responses is acquired and brought under control of antecedent stimuli, a verbal repertoire can expand rapidly and indefinitely. Verbal responses usually require little effort but can have great consequences, not just for the speaker, but for the listener and the entire culture, because verbally-governed behavior can short-circuit the process of shaping by inducing critical variations in behavior in a single step. Novel forms of adaptive behavior sweep rapidly through verbal communities. Because speakers are also typically listeners, sharp stimulus control of response form can be maintained "automatically," that is, without instruction. As a consequence very slight differences in response topographies can yield different response classes that are respected by nearly everyone within a verbal community. Verbal behavior is so efficient that novel verbal responses can be acquired in the apparent absence of contingencies of reinforcement, an illusion that arises form the privacy of the listener's responses and the subtlety of the reinforcing consequences.

The task of the behavior analyst is to offer an interpretation of this remarkable kind of behavior using only the concepts and principles that have emerged from experimental analyses of behavior, that is to say, those concepts and principles to which this volume is devoted. The interpretive task is formidable, for much human behavior is covert, we seldom know much about the histories of our subjects, and verbal behavior is almost always under control of multiple stimuli. Nevertheless, following Skinner, I have tried to show that our interpretive and analytical tools are versatile enough to offer speculative accounts of even the most baffling of verbal phenomena. Restricting ourselves to behavioral principles imposes a cost; our task would be much easier if we could invoke lexicons, grammatical modules, syntactic assembly processes, and so on, but our restraint has one advantage, and it is an overpowering one: The principles of behavior are not hypothetical. It may be that we have not yet settled on a final statement of these principles, but the reliability and validity of the data from which they arise compare favorably with those of competing interpretations of verbal behavior. It is just this consideration that justifies the present approach.

References

Baer, D. M., & Deguchi, H. (1985). Generalized imitation from a radical-behavioral viewpoint. In S. Reiss & R. R. Bootzin (Eds.), *Theoretical issues in behavior therapy* (pp. 179–217). New York: Academic Press.

Brown, R., & Hanlon, C. (1970). Derivational complexity and order of acquisition in child speech. In J. R. Hayes (Ed.), *Cognition and the development of language* (pp. 11–53). New York: John Wiley & Sons, Inc.

Carr, J. E., & Miguel, C. F. (2012). The analysis of verbal behavior and its therapeutic applications. In G. J. Madden, W. V. Dube, T. D. Hackenberg, G. P. Hanley, & K. A. Lattal (Eds.), *APA Handbook of Behavior Analysis*, Vol. 2 (pp. 329–352). Washington, DC: American Psychological Association.

Chomsky, N. (1959). Review of Skinner's *Verbal Behavior. Language, 35*, 26–58.

Chomsky, N. (1965). *Aspects of a theory of syntax.* Cambridge, MA: MIT Press.

Chomsky, N. (1975). *Reflections on language.* New York: Pantheon.

Chomsky, N. (1980). *Rules and representations.* New York: Columbia University Press.

degli Espinosa, F. (2011). *Verbal behaviour development for children with autism.* Unpublished Ph.D. thesis., University of Southampton, UK.

Donahoe, J. W., & Palmer, D. C. (2004). *Learning and complex behavior.* Richmond, MA: Ledgetop Publishing (originally published in 1994).

Dougher, M. J., Hamilton, D. A., Fink, B. C., & Harrington, J. (2007). Transformation of the discriminative and eliciting functions of generalized relational stimuli. *Journal of the Experimental Analysis of Behavior, 88*, 179–197.

Dugdale, N., & Lowe, C. F. (1990). Naming and stimulus equivalence. In D. E. Blackman & H. Lejeune (Eds.), *Behaviour analysis in theory and practice: Contributions and controversies* (pp. 115–138). Hove, UK: Erlbaum.

Emurian, H. H., & Weiss, S. J. (1972). Compounding discriminative stimuli controlling free-operant avoidance. *Journal of the Experimental Analysis of Behavior, 17*, 249–256.

Fabbro, F., & Darò, V. V. (1995). Delayed auditory feedback in polyglot simultaneous interpreters. *Brain and Language, 48*, 309–319.

Fadiga, L., Craighero, L., Bucchino, G., & Rizzolatti, G. (2002). Speech listening specifically modulates the excitability of tongue muscles: A TMS study. *European Journal of Neuroscience, 15*, 399–402.

Fodor, J. A. (1975). *The language of thought.* New York: Thomas Crowell.

Fodor, J. A. (1983). *The modularity of mind.* Cambridge, MA: MIT Press.

Goldberg, A. E., Casenhiser, D. M., & Sethuraman, N. (2004). Learning argument structure generalizations. *Cognitive Linguistics, 13*, 289–316.

Gordon, P. (1986). Level-ordering in lexical development. *Cognition, 21*, 73–93.

Greer, R. D., & Ross, D. E. (2008). *Verbal behavior analysis: Inducing and expanding new behavioral capabilities in children with language delays.* Boston, Pearson.

Hayes, S. C., Barnes-Holmes, D., & Roche, B. (2001). *Relational frame theory: A post-Skinnerian account of human language and cognition.* New York: Kluwer Academic/Plenum.

Holth, P., & Arntzen, E. (2000). Reaction times and the emergence of class consistent responding: A case for precurrent responding? *The Psychological Record, 50*, 305–337.

Horne P. J., & Lowe, C. F. (1996). Naming and other symbolic behavior. *Journal of the Experimental Analysis of Behavior, 65*, 185–241.

Jackendoff, R. (2002). *Foundations of language.* Oxford: Oxford University Press.

Krisjánsson, A., & Campana, G. (2010). Where perception meets memory: a review of repetition priming in visual search tasks. *Attention, Perception, and Psychophysics, 72*, 5–18.

Liberman, A. M., Cooper, F. S., Shankweiler, D. P., & Studdert-Kennedy, M. (1967). Perception of the speech code. *Psychological Review, 74*, 431–461.

Lieberman, P. (2000). *Human language and our reptilian brain.* Cambridge, MA: Harvard University Press.

Lieberman, P. (2006). *Toward an evolutionary biology of language.* Cambridge, MA: Harvard University Press.

Locke, J. L. (1993). *The child's path to spoken language.* Cambridge, MA: Harvard University Press.

Lowenkron, B. (1991). Joint control and the generalization of selection-based verbal behavior. *The analysis of verbal behavior, 9*, 121–126.

Lowenkron, B. (1998). Some logical functions of joint control. *Journal of the Experimental Analysis of Behavior, 69*, 327–354.

Lowenkron, B., & Colvin, V. (1992). Joint control and generalized non-identity matching: Saying when something is *Not. The Analysis of Verbal Behavior, 10*, 1–10.

MacCorquodale, K. (1970). On Chomsky's review of Skinner's *Verbal Behavior. Journal of the Experimental Analysis of Behavior,13*, 83–99.

Michael, J., Palmer, D. C., & Sundberg, M. L. (2011). The multiple control of verbal behavior. *The Analysis of Verbal Behavior, 27*, 3–22.

Miguel, C., Pétursdóttir, A. L., Carr, J. E., & Michael, J. (2008). The role of naming in stimulus categorization by preschool children. *Journal of the Experimental Analysis of Behavior,89*, 383–405.

Moerk, E. L. (1983). A behavioral analysis of controversial topics in first language acquisition: Reinforcements, corrections, modeling, input frequencies, and the three-term contingency. *Journal of Psycholinguistic Research, 12*, 129–155.

Neely, J. H. (1991). Semantic priming effects in visual word recognition: A selective review of current findings and theories. In D. Besner & G. W. Humphreys (Eds.,), *Basic processes in reading: Visual word recognition* (pp. 264–336). Hillsdale, NJ: Erlbaum.

Nearey, T. M. (1980). On the physical interpretation of vowel quality: Cinefluorographic and acoustic evidence. *Journal of Phonetics, 8*, 213–241.

Novak, G., & Pelaez, M. (2004). *Child and adolescent development: A behavioral systems approach.* Thousand Oaks, CA: Sage.

Østvik, L., Eikeseth, S., & Klintwall, L. (2012). Effects of modeling and explicit reinforcement in the establishment of verbal behavior in preschool aged children. *The Analysis of Verbal Behavior, 28*, 73–82.

Palmer, D. C. (1986). Chomsky's nativism: A critical review. In P. N. Chase & L. J. Parrott (Eds.), *Psychological aspects of language* (pp. 44–60). Springfield, IL: Thomas.

Palmer, D. C. (1991). A behavioral interpretation of memory. In L. J. Hayes & P. N. Chase (Eds.), *Dialogues on verbal behavior* (pp. 261–279). Reno, NV: Context Press.

Palmer, D. C. (1996). Achieving parity: The role of automatic reinforcement. *Journal of the Experimental Analysis of Behavior, 65*, 289–290.

Palmer, D. C. (1998). The speaker as listener: The interpretation of structural regularities in verbal behavior. *The Analysis of Verbal Behavior, 15*, 3–16.

Palmer, D. C. (2000). Chomsky's nativism reconsidered. *The Analysis of Verbal Behavior, 17*, 51–56.

Palmer, D. C. (2005). Ernst Moerk and the puzzle of zero-trial learning. *The Analysis of Verbal Behavior, 21*, 9–12.

Palmer, D. C. (2006). On Chomsky's appraisal of Skinner's *Verbal Behavior*: A half-century of misrepresentation. *The Behavior Analyst, 29*, 253–267.

Palmer, D. C. (2007). Verbal behavior: What is the function of structure? *European Journal of Behavior Analysis, 8*, 161–175.

Palmer, D. C. (2008). On Skinner's definition of verbal behavior. *International Journal of Psychology and Psychological Therapy, 8*, 295–307.

Palmer, D. C. (2009). Response strength and the concept of the repertoire. *European Journal of Behavior Analysis, 10*, 49–60.

Palmer, D. C. (2012). The role of atomic repertoires in complex behavior. *The Behavior Analyst, 35*, 59–73.

Panlilio, L. V., Weiss, S. J., & Schindler, C. W. (2000). Stimulus compounding enhances conditioned suppression produced by cocaine-paired stimuli. *Experimental and Clinical Psychopharmacology, 8*, 6–13.

Pavlov, I. P. (1927). *Conditioned reflexes: An investigation into the physiological activity of the cerebral cortex.* Oxford: Oxford University Press.

Pinker, S. (1989). *Learnability and cognition.* Cambridge, MA: MIT Press.

Pinker, S. (1994). *The language instinct.* New York: William Morrow & Co.

Randell, T., & Remington, B. (2006). Equivalence relations, contextual control, and naming. *Journal of the Experimental Analysis of Behavior, 86*, 337–354.

Schlinger, H. D. (1995). *A behavior analytic view of child development.* New York: Plenum Press.

Schlinger, H. D. (2008a). Conditioning the behavior of the listener. *The International Journal of Psychology and Psychological Therapy, 8*, 309–322.

Schlinger, H. D. (2008b). Listening is behaving verbally. *The Behavior Analyst*, *31*, 145–161.

Schlinger, H., & Blakely, E. (1987). Function-altering effects of contingency-specifying stimuli. *The Behavior Analyst*, *10*, 41–46.

Schoneberger, T. (2010). Three myths from the language acquisition literature. *The Analysis of Verbal Behavior*, *26*, 107–131.

Sherrington, C. S. (1906). *The integrative action of the nervous system*. New Haven, CT: Yale University Press.

Sidman, M. (1994). *Equivalence relations and behavior: A research story*, Boston: Authors Cooperative.

Sidman, M. (2000). Equivalence relations and the reinforcement contingency. *Journal of the Experimental Analysis of Behavior*, *74*, 127–146.

Silvestri, S. M., Davies-Lackey, A. J., Twyman, J. S., & Palmer, D. C. (2000). *The role of automatic reinforcement in the acquisition of an autoclitic frame*. Unpublished manuscript.

Skinner, B. F. (1953). *Science and human behavior*. New York: Macmillan.

Skinner, B. F. (1957). *Verbal behavior*. New York: Appleton-Century-Crofts.

Skinner, B. F. (1963). Operant behavior. *American Psychologist*, *18*, 503–515.

Skinner, B. F. (1969). *Contingencies of reinforcement: A theoretical analysis*. New York: Appleton-Century-Crofts.

Sundberg, M. L. (2008). *VB-MAPP: Verbal behavior milestones assessment and placement program*. Concord, CA: AVB Press.

Tomasello, M. (2003). *Constructing a language: A usage-based theory of language acquisition*. Cambridge, MA: Harvard University Press.

Tomasello, M. (2008). *Origins of human communication*. Cambridge, MA: MIT Press.

Van den Bussche, E., Noortgate van den, W., & Reynvoet, B. (2009). Mechanisms of masked priming: A meta-analysis. *Psychological Bulletin*, *135*, 452–477.

Van Houten, R. K., O'Leary, D., & Weiss, S. J. (1970). Summation of conditioned suppression. *Journal of the Experimental Analysis of Behavior*, *13*, 75–81.

Watkins, K. E., Strafella, A. P., & Paus, T. (2003). Seeing and hearing speech excites the motor system involved in speech production. *Neuropsychologia*, *41*, 989–994.

Weiss, S. J. (1964). Summation of response strengths instrumentally conditioned to stimuli in different sensory modalities. *Journal of Experimental Psychology*, *68*, 151–155.

Weiss, S. J. (1967). Free-operant compounding of variable-interval and low-rate discriminative stimuli. *Journal of the Experimental Analysis of Behavior*, *10*, 535–540.

Weiss, S. J. (1977). Free-operant compounding of low-rate stimuli. *Bulletin of the Psychonomic Society*, *10*, 115–117.

Wilson, S. M., Saygin, A. P., Sereno, M. I., & Iacoboni, M. (2004). Listening to speech activates motor areas involved in speech production. *Nature Neuroscience*, *7*, 701–702.

Wolf, M. M. (1963). Some effects of combined S^D*s*. *Journal of the Experimental Analysis of Behavior*,*6*, 343–347.

Wright, A. N. (2006). The role of modeling and automatic reinforcement in the construction of the passive voice. *The Analysis of Verbal Behavior*, *22*, 153–169.

Žinkin, N. I. (1968). *Mechanisms of speech*. The Hague: Mouton.

16

Animal Cognition

William A. Roberts

Historically, the modern interest in animal cognition arose with Charles Darwin's publication of his theory of evolution by natural selection (1872). In particular, his theory implied that humans had evolved from nonhuman ancestral species. Similarities between *Homo sapiens* and other primates seen in the structure of organ systems, physiological processes, and behavior were offered as evidence of continuity. Darwin (1871) was also concerned that there should be continuity of intelligence between humans and animals. Thus, he and his colleague, George J. Romanes (1882), collected and reported on numerous examples of animal behavior that seemed to reflect human-like intelligence in animals. This approach became known as the anecdotal method, and from our current point of view was seriously flawed. The veracity of reports was not checked, and alternative explanations were not explored.

An important counterweight to the anthropomorphic speculations contained in the anecdotal approach was proposed by C. Lloyd Morgan. In what has become known as *Morgan's Canon*, he proposed that "In no case may we interpret an action as the outcome of the exercise of a higher psychical faculty, if it can be interpreted as the outcome of the exercise of one which stands lower in the psychological scale" (Morgan, 1906, p. 53). Although Morgan was concerned with the application of an actual scale of psychological processes to animals (Burghardt, 1985), his canon has largely been used as the application of the law of parsimony. That is, simpler explanations of animal behavior should always be considered before considering cognitive processes.

For Morgan (1906), a lower psychical faculty that explained much of learned animal behavior was the association of ideas or representations of environmental stimuli. In North America, an even more direct form of association was proposed between stimuli or sensory neural impulses and responses or efferent neural impulses leading to action. Learning theorists such as Edward Thorndike (1911), John B.

The Wiley Blackwell Handbook of Operant and Classical Conditioning, First Edition.
Edited by Frances K. McSweeney and Eric S. Murphy.

Watson (1913), Clark Hull (1943), and Kenneth Spence (1956) formulated theories that varied in detail but had in common the idea that S-R learning was the basis of animal behavior. Only Edward Tolman (1932) proposed that animals could also learn by associating sensory events with one another (S-S theory), giving rise to numerous debates between the S-R and S-S camps.

The early 20th century psychology then was firmly planted in behaviorism, both as an empirical approach to measurement of learning and as a theoretical approach to what was learned. Skinner (1950) carried this approach a step further by eschewing internal associative processes and holding that the study of learning should be based only on the modification of behavior through the differential application of reinforcers. Needless to say, concerns about animal cognition were largely disregarded within this behaviorist framework.

It was only in the late 1960s and 1970s that a concerted interest in animal cognition began to reappear. It was undoubtedly spurred by the cognitive revolution in the study of human psychology. Early studies of animal cognition were particularly aimed at studies of memory in animals, both short-term memory (W. A. Roberts, 1972) and long-term memory (Spear, 1971, 1973). Studies of other cognitive processes followed, including language in animals, pattern learning, conceptual processes, spatial mapping, timing, and counting. Several early volumes of articles reported on these new investigations (Honig & James, 1971; Hulse, Fowler, & Honig, 1978; Medin, W. A. Roberts, & Davis, 1976). What should be kept in mind is that this renewed interest in animal cognition bore little resemblance to the earlier anecdotal approach. Most of the researchers interested in animal cognition came from the behaviorist learning tradition and brought all of the tools for studying operant and classically conditioned behavior to bear on their new studies. They were particularly concerned with controls for artifacts and alternate accounts of possible cognitive accounts of performance.

In the past 40 years, the field of animal cognition has been sustained and has grown considerably. All of the major journals concerned with animal behavior now contain numerous articles on animal cognition, and one journal, *Animal Cognition*, is totally devoted to the topic. The Comparative Cognition Society meets yearly, with its attendance and number of presentations having grown steadily over the 20 years since its inception. The society also publishes its own online journal, *Comparative Cognition and Behavior Reviews.*

In this chapter, I will not attempt a thorough review of the field of animal cognition, as space will not allow and there are available textbooks (Shettleworth, 2010) and recent handbooks (Vonk & Shackelford, 2012; Zentall & Wasserman, 2012) that cover the large variety of topics now studied by different investigators. Only selected topics then will be covered. Three areas of research will be covered in which cognitive processes in animals are widely accepted and considered non-contentious. These concern processing of basic dimensions of the world shared by humans and animals. These dimensions are time, space, and number. A number of studies have examined how animals keep track of time, how they navigate through spatial environments, and how they estimate the number of times an event or stimulus occurs. An interesting product of this work is that it has promoted research on these processes with humans and has led to interesting theoretical suggestions about similarities and differences in the ways humans and animals may encode time, space, and number.

Timing

Interval Timing

People frequently keep track of intervals of time. A person might put an egg on to boil and plan to return to take it out of the pot 5 minutes later. Another example would be parking your car at a meter, putting in enough money for 1 hour, and then returning when you believe an hour has elapsed. Even without using a watch, people can approximate these time intervals fairly accurately. We refer to this ability as *interval timing*, and we can ask if animals are capable of accurate interval timing.

One procedure for studying timing in animals is to study discrimination between two time durations. Suppose that a rat in an operant chamber is presented with tones that last for either 2 seconds or 8 seconds in a randomly changing sequence. Each tone presentation is defined as a trial because the rat is tested each time for its ability to detect the duration of the tone. After each tone has been played over a speaker, two levers are extended into the chamber. A press on one lever (say left) is correct after the 2-second tone and leads to delivery of a reward, usually the delivery of a food pellet in a tray situated between the levers. A press on the other lever (right), however, leads to no reward. After presentation of an 8-second tone, on the other hand, a press on the right lever yields a reward pellet, and a press on the left lever yields nothing. At the end of a trial, the levers are retracted and an interval lasting a few seconds follows (the intertrial interval); a new tone then is presented for the next trial.

Discrimination between short and long time intervals has been demonstrated repeatedly in rats and pigeons. As might be expected, the speed of learning is directly related to the amount of time separating the short and long intervals. However, a more important factor is the ratio between the short and long intervals. In general, the speed of learning is the same for constant ratios. Thus, it would take an equal number of trials to learn to discriminate between short and long intervals of 2 and 8 seconds, 4 and 16 seconds, and 16 and 64 seconds. Thus, temporal discrimination obeys Weber's law or the rule that equal ratios between stimulus strength or duration yield equal degrees of discrimination.

A further question of interest is where the subjective midpoint between two temporal intervals lies. In a discrimination between durations of 2 and 8 seconds, for example, how much time must elapse for the subject to judge that the time elapsed and the time left are equal or that it is equidistant from these durations? A psychophysical procedure is used to answer this question. After a rat has learned to discriminate between 2- and 8-second durations with a high degree of accuracy, probe trials are introduced on which probe durations of intermediate length are presented, as well as the training durations. Thus, durations of 2, 3, 4, 5, 6, 7, and 8 seconds are presented, and a press on either lever is reinforced. After a number of tests at each duration has been recorded, the average probability of choosing the lever correct after 8 seconds (choice of the long lever) is calculated over several subjects and plotted as a function of probe-trial duration. A curve plotting such a function is shown in Figure 16.1. It can be described as a psychophysical curve that is relatively flat over short and long durations but changes rapidly through the middle durations. The point at which the short and long levers are chosen equally often (50% choice of long

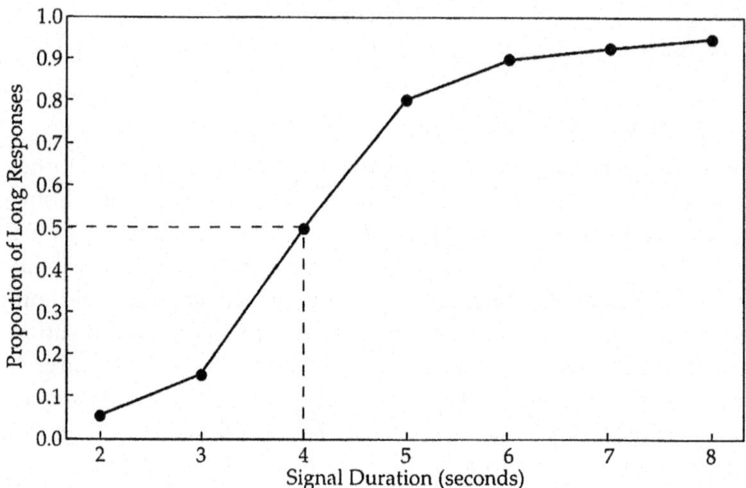

Figure 16.1 Psychophysical curve showing proportion of long signal lever presses at test signal durations of 2–8 seconds after training to discriminate between durations of 2 and 8 seconds.

lever) is the subjective midpoint and is found to be 4 seconds in the 2 versus 8 seconds discrimination. Notice that this value is not the arithmetic mean between 2 and 8 seconds, which is $(2 + 8)/2 = 5$ seconds. Rather, 4 seconds is the geometric mean of the short and long durations or the square root of $(2 * 8)$. Similarly, the judged midpoint between 4 and 16 seconds is 8 seconds, and the judged midpoint between 8 and 32 seconds is 16 seconds. Another way to view this finding is to note that the judged midpoint is at the same ratio to the short duration as the long duration is to the midpoint. This observation further suggests the importance of equal ratios in time discrimination.

A simple procedure for measuring interval timing in people is to ask a person to time a fixed interval from the onset of a signal. Thus, when a light cue comes on, a subject may be asked to indicate "time" when he/she judges that 60 seconds have gone by. An average of several such judgments would be an estimate of the real time that corresponds to the subject's subjective feeling of 60 seconds. Although animals cannot give us a verbal report of elapsed time, we can use their behavior to estimate their time judgments. Fixed-interval schedules of reinforcement have long been studied in the operant laboratory. A rat trained on a fixed-interval 30 seconds schedule would receive a food pellet for the first lever press made 30 seconds after the last reinforcer delivery. The pattern of responding that develops on such a fixed-interval schedule is low responding during the first half of the interval followed by acceleration of responding to a high level just before 30 seconds and delivery of the reinforcer. This pattern of responding suggested that the rat might be timing the fixed interval, thus saving its most vigorous responding for the end of the interval when the probability of reinforcement was high.

Clear evidence that animals time a fixed interval was found with the introduction of the *peak procedure* (Catania, 1970; S. Roberts, 1981). Suppose a rat has been

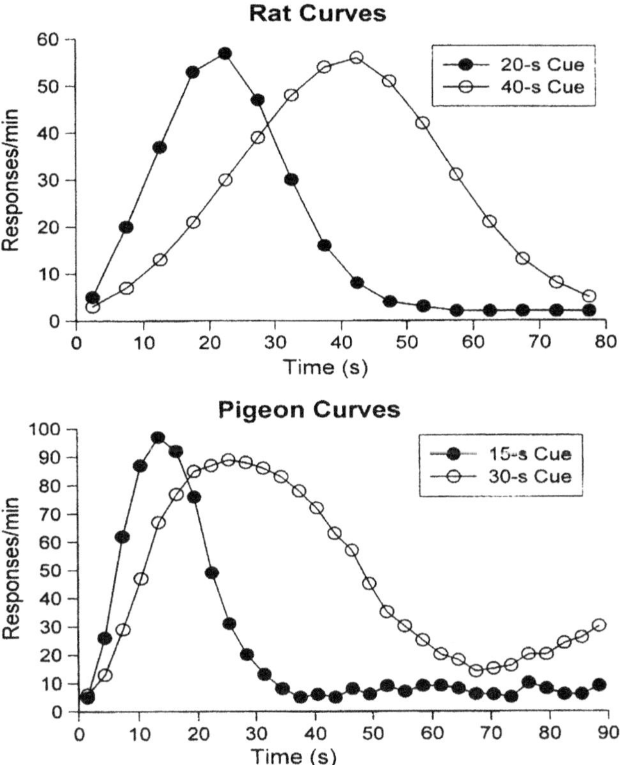

Figure 16.2 Peak-time curves from experiments with rats and pigeons. After training with light and sound cues that signaled fixed intervals of different length, peak-time curves were obtained on empty (non-reinforced) probe trials. From "Are animals stuck in time?," by W. A. Roberts (2002), *Psychological Bulletin, 128,* 473–489. Copyright 2002 by the American Psychological Association. Reprinted with permission.

trained to press a lever for reinforcement on a fixed-interval 30-second schedule that is signaled by the onset of a light cue. When the light cue comes on, the first lever press after 30 seconds yields a food reinforcer. After the rat is well trained on the fixed-interval schedule, so called *empty* probe trials are introduced. On these occasional probe trials, the light signal remains on for a period of 90 seconds, and no reinforcer is delivered for lever pressing. Rate of responding during successive time bins over the 90 seconds is recorded, and average response rate is then plotted for a number of probe trials. Curves obtained by this procedure for rats and pigeons are shown in Figure 16.2. Each curve contains two limbs. The left limb rises as the usual fixed-interval response curve, and the right limb shows a symmetrical decline in responding. Various analyses used to calculate the peaks of such curves show that they are very near the fixed intervals used on training trials.

It was suggested that discrimination between durations obeyed Weber's law because equal discrimination difficulty was found when the long interval held a constant ratio to the short interval. The operation of Weber's law may also be seen in the curves shown in Figure 16.2. If the fixed interval to be timed is increased from

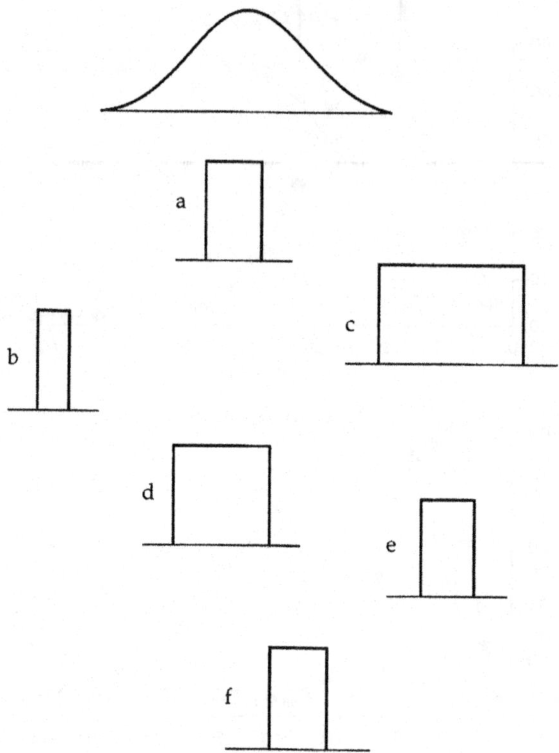

Figure 16.3 The a–e curves show rectangular break-run-break functions from different trials in which an animal started to respond early and stopped late (broad curves) or started late and stopped early (narrow curves). The Gaussian curve is a product of averaging the rectangular curves. From *Principles of animal cognition* (p. 263), by W. A. Roberts (1998), Boston, McGraw-Hill. Reprinted with permission.

20 seconds to 40 seconds (rat curves) or from 15 seconds to 30 seconds (pigeon curves), Weber's law suggests that the temporal distance at which proximity to the fixed interval can be detected should be increased. In agreement with this prediction, the peak-time curves shown in Figure 16.2 increase in width as the target fixed interval used in training increases. This property of peak-time curves is referred to as the *scalar property*.

The peak-time curves shown in Figure 16.2 approximate Gaussian or normal bell-shaped curves and suggest that rats and pigeons show a smooth gradual acceleration in responding to the peak and a smooth gradual deceleration of responding after the peak. In fact, this is not the case. When responding on single empty probe trials is examined, we find quite a different story. Animals show what are called break-run-break functions, curves that are rectangular rather than Gaussian. At the beginning of a probe trial, an animal does not respond at all. At some point before the fixed interval, it begins to respond at a high rate and continues to respond at this rate until it reaches a time longer than the fixed interval. At this point, it stops responding entirely. The curves a-e shown in Figure 16.3 are rectangles that vary in width and represent break-run-break curves obtained on different probe trials. The smooth Gaussian curves seen in Figure 16.2 are produced by averaging a number of these rectangular curves. A good measure of the peak of responding can be obtained by averaging the midpoints of these component rectangular curves. The scalar property of peak-time curves then arises from the fact that the width of the rectangular curves increases with longer training fixed intervals.

How do animals keep track of time intervals? Although a number of theories have been proposed, the most frequently examined theory has been *scalar timing theory* (Gibbon, 1977, 1991; Church, Meck, & Gibbon, 1994). This model of timing holds that time is represented by an accumulator that records the number of pulses emitted by an internal pacemaker during an interval to be timed. Thus, when the onset of an external signal indicates the beginning of a fixed interval, a switch closes allowing pulses to flow from the pacemaker to the accumulator. When the end of the fixed interval is indicated by the delivery of a reinforcer, the switch opens, leaving a fixed number of pulses trapped in the accumulator. This number of pulses is then stored in a reference memory as a representation of the fixed interval on that trial. Over repeated trials, a distribution of these representations is stored in memory. When empty probe trials are eventually presented, the model suggests that the number of pulses accumulating during a trial is monitored in working memory and continually compared with a representation of the fixed interval drawn from reference memory. The absolute difference between the reference memory representation and the accumulation in working memory indicates how close the elapsing interval is to the fixed interval. When the ratio between the absolute difference and the reference memory criterion drops below a threshold, responding is triggered. The animal continues to respond until this ratio exceeds the threshold, which happens when elapsing time has exceeded the fixed interval. In this way, a break-run-break response curve is generated that brackets the fixed interval. The scalar timing model accurately predicts that peak times calculated from the average midpoints of break-run-break functions closely approximate reinforced fixed intervals. This model also accurately predicts that the width of break-run-break functions and peak-time curves will obey Weber's law by increasing in proportion to the length of the fixed interval to be timed.

Detecting Time of Day

Experiments were carried out with birds, garden warblers, by Biebach, Gordijn, and Krebs (1989). Several birds were trained in an apparatus that consisted of a central chamber and four feeding rooms placed around it. Food then was made available in different rooms at different times of day. From 0600 to 0900, food was available in Room 1; a bird could fly to Room 1, open a feeder, and eat for 20 seconds. It then had to return to the central chamber for 280 seconds before it could visit the feeding room again. At the end of the availability of food in Room 1, food was available in Room 2 from 0900 to 1200, in Room 3 from 1200 to 1500, and in Room 4 from 1500 to 1800. Importantly, a bird could go to any of the four rooms at any time but could gain food from each room only during its designated period of food accessibility. Warblers learned to visit each room predominantly during the time of day when it yielded access to food. To control for the possibility that the birds just sampled rooms until they found the one that provided reward, test days were run in

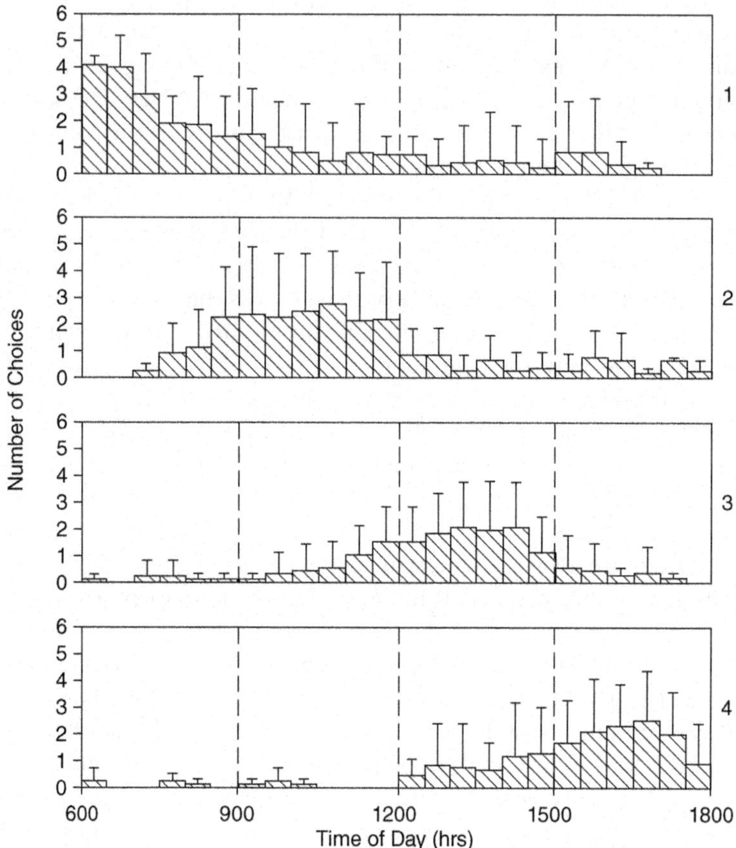

Figure 16.4 Frequency of choices by garden warblers of different rooms where reward could be obtained at different times of day. Rooms 1–4 delivered reward over successive 3-hour blocks from 6:00 to 18:00 hours. From "Are animals stuck in time?," by W. A. Roberts (2002), *Psychological Bulletin*, *128*, 473–489. Copyright 2002 by the American Psychological Association. Reprinted with permission.

which all four rooms contained food throughout the day. It can be seen in Figure 16.4 that warblers continued to make most of their choices of each room at the appropriate time of day. Another interesting aspect of these data is that birds showed anticipation and perseverance errors in timing. Notice on Figure 16.4 that birds began to pay visits to Rooms 2, 3, and 4 an hour or more before they provided food reward and persisted in visiting Rooms 1, 2, and 3 after they ceased to provide reward. As was the case in interval timing, animals approximate the correct time of day and show error responding both before and after the correct time window.

How do animals know what time of day it is? They, as well as humans, seem to rely on internal oscillators or circadian cues that wax and wane over time. A number of internal processes, such as temperature, rate of neural firing, and hormone concentration, rise and fall throughout daily cycles. These cycles adapt gradually to periods of light onset and offset. How might they control differential operant responding at different times of day? At least two mechanisms have been suggested (W. A. Roberts, 2002). One possibility is that the state of internal circadian oscillators at the moment a response is made and reinforced may form part of a stored memory of that event. When these oscillators are in a similar state on a subsequent day, they may act as retrieval cues for memory of the correct response and reward. As an alternative account, circadian cues might act as an occasion setter (Holland, 1992). Occasion setters in Pavlovian conditioning are background cues that do not directly elicit a response but set the occasion for a conditioned stimulus to be paired with an unconditioned stimulus. Thus, a unique daily internal state may signal the occasion for an operant response to a particular stimulus or place to be rewarded. The retrieval cue and occasion setting accounts seem highly similar, in that both rely on memory for previously formed hierarchical associations.

Numerical Estimation

Although the learned system we use for counting and numerical operations is exact, what many may not know is that an *approximate number system* (ANS; Merritt, DeWind, & Brannon, 2012) underlies our *precise number system*. People often estimate the number of objects seen in a set when they do not wish to take the time to count them. In experiments, a subject may be presented with a set of items and told not to count them with number symbols, either overtly or covertly (Cantlon & Brannon, 2006; Whalen, Gallistel, & Gelman, 1999). The items to be estimated may be presented sequentially, one at a time, or simultaneously on a screen. If the number is small, five or fewer, people can usually provide the exact number. This process is called *subitizing*. As the number of items becomes larger, however, reported totals are less accurate. They are not random, however; an average of such estimates may be close to the actual total, but show a Gaussian-like distribution of estimates around the mean. Thus, the ANS has properties similar to the internal timing system discussed in the preceding section.

Of interest here is that adult humans share the ANS with preverbal children and with animals. A good example of this point is found in the data from an experiment by Mechner (1958). A rat placed in an operant chamber with two levers, A and B, was given a series of trials on which a fixed number of presses was required on lever A in order to earn a reinforcer. On test trials randomly intermixed with the training trials, the rat had to complete at least the fixed number of presses on lever A and then press on lever B for its reward. If it exceeded the fixed number of presses on lever A by too many presses, it performed unnecessary work and delayed delivery of the reward. If it made fewer than the fixed number of presses on lever A before pressing on lever B, the trial terminated, and the rat had to start again on lever A. Rats were tested in different blocks of sessions with the fixed number set at 4, 8, 12, and 16.

Figure 16.5 shows the proportion of responses at each fixed number criterion that were made at the fixed number and at numbers surrounding it on test trials. Testing at each fixed number generated Gaussian-like curves with peaks that exceeded the fixed number by a few responses. This seems understandable, as the penalty for too few responses to lever A was higher than the penalty for too many responses. Clearly

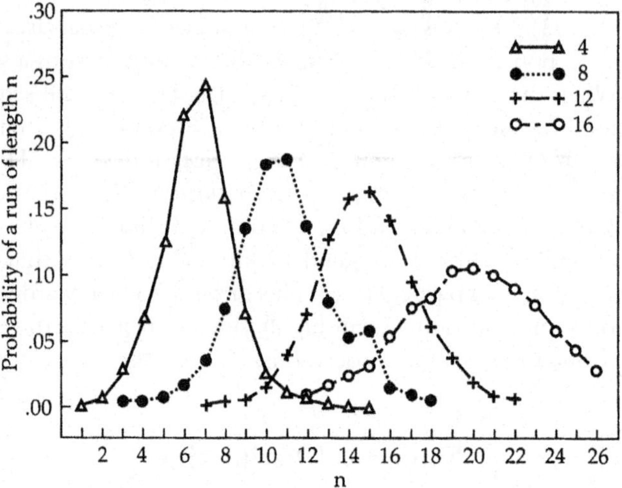

Figure 16.5 Relative probability of making *n* responses on Lever A before pressing Lever B. The curves show the distribution of frequencies when the criterion number of responses required on Lever A was at least 4, 8, 12, or 16 responses. From *Principles of animal cognition* (p. 316), by W. A. Roberts (1998), Boston, McGraw-Hill. Reprinted with permission.

the peaks of these curves increase as the fixed number requirement increases. Rats appeared to estimate the fixed number, with decreasing error in judgment as distance from the peak judgment increased. Notice that these curves also show the scalar property seen in timing. That is, the widths of the curves increased as the fixed number increased, indicating that error in judgment increased at higher numbers.

Numerical discrimination has been extensively studied in both nonhuman primates and birds. Brannon and Terrace (1998) presented two rhesus monkeys with four displays on a touchscreen monitor. The different displays contained 1, 2, 3, and 4 patterns, and the patterns shown varied in shape, color, size, and their arrangement. This constant variation in the visual characteristics of the patterns guaranteed that discrimination between them could be based only on the more abstract property of number. A reward was delivered when the monkey pressed the displays in numerical order from 1 to 4 patterns. Although their performance was initially low, they learned to respond in the correct order on about 50% of the trials, far above the chance level of 4%. The monkeys then were transferred to tests with pairs of displays that contained familiar 1–4 patterns and displays that contained novel 5–9 patterns. Although all possible pairs of the numbers 1–9 were shown, a reward was delivered only for pressing pairs containing the familiar quantities 1–4 (FF) in the correct order. Although the monkeys were not rewarded for responding on interspersed trials containing familiar and novel patterns (FN), they responded correctly by pressing the lower number display before the higher number display on over 90% of the tests. On nonrewarded novel-novel (NN) pair trials, their accuracy dropped to around 75%. Figure 16.6 shows the percent correct as a function of the numerical distance between patterns within a pair. Thus, a distance of one would be based on pairs that contained 1 and 2, 2 and 3, 3 and 4, etc., and a distance of four would be based on pairs that

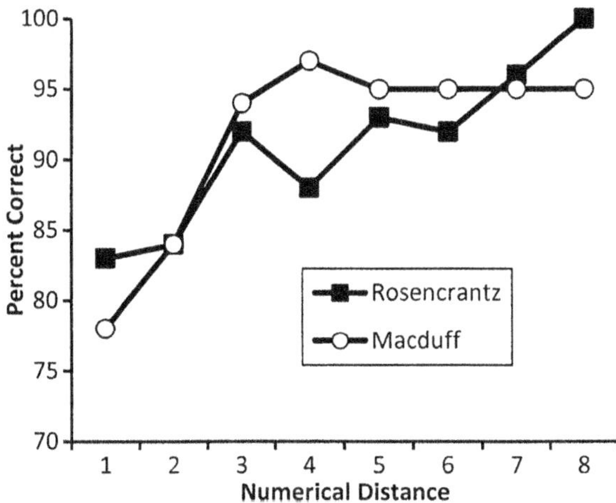

Figure 16.6 The percentage of correct trials (press smaller number display before larger number display) plotted over increasing numerical difference between displays for two rhesus monkeys. From "Ordering of the numerosities 1 to 9 by monkeys," by E. M. Brannon and H. S. Terrace (1998), *Science, 282*, 746–749. Reprinted with permission from AAAS.

contained 1 and 5, 2 and 6, 3 and 7, etc. The curves show an important property of numerical discrimination, *the distance effect*. That is, discrimination between numbers improves as the distance between them increases.

The distance effect does not explain why Brannon and Terrace's monkeys performed less accurately on NN pairs than on FF pairs, because the distances should have been comparable between displays on these tests. Although the difference might be attributed to the novelty of the NN pairs, another property of numerical discrimination can explain this finding. This is the *magnitude effect* and is essentially the operation of Weber's law. As the magnitude of the numbers to be discriminated increases, comparisons within displays of equal distance become more difficult. Thus, it is easier to discriminate between 1 and 2 than between 8 and 9. As in timing, the ratios between items to be discriminated are critical. As the ratio of the lower number to the higher number in a discrimination increases, discrimination accuracy decreases. Thus the ratio of 1/2 =.50 is lower than the ratio of 8/9 = .89. Because the NN pairs tested by Brannon and Terrace involved the numbers 5–9 and the FF pairs involved the numbers 1–4, the ratios among NN pairs would necessarily be higher than those among FF pairs of equivalent distance. The magnitude effect then may have been primarily responsible for the higher accuracy of numerical ordering seen with FF pairs than with NN pairs.

The ANS also may be used to estimate numbers of sequentially presented items. Chimpanzees were shown 1–10 food items (bananas or marshmallows) dropped into opaque containers by an experimenter (Beran, 2001, 2004; Beran & Beran, 2004). The time intervals between food placements varied so that total time duration of food deliveries could not be used as a reliable cue for choice of the larger amount. All possible pairs were tested on different trials, with more food placed in one container than the other. When given a choice between containers, chimpanzees chose the container with more food items accurately. Further, their accuracy was not related to the order in which the containers were baited; the container with the most food was chosen equally often when it was baited first and last. In addition, these experiments showed clear evidence of distance and magnitude effects, with choice of the correct container increasing as the difference in number of food items increased and decreasing as the small/large ratio increased.

Notice that distance and magnitude effects should not occur when we use precise verbal counting. That is, if we assign number symbols to items as we count them, we can order 8 and 9 as accurately as 5 and 9 or as 1 and 2. Weber's law effects are the hallmark of ANS numerical discrimination in both humans and animals. Libertus and Brannon (2009, 2010) presented 6-month-old infants with changing displays simultaneously on two screens. One display presented patterns with the same number of items on each presentation. The other screen presented displays that varied in number. Children showed increasing visual preference for the screen that changed in number as the ratio of the numbers went from 1:2 to 1:3 to 1:4. However, they showed no preference for the screen that changed in number when the ratio was 2:3. As in animal studies, preverbal children show the magnitude effect and appear to use the ANS to judge number quantities.

Current theory suggests that the precise number system emerges from the ANS as children develop language (Gelman & Butterworth, 2005; Gelman & Gallistel, 2004). As language develops in children, they learn to map ordinal number symbols onto successively viewed items and gradually become capable of precise counting. It appears that the ANS is phylogenetically old and that precise counting appears only ontogenetically in humans with the development of language. What kind of system could allow animals and preverbal children to estimate numbers of objects or events? One theoretical account suggests that the ANS arises from analog magnitude representation. That is, each item experienced adds to an increasing magnitude in the nervous system that represents a number estimate. A good example of such a mechanism is the scalar timing accumulator model discussed in the preceding section. Meck and Church (1983) suggested that this system can operate in two modes, a run mode for timing and an event mode for counting. In the event mode, the switch that closes to allow pulses to enter the accumulator stays closed only briefly each time an event occurs, allowing an approximately equal number of pulses to be recorded in the accumulator. The total pulses accumulated may then serve as a representation of the number of events experienced.

Spatial Cognition

In addition to tracking the time and the frequency with which events occur, virtually all species of animals show spatial competence. It is critical for an animal's survival that it know the locations of its home, water, foods, mates, and potential predators. Most animals also travel across spatial environments and thus must keep track of their own travels. For example, many foragers pursue a win-shift strategy, meaning that they do not return to patches or locations where they have exhausted the food supply.

In order to remember where previously visited patches are located, the animal must use *spatial memory.*

Two general areas of interest will be reviewed here. One area is the memory properties of spatial memory: How large is spatial memory? Are spatial memories forgotten? What factors affect retention versus forgetting in spatial memory? The other area is the nature of memory encoding. What features of their environment do animals store in memory that allow them to accurately navigate through space?

Spatial Memory on the Radial Maze

Mazes have been used to study operant learning in rodents since the beginning of the study of animal learning. These mazes often involved a long series of right and left turns that eventually led to a goal box containing food reward. Each choice point contained an incorrect turn that led to a blind alley. Rats proved to be particularly good at learning such mazes. Their skill on mazes may be traced to their evolutionary habitat of underground tunnels interconnected with one another. Thus, rats were genetically prepared to be particularly good maze learners (W. A. Roberts, 1992).

The *radial maze* was introduced by Olton and Samuelson (1976) and has become a particularly popular piece of equipment for the study of spatial memory in rats and other species. An eight-arm radial maze is shown in Figure 16.7. It consists of a central platform with eight arms that radiate out from it at equal angles. The maze is typically open and elevated, so that a rat has to run along arms that are some distance above the floor and return to the center of the maze between each visit. A small cup is placed at the end of each arm, with a small amount of food in it. Hungry rats are allowed initially to explore the arms of the maze and then to run down the arms to obtain food from the cups at the ends of the arms. After only a few trials of

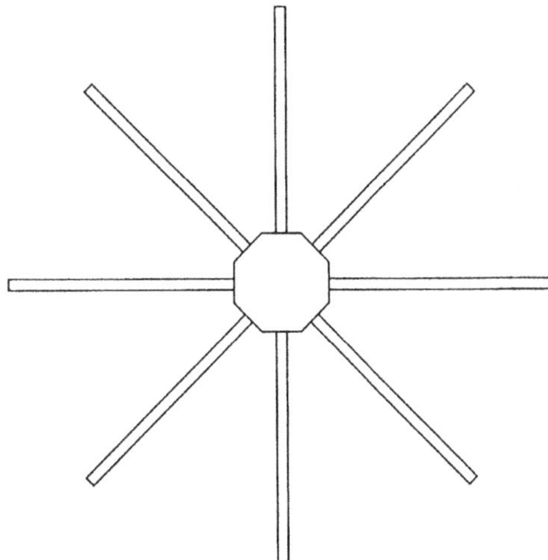

Figure 16.7 A top view of an 8-arm radial maze.

learning, rats tend to visit all of the arms on the maze with few re-visits to arms previously entered. If the number of correct (novel) arms visited in the first eight choices is counted as a measure of performance, rats make 7.5–8.0 correct choices. By chance alone, only 5.25 novel arm choices should be made over eight choices.

Olton and Samuelson suggested that rats were showing spatial memory by keeping track of the locations (arms) where they had exhausted the available food. One challenge to this conclusion was raised by the possibility that rats were using odor cues. Perhaps they left a slight scent on each arm entered and could detect that scent and avoid it on future choices. Various controls ruled out this possibility. Olton and Samuelson allowed a rat to enter half the arms on the maze. The rat was taken off the maze briefly, the entered and un-entered arms were interchanged with one another, and the rat was put back on the maze to complete its trial. If odor cues were the basis for rats' performance on the radial maze, when put back on the maze, the rat should visit spatial locations in the testing room where it had previously traveled because these arms would have no odor on them. Instead, rats visited novel locations where they had not gone previously on that trial, even though they entered arms on which they might have left an odor. As a further control for the possibility that rats could smell food in the cups at the end of the arms, Zoladek and W. A. Roberts (1978) showed that rats were highly accurate on the radial maze even when made temporarily anosmic.

One other possibility other than spatial memory was that rats were executing an algorithmic search process. For example, if a rat went around the maze in a clockwise or counter-clockwise manner, it could collect all the food items without repeating a visit to any arm. As a control for this possibility, rats were forced to visit four randomly chosen arms on the maze by closing doors to the other arms. The experimenter, and not the rat, then chose which arms the rat would enter initially. When rats were put back on the maze with all arms open and food placed only on the un-visited arms, rats selectively visited the arms they had not previously entered. All of these findings led to the conclusion that rats were indeed using spatial memory on the radial maze.

Spatial Memory Capacity

On an expanded 17-arm radial maze, Olton, Collison, and Werz (1977) found that rats could still choose un-visited arms correctly above chance accuracy. W. A. Roberts (1979) tested rats on a hierarchical maze that contained eight primary arms, as shown in Figure 16.7. Three branching secondary arms were attached to the end of each primary arm. The maze then contained a total of 24 arms. Within 10–20 trials on the maze, rats entered all of the primary and secondary arms with little repetition of arm visits. Finally, Cole and Chappell-Stephenson (2003) tested rats on a radial maze, with the number of arms gradually increased from 8 to 48 arms. Rats were able to choose correctly above chance up to 40 arms, but not with 48 arms. When 48 arms were placed on the maze, the arms were necessarily quite close to one another. The authors concluded that rats' spatial memory capacity may not be limited by a central storage capacity, but more likely by an inability to discriminate nearby locations in space.

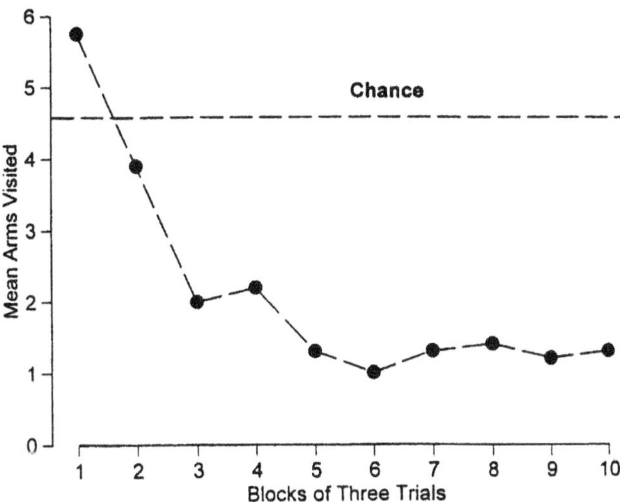

Figure 16.8 Curve shows the mean number of arms visited by rats to enter the arm containing reward over successive blocks of three trials. Rats quickly learned to enter the beacon (white) rewarded arm. Adapted from "Spatial localization of a goal: Beacon homing and landmark piloting by rats on a radial maze," by L. A. Hogarth, W. A. Roberts, S. Roberts, and B. Abroms (2000), *Animal Learning & Behavior, 28*, 43–58. Copyright 2000 by the Psychonomic Society, Inc. Reprinted with permission.

Retention of Spatial Memory

Olton (1978) described spatial memory performance on the radial maze by rats as *working memory,* equivalent to short-term memory found in humans. This seemed reasonable initially because rats had to remember locations just recently visited in order to avoid those locations. In subsequent experiments, Beatty and Shavalia (1980) forced rats to enter four randomly chosen arms and then returned them to the maze to choose among all eight arms several hours later. Over a 4-hour retention interval, rats showed no forgetting, selecting the correct un-entered arms at over 90% accuracy. After 24 hours, rats showed forgetting but still chose the correct arms significantly above chance accuracy. Clearly, spatial memory on the radial maze is not limited to short retention intervals of a few seconds or minutes.

Subsequent research with food-storing birds also showed excellent long-term memory. Black-capped chickadees, for example, cache a variety of foods in the wild and use spatial memory to retrieve their stored caches at a later point in time. In controlled experiments, chickadees cached food items in trees placed in an aviary and then were allowed to forage for them after different retention intervals. Hitchcock and Sherry (1990) found that chickadees accurately visited cache sites significantly more often than non-cache sites after a retention interval as long as 28 days.

How Are Locations in Space Encoded?

Research on spatial navigation in animals suggests that a variety of mechanisms are used to locate and travel to specific places. A given species may use several mechanisms that are organized hierarchically. Thus, a preferred mechanism will be used if possible, but if it cannot be used, alternative processes for spatial navigation come into play. Mechanisms that are based on internally generated cues are referred to as *egocentric*, and mechanism that utilize cues perceived outside the organism are referred to as *allocentric*. Path integration will be discussed as an egocentric mechanism, and beacon homing, the geometric module, and landmark piloting will be discussed as allocentric mechanisms.

Path Integration

Path integration, also called dead reckoning, is the ability to maintain an accurate heading and distance to a starting point while traveling a winding route away from that point. Thus, ants and other insects have been observed to leave their nest and search over distant territory by taking tortuous paths. Once a morsel of food is found, however, the ant moves in a very direct line toward its nest. After traveling a distance that approximates the distance to the nest, the ant will execute a systematic search in which it makes wider and wider loops until it finds the nest (Cheng, 2012). As more and more turns are made on its outward bound trip, error in calculating and maintaining an accurate heading and distance to the home nest accumulates. Nevertheless, path integration is quite accurate. The ratio between the distance traveled on homeward bound trips and the straight line distance between the start and end of the trip was only 1.06 (Wehner & Wehner, 1990).

Path integration arises from the use of internal cues supplied by the semicircular canals and by motor cues from kinesthetic receptors and efference copies. The vestibular sense in particular may provide information about direction by sensing degree of angular rotation. Distance can be sensed by proprioceptive feedback from locomotion. Detection of speed of movement and trip time may allow a calculation of distance traveled. In addition to return trips to a starting point, path integration may be used in a number of other spatial navigation tasks. For example, rats tested on a radial maze without vision or in darkness still show a high level of accuracy in choosing arms not previously visited (Brown & Moore, 1997; Zoladek & W. A. Roberts, 1978). When rats with vestibular lesions (labyrinthectomies) were tested, however, repeat visits to the same arms increased markedly compared to controls (Ossenkopp & Hargreaves, 1993).

Beacon Homing

In the natural world, an animal's home or the location of food or water may be near a distinctive landmark or beacon, such as a tree or large rock. As an example of beacon homing in the laboratory, Hogarth, W. A. Roberts, S. Roberts, and Abroms (2000) trained rats on an eight-arm radial maze with all of the arms painted black. Only one arm on the maze contained food on each trial, and this arm changed randomly between trials. A beacon was placed on the rewarded arm by placing a white metal cover over it. Performance on the maze is shown in Figure 16.8. The mean number of arms visited on a trial to enter the rewarded arm is plotted against blocks of three daily trials. By chance alone, the rewarded arm should be found in 4.5 arm entries. The number of arms visited on the first block of three days was somewhat above

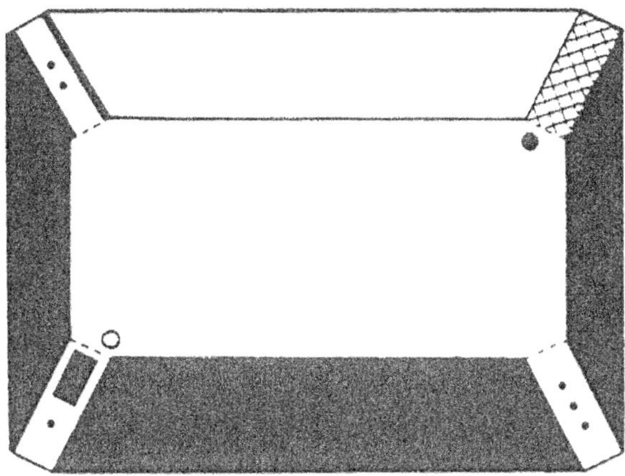

Figure 16.9 Rectangular arena used to study the geometric module in rats. Diagonally opposite corners are geometrically identical but have panels that provide different visual and olfactory cues. From "Spatial representation and the use of spatial codes in animals," by W. A. Roberts. In *Spatial schemas and abstract thought* (p. 29), by M. Gattis (Ed.) (2001), Cambridge, MA, MIT Press. Reprinted with permission.

chance. Thereafter, the curve drops, showing that by the fifth block and thereafter, rats were entering the rewarded arm in little over one choice. In other words, rats learned quickly to use the white arm as a beacon showing the way to reward.

The Geometric Module

Beacons may not always be available to indicate a vital location, and, in some cases, a beacon may not be the preferred cue. The geometric frame within which an organism finds itself may also provide important cues to location. For example, the walls of your office or your home may provide salient cues as to the location of objects in the room or home. In a classic study, Cheng (1986) trained rats to dig for a piece of food buried within bedding located in a dimly illuminated rectangular box. As shown in Figure 16.9, one long wall and two adjacent shorter walls were black, but the other long wall was white. Panels that differed in visual pattern and that contained different odors were placed in each corner. Food was buried at the location shown by the filled circle. Rats could then use a variety of visual and odor cues to locate the food. They could use the visual appearance of the panel in that corner or its odor as beacon cues. In addition, they could learn that food was buried in the corner with a white wall on the left and a black wall on the right. The results were surprising. Although rats learned to dig in the correct corner for food, they frequently made errors by searching in the diagonal corner (open circle). The frequency of these errors led Cheng to conclude that rats were using a geometric module, or finding food on the basis of the geometric structure of the box. Notice that what the two corners have in common is a long wall on the left and a short wall on the right. It appeared that this geometric structure was the primary cue used by rats.

Cheng's discovery has generated considerable research on both animals and people (Cheng & Newcombe, 2005; Kelly & Spetch, 2012). A prominent issue has been whether geometric information will always overshadow visual feature cues. Associative learning theories suggest that cues compete for attention or associative strength, and thus if one cue is dominant, the other must be weaker (Rescorla & Wagner, 1972; Miller & Shettleworth, 2007). However, some evidence suggests that both featural and geometric information may be encoded, although one type of information may be predominant. As an example, Kelly, Spetch, and Heth (1998) trained pigeons to find food in one corner of a rectangular arena. Visual cues placed in each corner were objects that varied in shape and color. After pigeons learned to always go to the correct corner for reward, the pigeons were tested with the cues rotated clockwise (affine transformation). The pigeons went to the new corner containing the positive feature on 76% of the test trials. On yet another test, all of the distinctive visual cues were removed. Now pigeons chose the rewarded corner on 44% of the trials and its diagonally opposite corner on 44% of the trials. Both corners were geometrically correct because they had a long wall on the left and a short wall on the right. Thus, without visual cues present, the correct geometric choice was made on 88% of the trials. Although visual cues dominated when present, tests without visual cues showed that pigeons had also encoded geometric information.

Piloting with Landmarks

In many cases, an animal may find itself flying over or locomoting through open space in search of a target location. A geometric frame is not available, and no landmark is near the target to serve as a homing beacon. Yet, the animal is able to pilot toward the target location using landmarks that may be present some distance from the target. How is this accomplished? One possibility is that the animal computes the distance and direction of a goal from a single landmark, using some background cue, such as a mountain range, as an orienting cue. The other possibility is that the animal computes the location of the goal relationally, such as midway between two landmarks.

Interesting experiments suggest that pigeons and humans use landmarks differently. In experiments carried out both with touchscreens (Spetch, Cheng, & MacDonald, 1996) and in arenas that required subjects to travel over a field (Spetch, Cheng, MacDonald, Linkenhoker, Kelly, & Doerkson, 1997), pigeons and people were trained with four landmarks arranged as the corners of a square. Responses to the center of the square (equal distance from all four landmarks) yielded reward. After learning to accurately respond to the center of the array, tests were given in which the landmarks were expanded horizontally, vertically, or diagonally. The findings are shown in Figure 16.10. Human subjects continued to respond to the center of the expanded landmarks, showing relational encoding of target location. Pigeons, on the other hand, responded to locations that were equal to the training distance from one of the landmarks. The landmark chosen varied among pigeons, but the pattern of results suggested that pigeons had encoded the goal as a specific direction and distance from a single landmark.

A variety of allocentric cues then seem to be available to animals for spatial travel that allow them to navigate successfully from one location to another. Which of these

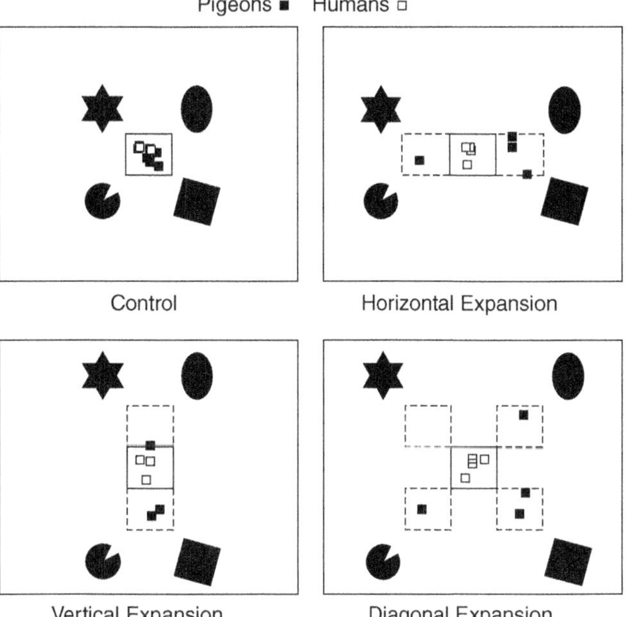

Figure 16.10 Small squares show areas of most concentrated searching for reward by pigeons and humans when the training (control) landmark array is expanded horizontally, vertically, or diagonally. Humans search in the middle, but pigeons search at a fixed distance and direction from one landmark. From "Spatial representation and the use of spatial codes in animals," by W. A. Roberts. In *Spatial Schemas and Abstract Thought* (p. 18), by M. Gattis (Ed.) (2001), Cambridge, MA, MIT Press. Reprinted with permission.

cues may be used appears to be determined by the situation faced by the animal. These cues may be encoded in a hierarchical fashion. Beacon homing or geometric encoding may be favored if these cues are available, but landmark piloting can be used if necessary. Although coding the absolute distance and direction from a single landmark takes priority if it will suffice, coding the relative distance from more than one landmark may be used if necessary.

Conclusions

The findings reviewed in this chapter suggest considerable continuity across species in ability to process dimensions experienced in common by virtually all animals. Thus, most animals tested, as well as humans, are able to keep track of intervals of time, to accurately approximate the frequency of a number of stimuli, and to encode and remember locations in space. Many of the mechanisms used to process time, number, and space may be common to different species of animals, as well as humans. A particularly good example is evidence for the ANS in pigeons, monkeys, preverbal children, and adults instructed not to use verbal counting. It is also clear that animals and humans use similar mechanisms to track positions in space, including path integration, beacon homing, the geometric module, and landmark piloting.

Although animals and humans share these basic abilities to process information about time, number, and space, humans appear to have made qualitative advances in the sophisticated use of these processes. Through the development of language and symbolic thought, humans map number symbols onto quantities, giving rise to precise counting without the scalar error found with use of the ANS. Because timekeeping involves counting units of time, our development of time technology (clocks and calendars) allows us to time far more precisely than is done with time estimation procedures such as the peak procedure. Finally, humans appear to encode locations in space in relation to several landmarks more readily than some animals. Although pigeons locate a goal as a fixed direction and distance from one landmark in an array, people encode the location as being in the middle of the array. The development of language may have led to the development of a concept of "middleness."

Acknowledgment

Support for preparation of this chapter was provided by a Discovery Grant from the Natural Sciences and Engineering Research Council of Canada.

References

Beatty, W. W., & Shavalia, D. A. (1980). Spatial memory in rats: Time course of working memory and effect of anesthetics. *Behavioral and Neural Biology*, *28*, 454–462.

Beran, M. J. (2001). Summation and numerousness judgments of sequentially presented sets of items by chimpanzees (*Pan troglodytes*). *Journal of Comparative Psychology*, *115*, 181–191.

Beran, M. J. (2004). Chimpanzees (*Pan troglodytes*) respond to nonvisible sets after one-by-one addition and removal of items. *Journal of Comparative Psychology*, *118*, 25–36.

Beran, M. J., & Beran, M. M. (2004). Chimpanzees remember the results of one-by-one addition of food items to sets over extended time periods. *Psychological Science*, *15*, 94–99.

Biebach, H., Gordijn, M., & Krebs, J. R. (1989). Time-and-place learning by garden warblers, *Sylvia borin*. *Animal Behaviour*, *37*, 353–360.

Brannon, E. M., & Terrace, H. S. (1998). Ordering of the numerosities 1 to 9 by monkeys. *Science*, *282*, 746–749.

Brown, M. F., & Moore, J. A. (1997). In the dark II: Spatial choice when access to extrinsic spatial cues is eliminated. *Animal Learning & Behavior*, *25*, 335–346.

Burghardt, G. M. (1985). Animal awareness: Current perceptions and historical perspective. *American Psychologist*, *40*, 905–919.

Cantlon, J. F., & Brannon, E. M. (2006). Shared system for ordering small and large numbers in monkeys and humans. *Psychological Science*, *17*, 402–407.

Catania, A. C. (1970). Reinforcement schedules and psychophysical judgments: A study of some temporal properties of behavior. In W. N. Schoenfeld (Ed.), *The theory of reinforcement schedules* (pp. 1–42). New York: Appleton-Century-Crofts.

Cheng, K. (1986). A purely geometric module in the rat's spatial representation. *Cognition*, *23*, 149–178.

Cheng, K. (2012). Arthropod navigation: Ants, bees, crabs, spiders finding their way. In T. R. Zentall & E. A. Wasserman (Eds.), *The Oxford handbook of comparative Cognition* (pp. 347–365). Oxford, UK: Oxford University Press.

Cheng, K., & Newcombe, N. S. (2005). Is there a geometric module for spatial orientation? Squaring theory and evidence. *Psychonomic Bulletin & Review*, *12*, 1–23.

Church, R. M., Meck, W. H., & Gibbon, J. (1994). Application of scalar timing theory to Individual trials. *Journal of Experimental Psychology: Animal Behavior Processes*, *20*, 135–155.

Cole, M. R., & Chappell-Stephenson, R. (2003). Exploring the limits of spatial memory in rats, using very large mazes. *Learning & Behavior*, *31*, 349–368.

Darwin, C. (1871). *The descent of man and selection in relation to sex*. London: John Murray.

Darwin, C. (1872, 6th edition). *Origin of species by means of natural selection or the perseveration of favoured races in the struggle for life*. London: John Murray (originally published in 1859).

Gelman, R., & Butterworth, B. (2005). Number and language: How are they related? *Trends in Cognitive Sciences*, *9*, 6–10.

Gelman, R., & Gallistel, C. R. (2004). Language and the origin of numerical concepts. *Science*, *306*, 441–443.

Gibbon, J. (1977). Scalar expectancy theory and Weber's law in animal timing. *Psychological Review*, *84*, 279–325.

Gibbon, J. (1991). Origins of scalar timing. *Learning and Motivation*, *22*, 3–38.

Hitchcock, C. L., & Sherry, D. F. (1990). Long-term memory for cache sites in the black-capped Chickadee. *Animal Behaviour*, *40*, 701–712.

Hogarth, L. A., Roberts, W. A., Roberts, S., & Abroms, B. (2000). Spatial localization of a goal: Beacon homing and landmark piloting by rats on a radial maze. *Animal Learning & Behavior*, *28*, 43–58.

Holland, P. C. (1992). Occasion setting in Pavlovian conditioning. In D. L. Meding (Ed.), *The psychology of learning and motivation* (Vol. 28, pp. 69–125). San Diego: Academic Press.

Honig, W. K., & James, P. H. R. (1971). *Animal memory*. San Diego: Academic Press.

Hull, C. L. (1943). *Principles of behavior: An introduction to behavior theory*. New York: Appleton-Century-Crofts.

Hulse, S. H., Fowler, H., & Honig, W. K. (1978). *Cognitive processes in animal behavior*. Hillsdale, NJ: Erlbaum.

Kelly, D. M., & Spetch, M. L. (2012). Comparative spatial cognition: Encoding of geometric information from surfaces and landmark arrays. In T. R. Zentall & E. A. Wasserman (Eds.), *The Oxford handbook of comparative cognition* (pp. 366–389). Oxford: Oxford University Press.

Kelly, D. M., Spetch, M. L., & Heth, C. D. (1998). Pigeons' (*Columba livia*) encoding of geometric and featural properties of a spatial environment. *Journal of Comparative Psychology*, *112*, 259–269.

Libertus, M. E., & Brannon, E. M. (2009). Behavioral and neural basis of number sense in infancy. *Current Directions in Psychological Science*, *18*, 346–351.

Libertus, M. S., & Brannon, E. M. (2010). Stable individual differences in number Discrimination in infancy. *Developmental Science*, *13*, 900–906.

Mechner, F. (1958). Probability relations within response sequences under ratio reinforcement. *Journal of the Experimental Analysis of Behavior*, *1*, 109–121.

Meck, W. H., & Church, R. M. (1983). A mode control model of counting and timing processes. *Journal of Experimental Psychology: Animal Behavior Processes*, *9*, 320–334.

Medin, D. L., Roberts, W. A., & Davis, R. T. (1976). *Processes of animal memory*. New York: Erlbaum.

Merritt, D. J., DeWind, N. K. & Brannon, E. M. (2012). Comparative cognition of number representation. In T. R. Zentall & E. A. Wasserman (Eds.), *The Oxford handbook of comparative cognition* (pp. 451–476). Oxford: Oxford University Press.

Miller, N. Y., & Shettleworth, S. J. (2007). Learning about environmental geometry: An associative model. *Journal of Experimental Psychology: Animal Behavior Processes, 33*, 191–212.

Morgan, C. L. (1906). *An introduction to comparative psychology.* London: Walter Scott.

Olton, D. S. (1978). Characteristics of spatial memory. In S. H. Hulse, H. Fowler, W. K. Honig (Eds.), *Cognitive processes in animal behavior* (pp. 341–373). Hillsdale, NJ: Erlbaum.

Olton, D. S., Collison, C., & Werz, M. A. (1977). Spatial memory and radial arm maze performance of rats. *Learning and Motivation, 8*, 289–314.

Olton, D. S., & Samuelson, R. J. (1976). Remembrance of places passed: Spatial memory in rats. *Journal of Experimental Psychology: Animal Behavior Processes, 2*, 97–116.

Ossenkopp, K.-P., & Hargreaves, E. L. (1993). Spatial learning in an enclosed eight-arm maze in rats with sodium arsanilate-induced labyrinthectomies. *Behavioral and Neural Biology, 59*, 253–257.

Rescorla, R. A., & Wagner, A. R. (1972). A theory of Pavlovian conditioning: Variations of effectiveness of reinforcement and non-reinforcement. In A. H. Black & W. F. Prokasy (Eds.), *Classical conditioning II: Current research and theory* (pp. 64–99). New York: Appleton-Century-Crofts.

Roberts, S. (1981). Isolation of an internal clock. *Journal of Experimental Psychology: Animal Behavior Processes, 7*, 242–268.

Roberts, W. A. (1972). Short-term memory in the pigeon: Effects of repetition and spacing. *Journal of Experimental Psychology, 94*, 74–83.

Roberts, W. A. (1979). Spatial memory in the rat on a hierarchical maze. *Learning and Motivation, 10*, 117–140.

Roberts, W. A. (1992). Foraging by rats on a radial maze: Learning, memory, and decision Rules. In I. Gormezano & E. A. Wasserman (Eds.), *Learning and memory: The behavioral and biological substrates* (pp. 7–23). Hillsdale, NJ: Erlbaum.

Roberts, W. A. (1998). *Principles of animal cognition.* Boston: McGraw-Hill.

Roberts, W. A. (2001). Spatial representation and the use of spatial codes in animals. In M. Gattis (Ed.), *Spatial schemas and abstract thought* (pp. 15–44). Cambridge, MA: MIT Press.

Roberts, W. A. (2002). Are animals stuck in time? *Psychological Bulletin, 128*, 473–489.

Romanes, G. J. (1882). *Animal intelligence.* London: Kegan Paul, Trench, & Co.

Shettleworth, S. (2010). *Cognition, evolution, and behavior.* Oxford: Oxford University Press.

Skinner, B. F. (1950). Are theories of learning necessary? *Psychological Review, 57*, 193–216.

Spear, N. E. (1971). Forgetting as retrieval failure. In W. K. Honig & P. H. R. James (Eds.), *Animal memory* (pp. 45–109). San Diego: Academic Press.

Spear, N. E. (1973). Retrieval of memory in animals. *Psychological Review, 80*, 163–194.

Spence, K. W. (1956). *Behavior theory and conditioning.* New Haven, CT: Yale University Press.

Spetch, M. L., Cheng, K., & MacDonald, S. E. (1996). Learning the configuration of a landmark array: I. Touchscreen studies with pigeons and humans. *Journal of Comparative Psychology, 110*, 55–68.

Spetch, M. L., Cheng, K., MacDonald, S. E., Linkenhoker, B. A., Kelly, D. M., & Doerkson, S. R. (1997). Use of landmark configuration in pigeons and humans: II. Generality across search tasks. *Journal of Comparative Psychology, 111*, 14–24.

Thorndike, E. L. (1911). *Animal intelligence: Experimental studies.* New York: Macmillan.

Tolman, E. C. (1932). *Purposive behavior in animals and men.* New York: Appleton-Century-Crofts.

Vonk, J., & Shackelford, T. K. (2012). *The Oxford handbook of comparative evolutionary psychology.* Oxford: Oxford University Press.

Watson, J. B. (1913). Psychology as the behaviorist views it. *Psychological Review, 20,* 158–177.

Wehner, R., & Wehner, S. (1990). Insect navigation: Use of maps or Ariadne's thread? *Ethology, Ecology, and Evolution, 2,* 27–48.

Whalen, J., Gallistel, C. R., & Gelman, R. (1999). Nonverbal counting in humans: The psychophysics of number representation. *Psychological Science, 10,* 130–137.

Zentall, T. R., & Wasserman, E. A. (2012). *The Oxford handbook of comparative cognition.* Oxford: Oxford University Press.

Zoladek, L., & Roberts, W. A. (1978). The sensory basis of spatial memory in the rat. *Animal Learning & Behavior, 6,* 77–81.

17

Instrumental and Classical Conditioning

Intersections, Interactions and Stimulus Control[1]

Stanley J. Weiss

In classical conditioning, a conditioned stimulus (CS) that reliably predicts the occurrence of an unconditioned stimulus (US) comes to elicit a conditioned response (CR) (Pavlov, 1927). For example, seeing (or even imagining) a fresh lemon being sliced (CS) causes a person to salivate (CR) because this sight has preceded sour juice (US) being taken into the mouth. In operant (also known as instrumental) conditioning, behaviors that produce a reinforcer (e.g., an attractive event such as food, approval or a safety signal) are strengthened while behaviors that produce an aversive situation (e.g., a repelling event such as shock, rejection or a time-out from reinforcement) are weakened (cf. Thorndike, 1898). Ferster and Skinner (1957) pioneered the systematic study of operant reinforcement contingencies—the specific relationships between behavior and its consequences that powerfully shape the patterns in which operant behavior occurs.

Given that behavior is affected by both classical and operant conditioning, it is natural to ask how these processes interact with each other. Two-process learning theory (e.g., Mowrer 1947, 1960 presented below) was an early attempt to answer this question. Experiments designed to test two-process theory primarily used the transfer-of-control paradigm in which operant and classical processes are established *independently* and then tested in combination by presenting the CS while the subject is working for the reinforcer. As will be discussed below, the transfer-of-control approach to the investigation of classical-operant interactions encountered certain problems primarily related to potential competition between the operant and CS-elicited behaviors.

The present chapter, derived from Fulbright Lectures the author delivered at Pavlov Medical University in St. Petersburg, Russia (*Operant and classical conditioning: A point of natural intersection*), argues that in non-laboratory environments most classical conditioning is actually due to associations that are embedded in

The Wiley Blackwell Handbook of Operant and Classical Conditioning, First Edition.
Edited by Frances K. McSweeney and Eric S. Murphy.

operant-conditioning situations that involve discrimination learning. In nature, environmental cues usually signal when a behavior will produce certain consequences and when it will not. For example, a speaker is likely to get an answer only when he/she has a listener's attention. This relationship is represented schematically by the three-term contingency: $S^D \bullet R \rightarrow S^r$. It symbolizes that a behavior (R), e.g., asking a question, emitted in the presence of a discriminative stimulus (S^D), e.g., an attentive-prepared listener, will produce a reinforcer (S^r), here, an answer—while R will not produce the S^r when the S^D is absent. This differential reinforcement creates operant *stimulus control* through which an S^D comes to occasion the behavior. The differential association of the S^D with reinforcement, a *by-product* of this *emergent* stimulus control, inherently produces a Pavlovian association, and this association can produce incentive-motivational effects that energize behavior. From this, it follows that a manipulation that decreases the incentive value of the outcome should also reduce the operant that produces it (e.g., Dickinson & Balleine, 1994).

Since it is natural for classical conditioning to be produced by reinforcement-related differences between stimuli in operant discriminative-learning situations, it is logical (and perhaps most valid) to study classical-operant interactions that are established *contemporaneously* in operant-discrimination experiments. This chapter will show that: (1) an S^D acquires both discriminative-response and incentive-motivational properties, (2) this can create situations where comparable-appearing behaviors are not under the same stimulus control, and (3) specialized behavioral assays (e.g., stimulus compounding, stimulus-generalization, stimulus-element tests) are required to reveal the underlying combination of these two processes.

A stimulus-control model based on the proposition that both processes operate during the typical three-term contingency is developed and empirically supported. The model is tested and confirmed in both positive and aversive situations in which all classical conditioning is a by-product of the three-term operant contingency. This model: (1) accounts for results reported in more than 50 stimulus-compounding experiments; (2) reconciles different stimulus-compounding test outcomes by behaviorally indistinguishable groups, and (3) can be successfully applied to seemingly unrelated phenomena such as stimulus-generalization peak shift and selective associations.

The stimulus-control model presented here also has many empirically supported practical implications and applications. These include environmentally-energized "drug seeking" and "loss of control" that produces self-injurious behavior in drug self-administration and shock-avoidance situations. This learning-based model also suggests ways to control these injurious behaviors and presents viable, credible treatment strategies. The rest of this chapter will develop and examine this model in more detail.

Two-Process Learning Theory

Explaining the maintenance of avoidance behavior challenged early learning theory because the aversive event was not presented when the organism was successful. Mowrer's (1947) answer to "How is avoidance behavior maintained?" was facilitated by his observation that classical contingencies were "embedded" in the discriminated-operant avoidance paradigm.

Mowrer postulated two-process learning theory because, in such situations

> conditioning of the visceral-vascular, or "diffuse," responses takes place first and that the accompanying emotional state provides the motivation, or problem, which produces the subsequently observed skeletal, or "precise, adaptive," reactions. (p. 127)

Therefore, the temporal dynamics create stimuli that: (1) become motivational mediators (e.g., elicitors of "fear") that are conditioned through the embedded warning-stimulus-shock classical contingency, and (2) become discriminative for operant behavior because a response is negatively reinforced by terminating the stimulus eliciting the negative emotional state of "fear" (Mowrer, 1960; Mowrer & Lamoreaux, 1942).

Trapold and Overmier (1972) represented this "embeddedness" schematically with S-R-S^r notation. This three-term contingency includes within it the operant (R-S^r) and classical (S-S^r) contingencies plus the resulting environmental operant control (S-R). But (as discussed later) the transfer-of-control design, as used to study two-process learning theory (e.g., Rescorla & Solomon, 1967), investigates the "mediation" of instrumental behavior by a classically-conditioned incentive-motivational state that is conditioned *independently* of the operant response and the discriminative stimuli that control it.

The present chapter argues that two-factor theory is better studied in discriminative-operant situations. In these situations, a discriminative stimulus (S^D) acquires two contingency-related properties that must be considered when predicting the stimulus' effect on behavior. The S^D's discriminative-response property is represented by the S-R unit of the three-term contingency and is produced by the response-reinforcer contingency in effect during the S^D. For simplicity, and illustrative purposes, this discriminative property will be described as controlling an increase (↑) in responding, a decrease (↓) in responding, or no change (=) in responding. In contrast, the classically-conditioned incentive properties are produced by the differential probability of a reinforcer during the components of multi-component operant schedules. They are represented by the S-S^r unit of the three-term contingency. However, it should be appreciated that in addition to

> [relative] reinforcement probability, factors such as schedule requirements, delay of reinforcement, reinforcement magnitude, effort, [plus] reinforcement predictability or periodicity can influence reinforcement value [and resulting incentive motivation associated with an S^D] in the instrumental situation. Determining the [relative] reinforcement value acquired by a schedule component requires a . . . [behavioral] . . . measure reflecting the organisms' integration of all these influences. Component preference could serve this function . . . (Weiss, 1978, p 363).

Brown (1961) and Logan and Wagner (1965) proposed that a subject's preference between goal objects indicates which has the greater incentive and reinforcement value. This was recently supported by Parkes and Balleine's (2013) elegant investigation of the role of the basolateral amygdala and insular cortex in incentive-related learning, memory and actions. They concluded that their "results provide the basis for elaborating an incentive memory system encoding the incentive value of the instrumental outcome to guide choice between goal-directed actions" (p. 8762).

With positive reinforcement, the preferred condition possesses the greater excitatory-incentive value because one is working to produce an "attractive" event. Negatively-reinforced behavior would be viewed symmetrically. Therein, the non-preferred condition possesses the greater excitatory-incentive value because one is working to remove a "repelling" event.

How incentive motivation energizes avoidance, and creates the opportunity for negative reinforcement was described above. Symmetrically, originally neutral environmental stimuli that are paired with positive reinforcers can create "needs" that energize behavior through appetitive incentive motivation. For example, you may be drawn into a bakery by the aroma of a favored pastry and purchase it even though immediately before sensing the aroma you did not desire it (or any kind of food) at all. Unfortunately, as will be demonstrated later, appetitive incentive motivation elicited by features of the environment that have been associated with tobacco or other drugs can dramatically increase incentive motivation for these substances—often to uncontrollable levels. This process might play a central role in addiction.

The discriminative-response and incentive-motivational properties acquired by an S^D co-vary in most operant situations, making the contribution of each process elusive and difficult to appreciate. Group A in Table 17.1 exemplifies this. On that three-component multiple-schedule, periods of tone, light, and the absence of tone and light ($\overline{T}\overline{L}$) were presented repeatedly during each training session. Lever pressing produced food on a variable-interval (VI) schedule when either the tone-or-light S^D was present. But food was unavailable (extinction) in $\overline{T}\overline{L}$. Here, the tone and light would *each*: (1) become discriminative for the lever pressing (S-R$\uparrow$) that was required for reinforcement, and (2) acquire excitatory-incentive-motivational properties ($S\text{-}S^r\uparrow$) through their association with an increase in the probability of receiving food (from 0% in $\overline{T}\overline{L}$ to nearly 100% when the tone or light was present).

On this, and most other three-component training schedules presented in this chapter, components alternated such that the tone-or-light S^D was equally likely after $\overline{T}\overline{L}$ while these S^Ds were always followed by $\overline{T}\overline{L}$—exemplified by: tone, $\overline{T}\overline{L}$, light, $\overline{T}\overline{L}$, light, $\overline{T}\overline{L}$, tone, $\overline{T}\overline{L}$, light $\overline{T}\overline{L}$, etc. Training continued until response rate in the tone and in the light were reliably at least 10 times the rate in $\overline{T}\overline{L}$. Then, a stimulus-compounding test was administered wherein the tone and light were presented *simultaneously* (T+L) for the *first* time. These tests contained 12–18 block-randomized, one-minute presentations of tone, light and T+L—each separated by one-minute of $\overline{T}\overline{L}$. A representative test block could be sequenced as: tone, $\overline{T}\overline{L}$, T+L, $\overline{T}\overline{L}$, light, $\overline{T}\overline{L}$. All stimulus-compounding tests, unless otherwise indicated, were conducted in extinction to preclude feeder-operation-elicited and reinforcer-related behaviors from influencing results.

After the multiple-schedule training described for Group A in Table 17.1, Weiss (1971, Experiment 2) reported that during the stimulus-compounding test, the T+L compound controlled about three-times the response rate of tone or light alone (Figure 17.1). Unfortunately, looking only at this experiment, the process(es) responsible for this three-fold response increase in responding are indeterminate because the discriminative-response (S-R) and incentive-motivational ($S\text{-}S^r$)

Table 17.1 Training and test conditions of groups that produced the instrumentally-derived incentive motivational function (S-R and S-S^r properties established to tone and to light S^Ds are indicated)*

		TRAINING		COMPOUNDING TEST		
		Tone/Light	$\overline{TL}$	Tone + Light		TL : T/L_{av}
		VI Food	EXT			Results
Group A	S-R	↑	*No Food*	↑	↑	
		$P(S^r \mid \text{tone or light}) > P(S^r \mid \overline{TL})$				**3: 1**
	S-S^r	↑		↑	↑	
		VI Food	*DRO*			
Group B	S-R	↑	*Food*	↑	↑	
		$P(S^r \mid \text{tone or light}) = P(S^r \mid \overline{TL})$				**2: 1**
	S-S^r	=		=	=	
		Chain VI	*DRO*			
Group C	S-R	↑	*Food*	↑	↑	
		$P(S^r \mid \text{tone or light}) < P(S^r \mid \overline{TL})$				**1: 1**
	S-S^r	↓		↓	↓	
	Cumulative Record	/	—			

*Group contingencies in tone, in light and their absence ($\overline{TL}$). (VI = variable interval; EXT = extinction; DRO = differential-reinforcement-of-other-behavior.) Probability equation reflects reinforcement (S^r) change, increase (↑), no-change (=) or decrease (↓), in tone and in light. In all groups these S^Ds occasioned response increase (S-R↑). Right: stimulus-compounding tests with S^D's S-R and S-S^r properties plus compound:single-stimulus-rate ratio. Cumulative records drawn to show that on all training schedules rats responded at moderate-steady rates in each S^D and ceased in $\overline{TL}$.

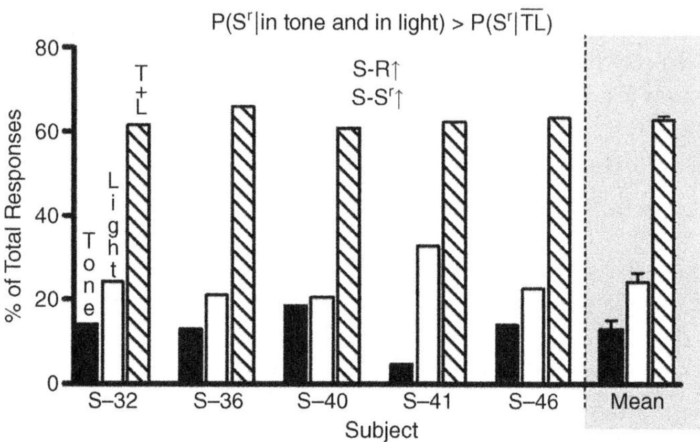

Figure 17.1 Results of Weiss' (1971, Exp. 2) stimulus-compounding test. Multiple-schedule trained rats earned food in tone and in light S^Ds, but not their absence ($\overline{TL}$). Tone-plus-light was presented for the *first* time on this test.

properties established to the compounded S^Ds co-varied. Therefore, the enhanced responding to T+L could be due to the fact that both elements of T+L: (1) signal the presence of food (the incentive-motivational process), (2) occasion a response-rate increase (the discriminative-response process), or (3) some combination of the two. The confounding of these processes in Group A of Table 17.1 is also common in most behavioral situations (Shettleworth & Nevin, 1965), but this confound must be broken to answer the question of how the classically-conditioned and operantly-conditioned properties of the training stimuli interrelate.

The Instrumentally-Derived Appetitive Incentive-Motivational Function

The confounded S-R and S-S^r properties of the S^D described above was broken by devising operant schedules in which: (1) for all three groups the tone-and-light S^Ds *each* occasioned a steady, moderate leverpress response that was ultimately maintained by food, but (2) each group had a different embedded classical-conditioning (S-S^r) contingency related to these S^Ds that made them excitatory, neutral, or inhibitory. These relationships are symbolically described in Table 17.2 (upper panel) and operationalized in Table 17.1. Here, and throughout this chapter, the discriminative-response as well as incentive-motivational properties to tone and to light S^Ds are described *relative* to what is happening in $\overline{T}\overline{L}$.

In Group A, the tone and the light were differentially associated with food (relative to $\overline{T}\overline{L}$) and thereby became excitatory CSs through this S-$S^r\uparrow$ relationship. Therefore, the tone-and-light components would be preferred over $\overline{T}\overline{L}$ (Holz, Azrin, & Ayllon, 1963). In Group C, because all food was received in $\overline{T}\overline{L}$ the tone and the light would be inhibitory, relative to $\overline{T}\overline{L}$, and non-preferred (Duncan & Fantino, 1972). In Group B, food was received in all three components of the training schedule, so tone and light were neutral and would be about equal to $\overline{T}\overline{L}$ in a preference test (Herrnstein, 1964). Such resulting component preferences would indicate that the appetitive incentive-motivational properties conditioned to the tone and the light S^Ds varied systematically across the three groups, from excitatory (S-$S^r\uparrow$) in Group A through neutral (S-S^r=) in Group B to inhibitory (S-$S^r\downarrow$) in Group C.

Briefly, these schedules were arranged as follows. In Group B, leverpressing produced food on a VI schedule when the tone or light were present, as in Group A (described above). But, in $\overline{T}\overline{L}$ food was delivered on a differential-reinforcement-of-other-behavior (DRO) schedule (see Table 17.1) in which food was received as long as leverpressing did *not* occur for a specified amount of time. This essentially eliminated leverpressing in $\overline{T}\overline{L}$. With probability of food in tone, light and $\overline{T}\overline{L}$ comparable, differential incentive-motivational properties should not have been conditioned to tone or light relative to $\overline{T}\overline{L}$.

Group C responded on a chained schedule (Table 17.1) where leverpressing in tone-or-light components cause the schedule to progress, on a VI schedule, to the $\overline{T}\overline{L}$ component, where food was presented for not responding (DRO). After a few minutes, the $\overline{T}\overline{L}$ terminated, with a tone-or-light component equally likely to appear. Here, food probability was zero in tone or light, but close to 100% in $\overline{T}\overline{L}$. Therefore, inhibitory appetitive-incentive-motivational properties (S-$S^r\downarrow$) should have been established to these S^Ds relative to $\overline{T}\overline{L}$.

Table 17.2 Designs eliminating co-variation of the incentive-motivational and response-discriminative properties established to S^Ds*

Experiments Generating Appetitive Incentive-Motivational Function
Properties established to tone and to light S^Ds

* S^D's Discriminative-response property comparable over groups; incentive-motive property systematically varied.

Group	Response-Discriminative	Incentive-Motive
A	↑	↑
B	↑	=
C	↑	↓

Experiments Generating Response-Discriminative Function
Properties established to tone and to light S^Ds

* S^D's incentive-motive property comparable over groups; discriminative-response property systematically varied.

Group	Response-Discriminative	Incentive-Motive
A	↑	↑
B	=	↑
C	↓	↑

Figure 17.2 contains representative cumulative records of subjects from Group C (chain VI DRO) and Group B (multiple VI DRO). With respect to the lever response, these subjects are behaviorally comparable, responding at steady-moderate rates in tone and in light (S-R↑) but not responding in $\overline{T}\overline{L}$. Except for hatch-marks showing that $\underline{S}$-203 received food in tone, light, and $\overline{T}\overline{L}$, while $\underline{S}$-201 received food only in $\overline{T}\overline{L}$, these records are *indistinguishable.* (To ensure that chain- and multiple-schedule-trained rats were comparably exposed to tone, light, and $\overline{T}\overline{L}$ components, respectively, Weiss and Van Ost (1974) "yoked" pairs of rats with respect to these durations.)

Despite these similarities in baseline behavior, the stimulus-compounding tests produced dramatically different results across the two groups. All multiple VI DRO-trained rats (Group B) responded at about twice the rate in T+L as in tone or light (Figure 17.3, left) while no chain VI DRO-trained rat (Group C) responded more in T+L than in tone or light (Figure 17.3, right). This revealed that: (1) the discriminative-response process alone was sufficient to double the rate of responding in T+L over responding in either tone or light alone, (2) this response

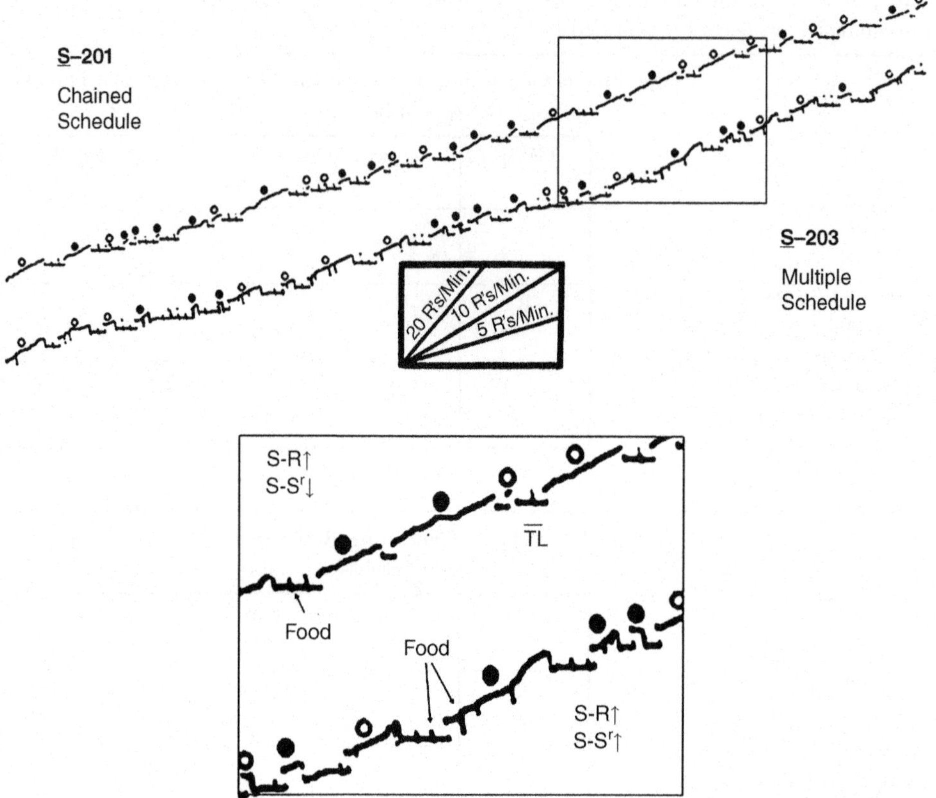

Figure 17.2 Cumulative records of chain-schedule-trained S-201 and multiple-schedule-trained S-203. S-201's leverpressing in tone (filled-circles) and light (open-circles) only produced $\overline{\text{TL}}$ (pen-depressed) wherein it received food (hatch-marks) for not responding—making $\overline{\text{TL}}$ preferred over tone or light. S-203's leverpressing earned food in tone and in light S^Ds, with comparable food in $\overline{\text{TL}}$ for not leverpressing. Adapted from Weiss and Van Ost (1974), Figure 1. Cumulative recorder paper slowly unrolls continuously, creating a time axis, and the pen is incrementally raised by every response. Therefore, the record's slope reflects overall response rate (see legend box) and its "fine=grain" how responses are distributed over time.

enhancement was less than the 3 : 1 increase T+L produced in Group A (Figure 17.1) where discriminative- and incentive-motivational processes were operating in concert (both increasing (S-R↑,S-S^r↑)), and (3) T+L did not enhance responding after chain VI DRO-training (Group C) even though tone and light *each* occasioned responding *indistinguishable* from Groups A and B. This failure of T+L to increase responding can be attributed to the chain-schedule arrangement producing conflicting discriminative-response and incentive-motivational properties (S-R↑,S-S^r↓) to the tone and the light S^Ds.

Figure 17.4 presents the percent of stimulus-compounding test responses to T+L by Groups A, B, and C in Table 17.1. With baseline behavior *indistinguishable* over groups (Figure 17.2), the stimulus-compounding assay was necessary to reveal the incentive-motivational contribution to underlying stimulus control in this *instrumentally-derived appetitive incentive-motivational function.* On these tests,

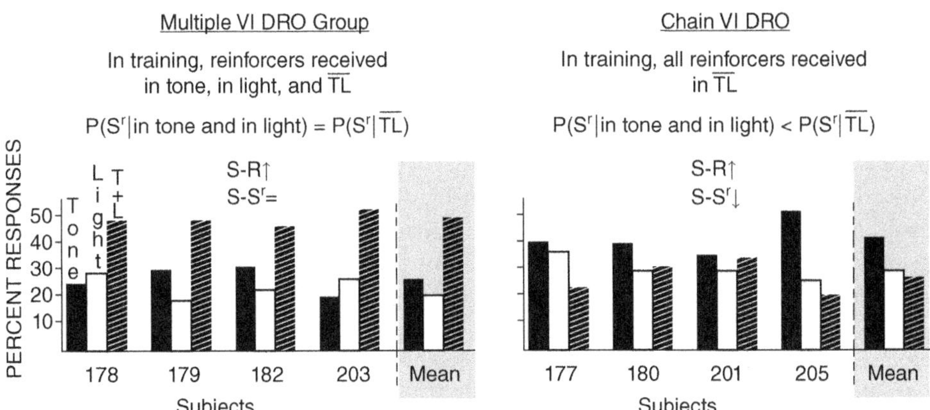

Figure 17.3 Stimulus-compounding tests of behaviorally-comparable groups that lever pressed in tone and in light S^Ds and ceased in $\overline{TL}$. With conflicting (S-R↑,$S\text{-}S^r$↓) properties established to S^Ds (chain-schedule), tone, light and T+L rates were comparable. With only S-R↑ established to tone and to light (multiple-schedule), T+L doubled responding. Adapted from Weiss and Van Ost (1974), Figure 2.

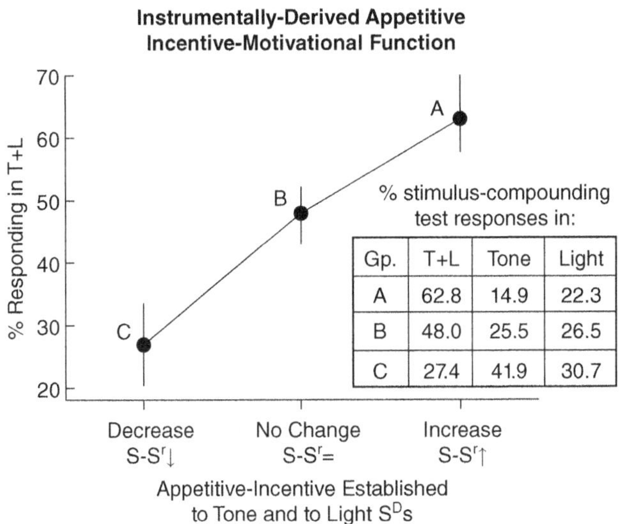

Figure 17.4 Instrumentally-derived appetitive incentive-motivational function. On stimulus-compounding tests, compared to tone or light alone, T+L tripled responding in Group A (S-R↑,$S\text{-}S^r$↑), doubled responding in Group B (S-R↑,$S\text{-}S^r=$) and did not change responding in Group C (S-R↑,$S\text{-}S^r$↓). Group A from Weiss (1969, 1971 Experiment 2). Groups B and C from Weiss (1971 Experiment 2) and Weiss and Van Ost (1974). (ANOVA of T+L% yields $F_{(2,21)} = 114.8$, $p < 0.001$, with Group A > Group B > Group C, $p < 0.001$. This is the first statistical comparison incorporating all three groups. Its validating rationale is described in the text.)

Group A (S-R↑,S-S^r↑) emitted more than 60% of its total responses in T+L, Group B (S-R↑,S-S^r=) about 50% and Group C (S-R↑,S-S^r↓) less than 30%. The absence of overlap between the three groups demonstrates the incentive-motivational processes' potency.

The results for different groups of subjects presented in Figure 17.4 were obtained from different experiments. Comparing results across studies is open to challenge because group differences might be produced by variation in subjects, apparatuses, procedures, etc., over studies, rather than by differences in the hypothesized processes. Nevertheless, the validity of the comparisons reported in Figure 17.4 are supported by the fact that: (1) each group contributing to the function was directly *replicated* in an experiment containing another group, with original-and-replicated groups indistinguishable (note Figure 17.4's narrow, non-overlapping range bars); (2) to control for differences in response rates across subjects, each was equally weighted in this and subsequent functions by converting its output to tone, light, and T+L test stimuli to a percentage of its total-test responses; and (3) all studies were conducted in the same laboratory and used the same operant enclosures, species, S^Ds, reinforcers, temporal parameters, etc.

A straightforward model combining the S^Ds' discriminative-response and incentive-motivational properties can be induced here. For illustration, assign an excitatory function (↑) a value of 1, an inhibitory function (↓) a value of −1, and a neutral function (=) a value of 0, with a simple combination assumption. Applying this model to Table 17.1's "Compounding-Test" section yields "4" for Group A ($1 + 1 + 1 + 1$), "2" for Group B ($1 + 1 + 0 + 0$) and "0" for Group C ($1 + 1 - 1 - 1$). This pattern resembles "% response to T+L," Figure 17.4's ordinate. Later, this model is extended to incorporate comparable baseline behavior in tone and in light S^Ds over groups.

Presenting T+L tripled Group A's responding—whose tone-and-light S^Ds *each* occasioned lever pressing (S-R↑) and were also associated with food increase (S-S^r↑). But, the part played by the appetitive-incentive-motivational process in this enhancement can only be appreciated in comparison to Group B—whose S^Ds occasioned lever pressing (S-R↑) without signaling reinforcement change (S-S^r=). In Group B, T+L only doubled response rate (Figure 17.3, left frame and Figure 17.4). This 2:1 response enhancement implies a simple additive summation when *only* the discriminative-response process (S-R↑,S-S^r=) is activated. That is especially intriguing in the context of the simple additive summation Pavlov reported (cited by Kimble (1961)) in a "pure" classical-conditioning situation. The odor of oil of camphor ordinarily evoked 60 drops of saliva and a mild shock usually produced 30 drops. Compounding these stimuli evoked 90 drops.

The Instrumentally-Derived Aversive Incentive-Motivational Function

The instrumentally-derived appetitive incentive-motivational function enhances our understanding of interactions between operant and classical conditioning. This would be deepened by demonstrating generality of these interactions with aversive-instrumental contingencies. Data relevant to the extreme points in Figure 17.4 are available and briefly described next. The tactics employed with shock-avoidance are conceptually the same as in the food-related experiments described above.

Emurian and Weiss' (1972) rats postponed shock on a free-operant-avoidance (FOA) contingency by lever pressing in tone and in light S^Ds, while $\bar{T}\bar{L}$ was shock-free. Figure 17.5 (upper record) shows that these rats lever pressed during S^Ds (S-R↑) and ceased in $\bar{T}\bar{L}$, indicating that these S^Ds each possessed a discriminative (S-R↑) property comparable to that in the food schedules (Groups A, B, and C, above). Additionally, by being differentially associated with shock, these S^Ds increased avoidance incentive (S-S^r↑) or, more colloquially, produced "fear." As expected, compounding aversive S^Ds with S-R↑,S-S^r↑ properties produced almost 2.5 times the avoidance responses as the highest-rate-single stimulus. Tone + light controlled 58.6% of total-test responses. (Figure 17.6, Point A).

Weiss (1976, Experiment 3, Phase 1) used the same training chambers, stimuli, species etc., as Emurian and Weiss (1972). Additionally, like in Emurian and Weiss' study, rats' lever pressing postponed shock on free-operant avoidance in tone and in light. But now shock-related contingencies were programmed in $\bar{T}\bar{L}$ to make it more aversive than tone or light. In $\bar{T}\bar{L}$, unsignaled-unavoidable shock was delivered intermittently and lever pressing produced immediate shock (punishment).

Effective avoidance (Figure 17.5, S-191) led to shock rates in tone or light (0.22 shocks/minute) being only half those in $\bar{T}\bar{L}$ (0.53 shocks/minute). Therefore, on the basis of relative-shock rate, presentation of tone or light should reduce (S-S^r↓) aversive incentive-motivation ("fear") *relative* to that in $\bar{T}\bar{L}$—even though shocks occurred during all three conditions. In addition, it follows from Badia and Culbertson (1972) that signaled-avoidable shock should be preferred to unsignaled-inescapable shock. That might have further reduced aversive incentive-motivation in tone and in light S^Ds where shock was: (1) "predictable" from time elapsing since S's response (Anger, 1963), and (2) "controllable" since it could be avoided. Contrast that with $\bar{T}\bar{L}$ in which shock was provided both independent of, and dependent on, responding. Therefore, shock predictability, controllability, and lower rate were all contributing to the tone and the light S^Ds reducing "fear."

The S-R↑,S-S^r↓ combination of S^D properties did not enhance responding with appetitive-related-compounded S^Ds (Group C, Figure 17.4). Here again, but in the aversive situation, when discriminative-response and incentive-motivational processes were conflicting, response rates during tone, light, and T+L were comparable. Tone-plus-light controlled only 35.3% of total-test responses (Point B, Figure 17.6). Nevertheless, S-191's cumulative record (Figure 17.5, bottom), shows behavioral control comparable to S-6's for whom T+L increased avoidance-rate 2.5 fold. The instrumentally-derived-aversive incentive-motivational function (Figure 17.6) is remarkably similar to Figure 17.4's based on appetitive control, supporting the incentive-motivational-processes generality. But, again, underlying stimulus control could not be appreciated from baseline-training behavior.

Transfer-of-Control Research: Overview and Discussion

Rescorla and Solomon's (1967) treatise supporting two-process learning theory was largely based on the three-stage transfer-of-control (TOC) paradigm that separates,

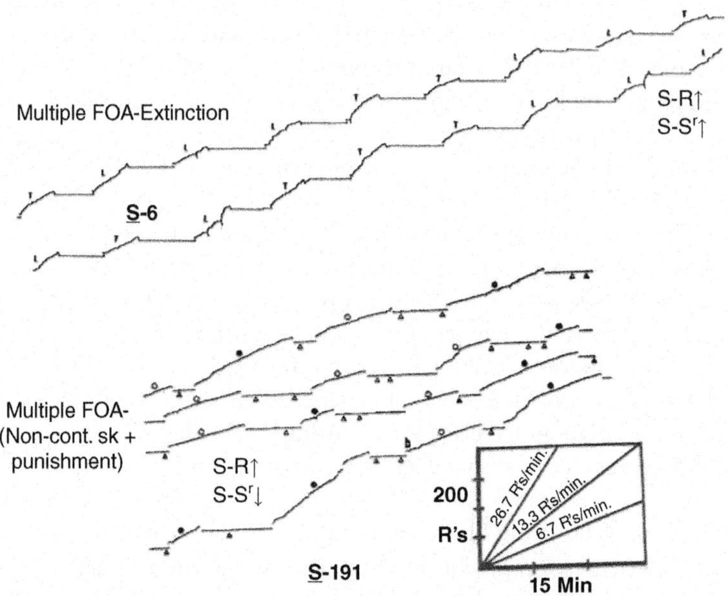

Figure 17.5 Cumulative records show these rats are behaviorally indistinguishable, with S-R↑ established to tone and to light S^Ds. Both lever pressed to postpone shock (hatch-marks) in tone (T-or-filled circles) and light (L-or-open circles) S^Ds. Pressing ceased when S^Ds were absent ($\overline{T}\overline{L}$) (pen depressed). But (see text) these S^Ds *increased* avoidance incentive (S-S^r↑) in S-6 and *decreased* it (S-S^r↓) in S-191. S-6 from Emurian and Weiss, (1972). S-191 from Weiss (1976, Experiment 3).

and then "synthesizes," the two processes Mowrer (1947, 1960) identified within discriminative-operant situations. In Phase 1 of a transfer-of-control experiment, Rescorla and LoLordo's (1965) dogs' hurdle-jumping postponed shock on a continuously-operating free-operant avoidance schedule. In Phase 2, inescapable shock followed CS+ but not CS−. In Phase 3, CS+ doubled jumping and CS− dramatically reduced it. These results were attributed to the excitatory-and-inhibitory motivational properties conditioned to the CSs in Phase 2 mediating avoidance-rate. Weisman and Litner (1969) systematically replicated this result with rats' wheel-turning postponing shock.

Applying transfer-of-control to appetitive situations was challenging and less successful. The problem is that a food-paired CS+ elicits behaviors that can (perhaps inevitably) compete with the operant response that is used as a dependent variable (DV)—unless the operant-and-elicited responses are similar (LoLordo, McMillan, & Riley, 1974). Overmier and Lawry (1979) described how, after CS+-food pairings, the CS could come to elicit both conditioned orienting and approach towards the food-associated stimulus ("sign-tracking") as well as orienting and approach to the food trough ("goal-tracking"). In addition, food-signaling stimuli become discriminative for food retrieval. *All* of these behaviors are *incompatible* with the operant DV in transfer-of-control studies. "Facilitation of instrumental behavior by an appetitive

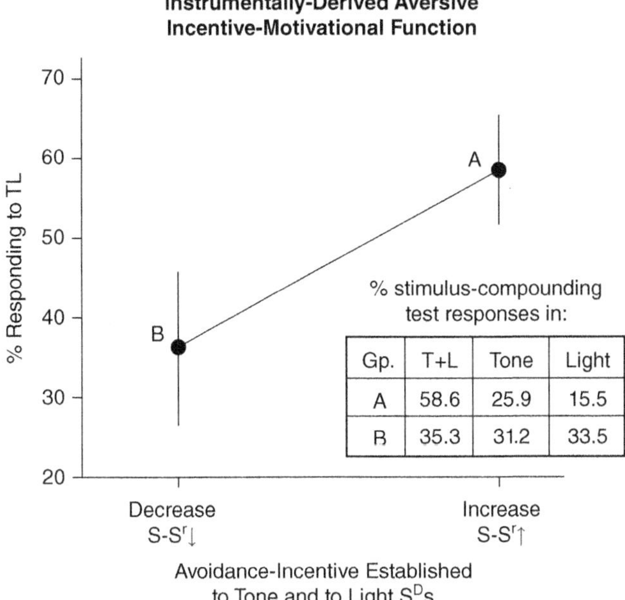

Figure 17.6 Instrumentally-derived aversive incentive-motivational function. On stimulus-compounding tests, compared to tone or light alone, T+L increased responding 2.5 fold in Group A (S-R↑,S-S^r↑) and did notchange responding in Group B (S-R↑,S-S^r↓). Range-bars again reveal non-overlapping groups. Group A from Emurian & Weiss (1972). Group B from Weiss (1976, Experiment 3, Phase 1). (Comparing T+L% over groups yields $t_{(4)} = 11.3$, $p < 0.001$. This is the first statistical comparison of these groups and its validating rationale is described in the text.)

CS has only been reported when the CS is relatively long . . . and the baseline rate of responding has been lowered . . ." (Lovibond, 1983, p. 236). Recently, Holmes, Marchand, and Coutureau (2010) comprehensively covered behavioral factors influencing transfer-of-control-related Pavlovian-to-instrumental transfer (PIT). They concluded their systematic ". . . analyses of data for individual groups in PIT studies suggested that competition between Pavlovian and instrumental responses is an important determinant of PIT [effects]" (p. 1283).

Elicited behavior(s) probably facilitated operant responding in the "successful" transfer-of-control studies where a shock-related CS+ increased avoidance responding. For example, jumping (Rescorla & LoLordo's (1965) operant) and running (which resembles Weisman & Litner's (1969) wheel-turning operant) are species-specific defense reactions (SSDRs, Bolles, 1970) in the dog and rat, respectively. Therefore, these behaviors elicited by shock-associated CS+ likely facilitated avoidance over what the CS+'s incentive-motivational properties alone would have produced.

That SSDRs likely contributed to this CS+-increased avoidance responding is analogous to a food-paired CS+ augmenting a food-maintained operant when the conditioned behavior it elicits is similar to the operant (LoLordo et al., 1974). The dynamics of Schwartz and Gamzu's (1977) additivity theory of behavioral contrast can be identified in these aversive and appetitive situations.

Behavioral contrast is observed when the reinforced operant in one component of a multiple schedule increases after reinforcement decreases in another component. In pigeons, the additivity theory attributes this response increase to elicited "autoshaped" pecks to the key color that now is differentially associated with food. However, the additivity theory does not easily account for behavioral contrast obtained when responses elicited by the food-signaling stimulus would not be congruent with the operant response, such as with rats lever pressing for food that Guttman (1977) reported. But, behavioral contrast in both congruent and non-congruent situations can be accounted for by the differential association of S+ with food creating an incentive-motivational state that energizes operant behavior. In congruent situations, such as with pigeons pecking a lighted key, the increased responding in S+ could be due to both increased incentive motivation and "autoshaped" pecks.

Notably, the procedures used to obtain the instrumentally-derived incentive-motivational functions described in Figures 17.4 and 17.6 were designed to deal with "competition-of-response" problems like those encountered in transfer-of-control experiments. In all instances, target incentive-motivational properties were produced *within* multi-component operant baselines through food- or shock-related changes in the tone and the light S^Ds relative to conditions in $\overline{T}\overline{L}$. But, in all groups these S^Ds always occasioned steady-moderate leverpressing that ceased in $\overline{T}\overline{L}$. Finally, the feeder-click, that could produce leverpress-competing behaviors, was not presented during the stimulus-compounding tests, which were performed in extinction.

Nevertheless, it is impossible to prove that something (here, behaviors that compete with lever pressing) do not occur. They could always be lurking somewhere, yet to be discovered. But, logically, they should not be a factor if a functional analysis showed that such potential, unidentified leverpress-competing behavior(s) would have led to different stimulus-compounding-test outcomes than the groups in Figure 17.4 produced.

Food-related, leverpress-competing behavior in tone or light are possible in Groups A and B of Figure 17.4 because in training both obtained food during those stimuli. But such competing behavior should be more likely in Group A, where the S^Ds *differentially* signaled food, than Group B where they did not (see Table 17.1). Nevertheless, T+L tripled the rate of lever pressing in Group A (relative to tone or light alone) while only doubling it in Group B—results inconsistent with potentially heightened response competition in Group A. Group C's results are even more compelling. Because Group C *never* received food in tone or light, leverpress-competing behavior should have been least likely therein for Group C. Nevertheless, T+L produced response rates that were no higher than in tone or light alone. That lever pressing was an "arbitrary operant" here probably contributed to within-group consistency (see range bars in Figures 17.4 and 17.6). In nature, rats do not leverpress for food or to avoid aversive situations.

The Discriminative-Response Function

Operant responses maintained by continuously-functioning variable interval or free-operant-avoidance contingencies are common DVs in transfer-of-control experiments. Because these operants were not explicitly under discriminative control of a

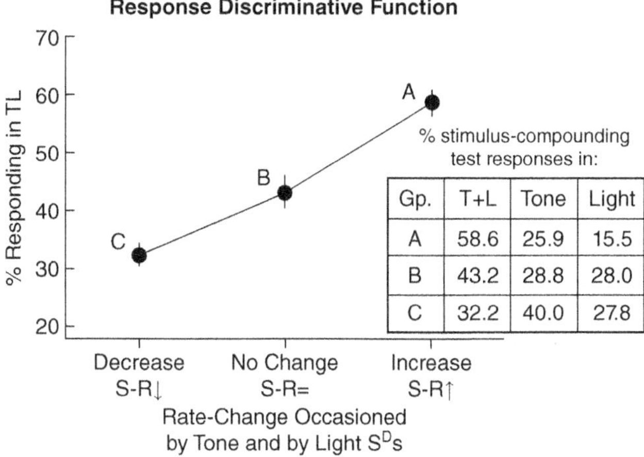

Gp.	T+L	Tone	Light
A	58.6	25.9	15.5
B	43.2	28.8	28.0
C	32.2	40.0	27.8

Figure 17.7 Discriminative-response function. All groups lever pressed comparably in tone and in light S^Ds to postpone shock, with $\overline{TL}$ shock-free. On stimulus-compounding tests, compared to tone-or-light alone, T+L increased responding 2.5 fold in Group A (S-R↑,S-S^r↑), 1.5 fold in Group B (S-R=,S-S^r↑), and did not change responding in Group C (S-R↓,S-S^r↑). Range-bars again reveal non-overlapping groups. Group A from Emurian & Weiss (1972). Group B from Weiss, (1977). Group C from Weiss (1976, Experiment 2, Phase 1). (ANOVA of T+L% yields $F_{(2,9)} = 62.4$, $p < .001$, with Group A > Group B > Group C, $p < .004$. This is the first statistical comparison incorporating all three groups and its validating rationale is described in the text.)

specified stimulus, the transfer-of-control design did not take into account: (1) the discriminative-response process, (2) how that process creates the conditions responsible for the instrumentally-derived incentive-motivational process, and (3) the resulting integrated stimulus control. The experiment in Table 17.2, lower panel, was designed to reveal the discriminative-response process' role in stimulus control.

These three groups lever pressed at steady-moderate rates in tone and in light S^Ds to postpone shocks for 25-sec on a free-operant-avoidance contingency. *Shock-free* $\overline{TL}$ periods separated these S^Ds. Therefore, tone and light *each* excited the avoidance incentive (S-S^r↑) in *all* groups. But the response-rate change (that reflects the discriminative-response process) occasioned by these S^Ds, relative to the rate in $\overline{TL}$, was systematically varied over groups. It increased (S-R↑) in Group A, was unchanged (S-R=) in Group B and decreased (S-R↓) in Group C. This is the mirror image of the experiment in the upper panel of Table 17.2 responsible for the instrumentally-derived incentive-motivational function (Figure 17.4).

Group A rats' lever pressing postponed shocks in tone and in light. In shock-free $\overline{TL}$ they ceased responding. Therefore, during these S^Ds the discriminative-responses process (S-R↑) and avoidance incentive (S-S^r↑) increased, relative to $\overline{TL}$. In testing, these rats responded 2.5-times faster in T+L than in tone or light, with T+L controlling 58.6% of total-test responses (Figure 17.7, Point A) (Emurian & Weiss, 1972).

Group B rats were also on free-operant avoidance in tone and in light, but comparable leverpressing rates were maintained in shock-free $\overline{TL}$ by a lean VI-food

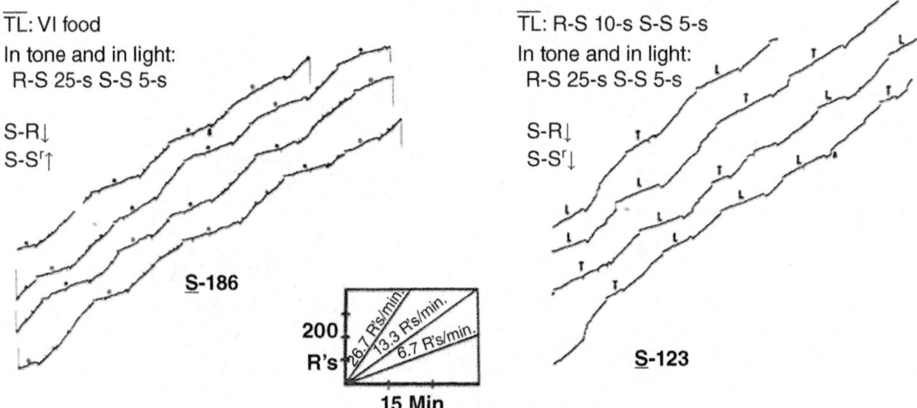

Figure 17.8 Cumulative records show these rats are behaviorally indistinguishable, with S-R↓ established in tone (T-or-filled circles) and light (L-or-open circles) where they avoided shock. But (see text), these S^Ds decreased S-123's avoidance incentive (S-S^r↓) and *increased* (S-S^r↑) S-186's. Tone-and-light-off (T̄L̄) contingencies (see figure and text) increased both rat's lever-pressing therein. From Weiss (1976) Experiments 1 and 2, respectively. [Two parameters define a free-operant avoidance contingency. These are the time a response postpones shock, the Response-Shock (R-S) interval, and the inter-shock time in the absence of responding, the Shock-Shock (SS) interval.]

schedule. Therefore, when entering tone-or-light S^Ds response rate did not change (S-R=), but avoidance incentive increased (S-S^r↑). In testing, these rats responded 1.5-times faster in T+L than in tone or light, with T+L controlling 43.4% of total-test responses (Figure 17.7, Point B) (Weiss, 1977).

Group C rats also postponed shock in tone and in light, but higher response rates were maintained in shock-free T̄L̄ by a rich VI-food schedule (left frame, Figure 17.8). Therefore, when entering an S^D, response rate decreased (S-R↓) but avoidance incentive increased (S-S^r↑). In testing, these rats responded comparably in tone, light and T+L, with T+L controlling only 32.2% of total-test responses (Figure 17.7, Point C) (Weiss, 1976, Experiment 2, Phase 1).

Across these three groups (Figure 17.7), manipulation of the discriminative-response process produced a function very similar to the incentive-motivational functions in Figures 17.4 and 17.6, with the rate of responding in the presence of the T+L compound a direct function of whether tone alone and light alone controlled an increase, no change, or a decrease in responding relative to the rate in T̄L̄. This comparability suggests that the discriminative and incentive-motivational processes combine and are comparably influencing behavior, at least in these experiments. It also supports that the increase in avoidance incentive upon entering tone or light was at least generally comparable over Figure 17.7's groups even though Groups B and C received food in shock-free T̄L̄ and Group A did not. But this remains to be further explored.

Taken together, the discriminative-response and incentive-motivational functions show that both processes increasing (S-R↑,S-S^r↑) produced T+L's largest (2.5–3 : 1) response enhancement over tone or light alone (Point A, Figures 17.4, 17.6, and 17.7). However, with only one process increasing (S-R↑,S-S^r = or S-R=,S-S^r↑), T+L produced a more modest (1.5–2 : 1) enhancement (Point B, Figures 17.4 and 17.7, respectively). Finally, when the processes established to an S^D conflicted (S-R↑,S-S^r↓ or S-R↓,S-S^r↑), tone, light and T+L controlled comparable responding (Point C of Figure 17.4, Point B of Figure 17.6, Point C of Figure 17.7). The lawfulness of this combination of S-R and S-S^r processes in the variety of contingency and incentive situations described above supports the proposed model that is more fully described next.

Responsive-Discriminative-by-Incentive-Motivational-Process Combination Matrix

Table 17.3 presents in a 3 × 3 matrix the response-discriminative (S-R) and incentive-motivational (S-S^r) variables manipulated to produce the functions in Figures 17.4, 17.6, and 17.7. The operant-contingency-related change in response rate occasioned by tone and by light S^Ds (reflecting the S^D's discriminative-response property) appears in the columns. The incentive-motivational property conditioned to these S^Ds (established through between-component reinforcement/contingency differences within the operant schedule) appears in the rows. This nine-cell matrix presents projected

Table 17.3 Stimulus compounding (generalization) test outcomes predicted to combinations of discriminative-response and incentive-motive properties established to S^DS

Incentive Change Established to Tone and to Light S^Ds relative to $\overline{TL}$ (Incentive Change Established to S_1 relative to S_2)	Response-Rate Change Occasioned by Tone and by Light S^Ds Relative to $\overline{TL}$ (Response-Rate Change Occasioned by S_1 Relative to S_2): Increase	No Change	Decrease
Increaseac	Maximum Response Enhancement (Positive Peak Shift)	Moderate Response Enhancement (Positive Peak Shift)	Minimal or No Effect
	↑ / ↑	= / ↑	↓ / ↑
No Change	Moderate Response Enhancement (Positive Peak Shift)	Minimal or No Effect	Moderate Response Reduction (Negative Peak Shift)
	↑ / =	= / =	↓ / =
Decrease	Minimal or No Effect	Moderate Response Reduction (Negative Peak Shift)	Maximum Response Reduction (Negative Peak Shift)
	↑ / ↓	= / ↓	↓ / ↓

* See text for matrix translation to stimulus-generalization results after intra-dimensional (S_1/S_2, e.g., 540/550 nm) training.

stimulus compounding assay outcomes assuming that discriminative-response and incentive-motivational properties established to the S^Ds combine (see last paragraph of "Appetitive Incentive-Motivational Function" section.)

Studies producing the instrumentally-derived incentive-motivational functions (appetitive in Figure 17.4 and aversive in Figure 17.6) are represented by the S-R, $S\text{-}S^r$ combinations in the three left-column cells. Studies producing the discriminative-response function (Figure 17.7) are represented by the three top-row cells. In addition, this matrix represents the results of more than 50 instrumental stimulus-compounding studies reported to date.[2]

Cells along the lower-left-to-upper-right diagonal are especially informative. As predicted, in stimulus-compounding tests, these conditions produced comparable response rates in tone, light, and T+L. But these equivalent test outcomes were produced by different combinations of discriminative-response and incentive-motivational properties in each instance. (For the bottom-left cell ($S\text{-}R\uparrow, S\text{-}S^r\downarrow$), see Group C, Figure 17.4 and Group B, Figure 17.6. For the top-right cell ($S\text{-}R\downarrow, S\text{-}S^r\uparrow$), see Group C, Figure 17.7.) Weiss (1977) confirmed the middle-cell ($S\text{-}R{=}, S\text{-}S^r{=}$) with non-differentially-trained groups for whom the same contingency (VI-food in an appetitive experiment and free-operant avoidance in an aversive experiment) maintained responding in all three components of the training schedule (tone, light, and $\overline{T}\overline{L}$).

This shows that stimulus compounding can produce *different* results when the training stimuli control similar leverpressing behavior across groups (left-column, Table 17.3) and similar results when the training stimuli control different leverpressing behavior across groups (lower-left-to-upper-right diagonal, Table 17.3). It all depends on the *combination* of discriminative-and-incentive-motivational properties established to the tone and the light S^Ds, relative to $\overline{T}\overline{L}$, in each group. The systematic nature of these results, and those discussed later, are consistent with the predictions of Table 17.3. They support the hypothesis that discriminative- and incentive-motivational processes combine, with sign relevant, to produce resultant behavior.

It is noteworthy that conflicting processes essentially neutralized each other in the studies satisfying the bottom-left and top-right cells of Table 17.3. That could be due to the possibility that a rather wide range of conflicting processes can essentially neutralize each other, the intrinsic variance in behavioral data and/or the "moderate" levels of each property established to the S^Ds in those studies. It is reasonable to assume that a particularly strong increase in one process might overpower a slight decrease in the other, yielding an inequality where Table 17.3 predicts equality. Therefore, these predictions of Table 17.3 would not be expected to hold if there is a wide disparity in the strength of opposing effects. Parametric research would be necessary to fill in details such as this on what is a first approximation of an induced combinational theory.

When processes operated in concert in tone and in light (Table 17.3, upper-left-and-lower-right cells) behavior in T+L is both substantially enhanced and very persistent—*even when that behavior produces self-injury.* On the positive side, recall Emurian and Weiss (1972) where T+L almost tripled avoidance-response rate on a stimulus-compounding test performed in extinction. Subsequently, these investigators administered 28 *maintenance* stimulus-compounding tests to each rat wherein the free-operant-avoidance contingency continued to operate in tone, light *and*

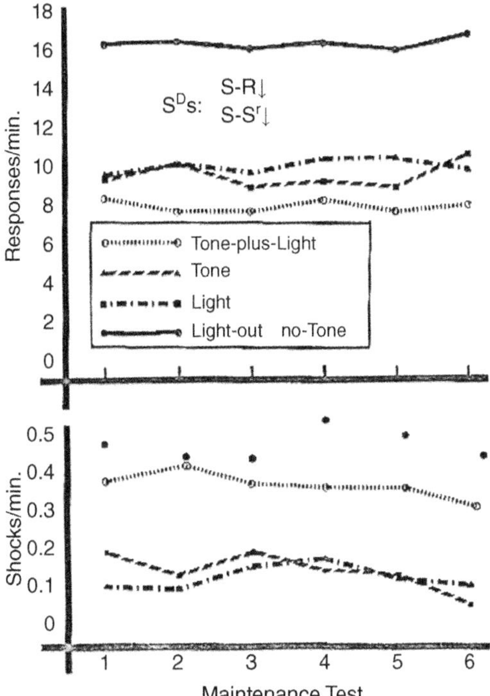

Figure 17.9 When decreased avoidance-rate (S-R↓) and incentive (S-S^r↓) properties were established to tone and to light S^Ds (e.g., see S-123, Figure 17.8), T+L significantly reduced avoidance rate therein over all successive maintenance-stimulus-compounding tests. This *tripled shock-rate* is a dramatic, painful example of environmentally-induced self-injurious loss-of-control. Amplification of data reported in Weiss (1976, Experiment 1, Phase 1).

T+L. On *all* 81 maintenance tests, shocks were more effectively avoided in T+L than tone or light.

Unfortunately, the behavior produced by stimulus compounding can be so robust that it is relatively insensitive to immediate, clearly maladaptive, consequences. Weiss (1976, Experiment 1, Phase 1) demonstrated this under conditions depicted in the lower-right cell of Table 17.3. In training, rats' lever presses postponed shock in $\overline{T}\overline{L}$ for 10 seconds and for 25 seconds in tone and in light. Therefore, avoidance responding decreased (S-R↓) upon entering tone or light and increased in $\overline{T}\overline{L}$ (right-record, Figure 17.8). Actual component-preference tests revealed a strong preference for the tone or light over $\overline{T}\overline{L}$—establishing that these S^Ds were less "feared" (S-S^r↓) than $\overline{T}\overline{L}$. On a stimulus-compounding test with shock discontinued, as Table 17.3 predicts, T+L controlled strong response reduction—half the avoidance-rate of tone or light alone. But would this occur if the avoidance contingency operated in testing so that reduced responding in T+L increased shock rate? Maintenance tests investigated this, with dramatic results.

Figure 17.9 shows the six maintenance tests performed on all nine rats. Horizontal, non-converging-parallel lines resulted when shock rates were plotted over days in tone, light, and T+L, respectively, indicating no change in the strength of the stimulus-compounding effect over the course of multi-day testing. Although the shock rate in T+L was triple that in tone or light, the low rate of avoidance responding the T+L compound controlled was sustained. Regrettably, only six maintenance tests were planned. When this sustained, maladaptive effect T+L engendered was noted, most subjects had progressed to their next phase. But, the few rats administered additional maintenance tests were still receiving more shocks in T+L than tone or light after 20+ tests, with little sign of the effect abating. They outlasted the experimenters.

This continuation of a behavioral pattern despite clearly adverse, self-destructive consequences would be colloquially labeled "loss of control" over the behavior. However, there is no question that the phenomenon is lawful (i.e., produced by specific, known variables). The evidence is strong that such self-destructive behavior is induced by environmental cues established though operant-discrimination learning with its embedded classical conditioning. As discussed in the next section, the author and his associates have investigated similar "loss of control" with operant schedules of drug self-administration in rats as a model of addiction in humans.

But prior to progressing to the next section, the dynamics presented in Table 17.3 should be placed in a larger historical context. Hull's (1952) *behavior system* included habit (sHr) and incentive motivation (sKr) among the factors combining to produce resulting excitatory potential (sEr). More recently, the Mathematical Principles of Reinforcement theory proposed that "Incentives invigorate responses, in particular those preceding and predicting the incentive" (Killeen & Sitomer, 2003, p. 49). And, of course, the role of incentive-motivation and its relation to behavior has received much attention (e.g., Bindra, 1969; Brown 1961; Gray, 1975; Konorkski, 1967; Logan, 1960; Mowrer, 1960; Rescorla & Solomon, 1967; Weiss, 1978; Weiss, Thomas, & Weissman, 1996). Thus, Table 17.3 with its associated supporting research extends and applies the existing knowledge/theory about these fundamental processes and their dynamics.

Environmentally Induced Increases in Drug Seeking: An Animal Learning Model of Drug Abuse and Loss of Control

Stimuli (e.g., specific people, places, and/or paraphernalia) associated with rewarding effects of drugs can produce drug-seeking and therefore play a major role in drug addiction (Robbins, Ehrman, Childress, & O'Brien, 1997; Markou et al., 1993; Robinson & Berridge, 1993). Further, drug cues not only increase drug craving but produce some of the same changes in brain activity as the drug itself—with this reaction more powerful in those severely addicted (Volkow et al., 2008). Relapse to drug use is also associated with heightened drug-cue response in several brain areas (Sinha & Li, 2007). Thus, drug-related cues appear to play a significant role in addiction, acting as both discriminative stimuli (guiding the behavior required to obtain, prepare and ingest the drug) and conditioned stimuli (having incentive-motivational effects that lead people to seek drugs). As described above, establishing S^Ds with S-R$\uparrow$,S-$S^r\uparrow$ properties and then presenting them in compound tripled the rate of food-seeking and shock-avoidance (Point A, Figures 17.4 and 17.6, respectively). Would a drug-seeking response also triple if such S^Ds for drug self-administration were established and then presented in compound?

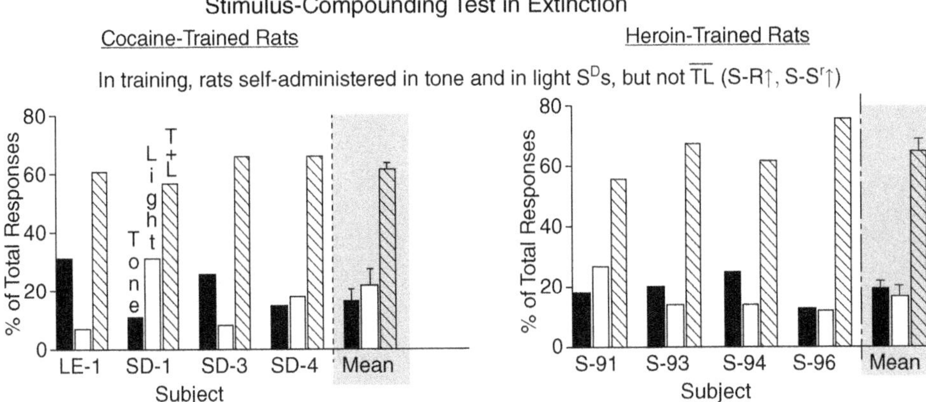

Maintenance Stimulus-Compounding Test

Drug earned in tone, light and T+L during this test directly related to response rate

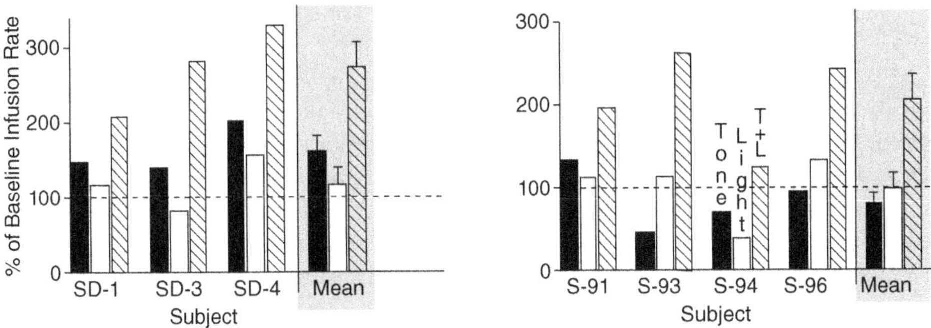

Figure 17.10 With S-R↑,S-S^{r}↑ properties established to tone and to light S^{D}s, on stimulus-compounding test performed in extinction T+L tripled drug-seeking in cocaine-trained (upper-left frame) and heroin-trained (upper-right frame) rats. On maintenance tests, that related response-and-infusion rates, T+L doubled infusion of cocaine and heroin over self-regulated baseline-training levels (lower-frames). Adapted from Panlilio, Weiss, and Schindler (1996, 2000).

Rats self-administered cocaine or heroin (Panlilio, Weiss, & Schindler, 1996, 2000) on a low variable ratio (VR) schedule in tone and in light, with drug unavailable in $\overline{TL}$. The VR schedule was used here so that: (1) the subject could regulate its drug intake to an "optimal" level of effect during training, and (2) increases in drug-seeking during stimulus-compounding tests conducted under maintenance conditions would increase drug intake. On a stimulus-compounding test performed in extinction, T+L overall *tripled* drug-seeking whether rats self-administered cocaine or heroin (upper frames, Figure 17.10) even though these drugs are distinctly different in their pharmacological mechanisms and behavioral effects (Wise, 1996). (For a detailed description of how stimulus control of drug self-administration was produced, and how cocaine-reinforced leverpressing can be indistinguishable from that created with food reinforcement under comparable three-component schedules of reinforcement, see Weiss, Kearns, Cohn, Schindler, & Panlilio (2003)).

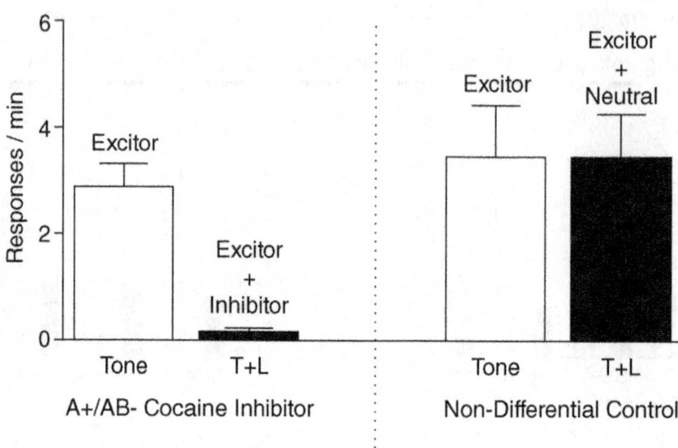

Figure 17.11 A conditioned inhibitor (CI) for cocaine created via A+/AB− procedure with operant contingencies reduced cocaine seeking by more than 90%. Adapted from Kearns et al. (2005).

On maintenance stimulus-compounding tests, in which rats received cocaine for every fifth response in tone, light, and T+L, the rate of cocaine intake in the presence of tone alone and light alone was about the same as in training (lower frames, Figure 17.10). But, the T+L compound doubled drug intake. This finding is significant because rats (Panlilio, Katz, Pickens, & Schindler, 2003) and humans (Sughondhabirom et al., 2005) normally self-regulate their drug intake within a fairly narrow range, and "loss of control" over this intake is a hallmark of addiction (American Psychological Association, Diagnostic and Statistical Manual-IV, 2007). Again, self-injurious behavior was the lawful, predictable outcome when discriminative-response and incentive-motivational properties of environmental conditions confronting the animal acted in concert—in this case both factors increasing (S-R↑,S-S^r↑). So, this procedure may model one mechanism by which human drug taking escalates from controlled, casual use to "uncontrollable" abuse. Clearly, drug-associated environmental stimuli increase the motivation to seek and consume abused drugs.

Kearns, Weiss, Schindler, and Panlilio (2005) subsequently reported that instrumentally-derived conditioned inhibitors dramatically decrease drug seeking. During training, rats self-administered cocaine in tone and in click while cocaine was unavailable in click-plus-light (C+L) or $\overline{T}\overline{L}\overline{C}$. On compounding tests, T+L reduced the cocaine-seeking that tone alone occasioned by more than 90% (Figure 17.11). This substantial cue-induced decreased drug seeking by a cocaine-based conditioned inhibitor suggests that conditioning-based treatments might be devised that help reduce drug seeking by addicts. Unfortunately, a direct application of the tactic used in this study with rats has limited treatment applications for humans because inhibitors lose effectiveness unless their related conditioned excitor is maintained (Lysle & Fowler, 1985). Here, the excitor is cocaine and it is undesirable to continue delivering cocaine.

Konorski's (1967) appetitive-aversive-interaction theory of motivation suggests a solution. It posits that reinforcers within the same incentive class (appetitive or

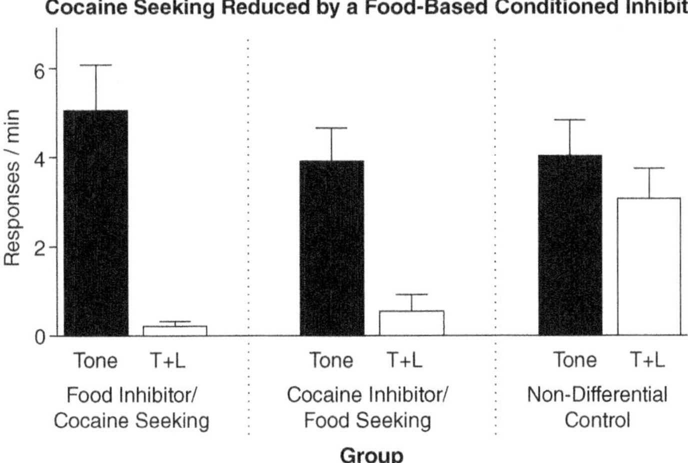

Figure 17.12 Left-frame: stimulus-compounding (summation) test results after leverpressing was maintained by cocaine self-administration in tone (T) and by food in click (C) while food was unavailable in click-plus-light. This made light (L) a food-based inhibitor through the A+/AB− paradigm. Tone-plus-light (T+L) reduced tone-occasioned cocaine seeking more than 90%. Middle-frame: comparable summation-test results after training symmetrical to that described above (see text). Right-frame: non-differential-comparison group. Adapted from Weiss et al. (2007).

aversive) have functionally comparable motivational properties (but see Balleine, 2005; Delamater & Holland, 2008). If so, excitatory cues for another, non-drug reinforcer from the appetitive class (e.g., food) could be established and used to inhibit drug-seeking. Weiss et al. (2007) investigated this possibility by using operant-baseline training to create a conditioned inhibitor for food. Their rats self-administered cocaine in tone and earned food in click. But, food was unavailable in click-plus-light (C+L), thus using the highly-effective A+/AB− conditioned-inhibition paradigm. In testing, presenting the food-based inhibitor (light) in compound with the discriminative stimulus for cocaine-seeking (tone) decreased responding by more than 90% compared to tone alone (Figure 17.12). Symmetrically, a cocaine-based inhibitor comparably reduced food seeking.

It is certainly possible, and even likely, that the S-R↓-property of the food-based inhibitor accounted for some of the reduced cocaine-seeking observed by Weiss et al. (2007). Nevertheless, food-based inhibition should also have contributed to this more than 90% reduction in cocaine-seeking because: (1) this reduction was equal to that of a cocaine-based inhibitor where both S-R↓,S-S^r↓ properties were operating (Figure 17.11), (2) the incentive-motivational property of an inhibitor can be manipulated independently of its discriminative-response property (Weiss, Thomas, & Weissman, 1996), and (3) comparable results were forthcoming in the symmetrically-trained Food-Seeking/Cocaine-Based-Inhibitor Group. This suggests that inhibitors based on non-drug appetitive reinforcers might be a practical method of reducing drug seeking in human drug abusers—a treatment derived from the appetitive-aversive-interaction theory of motivation. It remains to be seen whether this strategy can be adapted for clinical application, but it makes sense that if learning principles can account for environmentally-energized drug seeking, they might also offer leads for developing new treatments to reduce it.

Extending Discriminative-Response/Incentive-Motivational Combination Model to Stimulus-Generalization Peak Shift

Parsimonious explanation, accounting for the greatest variety of phenomena with the fewest variables, is a major goal of science. How the incentive-motivational and discriminative properties of stimuli interact to determine the effects of compounding S^Ds (Table 17.3) can also be applied to another phenomenon traditionally of interest to students of stimulus control, *generalization peak shift*,. In *positive peak shift*, after intra-dimensional (e.g. wavelength) S+/S– training, on a stimulus-generalization test maximum responding is controlled by a stimulus *removed from S+ in a direction away from S–* (extinction), rather than by S+ (cf. Hanson, 1959). Peak-shift research has substantially increased our understanding of how excitatory-and-inhibitory processes contribute to stimulus control (e.g., Spence, 1937; Hearst, 1968; Rilling, 1977; Weiss, 1978).

Demonstrating that comparable underlying processes contribute to stimulus-compounding's response enhancement and that of peak shift would be a substantial integration. (In both paradigms, maximum responding in testing is not controlled by the S+ training stimulus.) That integration could be achieved by ***dimensionalizing*** the stimulus-compounding paradigm's unitary-stimulus conditions (tone, light, $\overline{T}\overline{L}$) to create a functional equivalence with the intra-dimensional stimulus-generalization-peak-shift paradigm (Weiss, 1964, 1969, 1978; Wolf, 1963). Translating $\overline{T}\overline{L}$ to "zero-stimuli on," tone and light *each* to "one-stimulus on" and T+L to "two-stimuli on accomplishes this by creating a 0, 1, 2 *ordinal dimension.*

With this translation, enhancement of responding through stimulus compounding can be described as follows: *After intra-dimensional training (between S+ tone or light (one-stimulus-on) and S– $\overline{T}\overline{L}$ (no-stimuli-on)), during a stimulus-compounding test more responding is controlled by two-stimuli-on (T+L), the stimulus removed from S+ in a direction away from S–, than by S+ itself.* This parallels the peak-shift description, above. Likewise, *response reduction*, where T+L controls a lower rate than tone or light after training in which the high-rate stimulus is $\overline{T}\overline{L}$, can be considered analogous to *negative peak shift.* (In *negative peak shift*, minimum response rate on a generalization test is controlled by a stimulus removed from the lowest-rate training stimulus on in a direction away from the high-rate stimulus.)

This derived functional equivalence permits application of the combinational model to predicting stimulus-generalization-test results after intra-dimensional discrimination training. Table 17.3 does this with these simple substitutions: (1) "S_1" for "tone and for light S^Ds," (2) "S_2" for "$\overline{T}\overline{L}$," (3) "positive peak-shift" for "response enhancement in T+L," and (4) "negative peak-shift" for "response reduction in T+L." Now, the matrix can be applied to more than 70 intra-dimensional stimulus-generalization experiments: (1) organized with respect to the combination of discriminative-response (S-R) and incentive-motivational ($S\text{-}S^r$) properties training conditions should have established in S_1, and (2) with peak-shift predicted from these properties.

Although these more than 70 experiments were not specifically performed to test the combinational model, the degree of confirmation is considerable.[3] Guttman (1965) appreciated the possible comparability of component and wavelength situations, speculating that "wavelength stimulation produces an effect with several components . . . and it may well turn out that the results obtained with wavelength will be more readily generalizable to multidimensional-stimulus situations than to unidimensional cases" (p. 271). The Table 17.3 model supports Guttman, but going from multidimensional to unidimensional situations.

When compounded S^Ds each controlled response increase, but simultaneously signaled reinforcement decrease (S-R↑,S-S^r↓), T+L did not enhance responding (Weiss & Van Ost, 1974). Would positive peak shift also be absent on a stimulus-generalization test when intra-dimensional discrimination training established these properties to the S_1 wavelength? Weiss and Dacanay (1982) directly tested that. Their pigeons responded on a chained schedule in which treadle pressing during the S_1 keylight (572- or 580-nm, counterbalanced) produced the S_2 keylight on a VI schedule. During S_2,, treadle-press cessation was reinforced with grain on a DRO schedule. This established conflicting S-R↑,S-S^r↓ properties to S_1 (lower-left cell, Table 17.3). As predicted, no pigeon showed a peak shift in their generalization gradient (Phase 1, Figure17.13), even though S_1 occasioned treadle pressing and S_2 did not.

In Phase 2, treadle pressing in S_1 produced grain on a VI schedule, but S_2 signaled extinction. This established S-R↑,S-S^r↑ properties to S_1—the combination that should optimize positive peak shift (upper-left cell, Table 17.3). The stimulus-generalization test confirmed this prediction in all pigeons (Phase 2, Figure 17.13), even with S_1's inhibitory history. The response-discriminative-by-incentive-motivational combination model of stimulus control also predicts greater likelihood, and more substantial, peak shift when both S_1 properties are excitatory than when only one is. Weiss and Weissman (1992) supported this prediction.

Incentive Processes and a Biological-Constraint-on-Learning: Selective Associations

When a set of stimuli are given equal opportunity to control a response, the nature of the US may determine which stimulus is most effective (Garcia & Koelling, 1966). This was further investigated with pigeons (Foree & LoLordo, 1973) and rats (Schindler & Weiss, 1982) that avoided shock *or* earned food in T+L, with $\overline{TL}$ signaling extinction. On stimulus-element tests, for both species: (1) after appetitive training, the light exerted stronger control over responding than the tone, and (2) after avoidance training, the tone controlled more responding than the light (upper frames, Figure 17.14). Unfortunately, the nature of the events experienced in T+L (food or shock) are confounded with hedonic value conditioned to T+L—positive and negative, respectively. This could mean "preferred" T+L, not necessarily food association, favors light control while "non-preferred" T+L, not necessarily shock association, favors tone control.

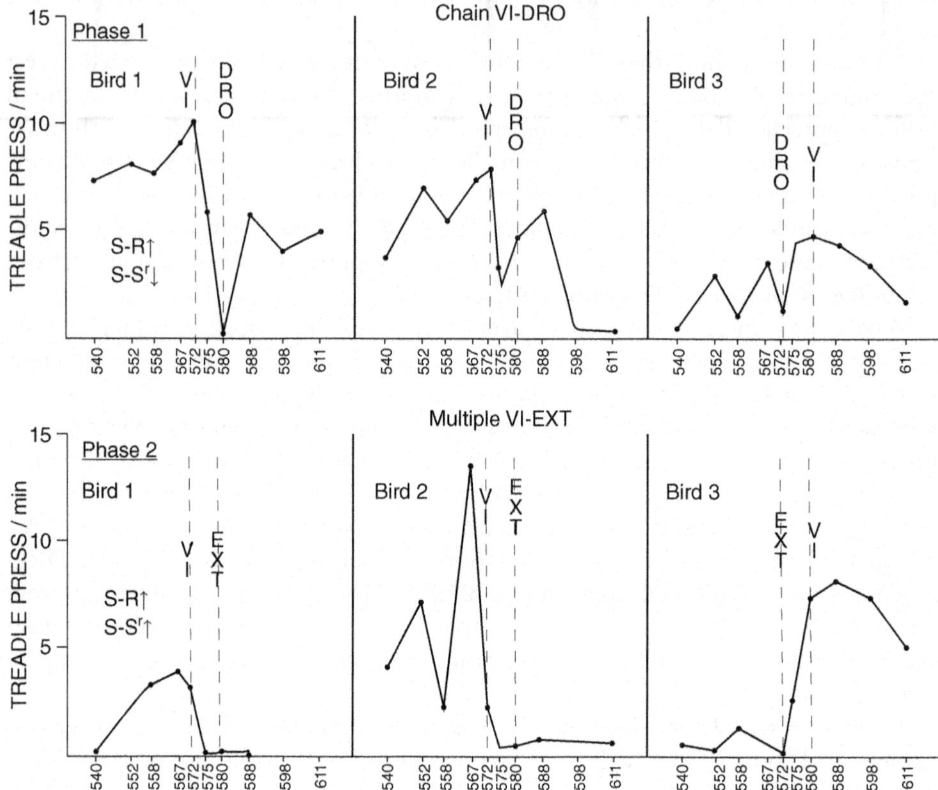

Figure 17.13 In Phase 1, with conflicting S-R↑,S-S^r↓ properties established to S_1 wavelength, treadle-pressing pigeons did not produce peak shift on a stimulus-generalization test. In Phase 2, when S-R↑,S-S^r↑ properties were established to S_1, all pigeons produced peak shift. Adapted from Weiss and Dacany (1982).

Konorski's (1967) appetitive-aversive-interaction theory of motivation offers a solution to this problem. It postulates that when behavior is maintained by one-class-of reinforcer (appetitive or aversive), it should be: (1) *energized* by a conditioned excitor for that system *or* by a conditioned inhibitor for the other, and (2) *weakened* by a conditioned inhibitor for that system *or by* a conditioned excitor for the other. Overall, Konorski's system is a credible, parsimonious and integrative hedonically-based theory that has stimulated research and much supporting evidence (e.g., Dickinson & Pearce, 1977; Holmes et al., 2010; Weiss & Schindler, 1989; Weiss, et al., 1996).

That food-withdrawal and shock both create *negative hedonic states* suggested a solution to the confounding of food/shock with positive/negative hedonic state described above. Weiss, Panlilio, and Schindler (1993) produced T+L conditions of positive or negative hedonic value with appetitive contingencies. Their T+L-Positive Group earned all VI-food reinforcers for lever pressing in T+L and none in $\overline{\text{TL}}$. In contrast, their T+L-Negative Group responded on a chained schedule where lever pressing during T+L produced $\overline{\text{TL}}$, on a VI schedule, in which all food was received

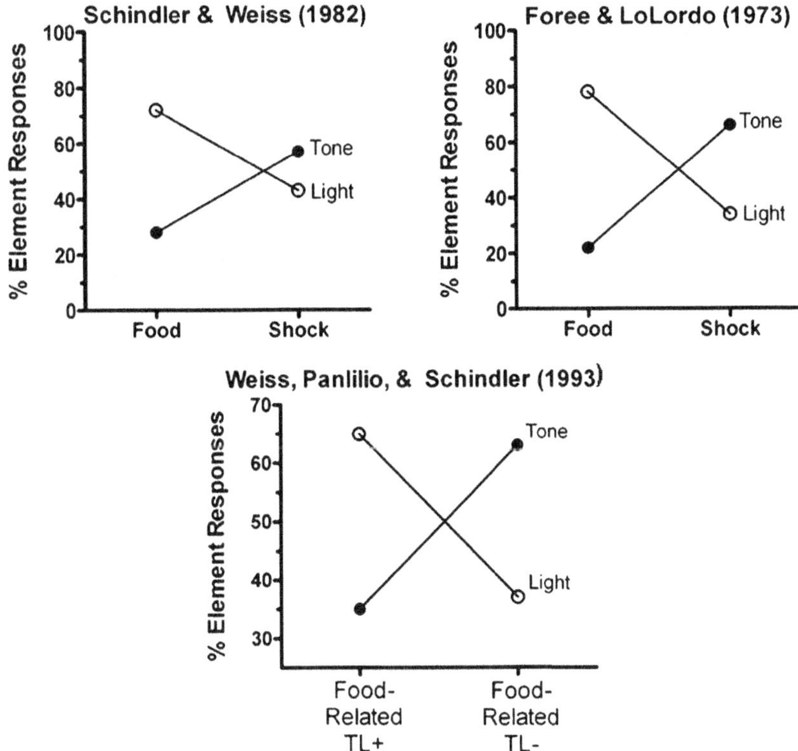

Figure 17.14 Upper-left frame. On a stimulus-element test, percent total-element-test responses emitted in tone and in light elements by rats earning food or avoiding-shock in tone-plus-light (TL) (Schindler & Weiss, 1982). Upper-right frame presents same measure for Foree-and-LoLordo's (1973) pigeons. Lower-frame: percent total-element-test responses emitted in tone and in light elements by food-related TL+ and food-related TL−Groups. Adapted from Weiss, Panlilio, and Schindler (1993).

for response cessation (DRO). These chained-schedule-trained rats worked to remove themselves from T+L, and enter $\overline{\mathrm{T}}\overline{\mathrm{L}}$, showing that T+L was negative (or at least substantially less positive) compared to $\overline{\mathrm{T}}\overline{\mathrm{L}}$. Nevertheless, the groups' lever-pressing behavior was indistinguishable, with both responding at steady-moderate rates in T+L and ceasing in $\overline{\mathrm{T}}\overline{\mathrm{L}}$. On a stimulus-element test, T+L-Positive rats emitted 65% of their responses in light while the T+L-Negative rats emitted a significantly lower 40% in light (lower frame, Figure 17.14). These T+L-Negative rats resembled those avoiding shock in T+L.

This study again produced incentive-motivational states through between-component reinforcement differences. It demonstrated for the first time that *hedonic processes*, not particular reinforcers, are responsible for *selective associations*, and supported Konorski's motivational theory. This raises selective associations to a higher level of processing, involving comparison of the relative hedonic value between situations, rather than hard-wired connections determined by the reinforcer's physical nature.

Reconciling Different Test Outcomes by Behaviorally Indistinguishable Groups: A Composite-Stimulus Control Analysis

As described above, the instrumentally-derived appetitive incentive-motivational function (Figure 17.4) was obtained with three groups whose leverpressing rates were indistinguishable. During training, all groups responded at moderate-steady behavior in tone and in light S^Ds and essentially ceased in $\bar{T}\bar{L}$. Nevertheless, T+L tripled Group A's rate, doubled Group B's and did not change Group C's.

A composite analysis of the stimuli that control behavior under the baseline conditions can provide insight into why the stimulus control that appears to be the same across groups can be revealed to be different by presenting the stimuli in compound. In this analysis, the tone and the light S^Ds are viewed in terms of the on-off states of their composite elements rather than as unitary stimuli. Within this reformulation: (1) tone-and-light *both* off is represented as "$\bar{T}\bar{L}$," (2) tone is represented as "tone-on and light-off" ($T\bar{L}$), 3) light is represented as "light-on and tone-off" ($L\bar{T}$), and 4) tone-and-light *both* on is "TL". (To simplify notation here, the "+" symbol is not inserted between "T" and "L".)

In a multi-component schedule comprised of $\bar{T}\bar{L}$, $T\bar{L}$, and $L\bar{T}$ components: 1) the subject is assumed to be sampling *both* modalities, and 2) behavior is a simple *resultant*, taking sign into account, of the discriminative-response (S-R) and incentive-motivational (S-S^r) properties established to *each* sampled composite-element. Therefore, properties established to $\bar{T}\bar{L}$ contribute to control exerted by tone ($T\bar{L}$) and light ($L\bar{T}$) when $\bar{L}$ and $\bar{T}$ elements, respectively, are sampled. [4]

Table 17.4 presents this composite representation for training and stimulus-compounding-test conditions of Groups A, B, and C of Figure 17.4, the instrumentally-derived appetitive incentive-motivational function. Equalities are generated to $T\bar{L}$ and $L\bar{T}$ over the three schedules in Table 17.4's "Training" section by applying the "composite-element sampling" and "combination" assumptions described above. This can be illustrated with the following surprisingly simple and straightforward translations where ↑ is assigned the value 1, ↓ is assigned the value −1, and = is assigned the value 0. Applying these translations yields comparable outcomes (zero) for $T\bar{L}$ and $L\bar{T}$ for Group A, B, and C's training conditions—ergo, comparable baseline behavior in "tone" and in "light" S^Ds.

These predictions of equal responding to the baseline-training composite stimuli were achieved with a post hoc application of the assumptions. They can be tested predicatively through recombination of the elements. The stimulus-compounding test accomplishes this because in TL the response and incentive properties acquired by $\bar{L}$ and $\bar{T}$ are not contributing to the "mix", as they are in $T\bar{L}$-and-$L\bar{T}$ composites. During TL, only the T and L elements can be sampled. Table 17.4's "Compounding-Test" column presents each group's response-and-incentive properties established to TL elements by the respective training contingencies. Within this schematic representation, an application of the attentional and combinational dynamics described above produce several clear, empirically-supported ordinal predictions:

Table 17.4 Composite representation of training and test conditions of Figure 17.4's S-R and S-S^r properties to each composite element (symbol translations in Table 17.1)

	Training					Compounding Test		Results
	Tone		Light		$\overline{TL}$	Tone + Light		TL:T/L_{av}
Group A	VI Food		VI **Food**		EXT			
Composite	T	$\overline{L}$	L	$\overline{T}$		T	L	
S-R	↑	↓	↑	↓	No Food	↑	↑	3:1
S-S^r	↑	↓	↑	↓		↑	↑	
Group B	VI Food		VI Food		DRO			
Composite	T	$\overline{L}$	L	$\overline{T}$		T	L	
S-R	↑	↓	↑	↓	Food	↑	↑	2:1
S-S^r	=	=	=	=		=	=	
Group C	Chain VI		Chain VI		DRO			
Composite	T	$\overline{L}$	L	$\overline{T}$		T	L	
S-R	↑	↓	↑	↓	Food	↑	↑	1:1
S-S^r	↓	↑	↓	↑		↓	↓	

1) After multiple VI EXT training (Group A), with four ↑ (resultant = 4), TL should control more responding than $T\overline{L}$ or $L\overline{T}$ which each contain two ↑ and two ↓ (resultant = 0).
2) After multiple VI-DRO training (Group B), with two ↑ and two = (resultant = 2), TL should control more responding than $T\overline{L}$ or $L\overline{T}$ which each contain one ↑, one ↓ and two = (resultant = 0).
3) With four ↑, TL in (1) should control greater response enhancement than TL in (2) which contains two ↑ and two =
4) After chained VI DRO training, TL, $T\overline{L}$, or $L\overline{T}$ should control roughly comparable response rates because each composite produces a 0 resultant generated by different combinations of two ↑ and two ↓.

In predicting these outcomes, the contribution of the discriminative-response and incentive-motivational properties established to these composites were treated equally in determining resultant behavior. Figure 17.4's instrumentally-derived appetitive incentive-motive function and the behavior represented by Figure 17.2's cumulative records support these predictions. The ***two-factor-combinational model of composite-stimulus control*** appears to handle both the training and test outcomes in "tone," "light," and TL here after training on *these* baselines. But, even in the context of these successful applications, as mentioned earlier, it is reasonable to assume that a particularly strong increase in one process might overpower a slight decrease in the other.

The author is not aware of another analysis that can handle this range of conditions and results. Moreover, a similar analysis can be successfully applied to the groups producing Figure 17.6's instrumentally-derived aversive incentive-motivational function and Figure 17.7's discriminative-response function. Thus, the combination model appears to apply over a rather wide range of response-discriminative and incentive-motivational values and manipulations. The breadth of situations this model handles, that span food and positive reinforcement, shock, and negative reinforcement as well as combinations of the two, plus its simplicity, is appealing and increases confidence in its validity.

Summary and Conclusion

On multi-component operant baselines, a discriminative stimulus (S^D) generally acquires two kinds of properties. The discriminative-response property results from the different contingencies operating in the diverse environmental conditions the organism encounters. It typically occasions an increase or decrease in response rate. In addition, the S^D becomes differentially associated with reinforcement. Through this embedded classical contingency the S^D also acquires incentive-motivational properties (to which factors such as reinforcer predictability, delay and schedule requirements, etc., would contribute). Because response-and-reinforcement rates usually co-vary, the contribution of each property to resulting stimulus control has often been neglected and challenging to study.

By systematically eliminating this co-variation, the research programs described in this chapter produced the ***instrumentally-derived*** incentive-motivational functions (Figures 17.4/17.6) and the discriminative-response function (Figure 17.7). From those functions, a two-process combinational stimulus-control model was induced (Table 17.3) that handled outcomes of more than 50 instrumental studies employing stimulus-compounding assays.[4] Translating the stimulus-compounding paradigm's "unitary" stimulus conditions (i.e., tone, light) to an ordinal dimension (i.e., the number of stimuli that are "on") extended the model to predicting peak shift after intra-dimensional-discrimination training. These predictions were highly successful with more than 70 stimulus-generalization studies.[3] Incorporating a "composite-stimulus-control" analysis provided a refined explanation for why groups that were indistinguishable with respect to their lever-pressing behavior during training can exhibit vastly different behavior during stimulus compounding, and vice-versa.

Table 17.3's upper-left and lower-right cells represent the co-varying response-discriminative/incentive-motive combinations most frequently encountered. The consistent, about 3:1 response enhancement when compounding stimuli with $S\text{-}R\uparrow, S\text{-}S^r\uparrow$ properties (whether the reinforcer is food, water, shock-avoidance, cocaine or heroin) suggests an important, central-motivational mechanism operating here. Unfortunately, such environmentally-induced "response enhancement" can produce self-injurious "loss of control." For example, presenting multiple stimuli, each occasioning drug-seeking, ***doubled*** cocaine- and heroin-infusions over the normal self-regulated levels. Conditions producing loss of control that tripled shock rate were also described. In both instances, the loss of control was lawful, and entirely predictable from the co-varying response-discriminative and incentive-motivational properties established to the ***environmental conditions*** confronting these subjects.

The operation of incentive-motivational processes in producing behavioral phenomena discussed in this chapter has often incorporated Konorski's (1967) appetitive-aversive-interaction theory of motivation. This theory based on "attractive" and "repelling" conditions is parsimonious and "psychological" because it treats the individual as a *hedonic comparator*. Creating hedonically negative conditions through food absence revealed that selective associations were based on positive and negative hedonic states, rather than specific events (e.g., food or shock)—elevating this biological-constraint-on-learning to a level where the organism is a hedonic comparator rather than just "hardwired." Applying Konorski's comparability assumption about inhibitors based on the same reinforcer class, it was discovered that a food-based inhibitor reduced cocaine seeking comparably to a cocaine-based inhibitor (Figure 17.12)—suggesting a drug-abuse treatment.

Starting out trying to tease apart the contributions of discriminative and incentive-motivational components of the two-factor learning model led the author through a number of interesting, challenging, and ultimately productive paths. They produced the instrumentally-derived incentive-motivational and discriminative- response functions for the first time—plus a combinational model of stimulus-control derived from these functions. Along the way, some principles of conditioning have appeared that seem to have wide generality and applications. The path eventually led to hypotheses relevant to 1) understanding, and even treating, drug abuse, and 2) self-destructive "loss of control" predictable from the discriminative and incentive-motivational properties established to the environmental conditions confronting the individual. Murray Sidman (1960) maintained that if one studies any behavioral phenomenon deeply enough, basic underlying mechanisms are discovered—mechanisms probably also responsible for other important phenomena that might not even directly resemble the original one. The research programs described herein have proved my mentor from afar correct.

Notes

1 Preparation of this chapter was supported by NIDA Award R01-DA008651. It is derived from Fulbright Lectures the author delivered at Pavlov Medical University (PMU) in St. Petersberg, Russia. At PMU he was affiliated with the Behavioral Pharmacology Laboratory directed by Professor Anton Bespalov who was a most stimulating colleague and generous, thoughtful host. It is solely the author's responsibility and does not necessarily represent official views of NIDA/NIH. The author appreciates the assistance of Leigh Panlilio, David Kearns, Björn Brembs, John Moore and Brendan Tunstall.

2 See Table 2 in Weiss (1978). Space limitations preclude presenting an updated table here. One is available from the author (sweiss@american.edu).

3 See Table 4 in Weiss (1978). Space limitations preclude presenting an updated table here. One is available from the author (sweiss@american.edu).

4 For additional composite-stimulus-control research and applications, see Weiss (1969, 1972, 1978), Weiss and Emurian (1970), Weiss and Schindler (1987), Tsai and Weiss (1977) and Weiss, Kearns, and Antoshina (2009).

References

American Psychiatric Association. (2007). *Diagnostic and statistical manual of mental disorders* (5th ed., text rev.). Washington, DC: American Psychiatric Association .

Anger, D. (1963). The role of temporal discriminations in the reinforcement of Sidman avoidance behavior. *Journal of the Experimental Analysis of Behavior, 6*, 477–506.

Badia, P., & Culbertson, S. (1972). The relative aversiveness of signaled versus unsignaled escapable and inescapable shock. *Journal of the Experimental Analysis of Behavior, 17*, 463–471.

Balleine, B. (2005). Neural bases of food-seeking: Affect, arousal, and reward in corticostriatolimbic circuits. *Physiology & Behavior, 86*, 717–730.

Bindra, D. (1969). The interrelated mechanisms of reinforcement and motivation, and the nature of their influence on response. In W. Arnold and D. Levine (Eds.), *Nebraska symposium on motivation*, Vol. 17 (pp. 1–33). Lincoln: University of Nebraska Press.

Bolles, R. (1970). The cue value of illumination change in anticipatory general activity. *Learning and Motivation, 1*, 177–185.

Brown, J. (1961). *The motivation of behavior.* New York: McGraw-Hill.

Delamater, A., & Holland, P. (2008). The influence of CS-US interval on several different indices of learning in appetitive conditioning. *Journal of Experimental Psychology: Animal Behavior Processes, 34*, 202–222.

Dickinson, A., & Balleine, B. (1994). Motivational control of goal directed action. *Animal Learning & Behavior, 22*, 1–18.

Dickinson, A., & Pearce, J. (1977). Inhibitory interactions between appetitive and aversive stimuli. *Psychological Bulletin, 84*, 690–711.

Duncan, B., & Fantino, E. (1972). The psychological distance to reward. *Journal of the Experimental Analysis of Behavior, 18*, 25–34.

Emurian, H., & Weiss, S. (1972). Compounding discriminative stimuli controlling free-operant avoidance. *Journal of the Experimental Analysis of Behavior, 17*, 249–256.

Ferster, C., & Skinner, B. (1957). *Schedules of reinforcement.* New York: Appleton.

Foree, D., & LoLordo, V. (1973). Attention in the pigeon: Differential effects of food-getting versus shock avoidance procedures. *Journal of Comparative and Physiological Psychology, 85*, 551–558.

Garcia, J., & Koelling, R. (1966). Relation of cue to consequence in avoidance learning. *Psychonomic Science, 4*, 123–124.

Gray, J. (1975). *Elements of two-process learning theory.* London: Academic Press.

Guttman, A. (1977). Positive contrast, negative induction, and inhibitory stimulus control in the rat. *Journal of the Experimental Analysis of Behavior, 27*, 219–233.

Guttman, N. (1965). Effects of discrimination formation on generalization measured from a positive-rate baseline. In D. Mostofsky (Ed.), *Stimulus generalization* (pp. 210–217). Stanford, CA: Stanford University Press.

Hanson, H. (1959). Effects of discrimination training on stimulus generalization. *Journal of Experimental Psychology, 58*, 321–334.

Hearst, E. (1968). Discrimination learning as the summation of excitation and inhibition. *Science, 162*, 1303–1306.

Herrnstein, R. (1964). Secondary reinforcement and the rate of primary reinforcement. *Journal of the Experimental Analysis of Behavior, 7*, 27–36.

Holmes, N., Marchand, A., & Coutureau, E. (2010). Pavlovian to instrumental transfer: A neurobehavioural perspective. *Neuroscience and Biobehavioral Reviews*, *34*, 1277–1295.

Holz, W., Azrin, N., & Ayllon, R. (1963). Elimination of behavior of mental patients by response-produced extinction. *Journal of the Experimental Analysis of Behavior*, *6*, 407–412.

Hull, C. (1952). *A behavior system*. New Haven,CT: Yale University Press.

Kearns, D., Weiss, S., Schindler, C., & Panlilio, L. (2005). Conditioned inhibition of cocaine self-administration. *Journal of Experimental Psychology: Animal Behavior Processes*, *31*, 247–253.

Killeen, P., & Sitomer, M. (2003). MPR. *Behavioral Processes*, *62*, 49–64.

Kimble, G. (1961). *Hilgard and Marquis' conditioning and learning*. New York: Appleton.

Konorski, J. (1967). *Integrative activity of the brain*. Chicago: University of Chicago Press.

Logan, F. (1960). *Incentive: How the conditions of reinforcement affect the performance of rats*. New Haven, CT: Yale University Press.

Logan, F., & Wagner, A. (1965) *Reward and punishment*. Boston: Allyn and Bacon.

LoLordo, V., McMillan, J., & Riley, A. (1974). The effects upon food reinforced key pecking and treadle pressing of auditory and visual signals for response independent food. *Learning and Motivation*, *5*, 24–41.

Lovibond, P. (1983). Facilitation of instrumental behavior by a Pavlovian appetitive conditioned stimulus. *Journal of Experimental Psychology: Animal Behavior Processes*, *9*, 225–247.

Lysle, D., & Fowler, H. (1985). Inhibition as a "slave" process: Deactivation of conditioned inhibition through extinction of conditioned excitation. *Journal of Experimental Psychology: Animal Behavior Processes*, *11*, 71–94.

Markou, A., Weiss, F., Gold, L., Caine, B., Schultiess, G., & Koob, G. (1993). Animal models of drug craving. *Psychopharacology*, *112*, 163–182.

Mowrer, O. (1947). On the dual nature of learning: A re-interpretation of "conditioning" and "problem solving." *Harvard Educational Review*, *17*, 102–148.

Mowrer, O. (1960). *Learning theory and behavior*. New York: Wiley.

Mowrer, O., & Lamoreaux, R. (1942). Avoidance conditioning and signal duration: A study of secondary motivation and reward. *Psychological Monography*, *54*(Whole No. 247), 1–34

Overmier, J., & Lawry, J. (1979). Pavlovian conditioning and the mediation of behavior. In G. Bower (Ed.), *The psychology of learning and motivation* (Vol. 13, pp. 1–55). New York: Academic.

Panlilio, L., Katz, J., Pickens, R., & Schindler, C. (2003). Variability of drug self-administrations in rats. *Psychopharmacology*, *167*, 9–19.

Panlilio, L., Weiss, S., & Schindler, C. (1996). Cocaine self-administration increased by compounding discriminative stimuli. *Psychopharmacology*, *125*, 202–208.

Panlilio, L., Weiss, S., & Schindler, C. (2000). Effects of compounding drug-related stimuli: Escalation of heroin self-administration. *Journal of Experimental Analysis of Behavior*, *73*, 211–224.

Parkes, S., & Balleine, B. (2013). Incentive memory: Evidence the basolateral amygdala encodes and the insular cortex retrieves outcome values to guide choice between goal-directed actions. *The Journal of Neuroscience*, *33*, 8753–8763.

Pavlov, I. (1927). *Conditioned reflexes*. New York: International Publishers.

Rescorla, R., & LoLordo, V. (1965). Pavlovian inhibition of avoidance behavior. *Journal of Comparative and Physiological Psychology*, *59*, 406–412.

Rescorla, R., & Solomon, R. (1967). Two-process learning theory: Relationship between Pavlovian conditioning and instrumental learning. *Psychological Review*, *74*, 151–182.

Rilling, M. (1977). Stimulus control and inhibitory processes. In W. Honig and J. Staddon (Eds.), *Handbook of operant behavior* (pp. 432–480). Englewood Cliffs, NJ: Prentice-Hall.

Robbins, S., Ehrman, R., Childress, A., & O'Brien, C. (1997). Relationships among physiological and self-report responses produced by cocaine-related cues. *Addictive Behaviour, 22*, 157–167.

Robinson, T., & Berridge, R. (1993). The neural basis of drug craving: An incentive-sensitization theory of addiction. *Brain Monograph, 84*, 180–195.

Schindler, C., & Weiss, S. (1982). The influence of positive and negative reinforcement on selective attention in the rat. *Learning and Motivation, 13*, 304–323.

Schwartz, B., & Gamzu, E. (1977). Pavlovian control of operant behavior: An analysis of autoshaping and its implications for operant conditioning. In W. K. Honig & J. E. R. Staddon (Eds.), *Handbook of operant behavior* (pp. 53–97). Englewood Cliffs, NJ: Prentice-Hall.

Shettleworth, S., & Nevin, J. (1965). Relative rate of response and relative magnitude of reinforcement in multiple schedules. *Journal of the Experimental Analysis of Behavior, 8*, 199–202.

Sidman, M. (1960). *Tactics of scientific research.* New York: Basic Books.

Sinha, R., & Li, C. (2007). Imaging stress-and-cue-induced drug and alcohol craving: association with relapse and clinical implications. *Drug and Alcohol Reviews, 26*, 25–31.

Spence, K. (1937). The differential response in animals to stimuli varying within a single dimension. *Psychological Review, 44*, 430–444.

Sughondhabirom, A., Jain, D., Gueorguieva, R., Coric, V., Berman, R., Lynch, W., Self, D., Jatlow, P., & Malison, R. (2005). A paradigm to investigate the self-regulation of cocaine administration in humans. *Psychopharmacology, 180*, 436–446.

Thorndike, E. (1898). *Animal intelligence: An experimental study of the association processes in animals. Psychological Review Monograph*, 2 (whole Vol. 8). New York: Columbia University Press.

Trapold, M., & Overmier, J. (1972). The second learning process in instrumental learning. In A. Black & W. Prokasy (Eds.), *Classical conditioning II. Current theory and research* (pp. 427–451). New York: Appleton.

Tsai, S., & Weiss, S. (1977). A further test of composite-stimulus control in additive summation. *Bulletin of the Psychonomic Society, 9*, 169–172.

Volkow, N., Wang, G., Telang, F., Fowler, J., Logan, J., Childress, A., Jayne, M., Ma, Y., & Wong, C. (2008). Dopamine increases in striatum do not elicit craving in cocaine abusers unless they are coupled with cocaine cues. *Neuroimage, 39*, 1266–1273.

Weisman, R., & Litner, J. (1969). The course of Pavlovian excitation and inhibition of fear in rats. *Journal of Comparative and Physiological Psychology, 69*, 667–672.

Weiss, S. (1964). The summation of response strengths instrumentally conditioned to stimuli in different sensory modalities. *Journal of Experimental Psychology, 68*, 151–155.

Weiss, S. (1969). Attentional processes along a composite stimulus continuum during free-operant summation. *Journal of Experimental Psychology, 82*, 22–27.

Weiss, S. (1971). Discrimination training and stimulus compounding: Consideration of non-reinforcement and response differentiation consequences of S^{Δ}. *Journal of the Experimental Analysis of Behavior, 15*, 387–402.

Weiss, S. (1972). Stimulus compounding in free-operant and classical conditioning: A review and analysis. *Psychological Bulletin, 78*, 189–208.

Weiss, S. (1976). Stimulus control of free-operant avoidance: The contribution of response-rate and incentive relations between multiple schedule components. *Learning and Motivation, 7*, 477–516.

Weiss, S. (1977). The isolation of stimulus-reinforcer associations established with multiple schedules. *Animal Learning & Behavior*, *5*, 421–429.

Weiss, S. (1978). Discriminated response and incentive processes in operant conditioning: A two-factor model of stimulus control. *Journal of the Experimental Analysis of Behavior*, *30*, 361–381.

Weiss, S., & Dacanay, R. (1982). Incentive processes and the peak shift. *Journal of the Experimental Analysis of Behavior*, *37*, 441–453.

Weiss, S., & Emurian, H. (1970). Stimulus control during the summation of conditioned suppression. *Journal of Experimental Psychology*, *85*, 204–209.

Weiss, S., Kearns, D., & Antoshina, M. (2009). Within-subject reversibility of the discriminative function in the composite-stimulus control of behavior. *Journal of the Experimental Analysis of Behavior*, *92*, 367–377.

Weiss, S., Kearns, D., Christensen, C., Huntsberry., Schindler, C., & Panlilio, L. (2007). Reduction of cocaine seeking by a food-based inhibitor in rats. *Experimental & Clinical Psychopharmacology*, *15*, 359–367.

Weiss, S., Kearns, D., Cohn, S., Schindler, C., & Panlilio, L. (2003). Stimulus control of drug self-administration. *Journal of the Experimental Analysis of Behavior*, *79*, 111–135.

Weiss, S., Panlilio, L., & Schindler, C. (1993). Selective associations produced solely with appetitive contingencies: The stimulus-reinforcer interaction revisited. *Journal of the Experimental Analysis of Behavior*, *59*, 309–322.

Weiss, S., & Schindler, C. (1987). The composite-stimulus analysis and the quantal nature of stimulus control: Response and incentive factors. *The Psychological Record*, *37*, 177–191.

Weiss, S., & Schindler, C. (1989). Integrating control generated by positive and negative reinforcement: Appetitive-aversive interactions. *Animal Learning & Behavior*, *17*, 433–446.

Weiss, S., Thomas, D., & Weissman, R. (1996). Combining operant-baseline-derived conditioned excitors and inhibitors from the same and different incentive class: An investigation of appetitive-aversive interactions. *The Quarterly Journal of Experimental Psychology*, *49B*, 357–381.

Weiss, S., & Van Ost, S. (1974). Response discriminative and reinforcement factors in stimulus control of performance on multiple and chained schedules of reinforcement. *Learning and Motivation*, *5*, 459–472.

Weiss, S., & Weissman, R. (1992). Generalization peak shift for operant and autoshaped keypecks. *Journal of the Experimental Analysis of Behavior*, *57*, 127–143.

Wise, R. (1996). Neurobiology of addiction. *Current Opinion in Neurobiology*, *6*, 243–251.

Wolf, M. (1963). Some effects of combined S^Ds. *Journal of the Experimental Analysis of Behavior*, *6*, 343–347.

Part IV

Applied Operant Conditioning

18

Modern Animal Training
A Transformative Technology

Karen Pryor and Kenneth Ramirez

The shortest path to intentional or deliberate operant behavior is the functionally appropriate use of a classically conditioned positive reinforcer, or event marker.
(Ogden Lindsley, n.d.)

Introduction

Animal training probably arose with the beginning of domestication of non-human species, currently thought to have occurred some 10,000 years ago (Diamond, 2002). Wherever humans exist, a tradition has evolved of specific methods and equipment for animal confinement and restraint, reinforcement, guidance, and aversive control, differing in accordance with the behavioral traits of each species (Krebs & Krebs, 2003). Conventional animal training has always been an artisanal craft or trade, based on traditional tools and methods, and augmented by apprenticeship, personal experience, and opinion. Modern training, in contrast, is based not on tradition and personal methods but on principles derived from three branches of science: behavior analysis, ethology, and neuroscience. Behavior analysis provides the principles of learning; ethology focuses on the innate behavior of animals. Careful observation can enable the trainer to interpret behavioral indications of internal affect and thus to modify training procedures to reduce stress and improve the rate learning. Neuroscience supplies the understanding of brain functions that explain underlying physical and chemical processes. Much aided by the Internet, the animal training community, worldwide, is in the process of evolving from methods-based traditional training to science-based modern training.

Zoologists, anthropologists, and historians differentiate between wild species, unmodified by human intervention, and domestic species, whose genome, appearance, and behavior have been modified by selective breeding (Coppinger & Coppinger,

The Wiley Blackwell Handbook of Operant and Classical Conditioning, First Edition.
Edited by Frances K. McSweeney and Eric S. Murphy.

2002; Diamond, 2002). Domestic cattle, for example, have reduced flight responses in comparison to, say, zebras, and thus can be herded without bolting or attacking. With modern training, however, all species become trainable, from killer whales to reptiles and insects (Pryor, 2009; Ramirez, 1999). Furthermore the behavioral skills one can select for are no longer limited to the conventional goals of obedience and compliance, but may include such natural components of animal behavior as initiative, exploration, and social interaction, as well as species-specific social behavior and signaling.

The historic difference between conventional training and modern training is that the first is based on methods, while the second is based on deliberate use of the underlying principles that govern behavior acquisition. Conventional training focuses on the antecedent, with the trainer attempting to elicit or prevent a desired action, while the modern technology focuses on the postcedent, increasing the occurrence of a particular behavior by providing desirable consequences contingent on selected movements or events. One outcome is that the training affects the learner differently: Conventional training makes use of punishment, avoidance conditioning, and negative reinforcement; modern training relies on conditioned and primary positive reinforcers and seeks to minimize aversive experiences for the learner.

Conventional Animal Training

People have been training animals—dogs, cattle, sheep, and goats, various beasts of burden for at least 10,000 years and probably longer (Diamond, 2002). Our behavioral interactions with animals have traditionally consisted of a mix of beneficial and aversive events. We control animals by aversive stimuli that generate behavior (herding, driving, prodding, leading) by restraint or confinement (using barns, corrals, pens, cages, hobbles, or tethers), and by punishment (whips, collars, bits, and spurs). In spite of the level of aversives sometimes employed, being under human control presents distinct benefits to the animal: a steady supply of food and water, the presence of conspecifics and breeding opportunities, and, probably best of all, protection from predators. Furthermore, humans and their domestic animals can form bonds of trust and even affection which are beneficial to both.

Over the millennia, many species have accepted the bargain (yaks, camels, horses) while other species have not (zebras, musk oxen, giraffes). Domestication of species that proved susceptible was probably at least partially a result of selection. The cow that moved quietly into the kraal was kept for her milk and her calves; the cow that repeatedly lowered her horns and charged the herders was featured at the next feast. The outcome is a population of neotenized, comparatively docile individuals in which fight-or-flight reactions are suppressed or remain relatively undeveloped, as would be normal in infants or juveniles of the species (Coppinger & Coppinger, 2002). Some species have been brought so far down the domestic path that they are incapable of surviving without human care (most sheep, for example, which do not shed their wool and must be shorn by people). Animals whose behavior has proved difficult to modify genetically are classified as "wild," regarded as untamable, and kept, if at all, in zoos.

Most domestic animals are selectively bred to be easy to manage. Almost anyone, even a child, can help herd cows, keep a dog as a pet, or take care of a flock of chickens. Going beyond simple care and management however, as when training animals to perform specific tasks, has always been something of a specialty. Some individuals see themselves and are seen by others as having a "natural gift" for working with animals, just as some might have a "gift" for dance or for violin-making. Alexander the Great went down in history as a gifted horse trainer, realizing that an unmanageable steed, Bucephalus, was panicked by the sight of its own shadow, and turning the horse to face the sun. In the U.S. in the 20th century circus trainer Gunther Gabel Williams was a famous innovator, for example training a giraffe to wear a halter, obey a lead rope, and walk in a circus parade.

Conventional training is an artisanal skill, a mix of accurate information, history, personal experience, and superstition. The tools, the methods, and the skills are transferred from expert to novice through instruction or apprenticeship, and honed by long practice and much repetition. Training methods and equipment differ for each species and each application. Horse trainers use the ancient tools of whip, bridle, harness, and spurs, oxen trainers the yoke, dog trainers the collar and leash. Methods and tools may also differ from one person to another. As with other artisanal trades, conventional animal trainers may regard some methods as "secret" or proprietary, keeping new ideas to themselves or within a private group or guild in order to reduce competition.

Many trainers are highly skilled, and few deliberately abuse animals or cause them random pain. Conventional training conforms to the laws of learning at least some of the time, or it would not work as well as it does. Almost all of the traditional equipment is punitive by design. Coercive training can be pretty rough on the animal; the more advanced the work, the higher the percentage of individuals that prove unable to meet the demands. And coercion definitely has its limits. Except for the domesticated species most mammals do not respond well to correction-based training. Cold-blooded species, such as reptiles, fish, and invertebrates, have traditionally been considered too limited in capabilities to be actually trained at all.

The Development of Modern Training

The principles of behavior analysis underlying modern training arose in the laboratories of B. F. Skinner, beginning in the 1930s. While Skinner was interested in potential applications and developed many himself, his primary focus was on the analysis of the underlying factors governing behavior acquisition. He refined our understanding of the difference between rewards (a class of events defined culturally) and what he named reinforcement (a class of events defined functionally). Did the behavior increase in frequency? Then it had been reinforced. Did it stay the same? Then reinforcement did not occur. He created a useful distinction between respondent conditioning, which may be involuntary, and what he named operant conditioning, the establishment of consciously learned and deliberately offered behavior. He recognized and defended the counterintuitive and often overlooked reality, underlying all of operant conditioning theory and practice, that it is not the antecedent but the postcedent event that governs the rise and persistence of new behavior. He studied and described a wide variety of schedules of reinforcement and their impact on the learning and maintenance of behavior. He developed the role of the *conditioned reinforcer* (a learned stimulus indicating that a reinforcer is coming), when presented during a specific movement, as having the additional function of indicating to the learner exactly which move triggered the coming benefit (Skinner's student Ogden Lindsley subsequently applied the term "event marker" to this function of a conditioned reinforcer).

Through this use of the conditioned reinforcer Skinner also discovered and described the procedure he called shaping. Conventional trainers over the centuries had relied on successive approximation, the technique of changing the environment in increments (for example literally "raising the bar" in the case of hurdles) to strengthen or extend a behavior. Through timing the click of the feeding mechanism with a pigeon's movements in pecking at a ball, Skinner discovered he could use a conditioned reinforcer as an event marker for incremental development of new behavior, without any other modification of the environment. He named this procedure shaping (Peterson, 2004). These scientific discoveries, and the positive-reinforcement-based applications that continue to arise from them, are the basis of modern training.

The Beginnings: Marine Mammals

The first broad-scale application of laboratory theories to animal training arose as a byproduct of bringing dolphins into captivity. An early public exhibit featuring marine mammals, Marine Studios, opened in St. Augustine, Florida, in 1938, with a single bottlenose dolphin (*Tursiops truncatus).* By the 1950s that exhibit, now renamed Marineland, featured a daily show of dolphins catching thrown fish and jumping to take fish from a person's hand. A second oceanarium, Marineland of the Pacific, opened in 1954 in California with more performing odontocetes, including dolphins, pilot whales (*Globicephala macrorhyncus)*, and, eventually, the first captive killer whales (*Orcinus orca*). The Miami Seaquarium and a chain of major oceanariums, all called Sea World, soon followed, along with other large and small marine mammal exhibits in many countries.

There are approximately 30 species of dolphins and small whales in the world's oceans. The coastal bottlenose dolphin was the easiest to collect, and was also unusually suitable for captive life. A highly opportunistic species, bottlenose dolphins could adapt to tank walls and gates and new sights and sounds. They also took with enthusiasm to finding ways to extract food from the trainers and their buckets of fish. Meanwhile physician John Lilly's *Man and Dolphin* and other books fired the public imagination with speculations about dolphin intelligence and possible language (Lilly, 1961).

Science-based training began to spread through the marine mammal-related community. In 1962, the U.S. Navy opened a research center in San Diego, initially studying dolphin sonar and hydrodynamics, but later developing procedures for training marine mammals to perform useful tasks in the open ocean. Two of B. F. Skinner's graduate students, Keller and Marian Breland, formed a company in Arkansas, Animal Behavior Enterprises, using operant conditioning to train birds and animals for television commercials and for military applications. Keller Breland served as consultant to the U.S. Navy's new dolphin research program. A Breland associate, Kent Burgess, became the first Sea World head trainer in 1963. In the same year

Kenneth S. Norris, a biologist and marine mammal specialist, and his associate Ronald Turner, a psychologist from Columbia University, brought operant conditioning principles to Sea Life Park and the related Oceanic Institute in Hawaii, where Karen Pryor was the first head trainer.

The International Marine Animal Trainers Association

As training of marine mammals became more popular through the growth and expansion of their exhibition in zoos, aquariums, and marine parks, the marine mammal trainers became more organized in their approach to using training technology. In 1971, the first meeting of marine mammal trainers from Navy labs and public facilities throughout North America took place in San Diego, California (Blanchard & Pepper, 1972). Over the next three years the group met annually and grew in size and scope, until 1973 when the group formalized and became the International Marine Animal Trainer's Association (IMATA) (Pepper, 1974). In 2012 IMATA held its 40th annual conference in Hong Kong and was recognized as a truly global organization, with members in more than 35 countries (IMATA, 2012).

IMATA focuses on the science of operant conditioning with an emphasis on optimal animal care and the use of positive reinforcement (IMATA, 2012). Through their conferences, website, and various publications, IMATA became one of the most influential organizations in spreading the technology to many countries outside of the United States. It was one of the first widespread examples of sharing of training techniques in the exotic animal world. Their members, and their many member organizations, also created many systems for teaching training and standardized many techniques that became commonplace in the marine mammal training community (Ramirez, 2012a).

IMATA has always focused on marine mammal training and husbandry. Another organization, the Animal Behavior Management Alliance (ABMA), was formed in 1990 to promote animal welfare and positive reinforcement training primarily in the zoological community, across all vertebrate species. Like IMATA, ABMA has become an important organization in promoting and spreading the science of operant conditioning throughout the zoological world (ABMA, 2012).

Meanwhile IMATA, as the first organization for modern trainers, produced, documented, and described in IMATA publications many technical advances which have become standard practice in modern training. Some examples are:

Husbandry Training IMATA members pioneered the use of operant training to teach animals to participate in their own medical care. The training of cooperative husbandry behaviors allowed voluntary blood sampling for regular health screenings, positioning for ultrasound exams and radiographs through the cage bars, and teaching animals to allow the insertion of endoscopes to examine stomach contents and perform various medical procedures (Ramirez, 1999).

Reinforcement Variety IMATA trainers with scientific backgrounds developed procedures and protocols for utilizing different types of reinforcers and reinforcement schedules. Watching a whale show at Sea World, for example, you may witness behaviors being reinforced with a whistle (the conditioned or secondary reinforcer) followed by the primary reinforcer of a fish, or followed by pats, tongue rubs, back or belly scratching, novel behavior such as jumping or waving on the part of the trainer, or a cue[1] for subsequent behavior. This variety and unpredictability of reinforcing events introduces novelty and maintains attention in the animals and trainers both. IMATA members also drafted explanations to assist less technically experienced trainers in understanding how to use a variety of schedules and reinforcers effectively (Ramirez, 1999).

Least Reinforcing Scenario IMATA members developed and published descriptions of a tool referred to as an LRS (Least Reinforcing Scenario). The LRS constitutes a reliable and safe method for dealing with animal errors, such as performing some unwanted behavior, or failing to respond to a cue. The procedure consists of continuing in what you were doing when the error occurred, until the animal gives you attention; then signaling for a simple and highly probable behavior, reinforcing that, and then re-introducing whatever cue was being disregarded or disobeyed previously. The LRS constitutes a relatively positive way to deal with incorrect responses from animals without falling back on the use of aversives or accidentally putting an animal into an extinction curve, both of which can be risky for the trainer when working with volatile learners such as killer whales (Scarpuzz et al., 1991, 1999).

Spread of IMATA Trainers to Other Environments The complexity of the training and the variety of species being trained in marine mammal exhibits produced many skilled IMATA trainers who began to move into other areas such as the domestic animal and zoological communities. The Association of Zoos and Aquariums (AZA) recognized the advances that were taking place in the marine mammal world and invited IMATA to make a presentation to their membership in 1989 (Pearson & Sullivan, 1989). This led to several key developments in the zoo world in the next two decades, including:

Protected Contact Protected contact management systems were developed by AZA and IMATA members to facilitate working with large and potentially dangerous animals safely and positively. For example, elephants, traditionally trained with physical restraints, compulsion, and pain-inducing metal hooks and prods, can be trained instead through the cage bars, using positive reinforcement and operant conditioning. With humans safely on one side of the barricade and animals safely on the other, elephants, tigers, great apes, and other animals learn to present body parts voluntarily, at or through the cage bars, for physical and medical care that was previously possible only through chemical or physical immobilization by means of dart guns or squeeze cages. By 2013 most American zoos had adopted protected contact and positive reinforcement techniques for husbandry care of many species. These techniques have been expanded and documented and are in widespread use across the world (Desmond & Laule, 1991; Priest et al., 1998; Belting et al., 1998; Ramirez, 2012b).

Enrichment Animals in confinement suffer from lack of stimulation leading to increased stress, stereotypy or repetitive movement, and self-injurious behavior such as feather-pulling or compulsive licking. Confinement-related stress can affect animals in zoos, kennels, stables, and laboratories (and humans in hospitals and prisons). The concept of providing environmental enrichment as an important element in a captive animal's wellbeing was first proposed by Hal Markowitz in the 1970s (Markowitz, 1981). The American Zoo and Aquarium Association (AZA) has mandated that its members implement enrichment programs for certain species such as primates and incorporate enrichment into a comprehensive behavioral management program (AZA, 2012; Bloomsmith, 1995).

All vertebrate species, including mice, rats, birds, reptiles, and fish, can benefit from an environment that provides interest and stimulation. Enrichment may include environmental additions such as toys, food-dispensing puzzles and games, nesting materials, wood to chew, branches to nibble on or drag around, new companions, or novel sights, smells, and sounds. Positive-reinforcement-based training, in which the animal has an opportunity to use its brain as well as its body, is a high-value enrichment experience in itself, reducing fear and stress, facilitating moving animals from place to place, and enabling the provision of good medical care. Modern training and environmental enrichment are also gradually bringing about changes in the world of laboratory animals. Improved laboratory animal well-being is not solely a moral issue; calm and stress-free animals can also provide more accurate research results.

A defining characteristic of any new technology is that it enables ordinary people, without extensive training, to accomplish things which were once the province of a few brilliant and rare individuals; or even things that were previously entirely impossible. In modern zoos, keepers using conditioned reinforcers teach elderly, hypertensive gorillas to calmly extend an arm through the bars for blood pressure testing and blood draws. Crocodiles follow targets from one enclosure to another on pool cleaning day. Hyenas lean on the bars and present the throat for blood draws from the jugular vein; and tiny marmosets, individually and on cue, jump on the scales to be weighed, a vital clue to general health. When caregivers are perceived as resources or even allies rather than as potential predators, fear and stress levels drop dramatically. One outcome is that some endangered or threatened species of animals and birds are more apt to reproduce successfully in captivity, contributing to conservation efforts worldwide (Mark, 2007; Maple, 2007).

Domestic Animals and the General Public

For nearly 30 years, from the early 1960s to 1992, these developments within the zoo and oceanarium communities made very little impression on the outside world. Behavior analysts, focusing on verbal instruction for humans, had moved away from the animal laboratory and its key tools of conditioned reinforcers and shaping. While many people were exposed to the training through seeing marine mammals perform in public exhibits, few made the mental leap to seeing how the same training might apply to their own pets, much less to themselves and other humans.

Punishment-Free Dog Training

In 1984 Karen Pryor authored a book, written with parents in mind, on applying operant conditioning and punishment-free teaching and training to behavioral events in one's own daily life. The publishers, Simon & Schuster, focusing on the absence of punishment in the new approach, titled the work *Don't Shoot the Dog!* (Pryor, 1984, 1999). As a result, while parents avoided the book, many dog trainers discovered the new approach and began trying it out. The technology spread among dog trainers by word of mouth, seminars, and the Internet. Dog trainers use whistles as commands, especially with hunting dogs; they did not want to use the dolphin trainer's whistle as a conditioned reinforcer. In an article in *Scientific American*, B. F. Skinner first suggested that a toy noisemaker called a clicker or cricket would make a good conditioned reinforcer for dogs (Skinner, 1951). These toys, small noisemakers containing a strip of spring steel which makes a click-click sound when bent and released, were available as novelty items. At a 1992 meeting of the Association for Behavior Analysis and at a subsequent two-day seminar for dog trainers, Pryor and several trainer colleagues gave away clickers imprinted with contact information. A police dog trainer, Kathleen Weaver, subsequently initiated an Internet dog training discussion list, click-l, focusing on the new training, and the technology acquired a name: clicker training. Horse trainer Alexandra Kurland and others began publishing and teaching clicker training procedures for horses, and other authors followed with publications and videos demonstrating clicker training for dogs, cats and other pets (Kurland, 1999; Pryor, 2001; Orr & Lewin, 2006).

It used to be said of conventional dog trainers that one thing you could be certain of is that no two trainers will ever agree about anything. That was true as long as the training was based on methods. After all, anyone can say "My method is better than yours." However the spread of clicker training in the dog world put an end to that joke. Conventional trainers argue about methods. Modern trainers share their experience and understanding based on the underlying principles.

The sharing of principles-based applications was facilitated by the 2003 launching of ClickerExpo, a teaching conference for the general public. Hosted by Karen Pryor Clicker Training (KPCT, www.clickertraining.com) a company founded by Pryor, the program was held in two (initially three) different U.S. cities yearly. Just as IMATA had created an annual forum for marine mammal trainers, ClickerExpo accomplished the same goal for dog trainers, providing consensus on the principles and a chance to keep pace with technological advances from year to year. An additional division of KPCT, Karen Pryor Academy, (www.karenpryoracademy.com), produces online instruction programs and associated workshops, bringing the technology to an international audience.

Crossing Over: Guide Dogs for the Blind

Newcomers to animal training can often get started with the modern training technology quickly and easily, partly because one's efforts, from the very start, are apt to be reinforced by success. It is a different matter for the conventional trainer, who may have years of experience and success with correction-based methods, making it more difficult to cross over to modern training. The advent of new technology can be disruptive to those using existing methods, provoking argument. Clicker trainers can find themselves caught in confrontation with a traditional trainer, or even a traditionalist who may not be a dog trainer at all, but one's veterinarian, family member, or simply a fan of some conventional trainer on television.

The change can be accomplished, however, and when it happens, it is permanent. Guide Dogs for the Blind (GDB), founded in 1942, is one of the largest and most successful guide-dog training organizations in the world, placing some 300 guide dogs a year. Based in San Rafael, California with a second campus in Oregon, GDB maintains a cadre of about 75 full-time trainers, working under strict and carefully designed protocols.

The training is not counted as successful until a dog has been through the program, passed its performance tests, been matched with a client, and has remained with that client for six months. From the founding until 1999 the training was traditional, using compulsion and physical correction along with verbal praise. Success rates ranged from 40% to 53% annually (not counting dogs that dropped out for health reasons). In the 1999–2000 season food rewards[2] were introduced, to supplement praise. Success rates jumped to 63%. Research director Michele Pouliot began introducing clicker training, including the use of the conditioned reinforcer as an event marker, in 2000. Clicker training was established as the standard training method in 2004. The success rate for dogs in the 2004 year class was 73%.

Through 2011 the success rates ranged between 65% and 75% annually, with the highest year's rate being 86%, a remarkable improvement in the organization's return on investment. Furthermore, modern training principles have been incorporated into the teaching program for blind clients, resulting in a shorter training schedule, fewer dropouts, and an increase in successful matches with the dogs.

These changes were a product of careful and respectful procedures for enabling the existing trainers to cross over to the new technology. GDB now exports their "crossover" training protocols to other guide-dog organizations through lectures, seminars, and an on-campus intensive training program. A potential exists for similar processes in any area where convention and tradition conflict with modern behavioral technology, including school teaching, sports coaching, and training of medical personnel.

Tools and Procedures

The following discussion of tools and procedures is not intended to provide the reader with a comprehensive training manual; descriptions of specific applications and procedures are available elsewhere (see Recommended Reading). Our intention, rather, is to give an overview of the technology, to point out some of the incompatibilities between modern training and conventional training, and to clarify some of the science that underlies the technology.

Tools: Reinforcement

Reinforcement refers to strengthening behavior by providing positive consequences (in this text the term reinforcement always refers to positive reinforcement unless negative reinforcement, the removal of an aversive stimulus, is specifically mentioned).

In behavior analysis literature the word "reinforce*ment*" refers to the process; the word reinforc*er* refers to the particular consequence itself. Reinforcers are identified not by their nature but by their outcome: a reinforcer strengthens the likelihood that a given behavior will occur more frequently in the future. Informally animal trainers define a reinforcer as anything the learner will work to get. What is reinforcing to one organism may not be reinforcing to another. "Rain is aversive to cats, reinforcing to ducks, and apparently a matter of indifference to cows" (Pryor, 1999). If the behavior you are paying for does not actually increase, your choice of consequences was not reinforcing (or not sufficiently reinforcing).

Common reinforcers for animals include food, water, toys, freedom, companionship, tactile stimulation (such as scratching or petting), warmth, companionship, and favored activities such as play, chasing, exploration and sex. Novelty is intriguing to some animals and may be used as a reinforcer.

Selecting Reinforcers The practical trainer keeps a variety of reinforcers in mind and on hand, ranging from low-value to high-value. One might reserve high-value treats for learning new behavior, for especially challenging work, or for working in stressful situations. One might end a session with an unusually high-value reinforcer, such as a new toy or a game of tug-o-war, to mitigate the disappointment that the session is over. One might rotate or vary reinforcers to raise the overall level of the reinforcing nature of the training experience itself.

Any individual may satiate or may lose interest in a specific reinforcer. Psitticines (birds of the parrot family) are eclectic feeders and may tire rapidly of previously high-value treats. A learner may prefer one reinforcer to another or may find very aversive something you intended to be pleasant (hugging a strange dog or petting it on the top of the head are notorious examples). Preferences may also change rapidly in young children. A simple precaution is to run a small preference test from time to time, presenting a selection of potential reinforcers and seeing which is currently being selected first.

Transferring and Fading Reinforcers Once a behavior has been learned, reinforcement of each occurrence is no longer necessary. In fact well-established behavior can be maintained more effectively by a random schedule of reinforcement than by continuous reinforcement. Inadvertent intermittent reinforcement is at the root of many problem behaviors in household pets. For example finding something delicious to steal off the kitchen counter may occur only sporadically, but that occasional reinforcer powerfully maintains the unwanted canine behavior called "counter surfing."

Environmental reinforcers may replace training reinforcers once a behavior has been learned. A dog's behavior of sitting quietly at the door, initially trained with clicks and treats, is now reinforced by opening the door and letting the dog go out. Behavior may be blended into other behaviors; permitting physical manipulation may become just one part of cooperating in veterinary procedures, with reinforcement provided only intermittently. Finally, behavior may be brought under stimulus control; the cue to perform the behavior becomes reinforcing in itself (see "Cues," this chapter).

Tools: The Conditioned Reinforcer or Marker

The conditioned reinforcer is perhaps the most essential and powerful tool in modern training. It might seem as if delivering food is a more powerful reinforcer than delivering a conditioned reinforcer first; but there is an important difference in the learning that results. The primary reinforcer (food, for example) paints with a broad brush: This circumstance is beneficial; this is a nice place; you (the giver) are a nice person (Holland, 2008). The learner becomes passive, awaiting the next pleasant event. In contrast, the secondary or conditioned reinforcer announces an available benefit, and at the same time identifies a specific action of the learner that will lead to that benefit. The learner becomes active, focused, and eager to try that behavior again. Modern animal training depends on the frequent use of a conditioned reinforcer, not to replace a primary reinforcer, as it was originally used in the laboratory, but both to signal the imminent arrival of a primary reinforcer and to identify the precise movement that caused that event.

Conditioned reinforcers are widespread in the natural environment. The stimulus might be chemical, visual, acoustic, or tactile; but if it indicates the availability of a benefit, and occurs simultaneously with a particular action, it will reinforce that action. Animals easily learn to engage in behavior that led to reinforcement the last time they heard that particular sound or smelled that special scent. Conditioned reinforcers show predators good ways to hunt and help foragers to find preferred foods. Falconers report that young red-tail hawks often fail in early hunting attempts. Once they successfully catch their first squirrel or pheasant, they will preferentially search for clues to that type of prey from then on.

Conditioned punishers also occur in nature, particularly in agonistic behavior between conspecifics (a warning growl, followed if necessary by a bite). Scent, sound, or movement indicating a predator in the neighborhood may also constitute conditioned punishers. Among conventional dog trainers the shouted word "No" or some other specific sound is often used as a conditioned punisher for an erroneous or undesirable behavior, to be followed immediately by physical punishment if the behavior does not change. Pet owners frequently repeat the verbal reprimand without associating it with an actual aversive, thereby in effect training the animal to ignore being scolded.

Conditioned punishers, which have been widely studied by neuroscientists, are processed through the amygdala, a primitive part of the brain, and produce specific results: rapid acquisition, sometimes in a single event; long retention; and production of an emotion: fear (Pryor, 2009, pp. 173–176; Ledoux, J. 1998). Conditioned reinforcers, once established, follow a similar path (although through a different part of the amygdala) and show the same characteristics: rapid acquisition, long, even permanent, retention, and production of an emotion: a sort of positive excitement that humans describe as elation or joy (Pryor, 2009, pp. 184–186; Panksepp, 2004).

Choosing a Conditioned Reinforcer to Use as an Event Marker A marker stimulus should be:

- easily delivered;
- easily perceived by both trainer and learner;
- brief (in order to isolate particular details of movement);
- obvious, standing out from the environment;
- novel;
- neutral.

Marker stimuli popular with animal trainers include clickers, whistles of all sorts, bells, vibration, and a blink or flash of light (especially useful for deaf animals, fish, and birds at a distance). Arbitrary stimuli are preferable to the human voice for this particular purpose. A short, sharp word can fulfill the first three requirements listed above; but the spoken word certainly is not novel. A word does not stand out clearly from the stream of words we produce daily. And spoken words are encumbered with a freight of other associations which may be far from neutral. Spoken words (praise, for example) can sometimes be used to maintain already established behavior. However even the most scrupulous use of a word as a marker (never using the word in casual conversation for example) increases the trials needed for behavior acquisition by roughly 50% (Wood, 2006).

Establishing the Marker Establishing a conditioned reinforcer requires associating the stimulus with a primary reinforcer through classical conditioning. Laboratory instructions for establishing a conditioned reinforcer sometimes recommend disassociating the stimulus from any accidental environmental stimulus or behavioral event by randomizing all aspects of the pairing (other than the arrival of the primary reinforcer) over a prescribed series of 200 or more trials.

In fact it is counterproductive to introduce a new learner to the conditioned reinforcer by extensive classical conditioning. One needs the classical connection of course; that is what gives the marker its value. However the crucial event for behavioral acquisition is the shift from respondent to operant conditioning, as the animal learns that its own behavior triggered the conditioned reinforcer. This connection may be made gradually, during several training sessions, or it can happen quite suddenly, sometimes in the first two or three clicks. The shift from respondent to operant learning is often accompanied by evidence of excitement such as barking or running around in circles (trainers call this "the lightbulb moment"). The laboratory practice of extended non-contingent pairing delays the forming of an association between behavior and marker, and in fact stands in its way, as the animal has already learned to ignore everything else that is happening when the stimulus arrives, including its own behavior.

Continuity Maintaining continuity within a training session is an important element of success. A training session is defined as a short period of dedicated time (perhaps no more than a few minutes) consisting entirely of a series of opportunities to earn reinforcers. A training session, once entered into, should be continuous. Providing continuous opportunities for reinforcement keeps the learner's attention and shortens the time needed for behavior acquisition. One might switch from one behavior to another, or one location to another, but with no gaps in the interaction. If a pause occurs, if for example the trainer removes attention from the learner to answer the phone or talk to a visitor, or even just to take notes or reload the food supply bag, the opportunity for reinforcement vanishes.

This removal of opportunity constitutes negative punishment. The delay is aversive to the learner, and especially so to naïve individuals who are just learning the system (or to any learner if delays become chronic). Displacement behaviors such as sniffing, yawning, scratching, or turning away indicate the resulting frustration. Repeated experiences may lead to increased latencies, extinction of the behavior currently being reinforced, or extinction of the attending response altogether: the learner leaves when the trainer approaches. "I don't know why, but this animal just won't work for me!" Of course correcting or punishing errors, rather than just ignoring them, also halts the session momentarily, and endangers cooperation and interest even more. (These responses are just as likely to occur in human learners, whether children or adults, as in animal subjects).

Conventional trainers often utilize prolonged repetition, with correction of errors throughout, in attempting to produce error-free performance. While repetition is useful in shaping extended duration of a behavior or in building physical strength and endurance, a principles-based trainer views repeated errors simply as information that the learner has not yet acquired some particular criterion. Rather than punishing errors, the modern trainer creates and trains additional criteria for the behavior needing improvement.

Tools: Shaping

Shaping starts by marking some already occurring behavior. Since behavior is always variable, one can then begin selectively marking variations in a desired direction toward the end goal. The behavior is marked during the movement, not on completion. Thus one is reinforcing a vector: the movement, and the direction of the movement. With each reinforced presentation of the movement, the behavior will tend to increase in both strength and duration. In selective reinforcement procedures the trainer is careful to raise criteria in small enough steps so that the learner has at least a 50% likelihood of earning reinforcement each time it tries.

The Shaping Plan: Breaking Behavior into Smaller Units Shaping begins with a behavioral goal: "I want this raccoon to go into a shipping crate voluntarily and stay there while I close the door." Breaking the goal down into small steps is an essential element of shaping. This task is composed of several behaviors: Go to the crate; go in the crate; come out of the crate; wait in the crate while the door is moved (instead of bolting through the opening). Each of those steps can also be broken down into many smaller steps: look at the crate, take one step towards the crate, and so on. Some steps must precede others in the goal performance: that is, shaping "staying in the crate" must be preceded by going in and out of the crate voluntarily. However, elements can be trained separately and then rearranged. For example "waiting quietly" can be shaped and brought under stimulus control as a separate unit, perhaps by training "sit on a box" or "lie on a mat", which can then be transferred to "wait in a crate."

Shaping starts at a point of success, reinforcing something the learner is already doing quite frequently, such as turning the head or moving a foot. When the movement is operant, that is, when the animal is offering it briskly and repeatedly, the trainer can raise criteria, selectively reinforcing turning the head further, or taking an actual step. As the behavior strengthens, criteria can be shifted, perhaps to taking several steps, or to doing the same thing but for a longer time. For example, the duration of the wait for the crate door to be closed (and opened again) can be shaped from, say, a portion of a second to a minute or more by withholding the click for a series of varying but gradually lengthening intervals. The more behaviors are shaped, the more sophisticated the animal (and trainer) become about guessing what to try next; what once seemed very time-consuming can become an almost magically quick process, shaping a new behavior in just a few clicks.

Any behavior an animal is physically capable of, including behaviors that might seem frightening or uncomfortable, can be shaped with positive reinforcement. This seems contrary to common sense, and is a common objection. For example, how can you possibly train an animal to endure, say, an injection or a blood draw for the small reward of a click and a food treat when the procedure itself is painful? It seems to the conventional trainer as if physical restraint is the only possibility in this circumstance.

If you walked up to an unprepared animal and stuck a needle in it the animal would almost certainly object. Instead, whether at the vet clinic with a dog or in the zoo with a tiger, trainers can develop voluntary cooperation with invasive medical procedures. The standard procedure utilizes a combination of shaping and successive approximation. For example, for immunizations and blood draws, the trainer might first shape the behaviors, "Come here, lie down, and hold still until clicked." Then, on the examining table (dog) or through the cage bars (tiger) the trainer sequentially introduces a new set of stimuli, clicking and rewarding several times at each level as criteria are met. The shaping plan might look like this:

- Step 1: Touch, press, and finally poke the injection site with a finger.
- Step 2: Repeat with a pencil point.
- Step 3: Repeat with an empty syringe.
- Step 4: Introduce and build tolerance for wiping the injection site with disinfectant.
- Step 5: Disinfect the site and introduce a syringe with a very fine needle, actually penetrating the skin.
- Step 6: Repeat step 5 using a larger needle and perhaps injecting a small amount of sterile saline solution.
- Step 7: Introduce the actual medical procedure. Continue to reinforce both practice and actual treatments in subsequent husbandry training sessions.

Shaping makes tolerating the various steps a predictable and rewarding experience, resulting in calm and cooperative acceptance of medical care, even when pain is unavoidable. Killer whales are vulnerable to tooth decay. Using shaping procedures, Sea World trainers and veterinarians have established voluntary cooperation in killer whales for dental treatments, using injected local anesthetics, up to and including poolside root canal surgery.

A high rate of reinforcement makes executing the final shaped behavior a reinforcing event in itself. Shaping can therefore be a useful procedure in overcoming learned fear, even when the fear is extreme. Students at the University of North Texas selected a group of horses that had repeatedly been loaded onto horse trailers by force involving ropes and whips. As a result they learned to resist so violently (whirling, rearing, going over backwards, risking injury to themselves and to the handlers) that they could no longer be loaded or transported at all, and were just turned out to pasture. By shaping the behavior of going to a target and touching it with the nose, the experimenters were able to get all five horses to voluntarily and calmly walk onto any horse trailer, to reach their target inside (Ferguson & Rosales-Ruiz, 2001).

Extinction in Shaping Extinction of a behavior occurs when a previously well-established reinforcement contingency is discontinued. In shaping, as new criteria are gradually added, the previous criterion fades out while the new criterion is established. Technically one can say that the previous version of the behavior is extinguished; however the change is gradual enough that the rate of reinforcement remains continuously high. One characteristic or element of the behavior is modified, but at no point is the whole behavioral response put into extinction (Peterson, 2006).

Beginning trainers working with a new animal sometimes accidentally do put the whole behavior into extinction. This abrupt cessation of all reinforcement can be highly stress-inducing and may evoke strong states of affect, evidenced by aggressive displays and actions (dolphins may ram a swimmer or soak bystanders with a big splash) or, in any species, by complete withdrawal, retreating from the training location, hiding in a corner and refusing food. (For a video of extinction-induced distress in a fish see http://reachingtheanimalmind.com/chapter_04.html.)

We all experience extinction events and the concomitant emotional states in daily life. The Coke machine takes your money but fails to deliver a soda and you hit or kick the machine; or you are headed for an important job interview and quite unexpectedly your car will not start, triggering feelings of anger and even panic. A common response is to repeat the unreinforced behavior rapidly and vigorously; put more quarters in the machine and hit it harder; or pump the gas and turn the ignition switch over and over. This is called an extinction burst; it too is a state of high affect, sometimes, in humans, manifested by cursing.

Some psychology and education textbooks recommend a variation of the shaping procedure consisting of deliberately inducing abrupt extinction of an existing behavior in order to trigger an extinction burst from which new or more intense behaviors might be selected. Modern animal trainers prefer to avoid putting an animal (or a human) into extinction mode. The aversive nature of the experience taints the training situation and reduces cooperation and participation. The aggression that can be triggered in, say, elephants or killer whales, is undesirable in the animals and potentially dangerous for people; and the stressful nature of extinction events can be deleterious to the training relationship and to the learner's wellbeing.

Extinction procedures can be useful: One can sometimes eliminate undesirable behavior simply by removing the reinforcer that maintains it. However, in real-life situations removing the stimuli and reinforcers for a behavior may not always be feasible. The dog barks out the window at passersby; the barking is self-reinforcing and the passersby are not under your control. Modern trainers often get rid of undesirable behavior such as nuisance barking by management (close the window curtains) or by reinforcing some incompatible behavior such as shutting the mouth on cue.

Since all behavior is fluid, one can always shape new behaviors. The previous version of the behavior, rather than extinguishing, incrementally becomes the new version. Julie Skinner Vargas offers a thorough discussion of shaping behavior in people in the classroom and in everyday life in her book *Behavior Analysis for Effective Teaching* (Vargas, 2013).

Punishment Punishment suppresses behavior. The conventional "obedience" class in your neighborhood park or pet store is designed to do exactly that. Undesirable but normal dog behaviors such as jumping on people, running around, barking, and pulling on the leash, are reduced by creating a whole set of suppressions: sit, (don't move) down, (don't move) stay, (don't move) heel (only move next to me) and come (only move directly to me). The training usually involves the use of "correction" in the form of a pain-inducing yank on the choking chain collar. Seeing the behavior stop, however briefly, may reinforce the punishing behavior of the handler. The procedure is widespread and harmful. In the U.S. many elderly dogs cough and wheeze because of a partially collapsed trachea, due to years of pulls and yanks on leash and collar.

To the conventional trainer, correcting errors seems to make sense: Telling the learner when a behavior is right is useful, but telling the learner when a behavior is wrong doubles the information, does it not. Does that not speed things up? In fact even mild correction can interrupt forward progress in learning. Avoiding the temptation to correct errors or punish undesired behavior during behavior acquisition is a key element of modern training.

The experience of searching for reinforcement opportunities constitutes self-directed learning, the process by which animals explore their environment in nature. Correction-based training constitutes directed learning, in which the organism is told what to do. The punishment shifts the learner's focus from exploring positive opportunities, as it would in nature, to waiting to be ordered or shown what to do, as one might do in some areas of human society. The reinforcement-trained animal is a free agent, willingly interacting with the trainer. The avoidance-trained animal is a "good soldier," focused largely on staying out of trouble.

Does this mean that the modern trainer never controls unwanted behavior? Not at all. The first step is to limit unwanted behavior by managing the environment. Fences, kennels, cages, corrals, tethers, may or may not be seen as aversive by the animal, and they do not teach the animal any new behavior; but they serve to keep the animal safe and out of mischief until training can be undertaken to counteract some particular problem behavior. Behavior may also be temporarily interrupted by reprimand, for example, saying "No" to a pet that is eyeing the cheese and crackers on the coffee table. However, the modern trainer is aware that while reprimands may interrupt behavior in the present, they have no guarantee of affecting behavior in the future or when you are not around.

Tools: The Cue, A Control for Learned Behavior

Conventional training begins with the antecedent, a command: The trainer tells the animal what to do, then makes it happen, through physical pressure, until the animal learns to give the correct response to the command in order to avoid being forced into the move. Commands thus are covert threats: Do this, or else. Once the behavior has been learned, however, commands can become indicators of negative reinforcement, that is, they offer a chance for successful avoidance of pressure. Conventional trainers can be highly successful due to this effect; in fact almost all horses are trained by fading punishment down into negative reinforcement for correct behavior.

The cue, in contrast, indicates an opportunity for positive reinforcement. (The term "cue" is taken from the stimulus that tells an actor in the theater when to begin a particular behavior on stage.) The antecedent, or cue, is not introduced until the behavior is established. The cue then becomes a discriminative stimulus, specific to that behavior, intended to indicate that the behavior is now—and only now—available for reinforcement.

The cue, like the marker, should be brief, simple, consistent, novel (i.e. easily distinguished from other stimuli) and neutral until established. While words do not make good markers, consistent words do make good cues. However the need for brevity and consistency runs somewhat contrary to typical human verbalizing: "Come here, here boy, come over, attaboy, hey, come back, bad dog!" Animals and people quickly learn to tune out such mixed messages.

Creating Cues For a naïve learner, understanding cueing begins with assimilating a new concept: This behavior earns reinforcement only if a particular event (the cue) happened first. Marine mammal trainers in the 1960s learned a common laboratory procedure for establishing cues, consisting of presenting the cue just before the animal offers the operant behavior, such as jumping in the air, which it has previously learned to associate with reinforcement. Then, after several to many repetitions, one withholds the cue, allowing the next repetition of the behavior to go unreinforced. By alternating successful (cued) responses with unsuccessful (uncued and unreinforced) responses, gradually the animal will learn the contingency that one circumstance predicts reinforcement and the other predicts extinction.

Extinction does bring about learning, but the procedure is time-consuming and can be aversive. Unless one is very careful to moderate the ratio of deprivation vs. reinforcement, extinction can have undesirable side effects.

The modern training community has developed many ways to establish correct response on cue and absence of the response in the absence of the cue without utilizing extinction procedures. For example one might introduce a previously learned cue and behavior (perhaps touching a target, in which presentation of the target is the cue) and alternate between offering the learned pair and the new pair until the animal learns to wait to see which cue is coming next, before offering the appropriate response. One can then introduce a brief pause before offering either cue; the contingent behavior in order to receive information about the next reinforcement might be described as "wait for the cue." The animal is engaged in a process of finding out what works; it is a choice procedure, not solely an extinction-based procedure.

When an incorrect behavior is offered, or when the behavior is offered in the absence of the cue, the trainer withholds the marker, but keeps the opportunity open for reinforcement by then providing a new opportunity to respond correctly to one cue or another. When the learner has acquired several cues for several behaviors (three is usually sufficient), the animal will have learned that each cue identifies a specific behavior as being presently available for reinforcement. Once this contingency is established, subsequent cues for additional behaviors can be learned rapidly.

Cues are not "written in stone." Once learned, one can easily replace a verbal cue with a hand signal, or transfer touching a target to touching an object next to or beneath the target. Cues can be transferred from a trainer to something in the environment, or gradually faded so as to remain obvious to the animal while being imperceptible to a bystander.

The number of cues that can be established is relatively open-ended. Counting environmental cues such as the doorbell or car keys jingling in a coat pocket a dog in an active, attentive household may acquire 100 or more cues in normal life, without extensive training. Some dogs in research settings have learned many more.

Cueing Concepts Reinforcement-based training may be thought of as establishing the learning of a series of contingencies between cues, responses, and reinforcers, including:

- Click means treat.
- I (the learner) can make the click happen by doing a particular behavior.
- Many different behaviors can make clicks happen.
- If a click doesn't happen, try again.

The first four contingencies listed below constitute what behavior analysts define as "stimulus control," the criteria necessary for secure attachment of a single cue to a single behavior (Pryor, 1999).

- This cue only "works" for this one behavior.
- The behavior does not lead to reinforcement in the absence of the cue (that is, reinforcement from the trainer; the learner may freely exhibit the behavior on its own time).
- No other cue works for this one behavior.
- This cue does not work for any other behavior.

The next three apply to all cues:

- New behaviors have new cues.
- Cues may only be available briefly; respond quickly (i.e. develop short latencies).
- Cues can happen anywhere, any time. (This concept builds focus on the human cue giver as a continuing potential source of good news. The resulting attentiveness is often a highly reinforcing surprise to novice pet owners developing their first clicker-wise pet.)

Cues as Reinforcers Once learned, cues also become conditioned reinforcers. The cue for one behavior can be used to reinforce a preceding behavior, as well as serving as the discriminative stimulus for the next behavior. This powerful aspect of cues enables one to link many behaviors together without the need to mark and reinforce each specific act. It is one reason why, in clicker training household pets in daily life, the actual marking and treating is no longer necessary once behaviors have been shaped and given cues. The dog that used to dash out into the street any time the door opened has learned behaviors which are now chained together by cues. Putting on the leash cues the behavior of going to the door. The closed door cues the dog to sit and wait while door is opened. The owner's voice or movement cues the behavior of going through the open door, and the ultimate reinforcer is the pleasure of being outside. This sequence of behaviors constitutes a behavior chain, in which each cue reinforces the previous behavior. This process, perhaps replacing the previous behavior of bolting out the door at the first opportunity, also instills in the animal the useful skill of impulse control.

The Poisoned Cue Once a cue is established and generalized to new environments and circumstances, responses will usually be predictable. Repeated failure to respond, or failure to respond correctly, is never the learner's fault; it just tells you to look for the antecedent. Perhaps the behavior or the cue response is not fully established. Perhaps some physical or environmental change is interfering, or some aspect of the training has been overlooked.

Unfortunately in this circumstance the human tendency is to blame the learner. Why is this happening? The animal "should know this by now." The animal (or human) is "disobeying!" The conventional trainer then "corrects" or punishes the behavior. Because a cue is an opportunity for reinforcement, not a message about avoiding trouble, to issue a cue and then punish the erroneous results confounds the message. Now this cue might lead to a reinforcer *or* to a punisher. One can easily see (and replicate) the result in dogs, with their expressive faces: doubt, stress, anxiety, hesitation: what to do? A simple "sit" becomes a quandary.

The ambiguous cue, named a poisoned cue by Pryor (Pryor, 2002b) can be the cause of prolonged response changes. For example the command "Come!" can easily become a poisoned cue, producing evasive maneuvers instead of compliance. The "cure" for a poisoned cue is to re-shape the behavior and attach a completely different cue.

Advanced Cueing Concepts

By freeing the animal up to engage in self-directed learning, modern training sets the stage for rapid acquisition and generalization of new contingencies and associations. Each concept, once taught, gives the animal new skills for analyzing and responding to the environment, thus providing precursor skills for more advanced concepts (meanwhile, in developing new concepts, the trainer is learning new skills too).

Some cueing concepts that can be established by careful shaping include:

- Modifier cues (left/right; up/down; big/small; over/under/through).
- Compound cues or "sentences" (nose-small-object-touch vs. paw-large object-knock over).
- Context cues (usually environmental cues, such as a special location or type of equipment, indicating that a particular class of behaviors such as tracking is about to start).
- Adduction: combining two cues for known behaviors to produce a third, new behavior.

With adroit shaping of cue responses one can take the concepts an animal is capable of learning very far indeed. Here are some categories of advanced cue responses, all with practical real-world applications, that are difficult, sometimes impossible, to obtain by conventional, directed-learning methods, but quite manageable by modern training technology. The trainer and learner both need good precursor skills but rare or unusual talent is not required in either trainer or learner; the protocol will usually produce the intended results.

Match to Sample The behavior is "Find and indicate the object which resembles the sample." The sample is commonly a visible object or pattern or a scent. Separately trained elements include establishing an indicator behavior for the choice the animal has made, back chaining the final behavior, and escalating criteria from familiar to novel objects or scents. Practical applications range from to finding one's glasses or keys to police work, tracking, and search and rescue.

Mimicry The final behavior is "Replicate the operant behavior exhibited by that other animal." Many animals, including horses, dogs, cats, birds, and some fish, exhibit allelomimetic behavior or social mimicry, copying the behavior of conspecifics without special training (Godfrey, 1979; Scott & Fuller, 1965). Understanding the function of the marker increases this tendency by enabling social animals such as horses to identify and repeat behavior they see other conspecifics getting clicked for, such as lowering the head, or lifting a hoof. The mimicry training procedure allows this capacity to be brought under stimulus control and extended to complex and novel behaviors.

An initial training objective (requiring at least two trainers) is to transfer the cue for a known behavior from the existing cue to the sight of another animal, the model, executing that behavior. With proper screening and monitoring for accidental cueing effects, cues are transferred for several behaviors known to both the model and the learner, to establish the concept. One then builds a context cue signaling "Mimic." When the context cue is established, and the mimic animal is fluent in reproducing whatever familiar behavior the model animal performs, the model animal is cued to present a behavior the mimic animal has not been trained to perform on cue. One reinforces the attempt to repeat the behavior, even if the first efforts are not fully accurate. The behavior is then refined, if necessary, through practice and shaping. Practical applications include short-cutting the time required to train challenging behavioral skills.

Preemptive Cues ("Intelligent Disobedience") Dogs for blind handlers must be taught to recognize hazards that the blind person is not aware of. The behavior to be learned is to halt at the hazard even if commanded to go forward. In conventional training this skill, called intelligent disobedience, is often taught by setting up an obstacle, and then ordering the dog forward until the handler pretends to blunder into the obstacle. The handler then cries out and mimes great fear and distress. The dog learns to pause at obstacles, regardless of orders to go forward, until the handler has investigated the problem manually. Unfortunately this aversive procedure may also produce a dog that decides to avoid the whole area, and can no longer be persuaded to go onto footbridges, or train platforms, or wherever the first exercise took place. Developing reliable "disobedience" by conventional methods may require months of repetition.

Trainers at Guide Dogs for the Blind (GDB) teach intelligent disobedience through establishing a new concept: Environmental cues can pre-empt the trainer's cues. Here is one method: two steel barrels are set on the sidewalk with a narrow gap between them. The trainer, playing the blind person, and the dog, in its guide-dog harness, proceed toward the gap. At the barrels the dog, noticing the gap that is scarcely wide enough for the dog alone, will hesitate. The handler clicks that instant of hesitation, and treats. After a few repetitions the "approach obstacle and pause" behavior is established. Now, when the dog pauses, the handler introduces a command to go forward, and clicks while the dog is still paused, reinforcing the dog for not moving.

After a few more repetitions the dog, usually with a gaily wagging tail, can stand still at the gap, no matter how vigorous the go-forward commands become. "Can't fool me!" The final step is to add a third cue: The trainer reaches out and feels the obstacle, showing awareness of the problem. The obstacle is moved away (by an assistant). The dog then responds to the forward commands and gets clicked for doing so.

The concept can now be applied to a new obstacle. A bar is set across the path, first at the dog's head height, then gradually raised by an assistant to the handler's head height. The dog is clicked at each level both for noticing the bar, and for stopping. The dog learns to look upward, and retains the concept of stopping, in spite of being ordered forward, until the handler has manually identified the overhead obstacle. The criteria remain the same; only the nature of the obstacle varies. Skill at spotting overhead obstacles, which are now clickable opportunities, can then be extended to tricky items such as dangling wires or the big side mirrors that stick out from buses and trucks. Training time: days, not weeks or months. Success rate: 100%.

Creativity or Innovative Behavior The behavior might be described as, "Think up a new behavior." At Sea Life Park in 1965, Pryor and head trainer Ingrid Kang taught a rough-toothed dolphin (*Steno bredanensis)* to offer new, previously untrained behavior on cue. The procedure was replicated with another animal of the same species (Pryor et al., 1969). Similar procedures have since been carried out successfully with many species. Training for innovative behavior begins with capturing a variety of random behaviors across several training sessions. A context cue is established for when experimentation will be reinforced and when it will not; this often turns the experimental sessions into a game, with strong play elements for animal and trainer too. Training for novel behavior has spread widely through the modern training community. A game for dogs ("101 things to do with a box") consists of presenting the dog with a cardboard box and then reinforcing any interactions that ensue, from glancing at the box to climbing in it, knocking it over, or dragging it around (Pryor, 2002a).

Zoo keepers have established innovative behavior games in a wide variety of species. Asking repeatedly for novel behavior that has not been previously reinforced can be a challenge even for humans (Maltzman, 1960); however the skill can be developed with practice. An African Painted Dog (*Lycaon pictus*) at the Denver zoo has come up with over 40 novel behaviors, many of them aerial. Zoo keepers in the United States frequently use the creative game to provide sorely needed mental exercise for potentially troublesome young male gorillas. In this application, the game is called "Show me something new" and the context cue is waggling both hands in the air, a version of the American Sign Language sign for "play" (Pryor, 2009, pp. 82–85; video at http://www.reachingtheanimalmind.com/chapter_05.html).

Practical uses of innovative behavior include advancing the learner's conceptual skills, reducing fear of novel objects and events, and discovering amusing new behaviors for performance purposes. One useful remedial application is establishing the skill of offering behavior in dogs that have become risk-averse due to correction-based histories (some retired police dogs, for example).

TAGteach: An Application for People

Many newcomers to marker-based training for animals ask the same question, usually with an anxious laugh: "Does this work with husbands (or wives, or kids, or bosses)?" Yes, of course, provided you understand the principles. However, the field of applied behavior analysis, where human applications naturally belong, has moved away from the original experimental work with animals that underlies all behavior acquisition. Some tools were no longer being taught to practitioners, such as the use of a conditioned reinforcer as a marker, shaping as an alternative or additional tool to direct instruction, and using the learner's emotional responses as information.

In 2006 gymnastics coach Theresa McKeon, who had learned clicker training with her horses, began using the clicker as a marker with her youngest gymnastics students. A click could capture an instant of movement, such as being truly vertical in a hand stand, while it was actually happening. The student could then recreate the bodily sensation of that instant, on the very next try. The click meant success. Backup reinforcers, points towards a pizza party, for example, were useful, but the most motivating reward was the thrill of being right.

The children loved it. It was fun to be right, over and over. They learned faster and with much better retention. They could work in pairs and click each other. Best of all, no one was scolding them and telling them they were wrong. The parents, however, objected to idea that their children were being "trained like dogs." McKeon renamed the clicker a "tagger" and called the process Teaching with Acoustic Guidance, or TAGteaching, a semantic ruse which solved the public relations issue.

The trade name TAGteach identifies a subset of applied behavior analysis that integrates the technology of modern training and the teaching of human skills. The specific applications—what is being taught—are up to the teacher. TAGteach principles may be applied to individual or group training or coaching, and can be tailored to classroom use (Vargas, 2013). The main goal is to change the behavior of the teacher him or herself. As with shaping, the desired goal behavior is broken down into single elements which are taught one at a time.

Language use is key. TAGteach protocols include giving instructions with no personal pronouns: saying "I want you to bend your knees" implies showing obedience to please the teacher, an unnecessary onus on the student. A simple instruction "bent knees" gives the student something purely positive: useful information about the "tag point," the descriptor of exactly what will be clicked. Concise non-perjorative instructions begin to function as markers and as cues, with all the concomitant benefits of rapid acquisition, long retention, and positive emotional response.

Tagpoints have been identified and reinforced in a wide range of situations requiring muscle control: singing; playing an instrument; dance; athletics; physical therapy;

rehabilitation; speech therapy; acquiring or losing an accent, or learning any new skill, from rock-climbing to administering lumbar punctures. In many cases, the actual use of a marker signal is not needed. New skills are acquired through the careful framing of instructions, the continuity of the learning experience, the absence of aversives, and forethought about introducing one criterion at a time.

TAG tools complement rather than replace the expertise of trained therapists such as behavior analysts. The procedures are simple solutions for behavioral change that can be accomplished without highly specialized education. TAGteach is particularly useful in situations where the learner is non-verbal or has other developmental deficits. Parents with difficult-to-manage children are using TAGteach methods to create better daily life skills, to the benefit of the whole family (Gabler, 2013).

TAGteach clients include the State of Arkansas school systems special needs division, and fishing companies in the Bering Sea, where TAG methodology improves safety and efficiency on factory ships with multinational crews. TAGteach is taught in online courses and hands-on-two-day seminars and certification programs (see www.tagteach.com).

The Question of Awareness

The nervous system of all animals is designed to enable the organism to respond to threats, of course, but also to useful information. That information often comes from a conditioned reinforcer, a signal about the availability of something good: a smell, a sound, a movement, a change in the environment. While responses to such stimuli are often innate and automatic, many have a learned element as well. The question of intelligence in this process is moot; the nervous system is designed to learn this way (Griffin, 1976).

Even invertebrates have awareness and capacities for learning that may exceed what we have allowed ourselves to notice. Many arthropods exhibit learned behavior, and octopi can innovate and problem-solve. Richard Herrnstein, a colleague of Skinner's, described to Pryor training a scallop to clap its shell for a food reward. Who knows what the mollusk made of that experience; but it was certainly aware enough to learn how to change its behavior in order to extract extra food from the environment.

The prevailing view in science and the humanities for perhaps a century or more seems to have been, "It would be wonderful if animals could ask questions and express opinions, but they cannot, and they never will." People who believe that are not yet ethologically sophisticated. Animals exposed to modern training understand our messages clearly. In the training process they emit messages too. Since we know the animal's reinforcement status and the internal states that are usually generated in that circumstance, we can learn to read and appreciate those messages. It is an eerie and moving experience to get a head turn, and a full strong binocular eye contact, conveying a question—"?"—from a guinea pig that is offering a new behavior and hoping for a click; or equally intense and deliberate eye contact conveying an opinion—"!"—from a turtle that has been given distasteful food. Is that awareness? Certainly. Is it communication? Yes, in a way; we are receiving the same display of an internal state of affect that a conspecific would receive in a parallel situation. Is it cognition? Not exactly; but whatever it is, the training opens the door and lets us see it happen. At all levels, animals seem to have capacities that deserve respect; that we share; and from which we have much to learn.

So where and when does cognition arise? There is much confusion in the psychology literature between cognition and operant behavior. The first is worthy of investigation; the second is often treated as if it were some obsolete mechanistic process unrelated to questions of cognition. To modern trainers, however, the two concepts are interdependent. We use operant procedures to build the skills that let the animal display its capacities, whatever they may be. Cognition is not only revealed but commonplace. And replicable. Anyone who wants to can learn how to open that door. The concept that one must have a "way with animals" or some special genius is moot.

That does not mean that individuality is not still in play. There will always be remarkably gifted individual trainers, both conventional and modern, who excel in observation, empathy, training skills, and creativity. The unusually gifted individual can occur on the animal side, too. In the "novel behavior" experiment at Sea Life Park with dolphins, Hou, the second animal trained, succeeded in meeting criterion by coming up with new behaviors on her own. Her behaviors were novel in that they had not been previously reinforced, but they were simple behaviors often seen in dolphins: spitting water; rising vertically half out of the water, as if to look around in the air, a behavior called "spyhopping;" slapping the tail on the water; resting the chin on the training platform; and clapping the jaws.

Malia, the first animal to be trained and the one who showed us that novelty could be a successful requirement, was different. Her behaviors were completely novel, never seen by us in any dolphin before or since. She created an arcing jump high above the water but upside down; swimming underwater in circles while revolving in a corkscrew manner; coasting under water at high speed but with her tail, held above the surface, gliding through the air; launching herself onto the training platform and sliding around on the concrete surface; and circling underwater upside down while, with the tip of her dorsal fin, she drew beautiful parabolic lines in the silt on the tank floor.

There was certainly a cognitive aspect to these events. Malia often exhibited unusual excitement in her holding tank when we arrived in the morning. (The excitement was not food-related; both animals received full rations every day.) Malia's holding tank was too small to practice any of these large-scale behaviors, and yet each of them was produced fully formed and complete on the first trial. It did seem as if Malia had amused herself by thinking up new behaviors overnight (Pryor et al., 1969).

Looking Forward

The whole question of animal welfare is much in the public mind at present. Many supporters focus on the animal's primary needs for food, water, shelter, and good health, while ignoring emotional health. The detrimental effects of lack of physical activity, especially in laboratory and zoo animals, have begun to be addressed. Mental activity, the chance to explore and learn, is not always seen as equally valuable. The concept of "training" still suggests, to many animal lovers, the use of force, physical abuse, and imposing one's will on the helpless captive; animal welfare organizations and some animal caregivers still assume that any kind of training interaction would be abusive rather than enriching.

Even in science, prejudice and tradition can persist. Many research laboratories retain the trappings of early operant research—the isolating chamber, the lever, some apparatus for dispensing the primary reinforcer of food or water, and a data recording system—while failing to make use of operant training when appropriate for gaining informative results. This can, of course, change. In 2012 at a southwestern neuroscience laboratory over 100 people were investigating motion control in the brains of cats. The cats were required to perform various tasks, such as walking down an indicated path or balancing on a wobbly platform. A company-wide study of a four-decades old book about dolphin training (Pryor, 1975) reportedly enabled the entire staff, from high school interns to senior scientists, to train their cats to do whatever the research required.

The modern training technology enhances positive experiences and reduces stress-inducing aversive events. All of the principles-based techniques described in this chapter, such as raising criteria in small increments, avoiding correction or punishment of errors when shaping new behavior, using high-value reinforcers in new or challenging situations, and so on, apply just as much to human learners as to animals. How best do we continue to expand the population of users of the new technology, whatever the species of the learner? It seems like a good thing to do, if only for the moral reason of reducing some of the gratuitous cruelty in the world. But it is a challenge. Books and writing help; but books can only capture the small accretion of facts and applications as we know them at the time of writing. Online instruction, if it is interactive and reinforcing, helps more, because one gets the "feel" as well as the information. The face-to-face seminar, with its guided exercises, seems to be the most powerful teaching device, but it is expensive and not always feasible. Online discussion lists, with people helping each other and sharing new ideas and developments, continue to be very valuable.

What we do know something about is what happens to the human users of the technology. Whether through animal training or through working with humans, absorbing these new skills often leads to a beneficial shift in one's outlook in general. Instead of complaining about unwanted behavior, arguing, nagging, worrying about why this or that is happening, and trying to force results (on oneself as well as others) we have new tools. We ask new questions: What do I want to change? What would I like to see instead? Where is the point of success at which that starts? How do I reinforce that?

The shift in one's worldview is both comforting and liberating. Once you see things from the angle of reinforcing what you want, instead of trying to control what you do not want, you can never quite go back to the way you were. We see the comments on the Internet and hear them from students, clients, colleagues, co-workers, family, and friends: "This changed my life." And it does.

Acknowledgments

Modern training is rooted in the fundamental science of operant conditioning. We would especially like to thank Julie Skinner Vargas and Ernest Vargas for their continuing friendship and guidance in that science.

The evolution of the science into an ever-improving technology is the product of a community of teachers and trainers fascinated by the technology they use. The growth of the technology continues to lead to new tools, applications, and insights for developing beneficial behavior in animals and humans. These new insights, of course, raise new questions for the basic science. Our gratitude to the marker-based training and teaching community is profound. It's a privilege to work with you, and a never-ending source of joy and amazement at what you continue to create and accomplish.

Notes

1 The word "cue" signifies a conditioned discriminative stimulus indicating both a specific behavior and also the opportunity for earning positive reinforcement by executing that behavior. This differentiates the term from the conventional trainer's word, "command," which indicates a specific behavior, but also carries the threat of punishment if the behavior is not executed correctly.

2 A food reward may or may not be a reinforcer. Food rewards are often delivered after a given behavior rather than during it, so they may not reinforce any particular behavior other than food seeking and consumption.

References

ABMA (2012). Mission Statement and values. Website of the Animal Behavior Management Alliance. Retrieved January 3, 2014 from http://www.theabma.org.

AZA (2012). AZA Accreditation Standards. Website of the Association of Zoos and Aquariums. Retrieved January 8, 2014 from http://www.aza.org/uploadedFiles/Accreditation/AZA-Accreditation-Standards.pdf.

Belting, T., Joseph, J., Messersmith, M., & Nordone, L. (1998). Teaching an old polar bear new tricks. *Soundings, 23*, 20–22.

Blanchard, R. E., & Pepper R. L. (1972). *Proceedings of the First Marine Mammal Trainer Workshop*. NURDC, San Diego, CA.

Bloomsmith, M. A. (1995). Evolving a behavioral management program. *The Shape of Enrichment, 4*, 7–10.

Coppinger, R., & Coppinger, L. (2002). *Dogs: A startling new understanding of canine origin, behavior, and evolution*. New York: Howell Book House, New York.

Desmond, T., & Laule, G. (1991). Protected contact elephant training. *Proceedings of the American Association of Zoological Parks and Aquariums Annual Conference*. AAZPA, Silver Spring, MD.

Diamond, J. (2002). Evolution, consequences, and future of plant and animal domestication. *Nature, 418*, 700–707.

Ferguson, D. L., & Rosales-Ruiz, J. (2001). Loading the problem loader: The effects of target training and shaping on trailer-loading behavior of horses. *Journal of Applied Behavior Analysis, 34*, 409–424.

Gabler, M. (2013). *Chaos to calm: Discovering solutions for living with autism*. Indian Trail, NC: TAGteach Press.

Godfrey, J. F. (1979 [2005]). *How horses learn: Equine psychology applied to training*. Lincoln, NE: Iuniverse.

Griffin, D. (1976). *The question of animal awareness: Evolutionary continuity of mental experience.* New York: Rockefeller University Press.

Holland, P. (2008). Department of Neuroscience, Johns Hopkins University. Pers. Com.

IMATA (2012a). International Marine Animal Trainers Association. Retrieved January 3, 2014 from http://www.imata.org.

IMATA (2012b). IMATA Mission Statement and Values. International Marine Animal Trainers Association. Retrieved 3 January, 2014 from http://www.imata.org.

Krebs, R. E., & Krebs, C. A. (2003). *Groundbreaking scientific experiments, inventions and discoveries of the ancient world.* Westport, CT: Greenwood Press.

Kurland, A. (1999). *Clicker training for your horse.* Waltham, MA: Sunshine Books.

Ledoux, J. (1998). *The emotional brain: The mysterious underpinnings of emotional life.* New York: Touchstone.

Lilly, J. (1961). *Man and dolphin: Adventures of a new scientific frontier* (1st ed.). Garden City, NY: Doubleday.

Maltzman, I. (1960). On the training of originality. *Psychological Review, 27,* 229–242.

Maple, T. L. (2007). Toward a science of welfare for animals in the zoo. *Journal of Applied Animal Welfare Science, 10,* 63–70.

Mark, E. (2007). Reducing stress in Northern bald ibis through training. *ABMA Journal, 4,* 23–35.

Markowitz, H. (1981). *Behavioral enrichment in the zoo.* New York: Van Nostrand Reinhold.

Orr, J., & Lewin, T. (2006). *Clicking with your rabbit.* Waltham, MA: Sunshine Books.

Panksepp, J. (2004). *Affective neuroscience: The foundations of human and animal emotions.* New York: Oxford University Press.

Pearson, J., & Sullivan T. (1989). Husbandry behaviors: A look at what is possible. *Proceedings of the American Association of Zoological Parks and Aquariums Annual Conference,* AAZPA, Silver Spring, MD.

Pepper, R. L. (1974). *Proceedings of the third marine mammal trainer workshop.* Honolulu, HI: NUC.

Peterson, G. (2004). A day of great illumination: B. F. Skinner's discovery of shaping. *Journal of Experimental Analytical Behavior, 84,* 317–328.

Peterson, G. (2006). Shaping. *Encyclopedia of Educational Psychology.* Thousand Oaks, CA: Sage.

Priest, G., Antrim, J., Gilbert, J., & Hare, V. (1998). Managing multiple elephants using protected contact at San Diego's Wild Animal Park. *Soundings, 23,* 20–25.

Pryor, K. (1975). *Lads before the wind.* New York: Harper & Row.

Pryor, K. (1984). *Don't shoot the dog: The new art of teaching and training.* New York: Bantam Books.

Pryor, K. (1999). *Don't shoot the dog: The new art of teaching and training* (rev. ed.). New York: Bantam Books.

Pryor, K. (2001). *Clicker training for cats.* Waltham, MA: Sunshine Books.

Pryor, K. (2002a). *Clicker training for dogs* (pp. 60–67). Lydney, UK: Ringpress Books.

Pryor, K. (2002b). The poisoned cue. *Teaching Dogs, 1,* 8–9.

Pryor, K. (2009). *Reaching the animal mind: What clicker training teaches us about all animals.* New York: Scribner.

Pryor, K., Haag, R., & O'Reilly, J. (1969). The creative porpoise: Training for novel behavior. *Journal of Experimental Analytical Behavior, 12,* 653–669.

Ramirez, K. R. (1999). Advanced techniques and concepts. In K. R. Ramirez (Ed.), *Animal training: Successful animal management through positive reinforcement.* Chicago: Shedd Aquarium Press.

Ramirez, K. R. (2012a). Husbandry training. In M. Irwin, J. Stoner, & A. Cobaugh (Eds.), *Zoo technology.* Chicago: University of Chicago Press.

Ramirez, K. R. (2012b). Marine mammal training: The history of training animals for medical behaviors and the keys to their success. *Veterinary Clinics of North America (Exotic Animal Practice—Exotic Animal Training and Learning), 15*, 413–423.

Ramirez, K. R. (2013). Husbandry training. In M. Irwin, J. Stoner, & A. Cobaugh, (Eds.), *Zookeping: An introduction to the science and technology* (pp. 424–434). Chicago: The University of Chicago Press.

Scarpuzzi, M. R., Lacinak, C. T., Turner, T. N., Tompkins, C. D., & Force, D. L. (1991). Decreasing the frequency of behavior through extinction: An application for the training of marine mammals. *Proceedings of the 19th Annual Conference of the International Marine Animal Trainers Association*. IMATA, San Diego.

Scarpuzzi, M. R., Turner, T. N., Tomkins, C. D., Force, D. L., Lacinak, C. T., & Kuczaj, S. A. (1999). The use of the least reinforcing scenario in a proactive training program. *Proceedings of the 27th Annual Conference of the International Marine Animal Trainers Association*, IMATA, Chicago.

Scott, J. P., & Fuller, J. L. (1965). *Genetics and social behavior of the dog*. Chicago: University of Chicago Press.

Skinner, B. F. (1951). How to teach animals. *Scientific American, 185*, 26–29.

Vargas, J. S. (2013). *Behavior analysis for effective teaching* (2nd ed.). New York: Routledge.

Wood, L. A. (2006). An analysis of the efficacy of bridging stimuli: Comparing the clicker to a verbal bridge. Unpublished master's thesis, Hunter College, City University of New York.

Recommended Reading

Dog Training Foundations. Online course. Retrieved 3 January, 2014 from www.karenpryoracademy.com.

Pryor, K. (1975). *Lads before the wind: Adventures in porpoise training*. New York: Harper & Row.

Pryor, K. (1999). *Don't shoot the dog! The new art of teaching and training*. Revised Edition. New York: Bantam Books.

Pryor, K. (2009). *Reaching the animal mind: What clicker training teaches us about all animals*. New York: Scribner.

Ramirez, K. (1999). *Animal training: Successful animal management through positive reinforcement*. Chicago: Shedd Aquarium Press.

Schneider, S. (2013). *The science of consequences: How they affect genes, change the brain, and impact our world*. Amherst, NY: Prometheus Books.

Vargas, J. S. (2013). *Behavior analysis for successful teaching*. (2nd ed.). New York: Routledge.

19

Autism and Behavior Analysis *History and Current Status*[1]

Travis Thompson

Antecedents to Applied Behavior Analytic Approach to Autism

The distinction between children and youth with intellectual delays and those with typical functioning dates to the Ancient Greeks and was recognized as well as throughout the Middle Ages (Walter, 2005; Paracelsus, 1951/1942). Autism was not acknowledged as a distinct condition from other differences among children until the late 1800s. John Haslam who was the apothecary of Royal Bethlehem Hospital noted two boys in 1809 with autism features (Vaillant, 1962), and Jean Itard (1802), a physician in southern France described a 12-year-old feral boy with unusual characteristics. These children exhibited typical fine motor skills, such as the ability to construct complex puzzles, but displayed little ability to interact with another person or to grasp the most basic social conventions. These boys appeared to lack familiarity with many daily aspects of the world around them. They were keen on dismantling mechanical devices and discovering how they worked, but had little interest in people. They appeared to have some characteristics of children with intellectual disabilities but others of typically developing children, and even unusual skills in some domains. It was not until 1943 that Leo Kanner gave this condition a name, *infantile autism* (Kanner, 1943). Because of this enigmatic combination of features, autism came to be iconically represented by the jigsaw puzzle piece, a symbol that grew out of a meeting among a group of parent advocates in London in February 1963. When attempting to identify an emblem to capture the essence of their children's unusual condition, they believed the puzzle piece was apt (Gasson, 2011, personal communication, June 17, 2011).

The Wiley Blackwell Handbook of Operant and Classical Conditioning, First Edition.
Edited by Frances K. McSweeney and Eric S. Murphy.

Jean Marc Gaspard Itard's Proto-behavioral Treatment of Victor

Jean Itard, a physician living in Aveyron in southern France who specialized in treating deaf children, encountered a boy estimated to be about 12 years old. The boy was brought to him in July, 1799 by the village constable. He had been pilfering fruit and vegetables from nearby farms. The constable believed the boy had some type of mental disorder and thought it inappropriate to treat him as a common criminal (Itard, 1802).

The boy was naked and described as feral with no speech but guttural sounds. He exhibited animal-like behavior. He had burn scars on his body suggesting possible prior encounters with people who may have tormented him. He exhibited unusual features, such as not understanding the communicative purpose of language or social gestures. He also exhibited rigid, non-functional, repetitive behavior patterns and violent emotional and behavioral outbursts.

After examining the boy, Itard and his housekeeper decided to take him into Itard's home to determine if they could cure him through training. They called the boy Victor. Itard speculated that Victor had grown up on his own without regular human contact. Perhaps Victor had been born with some type of disability, and his parents put him in the forest to fend for himself or die. It was common at the time to believe such a child had come from the devil. Returning him to the devil was considered appropriate.

Itard soon discovered Victor responded well to predictable routines and the use of simple spoken instructions combined with gestures and tangible rewards. When Itard or his housekeeper presented Victor with a spoken or gestural command and the boy responded appropriately, he was given a desired consequence. As a result, the boy began to learn. Today, we recognize that sequence as the most rudimentary form of operant learning. Perhaps most remarkably, the boy learned to make requests using two- and three-dimensional symbols or objects, using a method similar to the Picture Exchange Communication System (Bondy & Frost, 1994), which is now called Mand Training (Stafford, Sundberg, & Braam, 1988). Itard's hope for a cure was eventually dashed when it became apparent he was unable to overcome Victor's severe disability through training alone. Nonetheless, he reported his findings to the French Academy of Sciences (Itard, 1802).

Leo Kanner's First Clinical Description of Autism

Using observational and other clinical psychiatric methods considered new at that time at his clinic at Johns Hopkins University, Leo Kanner (1943) studied 11 children with a condition that had not been previously described in medical literature. Kanner, who had been trained as a pediatrician in Austria, correctly identified the main features of this new condition that he called *infantile autism:* Lack of social awareness and understanding, deficit or lack of communication, non-functional repetitive behavior, and fixed behavioral routines and insistence on sameness. His article describing this new condition was remarkably insightful.

Kanner concluded the condition was different from intellectual disability and likely congenital. Although parenting might be a contributing factor to some of the symptoms, he considered autism to be present at birth, not learned. He noticed that some of the same restricted interest and insistence on sameness were exhibited by their parents, but to lesser degrees. Kanner underestimated the ability of children with autism to profit from systematic teaching or therapy.

When Kanner published his findings, the professional world began realize there was order to be found in this very puzzling condition. However, autism research and practice languished for many years subsequent to Kanner's first clinical characterization of the syndrome that bore his name.

What is Autism?

Autism is a family of neurodevelopmental disabilities differing considerably among individuals, but sharing several common features: (1) Absence of language or effective functional use of spoken language; (2) Lack of social interest and social understanding; (3) Insistence on rigid routines and sequences of daily events and; (4) Emotional and behavioral outbursts and tantrums when expected routines are altered, or alarming stimuli are present (American Psychiatric Association, 2000; International Classification of Diseases, 2012).

People with autism vary widely in the degree to which each of these features is present, which is often troubling to family members, teachers, and practitioners. A subset of individuals with autism exhibits considerable speech and even some functional communication, while others display none. Some people with autism exhibit interest in social interactions but typically have limited understanding of others' feelings and motives. Such people often have difficulty maintaining close relationships. All of those with autism exhibit some degree of rigidity and a tendency to react negatively to disruptions or thwarting of expected routine events. Though not part of Kanner's original description, most people with autism also experience considerable social anxiety, sometimes including panic attacks and phobias.

Because of this range of features, autism was called an *Autism Spectrum Disorder* within the diagnostic system of the American Psychiatric Association in Diagnostic and Statistical Manual (DSM-IV, American Psychological Association, 2000) and the International Classification of Mental Disorders (ICD 10). For some years autism was divided into several diagnostic conditions (Autistic Disorder, Asperger Disorder, and Pervasive Developmental Disorder-Not Otherwise Specified) but with the 2013 revision of the American Psychiatric Association's DSM-5, those separate disorders will no longer be professionally recognized. There is considerable evidence that the three previously recognized conditions often occur within the same families, which should not be the case with qualitatively different disorders.

The status of Asperger Disorder continues to the controversial. Under the 2013 Diagnostic and Statistical Manual of the American Psychiatric Association (DSM-5), Asperger Disorder will now be considered a form of mild Autism Spectrum Disorder (American Psychiatric Association, 2010). Studies indicate that a substantial number of people who would have been labeled Asperger Disorder using the DSM-IV criteria will be excluded from the Autism Spectrum Disorder category due to specific changes in the diagnostic criteria (Matson, Kozlowski, Hattier, Horovitz, & Sipes, 2012; Tsai, 2012; McPartland, Reichow, & Volkmar, 2012). Their omission is likely to have implications for educational services and treatment, as well as for comparing results of earlier and later studies, because the samples will likely differ. Others contend only a small number of individuals with Asperger Disorder or Pervasive Developmental Disorder-Not Otherwise Specified will fail to meet the DSM-5 diagnostic criteria (Huerta, Bishop, Duncan, Hus, & Lord, 2012).

Early Behavioral Treatment of Autism

For nearly three decades after Kanner's classic article was published, most of the autism literature consisted of mistaken theories (Bettleheim, 1967; Spitz, 1945), diagnostic blind alleys (Bender, 1947; Silver, 1954) and misplaced approaches to intervention (Bender, Goldschmidt, & Siva, 1962). Some professionals recognized that autism probably has a biological foundation (e.g., Rimland, 1964; Rutter, 1971) but nonetheless, believed it was "incurable" despite its also often being viewed as a largely psychogenic disorder (Bettleheim, 1967).

Charles B. Ferster

Charles B. Ferster initially conducted research with B. F. Skinner in his Harvard Laboratory that led to the book *Schedules of reinforcement* (Ferster & Skinner, 1957). Ferster was among the first in the field of behavior analysis to explore the applicability of operant principles to the behavior of children with autism. In 1961, Ferster and DeMyer described operant performances of an 8-year-old boy and a 9-and-a-half-year old girl with what appears to be severe autism. The behavior Ferster studied was children pressing illuminated panels with their hands, using food, music, visual stimuli, trinkets and other tangible reinforcers contingent on performance under fixed-ratio and variable-interval schedules. Recordings of the children's test site performance were similar to those exhibited by laboratory nonhuman subjects (Ferster & DeMyer, 1961). Ferster (1961) also published a theoretical article describing the application of operant principles to teaching functional adaptive skills to children with autism.

Risley, Wolf, and Mees: At the University of Washington, Wolf, Risley, and Mees (1964) described procedures used to establish typical-appearing behavior by a child with autism who had resided in an institution. They collected no systematic data on speech nor on their efforts at training his parents to work with him. Subsequently, Risley and Wolf (1964) applied similar operant principles to working with a 6-year-old child with autism. The child exhibited non-functional, repetitive, mannerisms and repetitive vocal sounds (echolalia), and was withdrawn and inactive, with no functional speech. Although the child was brought to the Developmental Psychology Laboratory at the University of Washington for training, generalization tests confirmed the transfer of skills, including rudimentary speech, to the child's home.

Contributions by Other Researchers

Many of the earliest contributors to a behavior analytic approach to autism originated with academic professionals specifically trained in operant learning theory. Other advances emerged from work by other practitioner-professionals who learned operant principles on their own and incorporated those concepts in their own approaches to teaching children with autism. Frank Hewett (1964, 1965) described teaching reading and speech to children with autism using an operant reinforcement approach. His work later became the basis of *The engineered classroom*, a public school model for teaching children with autism (Hewett, 1969). About the same time, Carl Fenichel created the League School in Brooklyn, New York, which used a structured approach to learning among children with autism that resembled incidental learning (Fenichel, 1966). Hingten, Coulter, and Churchill (1967) described an operant approach to teaching motor, object, and vocal imitation in autism. The same year, Jensen and Womack (1967) reported use of operant learning principles to increase frequency of interactions with peers, use of language, and cooperation in play among children with autism.

Rosalind C. Oppenheim and the Rimland School In 1961, the parent of a child with autism, Rosalind C. Oppenheim, wrote an article for *Saturday Evening Post* (June 17, 1961) describing the progress she made with her son with autism using basic operant procedures. Ms. Oppenheim, a special education teacher, used principles she adapted from consulting with a special education faculty member at Purdue University. Oppenheim reported that she taught her nonverbal son, Ethan, reading, writing, spelling and arithmetic.

Rosalind Oppenheim started a day school for children with autism based largely on behavior analytic principles and her experience with her son Ethan. The idea for such a school had arisen from discussions with Bernald Rimland, the parent advocate from San Diego who was instrumental in founding the Autism Society of America. Løvaas sent two of his staff to work with Oppenheim for several weeks to assist her in starting up the school.

Rosalind Oppenheim published a book in 1973, *Effective teaching methods for autistic children*, which was based largely on operant learning principles (Oppenheim, 1973, Chapter 1). Oppenheim's book was adopted by emerging school autism programs, but it had limited impact among most behavior analysis professionals and researchers who were not familiar with her work.

Ivar Løvaas's Early Research

In 1965, Løvaas, Schaeffer, and Simmons published a report using foot shock with two 5-year-old twin boys with autism. The boys were placed barefoot in a room with a shock grid on the floor. The staff member made a verbal request, such as "come here." When the child did as requested, he avoided foot shock, and was given praise, hugs, and edible reinforcement. Both boys had previously exhibited frequent tantrums, aggression, and self-injury. These behaviors diminished when shock was provided contingent on such responses and the behaviors stopped when positive reinforcement was provided when the child complied with requests.

The article created a furor among advocates and practitioners alike who contended that the technique was unethical and amounted to child abuse (Akerley, 1976). Later, parents (Maurer, 1983) and professionals argued that using shock was inappropriate and unnecessary (Carr, Robinson, Taylor, & Carlson, 1990; Horner, Dunlap, Koegel, Carr, Sailor, Anderson, Albin, & O'Neill, 1990).

Løvaas conducted additional research into using positive reinforcement strategies to teach verbal imitation and rudimentary communication skills to several children with autism. The children became famous after their appearance in a film *Behavioral treatment of autistic children*, the script of which was written by Løvaas in 1988.

Løvaas (1967) and Simmons and Løvaas (1969) studied the use of other noxious stimuli combined with food reinforcement, to reduce intense self-stimulation and self-injury among several children with autism. They reduced repetitive and self-injurious behavior, and generally increased speech, but obtained no evidence of generalization to other contexts. That work was described in *Life Magazine* and became the face of behavioral treatment of autism for much of the world (Moser & Grant, 1965). For many readers, this was their only impression of applied behavior analysis.

The children with whom Løvaas initially worked had previously received many treatments for aggression and self-injury, including psychotherapy, play therapy, and various medications, but none of those treatments reduced the severe behavioral challenges. For some of the children, their behavior problems were all consuming, very severe and intractable, potentially physically damaging, and socially stigmatizing. For others, the self-injury was extreme and potentially disfiguring. There was a sense of urgency about finding a way to reduce or stop the dreadful self-injury.

The only alternative at that time was chronic physical restraint. Løvaas, Simmons and colleagues reasoned that delivering a brief painful skin shock, a relatively small number of times, would be less noxious to the child than his or her own striking his head against hard surfaces, hitting his face with his hands or biting himself, often hundreds of times per day. These self-inflicted blows produced bruises and lacerations and threatened loss of vision. Delivering shocks seemed to Løvaas and Simons to be less noxious than common medical procedures, such as surgery for congenital leg or foot disabilities, which usually involved weeks of discomfort. They believed their procedure was defensible as an ethical alternative, if it effectively reduced or stopped self-injury, as it did in many cases.

Critics not only viewed delivering shocks as inherently inhumane, but also believed more effective alternatives must exist to treat self-injury, even though none had been adequately demonstrated to that point. They argued that more attention should be paid to the conditions giving rise to and maintaining the problem behavior in the natural environment, and less to trying to simply stop it with punishment.

Eventually, some of the critics' arguments were confirmed by later results and Løvaas discontinued the use of physical punishment. Severe self-injury was often reduced by a combination of positive reinforcement to teach new skills to replace the self-injurious behavior, and minimally intrusive time out or extinction (planned ignoring) techniques to reduce the problematic behavior.

While Løvaas' initial use of punishment and avoidance procedures may have been understandable to some colleagues within the young field of applied behavior analysis, its use overshadowed the remarkable positive contributions applied behavior analytic methods had for children with autism. This legacy still hangs over the field today.

O. Ivar Løvaas Ole Ivar Løvaas was born on a farm in Lier, Norway not far from Oslo in 1927 and knew nothing of psychology early in his life. He experienced first hand Nazi oppression during World War II when Norway was occupied by Nazi

Germany. He attended a small American Midwestern college on a music scholarship, and later switched his specialty to psychology. On graduation, working as aide at a private mental hospital in the state of Washington, he became disenchanted with the care provided and lack of patient improvement. Though he had initially been drawn to psychoanalysis, the predominant therapeutical approach of that time, his interest shifted to the embryonic field of applied behavior analysis based on principles promulgated by B. F. Skinner. After completing his doctorate in 1958, Løvaas stayed at the University of Washington, where he worked alongside other applied behavior analysis pioneers such as Sidney Bijou, Donald Baer, and Todd Risley. Løvaas's approach was practical, much like that of farmers in Norway where he had grown up. He did what worked without too much theoretical concern for exactly how or the circumstances under which it was effective.

In 1961, Ivar Løvaas became a faculty member in the University of California at Los Angeles (UCLA) Psychology Department. He was soon placed in charge of a unit at UCLA's Neuropsychiatric Institute. Few professionals were familiar with autism at the time, but Løvaas was drawn to several children with autism who were being treated at UCLA and at the nearby Camarillo State Hospital. Those children did not speak, lacked typical social interest, and play. They rocked, twirled in circles, displayed repetitive non-functional rituals, and other rigid routines. Most disturbingly, they engaged in persistent and sometimes severe self-injurious behavior. Løvaas reasoned that if operant learning principles could be used to teach complex behavioral skills to rats and pigeons, surely those same principles could apply to human children, who had much larger brains and greater mental ability. Perhaps, Løvaas thought, he could even teach them to respond appropriately to adult requests, to learn basic skills, and even to talk. Most importantly at the time, he sought a way of overcoming their excruciating self-injury, for which there was no known treatment. His initial efforts included use of punishment, which was later eliminated from his overall treatment approach.

Unlike Piaget's (1936) and Vygotsky's (1986/1934) developmental theories which were primarily philosophically driven, Løvaas's behavioral approach was based on the assumption that operant learning principles could be used to teach young children with autism specific skills, such as communicating their needs, caring for themselves, and learning basic cognitive skills. His goals were unassuming. Neither Løvaas, nor most others using a behavior analytic approach, assumed they were treating a mental disorder called *autism*, nor planned to normalize social, communication, and behavioral functioning of an affected young child. They did not view themselves as treating a disability, rather they were teaching specific skills and reducing problematic behavior. They began with the assumption that one response exhibited by a child with autism was similar to any other response. They reasoned that if one could teach a child to follow a simple direction, "Come sit," followed by presentation of a reinforcer, the child might also be taught more complex responses using the same method. Perhaps it would also be possible to teach a child to respond to a question such as, "What did Mommy say?"

Initial studies demonstrated that children with autism could be taught relatively simple arbitrary responses using mechanical signals like tones or lights, as well as spoken requests (Ellis, Pryer, & Barnett, 1960; Ferster, 1961; Orlando & Bijou, 1960; Spradlin, 1959). These first efforts were followed by more complex studies.

Researchers were often surprised to discover that the principles from the laboratory also applied relatively well to people in applied settings. Increasingly, those laboratory principles proved effective in schools and residential settings with children and adolescents with developmental disabilities, some of whom had autism (Girardeau & Spradlin, 1964; Thompson & Grabowski, 1972).

Reducing Challenging Behavior

From the 1960s to 1980s, much of the field of behavior analysis and autism and related disabilities, focused on reducing behavioral challenges in adolescents and adults with severe autism. In many cases, behavior analysts working within, or consulting with, public treatment agencies had been presented with the most treatment-resistant individuals with long histories of severe self-injury. Previous efforts to use medication and psychological treatments had been unsuccessful in reducing the self-destructive behavior (National Institutes of Health, 1989). Limited attention was devoted to developing positive skills or to the possible factors that may have given rise to the behavioral challenges.

The initial impression that self-injury could not be changed using less intrusive methods was subsequently shown to be incorrect. In 1977, E. G. Carr published an article that for the first time seriously raised the question, "What is the motivation for self-injurious behavior?" He suggested that, in many instances, self-injury served a communicative request or Mand function (Skinner, 1957, p. 35). This posed the question, "If the person with autism who self-injures is doing so as a request or Mand (in Skinner's parlance), such as to stop an activity they found too difficult or unpleasant, why not teach the person another means of making that request instead of injuring themself?" Carr et al. (1990) followed up by reviewing a variety of positive alternatives to aversive methods. They reported that there were several other options that were effective in many cases.

The growth of the Positive Behavior Support (PBS) movement, based on principles of applied behavior analysis, began in 1990 with a publication by Carr et al. (1999) and another by Horner, Albin, Sprague, and Todd (1999). The publications promoted the use of positive-reinforcement-based instructional alternatives based on a functional assessment methodology. Others within applied behavior analysis, such as Fisher, Kuhn, and Thompson (1998), demonstrated that functional communication training plus extinction reduced destructive behavior to near-zero levels.

Despite the growing evidence that many behavior challenges could be reduced or eliminated by determining the functions of the behavior and by teaching alternatives, some professionals continued to argue that aversive consequences were often needed to reduce severe self-injury (Kahng, Iwata, & Lewin, 2002). The epitome of this disagreement played out in the case of the Judge Rotenberg Center in Massachusetts. The Center relied heavily on the use of painful skin shock to reduce intractable self-injury among adolescents and adults with autism, despite the lack of compelling evidence it was necessary. The U.S. Department of Justice eventually investigated the Center, resulting in the Director's resignation and changes in treatment policies and procedures (Perez, 2010).

Løvaas's 1987 Landmark Study

Had Ivar Løvaas's legacy been solely based on the use of punishment procedures to reduce destructive behavior in autism, few would remember him today. But he also undertook one of the more important treatment studies in the history of psychology. The study transformed the new field of applied behavior analysis. Løvaas concluded that the previous work he had done to teach skills to a small number of children with autism had begun too late (7 to 9 years of age) and was not sufficiently intense (e.g., a few hours per week) to produce substantial lasting improvements. As a result, in 1971, he established an outpatient clinic at UCLA to provide home-based one-on-one behavioral interventions for preschool age children with autism. The children participated based on having an autism diagnosis from a competent professional and parental agreement to having their child participate in 40 hours per week of home-based intervention. The children were not randomly selected. Instead, the sample consisted of whatever autistic children were self-referred by families in the Los Angeles area. Most of the hands-on therapists were undergraduate students at UCLA who Løvaas and his graduate student staff members (Robert Koegel, Laura Schreibman, John McEachin, Ron Leaf, Mitch Taubman and several others) trained and supervised in the use of his intervention methods. Initially the therapy was largely discrete-trial intervention. Over subsequent years, the therapy included simulation of play dates and classroom activities, observational learning and group instruction. The final year of a child's therapy focused on peer and sibling interactions and preparation for participation in school.

Over 14 years, Løvaas accumulated data from 19 children who had received 40 hours of one-on-one treatment for three years each. Løvaas's first attempt at publishing his findings in 1985 was unsuccessful because he did not have an untreated comparison group. Over the next two years, he gathered the comparison-group data that were included in a 1987 publication (Løvaas, 1987). One comparison group of children with autism had received standard community childcare for about 10 hours per week. The second comparison group received no supplementary childcare or intervention services.

There were no notable differences in outcomes for the two comparison groups, but very large differences from the intensive early behavioral intervention group. Follow-up data from the intensive behavioral intervention group ($n = 19$) showed that 47% scored intellectually within the low typical IQ range and were successfully included in regular first grade public school classrooms. Another 40% tested in the mildly cognitively-delayed range and were assigned to special classes for children with language delay or learning disability. Ten percent tested in the severe/profound intellectual disability range and were assigned to classes for autistic/intellectually disabled. In contrast, 2% of the comparison-group children ($n = 40$) achieved typical educational and intellectual functioning; 45% tested in the mild intellectual disability range and were placed in language-delayed or learning disability classes; and 53% tested in the severe intellectual disability range and were placed in classes for students with autism or intellectual disability.

When Løvaas published the results of this longitudinal study, objections erupted from the developmental and clinical psychology worlds. For the first time any psychological or educational early intervention method had been shown to be highly effective in reducing, and in some cases nearly eliminating, most autism symptoms in about half of the treated young children. The effects were durable and long lasting. Most troubling to many, the method used was based on operant learning principles, not developmental psychology theory. Løvaas's findings produced a seismic reaction throughout the developmental and clinical psychology communities, which had assumed early intervention methods were the exclusive province of psychologists trained in cognitive development and attachment theory (Gutstein & Sheely, 2002; Schopler, Short, & Mesibov, 1989).

Why Løvaas's Findings Were Troubling to Critics

Two aspects of Løvaas's (1987) findings were especially troubling to critics. The treatment effects were clinically large, more substantial than had been reported before. To many, this seemed implausible. Perhaps more dismaying, Løvaas's work did not begin with developmental theoretical assumptions. He did not assume children with autism had failed to develop social and communication skills because they had a flawed maternal attachment, as did Bowlby (e.g., 1969). Nor did he assume that intervention required developmentally age-matched guided autonomous cognitive exploration of the world around them in order to develop the basic skills he was trying to teach, as did Piaget (e.g., 1957). He did not assume a drive for autonomy was one of the most important aspects of children's early learning, as did Vygotsky (e.g., 1986/1934).

Løvaas and other early autism behavioral researchers and practitioners did not find such assumptions helpful in teaching young children with autism. Instead, they focused on using operant principles to teach basic skills (e.g., greeting, making eye contact) that were intended to make their daily lives a little better. Unlike Piaget, Vygotsky, and Bowlby, Ivar Løvaas had hardly had any theory at all, other than the limited assumption that children with autism could be taught specific skills using operant learning principles. He reasoned that when those skills were acquired, they could be combined to begin to resemble more typical functioning.

Løvaas's approach had been based on earlier observations that children with autism could be taught appropriate skills in controlled situations. This assumption did not require a major extrapolation from existing literature. The pragmatic principles involved in teaching these skills were derived from Skinner's analysis of operant behavior (Skinner, 1938, 1953; Holland & Skinner, 1961). A better understanding of typical processes of social and communication development may have improved progress using behavioral strategies (e.g., Landa, Holman, O'Neill, & Stuart, 2011; Dawson, Rogers, Munson, Smith, Winter, Greenson, Donaldson, & Varley, 2010; Prizant & Wetherby, 1998). Nevertheless, children were shown to be able to learn many of their lacking communication, social, and cognitive skills.

It seemed incomprehensible to some that such a relatively simple, pragmatic, and minimally theoretical approach had proven to be effective. For several years after Løvaas's (1987) paper, articles appeared in professional journals criticizing Løvaas's methods and claiming that such dramatic findings could not be replicated (e.g., Schopler et al., 1989; Gresham & McMillan, 1998). Nevertheless, many replications of Løvaas's findings were subsequently published (e.g., McEachin, Smith, & Løvaas,

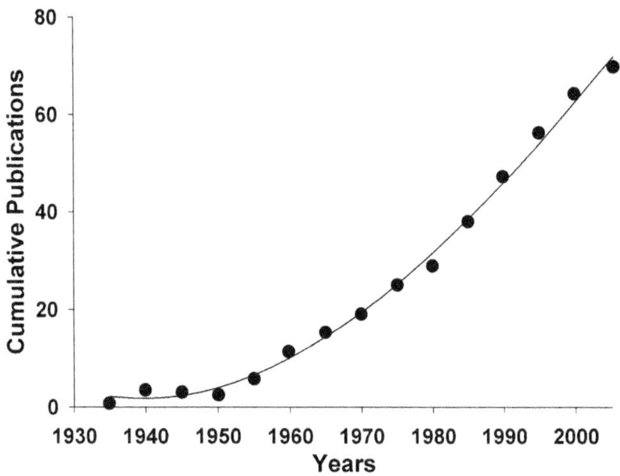

Figure 19.1 Cumulative autism research publications 1940–2010. (from T. Thompson (2013), "Autism research and services for young Children: History, progress and challenges," *Journal of Applied Research in Intellectual Disabilities*. John Wiley & Sons. Reprinted with permission.

1993; Remington, Hastings, Kovshoff, degli Espinosa, Jahr, Brown, Alsford, Lemaic, & Ward, 2007; Sallows & Graupner, 2005; Løvaas & Wright, 2006). In 2001, an expert panel of the U.S. National Research Council concluded that applied behavior analysis intervention was often effective, though it was unclear which aspects of the intervention were responsible for the main results (Lord & McGee, 2001). Criticisms about the effectiveness of the behavior analytic approach began to wane when it became apparent Løvaas's basic findings were robust.

Growth of Autism Research

Few behavioral research publications on autism appeared per year between the early studies in the 1960s and Løvaas's landmark longitudinal study of early intensive behavioral intervention (EIBI) in 1987. But, the rate of published behavioral autism research literally grew exponentially beginning with publication of Løvaas's 1987 follow-up study.

Figure 19.1 shows the overall growth of autism research from 1988, prior to publication of the first diagnostic test for autism (the Autism Diagnostic Observation Scale) to 2011. It reports an annual increase from 118 to 2,207 scientific articles in archival journals (Thompson, 2013). Behavior analytic research has comprised around 10% of that growth.

Figure 19.2 shows the growth of publications on autism in the *Journal of Applied Behavior Analysis* and the *Journal of the Experimental Analysis of Behavior* from 1983 through 2010. There were a total of 227 journal articles with 46% of them appearing between 2005 and 2010. The growth in published autism research is described by a power function.

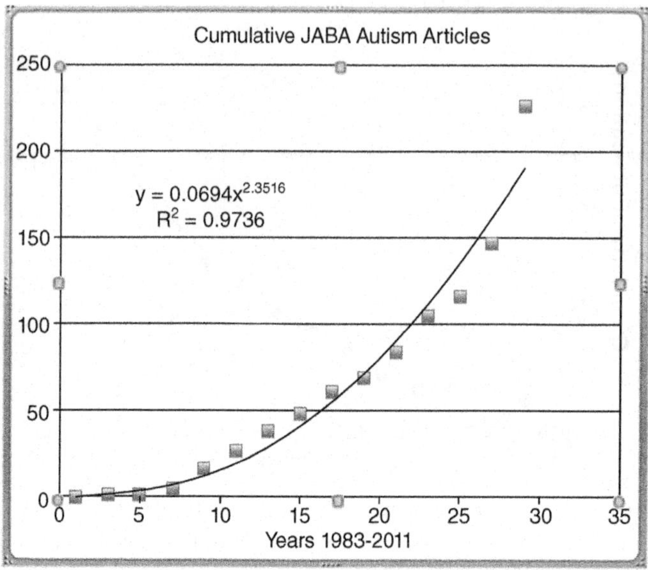

Figure 19.2 Autism publications in the *Journal of Applied Behavior Analysis,* 1981–2011.

Beginning in 2007, the Association for Behavior Analysis International has offered an annual Autism Conference. In 2011, more than 750 people attended the conference from 47 states and 17 countries, attesting to the growing interest in autism.

Comprehensive Early Intensive Behavioral Intervention

Several modifications of the discrete-trial approach developed by Løvaas beginning in 1975, and published in 1987 (Løvaas, 1987), have been used within the United States and other countries. The newer strategies begin with a criterion-based assessment of skills prior to beginning intervention. Two widely used tools are the Assessment of Basic Language and Learning Skills-Revised (ABLLS-R; Partington, 2007), and the Verbal Behavior Milestones Assessment and Placement Program (VBMAPP; Sundberg, 2008), both of which sample a wide array of skills based roughly on typical developmental skill sequences, though neither bases the order of the skills on Piaget's Developmental Stages. The VBMAPP differs from the ABLLS-R mainly in providing different skills sets for chronological age groups and in explicitly addressing barriers to implementing intervention. Recently, the ABLSS-R has included chronological developmental age norms, making it possible to compare scores on the scale with similar achievements of typically developing children. These instruments guide the selection of skills targeted for intervention, suggest intervention approaches, provide a way of monitoring progress, and graphically present outcomes to parents or other caregivers.

Though Løvaas's original Discrete Trial method (DTI) is based on operant learning principles, *it is not a free operant approach* similar to learning within typical nonhuman laboratory operant situations. Rather than waiting for the child to discover the teacher's or parents' preferred response on her or his own, the therapist verbally and manually guides the child to the correct response. The child is seated at a table across from the therapist in a room devoid of distractions, with limited learning materials (e.g., ball, cup), and usually consumable reinforcers in a container (e.g., pieces of fruit, cereal, sips of a preferred beverage). The therapist presents a verbal and gestural discriminative stimulus ("Point ball") and gently guides the child's hand to the ball if she does not respond. Immediately after the child's pointing, the therapist presents a small amount of the child's preferred reinforcer.

The reasoning behind the DTI approach is that it shortens the time for the child to begin responding to the therapist's (or parents') requests. In a few cases, the child may never respond correctly without manual guidance and frequent repetition. This procedure also reduces ambiguity about which are the relevant stimuli and which is the correct response. General skill acquisition in the course of DTI training is directly related to baseline intellectual functioning and language skills (Løvaas, 1987; Remington et al., 2007; Sallows & Graupner, 2005).

An alternative and widely used approach is called Incidental or Naturalistic Teaching. It has several variants (e.g., Pivotal Response Training, Naturalistic Intervention, Play-Based Behavioral Intervention, Blended Intervention). Incidental Teaching grew out of earlier work on Milieu Language Intervention (Hart & Risley, 1975), which involved a combination of basic operant techniques and developmental language concepts (McGee, Almeida, Sulzer-Azaroff, & Feldman, 1992). In Incidental Teaching, operant procedures are employed (embedded) within the context of ongoing play or educational activities. Instead of the highly structured approach of DTI, prompts are provided ("What is that?") and reinforcers are delivered ("That's right, good job.") as natural opportunities arise in the course of other activities. The most widely used Incidental Teaching approach, Pivotal Response Training (PRT) was developed by L. K. Koegel, R. L. Koegel, Harrower, and Carter (1999) and Schreibman, Stahmer, and Pierce (1996). Many studies have demonstrated the efficacy of PRT in general and of some of its components, especially natural language learning.

Incidental Teaching is a far more demanding approach than DTI for the therapists or teachers, requiring much more skill and training to deliver well. Like adjusting steering and pedaling as one rides a bicycle down a hill, a good Incidental Teaching therapist must be able to make moment-to-moment adjustments in the course of interacting with a child with autism. Incidental Teaching has the advantage that there is little need for training generalization. The skills are learned in the natural settings where they will be performed in the future.

Two therapies based on operant principles are both called "Verbal Behavior," one developed by Sundberg and colleagues (Stafford et al., 1988) and the other by Carbone (Carbone, 2007). Both employ Skinner's principles, but Sundberg's is a more comprehensive approach heavily drawing upon the theoretical analysis in Skinner's book, *Verbal behavior* (Skinner, 1957). There have been no comprehensive evaluations of the two Verbal Behavior approaches comparable to those that have been reported for various DTI strategies.

It has become increasingly clear that not all children require or learn equally well with DTI or Incidental Teaching. Sherer and Schreibman (2005) examined whether there were different profiles for children who responded favorably to PRT and those who did not. They selected six children, three predicted responders and three predicted nonresponders. Responders who received PRT had higher toy play scores, were more likely to approach the examiner, and were more likely to engage in verbal self-stimulation than those who did not receive PRT. Nonresponders who did not

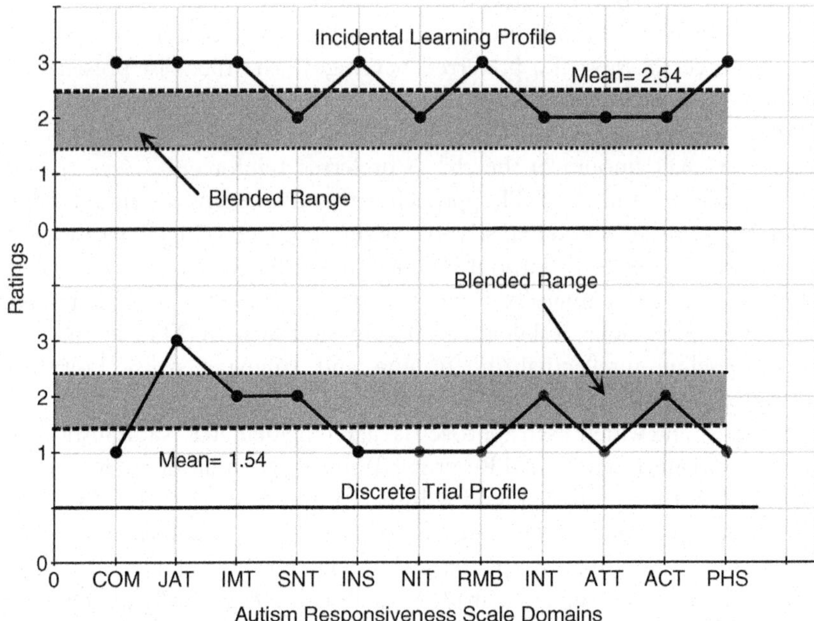

Figure 19.3 Typical Autism Intervention Responsiveness (AIRStm) profiles for a child who will most likely profit from an Incidental Teaching Strategy (top) and for a child who will most likely profit from a more structured Discrete Trial approach (bottom). Adapted from T. Thompson(2011), *Individualized autism intervention for young children: Blending discrete trial and naturalistic strategies.* Baltimore, MD: Paul H. Brookes Publishing Co., with Permission.

receive PRT were more socially avoidant and engaged in more nonverbal self-stimulation than those who did.

Thompson and colleagues examined predictors of response to EIBI varying in type and intensity (Thompson, 2011). Twenty-five children with autism (mean age = 44.7 months) received discrete trial, incidental, or blended intervention. Intensity varied from 10 to 35 hours per week (mean = 21.2 hours). The children were assigned by treatment teams to discrete trial, incidental intervention, or blended intervention using typical intake information and observations, including psychological test results and clinical observations. In addition, the Autism Intervention Responsiveness Scale™ (AIRS) was used to predict which children would be assigned by treatment teams to interventions. The AIRS is an 11-item rating scale that includes such variables as Communication, Imitation, Intellectual Ability, and Dysmorphic Features.

Figure 19.3 (top) shows a typical AIRS profile for a child who will most likely profit from an Incidental Teaching Strategy and the bottom for a child who will most likely profit from a more structured Discrete Trial approach. AIRS scores predicted accurately assignment to discrete-trial and incidental intervention but with less accuracy for blended intervention. After intervention, of 25 children, 16 were in regular education classrooms, 11 without additional support and five with paraprofessional support. Eight were in self-contained special education classrooms. Parents' symptom ratings of children who received EIBI, and a comparison group not receiving EIBI, revealed that those not receiving EIBI displayed more autism socialization deficits and repetitive behavior and fixed routines than those who did. Parent Treatment Acceptability Rating Form scores indicated a high degree of acceptability of their child's intervention, with some concerns about cost, disruption to routines, and time commitment.

Outcome of Early Intensive Behavioral Intervention

Twenty one studies listed in Table 19.1 have been published in peer-reviewed journals. They verify the effectiveness of EIBI in improving the core symptoms of autism and related behavioral cognitive skills.

Developing More Advanced Skills

Within the past decade, increasing research has focused on using behavior analytic strategies for teaching social and communication skills previously thought to be beyond the reach of EIBI methods. Most comprehensive approaches to EIBI have emphasized the language and cognitive skills necessary to succeed at home, in school, and in the community. More recently greater emphasis has been placed on the third leg of the autism diagnostic stool, lack of social skills.

Table 19.1 Empirical publications in peer-reviewed journals of effects of early intensive behavioral intervention on cognitive, social, language and intellectual functioning of young children with autism spectrum disorders.[1]

Anderson, S. R., Avery, D. L., DiPietro, E. K., Edwards, G. L., & Christian, W.P. (1987). Intensive home-based early intervention with autistic children. *Education and Treatment of Children, 10*, 352–366.

Bibby, P., Eikeseth, S., Martinc, N. T., Mudford, O. C., & Reeves, D. (2001). Progress and outcomes for children with autism receiving parent-managed intensive interventions. *Research in Developmental Disabilities, 22*, 425–447.

Birbrauer, J. S, & Leach, D. J. (1993). The Murdoch early intervention program after 2 years. *Behaviour Change, 10*, 63–74

Cohen, H., Amerine-Dickens, M., & Smith, T. (2006). Early intensive behavioral treatment: Replication of the UCLA model in a community setting. *Journal of Developmental and Behavioral Pediatrics, 27*(2 Suppl), S145–155.

Dawson, G., Rogers, S., Munson, J., Smith, M., Winter, J., Greenson, J., Donaldson, A., & Varley, J. (2009). Randomized, controlled trial of an intervention for toddlers with autism: The Early Start Denver Model. *Pediatrics, 125*, e17–e23.

(*Continued*)

Table 19.1 (*Continued*)

Eikeseth, S., Smith, T., Jahr, E., & Eldevik, S. (2002). Intensive behavioral treatment at school for 4- to 7-year-old children with autism. A 1-year comparison controlled study. *Behavior Modification, 26*, 49–68.

Eldevik, S., Eikeseth, S., Jahr, E., & Smith, T. (2006). Effects of low-intensity behavioral treatment for children with autism and mental retardation. *Journal of Autism and Developmental Disorders, 36*, 211–224.

Fenski, E. C., Zelenski, S., Krantz, P. J., & McClannahan, L. E. (1985). Age at intervention and treatment outcome for autistic children in a comprehensive intervention program. *Analysis and Intervention in Developmental Disabilities, 5*, 7–31.

Handleman, J. S., Harris, S. L., Celiberti, D., Lilleleht, E., & Tomchek, L. (1991). Devlopmental changes of preschool children with autism and normally developing peers. *Infant Toddler Intervention, 1*, 137–143.

Harris, S. L., Handleman, J. S., Gordon, R., Kristoff, B., & Fuentes, F. (1991). Changes in cognitive and language functioning of preschool children with autism. *Journal of Autism and Developmental Disorders, 21*, 281–290.

Harris, S. L., Handleman, J. S., Kristoff, B., Bass, L., & Gordon, R. (1990). Changes in language development among autistic and peer children in segregated and integrated school settings. *Journal of Autism and Developmental Disorders, 20*, 23–31.

Hastings, R. P., & Symes, M. D. (2002). Early intensive behavioral intervention for children with autism: Parental therapeutic self-efficacy. *Research in Developmental Disabilities, 23*, 332–341.

Howard, J. S., Sparkman, C. R., Cohen, H. G., Green, G., & Stanislaw, H. (2005). A comparison of intensive behavior analytic and eclectic treatments for young children with autism. *Research in Developmental Disabilities, 26*, 359–383.

Løvaas, O. I. (1987). Behavioral treatment and normal educational and intellectual functioning in young autistic children. *Journal of Consulting and Clinical Psychology, 55*, 3–9.

Løvaas, O. I., Koegel, R., Simmons J. Q., & Long, J. S. (1973). Some generalization and follow-up measures of autistic children in behavior therapy. *Journal of Applied Behavior Analysis, 63*, 131–166.

Perry, A., Cummings, A., Geier, J. D., Freeman, N. L., Hughes, S., LaRose, L., Managhan, T., Reitzel, T., & Williams, J. (2008) Effectiveness of intensive behavioral intervention in a large, community-based program. *Research in Autism Spectrum Disorders, 2*, 621–642.

Smith, T., Buch, G. A., & Gambya, T. E. (2000). Parent-directed, intensive early intervention for children with pervasive developmental disorder. *Research in Developmental Disabilities, 21*, 297–309.

Strain, P. S. & Bovey II, E. H. (2011). Randomized, controlled trial of the LEAP Model of early intervention for young Children with autism spectrum disorders. *Topics in Early Childhood Special Education,* 31, 133–154.

Smith, T., Gore, A. D., & Wynn, J. W. (2000). Randomized trial of intensive early intervention in children with pervasive developmental disorder. *American Journal of Mental Retardation, 105*, 269–285.

Sallows G. O., & Graupner, T. D. (2005). Intensive behavioral treatment for children with autism: Four-year outcome and predictors. *American Journal on Mental Retardation, 6*, 417–438.

Weiss, M. J. (1999). Differential rates of skill acquisition and outcomes of early intensive behavioral intervention for autism. *Behavioral Interventions, 14*, 3–22.

[1]The author is grateful to Dr. Wayne Fisher for his assistance in this review of the empirical autism early intervention literature.

Social Skills

Learning to look at what another person is observing is among the most basic social skills. It is called *social referencing*. Social referencing, a form of nonverbal communication, involves seeking out social discriminative stimuli in an ambiguous context in order to respond in a manner that produces reinforcement. Social referencing is absent or limited in individuals with autism.

Verbal, visual, and manual prompting and reinforcement were used to teach four children with autism to exhibit a social referencing response chain composed of an observing response and a conditional discriminative response in the presence of variants of standard academic materials. Observing involved looking at the experimenter when presented with unfamiliar handwriting materials, verbal models, and video models. Conditional discriminative responding involved completing the handwriting task or imitating the verbal and video models in the presence of a head nod and a smile. It also involved placing the handwriting materials aside, or remaining seated in a chair in the presence of a headshake and a frown. All four children learned to exhibit social referencing. The ambiguous materials were then interspersed among the standard materials. One of the children spontaneously showed discriminated social referencing, observing in the presence of the ambiguous stimuli and not in the presence of the standard materials. The other children had to be taught to discriminate (Brim, Townsend, DeQuinzio, & Poulson, 2009).

Another common limitation in autism, lack of perspective taking can be taught to many autistic children. Perspective taking refers to understanding another person's viewpoint and responding accordingly. This has been called "theory of mind," a hypothetical construct that has been questioned (Thompson, 2008). The deficit some have described as "mind-blindness" is present in most children with autism (Baron-Cohen, 1995).

LeBlanc, Coates, Daneshvar, Charlop-Christy, Morris, and Lancaster (2003) evaluated video modeling and reinforcement for teaching perspective-taking to three children with autism using a multiple baseline design. Video modeling and reinforcement were effective; however, only two children showed generalization to an untrained task. The findings suggest that video modeling may be an effective technology for teaching perspective taking but may require additional assistance to promote generalization.

Schrandt, Townsend, and Poulson (2009) taught *empathy* and empathetic responding to four children with autism using vignettes with dolls and puppets. The dolls and puppets showed various types of affect. The authors used prompt delay, modeling, manual prompts, behavioral rehearsals, and reinforcement to teach participants to perform empathetic responses. Responding generalized from training to nontraining probe stimuli for all participants. Generalization occurred from dolls and puppets to actual people in a nontraining setting for two participants.

Similar techniques have been used to teach generalized social helpfulness among children with autism. S. A. Reeve, K. F. Reeve, Townsend, and Poulson (2007) taught children with autism to be *socially helpful* (e.g., locating objects, putting away items, setting up an activity). Video models, prompting, and reinforcement were used during training. All children learned to help during training, and in the presence of untrained discriminative stimuli, during additional probe conditions. Helping also generalized across contexts. It increased in the presence of novel stimuli, in a novel setting, and with a novel adult caregiver.

Challenging Behavior in Autism Revisited

Reducing behavior challenges was the major focus of autism intervention early in the history of applied behavior analysis. Identifying the social functions of self-injury, aggression, tantrums, and other behavioral disturbances was successful in most cases, but it was entirely idiosyncratic. The unpredictability of such analyses was troubling in a field seeking simpler solutions to these difficult behavioral challenges. After E. G. Carr's (1977) article proposing social functions for self-injurious behavior, more systematic efforts emerged to identify the proposed functions of challenging behaviors (e.g., attention seeking, avoiding, or escaping from unwelcome caregiver demands). A third category, Automatic Reinforcement, referred to hypothetical unknown controlling consequences often assumed to be arising from self-stimulation (Iwata, Dorsey, Slifer, Bauman, & Richman, 1994).

Standardized protocols for conducting Analog Functional Analysis evaluations were reported. These protocols were often effective in predicting the causal variables maintaining challenging behavior (Hanley, Iwata, & McCord, 2003). The main advantage of this approach was that it required relatively little time, could be conducted in nearly any environment, and required minimal training for the staff. The main disadvantage of Analog Functional Analysis is that it posed ethical problems because it required exposing the client to conditions which were likely to provoke the behavioral problem which was to be reduced or eliminated (e.g., repeatedly making a demand that is likely to elicit self-injury). Although self-injurious behavior and aggression were blocked, the procedure was inherently provocative. Moreover, good practice would not require the individual to adjust his or her behavior to provocative environments (e.g., repeated demands that cannot be met). Rather, good practice would determine which aspects of the environment could be reasonably changed to reduce the problematic behavior (e.g., making the task easier to complete, teaching new skills, reducing size of demands).

About 60% of Functional Analyses yield "automatic reinforcement" as the function of the behavior, meaning the controlling factor is unknown. Although only a few undifferentiated cases have been reported in published journal articles on Functional Analysis (Hanley et al., 2003), undifferentiated outcomes are very common in practice (i.e., there is no clear single consequence that seems to be maintaining the challenging behavior). Recently, Dube, Schichenmeyer, Grant, and Roscoe (2012) described a combined experimental analog functional assessment and interview-based Idiosyncratic Functional Analysis method that overcomes some of these issues and appears to validly identify more idiosyncratic controlling variables.

As a result of limitations of Analog Functional Analysis, an alternative strategy has been devised that conducts Observational Functional Assessments in natural environments. Using a time sampling method, antecedent setting events (e.g., hunger, lack of sleep), the immediate trigger events (e.g., a demand), the type of usual response under these circumstances, and the consequence that typically follows (e.g., removing the unwelcome demand) are observed as they occur throughout the individual's day. Observational Funtional Assessment emphasizes identifying antecedent motivating events (e.g., being hungry), triggers (e.g., the specific way demands are stated) and response alternatives (e.g., asking for help). This functional assessment strategy is widely used in special education programs based on Positive Behavior Support approaches, which is a derivative of applied behavior analysis (Horner et al., 1990). In some settings, it may be more helpful to know what actually happens in the natural environment than what occurs under the controlled conditions of the Analog Functional Assessment, although there is evidence that the latter can effectively predict behavior under more natural conditions as well (Hanley et al., 2003).

Early Behavioral Intervention and Brain Development

Approximately half of the children in Løvaas's and most later EIBI studies exhibit dramatic improvement in autism symptoms and intellectual functioning, but the other half fail to show such dramatic improvement. While most of the latter group exhibit gains, they are typically less marked. Sallows and Graupner (2005) found that children with lower baseline IQs, lack of joint attention, and little or no motor or verbal imitation (at 2 to 3 years of age) and with autism diagnoses showed limited improvement in core autism symptoms over four years of more than 30 hours per week of EIBI.

That raises the question of why EIBI is especially effective with some children with autism but not with others. Whatever is different about the brain functioning of children with autism must be consistent with the EIBI evidence, namely that half of the children dramatically improve and half show limited gains using what appear to be the same behavioral intervention techniques. Children with autism diagnoses who are especially responsive to EIBI appear to have the potential to form synapses in brain areas known to be dysfunctional in autism. Those who profited less from EIBI have abnormalities in the same structures but could not form new synapses (Thompson, 2005).

EIBI involves repetitive training that can be accomplished only by enlisting the active engagement of those specific brain structures. By repeatedly requiring the child to perform such discriminative tasks, new synapses will probably be formed in that brain area. The more those skills are practiced, the more functionally consolidated or effective those synapses become, which is probably why the effects are permanent. In the absence of practice, as was common in the past when young children with autism were placed in sequestered residential or ineffective school settings, synapses failed to form, and the neurons that would normally have served that function regressed through disuse. Those structures became permanently non-functional.

Similarly, the difficulties that children and youth with autism encounter discriminating facial expressions are related to dysfunction in the amygdala and fusiform gyrus of the temporal lobe (Baron-Cohen et al., 1999). Experience in learning visual discriminations that require use of those structures can alter the responsiveness of neurons to such visual discriminations (such as faces) in the future (Grelotti, Gauthier, & Schultz, 2002). In other words, experience making visual discriminations that require use of those brain structures appears to promote synaptogenesis in those brain areas.

Why Do Some Children Greatly Benefit from EIBI and Others Do Not?

Those who do not benefit from EIBI may have dysfunction in some of the same brain structures as those who do, but the non-functional tissue may have arisen by a different mechanism, one that is not as amenable to correction by forming and consolidating new synapses. This possibility does not imply that children who are minimally responsive to EIBI should receive no intervention. However, it does suggest that we must understand better the mechanisms underlying their disability and determine which intervention strategies are most likely to ameliorate those limitations (Thompson, 2005).

Why "Cure" and "Recovery" Are Misnomers

Some advocates of EIBI have suggested that the changes obtained after behavioral treatment constituted "recoveries" or "cures" (e.g., Maurice, 1994). Other clinical researchers have said that, while the autistic children had clearly improved, claims of recovery or "cures" were exaggerated (Helt et al., 2008). Many of these children performed well in school in most respects and engaged in social activities with their peers. However, most continued to exhibit some language and social differences including difficulties with friendships (Sallows & Graupner, 2005). A significant percentage of treated individuals continued to exhibit differences from typical peers although they are able to lead productive and happy lives. There have been too few longitudinal studies to determine the adult adjustment of individuals who experienced EIBI as young children. In the absence of such information, it is ethically unsound to lead parents of children with autism spectrum disorders to believe that their child's later functioning will be indistinguishable from their typical siblings or other youngsters without autism.

Prognosis

The future for individuals with autism spectrum disorders is vastly more promising today than it was 50 or even 25 years ago. A longitudinal outcome study by M. K. DeMyer, Barton, W. E. DeMyer, Norton, Allen, and Steele (1973) found that "Most autistic children remained educationally retarded and 42% were institutionalized . . . [Their findings] indicated the following prognosis in autism: 1–2% recovery to normal, 5–15% borderline, 16–25% fair, and 60–75% poor." Higher functioning at intake, but nothing else, predicted a better outcome. In the 1980s, most children with autism were served in classrooms for children with intellectual disabilities and often severe behavior challenges, where they received few specific services addressing their needs. Most EIBI outcome studies conducted since the 1990s indicate roughly half of the children who have been recipients of EIBI function near the typical range of their peers although they often continue to exhibit some language and social deficits. Many of the remaining children experience marked improvements, but usually remain in special education classrooms for children with autism or language delays. They also have significant residual autism symptoms. I am aware of no other treatments for children with emotional and/or developmental disorders with such a remarkable pattern of outcomes.

Note

1 Portions of this manuscript are based in part on T. Thompson (2013) Autism research and services for young children: Progress and challenges. *Journal of Applied Research in Intellectual Disabilities, 6*(2) in press; reproduced with permission, John Wiley & Sons, Inc.

References

Akerley, M. S. (1976). Parents speak: Introduction; reactions to "employing electric shock with children." *Journal of Autism and Childhood Schizophrenia, 6*, 289–294.

American Psychiatric Association (2000). *Diagnostic and statistical manual of mental disorders DSM-IV-TR* (4th ed., text rev.). Washington, DC: American Psychiatric Publishing.

American Psychiatric Association (2010). *DSMV: The future of psychiatric diagnosis, DSM-5 development.* Washington DC. American Psychiatric Association. Retrieved June 21, 2012 from http://www.dsm5.org/Pages/Default.aspx. .

Baron-Cohen, S. (1995). *Mindblindness: An essay on autism and theory of mind.* Cambrdige, MA: MIT Press/Bradford Books.

Baron-Cohen, S., Ring, H. A., Wheelwright, S., Bullmore, E. T., Brammer, M. J., Simmons, A., & Williams, S.C. (1999). Social intelligence in the normal and autistic brain: an fMRI study. *European Journal of Neuroscience, 11*, 1891–898.

Bender, L. (1947). The visual motor gestalt test and its clinical use: One hundred cases of childhood schizophrenia treated with electric shock. *Transactions of the American Neurology Association, 72*, 165–169.

Bender, L., Goldschmidt, L., & Siva, D. V. (1962). Treatment of autistic schizophrenic children with LSD-25 and UML-49. *Recent Advances in Biological Psychiatry, 4*, 170–177.

Bettleheim, B. (1967). *The empty fortress.* New York: The Free Press.

Bondy, A. S., & Frost, L. A. (1994). The picture exchange communication system. *Focus on Autism, 9*, 1–19.

Bowlby, J. (1969). *Attachment (Volume I).* New York: Basic Books.

Brim, D., Townsend, D. B., DeQuinzio, J. A., & Poulson, C. L. (2009). Analysis of social referencing in autism. *Research in Autism Spectrum Disorders, 3*, 942–958.

Carbone, V. (2007). *Carbone Clinic.* New York: Valley Cottage. Retrieved November 17, 2012 from http://www.drcarbone.net/.

Carr, E. G. (1977). The motivation of self-injurious behavior: A review of some hypotheses. *Psychological Bulletin, 84*, 800–816.

Carr, E. G., Horner, R. H., Turnbull, A. P., Marquis, J. G., McLaughlin, D. M., McAtee, M. L., Smith, C. E., Ryan, K. A., Ruef, M. B., & Doolabh, A. (1999). *Positive behavior support for people with developmental disabilities: A research synthesis.* American Association on Mental Retardation Monograph Series. Washington, DC: American Association on Mental Retardation.

Carr, E. G., Robinson, S., Taylor, J. C., & Carlson, J. I. (1990). Toward a technology of "nonaversive" behavioral support. *Monograph of the Association for Persons with Severe Handicaps, Monograph No. 4*, 1–34.

Dawson, G., Rogers, S., Munson, J., Smith, M., Winter, J., Greenson, J., Donaldson, A., & Varley, J. (2010). Randomized, controlled trial of an intervention for toddlers with autism: The Early Start Denver Model. *Pediatrics, 125*, e17–23.

DeMyer, M. K., Barton, S., DeMyer, W. E., Norton, J. A., Allen, J., & Steele, R. (1973). Prognosis in autism: A follow-up study. *Journal of Autism Child Schizophrenia, 3*, 199–246.

Dube, W., Schichenmeyer, K., Grant, E., & Roscoe, E. (2012). *Functional analysis of problem behavior: A systematic approach to idiosyncratic variables.* Paper presented at the Annual Gatlinburg Conference for Research and Theory on Intellectual and Developmental Disabilities, March 8, 2012, Annapolis, MD.

Ellis, N. R., Pryer, M. W., & Barnett, C. D. (1960). Note on habit formation in normal and retarded subjects. *Psychological Record, 6*, 385–386.

Fenichel, C. (1966). Psychoeducational approaches for seriously disturbed children in the classroom. *Intervention approaches in educating emotionally disturbed children.* Syracuse Division of Special Education and Rehabilitation. Syracuse University.

Ferster, C. B. (1961). Positive reinforcement and behavior deficits of autistic children. *Child Development, 32*, 437–456.

Ferster, C. B., & DeMyer, M. K. (1961). The development of performances in autistic children in an automatically controlled environment. *Journal of Chronic Diseases, 13*, 312–314.

Ferster C. B., & Skinner, B. F. (1957). *Schedules of reinforcement.* New York: Appleton.

Fisher, W. W., Kuhn, D. E., & Thompson. R. H. (1998). Functional analysis and treatment of destructive behavior maintained by termination of "don't" (and symmetrical "do") requests. *Journal of Applied Behavior Analysis, 31*, 339–356.

Girardeau, F. L., & Spradlin, J. E. (1964). Token rewards in a cottage program. *Mental Retardation, 13*, 345–351.

Grelotti, D. J., Gauthier, I., & Schultz, R. T. (2002) Social interest and the development of cortical face specialization: What autism teaches us about face processing. *Developmental Psychobiology, 40*, 213–225.

Gresham, F. M., & MacMillan, D. L. (1998). Early Intervention Project: Can its claims be substantiated and its effects replicated? *Journal of Autism and Developmental Disorders, 28*, 5–13.

Gutstein, E., & Sheely, R. K. (2002). *Relationship development intervention with young children: Social and emotional development activities for Asperger Syndrome, Autism, PDD and NLD.* London: Jessica Kingsley Publishers.

Hanley, G. P., Iwata, B. A., & McCord, B. E. (2003). Functional analysis of problem behavior: A review. *Journal of Applied Behavior Analysis, 36*, 147–185.

Hart, B., & Risley, T. R. (1975). Incidental teaching of language in the preschool. *Journal of Applied Behavior Analysis, 8*, 411–420.

Helt, M., Kelley, E., Kinsbourne, M., Pandey, J., Boorstein, H., Herbert, M., & Fein, D. (2008). Can children with autism recover? If so, how? *Neuropsychological Review, 18*, 339–366.

Hewett, F. M. (1964). Teaching reading to an autistic boy through operant conditioning. *Reading teacher, 17*, 613–18.

Hewett, F. M. (1965). Teaching speech to an autistic child through operant conditioning. *American Journal of Orthopsychiatry, 35*, 927–936.

Hewett, F. M. (1969). *The Santa Monica Project: Demonstration and evaluation of an engineered classroom design for emotionally disturbed children in the public school; Phase two: Primary and secondary level. Final Report.* Department of Education, Bureau of Research Project (0EG-0-80071298-2799(032) ERIC 038809.

Hingten, J. N., Coulter S. K., & Churchill, D. W (1967). Intensive reinforcement of imitative behavior in mute autistic children. *Archives of General Psychiatry, 17*, 36–43.

Holland, J. G., & Skinner, B. F. (1961). *The analysis of behavior: A program for self-instruction.* New York: McGraw Hill.

Horner, R. H., Albin, R. W., Sprague, J. R., & Todd, A. W. (1999). Positive behavior support. In M. E. Snell & F. Brown (Eds.), *Instruction of students with severe disabilities* (5th ed.) (pp. 207–243). Upper Saddle River, NJ: Prentice Hall.

Horner, R. H., Dunlap, G., Koegel, R. L., Carr, E. G., Sailor, W., Anderson, J., Albin, W. R., & O'Neill, R. E. (1990). Toward a technology of "nonaversive" behavioral support. *The Journal of the Association for the Severely Handicapped, 15*, 125–132.

Huerta, M., Bishop, S. L., Duncan, A., Hus, V., & Lord, C. E. (2012). Application of DSM-5 criteria for Autism Spectrum Disorder to three samples of children with DSM-IV diagnoses of Pervasive Developmental Disorders. *American Journal of Psychiatry, 169*, 1056–1064.

International Classification of Diseases (WHO) (2012). Reactive attachment disorder. Retrieved February 25, 2012 from http://www.who.int/classifications/icd/en/.

Itard, M. E. (Jean) (1802). *An historical account of the discovery and education of a savage man: Or, the first developments, physical and moral, of the young savage caught in the woods near Aveyron in the year 1798.* London: Richard Phillips (Google eBook) Retrieved February 25, 2010 from http://books.google.com/books/about/An_Historical_Account_of_the_Discovery_a.html?id=F63cRcnV2hIC.

Iwata, B. A., Dorsey, M. F., Slifer, K. J., Bauman, K. E., & Richman, G. S. (1994). Toward a functional analysis of self-injury. *Journal of Applied Behavior Analysis, 27*, 197–209.

Jensen, G. D., & Womack, M. G. (1967). Operant conditioning techniques applied in the treatment of an autistic child. *American Journal of Orthopsychiatry, 37*, 30–34.

Kahng, S., Iwata, B. A., & Lewin, A. B. (2002). Behavioral treatment of self-injury, 1964 to 2000. *American Journal on Mental Retardation, 107*, 212–221.

Kanner, L. (1943). Autistic disturbances of affective contact. *Nervous Child, 12*, 217–250.

Koegel, L. K., Koegel, R. L., Harrower, J. K., & Carter, C. M. (1999). Pivotal response intervention I: Overview of approach. *The Journal of the Association for Persons with Severe Handicaps, 24*, 174–185.

Landa, R. J., Holman, K. C., O'Neill, A. H., & Stuart, S. A. (2011). Intervention targeting development of socially synchronous engagement in toddlers with autism spectrum disorder: A randomized controlled trial. *Journal of Child Psychology and Psychiatry, 52*, 13–21.

LeBlanc, L., Coates, A. M., Daneshvar, S., Charlop-Christie, M. H., Morris C., & Lancaster, B. M. (2003). Using video modeling and reinforcement to teach perspective-taking skills to children with autism. *Journal of Applied Behavior Analysis, 36*, 253–257.

Lord, C. E., & McGee, J. (2001). *Educating children with autism.* Committee on Educational Interventions for Children with Autism, National Research Council. Washington, DC: National Academies Press.

Løvaas, O. I. (1967). A behavior therapy approach to the treatment of childhood schizophrenia. *Minnesota Symposia on Child Psychology, 1*, 108–159.

Løvaas, O. I. (1987). Behavioral treatment and normal educational and intellectual functioning in young autistic children. *Journal of Consulting and Clinical Psychology, 55*, 3–9.

Løvaas, O. I. (1988). *Behavioral treatment of autistic children.* Motion Picture produced by Focus International, Huntington Station, NY; distributed as DVD Cambridge Center for Behavioral Studies, Cambridge, MA.

Løvaas, O. I., Schaeffer, B., & Simmons, J. Q. (1965). Building social behaviors in autistic children by use of electric shock. *Journal of Experimental Research in Personality, 1*, 99–109.

Løvaas, O. I., & Wright, S. (2006). A reply to recent public critiques. *Journal of Early Intensive Behavioural Intervention, 3*, 221–229.

Matson, J. L., Kozlowski, A. M., Hattier, M. A., Horovitz, M., & Sipes, M. (2012). DSM-IV vs DSM-5 diagnostic criteria for toddlers with autism. *Developmental Neurorehabilitation, 15*, 185–190.

Maurer, A. (1983). The shock rod controversy. *Journal of Clinical Child Psychology, 12*, 272–278.

Maurice, C. (1994). *Let me hear your voice: A family's triumph over autism*. New York: Random Hous.

McEachin, J. J., Smith, T., & Løvaas, O. I. (1993). Long-term outcome for children with autism who received early intensive behavioral treatment. *American Journal on Mental Retardation, 97*, 359–372.

McGee, G. G, Almeida, M. C, Sulzer-Azaroff, B., & Feldman, R. S. (1992). Promoting reciprocal interactions via peer incidental teaching. *Journal of Applied Behavior Analysis, 25*, 117–126.

McPartland, J. C., Reichow, B., & Volkmar, F. R. (2012). Sensitivity and specificity of proposed DSM-5 diagnostic criteria for autism spectrum disorder. *Journal of the American Academy of Child and Adolescent Psychiatry, 51*, 368–83.

Moser, D., & Grant, A. (1965). Screams, slaps & love: A surprising, shocking treatment helps far-gone mental cripples. *Life Magazine*, May 7, 1965.

National Institutes of Health (1989). *Treatment of destructive behaviors in persons with developmental disabilities*. NIH Consensus Statement Online 1989 September, 11–13. Retrieved June 21, 2012 from NIH web address: http://consensus.nih.gov/1989/1989DestructiveBehaviorsDevelopment075html.htm

Oppenheim, R. C. (1961). They said our child was hopeless. *Saturday Evening Post, 23*, 56–58, June 17, 1961.

Oppenheim, R. C. (1973). *Effective teaching methods for autistic children*. Springfield, IL: Charles C. Thomas Publishing Co.

Orlando, R., & Bijou, S. W. (1960). Single and multiple schedules of reinforcement in developmentally retarded children. *Journal of the Experimental Analysis of Behavior, 3*, 339–348.

Paracelsus, T. (1951/1942). *Paracelsus: Selected writings* (Norbert Guterman Trans.) (J. Jacobi ed.). Originally published in German as *Theophrastus Paracelsus: Lebendiges Erbe*, by Rascher Verlag, Zurich, 1942, Bollinger Series 28. New York: Pantheon Books.

Partington, J. W. (2007). *Assessment of basic language and learning skills—Revised (ABLLS-R)*. Walnut Creek, CA: The Behavior Analysts, Inc.

Perez, T. E. (2010). Remarks of Assistant Attorney General for Civil Rights Thomas E. Perez at the National Disability Rights Network Annual Conference. June 10, 2010. Los Angeles, CA. Retrieved June 22, 2012 from http://www.justice.gov/crt/speeches/perez_disability_conf.php.

Piaget, J. (1936). *Origins of intelligence in the child*. London: Routledge.

Piaget, J. (1957). *Construction of reality in the child*. London: Routledge.

Prizant, B. M., & Wetherby, A. M. (1998). Understanding the continuum of discrete-trial traditional behavioral to social-pragmatic developmental approaches in communication enhancement for young children with autism/PDD. *Seminars in Speech and Language, 19*, 329–352.

Reeve, S. A., Reeve, K. F., Townsend, D. B., & Poulson, C. L. (2007). Establishing a generalized repertoire of helping behavior in children with autism. *Journal of Applied Behavior Analysis, 40*, 123–136.

Remington, B., Hastings, R. P., Kovshoff, H., degli Espinosa, F., Jahr, E., Brown, T., Alsford, P., Lemaic, M., & Ward, N. (2007). Early intensive behavioral intervention: Outcomes for children with autism and their parents after two years. *American Journal on Mental Retardation, 112S*, 418–438.

Rimland, B. (1964). The etiology of infantile autism: The problem of biological versus psychological causation. In B. Rimland (Ed.). *Infantile autism* (pp. 39–66). New York: Appleton.

Risley, T. R., & Wolf, M. M. (1964). *Experimental manipulation of autistic behaviors and generalization into the home.* Paper presented at American Psychological Association, Los Angeles, September, 1964.

Rutter, M. (Ed.) (1971). *Infantile autism: Concepts, characteristics and treatment.* Edinburgh & London: Churchill Livingstone.

Sallows, G. O., & Graupner, T. D. (2005). Intensive behavioral treatment for children with autism: four-year outcome and predictors. *American Journal on Mental Retardation, 110,* 417–438.

Schopler, E., Short, A., & Mesibov, G. (1989). Relation of behavioral treatment to "normal functioning": Comment on Løvaas. *Journal of Consulting and Clinical Psychology, 57,* 162–164.

Schrandt, J. A., Townsend, D. B., & Poulson, C. L. (2009). Teaching empathy skills to children with autism. *Journal of Applied Behavior Analysis, 42,* 17–32.

Schreibman, L., Stahmer, A. C., & Pierce, K. (1996). Alternative applications of Pivotal Response Training: Teaching symbolic play and social interaction skills. In L. K. Koegel, R. L. Koegel, & G. Dunlap (Eds.), *Positive behavioral support: Including people with difficult behavior in the community* (pp. 353–371). Baltimore, MD: Paul H. Brookes Publishing Co.

Sherer, M. R., & Schreibman, L. (2005). Individual behavioral profiles and predictors of treatment effectiveness for children with autism. *Journal of Consulting and Clinical Psychology, 73,* 525–538.

Silver, A. A. (1954). Diagnosis of the various syndromes encountered in the retarded preadolescent child. *Quarterly Review of Pediatrics, 9,* 127.

Simmons, J. Q., & Løvaas, O. I. (1969). Use of pain and punishment as treatment techniques with childhood schizophrenics. *American Journal of Psychotherapy, 23*(1), 23–36

Skinner, B. F. (1938). *The behavior of organisms.* New York: Appleton.

Skinner, B. F. (1953). *Science and human behavior.* New York: Macmillan.

Skinner, B. F. (1957). *Verbal behavior.* New York: Appleton.

Spitz, R. A. (1945). Hospitalism: An inqury into the genesis of psychiatric conditions in early childhood. *Psychoanalytic Study of the Child, 1,* 53–74

Spradlin, J. E. (1959). *Effects of reinforcement schedules on extinction in severely mentally retarded children.* Doctoral dissertation. George Peabody College for Teachers, Nashville, TN.

Stafford, M. W., Sundberg, M. L., & Braam, S. (1988). A preliminary investigation of the consequences that define the Mand and the Tact. *The Analysis of Verbal Behavior, 6,* 61–71.

Sundberg, M. L. (2008). *Verbal behavior milestones assessment and placement program (VB-MAPP).* Concord, CA: Advancements in Verbal Behavior Press.

Thompson, T. (2005). Paul E. Meehl and B. F. Skinner: Autitaxia, autitypy and autism. *Behavior and Philosophy, 33,* 101–133.

Thompson, T. (2008). Self-awareness: Behavior analysis and neuroscience. *The Behavior Analyst, 31,* 137–144.

Thompson, T. (2011). *Individualized autism intervention for young children: Blending discrete trial and naturalistic strategies.* Baltimore, MD: Paul H. Brookes Publishing Co.

Thompson, T. (2013). Autism research and services for young children: Progress and challenges. *Journal of Applied Research in Intellectual Disabilities, 26,* 1–27.

Thompson, T., & Grabowski, J. G. (Eds.) (1972). *Behavior modification of the mentally retarded* (1st ed.). New York: Oxford University Press.

Tsai, L. Y. (2012). Sensitivity and specificity: DSM-IV versus DSM-5 criteria for autism spectrum disorder. *American Journal of Psychiatry*, *169*, 1009–1011.

Vaillant, G. E. (1962). John Haslam on early infantile autism. *American Journal of Psychiatry*, *119*, 376.

Vygotsky, L. (1986/1934). *Thought and language*. Cambridge, MA: MIT Press.

Walter, C. (2005). Teaching against idiocy, *Phi Delta Kappan*, *86*, 344.

Wolf, M. M., Risley, T., & Mees, H. (1964). Application of operant conditioning procedures to the behavior problems of an autistic child. *Behaviour Research and Therapy*, *1*, 305–312.

20

Parenting

Raymond G. Miltenberger
and Kimberly A. Crosland

Parenting may be one of the most challenging yet potentially rewarding long-term commitments one can make. Parents (hereafter, parent refers to parent or primary caretaker) play an important role in promoting children's health, development, and welfare. Parents promote learning and abate problems by creating positive learning environments and by effectively managing contingencies on child behavior. Parenting itself is a complex repertoire of behavior that is influenced by the parents' learning history and shaped by children's behavior (e.g., Carr, Taylor, & Robinson, 1991; Emery, Binkoff, Houts, & Carr, 1983) and other environmental factors (e.g., spouse behavior, advice, and contingencies from other influential adults, parenting programs, etc.). Effective parenting often is challenged by child variables such as the presence of severe behavior problems, developmental disabilities, autism, or other disorders that make greater demands on parents' behavioral resources. Parent-training programs based on the scientific principles of behavior have been shown to increase parental competence and improve child behavior (e.g., Egel & Powers, 1989; Smagner & Sullivan, 2005; Van Camp, Borrero, & Vollmer, 2003).

This chapter will first describe the role of operant conditioning as it applies to parenting. A description of the variables that may influence parent and child behavior (including problem behavior) will be presented. Next, parenting intervention strategies that have been empirically documented as successful will be discussed. More recently, efforts have been made to develop parent-friendly packaged approaches, many of which have been deemed evidence-based. These approaches along with a discussion of some barriers to successful parent training will be described.

Child Behavior and Development

Child development involves operant conditioning (learning) which produces changes in child behavior over time due to the reinforcing consequences that result from

The Wiley Blackwell Handbook of Operant and Classical Conditioning, First Edition.
Edited by Frances K. McSweeney and Eric S. Murphy.

interactions between the child and the people (mostly parents), objects, and activities in the environment (e.g., Bijou, 1976; Bijou & Baer, 1961). As the child engages in behavior that is reinforced, that behavior is more likely to occur in similar circumstances. The child's behavioral repertoire is expanded incrementally as each subsequent operant response is reinforced, forming new response classes that allow the child to interact effectively with people and the physical environment. Specific child responses may be more or less likely to occur depending on the child's current behavioral repertoire and current circumstances. For example, when a 6-month-old child engages in babbling, the parent is likely to react with attention, thus reinforcing the behavior.

Over time, parents differentially reinforce (shape) verbal utterances that more closely approximate language. Therefore, at 24 months of age, the child is likely to engage in more complex verbal behavior (naming objects or events, answering questions, asking for things) that produces reinforcement from the parents. Both responses, the rudimentary verbal utterance of babbling and the more refined verbal behavior of naming or asking, are products of the history of reinforcement by the parent that occur at different times in the child's life. As child development is comprised of a sequential learning process, the latter more complex responses depend on the development of the earlier rudimentary responses (Bijou, 1976; Bijou & Baer, 1961).

Some psychologists examine development from a chronological age perspective such as observing and describing the behavior of 2 year olds or 5 year olds (Gesell, 1954; Hurlock, 1977). This approach can appear too simplistic for those wanting to understand interactions between the child and the environment (Baer, 1970; Bijou, 1976; Schlinger, 1995). An alternative is to identify stages according to the types of interactions a child has and how those interactions contribute to development (Kantor, 1959). Although these stages represent periods of time in which certain types of interactions occur, they do not reflect any causal relationships between environmental events and behavior.

The search for causal relationships between environment and behavior started with Watson and progressed through Skinner and has continued with the legions of behavioral researchers that have embraced Skinner's operant perspective on learning (e.g., Fisher, Piazza, & Roane, 2011; Madden, 2012). Skinner (1938, 1953, 1974) focused his work primarily on operant conditioning, the basic process by which behavior is modified by its consequences. Operant behavior is influenced by its immediate consequences. Reinforcement strengthens behavior and punishment weakens behavior. For example, when an infant swats the mobile hanging in her crib and makes it move, she is more likely to swat the mobile when lying in her crib. On the other hand, when the infant swats the wooden bar in her crib and produces pain in her hand, she is less likely to swat the bar again. These examples show the effect of consequences produced by the behavior's direct effect on the physical environment. In contrast, some consequences are social—delivered by people. A child who receives praise for completing chores is more likely to do the chores; a child who loses privileges for hitting his brother is less likely to hit his brother. Although Skinner and behavior analysts in general do recognize that genes and biology play a role in behavior, they maintain that these factors merely set the limits within which behavior can be modified by environmental variables (Skinner, 1974).

From early on, behavior analysts adopted the operant conditioning approach to study basic principles of learning in children (Bijou, 1955, 1957, 1958; Bijou & Baer, 1961, 1963). This work led to the terms, behavior modification, and applied behavior analysis (Baer, Wolf, & Risley, 1968), and led to years of research on understanding and improving child and parent behavior.

A ground breaking study by Hart and Risley (1995) examined the acquisition of language in young children. This longitudinal study recorded the number of words spoken between parents and children in 42 families over a three-year period. The children were observed once a month for one hour from the time they were 7 to 9 months old until they reached 3 years of age. The researchers recorded more than 1,300 hours of interactions between parents and children and discovered that parents differed markedly in the amount that they talked to their children. Some parents spoke more than 2,000 words per hour while others spoke as few as 616 words per hour. The children were followed over time and language ability was assessed when they were 9 to 10 years of age. Hart and Risley's found that the children's vocabulary at 3 years was strongly associated with later intellectual achievement related to reading and spoken language ability.

Hart and Risley's results demonstrated the amount of talk between parent and child was directly linked to the child's rate of vocabulary growth and future academic achievement including IQ scores. This direct connection between the number of words heard and the number of words used by children clearly speaks to the incredible advantage that effective parenting can have on a young child's development. It speaks to the argument that a child's early environment can set the stage for later accomplishments. Likewise, impediments in the child's early environment can set the stage for poor performance in school and beyond.

Several other early studies examined the role of the environment in children's intellectual development (Heber, 1971; Skeels, Updegraff, Wellman, & Williams, 1938). The Glenwood State School project placed infants from an orphanage in the direct personal care of women who were residing at the Glenwood School, an institution for women with cognitive disabilities (Skeels et al., 1938). The 13 infants with the lowest IQ's (averaging 64) were placed on the active wards with the older, and relatively brighter, women residing at the institution. The "mothers" provided a loving, engaging environment. They were taught how to stimulate the intellectual abilities of the babies and how to evoke language. Each mother was taught how to provide basic care and attention for her baby including how to hold, feed, talk to, and stimulate the child. Books and toys were available and the babies were taken on outings. The children also attended a half-morning kindergarten program at the institution. The infants in the experimental group remained with the women at the Glenwood School until they were adopted or entered formal schooling. After 18 months, the average IQ of the children placed with the mothers increased 29 points and several years later a follow-up study showed that their average IQs were 101. The 12 children that stayed at the orphanage started with an average IQ of 87 and experienced a substantial decrease in IQ to an average of 66.

Heber (1971) also studied the effects of an enriched environment including intellectual stimulation on newborns that were born to mothers with low IQs in a low-income area of Milwaukee. Known as the Milwaukee Project, 40 newborns were randomly assigned, 20 to an experimental group and 20 to a control group. Mothers in the experimental group received extensive education and training including vocational rehabilitation and childcare. The children also attended a special education center that focused on language and cognitive development. The children attended the program 7 hours per day, 5 days per week, and the program was staffed by paraprofessionals who were chosen based on characteristics of being caring, warm, and having a significant language repertoire. As the children grew older, they received instruction from certified preschool teachers. The control group did not receive home-based training or educational enrichment. At age 6, the average IQ of children in the experimental group was 120.7 compared to the control group which was 87.2. Other measures showed that all of the children in the experimental group scored higher than those in the control group.

Clearly, the interactions between a parent and child are important influences on child development. Verbal abilities, reading, social interactions, and a myriad of adaptive behaviors are all operant in nature and are thus learned within the child's immediate environment. These behaviors are acquired and maintained via operant conditioning primarily through contingencies managed by parents.

Relationship Between Parent and Child Behavior

Learning and the development of appropriate and inappropriate behavior by children is a product of operant conditioning in which parental behavior plays a major role in the three-term contingency of reinforcement. Due to the extensive contact between parent and child from birth to young adulthood, parental behavior is the basis of many antecedents to child behavior and the basis of many consequences of child behavior. The functional antecedents in the three-term contingency are the discriminative stimuli (S^D) and establishing operations (EO) that evoke child behavior (response-R) and the reinforcing (S^R) consequences that strengthen child behavior.

$$EO / S^D \rightarrow R \rightarrow S^R$$

An antecedent stimulus that is present when a behavior is reinforced is known as a discriminative stimulus. For example, if a parent reinforces a child's problem behavior with attention, then the parent's presence is an S^D for the problem behavior. An establishing operation is an event that increases the potency of a particular reinforcer and evokes the behavior at a particular time. For example, if a child has not had attention from the parent in a long time, then the parent's attention is more reinforcing than if the child has had recent attention.

The essential feature of operant conditioning is the response strengthening power of reinforcement. It is often asserted that children learn much through observational learning in which they observe the behaviors of parents, teachers, and others around them then engage in similar behaviors (Bandura, 1977). Nevertheless, observational learning does not take place unless behavior is strengthened by the use of reinforcement. Many antecedents can influence child behavior, including observing models, but only those behaviors that are reinforced once they occur will continue and generalize to other contexts.

Reinforcement is a principle whereby an environmental event is contingent on a behavior and the frequency of that type of behavior increases in the future. Reinforcement from parents is ubiquitous in child learning and development. Reinforcement may occur naturally (e.g., an infant is more likely to smile or reach for the parent when parental smiling and attention are contingent on such behavior), or it might be programmed (e.g., a child is more likely to complete chores when the parent makes the opportunity to play a favorite video game contingent on completing the chore).

Antecedent variables also influence the acquisition and maintenance of child behavior. Antecedent variables, S^Ds and EOs, have an evocative function. An evocative function refers to the extent to which the presentation of a stimulus produces a momentary increase in behavior. Certain stimuli evoke or set the occasion for particular responses to occur by virtue of their relation to the reinforcer for the behavior. If a parent tells a child to put his dirty clothes in his laundry bin and the child immediately does so, then the demand evoked the child's behavior presumably because the parent previously reinforced the behavior in the presence of the demand. Many stimuli can acquire evocative functions as S^Ds and EOs by virtue of their temporal relation to behavior that is reinforced (Laraway, Snycerski, Michael, & Poling, 2003; Michael, 1982, 1993).

In everyday language, an S^D signals the availability of reinforcement or punishment. Technically, the S^D is the stimulus that was present when a behavior was reinforced, thus making the behavior more likely to occur in its presence. In this way, discriminative stimuli influence how children and adults behave. Stimulus control is achieved if reliable and predictable changes occur in behavior in the presence of the S^D.

Whereas an S^D signals reinforcement availability, an EO increases the effectiveness of a reinforcer and thus evokes the behavior that has produced that reinforcer. An EO is one type of a larger class of stimuli called motivating operations (MOs) that influence reinforcer effectiveness. MOs can either increase reinforcer effectiveness (EO) or decrease reinforcer effectiveness (abolishing operation or AO) and thus alter the frequency of the behavior that has been reinforced (Cooper, Heron, & Heward, 2007; Laraway et al., 2003). When a parent has not seen her children all day, interaction with her children will be more reinforcing and playing with them will be more likely. Not seeing her children for a long time is an EO that evokes playing with them. When a parent has recently had coercive interactions (such as arguing) with her children, she may be less likely to play with them. A coercive interaction is an AO that decreases the effectiveness of interactions with children as reinforcement and makes playing with the children less likely.

Schedules of reinforcement can have a major impact on how quickly behavior is acquired and which behaviors are strengthened. Continuous reinforcement, in which the parent reinforces every instance of a child's behavior, is used to help children acquire new behaviors. Intermittent schedules of reinforcement are used to maintain behavior once they are established and to enable the progression from reinforcement by the parent to naturally occurring reinforcement. Although the parent may reinforce such behaviors as cooperative play, sports activities, reading, toileting, and many others, ultimately these behaviors are maintained by naturally occurring reinforcers rather than parental reinforcement (e.g., reading an interesting book is naturally reinforcing).

Parent-training programs take into account the powerful influence of parental behavior on child behavior and they teach parents to manage the behavior that they direct towards their children. Parents are taught to manage influential antecedents and consequences to child problem behavior to make problem behavior less likely. They are also taught to reinforce desirable child behavior so that the desirable behavior is established to replace problem behavior (e.g., Hembree-Kigin & McNeil, 1995; Latham, 1990; McIntire, 1995).

Functional Analysis Technology

In behavior analysis, a dependent variable (behavior of child) and a given independent variable (environmental event; often the parent's behavior or an intervention procedure) are functionally related if the dependent variable changes systematically with changes in the value of the independent variable. A functional analysis examines the relationship between environmental events (antecedents and consequences) and the occurrence of the behavior to identify the environmental events that evoke and maintain the behavior (Iwata, Dorsey, Slifer, Bauman, & Richman, 1982; Iwata, Vollmer, & Zarcone, 1990; Iwata, Vollmer, Zarcone, & Rodgers, 1993). A functional analysis involves directly observing behavior while arranging antecedents that may evoke problem behavior and consequences that may increase the problem behavior in order to determine which variables influence the behavior. In a functional analysis, one or more variables are manipulated and the variables that produce differential responding (a level of behavior that is consistently higher than the level produced by the other variables or a control condition) are determined to be the variables that are evoking and/or maintaining the behavior.

Four main categories of maintaining variables have been identified through research utilizing functional analysis methods: social positive reinforcement in the form of attention or access to tangible items, social negative reinforcement in the form of escape from tasks or other aversive stimuli, automatic reinforcement in the form of sensory stimulation, and automatic negative reinforcement in the form of escape from aversive stimuli (Iwata et al., 1982, 1990, 1993). The majority of functional analyses (87 to 95%) have been found to yield differential responding useful for intervention planning (Hanley, Iwata, & McCord, 2003; Iwata et al., 1982; Kurtz et al., 2003)

Functional analysis can be advantageous as it allows for the development of behavioral interventions that are specific to the variables maintaining the problem behaviors exhibited by a particular child. Interventions based on functional analysis have been found to be more effective than those not based on functional analysis (Axelrod, 1987; Carr & Durand, 1985; Iwata, Pace, Cowdery, & Miltenberger, 1994; Repp, Felce, & Barton, 1988). These interventions are effective because the undesirable behavior is placed on extinction (does not receive reinforcement) while a desirable replacement behavior is differentially reinforced often with the reinforcer that was maintaining the problem behavior (Miltenberger, 2012). In addition specific antecedents (S^Ds and EOs), found to be functionally related to the problem behavior, are altered to influence the problem behavior (e.g., Dunlap, Kern-Dunlap, Clarke, & Robbins, 1991; Kennedy, 1994; Kennedy & Itkonen, 1993).

A functional approach to intervention typically includes three treatment components, with specific variations of each component determined by the functional analysis. Functional treatments include: (a) extinction, (b) differential reinforcement, and (c) antecedent manipulations (Miltenberger, 2012). To use extinction, parents are taught to withhold reinforcing consequences contingent on the occurrence of the problem behavior. To use differential reinforcement, parents are taught to provide the reinforcer contingent on more appropriate behavior to replace the problem behavior. These two procedures reverse the contingencies to favor desirable behavior over problem behavior. Finally, to use antecedent manipulations, parents are taught to alter the conditions or events that evoke problem behaviors (Iwata et al., 1993). Table 20.1 provides examples of these three functional intervention components applied to child behavior maintained by the different categories of reinforcement.

Function-based intervention has become the behavior analytic gold-standard in the areas of developmental disability and autism (Hanley et al., 2003). It has produced positive results in the treatment of serious problem behaviors such as self-injury (Vollmer, Marcus, & Ringdahl, 1995; Kahng, Iwata, & Lewin, 2002) and aggression (Fisher, Adelenis, Thompson, Worsdell, & Zarcone, 1998; Northup et al., 1991). Functional analysis and function-based intervention also has been shown to be effective in the treatment of child problem behaviors in home, school, and clinic settings (e.g., Arndorfer, Miltenberger, Woster, Rortvedt, & Gaffaney, 1994; Carr & Durand, 1985; Derby et al., 1992; Mace & Knight, 1986; Wright-Gallo, Higbee, Reagon, & Davey, 2006).

However, in the area of parenting typically-developing children who have challenging behavior, the combination of functional analysis and function-based treatment has not been as widely adopted. As Mullen and Scotti (2000) pointed out, the widespread adoption of such approaches would have ramifications for some of the most commonly implemented parenting programs. Most notably, parents would have to be trained to define behaviors operationally and make judgments with respect to possible function and appropriate responses to those behaviors. In other words, parents would be responsible for conducting some sort of functional assessment, identifying the function of their child's problem behavior, and choosing or developing treatments matched to the function. This is a complex activity that is probably out of the realm of what can realistically be expected of most parents.

Some parenting studies have employed functional analysis, however. Shayne and Miltenberger (2013) taught foster parents to conduct functional assessments and to choose appropriate treatments. However, the training was applied to video vignettes, rather than to actual child behavior problems. McNeill, Watson, Henington, and Meeks (2002) studied a competency-based training program to teach parents to define behavior, identify antecedents and consequences, teach replacement behaviors and implement procedures to decrease inappropriate behaviors. Results indicated that parents improved their skills in defining behaviors, identifying antecedents and consequences, and suggesting interventions.

The findings of Shayne and Miltenberger and McNeill et al. notwithstanding, empirically supported behavioral parenting programs typically do not proceed from a functional analysis to treatment development. Rather they provide a standard set of procedures that can be applied successfully to prevent and ameliorate child behavior problems. These programs are often described in a manual and they provide

Table 20.1 Functional treatments for child problem behaviors

Functions of Behavior	*Functional Treatment Components*		
	Extinction	*Differential Reinforcement*	*Antecedent Manipulations*
Attention	Withhold attention contingent on problem behavior (e.g., when child screams, parent no longer scolds child)	Provide attention contingent on a desirable behavior (e.g., when child plays quietly, parent provides attention)	Provide noncontingent attention (e.g., parent gives child attention frequently throughout the day)
Tangible	Withhold tangible item contingent on problem behavior (e.g., when child screams, parent no longer gives child cookie)	Provide tangible item contingent on a desirable behavior (e.g., when child asks appropriately, parent provides cookie)	Provide noncontingent access to the tangible item (e.g., parent provides access to preferred item frequently throughout the day)
Escape	Do not allow escape contingent on problem behavior (e.g., when child screams, parent no longer lets child out of doing chore)	Provide a brief break (escape) from the task contingent on a desirable behavior (e.g., when child finishes part of chore, parents give child a break); provide powerful positive reinforcer contingent on desirable behavior (e.g., when child finishes chore parent provides access to favorite video game)	Alter the aversive properties of the task (e.g., parent assigns child an easier task); provide assistance (e.g., parent works with child until child competent on the task); provide noncontingent escape (e.g., parent provides frequent breaks as child completes the task)
Sensory	Mask the stimulation produced by the behavior (e.g., when child sucks thumb, parent wraps thumb with gauze to alter the stimulation from thumb sucking)	Provide access to matched stimulation or highly preferred reinforcer contingent on desirable behavior (e.g., when child refrains from thumb sucking, parent provides lollipop)	Provide noncontingent access to matched stimulation (e.g., parent provides access to lollipops at various points during the day)

recommendations for altering antecedents and consequences of child problem behavior while promoting desirable behaviors to supplant problem behaviors. Therefore, these programs are based on behavioral research on the analysis and treatment of child problem behaviors and use empirically supported functional interventions even though an explicit functional analysis is not a part of the programs (e.g., Christophersen

& Mortweet, 2001; Hembree-Kigin, & McNeil, 1995; Latham, 1990; McIntire, 1995).

Parent-Training Programs

The objectives of parent training programs have been to identify and ameliorate child behavior problems in addition to improving social emotional development and even physical health (Kaminski, Valle, Filene, & Boyle, 2008; Reifsnider, 1998). Behavioral Parent Training (BPT) is a broad term that has been used to describe various training programs that are designed to have some positive effect on the behavior of children through operant techniques (Graziano & Diament, 1992). BPT focuses on parental behavior change that is widely viewed as socially significant such as: (a) the reduction of negative behaviors of parents in responding to inappropriate child behavior (e.g., coercive interactions that might evoke child problem behavior maintained by escape, or negative attention that might function to reinforce child problem behavior), and (b) the increase in positive interactions that might function to reinforce appropriate behavior (e.g., parental praise for child compliance), or as abolishing operations for attention- or escape-maintained problem behavior (e.g., noncontingent parent attention that makes attention-maintained or escape-maintained behavior less likely). The goal is to increase appropriate behavior of children as a result of effective interventions implemented by parents (Smagner & Sullivan, 2005; Wolfe, Sandler, & Kaufman, 1981).

BPT programs have taught parents to alter the nature of their interactions with the child (e.g., set clear expectations, provide noncontingent attention), to make problem behaviors less likely (Eyberg et al., 2001; Hembree-Kigin & McNeil, 1995), to reinforce appropriate child behaviors (O'Dell et al., 1982), to withhold reinforcement for inappropriate child behavior (Eyberg & Matarazzo, 1980) and, in some cases, to punish inappropriate behavior (Eyberg & Robinson, 1982). For example, parents have been taught to use reinforcement for compliance with requests, while ignoring noncompliance (Ducharme, Atkinson, & Poulton, 2001) and to use reinforcement for compliance combined with a time-out procedure for a failure to comply within a specified latency period (Forehand & King, 1974, 1977).

Some programs have involved teaching parents to use combinations of reinforcement, extinction, prompting, rule-stating and time-out depending on various dimensions of the child's behavior, such as whether or not it is potentially physically harmful to the child, others, or property (Van Camp et al., 2003, 2008). For example, the Tools for Positive Behavior Change Curriculum teaches parents to ignore minor child problem behavior so as to extinguish the behavior, but to use time-out procedures for child problem behavior that is potentially dangerous to minimize the harm that could befall the child or others (Crosland et al., 2008; Van Camp et al., 2003, 2008).

BPT programs have also taught specific interaction skills meant to improve relationships between the child and parent by altering the parent's verbal and nonverbal behaviors. For example, Van Camp et al. (2008) taught parents how to remove reinforcement when a child was engaging in problem behavior and to provide reinforcement when the child was engaging in appropriate behavior (i.e., differential reinforcement). They also taught parents to provide noncontingent reinforcement, which included asking open-ended questions and providing empathy, to enhance the parent-child relationship. Additionally, they taught skills such as how to set expectations for behavior(s) a child was expected to engage in to earn reinforcement and how to implement a time-out procedure.

In a similar fashion, as part of the Parent-Child Interaction Therapy program, the parent is taught to increase positive interactions with the child in the context of play by providing praise for appropriate behavior, reflecting and paraphrasing child language, imitating child play, describing the child's actions, and showing enthusiasm for the child's play (Hembree-Kigin & McNeil, 1995). Together, these positive interactions may influence child behavior in a number of ways such as establishing parental attention as a reinforcer so that parental proximity evokes positive child behavior, providing noncontingent reinforcement which functions as an AO for attention-maintained and escape-maintained problem behavior, and reinforcing appropriate child behavior, making the child less likely to engage in attention seeking behavior and less likely to try to escape from the parents' demands.

The formats for caregiver training programs can range from minimally intrusive web-based or DVD interactive multimedia (Pacifici, Delaney, White, Nelson, & Cummings, 2006) to multidimensional treatment plans involving intensive treatment interventions (Westermark, Hansson, & Vinnerljung, 2007). Common among many BPT training packages is the combination of didactic instruction (e.g., lecture or readings) with modeling, role-playing, and the contingent delivery of feedback based upon performance (Ducharme et al., 2001; Forehand & King 1977; Marcus, Swanson, & Vollmer, 2001; Sandler et al., 1978).

Training that employs instructions, modeling, role-playing, and the contingent delivery of feedback for correct and incorrect performance is known as Behavioral Skills Training (BST). It is typically used in cases where individuals must learn appropriate responses to situations that, due to their nature, often have to be staged or simulated (Poche, Brouwer, & Swearingen, 1981). BST has been used in training children to react to potentially dangerous situations such as the presence of fire (Jones, Kazdin, & Haney, 1981), a firearm (Himle, Miltenberger, Flessner, & Gatheridge, 2004), or a potentially abusive person (Poche, Yoder, & Miltenberger, 1988).

In addition to the use of BST for teaching skills to children, BST has been used in a large number of BPT programs for teaching parents to respond appropriately to child behavior (Ducharme et al., 2001; Eyberg & Robinson, 1982; Forehand & King, 1977; Wolfe et al., 1981; Van Camp et al., 2003). For example, Van Camp et al. (2008) described a BPT program that presented parents with nine techniques to use with children to reduce inappropriate behavior, teach appropriate alternative behavior, and improve the quality of parent/child interactions. During class sessions, the trainers demonstrated the techniques and then role-played with the parents using situations that were frequently encountered in the home environment. Correct responses were prompted as necessary during the role plays, with feedback delivered to identify which steps of the relevant technique were completed successfully and which were not. The goal of BPT is to foster the development of parenting skills with the expectation that the parents will use the skills during the appropriate situations at home with their children.

To foster the use of parenting skills with children in naturally occurring situations, some parent-training programs use the bug-in-the-ear approach (in which the therapist communicates with the parent via a wireless speaker) to coach parents as they engage in interactions with their children in real time (Hembree-Kigin & McNeil, 1995). The bug-in-the-ear approach promotes acquisition and generalization of parenting skills because the therapist prompts the parent to use a parenting skill when a natural opportunity arises (some aspect of the child behavior is an S^D for the parenting skill) and provides praise for the parent's use of the parenting skill as it occurs in the presence of the S^D (resulting in immediate reinforcement and the development of stimulus control). In a similar vein, Hupp and Allen (2005) used an audio cueing device to prompt a parent to provide attention to her oppositional child on a frequent basis as the parent played with the child. The cueing procedure helped the parenting skill generalize from the training setting to the parent's natural interactions with her child.

Parent-training can be delivered individually or in a group setting. The group setting can be advantageous as parents may benefit from sharing ideas or gaining support from other parents. Parents can benefit from seeing the feedback that other parents receive, from seeing multiple models of successful performance, and from analyzing other parents' performance and formulating feedback. It is also more cost effective to train a group of parents than to train them individually. Individual training may be warranted in cases where the parent is not available to participate in group training or if the child is engaging in serious problem behavior for which more individualized interventions may be necessary (Pfiffner & Kaiser, 2010).

Modes of Assessment of Parenting Programs

The most common way of assessing skills acquired after parent training is to administer written or verbal tests or questionnaires. Verbal assessments have been used to determine if parents understood the training information (Berard & Smith, 2008) and to identify changes in how parents view the intervention (Forehand et al., 1979; Leathers, Spielfogel, McMeel, & Atkins, 2011; Pacifici et al., 2006; Westermark et al., 2007). Verbal assessments are limted because a parent's knowledge may not correspond with the parent's ability to implement the skills.

To mitigate this limitation, demonstrative and applied assessments have been used to assess parental skill acquisition. Demonstrative assessments evaluate skills by setting up staged or role-play situations for parents to demonstrate their skills with the trainer acting as the child (Berard & Smith, 2008; Lafasakis & Sturmey, 2007; Stoutimore, Williams, Neff, & Foster, 2008). These assessments also allow for additional opportunities to practice the skills learned during the training. Demonstrative assessments evaluate skill acquisition but not generalization. After a demonstrative assessment, it is not known whether the parents' skills will generalize from the training environment to other settings or to the parents' interactions with their own children.

Applied assessments allow for direct observation of parents implementing the learned skills with their children in the settings in which the skills are to be used (i.e., home, community, Crosland et al., 2008; Smagner & Sullivan, 2005). These assessments are considered to be the most rigorous and to yield the most information regarding the extent to which parents perform the skills taught during training. However, applied assessments have their own limitations. Observer reactivity may occur in which parents may alter their performance when they are aware that they are being observed (Kazdin, 2011). Reactivity can be minimized by having observers enter the environment on a regular basis, using hidden cameras, or having observers unknown to the parent record behavior.

In situ assessments constitute the most valid form of assessment because assessment takes place in the natural environment under the natural stimulus control of the child's behavior without an observer present to generate reactivity (e.g., Gatheridge et al., 2004; Himle, Miltenberger, Gatheridge, & Flessner, 2004). In situ assessment of parenting skills consists of observing the parent-child interactions without the parents' and children's knowledge (e.g., via video, webcam, or participant observer).

In situ assessments have been used to assess the generalization of safety skills exhibited by children and by adults with intellectual disabilities (Gatheridge et al., 2004; Himle, Miltenberger, Flessner et al., 2004; Johnson et al., 2005, 2006; Lumley, Miltenberger, Long, Rapp, & Roberts, 1998; Miltenberger et al., 1999). This research shows that skills acquired through BST and demonstrated in the training setting through demonstrative assessments do not always generalize to the natural environment as assessed with in situ assessments. For example, Miltenberger et al. (1999) showed that women with intellectual disabilities demonstrated sexual abuse prevention skills during role-plays in the training setting but then failed to demonstrate the skills in the home environment when they did not know an assessment was taking place. These findings suggest that in situ assessments should be used whenever possible to assess the effects of BPT.

Meta-Analyses of Parent-Training Programs

Parent-training programs often include functional interventions established as effective in numerous studies (e.g., Hanley et al., 2003; Iwata et al., 1993; Lennox & Miltenberger, 1989). These interventions include teaching skills related to the use of: (a) antecedent procedures to prevent problem behavior, (b) instructional strategies to promote skill development, and (c) consequence strategies for responding to problem behavior. For ease and clarity, parenting programs often are packaged and marketed. Behavioral parent-training programs share characteristics with each other but may emphasize different content. They vary on dimensions such as typical child development, how to arrange environments to prevent problem behavior, delivery settings, or specific behaviors of concern such as sleep or toilet training. Because of the large number of multicomponent BPT programs, analysis of the effective components of these programs is warranted.

A meta-analysis examines the methodology and results of a body of literature to identify patterns of agreement and disagreement among studies. Meta-analyses allow for conclusions to be made regarding the relevant facets of the research (e.g., identifying effective treatment components). Several meta-analyses have been completed on parent-training research (Centers for Disease Control (CDC), 2009; Kaminski et al., 2008; Lundahl, Risser, & Lovejoy, 2006; Serketich & Dumas, 1996). In order to conduct meta-analyses, researchers treat each study or evaluation as one "case," break down all of the components of the parent-training interventions, and determine which components were the most effective across the different programs (CDC, 2009).

All of the known meta-analyses on parent training were conducted with studies that used an active learning approach similar to BST that included such procedures as modeling, practicing the skills with feedback, and assigning homework. These meta-analyses focused on active learning approaches because research has shown that active learning approaches are superior to passive learning approaches (e.g., Beck & Miltenberger, 2009; Gatheridge et al., 2004; Himle, Miltenberger, Gatheridge, et al., 2004; Salas & Cannon-Bowers, 2001; Swanson & Hoskyn, 2001). The components that were found to improve parent-child relationships and child behavior were: (a) teaching parents emotional communication skills such as active listening and labeling emotions (which may function as AOs for problem behaviors or EOs for desirable behavior), (b) teaching positive parent-child interaction skills such as providing positive attention (which may function as a form of differential reinforcement or noncontingent reinforcement), and (c) requiring parents to practice with their own child during the training sessions, rather than relying on role-playing with the trainer or failing to include practice. Requiring actual practice may enhance generalization of the skills from the training setting to the home (CDC, 2009).

Other components that were found to result in better outcomes specific to children's aggressive, hyperactive, and noncompliant behavior included teaching parents how to correctly implement time-out (as a form of extinction or negative punishment), how to respond consistently to problem behavior (to prevent accidental intermittent reinforcement), and how to react positively to appropriate behavior (to differentially reinforce desirable behavior).

Meta-analyses of parent-training research have been and will continue to be helpful in determining the types of interventions and the best possible combination of interventions that should be included to produce optimum results. Because most parent-training programs use a number of intervention components, researchers and practitioners should attend to the results of these meta-analyses when developing or changing programs.

Evidence-Based Practices

Evidence-Based Practice (EBP) has been defined as, "Practices that are informed by research in which the characteristics and consequences of environmental variables are empirically established and the relationship directly informs what a practitioner can do to produce a desired outcome" (Dunst, Trivette, & Cutspec, 2002, p. 3). EBP originated in the medical field and has since been embraced in education and psychology (Detrich, 2008; Metz, Espiritu, & Moore, 2007). Evidence-based programs refer to interventions that have multiple components with clear linkage to research that has shown that these components produce effective outcomes.

Typically, a program must have been tested experimentally using randomized controlled trials, often with replication in different settings, to be considered evidence based. A randomized controlled trial is an experiment in which participants are randomly assigned to an experimental group that receives the intervention or to a control group that does not receive the intervention or receives an alternative intervention. Outcomes are measured to determine if the outcome for the experimental, intervention, group is statistically different from the outcome for the control group. Randomized control trials require a large number of participants. Because of the significant number of participants needed and the stringent criteria for randomized controlled trials, some programs that do not yet meet these standards may be called promising practices or evidence supported programs if they have shown positive outcomes in a number of experimental studies.

One common characteristic of all evidence-based parent-training programs is a strong behavioral component. Although programs may have a different emphasis, they all incorporate basic behavioral principles. Some examples of well-known programs include the Teaching Family Model (Wolf, Kirigin, Fixsen, Blasé, & Braukman, 1995; Wolf et al., 1976), Parent-Child Interaction Therapy (PCIT) (Eyberg, 1988), Incredible Years (Webster-Stratton, 2001), Nurse-Family Partnership (Olds, 2002), and Triple P (Sanders, 1999).

The Teaching Family Model was developed more than 50 years ago by behavior analysts working with troubled youth living in residential settings (Wolf et al., 1976). The focus of the model is to teach pro-social and problem-solving skills and to use praise to reinforce desirable behaviors. A self-governance system is used to encourage active participation by all youth in teaching-family homes. The self-governance system consists of problem-solving family conferencing, a peer-reporting method, and a peer-leadership system.

Similar to the Teaching Family Model, PCIT was developed for younger children, ages 3 to 7, with emotional and behavioral disorders (Eyberg, 1988). PCIT emphasizes improving the relationship between the parent and child. The program teaches the parent to alter antecedents and consequences to promote appropriate child behavior and to decrease inappropriate child behavior. Therapists teach parents basic applied behavior analytic principles including positive reinforcement, extinction, and differential reinforcement. Parent are taught to give demands that are specific and appropriate to the child's current behavioral repertoire in order to improve compliance. They also use time-out when necessary. Finally, behavioral skills training provides the parent with coaching, modeling, and immediate feedback in the use of the behavioral techniques.

The Teaching Family Model and PCIT, along with the Triple P program, have been used extensively in the child-welfare system to improve caregiver competence and skills for managing problem behavior of youth in foster care. Several evidence-based programs have been developed specifically for child welfare because there are approximately 800,000 families in the child-welfare system that receive training each year (Barth et al., 2005). The Triple P-Positive Parenting Program is one of those programs designed specifically to prevent child maltreatment and target at-risk children and parents (Sanders, 1999). The program incorporates a tiered system including universal (population) prevention interventions and interventions tailored specifically for at-risk parents. Parents are taught skills to increase child appropriate behavior including providing reinforcement in the form of praise and attention, enriching the environment by involving reinforcing activities and interactions, modeling appropriate behavior, incidental teaching, setting rules and expectations, and prompting strategies to improve compliance. They also are taught skills to decrease inappropriate behavior including extinction or planned ignoring and time-out. The positive parenting component emphasizes parents providing safe, positive environments, decreasing the use of punishment, and learning realistic child expectations.

The other two programs mentioned earlier, the Incredible Years and the Nurse-Family Partnership are implemented with young children. The Incredible Years promotes social and emotional develop of young children by teaching positive and consistent discipline strategies to parents and teachers (Webster-Stratton, 2001). Discipline strategies include active listening, using praise and other incentives as reinforcers, modeling problem-solving skills, and setting limits and establishing household and classroom rules. The Nurse-Family Partnership is a home visiting program for low-income, first-time parents (Olds, 2002). Registered nurses begin home visits during pregnancy and continue through the first two years of the child's life. The nurses teach basic health, safety, child development, and parenting skills to mothers. Results of this program have shown improved prenatal health, fewer child injuries, and improved school readiness.

One advantage of adopting and implementing EBPs is the increased chance that the programs will be effective. Organizations can select from a growing number of EBPs that have well-packaged curricula and training instead of using their own resources for program development. Another advantage is that funding agencies and community stakeholders are aware of EBPs and may be more likely to financially support the implementation of these programs (Cooney, Huser, Small, & O'Connor, 2007). Obtaining financial support is crucial, as a major constraint of EBPs is the financial resources needed to implement these programs. The programs can be costly to purchase and often require personnel to attend specialized training. Cost-benefit analyses need to be conducted which may drive public policy towards implementing EBPs even though the initial costs may be high.

Barriers to Successful Parent Training

Parent training is not always successful despite the number of EBPs available to professionals who provide parent training, To be successful, parent training must result in *skill acquisition* and *adherence*. That is, the parents must learn the skills and implement the skills with the child in the home environment (Allen & Warzak, 2000). A number of reasons have been cited for a lack of successful implementation of parenting skills. Allen and Warzak (2000) identified the contingencies surrounding parental adherence and how they may influence parents' use of the skills learned during parent training. Their analysis identified four general categories of variables that influence adherence: establishing operations, stimulus generalization, response acquisition, and consequent events.

In the area of establishing operations, Allen and Warzak (2000) suggest that the failure to establish intermediate outcomes as reinforcers for parenting behavior may be a factor responsible for a lack of adherence. Continued use of the skills is less likely when immediate changes in child behavior do not occur. As a result, the parent does not contact reinforcement for implementing the learned skills. This could happen in the case of an extinction burst, when child behavior actually worsens before improving. In cases where extinction is used, the trainer or clinician should attempt to establish the extinction burst as a reinforcer by preparing parents for this phenomenon and suggesting that it is a sign of progress.

Stimulus generalization may be a factor influencing parental adherence and child behavior change if the training did not include strategies to promote generalization, such as training sufficient exemplars, training with a broad range of setting stimuli, or promoting caregivers' rule-following behavior. If generalization to the home environment is not specifically programmed during training, it might not occur and thus parents may be less likely to continue to use the parenting strategies with fidelity.

Allen and Warzak (2000) suggest that parental adherence also is influenced by the success of parenting skill acquisition. That is, the more fluent parents are in the skills taught, the more likely they are to use the skills in the home environment. Allen and Warzak advocate for: (a) careful selection of parenting skills that are not too complex for the particular parents, (b) the use of effective instructional techniques such as behavioral skills training procedures, and (c) management of the educational environment so that it is most conducive to learning (e.g., reducing distractions or competing contingencies).

Finally, Allen and Warzak (2000) recommend careful analysis of the consequences in the natural environment that might impede parents' use of the parenting skills. They suggest therapists take steps to help the parents identify and eliminate, to the extent possible, competing contingencies that: (a) punish parents' use of the parenting skills and (b) reinforce behaviors that interfere with the use of the parenting skills (e.g., missing a TV show or talking on the phone). Managing the contingencies that regulate the use of parenting skills in the natural environment, to the extent possible, is essential for maintaining adherence.

In addition to the problem of parental nonadherence, other factors may result in inadequate skill acquisition and/or increased rates of treatment drop out. These factors may include stressors that compete with treatment, negative perceptions of the treatment, high pessimism, and inadequate rapport between the parent and the therapist (Durand, 2007; Kazdin, 2000; Kazdin, Marciano, & Whitley, 2005; Nock & Kazdin, 2001). Socioeconomic disadvantages in the areas of family education, occupational status, and income may lead to increased drop out from parent training. In addition, black and Hispanic parents have higher drop-out rates than white families (Kazdin, Stolar, & Marciano, 1995; Santisteban et al., 1996), although the factors that contribute to racial differences in the success of parental training have not been thoroughly studied. Additionally, parental buy-in and the capacity to implement intervention programs are also key variables in determining whether parent training will result in positive outcomes (Durand, Hieneman, Clarke, & Zona, 2009). Parent training will become even more successful once the barriers to successful implementation are adequately understood and sufficiently addressed in parent-training programs.

Conclusion

Parent training incorporating basic behavioral principles has been used to teach parents how to decrease unwanted child behaviors and to increase desirable child behaviors. Interactions between parents and children are clearly important influences on child development. Although there are many effective parent-training programs, barriers do exist that may prevent parents from developing and maintaining the use of parenting skills. Therefore, BPT researchers have started to evaluate the reasons some parents are unable to fully implement interventions. In this regard, Allen and Warzak (2000) analyzed parental nonadherence and provided solutions geared to the reasons nonadherence may occur. Durand et al. (2009) found that adding a cognitive-behavioral component to standard BPT (optimism training) resulted in lower drop-out rates and improved child behavior. The optimism component encouraged parents to identify pessimistic beliefs and to dispute those beliefs while learning strategies to maintain positive verbal behavior. The positive verbal behavior (optimism) may function as an EO for continuing to use the parenting strategies that the parents learned in the program.

Understanding the principles of operant conditioning applied to child (and to parent) behavior can help parents to understand how to teach skills and manage contingencies that will result in improved child behavior, enhanced positive interactions, academic and social success, and successful transitions to adulthood. Standardized BPT programs that are cost effective, feasible, and replicable and that address barriers to treatment, are needed to further increase knowledge and skills for all parents.

References

Allen, K. D., & Warzak, W. J. (2000). The problem of parental nonadherence in clinical behavior analysis: Effective treatment is not enough. *Journal of Applied Behavior Analysis*, *33*, 373–391.

Arndorfer, R., Miltenberger, R., Woster, S., Rortvedt, A., & Gaffaney, T. (1994). Home based descriptive and experimental analysis of problem behavior in children. *Topics in Early Childhood Special Education*, *14*, 64–87.

Axelrod, S. (1987). Functional and structural analyses of behavior: Approaches leading to reduced use of punishment procedures. *Research in Developmental Disabilities*, *8*, 165–178.

Baer, D. M. (1970). An age-irrelevant concept of development. *Merrill-Palmer Quarterly of Behavior and Development*, *16*, 238–245.

Baer, D., Wolf, M., & Risley, T. (1968). Some current dimensions of applied behavior analysis. *Journal of Applied Behavior Analysis*, *1*, 91–97.

Bandura, A. (1977). *Social learning theory*. Englewood Cliffs, NJ: Prentice Hall.

Barth, R. P., Landsverk, J., Chamberlain, P., Reid, J. B., Rolls, J. A., Hurlburt, M. S., & Kohl, P. L. (2005). Parent-training programs in child-welfare services: Planning for a more evidence-based approach to serving biological parents. *Research on Social Work Practice*, *15*, 353–371.

Beck, K., & Miltenberger, R. (2009). Evaluation of a commercially-available abduction prevention program and in situ training by parents to teach abduction prevention skills to children, *Journal of Applied Behavior Analysis*, *42*, 761–772.

Berard, K. P., & Smith, R. G. (2008). Evaluating a positive parenting curriculum package: An analysis of the acquisition of key skills. *Research on Social Work Practice*, *18*, 442–454.

Bijou, S. W. (1955). A systematic approach to an experimental analysis of young children. *Child Development*, *26*, 161–168.

Bijou, S. W. (1957). Patterns of reinforcement and resistance to extinction in young children. *Child Development, 28*, 47–54.

Bijou, S. W. (1958). Operant extinction after fixed interval schedules with young children. *Journal of the Experimental Analysis of Behavior, 1*, 25–29.

Bijou, S. W. (1976). *Child development: The basic stages of early childhood.* Englewood Cliffs, NJ: Prentice Hall.

Bijou, S. W., & Baer, D. M. (1961). *Child development: A systematic and empirical theory.* Englewood Cliffs, NJ: Prentice Hall.

Bijou, S. W., & Baer, D. W. (1963). Some methodological contributions from a functional analysis of child development. In L. P. Lipsitt and C. S. Spiker (Eds.), *Advances in child development and behavior* (pp. 197–231). New York: Academic Press.

Carr, E. G., & Durand, V. M. (1985). Reducing behavior problems through functional communication training. *Journal of Applied Behavior Analysis, 18*, 111–126.

Carr, E. G., Taylor, J. C., & Robinson, S. (1991). The effects of severe behavior problems of children on the teaching behavior of adults. *Journal of Applied Behavior Analysis, 24*, 523–535.

Centers for Disease Control and Prevention (2009). *Parent irograms: Insight for practitioners.* Atlanta (GA): Centers for Disease Control and Prevention.

Christophersen, E. R., & Mortweet, S. L. (2001). *Treatments that work with children: Empirically supported strategies for managing childhood problems.* Washington, DC: American Psychological Association.

Cooney, S. M., Huser, M., Small, S. A., & O'Connor, C. (2007). Evidence-based programs: An overview. *What works, Wisconsin research to practice series, 6.* Madison: University of Wisconsin—Extension.

Cooper, J. O., Heron, T. E., & Heward, W. L. (2007). *Applied behavior analysis* (2nd ed.). New York: Macmillan.

Crosland, K. A., Dunlap, G., Sager, W., Neff, B., Wilcox, C., Blanco, A., & Giddings, T. (2008). The effects of staff training on the types of interactions observed at two group homes for foster care children. *Research on Social Work Practice, 18*, 410–420.

Derby, K. M., Wacker, D. P., Sasso, G., Steege, M., Northup, J., Cigrand, K., & Asmus, J. (1992). Brief functional assessment techniques to evaluate aberrant behavior in an outpatient setting: A summary of 79 cases. *Journal of Applied Behavior Analysis, 25*, 713–721.

Detrich, R. (2008). Evidence-based, empirically supported, or best practice? A guide for the scientist-practitioner. In J. K. Luiselli, D. C. Russo, W. P. Christian, S. M. Wilczynski (Eds.), *Effective practices for children with autism: Educational and behavioral support interventions that work* (pp. 3–26). New York: Oxford University Press.

Ducharme, J. M., Atkinson, L., & Poulton, L. (2001). Errorless compliance training with physically abusive mothers: A single-case approach. *Child Abuse and Neglect, 25*, 855–868.

Dunlap, G., Kern-Dunlap, L., Clarke, S., & Robbins, F. (1991). Functional assessment, curricular revision, and severe behavior problems. *Journal of Applied Behavior Analysis, 24*, 387–397.

Dunst, C. J., Trivette, C. M., & Cutspec, P. A. (2002). Toward an operational definition of evidence-based practices. *Centerscope, 1*, 1–10. Retrieved January 3, 2014 from http://www.evidencebasedpractices.org/centerscope/centerscopevol1no1.pdf.

Durand, V. M. (2007). Positive family intervention: Hope and help for parents with challenging behavior. *Psychology in Mental Retardation and Developmental Disabilities, 32*, 9–13.

Durand, V. M., Hieneman, M., Clarke, S., & Zona, M. (2009). Optimistic parenting: Hope and help for parents with challenging children. In W. Sailor, G. Dunlap, G. Sugai, & R. Horner (Eds.), *Handbook of positive behavior support* (pp., 233–256). New York: Springer.

Egel, A. L., & Powers, M. D. (1989). Behavioral parent training: A view of the past and suggestions for the future. In E. Cipani (Ed.), *The treatment of severe behavior disorders: Behavior analysis approaches* (pp. 153–173). Washington, DC: American Association on Mental Retardation.

Emery, R. E., Binkoff, J. A., Houts, A. C., & Carr, E. G. (1983). Children as independent variables: Some clinical implications of child-effects. *Behavior Therapy, 14*, 398–412.

Eyberg, S. M. (1988). Parent-child interaction therapy: Integration of traditional and behavioral concerns. *Child and Family Behavior Therapy, 10*, 33–46.

Eyberg, S. M., Funderbunk, B. W., Hembree-Kigin, T. L., McNeil, C. B., Querido, J. G., & Hood, K. (2001). Parent-child interaction therapy with problem behavior children: One and two year maintenance of treatment effects in the family. *Child and Family Behavior Therapy, 23*, 1–20.

Eyberg, S. M., & Matarazzo, R. G. (1980). Training parents as therapists: A comparison between individual parent-child interaction training and parent group didactic training. *Journal of Clinical Psychology, 36*, 492–499.

Eyberg, S. M., & Robinson, E. (1982). Parent-child interaction training: Effects on family functioning. *Journal of Clinical Child Psychology, 11*, 130–137.

Fisher, W. W., Adelenis, J. D., Thompson, R. H., Worsdell, A. S., & Zarcone, J. R. (1998). Functional analysis and treatment of destructive behavior maintained by termination of "don't" (and symmetrical "do") requests. *Journal of Applied Behavior Analysis, 31*, 339–356.

Fisher, W., Piazza, C., & Roane, H. (2011). *Handbook of applied behavior analysis.* New York: Guilford.

Forehand, R., & King, H. E. (1974). Pre-school children's noncompliance: Effects of short-term behavior therapy, *Journal of Community Psychology, 2*, 42–44.

Forehand, R., & King, H. E. (1977). Noncompliant children: Effects of parent training on behavior and attitude change. *Behavior Modification, 1*, 93–108.

Forehand, R., Sturgis, E. T., McMahon, R. J., Aguar, D., Green, K., Wells, K. C., & Breiner, J. (1979). Parent behavioral training to modify child noncompliance: Treatment generalization across time and from home to school. *Behavior Modification, 3*, 3–25.

Gatheridge, B. J., Miltenberger, R., Huneke, D. F., Satterlund, M. J., Mattern, A. R., Johnson, B. M., & Flessner, C. A. (2004). A comparison of two programs to teach firearm injury prevention skills to 6 and 7 year old children. *Pediatrics, 114*, e294–e299.

Gesell, A. (1954). *The ontogenesis of infant behavior.* In L. Carmichael (Ed.), *Manual of child psychology* (2nd ed.) (pp. 335–373). New York: John Wiley & Sons, Inc.

Graziano, A. M., & Diament, D. M. (1992). Parent behavioral training: An examination of the paradigm. *Behavior Modification, 16*, 3–38.

Hanley, G., Iwata, B. A., & McCord, B. E. (2003). Functional analysis of problem behavior: A review. *Journal of Applied Behavior Analysis, 36*, 147–185.

Hart, B., & Risley, T. R. (1995). *Meaningful differences in the everyday experiences of young American children.* Baltimore, MD: Brookes Publishing.

Heber, R. (1971). *Rehabilitation of families at risk for mental retardation: A progress report (for the Social Rehabilitation Service, Department of Health, Education, and Welfare, Washington, DC).* Madison: University of Wisconsin.

Hembree-Kigin, T. L., & McNeil, C. B. (1995). *Parent-child interaction therapy.* New York: Plenum.

Himle, M. B., Miltenberger, R. G., Flessner, C., & Gatheridge, B. (2004). Teaching safety skills to children to prevent gun play. *Journal of Applied Behavior Analysis, 37*, 1–9.

Himle, M., Miltenberger, R., Gatheridge, B., & Flessner, C. (2004). An evaluation of two procedures for training skills to prevent gun play in children. *Pediatrics, 113*, 70–77.

Hupp, S. D., & Allen, K. D. (2005). Using an audio cueing procedure to increase rate of parental attention during parent training. *Child and Family Behavior Therapy*, *27*, 43–49.

Hurlock, E. B. (1977). *Child development* (6th ed.). New York: McGraw-Hill.

Iwata, B. A., Dorsey, M. F., Slifer, K. J., Bauman, K. E., & Richman, G. S. (1982). Toward a functional analysis of self-injury. *Analysis and Intervention in Developmental Disabilities*, *2*, 3–20.

Iwata, B., Pace, G., Cowdery, G., & Miltenberger, R. (1994). What makes extinction work: An analysis of procedural form and function. *Journal of Applied Behavior Analysis*, *27*, 131–144.

Iwata, B. A., Vollmer, T. R., & Zarcone, J. R. (1990). The experimental (functional) analysis of behavior disorders: Methodology, applications, and limitations. In A. C. Repp & N. N. Singh (Eds.), *Perspectives on the use of nonaversive and aversive interventions for persons with developmental disabilities* (pp. 301–330). Sycamore, IL: Sycamore Press.

Iwata, B. A., Vollmer, T. R., Zarcone, J. R., & Rodgers, T. A. (1993). Treatment classification and selection based on behavioral function. In R. Van Houten, & S. Axelrod (Eds.), *Behavior analysis and treatment* (pp. 101–125). New York: Plenum.

Johnson, B. M., Miltenberger, R. G., Egemo-Helm, K., Jostad, C. M., Flessner, C., & Gatheridge, B. (2005). Evaluation of behavioral skills training for teaching abduction prevention skills to young children. *Journal of Applied Behavior Analysis*, *38*, 67–78.

Johnson, B. M., Miltenberger, R. G., Knudson, P., Egemo-Helm, K., Kelso, P., Jostad, C., & Langley, L. (2006). A preliminary evaluation of two behavioral skills training procedures for teaching abduction prevention skills to school children. *Journal of Applied Behavior Analysis*, *39*, 25–34.

Jones, R.T., Kazdin, A. E., & Haney, J. I. (1981). Social validation and training of emergency fire safety skills for potential injury prevention and life saving. *Journal of Applied Behavior Analysis*, *14*, 249–260.

Kahng, S., Iwata, B. A., & Lewin, A. B. (2002) Behavioral treatment of self-injury, 1964–2000. *American Journal on Mental Retardation*, *10*, 212–221.

Kaminski, J. W., Valle, L. A., Filene, J. H., & Boyle, C. L. (2008). A meta-analytic review of components associated with parent training program effectiveness. *Journal of Abnormal Child Psychology*, *36*, 567–589.

Kantor, J. R. (1959). *Interbehavioral psychology* (2nd rev. ed.). Bloomington, IN: Principia Press.

Kazdin, A. E. (2000). Perceived barriers to treatment participation and treatment acceptability among antisocial children and their families. *Journal of Child and Family Studies*, *9*, 157–174.

Kazdin, A. E. (2011). *Single-case research designs: Methods for clinical and applied settings* (2nd ed.). New York: Oxford University Press.

Kazdin, A. E., Marciano, P. L., & Whitley, M. K. (2005). The therapeutic alliance in cognitive-behavioral treatment of children referred for oppositional, aggressive, and antisocial behavior. *Journal of Consulting and Clinical Psychology*, *73*, 726–730.

Kazdin, A. E., Stolar, M. J., & Marciano, P. L. (1995). Risk factors for dropping out of treatment among white and black families. *Journal of Family Psychology*, *9*, 402–417.

Kennedy, C. (1994). Manipulating antecedent conditions to alter the stimulus control of problem behavior. *Journal of Applied Behavior Analysis*, *27*, 161–170.

Kennedy, C., & Itkonen, T. (1993). Effects of setting events on the problem behaviors of students with severe disabilities. *Journal of Applied Behavior Analysis*, *26*, 321–327.

Kurtz, P. F., Chin, M. D., Huete, J. M., Tarbox, R. S. F., O'Connor, J. T., Paclawskyj, T. R., & Rush, K. S. (2003). Functional analysis and treatment of self-injurious behavior in young children: A summary of 30 cases. *Journal of Applied Behavior Analysis, 36*, 205–219.

Lafasakis, M., & Sturmey, P. (2007). Training parent implementation of discrete-trial teaching: Effects on generalization of parent teaching and child correct responding. *Journal of Applied Behavior Analysis, 40*, 685–689.

Laraway, S., Snycerski, S., Michael, J., & Poling, A. (2003). Motivating operations and terms to describe them: Some further refinements. *Journal of Applied Behavior Analysis, 36*, 407–414.

Latham, G. I. (1990). *The power of positive parenting.* Logan, UT: P&T Ink.

Leathers, S. J., Spielfogel, J. E., McMeel, L. S., & Atkins, M. S. (2011). Use of a parent management training intervention with urban foster parents: A pilot study. *Children and Youth Services Review, 33*, 1270–1279.

Lennox, D. B., & Miltenberger, R. G. (1989). Conducting a functional assessment of problem behavior in applied settings. *Journal of the Association for Persons with Severe Handicaps, 14*, 304–311.

Lumley, V., Miltenberger, R., Long, E., Rapp, J., & Roberts, J. (1998). Evaluation of a sexual abuse prevention program for adults with mental retardation. *Journal of Applied Behavior Analysis, 31*, 91–101.

Lundahl, B. W., Risser, H. J., & Lovejoy, M. C. (2006). A meta-analysis of parent training: moderators and follow-up effects. *Clinical Psychology Review, 26*, 86–104.

Mace, F. C., & Knight, D. (1986). Functional analysis and treatment of severe pica. *Journal of Applied Behavior Analysis, 19*, 411–416.

Madden, G. (2012). *APA handbook of behavior analysis.* Washington, DC: American Psychological Association.

Marcus, B. A., Swanson, V., & Vollmer, T. R. (2001). Effects of parent training on parent and child behavior using procedures based on functional analyses. *Behavioral Interventions, 16*, 87–104.

McIntire, R. W. (1995). *Enjoy successful parenting: Practical strategies you can use today.* Colombia, MD: Summit Crossroads Press.

McNeill, S. L., Watson, T. S., Henington, C., & Meeks, C (2002). The effects of training parents in functional behavior assessment on problem identification, problem analysis, and intervention design. *Behavior Modification, 26*, 499–515.

Metz, A. J. R., Espiritu, R., & Moore, K. A. (2007). *What is evidence-based practice?* (Research-to-Results brief). Washington, DC: Child Trends. Retrieved January 3, 2014 from www.childtrends.org/Files//Child_Trends-2007_06_04_RB_EBP1.pdf.

Michael, J. (1982). Distinguishing between discriminative and motivational functions of stimuli. *Journal of the Experimental Analysis of Behavior, 37*, 149–155.

Michael, J. L. (1993). Establishing operations. *The Behavior Analyst, 16*, 191–206.

Miltenberger, R. G. (2012). *Behavior modification: Principles and procedures* (5th ed.). Belmont, CA: Wadsworth.

Miltenberger, R., Roberts, J., Ellingson, S., Galensky, T., Rapp, J., Long, E., & Lumley, V. (1999). Training and generalization of sexual abuse prevention skills for women with mental retardation. *Journal of Applied Behavior Analysis, 32*, 385–388.

Mullen, K., & Scotti, J. R. (2000). The educative approach to intervention with child excess behavior: Toward an application to parent training packages. *Child and Family Behavior Therapy, 22*, 1–37.

Nock, M. K., & Kazdin, A. E. (2001). Parent expectancies for child therapy: Assessment and relation to participation in treatment. *Journal of Child and Family Studies, 10*, 155–180.

Northup, J., Wacker, D., Sasso, G., Steege, M., Cigrand, K., Cook, J., & DeRaad, A. (1991). A brief functional analysis of aggressive and alternative behavior in an out clinic setting. *Journal of Applied Behavior Analysis, 24*, 509–522.

O'Dell, S. L., O'Quin, J. A., Alford, B. A., O'Briant, A. L., Bradlyn, A. S., & Giebenhain, J. E. (1982). Predicting the acquisition of parenting skills via four training methods. *Behavior Therapy, 13*, 194–208.

Olds, D. L. (2002). Prenatal and infancy home visiting by nurses: From randomized trials to community replication. *Prevention Science, 3*, 153–172.

Pacifici, C., Delaney, R., White, L., Nelson, C., & Cummings, K. (2006). Web-based training for foster, adoptive, and kinship parents. *Children and Youth Services Review, 28*, 1329–1343.

Pfiffner, L. J., & Kaiser, N. M. (2010). Behavioral parent training. In M. K. Dulcan (Ed.), *Dulcan's textbook of child and adolescent psychiatry* (1st ed.) (pp. 845–868). Washington, DC: American Psychiatric Publishing.

Poche, C., Brouwer, R., & Swearingen, M. (1981).Teaching self-protection to young children. *Journal of Applied Behavior Analysis, 14*, 169–176.

Poche, C., Yoder, P., & Miltenberger, R. (1988). Teaching self-protection to children using television techniques. *Journal of Applied Behavior Analysis, 21*, 253–261.

Reifsnider, E. (1998). Reversing growth deficiency in children: The effect of a community-based intervention. *Journal of Pediatric Health Care, 12*, 305–312.

Repp, A. C., Felce, D., & Barton, L.E. (1988). Basing the treatment of stereotypic and self-injurious behaviors on hypotheses of their causes. *Journal of Applied Behavior Analysis, 21*, 281–289.

Salas, E., & Cannon-Bowers, J. A. (2001). The science of training: A decade of progress. *Annual Review of Psychology, 52*, 471–499.

Sanders, M. R. (1999). Triple P-positive parenting program: Towards an empirically validated multilevel parenting and family support strategy for the prevention of behavioral and emotional problems in children. *Clinical Child and Family Psychology Review, 2*, 71–90.

Sandler, J., Van Dercar, C., & Milhoan, M. (1978). Training child abusers in the use of positive reinforcement practices. *Behaviour Research and Therapy, 16*, 169–175.

Santisteban, D. A., Szapocznik, J., Perez-Vidal, A., Kurtines, W. M., Murray, E. J., LaPerriere, A. (1996). Efficacy of intervention for engaging youth and families into treatment and some variables that may contribute to differential effectiveness. *Journal of Family Psychology, 10*, 35–44.

Schlinger, H. (1995). *A behavior analytic view of child development.* New York: Plenum.

Serketich, W. J., & Dumas, J. E. (1996). The effectiveness of behavioral parent training to modify antisocial behavior in children: A meta-analysis. *Behavior Therapy, 27*, 171–186.

Shayne, R., & Miltenberger, R. (2013). Evaluation of behavioral skills training for teaching functional assessment and treatment selection skills to parents. *Behavioral Interventions.*

Skeels, H., Updegraff, R., Wellman, B., & Williams, H. (1938). *A study of environmental stimulation: An orphanage preschool project, Vol. 15* (Iowa: University of Iowa Studies in Child Welfare), 1–191.

Skinner, B. F. (1938). *The behavior of organisms: An experi–mental analysis.* New York: Appleton-Century-Crofts.

Skinner, B. F. (1953). *Science and human behavior.* New York: Free Press.

Skinner, B. F. (1974). *About behaviorism.* New York: Knopf.

Smagner, J. P., & Sullivan, M. H. (2005). Investigating the effectiveness of behavioral parent training with involuntary clients in child welfare settings. *Research on Social Work Practice, 15*, 431–439.

Stoutimore, M. R., Williams, C. E., Neff, B., & Foster, M. (2008). The Florida child welfare behavior analysis services program. *Research on Social Work Practice, 18*, 367–376.

Swanson, H. L., & Hoskyn, M. A. (2001). A meta-analysis of intervention research for adolescent students with learning disabilities. *Learning Disabilities Research and Practice, 16*, 109–119.

Van Camp, C. M., Borrero, J. C., & Vollmer, T. R. (2003). The family safety/applied behavior analysis initiative: An introduction and overview. *The Behavior Analyst Today, 3*, 389–404.

Van Camp, C. M., Vollmer, T. R., Goh, H. L., Whitehouse, C. M., Reyes, J., Montgomery, J. L., & Borrero, J. C. (2008). Behavioral parent training in child welfare: Evaluations of skills acquisition. *Research on Social Work Practice, 18*, 377–391.

Vollmer, T. R., Marcus, B. A., & Ringdahl, J. E. (1995). Noncontingent escape as treatment for self-injurious behavior maintained by negative reinforcement. *Journal of Applied Behavior Analysis, 28*, 15–26.

Webster-Stratton, C. (2001). *The incredible years: Parents, teachers, and children training series. Leader's guide*. Seattle, WA: The Incredible Years, Inc.

Westermark, P. K., Hansson, K., & Vinnerljung, B. (2007). Foster parents in multidimensional treatment foster care: How do they deal with implementing standardized treatment components? *Children and Youth Services Review, 29*, 442–459.

Wolf, M. M., Kirigin, K. A., Fixsen, D. L., Blasé, K. A., & Braukmann, C. J. (1995). The teaching-family model: A case study in data-based program development and refinement (and dragon wrestling). *Journal of Organizational Behavior Management, 15*, 11–68.

Wolf, M. M., Phillips, E. L., Fixsen, D. L., Braukmann, C. J., Kirigin, K. A., Willner, A. G., & Schumaker, J. (1976). Achievement place: The teaching-family model. *Child Care Quarterly, 5*, 92–103.

Wolfe, D. A., Sandler, J., & Kaufman, K. (1981). A competency-based parent-training program for child abusers. *Journal of Consulting and Clinical Psychology, 49*, 633–640.

Wright-Gallo, G. L., Higbee, T. S., Reagon, K. A., & Davey, B. J. (2006). Classroom-based functional analysis and intervention for students with emotional/behavioral disorders. *Education and Treatment of Children, 29*, 421–436.

21

Behavior Analysis in Education

Janet S. Twyman

Foundations in Basic and Applied Science

"We know how to build better schools" (Skinner, 1989, p. 96). B. F. Skinner clearly saw the significance of basic work in solving real-world problems, stating "[t]he importance of a science of behavior derives largely from the possibility of an eventual extension to human affairs" (Skinner, 1938, p. 441). While basic principles were "discovered" in the laboratory with nonhumans, the first human operant study occurred in 1949, showing the conditioning of an arm raise by a previously unresponsive young man (Fuller, 1949). Studies involving human participants were included in the very first issues of the *Journal of the Experimental Analysis of Behavior*; however, these were less "applied" than they were experimental documentations of the effects of operant learning principles discovered with nonhumans to humans[1] (e.g., Bijou, 1958; Holland, 1958). Laboratories specifically studying the experimental analysis of human behavior began to emerge in the 1950s, and generally focused on extrapolation of issues such as reinforcement schedules or aversive control (Mace & Critchfield, 2010).

The first documentation of what could be considered "applied behavior analysis" (ABA) was the application of laboratory-verified behavioral techniques by psychiatric nurses with their patients (Ayllon & Michael, 1959). Early behavioral work on *addressing* human problems occurred mostly in therapeutic settings, involving individuals with chronic mental illness or "retardation" in institutions where lab-developed procedures could be more readily controlled (Honig, 1966). Not until the 1960s did behavioral psychologists and researchers begin systematically applying an operant science to the development of teaching methods. While experimental analysis of

The Wiley Blackwell Handbook of Operant and Classical Conditioning, First Edition.
Edited by Frances K. McSweeney and Eric S. Murphy.

behavior (EAB) researchers were beginning to look at operant learning with humans, B. F. Skinner, Fred S. Keller, and other early behaviorists began to consider what behavior analysis could offer education. Skinner's *Technology of teaching*, published in 1968, brought his theoretical perspective to long-standing problems in teaching and learning. Keller formulated the Personalized System of Instruction (PSI) for college teaching shortly after leaving Columbia University in the mid-1960s (Keller, 1968). In 1965 Ogden Lindsley went to the University of Kansas Medical Center to focus on applied research in (special) education, teacher training, and field-based educational research (Lindsley, 1970). At the same time Sidney Bijou initiated his groundbreaking work with children at University of Washington's Institute of Child Development, remarking that applied behavior analysis had much to offer educational and child development practices (Bijou & Baer, 1961). Ivar Løvaas began his early work applying known EAB principles to children with autism during this period, showing successful treatment gains against other treatments (Løvaas, 1987; Smith & Eikeseth, 2011). The effects of behavior analysis on socially significant, educationally relevant behavior were emerging, and other areas in education soon adopted behavioral procedures and tactics.

The plethora of studies showing the effectiveness of laboratory-derived behavioral principles to socially important human behavior led in 1968 to the creation of the *Journal of Applied Behavior Analysis (JABA)*. The inaugural article by Baer, Wolf, and Risley (1968) specified characteristics of applied behavior analysis (ABA) that have come to characterize the field: ABA is applied, behavioral, analytic, technological, conceptual, effective, and generalizable. As noted by Cooper, Heron, and Heward (2007):

> Applied behavior analysis is the science in which procedures derived from the principles of behavior are systematically applied to improve socially significant behavior to a meaningful degree and to demonstrate experimentally that the procedures employed were responsible for the improvement in behavior. (p. 14)

Cooper et al. (2007) identified six key aspects that also describe behavior analysis in education: (1) the methods of science are used to guide practice; (2) behavior change procedures are applied systematically and are technologically replicable; (3) only procedures conceptually derived from the basic principles of behavior are claimed or used; (4) socially significant behavior is the focus; (5) meaningful improvement in behaviors relevant to the individual is made; and (6) the factors responsible for improvement are analyzed. As Bushell and Baer (1994) noted, "close continual contract with the relevant outcome data is a fundamental, distinguishing feature of applied behavior analysis . . . [it] ought to be a fundamental feature of classroom teaching as well" (p. 7). The characteristics and features of ABA set the foundations for an evidence-base in education that seems unparalleled.

For over half a century, behavior analysts have been designing, developing, implementing, and testing numerous procedures that have produced substantial gains for all types of learners across a wide variety of behaviors. The history of behavior analysis in education is replete with meta-analyses, systematic reviews, studies, replications, and empirical demonstrations of effectiveness and social validity (see Axelrod, 1991; Heward, 1997).

Foundational Behavioral Units

Without doubt, many of the successful behavioral applications in education are rooted in the basic EAB work and further tested in applied settings. Numerous tactics used in behavioral education programs continue to be informed by basic operant work to this day (e.g., applications of the matching law (see Myerson & Hale, 1984; Saunders Saunders, & Marquis, 1998) or behavioral momentum (see Nevin, Mandell, & Atak, 1983; Tsiouri & Greer, 2003)). Ultimately the objective of behavioral research in education is the improvement of practice, resulting in improved outcomes and lives for our learners. ABA's strength is a focus on improving teaching and learning in ways that are direct, observable, measurable, and socially valid. As noted by Heward (2005), "[t]he primary goal of behavior analysts working in education should not be getting education to do more and better ABA; our goal should be helping education do better" (n.p.).

Principles and methods of behavior analysis underlie many of the effective procedures used in K-12 schools (Dunlap, Kern, & Worcester, 2001; Lovitt, 1976) and college teaching (see Austin, 2000). Embry and Biglan (2008) referred to procedures such as contingent reinforcement, timeout, and response cost as a few of the 52 "kernels" or underlying fundamental units of behavioral influence. Their notion of (1) discrete, foundational units of behavior change, (2) verified by experimental and applied analysis, (3) relatively easy to implement with (4) readily discernible outcomes across (5) relevant, socially valid behavior is compelling. Rogers (1995) noted educators are more likely to embrace a practice if it is simple to do, is easily tested, has readily observable effects, offers an advantage over current solutions, addresses an important problem, and is compatible with existing routines. Several strategies and tactics for accomplishing practical goals from the applied behavior analysis are available for all educators (Kimball, 2002). Table 21.1 presents a non-exhaustive list of such foundational units, noting that many items are interrelated. Previous publications of similar lists reflect the general agreement that these are hallmarks of effective behavioral education (e.g., Cooper et al., 2007; Greer, 2002; White, 1971). Also a number of books are devoted to a more in-depth analysis of their use in educational and treatment settings (see, for example, Alberto & Troutman (2012), Becker (1986), Lovitt (1994), Chance (2008), Cooper et al. (2007), Frederick, Deitz, Bryceland, & Hummel (2000), Greer (2002), Jenson, Sloane, & Young (1988), Latham (2002), Lovitt (1994), Malott & Trojan-Suarez (2004), Neef et al. (2004), Schloss & Smith (1997), Skinner (1968/2003), Sulzer-Azaroff & Mayer (1994), Vargas (2009), and Wolery, Bailey, & Sugai (1988)).

Behavioral Systems and Models

Successful strategies and tactics are often combined to build a system or model of practice. There are a number of educational systems, models, and frameworks that authentically indicate a path to more effective teaching, valid learning, and improved schooling. Some are fully based on ABA, while others combine behavioral technologies with methods, procedures, or perspectives associated with other closely related disciplines. The sampling of successful models and systems described below, while

Table 21.1 Behavioral tactics prevalent in education

Active Student Responding	Group Contingencies (Good Beh. Game)
choral responding	dependent
guided notes	independent
response cards	interdependent
Behavioral Momentum	Incidental Teaching
Behavioral Objectives	Modeling and Imitation
Chaining	Observational Learning
backward	Planned Ignoring
forward	Premack Principle
total task	Public Posting
Contingent Attention and Approval	Priming, Prompting, and Fading
Contingency Contract/Behavior Contract	Reinforcement Schedules
Data-based Decision Making	Response Cost
Differential Reinforcement	Shaping
Errorless Learning	Stimulus Control Procedures
Feedback (Immediate)	Stimulus Discrimination Procedures
Fluency	Task Analysis
General Case/Multiple Exemplar Training	Time Delay
	Timeout
Generalization	Token Economy

somewhat different all share foundational components from a science of behavior and reflect the six key aspects that characterize behavior analysis in education noted by Cooper et al. (2007). Presented alphabetically they are:

Class-wide Peer Tutoring (CWPT) is a peer-assisted instructional strategy that helps teachers individualize instruction while providing numerous opportunities for active student engagement. Class members form tutor/tutee pairs using fast-paced response trials or paired reading to practice and learn new material. Students change roles to foster positive social interaction, and earn points for competently completing each role. Decades of data indicate that students using CWPT acquired skills at a faster rate, retained more, and improved social competency when compared to previous classroom practices (Greenwood, 1997, 2006; Greenwood, Delquadri, & Hall, 1989).

The Competent Learner Model (CLM) emphasizes the development of repertoires required for individuals to become competent learners and competent instructors (e.g., teachers, para-educators, and parents), so that they can act effectively in novel circumstances. The CLM equips instructors with the "tools" (e.g., a framework and a curriculum) to engineer learning environments to bring about the required schedule of reinforcement to develop competent repertoires (e.g., learner as participator; learner as observer) (Tucci & Hursh, 1994; Tucci, Hursh, & Laitinen, 2004).

The Comprehensive Application of Behavior Analysis to Schooling (CABAS®) (www.cabasschools.org) originated to empirically develop a science of teaching based on learner-driven education. Practitioners of CABAS develop and run schools based entirely on the use of scientific procedures applied to classroom management, pedagogy, curriculum design, staff training, and parent education (Greer & Keohane, 2007). It is a data-driven system based on the "learn unit" as a standard measure of learning for both student and teacher behavior (Greer & McDonough, 1999). Continuous measurement of student behavior provides evidence of effectiveness of the system, and the model includes a sophisticated and extensive curriculum for training teachers to become "strategic scientists" of instruction (Greer, 2002).

Functional Behavior Analysis and Assessment (FBA) is a systematic process and set of strategies used to gather information on underlying function(s) of a behavior in relation to aspects of their environment, so that an effective intervention plan can be developed (Iwata, 1994; Gresham, Watson, & Skinner, 2001; O'Neill et al., 1997). Data collection is essential to the FBA process. Functional *assessment* focuses on gathering information that describes the problem behavior, identifying antecedent or consequent events that may influence the behavior, and conducting a series of environmental manipulations and measuring the results. A functional *analysis* considers the variables that influence the occurrence of problem behavior to derive a hypothesis of the function of the behavior. Assessment and analysis inform treatment plans. Well-conducted FBAs (Hanley, Iwata, & McCord, 2003) have shown such value that school-based teams are required conduct a FBA as part of the Individualized Education Plan (IEP) process (NASDSE, 1988).

The Morningside Model of Generative Instruction (www.morningsideacademy.org) is an empirically-based technology of instruction that combines carefully-sequenced and presented instructional materials, fast-paced classroom presentation, and focused practice to fluency, to produce expert and confident learners who apply skills and strategies to think about the world around them, continue to learn on their own, and combine skills to solve life's daily problems (Johnson & Layng, 1992, 1994; Johnson & Street, this volume). Generative instruction has been in use for decades at Morningside Academy in Seattle, WA and its more than 100 partner schools and agencies in the United States and several other countries (Johnson & Street, 2004).

Personalized System of Instruction (PSI), also known as the "Keller Plan," is a teaching plan composed of small, self-paced, modularized units of instruction (rather than traditional lectures), with study guides or proctors to direct learners through the modules until they demonstrate mastery (Buskist, Cush, & DeGrandpre, 1991; Keller, 1968). PSI has been used in thousands of college courses throughout the United States, and has been found "effective in fostering improved subject matter mastery over more conventional instructional approaches" (Pascarella & Terenzini, 1991, p. 91).

Precision Teaching (PT) uses precise and systematic methods of evaluating instructional tactics and curricula that base "educational decisions on changes in continuous self-monitored performance frequencies displayed on 'standard celeration charts'" (Lindsley, 1992, p. 51). As a discipline PT follows four guiding principles: Focus on directly observable behavior; use frequency as a measure of performance; display learning on the standard celeration charts, and ultimately, believe that "the learner knows best" (Kubina & Yurich, 2012; Lindsley, 1990, 1991, 1992; West &Young, 1992).

Programmed Instruction (PI) embodies specialized methods or teaching programs that present material to be learned in structured, logical, and systematic sequences featuring behavioral objectives, reinforcement, high rates of relevant activities, successive approximation, and mastery progression. Students move forward at their own pace, experiencing few errors, through incremental steps within units of study, immediately independently checking answers and moving on when "firm" (consistently correct) (Skinner, 1968/2003, 1986; Vargas & Vargas, 1991, 1992). Skinner developed the first PI programs in 1954. While initially delivered via "teaching machine" (Pressey, 1950) PI can be delivered via textbook (see Holland & Skinner, 1961), computer (see Bostow, Kritch, & Tompkins, 2005), or digital mobile devices. Instruction may be linear (following response feedback the learner goes to the next frame) or branching (the next frame is determined by the learner's previous response). PI continues to influence instructional design (Lazaru, 2009).

The Pyramid Approach and the Picture Exchange System (PECS) (www.pecs.com) were developed for individuals with developmental disabilities and/or learning impairments. The Pyramid Approach to Education is a teaching model that establishes effective structured learning elements such as functional activities, reinforcement systems, functional communication, and identification and replacement of contextually inappropriate behaviors. These instructional elements inform the creation of individualized lessons for each learner (Bondy & Sulzer-Azaroff, 2002; Frost & Bondy, 2002). PECS is an augmentative/alternative communication intervention package to teach functional verbal operants using prompting and reinforcement strategies, leading to independent communication (Bondy & Frost, 2001).

Schoolwide Positive Behavioral Supports (SWPBS) (www.pbis.org) provides an operational framework for ensuring all students have access to the most effective and accurately implemented instructional and behavioral practices possible. SWPBS provides a decision-making framework that includes systems level data-based decision making, local coaching and team led implementation, ongoing expert training with active leadership to guide the selection, integration, and implementation of evidence-based practices for all students (Dunlap, Carr, Horner, Zarcone, & Schwartz, 2008; Sugai & Horner, 2006).

Many other behavioral models and systems approaches predominantly serve learners with autism spectrum disorders, such as *Discrete Trial Teaching* (DTT), *Pivotal Response Training* (Koegel & Koegel, 2006) and *Early Intensive Behavioral Intervention* (EIBI), formerly known as the "Løvaas Method" (Løvaas, 1987; Maurice, Green, & Luce, 1996; Reichow & Wolery, 2009). Strong demand has resulted in their rapid growth. Further description may be found in the chapter on autism in this volume (Thompson, 2014), or the number of the extensive descriptions found elsewhere (e.g., Freeman, 2007; Reichow, Doehring, Cicchetti, & Volkmar, 2011).

Direct Instruction is another systematically designed framework and method of instruction so similar to applied behavior analysis that they are often considered together. Direct Instruction (DI) emphasizes carefully planned lessons designed around small learning increments and prescribed teaching tasks. In the early 1960s, Zig Engelmann began using scientific methodology to inform the development of efficient procedures to teach concepts and ideas, and with early colleagues, Carl Bereiter and Wes Becker, created the explicit, carefully-sequenced, scripted model of instruction known as "DI." The instructional principles are thoroughly described in Engelmann and Carnine's *Theory of instruction* (1982, 1991) and applications have been validated by numerous individual studies (see National Institute for Direct Instruction, 2011), meta-analyses (see Adams & Engelmann, 1996; Hattie, 2009), and the largest controlled educational experiment in history, "Project Follow Through" (see Association of American Educators, 1998).

Sharing the behavioral credo "the rat is always right" (attributed to Skinner; see Davidson Films, 1999; Lindsley, 1990) and restated by Fred S. Keller as "the student is always right" (see Sidman, 2006), ABA and the DI models are guided by the basic principle that when children are not learning, the fault lies not with them, but with the instruction (Crawford, Engelmann, & Engelmann, n.d.). ABA and DI share instructional characteristics such as multiple exemplars, clear antecedents (Carnine, 1980), reduced error learning, and task (and concept) analysis used to inform instructional sequencing (Kinder & Carnine, 2001). Engelmann and Carnine's (1991) principles of instruction provide insight for the behavioral areas of stimulus control, language of instruction, educational programming, and teaching arrangements. Explicit explanations, small instructional steps, frequent review, small group instruction, choral responding, high rates of teacher-student interactions, and specific and immediate feedback have become so ubiquitous to Direct Instruction that approaches featuring these characteristics are often referred to as "little di" (Rosenshine, 1976).

Several additional strategies appear to be rooted in behavior science, and have had robust effects when applied with fidelity. *Curriculum-Based Assessment* (CBA) and *Curriculum-Based Measurement* (CBM) link assessment with instruction and are used to determine student eligibility for certain curricula and to develop goals for instruction. The most salient feature is ongoing measurement of student progress within the curriculum, and includes other behavioral hallmarks such as defining observable target behaviors, frequent measurement of instruction, and data-based decision-making (Choate, Enright, Miller, Poteet, & Rakes, 1995).

A related framework is *Response to Intervention* (RtI), which evolved from the reauthorization of the Individuals with Disabilities Education Act (IDEA) 2004, as a system for instructional and eligibility decisions and to guide school districts in reducing the number of special education placements. RtI describes a three-tiered prevention model for use with all students (including general and special education), matching student needs to evidence-based interventions and measuring learning rates over time to make timely educational decisions (Jimerson, Burns, & VanDerHeyden, 2007; National Association of State Directors of Special Education, 2005).

Superior Instruction by Design

"How do we learn?" is an age-old question. Early theorists postulated that learning is primarily innate and the result of evolutionary biology's designed interaction of structure, function, and maturity (see Piaget, 1980 or Erikson, 1968). Most contemporary theorists recognize that learning is a result of the interplay between a biological organism (the learner) and the environment (both immediate and historical; Hofer & Pintrich, 1997). Thus basic behavioral research, which develops new knowledge by formulating, expanding, or evaluating theories on how behavior and the environment interact, has been useful when applied to education. Basic research has implications for altering practice, which applied research builds upon to find solutions to societal problems (Carnine, 1997). This synergy has given us many of today's effective procedures and holds the promise of discoveries to come.

In 1954, Skinner published *The science of learning and the art of teaching*, outlining a technology of instruction based on the behavioral principles of small, incremental steps, simple to complex sequencing, high rates of learner interaction, reinforcement of correct responses, and individual pacing. In the *Technology of teaching*, Skinner (1968/2003) started an instructional technology revolution featuring designed instruction, scientific validation, and mechanical delivery systems (Rumph et al., 2007). Several noted behaviorists assisted in the development of the teaching machine and programmed instruction, including Jim Holland (Holland & Skinner, 1961) and Susan Meyer Markle (Skinner, 1983; Vargas & Vargas, 1992). From this early heyday of teaching machine development, these and other behavioral instructional designers were explicit in stating that the program of instruction, not the machine, produced student learning (Skinner, 1958).

The instructional techniques developed are still in use today (Roblyer, 2006). The influence of behaviorism on instructional systems design can be seen in the prevalence of task analysis (Cooper et al., 2007), behavioral objectives (Mager, 1962/1984), programmed instruction (Skinner, 1986; Vargas & Vargas, 1992), frequent opportunities to respond (Heward, 1994), shaping (Issacs, Thomas, & Goldiamond, 1960), supplemental prompts and fading (Touchette & Howard, 1984), feedback for improving performance (Van Houten, 1980), individualized pacing (Keller, 1968), and a systems approach to the design of instruction (Burton, Moore, & Magliaro, 1996). As Burton et al. (1996) note: "behavioral theory is the basis for innovations such as teaching machines, computer-assisted instruction, competency-based education (mastery learning), instructional design, minimal competency testing, performance- based assessment, [and] 'educational accountability'" (p. 3). Walberg's (1984) meta-analysis of approximately 3,000 educational evidence studies found the largest effect sizes (i.e., learning gains) in programs that used reinforcement, cues and feedback, and mastery learning—all common facets of behavioral education.

Contemporary instructional theory is rooted both in behaviorism and the movement toward applying scientific approaches to the social sciences (Tennyson, 2010), placing an emphasis on the actual ***design*** of instructional sequences (rather than practices surrounding use of the materials). Instructional design is a process of, "systematically applying instructional theory and empirical findings to the planning of instruction" (Dick, 1987, p. 183), "in a consistent and reliable fashion" (Reiser & Dempsey, 2007, p. 11), to achieve dependable, effective results. It encompasses the entire process of analyzing learning needs, determining goals, and developing a delivery system to meet those goals. Good instructional design also incorporates ongoing evaluation of learner activities and outcomes.

Instructional design is not synonymous with "learning theory," which specifies a conceptual framework for interpreting the conditions of learning (Ertmer & Newby, 1993). For example, behavioral learning theory emphasizes outcomes indicated by observable, measureable behavior that is greatly influenced by environmental events. Cognitive learning theory focuses on the thought process behind the behavior, and constructivist learning theory follows the premise that experience and schemas (internal knowledge structures) allow one to construct an individual perspective of the world (see Ertmer & Newby, 1993 or Schunk, 2007). Instructional design also is not "instruction"—the actual teaching practices involved in the management and delivery of curriculum lessons to learners (Smith & Ragan, 2005; Driscoll, 1994)—although this is a crucial area and one in which behavior analysis has made tremendous contributions.

Effective instructional design produces learning through crafting interactions between the learner and the environment. Instructional designers learn what works from their learners. In *Good frames and bad*, Markle (1964) reminds us that there is no single best way to craft a well-designed instructional program. Instead, a careful "front end" analysis produces programs designed based on the nature of the skill involved and the best match for the context (Tiemann & Markle, 1983, 1990). The differences inherent in learning concepts, verbal skills, or motor skills require different types of programs (Markle, 1983/1990; Markle & Tiemann, 1970). For example, the design procedures "ruleg" and "egrul" (pronounced "rule eg" and "eg rule") are best used when verbal or cognitive subject matter is composed of rules and examples. Ruleg teaches learners to explain the "rule" (i.e., principle, postulate, formula, etc.) that underlies the topic and then identify "examples" and "non-examples" of the rule while egrul starts with examples and reverses the process by having learners discover the rule being exemplified. When requiring learners to make discriminations or generalizations or to learn chains of behaviors, mathetics—a concept developed by Gilbert (1962, 1969)—may be more efficacious. Using mathetics, instructional designers start with the end knowledge to be demonstrated by the learner and work backward, parsing instruction not into "small steps" but into the largest, meaningful steps that the learner can master. The specific teaching sequence of demonstration, prompt, and release (or criterion test) inherent to mathetics is now evident as the "model-lead-test" procedure used in Direct Instruction (Engelmann & Carnine, 1982) and numerous other procedures.

The scientific method should be applied to the design of effective instruction (Twyman, Layng, Stikeleather, & Hobbins, 2005). The valuable, yet underutilized, programming process described by Markle and Tiemann (1967) uses a scientific control analysis that considers all components of instructional design to determine whether or not a program will fulfill its goals, and can be updated and summarized as: (1) Perform a content analysis; (2) State the objectives; (3) Determine the criterion tests; (4) Establish the required entry behavior; (5) Build the instructional sequence; (6) Use performance data to continually adjust the instructional sequence (#5) until it meets the objectives (#2); and (7) Build in maintaining consequences (added from Goldiamond, 1974). This is the sequence for the *design* of a program. Learners who experience the program would progress differently, starting with their entry behavior (#4) and moving through the instructional sequence (#5) while performance data are being collected (#6). Via criterion tests (#3) they demonstrate mastery of the content (#1) and thereby meet instructional objectives (#2). Meanwhile program specific and program-intrinsic consequences maintain learner behavior (#7).

An instructional program is only as good as its outcomes. A program of instruction designed according to these principles differs from other teaching strategies by virtue of the rigor of testing and validation required (Markle, 1967). The empirical testing of instructional sequences or programs should occur at three phases: (a) the laboratory or developmental testing phase where program "kinks" or errors are worked out so that one ends up with a workable program; (b) the demonstration phase or validation testing which specifies how the program works under what conditions; and (c) the extension phase or field testing where the program is evaluated under widely varying "natural" conditions (Markle, 1967). These phases reveal what works, when, and under what conditions, and also provide information about what does not work (such as when designers teach faulty or incomplete discriminations, use unnecessary prompts, or overload learners with information) or where the program might break down (such as in a schoolwide implementation or with a different population of learners).

The design and analysis of curricula using this type of scientific control analysis have allowed behavior analysts to effectively increase repertoires previously considered outside the realm of a behavioral framework, such as concept formation (Layng, Sota, & Leon, 2011), reading comprehension, complex verbal relations, and theory of mind (Layng, 2007;), and the creation of new knowledge through generativity (Layng, Twyman, & Stikeleather, 2004b; Matos, Avanzi, & McIlvane, 2006). In *Designing teaching strategies*, Greer (2002) devotes a full chapter and extensive examples of a system to direct teach the repertoires of solving problems (e.g., authority, logic, and scientific procedures), stating, "[t]he thoroughgoing application of the science of pedagogy within behavioral systems will make teaching the repertoires of solving problems using the vocabularies of disciplines feasible goals of education" (pp. 184–185).

In addition, generative instruction is a method for fostering new knowledge and skills without direct teaching (i.e., a form of creativity) that grew out of basic and applied analysis of stimulus control (see Alessi, 1987; Epstein, 1985, 1990, 1991). In education, generative instruction focuses on the careful arrangement of teaching sets and on establishing and making fluent component skills so that new composite behaviors can emerge. When the environment requires something new, component behaviors can recombine in untaught ways that reveal a composite of higher-level complex skills (Johnson & Layng, 1992, 1994). As noted by Johnson and Street (2004), "[t]he elegance of an instructional program depends on the programmer's ability to detect and teach some minimal response or generative set which can combine and recombine into a universal set of all possible relationships" (p. 28). This provides not only gains in teaching (and learning) efficiency, but also engineers a form of "discovery learning" in which the principal content of what is to be learned is independently discovered by the learner (Layng, Twyman, & Stikeleather, 2004a).

Evidence of Effectiveness

With the certification of behavior analysts (Johnston & Shook, 2001) and the resulting increase in online and traditional behavior-analytic course sequences, the number of opportunities for educators to learn about behavior analysis is increasing dramatically. There appears to be an increase in behaviorally-oriented teachers and teacher education programs (e.g., Alber-Morgan, 2011; Greer, Singer-Dudek, & Du, 2011; Maheady, Harper, & Mallette, 2005), thus increasing ABA's visibility and potentiating its benefit to learners. The presence of applied behavior analysis in school psychologist training programs has expanded as well (Friman, 2006). We are fortunate to now have a number of successful schools based on thoroughgoing behavioral systems that not only benefit the children and families they serve, but also function as models for administrators and those interested in school reform (e.g., McDonough et al., 2005; Singer-Dudek, Speckman, & Nuzzolo, 2010; Twyman, 1998). While the change has been gradual, behaviorally-based systems are spreading to entire schools or even districts (e.g., Greer, Keohane, & Healy, 2002; Mattaini, 2001; Spaulding et al., 2010).

Federal legislation has emphasized the importance of scientific evidence to inform educational policy and practice, giving further credibility to the use of behavior analysis in education. The No Child Left Behind Act of 2001 (NCLB) and many federal K-12 grant programs require educators and school administrators to use "scientifically-based research" to guide their decisions about which interventions to implement (U.S. Department of Education, 2003). Funding received through NCLB required the use of instructional materials and education programs that have a foundation of evidence from scientifically-based research (NCLB, 2002). In 2002, the Institute of Education Sciences (IES) was established within the U.S. Department of Education to provide and support the use of rigorous evidence in schooling. In both the original and amended Individuals with Disabilities Education Act (IDEA 1997, 2004), Congress has mandated that special education referrals for learning disabilities include "data-based documentation of repeated assessment of achievement at reasonable intervals, reflecting formal assessment of student progress during instruction" (IDEA, 2004, p. 34) and explicitly noted the use of Positive Behavior Interventions and Supports to prevent exclusion and improve educational results (USDOE, 2004). The 2004 amendments also formally incorporated RtI models (IDEA, 2003) and mandates for functional behavioral assessments are yet another sign of the increased impact of ABA in education (Dunlap et al., 2001). Overall, recognition of behavior-analytic procedures has increased among groups external to the field, including the United States Surgeon General (1999) and the National Science Foundation (as cited by Dorsey, Weinberg, Zane, & Guidi, 2009).

The evidence-base for behavior analysis in education is extensive and robust (Baer & Bushell, 1981; Horner, 2008). There are clear indications that much of the impact comes from use of the foundational units described earlier (Kimball, 2002). Dunlap et al. (2001) noted that "the principles and methods of ABA have been extensively integrated into routine educational procedures" (p. 129), resulting in improved outcomes for a variety of learners. ABA is replete with examples of success in teaching individuals considered previously unteachable (Bijou, 2007; Heward, 1996; Miltenberger, 2008), and evidence of effectiveness has been documented in numerous education-themed books (e.g., Mitchell, 2007; Moran & Malott, 2004) and ones addressing autism, such as those by Freeman (2007), the NYSDOH (1999), and Reichow, Doehring, Cicchetti, and Volkmar (2011).

Despite the compelling body of research validating the principles and applications of behavior analysis, behavioral interventions seem to remain outside the mainstream (Horner, 2008; Skinner, 1984). Most of the fundamental strategies of ABA have been "visible and available to education" (Baer & Bushell, 1981, p. 260) for decades, but seemingly without notice (Lindsley, 1992). As stated by Dietz (1994), "[B]ehavior analysts have presented effective solutions to some of the most pressing problems of American education. Unfortunately for behavior analysts and educational consumers, almost no one is listening" (p. 33). Behavior analysis is viewed, at best, as a "bit player in our country's efforts to reform education" (Heward, 2008, n.p.), thus creating an "unfulfilled dream" (Hall, 1991).

Translating Research into Practice

Researchers, educators, and the U.S. Government have identified a gaping hole between evidence of effective instruction and what is actually implemented in most classrooms (Carnine, 1997, 2000; Hall, 1991; IDEA, 2004; No Child Left Behind (NCLB), 2001). Teachers have been found to be *less* likely to use evidence-based interventions than interventions for which there is little or no evidence of impact (Kazdin, 2000). Burns and Ysseldyke (2009) reported that special education teachers use *ineffective* interventions in about equal amount to their use of approaches with a strong research base. In some instances educators/practitioners may simply not be aware of available evidence-based interventions (Kratochwill, Albers, & Shernoff, 2004). Deemed the "research-to-practice gap" (or sometimes the "knowledge-to-practice gap"), this distance between knowing and doing is not singular to behavioral education but occurs also in fields such as medicine (Eaglstein, 2010), clinical psychology (Norcross, Karpiak, & Santoro, 2005), health and nutrition (Banker & Klump, 2009), human-computer interaction (Stokes, 1997), and science in general (Mosteller, 1981).

Theories to explain the gap are numerous (Gersten, 2001; Robinson, 1998). While encouraging results may emerge within a single research study, the verified practices are rarely brought to scale (i.e., sustained over an extended period of time across a wide array of settings, under conditions pre-existing in school environments; Stone, 1994). After reviewing the literature, Greenwood and Abbot (2001) surmised that research-to-practice gaps are caused largely by: (a) separate research and practice communities similar to the basic and applied distinction that behavior analysts often note (see Mace & Critchfield, 2010); (b) the perception of limited relevance to practitioners (the assumption that research is too conceptual); (c) research findings of little direct applicability; and (d) limited opportunities for professional collaboration, including opportunities for other than a top-down transmission of information to teachers (see Cole & Knowles, 1993). Behavioral "solutions" also need to be compatible with the existing context and behavior analysts must ensure that the conditions established in experimental and applied research are analogous to those found in actual practice (Malouf & Schiller, 1995).

Behavior Analysis' Impact in Education

Noted behavior analysts have attempted to provide either logical methods or well-conceived suggestions to address the gap between a science of behavior and its applications in education (see Axelrod, 1992; Carnine, 2000; Gersten, 2001; Smith, Richards-Tutor, & Cook, 2010). Many recommendations focus on dissemination and collaboration, and require behavior analysts to interact with those outside the field and spread the word (Binder, 1994; Foxx, 1996; Pennypacker & Hench, 1997). Technology transfer is critical for behavioral programs to achieve worldwide impact (Pennypacker, 1986). As cautioned by Horner (2008),"[c]onducting science to validate the principles and practices of behavior analysis is necessary but insufficient for large-scale social adoption of behavioral technology" (n.p.). He suggested we need targeted action with regard to understanding, planning for, and delivery of our technology at scale. Hall (1991) advocated that we develop procedures that fit the ecology of the regular classroom and publish the results in journals that teachers actually read, while also participating more actively in the training of undergraduate regular education teachers. Greater integration into the established educational community—achieved by actively collaborating more with any and all educators interested in improving academic performance (Stone, 1994) or spending more time within a school's culture supporting (and cultivating) the existing resources (Fantuzzo & Atkins, 1992)—may increase the acceptance of behavior analysis. On an even larger stage, Greer (1982) recommended strengthening ABA's presences at the national/political table and doing more to influence the research and teacher training agenda. The Association for Behavior Analysis International (ABAI) promotes evidence-based practices in its 1990 policy "Statement on Students' Right to Effective Education" (Barrett et al., 1991).

At ABAI's first ever conference dedicated solely to the topic of education (see Malott & Twyman, 2008), Bill Heward (2008) suggested that ABA is good for education for several reasons: ABA is meaningful, effective, focused, broadly relevant; self-correcting, accountable, public, doable, replicable, empowering, and optimistic, and it knows about motivation. He stated 14 reasons why ABAI is not broadly adopted, many pertaining to the public image of behavior analysis, and ended with a call to action to behavioral educators that remains relevant: (a) develop a technology of adoption to better understand and influence the sustained use of behavioral instructional practices; (b) keep telling our story, in a language understood by our larger culture; (c) maintain a realistic optimism, as behavior analysis continues to contribute with both new discoveries and new applications; and (d) keep nibbling, by reinforcing small changes or successive approximations towards a more global adoption of known effective teaching practices.

Horner (2008) provides additional direction on how to increase the utility of behavior analysis by implementing evidence-based practices at scale in schools across the nation. Based on decades of research and implementation in schools across the United States, he offers guidelines from lessons learned: (1) build behavioral interventions that are sufficiently comprehensive to produce change in very highly valued outcomes; (2) expand the unit of analysis to meet the level of societal significance; (3) collect and use data for decision-making; (4) make behavioral principles accessible; (5) implement behavioral technology with the same level of care and discipline that was used to build the technology; and (6) understand that the process of scaling-up effective practices is different from the process of initial implementation in demonstration contexts.

A Science of Implementation

In order to have robust effects in education, people need to know *how* and *when* to use *what* procedures (Neef, 1995). Evidence alone has failed to reliably produce widespread use of better practices and improved outcomes, partly because we have not paid enough attention to the variables critical to implementation (Grol, 2000; Dede, 2006). The study of the process of implementing evidence-based programs and practices is called the science of implementation (Fixsen, Naoom, Blase, Friedman, & Wallace, 2005). In a meta-analysis of implementation literature across human services delivery fields, Fixsen and colleagues (2009) identified six functional, non-linear stages of implementation: exploration, installation, initial implementation, full implementation, innovation, and sustainability. Implementation "drivers" include staff selection, preservice and in-service training, ongoing coaching and consultation, staff evaluation, decision support data systems, facilitative administrative support, and systems intervention.

With the numerous challenges inherent in system-wide change (Curtis, Castillo, & Cohen, 2008), a focus on implementation is seen as the critical link between evidence-based practices and positive outcomes (Fixsen & Blase, 1993; Odom, 2009). Behavior analysts should conduct more targeted research on scalable implementation variables, and apply what we already know about schoolwide applications (e.g., Page, Iwata, & Reid, 1982; Sugai & Horner, 2006) systems of schooling (e.g., Greer & Keohane, 2007; Lewis & Sugai, 1999), organizational behavior management (e.g., Houmanfar, Herbst, & Chase, 2003), and meta-contingencies (e.g., Glenn, 1988) to the problems of wide-scale implementation (Odom, 2009).

A Nonlinear Systems Approach

To improve the implementation and scalable dissemination of our teaching technologies, we need to actively concentrate efforts towards ***a thoroughgoing analysis of the contingencies related to wide-scale systems change***. The problems require "a contingency analysis of adoption and maintenance of innovation" (T. V. J. Layng, personal communication, August 18, 2012; see also Glenn & Malott, 2004; Mechner, 2008). The challenges to the American educational system (Aud et al., 2010) and the cycle of educational fads (Cuban, 1990) are more comprehensible when viewed through a contingency-analysis lens. This involves a functional analysis of variables not only related to the current "problem" but to the contingencies, both beneficial and costly, operating on alternative behaviors as well. Termed a "constructional approach," behavior is viewed as a function of multiple intersecting contingencies for occurrence and non-occurrence that interact and change over time (Goldiamond, 1974; Layng, 2009). For behavior analysts to make a salient, sustainable difference in education we must embark on this critical analysis of all the contingencies in operation—for students, teachers, administrators, district personnel, parents, and the community at large. The advantages of a nonlinear constructional approach for understanding behavior has been witnessed in the laboratory (Estes & Skinner, 1941; Sidman, 1960), clinical settings (Layng, 2006), and program design (Twyman et al., 2005) and is well suited to help solve the grand problems in education.

Behavioral Education in the Digital Age

Behavior analysis has a rich history of developing technology, in the design and production of hardware and apparatus as well as methods and practices. Skinner "constructed apparatus after apparatus as his rats' behavior suggested changes" in his attempt to relate behavior to environmental conditions (Vargas, 2005, n.p.), developing the cumulative recorder only after building and testing several different apparatuses (Skinner, 1956). From the early days of the teaching machine (Skinner, 1968/2003), through "Sniffy the Virtual Rat" (Graham, Alloway, & Krames, 1994), to the behavioral pedagogy-driven applications for Internet-based instruction such as Headsprout® *Early Reading* (Layng, Twyman, & Stikeleather, 2003), behavior analysts have been using hardware and computer-based mechanisms in the delivery of instruction. Current "new technologies" (e.g., computer-mediated instruction, virtual interaction, electronic sensors) provide abundant occasions for behavior analysts to continue to study these types of contingencies.

It is essential to note that neither the use of new technologies and devices, nor their novelty or popularity, automatically translates into educational outcomes. Despite the tremendous interest in the potential of computer games, to date there is little consistent evidence that games truly function as innovative educational tools (O'Neil, Wainess, & Baker, 2005). While there tends to be great hope for educational reform when a new technology takes hold in the classroom (as seen by the excitement generated in turn by the lectern, chalkboard, overhead projector, videos, desktop computers, and interactive white-boards, to name a few), ensuring that principles change outcomes; rather ensuring that principles of design are brought to bear on the medium and dissecting the contingencies of interaction between the learner and the medium are the keys to improved outcomes. As stated by Rumph et al. (2007):

> Not all computer-based learning products or even designed instructional products are effective in teaching students. Any computer-based instruction product is only as good as the instructional design within it. There are many poorly designed computer-based instructional products. Like any instructional product or model only scientific demonstration of effectiveness is an assurance of quality. It is important that the scientific evidence requirement be maintained. (pp. 48–49)

A behavioral approach holds promise for all areas of digital technology, from development and use to evaluation, yet digital programs are rarely designed with the benefit of a thoroughgoing behavioral framework and a contingency-analysis of behavior change (Twyman, 2011). Given the knowledge behavior analysts have of contingency arrangements and instructional sequences, and our understanding of the effects of contrived vs. natural (or program-extrinsic vs. program-intrinsic) and scheduling of consequences, behavior analysis could greatly influence the effectiveness and future of digital instructional technology. When coupled with the legacy of valuable instructional tools already gained from fundamental units, programmed instruction, and other applications of behavioral instruction, digital technologies provide opportunities for unheralded access, measurement, and analysis of an array of behavior in real time, across settings, and with great precision and control. The opportunity for behavior analysts to conduct research and further our understanding of how individuals and their environments interact is noteworthy. Discovery and change in these areas is going to happen, and it is already happening. Given what we know, we should be participating. As noted by B. F. Skinner (1972, p. 156):

> A failure is not always a mistake,
> it may simply be the best one can do under the circumstances.
> The real mistake is to stop trying.

Behavior analysis can make tremendous differences in education. Let us not make the real mistake.

Note

1 With the exception of Flanagan, Goldiamond, and Azrin's (1958) study exploring the operant control of stuttering.

References

Adams, G. L., & Engelmann, S. (1996). *Research on direct instruction: 25 Years beyond Distar.* Seattle, WA: Educational Achievement Systems.

Alber-Morgan, S. (2011). ABAI accredited graduate programs at the Ohio State University. *Inside Behavior Analysis, 3*(3). Retrieved January 3, 2014 from http://www.abainternational.org/ABA/newsletter/IBAvol3iss3/Programs/OSU.asp.

Alberto, P. A., & Troutman, A. C. (2012). *Applied behavior analysis for teachers.* Englewood Cliffs, NJ: Prentice Hall.

Alessi, G. (1987). Generative strategies and teaching for generalization. *The Analysis of Verbal Behavior, 5,* 15–27.

Ayllon, T., & Michael, J. (1959). The psychiatric nurse as a behavioral engineer. *Journal of the Experimental Analysis of Behavior, 2,* 323–334.

Association of American Educators (1998). *Project follow through.* Retrieved November 20, 1998 from http://www.aaeteachers.org/feature.html.

Aud, S., Hussar, W., Planty, M., Snyder, T., Bianco, K., Fox, M., & Drake, L. (2010). *The condition of education 2010 (NCES 2010-028).* National Center for Education Statistics, Institute of Education Sciences, U.S. Department of Education. Washington, DC.

Austin, J. L. (2000). Behavioral approaches to college teaching. In J. Austin and J. E. Carr (Eds.), *Handbook of applied behavior analysis* (pp. 449–472). Reno, NV: Context Press.

Axelrod, S. (1991). The problem: American education. The solution: Use behavior-analytic technology. *Journal of Behavioral Education, 1,* 275–282.

Axelrod, S. (1992). Disseminating effective educational technology. *Journal of Applied Behavior Analysis, 25,* 31–35.

Baer, D. M., & Bushell, D., Jr. (1981). The future of behavior analysis in the schools? Consider its recent past, and then ask a different question. *School Psychology Review, 10,* 259–270.

Baer, D. M., Wolf, M. M., & Risley, T. R. (1968). Some current dimensions of applied behavior analysis. *Journal of Applied Behavior Analysis, 1,* 91–97.

Banker, J. D., & Klump, K. L. (2009). Research and clinical practice: A dynamic tension in the eating disorder field. In I. F. Dancyger & V. M Fornari, (eds.), *Evidence based treatments for eating disorders: Children, adolescents, and adults* (pp. 71–86). Hauppauge, NY: Nova Science Publishers, Inc.

Barrett, B. H., Beck, R., Binder, C., Cook, D. A., Engelmann, S., Greer, R. D., & Watkins, C. L. (1991). The right to effective education. *The Behavior Analyst, 14,* 79–82.

Becker, W. C. (1986). *Applied psychology for teachers: A behavioral cognitive approach.* Chicago, IL: Science Research Associates.

Bijou, S. W. (1958). Operant extinction after fixed-interval reinforcement with young children. *Journal of the Experimental Analysis of Behavior, 1,* 25–29.

Bijou, S. W. (2007). *An open letter.* Retrieved January 3, 2014 from www.sidneybijou.com.

Bijou, S. W., & Baer, D. M. (1961). *Child development: A systematic and empirical theory.* New York: Appleton-Century-Crofts.

Binder, C. (1994). Measurably superior instructional methods: Do we need sales and marketing? In R. Gardner, D. Sainato, J. O. Cooper, T. E. Heron, W. L. Heward, J. Eshleman, & T. A. Grossi (Eds.), *Behavior analysis in education: Focus on measurably superior instruction* (pp. 21–31). Monterey, CA: Brooks-Cole.

Bondy, A. S., & Frost, L. (2001). The picture exchange communication system. *Behavior Modification, 25,* 725–744.

Bondy, A. S., & Sulzer-Azaroff, B. (2002). *The Pyramid Approach to education in autism.* Newark, DE: Pyramid Educational Products.

Bostow, D. E, Kritch, K. M., & Tompkins, B. F. (2005). Computers and pedagogy: Replacing telling with interactive computer-programmed instruction. *Behavior Research Methods, Instruments, and Computers, 27,* 297–300.

Burns, M. K., & Ysseldyke, J. E. (2009). Reported prevalence of evidence-based instructional practices in special education. *Journal of Special Education, 43,* 3–11.

Burton, J. K., Moore, D. M., & Magliaro, S. G. (1996). Behaviorism and instructional technology. In D. H. Jonassen (Ed.), *Handbook of Research for Educational Communications and Technology* (pp. 3–36). New York: Macmillan. Retrieved January 3, 2014 from http://www.aect.org/edtech/ed1/01.pdf.

Bushell Jr., D., & Baer, D. M. (1994). Measurably superior instruction means close, continual contact with the relevant outcome data: Revolutionary! In R. Gardner III, D. M. Sainato, J. O. Cooper, T. E. Heron, W. L. Heward, J. Eshleman, & T. A. Grossi (Eds.), *Behavior analysis in education: Focus on measurably superior instruction* (pp. 3–10). Monterey, CA: Brooks/Cole.

Buskist, W., Cush, D., & DeGrandpre, R. J. (1991). The life and times of PSI. *Journal of Behavioral Education, 1,* 215–234.

Carnine, D. W. (1980). Relationships between stimulus variation and the formation of misconceptions. *Journal of Educational Research, 74,* 106–110.

Carnine, D. W. (1997). Bridging the research-to-practice gap. *Exceptional Children, 63,* 513–521.

Carnine, D. W. (2000). *Why education experts resist effective practices: Report of the Thomas B. Fordham Foundation.* Washington, DC: Thomas B. Fordham Foundation.

Chance, P. N. (2008). *The teacher's craft: The 10 essential skills of effective teaching.* Long Grove, IL: Waveland Press Inc.

Choate, J. S., Enright, B. E., Miller, L. J., Poteet, J. A., & Rakes, T. A. (1995). *Curriculum-based assessment and programming* (3rd ed.). Boston: Allyn & Bacon.

Cole, A. L., & Knowles, J. G. (1993). Teacher development partnership research: A focus on methods and issues. *American Educational Research Journal, 30,* 473–495.

Cooper, J. O., Heron, T. E., & Heward, W. L. (2007). *Applied behavior analysis* (2nd ed.). Upper Saddle River, NJ: Pearson.

Crawford, D., Engelmann, K., & Engelmann, S. (n.d.). *Direct instruction.* Retrieved January 3, 2014 from http://www.education.com/reference/article/direct-instruction/.

Cuban, L. (1990). Reforming again and again and again. *Educational Researcher, 19,* 2–13.

Curtis, M. J., Castillo, J. M., & Cohen, R. M. (2008). Best practices in system-level change. In A. Thomas & J. Grimes (Eds.), *Best practices in school psychology V* (pp. 887–902). Bethesda, MD: National Association of School Psychologists.

Davidson Films. (1999). B. F. Skinner: A fresh appraisal (DVD). United States: Davidson Films. ISBN: 1-891340-68-9.

Dede, C. (2006). Scaling up: Evolving innovations beyond ideal settings to challenging contexts of practice. In R. K. Sawyer (Ed.), *Cambridge handbook of the learning sciences* (pp. 551–566). Cambridge: Cambridge University Press.

Dick, W. (1987). A history of instructional design and its impact on educational psychology. In J. A. Glover & R. R. Ronning (Eds.), *Historical foundations of educational psychology* (pp. 183–202). New York: Plenum Press. Retrieved January 3, 2014 from http://books.google.com/.

Dietz, S. (1994). The insignificant impact of behavior analysis in education: Notes from a Dean of education. In R. Gardner, D. Sainato, J. O. Cooper, T. E. Heron, W. L. Heward, J. Eshleman, & T. A. Grossi (Eds.), *Behavior analysis in education and public policy: Focus on measurably superior instruction* (pp. 33–41). Monterey, CA: Brooks-Cole.

Dorsey, M. F., Weinberg, M., Zane, T., & Guidi, M. M. (2009). The case for licensure of applied behavior analysts. *Behavior Analysis in Practice, 2*, 53–58.

Driscoll, M. P. (1994). *Psychology of learning for instruction.* Boston: Allyn and Bacon.

Dunlap, G., Carr, E. G., Horner, R. H., Zarcone, J., & Schwartz, I. (2008). Positive behavior support and applied behavior analysis: A familial alliance. *Behavior Modification, 32*, 682–698.

Dunlap, G., Kern, L., & Worcester, J. (2001). ABA and academic instruction. *Focus on Autism and Other Developmental Disabilities, 16*, 129–136.

Eaglstein, W.H. (2010). Evidence-based medicine, the research-practice gap, and biases in medical and surgical decision making in dermatology. *Archives of Dermatology, 146*, 1161–1164.

Embry D. D., & Biglan A. (2008). Evidence-based kernels: Fundamental units of behavioral influence. *Clinical Child and Family Psychology Review, 11*, 75–113.

Engelmann, S., & Carnine, D. (1982). *Theory of instruction: Principles and applications.* Eugene, OR: ADI Press.

Engelmann, S., & Carnine, D. (1991). *Theory of instruction: Principles and applications* (rev. ed.). Eugene, OR: ADI Press.

Epstein, R. (1985). The spontaneous interconnection of three repertoires. *The Psychological Record, 35*, 131–143.

Epstein, R. (1990). Generativity theory and creativity. In M. A. Runco & R. S. Albert (Eds.), *Theories of creativity.* Thousand Oaks, CA: Sage.

Epstein, R. (1991). Skinner, creativity, and the problem of spontaneous behavior. *Psychological Science, 6*, 362–370.

Erikson, E. H. (1968). *Identity: Youth and crisis.* New York: Norton.

Ertmer, P. A., & Newby, T. J. (1993). Behaviorism, cognitivism, constructivism: Comparing critical features from an instructional design perspective. *Performance Improvement Quarterly, 6*(4), 50–72.

Estes, W. K., & Skinner, B. F. (1941). Some quantitative properties of anxiety. *Journal of Experimental Psychology, 29*, 390–400.

Fantuzzo, J., & Atkins, M. (1992). Applied behavior analysis for educators: Teacher centered and classroom based. *Journal of Applied Behavior Analysis, 25*, 37–42.

Fixsen, D. L., & Blase, K. A. (1993). Creating new realities: Program development and dissemination. *Journal of Applied Behavior Analysis, 26*, 597–615.

Fixsen, D. L., Blase, K. A., Naoom, S. F., & Wallace, F. (2009). Core implementation components. *Research on Social Work Practice, 19*, 531–540.

Fixsen, D. L., Naoom, S. F., Blase, K. A., Friedman, R. M., & Wallace, F. (2005). *Implementation research: A synthesis of the literature* (FMHI #231). Tampa, FL: University of South Florida, Louis de la Parte Florida Mental Health Institute, The National Implementation Research Network. Retrieved January 3, 2014 from http://ctndisseminationlibrary.org/PDF/nirnmonograph.pdf.

Flanagan, B., Goldiamond, I., & Azrin, N. (1958). Operant stuttering: The control of stuttering behavior through response-contingent consequences. *Journal of the Experimental Analysis of Behavior, 1*, 173–177.

Foxx, R. M. (1996). Translating the covenant: The behavior analyst as ambassador and translator. *The Behavior Analyst, 19*, 147–161.

Frederick, L. D., Deitz, S. M., Bryceland, J. A., & Hummel, J. H. (2000). *Behavior analysis, education, and effective schooling.* Reno, NV: Context Press.

Freeman, S. K. (2007). The complete guide to autism treatments, a parent's handbook: Make sure your child gets what works! Langley, B.C. and Lynden, WA: SKF Books, Inc.

Friman, P. C. (2006). The future of applied behavior analysis is under the dome. *ABAI Newsletter, 29*(3). Retrieved January 3, 2014 from http://www.abainternational.org/aba/newsletter/vol293/Research.Friman.asp.

Frost, L. A., & Bondy, A. S. (2002). *The picture exchange communication system training manual* (2nd ed.). Newark, DE: Pyramid Educational Products Inc.

Fuller, P. R. (1949). Operant conditioning of a vegetative organism. *American Journal of Psychology, 62*, 587–590.

Gersten, R. (2001). Sorting out the roles of research in the improvement of practice. *Learning Disabilities Research and Practice, 16*, 45–50.

Gilbert, T. F. (1962) Mathetics: The technology of education. *The Journal of Mathetics, 1*, 7–73.

Gilbert, T. F. (1969). *Mathetics: An explicit theory for the design of teaching programmes*. London: Longmac

Glenn, S. S. (1988). Contingencies and metacontingencies: Toward a synthesis of behavior analysis and cultural materialism. *The Behavior Analyst, 11*, 161–179.

Glenn, S. S., & Malott, M. E. (2004). Complexity and selection: Implications for organizational change. *Behavior and Social Issues, 13*, 89–106.

Goldiamond, I. (1974). Toward a constructional approach to social problems: Ethical and constitutional issues raised by applied behavior analysis. *Behaviorism, 2*, 1–84.

Graham, J., Alloway, T., & Krames, L. (1994). Sniffy the virtual rat: Simulated operant conditioning. *Behavior Research Methods Instruments and Computers, 26*, 134–141.

Greenwood, C. R. (1997). Classwide peer tutoring. *Behavior and Social Issues, 7*, 55–57.

Greenwood, C. R. (2006). The Juniper Gardens children's project. In R. L. Schiefelbusch & S. R. Schroeder (Eds.), *Doing science and doing good* (pp. 327–349). Baltimore, MD: Brookes.

Greenwood, C. R., & Abbott, M. (2001). The research-to-practice gap in special education. *Teacher Education and Special Education, 24*, 276–289.

Greenwood, C. R., Delquadri, J., & Hall, R. V. (1989). Longitudinal effects of classwide peer tutoring. *Journal of Educational Psychology, 81*, 371–383.

Greer, R. D. (1982). Countercontrols for the American Educational Research Association. *The Behavior Analyst, 5*, 65–76.

Greer, R. D. (2002). *Designing teaching strategies: An applied behavior analysis systems approach*. New York: Academic Press.

Greer, R. D., & Keohane, D. (2007). CABAS®: The comprehensive application of behavior analysis to schooling. In J. Handleman (Ed.), *Preschool education programs for children with autism* (3rd ed.) (pp. 249–354). Austin, TX: Pro-Ed.

Greer, R. D., Keohane, D., & Healy, O. (2002). Quality and comprehensive applications of behavior analysis to schooling. *The Behavior Analyst Today, 3*, 120–132.

Greer, R. D., & McDonough, S. H. (1999). Is the learn unit the fundamental measure of pedagogy? *The Behavior Analyst, 22*, 5–16.

Greer, R. D., Singer-Dudek, J., & Du, L. (2011). Programs in applied behavior analysis at Teachers College and Graduate School of the Arts and Sciences of Columbia University. *Inside Behavior Analysis, 3*(3). Retrieved January 3, 2014 from http://www.abainternational.org/ABA/newsletter/IBAvol3iss3/Programs/Columbia.asp.

Gresham, F. M., Watson, T. S., & Skinner, C. H. (2001). Functional behavioral assessment: Principles, procedures, and future directions. *School Psychology Review, 30*, 156–172.

Grol, R. (2000). Implementation of evidence and guidelines in clinical practice: A new field of research? *International Journal for Quality in Health Care, 12*, 455–456.

Hall, R. V. (1991). Behavior analysis and education: An unfulfilled dream. *Journal of Behavioral Education, 1*, 305–316.

Hanley, G. P., Iwata, B. A., & McCord, B. E. (2003). Functional analysis of problem behavior: A review. *Journal of Applied Behavior Analysis, 36*, 147–185.

Hattie, J. (2009). *Visible learning: A synthesis of over 800 meta-analyses relating to achievement*. London and New York: Routledge.

Heward, W. L. (1994). Three "low-tech" strategies for increasing the frequency of active student response during group instruction. In R. Gardner III, D. M. Sainato, J. O. Cooper, T. E. Heron, W. L. Heward, J. Eshleman, & T. A. Grossi (Eds.), *Behavior analysis in education: Focus on measurably superior instruction* (pp. 283–320) Pacific Grove, CA: Brooks/Cole.

Heward, W. L. (1996). *Exceptional children: An introduction to special education* (5th ed.). Englewood Cliffs, NJ: Prentice Hall.

Heward, W. L. (1997). Four validated instructional strategies. *Behavior and Social Issues, 7,* 43–51.

Heward, W. L. (2005). Reasons applied behavior analysis is good for education and why those reasons have been insufficient. In W. L. Heward, T. E. Heron, N. A. Neef, S. M. Peterson, D. M. Sainato, G. Cartledge, R. Gardner III, L. D. Peterson, S. B. Hersh, & J. C. Dardig (Eds.), *Focus on behavior analysis in education: Achievements, challenges, and opportunities* (pp. 316–348). Upper Saddle River, NJ: Prentice Hall.

Heward, W. L. (2008). A place at the education reform table: Why behavior analysis needs to be there, why it's not as welcome as it should be, and some actions that can make our science more relevant. *ABAI Newsletter, 31*(3). Retrieved January 3, 2014 from http://www.abainternational.org/ABA/newsletter/vol313/Heward.asp.

Heward, W. L., Heron, T. E., Neef, N. A., Peterson, S. M., Sainato, D. M., Cartledge, G., Gardner III, R., Peterson, L. D., Hersh, S. B., & Dardig, J. C. (Eds.) (1994). *Focus on behavior analysis in education: Achievements, challenges, and opportunities.* Upper Saddle River, NJ: Prentice Hall.

Hofer, B. K., & Pintrich, P. R. (1997). The development of epistemological theories: Beliefs about knowledge and knowing and their relation to learning. *Review of Educational Research, 67,* 88–140.

Holland, J. G. (1958). Counting by humans on a fixed-ratio schedule of reinforcement. *Journal of the Experimental Analysis of Behavior, 1,* 179–181.

Holland, J. G., & Skinner, B. F. (1961). *The analysis of behavior.* New York: McGraw-Hill.

Honig, W. K. (1966). *Operant conditioning: Areas of research and application.* New York: Appleton-Century-Crofts.

Horner, R. H. (2008). Implementing evidence-based practices at socially important scales. *ABAI Newsletter, 31*(3). Retrieved January 3, 2014 from http://www.abainternational.org/ABA/newsletter/vol313/Horner.asp.

Houmanfar, R., Herbst, S., & Chase, J. (2003). Organizational change applications in behavior analysis: A review of the literature and future directions. *The Behavior Analyst Today, 4,* 59–67.

Issacs, W., Thomas, J., & Goldiamond, I. (1960). Application of operant conditioning to reinstate verbal behavior in psychotics. *Journal of Speech and Hearing Disorders, 25,* 8–12.

The Individuals With Disabilities Education Act (IDEA) Public Law 105–117 (1997).

The Individuals With Disabilities Education Act (IDEA), 20 U.S.C. § 1400 (2004).

Iwata, B. A. (1994). Functional analysis methodology: Some closing comments. *Journal of Applied Behavior Analysis, 27,* 413–418.

Jenson, W. R., Sloane, H. N., & Young, K. R. (1988). *Applied behavior analysis in education: A structured teaching approach.* Englewood Cliffs, NJ: Prentice Hall.

Jimerson, S., Burns, M. K., & VanDerHeyden, A. (Eds.). (2007). *Handbook of response to intervention: The science and practice of assessment and intervention.* New York: Springer.

Johnston J. M., & Shook, G. L. (2001). A national certification program for behavior analysts. *Behavioral Interventions, 16,* 77–85.

Johnson, K. R., & Layng, T. V. J. (1992). Breaking the structuralist barrier: Literacy and numeracy with fluency. *American Psychologist, 47,* 1475–1490.

Johnson, K. R., & Layng, T. V. J. (1994). The Morningside model of generative instruction. In R. Gardner, D. Sainato, J. O. Cooper, T. E. Heron, W. L. Heward, J. Eshleman, & T. A. Grossi (Eds.), *Behavior analysis in education: Focus on measurably superior instruction* (pp. 173–197). Monterey, CA: Brooks-Cole.

Johnson, K. R., & Street, E. M. (2004). The Morningside model of generative instruction: What It means to leave no child behind. Cambridge Center for Behavioral Studies.

Johnson, K. R., & Street, E. M. (2014). Precision teaching: The legacy of Ogden Lindsley. In F. K. McSweeney & E. S. Murphy (Eds.), *The Wiley-Blackwell Handbook of Operant Conditioning* (pp. 581–610). Oxford: Wiley-Blackwell.

Kazdin, A. E. (2000). *Psychotherapy for children and adolescents: Directions for research and practice.* New York: Oxford University Press.

Keller, F. S. (1968). Goodbye, Teacher. *Journal of Applied Behavior Analysis, 1,* 79–89.

Kimball, J. W. (2002). Behavior-analytic instruction for children with autism: Philosophy matters. *Focus on Autism and Other Developmental Disabilities, 17,* 66–75.

Kinder, D., & Carnine, D. (2001). Direct instruction: What it is and what it is becoming. *Journal of Behavioral Education, 1,* 193–213.

Koegel, R. L., & Koegel, L. K. (Eds.). (2006) *Pivotal response treatments for autism: Communication, social, and academic development.* Baltimore, MD: Paul H Brookes Publishing.

Kratochwill, T. R., Albers, C. A., & Shernoff, E. S. (2004). School-based interventions. *Child and Adolescent Psychiatric Clinics of North America, 13,* 885–903.

Kubina, R. M., & Yurich, K. K. L. (2012). *The precision teaching book.* Lemont, PA: Greatness Achieved.

Latham, G. I. (2002). *Behind the schoolhouse door: Managing chaos with science, skills and strategies* Logan, UT: P & T Ink.

Layng, T. V. J. (2006). Emotions and emotional behavior: A constructional approach to understanding some social benefits of aggression. *Brazilian Journal of Behavior Analysis, 2,* 155–170.

Layng, T. V. J. (2007, August). Complex verbal relations and theory of mind. Invited workshop presented at the National Autism Conference, Pennsylvania State University, University Park, PA.

Layng, T. V. J. (2009). The search for an effective clinical behavior analysis: The nonlinear thinking of Israel Goldiamond. *The Behavior Analyst, 32,* 163–184.

Layng, T. V. J., Sota, M., & Leon, M. (2011). Thinking through text comprehension I: Foundation and guiding relations. *The Behavior Analyst Today, 12,* 3–11.

Layng, T. V. J., Twyman, J. S., & Stikeleather, G. (2003). Headsprout Early Reading™: Reliably teaching children to read. *Behavioral Technology Today, 3,* 7–20.

Layng, T. V. J., Twyman, J. S., & Stikeleather, G. (2004a). Engineering discovery learning: The contingency adduction of some precursors of textual responding in a beginning reading program. *The Analysis of Verbal Behavior, 20,* 99–109.

Layng, T. V. J., Twyman, J. S., & Stikeleather, G. (2004b). Selected for success: How Headsprout Reading Basics™ teaches children to read. In D. J. Moran and R. W. Malott (Eds.), *Evidence based education methods* (pp. 171–197). San Diego, CA: Elsevier Academic Press.

Lazaru, B. D. (2009). Programmed instruction resources. In P. Rogers, G. Berg, J. Boettcher, C. Howard, L. Justice, & K. Schenk (Eds.), *Encyclopedia of distance learning* (2nd ed.) (pp. 1693–1699). Hershey, PA: Information Science Reference.

Lewis, T. J., & Sugai, G. (1999). Effective behavior support: A systems approach to proactive school-wide management. *Focus on Exceptional Children, 31,* 1–24.

Lindsley, O. R. (1971). Theoretical basis of behavior modification. In C. E. Pitts (Ed.), *Operant conditioning in the classroom: Introductory readings in educational psychology* (pp. 54–60). New York: Thomas Y. Crowell Co.

Lindsley, O. R. (1990). Precision teaching: By teachers for children. *Teaching Exceptional Children, 22*, 10–15.

Lindsley, O. R. (1991). Precision teaching's unique legacy from B. F. Skinner. *Journal of Behavioral Education, 1*, 253–266.

Lindsley, O. R. (1992). Why aren't effective teaching tools widely adopted? *Journal of Applied Behavior Analysis, 25*, 21–26.

Løvaas, O. I. (1987). Behavioral treatment and normal educational and intellectual functioning in young autistic children. *Journal of Consulting and Clinical Psychology, 55*, 3–9.

Lovitt, T. C. (1976). Applied behavior analysis techniques and curriculum research: Implications for instruction. In N. G. Haring & R. L. Schiefelbusch (Eds.), *Teaching special children* (pp. 112–156). New York: McGraw-Hill.

Lovitt, T. C. (1994). *Tactics for teaching* (2nd ed.). Englewood Cliffs, NJ: Prentice Hall.

Mace, F. C., & Critchfield, T. S. (2010). Translational research in behavior analysis: Historical traditions and imperative for the future. *Journal of the Experimental Analysis of Behavior, 93*, 293–312.

Mager, R. F. (1962). *Preparing instructional objectives.* Palo Alto, CA: Fearon Publishers.

Mager, R. F. (1984). *Preparing instructional objectives.* Belmont, CA: David S. Lake Publishers.

Maheady, L., Harper, G. F., & Mallette, B. (2005). Developing, implementing, and maintaining a responsive educator program for preservice general education teachers. In W. L. Heward, T. E. Heron, N. A. Neef, S. M. Peterson, D. M. Sainato, G. Cartledge, R. Gardner III, L. D. Peterson, S. B. Hersh, & J. C. Dardig (Eds.), *Focus on behavior analysis in education: Achievements, challenges, and opportunities* (pp. 139–153). Upper Saddle River, NJ: Prentice Hall.

Malott, R. W., & Trojan-Suarez, E. W. (2004) *Principles of behavior* (5th ed.). Upper Saddle River, NJ: Prentice Hall.

Malott, M. E., & Twyman. J. S. (2008). ABAI's dissemination of behavior analysis in education. *ABAI Newsletter, 31*(3). Retrieved January 3, 2014 from http://www.abainternational.org/ABA/newsletter/vol313/EdConf.asp#EducationPresentations.

Malouf, D. B., & Schiller, E. P. (1995). Practice and research in special education. *Exceptional Children, 61*, 414–424.

Martens, B. K., DiGennaro, F. D., Reed, D. D., Szczech, F. M., Rosenthal, B. D. (2008). Contingency space analysis: An alternative method for identifying contingent relations from observational data. *Journal of Applied Behavior Analysis, 41*, 69–81.

Markle, S. M. (1964). *Good frames and bad: A grammar of frame writing.* New York: John Wiley & Sons, Inc.

Markle, S. M. (1967). Empirical testing of programs. In P. C. Lange (Ed.), *Programmed instruction: Sixty-sixth yearbook of the National Society for the Study of Education: 2* (pp. 104–138). Chicago: University of Chicago Press.

Markle, S. M. (1983/1990). *Designs for instructional designers.* Seattle, WA: Morningside Press.

Markle, S. M., & Tiemann, P. W. (1967). Programming is a process. Sound filmstrip. Chicago: University of Illinois at Chicago.

Markle, S. M., & Tiemann, P. W. (1970). "Behavioral" analysis of "cognitive" content. *Educational Technology, 10*, 41–45.

Matos, M. A., Avanzi, A. L., & McIlvane, W. J. (2006). Rudimentary reading repertoires via stimulus equivalence and recombination of minimal verbal units. *The Analysis of Verbal Behavior, 22*, 3–19.

Mattaini, M. A. (2001). *Peace power for adolescents: Strategies for a culture of nonviolence.* NASW, 750 First St., NE, Suite 700, Washington, DC 20002–4241.

Maurice, C. Green, G., & Luce, S. (Eds.). (1996). *Behavioral intervention for young children with autism: A manual for parents and professionals.* Austin, TX: Pro-Ed.

McDonough, C. S., Covington, T., Endo, S., Meinberg, D. Spencer, T. D., & Bicard, D. F. (2005). The Hawthorne Country Day School: A behavioral approach to schooling. In W. L. Heward, T. E. Heron, N. A. Neef, S. M. Peterson, D. M. Sainato, G. Cartledge, R. Gardner III, L. D. Peterson, S. B. Hersh, & J. C. Dardig (Eds.), *Focus on behavior analysis in education: Achievements, challenges, and opportunities* (pp. 188–210). Upper Saddle River, NJ: Prentice Hall.

Mechner, F. (2008). Behavioral contingency analysis. *Behavioural Processes, 78*, 124–144.

Miltenberger, R. G. (2008). *Behavior modification: Principles and procedures* (4th ed.). Belmont, CA: Wadsworth/Thomson Learning.

Mitchell, D. (2007). *What really works in special and inclusive education: Using evidence-based teaching strategies*. New York: Routledge.

Moran, D. J., & Malott, R. W. (2004). *Evidence-based educational methods*. San Diego, CA: Elsevier.

Mosteller, F. (1981). Innovation and evaluation. *Science, 211*, 881–886.

Myerson, J., & Hale, S. (1984). Practical implications of the matching law. *Journal of Applied Behavior Analysis, 17*, 367–380.

National Association of State Directors of Special Education (NASDSE). (1988). *Guidance on functional behavioral assessments for students with disabilities*. Retrieved January 3, 2014 from http://www.p12.nysed.gov/specialed/publications/policy/functionbehav.htm.

National Association of State Directors of Special Education (NASDSE) (2005). *Response to intervention: Policy considerations and implementation*. Alexandria, VA: National Association of State Directors of Special Education, Inc.

National Institute for Direct Instruction (2011, October). *A bibliography of the direct instruction curriculum and studies examining its efficacy*. Eugene OR: National Institute for Direct Instruction. Retrieved January 3, 2014 from http://www.education-consumers.org/Reference%20List%2010.07.11..pdf.

Neef, N. A. (1995). Research on training trainers in program implementation: An introduction and future directions. *Journal of Applied Behavior Analysis, 28*, 297–299.

Neef, N. A., Iwata, B. A., Horner, R. H., Lerman, D., Martens, B. A., & Sainato, D. S. (Eds.) (2004). *Behavior analysis in education* (2nd ed., 1968–2002 *The Journal of Applied Behavior Analysis*. Reprint Series, Vol. 3. Lawrence, KS: University of Kansas, Society for the Experimental Analysis of Behavior.

Nevin, J. A., Mandell, C., & Atak, J. R. (1983). The analysis of behavioral momentum. *Journal of the Experimental Analysis Behavior, 39*, 49–59.

New York State Department of Health (NYSDOH), Early Intervention Program, U.S. Department of Education. (1999). *Clinical practice guideline: Report of the recommendations. Autism/pervasive developmental disorders: Assessment and intervention for young children (age 0–3 years)*. Retrieved January 3, 2014 from http://www.health.ny.gov/community/infants_children/early_intervention/disorders/autism/#acknowledgment.

No Child Left Behind (NCLB) Act of 2001, Pub. L. No. 107–110, § 115, Stat. 1425 (2002).

Norcross, J. C., Karpiak, C. P., & Santoro, S. O. (2005). Clinical psychologists across the years: The Division of Clinical Psychology from 1960 to 2003. *Journal of Clinical Psychology, 61*, 1467–1483.

Odom, S. L. (2009). The tie that binds: Evidence-based practice, implementation science, and outcomes for children. *Topics in Early Childhood Special Education, 29*, 53–61.

O'Neil, H. F., Wainess, R., & Baker, E. L. (2005). Classification of learning outcomes: Evidence from the computer games literature. *The Curriculum Journal, 16*, 455–474.

O'Neill, R. E., Horner, R. H., Albin, R. W., Sprague, J. R., Storey, K., & Newton, J. S. (1997). *Functional assessment and program development for problem behavior: A practical handbook* (2nd ed.). Pacific Grove, CA: Brooks/Cole.

Page, T. J., Iwata, B. A., & Reid, D. H. (1982). Pyramidal training: A large-scale application with institutional staff. *Journal of Applied Behavior Analysis, 15*, 335–351.

Pascarella, E. T., & Terenzini, P. T. (1991). *How college affects students*. San Francisco: Jossey Bass.

Pennypacker, H. S. (1986). The challenge of technology transfer: Buying in without selling out. *The Behavior Analyst, 9*, 147–156.

Pennypacker H. S., & Hench L. L. (1997). Making behavioral technology transferable. *The Behavior Analyst, 20*, 97–108.

Piaget, J. (1980). *Adaptation and intelligence: Organic selection and phenocopy*. Chicago: University of Chicago Press.

Pressey, S. L. (1950). Development and appraisal of devices providing immediate automatic scoring of objective tests and concomitant self-instruction. *Journal of Psychology, 29*, 417–447.

Reichow, B., Doehring, P., Cicchetti, D. V., & Volkmar, F. R. (Eds.) (2011). *Evidence-based practices and treatments for children with autism*. New York: Springer.

Reichow, B., & Wolery, M. (2009). Comprehensive synthesis of early intensive behavioral interventions for young children with autism based on the UCLA young autism project model. *Journal of Autism and Developmental Disorders, 39*, 23–41.

Reiser, R. A., & Dempsey, J. V. (Eds.) (2007). *Trends and issues in instructional design and technology* (2nd ed.). Upper Saddle River, NJ: Pearson Education.

Robinson, V. (1998). Methodology and the research-practice gap. *Educational Researcher, 27*, 17–26.

Roblyer, M. D. (2006). *Integrating educational technology into teaching* (4th ed.). Upper Saddle River, NJ: Pearson Education.

Rogers, E. M. (1995). *Diffusion of innovations* (4th ed.). New York: The Free Press.

Rosenshine, B. (1976). Recent research on teaching behaviors and student achievement. *Journal of Teacher Education, 27*, 61–64.

Rumph, R., Ninness, C., McCuller, G., Holland, J., Ward, T., & Wilbourn, T. (2007). Stimulus change: Reinforcer or punisher? Reply to Hursh. *Behavior and Social Issues, 16*, 47–49.

Saunders, M. D., Saunders, R. R., & Marquis, J. G. (1998). Comparison of reinforcement schedules in the reduction of stereotypy with supported routines. *Research in Developmental Disabilities, 19*, 99–122.

Schloss, P. J., & Smith, M. A. (1997). *Applied behavior analysis in the classroom* (2nd ed.). Boston: Allyn & Bacon.

Schunk, D. H. (2007). *Learning theories: An educational perspective* (5th ed.). Englewood Cliffs, NJ: Prentice Hall.

Sidman, M. (1960). Normal sources of pathological behavior. *Science, 132*, 61–68.

Sidman, M. (2006). Fred S. Keller, a generalized conditioned reinforcer. *The Behavior Analyst, 29*, 235–242.

Singer-Dudek, J., Speckman, J., & Nuzzolo, R. (2010). A comparative analysis of the CABAS® model of education at the Fred S. Keller School: A twenty-year review. *The Behavior Analyst Today, 11*, 253–264. Retrieved January 3, 2014 from http://www.baojournal.com/BAT%20Journal/VOL-11/BAT%2011-4.pdf.

Skinner, B. F. (1938). *The behavior of organisms: An experimental analysis*. New York: Appleton-Century-Crofts.

Skinner, B. F. (1954). The science of learning and the art of teaching. *Harvard Educational Review, 24*, 86–97.

Skinner, B. F. (1956). A case history in scientific method. *American Psychologist, 11*, 221–233.

Skinner, B. F. (1958). Teaching machines. *Science, 128*, 137–158.

Skinner, B. F. (1968/2003). *The technology of teaching*. New York: Appleton-Century-Crofts.

Skinner, B. F. (1972). *Beyond freedom and dignity*. New York: Bantam Vintage.

Skinner, B. F. (1983). *A matter of consequences: Part three of an autobiography*. New York: New York University Press.

Skinner, B. F. (1984). The shame of American education. *American Psychologist*, *39*(9), 947–954.

Skinner, B. F. (1986). Programmed instruction revisited. *The Phi Delta Kappan*, *68*(2), 103–110.

Skinner, B. F. (1989). The school of the future. In B. F. Sinner (Ed.), *Recent issues in the analysis of behavior* (pp. 85–96). Englewood Cliffs, NJ: Prentice Hall.

Smith, G., Richards-Tutor, C., & Cook, B. (2010). Using teacher narratives in the dissemination of research-based practices. *Intervention in School and Clinic*, *46*, 67–70.

Smith, P. L., & Ragan, T. J. (2005). *Instructional design* (3rd ed.). Hoboken, NJ: John Wiley & Sons Inc.

Smith, T., & Eikeseth, S. (2011). O. Ivar Løvaas: Pioneer of applied behavior analysis and intervention for children with autism. *Journal of Autism and Developmental Disorders*, *41*, 375–378.

Spaulding, S. A., Irvin, L. K., Horner, R. H., May, S. L., Emeldi, M., Tobin, T. J., & Sugai, G. (2010). Schoolwide social-behavioral climate, student problem behavior, and related administrative decisions: Empirical patterns from 1,510 schools nationwide. *Journal of Positive Behavior Interventions*, *12*, 69–85.

Stokes, D. E. (1997). *Pasteur's quadrant: Basic science and technological innovation*. Washington, D.C.: Brookings Institution Press.

Stone, J. E. (1994). Developmentalism's impediments to school reform: Three recommendations for overcoming them. In R. Gardner, III, D. M. Sainato, J. O. Cooper, T. E. Heron, W. L. Heward, J. Eshleman, & T. A. Grossi (Eds.), *Behavior analysis in education: Focus on measurably superior instruction* (pp. 57–72). Monterey, CA: Brooks/Cole.

Sugai, G., & Horner, R. H. (2006). A promising approach for expanding and sustaining school-wide positive behavior support. *School Psychology Review*, *35*, 245–259.

Sulzer-Azaroff, B., & Mayer, G. R. (1994). *Achieving educational excellence: Behavior analysis for achieving classroom and schoolwide behavior change*. San Marcos, CA; Westen Image.

Tennyson, R. D. (2010). Historical reflection on learning theories and instructional design. *Contemporary Educational Technology*, *1*, 1–16.

Thompson, R. H., & Iwata, B. A. (2007). A comparison of outcomes from descriptive and functional analyses of problem behavior. *Journal of Applied Behavior Analysis*, *40*, 333–338.

Thompson, T. (2014). Autism and behavior analysis: History and current status. In F. K. McSweeney & E. S. Murphy (Eds.), *The Wiley-Blackwell Handbook of Operant Conditioning* (pp. 483–508). Oxford: Wiley-Blackwell.

Tiemann, P. W., & Markle, S. M. (1983). *Analyzing instructional content: A guide to instruction and evaluation*. Champaign, IL: Stipes Publishing Co.

Tiemann, P. W., & Markle, S. M. (1990). *Analyzing instructional content: A guide to instruction and evaluation*. Seattle, WA: Morningside Press.

Touchette, P. E., & Howard, J. S. (1984). Errorless learning: Reinforcement contingencies and stimulus control transfer in delayed prompting. *Journal of Applied Behavior Analysis*, *17*, 175–188.

Tsiouri, I., & Greer, R. D. (2003). Inducing vocal verbal behavior in children with severe language delays through rapid motor imitation responding. *Journal of Behavioral Education*, *12*, 185–206.

Tucci, V., & Hursh, D. (1994). Developing competent learners by arranging effective learning environments. In R. Gardner, D. Sainato, J. O. Cooper, T. E. Heron, W. L. Heward, J. Eshleman, & T. A. Grossi (Eds.), *Behavior analysis in education: Focus on measurably superior instruction* (pp. 21–31). Monterey, CA: Brooks-Cole.

Tucci, V., Hursh, D. E., & Laitinen, R. E. (2004). The Competent Learner Model (CLM): A merging of applied behavior analysis, direct instruction, and precision teaching. In D. J. Moran & R. Malott (Eds.), *Evidence-based educational methods* (pp. 109–123). San Diego, CA: Elsevier, Inc.

Twyman, J. S. (1998). The Fred S. Keller School. *Journal of Applied Behavior Analysis, 31*, 695–701.

Twyman, J. S. (2011). Emerging technologies and behavioural cusps: A new era for behaviour analysis? *European Journal of Behavior Analysis, 2*, 461–482.

Twyman, J. S. (2012, April). *Getting into the game: Synergies between behavior analysis and gaming technology.* Keynote presentation at the 4th Annual convention of the Ireland Association for Behavior Analysis, Dublin, Ireland.

Twyman, J. S., Layng, T. V. J., Stikeleather, G. and Hobbins, K. A. (2005). A non-linear approach to curriculum design: The role of behavior analysis in building an effective reading program, In W. L. Heward, T. E. Heron, N. A. Neef, S. M. Peterson, D. M. Sainato, G. Cartledge, R. Gardner III, L. D. Peterson, S. B. Hersh, & J. C. Dardig (Eds.), *Focus on behavior analysis in education: Achievements, challenges, and opportunities* (pp. 55–68). Upper Saddle River, NJ: Prentice Hall.

U.S. Department of Education. (2003). *Identifying and implementing educational practices supported by rigorous evidence: A user friendly guide.* Washington, DC: U.S. Department of Education. Retrieved January 3, 2014 from http://www2.ed.gov/rschstat/research/pubs/rigorousevid/rigorousevid.pdf.

Van Houten, R. (1980). *Learning through feedback: A systematic approach for improving academic performance.* New York: Human Sciences Press.

Vargas, E. A., & Vargas, J. (1991). Programmed instruction: What it is and how to do it. *Journal of Behavioral Education, 1*, 235–251.

Vargas, E. A., & Vargas, J. (1992). Programmed instruction and teaching machines. In R. P. West & L. A. Hamerlynck (Eds.), *Designs for excellence in education: The legacy of B. F. Skinner* (pp. 33–69). Longmont, CO: Sopris West, Inc.

Vargas, J. S. (2005). A brief biography of B. F. Skinner. Retrieved January 3, 2014 from http://bfskinner.org/BFSkinner/AboutSkinner.html.

Vargas, J. S. (2009). *Applied behavior analysis for educators.* New York: Routledge.

Walberg, H. J. (1984). Improving the productivity of America's schools. *Educational Leadership, 41*(8), 19–27.

West, R. P., & Young, K. R. (1992). Precision teaching. In R. P. West & L. A. Hamerlynck (Eds.), *Designs for excellence in education: The legacy of B. F. Skinner* (pp. 113–146). Longmont, CO: Sopris West, Inc.

White, O. R. (1971). *A glossary of behavioral terminology.* Champaign, IL: Research Press Co.

Wolery, M., Bailey Jr., D. B., & Sugai, G. M. (1988). *Effective teaching: Principles and procedures of applied behavior analysis with exceptional students.* Boston: Allyn and Bacon, Inc.

22

Operant Conditioning in Developmental Disabilities

Jeffrey H. Tiger, Brittany C. Putnam, and Caitlin S. Peplinski

The term "developmental disabilities" refers to a large and diverse cluster of disorders that affects the normal growth and development of children. Individuals with developmental disabilities may have problems with communication, mobility, learning, social skills, self-help, and independent living that persist throughout their lives (Centers for Disease Control, 2012). These disorders may result from genetic inheritance (e.g., Angelman syndrome, Prader Willi syndrome), chromosomal mutations (e.g., Down's syndrome, Fragile X syndrome), acquired injury (e.g. cerebral palsy), or prenatal narcotics exposure (e.g., Fetal Alcohol Syndrome). The causes of some developmental disabilities (e.g., autism) are less clear.

Each disorder can be categorized by its genetic phenotype (i.e., characteristic genetic markers) and by its behavioral phenotype (i.e., characteristic behavior patterns). For instance, individuals with Prader Willi will display numerous physical markers of the disorder such as infantile hypotonia (i.e., low muscle tone), short stature, characteristic facial features, and increased risks of obesity as well as behavioral characteristics such as hyperphagia (i.e., excessive eating), food hoarding and food stealing, skin picking, stubbornness, obsessive and compulsive behavior, tantrums, disobedience, and talking too frequently (Dykens & Shah, 2003). Successful intervention for individuals with developmental disabilities will typically involve both medical and behavioral interventions.

Behavior analysts are involved frequently in developing treatment programs for individuals with developmental disabilities, especially individuals with autism spectrum disorders. These treatment programs, based predominantly upon operant conditioning, focus on arranging individuals' environments to: (a) reduce behavioral excesses, such as aggression, self-injury, property destruction, and repetitive behaviors that compete with skill acquisition and (b) increase their communicative, social, self-help, and leisure skills to promote normalcy, independence, and quality of life.

The Wiley Blackwell Handbook of Operant and Classical Conditioning, First Edition.
Edited by Frances K. McSweeney and Eric S. Murphy.

This chapter will provide an overview of how operant conditioning may be used in treatment programs for individuals with developmental disabilities. Given the variety of developmental disabilities with which a behavior analyst may be requested to work, it is important for behavior analysts to know the idiosyncratic behavioral characteristics and physical limitations associated with the developmental disorders they are serving. The Behavior Analyst Certification Board (2010) requires behavior analysts to seek expert consultation when serving cases with disorders with which they are not familiar.

Once a behavior analyst has accepted the case of an individual with developmental disabilities, the behavior analyst then devises an assessment and treatment plan based upon the presenting problems; these plans often involve both short- and long-term goals. We will broadly characterize these presenting problems as behavioral excesses targeted for reduction and behavioral deficiencies targeted for increase.

Operant Conditioning to Reduce Behavioral Excesses

Because the occurrence of problem behavior is a frequent impediment to effective teaching and the development of novel skills (Carr, Taylor, & Robinson, 1991; Dunlap, Dyer, & Koegel, 1983; Epstein, Doke, Sajwaj, Sorrell, & Rimmer, 1974; Koegel & Covert, 1972; Koegel, Firestone, Kramme, & Dunlap, 1974; Løvaas, Litrownik, & Mann, 1971; Morrison, & Rosales-Ruiz, 1997; Risley, 1968), it is common to reduce problem behavior prior to teaching novel skills. As such, we will discuss the treatment of problem behavior first.

Individuals with developmental disabilities present with a higher likelihood of problem behavior, such as aggression and self-injury, than do their typically developing peers. The predominant view is that these problem behaviors are learned through an individual's interaction with his or her environment via operant mechanisms. That is, when individuals engage in problem behavior, this behavior results in a change in his or her environment and that change may increase the occurrence of that behavior in the future. Take for example, a scenario in which a parent is attempting to brush the teeth of his or her young son with a developmental disability. While the child's teeth are being scrubbed, he flails his body and hits his head on the counter. He begins to cry loudly. The concerned parent then puts down the toothbrush, scoops up the child, and provides comfort (as most parents would in this situation). It is possible that the child with limited communicative abilities may have just learned that head-banging was an effective means of recruiting: (a) social positive reinforcement (attention) and (b) social negative reinforcement (termination of a non-preferred activity). This child may engage in head-banging in the future when deprived of attention or presented with non-preferred tasks.[1] In some cases, problem behavior may result in environmental changes that are not mediated (delivered) by another person. For instance, hand biting and hand mouthing may generate sensory stimulation to the hands or mouth that serve as reinforcers (Goh, Iwata, Shore, DeLeon, Lerman, Ulrich, & Smith, 1995). We refer to behavior that directly produces its own reinforcement as automatically reinforced (Vollmer, 1994).

Therefore, as initially posed by Carr (1977), problem behavior, including self-injury, likely serves one or more of four operant functions: (a) social positive reinforcement in the recruitment of attention, food, or leisure items, (b) social negative reinforcement in the termination of demands, self-care tasks, or other aversive events such as loud noises, (c) automatic positive reinforcement by generating stimulation, and (d) automatic negative reinforcement such as temporary pain attenuation (i.e., it is hypothesized that self-injury directed towards an existing injury may provide brief relieve from pain, similar to the manner in which applying pressure to the temples relieves discomfort associated with headaches). Further, these behaviors develop as a result of idiosyncratic learning histories. The form of the behavior (e.g., head-banging) tells us little about the sources of reinforcement that maintain the problem behavior, but if a therapist can identify the reinforcers for problem behavior, the likelihood of treatment success increases. The process for identifying those idiosyncratic sources of reinforcement for problem behavior is referred to as functional assessment.

Functional Assessment

There are several techniques for conducting functional assessments including indirect assessments, descriptive assessments, and "experimental" functional analyses.

Indirect Assessments. Indirect assessments include interviews, questionnaires, and rating scales completed with a client's caregivers. Two of the most common published tools are the Motivation Assessment Scale (MAS; Durand & Crimmins, 1988) and the Questions About Behavioral Function (QABF; Paclawskyj, Matson, Rush, Smalls, & Vollmer, 2000). These assessments require caregivers to rate 16 (Durand & Crimmins, 1988) or 25 (Paclawskyj et al., 2000) items on Likert scales. The rated items are intended to differentiate problem behavior maintained by: (a) attention (e.g., "Does the behavior occur whenever you stop attending to this person?" and "Does the person engage in the behavior to get a reaction out of you?"), (b) by escape from demands (e.g., "Does the behavior occur following a request to perform a difficult task?" and "Do they engage in the behavior when he/she does not want to do something"), and (c) automatic reinforcement (e.g., "Does it appear to you that the person enjoys doing the behavior?" and "Does the person engage in the behavior as a form of 'self-stimulation'?"). At the conclusion of this interview, scores for each item are added together and the category with the highest overall ranking is considered indicative of behavioral function.

Indirect assessments, such as those described, are generally quick and require little training to complete. However, there are great concerns regarding the validity (i.e., how well does a high-score in the attention category predict treatment success?) and reliability (i.e., how much correspondence would there be from two raters responding to the same questions about the same client) of such assessments. For instance, Zarcone, Rodgers, Iwata, Rourke, and Dorsey (1991) compared the inter-rater reliability for the MAS by having two staff members or two teachers complete the MAS for each subject. The authors then conducted an item-by-item analysis and found that raters were in very poor agreement. One cannot begin to ask questions regarding the validity of an assessment technique if the device cannot produce reliable ratings. For this reason, indirect assessment is not recommended as a stand-alone functional-assessment technique. However, idiosyncratic information gathered from indirect assessments may be used to inform more rigorous functional assessments, as we will describe more fully below.

Descriptive Assessments. Unlike indirect assessments that rely on a third-party report of the environmental events surrounding problem behavior, descriptive assessments involve the direct observation and repeated measurement of these events in the natural environment (Thompson & Borrero, 2012). Oftentimes, these assessments involve the recording of problem behavior and its correlation with time (i.e., scatterplots, Touchette, MacDonald, & Langer, 1985) or with antecedent and potential consequent events similar to those that would be manipulated in an experimental functional analysis (i.e., attention, the delivery and removal of instructions; see Piazza et al., 2003; Vollmer, Borrero, Wright, Van Camp, & Lalli, 2001 for some examples of descriptive assessments and read below for how consequences are arranged in experimental functional analyses).

As noted by Thompson and Borrero (2012), there are a number of uses for which descriptive assessments are extremely useful (e.g., identifying common contingencies in natural settings, establishing baseline levels of problem behavior, studying basic behavioral processes under naturally occurring circumstances, and studying quantitative models of behavior such as the matching law), but in terms of accurately identifying behavioral function, descriptive assessments are fundamentally flawed.

Descriptive assessments attempt to identify behavioral function by analyzing correlations between particular environmental events and the occurrence of problem behavior (e.g., attention delivery may be highly correlated with the occurrence of problem behavior or problem behavior may occur frequently following the delivery of an instruction).[2] However, correlation between two events does not imply causation and, unlike experimental approaches (described below), descriptive approaches cannot demonstrate functional relations between environmental events. For instance, if one was to conduct a descriptive assessment of the consequences of one's sneezing, there would likely be a strong correlation between the occurrence of a sneeze and members of the social environment saying, "bless you." It is absurd to suggest that saying "bless you" serves as a reinforcer for sneezing and, relatedly, if "bless you" was no longer said, sneezing would discontinue. Such claims, however, parallel the conclusions drawn from descriptive assessments.

Studies comparing the outcomes of descriptive techniques with more rigorous experimental functional analyses and have shown that descriptive assessment may nominate spurious events as potential reinforcers (Camp, Iwata, Hammond, & Bloom, 2009; St. Peter, Vollmer, Bourret, Borrero, Sloman & Rapp, 2005; Thompson & Iwata, 2007) and may fail to identify functional reinforcers that only occur intermittently following problem behavior in the natural environment (Lerman & Iwata, 1993). In particular, several studies have noted that attention delivery is a nearly ubiquitous response to problem behavior in natural environments (McKerchar & Thompson, 2004; Thompson & Iwata, 2001; VanDerHeyden, Witt, & Gatti, 2001) even under conditions in which attention does not serve as a reinforcer (St. Peter et al., 2005; Thompson & Iwata, 2007).

Descriptive assessments may still play a useful part of the functional-assessment process, although their utility as a stand-alone functional assessment is questionable. In particular, formal or informal descriptive assessments may help to identify unique or idiosyncratic events to include in experimental functional analyses that would not typically be included (Carr, Yarbrough, & Langdon, 1997; Bowman, Fisher, Thompson, & Piazza, 1997; Richman & Hagopian, 1999; Tiger, Fisher, Toussaint,

& Kodak, 2009; Tiger, Hanley, & Bessette, 2006). To ensure this benefit, descriptive assessments should allow the open-ended or narrative coding of environmental events (e.g., Groden, 1989) such that idiosyncratic events can be captured via the descriptive assessment. This unique information will be lost should the descriptive assessment utilize a close-ended code (i.e., if the data collector can only score those events that would be manipulated in a functional analysis).

Experimental Functional Analysis. Experimental functional analysis is characterized by not only the direct observation of problem behavior, but also by the systematic manipulation of environmental variables to determine their effects on the occurrence of problem behavior. The term "functional analysis" was derived from the mathematical meaning of function; that is, to show that behavior occurred as a function of certain environmental events (Skinner, 1957). Unlike indirect and descriptive assessments, functional analyses can show a cause-and-effect relationship between particular environmental variables and the occurrence of problem behavior (i.e., a functional analysis demonstrates that when a particular reinforcer is delivered for problem behavior that behavior increases, and when the reinforcer is delivered independently of that behavior the behavior decreases). For that reason, functional analysis serves as the "gold standard" of functional-assessment procedures (Hanley, Iwata, & McCord, 2003).

Iwata, Dorsey, Slifer, Bauman, and Richman (1982/1994) described the first comprehensive functional analysis of self-injurious behavior conducted with nine individuals with intellectual and developmental disabilities. This assessment procedure involved arranging a series of test conditions in which a particular source of reinforcement was withheld and delivered only following the occurrence of problem behavior. This assessment included: (a) a test for behavioral sensitivity to social reinforcement in the form of attention in which a therapist withheld attention except to deliver a brief reprimand (e.g., "Don't hit yourself, you might get hurt") following each instance of problem behavior, (b) a test for social negative reinforcement in which the therapist presented academic or self-care tasks and withdrew those tasks for a brief period following problem behavior, and (c) a test for automatic reinforcement in which the individual was placed in an austere environment and the therapist did not respond to problem behavior or waited outside the therapy room during sessions. Each of these test conditions were conducted repeatedly and compared to a control condition (frequently referred to as a toy-play condition) in which each source of reinforcement was delivered freely (i.e., the therapist provided frequent attention, withheld demands, and provided a variety of high-quality leisure items). These conditions were compared in a multi-element design until the levels of problem behavior in one or more test conditions regularly exceed the levels exhibited during the control condition.

In a review of the functional analysis literature, Hanley et al. (2003) reported that this basic framework for conducting functional analyses had been replicated in over 270 published studies, in 21 scholarly journals, and had been applied to children and adults with intellectual and developmental disabilities; these numbers are even greater now. These procedures have been implemented in hospitals, schools, institutions, homes, outpatient clinics, and vocational programs and have been applied to a variety of problem behaviors including self-injury, aggression, disruption, vocalizations, property destruction, stereotypy, noncompliance, tantrums, elopement, and pica.

Further, functional analyses have been modified to incorporate a number of additional test conditions based upon information obtained through indirect and descriptive assessments and for unusual topographies of problem behavior. For instance, Bowman et al. (1997) conducted a functional analysis of aggression using the standard conditions from the Iwata et al. (1982/1994) functional analysis model, but failed to occasion problem behavior (i.e., problem behavior occurred at very low levels across test conditions). Informal observation of the participant indicated that the individual would request his parents to engage in unusual activities (e.g., "pretend to walk a dog") and then engage in aggression if his request was not honored (i.e., the child engaged in problem behavior to increase the probability that his requests would be honored). Bowman et al. tested this hypothesis by conducting a modified functional analysis including a: (a) test condition in which the therapist refused the participant's requests, but complied with those requests for 30 s following an instance of aggression and (b) a control condition in which the therapist complied with all requests. This procedure systematically demonstrated that aggression was higher when it resulted in compliance with the child's requests.

Chapman, Fisher, Piazza, and Kurtz (1993) provide an example of how functional analyses can be modified to accommodate unusual behavior, in this case a boy who ingested prescription medication in his home. In this study, the experimenters baited the room with placebo pills placed in different colored pill bottles. Pill consumption from each bottle was associated with a different potential social consequence (i.e., parental attention, physician attention, and escape from a work task). The results of this analysis indicated that, in this case, pill consumption was maintained by escape from work tasks and a treatment based upon this outcome resulted in long-term decreases in pill consumption.

Function-Based Treatment

Function-based treatments are those that directly address the reinforcers maintaining problem behavior as identified by a functional assessment (preferably a functional analysis). The foundation of function-based treatment is to: (a) eliminate the source of reinforcement for problem behavior (termed extinction) and (b) arrange a novel contingency through which that reinforcer can be accessed either based upon the absence of problem behavior (termed a differential reinforcement of other behavior, or DRO procedure), delivered independent of behavior (termed a noncontingent reinforcement, or NCR, procedure), or delivered following a more desirable behavior (termed differential reinforcement of an alternative behavior, or DRA).

The value of matching behavioral function to treatment was highlighted by Iwata, Pace Cowdery, and Miltenberger (1994) who conducted functional analyses of the head-banging of three children with intellectual and developmental disabilities and then applied both indicated and contraindicated behavioral treatments based upon each functional analysis. Specifically, these experimenters designed three procedural variations of extinction. For head-banging maintained by attention, extinction would take the form of planned ignoring in which a therapist would withhold attention following head-banging (termed EXT (attention)). For head-banging maintained by escape from demands, extinction would take the form of presenting demands following an occurrence of head-banging (termed EXT (escape)). For head-banging maintained by the automatic sensory consequences of the behavior, extinction would take the form of presenting protective equipment (e.g., padded helmets) to mitigate the sensory consequences caused by head-banging. The experimenters found that in each case, only the treatment indicated by the functional analysis resulted in decreased head-banging; all contraindicated treatments resulted in no change in head-banging levels.

Although extinction alone has been found to be a successful treatment for problem behavior (and in many cases is the "operative" component of interventions in which extinction is combined with other procedures; Fisher, Piazza, Cataldo, Harrell, Jefferson, & Conner, 1993; Kahng, Iwata, Thompson, & Hanley, 2000; Mazaleski, Iwata, Vollmer, Zarcone, & Smith, 1993; Wacker et al., 1990; Zarcone, Iwata, Vollmer, Jagtiani, Smith, & Mazaleski, 1993), extinction implemented in isolation can result in temporary increases in problem behavior (termed the extinction burst) and can result in increased emotional and aggressive behavior; however, these side effects of extinction are minimized when the maintaining reinforcer is delivered either via DRO, NCR, or DRA procedures (Lerman, Iwata, & Wallace, 1999; Vollmer et al. 1998).

Differential Reinforcement of Other Behavior (DRO). DRO procedures involve the delivery of reinforcement contingent upon the omission (non-occurrence) of a target behavior. That is, a therapist determines an interval of time and if the individual has not engaged in problem behavior during that interval, then reinforcement is delivered. Vollmer, Iwata, Zarcone, Smith, and Mazaleski (1993) presented an example of DRO for problem behavior maintained by attention. These experimenters determined their initial DRO interval by calculating the mean inter-response times (IRTs) between instances of problem behavior and gradually increased the DRO interval as problem behavior became less frequent.

There have been a number of variations of DRO procedures described in the literature. Although here we describe the use of function-based DRO's (i.e., those that involve withholding the reinforcer that maintains problem behavior and delivering that same reinforcer only following the omission of problem behavior), many applications of DRO have involved the use of high-quality reinforcers that were not functionally related. For instance, Cowdery, Iwata, and Pace (1990) treated the self-injurious scratching of a 9-year-old boy by delivering token reinforcers (pennies) that could be exchanged for a variety of leisure items and snack foods while the reinforcement for self-scratching (in this case automatic reinforcers) remained intact.

DRO schedules can be highly effective, but they are difficult to implement because they require constant vigilance to ensure procedural integrity (i.e., an implementer must watch continuously to see whether or not reinforcement should be delivered in a given interval). More recent research on DRO schedules has examined means of making DROs more practical. One such variation has been referred to as a momentary DRO schedule. Momentary DROs operate similarly to regular (or whole interval) DROs except that the delivery of reinforcement is determined by the presence or absence of a target behavior only at the moment an interval ends. Lindberg, Iwata, Kahng, and DeLeon (1999) demonstrated the utility of momentary DROs in the treatment of self-injurious behavior maintained by attention (see also Hammond, Iwata, Fritz, & Dempsey, 2011 and Toussaint & Tiger, 2012).

Noncontingent Reinforcement (NCR). NCR involves delivering the reinforcer that maintained problem behavior independent of ongoing behaviors. That is, the reinforcer is delivered on a fixed or variable time schedule, whether problem behavior is occurring or not. Vollmer et al. (1993) provided one of the earliest demonstrations of this procedure in the treatment of self-injurious behavior exhibited by three children with developmental disabilities. Functional analyses in each case indicated that self-injury was maintained by attention, so the authors delivered attention based solely on the passage of time. The time schedule was then gradually reduced across time (i.e., reinforcement delivery became less frequent). This procedure resulted in effective reductions of self-injury in each case. NCR procedures have the relative advantage over DRO procedures in that they do not require constant monitoring of the participant in order to implement the contingencies with perfect integrity.

It should be noted, that as some instances of problem behavior may be followed by reinforcement when using NCR schedules, it is possible that problem behavior may persist in some cases. For instance, Vollmer, Ringdahl, Roane, and Marcus (1997) found this to be the case in the treatment of a 13-year old with developmental disabilities presenting with severe aggression. This child's aggression increased as the NCR schedule was thinned, suggesting that aggression was being inadvertently reinforced. The experimenters remediated this problem by including a brief omission contingency; the experimenter did not deliver the scheduled reinforcer if aggression occurred within 10 s of the scheduled delivery. With this addition, the authors were able to extend the NCR schedule out to 5 min while maintaining low levels of problem behavior.

Some researchers have also raised concerns over the extent to which: (a) NCR does not teach a novel behavior and (b) the extent to which delivering "free" reinforcement minimizes individuals' motivation to learn new skills to acquire that reinforcer (Shirley, Iwata, Kahng, Mazaleski, & Lerman, 1997).

Differential Reinforcement of Alternative Behavior (DRA). DRA involves delivering the reinforcer that maintains problem behavior contingent upon an alternative response. One of the most common versions of DRA is referred to as Functional Communication Training, or FCT (see Tiger, Hanley, & Bruzek, 2008 for a review). FCT is a function-based DRA procedure in which the alternative response is a form of communicative behavior (e.g., specifically teaching a child with attention-maintained problem behavior to recruit attention either vocally, through signed language, or through an alternative or augmentative communication system).

Carr and Durand (1985) provided the seminal demonstration of FCT in the treatment of problem behavior with four children with developmental disabilities who engaged in problem behavior. Their procedure involved teaching participants to engage in the vocal requests, "Am I doing good work?" and "I don't understand." to recruit attention and assistance with difficult tasks, respectively. Teaching this alternative response while extinguishing problem behavior is one of the most powerful treatments for problem behavior available (Fisher et al., 1993; Hagopian, Fisher, Sullivan, Acquisto, & LeBlanc, 1998; Wacker et al., 1990; Worsdell, Iwata, Hanley, Thompson, & Kahng, 2000). FCT is a powerful tool because it not only results in decreased levels of a maladaptive behavior (similar to DRO and NCR), but it also teaches a new skill and allows clients the autonomy to request reinforcers when they are most valuable and preferred (some preference assessments have indicated that children with and without disabilities prefer conditions in which DRA is arranged in lieu of NCR contingencies; see Hanley, Piazza, Fisher, Contrucci, & Maglieri, 1997 and Luczynski & Hanley, 2009).

Selecting a Function-Based Treatment

The decisions that go into selecting a function-based intervention depend in large part on the repertoires of the individual child and the resources in the natural environment to provide continuous monitoring. The total process for selecting treatments is beyond the scope of this chapter, so we refer readers to Fisher and Bouxsein (2011); Geiger, Carr, and LeBlanc (2010); Lerman and Toole (2011); Smith (2011); Tiger, Toussaint, and Kliebert (2010); and Vollmer and Athens (2011). It is also exceedingly important to ensure that the staff and/or caregivers that will be implementing the behavior plan are well-trained and supported with follow up feedback and consultation (see Reid, O'Kane, & Macurik, 2011). Research has shown suboptimal implementation of interventions can result in the reemergence of problem behavior in many situations (St. Peter-Pipkin, Vollmer, & Sloman, 2010; Vollmer, Roane, Ringdahl, & Marcus, 1999).

Operant Conditioning to Improve Skill Deficiencies

Once concerns regarding the occurrence of problem behavior are eliminated, or at least reduced, behavior analysts can then begin programming for the development of important life skills. The totality of skills that need to be addressed by a therapist can be vast and is certainly beyond the scope of this chapter. We recommend practicing behavior analysts consult available curricula to identify important start points (e.g., Assessment of Basic Language and Learning Skills or ABLLS-R, Partington, 2010; and the Verbal Behavior Milestones Assessment and Placement Program, VB-MAPP; Sundberg, 2008). Formalized curricula such as the ABLLS-R and VB-MAPP allow therapists to identify skills needing intervention and provide a cogent sequence for skills to be targeted.

Among the most common targets for the initial stages of intervention are learning prerequisites including making eye contact, imitating motor and vocal responses, complying with instructions, matching similar items, and developing early language skills (see Baer, Peterson, & Sherman, 1967; Garcia, Baer, & Firestone, 1971; Hanley, Heal, Tiger, & Ingvarsson, 2007; Stephenson & Hanley, 2010; Wilder, Myers, Fischetti, Leon, Nicholson, & Allison, 2012). The operant approach to teaching new skills requires that: (a) the learner can engage in necessary prerequisite behaviors, (b) the target behavior(s) occur at some level or can be brought about by the teacher, and (c) the teacher can deliver a stimulus that will serve as a reinforcer that will promote the occurrence of that skill in the future.

In arranging for programmed reinforcement to follow a targeted response, it is ideal if one can program a natural consequence to serve as a reinforcer (or one with a high probability of occurring in the natural environment without specific structuring). For instance, it is ideal if the natural reinforcer of saying, "Hello" to an adult entering a room (likely the adult also saying, "Hello") served as a reinforcer. However, it is frequently the case that individuals with intellectual and developmental disabilities are not sensitive to "typical" events as reinforcers. Therefore, effective teaching must often rely on contrived sources of high-quality reinforcement, at least during the initial stages of teaching a skill, to create appropriate motivation. It is common to conduct preference assessments prior to initiating treatment planning to ensure that a teacher has access to stimuli that are likely to serve as reinforcers.

Preference Assessments

The first step of conducting preference assessments is to interview caregivers to identify potentially preferred items and activities that may serve as reinforcers. One such standardized interview is the Reinforcer Assessment for Individuals with Severe Disabilities, or RAISD (Fisher, Piazza, Bowman, & Amari, 1996). This interview tool prompts caregivers to nominate stimuli that offer visual, auditory, olfactory, gustatory, tactile, and vestibular stimulation as well as social interaction. The information obtained from interviews such as the RAISD can then be included in a direct preference assessment. Unfortunately caregiver report alone is an unreliable indicator of reinforcer effectiveness (Cote, Thompson, Hanley, & McKerchar, 2007; Green, Reid, White, Halford, Brittain, & Gardner, 1988).

Systematic preference assessments involve presenting individuals with putative reinforcing stimuli and directly measuring their engagement with or consumption of those stimuli as an indicator of reinforcer strength (see also Tiger & Kliebert, 2011 for a "how to" guide to stimulus preference assessments). Stimuli may be presented either singly (Pace, Ivancic, Edwards, Iwata, & Page, 1985), in pairs (Fisher, Piazza, Bowman, Hagopian, Owens, & Slevin, 1992), or in larger arrays (DeLeon & Iwata, 1996). Stimuli are then rank ordered based upon the percentage of trials during which participants selected each item or the duration of time participants interacted with each item (DeLeon, Iwata, Conners, & Wallace, 1999; Roane, Vollmer, Ringdahl, & Marcus, 1998; Worsdell, Iwata, & Wallace, 2002). Those stimuli that have been identified as highly preferred tend to be more effective reinforcers than those identified as less preferred (Penrod, Wallace, & Dyer, 2008; Roane, Lerman, & Vorndran, 2001).

Reinforcer preferences are likely to change across time as a function of reinforcer satiation (Hanley, Iwata, & Roscoe, 2006) and access to those reinforcers outside of the therapeutic context (Roane, Call, & Falcomata, 2005). Several strategies have been recommended to maintain the strength of reinforcers used during therapeutic programming including restricting access to those stimuli outside of sessions (Kodak, Lerman, & Call, 2007; Roane et al., 2005), rotating the delivery of multiple reinforcing stimuli (Bowman, Piazza, Fisher, Hagopian, & Kogan, 1997; Egel, 1981), or providing a choice among an array of potential reinforcing stimuli (Tiger, Hanley, & Hernandez, 2006; Tiger, Toussaint, & Roath, 2010). In addition, preference assessments should be conducted periodically to "update" the array of stimuli delivered as reinforcers.

Teaching Procedures

Once a therapist has determined what skill should be taught and identified some potentially potent reinforcers, the next step is to determine how the skill shall be taught. Using an operant model, the target behavior must occur and then contact reinforcement. If the behavior occurs at some low level, it may be sufficient to simply arrange differential reinforcement by delivering a highly preferred stimulus after the occurrence of the behavior. For instance, Broden, Bruce, Mitchell, Carter, and Hall (1970) increased the attending behavior of two young boys in their school classroom simply by having the teacher intermittently provide praise when she noticed them attending. If the behavior does not occur with sufficient regularity to contact reinforcement, then a behavior analyst must use other procedures to bring the behavior about so it can then be reinforced.

Shaping. Shaping is sometimes referred to as the method of teaching by successive approximations. Shaping begins by reinforcing some behavior the individual currently exhibits that is an approximation of the target goal and then gradually reinforcing behaviors that are closer and closer to the goal (Miltenberger, 2012). Fleece, Gross, O'Brien, Kistner, Rothblum, and Drabman (1981) used shaping and visual feedback to increase the voice volume exhibited by a young child with developmental delays who engaged in very quiet speech. These authors presented a decibel meter that provided visual feedback (lights in the shape of a Christmas tree) when the child's speech exceeded a set decibel threshold. The experimenters gradually increased the threshold, which resulted in progressively louder speech that was not initially present. Shaping has often been referred to as more of an art than a science, as shaping typically relies on the recognition and reaction of the therapist (although see Athens, Vollmer & St. Peter-Pipkin, 2007 and Hall, Maynes, & Reiss, 2009 for some recent work on a more systematic approach to shaping). Shaping may be fairly slow and it can be extremely difficult to shape complex behaviors or behaviors involving multiple steps. Therefore, other strategies have been developed to "help along" more complex forms of behavior.

Task Analysis and Response Chaining. Conducting a task analysis involves identifying all component parts of a task, and their sequence, that must be completed. A thorough task analysis ensures that the trainer targets all relevant and important behaviors. One can develop a task analysis by either: (a) a therapist completing the behavior chain him- or herself and noting each of his or her own behaviors or (b) observing a competent model engage in the behavior chain. For instance, Jerome, Frantino, and Sturmey (2007) developed a task analysis to teach a 25-year man with mild mental retardation to access websites on a computer. This task analysis was divided into 13 steps including turning on the computer and the monitor, placing the hand on the mouse, moving the cursor to the Internet Explorer® icon, double-clicking the icon, moving the cursor to the Google® search box, left clicking the box, typing in a search topic, placing the hand back on the mouse, moving the cursor to the box labeled "search" and clicking, scrolling through website options, and clicking on the website of choice.

Once a therapist has developed a task analysis, he or she must then teach the component skills necessary to complete the task; collectively this is referred to as response chaining. There are three variations of chaining procedures. They are referred to as forward chaining (in which each component is taught sequentially until mastery, beginning with the initial step of the chain), backward chaining (in which each component is taught in reverse order until mastery, beginning with the terminal step of the chain), and the total task method in which the entire chain is taught simultaneously. Each of these chaining methods has proven successful in teaching self-care (Hagopian, Farrell, & Amari, 1996; Schuster, Gast, Wolery, & Guiltinan, 1988), leisure (Jerome et al., 2007; Luyben, Funk, Morgan, Clark & Delulio, 1986; Schleien, Wehman, & Kiernan, 1981), and vocational skills (e.g., Hur & Osborne, 1993). Research has suggested that each form of chaining is effective and comparative studies have indicated that the chaining techniques are of similar efficacy and efficiency (Slocum & Tiger, 2011). Similar to differential reinforcement alone, chaining alone will be most effective if the component behaviors occur at some existent level. If the component behaviors are not occurring, the behavior analyst may rely on shaping, but more often than not will resort to prompting and prompt fading procedures.

Prompting Strategies. Consider the notion that skill acquisition training involves presenting a target discriminative stimulus that should result in a target response. For instance, if we present colored shapes and the spoken discriminative stimulus "red," we hope the learner could point to the red shape. Before training, the target discriminative stimulus, in this case the red shape, does not occasion the target response. Prompting involves presenting an additional discriminative stimulus with a high probability of occasioning a target response (or a closer approximation to a target response). In our example, the teacher might provide a model prompt after saying "red" by pointing to the red shape, and then allowing the learner to imitate the pointing response. The prompted response will then be reinforced and the prompts can be gradually reduced across trials to transfer stimulus control from the model prompt to the target discriminative stimulus, "red."

There is a large variety of procedures for prompting and prompt fading. In addition to the model prompt described above, prompts can involve vocal stimuli (Ingvarsson & Hollobaugh, 2010), pictures (Phillips & Vollmer, 2012), text (Sarakoff, Taylor, & Poulson, 2001), or physical (hand-over-hand) stimuli (Thompson, Cotnoir-Bichelman, McKerchar, Tate, & Dancho, 2007). Prompts may involve manipulating characteristics of the target stimuli (Schilmoeller, Schilmoeller, Etzel, & LeBlanc, 1979) or highlighting important characteristics of the target stimuli (Osborne, Rudrud, & Zezoney, 1990). Prompts may be provided immediately following a target discriminative stimulus, following a fixed delay (e.g., 5 s after the target discriminative stimulus), or following a progressively increasing delay (1 s, then 2 s, then 3 s increasing across teaching trials; Ault, Gast, & Wolery, 1988; Walker, 2008). Prompts may be implemented with full intensity and gradually reduced (e.g., Fisher et al., 1993) or may be withheld and then gradually increased as necessary to occasion a target response (e.g., Shirley et al., 1997). The variety of prompting and prompt fading strategies is well beyond the scope of this chapter, but we recommend Wolery and Gast's (1984) review of prompting and fading procedures.

Programming of Generalization

One of the unique features of teaching children with developmental disabilities is that their behavior may come under faulty, or selective, stimulus control. That is, socially important behaviors may only occur in the presence of some stimuli that were not intended to control the response. For instance, Halle and Holt (1991) conducted an analysis of the stimulus control predicting the use of the word "please" on the requests of four children with moderate mental retardation. In this study, participants were sent on an errand by their teacher (Cathy) to request an item (a tape recorder) from another teacher (Connie) in a particular location (a vocational training room) using "please" in their request. Once participants were reliably using please in their requests, the experimenters examined the extent to which please would continue to occur if the situation varied in terms of the requester, the item requested, the person from whom they were requesting, and the setting in which they had to find the person. The authors found that for one participant, the teachers involved in initial training had acquired stimulus control over responding. Another participant did not use please if any single stimulus from the training environment was included in the generalization probe, but a complex of any two stimuli did occasion the target response.

Rincover and Koegel (1975) provided another important demonstration of selective stimulus control with children with autism. In one case, the authors taught the child to respond to the instruction, "touch your chin." After the child was responding to this instruction, the experimenters found that this response only occurred in the presence of one therapist, who emitted an inadvertent hand gesture when providing the instruction. The response had come under control of the hand gesture (only exhibited by one person) rather than the instruction, "touch your chin." The authors also reported that one child learned to respond to the instruction "touch your nose," but would only do so when the table and chairs from the training room were present.

These studies highlight that teaching procedures involving shaping, chaining, prompting, and differential reinforcement are likely not sufficient in developing useful skills in some proportion of children. That is, the goal of intervention is not that a child can carry on a conversation with the behavior analyst in the therapeutic environment, but rather that the child can also carry on a normal conversation with any person he or she encounters in any setting. Rather than teach a target behavior under one set of conditions and hope for the best, behavior analysts instead program and test for the generality of their interventions systematically across relevant settings and caregivers. Stokes and Baer (1977) wrote a seminal review on promoting generalization that continues to influence behavior analysts today. We will highlight some of their techniques that we have found most useful.

Training Multiple Exemplars. This technique involves systematically varying the training conditions and the target stimuli such that it becomes more likely the intended stimuli come to control responding. For instance, if we were to teach a child to label the color red, it would be desirable to not only teach him or her to respond to a red square (in which he or she may be responding to the shape or the texture of the paper), but also to respond in the presence of a red bear, a red car, a red shoe, a red shirt, a red block, etc. Further, we would want to present a number of other red objects that were not associated with instruction to ensure the child responds to the red quality of those stimuli as well (e.g., a red stapler). Similarly, it is worthwhile to introduce multiple therapists and training settings to promote generalization across environmental stimulus features.

Program Common Stimuli. The notion of programming common stimuli is to ensure the stimuli that should occasion responding in the natural environment are included in the training environment. For instance, in teaching individuals with mental retardation pedestrian skills, Page, Iwata, and Neef (1976) constructed a model city in which the participants were able to practice responding to street signs saying "Walk" or "Don't Walk" with a pedestrian doll. Instruction and acquisition of safe pedestrian behavior in the training environment with the model city resulted in safe pedestrian behaviors in the regular city environment for each of their five participants.

Programming common stimuli may also mean bringing the occurrence of a target behavior under the tight stimulus control of a contrived discriminative stimulus and then introducing that stimulus into the natural environment. For instance, in the treatment of cigarette pica (ingestion) exhibited by a young man with mental retardation and autism, Piazza, Hanley, and Fisher (1996) developed stimulus control over pica by: (a) presenting a colored card during some sessions in which the therapist observed the participant covertly from outside the session room and immediately upon an instance of pica entered and provided a mild reprimand (which had been demonstrated to be a punisher) and (b) by presenting another colored card during other sessions in which pica would not be disturbed. After repeated sessions of this procedure, the experimenters were able to control the occurrence of pica by presenting the colored cards in other environments, even when the reprimand could not be delivered.

Introduce Natural Maintaining Contingencies. Stokes and Baer (1976) also highlight a behavior that requires the delivery of contrived sources of reinforcement (e.g., edibles or leisure items) is unlikely to persist in the natural environment. That is, without retraining all (or at least most) of the adults with whom an individual may come in contact, the target behavior is likely to contact extinction and be weakened. Therefore, to the greatest extent possible, it is desirable to: (a) identify the natural reinforcers that typically maintain a behavior, (b) teach behavior that specifically recruits natural sources of reinforcement, and (c) minimize the use of contrived reinforcement (e.g., to teach students to request praise for completing high-quality work rather than to arrange edibles or activities for work completion; Stokes, Fowler, & Baer, 1978).

Conclusions

The understanding of operant learning and systematic application of operant principles has allowed behavior analysts to take a larger role in the treatment of individuals with developmental disabilities, in particular those with autism spectrum disorders (see also chapter by T. Thompson in this volume for a greater description of autism intervention). These treatments involve reducing problem behavior through extinction and differential reinforcement, teaching important novel communicative, social, and self-care behaviors, and ensuring those behaviors are under appropriate stimulus control in the natural environment. By altering environmental consequences, behavior analysts are able to engender lasting behavioral changes in populations that have historically been ignored or cast-away.

Notes

1 Empirical demonstrations of these learning histories promoting self-injury with humans cannot take place for obvious ethical reasons. However, Shaefer (1970) demonstrated the development of self-injurious head-banging in monkeys using similar social contingencies.

2 Although the measurement of descriptive data is relatively simple, the quantitative analysis of descriptive behavior is quite complex. We recommend Thompson and Borrero (2012) for strategies for analyzing descriptive data.

References

Athens, E. S., Vollmer, T. R., & St. Peter-Pipkin, C. C. (2007). Shaping academic task engagement with percentile schedules. *Journal of Applied Behavior Analysis*, *40*, 475–488. doi: 10.1901/jaba.2007.40–475.

Ault, M. J., Gast, D. L., & Wolery, M. (1988). Comparison of progressive and constant time-delay procedures in teaching community-sign word reading. *American Journal on Mental Deficiency*, *93*, 44–56.

Baer, D. M., Peterson, R. F., & Sherman, J. A. (1967). The development of imitation by reinforcing behavioral similarity to a model. *Journal of the Experimental Analysis of Behavior*, *10*, 405–416. doi: 10.1901/jeab.1967.10 405.

Behavior Analyst Certification Board (2010). *Guidelines for responsible conduct for behavior analysts*. Retrieved January 3, 2014 from http://www.bacb.com/Downloadfiles/BACBguidelines/1007guidelinesFpdf.pdf.

Bowman, L. G., Fisher, W. W., Thompson, R. H., & Piazza, C. C. (1997). On the relation of mands and the function of destructive behavior. *Journal of Applied Behavior Analysis*, *30*, 251–265. doi: 10.1901/jaba.1997.30-251.

Bowman, L. G., Piazza, C. C., Fisher, W. W., Hagopian, L. P., & Kogan, J. S. (1997). Assessment of preference for varied versus constant reinforcers. *Journal of Applied Behavior Analysis*, *30*, 451–458. doi: 10.1901/jaba.1997.30-451.

Broden, M., Bruce, C., Mitchell, M. A., Carter, V., & Hall, R. V. (1970). Effects of teacher attention on attending behavior of two boys at adjacent desks. *Journal of Applied Behavior Analysis*, *3*, 199–203. doi: 10.1901/jaba.1970.3-199.

Camp, E. M., Iwata, B. A., Hammond, J. L., & Bloom, S. E. (2009). Antecedent versus consequent events as predictors of problem behavior. *Journal of Applied Behavior Analysis*, *42*, 469–483. doi: 10.1901/jaba.2009.42-469.

Carr, E. G. (1977). The motivation of self-injurious behavior: A review of some hypotheses. *Psychological Bulletin*, *84*, 800–816. doi: 10.1037/0033-2909.84.4.800.

Carr, E. G., & Durand, V. M. (1985). Reducing behavior problems through functional communication training. *Journal of Applied Behavior Analysis*, *18*, 111–126. doi: 10.1901/jaba.1985.18-111.

Carr, E. G., Taylor, J. C., & Robinson, S. (1991). The effects of severe behavior problems in children on the teaching behavior of adults. *Journal of Applied Behavior Analysis*, *24*, 523–535. doi: 10.1901/jaba.1991.24-523.

Carr, E. G., Yarbrough, S. C., & Langdon, N. A. (1997). Effects of idiosyncratic stimulus variables on functional analysis outcomes. *Journal of Applied Behavior Analysis*, *30*, 673–686. doi: 10.1901/jaba.1997.30-673.

Centers for Disease Control and Prevention (2012) *Developmental disabilities*. Retrieved January 3, 2014 from http://www.cdc.gov/ncbddd/dd.

Chapman, S., Fisher, W., Piazza, C. C., & Kurtz, P. F. (1993). Functional assessment and treatment of life-threatening drug ingestion in a dually diagnosed youth. *Journal of Applied Behavior Analysis*, *26*, 255–256. doi: 10.1901/jaba.1993.26-255.

Cote, C. A., Thompson, R. H., Hanley, G. P., & McKerchar, P. M. (2007). Teacher report and direct assessment of preferences for identifying reinforcers for young children. *Journal of Applied Behavior Analysis*, *40*, 157–166. doi: 10.1901/jaba.2007.40-157.

Cowdery, G. E., Iwata, B. A., & Pace, G. M. (1990). Effects and side effects of DRO as treatment for self-injurious behavior. *Journal of Applied Behavior Analysis, 23*, 497–506. doi: 10.1901/jaba.1990.23-496.

DeLeon, I. G., & Iwata, B. A. (1996). Evaluation of a multiple-stimulus presentation format for assessing reinforcer preferences. *Journal of Applied Behavior Analysis, 29*, 519–533. doi: 10.1901/jaba.1996.29-519.

DeLeon, I. G., Iwata, B. A., Conners, J., & Wallace, M. D. (1999). Examination of ambiguous stimulus preferences with duration-based measures. *Journal of Applied Behavior Analysis, 32*, 111–114. doi: 10.1901/jaba.1999.32-111.

Dunlap, G., Dyer, K., & Koegel, R. L. (1983). Autistic self-stimulation and intertrial interval duration. *American Journal of Mental Deficiency, 88*, 914–202.

Durand, V. M., & Crimmins, D. B. (1988). Identifying the variables maintaining self-injurious behavior. *Journal of Autism and Developmental Disorders, 18*, 99–117. doi: 10.1007/BF02211821.

Dykens, E., & Shah, B. (2003). Psychiatric disorders in Prader Willi syndrome: Epidemiology and management. *CNS Drugs, 17*, 167–178.

Egel, A. L. (1981). Reinforcer variation: Implications for motivating developmentally disabled children. *Journal of Applied Behavior Analysis, 14*, 345–350. doi: 10.1901/jaba.1981.14-345.

Epstein, L. H., Doke, L. A., Sajwaj, T. E., Sorrell, S., & Rimmer, B. (1974). Generality and the side effects of overcorrection. *Journal of Applied Behavior Analysis, 7*, 385–390. doi: 10.1901/jaba.1974.7-385.

Fisher, W. W., & Bouxsein, K. J. (2011). Developing function-based reinforcement procedures. In W. W. Fisher, C. C. Piazza, and H. S. Roane (Eds.), *Handbook of applied behavior analysis* (pp. 335–347). New York: Guilford Press.

Fisher, W. W., Piazza, C. C., Bowman, L. G., & Amari, A. (1996). Integrating caregiver report with a systematic choice assessment to enhance reinforcer identification. *American Journal on Mental Retardation, 101*, 15–25.

Fisher, W., Piazza, C. C., Bowman, L. G., Hagopian, L. P., Owens, J. C., & Slevin, I. (1992). A comparison of two approaches for identifying reinforcers for persons with severe and profound disabilities. *Journal of Applied Behavior Analysis, 25*, 491–498. doi: 10.1901/jaba.1992.25-491.

Fisher, W., Piazza, C. C., Cataldo, M. F., Harrell, R., Jefferson, G., & Conner, R. (1993). Functional communication training with and without extinction and punishment. *Journal of Applied Behavior Analysis, 26*, 23–36. doi: 10.1901/jaba.1993.26-23.

Fleece, L., Gross, A., O'Brien, T., Kistner, J., Rothblum, E., & Drabman, R. (1981). Elevation of voice volume in young developmentally delayed children via an operant shaping procedure. *Journal of Applied Behavior Analysis, 14*, 351–355. doi: 10.1901/jaba.1981.14-351.

Garcia, E., Baer, D. M., & Firestone, I. (1971). The development of generalized imitations within topographically defined boundaries. *Journal of Applied Behavior Analysis, 4*, 101–112. doi: 10.1901/jaba.1971.4-101.

Geiger, K. B., Carr, J. E., & LeBlanc, L. A. (2010). Function-based treatments for escape-maintained problem behavior: A treatment-selection model for practicing behavior analysts. *Behavior Analysis in Practice, 3*, 22–32.

Goh, H., Iwata, B. A., Shore, B. A., DeLeon, I. G., Lerman, D. C., Ulrich, S. M., & Smith, R. G. (1995). An analysis of the reinforcing properties of hand mouthing. *Journal of Applied Behavior Analysis, 28*, 269–283. doi: 10.1901/jaba.1995.28-269.

Green, C. W., Reid, D. H., White, L. K., Halford, R. C., Brittain, D. P., & Gardner, S. M. (1988). Identifying reinforcers for persons with profound handicaps: Staff opinion versus systematic assessment of preferences. *Journal of Applied Behavior Analysis*, *21*, 31–43. doi: 10.1901/jaba.1988.21-31.

Groden, G. (1989). A guide for conducting a comprehensive behavioral analysis of a target behavior. *Journal of Behavior Therapy and Experimental Psychiatry*, *20*, 163–169.

Hagopian, L. P., Farrell, D. A., & Amari, A. (1996). Treating total liquid refusal with backward chaining and fading. *Journal of Applied Behavior Analysis*, *29*, 573–575. doi: 10.1901/jaba.1996.29-573.

Hagopian, L. P., Fisher, W. W., Sullivan, M. T., Acquisto, J., & LeBlanc, L. A. (1998). Effectiveness of functional communication training with and without extinction and punishment: A summary of 21 inpatient cases. *Journal of Applied Behavior Analysis*, *31*, 211–235. doi: 10.1901/jaba.1998.31-211.

Hall, S. S., Maynes, N. P., & Reiss, A. L. (2009). Using percentile schedules to increase eye contact in children with Fragile X syndrome. *Journal of Applied Behavior Analysis*, *42*, 171–176. doi: 10.1901/jaba.2009.42-171.

Halle, J. W., & Holt, B. (1991). Assessing stimulus control in natural settings: An analysis of stimuli that acquire control during training. *Journal of Applied Behavior Analysis*, *24*, 579–589. doi: 10.1901/jaba.1991.24-579.

Hammond, J. L., Iwata, B. A., Fritz, J. N., & Dempsey, C. M. (2011). Evaluation of fixed momentary DRO schedules under signaled and unsignaled arrangements. *Journal of Applied Behavior Analysis*, *44*, 69–81. doi: 10.1901/jaba.2011.44-69.

Hanley, G. P., Heal, N. A., Tiger, J. H., & Ingvarsson, E. I. (2007). Evaluation of a classwide teaching program for developing preschool life skills. *Journal of Applied Behavior Analysis*, *40*, 277–300. doi: 10.1901/jaba.2007.40-277.

Hanley, G. P., Iwata, B. A., & McCord, B. E. (2003). Functional analysis of problem behavior: A review. *Journal of Applied Behavior Analysis*, *36*, 147–185. doi: 10.1901/jaba.2003.36-147.

Hanley, G. P., Iwata, B. A., & Roscoe, E. M. (2006). Some determinants of changes in preference over time. *Journal of Applied Behavior Analysis*, *39*, 189–202. doi: 10.1901/jaba.2006.39-189.

Hanley, G. P., Piazza, C. C., Fisher, W. W., Contrucci, S. A., & Maglieri, K. (1997). Evaluation of client preference for function-based treatment packages. *Journal of Applied Behavior Analysis*, *30*, 459–473. doi: 10.1901/jaba.1997.30-459.

Hur, J., & Osbourne, S. (1993). A comparison of forward and backward chaining methods used in teaching corsage making skills to mentally retarded adults. *British Journal of Developmental Disabilities*, *39*, 108–117.

Ingvarsson, E. T., & Hollobaugh, T. (2010). Acquisition of intraverbal behavior: Teaching children with autism to mand for answers to questions. *Journal of Applied Behavior Analysis*, *43*, 1–17. doi: 10.1901/jaba.2010.43-1.

Iwata, B. A., Dorsey, M. F., Slifer, K. J., Bauman, K. E., & Richman, G. S. (1994). Toward a functional analysis of self-injury. *Journal of Applied Behavior Analysis*, *27*, 197–209. doi: 10.1901/jaba.1994.27-197.

Iwata, B. A., Pace, G. M., Cowdery, G. E., & Miltenberger, R. G. (1994). What makes extinction work: An analysis of procedural form and function. *Journal of Applied Behavior Analysis*, *27*, 131–144. doi: 10.1901/jaba.1994.27-131.

Jerome, J., Frantino, E. P., & Sturmey, P. (2007). The effects of errorless learning and backward chaining on the acquisition of internet skills in adults with developmental disabilities. *Journal of Applied Behavior Analysis*, *40*, 185–189. doi: 10.1901/jaba.2007.40-185.

Kahng, S., Iwata, B. A., Thompson, R. H., & Hanley, G. P. (2000). A method for identifying satiation versus extinction effects under noncontingent reinforcement schedules. *Journal of Applied Behavior Analysis*, *33*, 419–432. doi: 10.1901/jaba.2000.33-419.

Kodak, T., Lerman, D. C., & Call, N. (2007). Evaluating the influence of postsession reinforcement on choice of reinforcers. *Journal of Applied Behavior Analysis*, *40*, 515–527. doi: 10.1901/jaba.2007.40-515.

Koegel, R. L., & Covert, A. (1972). The relationship of self-stimulation to learning in autistic children. *Journal of Applied Behavior Analysis*, *5*, 381–387. doi: 10.1901/jaba.1972.5-381.

Koegel, R. L., Firestone, P. B., Kramme, K. W., & Dunlap, G. (1974). Increasing spontaneous play by suppressing self-stimulation in autistic children. *Journal of Applied Behavior Analysis*, *7*, 521–528. doi: 10.1901/jaba.1974.7-521-528.

Lerman, D. C., & Iwata, B. A. (1993). Descriptive and experimental analysis of variables maintaining self-injurious behavior. *Journal of Applied Behavior Analysis*, *26*, 293–319. doi: 10.1901/jaba.1993.26-293.

Lerman, D. C., Iwata, B. A., & Wallace, M. D. (1999). Side effects of extinction: Prevalence of bursting and aggression during the treatment of self-injurious behavior. *Journal of Applied Behavior Analysis*, *32*, 1–8. doi: 10.1901/jaba.1999.32-1.

Lerman, D. C., & Toole, L. M. (2011). Developing function-based punishment procedures. In W. W. Fisher, C. C. Piazza, and H. S. Roane (Eds.), *Handbook of applied behavior analysis* (pp. 348–369). New York: Guilford Press.

Lindberg, J. S., Iwata, B. A., Kahng, S., & DeLeon, I. G. (1999). DRO contingencies: An analysis of variable-momentary schedules. *Journal of Applied Behavior Analysis*, *32*, 123–136. doi: 10.1901/jaba.1999.32-123.

Løvaas, O. I., Litrownik, A., & Mann, R. (1971). Response latencies to auditory stimuli in autistic children engaged in self-stimulatory behavior. *Behavior Research and Therapy*, *9*, 39–49. doi: 10/1-16/0005-7967(71)90035-0.

Luczynski, K. C., & Hanley, G. P. (2009). Do children prefer contingencies? An evaluation of the efficacy of and preference for contingent versus noncontingent social reinforcement during play. *Journal of Applied Behavior Analysis*, *42*, 511–525. doi: 10.1901/jaba.2009.42–511.

Luyben, P. D., Funk, D. M., Morgan, J. K., Clark, K. A., & Delulio, D. W. (1986). Team sports for the severely retarded: Training a side-of-the-foot soccer pass using a maximum-to-minimum prompt reduction strategy. *Journal of Applied Behavior Analysis*, *19*, 431–436. doi: 10.1901/jaba.1986.19-431.

Mazaleski, J. L., Iwata, B. A., Vollmer, T. R., Zarcone, J. R., & Smith, R. G. (1993). Analysis of the reinforcement and extinction components in DRO contingencies with self-injury. *Journal of Applied Behavior Analysis*, *26*, 143–156. doi: 10.1901/jaba.1993.26-143.

McKerchar, P. M., & Thompson, R. H. (2004). A descriptive analysis of potential reinforcement contingencies in the preschool classroom. *Journal of Applied Behavior Analysis*, *37*, 431–444. doi: 10.1901/jaba.2004.37-431.

Morrison, K., & Rosales-Ruiz, J. (1997). The effect of object preferences on task performance and stereotypy in a child with autism. *Research in Developmental Disabilities*, *18*, 127–137. doi: 10-1016/S0891-4222(96)00046-7.

Osborne, K., Rudrud, E., & Zezoney, F. (1990). Improved curveball hitting through the enhancement of visual cues. *Journal of Applied Behavior Analysis*, *23*, 371–377. doi: 10.1901/jaba.1990.23-371.

Paclawskyj, T. P., Matson, J. L., Rush, K. S., Smalls, Y., & Vollmer, T. R. (2000). Questions about behavioral function (QABF): A behavioral checklist for functional assessment of aberrant behavior. *Research in Developmental Disabilities*, *21*, 223–229. doi: 10.1016/S0891-4222(00)00036-6.

Pace, G. M., Ivancic, M. T., Edwards, G. L., Iwata, B. A., & Page, T. J. (1985). Assessment of stimulus preference assessment and reinforcer value with profoundly retarded individuals. *Journal of Applied Behavior Analysis, 18*, 249–255. doi: 10.1901/jaba.1985.18-249.

Page, T. J., Iwata, B. A., & Neef, N. A. (1976). Teaching pedestrian skills to retarded persons: Generalization from the classroom to the natural environment. *Journal of Applied Behavior Analysis, 9*, 433–444. doi: 10.1901/jaba.1976.9-433.

Partington, J. W. (2010). *The assessment of basic language and learning skills-revised.* Pleasant Hill, CA: Behavior Analysts, Inc.

Penrod, B., Wallace, M. D., & Dyer, E. J. (2008). Assessing reinforcer potency of high- and low- preference reinforcers with respect to response rate and response patterns. *Journal of Applied Behavior Analysis, 41*, 177–188. doi: 10.1901/jaba.2008.41-177.

Phillips, C. L., & Vollmer, T. R. (2012). Generalized instruction following with pictorial prompts. *Journal of Applied Behavior Analysis, 45*, 37–54. doi: 10.1901/jaba.2012.45-37.

Piazza, C. C., Fisher, W. W., Brown, K. A., Shore, B. A., Patel, M. R., Katz, R. M., & Blakely-Smith, A. (2003). Functional analysis of inappropriate mealtime behaviors. *Journal of Applied Behavior Analysis, 36*, 187–204. doi: 10.1901/jaba.2003.36–187.

Piazza, C. C., Hanley, G. P., & Fisher, W. W. (1996). Functional analysis and treatment of cigarette pica. *Journal of Applied Behavior Analysis, 29*, 437–450. doi: 10.1906/jaba.1996.29-437.

Reid, D. H., O'Kane, N. P., & Macurik, K. M. (2011). Staff training and management. In W.W. Fisher, C. C. Piazza, and H. S. Roane (Eds.), *Handbook of Applied Behavior Analysis* (pp. 281–294). New York: Guilford Press.

Richman, D. M., & Hagopian, L. P. (1999). On the effects of "quality" of attention in the functional analysis of destructive behavior. *Research in Developmental Disabilities, 20*, 51–62. doi: 10.1016/S0891-4222(98)00031-6.

Rincover, A., & Koegel, R. L. (1975). Setting generality and stimulus control in autistic children. *Journal of Applied Behavior Analysis, 8*, 235–246. doi: 10.1901/jaba.2012.8-235.

Risley, T. R. (1968). The effects and side effects of punishing the autistic behaviors of a deviant child. *Journal of Applied Behavior Analysis, 1*, 21–34. doi: 10.1901/jaba.1968.1-21.

Roane, H. S., Call, N. A., & Falcomata, T. S. (2005). A preliminary analysis of adaptive responding under open and closed economies. *Journal of Applied Behavior Analysis, 38*, 335–348. doi: 10.1901/jaba.2005.38-335.

Roane, H. S., Lerman, D. C., & Vorndran, C. M. (2001). Assessing reinforcers under progressive schedule requirements. *Journal of Applied Behavior Analysis, 34*, 145–167. doi: 10.1901/jaba.2001.34-145.

Roane, H. S., Vollmer, T. R., Ringdahl, J. E., & Marcus, B. A. (1998). Evaluation of a brief stimulus preference assessment. *Journal of Applied Behavior Analysis, 31*, 605–620. doi: 10.1901/jaba.1998.31-605.

Sarakoff, R. A., Taylor, B. A., & Poulson, C. L. (2001). Teaching children with autism to engage in conversational exchanges: Script fading with embedded textual stimuli. *Journal of Applied Behavior Analysis, 34*, 81–84. doi: 10.1901/jaba.2001.34-81.

Schaefer, H. H. (1970). Self-injurious behavior: Shaping "head-banging" in monkeys. *Journal of Applied Behavior Analysis, 3*, 111–116. doi: 10.1901/jaba.1970.3-111.

Schilmoeller, G. L., Schilmoeller, K. J., Etzel, B. C., & LeBlanc, J. M. (1979). Conditional discrimination after errorless and trial-and-error training. *Journal of the Experimental Analysis of Behavior, 31*, 405–420. doi: 10.1901/jeab.1979.31-405.

Schleien, S. J., Wehman, P., & Kiernan, J. (1981). Teaching leisure skills to severely handicapped adults: An age-appropriate darts game. *Journal of Applied Behavior Analysis, 14*, 513–519. doi: 10.1901/jaba.1981.14.513.

Schuster, J. W., Gast, D. L., Wolery, M., & Guiltinan, S. (1988). The effectiveness of a constant time-delay procedure to teach chained responses to adolescents with mental retardation. *Journal of Applied Behavior Analysis, 21*, 169–178. doi: 10.1901/jaba.1988.21-169.

Shirley, M. J., Iwata, B. A., Kahng, S., Mazaleski, J. L., & Lerman, D. C. (1997). Does functional communication training compete with ongoing contingencies of reinforcement? An analysis during response acquisition and maintenance. *Journal of Applied Behavior Analysis, 30*, 93–104. doi: 10.1901/jaba.1997.30-93.

Slocum, S. K., & Tiger, J. H. (2011). An assessment of the efficiency of and child preference for forward and backward chaining. *Journal of Applied Behavior Analysis, 44*, 793–805. doi: 10.1901/jaba.2011.44-793.

Smith, R. G. (2011). Developing antecedent interventions for problem behavior. In W.W. Fisher, C. C. Piazza, and H. S. Roane (Eds.) *Handbook of applied behavior analysis* (pp. 297–316). New York: Guilford Press.

Stephenson, K. M., & Hanley, G. P. (2010). Preschoolers' compliance with simple instructions: A descriptive and experimental evaluation. *Journal of Applied Behavior Analysis, 43*, 229–247. doi: 10.1901/jaba.2010.43-229.

Stokes, T. F., & Baer, D. M. (1977). An implicit technology of generalization. *Journal of Applied Behavior Analysis, 10*, 349–367. doi: 10.1901/jaba.2012.10-349.

Stokes, T. F., Fowler, S. A., & Baer, D. M. (1978). Training preschool children to recruit natural communities of reinforcement. *Journal of Applied Behavior Analysis, 11*, 285–303. doi: 10.1901/jaba.1978.11-285.

St. Peter, C. C., Vollmer, T. R., Bourret, J. C., Borrero, C. S. W., Sloman, K. N., & Rapp, J. T. (2005). On the role of attention in naturally occuring matching relations. *Journal of Applied Behavior Analysis, 38*, 429–443. doi: 10.1901/jaba.2005.38-429.

St. Peter-Pipkin, C. C., Vollmer, T. R., & Sloman, K. N. (2010). Effects of treatment integrity failures during differential reinforcement of alternative behavior: A translational model. *Journal of Applied Behavior Analysis, 43*, 47–70. doi: 10.1901/jaba.2010.43-47.

Sundberg, M. L. (2008). *Verbal Behavior Milestones Assessment and Placement Program: A language and social skills assessment program for children with autism and other developmental disabilities.* Concord, CA: AVB Press.

Thompson, R. H., & Borrero, J. C. (2012). Direct observation. In W. W. Fisher, C. C. Piazza, & H. S. Roane (Eds.), *Handbook of applied behavior analysis* (pp. 191–205). New York: Guilford Press.

Thompson, R. H., Cotnoir-Bichelman, N. M., McKerchar, P. M., Tate, T. L., & Dancho, K. A. (2007). Enhancing early communication through infant sign training. *Journal of Applied Behavior Analysis, 40*, 15–23. doi: 10.1901/jaba.2007.40-15.

Thompson, R. H., & Iwata, B. A. (2001). A descriptive analysis of social consequences following problem behavior. *Journal of Applied Behavior Analysis, 34*, 169–178. doi: 10.1901/jaba.2001.34-169.

Thompson, R. H., & Iwata, B. A. (2007). A comparison of outcomes from descriptive and functional analyses. *Journal of Applied Behavior Analysis, 40*, 333–338. doi: 10.1901/jaba.2007.40-333.

Thompson, T. (2014). Autism and behavior analysis: History and current status. In F. K. McSweeney & E. S. Murphy (Eds.), *The Wiley-Blackwell Handbook of Operant Conditioning* (pp. 483–507). Oxford: Wiley-Blackwell.

Tiger, J. H., Fisher, W. W., Toussaint, K. R., & Kodak, T. (2009). Progressing from initially ambiguous functional analyses: Three case examples. *Research in Developmental Disabilities, 30*, 910–926. doi: 10.1016/j.ridd.2009.01.005.

Tiger, J. H., Hanley, G. P., & Bessette, K. K. (2006). Incorporating descriptive assessment outcomes into the design of functional analysis: A case example. *Education and Treatment of Children, 29*, 107–124.

Tiger, J. H., Hanley, G. P., & Bruzek, J. (2008). Functional communication training: A review and practical guide. *Behavior Analysis in Practice, 1*, 16–23.

Tiger, J. H., Hanley, G. P., & Hernandez, E. (2006). An evaluation of the value of choosing with preschool children. *Journal of Applied Behavior Analysis, 39*, 1–16. doi: 10.1901/jaba.2006.39-1.

Tiger, J. H., & Kliebert, M. L. (2011). Stimulus preference assessment. In J. K. Luiselli (Ed.), *Teaching and behavior support for children and adults with autism spectrum disorder: A practitioners guide* (pp. 30–37). New York: Oxford.

Tiger, J. H., Toussaint, K. A., & Kliebert, M. L. (2010). Rituals and stereotypies. In J. L. Matson (Ed.), *Applied behavior analysis for children with autism spectrum disorders* (pp. 145–155). New York: Springer.

Tiger, J. H., Toussaint, K. A., & Roath, C. T. (2010). An evaluation of the value of choice-making opportunities in single-operant arrangements: Simple fixed- and progressive-ratio schedules. *Journal of Applied Behavior Analysis, 43*, 519–524. doi: 10.1901/jaba.2010.43-519.

Touchette, P. E., MacDonald, R. F., & Langer, S. N. (1985). A scatter plot for identifying stimulus control of problem behavior. *Journal of Applied Behavior Analysis, 18*, 343–351. doi: 10.1901/jaba.1985.18-343.

Toussaint, K. A., & Tiger, J. H. (2012). Reducing covert self-injurious behavior maintained by automatic reinforcement through a variable momentary DRO procedure. *Journal of Applied Behavior Analysis, 45*, 179–184. doi: 10.1901/jaba.2012.45-179.

VanDerHeyden, A. M., Witt, J. C., & Gatti, S. (2001). Descriptive assessment method to reduce overall disruptive behavior in a preschool classroom. *School Psychology Review, 30*, 548–567.

Vollmer, T. R. (1994). The concept of automatic reinforcement: Implications for behavioral research in developmental disabilities. *Research in Developmental Disabilities, 15*, 187–207. doi: 10.1016/0891-4222(94)90011-6.

Vollmer, T. R., & Athens, E. (2011). Developing function-based extinction procedures for problem behavior. In W. W. Fisher, C. C. Piazza, and H. S. Roane (Eds.), *Handbook of Applied Behavior Analysis* (pp. 317–334). New York: Guilford Press.

Vollmer, T. R., Borrero, J. C., Wright, C. S., Van Camp, C., & Lalli, J. S. (2001). Identifying possible contingencies during descriptive analysis of severe behavior disorders. *Journal of Applied Behavior Analysis, 34*, 269–287. doi: 10.1901/jaba.2001.34-269.

Vollmer, T. R., Iwata, B. A., Zarcone, J. R., Smith, R. G., & Mazaleski, J. L. (1993). The role of attention in the treatment of attention-maintained self-injurious behavior: Noncontingent reinforcement and differential reinforcement of other behavior. *Journal of Applied Behavior Analysis, 26*, 9–21. doi: 10.1901/jaba.1993.26-9.

Vollmer, T. R., Progar, P. R., Lalli, J. S., Van Camp, C. M., Sierp, B. J., Wright, C. S., & Eisenschink, K. J. (1998). Fixed-time schedules attenuate extinction-induced phenomena in the treatment of severe aberrant behavior. *Journal of Applied Behavior Analysis, 31*, 529–542. doi: 10.1901/jaba.1998.31-529.

Vollmer, T. R., Ringdahl, J. E., Roane, H. S., & Marcus, B. A. (1997). Negative side effects of noncontingent reinforcement. *Journal of Applied Behavior Analysis, 30*, 161–164. doi: 10.1901/jaba.1997.30-161.

Vollmer, T. R., Roane, H. S., Ringdahl, J. E., & Marcus, B. A. (1999). Evaluating treatment challenges with differential reinforcement of alternative behavior. *Journal of Applied Behavior Analysis, 32*, 9–23. doi: 10.1901/jaba.1999.32-9.

Wacker, D. P., Steege, M. W., Northrup, J., Sasso, G., Berg, W., Reimers, T., & Donn, L. (1990). A component analysis of functional communication training across three topographies of severe behavior problems. *Journal of Applied Behavior Analysis, 23*, 417–429. doi: 10.1901/jaba.1990.23-417.

Walker, G. (2008). Constant and progressive time delay procedures for teaching children with autism: A literature review. *Journal of Autism and Developmental Disorders*, *38*, 261–275. doi: 10.1007/s10803-007-0390-4.

Wilder, D. A., Myers, K., Fischetti, A., Leon, Y., Nicholson, K., & Allison, J. (2012). An analysis of modifications to the three-step guided compliance procedure necessary to achieve compliance among preschool children. *Journal of Applied Behavior Analysis*, *45*, 121–130. doi: 10.1901/jaba.2012.45-121.

Wolery, M., & Gast, D. L. (1984). Effective and efficient procedures for the transfer of stimulus control. *Topics in Early Childhood Special Education*, *4*, 52–77. doi: 10.1177/027112148400400305.

Worsdell, A. S., Iwata, B. A., Hanley, G. P., Thompson, R. H., & Kahng, S. (2000). Effects of continuous and intermittent reinforcement for problem behavior during functional communication training. *Journal of Applied Behavior Analysis*, *33*, 167–179. doi: 10.1901/jaba.2000.33-167.

Worsdell, A. S., Iwata, B. A., & Wallace, M. D. (2002). Duration-based measures of preference for vocational tasks. *Journal of Applied Behavior Analysis*, *35*, 287–290. doi: 10.1901/jaba.2002.35-287.

Zarcone, J. R., Iwata, B. A., Vollmer, T. R., Jagtiani, S., Smith, R. G., & Mazaleski, J. L. (1993). Extinction of self-injurious escape behavior with and without instructional fading. *Journal of Applied Behavior Analysis*, *26*, 353–360. doi: 10.1901/jaba.1993.26-353.

Zarcone, J. R., Rodgers, T. A., Iwata, B. A., Rourke, D. A., & Dorsey, M. F. (1991). Reliability analysis of the Motivation Assessment Scale: A failure to replicate. *Research in Developmental Disabilities*, *12*, 349–362. doi: 10.1016/0891-4222(91)90031-M.

23

Precision Teaching
The Legacy of Ogden Lindsley

Kent Johnson and Elizabeth M. Street

What Is Precision Teaching?

Precision Teaching (PT) is a monitoring, practice, and decision-making technology for improving performance of any kind. Ogden Lindsley and his students at the University of Kansas developed PT in the 1960s. However, its seed had been planted during and immediately after Lindsley's time as a student in B. F. Skinner's laboratory at Harvard in the 1950s (Potts, Eshleman, & Cooper, 1993).

PT technology sets frequency goals or *aims* for individual student performance on well-calibrated curriculum *pinpoints*. Learners then practice the performance specified by the pinpoint in a series of *timings*. Typically 1–5 minutes in length, timings of performance on academic skills[1] may be as short as 10 seconds (sometimes called a *sprint*) or as long as 15 minutes or more. The frequency of performance that occurs in a timing is plotted on a specialized graph. Teachers, peers, and learners themselves observe performance over a series of timings to assess the impact of interventions, review performance *celeration*—the rate of change in performance across time—and make further instructional or practice modifications based on the degree to which the learner is making progress toward frequency and celeration aims.[2]

Johnson and Street (2013) have expanded a motto developed by Lindsley (1972, 1990)—pinpoint; measure; chart; decide; try, try again—to describe the steps in the pure, general case of PT. They include: (1) specifying a learning objective or pinpoint, (2) arranging materials and procedures for learning and practicing the pinpoint, including slicing the pinpoint into smaller sub-skills as necessary, (3) timing the learner's performance and counting its frequency, (4) charting the learner's performance, (5) reviewing performance trends on the chart, and (6) making decisions about interventions as needed to improve its growth in frequency and celeration.

Behavior analysts and psychologists may be confused about the definition of the term frequency in PT. It is primarily a semantic issue. Whereas Skinner used the more

The Wiley Blackwell Handbook of Operant and Classical Conditioning, First Edition.
Edited by Frances K. McSweeney and Eric S. Murphy.

conventional term *rate* to mean number of occurrences over time, Lindsley preferred the term *frequency* to mean number over time. For the purposes of this chapter, we use Lindsley's term, recognizing that it departs from standard usage in both psychology and behavior analysis.

Lindsley selected the name PT consistent with his belief that the system would enable teachers to be much more precise in their work (Lindsley, 1997). PT's primary tool is a standard graph called the Standard Celeration Chart. Although there have been refinements since its beginning, the broad parameters of PT continue today much as Lindsley envisioned them.

The Standard Celeration Chart

There are eight charts that currently make up Lindsley's family of standard celeration charts. They include the Daily count per minute and associated Timings Charts, Daily per day, Weekly per week, Median count per minute per week, Monthly per month, Median count per minute per month, and Yearly per year charts.[3] Of these, the Daily per minute and Timings Charts are the most commonly used.

The Daily per minute Standard Celeration Chart (Figure 23.1), hereafter SCC, provides uniformity for seeing and comparing two features—frequency and celeration—of student progress. *Frequency* is a measure of student *performance* at a particular point in time, whereas *celeration* is a measure of *learning* that reveals how quickly desirable behaviors increase in frequency (*ac*celeration) or unwanted behaviors decrease in frequency (*de*celeration). The SCC was designed in such a way that the slope or steepness of the trajectory of change across time reveals behavioral celeration, serving much the same function for reflecting human behavior in an applied setting as Skinner's cumulative record did for reflecting animal behavior in an experimental setting.[4] Proponents of PT believe the SCC is the most effective and efficient way to track performance *fluency* and *agility*.

According to Johnson and Layng (1996), fluency refers to performance that is quick, effortless, flowing, well-practiced, and accurate. Johnson and Street (2013) add to the definition the words flexible, errorless, automatic, confident, second nature, and masterful. Binder (1996) noted that fluency is "the fluid combination of accuracy plus speed that characterizes competent performance" (p. 164). The terms *fluent performance* and *expert performance* are often used synonymously.

Agility is the ability of individuals to quickly learn a new behavior or performance allowing them to change direction and increase speed of learning as needed to accommodate to a rapidly changing world (Lindsley, 2001b). Said another way, the more quickly a person learns a new skill, the more agile they are in adapting to change. Growth in agility is reflected on the SCC when the slope of the *ac*celeration and *de*celeration lines for each subsequent task becomes steeper (Lindsley, 2001a).

At least five features distinguish the SCC from typical graphical displays of human performance data:

1. **It records frequency.** As we have already discussed, PT is concerned with frequency or number per unit of time as its major datum.

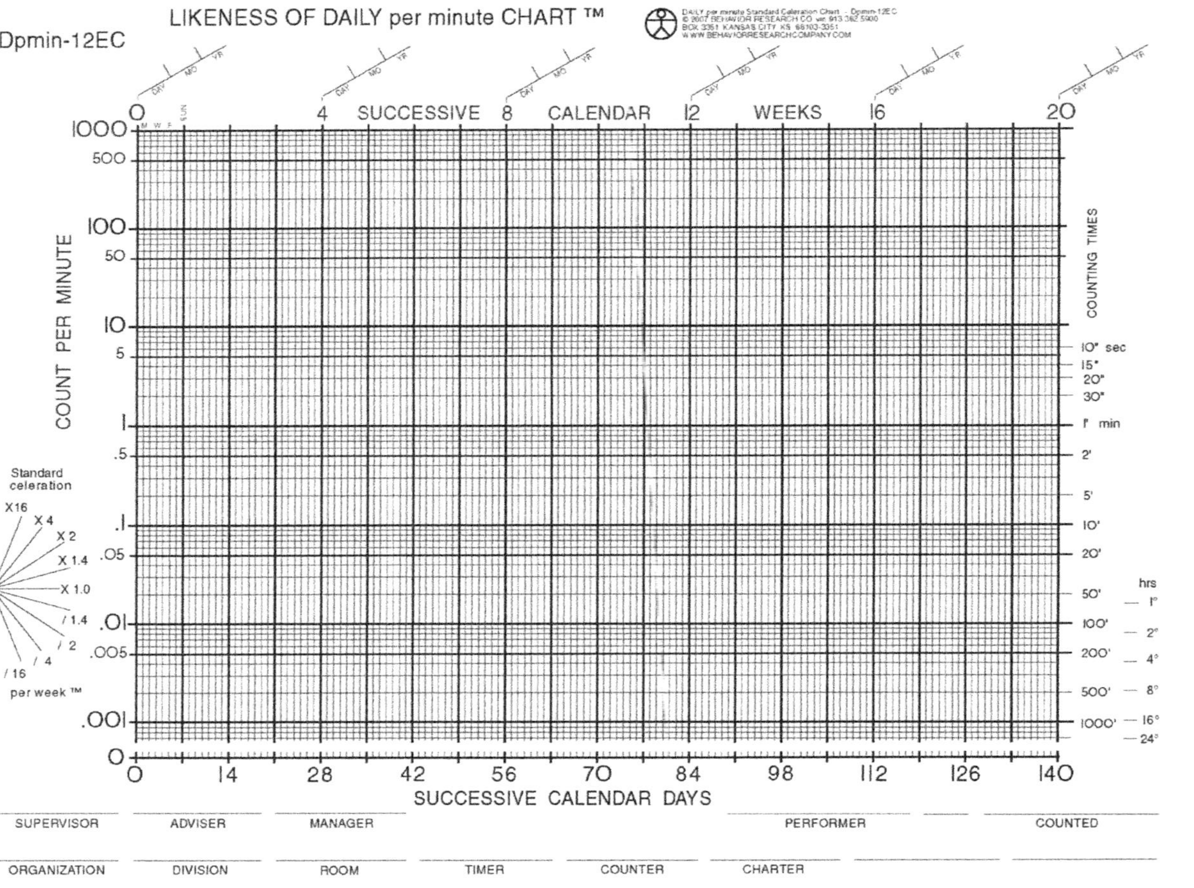

Figure 23.1 A likeness of a Daily per minute Standard Celeration Chart © The Behavior Research Company website (http://www.behaviorresearchcompany.com/). Reproduced with permission.

2. **It uses a standardized format to facilitate efficient communication of results.** Lindsley designed a universal, standardized chart to make communication of results quick and efficient. Standardization also made it possible to compare charts, to observe differences in learning as a function of pinpoints and procedures, and to evaluate the effects of learning one performance on subsequent learning (Pennypacker, Gutierrez, & Lindsley, 2003).
3. **It uses a *ratio* scale on the *y-axis*.** This is the most unique characteristic of the SCC, one that sets it apart from other instruments designed to track changes in human behavior. It contrasts with most other graphs designed for the same purpose which display growth in equal intervals based on an assumption that behavior ebbs and flows in an additive (or subtractive) manner. Expressing growth by showing how much is added or subtracted is called *absolute change* (White & Haring, 1980). Lindsley believed that behavior, like other natural phenomena, changes multiplicatively, proportionately, or relatively, rather than additively or absolutely. He also believed that a measurement system that reflects proportional or *relative change* would lead to better decisions about the effectiveness of an instructional program. Last, he believed that *relative change* is more accurately represented on a ratio scale. To that end, he designed a ratio scale like those used in the natural sciences and economics (Pennypacker et al., 2003). Characteristic of a ratio scale, distances between 1 and 10, between 10 and 100, and between 100 and 1,000 are the same. From a practical standpoint, the value of looking at relative change makes sense. For example, parents are captivated and their baby appears pleased when he or she improves from walking four steps to eight steps without falling but neither parents nor child appear to notice improvements from 500 to 504 steps, even though the absolute improvement is four steps in both cases.

   Most measurement in the physical sciences and engineering uses ratio scales, not interval scales. Lindsley believed that behavior was as natural a phenomenon as energy, electric charge, and other phenomena measured by ratio scales. Ratio scales allow more complex measures and analyses of behavior than interval scales, such as using geometric means to measure relative change of two or more behaviors. Thus, Lindsley was convinced that the ability to depict relative change on the SCC provided a more accurate picture of the power of an intervention than did absolute change. An examination of Figure 23.2, which compares the same data plotted on an equal interval scale and a ratio scale, reveals why this is so. The data path on the equal interval scale (left graph's y-axis) underestimates the effects of an intervention when performance is occurring at low frequencies, and overestimates the effects of an intervention when performance is occurring at higher frequencies (Giesecke et al., 2001; Johnson & Street, 2013; Schmid & Schmid, 1979). On the equal interval scale, low-frequency increases in performance appear to be barely changing, thus calling for changes in intervention procedures. However, when these same data are plotted on a ratio scale, the growth curve suggests that adequate growth is occurring and no further intervention is needed. Likewise, on the equal interval scale, higher frequency increases in performance look quite adequate, suggesting no further intervention is needed. However when these same data are plotted on a ratio scale (right graph's y-axis),

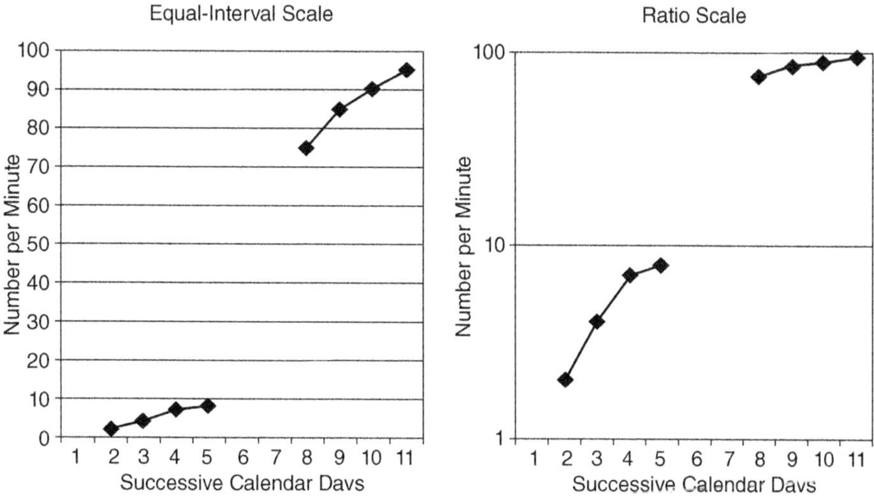

Figure 23.2 Comparing absolute and relative charts of the same data.

the resulting growth curves call for additional intervention (Johnson & Street, 2013; White & Haring, 1980).

Johnson and Street (2013) note another advantage of the ratio scaling of the *y-axis*. Because the chart uses six equal ratio cycles, behaviors of widely varying frequencies will fit on the same chart and more easily reveal relations between them. Thus, one can compare a learner's rate of classroom talk-outs to his or her rate of correct math facts answers on the same chart.

4. **It is calendar-based.** Every day is included whether or not there is an opportunity to respond. Lindsley preferred a calendar-based chart over a session-based chart because it makes clear how much unobserved time passed between observations (Pennypacker et al., 2003). This allows one to see performance across time and growth as a function of time as well as the effects of a program or procedure when it is in place and when it is not. After trying several options, Lindsley designed the chart to record data on a single pinpoint at a time for 140 days (20 weeks or half a school year).
5. **It provides a full picture of progress.** By focusing on celeration—growth, change, or progress over time—not just performance frequency on a given day, learning and performance become two ways in which the efficacy of a program is judged.

Outcomes of Fluent Performance

Fluency is an elusive property of behavior that is hard to establish directly. Fluency is not a quantity, but rather an idealized concept. In the late 1970s, Eric Haughton (1981) began to discuss fluency in terms of performance frequency. On the basis of informal evidence, he asked teachers to work toward two outcomes—retention and application—that he believed were related to fluency. He challenged them to arrange practice that built performance frequency and ultimately enabled their students to achieve these outcomes. He coined the acronym RA/PS—***Retention*** and ***Application*** **P**erformance **S**tandards—to remind teachers to teach to *performance standards* that produced retention and application. Haughton and others had observed that when a specified frequency range was obtained during practice, one could predict with some confidence that the learner would retain and apply what they had learned—for example, addition facts—for a substantial period of time without systematic practice. Subsequently, the specified frequency range became a retention and application performance standard for others to meet. Haughton (1972) also championed high frequencies because he believed that skills at high frequencies would be useful—readily available when needed—and would facilitate the growth of components or composites of which the current skills were a part.

Over time, as new evidence has emerged, PT proponents have expanded the list of outcomes that characterize expert or fluent performance and have identified, on the basis of soft empirical evidence, frequency ranges for different skills that are sufficient to predict these outcomes. Carl Binder (1993, 1996), for example, added *endurance* based on evidence from his dissertation that learners who wrote numbers at higher rates during 1-minute timings tended to maintain accuracy and frequency when the timing period was extended compared to those who wrote numbers at low rates. Still later, Johnson and Layng (1992, 1994, 1996) separated *stability* from the original definition of endurance, and added *adduction*[5] to the formula. Stability refers to the learner's ability to maintain his or her performance rate in the face of distraction. Adduction refers to circumstances in which "new contingencies or performance requirements recruit performances learned under other contingencies" (Johnson & Street, 2004b, p. 251).

Since that time, Johnson and colleagues at Morningside Academy (MA) have replaced the term *retention* with the more active term *maintained*. They have also replaced the term *adduction* with *generative*, a term coined by Robert Epstein and B. F. Skinner, which they defined as the unprompted interconnection of existing repertoires to solve (novel) problems (Epstein, 1991; Epstein, Kirshnit, Lanza, & Rubin, 1984).

Currently, these five outcomes are included among those thought to occur when behavior is fluent:

- it **m**aintains over time without additional practice;
- it **e**ndures for lengths of time that real world conditions require;
- it is **s**table in the face of distraction;
- it is **a**pplied correctly to other similar situations; and
- it is **g**enerative, that is, it readily combines with other skills to produce new learning in dissimilar contexts without explicit instruction.

Johnson coined the acronym *MESsAGe* to remind teachers to "get the MESsAGe" when employing PT technology (Johnson & Street, 2012, 2013).

Precision teachers have adopted a variety of procedures to identify frequencies that are sufficient for various skills and concepts to reveal MESsAGe outcomes. Many still use an early method that supposed that the frequencies of typical learners in a given population indicate the frequency aims that should be used when deficient learners practice. Others use the frequencies achieved by their very best students. Still others use their own performance frequencies or those of content experts as their norms. Normative approaches, while useful in establishing the general ballpark of a frequency aim, may not predict MESsAGe outcomes. An empirical approach in which various frequencies are checked for MESsAGe outcomes is more precise. Many frequency aims currently used at MA (Johnson & Street, 2004a, 2012, 2013) have been empirically verified. In addition, Fabrizio and Moors (2003) have detailed an empirical method for verifying frequency aims for children with autism.

Of course fluency is not solely synonymous with building high frequencies; multiple practice procedures produce fluency. Making contexts for practice plentiful and varied, approximating those in which the performance is to occur, improves fluency as well (Haughton, 1980). Practicing with chunks or curriculum slices of optimal size is also important, as is beginning practice sessions with massed practice followed by distributed practice—lessons learned from the verbal learning research of the functional school of psychology in the mid-20th century (Hilgard & Bower, 1964). Still, building frequencies to levels that predict MESsAGe remains the focus for most precision teachers.

Celeration and Agility

While frequency is a measure of performance, *celeration* is a measure of learning, or growth in frequency of performance over time. It is a measure of how timely a learner reaches a frequency aim. To quantify celeration, precision teachers draw a "line of best fit" through the trajectory of plotted frequencies over time on an SCC, and the resulting slope is stated as a multiplier. The convention is to specify celeration as the increase in frequency across one week. For example, a doubling of frequency in a week is ×2 (read "times two"; e.g., from 5 to 10 or 50 to 100); a cutting in half of frequency in a week is ÷2 (read "divide by two"; e.g., from 20 to 10, 100 to 50, 600 to 300).

A *celeration aim* can also be prescribed for each pinpoint, represented by a line that is extended from the first data point at the appropriate angle represented by the celeration aim until it crosses the frequency line representing the frequency aim (Johnson & Street, 2013). Precision teachers can then monitor frequency building and provide *celeration interventions* to increase growth.

As we have said earlier, Lindsley (1999) chose the term *agility*—the learner's ability to adapt to changing learning requirements—to describe a fast, accurate learner, one who is able to respond quickly to the unfolding events involved in learning something new. Lindsley then quantified agility in relation to the actual celeration of a learner's performance over time. Steep slopes on SCCs indicate agile performances. Successively steeper celeration slopes show growth in agility. Figure 23.3 illustrates an SCC that shows increasing agility, indicated by successive increases in celeration across phonics curriculum slices. Business leaders use agility to mean the capacity of their organizations and employees to respond to changes in the marketplace and culture, and create products that capitalize on those changes. In a school setting, agile learning refers to "the ability to learn new skills and concepts quickly and to adjust performance on the basis of new information" (Johnson & Street, 2013, p. 37). Examining learners'

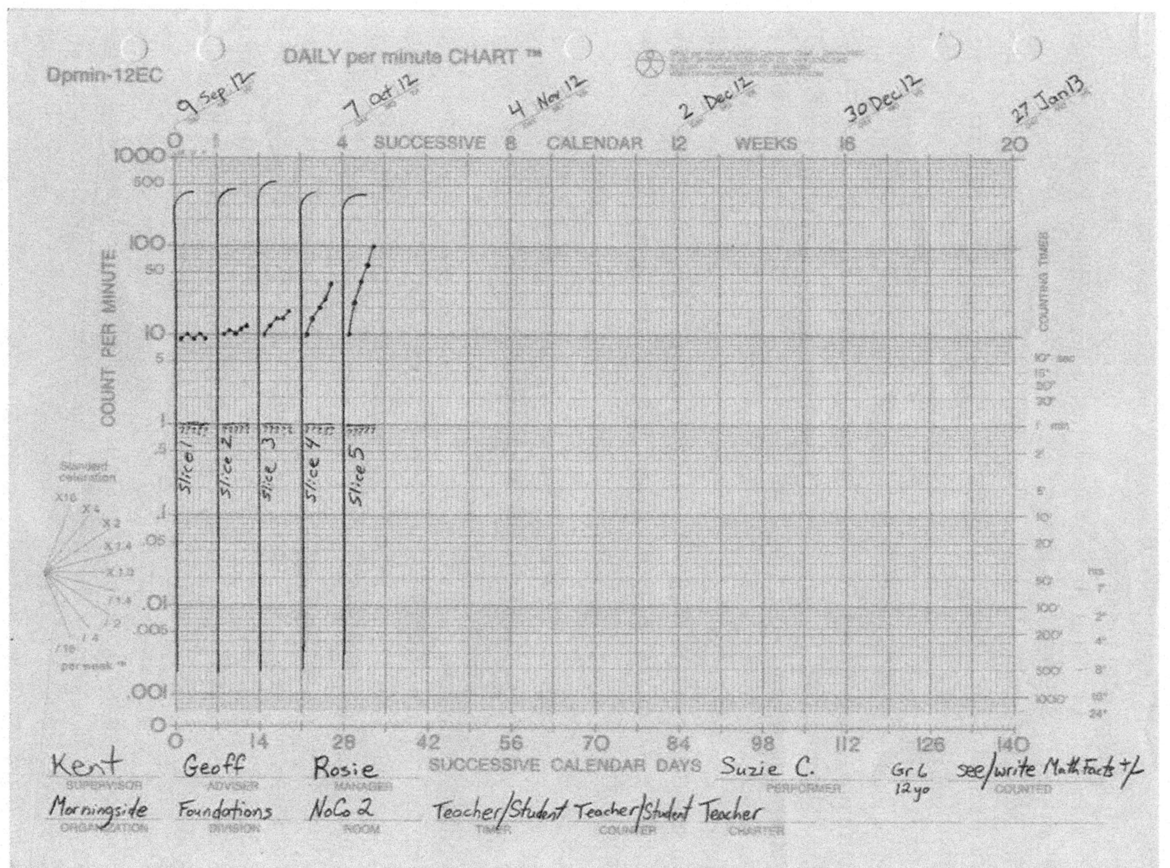

Figure 23.3 A Daily per minute Chart showing increasing agility as steepening celerations across slices of a curriculum. © The Behavior Research Company website (http://www.behaviorresearchcompany.com/). Reproduced with permission.

typical celerations when learning new pinpoints, as well as changes in those celerations across successive pinpoints, provides a more accurate picture of learning potential than do standardized test scores taken at a single point in time, if by "learning potential" we mean rate of learning or growth patterns of behavior across time. Celerations help those in classrooms, workplaces, and clinical settings to identify when to focus upon learning skills, learning to learn, and performance flexibility in addition to content aims. We have accelerated many students' academic progress by addressing problems in their growth patterns with supplemental instruction in learning skills.

Despite Lindsley's call for measuring celeration, even changing the name of the SCC from the Standard Behavior Chart to the Standard Celeration Chart, performance, not celeration, was the focus for the first 20 or so years of PT. A single daily timing on each important pinpoint was fairly typical. Performance was observed, typically daily, during a 1-minute or longer timing and the resulting frequency was plotted on the Daily per minute SCC. An *aim star* (Haughton, 1972) identified the desired frequency, and students continued to practice—once a day—until it was achieved. Teachers were encouraged to intervene to ensure that students' trajectories were in the right direction and "appropriately" steep. The "perfect" learning picture was one in which errors were going down and corrects were going up at about ×1.25, a number taken from Kathleen Liberty's calculation of median growth per week from over 600 projects (Lindsley, 2001b). That meant, for example, that a learner reading 100 wpm on a Monday would be able to read 125 wpm the following Monday. However, several other learning pictures were possible; for example, some projects showed corrects remaining flat with errors increasing; others showed corrects increasing but with an unusually high degree of variability or bounce in the data. Haring, Liberty, and White (1980) developed intervention recommendations for teachers based on these less than desirable learning pictures that, when implemented with fidelity, typically changed the behavior's trajectory and resulted in performance frequencies that were thought at the time to correlate with fluency.

Two things happened to change this approach. First, based on evidence from Marilyn Chapel whose second graders grew at ×2 on multiply facts without instruction, Lindsley (2001b) became convinced that a 1.25 celeration underestimated learner potential. Subsequently, he began to encourage ×2 celerations. Second, with a focus on celeration in the early 1990s, MA was experimenting with setting daily goals based on a prescribed celeration line. Students would read their expected aim by looking at where their anticipated celeration crossed the day line on their Daily per minute SCC. Then working with peers in a *peer-coaching model* (Johnson & Street, 2013), learners would practice several times each day to meet the goal, posting their teacher-verified personal best on the Daily per minute SCC. Multiple timings during a single practice session greatly improved speed or celeration of skill acquisition. This approach, which mimicked what Haughton, Maloney, and Desjardins (1980) had reported, set in motion the recommendations from which Lindsley developed the *Timings Chart* (Figure 23.4) for the purpose of recording the frequencies obtained during multiple timings in a single practice session. Users plot each timing completed in a session and focus upon increasing performance across timings—celeration—until the performance meets some predetermined goal or aim for the day as specified on the Daily per minute Chart. Over time, explicit instructions have developed to encourage a standard protocol for timings (Johnson & Street, 2013).

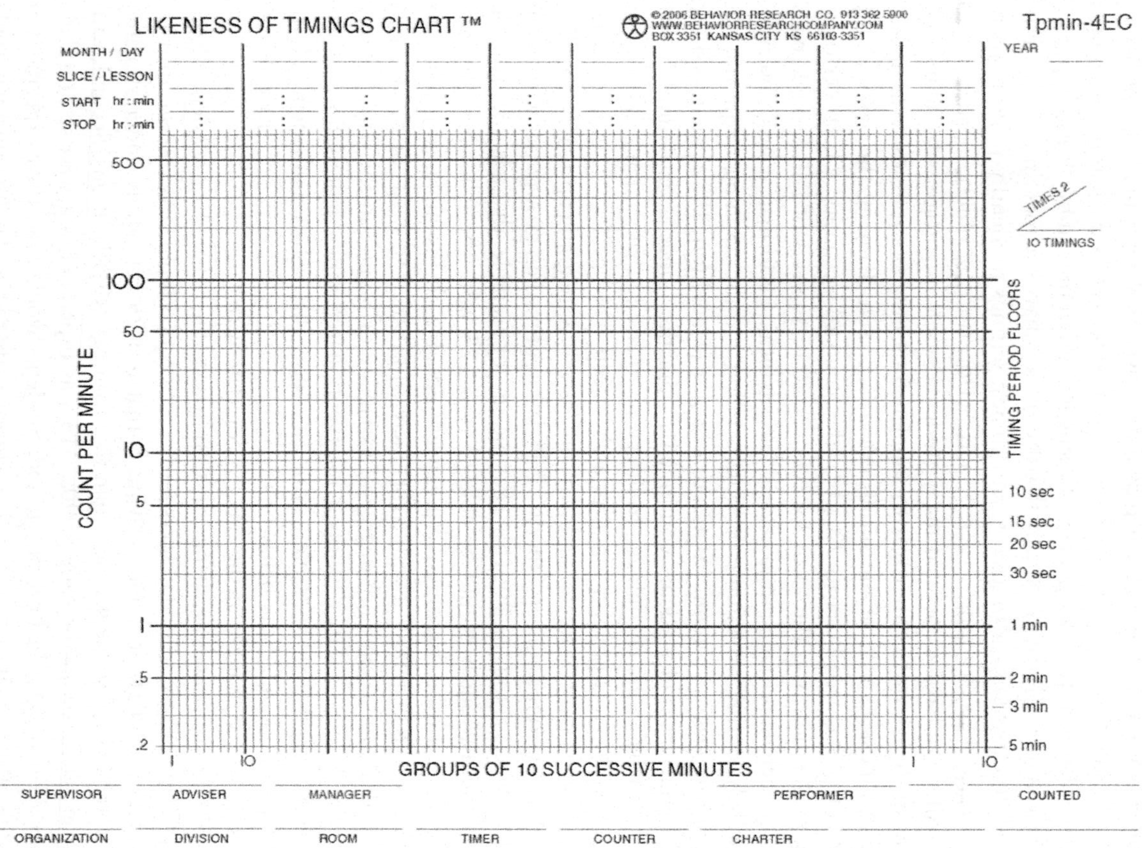

Figure 23.4 A likeness of a Timings Chart. © The Behavior Research Company website (http://www.behaviorresearchcompany.com/). Reproduced with permission.

The Timings Chart features a ratio scale on the *y*-axis, but it divides the *x*-axis into 10 segments of 10 lines each for daily practice. Precision teachers examine a Daily per minute Chart each day to determine what frequency the learner should attain on that day to remain on his or her celeration line. This intermediate aim is then marked on a Timings Chart. After the first timing, a celeration line is drawn from the resulting frequency to this intermediate frequency aim. Figure 23.5 illustrates how the Daily per minute and Timings Charts are coordinated in a practice session. Within-session frequency building is monitored and, when performance falls below that celeration line, celeration interventions are provided to keep the learner growing to meet the frequency requirement specified by the Daily per minute Chart (Johnson & Street, 2013).

When teachers or peer coaches at MA intervene between timings during a single practice session, celerations show even greater improvement. In fact, MA now recommends a minimum ×2 celeration for most of the approximately 75 pinpoints it has identified for reading, writing, and arithmetic. When tasks on practice sheets increase in difficulty over the period of time learners are practicing (for example, when building fluency of passage reading across a second grade reading curriculum which advances from first grade level passages to early third grade level passages), MA recommends a celeration of ×1.25.

An area ripe for PT research is the investigation of effective celeration interventions. Informally, precision teachers have used the following strategies, among others:

- Providing sprints—briefer timings—as warm-ups before official timings begin.
- Systematically increasing timing durations (Binder, Haughton, & Van Eyk, 1990).
- Arranging practice for deficient tool skills prior to practicing a pinpoint that depends on them.

F. Hyde and D. Brown (personal communication, July 22, 2011) have designed a formal *celeration shaping* procedure. After determining a learner's baseline celeration, successive celeration approximations to the desired celeration aim are introduced until the learner reliably celerates at the desired slope.

Just as multiple practice procedures produce fluency in addition to frequency building, multiple practice procedures in addition to celeration building are thought to produce agility. Among other variables, the sequence of tasks approximating newer and more difficult performance requirements is also thought to be relevant. This is another area ripe for research.

Quantitative Analyses with Chart Data

Since the advent of standard celeration charting, a number of analytical procedures have emerged to quantify the outcomes of charted data. For example, to reveal how much change is represented by the difference between one frequency and another, one can calculate *frequency multipliers*, literally the distance between the two. Thus, the difference between the frequencies of one and ten is ×10. Similarly, a frequency multiplier of ÷20 quantifies the difference between a frequency of 1 per minute and a frequency of .05 per minute. An *accuracy ratio* is one type of frequency multiplier

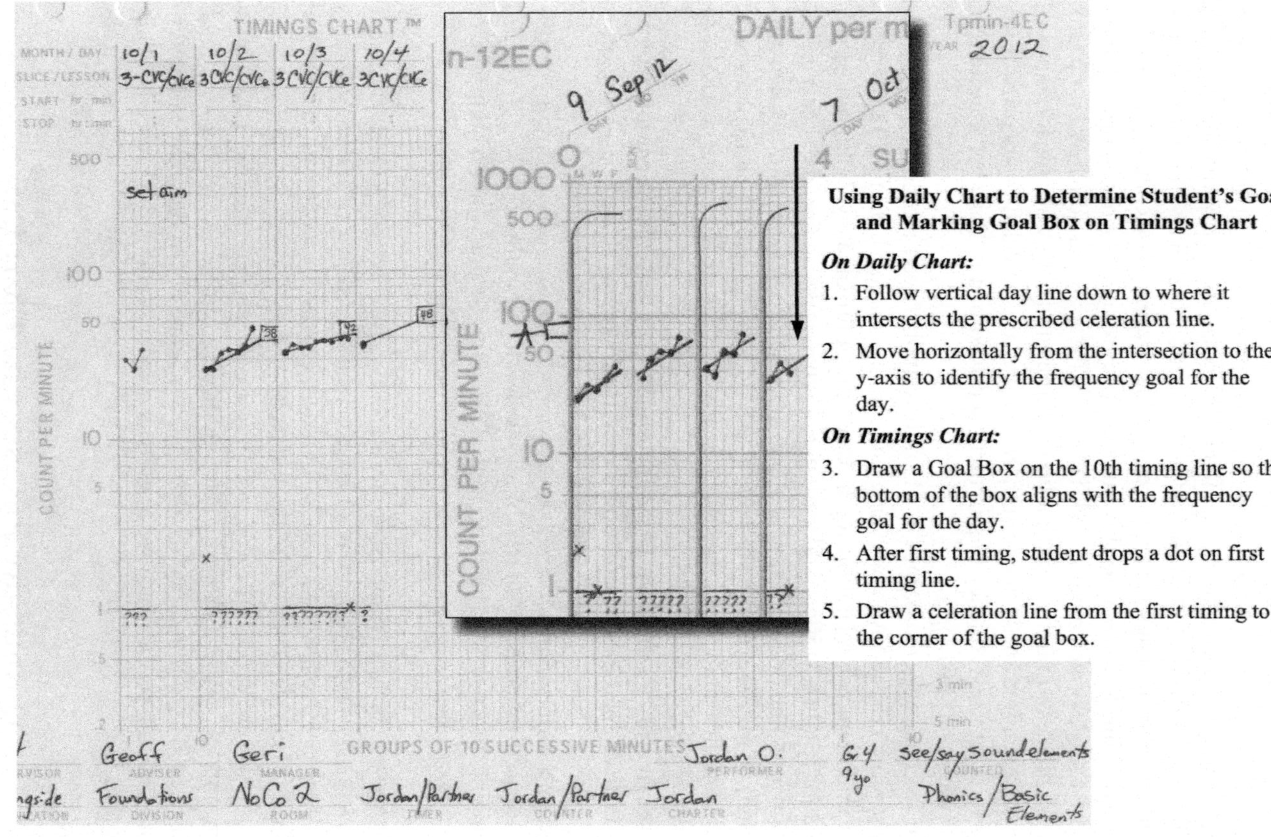

Figure 23.5 A segment of a Daily per minute Chart and a segment of a Timings Chart, illustrating how the two charts are coordinated during a practice session. © The Behavior Research Company website (http://www.behaviorresearchcompany.com/). Reproduced with permission.

calculated to determine whether quality is improving or getting worse. In this case, we find the distance between simultaneous correct and error performance frequencies. For example, if correct performance frequency is 8 and incorrect frequency is 2, the accuracy ratio is ×4. For more detail, see Pennypacker, et al. (2003.)

To compare the effectiveness of two behavior change procedures, we calculate a *celeration multiplier* by multiplying or dividing two celerations. This answers the question: By what value must I multiply (or divide) the first celeration to obtain the second celeration? If one procedure produces a ×10 celeration in performance and the second procedure produces a ×2 celeration, the celeration multiplier for the first procedure is ×5 compared to the second procedure, and the celeration multiplier for the second procedure is ÷5 compared to the first procedure. As Pennypacker et al. (2003) note, these quantities combined with cost figures provide a precise accountability statement.

The variability or *total bounce* of SCC data is quantified by finding the largest and the smallest frequencies in a set of data and forming a ratio by placing the larger over the smaller number. Chart researchers have also calculated *bounce due to celeration*, *bounce around celeration*, *up bounce*, *down bounce*, and a *verge index* between converging corrects and errors, the details of which are beyond the scope of this chapter. Pennypacker et al.'s (2003) handbook describes these and other analytical procedures in detail.

Current Practice Procedures

A PT classroom is distinctly different than virtually any other classroom as Ogden Lindsley described in a 1992 article in the *Journal of Applied Behavior Analysis.*

> The only adult in the classroom seems to be loitering. She is not standing in the front lecturing, or sitting at the teacher's desk reading to the class, or grading papers. She is moving about the classroom from student to student, answering a question with a whisper here, offering a quiet suggestion there, helping with a chart decision here, and giving a pat and a smile of appreciation there. . . . The students are busy at their desks, in teams of two, timing each other's practice. . . . The students are noisy, shouting correct answers as fast as they can at 200 words a minute, several shouting at once at neighboring desks. It sounds more like an adult cocktail party or a school recess, than a school classroom. . . . The "precision teacher" performs like a coach, an advisor, and an online instructional designer. She arranges materials and methods for the students to teach themselves, including self-counting, timing, charting, and one-on-one direction and support. (p. 51)

This ambience is the most noticeable feature of a classroom PT practice session, but there are other features that distinguish a PT practice regimen as well. For example, it is becoming increasingly common to combine PT with peer-coaching procedures. A major advantage of peer coaching is that it multiplies the number of monitored practice sessions in a class period and also teaches other learners to serve in a teaching role by providing feedback on the learner's performance. Johnson and Street (2013) provide a more complete account of peer coaching and practice procedures.

Who Has Used PT?

A wide variety of professionals have used PT. Salespeople have measured the effectiveness of different sales campaigns (e.g., Binder & Sweeney, 2002). Administrators, CEOs, planners, policy makers, politicians, and futurists have detected historical and economic trends and projected future conditions (Pennypacker et al., 2003). Caregivers have used PT in agencies for children and adults with developmental disabilities and autism (e.g., Barrett, 1977, 1979), cerebral palsy (Timmons, McLaughlin, & Kinakin, 1995), Alzheimer's disease (Johnson-Talbert & Cooper, 1992), and traumatic brain injuries (Kubina, Aho, Mozzoni, & Malanga, 1998). Nurses, speech pathologists, and psychiatric social workers have used PT with their patients and clients (e.g., Pierce, 1992). Parents have used PT to track and modify programs to help their children, and teenagers themselves have used PT to modify their own behavior (Duncan, 1969). PT has been used in sports and fitness programs (e.g., McGreevy, 1984). Even marriage counselors have helped couples track progress in their relationships and decide whether to make life changes with PT (Pennypacker et al., 2003). However, the majority of professionals who use PT work in schools as teachers, school psychologists (e.g., Alper & White, 1971), or teacher trainers (e.g., Caldwell, 1972). PT has been used with a variety of students, including learners in general education classrooms, emotionally disturbed children, children with severe disabilities, children with autism, and children with learning disabilities and attention deficit disorders (e.g., Fabrizio & Moors, 2003; Johnson & Street, 2013; Liberty & Paeth, 1995; Lovitt, 1977).

Since 1969, at least 11 PT researchers have studied 1,048 charts of *inner behaviors*, including thoughts, feelings, and urges, managed by over 540 individuals. These behaviors have been defined, counted, charted, and, in most cases, modified. Calkin's (2009) summary of most of these projects concludes that inner behaviors show the same patterns as outer behaviors, supporting Skinner's contentions (Skinner, 1953, 1957, 1969); however, additional research is needed to clarify the relation between inner and outer behavior, patterns of celeration of inner behavior, and the variability of inner behavior frequency and celeration.

Although not chart based, fluency building in sales knowledge in business and industry has been implemented with bank cash management executives, software sales professionals, phone center customer service representatives, interstate truck drivers, and insurance salespeople (Binder & Bloom, 1989). These results are so remarkable that a company, Product Knowledge Systems, Inc., was formed to train corporations and other organizations in implementing knowledge fluency systems (Binder & Sweeney, 2002).

A Brief History of the Development of Precision Teaching

Three articles (Binder, 1996; Potts et al., 1993; White, 1986) provide excellent background for understanding the early history of PT. A doctoral student in B. F. Skinner's laboratory at Harvard where he received his doctoral degree in 1957, Lindsley learned and subsequently borrowed important tenets from Skinner's experimental analysis of behavior, virtually all of which were instrumental in the development of PT. Of prime importance to Lindsley was Skinner's use of frequency measurement. Lindsley grasped that the frequency measure best approximates a natural science of behavior because it provides a direct measure of behavior in time. It stands in contrast to indirect measures such as percent correct, percent of intervals, and time samples, all of which either disguise the number of attempts the learner makes or count only a portion of those attempts.

Lindsley also believed that frequency was a very sensitive measure of behavior, readily distinguishing changes in performance produced by independent manipulations. Kozloff, LaNunziata, Cowardin, and Bessellieu (2000/2001) noted that Lindsley based PT on Skinner's discovery that the rate of a behavior is a fundamental property or *dimension* of a behavior, not just its dependent measure. That is, frequency itself can be manipulated as an independent variable to determine its impact on other variables; for example, one can judge the impact of different frequencies of "see/say sounds" on an individual's abilities to "see/say words." In addition, when one combines this notion with the ordinary language notion of frequency as an indication of the strength of behavior (Ryle, 1949/1984; Wittgenstein, 1958), PT characterizes behavior at high frequencies as fundamentally different from behavior at low frequencies. For example, PT proponents argue that high frequency behavior is more streamlined and less dependent on prompted contexts or collateral behavior (e.g., mnemonics) than is low-frequency behavior.

Another tenet that Lindsley learned in Skinner's laboratory and which he adapted to PT technology was the importance of free-operant performance. Free-operant performance in which an organism is able to operate on the environment unencumbered is distinguished from discrete trial performance constrained by the experimenter's control. The free operant removes restrictions on the frequency with which a response can occur and permits the observation of moment-to-moment changes in frequency, key advantages in detecting the occasions that give rise to a behavior (Ferster, 1953).

Lindsley's initial perspective was that behavioral probabilities could be obtained only from continuous monitoring. In a 1995 publication, he described his initial discomfort when Eric Haughton and his students Clay and Ann Starlin discontinued continuous measurement in favor of 10-minute samples a day initially and later 1-minute timings for each pinpoint. However, he eventually embraced the procedure for those pinpoints for which *ac*celeration was sought.

Lindsley did, however, insist that these abbreviated timings be structured consistent with free-operant methodology, believing that the learner's optimum performance frequency should not be constrained by arbitrarily imposed ceilings. Binder (1996) summarized four such ceilings that precision teachers are encouraged to avoid: measurement-imposed ceilings, procedure-imposed ceilings, deficit-imposed ceilings, and handicap-imposed ceilings.

Despite Skinner's focus on rate of response in the experimental analysis of behavior and his later assertion that his adoption of rate of responding as the primary dependent variable was one of his most important contributions to the experimental analysis of behavior (Evans, 1968), he abandoned rate of response for more conventional percent-correct measures when he turned his attention to programmed instruction (Binder, 1996). However, when Lindsley established the first human operant laboratory at Metropolitan State Hospital in Waltham, Massachusetts, he saw firsthand the sensitivity of rate (Skinner's preferred term) or frequency (Lindsley's preferred term) of responding as a dependent variable to test the effects of drugs on the behavior of patients with schizophrenia and for all human behavior (Potts et al., 1993).

In recent years, scholars in the curricular areas of literacy and numeracy have shown increasing interest in behavioral fluency, which in virtually every case is translated as rate or frequency of behavior over time (Armbruster, Lehr, & Osborn, 2001; National Mathematics Advisory Panel, 2008). The currently popular Response to Intervention (RTI) framework takes a similar stance, in part because, as Ysseldyke, in his foreword to VanDerHeyden and Burns (2010) noted, "RtI has its roots in the work on diagnostic teaching, and specifically in Ogden Lindsley's (1972) work on precision teaching" (p. xii). Similarly, curriculum-based measurement (CBM; Deno, 1985, 2003)—also an outgrowth of PT and one of the most commonly used approaches to school-based progress monitoring—uses learners' speed as well as accuracy during several assessments throughout the year to predict performance on high-stakes, end-of-year tests.

This was not, however, the view that prevailed among mainstream educators in 1965 when Ogden Lindsley accepted a position at the University of Kansas as professor of special education. By this time, Lindsley was fully committed to frequency as the most sensitive measure of behavior change, and began to search for a standard format for the display of data. Lindsley's original intent was to provide teachers with a format from which they could share data and receive feedback efficiently (Lindsley, 1971). Working with a team that included most notably his student Eric Haughton, he developed the parameters of the standard format which eventually became known as the SCC.

Early on, Lindsley did not see the value in combining PT with other instructional procedures, instead seeing the technology as sufficient unto itself. For that reason, in the early days, so-called *crossover jaws* appeared on many charts (e.g., McGreevy, 1980). "Jaws" reflected that early in practice, errors considerably outnumbered correct responses. After a number of practice sessions, there was a "crossover"—the point when correct responses exceeded errors. However, as Lindsley learned more about well-designed instructional sequences such as those in Siegfried Engelmann's Direct Instruction programs (e.g., Engelmann, 2008; Engelmann, Engelmann, Davis, & Hanner, 1998; Engelmann & Osborn, 2008a, 2008b), he became a proponent of Direct Instruction as the instructional front-end to improve a learner's first charted practice.

Lindsley developed a disdain for publication that was matched by mainline behavioral journals' reluctance to publish papers whose authors displayed data on SCCs (Binder, 1996). Although the journals' reluctance may have been, in part, a function of the failure of many studies in PT to use acceptable standard single-subject designs that met the requirements of baseline logic (Cooper, Heron, & Heward, 2007), it left a bad taste in the mouths of PT enthusiasts. Instead, the PT community focused upon sharing charts with brief reports at conferences and local gatherings. Carl Binder (1977–1982) began publishing the *Data-Sharing Newsletter* which reported on chart-sharing sessions held by Bea Barrett and colleagues at the Fernald State School in Waltham, Massachusetts. The *Journal of Precision Teaching and Celeration* began in 1980, providing a central forum for communication about PT.

PT's Relation to Instructivist Educational Philosophy

Within educational philosophies, PT is most closely aligned with the instructivist approach to teaching, "a set of educational practices consistent with the findings of behavioral psychologists . . . [It] favors thorough content analysis, identification of tool and component skills, carefully crafted educational sequences that build elemental knowledge into complex wholes, and an emphasis on building fluency of component skills as a way to encourage the emergence of untaught behaviors" (Johnson & Street, 2004a, p. 22).

PT fits squarely into the instructivist approach in several ways, but none more convincingly than the technology it provides for practice. Practice is the second of three components of an instructional hierarchy, initially proposed by Haring, Lovitt, Eaton, and Hansen (1978), that begins with skill acquisition and ends with application and opportunities for generalization. Martens, Daly III, Begeny, and VanDerHeyden (2011) describe Haring et al.'s hierarchy as "a dynamic teaching model that involves closely monitoring the proficiency level with which a skill is performed, then tailoring instruction to promote further skills mastery at that and subsequent levels" (p. 386). PT technology provides a systematic methodology for monitoring a skill's proficiency level.

PT also builds on the instructivist approach to curriculum and instructional design when it uses a specialized kind of task analysis known as *component/composite analysis*, situates tasks within a knowledge hierarchy, and takes advantage of a *learning channel analysis*. First, dependent on the incoming repertoire of the learner, skills are identified as being members of one of three categories: tool skills, component skills, or composite skills. According to Johnson and Street (2013), *tool skills* are those at the core of virtually all skills and concepts in a content area while *component skills* are intermediate-level skills that depend upon one or more tool skills and serve as the building blocks for engaging in composite repertoires. *Composite skills* are high-level performances that provide social validation of the learner's mastery of a content area (see Table 23.1). PT focuses on building to frequency aims the tool and component skills that comprise the authentic performances within a field of study.

Table 23.1 Examples of the relativity of tool, component, and composite skills

Tool Skills	*Component Skills*	*Composite Skills*
Typing words	Selecting words or grammatical constructions that correctly convey intended meaning	Writing a composition
Math facts	Arithmetic computation skills	Solving simple 3-term equations
Decoding words	Identifying who or what is talked about most in a paragraph	Identifying the main idea of a paragraph
Decoding words	Retelling what has been read	Critically evaluating two different explanations of a concept
Skating to an abrupt stop	Completing a figure 8	Skating in rhythm to a musical piece

PT also benefits from the use of a knowledge taxonomy that differentiates tasks into types according to the procedures required for instruction and practice (Johnson & Street, 2013). Tiemann and Markle's (1990) *kinds of learning* analysis serves this function particularly well because it differentiates between objectives in which what is taught is identical to what is assessed (so-called "simple cognitive" learning) and those in which examples used in instruction must be different from those used in assessment ("complex cognitive" learning; Johnson and Street's (2013) "generative performances").

Last, PT employs a *learning channel analysis*, an approach championed by Eric Haughton and his colleagues (Haughton, 1980), in which naturally occurring "inputs" and "outputs" for each objective are identified. Inputs or sensory dimensions of the discriminative stimulus are described in everyday language as *see, hear, touch, smell*, and *taste*; outputs or topographic dimensions of the response include, among others, *writing, pointing, saying*, and *marking* (Johnson & Layng, 1996). Haughton and others have argued that, absent practice on all relevant channels, students' proficiency with any one *channel*—for example, "see/say"—does not necessarily produce proficiency with other channels—for example, "hear/write"—that real world problem solving may require. Thus, instructional objectives or *pinpoints* in PT include a learning channel in addition to the conditions under which the learner will perform, the expected performance, and a frequency criterion. For example, the learner will *see/say* the correct place value of a number at 60–80 per minute.

Research Supporting Precision Teaching and Remaining Questions

It is clear that PT, done as recommended, produces measurably improved results. The *Journal of Precision Teaching and Celeration*[6] is the landmark journal in the field; it has published hundreds of studies that document improvements in learning as a function of the use of PT technology. In this section, we review the evidence of effectiveness of the technology and describe research questions yet to be answered.

As early as the mid-1950s, Lindsley (1956) asserted that "true mastery" required perfect accuracy which could be maintained over time without practice and which could be applied in new ways, a precursor of RA/PS. From the start, he was interested in compiling evidence of the technology's effectiveness in improving learning and, to that end, Lindsley (1990) and his colleagues established a "behavior bank" in 1967. The bank was a depository into which teachers could deposit behavior frequencies and describe procedures that had been used to achieve celerations. The result was a collection of more than 32,000 projects that provided access by interested parties to measurably effective instructional procedures that had been used to improve performance on a wide range of academic and social behaviors (Potts et al., 1993). Although teachers and researchers deposited data, they neither referred questions to the bank nor consulted its findings and Lindsley (1990) listed the behavior bank among the technology's failures. Even so, the bank provided evidence that when frequency-building exercises were added to existing teaching procedures, student performance dramatically improved.

The first large-scale study of the effects of PT on learner performance was the Sacajawea Precision Teaching Project in Great Falls, Montana under the direction of Ray Beck (1979). The project, which targeted both elementary and secondary students in general education classrooms and students with mild disabilities, created more than 10,000 practice sheets, used daily 1-minute assessments of basic academic skills, employed moderately high instructional aims (e.g., 70—90 correct digits per minute in math and 180–200 words per minute for oral reading), required daily charting, and made data-based instructional decisions (Beck & Clement, 1991). Despite the fact that many of the procedural improvements precision teachers have access to today had not been implemented, the United States Office of Education's Joint Dissemination Review Panel found that in the large majority of classrooms and in some entire schools, students who participated in the project significantly outperformed students in matched control groups. Students who caught up with same aged peers and were reassigned to regular education classrooms were reevaluated in 1977 using standardized achievement tests, classroom performance, and teacher judgments, all of which "supported the conclusion that these students were still academically successful" (Potts et al., 1993, p. 187).

The Sacajawea project is somewhat unique among PT demonstration projects because it is one of the few that uses a group design to compare performance of program participants with a matched control group. Other large-scale projects show their effectiveness by demonstrating change in students' learning trajectories as a result of program participation. MA is one such project. MA has benefited from and helped to evolve the PT technology for more than 30 years (Johnson & Layng, 1992, 1994; Johnson & Street, 2004a, 2004b, 2012, 2013). The very large majority of students at MA failed to stay on pace academically with their classmates prior to enrolling at the Academy. Similar to the Sacajawea Project, MA teachers have created frequency-building activities in many academic areas including mathematics, reading, and grammar. In addition, they layer PT on top of empirically validated curriculum and instructional protocols. When a student's failure to progress calls for it, faculty at MA provide additional instruction or design new frequency-building sheets that slice the curriculum into finer response requirements. The payoff has been tremendous. For much of its history, MA has offered a money-back guarantee to parents of students who fail to progress at least two years per year of instruction in their area of greatest deficit on high stakes, standardized, end-of-year tests. During that time, MA has returned less than 1% of tuition dollars to parents. The results of an 11-year study of its students' mean standardized test score gains are reported in Johnson and Layng (1992). Students averaged approximately 2.5 years growth in reading for each year of participation and, by the end of the study, growth in mathematics was approximately 3 years per year of instruction.

Morningside Academy has also collected considerable data from its outreach arm—Morningside Teachers' Academy (MTA). MTA consultants have worked with teachers throughout the United States and Canada as well as in Europe, Africa, Australia, and the Middle East to improve student achievement. Their results demonstrate that, in combination with empirically validated curricula, PT changes the trajectory of student learning (Johnson & Street, 2012). Learners who appear to be well behind same aged peers catch up and move ahead. In fact, at Ft. Frasier

Elementary School in British Columbia, Canada—a school where 98% of students were First Nation members—the growth was so exceptional that 15 other schools in the district asked to be included in the project.

Energy directed toward establishing procedures that yield speedier growth in rates of behavior correlated with fluency has paid off in improved learning by students of all ages. Even so, as Cooper and Eshleman (1991) and Cooper et al. (2007) pointed out, only rarely do these demonstrations use a true experimental design or in any way address the requirements of baseline logic that single-subject designs require.

Much of the evidence that does exist comes from field-based schools that combine PT with other behavioral practices, such as those described in Tiemann and Markle's (1990) *Analyzing Instructional Content* and in Engelmann and Carnine's (1991) *Theories of Instruction*, which describes the technology that underlies Direct Instruction. Rarely do such schools test individual elements of their curricular and instructional protocols, nor do they systematically vary procedures in a rigorous experimental design. Even the impressive Sacajawea Project in the 1970s did not hold constant variables such as the number of trials or number of reinforcers provided during PT episodes. Similarly, MA, which has incorporated PT in its school-based program for more than 30 years, has done so in combination with other empirically supported curricula and instructional strategies, rendering judgment about the role of PT in producing its outstanding results challenging. Like the Sacajawea Project, MA does not hold constant variables that may co-vary with the primary independent variable.

Thus, neither of these projects has the kind of experimental control to demonstrate that rate of responding is at the heart of their impressive results. Nor is that their purpose. As Johnston (1996) notes, the primary contingencies for such programs are established by their clients—in this case, the parents of learners—and are based on shared goals—in this case, learner performance on high-stakes tests. Success or failure is viewed as a function of an organization's ability to achieve or surpass pre-specified levels or to do better than a control group that does not have access to the intervention. Thus, the contingencies that operate on what Johnston calls third-level field-based laboratory schools work in opposition to a procedure in which program officials systematically deconstruct instructional packages to test the effectiveness of one or more instructional materials or procedures. Johnston contends that this work is left to research organizations at the first and second levels, which operate under contingencies more conducive to answering the kinds of questions that are of interest. Two studies provide examples of this kind of research, one by Bucklin, Dickinson, and Brethower (2000) and the second by Berens, Boyce, Berens, Doney and Kenzer (2003).

Bucklin et al. (2000) observed that "if the benefits of fluency training can be documented experimentally, arguments for its adoption would be more persuasive, perhaps leading to greater use by educators and trainers" (p. 141). To provide an experimental demonstration, the authors compared the effects of fluency training and accuracy training on application and retention using a contrived task with college students who were randomly assigned to one of two training scenarios. The task required participants to learn associations between Hebrew symbols and nonsense syllables and between nonsense syllables and Arabic numerals, either to an accuracy criterion (100% for each set of associations) or to a fluency criterion (100 correct responses per minute for the nonsense syllable-Arabic number association and 50 correct responses per minute for the Hebrew symbol-nonsense syllable association). Participants were tested for accuracy and rate per minute for retention and application (presenting arithmetic problems written as Hebrew symbols and requiring answers in Arabic numerals). Those in the fluency condition performed the math worksheet significantly faster than those in the accuracy condition. While those in the fluency condition also had higher accuracy than those in the accuracy condition, the differences weren't significant. In follow-up testing after 2 or 4 weeks and again at 16 weeks, performance rate was not significantly different for the groups but the fluency group had significantly better accuracy. The authors concluded that "fluency training can aid the acquisition of a higher level skill and increase . . . accuracy for both the component and composite skills" (p. 140).

In a similar attempt to bring the benefits of experimental design to PT, Berens et al. (2003) described a design technology intended to "systematically evaluate relations between response frequency and academic performance outcomes. . . . retention, endurance, and application" (p. 20). They reported on three studies, each related to a different outcome that used the design technology. Five (Study 1), seven (Study 2), and eight (Study 3) students ranging from Grade 4 to Grade 10 served as participants. Students' responses to basic computation flashcards served as the dependent variable. Rewards were available to students for improved performance and, in one case, for staying on task. Retention was assessed following a 1-month break between semesters. The authors found a positive relation between students' median training frequencies and the proportion of previous performance retained; however, at the same time, they found a negative relation between total number of responses emitted and retention of previous performance. Similar results were obtained during the second study that focused on endurance. Here the task was "see/say Arabic numbers" from single numbers up through numbers in the millions. To test endurance, the authors increased the timing length from 1 minute to 4 minutes. The authors noted that these findings contradict much of the classic literature on overlearning which reports better performance as the number of trials increases. The third study focused on application. The task for this study was "see/say the place value of a number highlighted within a larger number." To assess for application, if the students' current levels were at numbers up to thousands, the application test presented them with numbers up to ten thousands with which they had no previous experience. Speedier performance on the first task resulted in speedier and more accurate performance on the application task.

While these studies hold promise, none of them holds constant all other variables that could co-vary with the independent variable—in the case of PT, either rate building or celeration. In fact, to date, no study has provided the kind of control necessary to answer two important questions:

- Is frequency and frequency alone a necessary and sufficient condition to achieve the outcomes thought to correlate with fluency?
- What is the relation of celeration to the outcomes of fluency?

The dearth of experimentally controlled data on the components of PT has led some behavior analysts to question the degree to which its rate-building aspect is instrumental to educationally important outcomes. For example, Doughty, Chase, and O'Shields (2004) examined 29 peer-reviewed empirical studies of rate-building techniques. They concluded that the research on PT is confounded because, in most cases, the rate-building aspect of the intervention is combined with other effective methods of instruction and by differential but unspecified rates of practice and reinforcement. In other words, while they appreciate the impact of the combination of rate building with effective instruction, reinforcement, and multiple practice opportunities, they assert that there is little evidence of the contribution of rate building alone to the five outcomes of maintenance, endurance, application, stability, and generativity. Reflecting on Binder's (2004) and Kubina's (2005) replies to the Doughty et al. (2004) publication, Chase, Doughty, and O'Shields (2005) responded that a lucid argument from authorities on the logic underpinning PT has stood for too long in place of experimental evidence.

Heinicke, Carr, LeBlanc, and Severtson (2010) take a different tack, arguing that empirical evidence of the effectiveness of fluency-building practices for individuals with autism does not exist and calling its use with this population premature. These authors suggest four areas of research that could—should positive results emerge—justify PT interventions with this population. Specifically, they recommend research which focuses on determining the degree to which fluency approaches produce better outcomes than more traditional instruction for the population of individuals with autism, clarifying which early and intensive behavioral intervention (EIBI) outcomes are well served by a rate-building approach, identifying which rate-building procedures best serve the population of individuals with autism, and determining the degree to which rate-building interacts with escape-maintained problem behaviors which are chronic in this population.

Johnson and Street (2004a, 2012) agreed that research lags considerably behind implementation, and have suggested a number of controls that are necessary to empirically validate the relative effectiveness of building frequency. They have identified critical questions that need to be answered related to the efficacy of and best practice related to frequency building.

A recent laboratory study by Porritt, Van Wagner, and Poling (2009) provides a research prototype for studying frequency and celeration building with nonhuman animals, but which could also be applied with humans. Their research was specifically designed to identify if subsequent accuracy was higher under training conditions "that generated a higher rate of responding without altering the rate of reinforcement or number of trials arranged" (p. 297). The use of a variable interval 50-s schedule to arrange food deliveries ensured approximately equal rates of reinforcement under all training procedures. Porritt et al. had pigeons learn chains of pecking three response keys in which the reinforced key sequence was contingent on the color of the illuminated keys. The number of trials, rate of reinforcement, task difficulty, and motivating operations were held constant but the *rate of responding* was varied across three experimental conditions by imposing 5-s delays between each stimulus presentation and response within a chain, 15-s delays between chains, or no delays. Porritt et al. found significantly more accurate retention of previously learned chains and more accurate acquisition of new chains when there were no delays either between the chains or between each stimulus presentation within a chain. In other words, when delays were imposed within or between chains, acquisition and retention were impaired. In addition, the authors cited and controlled for several potential confounds and described a confound-free path for additional research to determine the efficacy of frequency building. In conclusion, until the large number of case studies and A-B designs demonstrating the effectiveness of PT are accompanied by evidence that derives from a rigorous experimental design, there will continue to be those who doubt the importance of frequency building, and efforts toward wide-scale adoption may be unsuccessful.

Where to Learn More

Readers wishing to learn the intricacies of PT are referred to the second edition of White and Haring's (1980) classic text, *Exceptional Teaching*. A more recent option is Kubina and Yurich's (2012) *The Precision Teaching Book*. Another valuable resource is the deluxe edition of Pennypacker et al.'s (2003) *Handbook of the Standard Celeration Chart*, the classic procedural handbook. Graf and Lindsley (2002) wrote a reference manual, *Standard Celeration Charting 2002*, recently remade available from www.behaviordevelopmentsolutions.com. White and Neeley (2012) have written a very thorough procedural manual, *The Chart Book*, available at http://education.washington.edu/areas/edspe/white/precision/readings/chartbook.pdf and White (2012) also wrote an excellent manual, *The Finder Book*, explaining a chart tool. It is available at http://education.washington.edu/areas/edspe/white/precision/readings/finderbook.pdf. Readers may also benefit from attending the annual conference of the Standard Celeration Society (http://celeration.org/conference-mainmenu-39130) that convenes in autumn each year. It provides opportunities for novices to learn more about the chart, specifically, and about PT generally.

Afterword

Fluency is not only a matter of interest to behavioral psychologists. It has also drawn the attention of cognitive psychologists, information-processing psychologists, and neuropsychologists, whose findings align with those of PT proponents. For example, in their landmark article written from an information-processing perspective, neuropsychologist David LaBerge and educational psychologist S. Jay Samuels (1974) found that automaticity of components of reading words was critical to comprehension. They attributed this to the fact that the automatic processing of words freed the reader's attention, which they argue is limited, to fully engage in the comprehension act.

Similarly, the well-known cognitive psychologist, K. Anders Ericsson, and colleagues in their often-cited paper asserted that "from our search for immutable characteristics corresponding to innate talent, we conclude that individuals acquire virtually all of the distinguishing characteristics of expert performers through relevant activities (deliberate practice)" (Ericsson, Krampe, & Tesch-Römer, 1993, p. 397). They also note that

> To assure effective learning, subjects ideally should be given explicit instructions about the best method and be supervised by a teacher to allow individualized diagnosis of errors, informative feedback, and remedial part training. The instructor has to organize the sequence of appropriate training tasks and monitor improvement to decide when transitions to more complex and challenging tasks are appropriate. (p. 367)

In addition, cognitive psychologists and neuroscientists have concluded that images of the brain (e.g., MRIs) change as a function of increased practice as well as when individuals develop behaviors that correspond to the definition of fluency; for example, improved ability to respond correctly in the face of distraction (Poldrack et al., 2005).

Two popular books reflect variables explored in PT. In *Outliers: The Story of Success*, Malcolm Gladwell (2008) argued that successful people share 2 important characteristics—opportunity plus 10,000 hours of practice. In *The Power of Habit, New York Times* reporter Charles Duhigg (2012) provides numerous illustrations of the power of practicing specific keystone habits, consisting of cue-routine-reward habit loops, until no thinking or second-guessing occurs. Case studies range from personal habits, to the habits of successful organizations, to the habits of societies.

PT provides a technology through which deliberate practice can change the trajectory of a person's learning. Further, proponents believe that PT has been and can continue to be the vehicle through which all individuals, including those who are otherwise disadvantaged, can be given the opportunity and practice required to fulfill their goals.

Acknowledgment

The authors are indebted to Warren R. Street for his careful reading and expert editing of this chapter.

Notes

1 Some behaviors may be observed and counted for 24 hours per day. Although this is more typical for behaviors targeted for *de*celeration such as swearing or fingernail biting, in some circumstances behaviors targeted for *ac*celeration may also be observed for the entire day, for example, the number of positive comments made.

2 Based on the data compiled from more than 3,000 learners, Morningside Academy, a laboratory school program in Seattle, Washington that has used PT technology to improve student learning for more than 30 years, has compiled frequency and celeration aims for reading, writing, and arithmetic curriculum objectives or pinpoints (see Johnson & Street, 2013).

3 The Behavior Research Company website (http://www.behaviorresearchcompany.com/) provides greater detail and an opportunity to inspect each of these charts.

4 Ferster (1953) observed that: "The virtue of the cumulative record is . . . that it emphasizes changes in rate which can be seen in the curvatures of the record" (p. 267).

5 Paul Andronis, T. V. Joe Layng, and Israel Goldiamond (1997) coined the term adduction, or more fully, *contingency adduction*.

6 Prior to 1995, the journal was known as the *Journal of Precision Teaching*.

References

Alper, T., & White, O. (1971). Precision Teaching: A tool for the school psychologist and teacher. *Journal of School Psychology*, *9*, 445–454.

Andronis, P. T., Layng, T. V. J., & Goldiamond, I. (1997). Contingency adduction of "symbolic aggression" by pigeons. *The Analysis of Verbal Behavior*, *14*, 5–17.

Armbruster, B. B., Lehr, F., & Osborn, J. (2001). *Put reading first—The research building blocks for teaching children to read: Kindergarten through grade 3.* Washington, DC: The Partnership for Reading. Retrieved January 3, 2014 from www.nichd.nih.gov/publications/pubs/upload/PRFbooklet.pdf .

Barrett, B. H. (1977). Behavior analysis. In J. Wortis (Ed.), *Mental retardation and developmental disabilities* (Vol. 9, pp. 141–202). New York: Brunner/Mazel.

Barrett, B. H. (1979). Communitization and the measured message of normal behavior. In R. York & E. Edgar (Eds.), *Teaching the severely handicapped* (Vol. 4, pp. 301–318). Columbus, OH: Special Press.

Beck, R. (1979). *Report for the Office of Education joint dissemination review panel.* Great Falls, MT: Precision Teaching Project. (Available from Ray Beck, Sopris West, 1140 Boston Ave., Longmont, CO 80501.)

Beck, R., & Clement, R. (1991). The Great Falls Precision Teaching Project: An historical examination. *Journal of Precision Teaching*, *8*, 8–12.

Berens, K. N., Boyce, T. E., Berens, N. M., Doney, J. K., & Kenzer, A. L. (2003). A technology for evaluating relations between response frequency and academic performance outcomes. *Journal of Precision Teaching and Celeration*, *19*, 20–34.

Binder, C. (1977–1982). *The data-sharing newsletter.* Waltham, MA: Behavior Prosthesis Laboratory, Walter E. Fernald State School. Retrieved January 3, 2014 from http://fluency.org/Data-sharingNewsletter.pdf .

Binder, C. (1993). Behavioral fluency: A new paradigm. *Educational Technology*, *33*, 8–14.

Binder, C. (1996). Behavioral fluency: Evolution of a new paradigm. *The Behavior Analyst*, *19*, 163–197.

Binder, C. (2004). A refocus on response-rate measurement: Comment on Doughty, Chase, and O'Shields. *The Behavior Analyst*, *27*, 281–286.

Binder, C., & Bloom, C. (1989). Fluent product knowledge: Application in the financial services industry. *Performance and Instruction*, *28*, 17–21.

Binder, C., Haughton, E., & Van Eyk, D. (1990). Increasing endurance by building fluency: Precision Teaching attention span. *Teaching Exceptional Children*, *22*, 24–27.

Binder, C., & Sweeney, L. (2002). Building fluent performance in a customer call center. *Performance Improvement*, *41*, 29–37.

Bucklin, B. R., Dickinson, A. M., & Brethower, D. M. (2000). A comparison of the effects of fluency training and accuracy training on application and retention. *Performance Improvement Quarterly*, *13*, 140–163.

Caldwell, T. (1972). Teacher training tools for precision. In J. B. Jordan & L. S. Robbins (Eds.), *Let's try doing something else kind of thing* (pp. 110–117). Arlington, VA: Council for Exceptional Children.

Calkin, A. (2009). An examination of inner (private) and outer (public) behaviors. *European Journal of Behavior Analysis*, *10*, 61–75.

Chase, P. N., Doughty, S. S., & O'Shields, E. M. (2005). Focus on response rate is important but not sufficient: A reply. *The Behavior Analyst*, *28*, 163–168.

Cooper, J. O., & Eshleman, J. W. (1991). Suggestions for presenting multiple baseline analyses on standard celeration charts. *Journal of Precision Teaching*, *8*, 48–57.

Cooper, J. O., Heron, T. E., & Heward, W. L. (2007). *Applied behavior analysis* (2nd ed.). Upper Saddle River, NJ: Pearson.

Deno, S. L. (1985). Curriculum-based measurement: The emerging alternative. *Exceptional Children, 52*, 219–232.

Deno, S. L. (2003). Developments in curriculum-based measurement. *Journal of Special Education, 37*, 184–192.

Doughty, S. S., Chase, P. N., & O'Shields, E. M. (2004). Effects of rate building on fluent performance: A review and commentary. *The Behavior Analyst, 27*, 7–23.

Duhigg, C. (2012). *The power of habit.* New York: Random House.

Duncan, A. D. (1969). Self-application of behavior modification techniques by teenagers. *Adolescence, 6*, 541–556.

Engelmann, S. (2008). *Reading mastery signature edition* [Curriculum program]. Columbus, OH: McGraw-Hill Education.

Engelmann, S., & Carnine, D. W. (1991). *Theory of instruction: Principles and applications.* Eugene, OR: ADI Press.

Engelmann, S., Engelmann, O., Davis, K. L. S., & Hanner, S. (1998). *Horizons: Reading to learn* [Curriculum program]. Columbus, OH: Science Research Associates.

Engelmann, S., & Osborn, J. (2008a). *Language for learning* [Curriculum program]. Columbus, OH: McGraw-Hill Education.

Engelmann, S., & Osborn, J. (2008b). *Language for thinking* [Curriculum program]. Columbus, OH: McGraw-Hill Education.

Epstein, R. (1991). Skinner, creativity, and the problem of spontaneous behavior. *Psychological Science, 2*, 362–370.

Epstein, R., Kirshnit, R., Lanza, R., & Rubin, R. (1984). "Insight" in the pigeon: Antecedents and determinants of an intelligent performance. *Nature, 308*, 61–62.

Ericsson, K. A., Krampe, R. T., & Tesch-Römer, C. (1993). The role of deliberate practice in the acquisition of expert performance. *Psychological Review, 100*, 363–406.

Evans, R. I. (1968). *B. F. Skinner: The man and his ideas.* New York: Dutton.

Fabrizio, M. A., & Moors, A. L. (2003). Evaluating mastery: Measuring instructional outcomes for children with autism. *European Journal of Behavior Analysis, 3*, 23–36.

Ferster, C. B. (1953). The use of the free-operant in the analysis of behavior. *Psychological Bulletin, 50*, 263–274.

Giesecke, F. E., Mitchell, A., Spencer, H. C., Hill, I. L., Loving, R. O., Dygdon, J. T., & Novak, J. E. (2001). *Engineering graphics* (8th ed.). Upper Saddle River, NJ: Prentice Hall.

Gladwell, M. (2008). *Outliers: The story of success.* New York, NY: Little, Brown.

Graf, S., & Lindsley, O. (2002) *Standard celeration charting 2002.* Retrieved January 3, 2014 from www.behaviordevelopmentsolutions.com.

Haring, N., Liberty, K., & White, O. (1980). Rules for data-based strategy decisions in instructional programs: Current research and instructional implications. In W. Sailor, B. Wilcox, & L. Brown (Eds.), *Methods of instruction for severely handicapped students* (pp. 159–192). Baltimore, MD: Brookes.

Haring, N. G., Lovitt, T. C., Eaton, M. D., & Hansen, C. L. (1978). *The fourth R: Research in the classroom.* Columbus, OH: Merrill.

Haughton, E. C. (1972). Aims: Growing and sharing. In J. B. Jordan & L. S. Robbins (Eds.), *Let's try doing something else kind of thing* (pp. 20–39). Arlington, VA: Council for Exceptional Children.

Haughton, E. C. (1980). Practicing practices: Learning by activity. *Journal of Precision Teaching, 1*, 3–20.

Haughton, E. C. (1981, March). R/APS and REAPS. *Data-Sharing Newsletter, 35*, 3. Retrieved from http://fluency.org/Data-sharingNewsletter.pdf.

Haughton, E. C., Maloney, M., & Desjardins, A. (1980). The tender loving care chart. *Journal of Precision Teaching, 1*, 22–25.

Heinicke, M. R., Carr, J. E., LeBlanc, L. A., & Severtson, J. M. (2010). On the use of fluency training in the behavioral treatment of autism: A commentary. *The Behavior Analyst, 33*, 223–229.

Hilgard, E., & Bower, G. (1964). *Theories of learning*. New York: Appleton-Century-Crofts.

Johnson, K., & Layng, T. V. J. (1992). Breaking the structuralist barrier: Literacy and numeracy with fluency. *American Psychologist, 47*, 1475–1490.

Johnson, K., & Layng, T. V. J. (1994). The Morningside Model of Generative Instruction. In R. Gardner, D. Sainato, J. Cooper, T. Heron, W. Heward, J. Eshleman, & T. Grossi (Eds.), *Behavior analysis in education: Focus on measurably superior instruction* (pp. 173–197). Belmont, CA: Brooks-Cole.

Johnson, K. R., & Layng, T. J. V. (1996). On terms and procedures: Fluency. *The Behavior Analyst, 19*, 281–288.

Johnson, K., & Street, E. M. (2004a). *The Morningside Model of Generative Instruction: What it means to leave no child behind*. Concord, MA: Cambridge Center for Behavioral Studies.

Johnson, K. R., & Street, E. M. (2004b). The Morningside Model of Generative Instruction: An integration of research-based practices. In D. J. Moran & R. Malott (Eds.). *Empirically supported educational methods* (pp. 247–265). St. Louis, MO: Elsevier Science/Academic Press.

Johnson, K., & Street, E. M. (2012). From the laboratory to the field and back again: Morningside Academy's 32 years of improving students' academic performance. *The Behavior Analyst Today, 13*, 20–40.

Johnson, K., & Street, E. M. (2013). *Response to intervention and Precision Teaching: Creating synergy in the classroom*. New York: Guilford.

Johnson-Talbert, C., & Cooper, J. O. (1992). Precision teaching and Alzheimer's. *Journal of Precision Teaching, 10*, 53–72.

Johnston, J. A. (1996). Distinguishing between applied research and practice. *The Behavior Analyst, 19*, 35–47.

Kozloff, M. A., LaNunziata, L., Cowardin, J., & Bessellieu, F. B. (2000/2001). Direct instruction: Its contributions to high school achievement. *High School Journal, 84*, 54–71.

Kubina, R. M. (2005). The relations among fluency, rate building, and practice: A response to Doughty, Chase, and O'Shields (2004). *The Behavior Analyst, 28*, 73–76.

Kubina, R. M., Aho, D., Mozzoni, M. P., & Malanga, P. (1998). A case-study in re-teaching a traumatically brain injured child handwriting skills. *Journal of Precision Teaching and Celeration, 15*, 32–40.

Kubina, R. M., & Yurich, K. K. L. (2012). *The Precision Teaching book*. Lemont, PA: Greatness Achieved.

LaBerge, D., & Samuels, S. J. (1974). Toward a theory of automatic information processing in reading. *Cognitive Psychology, 6*, 293–323.

Liberty, K. A., & Paeth, M. A. (1995). Self-recording for students with severe and multiple handicaps. *Journal of Precision Teaching, 12*, 63–66.

Lindsley, O. R. (1956). Operant conditioning methods applied to research in chronic schizophrenia. *Psychiatric Research Reports, 5*, 118–139.

Lindsley, O. R. (1971). Precision Teaching in perspective: An interview with Ogden R. Lindsley. Ann Duncan, interviewer. *Teaching Exceptional Children, 3*, 114–119.

Lindsley, O. R. (1972). From Skinner to Precision Teaching: The child knows best. In J. B. Jordon & L. S. Robbins (Eds.), *Let's try doing something else kind of thing* (pp. 1–11). Arlington, VA: Council on Exceptional Children.

Lindsley, O. R. (1990). Precision Teaching: By teachers, for children. *Teaching Exceptional Children, 22*, 10–15.

Lindsley, O. R. (1992). Precision Teaching: Discoveries and effects. *Journal of Applied Behavior Analysis, 25*, 51–57.

Lindsley, O. R. (1995). Ten products of fluency. *Journal of Precision Teaching and Celeration, 13*, 2–11.

Lindsley, O. R. (1997). Precise instructional design: Guidelines from Precision Teaching. In C. Dills & A. Romiszowski (Eds.), *Instructional development paradigms* (pp. 537–554). Engelwood Cliffs, NJ: Educational Technology Publications.

Lindsley, O. (1999, November). *Celeration and agility for the 2000s.* Paper presented at the International Precision Teaching and Standard Celeration Conference, Provo, UT.

Lindsley, O. R. (2001a). Celeration and agility for the 2000's [sic]. *Journal of Precision Teaching and Celeration, 17*, 107–111.

Lindsley, O. R., (2001b). Do times two, then go for four or more: Precision teaching aims for the 21st century. *Journal of Precision Teaching and Celeration, 17*, 99–102.

Lovitt, T. (1977). *In spite of my resistance I've learned from children.* Columbus, OH: Merrill.

Martens, B. K., Daly III, E. J., Begeny, J. C., & VanDerHeyden, A. (2011). Behavioral approaches to education. In W. W. Fisher, C. C. Piazza, & H. S. Roane (Eds.), *Handbook of applied behavior analysis* (pp. 385–401). New York: Guilford.

McGreevy, P. (1980). Hard to do becomes easy to learn. *Journal of Precision Teaching, 1*, 27–29.

McGreevy, P. (1984). From 1–1/4 miles to a marathon: Monitoring running on the standard celeration chart for 31 months. *Journal of Precision Teaching, 4*, 86, 89–91.

National Mathematics Advisory Panel. (2008). *Foundations for success: The final report of the National Mathematics Advisory Panel.* Washington, DC: U.S. Department of Education. Retrieved January 3, 2014 from www2.ed.gov/about/bdscomm/list/mathpanel/report/final-report.pdf.

Pennypacker, H. S., Gutierrez, A., & Lindsley, O. R. (2003). *Handbook of the standard celeration chart, deluxe edition.* Concord, MA: Cambridge Center for Behavioral Studies.

Pierce, G. (1992). Implementation of precision teaching by the speech-pathologist. *Journal of Precision Teaching, 9*, 24–25.

Poldrack, R. A., Sabb, F. W., Foerde, K., Tom, S. M., Asarnow, R. F., Bookheimer, S. Y., & Knowlton, B. J. (2005). The neural correlates of motor skill automaticity. *Journal of Neuroscience, 25*, 5356–5464.

Porritt, M., Van Wagner, K., & Poling, A. (2009). Effects of response spacing on acquisition and retention of conditional discrimination. *Journal of Applied Behavior Analysis, 42*, 295–307.

Potts, L., Eshleman, J. W., & Cooper, J. O. (1993). Ogden R. Lindsley and the historical development of Precision Teaching. *The Behavior Analyst, 16*, 177–189.

Ryle, G. (1949/1984). *The concept of mind.* Chicago, IL: University of Chicago Press.

Schmid, C. F., & Schmid, S. E. (1979). *Handbook of graphic presentation* (2nd ed.). New York: John Wiley & Sons, Inc.

Skinner, B. F. (1953). *Science and human behavior.* New York: Macmillan.

Skinner, B. F. (1957). *Verbal behavior.* New York: Appleton-Century-Crofts.

Skinner, B. F. (1969). *Contingencies of reinforcement: A theoretical analysis.* New York: Appleton-Century-Crofts.

Tiemann, P. W., & Markle, S. M. (1990). *Analyzing instructional content: A guide to instruction and evaluation.* Seattle, WA: Morningside Press.

Timmons, V., McLaughlin, T. F., & Kinakin, V. (1995). The effect of music on head posturing of a student with cerebral palsy: A case study. *Journal of Precision Teaching and Celeration, 13*, 35–46.

VanDerHeyden, A. M., & Burns, M. K. (2010). *Essentials of response to intervention.* Hoboken, NJ: John Wiley & Sons, Inc.

White, O. R. (1986). Precision teaching: Precision learning. *Exceptional Children, 52,* 522–534.
White, O. (2012). *The finder book.* Retrieved January 3, 2014 from http://education.washington.edu/areas/edspe/white/precision/readings/finderbook.pdf.
White, O. R., & Haring, N. G. (1980). *Exceptional teaching* (2nd ed.). Columbus, OH: Merrill.
White, O., & Neeley, M. (2012). *The chart book.* Retrieved January 3, 2014 from http://education.washington.edu/areas/edspe/white/precision/readings/chartbook.pdf.
Wittgenstein, L. (1958). *Philosophical investigations* (G. E. M. Anscombe, trans.). New York: Macmillan.

24

Behavioral Pharmacology
A Brief Overview

John M. Roll

Behavioral pharmacology is concerned with the interactions between drugs, organisms, and the environment. In other words, it is a specific offshoot of behavioral psychology that includes drugs as a defining feature. In this context, drugs should not be construed to mean only illicit or intoxicating drugs (e.g., cocaine, alcohol, and nicotine), but also those pharmaceuticals intended to treat a physical or mental complaint (e.g., antipsychotics, antimalarial agents, and drugs designed to treat pain), as well as those intended to enhance performance (e.g., some classes of steroids). Some may also include a type of substance known as a biologic agent in the subject matter of behavioral pharmacology. The National Cancer Institute (NCI) defines a biologic agent as a substance that is made from a living organism or its products and is used in the prevention, diagnosis, or treatment of cancer and other diseases. According to NCI biologic agents may include antibodies, interleukins, and vaccines (http://www.cancer.gov/dictionary). While I will not focus on biologics in this chapter, the application of behavioral pharmacology to their study promises to be an exciting new opportunity in the field of behavioral pharmacology.

This chapter provides an opportunity to present a brief and illustrative overview of what is a dynamic field of scientific and clinical effort. Table 24.1 also lists a small selection of some of the most influential books, chapters, and review articles addressing the field. This chapter commences with an overview of some of the crucial historical underpinnings of behavioral pharmacology. Following this, behavioral pharmacology is defined in more detail, and is contrasted with other fields (i.e., psychopharmacology and neuropharmacology). Examples are included throughout that illustrate behavioral pharmacology protocols conducted with animals and humans. The chapter then presents an example of a how a single behavioral principle, or observation, can be used to address many different topic areas (e.g., understanding, treatment, and prevention) in behavioral pharmacology. The chapter concludes with a section on the clinical application of behavioral pharmacology.

The Wiley Blackwell Handbook of Operant and Classical Conditioning, First Edition.
Edited by Frances K. McSweeney and Eric S. Murphy.

Table 24.1 Suggested readings—complete references in reference section

- *Cocaine abuse*—Higgins & Katz (1998).
- *Contingency management for substance abuse Treatment: A guide to implementing this evidence-based practice*—Petry (2011).
- *Behavior analysis of drug action*—Harvey (1971).
- *Behavioral pharmacology*—Thompson & Schuster (1968).
- *Introduction to Behavioral pharmacology*—Poling & Byrne (2000).
- *Contingency management in substance abuse treatment*—Higgins, Silverman, & Heil. (2008).
- *Guidelines and methodological reviews concerning drug abuse liability assessment*—Balster & Bigelow (2003).
- *Handbook of research methods in human operant behavior*—Lattal & Perone, (1998).
- *Motivating behavior change among illicit-drug abusers*—Higgins & Silverman (1999).
- *Reinforcement-based treatment for substance use disorders: A comprehensive behavioral approach*—Tuten, Jones, Schaffer, & Stitzer (2012).
- *Replacing relative reinforcing efficacy with behavioral economic demand curves*— Johnson & Bickel (2006).
- Special issue on the behavior analysis and treatment of drug addiction, *Journal of Applied Behavior Analysis*—Silverman, Roll, & Higgins (2008).
- *The pharmacology of cocaine related to is Abuse*—Johanson & Fischman (1980).

Historical Underpinnings of Behavioral Pharmacology

Animals often seek out fermenting fruit and consume it in large quantities, some even return to the same place each year, apparently to obtain the intoxicating food and experience its postingestive effects. People have been using drugs to alter their behavior since the earliest historical accounts (Courtwright, 2001). The Bible and other early documents are rife with accounts of the use of alcohol and others drugs that today we classify as drugs with abuse potential. Given this long relationship with drugs, it is admittedly arbitrary to provide a specific starting point for the field of behavioral pharmacology. Instead, I will describe what I perceive to be the major scientific accomplishments that set the stage for the modern field of behavioral pharmacology to emerge. Some of these you will recognize as underpinning other seminal areas of the Experimental Analysis of Behavior.

Law of Effect

Thorndike's *Law of Effect* was one of the first formally presented observations of the relationship between behavior and its consequences (e.g., Clifford, 1984). Thorndike observed that those activities followed by satisfying occurrences (satisfiers) increase in frequency while those that are followed by unsatisfying occurrences (annoyers) decrease in frequency. One key area of study in behavioral pharmacology is to explore the ways in which drugs can alter the ability of satisfiers and annoyers to influence behavior. For example, no less a personage than Sigmund Freud described, from his personal experience, how cocaine impacted the sensory characteristics of drinking water (a satisfier) (Freud, 2011). Experimental psychology has matured considerably since Freud conducted his introspective approaches to understanding the impact of cocaine on human behavior. However, it is still an active area of research to try to understand how drugs may influence an organism's reaction to positive or aversive experiences. Additionally, drugs themselves can function as satisfiers and annoyers. Today we would most likely describe these drugs in terms of reinforcers (e.g., cocaine—something an organism engages in behavior to receive) or punishers (e.g., ipecac—something an organism would engage in behavior to avoid).

Pavlovian Conditioning

Behavioral pharmacology also builds on the work of the Russian physiologist I. P. Pavlov (e.g., Gibbons, 1955) by investigating how drugs impact the conditioning processes so familiar to undergraduate psychology students. Additionally, behavioral pharmacologists are interested in how drugs can function as both conditioned and unconditioned stimuli in Pavlovian conditioning paradigms. Building on the work of Johanson and Schuster (e.g., Johanson, Mattox, & Schuster, 1995), my team has conducted several experiments to understand the extent to which drugs can apparently be conditioned in a Pavlovian paradigm so that they confer greater reinforcing efficacy—or exert stronger control over behavior (see below) than can be accounted for by their pharmacology alone (Alessi, Roll, Reilly, & Johanson, 2002; Roll, Reilly, Chudzynski, & Mercado, 2009).

In the study led by Alessi (Alessi et al., 2002), we provided recreational drug users (i.e., participants who used illicit drugs in a manner that did not meet dependence criteria) with placebo and diazepam (a tranquilizer) capsules on different days and had them rate how much they valued each. Almost all participants valued the placebo more than the diazepam presumably because they did not like the feeling of sedation the diazepam occasioned in our research setting. Following these initial sampling sessions, we arranged a paradigm in which participants thought they could earn money based on their performance of a complex, ambiguous cognitive/motor task in which moving stimuli were tracked on a computer screen. In fact, the results of the task were not related to the amount of money a participant received. Instead, we manipulated the outcome of the task by providing feedback that indicated either strong or weak performance so that following the ingestion of diazepam, participants earned more money than they did following ingestion of placebo. The participants were not aware of the noncontingent relationship between their performance and earnings. In this paradigm, one could consider the drugs (placebo and diazepam) to be conditioned stimuli (CS- i.e., a stimulus that evokes a response only when repeatedly paired with a stimulus that is salient to the organism) and the monetary consequences to be unconditioned stimuli (US- a salient stimulus, often having biological relevance.) (Note other conceptualizations of this paradigm are also valid. See Bouton,

2000.) Following a number of CS and US pairings, we reassessed the value of both placebo and diazepam to the participants. Participants mostly reversed their original preferences and reported that the diazepam was now more valuable to them than the placebo.

While this is a neat bit of conditioning prestidigitation, it also may have considerable real world significance in explaining the genesis of illicit-drug use as suggested by Alessi et al. (2002) and Roll (2013). Consider the following hypothetical situation. A new family with a 14-year-old son moves into a neighborhood in which the son does not know anyone. He desires, quite naturally, to be part of a social group—to have friends—a powerful source of reinforcement. There is a group of 14-year olds in the neighborhood but, unfortunately, they all smoke marijuana when they are together and they are uncomfortable having anyone around them who does not smoke marijuana. So, in order to gain access to the social group, the new boy—who has not smoked marijuana before—begins to smoke marijuana. The satisfaction he gains from smoking the marijuana is realized in part because of the pharmacology of the drug and its interaction with the boy's nervous system. However, this satisfaction is augmented (I would argue through a conditioning process) by the fact that it also allows him to gain access to a social group, which in and of itself is a powerful source of positive reinforcement. Thus, the marijuana has greater value to the boy than can be accounted for by the drug's pharmacology alone. The value has been augmented by a conditioning procedure in which the drug functioned as a CS and the social group functioned as a US.

As a slight aside, to the extent the above hypothetical situation is correct, it has profound treatment implications. It suggests that a treatment (pharmacotherapy or immunotherapy) that only addresses the drug (marijuana) receptor interaction will not be entirely successful as that may be unlikely to impact the reinforcing efficacy of the marijuana that has accrued via the above associative process.

Operant Psychology of B. F. Skinner

Behavioral pharmacology became a field in its own right—as opposed to an offshoot of other fields—once operant approaches to studying behavior became well accepted. It is difficult to imagine a richer, more scientifically supported approach to understanding behavior than that popularized by B. F. Skinner (see Skinner, 1938 for an introduction to his influential work). As eloquently described in his own and others' writing, Skinner's work was not so much theoretically novel as it was systematizing or organizing into a coherent framework, and extending to a logical pinnacle, the work of his scientific predecessors (e.g., Darwin, Morgan, Thorndike, Pavlov, Sherrington, Magnus and many others).

The development of laboratory preparations for the easy (relatively!) study of operant psychology (e.g., the Skinner Box preparation) was of great significance for the development of behavioral pharmacology. The operant chamber opened many possibilities for the study of how drugs altered behavior. Some of the earliest examples of this work were conducted by Skinner and Heron (1937) who examined how caffeine and amphetamine (benzadrine) transformed food reinforced behavior and extinction. They reported that mean cumulative responding by rats increased under drug conditions relative to control conditions. This has become a classic study in the history of behavioral pharmacology (see Poling & Byrne, 2000 for a detailed discussion). The study unambiguously demonstrated how the operant chamber preparation could be used to effectively gather replicable, stable data describing the impact of drugs on behavior.

A perhaps equally important occurrence in the development of behavioral pharmacology was the demonstration that naïve animals would self-administer drugs which are routinely abused by humans. In an early study utilizing an indwelling intravenous catheter attached to a drug pump, Thompson and Schuster demonstrated that drug-naïve monkeys would self-administer morphine (Thompson & Schuster, 1968). This was a seminal demonstration that drugs of abuse could serve as positive reinforcers analogous to other positive reinforcers like food and water. It also provided an intuitive model for the relatively parsimonious study of human behavior. This observation has resulted in a tremendous amount of research in which drugs are provided to organisms (human and nonhuman) contingent on an operant response in a self-administration paradigm. A recent Pub Med search of the term self-administration resulted in 48,702 publications (July 23, 2012) suggesting that the use of this procedure has been widely adopted in the study of behavioral pharmacology and related fields.

The observation that drugs of abuse serve as powerful sources of reinforcement has been a unifying concept in behavioral pharmacology. In fact, scholars from temporally—and perhaps philosophically—different perspective have endorsed the notion that drug reinforcement is the hallmark of addiction and that a corollary of this is that reducing the efficacy of the abused drug is the hallmark of a successful treatment effort. Many ways have been investigated to reduce the reinforcing efficacy of a drug of abuse (e.g., *cognitive* restructuring, arranging environments so that nondrug sources of reinforcement compete with drug-derived reinforcement, immunotherapeutic preparations in which a drug is degraded before it can bind to a receptor to initiate a pharmacologic response, and pharmacotherapy in which a drug is administered to block or modify the effects of an abused drug).

Development of Antipsychotic Drugs

Another seminal occurrence in the development of behavioral pharmacology was the explosion of pharmacotherapy for psychiatric conditions. Especially during the 1950s, drugs became available for the management of serious and persistent mental illness. In particular, chlorpromazine reduced the psychotic behavior of institutionalized individuals who had previously been resistant to all treatment approaches (Anton-Stephens, 1954). This observation demonstrated how pharmacologic preparations could be used to treat mental health concerns and fueled a search that continues to this day to screen and develop additional behaviorally-active compounds for use in the management of mental health (e.g., antidepressants, anxiolytics, and antipsychotics). This ongoing search has cemented a role for behavioral pharmacologists in the pharmaceutical industry and fueled a great many innovations in drug screening and classification paradigms. These include drug discrimination studies (e.g., Kamien, Bickel, Hughes, Higgins, & Smith, 1993) in which the stimulus properties of drugs are compared to those of other drugs and assessments of the direct effects of drugs, such as the drug's ability to produce ataxia, cataplexy, and other states that impact behavior (e.g., Kuribara, Asami, Ida, & Tadokoro, 1992).

Drug discrimination is an important technique employed in behavioral pharmacology with both human and nonhuman participants. As with most areas of behavioral pharmacology, it is covered in the excellent book, *Introduction to behavioral pharmacology*, edited by Poling and Byrne (2000). Interested readers may also wish to consult the chapter by Higgins and Hughes on human operant psychology that occurs in Lattal and Perone (1998). Briefly, a basic drug discrimination procedure involves training an organism that reinforcement is available when a certain drug is administered (e.g., morphine) and not available when placebo or another drug is administered. For example, a rat might be trained to respond on a lever in an operant chamber for food reinforcement in the presence of heroin but not in the presence of a placebo. Once this discrimination training had occurred, the investigator could administer another drug such as cocaine to see how the rat would respond. In this case, the rat would likely not respond in the presence of cocaine because the interoceptive stimulus state occasioned by the cocaine would be sufficiently unlike that produced by the heroin. However, if morphine were administered to the rat, it would probably respond because the interoceptive state produced would be similar to that produced when heroin is administered. This procedure is a sensitive assay that allows investigators to ascertain the degree of similarity between drugs. It has also been demonstrated that the neuropharmacology underpinning various drug states can be usefully compared with this procedure.

Modern Behavioral Pharmacology

All of these occurrences (delineation of the Law of Effect, *Description of Pavlovian conditioning, Development of operant psychology* by B. F. Skinner and others, and the development of drugs to treat mental health concerns) set the stage for behavioral pharmacology to be the diverse, vibrant field it is today. The National Institutes of Health (NIH) has institutes that focus almost entirely on the field (e.g., the National Institute on Drug Addiction and the National Institute on Alcoholism and Alcohol Abuse), and many others also fund research on the topic (e.g., National Institutes of: Mental Health; Complementary and Alternative Medicine; Nursing Research; Cancer; and Minority Health and Disparities). Many journals are devoted to the topic; it is a recognized specialty track by the Association for Behavior Analysis International and has one professional society that is eponymous: the Behavioral Pharmacology Society, as well as the International Society Investigating Drugs as Reinforcers, which are devoted to its topic matter. Many other professional meetings include behavioral pharmacology as a track. It is possible to get undergraduate, graduate, and postgraduate training in the discipline, and practitioners readily employ many of the field's findings to the direct benefit of those they serve and society in general.

The topic matter of behavioral pharmacology is vast and ranges from gene-level to population-level analyses. Preventing, understanding, and treating drug abuse are all vibrant areas of research, as is the discovery and classification of new drugs for use in modifying a person's behavior (e.g., antipsychotics, sleep aids, weight loss medications, medication to treat impulse control disorders like gambling and even medications to treat addictions to illicit drugs).

Before continuing with some additional specific examples of behavioral pharmacology, let us take a moment to compare behavioral pharmacology to a similar field—psychopharmacology. My belief is that most researchers and clinicians identifying with these fields would be fairly comfortable using the terms interchangeably. I, however, have always considered the proper subject matter of psychopharmacology to be the cognitive outcomes of drug-organism interactions which must be inferred and cannot be directly observed. This includes those items measured by subjective effects questionnaires about how someone feels (e.g., anxious, happy, hostile, etc.). This is the proper realm of psychopharmacology. Behavioral pharmacology should have as main dependent measures hard behavioral endpoints which can be directly observed such as number of self-administrations, percent of positive urine drug tests, or percent of choices for drug relative to another positive reinforcer. That said, the distinction may not be all that important but I believe that by using the term behavioral pharmacology to refer to research or clinical interventions with behavioral endpoints we are signaling to those who follow us that our protocols are based on behavioral, as opposed to cognitive, principles.

Certainly, both behavioral pharmacology and psychopharmacology are important areas of inquiry. In practice, the two approaches are often found in the same experimental preparation. For example, in a recent study conducted by my team (Roll et al., 2012) in which we investigated the ability of Gamma Hydroxy Butyrate (GHB) to function as a positive reinforcer in human participants, we measured self-administration rates and the percent of choices for GHB relative to monetary reinforcement (behavioral outcomes). We also measured subjective effects of GHB (cognitive outcomes) with questionnaires. I consider myself to be a behavioral pharmacologist, but I do not hesitate to borrow from other fields such as psychopharmacology when it allows me to better understand the topic under study. In fact, I would argue that a dogmatic approach to the topic matter is counterproductive. When you are working with human participants who have consented to participate in relatively inconvenient research protocols, I believe you owe it to them to obtain as much data as you can, without overburdening them, while maintaining them in the research protocol.

Another related field is neuropharmacology. Neuropharmacologists employ many of the same behavioral techniques as do behavioral pharmacologists, but their primary interest is in understanding the site and mechanism of action of specific drugs or combinations of drugs with a focus on understanding central nervous system mechanisms. Neuropharmacologists often make use of cellular recording or microscopic visualization techniques when working with nonhuman participants and neuroimaging technology when working with live humans. Often, these imaging preparations borrow heavily from psychopharmacology too, especially if the purpose is to isolate a brain area involved in a cognitive task and to understand how drug use alters the central nervous system processing needed to complete the cognitive task. Neuropharmacologists also utilize human brain tissue when postmortem analyses are being conducted to isolate brain regions that may have been altered through prolonged drug exposure. As with psychopharmacology, neuropharmacology is quite compatible with behavioral pharmacology and employs many of the same techniques (e.g., self-administration preparations).

What Do Behavioral Pharmacologists Do?

With an appreciation of the origins of behavioral pharmacology, the next question is what do behavioral pharmacologists do. Behavioral pharmacologists study interactions between drugs, organisms, and environments. We know what drugs are and we know what organisms are, but what are environments? I have recently argued for an expanded conceptualization of environments in understanding drug-organism interactions (Roll, 2013). I have suggested that to address the complexities of behavioral pharmacology, environment not only be construed to include the external environment—things like temperature, density of reinforcement available, light level, and noise level—but also could/should include an internal environment and a genetic environment. According to this conceptualization, the internal environment is composed of factors like receptor density in specific brain regions, deprivation state, and anxiety level. The genetic environment is composed of an individual's unique genetic makeup which may include predispositions to respond in different fashions to different drug classes relative to someone with a different genetic environment. I argued that in order to obtain a clear understanding of drug-organism-environment interactions one needs to account for all of the above and that by expanding the way we conceptualize environment, we can more easily accommodate the genetic and internal factors contributing to behavior. Regardless of the veracity of my claim or the persuasiveness of my argument, it does further illustrate the complexity of the topic matter when one needs to consider the pharmacologic action of a drug, the history of the organism experiencing the drug, the external environment in which the drug is experienced, the internal status of the organism and the genetic makeup of the organism in order to even begin to have a complete appreciation for the impact of the drug on the organism's behavior.

Adding to the complexity, one can engage in scholarly work in behavioral pharmacology with different goals and behavioral endpoints (e.g., dependent variables). You could work to understand how drug addiction begins (e.g., first self-administration), what maintains addiction (e.g., continued administration), what terminates it (e.g., cessation of self-administration). You could devote yourself to devising methods for preventing addiction (e.g., relative rate of initial self-administration in a given population), you could develop screening techniques to isolate compounds that may be useful in treating mental health concerns (e.g., impact on activities of daily living among those afflicted), or you might find yourself working with genetically engineered mice to try to understand how certain genetic manipulations impact self-administration variables such as rate or pattern. The list of possibilities may, in fact, be endless.

Can one person be an expert in all of these arenas? Just as in other areas of psychology, individual researchers and clinicians tend to specialize in a few related areas. This is largely why there is a current emphasis on multidisciplinary approaches to much of science, including studies striving to understand, treat, and prevent addiction. No one person is going to have all of the knowledge needed. Instead, a team of collaborative scientists and clinicians, each with different expertise may pose the best likelihood for moving any field of inquiry forward. However, a word of caution may be in order here. To be a good collaborator in a multidisciplinary team, it is crucial that you be an expert in your own chosen area of expertise.

Transitivity of Behavioral Observations

Luckily though, certain behavioral observations are so powerful that, by studying them, an individual may make contributions to many aspects of behavioral pharmacology. For example, Nader and Woolverton conducted a study in which they allowed rhesus monkeys to make exclusive choices between intravenously delivered cocaine and food (Nader & Woolverton, 1991). When the choice was between cocaine and one pellet of monkey food, the monkeys tended to self-administer the cocaine. However, when the dose of cocaine was held constant and the magnitude of the alternative source of reinforcement (monkey pellets) was increased to four per choice, the monkeys chose to self-administer cocaine on fewer trials. In the final condition, the magnitude of the alternative reinforcer was increased to 16 monkey pellets per choice. In this condition, the monkeys chose the alternative reinforcer, food, more than in other conditions. This elegant experiment demonstrates the powerful impact of arranging an environment so that the organism needs to make choices between a drug and a salient, high magnitude, alternative source of reinforcement. This finding has been reported by many investigators working with different drugs, different alternatives and different animal species (e.g., Carroll, Lac, & Nygaard, 1989). When the magnitude of the alternative source of reinforcement is weak, the drug has a powerful reinforcing efficacy, that is, it exerts strong control over the organism's behavior. However, the reinforcing efficacy of the drug can be reduced to such a low level that it is not self-administered simply by increasing the magnitude of the available alternative sources of reinforcement.

Monkeys in operant chambers are one thing, but how about humans? Higgins and colleagues conducted an analogous study with human volunteers in which they investigated the impact of manipulating the magnitude of alternative reinforcers on cocaine self-administration (Higgins, Bickel, & Hughes, 1994). In this protocol, recreational cocaine users were recruited to participate in an outpatient study. Participants came to the laboratory where they made 10 choices between cocaine and money on a given day. Cocaine dose was held constant throughout the study. Money was used as an alternative source of reinforcement and was provided at four different levels: $0.00 $0.50, $1.00, and $2.00. During a given session, monetary value was held constant. In a session, a participant made 10 choices between cocaine and money. When the monetary value was low, participants elected to self-administer cocaine exclusively. As the value of the alternative source of reinforcement increased, participants elected to receive less of the cocaine doses and when the magnitude of the alternative was increased to $2.00, participants elected to forgo cocaine and receive only money. This procedure has been replicated with many other types of drugs besides cocaine (e.g., Roll & Newton, 2008; Roll, Reilly, & Johanson, 2000). Exactly as in the Nader and Woolverton (1991) study with monkeys, the proclivity

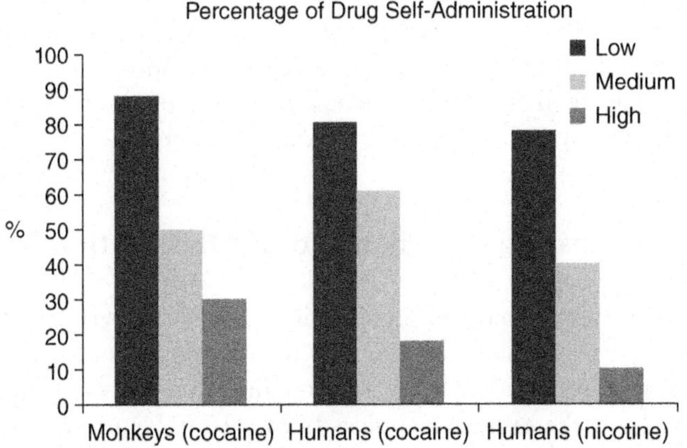

Figure 24.1 This figure depicts data gathered from published results of three studies depicting the influence of the magnitude of alternative reinforcement on drug self-administration. The left bars represent data form Nader and Woolverton (1991) in which monkeys responded for food pellets or 0.3 mg/kg cocaine infusions. The low magnitude was one food pellet, the medium four pellets and the high 16 pellets. In the middle bars, humans choosing between money and cocaine (10 mg unit doses) are depicted (Higgins, Roll, & Bickel, 1996). The low magnitude was \$0.05, the medium \$1.00, and the high \$2.00. The right bars present data from Roll, Reilly, and Johanson (2000) in which nicotine-deprived humans made choices between nicotine cigarette puffs and money. Low magnitude money value was \$0.10, medium was \$1.00, and high was \$2.00. These data are gleaned from published accounts that should be consulted for a complete examination of the data.

for humans to self-administer cocaine decreased in an orderly fashion as the magnitude of the alternative source of reinforcement increased. Figure 24.1 presents data from three studies illustrating the consistency of this finding.

As noted above, the hallmark of the successful treatment of drug addiction is the reduction of a drug's reinforcing efficacy to such a low level that the drug is not self-administered when it is available. The observation that providing a salient alternative source of reinforcement of sufficient magnitude reduces a drug's reinforcing efficacy has many implications. One of these implications is that arranging an addict's environment so that it provides a choice between drug-derived reinforcement and other types of reinforcement (i.e., alternative sources of reinforcement) should reduce the reinforcing efficacy of the abused drug and result in the termination of the drug-using behavior—also known as treatment. This is exactly the approach used in the contingency management interventions. This class of intervention is widely acknowledged to be one of the most powerful behavioral treatment modalities available and has been studied extensively and employed successfully in the treatment of many types of addictions (e.g., Dutra et al., 2008; Lussier, Heil, Mongeon, Badger, & Higgins, 2006; Prendergast, Podus, Greenwell, Finney, & Roll, 2006). This type of treatment approach is described in detail in this book in the chapter by Andrade and Petry. For our purposes though, please note that the heart of the contingency management interventions is the observation that alternative sources of reinforcement, when available in sufficient magnitude and arranged in a schedule that is incompatible with drug use, decrease the proclivity of addicts to use the drug.

Studying the impact of alternative reinforcement on drug self-administration allows us to gain a fuller appreciation of one reason why people may use drugs—a dearth of other sources of reinforcement or an inability to access available reinforcement— and provides a framework for the design of effective treatment protocols for all types of addiction. What else can we do with this powerful observation? At least one other area in which this observation may have profound implications is in terms of the prevention of drug addiction.

Undoubtedly, there are multiple paths to drug addiction. One that I am confident exists is the following. Consider an impoverished, homeless man living on the streets of any urban center in the world. Suppose that he not a drug user. As time passes his despair grows. He does not have sufficient food or even water. He has no facilities to take care of his personal needs. His health begins to deteriorate. He is beaten and robbed of his meager possessions with predictable regularity. He exists in an environment that offers him little in the way of reinforcement. His time horizon is severely truncated. He does not plan for the future; he just tries to survive the day, or moment. He is living in an environment that has minimal, if any, alternative sources of reinforcement. If he is introduced to drugs, I believe it is almost certain that he will become dependent on them. When he places a needle in his arm and injects heroin, it will be an extremely powerful source of reinforcement that he can access. One could even suggest that under the circumstances described it is understandable from an evolutionary point of view why someone would engage in drug abuse behaviors. The drug provides a dependable source of reinforcement in an environment with little or no chance to obtain other sources of reinforcement.

The obvious social solution to this plight would be for outside agents to provide the man with stability by supplying him with the basic necessities of life and opportunities to remove himself from the chaotic environment. If this effort succeeds, the alternative sources of reinforcement will increase in his environment and the reinforcing efficacy of the drug will diminish. This approach is one used by social service agencies throughout much of the world with some success (e.g., Thompson, Sowell, & Roll, 2009). Unfortunately, these agencies are often underfunded and unable to reach many of those most in need of their services. However, epidemiologic data support the notion that if we can prevent individuals from entering the morass of our hypothetical man, we can prevent them from drifting into a lifestyle characterized by addiction (e.g., Chilcoat & Johanson, 1998). As noted above, this is only one of many potential avenues leading to drug addiction. People living in environments that are rich in potential reinforcement may still develop addictions. However, just because your environment has reinforcement available does not guarantee that you will have the skills needed to gain access to the reinforcers. The forgoing is meant to be illustrative of one pathway to addiction and the role reinforcement plays in the pathway. I believe it is a common pathway, but clearly it is not the only pathway.

To reiterate, one observation—that providing high magnitude alternative sources of reinforcement decreases the proclivity of organisms to self-administer drugs of abuse—leads to an enhanced understanding of why drug addiction occurs, points the way towards an effective set of treatment modalities, and suggests potentially fruitful avenues for preventing, at least some, addiction in the first place. When you first encounter a phenomenon, you likely will not know what its full range of implications is going to be. However, in the field of the Experimental Analysis of Behavior and Behavioral Pharmacology it is likely that replicable, robust observations that transcend species, environments, and organisms will have profound effects for many clinical and research efforts.

Clinical Application

Behavioral pharmacology readily crosses from the research realm into the clinical realm in many ways. Drugs selected for development based, in part, on the screening work of behavioral pharmacologists are routinely employed to treat human and animal ailments as well as to enhance performance. Treatment modalities, such as contingency management, designed to reduce the reinforcing efficacy of an abused drug, are routinely employed in the treatment of substance abuse disorders. The translational research enterprise in behavioral pharmacology is quite robust, rivaling that in any other area of applied behavior analysis. Many of the clinical researchers in behavioral pharmacology are themselves clinicians or, at least, they work closely with clinicians actively engaged in the day-to-day treatment of addiction or behavioral health concerns. This provides an ideal crucible in which bidirectional research efforts can be implemented. By this I mean researchers and clinicians can collaborate and inform each other in the development of potential treatment efforts (Roll, Madden, Rawson, & Petry, 2009). Through this collaborative process clinicians and researchers can exchange ideas and observations based on replicable data and clinical experience. This process may enhance the likelihood that clinical research efforts will result in pragmatic, effective, and sustainable treatment modalities by ensuring that those who will employ the treatment—the clinicians—are active participants in the development of the protocols.

A logical extension of this bidirectional framework is that those who have recovered from an addiction—and maybe their families—might also be usefully involved in the development of clinical protocols because their unique, firsthand, experience may be valuable in framing new treatment approaches. This use of patient advocates is common in many medical fields (e.g., cancer research) but has not gained widespread acceptability in the field of behavioral pharmacology, perhaps because of the stigmatizing nature of drug addiction and mental health concerns in general. Unfortunately, many still place the blame for addiction and, more generally, mental health on those who suffer from the affliction and their families. This is largely unfounded and serves only to discourage those who need help from seeking the help that may be available. The inclusion of patient advocates in our research efforts may help ameliorate this state of affairs.

Conclusion

This brief and selective survey attempts to place behavioral pharmacology in its intellectual context as a subspecialty of the Experimental Analysis of Behavior. Certainly there is more than has been presented. In this chapter, I have tried to demonstrate how the power of behavioral observations which result from rigorous experimental control can have profound implications for many aspects of behavioral pharmacology. For those of you who are experts in the field, I am sure you would have selected different examples and organized things otherwise, but I hope you will find that my presentation has merit. For those of you just staring out in the field, I hope something in this chapter may have piqued your curiosity and challenged you to dig deeper. It has been my observation that, in behavioral pharmacology, Behavior Analysis has come the closest to realizing the full potential to impact society that Skinner foresaw (Skinner, 1953). I strongly encourage you to consult the sources listed in Table 24.1. They will point the way for a fuller appreciation of behavioral pharmacology.

References

Alessi, S. M., Roll, J. M., Reilly, M. P., & Johanson, C. E. (2002). Establishment of a diazepam preference in human volunteers following a differential-conditioning history of placebo versus diazepam choice. *Experimental Clinical Psychopharmacology*, *10*, 77–83. doi: 10.1037//1064-1297.10.2.77.

Andrade, L., & Petry, N. M. (2014). Contingency management treatments for substance-use disorders and healthy behaviors. In F. K. McSweeney & E. S. Murphy (Eds.), *The Wiley-Blackwell Handbook of Operant Conditioning* (pp. 627–644). Oxford: Wiley-Blackwell.

Anton-Stephens, D. (1954). Preliminary observations on the psychiatric uses of chlorpromazine (Largactil). *The British Journal of Psychiatry*, *100*, 543–557.

Balster, R. L., & Bigelow, G. E. (2003). Guidelines and methodological reviews concerning drug abuse liability assessment. *Drug and Alcohol Dependence*, *7*, 13–40.

Bouton, M. E. (2000). A learning theory perspective on lapse, relapse, and the maintenance of behavior change. *Health Psychology*, *19*, 57–63.

Carroll, M. E., Lac, S. T., & Nygaard, S. L. (1989). A concurrently available nondrug reinforcer prevents the acquisition or decreases the maintenance of cocaine-reinforced behavior. *Psychopharmacology*, *97*, 23–29.

Chilcoat, H. D., & Johanson, C. (1998). Vulnerability to cocaine abuse. In S. T. Higgins & J. L. Katz, (Eds.), *Cocaine abuse: Behavior, pharmacology, and clinical applications* (pp. 313–330). San Diego, CA: Academic Press.

Clifford, G. J. (1984). Edward Thorndike: *The sane positivist*. Middletown, CT: Wesleyan University Press.

Courtwright, D. (2001). *Forces of habit: Drugs and the making of the modern world*: Cambridge, MA: Harvard University Press.

Dutra, L., Stathopoulou, G., Basden, S. L., Leyro, T. M., Powers, M. B., & Otto, M. W. (2008). A meta-analytic review of psychosocial interventions for substance use disorders. *American Journal of Psychiatry*, *165*, 179–187. doi: 10.1176/appi.ajp.2007.06111851.

Freud, S. (2011). *Beyond the pleasure principle*. Canada: Broadview Press.

Gibbons, J. (1955). *I. P. Pavlov: Selected works*. Moscow: Foreign Languages Publishing House.

Harvey, J. A. (1971). *Behavioral analysis of drug action: Research and commentary*: Glenview, IL: Scott, Foresman.

Higgins, S. T., Bickel, W. K., & Hughes, J. R. (1994). Influence of an alternative reinforcer on human cocaine self-administration. *Life Sciences*, *55*, 179–187.

Higgins, S. T., & Hughes, J. R. (1998). Human behavioral pharmacology: An overview of laboratory methods. In K. A. Lattal & M. Perone (Eds.), *Handbook of research methods in human operant behavior* (pp. 579–618). New York: Plenum Press.

Higgins, S. T., & Katz, J. L. (1998). *Cocaine abuse: Behavior, pharmacology, and clinical applications.* San Diego, CA: Academic Press.

Higgins, S. T., Roll, J. M., & Bickel, W. K. (1996). Alcohol pretreatment increases preference for cocaine over monetary reinforcement. *Psychopharmacology, 123*, 1–8.

Higgins, S. T., & Silverman, K. (1999). *Motivating behavior change among illicit-drug abusers: Research on contingency management interventions.* Washington, DC: American Psychological Association.

Higgins, S. T., Silverman, K., & Heil, S. H. (2008). *Contingency management in substance abuse treatment.* New York: The Guilford Press.

Johanson, C. E., & Fischman, M. W. (1989). The pharmacology of cocaine related to its abuse. *Pharmacological Reviews, 41*, 3–52.

Johanson, C. E., Mattox, A., & Schuster, C. R. (1995). Conditioned reinforcing effects of capsules associated with high versus low monetary payoff. *Psychopharmacology, 120*, 42–48.

Johnson, M. W., & Bickel, W. K. (2006). Replacing relative reinforcing efficacy with behavioral economic demand curves. *Journal of the Experimental Analysis of Behavior, 85*, 73–93.

Kamien, J. B., Bickel, W. K., Hughes, J. R., Higgins, S. T., & Smith, B. J. (1993). Drug discrimination by humans compared to nonhumans: Current status and future-directions. *Psychopharmacology, 111*, 259–270. doi: 10.1007/Bf02244940.

Kuribara, H., Asami, T., Ida, I., & Tadokoro, S. (1992). Characteristics of the ambulation increasing effect of the noncompetitive nmda antagonist mk-801 in mice: Assessment by the coadministration with central-acting drugs. *Japanese Journal of Pharmacology, 58*, 11–18. doi: 10.1254/Jjp.58.11.

Lattal, K. A., & Perone, M. (1998). *Handbook of research methods in human operant behavior.* New York: Plenum Press.

Lussier, J. P., Heil, S. H., Mongeon, J. A., Badger, G. J., & Higgins, S. T. (2006). A meta analysis of voucher-based reinforcement therapy for substance use disorders. *Addiction, 101*, 192–203. doi: 10.1111/j.1360-0443.2006.01311.x.

Nader, M. A., & Woolverton, W. L. (1991). Effects of increasing the magnitude of an alternative reinforcer on drug choice in a discrete-trials choice procedure. *Psychopharmacology, 105*, 169–174. doi: 10.1007/Bf02244304.

Petry, N. (2011). *Contingency management for substance abuse treatment: A guide to implementing this evidence-based practice.* New York: Taylor and Francis Group.

Poling, A., & Byrne, T. (2000). *Introduction to behavioral pharmacology.* Reno, NV: Context Press.

Prendergast, M., Podus, D., Greenwell, L., Finney, J., & Roll, J. (2006). Contingency management for treatment of substance use disorders: A meta-analysis. *Addiction, 101*, 1546–1560. doi: 10.1111/j.1360-0443.2006.01581.x.

Roll, J. M. (2013). Contextual factors in addiction. In P. M. Miller, A. Blume, K. Kavanagh, K. Kampman, M. Bates, M. Larimer, N.M. Petry, P. de Witte, & S. A. Ball (Eds.), *Principles of addiction: Comprehensive addictive behaviors and disorders* (pp. 243–248). San Diego, CA: Academic Press.

Roll, J. M., Madden, G. J., Rawson, R., & Petry, N. M. (2009). Facilitating the adoption of contingency management for the treatment of substance use disorders. *Behavior Analysis in Practice, 2*, 4–13.

Roll, J. M., & Newton, T. (2008). Contingency management for the treatment of methamphetamine use disorders. In S. T. Higgins, K. Silverman, & S. H. Hiel, (Eds.), *Contingency management in the treatment of substance use disorders: A science-based treatment innovation* (pp. 80–99). New York: The Guilford Press.

Roll, J. M., Newton, T., Chudzynski, J., Cameron, J. M., McPherson, S., Fong, T., & Torrington, M. (2012). Preference for gamma-hydroxybutyrate (Ghb) in current users.

Journal of the Experimental Analysis of Behavior, 97, 323–331. doi: 10.1901/jeab.2012.97-323.

Roll, J. M., Reilly, M. P., Chudzynski, J., Mercado, P. (2009). Modulating the reinforcing effects of alcohol in humans. *Psychological Record, 59*, 335–346.

Roll, J. M., Reilly, M. P., & Johanson, C. E. (2000). The influence of exchange delays on cigarette versus money choice: A laboratory analog of voucher-based reinforcement therapy. *Experimental and Clinical Psychopharmacology, 8*, 366–370.

Silverman, K., Roll, J. M., & Higgins, S. T. (2008). Introduction to the special issue on the behavior analysis and treatment of drug addiction. *Journal of Applied Behavior Analysis, 41*, 471–480. doi: 10.1901/jaba.2008.41-471.

Skinner, B. F. (1938). *The behavior of organisms: An experimental analysis.* Acton, MA: Copley Publishing Group.

Skinner, B. F. (1953). *Science and human behavior.* New York: Macmillan

Skinner, B. F., & Heron, W. T. (1937). Effects of caffeine and benzedrine upon conditioning and extinction. *The Psychological Record, 1*, 340–346.

Thompson, L., Sowell, S., & Roll, J. M. (2009). Effects of methamphetamine on communities. In J. Roll, R. Rawson, W. Ling, & S. Shoptaw (Eds.), *Methamphetamine addiction: From basic science to treatment* (pp. 172–184). New York: The Guilford Press.

Thompson, T., & Schuster, C. R. (1968). *Behavioral pharmacology.* Englewood Cliffs, NJ: Prentice Hall.

Tuten, L. M., Jones, H., Schaffer, C., Stitzer, M. (2012). Reinforcement-based treatment for substance use disorders: A comprehensive behavioral approach. *The American Journal on Addictions, 21*, 499–500.

25

Contingency Management Treatments for Substance-Use Disorders and Healthy Behaviors

Leonardo F. Andrade and Nancy M. Petry

Drug use and abuse can be conceptualized as an operant behavior. Implicit in this definition is that drug use is under the control of environmental events, and therefore it can be initiated, maintained, and modified via the manipulation of external variables. Numerous studies conducted in controlled laboratory settings using nonhuman and human subjects have shown that drugs of abuse are positively reinforcing. For instance, laboratory animals, such as rats and monkeys, learn arbitrary operant responses when the behavior emitted produces a dose of morphine, amphetamine, or cocaine (e.g., Deneau, Yangita, & Seevers, 1969; Weeks, 1962).

In addition to the positive reinforcing function produced by the drug itself (e.g., euphoria), other consequences produced by drug use function as positive reinforcers, such as fitting in with others at social events. For those physiologically dependent, drugs also serve as negative reinforcers because their use remove withdrawal symptoms (e.g., Koob, Sanna, & Bloom, 1998; Skinner, 1953).

In this chapter we describe an evidenced-based behavioral treatment for drug abuse often referred to as contingency management (CM). The theoretical foundation of CM is based on the principles of operant conditioning. In this type of treatment, contingencies associated with drug use are manipulated to reduce the frequency of drug use. The core tenets of CM (Petry, 2000) are that the environment should be arranged in a manner that (1) the target behavior is objectively monitored; (2) tangible reinforcers are delivered contingent upon the detection of the target behavior, and (3) reinforcers are withheld when the target behavior is not emitted.

This chapter is structured in six parts. In "Historical Background of Contingency Management", we describe the initial studies and development of this approach, and in "Voucher-based Contingency Management" and "Prize-based Contingency Management", we describe the efficacy and applicability of voucher- and prize-based CM, respectively, as treatment approaches to promote abstinence in substance abusing populations. "Fundamental Elements and Parameters of CM" explains some of the

The Wiley Blackwell Handbook of Operant and Classical Conditioning, First Edition.
Edited by Frances K. McSweeney and Eric S. Murphy.

most important behavioral components embedded in effective CM interventions. In "Applying CM Toward Modification of other Behaviors", we go beyond abstinence-based reinforcement CM and describe how CM can be implemented to change other behaviors, including behaviors outside the substance abuse research arena. The final section of the chapter, "Incorporating New Technology into CM Programs" discusses the advent of new technology into CM programs and how it may facilitate its implementation and enhance its treatment effects.

Historical Background of Contingency Management

Early studies using contingency contracting show the effectiveness of operant conditioning principles in modifying substance use. Some initial studies were conducted in smokers enrolled in cessation treatment programs who received back monetary deposits contingently upon not smoking (Elliot & Tighe, 1968; Paxton, 1980, 1981). Stitzer and Bigelow (1982) used a within-subject reversal design (A-B-A) to evaluate the effect of monetary payments delivered contingently upon the objective verification of reductions in carbon monoxide (CO) levels. CO readings decreased from initial baseline levels when patients earned $5 per day for reductions in CO levels, and even after the contingencies were removed, smoking remained below baseline levels. Average expired CO levels during initial baseline, contingent reinforcement phase, and post-reinforcement phase were 28.0 parts per million (ppm), 17.3 ppm, and 18.2 ppm, respectively.

Miller (1975) applied reinforcement procedures to reduce drinking in chronic recidivist alcoholics. Twenty men, with long histories of drinking and multiple arrests for public drunkenness, were randomly assigned to a behavioral treatment or control condition. Patients in the behavioral treatment received goods and services from community agencies, such as clothing, meals, and employment, contingent on sobriety, whereas those in control group were provided the same services on a non-contingent basis. Alcohol use was accessed via observation of gross intoxication and alcohol breath tests conducted on a random basis. Among those in the contingent reinforcement group, reductions in public drunkenness arrests and alcohol consumption were noted, along with an increase in number of hours employed, compared to those in the control group. These initial studies showed that substance use could be changed by applying operant behavioral principles.

Voucher-Based Contingency Management

In the early 1990s, behavioral interventions termed contingency management were applied to cocaine abusing patients. Rather than relying upon monetary deposits or community services, Higgins and colleagues (1991, 1993) developed a voucher-based reinforcement system. In this system, patients earn vouchers worth a certain amount of money, and the vouchers are exchangeable for items of monetary value, such as sports equipment, electronics, clothing, etc. Vouchers are contingent upon submission of drug negative urine specimens.

The first study of voucher-based CM (Higgins et al., 1991) compared the efficacy of a multi-component behavioral treatment comprised of CM and community reinforcement approach therapy to 12-step counseling. The community reinforcement approach is a program grounded on operant principles which focuses on re-arranging naturalistic reinforcers associated with non-drug related behaviors to compete with the reinforcers produced by drug use. Higgins et al.'s (1991) clinical trial involved 25 consecutive admissions to an outpatient cocaine treatment program; the first 13 cocaine-dependent patients were assigned to the behavioral treatment, and the following 15 patients were offered 12-step oriented counseling. Treatment retention and abstinence was significantly higher for the patients receiving the behavioral treatment package compared to the 12-step counseling. More specifically, 85% of patients receiving the behavioral treatment remained in treatment throughout a 12-week period, whereas only 42% receiving the alternative treatment did. Longer duration of abstinence was also observed in patients receiving the behavioral treatment relative to the 12-step counseling. The proportion of patients in the behavioral treatment who achieved four and eight weeks of continuous abstinence was 77% and 46%, respectively, whereas the proportion of patients who attained four and eight weeks of continuous abstinence on the other group was 25% and 0%, respectively.

Following this study, Higgins and colleagues (1993) conducted a randomized clinical trial comparing the same two treatments, and the positive results of the CM intervention were replicated. In this trial, 19 cocaine-dependent patients were assigned to each treatment condition. Of those assigned to CM and community reinforcement approach treatment, 58% were retained through the 24-week treatment period, whereas only 11% of those assigned to 12-step treatment remained through the entire treatment period. Again, rates of continuous abstinence were significantly different between the two groups. Sixty-eight percent of the patients who received behavioral treatment achieved at least eight weeks of continuous abstinence, compared to only 11% of the patients receiving the alternative treatment. Importantly, follow-ups conducted at six, nine, and 12 months later showed that the patients from the voucher group were more likely to report abstinence from cocaine in the previous month as well as submit negative cocaine urine samples relative to patients from the 12-step counseling group (Higgins et al., 1995).

These two clinical trials show compelling evidence that a multi-component behavioral treatment, comprised of both CM and community reinforcement approach treatment, is more effective than usual standard counseling. These earlier studies, however, did not allow the evaluation of each component of the behavioral treatment package. To assess the unique contributions of CM, Higgins et al. (1994) conducted a subsequent trial in which cocaine dependents were randomly assigned to one of two treatment groups: community reinforcement approach treatment combined with CM or community reinforcement approach treatment alone. The study lasted for 24 weeks, but CM was in effect for only the first 12 weeks of the study. Treatment completion rates at 12 and 24 weeks for patients in the CM group were 90% and 75%, respectively, whereas completion rates in the non-CM group during the same periods were 65% and 40%. In regards to abstinence, 55% of the patients in the CM group achieved at least 10 continuous weeks of abstinence compared to only 15% in the group without CM. Further, the average duration of continuous abstinence across 12 and 24 weeks was approximately two times longer in the CM group compared to non-CM. During the first 12 weeks, duration of continuous abstinence were 7.2

vs. 3.9 weeks for the CM and non-CM groups, respectively; during the entire 24-week period, it was 11.7 vs. 6.0 weeks in the two respective groups.

In addition to cocaine, contingency management has demonstrated efficacy for promoting abstinence from a wide range of substances, such as alcohol, opioid, marijuana, methamphetamines, and tobacco (see Budney & Stanger, 2008; Epstein & Preston, 2008; Roll & Newton, 2008; Sigmon, Lamb, & Dallery, 2008; and Wong, Silverman, & Bigelow, 2008, for reviews). Meta-analyses of CM interventions also find strong benefits of CM compared to non-CM interventions (Lussier et al., 2006; Prendergast et al., 2006). A meta-analytical analyses of psychosocial treatments for substance-use disorders concluded that CM is the most efficacious intervention (Dutra et al., 2008).

Despite its empirically demonstrated efficacy in treating substance abuse, voucher-based CM has been rarely implemented in clinical practice. A primary issue hindering its implementation into drug abuse treatment programs is its high cost. In effective voucher CM interventions, patients can earn up to $1,200 over the course of a 12-week treatment period (Higgins et al., 1991, 1993, 1994; Silverman et al., 1996), and on average, patients' earnings are about $600 (Higgins et al., 1994; Silverman et al., 1996). Reducing the magnitude of voucher reinforcers available decreases the efficacy of the procedure (Dallery et al., 2001; Silverman et al., 1999). Thus, novel CM approaches are needed to extend this efficacious intervention to clinical treatment settings.

Prize-Based Contingency Management

Petry et al. (2000) developed a prize-based CM intervention that retains the benefits of voucher CM at lower costs. In prize-based CM, every time the target behavior is objectively demonstrated, patients have the opportunity to draw from a bowl and earn prizes. Typically, three magnitudes of prizes are available: "small," "large," and "jumbo." Small prizes are prizes that cost about $1, such as bus tokens, food items, toiletries, and $1 gift certificates. Large prizes cost up to $20, and they consist of items such as sporting goods, clothing, DVD/blue ray discs, watches, and gift cards to stores and restaurants. The jumbo prize is worth up to $100, and consists of items such as TVs, e-readers, gift cards, and/or combination of smaller magnitude prizes. The probability of drawing each kind of prize is inversely related to its magnitude. Typically, there are 500 slips of papers in the fishbowl, from which 50% are "winning" slips. Of these, 209 slips are small (41.8%), 40 are large (8.0%), and 1 is jumbo (0.2%). The other 250 non-winning prizes are comprised of an encouraging message, such as "good job!"

One of the main features of the prize system is that the patient has the chance of obtaining a reinforcer of high value in each draw, but the overall earnings (i.e., overall reinforcement rate) throughout the entire treatment is relatively low. In a 12-week treatment period, the maximal reinforcement programmed is on average about $250 to $400. Usually, patients' earnings during treatment are about half of the overall programmed reinforcement.

Because not every instance of the target behavior is reinforced with a tangible reinforcer, prize-CM can be conceptualized as an intermittent schedule of tangible reinforcement. Voucher-based CM, on the other hand, can be considered a fixed ratio schedule of reinforcement (or continuous rate of reinforcement, CRF) because each instance of the target behavior is reinforced with a tangible voucher. Compared to continuous reinforcement schedule, intermittent schedules typically generate greater rates of response and higher resistance to extinction (Ferster & Skinner, 1957; Nevin & Grace, 2000). The variable reinforcement nature of prize-CM is probably the feature responsible for promoting and sustaining high rates of the target behavior under a relatively lean schedule of reinforcement.

The first study evaluating prize CM was conducted by Petry et al. (2000). Forty-two alcohol-dependent men enrolled in a Veterans Affairs (VA) outpatient substance abuse treatment program were randomly assigned to standard care, consisting of relapse prevention, 12-step meetings, coping skills training, and AIDS education, or standard care combined with prize-CM. Patients from both groups submitted breath-alyzer samples at each daily visit to the VA, but only those from the CM group who provided negative sample were reinforced with the opportunity to draw for prizes. During the eight weeks of the study, 84% of patients in the prize-CM were retained, whereas only 22% in standard care remained in treatment during this period. Regarding alcohol use, 69% of those in the CM group remained abstinent throughout treatment versus 39% of those in the standard care. Patients receiving prize-CM were also less likely to relapse to heavy alcohol drinking by the end of the study than patients receiving standard care (26% vs. 61%). Patients in the CM group earned an average $200 worth of prizes.

Petry, Alessi, and colleagues (2005) compared this approach to voucher CM in cocaine-dependent patients. In this trial, 142 cocaine-dependent outpatients were randomly assigned to one of three conditions: standard care, standard care with prize CM or standard care with voucher CM. As expected, patients assigned to prize- or voucher-based CM remained in treatment longer and achieved longer duration of abstinence than the ones assigned to standard care alone. Individuals who received standard care only remained in treatment for 5.5 weeks, whereas the ones receiving prize- and voucher-based CM were retained in treatment for 9.3, and 8.2 weeks, respectively. Patients in standard care achieved 4.6 weeks of abstinence, and patients in the prize and voucher conditions attained 7.8 and 7.0 weeks, respectively.

These encouraging results prompted the National Institute on Drug Abuse Clinical Trials Network (CTN) to evaluate prize CM in community-based substance abuse treatment clinics across the country (Peirce et al., 2006; Petry, Peirce et al., 2005). These studies conducted in 14 community settings with over 800 stimulant abusing patients confirmed earlier results. Patients randomly assigned to CM remained in treatment longer and exhibited longer duration of abstinence than patients assigned to standard care. On average, patients earned between $120 and $203 in reinforcers, depending on the type of clinical setting (methadone vs. non-methadone). These studies demonstrate the efficacy of prize CM generalizes across different patient populations and settings.

Subsequent studies of prize CM have shown that its effects extend to opioid dependent (Petry et al., 2007; Petry & Martin, 2002), polydrug using (Petry, Weinstock, & Alessi 2011; Petry et al., 2011), and nicotine-dependent patients as well (Alessi, Petry, & Urso; 2008). A number of treatment programs have begun adopting and implementing prize CM in the context of clinical care (Kellogg et al.,

2005; Lott & Jencius, 2009; Squires, Gumbley, & Storti, 2008), and the VA began implementing CM interventions throughout its substance abuse treatment programs nationwide in 2011.

Fundamental Elements and Parameters of CM

Given that CM is an intervention based on operant conditioning principles, variables associated with behavior-analytic principles should be considered when designing a CM intervention. Below is a description of some of the most important behavioral components embedded in a CM intervention designed to reduce substance use (see also Petry, 2000, 2011).

Objective Verification of Behavior

As in any behavioral intervention, it is essential that the behavior targeted for reinforcement is clearly defined and objectively verifiable. Although verbal reports are an important component of the clinical process (Petry, Alessi, et al., 2010), tangible reinforcement should be delivered contingent on the objective demonstration of the target behavior (or the by-products of the target behavior). If the target behavior is abstinence from alcohol or drugs, the absence of substance consumption must be verified via some kind of biological test that produces reliable and valid readings of abstinence. Technically, CM for substance-use disorders is a differential reinforcement of other behavior (DRO).

Schedule/Frequency

The frequencies at which the target behavior is emitted, as well as the monitoring and reinforcement schedules, are also important features that greatly impact the effectiveness of the contingency. The target behavior should be one that occurs relatively frequently; otherwise, the reinforcement contingency is likely to be ineffective. If a patient uses cocaine only once every six months, for instance, it is unlikely that CM will produce meaningful changes in cocaine use.

The monitoring schedule also plays a prominent role in CM interventions. Ideally, a monitoring schedule for drug use should be arranged such that it can detect all instances of the target drug. Detection systems vary vastly across drugs of abuse. For example, alcohol and CO can only be detected over brief periods of time (i.e., a few hours; Lands, 1998; SRNT Subcommittee on Biochemical Verification, 2002), while cocaine and opioids remain detectable for about three days using standard urine testing procedures (Cone & Dickerson, 1992; Saxon, Calsyn, Haver, & Delaney, 1988). Thus, in CM interventions targeting alcohol or nicotine use, breath samples need to be monitored daily or even more frequently. In CM interventions for cocaine and opioid use, urine samples are usually collected two to three times per week. At the other end of the spectrum, marijuana remains detectable for one to three weeks in chronic marijuana users (Budney & Stanger, 2008; Johansson & Haldin, 1989). As a result, CM interventions for marijuana abstinence are more challenging to design and implement, because patients must be abstinent for several weeks in order to receive abstinence-based reinforcement.

Delay to Reinforcement

Numerous experimental studies conducted in nonhuman and human subjects show that delay to reinforcement greatly impacts reinforcement effectiveness. There is a vast body of literature, for example, providing compelling evidence that the value of a reinforcer not only decays in relation to the delay to its occurrence, but that it decays hyperbolically—meaning that the value decreases more sharply in the short run compared to the long run (see Green & Myerson, 2004, for a review of delay discounting).

Voucher CM can be conceptualized as a form of token economy system in which conditioned reinforcers are earned, accumulated, and exchanged for the final preferred reinforcers (e.g., the clothing or power tools). From this perspective, there are two interconnected reinforcement delays embedded into this system: the delay to the conditioned reinforcer (e.g., receipt of the voucher), and the delay to the exchange of the conditioned reinforcer for the preferred reinforcer (e.g., the goods or services). Both delays are important components of the overall contingency of reinforcement. Roll, Reilly, & Johanson (2000), for example, examined the control exerted by the voucher-exchange delays on smokers' choice between money and drugs using a laboratory-analog of voucher-based CM. Longer voucher-exchange delays produced increased preference for drug over money. The effect of the exchange immediacy was also demonstrated by Rowan-Szal et al. (1994) in a study in which methadone- maintained patients were reinforced with stars exchangeable for retail items after providing negative urine samples. Individuals who were exposed to a condition in which stars could be exchanged sooner provided more negative samples than ones who had to wait longer for the exchange period. Overall, CM interventions that provide more immediate exchange opportunities are more efficacious. A meta-analysis of CM studies also revealed that more immediate voucher-delivery was associated with significantly larger effect sizes (Lussier et al., 2006).

A main feature of prize CM is that prizes are kept onsite, so when patients draw a winning slip (the conditioned reinforcer) they exchange it immediately for their preferred tangible item. In voucher-based CM, however, the exchange of vouchers for retail items usually occurs with a delay of two to three days after the patient makes a request for voucher spending. Although the delay between non-drug using behaviors and the conditioned reinforcer delivery is similar in both CM systems, the delay to exchange the conditioned reinforcer for the preferred reinforcer is generally shorter in prize-based CM compared to voucher.

Magnitude

Behavior is also greatly impacted by reinforcement magnitude (e.g., Catania 1966). Nicotine abstinence, for example, increases as a direct function of the amount of monetary reinforcement available (Stitzer & Bigelow, 1983, 1984). Silverman et al. (1999) also reported that cocaine-dependent methadone patients who were resistant to treatment at the usual voucher amount achieved abstinence if amounts were tripled to $3000 over a 12-week period. In the context of prize-based CM, Petry et al. (2004) compared the efficacy of two prize magnitudes and also found that higher magnitude prizes were associated with greater abstinence. In a meta-analysis, Lussier et al. (2006) found that reinforcement magnitude impacted effect sizes of CM interventions.

Another important feature of CM interventions is escalating reinforcer magnitude for sustained behavior change. The magnitude of the vouchers increases as patients achieve consecutive periods of abstinence. For example, the first negative specimen submitted results in a $2.50 voucher, and voucher amounts increase by $1.25 for each subsequent consecutive negative specimen (Higgins et al. 1994). In addition, patients earned a bonus of $10 for each three consecutive negative specimens. Whenever a specimen was positive or the patient failed to submit a sample, the value of vouchers was reset to its initial value (i.e., $2.50). To illustrate the escalating procedure, a patient who remained abstinent for six consecutive tests, then provided a positive sample on the seventh test, and then two more negative samples would earn the following vouchers: $2.50, $3.75, $15.00 ($5 + $10 bonus), $6.25, $7.50, $18.75 ($8.75 plus $10 bonus), $0, $2.50, and $3.75.

Similar to voucher-based CM, prize-based CM also incorporates escalating reinforcement for consecutive negative samples to promote sustained behavior change. For instance, patients in the CTN studies earned increasing draws based on the number of weeks of consecutive abstinence (Peirce et al., 2006; Petry, Peirce et al., 2005. In many prize CM studies (e.g., Petry et al., 2012), draws increase by one for each consecutive negative sample submitted, but cap at a particular number (e.g., 10 draws) to contain costs.

Roll, Higgins, and Badger (1996) compared an escalating versus a fixed rate of reinforcement in cigarette smokers. Patients were assigned to one of three conditions. Condition 1 was comprised of three CO tests for smoking per day, and each negative breath test was reinforced with a fixed monetary amount of $9.80 in vouchers. Condition 2 was comprised of the same smoking test frequency, but each negative sample was reinforced with an escalating monetary amount in vouchers. Starting with $3.00 for the first negative test, vouchers increased by $ 0.50 each consecutive negative test with an additional bonus of $10 for every three negative tests in a row. Condition 3 was a yoked-control condition comprised of the same testing schedule in which vouchers were received non-contingently on the sample test results. All three conditions arranged the same overall magnitude of reinforcement. Patients in the escalating voucher condition were less likely to relapse to smoking than those in the other conditions, suggesting that the escalating system is an important feature in CM treatment.

Shaping

A concern related to CM interventions in treatment populations is that some patients do not achieve a long enough period of abstinence to test negative, and thus do not contact the reinforcement contingency. Iguchi et al. (1996), for example, reported that more than 45% of methadone-maintained substance abusing patients who were assigned to the CM condition did not earn a single reinforcer. One possible explanation for the non-responsiveness is that the value of the reinforcers used in the early stages of CM may be too small to compete efficiently with the reinforcers associated with drug use. Another possibility is that is that the requirement associated with the target response may be too high (e.g., one must achieve two to three days of abstinence prior to testing negative for cocaine or opioids).

The use of reinforcement for successive approximations (i.e., shaping) may be useful in this context. Instead of providing reinforcement contingently upon complete abstinence, a contingency can be arranged such that reinforcers are delivered contingently upon gradual approximations toward abstinence or treatment goals. To encourage attempts to abstain from cocaine, for instance, Elk et al. (1995) reinforced reductions in benzoylecgonine metabolites. In a similar vein, Dallery, Glenn, and Raiff (2007) shaped gradual reductions of CO levels in 20 heavy smokers for four days before starting the main abstinence-based reinforcement phase (see also Lamb et al., 2004, 2005). Although studies have used shaping to initiate abstinence, commonly used onsite testing systems for many illicit drugs of abuse provide only qualitative indices of substance use, precluding the use of shaping with some populations in typical clinical settings.

In sum, variables associated with behavior-analytic principles have great impact in determining the effectiveness of the contingency of reinforcement and thus must be considered carefully when designing and implementing a CM program. Although these variables were described mainly within the context of substance-use research targeting abstinence, their relevance extends to any response class, including behaviors outside the substance abuse research arena. Indeed, an increasing number of studies are implementing CM to modify other behaviors, some of which are described below.

Applying CM Toward the Modification of Other Behaviors

Compliance with Treatment Goals

Most studies implementing CM programs to treat substance abusers provide reinforcers contingent upon drug abstinence (i.e., DRO). An alternative or complementary approach is the implementation of a CM program to reinforce other treatment-related behaviors that compete or that are incompatible with drug use. Several studies have reinforced compliance with steps toward treatment goals, and results indicate that this procedure might improve treatment outcomes (Bickel et al., 1997; Iguchi et al., 1997; Petry et al., 2000, 2004; Petry, Alessi et al., 2005). In these studies, patients selected three activities to be completed per week based on his/her treatment goal(s). If the goal was to obtain employment, for example, a patient's activity could be attending an appointment with a job counselor. If the goal was to improve relationship with relatives, the activity could be going out on a social event with a specific relative (for a list of activities, see Petry, Tedford, & Martin, 2001). Contingent upon the successful completion of the established activity and provision of verifiable evidence, such as a receipt, patients earned vouchers or chances to draw prizes.

Bickel et al. (1997) used this approach to treat opioid dependent patients. Of the patients assigned to a voucher-based CM treatment package (comprised of CM for abstinence + CM for activities), 53% completed treatment compared to 20% of the patients in the standard treatment. Duration of continuous abstinence was also longer in the CM group compared to standard treatment. The percentage of patients assigned to CM who were able to achieve continuous abstinence through weeks 4, 8, 12, and 16 were 68%, 47%, 26%, and 11%, respectively. Among those assigned to standard care, only 55%, 15%, 5%, and 0% achieved these durations of abstinence. The correlation between the number of activities completed and weeks of continuous abstinence was .76, suggesting a strong association between completing activities and achieving abstinence.

However, in a study comparing directly the efficacy of a CM intervention that reinforced activity completion to one that reinforced abstinence, Petry et al. (2006) found that reinforcing abstinence engendered better effects than reinforcing completion of goal-related activities. Substance abusers who were assigned to an abstinence-based CM condition completed a median of 10.5 weeks of treatment, whereas those assigned to an activity-based CM condition completed 6.0 weeks. In regards to the number of negative samples, the same two groups submitted an average of 12.0 and 9.4 negative samples during the 12-week treatment period. These findings contrast with those of Iguchi et al. (1997), who found that a CM condition that reinforced activity completion promoted greater reductions in drug use in methadone patients than a CM condition that reinforced abstinence only. The differences between studies may relate to patient populations or procedural differences, but studies reviewed above nevertheless suggest that interventions that reinforce both abstinence and activity completion are efficacious. Additional research is investigating other objective behaviors to target in the context of substance abuse treatment, as outlined below.

Attendance at Treatment Programs

Up to 60% of scheduled appointments are not attended in substance abuse treatment programs (Lefforge, Donohue, & Strada, 2007). Many investigations have demonstrated that voucher- and prize-based CM programs are effective in increasing attendance (e.g., Petry, Martin, & Simcic, 2005; Ledgerwood et al., 2008; Sigmon & Stitzer, 2005). Ledgerwood et al. (2008), for example, evaluated the effectiveness of prize-CM in four community-based substance abuse clinics to increase attendance. The percentage of therapy sessions attended by substance abusers in CM groups was significantly higher (80%) than patients in the standard care non-CM groups (69%).

Petry et al. (2012) directly compared a CM intervention that reinforced attendance to one that reinforced abstinence in cocaine-dependent outpatients. Both CM interventions were equally efficacious in promoting longer durations of abstinence than a usual care, non-CM condition. Patients in the attendance reinforcement condition attended the greatest number of sessions and provided the most urine samples; however, the proportion of submitted samples that tested negative was lowest in this group (84% vs. >90%), suggesting that patients reinforced for attendance alone were either more likely to re-engage in treatment after a drug lapse or they used more drugs during treatment than those in other conditions. Concurrently reinforcing both attendance and substance abstinence, on the other hand, has clear benefits for increasing both behaviors (Petry, Weinstock, & Alessi, 2011).

Further research is necessary to assess the impact of reinforcing attendance exclusively on a wide variety of substance-use outcomes in these populations. Clearly, in behavior analyses, reinforcing any particular behavior is most likely to impact changes in the behavior targeted for change, while alterations in other related (or competing) behaviors may or may not occur. The next subsections describe other clinically relevant behaviors that can be modified using CM techniques.

Compliance with Medication

Compliance with medication is another response class that has been effectively modified via reinforcement in CM programs. A recent meta-analysis (Petry et al., 2012) identified 21 trials that compared reinforcement approaches to non-reinforcement approaches with respect to improving adherence to medications. Medication adherence was reinforced across a variety of patient conditions including substance abuse, tuberculosis, HIV, schizophrenia, hepatitis, and stroke prevention. This analysis found that CM interventions substantially improved compliance to medication relative to control conditions, with an overall effect size of 0.77. Studies that arranged for higher magnitude reinforcers, and more frequent reinforcement, yielded significantly larger effect sizes than those that provided lower magnitude and less frequent reinforcement.

Arranging a CM intervention to improve medication adherence, however, can be challenging due to difficulties in objectively monitoring medication adherence. In most populations and settings, direct observation is not possible, and delays between medication ingestion and reinforcement can reduce effectiveness. Innovative methods for monitoring behaviors directly or indirectly (via by-products of the behavior) have been developed using new technology, a point considered more fully in the last section of this chapter.

Exercise and Weight Loss

Contingency management has also been used to increase adherence to exercise and weight-loss regimens. We recently completed a pilot study in which older adults (55 years of age or older) wore pedometers for 12 weeks. Half were assigned to a monitoring and verbal encouragement alone intervention, and the other half to that same treatment plus chances to draw for prizes contingent on gradually increasing walking up to 10,000 steps per day. Those in the CM intervention walked an average of 9,276 steps per day compared with 7,576 among those assigned to the non-CM intervention, and these differences were statistically significant (Petry, Andrade, Barry, & Byrne, 2013).

Petry et al. (2011) evaluated the efficacy of a prize-CM program that provided reinforcers contingently upon losing weight. In this study, obese patients were randomly assigned to a well-validated weight-loss intervention alone or with CM. The patients exposed to CM as an adjunct to the weight-loss intervention lost significantly more weight on average (6.1 kg) than patients that were assigned to the weight-loss intervention program alone (2.7 kg). In another study, Volpp et al. (2008) similarly found that a reinforcement condition was more efficacious than a monitoring only control condition in enhancing weight loss.

In brief, an increasing number of studies are now implementing CM toward the modification of other behaviors. In this section, a few examples of this application were described, ranging from compliance with treatment goals and medication, to attendance to treatment and exercise programs, but this list is by no means exhaustive. The range of potential responses on which CM can be implemented effectively is expanding with the advent of new technology, a point addressed more fully in the next section.

Incorporating New Technology into CM Programs

Technology is changing at an incredibly fast-pace, and the incorporation of technological innovations into CM programs offers a range of unique opportunities to improve patient outcomes across a number of dimensions. Technology has great potential to facilitate CM implementation, enhance its treatment effects, and improve its dissemination as exemplified below.

One of the greatest advantages of the use of modern technology in the context of CM is that it can minimize the delay between behavior and reinforcement, as well as inconveniences associated with frequent clinic attendance for monitoring and reinforcement purposes. As noted earlier, abstinence-based reinforcement is especially challenging when the target behavior involves substances with short elimination half-life, such as nicotine and alcohol. The application of CM to promote reductions of alcohol and nicotine use using breathalyzers for alcohol and CO readings for smoking is onerous because testing should occur multiple times per day to ensure and reinforce total abstinence.

Dallery, Glenn, and Raiff (2007) used Internet technology to minimize burdens associated with CO monitoring. They implemented an Internet-based voucher program to promote nicotine abstinence using a home-based computer system and a website. Twenty patients were loaned CO monitors and computers equipped with web-cameras, and they were instructed to make videos of themselves providing CO samples twice per day. The videos, which depicted patients fully exhaling into the portable CO monitor and showing the final CO reading to the camera, were sent electronically to the smoking clinic so that the target behavior could be verified and reinforced. Significant decreases in CO levels were observed during the reinforcement phase relative to the baseline. In addition, high rates of overall sample collection was observed. Of the 1,120 samples scheduled, 1,092 (98%) were collected. Importantly, patients did not need to attend the clinic multiple times per day for monitoring, and reinforcement—or its proxy (e.g., notifications of voucher earnings)—could be delivered immediately over email (for a review of Internet-based CM to promote smoking cessation, see Dallery & Raiff, 2011).

The burden that frequent monitoring imposes on patients and treatment providers can be reduced even further with the use of smartphones. These devices have the advantage of even greater portability; they also can capture videos of sample testing, which can be sent remotely and reinforced nearly immediately. Alessi and Petry (2013) conducted a pilot study in which patients carried cellphones. Patients were randomly prompted to submit alcohol breath samples on hand-held breathalyzers while using the video function of the phone. All were modestly compensated for compliance with the monitoring procedure, and over 1,199 of 1,239 (90%) requested breath results were sent. Half of the participants received only compensation for submission of samples, and half were randomly assigned to a condition in which they also received reinforcement for breathalyzer results indicative of non-drinking. The percentage of abstinence days was 87% in those contingency reinforced for non-drinking vs. 67% for those in the monitoring only condition. These data suggest the feasibility and efficacy of using cell phone video recordings in conjunction with portable breathalyzers within a CM program.

Another illustrative example of the incorporation of new technology within the context of CM interventions relates to transdermal alcohol detection (Barnett et al., 2011). The Secure Remote Alcohol Monitoring Bracelet (SCRAM, Alcohol Monitoring Systems, Highlands Ranch, CO) is used to reduce recidivism among court-mandated driving while intoxicated offenders. This technology contains sensors that take frequent readings (about every 30 minutes) and are automatically transferred to a modem to a central monitoring system. Barnett et al. (2011) assessed the feasibility of this device as a part of a voucher-based CM intervention aimed at reducing drinking. After one week of baseline, 20 heavy drinkers were exposed to two weeks of CM in which monetary reinforcers were delivered contingently on abstinence as assessed by SCRAM. During the reinforcement phase, patients reduced their alcohol use substantially. The percentage of abstinence days in baseline was 9% versus 67% during the CM period.

The use of remote technology, including Internet, cell phones, and SCRAM, might also enhance CM accessibility across a wider range of populations, including those with difficulty accessing treatment providers. Stoops et al. (2009), for example, evaluated an Internet-based CM treatment (similar to that described earlier by Dallery, Glenn, & Raiff, 2007) in 68 smokers from rural areas of the United States. Patients were randomly assigned to voucher-based CM or a yoked-control condition, and results again showed that smokers in the CM condition were more likely to submit negative samples and achieve continuous abstinence than patients in the control group.

Extending beyond substance-use behaviors, technology is also widening the range of patient behaviors that can be objectively monitored and thus effectively modified in CM programs. Raiff and Dallery (2010) used an Internet-based CM intervention to increase adherence with blood glucose testing in adolescents with Type 1 diabetes. Patients earned vouchers contingent on testing and submitting videos via the Internet at least four times per day. During baseline condition, contingent-reinforcement-phase, and post-reinforcement phase, patients submitted on average 1.7, 5.7, and 3.1, respectively. Similarly, pedometer readings could be downloaded remotely to reinforce walking, and we have an ongoing pilot study using cell phone procedures to monitor and reinforce medication adherence remotely (Petry, 2012).

Conclusion

CM is an evidence-based behavioral treatment which is highly efficacious in promoting behavior change across populations and target behaviors. This chapter has briefly described the evolution of this behavioral treatment starting with early studies providing evidence that substance use is controlled by external variables to more advanced and sophisticated procedures that are now being widely applied in treatment settings across the nation. This chapter has also described the most fundamental components embedded in a successful CM program and how versatile CM interventions are in modifying behaviors. Finally, we discussed how the incorporation of new technology is revolutionizing CM by providing new ways to monitor and reinforce behavior more effectively.

References

Alessi, S. M., & Petry, N. M. (2013). A randomized study of cellphone technology to reinforce alcohol abstinence in the natural environment. *Addiction. 108*, 900–909. doi: 10.1111/add.12093

Alessi, S. M., Petry, N. M., & Urso, J. (2008). Contingency management promotes smoking reductions in residential substance abuse patients. *Journal of Applied Behavior Analysis, 41*, 617–622.

Barnett, N. P., Tidey, J., Murphy, J. G., Swift, R., & Colby, S. M. (2011). Contingency management for alcohol use reduction: A pilot study using a transdermal alcohol sensor. *Drug and Alcohol Dependence, 118*, 391–399.

Bickel, W. K., Amass, L., Higgins, S. T., Badger, G. J., Esch, R. A. (1997). Effects of adding behavioral treatment to opioid detoxification with buprenorphine. *Journal of Consulting and Clinical Psychology, 65*, 803–810.

Budney, A. J., & Stanger, C. (2008). Marijuana. In S. T. Higgins, K. Silverman, & S. H. Heil (Eds.), *Contingency management in substance abuse treatment* (pp. 61–79). New York: Guilford Press.

Catania, A. C. (1966). Concurrent operants. In W. K. Honig (Ed.), *Operant Behavior: Areas of research and application* (pp. 213–270). New York: Appleton-Century-Crofts.

Cone, E. J., & Dickerson, S. L. (1992). Efficacy of urinalysis in monitoring heroin and cocaine abuse patterns: Implications in clinical trials for treatment of drug dependence. In Jain, R. B. (Ed.), *Statistical issues in clinical trials for treatment of opioid dependence, National institute on Drug Abuse Research Monograph 128, DHHS Pub No. (ADM) 92-1947* (pp. 46–58). US Government Printing Office, Washington, DC.

Dallery, J., Glenn, I. M., & Raiff, B. R. (2007). An Internet-based abstinence reinforcement treatment for cigarette smoking. *Drug and Alcohol Dependence, 86*, 230–238.

Dallery, J., & Raiff, B. (2011). Contingency management in the 21st century: Technological innovations to promote smoking cessation. *Substance Use and Misuse, 46*, 10–22.

Dallery, J., Silverman, K., Chutuape, M. A., Bigelow, G. E., & Stitzer, M. L. (2001). Voucher-based reinforcement of opiate plus cocaine abstinence in treatment-resistant methadone patients: Effects of reinforcer magnitude. *Experimental and Clinical Psychopharmacology, 9*, 317–325.

Deneau, G., Yangita, T., & Seevers, M. H. (1969). Self-administration of psychoactive substances by the monkey. *Psychopharmacologia, 16*, 30–48.

Dutra, L., Stathopoulou, G., Basden, S. L., Leyro, T. M., Powers, M. B., & Otto, M. W. (2008). A meta-analytic review of psychosocial interventions for substance-use disorders. *The American Journal of Psychiatry, 165*, 179–187.

Elliott, R., & Tighe, T. (1968). Breaking the cigarette habit: Effects of a technique involving threatened loss of money. *The Psychological Record, 18*, 503–513.

Epstein, D. H., & Preston, K. L. (2008). Opioids. In S. T. Higgins, K. Silverman, & S. H. Heil (Eds.) *Contingency management in substance abuse treatment* (pp. 42–60). New York: Guilford.

Ferster, C. B., & Skinner, B. F. (1957). *Schedules of reinforcement.* New York: Appleton-Century-Crofts.

Green, L., & Myerson, J. (2004). A discounting framework for choice with delayed and probabilistic rewards. *Psychological Bulletin, 130,* 769–792.

Higgins, S. T., Budney, A. J., Bickel, W. K., & Foerg, F. E. (1994). Incentives improve outcome in outpatient behavioral treatment of cocaine dependence. *Archives of General Psychiatry, 51,* 568–576.

Higgins, S. T., Budney, A. J., Bickel, W. K., Badger, G. J., Foerg, F. E., & Ogden, D. (1995). Outpatient behavioral treatment for cocaine dependence: One-year outcome. *Experimental and Clinical Psychopharmacology, 3*: 205–212.

Higgins, S. T., Budney, A. J., Bickel, W. K., & Hughes, J. R. (1993). Achieving cocaine abstinence with a behavioral approach. *The American Journal of Psychiatry, 150,* 763–769.

Higgins, S. T., Delaney, D. D., Budney, A. J., & Bickel, W. K. (1991). A behavioral approach to achieving initial cocaine abstinence. *The American Journal of Psychiatry, 148,* 1218–1224.

Iguchi, M. Y., Belding, M. A., Morral, A. R., Lamb, R. J., & Husband, S. D. (1997). Reinforcing operants other than abstinence in drug abuse treatment: An effective alternative for reducing drug use. *Journal of Consulting and Clinical Psychology, 65,* 421–428.

Iguchi, M. Y., Lamb, R. J., Belding, M. A., Platt, J. J., Husband, S. D., & Morral, A. R. (1996). Contingent reinforcement of group participation versus abstinence in a methadone maintenance program. *Experimental and Clinical Psychopharmacology, 4,* 315–321.

Johansson, E., & Haldin, M. M. (1989). Urinary excretion half-life of D1-tetrahydrocannabinol-7-oic acid in heavy marijuana users after smoking. *Journal of Analytical Toxicology, 13,* 218–223.

Kellogg, S. H., Burns, M., Coleman, P., Stitzer, M., Wale, J. B., & Kreek, M. J. (2005). Something of value: The introduction of contingency management interventions into the New York City Health and Hospital Addiction Treatment Service. *Journal of Substance Abuse Treatment, 28,* 57–65.

Koob, G. F., Sanna, P. P., & Bloom, F. E. (1998). Neuroscience of addiction. *Neuron, 21,* 467–476.

Lamb, R. J., Kirby, K. C., Morral, A. R., Galbicka, G., & Iguchi, M. Y. (2004). Improving contingency management programs for addiction. *Addictive Behaviors, 29,* 507–523.

Lamb, R. J., Morral, A. R., Galbicka, G., Kimberly C. Kirby, K. C., & Iguchi, M. Y. (2005). Shaping reduced smoking in smokers without cessation plans. *Experimental and Clinical Psychopharmacology, 13,* 83–92.

Lands, W. E. (1998). A review of alcohol clearance in humans. *Alcohol, 15,* 147–160.

Ledgerwood, D. M., Alessi, S. M., Hanson, T., Godley, M. D., & Petry, N. M. (2008). Contingency management for attendance to group substance abuse treatment administered by clinicians in community clinics. *Journal of Applied Behavior Analysis, 41,* 517–526.

Lefforge, N. L., Donohue, D., & Strada, M. J. (2007). Improving session attendance in mental health and substance abuse settings: A review of controlled studies. *Behavior Therapy, 38,* 1–22.

Lott, D. C., & Jencius, S. (2009). Effectiveness of very low-cost contingency management in a community adolescent treatment program. *Drug and Alcohol Dependence, 102,* 162–165.

Lussier, J. P., Heil, S. H., Mongeon, J. A., Badger, G. J., & Higgins, S. J. (2006). A meta-analysis of voucher-based reinforcement therapy for substance-use disorders. *Addiction, 101,* 192–203.

Miller, P. M. (1975). A behavioral intervention program for chronic public drunkenness offenders. *Archives of General Psychiatry*, *32*, 915–918.

Nevin, J. A., & Grace, R. C. (2000). Behavioral momentum and the law of effect. *Behavioral and Brain Sciences*, *23*: 73–130.

Paxton, R. (1980). The effects of a deposit contract as a component in a behavioural programme for stopping smoking. *Behaviour Research and Therapy*, *18*, 45–50.

Paxton, R. (1981). Deposit contracts with smokers: Varying frequency and amount of repayments. *Behaviour Research and Therapy*, *19*, 117–123.

Peirce, J. M., Petry, N. M., Stitzer, M. L., Blaine, J. Kellogg, S., Satterfield, R., Li R. et al. (2006). Effects of lower-cost incentives on stimulant abstinence in methadone maintenance treatment: A national drug abuse treatment clinical trials network study. *Archives of General Psychiatry*, *63*, 201–208.

Petry, N. M. (2000). A comprehensive guide to the application of contingency management procedures in clinical settings. *Drug and Alcohol Dependence*, *58*, 9–25.

Petry, N. M. (2011). *Contingency management for substance abuse treatment: A guide to implementing evidence-based practice*. New York: Routledge.

Petry, N. M. (2012). Anti-retroviral medication adherence and secondary prevention of HIV. Unpublished manuscript.

Petry, N. M., Alessi, S. M., Carroll, K. M., Hanson, T., MacKinnon, S., Rounsaville, B., & Sierra, S. (2006). Contingency management treatments: Reinforcing abstinence versus adherence with goal-related activities. *Journal of Consulting and Clinical Psychology*, *74*, 592–601.

Petry, N. M., Alessi, S. M., Hanson, T., & Sierra, S. (2007). Randomized trial of contingent prizes versus vouchers in cocaine-using methadone patients. *Journal of Consulting and Clinical Psychology*, *75*, 983–991.

Petry, N. M., Alessi, S. M., Ledgerwood, D. M., & Sierra, S. (2010). Psychometric properties of the Contingency Management Competence Scale. *Drug and Alcohol Dependence*, *109*, 167–174.

Petry, N. M., Alessi, S. M., Marx, J., Austin, M., & Tardif, M. (2005). Vouchers versus prizes: Contingency management treatment of substance abusers in community settings. *Journal of Consulting and Clinical Psychology*, *73*, 1005–1014.

Petry, N. M., Andrade, L. F., Barry, D., Byrne, S. (2013). A randomized study of reinforcing ambulatory exercise in older adults. *Psychology and Aging*, *28*, 1164–1173.

Petry, N. M., Barry, D., Alessi, S. M., Rounsaville, B. J., & Carroll, K. M. (2012). A randomized trial adapting contingency management targets based on initial abstinence status of cocaine-dependent patients. *Journal of Consulting and Clinical Psychology*, *80*, 276–285.

Petry, N. M., Barry, D., Pescatello, L., White, W. B. (2011). A low-cost reinforcement procedure improves short-term weight loss outcomes. *The American Journal of Medicine*, *124*, 1082–1085.

Petry, N. M., & Martin, B. (2002). Low-cost contingency management for treating cocaine- and opioid-abusing methadone patients. *Journal of Consulting and Clinical Psychology*, *70*, 398–405.

Petry, N. M., Martin, B., Cooney, J. L., & Kranzler, H. R. (2000). Give them prizes and they will come: Contingency management for treatment of alcohol dependence. *Journal of Consulting and Clinical Psychology*, *68*, 250–257.

Petry, N. M., Martin, B., & Simcic Jr., F. (2005). Prize reinforcement contingency management for cocaine dependence: Integration with group therapy in a methadone clinic. *Journal of Consulting and Clinical Psychology*, *73*, 354–359.

Petry, N. M., Peirce, J. M., Stitzer, M. L., Blaine, J., Roll, J. M., Cohen, A. , Li, R. et al. (2005). Effect of prize-based incentives on outcomes in stimulant abusers in outpatient psychosocial treatment programs: A national drug abuse treatment clinical trials network Study. *Archives of General Psychiatry, 62*, 1148–1156.

Petry, N. M., Rash, C. J., Byrne, S., Ashraf, S., & White, W. B. (2014). Financial reinforcers for improving medication adherence: Findings from a meta-analysis. *American Journal of Medicine,125*, 888–896.

Petry, N. M., Tedford, J., Austin, M., Nich, C., Carroll, K. M., & Rounsaville, B. J. (2004). Prize reinforcement contingency management for treating cocaine users: How low can we go, and with whom? *Addiction, 99*, 349–360.

Petry, N. M., Tedford, J., & Martin, B. (2001). Reinforcing compliance with non-drug-related activities. *Journal of Substance Abuse Treatment, 20*, 33–44.

Petry, N. M., Weinstock, J., & Alessi, S. M. (2011). A randomized trial of contingency management delivered in the context of group counseling. *Journal of Consulting and Clinical Psychology, 79*, 686–696.

Petry, N. M., Weinstock, J., Alessi, S. M., Lewis, M. W., & Dieckhaus, K. (2010). Group-based randomized trial of contingencies for health and abstinence in HIV patients. *Journal of Consulting and Clinical Psychology, 78*, 89–97.

Prendergast, M., Podus, D., Finney, J., Greenwell, L., & Roll, J. (2006). Contingency management for treatment of substance-use disorders: A meta-analysis. *Addiction, 101*, 1546–1560.

Raiff, B. R., & Dallery, J. (2010). Internet-based contingency management to improve adherence with blood glucose testing recommendations for teens with Type 1 diabetes. *Journal of Applied Behavior Analysis, 43*, 487–491.

Roll, J. M., Higgins, S. T., & Badger, G. J. (1996). An experimental comparison of three different schedules of reinforcement of drug abstinence using cigarette smoking as an exemplar. *Journal of Applied Behavior Analysis, 29*, 495–505.

Roll, J. M., & Newton, T. (2008). Methamphetamines. In S. T. Higgins, K. Silverman, & S. H. Heil (Eds.), *Contingency management in substance abuse treatment* (pp. 80–98). New York: Guilford Press.

Roll, J. M., Reilly, M. P., & Johanson, C-E. (2000). The influence of exchange delays on cigarette versus money choice: A laboratory analog of voucher-based reinforcement therapy. *Experimental and Clinical Psychopharmacology, 8*, 366–370.

Ronith, E., Schmitz, J., Spiga, R., & Rhoades, H. (1995). Behavioral treatment of cocaine-dependent pregnant women and TB-exposed patients. *Addictive Behaviors, 20*, 533–542.

Rowan-Szal, G., Joe, G. W., Chatham, L. R., & Simpson, D. D. (1994). A simple reinforcement system for methadone clients in a community-based treatment program. *Journal of Substance Abuse Treatment, 11*, 217–223.

Saxon, A. J., Calsyn, D. A., Haver, V. M., & Delaney, C. J. (1988). Clinical evaluation of urine screening for drug abuse. *The Western Journal of Medicine, 149*, 296–303.

Sigmon, S. C., Lamb, R. J., & Dallery, J. (2008). Tobacco. In S. T. Higgins, K. Silverman, & S. H. Heil (Eds.), *Contingency management in substance abuse treatment* (pp. 99–119). New York: Guilford Press.

Sigmon, S. C., & Stitzer, M. L. (2005). Use of low-cost incentive intervention to improve counseling attendance among methadone maintained patients. *Journal of Substance Abuse Treatment, 29*, 253–258.

Silverman, K., Chutuape, M. A., Bigelow, G. E., & Stitzer, M. L. (1999). Voucher-based reinforcement of cocaine abstinence in treatment-resistant methadone patients: Effects of reinforcement magnitude. *Psychopharmacology, 146*, 128–138.

Silverman, K., Higgins, S. T., Brooner, R. K., & Montoya, I. D. (1996). Sustained cocaine abstinence in methadone maintenance patients through voucher-based reinforcement therapy. *Archives of General Psychiatry, 53*, 409–415.

Skinner, B. F. (1953). *Science and human behavior.* New York: Macmillan.

Squires, D. D., Gumbley, S. J., & Storti, S. A. (2008). Training substance abuse treatment organizations to adopt evidence-based practices: The Addiction Technology Transfer Center of New England Science to Service Laboratory. *Journal of Substance Abuse Treatment*, *34*, 293–301.

SRNT Subcommittee on Biochemical Verification. (2002). Biochemical verification of tobacco use and cessation. *Nicotine and Tobacco Research*, *4*, 149–159.

Stitzer, M. L., & Bigelow, G. E. (1982). Contingent reinforcement for reduced carbon monoxide levels in cigarette smokers. *Addictive Behaviors*, *7*, 403–412.

Stitzer, M. L., & Bigelow, G. E. (1983). Contingent payment for carbon monoxide reduction: Effects of pay amount. *Behavior Therapy*, *14*, 647–656.

Stitzer, M. L., & Bigelow, G. E. (1984). Contingent reinforcement for carbon monoxide reduction: Within-subject effects of pay amount. *Journal of Applied Behavior Analysis*, *17*, 477–483.

Stoops, W. W., Dallery, J., Fields, N. M., Nuzzo, P. A., Schoenberg, N. E., Martin, C. A., Casey, B., & Wong, C. J. (2009). An internet-based abstinence reinforcement smoking cessation intervention in rural smokers. *Drug and Alcohol Dependence*, *105*, 56–62.

Volpp, K. G., John, L. K., Troxel, A. B., Norton, L., Fassbender, J., & Loewenstein, G. (2008). Financial incentive-based approaches for weight loss: A randomized trial. *Journal of the American Medical Association*, *300*, 2631–2637.

Weeks, J. R. (1962). Experimental morphine addiction: Method for automatic intravenous injections in unrestrained rats. *Science*, *138*, 143–144.

Wong, C. J., Silverman, K., & Bigelow, G. E. (2008). Alcohol. In S. T. Higgins, K. Silverman, & S. H. Heil (Eds.), *Contingency management in substance abuse treatment* (pp. 120–139). New York: Guilford Press.

26

Organizational Behavior Management

Past, Present, and Future[1]

William B. Abernathy and Darnell Lattal

Overview of Chapter

Organizational behavior management (OBM) is the application of the science of behavior analysis in the workplace. OBM practitioners strive to improve the performance of individuals and groups by using direct observation of behavior and related measures of results. Practitioners identify and apply contingencies of reinforcement to achieve immediate and long-term behavior change through direct intervention and by transferring behavior-analytic skills to members of organizations. Individual performers' progress in achieving desired results is the core metric by which OBM's success is measured.

The domains of OBM are the structures, systems, processes, and related behavior patterns of individuals and groups within organizations. Although the techniques apply to any system of work, such as a classroom, volunteer group, or public enterprise, most of what OBM practitioners do, and the majority of reported research and case studies, take place in for-profit corporations.

Areas of focus across OBM encompass a range of organizational issues, including but not limited to:

- organizational strategic and tactical alignment to achieve desired outcomes;
- individual and group behavior change (coaching, training, computer-based instruction);
- performance improvement (selection, retention, development, fluency, quality, sales, service, instructional design, and design of motivational systems);
- safety (behavior-based, front line; safety leadership; total safety systems);
- organizational change (analysis, strategy implementation, leadership effectiveness);
- health and wellness (tactics, feedback, systems for worker and patient health).

The Wiley Blackwell Handbook of Operant and Classical Conditioning, First Edition.
Edited by Frances K. McSweeney and Eric S. Murphy.

The 21st century conditions of work are rapidly adapting to advanced technology changes taking the place of routine practices of the last century. More highly skilled workers are needed in almost every industry. Populations of well-trained workers in the United States are aging, with retirement looming. The need to replace skilled workers places a premium on hiring people who adapt and learn quickly. The lessons of the recent recession, caution in hiring, and getting more from less, are shaping a leaner workplace. Tools to facilitate new learning are increasingly in demand. Technological advances provide ease in entering international marketing and sales, training of employee groups, obtaining and serving distant customers, and setting up satellite offices.

The laws of behavior remain the same regardless of approaches within or across businesses. Consultants will be at a premium who design fluency into evolving content, help companies adapt to innovative practices, and stabilize a diverse workforce while achieving results. All these skills are present in the OBM tool chest.

As we move into the 21st century, practitioners of OBM are designing solutions that are sustainable. Such solutions need to pinpoint, measure, and reinforce the right skills of employees. These solutions build systems of consequences into the fabric of work, placing a premium on reinforcers available in the workplace to create enduring patterns of high performance and business success. Work need not be punishing. Twenty-first century workplaces can build in reinforcement systems such that employees "know no distinction between working and playing" (Jacks, 1932).

The chapter has four sections. Section 1 begins with a reexamination of Skinner's rarely quoted and valuable writings about what work and the workplace can be. We describe how management practices have evolved in the 20th century. The section ends with selected early behavior-analytic efforts to shape workplace practices. Section 2 highlights core skills required to practice OBM. Section 3 examines how human resource systems define the culture of the workplace through a range of reinforced behavior patterns. The authors suggest that principles of behavior analysis be designed directly into the framework of an organization's structures and processes to sustain individual and group efforts to achieve performance excellence. Section 4 discusses the emerging behavior systems perspective that moves beyond linear views of systems control. This behavior systems perspective is horizontal (work flow) and vertical (contingencies of reinforcement). The authors promote a new contextual view that sustains effective and fluent workplace behavior without the need for most of the current manager-led processes of supervision that are intended to guide workplace behavior today.

An Annotated History of OBM and its Historical Roots

Back to the Future. Skinner's early, sometimes seemingly offhanded, insights into workplace behavior are stunning, seminal, and lasting. Skinner's writings are rarely explored for the directional and design significance that they hold for OBM practices today as illustrated by this small sample of his writings.

Skinner's writings from 1948 onward emphasized designing systems that allow behavior to find its purpose through contingencies of reinforcement. Behavior systems management or contingency management is a better term for the application of

Skinner's theory of organizations, rather than behavior management or behavior modification.

Many things that Skinner wrote are as fresh today as when they were written, up to seven decades ago. Other ideas have been supplemented and elaborated in directions he probably did not anticipate. Skinner discovered fundamental behavioral processes, not mere social constructions. These processes have a basis in reality to the same extent that fundamental laws of physics are universal. Skinner's insights have contemporary relevance because the principles of behavior he articulated (his "truths") are scientific truths that have weathered the test of time and situational generality.

Skinner did not write much about the application of his principles to existing organizations. Nevertheless, he often proposed that the best policies for individual success in organizations were those that eliminated coercion, direct supervision, and restrictive rules. Contingency-shaped, fluent, behavior patterns (sometimes called self-managed patterns) allow the performer to achieve worthy performance primarily through natural reinforcers of work. He was not particularly interested in designing workplaces to implement rules of conduct that limited adaptive patterns, but rather in designing a workplace that reinforced the adaptive behavior patterns that were most effective or efficient for a given situation. When dealing with behavior in the context in which it occurs, Skinner (1953) stated:

> Behavior is a difficult subject matter, not because it is inaccessible, but because it is extremely complex. Since it is a process, rather than a thing, it cannot be held still for observation. It is changing, fluid, evanescent . . . But there is nothing insolvable about the problems that arise from this fact. (p. 15)

Skinner (1987) had much to say about coercive management and wrote that pay by the day or week is often mistakenly called positive reinforcement. Instead, its real function is to establish a standard of living from which the worker can be cut off. As he saw it, production in industry depends in great part on subordination, discipline, and acceptance of managerial authority. Traditional management approaches, natural or contrived, do little to establish positively reinforcing consequences. Conventional wage and salary systems pay for time. There are time clocks and time sheets, part-time and full-time employees, overtime, under-time, vacation time, and sick time. In Skinner's view, people should be paid for what they produce. As productivity improves, the time at work should decrease. He would not set hours or time as a condition for pay. Skinner cared more about contingency and effect.

With respect to direct supervision, Skinner wrote "that we cannot foresee" all future circumstances (1948). "You do not know what will be required. Instead, you set certain behavioral processes which lead the individual to design his own 'good conduct' when the time comes (1948)." In general, by allowing natural consequences to take control whenever possible, appropriate behavior is more likely to occur. Skinner (1987) argued that we promote the survival of the individual, the culture, and the species by allowing natural consequences to prevail.

Contrived reinforcers must eventually be terminated as natural reinforcers take over in both education and therapy. Skinner (1987) argued that the teacher or therapist must be able to withdraw from the life of the student or client before teaching or therapy can said to be complete. In the same vein, the manager as traditional overseer will no longer be needed to maintain employee performance. Rather naturally occurring reinforcers will replace the manager's work to a large extent.

Skinner (1948) examined competition between workers. Philosophically, he argued that recognizing and admiring the exceptional achievement of one person over another was the wrong strategy if ". . . it points up the unexceptional achievements of others. We are opposed to personal competition." Daniels (2009) has written of the pitfalls of "employee of the month" recognition and other awards that pit performers against one another. Such strategies set up competition that can suppress, not promote, accomplishment, thus limiting performance (Hake & Olvera, 1978; Hake, Olvera, & Bell, 1975).

Skinner (1969) drew a distinction between rule-governed and contingency-shaped behavior. He wrote:

- Contingency-shaped behavior has many fewer unwanted by-products.
- The person feels free . . . doing what he/she [needs] wants to do.
- Behavior that can be shaped by nonsocial contingencies is as universal as those contingencies themselves.
- Contingency-shaped behavior is more likely to be associated with joy.
- Contingency-shaped behavior is likely to have a greater variety or richness.
- Contingencies contain reasons which rules can never specify.

Skinner had much to say about rule-governed behavior. For example, the likelihood of following a rule is mainly controlled by the consequences that follow it. Rules of conduct civilize us in many ways, but contingency-shaped responses both control the likelihood of rule following and provide flexibility and fluidity in responding to demands of the workplace. Understanding the dynamic relationship between behavior and reinforcement is critical to establishing and maintaining rules in settings where it is imperative that rules are followed (i.e., high hazard conditions).

Skinner also was concerned about entropy in which management moves from positive reinforcement, with minimal direct supervision and rules, back to the traditional coercive, closely supervised, rule-governed organization. As units expand in size, an absence of skill in how to manage many people may reinforce coercive strategies.

In a Skinnerian style of management, day-to-day management is performed by self-managed individual employees or by employee teams. Skinner's Walden Two Planners (those we call executives and their support teams today) connect the employee teams to the external environment or meta-contingencies. Organizational goals developed by the planners cascade with increasing specificity through middle and line management to individual workers and work teams. Each performer is connected to and informed of, the outcomes needed to sustain the business and/or its culture. Planners analyze revenue and conditions (e.g., consumer preferences, the market, resources, governmental regulations, competition, changes in technology) to increase profits. Behavior Systems Analysts (human resource specialists) translate the planners' strategies into employee motivational systems and performance measures. They also identify and remove constraints on performance such as poor scheduling or work methods. Mentors or coaches (managers or supervisors) help employees gain skills and guide their development along a number of dimensions. In the best

Skinnerian future, systems are designed to recognize mentors (today's supervisors) for ensuring that their employees succeed. In that future, systems that reinforce effective employee behavior are central to company success.

Early Management Experts. There was no Burrhus Frederick Skinner at the turn of the 20th century and thus no behavior analysis as known today. But there were skillful people applying technology that changed human behavior. Several early American management experts systematically observed behavior and applied new methods for doing work.

Frederick Winslow Taylor (1911) introduced the time card, functional oversight of workers' performance, differential piece-rate compensation, and other methods of decreasing cost and increasing productivity and wages. He introduced aligning specific behaviors with desired results. Even though he was a controversial figure (Stewart, 2009), many elements of his efforts made significant changes in production. These elements continued to evolve and later were directly adopted by Toyota as part of its approach to manufacturing. To this day, his work is considered the beginning of much of modern management. He stated that managers should:

1. Replace rule-of-thumb work methods with a scientific study of the tasks.
2. Scientifically select, train, and develop employees rather than having them train themselves.
3. Provide detailed instruction and supervision to each worker on that worker's discrete task.
4. Divide work between managers and workers with managers applying scientific management principles to plan the work and workers performing related tasks.

Taylor was influenced by the technological revolution seen in the industrial revolution of the early 20th century. His dictate that man was second to the system was just one of the fallacies that guided his assumptions about behavior. Nevertheless, before him, the system of how work was to be done was ill formed and often illogical.

Taylor insisted on minute examination and reexamination of behavior at each step required to achieve particular outcomes. The process of defining critical tasks by refining pinpointed behaviors was done through a process that looks very much like backward chaining today (Keller & Schoenfeld, 1950). Kaplan and Norton (1996), Daniels and Daniels (2004), and Abernathy (2011), among others, have continued to refine this analysis of behavior at each organizational level.

Other early management experts, Gilbreth and Gilbreth (1917), advocated that workers engage in the smallest, most effective behavioral unit possible. The work of the Gilbreths, along with that of others, increased attention to efficiency (minimal time and effort to achieve a result) and effectiveness (the quality or effect of the behavior). The technology of machinery shaped the emergence of these new management practices. For example, the growth of assembly lines required a focus on efficiency, time, motion, and related elements of human performance.

Quality guru W. Edwards Deming found an audience in Japan after World War II to introduce more effective manufacturing processes. He gained ground in the United States where his quality approaches (Deming, 1986) were widely adopted. They are used in almost all manufacturing plants today. OBM practitioners in manufacturing settings should understand the quality processes (e.g., statistical processes) that grew from Deming's advocacy (Mawhinney, 1987). Lean, Six Sigma, Kaizen, Total Quality Management, and other engineering management processes, provide useful approaches for effective technical process management. However, such linear designs rarely take into account the effects of contingencies of reinforcement occurring along the way. Examining these engineering processes provide behavior analysts a starting place for identifying naturally occurring contingencies of reinforcement that could be built into the process to achieve the desired effect.

Near the end of his life, Deming indicated that manpower, a component of his analysis, was critical to the rest of the quality chain, but he acknowledged knowing little about how to motivate behavior. Today OBM practitioners add value by addressing motivating elements, such as behavioral drift and unintended consequences, that arise even from well-designed process flow maps and quality tools (McCarthy, 2011). Still, the science of behavior analysis remains outside the purview of many who design improvement processes. In addition, some in OBM are unaware of the highly refined tools of quality and process engineering that can help to clarify and sustain well-designed systems of motivation.

Initial OBM Applications. Early applications of behavior analysis in the 1950s, 1960s, and 1970s influenced OBM methods today. In the interest of brevity, the authors encourage the reader to explore the workplace-changing strategies of applied behavior analysis pioneers whose work gave rise to OBM. Sources include Balcazar, Hopkins, and Suarez (1985), Andrasik (1989), Dickinson (2000), Alvero, Bucklin, and Austin, (2001), and Abernathy (2012a). Compilations of readings in OBM are available in the works of Austin, Clayton, Houmanfar, and Hayes (2001), O'Brien, Dickinson, and Rosow (1979), and Frederiksen (1982).

Owen Aldis (1961) is considered to be the first to expose a broad American business readership to how managers could use operant principles to address workplace issues in his *Harvard Business Review* (HBR) article entitled "Of Pigeons and Men." Aldis's piece, however, had no demonstrable effect on the business community nor in demand for future articles on OBM in the HBR.

Tom Gilbert (2011) was probably the first behavior analyst to conduct actual behavioral observations in typical work settings. In the late 1950s and 1960s, he observed how candy and pharmaceutical sales representatives, forklift truck and yellow pages salesmen, interacted with customers. Quotable advice offered by Gilbert include: "Look before you listen" (observe before you interview) and "Observe accomplishments" (find examples of successful behavior). Such advice is essential for good practice today. In addition, Gilbert identified how to operationalize worthy performance. He compared the accomplishments of the one who achieves the strongest result (sales, production, quality, efficiency) in a given setting (the exemplar), with what is possible for all performers in that environment.

Ayllon and Azrin (1965) applied operant principles to a closed psychiatric ward at Anna State Hospital. Their application contains many elements relevant to OBM today. They removed psychotropic medication from psychiatric patients in an enclosed area of the hospital while persuading leadership of the hospital to sponsor the program, and remove institutional barriers to setting up a token economy for some patients. Reinforcement was provided when behavior occurred in desired, directionally correct, ways. The patients were not getting dressed, so getting dressed was one of the behaviors that earned tokens which were exchanged for back-up reinforcers.

Working as a tour guide and working at a mini-store on the ward, earned tokens. Those behaviors were not artificial, but functional, skills that were adaptive to life outside the institutional environment.

Over time, as the individual's behavior came under environmental control, the reinforcers were changed to choices made by the individual such as time outside by oneself, choice of clothing and décor, selection of roommates or a room alone, and conversational events in social settings (Ayllon, personal communication, November 2012).

Ayllon and Azrin's token economy was an example of how to arrange working conditions to shape desired behavior. It introduced a unit-wide system of behavior control inside a hospital workplace (in effect, the company) that changed many patterns of behavior through the appropriate arrangement of consequences in the form of individually-selected reinforcers. As in any work setting, people got paid (the token) as they exhibited specific patterns required to do their "job" of adapting. Ayllon and Azrin's work stands as a uniquely designed demonstration of and, profound respect for, how organizational environments can be arranged to help people make good behavioral choices that advance their freedom and dignity.

In the mid-1960s, Aubrey Daniels' implementation of a similar token economy system in a hospital system prepared him for applications of this technology in business. He used the term *performance management* in his introduction of behavior analysis to the workplace and in the first edition of his textbook in the 1980s (Abernathy, 2012a; Daniels & Daniels, 2004). Daniels was the founding editor of the *Journal of Organizational Behavior Management (JOBM)*. He continues to champion the notion that managers and supervisors should use positive reinforcement strategies to influence employee behavior whenever possible. His insistence on teaching managers to use positive reinforcement as their core methodology to help employees achieve rapid and sustained behavior change continues to find practitioners in countries around the world. Those practitioners report that the concept is revolutionary compared to conventional management practices, which are often based on techniques of aversive control and extinction.

Edward J. Feeney had no formal training in behavior analysis. He attended a seminar on the topic and applied his new knowledge at his organization, Emery Airfreight. The successful projects were reported in the 1972 *Business Week* article "Where Skinner's Theories Work." The result was an increased interest in OBM in the business community.

Dale Brethower (1972) introduced a different kind of analysis to arrange and control behavior, from a focus on shaping individual behavior to producing well-designed behavior systems. Behavior systems analysis improves traditional work process systems involving input, throughput, and output to more effectively address performance. It is one of those early prescient indications of what would become a 21st century call to action to help clients achieve long-term OBM success.

In 1978, West Virginia University's (WVU) Psychology Department was the first to offer a subspecialty in behavioral systems when it introduced a behavioral systems track into its Ph.D. program (Hawkins, Chase, & Scotti, 1993). The faculty, many of whom went on to consult in applied business practices (e.g., Krapfl, Maley, Noah, Harshbarger), encouraged the examination of the contingencies of reinforcement present in the context of work as the source for guiding individual achievement.

Faculty at WVU encouraged their students to consider the cultural context and contingencies that may not be directly apparent in the work that is performed. Today, the context of work is still rarely explored closely enough to understand the controlling variables that operate on classes of behavior. A systems approach relies less on rules of conduct by which behavior is initiated than on exploring the unintended contingencies of reinforcement that maintain counterproductive patterns. By introducing a larger framework for individual performers, they introduced an approach to behavior change that was similar to the earlier work by Ayllon and Azrin, among others. They also exhibited an interest in the controlling variables found in verbal behavior and private events. Since this initial work, some of the faculty of that era have gone on to suggest an even more robust system of contextual control, described at the end of this chapter (Harshbarger & Maley, 1974).

OBM Practices and Research

Essential OBM Consulting Skills. Many variables contribute to effective consulting. First and foremost, continuous education in behavior analysis—basic, applied, and conceptual—is essential to deriving novel solutions to novel problems and to enhancing the everyday experiences of employees at all levels of operational authority. Although such knowledge is necessary, it is not sufficient to produce a successful practitioner. We highlight four areas important to long-term success: (1) functional analysis, (2) shaping, (3) relationship skills, and (4) ethical behavior.

Skills in Functional Analysis. As originally used by Skinner (1938), functional analysis refers to identifying the conditions in the environment that establish both antecedent and consequence control over behavior. One cannot solve behavioral problems without a functional analysis. OBM practitioners consider how systems, processes, and conditions of work affect individual performers to become antecedent and consequence sources of behavior change. Providing a functionally-analytic perspective in explaining why people do what they do helps clients see how to evaluate environmental controls to develop and sustain desired behavior patterns.

Shaping: The Wellspring of OBM Success. Shaping involves differentially reinforcing successive approximations to the goal or target behavior. Nothing is more important than doing just that—reinforcing directionally correct patterns of behavior through the precise application of shaping. While many people are creative, adaptive, and successful in shaping behavior without behavior analysts as guides, introducing managers to the rigors of technically correct shaping provides insights that enhance their ease in managing other's successful acquisition of skills.

Relationship Skills. Agnew (2012) proposed that how well the consultant serves as a potential reinforcer for client behaviors is important. She meant that relationships, how likeable the consultant coach is, matters to his or her success. Because behavior analysts are often involved in coaching others, and clients select those they want to work with, positive social skills help to maintain relationships and increase the opportunity to shape success. While not the only factor in success, such positive relationships increase the likelihood that the client does the work required to achieve behavior change.

Among the interpersonal skills that Bailey and Burch (2010) considered useful were networking, behaving ethically, gaining influence, handling power, and what they called demonstrating broad curiosity about the behavioral world around them. These qualities can help to strengthen work in companies and they increase the probability of returning the next morning to do it again. Being alert to one's own effects is a large and never ending obligation of an OBM consultant.

Ethical Behavior: Slippery Slopes and Unintended Consequences. OBM practitioners are not immune from the effects of the businesses in which they work. We need to be alert to the slippery slope of reciprocal relationships. Ethics is defined as a system of moral principles and rules of conduct with respect to a particular class of human actions or by a particular group or culture. It also refers to the moral principles by which individuals evaluate their own conduct. What is ethical is most often defined by the effects of behavior on outcomes, both short- and long-term, not simply by the intention to do good.

Determining what is ethical is not easy. Ethical actions are defined by prevalent values of society and sometimes by subgroup values within that society (Lattal & Clark, 2007). America is a pluralistic society so it is difficult to take one principle (e.g., the Golden Rule) as sufficient to define what is ethical in a given situation. The ethical impact of a behavior may occur long after the original behavior. It is also rare that absolute definitions of ethical actions exist outside of the specific context in which they occur. Finally, ethical conduct may be difficult for the performer to determine. We often do not see the effect of what we do (versus what we say we *intend* to do).

The use of positive reinforcement does not imply that the reinforced behavior will be positive. The immoral actions of storm troopers, Enron executives, and Bernie Madoff were highly reinforced. Likewise, business behaviors that are reinforced can produce great good or great bad. OBM practitioners need a set of externally generated values that guide what they will and will not do inside companies. That is easy to say but hard to do because we are often not alert to the contingencies in place until long after our actions have had an impact.

All too often, daily choices to beat the competition to market with a new product, or to overlook the team leader who fails consistently to do a safety check at the start of a procedure, may not seem like unethical actions. They are often not evaluated in that way until their impact is felt. The outcomes of today's actions are often delayed and less than certain, making them more difficult to control. Workplace rules of conduct are often too narrow for the circumstances that arise. In many ways, that narrow definition of ethics, the reliance on individual's justifying their actions in terms of their intention instead of analyzing their choices by looking ahead (often "guessing") as to the impact on others, is the hardest part of ensuring that we are behaving ethically. *Striving to be ethical*, and discussing and reviewing what we do and its potentially distant effect, helps us be alert to potentially slippery slopes and to walk carefully when near them.

The authors recommend that students who enter the workplace learn what they can about the ethical dilemmas faced by those businesses. Dilemmas of the workplace may set up unintended consequences or encourage deliberate and obviously unethical outcomes. Over the years, OBM practitioners have worked with behavior on oil and gas rigs, in deep mines, in nuclear facilities, in chemical manufacturing plants, in textile factories, in food-producing industries, and in insurance and pharmaceutical companies. All of these industries have had ethical problems in serving the public good while seeking to extract maximum profit. OBM practitioners should establish a dialogue with clients to discuss the longer term impact of actions designed to serve an immediate and desired outcome.

Concern For the Whole Person. OBM practitioners define a trait as a series of observable behaviors. These behaviors sum to the label applied to the person. Translating traits into behaviors helps to convert everyday terms into robust behavioral concepts and avoids stereotyping that limits the "potential" of individuals to that of their labels (e.g., lazy, shy, uncommitted, hostile, etc.). Everyday terms are important because people use the only words that they have to describe things. It can be exhausting to constantly explain to clients that behavior is shaped by external circumstances. For many, "mechanistic" descriptions of behaviors can make the OBM practitioner appear to be narrowly informed about what makes people do what they do. Dan Pink's (2011) book, *Drive*, became a best seller partly because his views about motivation resonated with so many, not because of the truth of the science he espoused. Even though the work OBM offers is rich and full of wisdom, our language can create a communications barrier between the OBM practitioner and the client.

The words people use exert powerful control over their sense of wellbeing, their assessment of their capabilities, and how they describe what they say and do. That language includes words such as good decision-making, wise judgment, socially responsible, excellent self-control, wisdom, and maturity. For OBM practitioners, the philosophy of behaviorism provides a depth of behavioral meaning for everyday terms, such as competencies and character. Translating findings from the science provides models for understanding behavioral processes. Together, the philosophy of behaviorism and the science of behavioral processes provide clarity and connection to socially-valued words in applied settings. We have the tools to develop the wise leader, the persistent tool maker, or the creative designer.

Social psychologists, such as Eisenberger (1992), use learning concepts to explain in behavioral terms the development and maintenance of such commonly valued traits as persistence. Latane and Steve (1981) conducted applied research on the conditions that produce behavior demonstrating social responsibility in the natural environment. Understanding what research can offer in predicting when asking for, or giving of, help will occur, helps companies arrange such conditions to increase both business and social responsibility.

The conditions surrounding behavior at work are complex and OBM does not always include all operating contingencies in its analysis. Clinical behavior analysts deal with what people say about their values, beliefs, and actions in ways that OBM does not. They offer insights into dealing with rule-governed behaviors and often address needed changes in an individual's verbal repertoire to open new ways of doing things.

Acceptance and Commitment Therapy (ACT) addresses rule-driven approaches to acceptable patterns of behavior (Hayes, Strosahl, & Wilson, 1999). ACT gives behavioral descriptions for internal states of causality that are traditionally used to explain behavior. All such work provides concepts and tools for behavior analysts to share with clients. The work also reduces the control for the performer that trait labels have on limiting employees' perceived workplace potential.

Researchers such as Holland (1958) on signal detection and Hursh (2011) on fatigue also expanded the landscape of operating contingencies. They increased the understanding of the conditions that affect front-line performance and performer vigilance which is particularly important in OBM's work in behavior-based safety. The airline, mining, nuclear power, and oil and gas industries all have stories of catastrophes related to fatigue. In their "blame-the-workers" approach, management often interprets the failure of vigilance as related to faulty or bad character, internal to the person, and not *fixable* through behavioral interventions. The findings of Holland and Hursh give specialists in safety fixable behavioral explanations for these failures.

OBM has added clarity to understanding safety in the workplace. Cultural and business practices often establish unintended consequences to behaving safely. OBM practitioners have built a reputation for identifying and addressing factors that lead to safe practice.

It is difficult to pinpoint precisely the beginning of the field of behavior-based safety. The work appears to have started in the early 1970s. Fox, Hopkins, and Anger (1987) used a token economy to improve safety in open-pit mining in Utah, starting in 1972. The good results were maintained for more than 12 years. Komaki, Barwick, and Scott (1978) showed positive effects of feedback and reinforcement on the safety of bakery workers. Sulzer-Azaroff published her first behavior-based safety article in *JOBM* in 1978. Her chapter in the *Handbook of organizational behavior management* remains one of the best explanations of behavioral safety (Sulzer-Azaroff, 1982). Many others have contributed to the evolution of the practice. McSween (1995), and Geller (2001), Agnew and Snyder (2008), and Agnew and Daniels (2010) all had a significant impact on the field. Petersen, a safety professional, wrote 17 safety books and introduced the term behavior-based safety. This socially significant issue of safety at work is an area in need of future OBM practitioners (Johnson, Dakens, Edwards, & Morse, 2008).

OBM practitioners are asked about promoting self-control, defined as choosing larger, later, rewards over smaller, immediate, rewards (Eisenberger, 1989). The ability to delay rewards is often regarded as part of the definition of a mature person. When OBM coaches help to arrange conditions that promote behavior patterns that are indicative of self-control, persistence, judgment, and wise decision-making, they are addressing maturity. The more we are seen as promoting qualities equated with wisdom, the more our work takes on larger social and cultural relevance. We do not advertise our effectiveness with such socially-relevant concepts as self-control as much as we could. However, Hyten suggested to Lattal (Hyten, personal communication, 2012) that OBM strategies seem to focus not on the long term, but on finding different immediate reinforcers to steer behavior away from problematic immediate reinforcers. He suggested that is it hard to imagine a design where practitioners promote control by a series of delayed reinforcers themselves. "So I don't think we actually promote self-control; we just switch impulsive reinforcers." This is a worthy topic for OBM to explore.

OBM and Human Resources Management

OBM practitioners address how work is designed, a topic which is currently in the domain of human resource offices. Human resource professionals supply the processes to select, retain, promote, recognize, and fire employees. Abernathy (2012b) and Austin and Carr (2000) have described relationships between human resources and OBM. Although there are many areas that could be the focus of OBM applications, nothing is more important than the motivational structures and processes that surround employees at work, typically termed Human Resource (HR) Management. OBM brings significant clarity to those practices.

Traditional HR management involves assumptions about how human behavior works. These assumptions, while well-meaning, are based more on anecdotal rather than scientifically-determined principles of human behavior. Daniels (2009) describes many traditional HR systems that are based on a flawed understanding of motivation. In many ways, HR practices are extremely rule-governed. Its rules are often externally mandated to ensure equity and equality of practices. One advantage of adopting the full array of behavior-analytic techniques is that those techniques create HR functions that support performance excellence (Snyder, 1995).

Organizational human resource management functions typically include: job analysis, selection, training, performance appraisal, compensation, reducing unintended consequences, and reducing constraints on performance. Each is described below.

Job Analysis. A job analysis describes the oversight, functions and tasks of a job. Crowell, Hantula, and McArthur (2011) and Langeland, Johnson, and Mawhinney (1997) synthesized OBM performance measurement techniques with industrial/organizational job analysis methods. Daniels and Daniels (2004) distinguished between behaviors and results in detail. They argued that, when possible, tasks or activities should be defined by their outcomes. Describing activities in terms of results provides the employee flexibility in choosing the specific response that will achieve needed outcomes. Instead, traditional managers might prescribe a specific sequence of behaviors in which the employee hands a customer a brochure first before addressing the customer's questions. In contrast, in a results-driven version, the employee is asked to produce customer satisfaction through the quality of the interactions while ensuring that needed materials are delivered. The employee can then respond based on what a customer says and does. He or she still delivers needed materials but in a way that allows a choice of effective methods of interacting with a specific customer. Measuring the number of accounts each customer opens provides a higher-level business result which gives the employee greater flexibility than a task-level result.

A second purpose of describing outcomes, rather than tasks or behaviors, is to express the task in a manner that is measurable. Observing and counting behaviors is a difficult and time-consuming process. In contrast, measuring results is usually less subject to observer error or bias.

Abernathy (2011) described five characteristics of effective performance measures:

1. Objective (numeric data)—measuring results should ensure objectivity and ease in counting the task measure.
2. Actionable (influenced by the employee)—the results defined in the behavioral job description should be under the control of the employee.
3. Focused (individual or small team)—the results should be measured for an individual or, in some cases, a small team.
4. Aligned—each measure should promote organizational objectives.

5. Balanced—success on one measure should not lead to poor outcomes in other job dimensions. That is, the result should be balanced against other objectives.

Individual behaviors should be plotted along a continuum of change. This will help the performer to document progress. While measuring results is important, reinforcing successive approximations to the goal requires that the performance be aligned with the contingent reinforcement. The manager as mentor can help to ensure accuracy and ease of responding, celebrate steps along the way, provide positive reinforcement as steps are mastered, and help the performer to achieve high and steady rates of behavior (fluency).

Performance Matrix. Unfortunately, a simple list of the tasks associated with a job does not ensure balanced performance, nor does it prioritize those tasks. The Performance Matrix, first proposed by Felix and Riggs (1986, see Figure 26.1), is a proven solution for these issues. Their Performance Matrix converts different measures' raw scores to a common scale. Each measure is weighted by priority. The converted score is multiplied by the weight to compute a weighted converted score. These weighted scores are then summed to compute a "performance index," which represents the employee's overall performance. The construction of performance matrices has been described by Abernathy (2011).

For example, in the above performance matrix the gross revenue for the month was $10,000. This converts to a performance scale score of −20. The measure's priority weight is 20%. The scale score times the priority weight (−20 × 20% = −4%) equals the measure's weighted score. Each of the four measure's weighted scores are computed and the summed to produce the "Performance Index" of 36% on a scale that ranges from −20% to 100%.

Points Method. Another method for weighting results and aggregating them to compute an employee's overall performance is the assignment of a point value to each result. This approach was described by Skinner (1948) in *Walden Two.* Points can be determined by a committee that is familiar with the job (subject matter experts or SMEs). The assignment of points can take into account time, priority, skill level, and task desirability. This method does not ensure balance as the matrix does,

Performance Matrix

	Performance Scales												
MEASURES	−20	−10	MIN 0	10	20	30	40	50	60	80	MAX 100	WT	WTD SCORE
Gross Revenue DATA: 10K	10K	15K	20K	25K	30K	35K	40K	45K	50K	55K	60K	.20	−4.0
Gross Profit Margin% DATA: 10%	9.0	9.5	10.0	10.5	11.0	11.5	12.0	12.5	13.0	13.5	14.0	.20	0.0
% Project Milestones DATA: 85%	50	55	60	65	70	75	80	85	90	95	100	.40	20.0
Customer Survey DATA: 9.0	4.0	4.5	5.0	5.5	6.0	6.5	7.0	7.5	8.0	8.5	9.0	.20	20.0

Performance Index 36

Figure 26.1 The Performance Matrix © Aubrey Daniels International 2011.

however. The performer can increase production by ignoring other performance dimensions such as accuracy or timeliness.

Converting traditional job descriptions to behavioral results improves the validity of the description. It also provides employees more flexibility in how they achieve the results, enables objective and frequent feedback, and can ensure prioritized and balanced performances (e.g. efficiency vs. quality).

Employee Selection. The quality and commitment of new employees is critical to an organization's success. As a result, the recruitment and selection of new employees is a key HR function. Jones and Azrin (1973) analyzed job-finding behaviors and implemented a program that rewarded local residents for reporting available jobs to an organization's human resources department. They reported that ten times as many job leads, and eight times as many placements, occurred as occurred in this situation under traditional employee recruiting procedures.

The job interview is the most common tool for selecting new employees. Job interviews may be unstructured or structured. Unstructured interviews leave the order and content of the questions up to the interviewer. Structured interviews involve a predetermined set of interview questions. The predictive validity of a selection tool is determined by correlating interview scores with job performance scores. Traditional, unstructured interviews yield a correlation of around 0.20 while structured behavioral interviews yield an average 0.53 predictive correlation across all published studies (Janz, 1982).

OBM can assist in improving and validating behavioral interviewing by moving from traits to behavioral interviewing. OBM also provides a wealth of information about how to objectively define situations, goals, behaviors, and results. Two critical research questions regarding behavioral interviewing are first, how reliably does past behavior predict future behavior? Second, how valid are interviewee's recollections of past situations and behaviors?

The operant concepts of response hierarchies and motivating operations can also be used to conceptualize, analyze, and improve the behavioral interviewing process. Response hierarchies are unique to each individual and they may change in different situations. The interview environment (location, interviewer, light, temperature, etc.), the situation and task described in the questions, and establishing operations can alter the applicant's verbal response hierarchy. Finally, certain words or phrases, or the manner in which they are presented, may evoke specific *tacts* and *intraverbals* (Skinner, 1991).

Other behavioral approaches to employee selection include work simulations, work samples, and assessment centers. In contrast to behavioral interviews, the applicant engages in actual or simulated tasks related to the job. The effects of prompts, feedback, and consequences during the simulations impact the applicant's performance on these tasks.

Employee Training. Improving employees' mastery of skills and fluency is a much needed area of growth for OBM in the 21st century. The application of behavior analysis to teaching can be traced back to Skinner's (1954) and (1958) articles. He summarized his techniques for improving teaching in *The Technology of Teaching* (1968). Today, instructional designers, working side-by-side with their web-based colleagues, use programmed instruction, computer assisted instruction (CAI), computer-based instruction, and direct instruction to train employees.

Mager (1997) applied behavioral principles specifically to employee training throughout a long career. He described useful instructional objectives as having three characteristics:

- Performance. What a learner is expected to be able to do or the result of the doing.
- Conditions. The important conditions (if any) under which the performance is to occur.
- Criterion. How well the learner must perform for performance to be considered acceptable.

Mager named his instructional design Criterion Referenced Instruction (CRI). Some of the critical aspects include goal/task analysis, performance objectives, criterion referenced testing, and development of learning modules tied to specific objectives.

Performance Appraisal. Performance appraisal is used both administratively and developmentally. Administrative uses include awarding annual pay increases and promotions, and placing people on probation. Developmental uses include performance feedback, improvement, and coaching. Infrequent and inconsistent applications of these activities reduce their effectiveness through the loss of feedback and reinforcement. Waiting until the quarter end, or worse, until year end, removes the opportunity to improve. Waiting reduces performance appraisal mainly to catching people doing things wrong and fails to help people achieve the excellence that they can achieve. Traditionally designed performance appraisals that neglect shaping and reinforcement remain one of the largest problems in motivating employees' best efforts.

Developmental Appraisals. OBM has been primarily concerned with developmental appraisals. DeNisi (2011) and Gravina and Siers (2011) argue that improved performance results from viewing performance appraisals in the context of a larger performance management system. Pinpointing potentials, analyzing constraints, and designing and implementing improvement plans can all be used to improve performance. David Uhl described how these behavior-based performance targets, when compared in six-month follow-ups, often correlate highly with business success and with cultural measures of employee satisfaction such as the Gallup Q12 (Uhl, personal communication to author, August 2008).

Pinpointing Improvement Potentials. A typical method for identifying employee opportunity for improvement involves the manager selecting an improvement target or targets for each subordinate. Measures are designed and data are collected for each pinpoint. Targets that display negative trends, high variability, or performance below goal are selected for improvement projects.

A second strategy for improvement pinpointing was proposed by Tom Gilbert (1978). Gilbert computed key job measures' performance-improvement potentials (PIPs) by dividing the exemplar's (best performance) by the average performance. The highest ratios were considered for improvement projects.

A third method is to administer a management practices survey across the organization (Abernathy, 2010). Performances affected by deficient management practices are then measured. The assumption is that deficient management practices often lead to poor performances. The improvement opportunity lies with managers learning to manage behavior more effectively.

Implementing an organization-wide performance scorecard system provides a fourth method (Abernathy, 2011; Daniels & Daniels, 2004). Potential for improvement is pinpointed based on monthly measurement of levels, trends, and variability in performance. Although this method is the most difficult to design and maintain, it provides a basis for an ongoing performance-improvement program because data are collected and analyzed every month.

Analyzing Performance Constraints. The performance constraint analysis methodologies of the Behavior Engineering Model (Gilbert, 1978), the Performance Analysis Flowchart (Mager & Pipe, 1997), the Vantage Analysis Chart (Smith & Chase, 1990), the PIC/NIC Analysis® (Daniels & Daniels, 2004), and the OCC Analysis (Abernathy, 2012b) are described below.

Behavioral Engineering Model. Tom Gilbert (1978) proposed two sources of performance constraints: environmental and individual. Environmental constraints included stimuli (e.g., job descriptions, guides, feedback), responses (e.g., tools, time, materials, processes), and consequences (e.g., incentives, career development, aversive consequences for poor performance). Individual constraints include stimuli (e.g. knowledge, training), responses (e.g., capacity, selection, scheduling, job aids), and consequences (e.g., motives in the form of reinforcement history, the recruitment process).

Performance Analysis Flowchart. Mager and Pipe (1997) presented a performance analysis decision tree. The components of the tree are: Expectations clear? (Yes/No). If no, clarify expectations. Resources sufficient? (Yes/No). If no, provide more resources. Feedback present? (Yes/No). If no, provide feedback. Desired performance punished? (Yes/No). If yes, remove punishers. Poor performance rewarded? (Yes/No). If yes, remove rewards. Effective consequences? (Yes/No). If no, implement positive reinforcement. Skill deficiency? (Yes/No). If yes, improve skills. Task simplification? (Yes/No). If no, simplify task. Person's potential? (Yes/No). If no, improve procedures for employee selection.

Vantage Analysis Chart (VAC). The VAC (Smith & Chase, 1990) provides six vantage points from which to analyze an organization: philosophical, social, organizational, departmental, individual outcomes, and individual activities. The VAC is used by performance engineers to: (1) gather information at all vantage levels, (2) use that information to analyze problems, and (3) develop interventions consistent with the values at all vantage levels.

PIC/NIC Analysis®. This analysis, described by Daniels and Daniels (2004), is concerned with the consequences (reinforcement) of performance. Highly effective consequences are positive, immediate, and certain (PIC). They promote behavior that is likely to reoccur. Less effective consequences are negative, future, and uncertain (NFU). Consequences that punish behavior are negative, immediate, and certain (NIC).

The approach also presents the A-B-C model of behavior analysis. Behavior (B) is a function of its antecedents (A) and its consequences (C). Behaviors with many or clear antecedents are more likely to occur than behaviors with few antecedents. Examples of antecedents include cues or prompts (e.g., training), communication, knowledge, direction, and, more broadly, the setting events of how work is done. These factors have been put into the PIC/NIC Analysis®, a popular tool for analyzing why behaviors occur. PIC/NIC Analysis is used in making decisions about structures, management processes and systems, that impede or enhance behaviors that contribute to desired business outcomes.

OCC Analysis™. This model, (Abernathy, 2012b), analyzes performance "constraints." The constraints are categorized as Opportunity, Capability, and Context. The analysis proceeds from left to right. That is it asks: Does the employee have a consistent opportunity to perform (i.e. time, input)? Does the employee have the capability to perform (i.e., competence, resources, processes)? And, finally, does the employee perform in a supportive context (i.e., prompts, feedback, consequences)? Each category and subcategory directs the analyst to several improvement strategies.

Designing and Implementing Performance Improvement Plans. Most OBM performance-improvement projects involve restructuring antecedents, feedback, and/or consequences. Alvero et al. (2001) reviewed the literature and found that 29.7% of OBM projects focused exclusively on improving feedback to employees. 18.8% of the projects improved feedback and consequences. Twenty-three-point-four percent of the projects improved feedback, goal setting, and consequences. Improving feedback alone produced consistent improvements in 47% of the projects. Projects involving feedback and consequences yielded consistent improvements 58% of the time. Feedback, goal setting, and consequences produced consistent improvements in 67% of the projects. However, projects involving the restructuring of antecedents, goal setting, feedback and consequences produced consistent positive results in 100% of the cases.

Abernathy (2012a) reviewed the literature published in *JOBM* and computed improvement percentages for OBM projects. The 68 projects that reported data on improvement yielded an average 90.4% improvement. The 16 projects that addressed antecedents yielded a 78.1% improvement. The 28 projects that addressed feedback yielded a 120% improvement. The 23 studies that employed monetary consequences yielded a 63.3% average improvement.

Compensation. Wages and salaries make up the conventional compensation system. An organization first conducts a job analysis as described previously. This is followed by a *job evaluation* to determine the appropriate levels of compensation. Job evaluation methods include ranking, classification, factor comparison, and the point method. A market survey in which wages and salaries are adjusted to regional or national averages is typically also conducted. Wages and salaries are reviewed annually and adjusted for the employee's performance (merit pay) and inflation (cost of living adjustment or COLA). Dickinson and Gillette (1993), Smoot and Duncan (1997), Thurkow, Bailey, and Stamper (2000), and Bucklin and Dickinson (2001), among others, have investigated the effects of monetary incentives on employee performance.

The conventional wage and salary system views employees as commodities with a market determined value. From a *metasystem* view, wages and salaries are antecedents for recruiting and retaining employees in the society at large. However, within the organization, wages and salaries often function as negative reinforcers. Murray Sidman (2001) devoted his book, *Coercion and its fallout*, to the issues associated with the widespread application of negative reinforcement. Traditional HR structures, the often overbearing or neglectful management oversight, and the application of the wage system, create a demotivating workplace. Abernathy (1996) argues that the wage and salary system must be replaced or significantly augmented before a culture based on positive reinforcement and on Skinner's science of behavior can be fully established.

Reducing Unintended Consequences. Negative reinforcers are operationally defined as any events, which increases the probability of behaviors that remove or prevent those events. When an employee works to avoid losing a wage or salary, rather than to earn it, the employee is operating under negative reinforcement, a type of aversive control. The potential or actual application of aversive control creates fear. This emotional state consists of rapid breathing, increased heart rate, pupil dilation, and other biological responses. Fear makes it difficult to perform complex or precise behaviors. Aversive control also prompts escape and avoidance (tardiness, long breaks, leaving early, and absenteeism). Aversive control constricts an employee's range of behaviors (innovation and creativity), particularly if the behaviors that produce the aversive event are not clearly specified. Finally, aversive control can reduce the employee's discretionary effort (likelihood of exceeding minimum requirements).

Extinction occurs when a reinforcer that supported a behavior is removed and the behavior no longer occurs. Introducing extinction (e.g., the removal of attention or other events that were once reinforcing) may not be neutral to the performer. Inadvertently placing a behavior on extinction (e.g., a busy manager fails to ask an employee to chat) can have a negative effect on behavior. It may "feel" like punishment (*rejection* to use the vernacular). Such inadvertent use of extinction at work can lead to "shame, guilt, and anger" as described by workers. Postal workers who "go postal" have reported being "ignored" and passed over when once they were valued. Extinction, when applied to adult behaviors, is often unnecessary and may have side effects because of the ways in which the performer attaches meaning to "being ignored."

Given these problems, why do many managers and supervisors resort to aversive control (threats, intimidation, embarrassment, poor reviews)? To positively reinforce improved or exceptional performances, beyond simple *atta boy* statements, the manager must have timely, objective performance data for each subordinate. They rarely gather such data from frequent visits to observe behavior in action or through discussions with the performer. Few organizations provide these data, opting for subjective annual performance reviews because they are easy to design and administer. Managers are often forced to evaluate their subordinates subjectively because they lack objective results (Abernathy, 1996).

Managers, and their leaders, often lack knowledge about the *potential* of their workers. They fail to understand discretionary effort, defined as conditions in which the employee *wants to* (because the behavior is reinforced positively) work as opposed to condition in which the employees *have to* work (because of threat or fear). Discretionary effort is often seen as unique to a particular person, not as promoted by the work environment. This is partly because "motivation" is seen as private and beyond the reach of the manager. However, managers can embed motivational factors in the conditions and consequences of employee behavior. If they do not do this, exceptions to expected patterns of behavior (mistakes), are usually addressed by negative reinforcement (e.g., "Do it or else"), rather than by reinforcing improvements. To address this problem, OBM needs to define objective measures with clients and help them observe and to track behavior change, capturing such change through data charts and graphs.

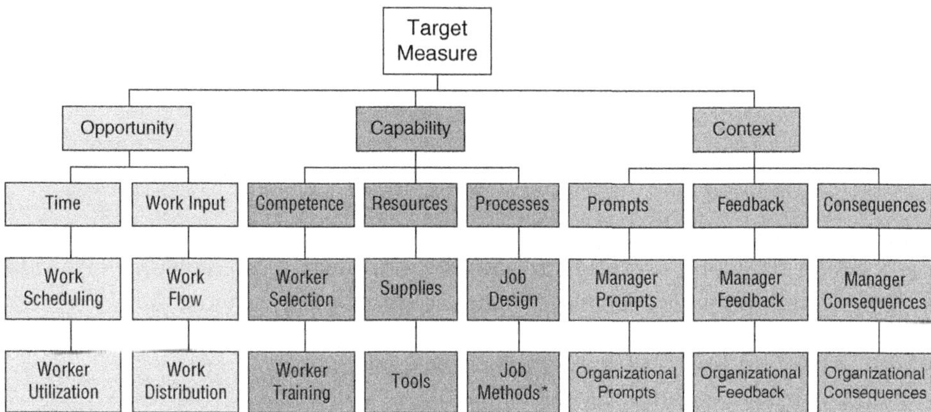

Figure 26.2 Performance Constraint Analysis (Abernathy, 2012b).

Reducing Constraints on Performance. OBM should aim at reducing constraints and at increasing opportunities for reinforcement in the workplace. By expanding their tool box to include concepts and techniques from other applied sciences, including industrial/organizational psychology, industrial and systems engineering, and managerial accounting, OBM can provide a full, functionally-analytic, approach to change, involving the individual, the unit, the levels of management, the customer the supplier, the community and beyond (Crowell et al., 2011; DeNisi, 2011; Gravina & Siers, 2011).

As described above (Figure 26.2), Abernathy (2012b) categorized performance constraints (opportunity, capability, and context constraints) in his multidisciplinary approach to performance improvement. Basically, the analysis asks three questions: Is there an opportunity to perform? Do the employees have the capability to perform? And, if there is opportunity and capability, does the work context guide, promote, and reinforce performance?

Industrial engineering is primarily concerned with the opportunity to perform including work scheduling, worker utilization, work flow, and work distribution. It also focuses on improving job methods. In contrast, Industrial/Organizational Psychology has been more concerned with the capability to perform, including worker selection, worker training, and job design. OBM looks at the context and behavioral contingencies that operate on the performer including antecedent conditions surrounding behavior (e.g., prompts, feedback, and consequences).

It makes little sense to analyze employee capability or context if there is no opportunity to perform. The tunnel vision that operates on these disciplines must be overcome to optimize performance. The analyst, regardless of background, must be familiar with techniques in all three disciplines and how they can enrich one another's approach to optimizing human behavior.

Analyzing the context of work has been of increasing importance in sustaining change across complex systems. Redesigning formal structures of work is often left to industrial engineers, organizational psychologists, HR specialists, or business systems analysts. Behavior analysts rarely approach opportunity in the workplace as workplace architects. In the past five years, interest in the behavior systems perspective has increased dramatically in no small part because of the influential writers and researchers whose behavior systems work was captured in the special issue of *JOBM* in 2009.

Behavior Systems Management

OBM has a strong research foundation, solid methods for increasing positive behavior, tools for designing systems that can allow individuals to accomplish worthwhile objectives, and techniques to create fluency across new and required skills. The early management engineers and behavior-analytic designers, created a roadmap to the future as they began to address workplace performance.

OBM is gaining traction in implementing its technology across wider spans of organizational management. The field has developed systems approaches that remove the restrictive rules that put the control of employee behavior in the hands of others. We are much more equipped to change behavior for the better, arranging the broad context of work so that it reinforces excellent behavior. Skinner (1948) suggested that to design systems that support behavior without unnecessary control is to "free up" the worker to achieve astonishing outcomes.

Abernathy (1996) argued that we can make the workplace more productive and reduce strife if we change the compensation system to use positive strategies of management. As OBM practitioners extend their reach to larger and larger organizational units, it is more evident that we need carefully crafted, systemic, designs to influence behavior. OBM is often asked to examine whole systems of a corporation in preparing for large-scale change. Glenn (2003) has broadened the scope of the analysis through her work with the larger cultural landscape, identifying meta- and mega- contingencies and interlocking organizational and societal systems.

OBM should strive to create such contingency-shaped workplaces for the future. To the authors' knowledge, only one company in the United States with more than 1,000 employees has approximated Skinner's vision. Lincoln Electric is a Fortune 500 company in Cleveland, Ohio, It manufactures arc welders. In 1895, James Lincoln started the company with piece-rate and profit-sharing, rather than wages, for his factory workers. The results then, and still reported at least through the 1990s, were life-time employment, 0.5% turnover after the first 90 days on the job, the highest paid factory workers in the world, and 100 employees per manager (Lincoln, 1951).

In our vision, OBM should fulfill Skinner's *Walden Two* vision and the visions of those who have come after him. We should move from coercive management practices to positive reinforcement through pay for performance, through developing performance measures that allow the individual to gauge and refine his or her own behaviors, and through removing constraints by artificial rules that impede actions in how the work is done. Applying science to advance the skills and wisdom of workers across our society would be an accomplishment that would establish new definitions for both freedom and dignity, returning control for such advances to the natural conditions of the environment.

> Imagine an input-throughput-output model that is embedded in a complex architecture that rises above and below the flow—architecture that structures and shapes flow, creates and limits possibilities and outcomes. And all of this travelling forward in time. Or, as historians, we can look back and retrospectively examine the three dimensional architecture, structure and flow of an organization's life. (Harshbarger, personal communication, July 2012)

Such a vision is exciting and possible.

Note

1 The authors wish to thank Aubrey Daniels for an early review of the chapter and Andy Lattal and Cloyd Hyten for a detailed critique of the manuscript through several iterations.

References

Abernathy, W. B. (1979). A bank-wide performance system. In R. O'Brien, A. Dickenson, & M. Rosow (Eds.), *Case studies in organizational behavior management*. New York: Prentice Hall.

Abernathy, W. B. (1996). *The sin of wages: Where the conventional pay system has led us, and how to find a way out*. Atlanta, GA: Performance Management Publications.

Abernathy, W. B. (2010). A comprehensive performance analysis and improvement method. *Performance Improvement*, *49*, 5–17.

Abernathy, W. B. (2011). *Pay for profit: Designing an organization-wide performance-based compensation system*. Atlanta, GA: Performance Management Publications.

Abernathy, W. B. (2012a). Behavioral approaches to business and industrial problems: Organizational behavior management. In G. Madden (Ed.), *APA handbook of behavior analysis* Washington, DC: American Psychological Association.

Abernathy, W. B. (2012b). *Performance diagnostics: A multidisciplinary approach to employee performance analysis and improvement*. Atlanta, GA: Performance Management Publications.

Agnew, J. (May 2012). Relationship development as an MO in safety. PowerPoint presented at the Association for Behavior Analysis Annual Convention, Seattle, WA.

Agnew, J., & Daniels, A. (2010). *Safe by accident? Take the luck out of safety*. Atlanta, GA: Performance Management Publications.

Agnew, J., & Snyder, G. (2008). *Removing obstacles to safety*. Atlanta, GA: Performance Management Publications.

Aldis, O. (1961). Of pigeons and men. *Harvard Business Review*, *39*, 297–300.

Alvero, A. M., Bucklin, B. R., & Austin, J. (2001). An objective review of the effectiveness and essential characteristics of performance feedback in organizational settings. *Journal of Organizational Behavior Management*, *21*, 3–29.

Andrasik, F. U. (1989). Organizational behavior modification in business settings: A methodological and content review. *Journal of Organizational Behavior Management*, *10*, 59–77.

Austin, J., & Carr, J. (2000). *Handbook of applied behavior analysis.* Oakland, CA: Context Press.

Austin, J., Clayton, M. R., Houmanfar, R., & Hayes, L (2001). *Organizational change.* Reno, NV: Context Press.

Ayllon, T., & Azrin, N. H. (1965). The measurement and reinforcement of behavior of psychotics. *Journal of the Experimental Analysis of Behavior, 8*, 357–383.

Bailey, J. S., & Burch, M. R. (2010). *25 essential skills and strategies for the professional behavior analyst: Expert tips for maximizing consulting effectiveness.* New York: Taylor and Francis.

Balcazar, F., Hopkins, B. L., & Suarez, Y. (1985). A critical, objective review of performance feedback. *Journal of Organizational Behavior Management, 7*, 65–89.

Brethower, D. M. (1972). *Behavioral analysis in business and industry: A total performance system.* Kalamazoo, MI: Behaviordelia.

Bucklin, B. R., & Dickinson, A. M. (2001). Individual monetary incentives: A review of different types of arrangements between performance and pay. *Journal of Organizational Behavior Management, 21*, 45–137.

Crowell, C. R, Hantula, D. A., & McArthur, K. L. (2011). From job analysis to performance management: A synergistic rapprochement to organizational effectiveness. *Journal of Organizational Behavior Management, 31*, 316–332.

Daniels, A. C. (2009). *Oops: 13 management practices that waste time and money (and what to do instead).* Atlanta, GA: Performance Management Publications.

Daniels, A. C., & Daniels, J. E. (2004). *Performance management: Changing behavior that drives organizational effectiveness* (4th ed). Atlanta, GA: Performance Management Publications.

Deming, E. (1986). *Out of the crisis.* Cambridge, MA: MIT Press.

DeNisi, A. S. (2011). Managing performance to change behavior. *Journal of Organizational Behavior Management, 31*, 262–276.

Dickinson, A. M. (2000). The historical roots of organizational behavior management in the private sector: The 1950s–1980s. *Journal of Applied Behavior Analysis, 20*, 9–58.

Dickinson, A. M., & Gillette, K. L. (1993). A comparison of the effects of two individual monetary incentive systems on productivity: Piece rate pay versus base pay plus monetary incentives. *Journal of Organizational Behavior Management, 14*, 2–82.

Eisenberger, R. (1989). *Blue Monday: The loss of the work ethic in America.* New York: Paragon House.

Eisenberger, R. (1992). Learned industriousness. *Psychological Review, 99*, 248–267.

Feeney, E. J. (December 2, 1972). Where Skinner's theories work. *Business Week*, 64–65.

Felix, G. H., & Riggs, J. L. (1986). *Productivity by the objectives matrix.* Corvalis, OR: Oregon Productivity Center.

Fox, D. K., Hopkins, B. L., & Anger, W. K. (1987). The long-term effects of a token economy on safety performance in open-pit mining. *Journal of Applied Behavior Analysis, 20*, 215–224.

Frederiksen, L. W. (Ed.) (1982). *Handbook of organizational behavior management.* New York: John Wiley & Sons, Inc.

Geller, E. S. (2001). *Working safe: How to help people actively care for health and safety.* Boca-Raton, LA: CRC Press.

Gilbert, T. F. (1978). *Human competence: Engineering worthy performance.* New York: McGraw-Hill.

Gilbert, T. F. (2011). *Human incompetence: Confessions of a psychologist.* Atlanta, GA: Performance Management Publications.

Gilbreth, F. B., & Gilbreth, L. M. (1917). *Applied motion study: A collection of papers on the efficient method to industrial preparedness.* New York: Sturgis and Walton Company.

Glenn, S. S. (2003). Operant contingencies and the origin of cultures. In K. A. Lattal, & P. N. Chase (Eds.), *Behavior theory and philosophy* (pp. 223–242). New York: Plenum Publishers.

Gravina, N. E., & Siers, B. P. (2011). Square pegs and round holes: Ruminations on the relationship between performance appraisal and performance management. *Journal of Organizational Behavior Management, 31*, 277–287.

Hake, D. F., & Olvera, D. (1978). Cooperation, competition, and related social phenomena. In A. C. Catania & T. A. Brigham (Eds.), *Handbook of applied behavior analysis: Social and institutional processes* (pp. 208–245). New York: Irvington.

Hake, D. F., Olvera, D., & Bell, J. C. (1975). Switching from competition to sharing or cooperation at large response requirements: Competition requires more responding. *Journal of the Experimental Analysis of Behavior, 24*, 343–354.

Harshbarger, D., & Maley, R. F. (1974). *Behavior analysis and systems analysis: An integrative approach to mental health programs.* Kalamazoo, MI: Behaviordelia.

Hawkins, R. P., Chase, P. N., & Scotti, J. R. (1993). Applied behavior analysis at West Virginia University: A brief history. *Journal of Applied Behavior Analysis, 26*, 573–582.

Hayes, S. C., Strosahl, K. D., & Wilson, K. G. (1999). *Acceptance and commitment therapy: An experiential approach to behavior change.* New York: Guilford Press.

Holland, J. G. (1958, July 11). Human vigilance. *Science, 128*, 61–67.

Hursh, S. R. (2011). *Evidence-based fatigue management as a continuous performance improvement process* (PDFe-Publisher). Baltimore: Institute for Behavioral Resources.

Jacks, L. P. (1932). *Education through recreation.* London: Harper and Brothers.

Janz, T. (1982). Initial comparisons of patterned behavior description interviews versus unstructured interviews. *Journal of Applied Psychology, 67*, 557–580.

Johnson, J., Dakens, L., Edwards, P., & Morse, N. (2008). *SwitchPoints: Culture change on the fast track for business success.* Hoboken, NJ: John Wiley & Sons, Inc.

Jones, R. J., & Azrin, N.H. (1973). An experimental application of a social reinforcement approach to the problem of job-finding. *Journal of Applied Behavior Analysis, 6*, 345–353.

Kaplan, R. S., & Norton, D. P. (1996). *The balanced scorecard: Translating strategy into action.* Boston: Harvard Business School Press.

Keller, F. S., & Schoenfeld, W. N. (1950). *Principles of psychology: A systematic text in the science of behavior.* New York: Appleton-Century-Crofts.

Komaki, J., Barwick, K. D., & Scott, L. R. (1978). A behavioral approach to occupational safety: Pinpointing and reinforcing safe performance in a food manufacturing plant. *Journal of Applied Psychology, 63*, 424–445.

Langeland, K. L., Johnson, C. M., & Mawhinney, T. C. (1997). Improving staff performance in a community mental health setting. *Journal of Organizational Behavior Management, 18*, 21–43.

Latane, B., & Steve, N. (1981). Ten years of research on group size and helping. *Psychological Bulletin, 89*, 308–324.

Lattal, A. D., & Clark, R. (2007). *A good day's work: Sustaining ethical behavior and business success.* New York: McGraw-Hill.

Lincoln, J. F. (1951). *Incentive management.* Cleveland, OH: The Lincoln Electric Company.

Mager, R. (1997). *Preparing instructional objectives.* Atlanta, GA: The Center for Effective Performance.

Mager, R., & Pipe, P. (1997). *Analyzing performance problems.* Atlanta, GA: The Center for Effective Performance.

Mawhinney, T. C. (1987). OBM, SPC, and Theory D: A brief introduction. *Journal of Organizational Behavior Management, 8*, 89–106.

McCarthy, M. (2011). *Sustain your gains.* Atlanta, GA: Performance Management Publications.

McSween, T. E. (1995). *The Values-Based Safety Process: Improving your safety culture with a behavioral approach.* New York: Van Nostrand Reinhold.

O'Brien, R., Dickinson, A., & Rosow, M. (Eds.) (1979). *Case studies in organizational behavior management.* New York: Prentice Hall.

Pink, D. H. (2011). *Drive: The surprising truth about what motivates us.* New York: Riverhead Books.

Sidman, M. (2001). *Coercion and its fallout.* Boston: Authors Cooperative.

Skinner, B. F. (1938). *The behavior of organisms: An experimental analysis.* New York: Appleton-Century-Crofts.

Skinner, B. F. (1948). *Walden two.* Indianapolis: Hackett Publishing.

Skinner, B. F. (1953). *Science and human behavior.* New York: Macmillan.

Skinner, B. F. (1954). The science of learning and the art of teaching. *Harvard Educational Review*, *24*, 86–97.

Skinner, B. F. (1958). Teaching machines. *Science*, *128*, 969–977.

Skinner, B. F. (1968). *The technology of teaching.* New York: Appleton-Century-Crofts.

Skinner, B. F. (1969). *Contingencies of reinforcement: A theoretical analysis.* New York: Appleton-Century-Crofts.

Skinner, B. F. (1987). *Upon further reflection.* New York: Prentice Hall.

Skinner, B. F. (1991). *Verbal behavior.* Ann Arbor, MI: Copley Publishing Group.

Smith, J. M., & Chase P.N. (1990). Using the Vantage Analysis Chart to solve organization-wide problems. *Journal of Organizational Behavior Management*, *11*, 127–148.

Smoot, D. A., & Duncan, P.K. (1997). The search for optimum individual monetary incentive pay system: A comparison of the effects of flat pay and linear and non-linear pay systems on worker productivity. *Journal of Organizational Behavior Management*, *17*, 5–75.

Snyder, G. (Summer 1995). The compensation and performance link: An overall system at Techneglas. *Performance Management Magazine*, *13*, 14–25.

Stewart, M. (2009). *The management myth: Why the experts keep getting it wrong.* New York: Norton.

Sulzer-Azaroff, B. (1978). Behavioral ecology and accident prevention. *Journal of Organizational Behavior Management*, *2*, 11–14.

Sulzer-Azaroff, B. (1982). Behavioral approaches to occupational health and safety. In L. W. Frederiksen (Ed.), *Handbook of Organizational Behavior Management* (pp. 505–538). New York: John Wiley & Sons, Inc.

Taylor, F. W. (1911). *Principles of scientific management.* New York and London: Harper and Brothers.

Thurkow, N. M., Bailey, J. S., & Stamper, M. R. (2000). The effects of group and individual monetary incentives on productivity of telephone interviewers. *Journal of Organizational Behavior Management*, *20*, 3–26.

27

Clinical Behavior Analysis

William C. Follette and Sabrina M. Darrow

Behavior analysis derives from B. F. Skinner's emphasis on the study of behavior in its own right rather than as a proxy for some more fundamental, unobservable process in the mind, brain, or psychic structure. Skinner's work, *The Behavior of organisms* (1938) and *Schedules of reinforcement* (Ferster & Skinner, 1957), formed the basis for applied behavior analysis, the application of the principles of reinforcement to changing human behavior. The results of applying principles of reinforcement to treating conditions that significantly limit human functioning have been profound. Childhood autism has been among the notable problems that have responded to behavior analytic treatment, starting with the work of Wolf, Risley, and Mees (1963) under the supervision of Sid Bijou. In 1968, Allyon and Azrin published their work on the effects of implementing a token economy that dramatically altered the way inpatient psychotic individuals could be treated. That work was elaborated further by Gordon Paul in his work on psychosocial interventions for chronic mental patients (Paul & Lentz, 1977).

Though these and other applications of behavioral principles remain as powerful examples of the utility of bringing principles of behavior analysis to bear on important behavioral problems, many of the early applications occurred in restricted environments in which there was a great deal of control over the contingencies delivered over long periods of time. The individuals being treated often had little time outside the influence of the behavior analyst and the contingencies the analyst arranged.

Clinical behavior analysis (CBA) ventures into less controlled environments. Though still generally adhering to behavioral principles, "clinical behavior analysis focuses on the use of verbally based interventions to verbally competent clients who seek outpatient treatment" (Dougher, 2000, p. v). In so doing, clinical behavior analysis has had to develop new tools and perspectives that are not without controversy.

The Wiley Blackwell Handbook of Operant and Classical Conditioning, First Edition.
Edited by Frances K. McSweeney and Eric S. Murphy.

Initial Successful Applications of Behavioral Principles

While many contributed to moving behavior analysis into the clinical arena, Charles Ferster (1972) opened the door even wider to studying clinical problems from a behavior analytic perspective. He and others did so by offering functional analyses of depression. Their analysis suggested that depressive behaviors could be understood by examining the history of the person and the current environmental contingencies that might produce or maintain those behaviors, including the social influences of depressive behavior on others (Ferster, 1973). Contemporaneously, Lewinsohn (1974) posited that depression was maintained by low levels of response-contingent reinforcement. More recently, Martell and colleagues (Martell, Addis, & Jacobson, 2001) have shown the utility of having depressed individuals contact reinforcing contingencies in their environment (i.e., behavioral activation procedures) in a way similar to Lewinsohn.

As the clinical behavior analyst ventured away from treating people with restricted verbal behavior in the confines of highly controlled environments, much of the initial work focused on relatively straightforward clinical problems. These efforts included successful interventions for such problems as phobias and other anxiety-related behaviors that were thought to limit successful social functioning. The initial efforts to apply basic learning principles, either operant or respondent (e.g., Wolpe, 1958), were seen as innovative applications that were parsimonious in how they approached clinical issues previously considered complex (Lang & Lazovik, 1963). The application of habituation procedures produced sustained reduction in fearful/anxious responding in persons with snake phobias. These procedures sat in stark contrast to Freud's psychoanalytic interpretation of the famous "Little Hans" horse phobia case that introduced the Oedipal complex. Lang and colleagues later automated systematic desensitization so that the therapist need not even be present (Lang, Melamed, & Hart, 1970).

With these procedures, behavior therapy began to address the behavior of higher functioning, verbal subjects. Nevertheless, these initial procedures involved little interpersonal interaction between the therapist and client. They also failed to focus on language or the social contexts in which problematic behaviors occurred and were treated. In spite of these limitations, exposure treatments based on learning principles became firmly established as useful interventions for problems that had previously been difficult to treat using psychoanalytic procedures. This first generation or wave of clinical behavior analysis stayed relatively close to behavioral principles but remained, with some exceptions, relatively distant from cognitions and language as a subject matter in higher functioning individuals.

Eventually, it became apparent to those working with highly verbal outpatients that much of what concerned clients was what and how they "thought or felt". The natural language of our culture supports thoughts and feelings as causes. We learn to say, "I did it because I was mad," or, "I don't want to feel this way anymore." To ignore the language in which the client frames a problem fails to understand the context in which a client acts, including the client's thoughts and feelings. In fact, between 1945 when Skinner began to speculate about the nature of private events and verbal behavior (Boring, Bridgman, Feigl, Pratt, & Skinner, 1945; Skinner,

1945), until his book *Verbal behavior* appeared 12 years later (Skinner, 1957), Skinner tried to find a functional way of understanding and describing thoughts, feelings, emotions, and private events. Not only did his attempt spark significant controversy with the linguistic structuralists of the day (e.g., Chomsky) but it caused a delay in clinical behavior analysts' ability to apply this analysis to clinical problems.

As a result, cognitive behavior therapy and social learning theory emerged only in the 1960s and 1970s, marking the second wave of behavior therapy (e.g., Bandura, 1977; Mahoney, 1974). The rise of cognitive therapy occurred as therapists and researchers recognized that modeling, observational learning, and rule-governed behavior could occur without a person experiencing direct reinforcement contingencies. Rather, behavior was acquired by observing behaviors or being told of these behaviors. Thus, clients behaved as if they had acquired the behaviors through direct contact with the contingencies even though they had never experienced these contingencies. Additionally, behavioral problems were increasingly seen as being caused by faulty cognitive processes rather than by problematic learning histories (e.g., Beck, Rush, Shaw, & Emery, 1979).

There was considerable Sturm und Drang as debates raged about the relative merits of a cognitive versus behavioral account of behavior change (cf., Lonigan, 1990; Mahoney, 1989; Skinner et al., 1992; Wyatt, 1990). The cognitivist position seemed to expand the domains of behavior therapy, but it also threatened some of the important philosophical positions held by the pioneering behavior analysts. One philosophical problem arose from seeing cognitions as causes of behavior, as opposed to Skinner's view of cognitions and emotion as important behaviors to be understood. Skinner stated, "We explicitly undertake to predict and control the behavior of the individual organism. This is our 'dependent variable'—the effect for which we are to find the cause" (Skinner, 1953, p. 53). Hayes and Brownstein (1986) recognized that this charge requires that the behavior analyst can manipulate those aspects of the world that stand outside of the behavior itself. Viewing cognitions as causes of behavior led to what was termed "behavior-behavior relations." This view was criticized as leaving no room for control because control, from a behavior analytic perspective, is exerted by discriminative or reinforcing stimuli.

During the 1980s and early 1990s, the debate about basic epistemology continued. As the 1990s wound down, clinical behavior analysts pointed to differing preanalytic assumptions held by each camp in order to partially resolve the debate. This resolution granted that such differences would not be resolved by data because the meaning and interpretation of the data differed depending on the assumptions held by the different camps (see Dougher, 1997 for an introduction to a special series of articles on this issue).

From the late 1980s until the present, clinical behavior analysis has been trying to provide a more complete account of verbal behavior that has clinical utility while respecting the operant tradition. The inclusion of these analyses of language and cognition marks a third wave of behavior therapy. The remainder of this chapter describes how clinical behavior analysts make use of core behavioral notions, including these analyses of verbal behavior, in clinical settings. Two specific applications of clinical behavior analytic principles are also described: one that emphasizes the social context (Functional Analytic Psychotherapy) and one that focuses on the role of language and cognition (Acceptance and Commitment Therapy).

The Application of Familiar Behavioral Principles

Clinical behavior analysts may employ techniques that are foreign to behavior analysts when dealing with the verbal behavior of outpatients of normal intellectual functioning. Nevertheless, clinical behavior analysis has tried to be as consistent with the operant tradition as possible. Below we highlight some of the important principles and assumptions that are common to behavior analysts and clinical behavior analysts alike.

The Unit of Analysis

One hallmark of clinical behavior analysis is a focus on the act in context as the appropriate unit of analysis of behavior. That is, clinical behavior analysis assumes that a behavior cannot be fully understood unless one understands the conditions under which the behavior occurs (the discriminative stimuli, S^D), the behavioral response itself (R), and the contingencies of reinforcement (S^R) that affect the rate of the behavior. This is the traditional three-term contingency. It may be supplemented by Michael's (1993) introduction of the establishing operations (EO) that change the reinforcing properties of the reinforcer. The familiar unit of analysis is:

$$\begin{gathered}\mathrm{EO} \\ S^D \cdot R \rightarrow S^R\end{gathered}$$

In which the dot denotes some probability that the response will occur in the presence of the discriminative stimulus, and the horizontal arrow indicates the response will be followed by some contingency that affects the likelihood of the same or similar behavior occurring again in the same or similar conditions.

Whether one includes the establishing operation is partly a matter of explanatory preference. The primary point is that behavior can only be understood in the context of the conditions that precede and follow it. When behavior affects the environment such that the consequences of that behavior are reinforced, the behavior is an "operant." Any other interpretation of behavior misses the context and subsequently the function of behavior. In clinical behavior analysis, knowing the context is essential in order to understand the behavior.

Stimulus and Response Classes

Another key notion in clinical behavior analysis is that there are multiple stimulus conditions that can occasion the same response. When this is the case, those conditions are referred to as a *stimulus class.* In some instances, formation of a stimulus class can be explained in terms of stimulus generalization in which new stimuli share the formal properties of the original stimulus and, therefore, elicit the same response. However, verbal organisms (i.e., humans) can derive stimulus classes across stimuli that are much more complex and do not share formal physical properties. A description of this phenomenon (but not an explanation how it emerges) is provided by Sidman (see Sidman, 1994 for an historical account). For now, it important to appreciate that different stimuli can give rise to the same behavior.

Similarly, very different behaviors, or responses, can have the same function. When that is the case, the behaviors form a *response class*. A rat in a Skinner box might receive a food pellet after pressing a bar. The same rat would also receive the food after a running somersault that landed it head first on the bar. In that case, the lever press and the somersault would form a response class.

The Case Conceptualization

An important contribution of clinical behavior analysis to clinical phenomena has been de-pathologizing problem behaviors and the emphasis on building effective behavioral repertoires from existing behaviors (Goldiamond, 1974, 1975; Hawkins, 1986). In spite of the caricatures of behaviorists as uncaring and goal-directed with little regard for the humanity involved in the therapeutic change process, Skinner's preference for the use of positive reinforcement and his demonstrations of shaping complex behavioral repertoires set a positive tone for how cases were conceptualized (cf. Skinner, 1948, 1971 for exposition in both fictional and popular writings).

When a client presents for treatment, the clinical behavior analyst has two initial tasks. The first is to determine the goals of the client including both proximal and distal targets for behavior change. The distal targets are determined by what the client values. The behavior analyst then determines how to bring about the required behavior change. The clinical behavior analyst uses a functional analysis to achieve this goal. During a functional analysis, the clinician manipulates potential controlling variables (i.e., antecedent and consequential stimuli) of target behaviors and observes whether changes in the target behavior result. A case conceptualization results from completing these tasks.

It may seem that a functional analysis ought to be central to any behavioral therapy. However, when the American Psychological Association (APA) began an effort to identify efficacious treatment for clinical problems, it commissioned a task force to identify treatments that worked for a variety of clinical problems (see Chambless & Ollendick, 2001). In many instances, empirically based treatments were described for categories of clinical problems (e.g., depression, agoraphobia, etc.). Problems were not assessed based on the functional analysis more familiar to behavior analysts (cf. Hayes & Follette, 1993; Kanfer & Saslow, 1969). The traditional, nomothetic perspective based on categories of disorders left little need for functional analysis. If a diagnosis of depression was made, then one of the depression treatments was delivered. More attention was given to adherence to a specific treatment protocol than to tailoring the treatment to the particular characteristics of a specific patient's environment or history as would be the case in the idiographic view taken in functional analysis. If treatments do not vary once an initial diagnosis has been made, then a functional analysis can have no treatment utility.

However, the utility of the nomothetic perspective in matching clients to effective treatments has not been as useful as hoped. As the fifth version of the Diagnostic and Statistical Manual (DSM-5) emerges (American Psychiatric Association, 2013), there is an opportunity to distinguish clinical behavior analysis from much of clinical psychology by extending the role of idiographic functional analysis. This approach may yield better results for people seeking behavior change because it will identify and apply appropriate behavioral principles to presenting problems (Follette, Naugle, & Linnerooth, 2000).

Identifying Targets. As we will discuss later, there are several ways to construe behavioral targets for change. Commonly clients present to therapy when they are experiencing distress or something interferes with their ability to perform their chosen roles such as partner, parent, employee, etc. Many clients are familiar with some of the terminology in DSM and will say that they are depressed or anxious or that they engage in self-injurious behavior. Clients may say that they do not want to feel a particular affective response such as depression, anxiety, loneliness, etc. These initial presenting concerns are not ignored. Instead, they are understood as proximal targets for change. Often, therapists may agree to target these behaviors using constructionalist approaches (Goldiamond, 1974, 1975; Hawkins, 1986). However, contemporary clinical behavior analysis increasingly emphasizes identifying and building the clients' repertoires toward more distal goals. Such goals focus on what the client values. They exceed merely removing symptoms so that a diagnosis is no longer present.

Behavior analysis has always aspired to apply behavioral principles in the service of improving the human condition. *Walden Two* was an attempt to describe how behavioral principles could be used to produce a more equitable, prosocial culture (Skinner, 1948). In many instances, clinical behavior analysts spend significant time helping clients define their personal *values*. While humanistic psychologists have long thought this to be an important issue, contemporary clinical behavior analysis has taken the analysis from discussions of values as commonly understood to conceptualizing values as establishing operations for behavior change. Furthermore, clinical behavior analysis frames values in terms of improving the quality of the larger environment in which we all function (cf. Biglan & Hinds, 2009; Bonow & Follette, 2009; Leigland, 2005; Plumb, Stewart, Dahl, & Lundgren, 2009). Part of the utility of focusing on distal targets defined by the clients' values is that it allows the client to see beyond the amelioration of distressing symptoms. It also allows clients to generate criteria by which to evaluate their own behavioral choices by asking themselves, "Is this consistent with my values?"

Functional Analysis. In traditional functional analysis, an individual's behavior is considered in the context of the person's current environment and history. Data about potential functional relationships are gathered using interviews and observation. Hypotheses are formed about the possible controlling variables and subsequent treatment plans are developed to change the behaviors of interest for a particular client. The last step in the initial analysis is to manipulate the relevant hypothesized variables and to evaluate whether they alter the clinical problem. If not, the process repeats until a useful functional relationship emerges in which the clinical behavior analyst identifies controlling variables, manipulates them, and observes clinically significant change. Observing clinically significant changes is the hallmark of an idiographic approach to behavior change.

Unfortunately, there is not a practical, standardized way of conducting a functional analysis for normal verbal adults (Hayes & Follette, 1992a, 1992b). Haynes and O'Brien (1990) offered helpful guidelines for clinical assessment. They suggested attending to those variables that are causal (variables that reliably covary), important (variables that account for a large amount of the variance in behavior) and changeable (conditions that exist in the current environment that can be altered rather than, for example, historical facts that cannot be undone). They also presented a thorough, though somewhat complex, methodology for developing and testing the utility of a functional analysis (Haynes & O'Brien, 2000). An abstracted review of the heuristic approach used in the context of clinical behavior analysis is presented below. This approach is convenient and manageable if not comprehensive (taken from Follette et al., 2000).

It is natural and productive for clinical behavior analysts to think about assessing client problems using the heuristic of the three-term contingency referenced earlier. One can listen to and interact with clients and organize the information so that it fits into the contingency framework. Thus, one can form the case conceptualization by assessing each of the elements that follow.

Antecedents

Inadequate Antecedents. For our immediate purposes "inadequate antecedents" refers to environments that contain few opportunities for reinforcement. This is an easy situation to overlook and instead find the cause of distress in the individual's dysfunctional repertoire. However, it is important to evaluate how a person's social repertoire may be successful in other environments and examine why there seems to be a lack of fit between the individual's repertoire and current environment. A client may describe a job that forces isolation because of location or timing (works nights), a recent divorce that disrupts a social network, or going back to school where few peers can be found. Such conditions signal the need to assess how frequently reinforcing opportunities occur in the client's environment.

Poor Discriminative Control. In this instance, the problem may not be that a client's behavior is problematic , but rather that the behavior is emitted in the wrong circumstances. For example, one partner in a relationship may describe a troubling situation at work in order to seek comfort and understanding. The other partner may offer a solution to the problem instead. The solution may be a good one but come at the wrong time. Offering the solution may lead the partner to feel misunderstood. In this example, the client did not discriminate that the response that would be reinforced was sympathy and evidence of listening. Later, problem-solving might have been appreciated.

Inappropriate Discriminative Control. Some clients describe behaviors that lead to distancing from important others because those behaviors are not appropriate in the context in which they are emitted. For example, it is never useful to attack a partner in an intimate relationship with ad hominem critical statements even though these critical statements may succeed in terminating an aversive interaction. This example may be exacerbated by a response deficit as well (e.g., not knowing how to effectively ask a partner to change his behavior). Nevertheless, such behavior indicates a lack of recognition that this response will not lead to positive outcomes in the long term.

Responses (Behaviors)

Clients often complain about what is not working in their lives. The client's description of the problem may not use specific technical terminology, but the clinician often listens for descriptors or observes behaviors during a session that would qualify as behavioral excesses, deficits, or behaviors that interfere with or prevent more useful behaviors from emerging.

Behavioral Excesses. Behavioral excesses are just that—behaviors that the client emits at a higher rate than would lead to optimal opportunities for reinforcement. Behavioral excesses in an institutionalized child are simple to identify based on their undesirable, injurious topography (e.g., head banging behaviors). In contrast, identifying a functionally important excess is sometimes difficult in a normal adult. For example, a client might describe how much she likes to tell her partner that she loves him. At first inspection this sounds like a behavior that will enhance intimacy. However, it might become apparent that the frequency of these expressions signals insecurity and a need for reassurance that the partner finds unappealing. In another example, a client may be excessively verbal. Others, including the therapist, may find the level of verbal behavior disturbing. The function served by the excessive talking remains to be determined. Hypotheses could include reduction of anxiety or preventing criticism from others among many other possibilities.

Behavioral Deficits. Behavioral deficits occur when a client does not exhibit functional behavior in an adequate form or quantity to lead to optimal rates of reinforcement given the client's valued goals. The inability to express emotion is often described as a problem in relationships hindering intimacy in couples.

It is generally easy for clinicians to see clinical problems as either an excess or a deficit. For example, a clinician may conceptualize a problem as talking too much or listening too little. The "correct" analysis is the one that provides the clinician and client with the most useful intervention strategy.

Interfering, Controlling, or Obstructing Behaviors. In some instances, behaviors may function in ways that make treatment impossible until those behaviors are addressed. Behaviors that impede the therapeutic relationship and treatment may be dramatic. For example, parasuicidal behavior may get the attention of the clinician in such a way that it derails treatment.

The problematic behaviors may also be excessive passivity or prolonged silences with few clear antecedents. Often such behaviors function to control demands for change, to regulate emotional responding, or to avoid or escape topics being examined in sessions. The clinician can analyze these behaviors as excesses or deficits, but these behaviors are given particular attention here because they directly impede effective treatment.

Consequences

Lack of Appropriate Consequential Control. In interpersonal relationships, some highly valued behaviors are emitted at a low level because they are not reinforced by the client's natural environment. The result can vary from depression to the escalation of dramatic behavior to gain some apparent control over the environment (valued people). The clinician may have good access to relevant information when analyzing apparent deficits in reinforcers in the environment during couples or family interventions. In contrast, when only the client is in treatment, the clinician may be told something like, "My partner didn't compliment me on dinner (or some other task)." The clinician might then ask if the client inquired whether her partner liked the dinner. Often times the client will then say the equivalent of, "No, but he (or she) should have known that I worked hard and would like to have received some sign of appreciation." In this case, there are different treatment implications depending on whether the partner is unresponsive or unaware. The environment may need to be changed in extreme cases in which the client has essentially no control over the environment (i.e., no or very little reinforcement for valued behavior). The client may need to consider a job change, a move to a new neighborhood or city, or even a new partner. Such changes are not decisions to be made lightly, but they may be necessary.

Competing Consequences. As one moves from childhood to adulthood, the sources and agents of reinforcement become more complex and may compete. A client who experiences high levels of competing contingencies may observe that his behavior is unpredictable, a condition upsetting to the client and to those around him. Similarly, the client may not know what to do when the same behavior is reinforced by some people and ignored or punished by others. For example, the client may value hard work and good pay. His employer and spouse may initially support such behavior. If, however, the spouse begins to resent the client's long working hours, the contingencies brought to bear by the spouse may compete with those of the employer and perhaps with the client's own values.

Inappropriate Consequential Control. One clinical problem that is particularly difficult to treat is when a client's behavior is under inappropriate stimulus control. In the case of illegal sexual preferences, both the clinical behavior analyst and the client can identify the problem, but there is a lack of technology to change such preferences. No one has yet reported a randomized clinical trial of a successful technology for treating sexual offenders without using aversive control or response prevention strategies. In other cases, inappropriate contingencies might be appropriate if accessed infrequently (e.g., alcohol or illicit substances). In these cases, contingency management and harm reduction programs can successfully change the frequency or intensity of abuse (for descriptions of each approach see Collins et al., 2012; Petry, 2012). Though not generally discussed in behavior analytic terms (Apodaca & Longabaugh, 2009), motivational interviewing is an approach to altering the reinforcing function of alcohol, illicit substances, smoking or gambling (Miller & Rollnick, 2013). It can be conceptualized as altering either consequential control or motivating operations in stimulus equivalence and transformation of functions (Christopher & Dougher, 2009).

Two Important Verbal Behaviors: Tacts and Mands. When the clinician cannot be present to count the occurrences of behaviors, she may listen for labels that the client relates for seemingly private events. For example, the client might say, "I feel like a failure if I ask for help." The label of "failure" is a tact, which Skinner described as verbal behavior controlled by nonverbal antecedent stimuli. The tact is maintained by generalized conditioned reinforcers. That is, the label of being a failure (the tact) is used because it is understood by the verbal community (Skinner, 1957, pp. 81–82). To achieve satisfying interpersonal relationships, clients must be able to properly label (tact) how they react to events in relationships. A tacting deficit leads to an unresponsive environment and a feeling of being misunderstood by those who matter.

A mand is a verbal operant reinforced by that which is specified in the verbal behavior (Skinner, 1957, pp. 35–36). "Scratch my back," is a mand that is reinforced by someone scratching the person's back. The reinforcer is specified in the verbal utterance itself.

Tacts and mands may be hard to distinguish from one another. However, using tacts and mands appropriately is an essential skill for stating preferences and for reacting to the actions of others. These two repertoires are often inadequate in clients who complain about not being understood. If a client cannot label the impact of an interaction with other people, then others cannot know what matters to the client. If the client cannot or does not mand for things she finds reinforcing, then the people in the client's environment cannot know what would be pleasing or aversive. There are a variety of other verbal behaviors that occur in therapy that can be maladaptive and thus require attention (Glenn, 1983), but tacts and mands are especially important for successful interpersonal relations.

The Challenge of Applying Principles In Clinical Settings

The functional analysis and resulting case conceptualization just described is as essential for treatment planning in clinical settings as it is in other applied settings. While the link between the description of this process and behavioral principles is relatively straightforward, putting it into practice is extremely challenging.

A disadvantage of clinical work with normal adults, living in naturalistic (as opposed to an institutional) settings, is that most therapy occurs in a traditional one-on-one environment. However, this way of conducting sessions is not ideal for observing and testing hypotheses about environmental controlling variables. In most states, laws that protect the confidentiality of therapist-client interactions apply to these types of sessions and do not extend to non-private sessions or observations. Thus, a clinician must possess the ability to be a keen observer of client behavior, including the consequences of the client's behavior on herself. The clinician must also assess her own stimulus functions on the client in real time. This set of observational skills, along with an awareness of one's own history, is complex contingency-shaped behavior, the acquisition of which often requires extensive supervision.

Distinguishing between Function and Topography

It is crucial for the clinician to understand the difference between the topography of a behavior and its function when observing and building a case conceptualization (Follette & Darrow, 2010). Failing to do so can lead to serious missteps during interventions. Topography is what a behavior looks like. The topography of crying is tears running down the cheeks, perhaps accompanied by sobs or whimpers. The clinician may assume that crying is an emotional conditioned response to a sad or distressing situation. However, the function of crying is an empirical question. Crying might be a conditioned emotional response or it might develop operant qualities, known or unknown to the client, if it has an effect on the people around the client (in this case the clinician). When crying occurs and how it functions should be carefully observed.

Behaviors may also have multiple functions. A clinician might observe that a client's crying increases when discussing how difficult behavior change might be. The client may well become distressed by the difficulty of changing behavior. In that case, crying is properly understood as an emotional reaction. However, the clinician or others in the client's environment may also establish an additional function for crying. The clinician might negatively reinforce crying by changing the topic from a request for behavior change whenever crying occurs. Concomitantly, the clinician may also positively reinforce crying by providing comfort to the crying client. These natural responses are easy to understand.

If, however, the clinician notices that little progress occurs during sessions, even though the sessions seem full of emotional content, a different analysis and way of responding may be warranted. The clinician may be contributing to the development and maintenance of this behavior in a way that is not effective in helping the client reach his or her behavior change goals. The clinician could implement an alternative treatment design to evaluate her hypotheses about the factors maintaining the behavior. She might vary how she responds to the crying and determine whether the different ways of responding, or intervening, change the rate of crying and, in turn, the progression of therapy.

Distinguishing Response Classes

Additionally, many different response topographies can serve the same function. Thus, it is important for clinicians to group these topographies into response classes based on function. Clients may have difficulty altering long-standing behavioral patterns even though those patterns may be preventing other, ultimately more reinforcing behaviors, from developing. Avoidance behaviors are a commonly observed response class in sessions. When a clinician sets the stage for change, clients may exhibit a wide variety of responses that all serve the function of avoiding an emotional response or having to initiate a new behavior. As crying is eliminated, other behaviors that serve the same function may emerge, thus forming a functional class. This class could include anger, prolonged silences, and effusive praise for the clinician, etc.

Properly understanding the function of broad response classes can be challenging. For example, it is hard not to be distracted by the dramatic response topography if a client begins talking about suicidal ideation and intent. Ethical and legal obligations may appropriately lead the clinician to focus on the suicidal content of the client's verbal behavior. Yet, the clinician should provide alternative behavioral pathways for the client to tolerate the session content and process, thus reducing the likelihood of the client bringing up suicidal ideation as a means of controlling the session.

Clinician as Context

Suppose that the clinician tries to change the apparent functional contingencies that follow crying, but the behavior does not change. In that case, the functional analysis should be reconsidered. A key complexity of clinical behavior analysis is that the clinician is an active part of context in which the behavior of interest occurs. The clinician is not an outside consultant attempting to identify the function of behaviors by observation. This can make it difficult for clinicians to identify all the controlling variables.

Consider an instance where the client's crying serves multiple functions. One function may be that crying results in the clinician comforting the client. The clinician's comforting behavior may, in turn, be positively reinforced by her ability to soothe the client. Additionally, the clinician's comforting behavior may be negatively reinforced by the reduction of the clinician's discomfort when the client stops crying. This contingency can make it difficult for clinicians to behave in different ways that might be necessary for client behavior change. Close attention to one's behavior is required for a clinician to become skillful at observing both her own responses and those of the client. New clinicians may benefit from experiential exercises designed to promote discrimination of their own private events that might be important sources of control for their in-session behavior, but that are not in the best interests of the client.

Natural Versus Arbitrary Reinforcement

Ferster (1967) raised the important distinction between natural and arbitrary reinforcement. Behavior analysts often use arbitrary reinforcement to establish behaviors in impaired or young populations. As an example, when a parent tells a child to put on his warm coat before going outside and praises the child for doing so, the praise is an arbitrary reinforcer. Others in the child's environment will not usually praise the child for putting on his coat. However, if putting on a coat occurs because it is initially followed by praise, other naturally-occurring reinforcers may help to maintain the behavior (e.g., staying warm). That contingency will occur in the child's natural environment regardless of whether a parent is there to prompt and reinforce the behavior in the future.

An additional feature of arbitrary reinforcement is that the delivery of the reinforcer also reinforces the behavior of the deliverer, in this case the parent. Asking the child to wear his warm coat is reinforced by the child's compliance with the parent's request.

The distinction between arbitrary and natural reinforcers is useful to the clinical behavior analyst. First, the clinician should ask, what reinforcers occur in session? Second, she should ask, what reinforcers occur in the natural environment? Natural reinforcers will be needed so that the change in behavior will generalize to the natural environment.

Requisite Interpersonal Skills for the Clinical Behavior Analyst

There are many sources of psychological distress that may lead a client to seek the services of a clinical behavior analyst. One major source of distress derives from the client's low rate of success (reinforcement) when attempting to effectively interact with those in his environment to attain valued sources of reinforcement. That is, the person is socially ineffective at getting what is valued. To address this issue, the clinician must possess complex social skills herself.

It is very useful for the clinician to have a strong background in basic applied behavior analysis. Such knowledge is helpful in understanding the issues described so far including the notion of a functional analysis, sensitivity to function rather than topography, functional classes, schedule effects, etc. However, the clinician's interpersonal repertoire is critically important when trying to facilitate change in normal adult outpatients. As mentioned above, the clinician is now part of the context in which behavior is observed and assessed, and in many cases the clinical behavior analyst mediates the reinforcers most critical for change. For social reinforcers to be effective, the clinician and client must actually matter to each other. The clinician must be able to recognize the legitimacy of valued behaviors that the client describes and that may not be the same as those the clinician may value, given the client and clinician's different histories or cultural backgrounds. It is much easier to teach behavioral principles to a naturally empathetic, courageous, and evocative clinician than to teach these latter skills to someone whose natural environment has not shaped them.

Among those qualities that the clinician must possess is the ability to participate and observe herself and the client in real time to assess the behaviors and effects each person is having on the other during a session. The clinician must also have the courage to care enough about the client and the process such that she can actually and genuinely matter to the client so that the clinician's reactions can reinforce the client's behavior. That is, the clinician should allow herself to supply meaningful, natural reinforcement. This same stance is necessary for a clinician to reformulate a case conceptualization when it no longer works, to phase out reinforcement when it is time to ask more of the client, and to risk feeling distress when the client is unsuccessful at times.

Suppose a clinician has developed a case conceptualization that suggests that a client has a deficit in empathy and perspective-taking. These deficits interfere with developing deep, meaningful relationships. What skills and stimulus properties would help such a therapist to establish this repertoire in a client? The clinician would need to be able to discriminate behaviors belonging to these response classes (i.e., empathy and perspective-taking) and approximations to them. The client's efforts to develop this repertoire would allow the clinician to exhibit such behaviors herself as the client struggled and failed on the way to making improvements. If the clinician did not possess that behavioral repertoire, modeling, reinforcing or shaping this complex class of behaviors is unlikely to be successful. In the worst case, the clinician might not identify her lack of these behaviors as the problem. A successful piano teacher might not play as well as her prodigies, but the teacher could not be tone deaf.

Similarly, clinicians may have repertoires of behaviors that are appropriate for close or intimate relationships, but feel uncomfortable emitting those behaviors with a client. However, to be optimally effective as a mediator of social reinforcement, the clinician must be able to display in therapy the behaviors that she exhibits in her closest interpersonal relationships. This may be the greatest difference between the clinical role and the consultant role taken by behavior analysts when they explain how to arrange environmental contingencies to effectively shape behavior or when they use arbitrary reinforcers with less functional populations (e.g., autistic children).

When targeting the interpersonal repertoire of clients, the clinician has to establish different functions for the therapeutic relationship as therapy begins and progresses (Follette, Naugle, & Callaghan, 1996). Initially, the clinician recognizes that the mere act of starting therapy is often challenging to clients. In the psychotherapy outcome literature, the most common number of sessions is one (assuming clients actually make it to a first session after the initial phone contact). Although there might be many reasons for this, establishing therapy as a safe and useful place is likely to be important regardless of why a client presents for change. The clinician must reinforce the general class of behaviors related to attending sessions by acknowledging the effort it took to make the decision to attend, building a collaborative set that would allow the client to predict a successful outcome, and minimizing the aversive aspects of the initial few sessions. Often, as in traditional therapy, information is gathered during initial sessions and disclosure, attending, scheduling and effort is reinforced. Within the first two to four sessions, an initial case conceptualization is presented. The clinician and client should agree that this conceptualization is a reasonable initial understanding of treatment targets and that the case conceptualization will evolve.

As therapy progresses, the rich reinforcement schedule for actively engaging in therapy is reduced and the clinician begins shaping more complex social interactions. It can be difficult to know exactly when to fade reinforcers and how to select the next approximation of some ultimately final target behavior. One common error is to continue to reinforce intermediate approximations of target behaviors. For example, a therapist might have targeted self-disclosure as a part of a class of intimacy-building behaviors. Since therapy is an intense collaboration between client and clinician, it is easy for the therapist to read more into a client's self-disclosure than is actually stated. As a result, the clinician may respond accurately to the disclosure even though the self-disclosure would not be understood by a person without a long history of interacting with the client. Essentially the clinician is relying on her history with the client rather than on the likely effectiveness of the client's behavior in the natural environment.

Also, both clinicians and clients may become comfortable with the status quo. Thus, clinicians can be reluctant to reduce the reinforcement of behavior that is successful in the session in the service of shaping responding that will be more effective outside of the session. A leaner reinforcement schedule can be aversive to the client if not handled properly. In short, all the schedule effects that occur in other settings are present in the clinical realm with the added difficulty that it may be hard to know when to increase demands in the behavioral repertoire when the clinician is part of the context.

Use of Molar Functional Relations

Although other therapeutic approaches will call a client "resistant," clinical behavior analysts try to identify competing contingencies or alternative conceptualizations. These situations often require a clinician to broaden the scope of her analysis to consider ways in which a target behavior relates to other behaviors and sources of reinforcement in the client's environment. Re-conceptualizing cases using molar functional relations can be helpful in these instances. Although all functional relations (e.g., reinforcement) are molar in that they refer to contingencies over time, it is easy to speak about them as instances. On the other hand, some functional relations are not easy to characterize in this way; it is these that are referred to as "molar." This section will briefly describe the utility of a few molar relations including matching, momentum, and discounting (see Plaud & Plaud, 1998; Waltz & Follette, 2009 for further applied descriptions of these relations).

Probably the most well-known molar functional relation is that described by the matching law (Davison & McCarthy, 1988; Herrnstein, 1997). While the matching law is the basis of the behavioral activation approach for depression, it is useful in many clinical scenarios. The matching law defines a relationship that states that the relative rate of a certain behavior can be predicted by the ratio of the rate of reinforcing contingencies for that behavior to the rate of reinforcing contingencies available for all other behaviors in that same situation. In its simplest form the equations is:

$$\frac{R_T}{R_T + R_e} = \frac{r_T}{r_T + r_e}$$

where R_T is the time spent engaging in the clinical target behavior and R_e is the time spent in all other concurrently available extraneous activities. The term r_t is the rate of reinforcement for the clinical target, and r_e is the rate of reinforcement for all other concurrently available activities (Waltz & Follette, 2009, pp. 52–53). This implies that clinicians should track not only problematic behavior but also those behaviors that would be more effective in a given situation.

The matching law suggests two different treatment pathways to decrease problem behavior in addition to directly targeting the reinforcing contingencies for that behavior: increase the reinforcement available for alternate responses and increase the rate of non-contingent reinforcement. These strategies are particularly useful in situations where it is not easy to intervene on the direct contingencies (e.g., it is difficult to decrease the reinforcing properties of illegal substances). The matching law provides a strong rationale for constructive approaches to intervention where the goals of therapy include both decreasing problematic behavior as well as increasing alternative adaptive behaviors.

Conceptualizing a client's behavior using the principle of behavioral momentum may also be useful (Nevin, 1992; Plaud & Gaither, 1996). Momentum characterizes how long a behavior will persist when there is a change in contingencies. Momentum is determined by the response rate and rate of reinforcement. If two behaviors occur at the same rate, the behavior that has a higher rate of reinforcement will persist for longer. Alternatively, if two behaviors have the same rate of reinforcement, the behavior that occurs with the greatest frequency will persist longer.

Understanding the principle of momentum may increase the empathy of a clinician toward a client who continues to behave in ways that do not work in his current environment. For example, a client may seem committed to changing interactions with his spouse while in session but continues to report fights in subsequent sessions. It could be that his partner has inadvertently reinforced the escalation of arguments and the rate of reinforcement supplied in therapy for changing this pattern cannot compete with the rich rate of reinforcement that has occurred at home.

Behavioral momentum is also a useful heuristic when shaping a new repertoire. Consider a client who has a limited repertoire for tacting emotions. It is likely that the client's attempts to tact emotions with his partner may not be reinforced as this repertoire is being shaped. The clinician will have to provide an environment that is rich in reinforcement for these attempts, however awkward, in order to build behavioral momentum. This can include non-contingent reinforcement, or reinforcement based on generally engaging in treatment. Furthermore, the clinician should attend to the rate that the client exhibits this new behavior. Providing a lot of opportunities for the client to tact emotion will be important to increase the likelihood this new behavior will persist in environments with fewer opportunities and a leaner schedule of reinforcement.

Similarly, the principle of discounting may provide a clinician with many alternative treatment pathways (Ainslie & Haslam, 2001; Bickel & Marsch, 2001; Critchfield & Kollins, 2001). Discounting characterizes patterns of choice behavior and how preferences may change when some inconvenience (e.g., delay, risk/uncertainty) is encountered. Although the largest outcome is preferred under most circumstances, there is some point where individuals choose the smaller, sooner consequence compared to the larger, later consequence. This switching point varies by person; those who choose the smaller, sooner consequence at an earlier time point are often called impulsive. Impulsivity is associated with many clinical problems (e.g., substance use, obsessive-compulsive disorder, and attention deficit and hyperactivity disorder).

One strategy suggested by an understanding of discounting involves building more proximal consequences (i.e., opportunities for positive reinforcement in the short term) related to the larger, later outcome. A verbal commitment to losing weight can impose a social contingency on making health food choices and exercising. Additionally, discussion regarding what makes a certain outcome (e.g., remaining substance free) important to the client may increase the value of that outcome. This may function to broaden the response class associated with the desired outcome and thus, increase the opportunities for reinforcement related to it. Alternatively, a clinician may try to decrease the aversive function of the inconvenience (e.g., improve a client's distress tolerance skills so that cravings do not lead to substance use).

There are many other ways that an understanding of molar functional relations may be useful clinically. The last sections focus on theory-based treatment packages that do not explicitly discuss these principles. However, an understanding of them is likely to enhance a clinician's effectiveness and more research is needed to support the use of these molar relations in applied/clinical settings.

Functional Analytic Psychotherapy

Functional Analytic Psychotherapy (FAP) was first described in 1991 and has been elaborated subsequently (Kohlenberg & Tsai, 1991; Tsai et al., 2009). FAP is perhaps the most straightforward translation of behavior analytic principles into clinical behavior analysis. An assessment and case conceptualization examines all the sources of behavioral control. For purposes of simplifying the presentation to the client, FAP primary discusses problematic behavioral excesses and deficits as clinically relevant behaviors 1 (CRB1). Improvements that lead to more functional behaviors are described as clinically relevant behaviors 2 (CRB2).

A key assumption of FAP is that the problematic behaviors that occur between the client and others will also occur between the client and the clinician in therapy. As a result, the behavior and the interpersonal conditions that give rise to problematic behaviors can be observed in therapy. Alternative, more useful behaviors can be tried and shaped in the context of the caring therapeutic relationship. There is no presumption that the therapeutic relationship and the clinically relevant behaviors observed are metaphorical for any other relationship. Instead, they are viewed as genuine responses to the client-clinician dyad.

The earlier discussion about the interpersonal repertoire of the clinical behavior analyst is most relevant for FAP. Correctly functionally analyzing the client's problematic and goal behaviors can be done only if the clinician does not distort the clinically relevant behaviors because of behavioral excesses or deficits of her own.

FAP is appropriate as a clinical behavior analytic technique when client dysphoria results from ineffective responding in his or her social environment. The term "ineffective" is not entirely appropriate because behavior evolves for a purpose in the context in which it is emitted. Understanding the context can dramatically alter a case conceptualization. For example, Hops and colleagues have shown that depressive behaviors can function to control aversive behaviors from other family members (Hops et al., 1987). FAP is appropriate when it is possible to establish conditions in therapy that are functionally equivalent to those conditions where the problematic behaviors are emitted in the outside environment and more functional alternatives can be shaped. FAP can be a powerful example of applying the principles of behavior analysis to outpatient normal adults to produce beneficial change.

FAP has five basic rules. The rules make sense to any behavior analyst, but implementing those rules may require a great deal of training because so much of the clinical behavior analyst's own behavior affects what happens in therapy and why.

Rule 1 is to watch for clinically relevant behaviors (CRB1s and CRB2s). The relevant behaviors are identified through sophisticated observation by the clinician and the development of a useful case conceptualization.

Rule 2 is to evoke clinically relevant behaviors. This allows problematic behaviors to be emitted and provides opportunities for the clinician to reinforce approximations of improvement.

Rule 3 is to reinforce improvements. As mentioned earlier, the behavior that is reinforced changes as one improvement plateaus and it is time to shape further improvements. This rule requires the clinician to notice improvements. Sometimes it may be necessary to reinforce any behavioral change.

Rule 4 is to observe the reinforcing effects of the clinician's responding on clinically relevant behavior. The clinician must supply effective reinforcers when the client's behavior begins to change. Reinforcement is only said to occur when the contingency alters the rate of behavior, not necessarily when the clinician intends to reinforce behavior. It can be disconcerting for a clinician to find that her efforts at reinforcement are not affecting the rate of improvement. In that case, the clinician must identify an effective reinforcement strategy. The strategy may change over time as familiarity grows in the dyad and the nature of what is reinforcing to the client evolves.

Rule 5 is to provide explanations of variables that affect client behavior as a way to promote generalization. In other words, a FAP clinician tries to help clients understand the functional relations that exist in their environments. In this way, FAP tries to provide an experience that will serve the client more broadly as important aspects of his or her life change. If the client can become his own behavior analyst, he will notice the impact of his behavior on others and vice versa. It is common for some

FAP clinicians to ask clients to act or react with intention and then determine if their behavior had the impact that they intended.

Blending and Distinguishing Principles

Many problems seen by the contemporary clinical behavior analysts initially have strong components of anxiety and avoidance. Though we have resisted using diagnostic labels, for the purposes of convenience, many anxiety disorders in DSM can be usefully conceptualized and treated by assuming that anxiety is the result of a respondent learning history and that subsequent avoidance was operantly conditioned by the negative reinforcer of reduction of that anxiety. This model, the two-factor theory of Mowrer (1939), is a useful way of understanding many treatments for anxiety disorders whether it is fully accurate or not. The basic treatment for the anxiety and related avoidance behavior is exposure and response prevention. That is, the client is gradually exposed to the aversive stimulus without being given the opportunity to escape or avoid it. This approach has been used to treat obsessive-compulsive disorders for many years (Foa, Steketee, & Milby, 1980; Whittal, Thordarson, & McLean, 2005). Exposure along with response prevention is a large component of treatments for posttraumatic stress disorder, phobias, and panic disorders.

Alternatively, avoidance behavior may be conceptualized as rule-governed behavior. For example, a client may follow the rule, "Telling people how you feel makes you weak and vulnerable" and subsequently avoid all expressions of emotion. The principle of exposure is equally useful in this case. The clinician can ask the client to try behaving in emotionally appropriate ways in order to contact different contingencies (i.e., attempt to bring behavior under the control of natural contingencies rather than arbitrary rules).

Clinical behavior analysts readily understand exposure as an intervention for avoidance. However, decreasing avoidance behavior may result in a deficit in a client's repertoire that must be replaced with behaviors that will lead to reinforcement. Problems related to anxiety can exist for many years and can interfere with the natural development of effective social behaviors. Therefore, even if exposure or other behavioral interventions are successful at eliminating avoidance behavior, additional interventions are often helpful to efficiently develop a social repertoire. This is when FAP can be useful.

FAP can be useful in shaping complex social repertoires that are not targeted by most other therapeutic approaches. It is much like functional analysis in that the principles are readily understood, but the implementation is not easy. There is not a single algorithm on how to proceed with either the case conceptualization or the intervention. As a result of not being easily described, it is not easy to develop a manual for conducting FAP. As a result, disseminating FAP is challenging.

One of the basic tenets of behavior analysis is that there are many ways to achieve a function. Someone may be attractive because she is effusive and sociable while someone else may be attractive because she is aloof and mysterious. Someone may be able to ask questions directly because of his earnest style while someone else may need to more circumspect when asking the same questions. The point is that different clinicians have different stimulus properties and repertoires for accomplishing the same task. Clinicians must learn to be effective, just as clients must. Clients have multiple ways to accomplish an interpersonal goal. Clinicians can also use many different response topographies to be successful. Therefore, one particular response topography cannot be prescribed.

Complicating the matter further is that clients do not have the same preference for the pace of change. A client may need to make small initial changes because he finds making large, rapid changes to be stressful. Other clients may be impatient with a slower pace. This flexibility does not mean that FAP allows all approaches to therapy. If the clinician has major interpersonal deficits of her own, treatment will not be effective. That said, FAP clearly follows principles familiar to behavior analysts. The difficulty in disseminating FAP so far is that it is a contingently shaped complex behavior that does not lend itself to rule-governed ways of training.

Cognitions, Relational Frame Theory and Acceptance and Commitment Therapy

As mentioned earlier, Skinner's (1945, 1957) account of verbal behavior and private events is creative yet incomplete. He clearly recognized the importance of treating thoughts, feelings, and emotions as events to be explained. However, his attempt to explain verbal behavior was difficult and did not provide clinicians with ways to easily translate his analysis into applied change strategies. His 1957 book is full of definitions and exemplars, but it is short on experimental findings and an account of how verbal stimuli become related. Sidman (see 1994 for an extensive history) offered a descriptive account of stimulus equivalence in which one stimulus or class of stimuli produces responses made to other stimuli without direct training of all relations (i.e., reflexivity, symmetry, and transitivity). Later, Sidman suggested how relations might emerge, but empirical challenges to his ideas soon appeared (cf. Minster, Jones, Elliffe, & Muthukumaraswamy, 2006; Sidman, 2000).

An analysis of verbal behavior that was readily translated into clinical practice appeared in 2001. This culmination of many years of research was introduced under the name of Relational Frame Theory (RFT) (Hayes, Barnes-Holmes, & Roche, 2001). While too complex and nuanced to discuss fully here, RFT describes verbal behavior as "the behavior of relating stimuli or events in a particular way" (Törneke, 2010, p. 68). It provides an operant account of how stimuli become related in the absence of direct contact with contingencies.

RFT describes relational networks in which one can learn, for example, "larger than" relations in which A is larger than B, and B is larger than C. Without any direct experience, people can derive that A is larger than C. This is transitivity when observed experimentally or clinically. One can readily see that as relational networks are established (e.g., "worse than"), people can respond without direct experience with the stimuli involved.

Of particular clinical importance is the notion of derived relational responding. Such responding can be observed during name—object learning. The sequence might go, see Bob → hear name → repeat name (Barnes-Holmes, Barnes-Holmes, McHugh, & Hayes, 2004, pp. 391–392). After some repetitions the child can point to the appropriate person when asked, "Where is Bob?" RFT terms this a derived relation because there is no direct history of being reinforced for pointing to Bob. This is a generalized operant brought under the control of contextual cues through differential reinforcement. After many such naming exemplars are reinforced, the response will eventually emerge to novel stimuli in the absence of differential reinforcement.

Other stimulus relations can be trained including arbitrary applicable relational responding (Törneke, 2010, pp. 83–86). Arbitrary refers to relations that initially are trained to one feature of relational responding and then are applied to other features that do not share the original formal properties. Larger-smaller can be initially trained to the physical size of objects. It can then be transferred to more abstract features as relational responding continues. In this way, a dime can be considered "larger than" a nickel even though the nickel is physically larger than the dime.

Transformation of function is at the heart of RFTs' link to psychopathology. Without needing to understand the complexity of RFT, it is easy to appreciate that, after an experience that associates a doctor with discomfort, a client may also experience anxiety in the presence of a dentist, who is also called a doctor. This phenomenon represents a "relation of coordination or equivalence." Stimuli can be members of more than one equivalence class making it difficult for anyone to completely predict the ways in which a stimulus will function.

Acceptance and Commitment Therapy (ACT) (Hayes, Strosahl, & Wilson, 1999, 2012) is a treatment approach derived from RFT that has evolved over time. Initially ACT emphasized acceptance, "defusion," and values. Now, ACT focuses on enhancing "psychological flexibility" and includes six core processes: acceptance, cognitive defusion, contact with the present moment, self as context, values, and committed action. The first three processes (acceptance, cognitive defusion, and contact with the present moment) are referred to as acceptance and mindfulness processes. A variety of exercises are implemented to improve psychological flexibility or break up relational framing that is functioning as a barrier to important behavior change.

Hayes and colleagues coined the term "defusion" to help clients make the distinction between thoughts, language and reality (Hayes et al., 1999, 2012). A function of defusion techniques is to emphasize that words and thoughts are not things even if someone has a long history of having a word and a thing function in the same relational network. The ACT therapist may shape clients' behavior into recognizing the different effect of saying, "I am having the thought that I'm a failure" compared to, "I am a failure."

Another exercise that may clarify the defusion process is having the client say a word over and over such that the word becomes a sound and loses correspondence with the thing to which it originally referred. The late comedian George Carlin stumbled on this notion years ago with his act that demonstrated the pointlessness of having seven words you cannot say on television. Most of these words were slang for parts of the anatomy or descriptors of intercourse. When Carlin first said these words in his act, they had clear shock value. (This was many years ago.) He then proceeded to repeat each word over and over so that even the initially most shocked audience member got the point that the words were just words. Blackledge (2007) has provided a summary of defusion exercises.

Mindfulness techniques have been increasingly incorporated into third-wave behavior therapies including ACT. While there are many different theoretical understandings of how and why mindfulness techniques are helpful, ACT purposes that these exercises help increase acceptance and cognitive defusion (see Fletcher & Hayes, 2005 for a comprehensive description).

The second set of core processes (self as context, values, and committed action) are commitment and behavior change processes. The goal of these is to help the client live a valued life. Significant time is spent helping a client to identify the hierarchy of what he truly values in life and making the changes necessary to behave in ways consistent with his values. Acceptance and change toward a valued goal go hand and hand. Acceptance without change makes little sense, and change entails acceptance.

There is a linkage between each of the core processes and RFT. However, RFT and particularly the experimental preparations testing RFT are difficult to understand. As ACT has been empirically supported, disseminated, and increasingly widely adopted, these terms have been developed as middle-level shorthand. Just as FAP is difficult to disseminate because it relies on the dynamic application of principles and a flexible therapist repertoire, ACT and RFT researchers have developed this vocabulary to ease dissemination. The goal is for clinicians to implement important RFT principles in therapy without necessarily understanding the primary RFT literature. Many ACT clinicians can move from these terms to techniques to an overarching philosophy. A smaller subset of people can move from the basic science, through the middle-level terms, to practice and back again.

Summary

Clinical behavior analysis has progressed enormously. From the Little Albert demonstration that fear could result from classical conditioning (Watson & Rayner, 1920), through systematic desensitization, to the development of a psychotherapy based firmly on behavior analytic principles, clinical behavior analysis has dramatically expanded the audience that can benefit from its application. With the advent of Relational Frame Theory, clinical behavior analysis tried to address the thorny issues of cognition and emotion while remaining consistent with the values of behaviorism as the behavior analyst understands it.

The ability of clinical behavior analysts to address issues that for a long while seemed outside the scope of applied behavior analysis is exciting and challenging. Yet the vast majority of distress and desire for change lies in people who are not confined to highly restricted settings. Clinical behavior analysis is responding to the challenges inherent in reaching these people.

References

Ainslie, G., & Haslam, N. (2001). Hyperbolic discounting. In G. Loenstein & J. Elster (Eds.), *Choice over time* (pp. 57–92). Thousand Oaks, CA: Sage.

Allyon, T., & Azrin, N. H. (1968). *The token economy: A motivational system for therapy and rehabilitation.* New York: Appleton-Century-Crofts.

American Psychiatric Association. (2013). *Diagnostic and statistical manual of mental disorders* (5th ed.). Washington, DC: American Psychiatric Association.

Apodaca, T. R., & Longabaugh, R. (2009). Mechanisms of change in motivational interviewing: a review and preliminary evaluation of the evidence. *Addiction, 104*, 705–715.

Bandura, A. (1977). *Social learning theory*. Englewood Cliffs, NJ: Prentice Hall.

Barnes-Holmes, Y., Barnes-Holmes, D., McHugh, L., & Hayes, S. C. (2004). Relational Frame Theory: Some implications for understanding and treating human psychopathology. *International Journal of Psychology and Psychological Therapy, 4*, 355–375.

Beck, A. T., Rush, A. J., Shaw, B. F., & Emery, G. (1979). *Cognitive therapy of depression*. New York: Guilford.

Bickel, W. K., & Marsch, L. A. (2001). Toward a behavioral economic understanding of drug dependence: Delay discounting processes. *Addiction, 96*, 73–86.

Biglan, A., & Hinds, E. (2009). Evolving prosocial and sustainable neighborhoods and communities. *Annual Review of Clinical Psychology, 5*, 169–196.

Blackledge, J. T. (2007). Disrupting verbal processes: Cognitive defusion in acceptance and commitment therapy and other mindfulness-based psychotherapies. *The Psychological Record, 57*, 555–576.

Bonow, J. T., & Follette, W. C. (2009). Beyond values clarification: Addressing client values in clinical behavior analysis. *Behavior Analyst, 32*, 69–84.

Boring, E. G., Bridgman, P. W., Feigl, H., Pratt, C. C., & Skinner, B. F. (1945). Rejoinders and second thoughts. *Psychological Review, 52*, 278–294.

Chambless, D. L., & Ollendick, T. H. (2001). Empirically supported psychological interventions: Controversies and evidence. *Annual Review of Psychology, 52*, 685–716.

Christopher, P. J., & Dougher, M. J. (2009). A behavior-analytic account of motivational interviewing. *Behavior Analyst, 32*, 149–161.

Collins, S. E., Clifasefi, S. L., Logan, D. E., Samples, L. S., Somers, J. M., & Marlatt, G. A. (2012). Current status, historical highlights, and basic principles of harm reduction. In G. A. Marlatt, M. E. Larimer, & K. Witkiewitz (Eds.), *Harm reduction: Pragmatic strategies for managing high-risk behaviors* (2nd ed.). (pp. 3–35). New York: Guilford Press.

Critchfield, T., & Kollins, S. (2001). Temporal discounting: basic research and the analysis of socially important behavior. *Journal of Applied Behavior Analysis, 34*, 101.

Davison, M., & McCarthy, D. (1988). *The matching law: A research review*. Hillsdale, NJ: Erlbaum.

Dougher, M. J. (1997). Cognitive concepts, behavior analysis, and behavior therapy. *Journal of Behavior Therapy and Experimental Psychiatry, 28*, 65–70.

Dougher, M. J. (2000). *Clinical behavior analysis*. Reno, NV: Context Press.

Ferster, C. B. (1967). Arbitrary and natural reinforcement. *The Psychological Record, 22*, 1–16.

Ferster, C. B. (1972). An experimental analysis of clinical phenomena. *The Psychological Record, 22*, 1–16.

Ferster, C. B. (1973). A functional analysis of depression. *American Psychologist, 28*, 857–870.

Ferster, C. B., & Skinner, B. F. (1957). *Schedules of reinforcement*. New York: Appleton-Century-Crofts.

Fletcher, L., & Hayes, S. C. (2005). Relational frame theory, acceptance and commitment therapy, and a functional analytic definition of mindfulness. *Journal of Rational-Emotive and Cognitive-Behavior Therapy, 23*, 315–336.

Foa, E. B., Steketee, G., & Milby, J. B. (1980). Differential effects of exposure and response prevention in obsessive-compulsive washers. *Journal of Consulting and Clinical Psychology, 48*, 71–79.

Follette, W. C., & Darrow, S. M. (2010). The function and topography of behavior: Things aren't always as they seem. *European Psychotherapy, 9*, 81–92.

Follette, W. C., Naugle, A. E., & Callaghan, G. M. (1996). A radical behavioral understanding of the therapeutic relationship in effecting change. *Behavior Therapy*, *27*, 623–641.

Follette, W. C., Naugle, A. E., & Linnerooth, P. J. N. (2000). Functional alternatives to traditional assessment and diagnosis. In M. J. Dougher (Ed.), *Clinical behavior analysis* (pp. 99–125). Reno, NV: Context Press.

Glenn, S. S. (1983). Maladaptive functional relations in client verbal behavior. *The Behavior Analyst*, *6*, 47–56.

Goldiamond, I. (1974). Toward a constructional approach to social problems: Ethical and constitutional issues raised by applied behavior analysis. *Behaviorism*, *2*, 1–84.

Goldiamond, I. (1975). Insider-outsider problems: A constructional approach. *Rehabilitation Psychology*, *22*, 103–116.

Hawkins, R. P. (1986). Selection of target behaviors. In R. O. Nelson & S. C. Hayes (Eds.), *Conceptual foundations of behavioral assessment* (pp. 331–385). New York: Guilford.

Hayes, S. C., Barnes-Holmes, D., & Roche, B. (Eds.). (2001). *Relational frame theory: A post-Skinnerian account of human language and cognition*. New York: Kluwer.

Hayes, S. C., & Brownstein, A. J. (1986). Mentalism, behavior-behavior relations, and a behavior-analytic view of the purposes of science. *The Behavior Analyst*, *9*, 175.

Hayes, S. C., & Follette, W. C. (1992a). Behavioral assessment in the DSM era. *Behavioral Assessment*, *14*, 293–295.

Hayes, S. C., & Follette, W. C. (1992b). Can functional analysis provide a substitute for syndromal classification? *Behavioral Assessment*, *14*, 345–365.

Hayes, S. C., & Follette, W. C. (1993). The challenge faced by behavioral assessment. *European Journal of Psychological Assessment*, *9*, 182–188.

Hayes, S. C., Strosahl, K. D., & Wilson, K. G. (1999). *Acceptance and commitment therapy: An experiential approach to behavior change*. New York: Guilford Press.

Hayes, S. C., Strosahl, K. D., & Wilson, K. G. (2012). *Acceptance and commitment therapy: The process and practice of mindful change* (2nd ed.). New York: Guilford Press.

Haynes, S. N., & O'Brien, W. H. (1990). Functional analysis in behavior therapy. *Clinical Psychology Review*, *10*, 649–668.

Haynes, S. N., & O'Brien, W. H. (2000). *Principles and practice of behavioral assessment*. New York: Plenum Press.

Herrnstein, R. J. (1997). *The matching law: Papers in psychology and economics*. Cambridge, MA: Harvard University Press.

Hops, H., Biglan, A., Sherman, L., Arthur, J., Friedman, L., & Osteen, V. (1987). Home observations of family interactions of depressed women. *Journal of Consulting and Clinical Psychology*, *55*, 341–346.

Kanfer, F. H., & Saslow, G. (1969). Behavioral diagnosis. In C. M. Franks (Ed.), *Behavior therapy: Appraisal and status* (pp. 417–444). New York: McGraw-Hill.

Kohlenberg, R. J., & Tsai, M. (1991). *Functional analytic psychotherapy*. New York: Plenum Press.

Lang, P. J., & Lazovik, A. D. (1963). Experimental desensitization of phobia. *Journal of Abnormal and Social Psychology*, *66*, 519–525.

Lang, P. J., Melamed, B. G., & Hart, J. (1970). A psychophysiological analysis of fear modification using an automated desensitization procedure. *Journal of Abnormal Psychology*, *72*, 220–234.

Leigland, S. (2005). Variables of which values are a function. *The Behavior Analyst*, *28*, 133–142.

Lewinsohn, P. M. (1974). A behavioral approach to depression. In R. M. Friedman & M. M. Katz (Eds.), *The psychology of depression: Contemporary theory and research* (pp. 157–185). New York: John Wiley & Sons, Inc.

Lonigan, C. J. (1990). Which behaviorism? A reply to Mahoney. *American Psychologist, 45*, 1179–1181.

Mahoney, M. J. (1974). *Cognition and behavior modification.* Cambridge, MA: Ballinger.

Mahoney, M. J. (1989). Scientific psychology and radical behaviorism: Important distinctions based in scientism and objectivism. *American Psychologist, 44*, 1372–1377.

Martell, C. R., Addis, M. E., & Jacobson, N. S. (2001). *Depression in context: Strategies for guided action.* New York: Norton.

Michael, J. (1993). Establishing operations. *Behavior Analyst, 16*, 191–206.

Miller, W. R., & Rollnick, S. (2013). *Motivational interviewing: Helping people change* (3rd ed.). New York: Guilford Press.

Minster, S. T., Jones, M., Elliffe, D., & Muthukumaraswamy, S. D. (2006). Stimulus equivalence: Testing Sidman's (2000) theory. *Journal of the Experimental Analysis of Behavior, 85*, 371–391.

Mowrer, O. H. (1939). A stimulus-response analysis of anxiety and its role as a reinforcing agent. *Psychological Review, 46*, 553–565.

Nevin, J. A. (1992). An integrative model for the study of behavioral momentum. *Journal of the Experimental Analysis of Behavior, 57*, 301–316.

Paul, G. L., & Lentz, R. (1977). *Psychosocial treatment of the chronic mental patients.* Cambridge, MA: Harvard University.

Petry, N. M. (2012). *Contingency management for substance abuse treatment: A guide to implementing this evidence-based practice.* New York: Routledge.

Plaud, J. J., & Gaither, G. A. (1996). Human behavioral momentum: Implications for applied behavior analysis and therapy. *Journal of Behavior Therapy and Experimental Psychiatry, 27*, 139–148.

Plaud, J. J., & Plaud, D. M. (1998). Clinical behavior therapy and the experimental analysis of behavior. *Journal of Clinical Psychology, 54*, 905–921.

Plumb, J., Stewart, I., Dahl, J., & Lundgren, T. (2009). In search of meaning: Values in modern clinical behavior analysis. *Behavior Analyst, 32*, 85–103.

Sidman, M. (1994). *Stimulus equivalence: A research story.* Boston: Authors Cooperative.

Sidman, M. (2000). Equivalence relations and the reinforcement contingency. *Journal of the Experimental Analysis of behavior, 74*, 127–146.

Skinner, B. F. (1938). *The behavior of organisms: An experimental analysis.* Englewood Cliffs, NJ: Prentice Hall.

Skinner, B. F. (1945). The operational analysis of psychological terms. *Psychological Review, 52*, 270–277.

Skinner, B. F. (1948). *Walden two.* New York: Macmillan.

Skinner, B. F. (1953). *Science and human behavior.* New York: Free Press.

Skinner, B. F. (1957). *Verbal behavior.* New York: Appleton-Century-Crofts.

Skinner, B. F. (1971). *Beyond freedom and dignity.* New York: Knopf.

Skinner, B. F., Mahoney, M. J., Day, W. F., Woolfolk, R. L., Richardson, F. C., Kitchener, R. F., et al. (1992). Peaceful coexistence in psychology. In R. B. Miller (Ed.), *The restoration of dialogue: Readings in the philosophy of clinical psychology.* (pp. 101–168). Washington, DC: American Psychological Association.

Törneke, N. (2010). *Learning RFT: An introduction to relational frame theory and its clinical application.* Oakland, CA: Context Press/New Harbinger Publications.

Tsai, M., Kohlenberg, R. J., Kanter, J. W., Kohlenberg, B., Follette, W. C., & Callaghan, G. M. (2009). *A guide to functional analytic psychotherapy: Awareness, courage, love and behaviorism.* New York: Springer.

Waltz, T. J., & Follette, W. C. (2009). Molar functional relations and clinical behavior analysis: Implications for assessment and treatment. *Behavior Analyst, 32*, 51–68.

Watson, J. B., & Rayner, R. (1920). Conditioned emotional reactions. *Journal of Experimental Psychology*, *3*, 1–14.
Whittal, M. L., Thordarson, D. S., & McLean, P. D. (2005). Treatment of obsessive-compulsive disorder: Cognitive behavior therapy vs. exposure and response prevention. *Behaviour Research and Therapy*, *43*, 1559–1576.
Wolf, M., Risley, T., & Mees, H. (1963). Application of operant conditioning procedures to the behaviour problems of an autistic child. *Behaviour Research and Therapy*, *1*, 305–312.
Wolpe, J. (1958). *Psychotherapy by reciprocal inhibition*. Stanford, CA: Stanford University.
Wyatt, W. J. (1990). Radical behaviorism misrepresented: A response to Mahoney. *American Psychologist*, *45*, 1181–1183.

28

Aging

Jonathan C. Baker and Linda A. LeBlanc

Behavioral gerontology refers to the application of the principles of operant and respondent conditioning to understanding and treating a wide range of socially important needs of older adults (Adkins & Mathews, 1999; Burgio & Burgio, 1986). Behavior analysts have explained the advantages of a behavioral approach to aging in both behavior analytic and non-behavior analytic journals. This chapter provides an overview of the broad conditioning literature on aging. The small but consistent literature of studies on basic respondent and operant conditioning is described, but the primary focus is on applied operant conditioning. This literature has created a framework for applied behavior analysts to improve the lives of older adults.

Interest in the behavior of aging adults has increased since the early 20th century with researchers proposing "age-change" theories to address the changes that human beings experience throughout the lifespan (Belsky, 1999, p. 41; Hendricks & Achenbaum, 1999). Such theories typically focus on specific, age-related events (e.g., Erikson's Psychosocial Crises; Erikson, 1959). In contrast, a behavior analytic account of aging focuses on the principles of respondent and operant conditioning that affect behavior in lawful ways across the life span (e.g., Durkin, Prescott, Furchtgott, Cantor, & Powell, 1993; Plaud, Plaud, & Von Duvillard, 1999). In spite of the general applicability of these principles of behavior, research suggests that certain changes in behavior and conditioning processes can only be accounted for by age. For example, age-related differences have been noted in response persistence (Plaud et al., 1999), stimulus control (Plaud, Gillund, & Ferraro, 2000), and the eliciting effects of conditioned stimuli (Woodruff-Pak & Thompson, 1988).

The reasons for these age-related changes to operant and respondent conditioning are not fully understood. Some potential explanations for age-related differences include biological changes (e.g., functional decline, cerebellar changes; Cheng, Faulkner, Disterhoft, & Desmond, 2010) and environments that select certain patterns of responding or non-responding (e.g., differential reinforcement of dependence through excessive helping). It is not clear why the salience of discriminative

The Wiley Blackwell Handbook of Operant and Classical Conditioning, First Edition.
Edited by Frances K. McSweeney and Eric S. Murphy.

stimuli decreases with age (i.e., stimuli associated with the differential availability of reinforcers no longer control differential responding). These changes commonly occur in later life (i.e., 60 years or older) and impact the person-environment interaction (Skinner, 1983). Dementia can drastically worsen these changes (LeBlanc, Raetz, & Feliciano, 2011).

The term dementia refers to a common pattern of deficits that negatively impact remembering (e.g., recalling information, recognizing people) and other aspects of functioning. Language deficits, such as the inability to name objects which may result in over use of vague substitutions like "'thing' or 'it'," are common (American Psychiatric Association, 2000, p. 148). Other deficits include problems initiating activities (i.e., failed stimulus control), planning and executing complex activities (i.e., completion of behavioral chains), and difficulties engaging in motor tasks despite intact motor and sensory skills. These deficits can be caused by several disease processes (American Psychiatric Association, 2000) and sometimes, the cause for the cognitive decline is not readily discernible.

Although there are many causes of dementia, the most common is Alzheimer's Disease (AD). There are 5.1 million Americans with AD today and there will be as many as 7.7 million by 2030 (Alzheimer's Association, 2011). The chances of developing Alzheimer's Disease double every five years beyond the age of 65. Those age 85 and over (approximately 9 million people by 2030) have almost a 50% chance of developing the disease.

In addition to the scientific value of identifying the impact of age-related changes on basic conditioning processes, changing global and national demographics are creating a social need to identify ways to improve the quality of later life (Kinsella & He, 2009; United States Census Bureau, 2010). The United States Census Bureau (2010) reports that currently approximately 40 million Americans are 65 years or older (about 34.4 million between 65 and 85 years of age, and about 5.6 million over the age of 85). Over the next 19 years, that number is expected to almost double, increasing to as many as 72 million older adults as the baby boom ages. Those over the age of 85 will number almost 9 million.

The group aged 85 and older, referred to as the oldest-old, is growing faster than any other demographic group, with a disproportionate increase for women and minority groups (United States Census Bureau, 2010). These rapidly increasing demographic groups are most likely to develop AD along with other health conditions and sensory deficits. AD is costly, debilitating, and potentially socially isolating (Alzheimer's Association, 2011; Belsky, 1999; Kinsella & He, 2009).

The infrastructure for providing effective support services is unprepared for the shifting demand from traditional palliative care nursing environments to community-based care (Molinari et al., 2003). The growing discrepancy among needs, infrastructure, and the published research base have created tremendous opportunities for behavior analysts interested in working with older adults.

Basic Conditioning Research on Aging

Basic research on aging usually focuses on changes in memory, perhaps the most salient age-related change (Dixon, Rust, Feltmate, & Kwong See, 2007). Research with both human and nonhuman animals tries to understand how memory and intellectual functioning change with age. Only a small portion of the basic research on aging focuses on conditioning (Derenne & Baron, 2002). Despite the relatively small body of basic research, some general findings have been reported. The following section reviews the basic research on both respondent and operant conditioning and summarizes the general findings.

Respondent Conditioning

A series of studies has documented clear age- and dementia-related changes in classically conditioned responding (Cheng et al., 2010). The eyeblink is probably the most common procedure for evaluating age-related differences in classical conditioning. In this procedure, an auditory stimulus is often presented followed by a puff of air to the participant's eye (Woodruff-Pak & Thompson, 1988).

Woodruff-Pak and Thompson (1988) compared the acquisition of a conditioned response (CR; an eyeblink) when a neutral stimulus (NS; a 500 ms tone) was presented 400 ms before an unconditioned stimulus (US; a puff of air). Four age groups of healthy participants were studied: (a) 18–27 year olds, (b) 40–49 year olds, (c), 50–59 year olds, and (d) 60–83 year olds. A 30–39 year old group was not included in most statistical analyses because it contained too few participants. CRs were defined as eye blinks of 0.5 mm or more that occurred within 25–399 ms after the onset of the tone.

Several age-related differences in CRs were observed. For example, when comparing the percentage of CRs across groups, the 50–59 year olds and the 60–83 year olds emitted a CR during fewer than 40% of the tones; the 40–49 year olds emitted a CR in 56 to 58% of tones; and the 18–27 year olds emitted a CR in more than 60% of the tones. Similar results were obtained for the number of trials required to meet the criterion of CRs during eight of nine tones. The 60–83 year olds required almost twice as many trials to meet the criterion as the two youngest groups.

The age-related differences observed by Woodruff-Pak and Thompson have been replicated several times over the past 30 years (e.g., Cheng et al., 2010). This research suggests that people begin to experience deficits in acquiring CRs as early as age 40. Age-related differences in the responding of healthy adults have also been observed for another CR, heart rate. Durkin et al. (1993) reported that two older groups (i.e., 50–63, 66–78) showed impaired acquisition of both classically conditioned eyeblink and heart-rate responses compared to two younger groups (a young group, ages 19–33, and a young middle-aged, ages 35–48), but the older groups showed greater conditioning than a no-trials control group.

Although most individuals experience changes in classically conditioned response acquisition as they age (Finkbiner & Woodruff-Pak, 1991; Woodruff-Pak & Thompson, 1988; Woodruff-Pak & Jaeger, 1998), the presence of dementia, and specifically AD, exacerbates the acquisition deficits. Woodruff-Pak, Finkbiner, and Sasse (1990) found that older adults with probable AD (ages 72–100) emitted even fewer CRs (i.e., a CR on only 10.77% of the total trials) than older adults with no dementia (i.e., a CR on 31.54% of the total trials).

Finally, the acquisition of CRs among older adults with AD differs from the acquisition of CRs by older adults with other types of dementia (Woodruff-Pak, 2001;

Woodruff-Pak, Papka, Romano, & Li, 1996) and with other neurological disorders (Woodruff-Pak, 2001). Poor acquisition of CRs (CRs during fewer than 25% of trials) can also predict the later onset of Alzheimer's Disease, even when symptoms are not yet present (Woodruff-Pak, 2001).

Operant Conditioning

The basic operant literature on aging has focused on two topics: sensitivity to schedules of reinforcement and stimulus control. Sensitivity to schedules of reinforcement refers to whether an organism's behavior is "responsive to consequences" (Plaud et al., 2000, p. 74), resulting in differential increases in behavior for different schedules of reinforcement. Sensitivity to reinforcement also refers to the cessation of behavior under extinction. Stimulus control refers to whether an organism's behavior differs during stimuli that have been associated with differential consequences (e.g., reinforcement, extinction). Researchers have noted that sensitivity to reinforcement and stimulus control play crucial roles in the three-term contingency (Plaud et al., 2000).

Sensitivity to Schedules of Reinforcement. Mixed results about age-related changes in sensitivity to reinforcement have been reported. Fisher and Noll (1996) compared the responding of five young (ages 19–23) and four elderly (ages 67–80) participants who responded on concurrent variable interval (VI) schedules (i.e., a two choice operant task). Matching is said to occur when the ratio of the rates of responding for two alternatives equals the ratio of the rates of reinforcement obtained from those alternatives. Overmatching refers to a greater preference for the alternative that provides the higher rate of reinforcement than would be predicted by the ratio of the rates of reinforcement obtained from those alternatives (Herrnstein, 1970; Baum, 1974). A within session analysis of the data indicated that the younger adults matched the schedule more quickly than the older adults. However, the older adults matched the schedules more consistently (i.e., less overmatching than the younger adults) once matching occurred. Older adults required 6–8 trials into a session before their responding matched the schedule of reinforcement for each operant, whereas the two younger groups required only 1–3 trials before their responding matched the schedule.

Two studies examined age-related changes in performance on signal detection tasks. Tripp and Alsop (1999) compared 32 children (ages 8–9), 31 young adults (ages 18–26), and 31 older adults (ages 66–89) who responded on a signal detection task that required discrimination between two patterns delivered according to fixed ratio (FR) 1 and FR 3 schedules. The authors used circles and squares as the patterns and participants were required to indicate whether there were more circles or squares on the screen. Two levels of difficulty were used: an "easy" condition where there were 66 of one shape and 78 of the other, and a "difficult" condition where there were 70 of one and 74 of the other. Relative to the children and young adults, the older adults had the slowest reaction times and the lowest bias toward the higher-ratio stimuli, suggesting decreased sensitivity to the frequency of reinforcement.

Plaud et al. (2000) also evaluated of the effects of reinforcement and stimulus control on older adult participants (ages 62–74) using signal detection preparations. All of the participants responded when that responding was reinforced (i.e., reinforcement effect), but three of the six responded more frequently to the denser schedule (i.e., the VI 30 s) and two responded more to the leaner schedule (i.e., the VI 60 s). The final participant did not respond differently to the two schedules.

Plaud et al. (1999) reported slightly different results when studying the responding of older adults (ages 60–79) on a computer-based task in which the size of the reinforcer differed for two possible responses (1 token vs. 10 tokens) but identical schedules delivered those reinforcers. When the schedules were subsequently changed, older adults altered their responding accordingly indicating that they were sensitive to changes in schedules of reinforcement. However, they also demonstrated a bias toward the response with a history of a higher magnitude of reinforcement, as would be predicted by behavioral momentum theory (Nevin, Mandell, & Atak, 1983). Their pattern of responding was similar to that of college students in previous studies with the exception that a greater number of older adults showed a response bias toward the key previously associated with the more dense schedule of reinforcement, even when contingencies were changed.

Spira and Edelstein (2007) extended the research on sensitivity to reinforcement to four older adults with mild or moderate dementia (ages 68–86), comparing their performance on a button-pressing task to the performance of four older adults with no memory impairment (ages 70–81). Participants received 5-cent coins for responding under FR and fixed interval (FI) schedules. No coins were available during extinction. Three of the four participants with dementia acquired the operant task and met the extinction criteria compared to all four of the healthy older adults. Interestingly, the older adults with dementia exhibited greater sensitivity to the change from the FI schedule of reinforcement to extinction than older adult counterparts without dementia. Additionally, older adults without memory impairment exhibited spontaneous recovery during extinction, whereas older adults with dementia did not.

Stimulus Control. Several studies reported weaker formation of stimulus equivalence classes for older than for younger adults. Studies on stimulus equivalence typically use a preparation referred to as matching to sample (MTS) in which one stimulus is presented as a sample and an array of a few stimuli are presented as comparisons for a selection. Often times the stimuli do not share any visual similarities and are designed to have no preexperimental meaning (e.g., non-sense syllables, 2-dimensional drawings). Conditional discriminations are established by differentially reinforcing the selection of a certain comparison in the presence of a given sample (e.g., hear "rooka," select ••). Stimulus equivalence refers to a summary of observed regularities in responding where the training of a few conditional discriminations results in the emergence of several untaught conditional discriminations (Sidman,1997; Sidman, Wayne, Macguire, & Barnes, 1989) that follow the mathematical properties of reflexivity, symmetry, and transitivity.

A person can be taught conditional discriminations using a set of three stimuli (i.e., stimuli A, B, and C) such that when A is presented as a sample they select B from a comparison array (given A, select B often noted as A = B) and when B is presented, select C (B = C). In addition to these two mastered conditional discriminations, several other responses can occur without a direct history of reinforcement for the responses (i.e., emergent or untrained relation). Reflexivity refers to the identity relation such that the person could select the same stimulus from a comparison array when presented with the sample (i.e., A = A, B = B, and C = C) without any direct reinforcement history for that relation (Sidman & Tailby, 1982). Symmetry is demonstrated when the person who has learned that A = B can also respond effectively with no explicit training when the reverse relation, B = A, is presented (i.e., B is the sample and A must be selected from the comparisons). Transitivity is demonstrated when the mastered trained relations of A = B and B = C result in emergent relations that combine the two relations (i.e., A = C, C = A).

Wilson and Milan (1995) reported slower response times and poorer performance on post-tests of equivalence relations for older adults (ages 62–81) compared to younger adults (ages 19–22). Perez-Gonzalez and Moreno-Sierra (1999) used a single-subject design to examine equivalence class formation. They reported slightly better formation of equivalence classes in older adults (ages 66–74) than Wilson and Milan, but equivalence class formation was still impaired in older adults relative to teenagers and younger adults (ages 13–53). Saunders, Chaney, and Marquis (2005) attempted to demonstrate equivalence in 12 healthy older adults (ages 58–89). Following training, nine of the 12 participants demonstrated equivalence. In a second experiment, six additional older adults (58–75) were trained using a 0-s delay following the presentation of the sample stimulus. That is, when the individual touched the sample stimulus, the sample stimulus was removed and the choice stimuli were immediately presented (i.e., 0-s later). This procedure is contrasted with the original procedure, in which the sample stimulus remained present when the choice stimuli were presented. Adding the 0-s delay resulted in fewer trials needed to demonstrate equivalence than when the sample stimulus was present along with the choice stimuli.

More recently, researchers have looked at the formation of stimulus equivalence classes in MTS preparations with older adults with dementia. Gallagher and Keenan (2009) evaluated the performance of older adults (ages 67–94) with varying levels of cognitive impairment as measured by the Mini-Mental Status Exam (MMSE). They established three-member equivalence classes in three different experiments and found that 90% of cognitively-intact individuals with scores of 27 or higher (n = 30) formed equivalence classes. All participants with an MMSE score below 27 (n = 16) failed to form such classes.

In a set of studies, Steingrimsdottir and Arntzen (2011a, 2011b) evaluated the performance of two older adults with dementia on identity MTS tasks (i.e., choose the comparison that is identical to the sample). Steingrimsdottir and Arntzen (2011a) reported that an 80-year-old-male with severe dementia selected the correct comparison stimulus when two, but not three, comparison stimuli were used. They also showed that adding a 0-second delay reduced responding to below chance level, contrary to prior results showing that healthy older adults benefited from inclusion of a 0-s delay when responding on these procedures (Saunders et al., 2005). Steingrimsdottir & Arntzen, 2011b reported that an 84-year-old woman with mild dementia was able to select the correct comparison stimulus from three alternatives. Additionally, she was able to select the correct comparison stimulus with 100% accuracy when 0- and 3-second delays separated the presentation of the stimulus from the presentation of the alternatives. She selected the correct stimulus 89% of the time when 6- and 9-second delays separated the stimulus from the choices. A comparison of the results of these two studies suggests that greater cognitive impairment leads to poorer performance on equivalence formation tasks. The studies also show that some aspects of common MTS preparations may improve or detract from accurate performance.

Taken together, these basic research studies on sensitivity to reinforcement and stimulus control illustrate age-related differences in operant conditioning. Older adults' behavior is sensitive to reinforcement, supporting the "age-irrelevant" nature of behavior analytic principles. However, responding may be more (e.g., Spira & Edelstein, 2007) or less sensitive (e.g., Tripp & Alsop, 1999) to operant contingencies depending on the level of functioning in individuals with cognitive impairments. Additionally, it appears that the behavior of older adults is less sensitive to controlling stimuli than the behavior of younger adults (Perez-Gonzalez & Moreno-Sierra, 1999; Plaud et al., 2000, Saunders et al., 2005; Wilson & Milan, 1995) although accommodations can be made to enhance stimulus control (Steingrimsdottir & Arntzen, 2011a, 2011b).

Applied Conditioning Literature on Aging

Most of the conditioning research conducted with older adults falls under the classification of applied research. Baer, Wolf, and Risley (1968) provided a succinct explanation of the difference between applied and non-applied (or basic) research, noting that in applied research, the behavior, stimuli, or organism are chosen because of their importance to society. For example, an applied researcher might study older adults with dementia (as opposed to older adults with little or no cognitive impairment) living in nursing homes (rather than community dwelling) who wander. The applied researcher would study these subjects specifically because of the challenges to society inherent in maintaining and treating aging nursing home dwelling elders with dementia (e.g., risk of fall, injury, exiting the facility). That is, the participants in applied research are chosen because of their behavior, rather than because of the convenience of the sample or the advantages of internal validity and experimental control for the researcher.

In their review of the applied behavioral literature, Williamson and Ascione (1983) classified the applied conditioning literature on aging into three treatment-based categories: (a) antecedent-stimulus control based interventions that involve altering the physical environment and/or training staff on how to work with aging populations; (b) contingency management-based interventions where specific consequences are programmed for behaviors in an effort to change the future frequency of those behaviors; and (c) combinations of the two. Antecedent-stimulus control procedures typically involve introducing discriminative stimuli that can evoke responses (e.g., placing a picture of the person on the door to facilitate finding the room). Contingency management-based interventions often involve adding reinforcers to strengthen behaviors (e.g., providing praise for independent dressing) or altering the consequences of behaviors that interfere with rehabilitative efforts or with care by others (e.g., providing breaks at fixed times to reduce combative behaviors during daily activities).

Rehabilitation—Reestablishment of Skills

As individuals age, many previous skills decline and may be lost. Cognitive responses (e.g., remembering) and functional independence in tasks (e.g., dressing) decline with age and dementia (Alzheimer's Association, 2011; Belsky, 1999; Cheng et al., 2010; Kinsella & He, 2009). As noted earlier, declines in functioning often result from a combination of physical and environmental changes. As a result, rehabilitative research on the reestablishment of skills has generally focused on environmental factors that can be modified to slow the decline and perhaps rebuild the skills.

Memory. Older adults with dementia have difficulty initiating and maintaining conversations, partly because of difficulty remembering details about familiar people and places. These details are critical to engaging in effective conversation. Improved conversation skills make it more enjoyable for loved ones and caregivers to interact with people with dementia.

Bourgeois (1990) evaluated the use of memory wallets to improve the conversational skills of nursing home residents with dementia. These memory wallets contained as many as 30 stimuli, each of which displayed pictures of family members along with text about them. Other topics in the memory wallet included information about the individual, her life, and her day. Three older adults with dementia aged 59–66 made a larger number of topic statements to either a cognitively-intact partner or to the experimenter when the memory wallet was present than when it was not. Bourgeois (1993) extended this finding to include dyads of older adults ages 74–88, both of whom had dementia. He found that the memory aids increased on-topic and novel utterances for both members of three of four dyads.

Another approach to improving remembering is the spaced retrieval technique (Cherry, Simmons, & Camp, 1999). Research using this technique has been conducted within a cognitive theoretical framework, but the procedure is a behavioral conditioning preparation, perhaps involving shaping or errorless learning (Bourgeois et al., 2003). The spaced retrieval procedure involves presenting information (e.g., a verbal, pictorial, tangible stimulus) and asking the individual to respond to a question about it. After a correct response, the delay between the presentation of the stimulus and the request to respond is gradually increased across trials. This procedure increased the accuracy of responding over intervals of several days (Bourgeois et al., 2003). Bourgeois et al. (2003) also showed that a combination of memory wallets (an antecedent-based stimulus control procedure) and spaced retrieval procedures (contingency management) helped older adults with dementia to converse more effectively than when those stimuli and procedures were absent.

Dixon, Baker, and Sadowski (2011) used an antecedent-stimulus control procedure to improve recall among older adults with dementia (ages 84–91). Participants viewed a series of pictures that were selected from different categories (e.g., tools). The pictures were presented on a computer screen with each item on one of two colored backgrounds. When a picture appeared on one of the colored backgrounds, Dixon et al. provided an echoic prompt ("Say, '________'") as an antecedent stimulus to have the participants name the item. Once the participant stated the name of the item, the researcher provided a question about the item. For example, if the item presented was a tool, the researcher might ask the participant how that tool could be used. When a picture appeared on the other background color, the researcher said nothing (i.e., no echoic prompt or question). Immediately after seeing all of the stimuli, and one week later, the participants were asked to list as many of the stimuli from the categories as they could recall. Dixon et al. sought to evaluate whether the prompt to name the item, and to answer a question about the item's use, might lead to a greater probability of the category name evoking the item name. Participants were indeed able to recall more target items associated with the echoic and intraverbal prompts than items for which the researcher remained silent both immediately and at one week follow up.

Independence. Research suggests that independence declines as people age, which may lead to the placement of older adults in long-term care settings. Declines in independent dressing, continence, and other activities of daily living are often created or exacerbated by contingencies that support dependent behaviors (Burgio & Burgio, 1986). As a result, many antecedent-based stimulus control and contingency management procedures have been used to reestablish functional independence.

Antecedent-stimulus control procedures have proven effective at increasing continence (Burton, Pearce, Burgio, Engel, & Whitehead, 1988), wayfinding (Nolan, Mathews, & Harrison, 2001), and activity engagement (Altus, Engelman, & Mathews 2002; Jenkins, Felce, Lunt, & Powell, 1977). For example, Nolan et al. (2001) posted a sign (i.e., this is ______'s room) and a photograph of the individual on the bedroom door of residents in nursing homes. Elderly individuals with dementia (ages 84–90) were able to find their own room upon request 48–56% more often when signs and photographs were posted on their doors than when they were not.

Engelman, Altus, Mosier, and Mathews (2003) provided a contingency management strategy for improving independence. They trained staff to use a system of gradually increasing prompts when aiding residents in self-care tasks. Specifically, staff members were taught to provide verbal prompts, then gestural prompts, and finally physical prompts until the older individual completed each relevant task. Staff members also praised the individuals for complying with the prompt within 5 seconds. This combination of an antecedent-stimulus and contingency-based strategy required no increased staff time but increased independence for all three participants relative to the baseline condition in which staff completed all tasks for the participants or used physical guidance prompts.

Many other researchers have incorporated combinations of antecedent interventions and altered contingencies when treating independence (e.g., Burgio, Burgio, Engel, & Tice, 1986; Burgio, Engel, McCormick, Hawkins, & Scheve, 1988; Burgio, Westley, & Voss, 1989; Engelman, Altus, & Mathews, 1999; Engelman, Mathews, & Altus, 2002; Fantl, Wyman, Harkins, & Hadley, 1990; Jeffcoate, 1961). For example, Altus et al. (2002) compared the percentage of participation in mealtime activities when meals were served on prepared plates to when meals were served family style. The monitored mealtime activities included preparation, serving and passing food, taking additional helpings of food, and clean-up. Each task was split into small steps and the percentage participation measure was based on the percentage of steps completed. During the prepared-plates condition, meals were prepared in the facility's traditional form with pre-portioned food on plates. Participation in mealtime activities during this condition was then compared to participation during a treatment package which contained antecedent-stimulus components such as putting food into communal dishes and providing the necessary utensils/dishes. The staff members were also trained to use a system of least to most supportive prompts to provide opportunities for involvement, and to praise participation. Participation increased from less than 20% during prepared meals to more than 60% during family-style meals which used the treatment package.

Activity Engagement. Much applied aging research has focused on increasing engagement in leisure activities (LeBlanc et al., 2011; Williamson & Ascione, 1983). Workers in aging care settings (e.g., day programming, assisted living, residential care) usually try to increase participation in, and enjoyment of, activities, rather than to teach patients new skills. Increasing activity engagement helps to improve quality of life, maintain functioning, and deter depression (Engelman et al., 1999; LeBlanc et al., 2011; Teri, 1991). For older adults with dementia, increased engagement in leisure activities also reduces agitation and aggression (Feliciano, Steers, Elite-Marcandontou, McLane, & Arean, 2009). Combinations of prompts/offering items, and praising selections and engagement, have increased participation in activities. However, until recently, relatively little attention focused on identifying individually-selected leisure activities that would be most effective for increasing engagement. Recently, researchers have used both indirect and direct preference assessments to achieve this goal.

The Pleasant Events Schedule—Alzheimer's Disease (PES-AD; Teri & Logsdon, 1991; Logsdon & Teri, 1997) is an indirect assessment in which a caregiver is asked to identify examples of potentially preferred activities. The shortened version of the PES-AD (Logsdon & Teri, 1997) can also be used to ask the individual for his or her preferences. However, administering the PES-AD as a verbal assessment may result in false positives (LeBlanc, Raetz, Baker, Strobel, & Feeney, 2008). That is, individuals may not actually engage in preferred activites more than non-preferred activities. Verbal assessments do not always accurately identify the value of items as reinforcers for operant purposes.

Because of the limitations of indirect survey assessments, researchers have begun to use direct observations of selections between currently available stimuli to assess preferences. These selection-based procedures have been studied extensively with individuals with intellectual disabilities and autism. The paired stimulus (PS) procedure involves presenting a series of trials with an opportunity to select between two stimuli at a time (Fisher et al., 1992). A selection results in brief access to the item. Typically, eight to 16 items are included in the assessment and all possible combinations of pairs are presented. An index of preference is calculated for each item by dividing the number of selections by the total number of presentations of that item. The multiple stimulus without replacement (MSWO; DeLeon & Iwata, 1996) procedure involves presentation of all of the items at the same time in an array. The individual has an opportunity to select an item resulting in brief access. That item is then removed from the array and ranked as 1 while the remaining items are rearranged for a subsequent selection from the remaining items. When all items have been selected or no additional selections occur, the array is completed. This is repeated 2–4 more times and the average ranking is calculated for each item as an index of preference.

These preference assessment methodologies produce preference hierarchies that can accurately predict the beneficial effects of those items when they are subsequently provided in behavioral programming. Higher preference items are more effective than lower preference items at increasing a targeted response when provided contingently (Hagopian, Long, & Rush, 2004). In addition, higher preference items result in higher levels of engagement and positive affect compared to lower preference items when provided noncontingently in an enriched environment preparation (Hagopian et al., 2004; Vollmer et al., 1994). Both of these uses have been examined with individuals with dementia and the results support their utility for identifying items to incorporate in programming (LeBlanc, Cherup, Feliciano, & Sidener, 2006; Raetz, LeBlanc, Baker, & Hilton, 2013; Virues-Ortega, Iwata, Nogales-González, and Frades, 2012).

LeBlanc et al. (2006) compared PS preference assessments (i.e., only two items presented on each trial) that used different formats for presentation of the items (i.e., tangible presentations, pictorial representations, printed text names, vocally presented names). For each of her four participants (pages 62–89), one of those methods produced the greatest correlation with measures of subsequent engagement (i.e., more accurately predicted subsequent levels of engagement in an enriched environment arrangement). Tangible presentations worked best for only one participant while vocal presentations were best for the other three. This finding contrasts starkly with the findings obtained with individuals with intellectual disabilities and autism for whom tangible presentations are typically the only format to prove predictive of subsequent intervention effects (Conyers, Doole, Vause, Harapiak,Yu, & Martin, 2002).

Virues-Ortega et al. (2012) used PS assessments to identify leisure activities and edible items that could be used as reinforcing stimuli for both arbitrary (e.g., pressing a lever), and socially important (e.g., responses in a physical therapy regimen) responses for older adults with dementia. Interesting, the well-established "displacement effect" (i.e., selecting edibles over preferred leisure items when both are available) did not occur for their participants with dementia even though it reliably occurs for participants with intellectual disabilities and autism. Feliciano et al. (2009) also illustrated the utility of PS preference assessments by providing preferred items contingently as part of a multi-component behavioral intervention plan to decrease depression and agitation in older adults with dementia.

Raetz et al. (2013) examined the predictive utility of a brief MSWO assessment (i.e., three presentations of multiple item arrays) with older individuals with dementia. The results of the MSWO preference assessment generally predicted the level of subsequent engagement but with some unusual patterns observed. Items identified as high preference in the MSWO assessment resulted in high levels of engagement when provided noncontingently in an enriched environment preparation. However, many low preference items also resulted in high levels of engagement as well. This finding contrasts with findings with individuals with intellectual disabilities and autism that noncontingent access to low preference items typically does not result in significant engagement (Vollmer et al., 1994; Hagopian et al., 2004). The MSWO assessments were repeated every two weeks over a 3–5-month period and preference remained stable for more than half of the participants across that time frame. Together these findings indicate that the PS and MSWO preference assessment procedures can be used to identify highly preferred items that can be incorporated into behavioral interventions for various therapeutic purposes (e.g., increased activity engagement, increased motor behaviors in rehabilitative regimens, decreased depression and agitation).

The above sections related to memory, independence, and activity engagement demonstrate how operant conditioning procedures have been used to successfully target rehabilitation of several socially important repertoires in older adults with cognitive impairments and significant health problems. These procedures have been studied often in nursing homes, but a growing number of studies also show that these procedures will allow individuals with dementia to succeed in community-based settings when more restrictive long-term care settings would otherwise be the only option (LeBlanc, 2010). To reduce the use of more restrictive placements and procedures, efforts at reestablishing engagement and independent responding are often accompanied by operant conditioning procedures that are designed to manage problematic behaviors. This idea is discussed below.

Management of Problematic or Unsafe Behavior

Before the last decade, most research on the management of problematic behaviors for individuals with dementia was not based on a functional assessment. Functional assessments explicitly identify the variables maintaining the problematic behavior and then use that assessment to guide subsequent treatment. For example, Lundervold and Jackson (1992) developed a treatment consisting of contingent restraint and differential reinforcement of behavior that was incompatible with agitation, paranoia, and aggression (DRI). Although the authors anecdotally reported that aggressive behavior was probably maintained by escape from demands by staff members, they did not perform a functional analysis that manipulated the environment (i.e., experimental functional analysis) to test for the response-reinforcer relation or to ensure that no other contingencies also influenced the behavior. As a result, their DRI contingency may have been superimposed on an ongoing contingency that maintained the problematic behaviors and therefore, reduced the effectiveness of their intervention. The authors report that levels of aggression averaged 1.07 aggressive episodes per month during baseline and 1.16 aggressive episodes per month during the 12-month intervention to reduce aggression. However, only one aggressive episode occurred during the last seven months of the 12-month intervention.

More recently, researchers have used functional assessments and function-based treatments (i.e., treatments that involve the manipulation of the response-reinforcer relation that maintains the behavior) to address problematic or unsafe behaviors. Researchers have reported that function-based treatments more effectively reduce problematic or unsafe behaviors than non-function-based interventions (Iwata, Pace, Cowdery, & Miltenberger, 1994).

Several studies used functional assessments (e.g., interviewing staff, direct observation, or experimental functional analysis) to guide the development of function-based treatments for older adults with dementia (e.g., Baker, Hanley, & Mathews, 2006; Baker, LeBlanc, Raetz, & Hilton, 2011; Buchanan & Fisher, 2002; Burgio, Scilley, Hardin, Hsu, & Yancey, 1996; Dwyer-Moore & Dixon, 2007; Heard & Watson, 1999; Moniz-Cook, Stokes, & Agar, 2003; Moniz-Cook, Woods, & Richards, 2001). Functional assessments have identified several different types of reinforcers for problematic behaviors. The reinforcers may be socially mediated such as attention (e.g., Buchanan & Fisher, 2002; Dwyer-Moore & Dixon, 2007); access to tangibles (e.g., Heard & Watson, 1999) or escape from staff proximity (e.g., Baker et al., 2006). Researchers have also developed hypothesis-based interventions to address problematic behaviors maintained by non-social consequences. Such interventions may reduce problematic behaviors by delivering non-problematic items that produce sensory experiences that are similar to those that are automatically produced by engaging in the problem behaviors (e.g., Baker et al., 2011; Burgio et al., 1996).

Function-based treatments may provide noncontingent delivery of the reinforcer at pre-set intervals (e.g., Baker et al., 2006, Buchanan & Fisher, 2002). They may also teach socially appropriate, responses to produce the reinforcer (i.e., Differential Reinforcement of Alternative behaviors; DRA), while also withholding the reinforcer following problematic behavior (i.e., extinction; Dwyer-Moore & Dixon, 2007). Function-based treatments have effectively reduced many problematic behaviors, including wandering (e.g., Dwyer-Moore & Dixon, 2007; Heard & Watson, 1999), aggression (Baker et al., 2006), disruptive vocalizations (Buchanan & Fisher, 2002), hoarding (Baker et al., 2011), and non-compliance (Moniz-Cook et al., 2003).

Operant contingencies often directly reduce problematic behaviors in aging individuals, just as they do for other populations. Reducing problematic behavior usually lowers the cost of care (i.e., reduced staffing, fewer worker injuries) and increases the quality of life for nursing- home residents. In addition, reducing problematic behavior of community-dwelling individuals may delay admission to more restrictive care settings, allowing people to remain at home longer with natural caregivers before entering nursing care with its substantial impact on the costs and quality of life.

Summary and Conclusions

Although the principles of conditioning are usually thought of as universal, a combination of biological and environmental factors can affect the aging person's reaction to environmental stimuli. The purpose of the present review was two pronged. First, we provided information about how basic operant and respondent processes are affected by both typical aging and disease processes common in aging. Second, we described the literature that evaluates the utility of operant conditioning procedures for enhancing the wellbeing of older adults who experience both typical aging and disease pathologies.

Evidence suggests that biological changes can decrease performance on basic operant and respondent conditioning tasks (e.g., changes in the cerebellum; Cheng et al., 2010). Specific behavioral deficits can be associated with specific pathologies, even when these pathologies are only identifiable with an autopsy after death (e.g., Gallagher & Keenan, 2009; Woodruff-Pak, 2001). Nevertheless, modifications in the environment, including introducing conditioning procedures, may improve behavior even when the deficits in performance are caused by physiological changes that are irreversible. Research has shown that these deficient performances (e.g., the lack of emergent relations using traditional stimulus equivalence procedures) can be altered by slight modifications in typical procedures (e.g., incorporating a 0-s delay, altering the number of stimuli in the array or reducing the number of sample stimuli in delayed matching to sample procedures; e.g., Steingrimsdottir & Arntzen, 2011a). More studies are needed using both basic respondent and operant procedures to identify other procedural changes that might improve the performance of older adults.

Basic research on aging-related changes in conditioning processes could inform applied work with older adults. For example, research by Plaud et al. (2000) indicated that the behavior of older adults is sensitive to extinction, suggesting that function-based interventions will be effective when they incorporate extinction. To date, except for the studies that have provided time-based delivery of putative reinforcers (i.e., noncontingent reinforcement), relatively few studies have evaluated the use of extinction with older adults with dementia (but see Dwyer-Moore & Dixon, 2007, for an exception). Some researchers have even suggested that extinction should not be used when treating aging participants diagnosed with dementia because of the potential for brief increases in the undesirable responding when extinction is first introduced (i.e., extinction bursts; Baker et al., 2006). Other research also suggests that older adult behavior may be resistant to extinction under some conditions (Plaud et al., 1999). These studies suggest that extinction must be supplemented by other procedures to effectively alter behavior and that schedule correlated stimuli (i.e., a stimulus associated with periods of extinction, a stimulus associated with periods of reinforcement for other behavior) should be employed to enhanced treatment effects.

Applied research also supports using experimental functional analyses with older adults with dementia. Basic research on stimulus control illustrated that older adults with dementia were less sensitive to differences in reinforcement schedules than younger adults (e.g., Plaud et al., 2000). This finding suggests that schedule correlated stimuli should be programmed to enhance stimulus control when working with older adults. If this is not done, a functional analysis may not produce clear differentiation between test and control conditions even when the functional analysis has been accurately designed to test the right hypotheses about the function of problem behavior.

As more basic and applied research on conditioning is conducted with older adults, behavior analysts will be uniquely situated to play a key role in the broader arena of gerontology or applied aging. Gerontology is an area in which behavior analysis can and has had an impact (Burgio & Kowalkoski, 2011). However, only a small group has been conducting research in this area and behavior analysis has not yet transformed elder care or created a community of young professionals that are eager to conduct research in the area. Nevertheless, interested professionals will have opportunities to make meaningful and culturally significant social and economic contributions on a very large scale. By further understanding the operant and classical relations between environmental stimuli and the aging organism, behavior analysts will be able to provide needed basic knowledge and applied treatments that will have lasting effects (Baker & LeBlanc, 2011). The time to act is now and the opportunities are abundant given the growing need to provide care and to answer questions about our aging population (LeBlanc, Heinicke, & Baker, 2012).

References

Adkins, V., & Mathews, M. (1999). Behavioral gerontology: State of the science. *Journal of Clinical Geropsychology, 5*, 39–49.

Altus, D. E., Engelman, K. K., & Mathews, R. M. (2002). Increasing mealtime participation and communication of persons with dementia. *Journal of Gerontological Nursing, 28*, 47–53.

Alzheimer's Association (2011). 2011 Alzheimer's disease facts and figures. Retrieved January 3, 2014 from http://www.alz.org/downloads/Facts_Figures_2011.pdf.

American Psychiatric Association (2000). *Diagnostic and statistical manual of mental disorders* (4th ed., text rev.). Washington, DC: American Psychiatric Association.

Baer, D. M., Wolf, M. W., & Risley, T. R. (1968). Some current dimensions of applied behavior analysis. *Journal of Applied Behavior Analysis, 1*, 91–97.

Baker, J., Hanley, G. P., & Mathews, R. M. (2006). Staff administered functional analysis and treatment of aggression by an elder with dementia. *Journal of Applied Behavior Analysis, 39*, 469–474.

Baker, J. C., & LeBlanc, L. A. (2011). Acceptability of interventions for aggressive behavior in long-term care settings: Comparing ratings and hierarchical selection. *Behavior Therapy, 42*, 30–41.

Baker, J. C., LeBlanc, L. A., Raetz, P. B., & Hilton, L. C. (2011). Assessment and treatment of hoarding in an individual with dementia. *Behavior Therapy, 42*, 135–142.

Baum, W. M. (1974). On two types of deviation from the matching law: Bias and undermatching. *Journal of the Experimental Analysis of Behavior, 22*, 231–242.

Belsky, J. (1999). *The psychology of aging: Theory, research, and interventions.* Belmont, CA: Brooks/Cole Publishing.

Bourgeois, M. (1990). Enhancing conversation skills in patients with Alzheimer's disease using a prosthetic memory aid. *Journal of Applied Behavior Analysis, 23*, 29–42.

Bourgeois, M. (1993). Effects of memory aids on the dyadic conversations of individuals with dementia. *Journal of Applied Behavior Analysis, 26*, 77–87.

Bourgeois, M. S., Camp, C. J., Rose, M., White, B., Malone, M., Carr, J., & Rovine, M. (2003). A comparison of training strategies to enhance use of external aids by persons with dementia. *Journal of Communication Disorders, 36*, 361–378.

Buchanan, J. A., & Fisher, J. E. (2002). Functional assessment and noncontingent reinforcement in the treatment of disruptive vocalization in elderly dementia patients. *Journal of Applied Behavior Analysis, 35*, 99–103.

Burgio, L. D., & Burgio, K. L. (1986). Behavioral gerontology: Application of behavioral methods to the problems of older adults. *Journal of Applied Behavior Analysis, 19*, 321–328.

Burgio, L. D., Burgio, K. L., Engel, B. T., & Tice, L. M. (1986). Increasing distance and independence of ambulation in elderly nursing home residents. *Journal of Applied Behavior Analysis, 19*, 357–366.

Burgio, L., Engel, B., McCormick, K., Hawkins, A., & Scheve, A. (1988). Behavioral treatment for urinary incontinence in elderly inpatients: Initial attempts to modify prompting and toileting procedures. *Behavior Therapy, 19*, 345–357.

Burgio, L., & Kowalkoski, J. D. (2011). Alive and well: The state of behavioral gerontology in 2011. *Behavior Therapy, 42*, 3–8.

Burgio, L., Scilley, K., Hardin, J. M., Hsu, C., & Yancey, J. (1996). Environmental "white noise": An intervention for verbally agitated nursing home residents. *Journal of Gerontology, 51B*, 364–373.

Burgio, K., Westley, F., & Voss, D. (1989). Increasing ambulation in elderly clients of an adult day care center. *Clinical Gerontologist, 8*, 57–67.

Burton, J., Pearce, L., Burgio, K., Engel, B., & Whitehead, W. (1988). Behavioral training for urinary incontinence in the elderly ambulatory patient. *Journal of the American Geriatrics Society, 36*, 693–698.

Cheng, D. T., Faulkner, M. L., Disterhoft, J. F., & Desmond, J. E. (2010). The effects of aging in delay and trace human eyeblink conditioning. *Psychology and Aging, 25*, 684–690.

Cherry, K. E., Simmons, S. S., & Camp, C. J. (1999). Spaced retrieval enhances memory in older adults with probably Alzheimer's disease. *Journal of Clinical Geropsychology, 5*, 159–175.

Conyers, C., Doole, A., Vause, T., Harapiak, S., Yu, D. C., & Martin, G. L. (2002). Predicting the relative efficacy of three presentation methods for assessing preferences of persons with developmental disabilities. *Journal of Applied Behavioral Analysis, 35*, 49–58.

DeLeon, I. G., & Iwata, J. C. (1996). Evaluation of a multiple-stimulus presentation format for assessing reinforcer preferences. *Journal of Applied Behavior Analysis, 29*, 519–533.

Derenne, A., & Baron, A. (2002). Behavior analysis and the study of human aging. *Behavior Analyst, 25*, 151–160.

Dixon, M., Baker, J. C., & Sadowski, K. A. (2011). Applying Skinner's analysis of verbal behavior to persons with dementia. *Behavior Therapy, 42*, 120–126. doi: 0005-7894/10.

Dixon, R. A., Rust, T. B., Feltmate, S. E., & Kwong See, S. (2007). Memory and aging: Selected research directions and application issues. *Canadian Psychology, 48*, 67–76. doi: 10.1037/cp2007008.

Durkin, M., Prescott, L., Furchtgott, E., Cantor, J., & Powell, D. A. (1993). Concomitant eyeblink and heart rate classical conditioning in young, middle-aged, and elderly human subjects. *Psychology and Aging, 8*, 571–581.

Dwyer-Moore, K. J., & Dixon, M. R. (2007). Functional analysis and treatment of problem behavior of elderly adults in long-term care settings. *Journal of Applied Behavior Analysis, 40*, 679–684.

Engelman, K., Altus, D., & Mathews, M. (1999). Increasing engagement in daily activities by older adults with dementia. *Journal of Applied Behavior Analysis, 32*, 107–110.

Engelman, K. K., Altus, D. E., Mosier, M. C., & Mathews, R. M. (2003). Brief training to promote the use of less intrusive prompts by nursing assistants in a dementia care unit. *Journal of Applied Behavior Analysis, 36*, 129–132.

Engelman, K., Mathews, R. M., & Altus, D. (2002). Restoring dressing independence in persons with Alzheimer's disease: A pilot study. *American Journal of Alzheimer's Disease and Other Dementias, 17*, 37–43.

Erikson, E. H. (1959). *Identity and the life cycle: Selected papers.* New York: International Universities.

Fantl, J. A., Wyman, J. F., Harkins, S. W., & Hadley, E. C. (1990). Bladder training in the management of lower urinary tract dysfunction in women: A review. *Journal of the American Geriatrics Society, 38*, 329–332.

Feliciano, L., Steers, M. E., Elite-Marcandontou, A., McLane, M., & Areán, P. A. (2009). Applications of preference assessment procedures in depression and agitation management in elders with dementia. *Clinical Gerontologist, 32*, 239–259. doi: 10.1080/07317110902895226.

Finkbiner, R., & Woodruff-Pak, D. (1991). Classical eyeblink conditioning in adulthood: Effects of age and interstimulus interval on acquisition in the trace paradigm. *Psychology and Aging, 6*, 109–117.

Fisher, J. E., & Noll, J. (1996). Age-associated differences in sensitivity to reinforcement frequency. *Journal of Clinical Geropsychology, 2*, 297–306.

Fisher, W., Piazza, C. C., Bowman, L. G., Hagopian, L. P., Owens, J. C., & Slevin, I. (1992). A comparison of two approaches for identifying reinforcers for persons with severe and profound disabilities. *Journal of Applied Behavior Analysis, 25*, 491–498.

Gallagher, S. M., & Keenan, M. (2009). Stimulus equivalence and the Mini-Mental Status Examination in the elderly. *European Journal of Behavior Analysis, 10*, 159–165.

Hagopian, L. P., Long, E. S., & Rush, K. S. (2004). Preference assessment procedures for individuals with developmental disabilities. *Behavior Modification, 28*, 668–677.

Heard, K., & Watson, T. S. (1999). Reducing wandering by persons with dementia using differential reinforcement. *Journal of Applied Behavior Analysis, 32*, 381–384.

Hendricks, J., & Achenbaum, A. (1999). Historical development of theories of aging. In V. L. Nengston & K. W. Shaie (Eds.), *Handbook of theories of aging* (pp. 21–39). New York: Springer.

Herrnstein, R. J. (1970). On the law of effect. *Journal of the Experimental Analysis of Behavior, 13*, 243–266.

Iwata, B. A., Pace, G. M., Cowdery, G. E., & Miltenberger, R. G. (1994). What makes extinction work: An analysis of procedural form and function. *Journal of Applied Behavior Analysis, 27*, 131–144.

Jeffcoate, T. N. (1961). Functional disturbances of the female bladder and urethra. *Journal of the Royal College of Surgeons of Edinburgh, 7*, 28–47.

Jenkins, J., Felce, D., Lunt, B., & Powell, L. (1977). Increasing engagement in activity of residents in old people's homes by providing recreational materials. *Behavior Research and Therapy, 15*, 429–434.

Kinsella, K., & He, W. (2009). *An aging world: 2008*. Washington, DC: US Government Printing Office.

LeBlanc, L. A. (2010). Integrating behavioral psychology services into adult day programming for individuals with dementia. *Behavior Modification, 34*, 443–458.

LeBlanc, L. A., Cherup, S. M., Feliciano, L., & Sidener, T. M. (2006). Using choice-making opportunities to increase activity engagement in individuals with dementia. *American Journal of Alzheimer's Disease and Other Dementias, 21*, 318–325. doi: 10.1177/1533317506292183.

LeBlanc, L. A., Heinicke, M. H., & Baker, J. C. (2012). Expanding the consumer base for behavior analytic services: Meeting the needs of consumers in the 21st century. *Behavior Analysis in Practice, 5*, 4–14.

LeBlanc, L. A., Raetz, P. B., Baker, J. C., Strobel, M. J., & Feeney, B. J. (2008). Assessing preference in elders with dementia using multimedia and verbal Pleasant Events Schedules. *Behavioral Interventions, 23*, 213–225. doi: 10.1002/bin.266.

LeBlanc, L. A., Raetz, P. B., & Feliciano, L. (2011). Behavioral gerontology. In W. W. Fisher, C. C. Piazza, & H. S. Roane (Eds.), *Handbook of applied behavior analysis* (pp. 472–486). New York: Guilford Press.

Logsdon, R. G., & Teri, L. (1997). The pleasant events schedule—AD: Psychometric properties and relationship to depression and cognition in Alzheimer's Disease patients. *The Gerontologist, 37*, 40–45.

Lundervold, D. A., & Jackson, T. (1992). Use of applied behavior analysis in treating nursing home residents. *Hospital and Community Psychiatry, 43*, 171–173.

Molinari, V., Karel, M., Jones, S., Zeiss, A., Cooley, S. G., Wray, L., et al. (2003). Recommendations about the knowledge and skills required of psychologists working with older adults. *Professional Psychology: Research and Practice, 34*, 435–443.

Moniz-Cook, E., Stokes, G., & Agar, S. (2003). Difficult behaviour and dementia in nursing homes: Five cases of psychosocial intervention. *Clinical Psychology and Psychotherapy, 10*, 197–208.

Moniz-Cook, E., Woods, R. T., & Richards, K. (2001). Functional analysis of challenging behaviour in dementia: The role of superstition. *International Journal of Geriatric Psychiatry, 16*, 45–56.

Nevin, J. A., Mandell, C., & Atak, J. C. (1983). The analysis of behavioral momentum. *Journal of the Experimental Analysis of Behavior, 53*, 49–59.

Nolan, B., Mathews, M., & Harrison, M. (2001). Using external memory aids to increase room finding by older adults with dementia. *American Journal of Alzheimer's Disease and Other Dementias, 16*, 251–254.

Perez-Gonzalez, L. A., & Moreno-Sierra, V. (1999). Equivalence class formation in elderly persons. *Psicothema, 11*, 325–336.

Plaud, J. J., Gillund, B., & Ferraro, F. R. (2000). Signal detection analysis of choice behavior and aging. *Journal of Clinical Geropsychology*, *6*, 73–81.

Plaud, J. J., Plaud, D. M., & Von Duvillard, S. (1999). Human behavioral momentum in a sample of older adults. *Journal of General Psychology*, *126*, 165–175.

Raetz, P. B., LeBlanc, L. A., Baker, J. C., & Hilton, L. C. (2013). Utility of the multiple stimulus without replacement procedure and stability of preferences of older adults with dementia. *Journal of Applied Behavior Analysis*, *46*, 765–780. doi: 10.1002/jaba.88.

Saunders, R. R., Chaney, L., & Marquis, J. G. (2005). Equivalence class establishment with two-, three-, and four-choice matching to sample by senior citizens. *The Psychological Record*, *55*, 195–214.

Sidman, M. (1997). Equivalence relations. *Journal of the Experimental Analysis of Behavior*, *68*, 258–266.

Sidman, M., & Tailby, W. (1982). Conditional discrimination vs. matching to sample: An expansion of the testing paradigm. *Journal of the Experimental Analysis of Behavior*, *36*, 5–22.

Sidman, M., Wayne, C. K., Macguire, R. W., & Barnes, T. (1989). Functional classes and equivalence relations. *Journal of the Experimental Analysis of Behavior*, *52*, 261–274.

Skinner, B. F. (1983). Intellectual self-management in old age. *American Psychologist*, *38*, 239–244.

Spira, A. P, & Edelstein, B. A. (2007). Operant conditioning in older adults with Alzheimer's disease. *The Psychological Record*, *57*, 409–427.

Steingrimsdottir, H. S., & Arntzen, E. (2011a). Identity matching in a patient with Alzheimer's disease. *American Journal of Alzheimer's Disease and Other Dementias*, *26*, 247–253. doi: 10.1177/1533317511402816.

Steingrimsdottir, H. S., & Arntzen, E. (2011b). Using conditional discrimination procedures to study remembering in an Alzheimer's patient. *Behavioral Interventions*, *26*, 179–192. doi: 10.1002/bin.334.

Teri, L. (1991). Behavioral assessment and treatment of depression in older adults. In P. Wisocki (Ed.), *Handbook of Clinical Behavior Therapy with the Elderly Client* (pp. 225–240). New York: Plenum Press.

Teri, L., & Logsdon, R. G. (1991). Identifying pleasant activities for Alzheimer's disease patients: The pleasant events schedule—AD. *The Gerontologist*, *31*, 124–127.

Tripp, G., & Alsop, B. (1999). Age-related changes in sensitivity to relative reward frequency. *New Zealand Journal of Psychology*, *28*, 30–36.

United States Census Bureau (2010). *Table 2. Annual Estimates of the Resident Population by Sex and Selected Age Groups for the United States: April 1, 2000 to July 1, 2009 (NC-EST2009-02)*. Retrieved January 3, 2014 from: http://www.census.gov/popest/national/asrh/NC-EST2009/NC-EST2009-02.xls.

Virues-Ortega, J., Iwata, B. A., Nogales-González, C. & Frades, B. (2012). Assessment of preference for edible and leisure items in individuals with dementia. *Journal of Applied Behavior Analysis*, *45*, 839–844.

Vollmer, T. R. Marcus, B. A., & LeBlanc, L. A. (1994). Treatment of self-injury and hand mouthing following inconclusive functional analyses. *Journal of Applied Behavior Analysis*, *27*, 331–344.

Williamson, P. N., & Ascione, F. R. (1983). Behavioral treatment of the elderly: Implications for theory and therapy. *Behavior Modification*, *7*, 583–610.

Wilson, K. M., & Milan, M. A. (1995). Age differences in the formation of equivalences classes. *Journal of Gerontology: Series B: Psychological Sciences and Social Sciences*, *50B*, 212–218.

Woodruff-Pak, D. (2001). Eyeblink classical conditioning differentiates normal from Alzheimer's disease. *Integrative Psychological and Behavioral Science*, *36*, 87–108.

Woodruff-Pak, D. S., Finkbiner, R. G., & Sasse, D. K. (1990). Eyeblink conditioning discriminates Alzheimer's patients from non-demented aged. *Neuroreport: An International Journal for the Rapid Communication of Research in Neuroscience, 1*, 45–48.

Woodruff-Pak, D., & Jaeger, M. (1998). Predictors of eyeblink classical conditioning over the life span. *Psychology and Aging, 13*, 193–205.

Woodruff-Pak, D., Papka, M., Romano, S., & Li, Y. (1996). Eyeblink classical conditioning in Alzheimer's disease and cerebrovascular dementia. *Neurobiology of Aging, 17*, 505–512.

Woodruff-Pak, D., & Thompson, R. (1988). Classical conditioning of the eyeblink response in the delay paradigm in adults aged 18–23 years. *Psychology and Aging, 3*, 219–229.

Index

The Wiley Blackwell Handbook of Operant and Classical Conditioning, First Edition.
Edited by Frances K. McSweeney and Eric S. Murphy.

CPSIA information can be obtained at www.ICGtesting.com
Printed in the USA
BVOW09*1124261015

423577BV00016B/90/P